HANDBOOK OF EFFECTIVE INCLUSIVE ELEMENTARY SCHOOLS

Now in its Second Edition, this seminal handbook offers a comprehensive exploration of how students with disabilities might be provided classrooms and schools that are both inclusive and effective. With an enhanced focus on the elementary level, this new edition provides readers with a richer, more holistic understanding of how inclusive settings operate in K-6, featuring expanded chapters on principal engagement, teacher preparation, district-level support, school-based improvement practices, and more. Fully revised and updated to reflect changes in the field, each chapter synthesizes the research, explores if and how this knowledge is currently used in schools and addresses the implications for practice and directions for future research.

James McLeskey is Professor in the School of Special Education, School Psychology, and Early Childhood Studies at the University of Florida and a project faculty member and state lead for the CEEDAR Center. His research interests include effective methods for achieving school change/ improvement; the role of the principal in developing effective, inclusive schools; and issues that influence teacher learning and the translation of effective instructional methods into practice.

Fred Spooner is Professor in the Department of Special Education and Child Development at the University of North Carolina at Charlotte, USA. He is known for his writing in the area of severe disabilities, specifically in teaching academic content to this population. He has published over 125 professional publications on teaching individuals with severe disabilities. Recent research has appeared in *Research and Practice for Persons with Severe Disabilities, Remedial and Special Education, Journal of Autism and Developmental Disorders, and Exceptional Children.*

Bob Algozzine is Professor Emeritus at the University of North Carolina at Charlotte, where he served as Director of the Behavior and Reading Improvement Center, Coordinator of the Research Program in the Department of Educational Leadership, and Research Mentor for the faculty in the Cato College of Education. He was a special education teacher and college professor for more than 40 years. His continuing research interests include assessment and evaluation, data-based decision making, and effective academic and behavior instruction for all students.

Nancy L. Waldron is Professor in the School of Special Education, School Psychology, and Early Childhood Studies at the University of Florida, USA. Her research and professional interests include school improvement to enhance inclusive education, school consultation and teacher learning, and school psychology training and credentialing.

Handbook of Effective Inclusive Elementary Schools

Research and Practice

2nd Edition

Edited by James McLeskey, Fred Spooner, Bob Algozzine, and Nancy L. Waldron

Routledge
Taylor & Francis Group
NEW YORK AND LONDON

Second edition published 2022
by Routledge
605 Third Avenue, New York, NY 10158

and by Routledge
2 Park Square, Milton Park, Abingdon, Oxon, OX14 4RN

Routledge is an imprint of the Taylor & Francis Group, an informa business

First edition published by Routledge 2014

Library of Congress Cataloging-in-Publication Data
A catalog record has been requested for this book

ISBN: 978-0-367-48999-1 (hbk)
ISBN: 978-0-367-48677-8 (pbk)
ISBN: 978-1-003-04387-4 (ebk)

DOI: 10.4324/9781003043874

Typeset in Bembo
by MPS Limited, Dehradun

Contents

Contributors

Bob Algozzine (Ph. D., Penn State University) is Professor Emeritus at the University of North Carolina at Charlotte, where he served as Director of the Behavior and Reading Improvement Center, Coordinator of the Research Program in the Department of Educational Leadership, and Research Mentor for the faculty in the Cato College of Education. He was a special education teacher and college professor for more than 40 years. His continuing research interests include assessment and evaluation, data-based decision making, and effective academic and behavior instruction for all students.

Kristen Apraiz (Ph.D., University of Florida) is a Clinical Assistant Professor of Mathematics Education and the UFTeach Mathematics Coordinator in the School of Teaching and Learning at the University of Florida. Her research interests include preservice teachers' mathematical task knowledge, technology integration, and program development in secondary mathematics teacher preparation.

Dr. Elizabeth Bettini is an Assistant Professor of Special Education at Boston University's Wheelock College of Education and Human Development. Her research examines factors shaping the special education teacher workforce, especially the role working conditions play in instruction and retention. Her work has been funded by the Institute of Education Sciences and the Spencer Foundation, among others.

Elizabeth E. Biggs, Ph.D., is an Assistant Professor in the Department of Special Education at Vanderbilt University. Her research and teaching focus on promoting the flourishing and inclusion of children and youth with severe disabilities within their schools and communities. She is particularly interested in practices to improve social, communication, and language/literacy outcomes for students with complex communication needs who use various forms of augmentative and alternative communication (AAC). She has published widely in the areas of AAC, peer support, peer interactions and friendships, and inclusive education, and she was recognized as an emerging leader in the field of severe disabilities by receiving the Alice H. Hayden Emerging Leader award from TASH.

Bonnie Billingsley, Ed.D., is a professor in the School of Education at Virginia Tech. Her research focuses on inclusive leadership, induction, and the working conditions that support teacher retention and effectiveness.

Stacie Brady, M.S., CCC-SLP, is a doctoral student at George Mason University (GMU). Her dissertation research focuses on morphological awareness. Prior to beginning the doctoral program, Ms. Brady was a trainer for the Accessible Instructional Materials Center, a Virginia

Department of Education funded center, where she provided professional development in the benefits of accessible reading and how to use assistive technology. She is a former speech language pathologist using evidence-based reading programs to address student's significant reading needs.

Dr. Nelson Brunsting is a Research Associate Professor of International Studies at Wake Forest University. His research focus is the well-being of diverse populations in academic contexts. His research has received funding from the Spencer Foundation.

Shannon Budin (Ph. D., Penn State University) is a Professor in the Exceptional Education Department at SUNY Buffalo State, where she also serves as Assistant Dean for Assessment and Accreditation for the Teacher Education Unit. Her research and scholarly interests focus on improving teacher use of research-validated, high-leverage practices in the classroom as well as the use of simulation activities to improve teacher candidates' knowledge and skills.

Shweta Chandrashekhar is a doctoral student in the Department of Rehabilitation Psychology and Special Education at the University of Wisconsin-Madison. Her research interests are in educator preparation for secondary teachers' collaborative practices and practitioner inquiry. Shweta previously worked in South India at a non-for-profit remedial center with students with high incidence disabilities and was involved in developing, executing, and teaching special and inclusive teacher education programs.

Erin A. Chaparro (Ph.D., University of Oregon) is a Research Assistant Professor at the University of Oregon's Educational and Community Supports Research Center. Dr. Chaparro has worked in schools in a variety of positions, including as a school psychologist, a special education teacher, and a high school counselor. Dr. Chaparro is the principal investigator or co-principal investigator on three Institute of Education Science research grants totaling over $6,000,000. The federally-funded projects make contributions in the areas of effective instruction for English learners, data-based decision making and teaming, and online professional development for teachers in rural settings. A theme of Dr. Chaparro's research is assisting school systems to efficiently and effectively scale up and use evidence practices within the context of multi-tiered systems for behavior and academics.

Ginevra Courtade is a Professor of Special Education at the University of Louisville. She has worked to support students with extensive support needs for over 20 years. Her work focuses specifically on teaching academics to students with moderate and severe intellectual disabilities and preparing teachers to provide meaningful academic instruction using evidence-based practices. She has authored over 50 publications, including peer-reviewed journal articles, books, book chapters, and curricula related to these areas. Dr. Courtade was recently recognized by her college for service to the profession.

Dale L. Cusumano (Ph.D., University of South Florida) is a Senior Implementation Specialist for the National Implementation Research Network (NIRN) at Frank Porter Graham Child Development Institute at UNC Chapel Hill. Throughout her career, she has supported system level implementation of evidence-based practices through her work with NIRN where she served as the Co-Director of the State Implementation of Evidence-based Practices (SISEP) center. She has also worked at the district and school level as a school psychologist collaborating with educators to adopt, scale and sustain effective instructional and behavior practices within a multi-tiered model of supports. Her interests include multi-tiered systems of support, data-based problem solving, coaching, and supporting effective implementation and scaling of evidence-based practices.

Shawn Datchuk (Ph.D., The Pennsylvania State University) is an Assistant Professor of Special Education at the University of Iowa. Dr. Datchuk is a former K-12 special education teacher and director. His research interests include writing development, writing interventions for students with disabilities, and data-based decision making.

Dr. Pixita del Prado Hill is a Professor in the Elementary Education, Literacy, and Educational Leadership Department and Co-director of the Professional Development Schools Consortium at Buffalo State College. Her research, teaching, and service interests include school-university partnerships, content literacy, and international education.

David DeMatthews, Ph.D., is an associate professor in the Department of Educational Leadership and Policy at the University of Texas at Austin. His research focuses on issues related to K-12 school leadership, educational policy, and equitable school improvement in urban schools and districts.

Sophia Farmer is an Implementation Specialist at the National Implementation Research Network. She provides support to state and local departments of education to utilize implementation and improvement sciences to ensure that all students have access to equitable, evidence-based instruction and interventions. Sophia has extensive experience in K-12 education as a special educator, district leader, regional technical assistance provider and state leader in MTSS.

Dr. Claudia Flowers is a professor of research, statistics, and measurement at the University of North Carolina at Charlotte and former chairperson of the Department of Educational Leadership. She has over 100 publications in the areas of assessment, measurement, and applied research methods. Her current research interests include exploring evidence of the technical quality of assessments for students with significant cognitive disabilities and testing accommodations.

Malinda Forsberg is a doctoral student in the Department of Rehabilitation Psychology and Special Education at the University of Wisconsin-Madison. She has extensive experience teaching students with emotional and behavioral disorders, and her research interests include restorative practices, inclusive education, and teacher education.

Megan Foster is an Associate Professor in the Teacher Preparation Program at Utica College in Utica, NY. Her research agenda is focused on access to the general education content and context for students with extensive support needs. Specifically, she has focused on the areas of (a) literacy, (b) assistive technology, (c) curriculum alignment and (d) policy. Prior to pursuing her Ph.D., she was a classroom teacher working with school-aged students with extensive support needs. She has co-authored book chapters and articles within the field of special education.

Ronda Fritz (Ph.D., University of Oregon) is an Associate Professor of Education at Eastern Oregon University. She teaches early literacy methods, emergent literacy, exceptionalities, and classroom management. Ronda has been an elementary general education teacher and reading specialist for 19 years and a college professor for 7 years. Her research interests include prevention and intervention of learning difficulties in reading, using observation feedback to improve intervention instruction, and literacy teacher preparation in both general and special education.

Dr. Keli Garas-York is a Professor in the Department of Elementary Education, Literacy, and Educational Leadership and Co-director of the Professional Development Schools Consortium at Buffalo State College. Her scholarly interests include school-university partnerships, online instruction, and literacy.

Heather Peshak George (Ph.D., Louisiana State University) is a Research Professor in the Department of Child & Family Studies at the University of South Florida within the Florida Center for Inclusive Communities (FCIC; www.flcic.org), a University Center for Excellence in Developmental Disabilities (UCEDD). She is also the Co-Director of the *National Technical Assistance Center on Positive Behavior Interventions and Supports* (PBIS; www.pbis.org) and *Florida's Positive Behavior Interventions and Support Project* (FLPBIS; www.flpbis.org), and an Ex-Officio and Past President of the international *Association for Positive Behavior Support* (APBS; www.apbs.org).

Cynthia C. Griffin (Ph.D., Purdue University) is Professor at the University of Florida in Gainesville, where she has served as Principal Investigator on several research and personnel preparation grants funded by the Institute of Education Sciences (IES) and the Office of Special Education Programs. Her current IES project provides funding to study *Prime Online*, an online teacher professional development program that targets elementary school teachers and the teaching of students with mathematics learning disabilities. She is also Co-Editor of *Teacher Education and Special Education*, the journal of the Teacher Education Division of the Council for Exceptional Children.

Nancy E. Harayama is a Lecturer in the Special Education Program at Boston University. She teaches courses on the assessment and instruction of students with disabilities. Her interests include the inclusion of students with severe disabilities who use augmentative alternative communication systems and have intensive behavioral support needs. She has co-authored a book chapter and articles.

Beth Harn (Ph.D., University of Oregon) is an Associate Professor within the Special Education program at the University of Oregon. She teaches classes including instructional design, history of special education, educational assessment, introduction to learning disabilities, and systems-level academic interventions. Her broad research interests focus on early intervention for students with reading and learning difficulties by implementing schoolwide, coordinated instructional and assessment practices, and designing and evaluating intensive interventions. Current efforts focus on the assessment and evaluation of intervention implementation to improve the delivery of tier 2 interventions and positive impact student outcomes.

Dr. Andrew Hashey is an Assistant Professor in the Exceptional Education Department at SUNY Buffalo State College, where his work is centered on special education teacher preparation in the areas of literacy and instructional design. Dr. Hashey's research interests include writing intervention, special education teacher preparation, and new literacies.

Rob Horner (Ph.D., University of Oregon) is an emeritus professor of special education at the University of Oregon. His research has focused on applied behavior analysis, positive behavior support, multi-tiered instructional systems, equity in education, and systems change. He has worked for 20 years with George Sugai in the development and implementation of school-wide positive behavioral interventions and supports (PBIS). Over 29,000 schools are implementing PBIS nationally. Dr. Horner has been the editor of the *Journal of the Association for Persons with Severe Handicaps*, co-editor of the *Journal of Positive Behavior Interventions,* and associate editor for both the *Journal of Applied Behavior Analysis* and the *American Journal on Mental Retardation*. Dr. Horner is the recipient of multiple awards, including the 2002 AAMR *Education Award,* the 2006 ABA *Public Service in Behavior Analysis Award,* the 1996 APA *Fred Keller Educational Researcher Award,* the 2014 *AERA Distinguished Researcher Award,* and the 2020 *Association of Positive Behavior Support Leadership Award.*

Melissa E. Hudson, Ph.D., is an Associate Professor in the Department of Special Education, Foundations, and Research at East Carolina University in Greenville, North Carolina. Her research and teaching focus on general curriculum access and inclusive education for learners with severe disabilities. She is also on the leadership team for Project CONVEY, a 5-year, $1.25 million grant from the U.S. Department of Education, Office of Special Education Programs, to collaboratively prepare Special Education, School Psychology, and Speech-Language Pathology graduate students to work together to improve outcomes for learners with significant support needs.

Dr. Tanya Ihlo is a Senior Implementation Specialist at the National Implementation Research Network (NIRN) at the Frank Porter Graham Child Development Institute at the University of North Carolina at Chapel Hill. Dr. Ihlo provides technical assistance (TA) support for education agencies in the application of equitable implementation practices for selection, implementation support planning, sustained use, and continuous improvement of evidence-based practices to achieve success for students, in particular students who have been farthest from opportunity. Her current projects focus on partnering to support Charter Management Organizations aiming to improve outcomes for students with disabilities who are Black, Latinx, or from under-resourced communities; providing technical assistance (TA) through the OSEP-Funded State Implementation and Scaling-up of Evidence-based Practices (SISEP) Center; and providing support for pairs of TA Providers and local education agencies in the development of implementation and measurements plans for us of high-quality math curricula for students in the middle grades who are Black, Latinx, or from under-resourced communities.

Maya Israel, Ph.D., is an associate professor of Educational Technology at the University of Florida. Her research focuses on the design and implementation of inclusive and accessible science, technology, engineering, and mathematics (STEM) K-8 instruction with a specific focus on Universal Design for Learning applications within computer science and computational thinking instruction.

Dr. Dia Jackson is a Senior Researcher at American Institutes for Research (AIR) with expertise in educator professional development, special education instructional practices, Response to Intervention (RTI)/Multi-tiered Systems of Support (MTSS), disproportionality and culturally responsive pedagogy. Dr. Jackson was a co-author of CEC/CEEDAR's High-Leverage Practices (HLPs) for Special Educators (2017) and provided national leadership and technical assistance to federal, state and district clients on HLPs, RTI/MTSS and equity in education. Additionally, Dr. Jackson conducts special education research on NAEP process data, district response to COVID and special education program evaluations.

Dr. Kathleen Ryan Jackson is an Implementation Specialist at NIRN and the founder of the Western Implementation Society for Practice and Research. She has 20 years of experience in organizational and system change in the field of education, PreK through adult living, place-based partnerships, and juvenile justice. Kathleen is passionate regarding the co-creation of a collective commitment for continuous improvement, so policy will support and sustain an effective practice that improves population outcomes.

Lebon Daniel James III is a Ph.D. student in the Educational Policy and Planning program in the Department of Educational Leadership and Policy Studies at the University of Texas at Austin. His research focuses on K-12 school leadership, principal preparation programs, and the intersection of schools and communities.

Bree A. Jimenez is an Associate Professor of Special Education at the University of Texas at Arlington. Her research and teaching focus is on general curriculum access and assessment for students with intellectual disabilities and autism. Specifically, Dr. Jimenez's research focuses on math, science, and STEM instruction for students with extensive support needs. She is the author/co-author of over 20 peer-reviewed journal articles, multiple book chapters, and five books on strategies to support academics for students with disabilities.

Lindsey Kaler is a doctoral student in Educational Studies at Boston University. Her research interests center around education policy, trauma, and special education, with a particular focus on how those topics intersect for students identified with emotional and behavioral disorders. Prior to her doctoral studies, Lindsey was a special education teacher in Washington, D.C. and Virginia.

Dr. Meagan Karvonen is Director of ATLAS (Accessible Teaching, Learning, and Assessment Systems), a research center at the University of Kansas. Her research focuses on assessment design, instructional strategies, and professional development for teachers who provide academic instruction for students with significant cognitive disabilities. Dr. Karvonen has served as PI or co-PI on projects totaling more than $60 million. She has co-authored more than 200 articles, book chapters, technical reports, and presentations.

Craig H. Kennedy is a Professor in the Departments of Educational Psychology and Pediatrics at the University of Connecticut. His research focuses on intensive behavioral supports, health conditions, and people with neurodevelopmental disabilities. He has co-authored over 160 research articles and book chapters, as well as six books.

Angus Kittelman, Ph.D., is a Postdoctoral Scholar at the University of Oregon and the Evaluation Coordinator for Educational and Community Supports, a research unit in the College of Education. His research interests include positive behavioral interventions and supports, implementation science, and vocational rehabilitation.

Jemma Bae Kwon (Ph.D., University of Florida) is Assistant Professor at the California State University, Sacramento. She teaches courses in curriculum and instructional strategies to prospective special education teachers and in mathematics teaching and inclusive education to both K-8 general education and special education teacher candidates. Her continuing research interests include teacher preparation and professional development for effectively teaching mathematics to students with special needs. Other research interests include technology-enhanced special education practices to support both special education teachers and students.

Donna Lehr is an Associate Professor in the Special Education Program at Wheelock College of Education and Human Development at Boston University. Dr. Lehr has focused her teaching and scholarship on issues and practices related to educational services for students of all ages who have severe handicaps, with a particular emphasis on those who challenge educational systems. Dr. Lehr has directed national projects that have developed and demonstrated innovative educational programs for children with extensive support needs and their families. Currently, Dr. Lehr's work focuses on including students with severe disabilities in general education and policies, issues, and practices in educating students with complex learning and health care needs.

Melinda Leko is a Professor in the Department of Rehabilitation Psychology and Special Education at the University of Wisconsin-Madison. Her research and educator preparation efforts have been funded by the U.S. Department of Education, the Office of Special Education Programs (OSEP), and the Institute of Education Sciences (IES) and focus on educator preparation to promote inclusive and equitable practices for students with disabilities, evidenced-based practices in reading for adolescents with disabilities, and teachers' implementation of evidence-based practices.

Timothy J. Lewis, Ph.D., is a Curators' Distinguished Professor of Special Education and Director of the University of Missouri Center for School-wide Positive Behavior Support. He is Co-Director of the Center for PBIS. His research interests include functional behavioral assessment, social skill instruction and early intervention and prevention through school-wide systems of positive behavior support.

Jennifer Lillis is a doctoral student at Boston University. She studies secondary transition and her dissertation research focuses on how practitioners share responsibility for transition planning and service delivery. Before pursuing her doctorate, she taught special education and served as the Director of College Access and Alumni Engagement for a sport-based youth development program in Boston. Jenn is passionate about ensuring equitable access to postsecondary opportunities for all students and helping young adults identify and pursue their life goals.

Dr. Sylvia Linan-Thompson is an Associate Professor in the Department of Special Education and Clinical Sciences and is affiliated with the Center on Teaching and Learning at the University of Oregon. Her primary research interests are examining appropriate instructional and assessment practices for English learners (ELs). She has been PI or Co-PI of longitudinal intervention research projects that developed and examined reading interventions for struggling readers who are monolingual English speakers, English language learners and bilingual students acquiring Spanish literacy, and has examined the English writing development of ELs with and without learning disabilities. Additionally, Dr. Linan-Thompson has also examined the implementation of RtI with English language learners in dual language schools. She has published widely on these topics.

Lawrence Maheady (Ph. D., University of Pittsburgh) is Distinguished Professor and Horace Mann Endowed Chair in the Exceptional Education Department at SUNY Buffalo State College. His scholarly interests include teacher preparation for inclusive educational settings, classroom-based interventions and peer-mediated instruction.

Dr. Matthew Marino is a professor of Exceptional Education at the University of Central Florida. His research examines the design, implementation, and educational outcomes associated with technology-enhanced curricular materials. A majority of his research is focused on Science, Technology, Engineering, and Mathematics (STEM) instruction using the Universal Design for Learning framework.

Linda H. Mason (Ph.D., University of Maryland) is a Professor and the Endowed Director of the Helen A. Kellar Institute for Human disAbility at George Mason University. Dr. Mason conducts research in reading comprehension and writing instruction, instruction that provides intensive support and that supports learning in inclusive classrooms. She was award the Distinguished Early Career Research Award, Division for Research, in 2011 and received the Council for Exceptional Children's Research Award in 2021.

Addie McConomy is currently a doctoral student in Special Education at Florida State University. Prior to enrolling in this program, she worked as a classroom teacher and district professional development trainer for 9 years. Addie earned her B.S. from the University of South Florida in Special Education and is a National Board Certified teacher. Addie is supported by Project RAISE (Research-based Academic Interventions for Students with Extensive Support Needs). Her area of research interest is the implementation fidelity of high-leverage and evidence-based practices in classroom settings.

Dr. Erica D. McCray is an Associate Professor of Special Education and Director of the School of Special Education, School Psychology, & Early Childhood Studies at the University of Florida. She is a Co-PI for the CEEDAR Center, an OSEP-funded technical assistance center, and PI on the MARC Project at UF designed to support including antiracism content across the undergraduate curriculum. Dr. McCray has been recognized on multiple levels for her teaching and research, which emphasize the influence of diversity on educational practice and policy.

Kent McIntosh, Ph.D., is the Philip H. Knight Chair of Special Education at the University of Oregon and Director of Educational and Community Supports, a research unit in the College of Education. He is Co-Director of the *Center on Positive Behavioral Interventions and Supports*. His research interests include implementation science, multi-tiered systems of support, and racial equity in school discipline.

James McLeskey (Ph.D., Georgia State University) is a Professor in the School of Special Education, School Psychology, & Early Childhood Studies at the University of Florida and a project faculty member and state lead for the CEEDAR Center. His research interests include effective methods for achieving school change/improvement; the role of the principal in developing effective, inclusive schools; and issues that influence teacher learning and the translation of effective instructional methods into practice.

Dr. Hannah Morris Mathews is an Assistant Professor in Special Education at University of Florida. Her research focuses on the professional socialization and role development of beginning special educators. This includes examining varied perspectives on role (e.g., special educators, teacher educators, administrators) and the various settings in which role is negotiated and enacted.

Kathryn M. Meyer is a doctoral student in Educational Studies with a specialization in special education at Boston University's Wheelock College of Education and Human Development. Her research interests include studying how school turnaround and state takeover policies impact special educators and students with disabilities. Before her doctoral studies, Kathryn worked as a special education teacher.

Kelsey Morris, EdD, is an Assistant Research Professor in the Department of Special Education in the College of Education at the University of Missouri (MU). He is Co-Director of the MU

Center for School-wide Positive Behavior Support. His research interests include classroom management and function-based thinking, targeted interventions, and data-based decision making.

Rhonda N. T. Nese, (Ph.D., University of Oregon) is an Assistant Professor in the Department of Special Education and Clinical Sciences at the University of Oregon and a Principal Investigator within Educational and Community Supports, a research unit housed in the College of Education. Dr. Nese currently serves as the Director of an IES grant to refine and test an intervention to reduce exclusionary discipline practices, improve student behavior and student-teacher relationships, and increase instructional time for students in secondary settings. Dr. Nese also provides technical assistance on preventative practices, including addressing implicit bias in school discipline, effective classroom behavior management strategies, bullying prevention, and alternatives to exclusionary discipline practices through the OSEP-funded National TA-Center on PBIS. Dr. Nese's research involves equitable intervention delivery within a multi-tiered behavior support framework focused on preventative strategies for improving student outcomes.

Angela L. Patti (Ph.D., University at Buffalo) is an Associate Professor in the Exceptional Education Department at SUNY Buffalo State. Prior to working in higher education, she was a special education teacher and Committee on Special Education Chairperson. Her scholarly interests include high-leverage practices, co-teaching, and developing teacher candidates' cross-cultural competency through faculty-led study abroad programs.

Robert C. Pennington, Ph.D., BCBA-D, is a Professor and the Lake and Edward J. Snyder, Jr. Distinguished Scholar in Special Education at UNC Charlotte. He has over 30 years of experience working with individuals with disabilities, their families, and teachers. His work has centered on the application of behavioral principles and procedures to improve outcomes for students with intellectual and developmental disabilities and their teachers. Recently, he has published numerous articles and chapters related to teaching written expression to students with IDD.

Angela I. Preston (Ph.D., University of North Carolina at Charlotte) is a K-3 Literacy Consultant for the District and Regional Support Team at the North Carolina Department of Public Instruction. Throughout her career, she coached leaders and teachers in support of early literacy instruction, taught courses in special education as an adjunct instructor, and supported the implementation of evidence-based practices as an implementation specialist. She began her career as a special educator in an elementary school. Her interests include effective instruction in early literacy, multi-tiered systems of support, implementation science, and special education.

Rebecca Raab, Ph.D., is an instructor in the Department of Special Education at Radford University. Her research focuses on K-12 English to speakers of other languages, teacher induction, and the intersection of special education and ESOL programs for dually identified learners.

Lisa A. Rafferty (Ph.D., University at Buffalo) is a Professor in the Exceptional Education Department at SUNY Buffalo State. Her research interests emanate from her earlier work as a teacher and behavior support specialist. Her most recent scholarly work has focused upon teacher-education program reform to help prepare candidates who can effectively implement high leverage practices that will result in positive outcomes for all students, including those with and at-risk for disabilities, through high-quality, clinically rich programming.

Carly Roberts is an Associate Professor in the College of Education at the University of Washington in Seattle. Her research and educator preparation efforts have been funded by the U.S. Department of Education, the Office of Special Education Programs (OSEP), and the Institute of Education Sciences and focus on teacher identity and learning, students with intellectual and developmental disabilities' literacy instruction and learning, and teacher preparation to advance inclusive and equitable practices.

Jenny R. Root is an Associate Professor of Special Education in the School of Teacher Education at Florida State University. Her research focuses on promoting meaningful academic learning for students with extensive support needs, particularly in the area of mathematics. She has authored over 30 publications in the area of instruction and assessment of students with disabilities, including *Mathematics Education and Students with Autism, Intellectual Disability, and Other Developmental Disabilities* (Division on Autism and Developmental Disabilities).

Elizabeth Burnett Rossi, M.Ed., is a doctoral student in the Department of Special Education at Vanderbilt University. Her research focuses on advancing meaningful social and engaging academic opportunities for students with severe disabilities in inclusive settings. An experienced general and special educator, she holds an M.Ed. from Vanderbilt University and a B.S. from Indiana University.

Lindsay Ruhter is a doctoral student in Special Education at the University of Kansas. Her research interests include building teacher capacity to use data to inform their teaching in inclusive settings through professional development. She also works on IES- and OSEP- funded projects to design, implement, and evaluate professional learning models for teachers of students with significant cognitive disabilities.

Diane Ryndak is a Professor in the Department of Specialized Education Services at the University of North Carolina Greensboro. Her research and teaching focus on (a) inclusive education practices that facilitate access to effective instruction on general education content standards in grade-appropriate classes and other inclusive settings for students with severe disabilities, and (b) strategies for transforming education systems at multiple levels (i.e., state, district, school and education teams) to increase opportunities for students with severe disabilities to learn general education content and embedded essential skills along with their general education classmates. She has co-authored books, chapters and articles; has completed a Fulbright International Research Fellowship; and serves on several editorial boards for peer-reviewed professional journals.

John Samuels is a former elementary school teacher and current doctoral student in Curriculum and Instruction at the University of Florida. He teaches technology integration to preservice elementary teachers.

Tashnuva Shaheen is a doctoral student in Educational Studies at Boston University with a focus on special education. Her research interests focus on how special and general educators are prepared to collaborate in service of students with disabilities, and particularly how they develop shared understandings of effective instructional practice. Prior to her doctoral studies, Tashnuva worked as a literacy specialist in Brooklyn, NY.

Karrie A. Shogren is Director of the Kansas University Center on Developmental Disabilities (a University Center for Excellence in Developmental Disabilities), Senior Scientist at the

Schiefelbusch Life Span Institute, and Professor in the Department of Special Education, all at the University of Kansas. Dr. Shogren's research focuses on assessment and intervention in self-determination and supported decision making for people with disabilities. Dr. Shogren has published over 180 articles in peer-reviewed journals, is the author or co-author of 10 books, and is the lead author of the Self-Determination Inventory (www.self-determination.org), a recently validated assessment of self-determination.

Brandi Simonsen (Ph.D., University of Oregon) is a professor of Special Education and the Co-Director of the Center for Behavioral Education and Research (CBER; www.cber.org) at the University of Connecticut. She is also the Co-Director of the *National Technical Assistance Center on Positive Behavior Interventions and Supports* (PBIS; www.pbis.org), Co-Principal Investigator of the *National Multi-Tiered System of Supports Research Network* (www.mtss.org), and a Senior Advisor to the *National Center on Intensive Interventions* (intensiveintervention.org).

Fred Spooner (Ph.D., University of Florida) is a Professor in the Department of Special Education and Child Development. He is known for his writing in the area of severe disabilities, specifically in teaching academic content to this population. He has published over 125 professional publications on teaching individuals with severe disabilities. Recent research has appeared in *Research and Practice for Persons with Severe Disabilities, Remedial and Special Education, Journal of Autism and Developmental Disorders,* and *Exceptional Children.*

Anne W. Todd, (M.S., University of Oregon), is Faculty Emeritus at the University of Oregon, where she served as instructor, teacher trainer, and researcher. Ms. Todd's experiences span 40 years and include special education teacher and developer of school-wide programs that are team-based, data-based, and focused on systems change and sustainability variables in the area of positive behavioral support. Her most current research and training contributions are in the area of using data for progress monitoring and decision-making using the Team-Initiated Problem Solving (TIPS) model. Her work has been recognized and used in local, national, and international schools.

Jessica R. Toste is an Associate Professor in the Department of Special Education at The University of Texas at Austin and the Meadows Center for Preventing Educational Risk. Her research and teaching focus on how best to support struggling readers. She investigates methods to intensify interventions for elementary students with reading disabilities, including data-based instruction and psychosocial processes (such as motivation and self-determination). Toste has been principal investigator on grants from Institute for Education Sciences (IES) and findings from her research have resulted in more than 50 peer-reviewed publications.

Dr. Shawnee Wakeman is a Clinical Associate Professor in the Department of Special Education and Child Development at the University of North Carolina at Charlotte. Her research interest includes access to the general curriculum and how it is enacted for students with significant cognitive disabilities in a variety of settings and special education teacher preparation, including edTPA. Dr. Wakeman is currently the Principal Investigator or Co-PI on several federally funded projects, including Project IMPACT: Inclusion Made Practical for All Children and Teachers and The TIES Center: Increasing Time, Instructional Effectiveness, Engagement, and State Support for Inclusive Practices for Students with Significant Cognitive Disabilities.

Nancy L. Waldron (Ph.D., Indiana University) is a Professor in the School of Special Education, School Psychology, & Early Childhood Studies at the University of Florida. Her research and professional interests include school improvement to enhance inclusive education, school consultation and teacher learning, and school psychology training and credentialing.

Dr. Caryn Ward is the Associate Director for Education and Measurement of the National Implementation Research Network (NIRN) at Frank Porter Graham Child Development Institute within UNC-Chapel Hill. At NIRN, she is the Director of the State Implementation and Scaling up of Evidence Based Practices (SISEP) Center funded by the US Department of Education. In addition, Dr. Ward leads several other K-12 implementation capacity development projects funded by the Bill & Melinda Gates Foundation, Department of Education, and various state and regional contracts.

Lauren N. Wong (M.Ed., University of Florida) is a doctoral student and research assistant in special education at the University of Florida. She was a special and general education teacher for three years. Her research interests include response to intervention and the identification of specific learning disabilities.

Leah Wood is an Associate Professor of Special Education at California Polytechnic State University at San Luis Obispo. Dr. Wood earned her Ph.D. from UNC Charlotte in 2014 in Special Education with an emphasis on moderate and severe disabilities. She is a Board Certified Behavior Analyst (BCBA-D) and specializes in the application of systematic instruction to teach academic content and skills to students with intellectual disability and autism spectrum disorder. As a classroom teacher, Dr. Wood taught students with mild to severe intellectual disabilities for six years. As the lead Graduate Research Assistant for the GoTalk Phonics IES grant, and coauthor of the *Early Reading Skills Builder* curriculum, Dr. Wood has contributed to research studies across a variety of paradigms (i.e., single case, randomized control, qualitative). At Cal Poly, Dr. Wood particularly enjoys teaching about single-case design research and evidence-based practices. In her own research, Dr. Wood is examining academic interventions for students with developmental disabilities, both with and without the application of technology. Specifically, she develops interventions intended to promote comprehension of text across content and formats and the acquisition of science and engineering practices.

Wei Yan is a doctoral student at University of Florida, majoring in Educational Technology. Her research interests include computational thinking integration into elementary education, computational thinking assessment, students' debugging behaviors, and computer-supported collaborative learning (CSCL).

Lauren Zepp is a doctoral student in the Department of Rehabilitation Psychology and Special Education at the University of Wisconsin-Madison. Her research interests include secondary special education teacher preparation, preservice teacher knowledge and skills for reading instruction, and adolescent literature and literacy.

Kathleen N. Zimmerman is an Assistant Professor in the Department of Special Education at the University of Kansas and Early Childhood Institute Director at the Kansas University Center on Developmental Disabilities. Her research and teaching focus on promoting strategies to enhance children's engagement in inclusive classrooms for children with behavioral support needs, coaching educational staff to implement effective instructional strategies in inclusive settings, and enhancing the rigor of single-case design studies and syntheses.

Acknowledgements

This Handbook was a collective effort of many scholars with expertise in a range of critical areas that are needed to support effective inclusive schools. We would like to thank the chapter authors for working with us to complete this endeavor. We are especially grateful that they worked without compensation so that all of the royalties from this Handbook could be used to support the work of the Council for Exceptional Children. We also would like to thank others who provided us with support as work on the Handbook progressed. In particular, we very much appreciate the support provided by our editor at Routledge, Misha Kydd. Misha encouraged us to make substantial changes in this second edition of the Handbook so that we could provide deeper coverage of the most critical issues related to developing, supporting, and sustaining effective inclusive schools. She also provided encouragement, support and direction as this project proceeded. As chapters were completed, Olivia Powers at Routledge took over and did a fine job in moving these documents to a final product. Many thanks for your support, Olivia. We would also like to thank anonymous reviewers of the first edition of the Handbook who provided us with valuable feedback regarding how we might improve this second edition, as well as anonymous reviewers of several chapters for this edition who provided feedback. Finally, we would like to thank Lynette Beacher from the University of Florida, who provided assistance to ensure the accuracy of references in several chapters.

Section I

Developing and Supporting Effective Inclusive Elementary Schools

James McLeskey and Nancy L. Waldron

While some progress has been made toward developing schools that are inclusive and effective for all students, including those with disabilities, much progress remains to be made. A consensus seems to be emerging that for progress to occur, large-scale changes are required that address systemic improvements, including school-wide change and the development of effective system-wide supports at district, state, and federal levels. More specifically, the development of schools that are inclusive and effective and the large-scale use of effective instructional and behavioral practices (e.g., high leverage practices, evidence-based practices, Positive Behavioral Interventions and Supports (PBIS)) in classrooms requires substantial changes in the culture and structure of schools (Bryk et al., 2015; Fixsen et al., 2015; Fullan, 2016; McIntosh et al., 2018).

This section includes five chapters that address key topics related to developing and systemically supporting effective inclusive schools. Given the continuing controversy surrounding inclusive schools, Chapter 1 provides our perspective on just what effective inclusive schools are and why a balance must be struck between inclusive placements and improved student outcomes. This chapter also reviews trends in academic and post-school outcomes, which remain lower than desirable for students with disabilities. The chapter concludes with a discussion of emerging directions related to school improvement that show promise for supporting the broad development of effective inclusive schools that meet the needs and improve outcomes for all students, including those with disabilities.

Chapter 2 then addresses the critical role that school principals play in supporting the development of effective inclusive schools that are sustained over time. Through a systematic review of case studies of effective inclusive schools, the authors identify the specific actions that principals engage in to develop and support the successful inclusion of students with disabilities. The chapter concludes with a description of how these findings inform a course of action for principal leadership and preparation, as well as future research.

Chapter 3 provides a review of research and practice related to teachers' roles in supporting students in inclusive elementary schools. The authors address how scholars and policy makers have conceptualized these roles, as well as what research tells us about the roles that teachers assume in inclusive schools. The authors then propose a path forward, discussing avenues for changing individual and collective beliefs about special and general educators' roles in inclusive schools for the purpose of improving how schools support the inclusion of students with disabilities.

Chapter 4 then addresses the importance of high quality-preparation of teachers to ensure that they are well prepared for working in effective inclusive schools. This chapter initially describes how

DOI: 10.4324/9781003043874-101

teacher education practices have evolved in response to changes in inclusive schools and reviews research findings related to more effective approaches to preparing teachers for effective inclusive schools. The chapter then addresses notable organizational, pedagogical, and empirical challenges to improving teacher preparation, followed by a descriptive case example that shows how faculty from one educator preparation program responded to these concerns.

Finally, Chapter 5 addresses the role of effective professional development (PD) in preparing teachers to effectively include and instruct elementary students with disabilities. The authors initially provide a description of the features of effective professional development. This is followed by a review of research related to professional development, including how teachers' beliefs and attitudes toward inclusion influence their practice. The authors then review research on effective professional development related to literacy, mathematics, collaboration and co-teaching, classroom management, and the use of technology to support teacher professional development. The chapter then concludes with recommendations regarding gaps in research and practice related to professional development that must be addressed if effective inclusive schools are to become a reality for all students.

These chapters are intended to provide readers with in-depth background information related to critical areas that need to be addressed systemically to ensure that schools have the capacity to become effective and inclusive. This includes principals who are well prepared to support the development of effective inclusive schools and teachers who are well prepared to fulfill appropriate roles as they support the diverse needs of students with disabilities and others who struggle to learn.

References

Bryk, A. S., Gomez, L., Grunow, A., & LeMahieu, P. (2015). *Learning to improve : How America's schools can get better at getting better.* Harvard Education Publishing.

Fixsen, D. L., Blase, K. A., Metz, A., & Van Dyke, M. (2015). Implementation science. In J. Wright (Ed.), *International encyclopedia of the social & behavioral sciences* (2nd ed., pp. 695–702). Elsevier.

Fullan, M. (2016). *The new meaning of educational change* (5th ed.). Teachers College Press.

McIntosh, K., Mercer, S. H., Nese, R. N. T., Strickland-Cohen, M. K., Kittelman, A., Hoselton, R., & Horner, R. H. (2018). Factors predicting sustained implementation of a universal behavior support framework. *Educational Researcher, 47*(5), 307–316. 10.3102/0013189X18776975

1

Time to Support Inclusion and Inclusive Schools

James McLeskey[1], Nancy L. Waldron[1], Fred Spooner[2], and Bob Algozzine[3]

[1]SCHOOL OF SPECIAL EDUCATION, SCHOOL PSYCHOLOGY, & EARLY CHILDHOOD STUDIES, UNIVERSITY OF FLORIDA

[2]SPECIAL EDUCATION, UNIVERSITY OF NORTH CAROLINA AT CHARLOTTE

[3]PROFESSOR EMERITUS EDUCATIONAL LEADERSHIP, UNIVERSITY OF NORTH CAROLINA AT CHARLOTTE

Setting the Stage

Historically exclusion and stigma have been part of the lives of persons with disabilities (Conrad, 2020). Over at least the last 50 years (Deno, 1970; Dunn, 1968), educators in the U.S. have worked to enact concepts such as mainstreaming, the Regular Education Initiative, integration, and, most recently, inclusion in an attempt to address these problems and more fully support students with disabilities as active, accepted participants in the same schools as their neighbors and peers without disabilities (McLeskey et al., 2018). While most people agree with the concept of inclusion and the need to ensure human rights for persons with disabilities, they have not been able to agree on the particulars regarding what inclusion is and how to make it happen (Ainscow et al., 2006; Kauffman et al., 2020; McLeskey & Waldron, 2011a).

Much of the controversy regarding how inclusion should be defined and enacted in practice has related to how much emphasis professionals place on whether schools should be equitable, e.g., students with disabilities should be included as valued participants in the school community, versus whether they should be excellent, e.g., the need to provide effective instruction that improves outcomes for students with disabilities (Fuchs & Fuchs, 1994; Kauffman et al., 2020; McLeskey & Waldron, 2011a; Peurach et al., 2019). In short, when addressing the needs of students with disabilities, should more emphasis be placed on the inclusiveness or the effectiveness of a school? We take the position that schools must equally emphasize both equity and excellence; otherwise, they will not achieve the primary aims of education to become both effective and inclusive for all of their students. The chapters in this Handbook are intended to provide information regarding how this might be achieved.

In this chapter, we provide a context for the chapters that follow. Initially, we review trends related to how inclusion is defined and enacted in practice. We then provide data on how schools in the U.S. have changed over the last three decades, as increasing numbers of students with disabilities are educated in general education classrooms for much of the school day. This is followed by a

DOI: 10.4324/9781003043874-1

review of trends in academic and post-school outcomes for students with disabilities and emerging directions related to school improvement that show promise for supporting the broad development of effective inclusive schools that meet the needs and improve outcomes for all students, including those with disabilities.

Current Trends Regarding Inclusion

Considerations Regarding the Definition of Inclusion

As we solicited lead authors for chapters in this Handbook, we did not ask them to use a standard definition of inclusion. We did this because we recognized that while most educators support the concept of inclusion, there is no agreement about what inclusive education means in practice. As Ainscow et al. (2006) have noted, there are many different perspectives on inclusion in the field, resulting in a lack of agreement on what inclusion is across countries and schools. Ryndak et al. (2001) similarly noted that while "The term inclusion has many uses in the literature…researchers have begun to use the term without an explicit definition, leaving the reader to determine the meaning of the word" (p. 102).

Given the lack of consensus regarding how inclusion should be defined and enacted, we provided authors with a very general definition of inclusive schools that addressed core features and was agreed upon by the editors of this Handbook. For this purpose, we described inclusive schools as places where students with disabilities are valued and active participants and where they are provided supports needed to succeed in the academic, social, and extra-curricular activities of the school. In the most basic sense, this suggests that inclusion may be defined as educating students with disabilities in the same classrooms and schools as their same-age neighbors and peers. Effective inclusive schools are then those with classrooms where students with disabilities succeed in academic, social, and extra-curricular activities.

We understand that this is a general definition and does not address and deeply examine every aspect of effective inclusive schools. The difficulty in defining effective inclusive schools is reflected in the considerable variability that exists in how these schools have been enacted across settings, suggesting that there are many paths for a school to follow to become both effective and inclusive (Dyson et al., 2004; Hehir & Katzman, 2012; Hoppey et al., 2018; McLeskey et al., 2014; Rouse & Florian, 1996). While there is much variability in the characteristics of effective inclusive schools, there are nonetheless guiding concepts that are important to consider when we address how a school may become more effective and inclusive. To address these key concepts, we build on our general definition of effective inclusive schools to offer what Ryndak et al. (2001) have called a working definition of inclusion and inclusive practice. This working definition is taken from a number of sources that have identified key concepts that are generalizable across inclusive settings (Booth & Ainscow, 2002; McLeskey & Waldron, 2006, 2011a; McLeskey et al. 2014; Ryndak et al., 2001; UNICEF, 2017). The components of this working definition include the following:

- *Effective inclusive schools provide comprehensive and ongoing support to meet the needs of a diverse range of students.* This includes sustained engagement of a large proportion of the school administration, staff, and other stakeholders in whole school improvement resulting in substantial alterations in the school related to curriculum, instruction, school organization, teacher roles, and beliefs and attitudes among school staff and administration. This is done while recognizing that developing effective inclusive schools is a never-ending process of improving supports to meet the evolving needs of all students.
- *The entire school community supports inclusion and equity for all students.* This support is enacted as students with disabilities are valued members of the school community who are accepted by

both their peers and adults. In these settings, diversity is valued and appreciated, all students are welcomed, and diversity is perceived as a valued and beneficial part of the school community.

- *Students are educated together.* A strong emphasis is placed on all students learning together during both academic and non-academic activities. This occurs throughout the school community, allowing students with and without disabilities to interact positively and actively participate with other students socially, physically, and academically.
- *Students are educated in natural settings that are highly effective in meeting their needs.* Schools actively seek to increase the participation of students with disabilities in natural settings and activities while also seeking to reduce placements in separate settings. This includes placement in age-appropriate general education classrooms that are located in schools they would attend if they did not have a disability. This does not preclude the use of separate settings for specialized instruction that may be needed to meet the needs of individual students. Regardless of the placement setting, all students are provided with high-quality instruction that leads to the achievement of desired outcomes on a range of academic and social measures that address challenging curricular standards.
- *Professionals work collaboratively to provide support and effective instruction.* Educators collaborate to plan, implement, and evaluate instruction based on each student's progress. Furthermore, services and supports for students with disabilities and those who struggle are seamlessly integrated within general education activities that are provided for all students.
- *Students are provided supports to meet individual needs and achieve valued learner outcomes.* This includes needed supports for both students and teachers that are intended to remove barriers and address necessary adaptations of curriculum, instruction, and assessment. These supports also include specialized instruction that is tailored to meet individual needs and ensure effective instruction for all students. Finally, these supports are provided to ensure meaningful participation in school routines and activities, allowing all students to make real, meaningful contributions that they value and that are recognized and valued by their teachers, peers, and families.

These six components of a working definition of inclusion are intended as a framework related to the development of effective inclusive schools that serve all students well, including those with disabilities. As we noted previously, these components embody the core elements of inclusion and effective inclusive schools—that is, students with disabilities are valued members of the school community who participate with peers without disabilities in academic, social, and extracurricular activities before, during, and after the school day. At the same time, these students are provided supports and effective instruction that result in the achievement of desired student outcomes. The chapters in this Handbook are intended to provide descriptions of effective practices that can be used to ensure that these guiding principles are enacted in schools that are both effective and inclusive.

In the next section, we examine data related to the extent to which students with disabilities are included in general education classrooms in the U.S. Because students with disabilities were historically educated in segregated schools or special classrooms, placement has been used as a proxy for change and inclusion in U.S. schools. We begin by reviewing changes that have occurred in placement practices over the last three decades. We then examine placement practices for disability categories and discuss trends related to these data that help to frame contemporary practices.

The Current Status of Inclusive Placements in the U.S.

Since 1990, the context for the education of students with disabilities in the U.S. has changed substantially (Williamson et al., 2020). This has happened primarily as a result of mandates in federal laws (i.e., the No Child Left Behind Act of 2001 [NLCB, 2006], the Individuals with Disabilities Education Act [Individuals with Disabilities Education Improvement Act, 2004]), and the Every Student

Table 1.1 Placement of All Students with Disabilities in General Education Classrooms—1990 and 2015 (Williamson et al., 2020)

Year	*Percent of Time in General Education Classroom*		
	>79%[1]	40–79%	<40% or SS[2]
1990	34%	36%	29%
2015	64%	19%	19%

Notes

1 These percentages indicate the percentage of the school day students with disabilities are placed in general education classrooms. For example, greater than 79% is used for students who spend 80% or more of the school day in general education classrooms.

2 Separate School (SS) includes public, private separate or residential facilities, and homebound or hospital programs.

Succeeds Act (Every Student Succeeds Act ESSA, 2015) ensuring that local schools will be held accountable for providing students with disabilities access to the general education curriculum, and ensuring that these students make adequate yearly progress relative to this curriculum. This context includes a longstanding mandate from reauthorized versions of the IDEA, which requires that students with disabilities be educated in the least restrictive environment, creating a clear preference for educating these students in general education classrooms (Turnbull et al., 2020) to the extent that their needs can be met in these settings. These mandates have resulted in pressure to develop schools that are both inclusive and effective in meeting the needs of all students (McLeskey et al., 2018).

Systematically collected data are not available in the U.S. regarding the extent to which inclusive schools are effective (McLeskey et al., 2014); however, data are available regarding the extent to which schools are educating students with disabilities in general education classrooms. These data are provided each year by the U.S. Department of Education to ensure that states are addressing the Least Restrictive Environment mandate of IDEA. Table 1.1 includes data on changes in the placement of all students with disabilities in general education classrooms between 1990 and 2015 (Williamson et al., 2020). Data from this table reveal substantial progress toward educating students with disabilities for most (i.e., 80% or more) of the school day in general education classrooms. For example, in 1990, only 34% of all students with disabilities were included in general education classes for most of the school day. This percentage almost doubled to 64% by 2015. Coupled with this increase was a substantial decrease in placements of students with disabilities in settings where they were segregated from general education classrooms for most of the school day. In 1990, 29% of all students with disabilities were educated in these settings. This percentage decreased to 19% by 2015.

These data reveal substantial progress toward educating students with disabilities in general education classrooms for much of the school day. However, it is noteworthy that about 1 in 5 students with disabilities continue to be largely segregated from their general education peers for most of the school day. These students are either educated in separate schools that are removed from their neighborhood schools or are educated in a local school but in a separate special education classroom for much of the school day. Further examination of data on placement patterns across categories of disabilities provides insight into the extent to which different groups of students are benefitting from the progress that has been made toward educating students with disabilities in more inclusive settings, as well as categories in which many students continue to be educated in largely separate settings.

Previous research has revealed that while the move toward educating students in less restrictive settings occurred across all disability categories, most of the change that occurred between 1990 and 2015 may be attributed to changes in placement patterns for students with relatively mild disabilities (i.e., learning disabilities, other health impairments, McLeskey et al., 2011, 2012). This research also

Table 1.2 Placement Patterns Across Selected Disability Categories—2015 (Williamson et al., 2020)

Disability Category	*Placement Setting*	*Percentage of Students*
Learning Disabilities	>79%	70%
	40–79%	23%
	<40% or SS	7%
Speech/Language Impairments	>79%	87%
	40–79%	5%
	<40% or SS	8%
Other Health Impairments	>79%	66%
	40–79%	21%
	<40% or SS	13%
Emotional Disturbance	>79%	49%
	40–79%	18%
	<40% or SS	35%
Autism	>79%	41%
	40–79%	18%
	<40% or SS	41%
Intellectual Disabilities	>79%	17%
	40–79%	28%
	<40% or SS	55%

revealed substantial differences in placement patterns across categories. Table 1.2 provides data regarding placement patterns across the disability categories that include the highest number of students with disabilities, accounting for about 93% of these students (Williamson et al., 2020). Categories are listed in this table based on the percentage of students who are educated in largely segregated settings, beginning with the category with the fewest students in these settings (i.e., learning disabilities).

As Table 1.2 reveals, students with some disabilities (i.e., learning disabilities, speech/language impairments, and other health impairments [including students with ADHD]) are likely to be educated for much of the school day in general education settings, and a relatively small proportion of these students are educated in predominantly separate settings. In contrast, students with disabilities whose characteristics more often result in substantial academic and/or behavioral challenges (i.e., intellectual disabilities, autism, and emotional disturbance) are much more likely to be educated in separate classes or separate school settings. More specifically, from 35% to 55% of students with substantial academic and behavioral challenges are educated in separate settings for much of the school day, compared to 7–13% of students with relatively mild disabilities.

This pattern is supported by previous research, which has documented that most teachers are generally supportive of including students with relatively mild disabilities in general education classrooms but tend to be less supportive of including students with more substantial academic or behavioral difficulties (Monsen et al., 2014; Waldron, 2007). The pattern toward educating students in more restrictive settings is perhaps most understandable for students from categories such as emotional disturbance and autism who exhibit challenging behaviors, as many teachers and researchers take the position that the needs of these students are often too complex to manage successfully in a general education classroom for substantial portions of the school day (Kauffman & Landrum, 2018). Thus, a higher proportion of these students are placed in separate settings, as teachers provide highly specialized instruction and programs that are designed to meet these students' individual needs (Walker & Gresham, 2014).

In contrast, it is much more difficult to understand placement patterns for students with intellectual disabilities (Agran et al., 2020; Williamson et al., 2006). As Table 1.2 reveals, only 17% of these students are educated in general education settings for most of the school day, while 55% are educated for much or all of the school day in separate settings. This placement pattern has occurred in spite of the fact that research that has been conducted for over 50 years has indicated that these students can be successfully included in general education classrooms and often benefit academically and socially from well-designed inclusive placements (e.g., Agran et al., 2020; Freeman & Alkin, 2000; Johnson, 1962). This finding suggests that perhaps more than any other disability category, much progress remains to be made in providing effective, inclusive programs for students with intellectual disabilities (Agran et al., 2020).

Overall, data on the extent to which students with disabilities are educated in general education classrooms provide positive information regarding the extent to which these students are being educated for more of the school day in general education classrooms and suggest that general educators are assuming more responsibility for the education of these students. Of course, placement in general education classrooms does not ensure that students with disabilities are valued, actively participating members of these classrooms and schools. Furthermore, this placement is not evidencing that the instructional programs and supports provided in these classrooms and schools are effective or that students with disabilities are making adequate yearly progress on academic and social benchmarks. The chapters that follow in this handbook are intended to address a range of important topics to consider as educators ensure that these issues are addressed and that their schools are both effective and inclusive. In the next section of this chapter, we examine critical outcomes of schooling for students with disabilities.

Academic and Post-School Outcomes for Students with Disabilities

The information provided in this Handbook is guided by three stark realities faced by schools in the U.S. and many other countries. First, most students with disabilities spend most of the school day in general education classrooms. Second, given these placement patterns, general and special education teachers share responsibility for educating these students. Third, local schools and their teachers are held accountable for ensuring that students with disabilities receive a high-quality education that enables them to attain proficiency related to challenging standards, just like their neighbors and peers without disabilities. In short, federal mandates in the U.S. and other countries require that schools are both inclusive and effective, and school professionals (i.e., teachers and administrators) must seek methods that support the achievement of these goals.

Limited research suggests that some schools have made substantial progress toward achieving these goals (Hehir & Katzman, 2012; Hoppey et al., 2018; McLeskey et al., 2014; Rouse & Florian, 1996). However, evidence also suggests that most inclusive schools are not as effective as they need to be (Dyson et al., 2004; Farrell et al., 2007; McLeskey & Waldron, 2011a,b). While the outcomes in these settings are often as good as or better than outcomes for students with disabilities who are educated in separate settings (Freeman & Alkin, 2000; Lindsay, 2007; McLeskey & Waldron, 2011b), available data reveal that most students with disabilities do not graduate from high school with skills that are needed for work or additional training that prepares them well for a successful life after school (National Council on Disability [NCD, 2018]).

For example, a substantial achievement gap exists between students with and without disabilities in reading and mathematics in grades 4 and 8 on the National Assessment of Educational Progress (NAEP). In 2019 30% of 4th grade students with disabilities scored at a basic achievement level or above in reading, while 72% of their peers without disabilities scored at this level. At the 8th grade level, 37% of students with disabilities scored at a basic level or above in reading, compared to 78% of their peers without disabilities. Similarly, while 50% of 4th grade students with disabilities scored at a basic level or above in mathematics, 86% of their peers without disabilities scored at this level; while in

8th grade, 32% of students with disabilities scored at a basic level or above, compared to 75% of their peers without disabilities. While both students with and without disabilities have seen modest improvements in reading and mathematics achievement over the last 20 years, the magnitude of this gap has remained largely unchanged during this time (NAEP, 2019). Given these low achievement levels, it is not surprising that students with disabilities are more than twice as likely to drop out of school before receiving their diploma when compared to their peers without disabilities, and these dropouts then face poorer subsequent educational and employment outcomes (Hussar et al., 2020).

These poor school outcomes often translate into limited success in post-secondary and work settings after high school for persons with disabilities. For example, in 2017, the unemployment rate among youth with disabilities who were seeking a job was 12.1%, more than twice the rate of youth without a disability (National Council on Disability (NCD), 2018). Furthermore, the workforce participation rate of persons with disabilities (those working or seeking work) was 32.6%, compared to 75.8% of the general population (NCD), indicating vast disparities faced by persons with disabilities when compared to those without disabilities related to employment outcomes.

Thus, in spite of an increased emphasis on inclusive placements in the U.S. over the last several decades, academic and employment outcomes for persons with disabilities have improved only slightly or remain unchanged and continue to be less than desirable. This suggests that we must continue to seek approaches to substantially improve educational programs for students with disabilities to levels that improve educational outcomes and offer these individuals more opportunities for success in their post-school years. In short, inclusive schools must be developed that focus on continuous improvement and use the most effective practices that result in substantially improved student outcomes (McLeskey & Waldron, 2011a). Fortunately, emerging trends hold substantial promise for supporting the development of effective inclusive schools, the implementation of effective practices in these settings, and the scaling up of these schools across different school contexts. In the following section, we briefly describe emerging directions related to school improvement and then briefly address strategies for scaling up these changes across multiple settings (i.e., schools, school districts and states).

Emerging Directions Related to School Improvement

In this Handbook, many of the issues that schools face in becoming effective and inclusive are addressed, and information related to effective practices that may be used to support students in these settings is provided. On the other hand, considerable evidence indicates that many of these effective practices, in particular evidence-based practices, are seldom used in schools (Cook & Odom, 2013; Grima-Farrell et al., 2011; Smith et al., 2013). Given this widely acknowledged research-to-practice gap, perhaps the most important issue facing schools as they seek to become effective and inclusive relates to how they engage in the major changes that are needed to successfully implement and sustain the use of effective practices related to instruction, social support, and inclusive education.

Elmore (1996) has noted that through much of the history of school improvement, professionals have expected that good ideas would "travel of their own volition" (p. 10) into schools. We now know that this does not occur, as even the best of ideas requires careful planning and collective action to change classroom and school practices (Fullan, 2016). Furthermore, we know that effective practices are not translated into practice by commonly used methods. As Fixsen et al. (2005) point out, "the best evidence points to what does not work with respect to implementation…including the two most widely used methods for attempting implementation" (p. 70). These methods are:

- Information dissemination alone (research literature, mailings, promulgation of practice guidelines) is an ineffective implementation method, and
- Training (no matter how well done) by itself is an ineffective implementation method. (p. 70).

Evidence from a variety of sources (Fixsen et al., 2005, 2013; Fullan, 2011, 2016; McKenna & Walpole, 2010; McLeskey & Waldron, 2000, 2006; Waldron & McLeskey, 2010) supports the perspective that systematic school improvement is required to successfully implement the changes in practices that are used to support effective inclusive schools, such as those that are described throughout this Handbook. For example, Fixsen et al. (2005) state "there is good evidence that successful implementation efforts designed to achieve beneficial outcomes for consumers require a longer-term multilevel approach" (p. 70).

Research on school improvement suggests that there are several core features that must be evident if a change is to be successful as effective inclusive schools are developed. These include:

1. *School improvement must be systemic and result in changes in the entire school.* School improvement is "extraordinarily complex and notoriously difficult to achieve, even under the best of circumstances" (McLeskey & Waldron, 2002, p. 66). If changes are to be sustained over time, they cannot address a small part of the school (e.g., only students with disabilities). Sarason (1995) has noted that it is impossible to change only one thing in a school because changes are "so embedded in a system of interacting parts that if (one thing) is changed, then changes elsewhere are likely to occur" (p. 16). Thus, if school improvement is to be effective and sustained over time, it must address the entire school and transform current practice (i.e., changes must be systemic and change school culture). When this occurs, areas that are changed include the beliefs and values of teachers and other stakeholders; curriculum and related instructional practices; how the school is organized; and the roles and responsibilities of teachers and other school professionals (Fullan, 2016; McLeskey & Waldron, 2000, 2002, 2006, 2010).
2. *The focus of school improvement should be coherent, clear to teachers and other stakeholders, and address areas that teachers are motivated to improve.* Coherence involves prioritizing and focusing on a limited number of issues that teachers and administrators can understand and reasonably manage. Fullan (2016) suggests that change should initially focus on improving some combination of literacy, numeracy, and student wellbeing. These areas are clearly important to teachers and also can provide coherence and focus for change. This also ensures that the school improvement activities engaged in by staff are manageable, and "the focus of decision-making remains on improving teaching practice and student outcomes as agreed upon by stakeholders in the school" (Waldron & McLeskey, 2010, p. 67).
3. *Sufficient time for planning should be provided before changes are implemented.* Some have recommended that from 3 to 6 months should be provided for teachers and stakeholders to understand the purpose of change, examine alternatives for change, visit other schools that have engaged in similar changes, learn to collaborate and trust their colleagues, develop a plan for change, and engage in initial professional development activities (McLeskey 2000, 2006). While planning time is important, Fullan (2016) recommends not spending too much time planning because any plan for school improvement must be a 'work in progress' as teachers implement changes and learn by doing as this occurs (see also Bryk et al., 2015). This suggests the need for ongoing planning time after changes in a school have been implemented to determine the effectiveness of the changes, identify where alterations in the plan for change should be made, and to continue to build capacity within the school for improving student outcomes.
4. *Change should continually focus on improving teacher practice and building the capacity of teachers for delivering high-quality instruction.* Capacity building is the "infrastructure and resources available within a school to address student needs" (Waldron & McLeskey, 2010, p. 26). A key aspect of capacity building is improving teacher practice through high-quality professional development. Evidence suggests that high-quality professional development is job-embedded, and

"teachers are active participants in identifying, learning about, adapting, and using instructional strategies to improve classroom practice" (McLeskey, 2011, p. 28). Furthermore, this professional development is best supported by a community of learners in a school, which supports teachers in learning from one another as they develop and use more effective practices (McLeskey et al., 2014; Waldron & McLeskey, 2010). This suggests that important aspects of school improvement are high-quality professional development and a group of teachers who form a community of learners as ongoing components of developing and sustaining improved school practices.

5. *School improvement requires strong leadership from the principal and other stakeholders.* Much research has revealed that the key leader or lead learner (Fullan, 2016) for school improvement in effective inclusive schools is the building principal (DeMatthews et al., 2020; Hoppey & McLeskey, 2013; Waldron et al., 2011). Key roles for principals in these settings include: (a) setting the direction for school improvement and inclusive practice; (b) promoting teacher growth; (c) using data for decision making regarding goals, use of resources, program changes, and so forth; (d) redesigning the organization; (e) buffering teachers and other stakeholders from external pressures that would impede school improvement; and, perhaps most importantly, (f) sharing or distributing leadership, as teachers and other professionals are engaged in taking on leadership roles that allow them to develop and use their expertise to support the goals of school improvement.
6. *School improvement is iterative and requires continuous use of formative and summative assessments to fully support learning for all students.* As the previous features suggest, school improvement is an ongoing process with the principal serving in the role as the lead learner (Fullan, 2016), modeling the need for continuous learning and school-wide improvements as the needs of students and their teachers evolve over time. A key component of this continuous improvement must be data-based decision making. That is, schools must have available data related to the critical components of change that are trusted by administrators and teachers in a school as relevant and accurate in reflecting needed areas of school improvement. This then allows stakeholders to use these data to reach a consensus on key areas for improvement and gather broad-based support for moving forward to ensure that the most impactful changes occur.

Research and Practice Related to District-Wide School Improvement

While research on school improvement has shown great promise in providing direction for improving and sustaining school practices and improving student outcomes on a school-by-school basis, some have suggested that approaches must be developed that allow for more quickly scaling up effective practices across large numbers of schools. While this research has begun in the last two decades (Barab & Squire, 2004; Peurach et al., 2019), promising frameworks have been identified to support the scaling up of practices across school districts (Fixen et al., 2013; Fullan, 2011, 2016). For example, Fullan has reported on scaling up school improvement and communities of learners in school districts in Canada and the U.S. and also has examined factors that have influenced improved student outcomes across several high-performing countries (Fullan, 2008, 2011, 2016). Through this work, he has identified over-arching policy and strategy levers or 'drivers' that may be used by policy makers to successfully scale up reform across an entire school district, province/state, or country. These drivers serve to directly change the culture of schools (i.e., norms, values, practices, skills, relationships), and foster teachers' and students' intrinsic motivation, and include:

- A focus on capacity building to develop new skills among teachers and leaders that generate deep motivation;
- Providing structures for teachers and leaders to work collectively (as part of learning communities) to support one another as they improve practice;

- A focus on improving instructional practices in classrooms;
- The use of systemic strategies to support capacity building, group work, and the development of deep knowledge and skill related to instruction.

Fullan (2011) contends that these strategies are effective because the energy or motivation of students and teachers needs to be the central driving force behind change. The goals of reform must thus be aligned with the intrinsic motivation of teachers and students if reform is to succeed. "Intrinsic energy derives from doing something well that is important to you and to those with whom you are working. Thus, policies and strategies must generate the very conditions that make intrinsic motivation flourish" (p. 3). For a more extensive discussion regarding the importance of district-level support in scaling up effective practice across schools district-wide, see Chapter 20 in this Handbook.

While Fullan has identified overarching, policy-based strategies to support scaling up change, other researchers have begun to address more specific strategies for scaling up changes that lead to more effective practice and improved student outcomes across many schools (Fixen et al., 2013; Fullan, 2011; Levin, 2013; McKenna & Walpole, 2010; Penuel et al., 2011; Peurach et al., 2019). For example, Fixsen and colleagues (Fixsen et al., 2005, 2013) have reviewed a broad range of investigations to identify strategies that are part of implementation science and are needed to successfully implement and sustain use of effective practices in many schools. Evidence from this research points to the need for a combination of factors to support these activities, including "practice-based practitioner selection, skill-based training, practice-based coaching, practitioner performance evaluation, program evaluation, facilitative administrative practices, and methods for systems interventions" (Fixsen et al., 2005, p. 70). For a more extensive discussion of implementation science, see Chapter 21.

While these strategies have only recently emerged, they offer promise for broad-based improvement of teacher practice, ensuring that effective instructional strategies are used in schools and improving academic and social/behavioral outcomes for all students, including those with disabilities. As important, a district-wide approach to change has the potential to support the sustained use of practices over time (Fullan, 2016) to ensure that schools remain excellent and equitable in meeting the needs of all students.

Conclusion

In this chapter, we provide a broad context for the chapters that follow, as we address issues related to how inclusion is defined and enacted in practice and review data on how schools in the U.S. have changed and moved toward more inclusive placements over the last two decades. We conclude the chapter by addressing future directions regarding the types of changes needed to develop schools that are both effective and inclusive and the need to develop methods to scale up and sustain these changes across large numbers of schools and school systems.

While much progress has been made in educating increasing numbers of students with disabilities in inclusive settings and providing these students with quality education, the current emphasis on accountability for student outcomes in the U.S. and many other countries has revealed that more progress must be made. This progress is needed to ensure that educational and social outcomes for students with disabilities continue to improve and to provide these students with increasing options for success after graduating from high school. The chapters in this Handbook are intended to provide the most current information regarding effective practices and how they may be used as educators continuously improve schools to meet the changing needs of all students who struggle in schools, including those with disabilities.

References

Ainscow, M., Booth, T., & Dyson, A. (2006). Inclusion and the standards agenda: Negotiating policy pressures in England. *International Journal of Inclusive Education, 10*(4-5), 295–308.

Agran, M., Jackson, L., Kurth, J. A., Ryndak, M., Burnette, D., Jameson, M., Zagona, A., & Wehmeyer, M. (2020). Why aren't students with severe disabilities being placed in general education classrooms: Examining the relations among classroom placement, learner outcomes, and other factors. *Research and Practice for Persons with Severe Disabilities, 45*(1), 4–13.

Barab, S., & Squire, K. (2004). Design-based research: Putting a stake in the ground. *The Journal of Learning Sciences, 13*(1), 1–14.

Booth, T., & Ainscow, M. (2002). *Index for inclusion: Developing learning and participation in schools*. Centre for Studies on Inclusive Education.

Conrad, J. (2020). On intellectual and developmental disabilities in the United States: A historical perspective. *Journal of Intellectual Disabilities, 24*(1), 85–101.

Cook, B., & Odom, S. (2013). Evidence-based practices and implementation science in special education. *Exceptional Children, 79*(2), 135–144.

DeMatthews, D., Billingsley, B., McLeskey, J., & Sharma, U. (2020). Principal leadership for students with disabilities in effective inclusive schools. *Journal of Educational Administration, 58*, 539–554.

Deno, E. (1970). Special education and developmental capital. *Exceptional Children, 37*(3), 229–237.

Dunn, L. (1968). Special education for the mildly retarded—is much of it justifiable? *Exceptional Children, 35*(1), 5–22.

Dyson, A., Farrell, P., Polat, F., Hutcheson, G., & Gallannaugh, F. (2004). *Inclusion and pupil achievement*. Research report RR578. DfES. Retrieved from www.education.gov.uk/publications/eOrderingDownload/RR578.pdf

Elmore, R. (1996). Getting to scale with good educational practice. *Harvard Educational Review, 66*(1), 1–26.

Every Student Succeeds Act (ESSA), Pub. L. No. 114-95 (2015).

Farrell, P., Dyson, A., Polat, F., Hutcheson, G., & Gallannaugh, F. (2007). Inclusion and achievement in mainstream schools. *European Journal of Special Needs Education, 22*(2), 131–145.

Fixsen, D., Blasé, K., Metz, A., & Van Dyke, M. (2013). Statewide implementation of evidence-based programs. *Exceptional Children, 79*(2), 213–230.

Fixsen, D. L., Naoom, S. F., Blase, K. A., Friedman, R. M. & Wallace, F. (2005). *Implementation research: A synthesis of the literature*. University of South Florida, Louis de la Parte Florida Mental Health Institute, The National Implementation Research Network (FMHI Publication #231).

Freeman, S., & Alkin, M. (2000). Academic and social attainments of children with mental retardation in general education and special education settings. *Remedial and Special Education, 21*, 3–18.

Fuchs, D., & Fuchs, L. (1994). Inclusive schools movement and the radicalization of special education reform. *Exceptional Children, 60*(4), 294–309.

Fullan, M. (2016). *The new meaning of educational change* (5th ed.). Teachers College Press.

Fullan, M. (2011). *Choosing the wrong drivers for whole school reform*. Centre for Strategic Education.

Fullan, M. (2008). *The six secrets of change: What leaders do to help their organization survive and thrive*. Jossey-Bass.

Grima-Farrell, C., Bain, A., & McDonagh, S. (2011). Bridging the research-to-practice gap: A review of the literature focusing on inclusive education. *Australasian Journal of Special Education, 35*(2), 117–136.

Hehir, T., & Katzman, L. (2012). *Effective inclusive schools: Designing successful schoolwide programs*. Jossey-Bass.

Hoppey, D., Black, W., & Mickelson, A. (2018). The evolution of inclusive practice in two elementary schools: Reforming teacher purpose, instructional capacity, and data-informed capacity. *International Journal of Educational Reform, 27*(1), 22–45.

Hoppey, D., & McLeskey, J. (2013). A case study of principal leadership in an effective inclusive school. *The Journal of Special Education, 46*(4), 245–256.

Hussar, B., Zhang, J., Hein, S., Wang, K., Roberts, A., Cui, J., Smith, M., Bullock Mann, F., Barmer, A., & Dilig, R. (2020). *The condition of education 2020* (NCES 2020-144). U.S. Department of Education. National Center for Education Statistics. Retrieved from https://nces.ed.gov/pubsearch/pubsinfo.asp?pubid=2020144

Individuals with Disabilities Education Improvement Act. (2004). Pub. L. No. 108-446. Retrieved from http://idea.ed.gov/download/statute.html

Johnson, G. O. (1962). Special education for the mentally handicapped: A paradox. *Exceptional Children, 29*(2), 62–69.

Kauffman, J. (2020). *On educational inclusion*. Taylor & Francis/Routledge.

Kauffman, J., & Landrum, T. (2018). *Characteristics of emotional and behavioral disorders of children and youth*. Pearson.
Levin, B. (2013). *What does it take to scale up innovations?* National Educational Policy Center.
Lindsay, G. (2007). Educational psychology and the effectiveness of inclusive education/mainstreaming. *British Journal of Educational Psychology*, 77(1), 1–24.
McKenna, M., & Walpole, S. (2010). Planning and evaluating change at scale: Lessons from Reading First. *Educational Researcher, 39*(6), 478–483.
McLeskey, J. (2011). Supporting improved practice for special education teachers: The importance of learner centered professional development. *Journal of Special Education Leadership, 24*(1), 26–35.
McLeskey, J., Landers, E., Hoppey, D., & Williamson, P. (2011). Learning disabilities and the LRE mandate: An examination of national and state trends. *Learning Disabilities Research & Practice, 26*(2), 60–66.
McLeskey, J., Landers, E., Williamson, P., & Hoppey, D. (2012). The Least Restrictive Environment mandate of IDEA: Are we moving toward educating students with disabilities in less restrictive settings? *The Journal of Special Education, 36*(3), 131–140.
McLeskey, J., Rosenberg, M., & Westling, D. (2018). *Inclusion: Effective practices for all students* (3rd ed.). Pearson Education.
McLeskey, J. & Waldron, N. (2000). *Inclusive schools in action: Making differences ordinary*. ASCD.
McLeskey, J. & Waldron, N. (2002). Inclusion and school change: Teacher perceptions regarding curricular and instructional adaptations. *Teacher Education and Special Education, 25*(1), 41–54.
McLeskey, J., & Waldron, N. (2006). Comprehensive school reform and inclusive schools: Improving schools for all students. *Theory into Practice, 45*(3), 269–278.
McLeskey, J., & Waldron, N. (2011a). Educational programs for elementary students with learning disabilities: Can they be both effective and inclusive? *Learning Disabilities Research & Practice, 26*(1), 48–57.
McLeskey, J., & Waldron, N., (2011b, April). *Full inclusion programs for students with learning disabilities: Can they meet student needs in an era of high stakes accountability*? Paper presented at the Council for Exceptional Children Convention, National Harbor, MD.
McLeskey, J.,Waldron, N., & Redd, L. (2014). A case study of a highly effective inclusive elementary school. *The Journal of Special Education, 48*(1), 59–70.
Monsen, J., Ewing, D., & Kwoka, M. (2014) Teachers' attitudes towards inclusion, perceived adequacy of support and classroom learning environment. *Learning Environments Research, 17*(1), 113–126.
National Council on Disability. (2018). *National disability employment policy—from the new deal to the real deal: Joining the industries of the future*. NCD.
National Assessment of Educational Progress (NAEP). (2020). *The nation's report card*. Retrieved from https://nces.ed.gov/nationsreportcard/.
No Child Left Behind Act of 2001, 20 U.S.C. § 6301 *et seq*. (2006).
Penuel, W., Fishman, B., Cheng, B., & Sabelli, N. (2011). Organizing research and development at the intersection of learning, implementation, and design. *Educational Researcher, 40*(7), 331–337.
Peurach, D. J., Yurkofsky, M., & Sutherland, D. (2019). Organizing and managing for excellence and equity: The work and dilemmas of instructionally focused education systems. *Educational Policy, 33*(6), 812–845.
Rouse, M., & Florian L. (1996). Effective inclusive schools: A study in two countries. *Cambridge Journal of Education, 26*(1), 71–86.
Ryndak, D., Jackson, L. & Billingsley, F. (2001). Defining inclusion for students with severe disabilities. What do experts say? *Exceptionality, 8*(2), 101–116.
Sarason, S. (1995). *School change: The personal development of a point of view*. Teachers College Press.
Smith, G., Schmidt, M., Edlelen-Smith, P., & Cook, B. (2013). Pasteur's quadrant as the bridge linking rigor with relevance. *Exceptional Children, 79*(2), 147–161.
Turnbull, A., Turnbull, R., Wehmeyer, M., & Shogren, K. (2020). *Exceptional lives: Special education in today's schools* (9th ed.). Pearson Education.
UNICEF. (2017). *Inclusive education—including children with disabilities in quality learning; What needs to be done?* Retrieved from https://www.unicef.org/eca/sites/unicef.org.eca/files/IE_summary_accessible_220917_brief.pdf.
Waldron, N. (2007). Teacher attitudes toward inclusion. In J. McLeskey (Ed.), *Reflections on inclusion: Classic articles that shaped our thinking* (pp. 161–187). CEC.
Waldron, N., & McLeskey, J. (2010). Establishing a collaborative school culture through comprehensive school reform. *Journal of Educational and Psychological Consultation, 20*(1), 58–74.

Waldron, N., McLeskey, J., & Redd, L. (2011). Setting the direction: The role of the principal in developing an effective, inclusive school. *Journal of Special Education Leadership, 24*(2), 51–60.

Walker, H., & Gresham, F. (Eds.) (2014). *Handbook of evidence-based practices for emotional and behavioral disorders.* Guilford.

Williamson, P., Hoppey, D., McLeskey, J., Bergmann, & Moore, H. (2020). LRE placement rates in the U.S.: Where are we now? *The Journal of Special Education, 53*(4), 236–244.

Williamson, P., McLeskey, J., Hoppey, D., & Rentz, T. (2006). Educating students with mental retardation in general education classrooms: An analysis on national and state trends. *Exceptional Children, 72*(3), 347–361.

2

Principal Actions in Effective Inclusive Schools: A Review of Elementary Case Studies

Bonnie Billingsley[1], David DeMatthews[2], Rebecca Raine Raab[3], and Lebon James[4]

[1]VIRGINIA TECH

[2]THE UNIVERSITY OF TEXAS AT AUSTIN

[3]RADFORD UNIVERSITY

[4]UNIVERSITY OF TEXAS AT AUSTIN

Setting the Stage

Principals play a crucial role in creating and sustaining effective schools that meet the diverse needs of all students. Although the administrative functions of the principalship are relatively the same across the nation's approximately 100,000 schools, principals need to understand and adapt to the local context in order to support teachers, students, and families. Each school is different because it operates in different communities, with different conditions and histories, and under the policies and administration of different local and state governments. Researchers have found a common set of skills or repertoire that effective leaders rely on and adapt to fit their school community's context (Hitt & Tucker, 2016; Leithwood et al., 2008). These skills tend to focus on improving organizational conditions and teacher capacity to increase student achievement. Teachers, families, staff, and community members often play critical leadership and support roles to improve schools.

Researchers have paid less attention to how principals support students with disabilities and create inclusive schools and classrooms. A growing body of literature has found that principals can be effective at increasing achievement and inclusive opportunities for students with disabilities (Billingsley et al., 2019; DeMatthews et al., 2020; Hoppey & McLeskey, 2014; Mayrowetz & Weinstein, 1999; Theoharis, 2007; Waldron et al., 2011). Not surprisingly, effective principals who create and sustain high-performing inclusive schools draw upon their knowledge of disability, special education policies, and inclusive practices to improve organizational conditions and the professional capacity of others to meet the needs of all students, including those with disabilities. Given the

DOI: 10.4324/9781003043874-2

crucial role of the principal, our purpose is to identify principals' actions as they supported effective inclusive schools, using case studies of elementary principals.

Special Education Policy in the U.S.

Effective leadership practice is of critical importance for supporting students with disabilities, partly because most public schools were not initially designed with students with disabilities in mind. Prior to the enactment of the Education for All Handicapped Children Act of 1975 (EAHCA), states could deny access to public education for students with disabilities. As a result, some states and districts developed special education programs to support or include students with disabilities, while others denied access to the general education classroom or public schools entirely to students with certain types of disabilities. EAHCA and subsequent reauthorizations under the Individuals with Disabilities Education Act (IDEA, 2004) provided funding for special education and a set of educational rights that included (a) the right of all students to a Free and Appropriate Public Education (FAPE) in the Least Restrictive Environment (LRE); (b) the right to due process and procedural safeguards for families; and (c) an Individualized Educational Program (IEP) developed by a committee of teachers, related services providers, family, and the student. Since the initial passage of EAHCA, consistent progress toward including students with disabilities in general education and improving educational outcomes (e.g., achievement, graduation) have been made (McLeskey et al., 2012; U.S. Department of Education, 2019; Williamson et al., 2019).

The LRE policy created a strong regulatory preference that students with disabilities be educated within the general education classroom. The law requires that states and districts provide a continuum of placements. Specifically, the LRE provision requires that:

> To the maximum extent appropriate, children with disabilities, including children in public or private institutions or other care facilities, are educated with children who are not disabled, and that special classes, separate schooling or other removal of children with disabilities from the regular educational environment occurs only when the nature or severity of the disability is such that education in regular classes with the use of supplementary aids and services cannot be achieved satisfactorily. (IDEA, 2004, Sec. 300.114 (a)B))

Although the LRE provision represents a strong preference for inclusion, the word inclusion is not in the law. Instead, schools are expected to reconvene at least annually with families to make placement decisions. In some instances, the decision to remove a student with a disability from the general education classroom can be made if it is based on the student's needs and justified in the IEP.

Defining Inclusion and Inclusive Leadership

Inclusion and several other terms have been used in many ways to describe how students with disabilities are educated in schools. Prior to EAHCA and the LRE provision, students with disabilities were primarily educated in a separate parallel education system. By the early 1980s, "mainstreaming" and "integration" were key terms used to support increased opportunities for students with disabilities to be educated with their peers, especially in "peripheral regular education classes such as music, art, physical education, electives, and/or lunch" (Pazey & Yates, 2019, p. 31). The Regular Education Initiative (REI) increased calls for access to the general education classroom and partnerships between regular and special education. Policymakers and practitioners have also used "inclusion" and "full inclusion" to describe educational reforms that provide more or full access to the general education classroom and neighborhood school to students with disabilities. Often, inclusion is defined as a place (e.g., the general education classroom) rather than considering the place and the supports, services, and surrounding culture within classrooms and schools.

Definitions of inclusion can also be value-driven or philosophical in nature. For example, Katzman (2007) defined inclusion as "an educational philosophy that calls for schools to educate all learners—including students with disabilities and other special needs—together in high-quality, age appropriate general education classrooms in their neighborhood schools" (p. 129). Osgood (2005) drew upon a historical analysis of special education in the US to argue that inclusion is "more of an ideal than an idea, one to which schools should continually aspire but also one that remains unobtainable in the foreseeable future" (p. 200). More recently, calls for inclusion have taken on an intersectional focus recognizing disability, but also race, sexual orientation, class, language, country of origin, and other groups of people historically marginalized and denied full access to public institutions (Annamma et al., 2013).

For the purpose of this article, we define inclusion in the context of IDEA (2004) and the LRE policy and in full recognition that students with disabilities have been historically denied access to critical academic, social, and emotional opportunities within school communities and society. We recognize that inclusion is more than a place and that all students deserve equitable access to their neighborhood schools, general education classrooms, resources, and opportunities available in classrooms, schools, and communities. From this perspective, inclusive leadership requires sustained commitment and collaboration to establish a school culture and organization that values all students, recognizes their unique assets and identities, and rejects segregation and all forms of inequitable treatment. However, given the history of segregation, we also recognize that under certain conditions, inclusive leadership will take time and require strategic and careful consideration of context and potential barriers to inclusion.

Potential Barriers to Inclusion

Barriers to inclusion are largely related to the unique context and histories surrounding a given school. Some districts and states have long prioritized inclusive initiatives while others have not. Given that public education systems were not initially designed or funded with students with disabilities in mind, principals who seek to create and sustain effective inclusive schools can confront a wide array of barriers. Depending on the surrounding working conditions and policy context, principals may face huge hurdles, especially when working in a district or school that has not traditionally valued students with disabilities or inclusive education.

At the state level, policy makers and university-based teacher and principal preparation programs may not provide sufficient attention and resources to ensure that school staff are prepared to teach and support students with disabilities and their families (DeMatthews et al., 2019; Lynch, 2012; Pazey & Cole, 2013). As a result, teachers and staff may enter the building under-prepared to take the necessary steps to support inclusion, which increases the difficulty and resources needed to create inclusive schools. At the district level, superintendents and district administrators might not fully support inclusion or may not actively prioritize special education and the needs of students with disabilities. In some instances, districts can be generally supportive of inclusion but require principals and schools to comply with burdensome bureaucratic processes that can slow or reduce opportunities for inclusion on campus (Theoharis, 2007). Districts may opt to keep self-contained special education programs on campus and continuously replace students with disabilities from outside of the school's boundaries when another student is moved from the class into an inclusive placement (DeMatthews & Mawhinney, 2013).

Principals may also confront barriers to inclusion at the school level. School personnel come from diverse backgrounds and may have different perspectives related to who should and should not be included. Researchers have found that some teachers may undervalue students with disabilities or reject a school's inclusive mission (DeMatthews, 2015b; Cameron & Cook, 2013; MacFarlane & Woolfson, 2013). Teachers may even reject inclusion outright and challenge a principal's legitimacy when enacting such reform efforts (DeMatthews, 2015b). Families may distrust school officials and principal efforts when districts and schools have historically devalued students with disabilities or have not appropriately adhered to IDEA (2004) requirements. Families may initially reject inclusion out of fear or caution that hard-fought services or placements are now being taken away from their child (DeMatthews & Mawhinney, 2014). Within schools, barriers can also be physical and structural. Outdated or poorly designed schools may make inclusion difficult for students with disabilities as they navigate classrooms and common spaces (Pivik et al., 2002). Physical and structural improvements can be costly and potentially outside of the control of principals.

What Do We Know Based on Research?

As the above suggests, inclusion may not be a priority in some districts and schools, and research about how principals lead and support inclusive schools is still emerging (DeMatthews & Mawhinney, 2014). Studies of inclusive leadership have focused on the state (e.g., Ryndak et al., 2007), district (e.g., Burstein et al., 2004; Causton-Theoharis et al., 2011; DeMatthews & Mawhinney, 2013; Dentith et al., 2013; Ryndak et al., 2007), and principals' efforts (e.g., DeMatthews, 2015a; Shogren et al., 2015) as they prepared for, implemented, and worked to sustain inclusion.

Although researchers described positive examples of inclusive leadership (e.g., Causton-Theoharis et al., 2011; Guzmán, 1997), some inclusive efforts stalled (e.g., Mayrowetz & Weinstein, 1999), failed (e.g., Fox & Ysseldyke, 1997), or were not sustained over time (e.g., Sindelar et al., 2006). Research on leadership for inclusive schools also vary in terms of scope (e.g., studying single versus multiple schools), settings studied (e.g., urban, rural, elementary, secondary), and methods employed (e.g., use of surveys, interviews, observations, mixed methods).

In this chapter, we identify the actions of elementary principals as they supported the inclusion of students with disabilities in their schools. In the next section, we review the selection criteria for this review, our criteria and procedures for selecting the case studies, and describe how we analyzed them. In the findings section, we present the five overarching themes that resulted from our analyses, with a conclusion at the end connecting these findings to the broader literature. Finally, we provide implications for practice, preparation, and future research.

Method

Selection Criteria

We sought peer-reviewed case studies that described principal leadership for inclusion in elementary schools from 1995 to 2020. We limited the case studies to U.S. schools, given variability in educational policy, special education, and service delivery models across countries (UNESCO, 2018).

Definition of Inclusive Principal

We sought studies that described the work of principals and/or assistant principals as they supported inclusion. We did not use a specific definition of inclusion to identify or exclude studies; however, we sought case studies in which the principal clearly made progress in moving the school toward greater inclusion for students with disabilities (DeMatthews, 2015a; Keyes et al., 1999) and/or how the principal supported schools that were inclusive at the time of the study (e.g., McLeskey et al., 2014; Waldron et al., 2011). To be included, the case study needed to describe the actions of the principal as they conceptualized, initiated, supported, problem-solved and/or monitored efforts toward greater inclusion in the school. Conversely, we excluded case studies that did not clearly describe the principal's role within a school or in which the principal was ineffective.

Definition of Case Study

We included articles that included more than one case study, as long as each met criteria (i.e., DeMatthews & Mawhinney, 2014; Hoppey et al., 2018; Mayrowetz & Weinstein, 1999). We also included studies that focused on secondary and elementary schools, as long as the findings of elementary schools could be disaggregated from secondary schools (e.g., Mayrowetz & Weinstein, 1999).

Search Criteria and Procedures

We employed a systematic electronic search to identify empirical articles about effective inclusive leadership that met the above selection criteria using a Boolean phase to search the literature using EBSCOhost's Education Research Complete from January 1995 to April 20, 2020, using the *Education* subject specific database. The Boolean phrase included the following: lead* OR principal* OR "school lead*" OR admin* AND "student* with disab*" OR "special educat*" or special need* AND inclus* OR "inclus* educat*" OR "inclus* class*" or "inclus* school." This electronic search resulted in 3,212 results after exact duplicates were removed.

To identify case studies, we completed a sub-search of the initial 3,212 articles, using the phrase "case stud*," which resulted in 261 articles from the 3,212 electronic articles. Second, we read the titles and abstracts of each of the 261 articles, eliminating 246 that did not meet the selection criteria (e.g., international studies [Sperandio & Klerks, 2007]; secondary schools [Olson et al., 2016]). In the third and final step, we eliminated seven additional articles after reviewing the purpose and methods sections of each article, as four focused on teachers with minimal information about the principal's role in inclusion (i.e., Causton-Theoharis et al., 2011; Downing et al., 2004; Fisher et al., 2000; Ryndak et al., 2007), one aggregated findings across case studies (Guzmán, 1997), and two focused on ineffective leaders (i.e., DeMatthews, 2015b; Mamlin, 1999). Thus, eight articles met the selection criteria. Three of the eight articles included two case studies (e.g., DeMatthews and Mawhinney, 2014, Hoppey et al., 2018, Mayrowetz & Weinstein, 1999[1]), for a total of 11 cases across the eight articles. Finally, we conducted an ancestral search, reviewing the reference list of each article and no additional studies were found.

Case Study Analyses

In the first reading of each case study, we identified actions that principals made to support inclusion (e.g., stated a 'moral purpose' for inclusion, "embedded professional development (PD) in 30 minute daily meetings," "progress monitoring," "teacher planning teams") across each study. Next, we reorganized these actions conceptually around five actions (see findings below). In this second stage, we reread each of the 11 case studies and recorded specific principal actions for each case study in an analysis chart by theme. For example, in analyzing the action "increasing capacity," the 11 case studies were listed, and actions related to building capacity were recorded for each case study. These charts provided the data for each finding.

Overview of Studies

These case studies included descriptions of principal leadership in inclusive elementary schools. Table 2.1 provides an overview of each case study, outlining the characteristics of each school.

Three of the schools served urban communities and the majority of students in these schools received Free and Reduced Meals (FARMs) (e.g., DeMatthews & Mawhinney, 2014; Hoppey et al., 2018). Other schools had a relatively small percentage of students receiving FARMs: 6% (DeMatthews, 2015a), 16% (Hoppey et al., 2018), and 28% (Mayrowetz & Weinstein, 1999). One school was characterized as a suburban school (McLeskey et al., 2014), another as a rural school (Hoppey & McLeskey, 2013), and some were described as a small school district (Mayrowetz & Weinstein, 1999), or a small school in a low populated area (e.g., Waldron et al., 2011).

Schools also varied in diversity, with some serving all or a vast majority of students of color (DeMatthews & Mawhinney, 2014), while others were less diverse, with about 25% students of color (e.g., Hoppey et al., 2018). Most of the schools that reported state grades had "A" ratings (DeMatthews et al., 2015a; Hoppey et al., 2018; McLeskey et al., 2014) or A and B ratings (Hoppey & McLeskey, 2013), while two schools had "F" ratings when the principals began, and one was characterized as "unfixable" (DeMatthews & Mawhinney, 2014, p. 857).

Researchers used varied theories or frameworks to situate their studies, including social justice leadership (DeMatthews & Mawhinney, 2014), cultural and organizational theory of schools (Hoppey et al., 2018), Heller and Firestone's (1995) leadership function theory and distributed leadership (Mayrowetz & Weinstein, 1999), and leadership frameworks (Hoppey & McLeskey, 2013; McLeskey et al., 2014; Waldron et al., 2011). All studies incorporated interviews and observations of meetings and/or classrooms and some included documents, such as agendas or minutes of meetings (e.g., DeMatthews, 2015a; DeMatthews & Mawhinney, 2014). Qualitative analyses included phenomenology (Hoppey & McLeskey, 2013), Patton's (2002) theme identification (McLeskey et al., 2014; Waldron et al., 2011), and leadership actions and interactions (e.g., DeMatthews, 2015a), among others.

Findings: Principal Actions that Support Inclusive Schools

Principals engaged in varied and complementary actions as they supported inclusion for students with disabilities. They (1) shared their commitment to an inclusive school, (2) redesigned the school for inclusion, (3) increased capacity for inclusion, (4) supported professional collaboration and effective instruction, and (5) monitored inclusive progress and outcomes while addressing challenges. These five actions were not discrete or sequential, rather they occurred in unique ways depending on the context and needs of the specific schools. For example, building capacity occurred throughout the year as teams redesigned the school for inclusion and as they began to use new practices (DeMatthews & Mawhinney, 2014; Mayrowetz & Weinstein, 1999). These actions and specific examples of each are summarized in Table 2.2.

Across all studies, principals worked to develop positive and trusting relationships with others as they engaged in these five inclusive actions. They also relied on others' expertise and sought to encourage teacher leadership (e.g., DeMatthews, 2015a; Mayrowetz & Weinstein, 1999; McLeskey et al., 2014) by engaging others in inclusive planning, decision-making, and problem-solving. As we describe the actions of principals, we refer to them by the name used in the case study (e.g., Principal Kraft, Principal Charlene). Given that Mayrowetz and Weinstein did not use names, we refer to the principals as the primary (grades K-2) or the intermediate principal (grades 3–6).

Shared Their Commitment to an Inclusive School

The moral and ethical dimensions of leadership (Sergiovanni, 1996) were evident as principals across these studies viewed inclusion as the right thing to do (e.g., Hoppey & McLeskey, 2013; Hoppey et al., 2018; Keyes et al., 1999; McLeskey et al., 2014; Waldron et al., 2011), and openly voiced their commitment to others, including parents, teachers, and the school community. Principals'

Table 2.1 Context of Elementary Case Studies: Purpose, Theoretical Model, Settings, and Methods

	Purpose/theoretical model	*Context, setting, and respondents*	*Methodology*
DeMatthews, 2015a	Examined how a principal and a teacher team "engaged in leadership activities to increase inclusivity and academic performance..." (p. 1011) Theoretical model/framework: Distributed leadership and collaboration	High-performing, well-resourced, diverse, school in high-income neighborhood in large urban district; recognized for inclusion. One leader of larger study of 5 principals met criteria: (1) committed to inclusion, (2) used distributed leadership, (3) effectively supported SWD. Dewey Elementary School, about 280 students 28% students of color, 4% of students eligible for FARM "A" rating	Qualitative case study (in-depth interviews of principal and staff over school year, multiple observations in varied settings, e.g., classrooms, meetings) in presence of principal. Documents; Identified leader actions, approaches, orientations, communication, and technical skills Analysis: Nvivo 9 software used to code date related to: 1) school administration practices, 2) school administration philosophies, 3) connections and rapport with employees, 4) knowledge and implementation of including students with disabilities
DeMatthews & Mawhinney, 2014	Studied "how two principals enacted social justice leadership" (p. 844) to support inclusion; Investigated principals' sense-making about inclusion Theoretical model/framework: Social justice and inclusion leadership	Two urban elementary schools in low income areas with frequent crimes. Lane Elementary, about 230 students 100% of color, and >90% of students eligible for FARM "F" rating year before study Hall Elementary, about 250 students 95% students of color, and >90% of students eligible for FARM "F" rating year before study	Qualitative case studies Multiple interviews of principals, document analysis (e.g., agendas, policies); Multiple observations of principals/staff (e.g., classrooms, IEP meetings, conferences, community); Analysis: Nvivo 9 software to code data related to 1) tangible practices of inclusion, 2) leaders' dedication and relationship to inclusion, 3) connections and rapport with employees, 4) knowledge and implementation of including students with disabilities, and 5) school district's guidelines, previous practices, and inclusion strategies
Hoppey, Black & Mickelson, 2018	Reviewed characteristics of two inclusive schools as they worked toward becoming more inclusive Framework: Cultural and organizational qualities of inclusive schools	Two high-performing elementary schools that had improved inclusive services selected from a metropolitan district with 68,000 students. Clark School, about 850 students 25% students of color, and 75% of students eligible for FARM "A"	Qualitative case studies Semi-structured interviews with principals; Focus group interviews with staff with varied orientations toward inclusion (14 participants at one school, 11 participants at another school);

		rating for most years Early adoptor of RtI and PBS Shady Lake about 750 students 26% students of color; 16% eligible for FARM "A" rating for 8 of 10 last years	Classroom practices observed for 96 hours; Analysis: Wolcott three pronged method
Hoppey & McLeskey, 2013	Examined role of principal in school change to support inclusion. Framework: Key elements of effective principal leadership that supports inclusive leadership and change	Rural elementary school in Florida with an exemplar of inclusion practices. Hawk's Nest Elementary, about 460 students 39% students of color 54% eligible for FARM Repeated "A" or "B" ratings from state	Qualitative case study over 1 year focused on principal's lived experiences and included interviews, observations throughout school year. In-depth interviews and weekly observations were frequent throughout data collection. Analysis: phenomenology used to analyze the principal's actions and make meaning of the data and draw conclusions
Keyes et al. 1999	Explored and depicted "the role of administrative leadership within an inclusive elementary school" (p. 206). Theoretical framework: Spirituality and organizational leadership	Elementary school in a midwest, moderate-sized urban school district with a high number of students from low socioeconomic backgrounds Woodland Hills Elementary, about 480 students 38% students of color	Critical ethnology, "built on active participation of the researched and the researcher" (p. 207) 38 participant interviews 27 classroom observation days, including 3 staff development sessions about inclusion Data gathered at additional events (e.g., graduation). Analysis: Transcripts of discussions discussed with participants data analyzed to generate an original theory
Mayrowetz & Weinstein, 1999	Examined distributed leadership for inclusive school reform Theoretical framework: Heller and Firestone's (1995) "leadership function theory"	"Small [school] district in central New Jersey" (p. 428) well known for its inclusion efforts District served 1450 students 39% students of color 28% eligible for FARM	Qualitative case study 25+ semistructured interviews, 12 formal and informal staff meeting observations, 4 student case studies, and document analysis Analysis: NUD*IST software used to code data related to leadership attributes, type of school, and job position of participants
McLeskey et al. 2014	Examined the qualities that supported high student achievement in an inclusive elementary school	Small elementary school located in low populated area in Florida Creekside Elementary School, about 480 students 32% students of color	Qualitative case study 22 interviews with teachers and administrators who applied the inclusive program.

(*Continued*)

Table 2.1 (Continued)

	Purpose/theoretical model	*Context, setting, and respondents*	*Methodology*
	Framework: Inclusion and excellent outcomes can co-exist	52% eligible for FARM "A" rating from state	• 13 initial interviews • 9 follow-up interviews, 10 observations of inclusive teaching Analysis: Patton's (2002) theme identification process which involved 4 cycles of theme development
Waldron et al., 2011	Examined the role of the principal in "developing and sustaining a highly effective, inclusive school" (p. 52) Framework: Principal plays a key role in ensuring students receive an inclusive and quality education-	Small elementary school located in low populated area Creekside Elementary School, about 480 students 32% students of color	Qualitative case study Interviewed teachers, administrators Observed classrooms Examined documents (e.g., school improvement plan, state and federal accountability reports) Analysis: Patton's (2002) theme identification process which involved 4 cycles of theme development

Table 2.2 Principals' Actions to Support Inclusive Schools

Actions	*Examples from Case Studies*
Shared their commitment to an inclusive school	• Voiced their commitment to an inclusive school and a quality education for students with disabilities • Identified the lack of inclusive opportunities and inadequate instruction for students with disabilities • Discussed concerns about the progress of students with disabilities and the need for change • Challenged beliefs about students with disabilities and inclusion
Redesigned the school for inclusion	• Created planning teams of teachers, staff, and stakeholders to lead, design, and support inclusion • Developed a vision to guide inclusion • Recruited specific teachers for initial inclusive placements • Identified students with disabilities to be included, revised IEPs, and created class rosters • Created schedules to support teacher collaboration and co-teaching • Developed inclusive models and teacher and paraeducators' roles • Encouraged continued conversations about inclusion, encouraged staff input and listened to concerns
Increased capacity for inclusion	• Focused on recruitment and retention of teachers to support inclusion • Set priorities for professional development (e.g., behavior management, differentiation, co-teaching) • Used varied approaches, including formal and informal opportunities for PD • Encouraged informal teacher learning, professional learning communities, and teacher leadership • Engaged academic coaches for Response-to-Instruction (RtI) • Supported participation in formal PD and coursework
Supported professional collaboration and effective instruction	• Supported collaborative planning and co-teaching • Created an environment of high expectations for student learning • Incorporated RtI and Positive Behavioral Supports (PBS) to monitor student progress and support instructional decision-making • Listened to teachers and supported high-quality instruction through specific supports (e.g., behavior, materials)
Monitored inclusive progress and outcomes	• Informally gathered data about inclusive progress by communication with staff and parents • Tracked student progress and performance on state tests over time • Monitored inclusive placements and dealt with problems and constraints

commitment to inclusion was evident in three of the principals who were former special educators, as they were knowledgeable about inclusive education (i.e., DeMatthews & Mawhinney, 2014; Keyes et al., 1999), as well as those principals who were just learning about inclusion (e.g., Mayrowetz & Weinstein, 1999).

Principals expressed their commitments in varied ways. Principal Smith stated, "whatever student that comes to our door…regardless of disability…we will serve him or her well…" (DeMatthews, 2015a p. 1017). Principal Kraft believed "a school can serve all students in the regular class if they are thoughtful, have a strong team, and use data to drive their instruction" (DeMatthews & Mawhinney,

2014, p. 858). Principal Richards stated a broader goal, to "meet *all* kid needs…it didn't turn into a *program* or a *fix* for one group, but how to meet the needs of *all* students and make everyone successful" (McLeskey et al., 2014, p. 63).

In schools documenting inclusive change, principals observed both the lack of inclusive opportunities and inadequate instruction for students with disabilities. Principal Richards stated that she observed students leave an effective general education classroom to go to an "ineffective situation [in a separate class] where they misbehaved, where they just got rote skills" (McLeskey et al., 2014, p. 64). Principal Kraft recognized that students with disabilities were taught primarily in segregated classrooms, and she expressed concerns about identical IEPs, low test scores, and the lack of differentiation, stating "these kids had been getting the short end of the stick" (DeMatthews & Mawhinney, 2014, p. 859). She also challenged teachers who believed that children with disabilities should be taught separately. Principal Jackson was concerned with the segregation of students with disabilities and the need to improve inclusive opportunities, stating, the typical classroom was "inflexible" and "overly focused on the kids who are at or near grade level" (DeMatthews & Mawhinney, 2014, p. 866). Principal Charlene observed that some teachers believed students with disabilities needed segregated classrooms and that "students needed to be ready for or worthy of inclusion" (Hoppey et al., 2018, p. 30).

Principals were strategic in how they began to move inclusion forward. Principal Charlene shared data with teachers, emphasizing the lack of improvement in students with disabilities and the need to try something different (Hoppey et al., 2018). She also involved teacher leaders in challenging the belief that "students needed to be ready for or worthy of inclusion" and argued that placing students in separate classrooms was not working as their "test scores were not improving" (Hoppey et al., 2018, p. 31). Principal Marta clearly shared her commitment to an inclusive school with school staff at the beginning of the year, then "allowed staff attrition and new hires to help create a supportive environment" (Keyes et al., 1999, p. 219).

In conclusion, principals across these effective inclusive schools were firmly committed to inclusion and identified concerns about the lack of inclusive opportunities as well as how some students with disabilities were taught. They shared their commitment to inclusion with staff and parents, challenging their assumptions and beliefs. These actions are consistent with "modelling aspirational and ethical practices" (Hitt & Tucker, 2016, p. 543) and were important to the initiation of inclusive change.

Redesigned the School for Inclusion

Principals gave time and energy to redesigning their school in ways that were consistent with and supportive of inclusion. In part, principals worked to help school staff understand what inclusion "meant for them in their context" (Hoppey et al., 2018, p. 31). Some principals created teams made up of varied individuals (e.g., general and special educators, parents, university faculty) to plan inclusion, set goals, problem-solve, and address concerns (e.g., DeMatthews & Mawhinney, 2014; Hoppey et al., 2018; Mayrowetz & Weinstein, 1999; McLeskey et al., 2014). Teachers often exercised leadership in these teams and helped shape inclusion in the school.

A few of the case studies suggested a specific vision that guided inclusion. Waldron et al. (2011) stated the vision was meeting the needs of all students, including those with disabilities, and including them in general education whenever possible. Mayrowetz and Weinstein (1999) described how "an enthusiastic group of state-trained supporters was responsible for selling the vision at the primary and intermediate schools" (p. 433). The vision at the primary school described how the plan for inclusion would unfold and the procedures necessary for getting started (e.g., begin with a volunteer, include a child they felt would be successful). Although there was evidence that school staff across the case studies became committed to inclusion, a vision was not always explicitly addressed (e.g., DeMatthews, 2015a; DeMatthews & Mawhinney, 2014).

Principals also sought the support of teachers who were willing to teach in inclusive classrooms. Principal Kraft faced challenges because teachers did not want to change their practices, so she recruited a teacher at each grade level willing to work to develop an inclusive model (McLeskey et al., 2014). One teacher did not see herself as being able to meet the needs of students with disabilities, but Principal Marta was able to convince her to participate (Keyes et al., 1999). Principal Beverly asked specific teachers to help her envision how they might include a student with behavior challenges prior to discussions with the entire staff (Hoppey et al., 2018).

School teams also made decisions about which students with disabilities would participate in inclusive classrooms as they hoped to create successful experiences for students and teachers. In primary school, they initially included a first grader with academic strengths and physical disabilities. Later, they included students with academic and behavior challenges and, eventually, students who were two or more years behind their assigned grade level (Mayrowetz & Weinstein, 1999). In another school, Principal Jackson worked with a special and general education teacher team to review the data of students in self-contained classrooms to determine which students could immediately benefit from inclusion and they revised their IEPs to reflect these new placements (DeMatthews & Mawhinney, 2014).

Creating an inclusive school required revision of schedules to support collaboration and co-teaching. Principal Kraft created a time when special educators and general education teachers could collaborate "to develop new class rosters, a new bell schedule to allow for co-planning and co-teaching, and the development of new teacher expectations for how inclusion would strengthen instructional delivery" (DeMatthews & Mawhinney, 2014, p. 860). McLeskey et al. (2014) found that effective use of the schedule increased staff transparency regarding co-teaching assignments, co-planning times, and equitable resource distribution based on students' needs. Additionally, some principals reorganized the school schedule to provide more time for co-teaching and to support data-driven decision-making processes (Hoppey & McLeskey, 2013).

Some of the case studies described new and changing inclusive models and teacher roles. McLeskey et al. (2014) described how special education teachers and paraeducators who previously taught in separate special education classrooms were reassigned to inclusive classrooms to support students who needed instruction in reading, math, and writing. These special and general educators worked collaboratively with general educators, supporting all students struggling with basic academic skills. Principal Charlene and teacher leaders initially created an inclusive model that clustered support for students with disabilities in selected classrooms (Hoppey et al., 2018). In this arrangement, specific general education classrooms were assigned high proportions of children with disabilities, with the idea that they could use staff resources efficiently in these classrooms. However, eventually, they decided to move toward natural proportions, placing students with disabilities in classrooms across the school. In this revised arrangement, general educators worked together to address student needs using Response to Intervention (RtI)[2] and Positive Behavioral Supports (PBS), with special educators providing additional help.

Teachers did not always welcome inclusive changes, and some of those at high-rated schools did not welcome change (DeMatthews, 2015a; Hoppey et al., 2018). Principals created opportunities for teachers to voice their concerns and discussed ways of addressing them (e.g., DeMatthews, 2015a; DeMatthews & Mawhinney 2014; Mayrowetz & Weinstein, 1999). Some principals made it clear that inclusion was not negotiable; however, they sought cooperation from teachers and allowed flexibility in determining how inclusion worked within the school (e.g., Keyes et al., 1999; Waldron et al., 2011). Many teachers who initially resisted inclusion came to support it over time, while in the intermediate school, several people continued to have "misgivings" about inclusion (Mayrowetz & Weinstein, 1999, p. 442).

In conclusion, principals worked with teams to redesign the school to include students with disabilities. Some started with small goals, such as including one student, and then gradually increased the number of students with more complex needs over time (Mayrowetz & Weinstein, 1999). Similarly, others recruited volunteers (DeMatthews & Mawhinney, 2014) or persuaded reluctant teachers to try inclusion (Keyes et al., 1999). Clearly, moving to more inclusive environments required changes in IEPs, schedules, teaching arrangements, teacher roles, and the distribution of special education teachers and paraprofessionals across inclusive classrooms. Throughout the redesign process, principals demonstrated a high level of consideration for staff by being available, listening to their concerns, participating in meetings, and giving them a voice in defining what inclusion looked like in the school.

Increased Capacity for Inclusion

A key responsibility of inclusive leaders is to ensure that teachers and paraprofessionals are ready to teach diverse students, including those with disabilities. As initiators of inclusive reform, principals were the architects of the planning process, as they worked with others to build capacity among faculty and staff. Effective principals used multifaceted approaches to build capacity for inclusion focusing on teacher hiring and retention, supporting both individual teachers and larger groups (e.g., all special education and general education teachers, grade level teams), and incorporating both informal and formal professional development (PD). Although most PD was school-based, staff sometimes participated in formal PD through conferences or university coursework.

Several principals recognized the importance of building capacity through hiring teachers, paraprofessionals, and staff who were open to inclusion. For example, Principal Smith emphasized selective recruiting and hiring and the need to retain teachers and related services personnel (DeMatthews, 2015a). Another principal emphasized the importance of hiring teachers and paraprofessionals who were a "good fit" for the school's shared vision of inclusion (Waldron et al., 2011, p. 55). Principal Marta also discussed the importance of attracting and retaining staff who were "able to see each child's gifts, and in turn develop opportunities for these gifts to be shared with other members of the school community" (Keyes et al., 1999, p. 218).

To increase teacher capacity for inclusion, principals did not wait for teachers to come to them with requests for PD, rather they were observant and decisive about setting priorities to create conditions that would support inclusion. For example, Principal Kraft quickly recognized that student discipline and classroom management would impede progress toward inclusion and began the year with an intensive focus of time and resources on supporting positive student behavior (DeMatthews & Mawhinney, 2014). She also observed students who were disruptive in general education classrooms and believed some of the behavior stemmed from instruction that was inappropriate for their needs. She worked with the district and other schools to support PD that addressed differentiated instruction, developed a teacher resource library, and brought staff from other schools to support those learning to co-teach. In addition to differentiated instruction and co-teaching, other schools addressed evidence-based teaching practices, multi-tiered supports, literacy, writing, and mathematics, among others (e.g., DeMatthews, 2015a; Hoppey et al., 2018; Hoppey & McLeskey, 2013; Keyes et al., 1999).

Principals encouraged the development of learning communities that supported ongoing, informal opportunities for teachers to learn from each other. In these schools, teachers shaped their own development by addressing challenges that were part of their daily work through learning together, sharing new strategies for teaching, reviewing student data to inform their instructional decisions, and engaging in problem-solving (e.g., Hoppey & McLeskey, 2013; McLeskey et al., 2014; Waldron et al., 2011). Principals also viewed these collaborative efforts as an opportunity to build teacher leadership so teachers could proactively identify and solve instructional challenges and other problems (e.g., Mayrowetz & Weinstein, 1999; DeMatthews, 2015a).

Principals also created other informal opportunities for teachers to learn. Principal Marta created spaces for teacher conversations regarding the use of instructional practices, such as Cognitively Guided Instruction (CGI) in math (Keyes et al., 1999). Principal Keys dedicated faculty meetings as a time for teachers to share teaching strategies (e.g., Keyes et al., 1999, p. 221). Principal Smith encouraged teachers to observe and coach each other (DeMatthews, 2015a). Other principals supported teachers by maintaining open-door policies, responding to teachers in impromptu inquiries about effective and ineffective practices (e.g., DeMatthews, 2015a; Keyes et al., 1999). As a result, principals were able to learn about teachers' needs and connect them to learning resources.

In a few schools, coaches and specialists were hired to support teachers. In one district, academic coaches were allocated to support teacher learning as they began to use RtI. As Hoppey et al. (2018) emphasized, these coaches were important to helping teachers understand and learn how to use new data tools to make instructional decisions and incorporate new teaching practices. In addition, ongoing teacher conversations about data were part of this PD effort as they worked together to plan instruction for students in general education classrooms. As Hoppey et al. (2018) stated, "making instructional changes to the ways teaching and learning are implemented in classrooms is paramount and at the core of successful inclusive reform" (p. 32). Principal Jackson secured funding to hire PD specialists to provide teachers with specific preparation in differentiated instruction, co-teaching, assessment systems, among others. These specialists observed and provided teachers with feedback on a monthly basis.

Although PD was often informal and school-based, others attended conferences or completed relevant university courses. Mayrowetz and Weinstein (1999) described how teams comprised of individuals with varied roles (e.g., principal, teachers, parent, school psychologist) participated in a State Department of Education program about inclusion. Individual teachers were asked to return to campus and provide PD at their schools. Principal Tom worked with a local university to design an advanced degree program that fostered teacher leadership, reflection about teaching practices and provided a path to national board certification (Hoppey & McLeskey, 2013).

In conclusion, developing capacity for inclusion was a priority for principals and they provided formal, informal and impromptu actions to support teacher learning. In some instances, principals' observations led them to identify areas of improvement and take immediate next steps. Principals often participated in PD with teachers, demonstrating their commitment to inclusion and their own learning (e.g., DeMatthews, 2015a; Mayrowetz & Weinstein, 1999; Waldron et al., 2011). In other cases, principals engaged in conversations with teachers to identify areas for PD. As part of these activities, principal worked to build trust and positive relationships as they supported staff learning.

Supported Collaboration and Effective Instruction

Principals recognized the importance of collaboration for effective instruction, supporting special and general education teachers' joint planning and co-teaching to meet the instructional and behavioral needs of students with disabilities. An initial challenge was creating opportunities for collaboration as some teachers either did not collaborate or were reluctant to do so (e.g., DeMatthews & Mawhinney, 2014). Principal Kraft met regularly with the special and general educators who co-taught to see how collaboration was progressing, giving them an opportunity to discuss their needs and express concerns. Principal Jackson set new expectations, encouraging teachers to share lessons and give each other feedback to create an environment where they would feel comfortable working together (DeMatthews & Mawhinney, 2014).

Collaboration was an integral part of a high-quality instructional program at Creekside Elementary, where Principal Richards and the staff worked in a supportive community, held high expectations for student learning, and engaged in ongoing conversations to address the needs of challenging students (McLeskey et al., 2014). At Creekside, high-quality instruction included well-prepared teachers with clear learning objectives and well-behaved students who participated in varied and engaging activities. Principal Richards explained that instructional support was provided not just to students with disabilities but also to all students who struggled in the classroom. She stated: "support might include providing explicit instruction to a small, homogeneous group of students...supporting students working in collaborative groups as part of station teaching...or teaching a large group while the classroom teacher provided this small-group support" (McLeskey et al., 2014, p. 64).

Principals in several inclusive schools used progress monitoring to gather data about how students were progressing over time (e.g., Hoppey et al., 2018; McLeskey et al., 2014; Waldron et al., 2011). Principal Charlene supported universal screening, RtI, and PBS, stating, "RtI and inclusion are one and the same" (Hoppey et al., 2018, p. 35), as it provided a shared language, brought staff together, and allowed them to monitor progress and respond to individual student needs. Hoppey et al. (2018) stated that "teacher leadership, collaborative planning, and data-informed decision making" took root as teachers had tools to identify "what the discrepancies are with students" (p. 36). McLeskey et al. also described how Principal Richards worked with staff to create their own data system based on their own curricular expectations, allowing them to monitor student progress across time. Thus the data system was used by all teachers and "changed the frame of reference" (McLeskey et al., 2014, p. 68) as they were expected to look at every child's gains and make instructional decisions accordingly. Principal Richards also used progress monitoring data to distribute resources in areas they were most needed (i.e., placement of co-teachers, paraeducators) and to determine PD priorities (Waldron et al., 2011). She also shared data with parents, showing what was working well and celebrating children's progress.

Supporting positive student behavior was also a major challenge for principals and teachers. In addition to PD focused on behavior, principals worked individually with some teachers to coach them and develop their confidence related to classroom management (e.g., DeMatthews, 2015a; DeMatthews & Mawhinney, 2014; Hoppey et al., 2018). Principal Marta developed a support team, called the Eagle Team, to support teachers who struggled with students with behavioral problems. The Eagle Team was comprised of staff without direct student contact and members could be called to a classroom and "substitute for the teacher, who could leave the room with the student to develop a solution" (Keyes et al., 1999, p. 220).

Principals communicated with staff informally about collaboration, instruction, and student behavior through individual discussions and varied types of meetings. Principal Kraft met regularly with teachers who co-taught to discuss their progress and concerns, which allowed her to learn how she could support them (DeMatthews & Mawhinney, 2014). Listening to teachers was also important as teachers moved toward data-based instruction and as they shared their struggles and questions (Hoppey et al., 2018). Teachers also felt Principal Richards was responsive to their concerns and needs, as she was prompt in providing supports, such as additional resources (Waldron et al., 2011).

In conclusion, principals sought to support teacher collaboration for effective instruction as all in the school shared the responsibility of teaching students with disabilities. Increasing expectations for students with disabilities was a priority as staff learned to address students' needs in inclusive classrooms. About half of the case studies described incorporating progress monitoring systems, which helped inform instructional decisions. Principals also supported collaboration and instruction by listening, meeting regularly, and helping teachers acquire the resources they needed.

Monitored Inclusive Progress and Outcomes

In addition to the use of ongoing progress monitoring to gather data and adjust students' programs as described above, principals monitored outcomes by: (1) gathering information about how inclusion was proceeding through informal communication and regularly scheduled meetings, (2) comparing students' with disabilities performance on state assessments before and after inclusion, and (3) monitoring changes in inclusive placements and making adjustments as needed. Monitoring was a crucial dimension of leadership, as it provided leaders with information about how inclusion was progressing, allowed them to identify needs, and consequently to determine how to support staff (Waldron et al., 2011). Some of these monitoring activities involved ongoing communication allowing for the constructive resolution of conflicts (Mayrowetz & Weinstein, 1999). In addition to monitoring, we describe positive and negative outcomes that occurred inclusive change.

Principals communicated with staff and parents informally through individual discussions and varied types of meetings. Mayrowetz and Weinstein (1999) provided an in-depth description of how monitoring was distributed across all school staff as principals, teachers, parents, special services personnel, and paraeducators (or paraprofessionals) shared in this responsibility. These researchers found that teachers "kept an ear to the ground"..."the principal monitored the parents of non-disabled children for complaints,"...and the psychologist "looked after the kids [who were included]" (p. 439). The psychologist in the primary school also held meetings every six weeks to evaluate the progress of each included child, and similar meetings occurred in the intermediate school. The intermediate principal also established regular action team meetings and monthly meetings to monitor inclusion and student progress (Mayrowetz & Weinstein, 1999). Action team meetings involved the parents, teacher, case manager, and principal in discussing student progress and reviewing students' plans in alignment with IEPs. Paraprofessionals (or paraeducators) also participated in monitoring through informal exchanges with teachers and parents, with some sending a daily journal to parents who responded with suggestions, queries, and questions (Mayrowetz & Weinstein, 1999).

A few studies documented the academic performance of students on state tests. McLeskey et al. (2014) studied Creekside Elementary because it was more inclusive than other schools in the district and state. In addition, the achievement of students with disabilities at Creekside Elementary exceeded local district and state averages, as did the achievement of students who were eligible for free or reduced lunch (52% of all students at Creekside). Comparing data from 2005–2006 to 2008–2009, students with disabilities' proficiency rates in reading increased from 30% to 69% and their proficiency rates in mathematics increased from 33% to 58%. DeMatthews and Mawhinney (2014) also included comparisons of students' performance on state achievement tests before and after inclusion. Although Principal Jackson noted some improvement on students' state tests after inclusion, she was not satisfied, yet still expressed optimism:

> "kids are happier and more kids are learning. Some of our kids are so low [on reading and mathematics assessments] that even a year and a half's worth of growth would not yield growth on the test after a year, but the test scores will come if we stay focused" (DeMatthews & Mawhinney, 2014, p. 869).

Although these case study schools showed progress toward inclusion, only a few researchers documented changes in service delivery (i.e., DeMatthews & Mawhinney, 2014; McLeskey et al., 2014; Waldron et al., 2011). The extent to which each school became more inclusive likely varied over time as students were both moved to or removed from inclusive settings. For example, some students with emotional and behavioral disorders (EBD) were moved back to special education settings as they were not responding to interventions and continued to disrupt classrooms (DeMatthews & Mawhinney, 2014). In some cases, students with disabilities were not given inclusive opportunities, as parents would not agree to inclusive placements (DeMatthews & Mawhinney, 2014).

It is encouraging that schools experienced other positive outcomes beyond those described above. These case studies document the development of caring schools (Hoppey & McLeskey, 2013), collaborative cultures (Hoppey & McLeskey, 2013; McLeskey et al., 2014; Waldron et al., 2011), and ongoing opportunities for teacher learning (DeMatthews & Mawhinney, 2014; McLeskey et al., 2014; Waldron et al., 2011).

At the same time, some principals encountered problems that interfered with their inclusive goals. Although some schools received substantial district support (Mayrowetz & Weinstein, 1999), other principals reported that district policies and conditions interfered with progress toward inclusion. Hoppey et al. (2018) described how staff at two schools were concerned about the placement of district self-contained classes for students with EBD and autism in their schools, as these segregated settings were inconsistent with their inclusive philosophy. To create more inclusive opportunities for these self-contained students, teachers would include them on a trial basis to see if they could be successful in an inclusive setting. Unfortunately, when trial inclusive placements were successful, the district required that these students be returned to their "home" schools, where they had previously been unsuccessful.

Problems with increasing enrollments also created problems for schools. Principal Kraft observed that new students enrolling throughout the year made it difficult to adequately serve these additional students, creating a stressful situation for teachers (DeMatthews & Mawhinney, 2014). This led Principal Kraft to encourage parents of prospective students to enroll their children in other schools. Although this was not consistent with Principal Kraft's inclusive values, she believed it was the best option given the constraints they faced.

Principal Beverly's fear of losing a teacher became a reality because they identified fewer students with disabilities, leading to the reduction of one teacher. Although RtI was successful in increasing the ability of classroom teachers to meet students' needs, it did not reduce the teacher support needed to implement RtI (Hoppey et al., 2018). Budget constraints also forced other principals to make difficult choices (e.g., DeMatthews, 2015a; Hoppey et al., 2018), such as giving up an assistant principal to keep a teacher (DeMatthews & Mawhinney, 2014). Even with difficult challenges, principals and staff remained committed to inclusion.

In conclusion, these case studies provide examples of how principals used informal and formal monitoring to examine how inclusion was progressing, monitor student learning, and adjust service delivery. Other outcomes that were mentioned briefly included the development of caring schools, a collaborative culture, and ongoing opportunities to learn through informal and formal PD. At the same time, some of the case studies described problems and constraints that kept schools from meeting their goals, yet, the principals and staff persisted despite these challenges, sometimes making difficult compromises. As DeMatthews and Mawhinney (2014) stated, change may be slow: "…the gritty experiences of social justice work, particularly under the most difficult circumstances, do not always result in positive outcomes, at least not in the short term" (p. 875).

Discussion

In summary, principals engaged in similar actions as they set a course for effective inclusion, even though the school contexts varied substantially. They shared their commitment to an inclusive school with teachers and parents, often challenging others' assumptions about students with disabilities. They redesigned the school for inclusion, facilitating buy-in from others, forming planning teams, and creating the structures needed to implement inclusion (e.g., co-teaching schedules, modifying teacher roles). They listened to teachers' and parents' concerns and worked with them to solve problems. Each principal realized the importance of teachers who were willing and ready to teach students with disabilities in inclusive classrooms. Thus they recruited teachers who were prepared for and/or would support inclusion. Principals also worked to increase capacity within their schools by supporting informal learning and formal PD in a range of areas, such as co-teaching, managing behavior, multi-tiered supports (RtI, PBS), and differentiating instruction. Principals supported instructional effectiveness by increasing expectations for students with disabilities, facilitating ongoing teacher collaboration and co-teaching, supporting the use of differentiated instruction, and using progress monitoring to support instructional decisions. Finally, principals monitored the progress and outcomes of inclusion by formally and informally assessing how inclusion was proceeding in the school, troubleshooting when problems occurred, and assessing how inclusion was influencing individual students and achievement outcomes over time (DeMatthews & Mawhinney, 2014; McLeskey et al., 2014; Waldron et al., 2011). Principals engaged others as they led, encouraging them to help shape inclusion in the school. They were firm about supporting inclusion and engaging with staff in positive ways, even when there were disagreements.

The above actions of the Principal are consistent with leadership syntheses about effective principal leadership (e.g., Hitt & Tucker, 2016; Leithwood et al., 2008) and current guidance about inclusive schools. Principals' actions were consistent with at least some of the recommended practices outlined by the Professional Standards for Educational Leaders (Council of Chief State School Officers (CCSSO) & CEEDAR Center, 2015; National Policy Board for Educational Administration, 2015) and the guidance document about leadership for inclusive schools (see link in Table 2.3). The latter was developed by the Council of Chief State School Officers (CCSSO) and the Collaboration for Effective Educator Development, Accountability, and Reform (CEEDAR). Evidence from these case studies suggests that principals worked to "ensure a commitment" to students with disabilities, possessed an "ethical mindset to identify, interpret, and manage the ethical dilemmas in leadership for students with disabilities" (PSEL 2), held "asset-based rather than deficit-based perspectives of students" (PSEL 3), and "gave student with disabilities opportunities to achieve within the general education curriculum using a multi-tiered system of support" (PSEL 4).

Moving an inclusive agenda forward also requires interpersonal skills, which are consistent with PSEL 2. Principals were visible in the inclusive effort and developed productive and trusting relationships with others (PSEL standard 2). In one example, Hoppey and McLeskey (2013) described how Principal Tom sought to "lubricate the human machinery" as he personally invested in teachers and sought to "improve the lives of teachers and students so they can do their best work" (p. 253). Principal Marta's leadership was described by staff as empowering as well as "ethical, caring, humble, patient, and loving" (Keyes et al., 1999, p. 221), which is consistent with her belief in spirituality as the core of her leadership. DeMatthews (2015a) described how Principal Smith was highly visible in the school, checking in with teachers frequently to understand their views and support positive relationships. She also demonstrated transparent leadership, supported democratic decision-making and teacher leadership, and had an open-door policy that allowed teachers and staff access to her during school or after hours.

Although some principals received district support (e.g., Mayrowetz & Weinstein, 1999), others struggled with district policies and practices over which they had little control. Hoppey et al. (2018) described the placement of district-self-contained classes in their schools that were in opposition to their inclusive philosophy. They also experienced a reduction in staff due to success with RtI, losing a teacher that supported the program. In addition, growth in the school population added to teachers' responsibilities, but resources were not provided to support additional students. Budget constraints forced difficult choices because two schools were less resourced than the others included in this review (e.g., DeMatthews & Mawhinney, 2014). Given that challenges will inevitably occur, it is important to note that principals created opportunities to celebrate successes, as noting successes may help motivate staff to continue their inclusive work (Waldron et al., 2011). Mayrowetz and Weinstein (1999) also described the way parents, teachers, principals, and aides worked together in the primary and intermediate schools, encouraging each other, and recognizing each other's efforts. This collaboration was an important form of support that helped school community members through trying times.

Table 2.3 Open Educational Resources Relevant to Inclusive Leadership

Type	*Resource & Source*	*Purpose & Description*	*URL*
Standards for inclusive leadership	**PSEL 2015 and Promoting Principal Leadership (PSEL) for the Success of Students with Disabilities**	Interprets the PSEL standards, outlining their meaning for principal leadership	Guidance Document URL https://www.ccsso.org/sites/default/files/2017-10/PSELforSWDs01252017_0.pdf
	Developed through collaboration between Council of Chief State School Officers (CCSSO) and the Collaboration for Effective Educator Development, Accountability, and Reform (CEEDAR) National Center	Executive summary and user guide outline applications of the PSEL guidance document for inclusive leadership, including State Education Agencies, educator effectiveness, regional centers, and leadership preparation programs	Executive Summary and User Guide https://ccsso.org/sites/default/files/2017-10/PSELforSWDsExecSummaryandUserGuide01252017_0.pdf
Leadership practices	**IRIS Module: Creating an inclusive school environment**	Defines inclusion and why it is important, provides models and actions that leaders can take to create and sustain inclusive environments.	IRIS Centerhttps://iris.peabody.vanderbilt.edu
	IRIS is a National Center that offers open educational resources that translate research to practice that focus on improving outcomes, especially for struggling learners and those with disabilities	Includes numerous other modules relevant to inclusive leadership	
	Swift Education Center National technical assistance center that builds whole system capacity to improve outcomes for all students.	Addresses policy structure and practice that supports inclusive schools, including administrative leadership, multi-tiered systems of support, among others.	https://swiftschools.org
Leadership preparation	**School leadership for students with disabilities, content enhancement module (CEM)** Developed through the CEEDAR National Center	This seven-part resource addresses school leadership for effective inclusive schools so students with disabilities have opportunities to achieve positive life outcomes. This resource includes course materials in seven areas and may be used in university courses, PD, or for self-study.	CEEDAR innovation configurationhttps://ceedar.education.ufl.edu/cems/leadership/ Other CEM modules are also relevant to inclusive leadership

Teaching practices for students with disabilities	**High leverage practices for teachers of students with disabilities** Council for Exceptional Children writing team and approved through CEC	These are 22 effective practices for teaching students with disabilities in the four areas of:collaboration, assessment, social/ emotional/ behavioral, instruction	https://ceedar.education.ufl.edu/wp-content/uploads/2017/07/CEC-HLP-Web.pdf
	IRIS Resource on High Leverage Practices	This resource links specific high leverage practices to IRIS resources, which provide relevant material to understanding and using these practices	https://iris.peabody.vanderbilt.edu/resources/high-leverage-practices/

At the same time, descriptions about service delivery and improved student achievement do not really help us understand how inclusion made a difference to individual students. The lack of knowledge about the specific impact of inclusion on students is perhaps not surprising, given this is a leadership study. A strength of the Mayrowetz and Weinstein (1999) study is that they provided a description of how shared leadership, expertise, resources, and professional and family collaboration made a difference for three children in the two elementary schools over time, considering these students' experiences and progress.

These case studies demonstrated actions principals took to move the inclusive agenda forward, as they competently assessed their current contexts and worked with teacher leaders in determining how to proceed. We cannot assume these case study principals are typical, as prior research suggests some principals are not prepared for (e.g., Billingsley & Banks, 2019; Fowler et al., 2019; Williams et al., 2013), are confused about, and/or are reluctant to engage in inclusive leadership (Sumbera et al., 2014).

Setting the Course for Effective Inclusion

Implications for Leadership and Teacher Preparation

Principals, district, and state education agency (SEA) leaders need opportunities to understand the meaning of inclusion, why it is important, and understand what is known about promoting inclusion and high-quality instruction for students with disabilities, including the use of RtI and PBS. Teachers also need opportunities to learn about supporting inclusion and how to collaborate to address the needs of students with disabilities and other struggling learners. We consider the implications of these case studies for leadership preparation and PD for each of these groups.

Principal Preparation

These case studies have important implications for how principals are professionally prepared and supported. In addition to identifying a repertoire of leadership actions that facilitated inclusive schools, these case studies illustrate how principals used these actions within specific contexts and how they worked with others to solve problems. Unfortunately, many principals still report learning about special education, disability, and inclusive practices on the job (Wakeman et al., 2006). Thus, principal preparation program faculty need to more comprehensively integrate special education and inclusion content into their coursework and clinical experiences. Rather than only covering special education-related topics in an educational law course, preparation programs should audit their entire program of study to ensure that students learn about addressing the needs of students with disabilities in inclusive settings through school improvement teacher supervision and other related coursework and field experiences.

Given that each of these principals firmly supported inclusion, preparation program faculty need to evaluate how well they are preparing principals to take leadership to support inclusive schools. Recent findings suggest that leadership preparation can make a difference in helping principals develop inclusive values. Sumbera et al. (2014) found that principals who successfully implemented the LRE mandate of IDEA (2004) attributed their success to university programs, stating that preparation helped shape their philosophies, attitudes, and abilities, which helped them enact these mandates. Similarly, DeMatthews et al. (2019) found that six practicing principals "recognized how students with disabilities were marginalized," and credited their preparation programs for helping them develop inclusive beliefs and values. As one principal stated, "I learned that inclusion was not just about students, but about teachers and parents too. That was a big take away…it's hypocritical to exclude voices when you are trying to include students" (DeMatthews et al., 2019, p. 9).

Principal preparation program faculty should consider how clinical experiences and internships can provide aspiring leaders with opportunities to broaden their knowledge and experience in special education and how to lead inclusive schools. To do so, principal preparation faculty may need to consider collaboration and co-teaching with faculty in special education departments. In addition, university-district partnerships that focus on supporting students with disabilities can generate opportunities for aspiring leaders to gain clinical experiences and mentoring in inclusive schools, rather than at a random site or where the aspiring leader currently works. Prior research focused on university-district partnerships has highlighted the many benefits of collaboration and how such partnerships can support leadership development (Causton-Theoharis et al., 2011).

School districts can play a crucial role in supporting principals who may require support within their learning communities. As we noted in our review, many principals confronted unanticipated challenges and had to learn on the job and adjust their plans. They often relied on teachers, families, or consultants. District administrators can support principal learning by creating learning communities where principals can engage in collaborative inquiry around problems of practice that emerge during inclusive reforms. Such efforts can not only allow principals to investigate critical issues and learn about effective practices in other schools but can also build community and a support network for principals who struggle, confront resistance, or be forced to manage setbacks and disappointments. As a consequence, principals may be more likely to stay the course and persist given their support group and the added expertise that it provides.

Given that principals may have a limited background in teaching students with disabilities, they may benefit from understanding the special education teacher's high leverage practices. These 22 practices are designed to improve student achievement and are organized under four areas for K-12 teaching: Collaboration, Assessment, Social/Emotional/Behavioral, and Instruction (McLeskey et al., 2017). These practices provide a starting point for discussing collaboration and instruction for students with disabilities and other students who struggle to learn and may provide a shared language for teachers as they work together to include and teach students with disabilities.

District and State Leaders

Policymakers in state education agencies (SEAs) and district administrators can also support aspiring and current principals. SEAs set criteria for principal certification and have some oversight responsibilities over principal preparation programs. Several SEAs offer grants or incentives for programs to adopt residencies or new initiatives. SEAs could provide incentives for principal preparation programs to add components of leadership development that support inclusive reforms. In addition, superintendent certifications and doctoral programs can also be encouraged or incentivized to adopt similar programmatic adaptations. SEAs can also support inclusion by setting higher expectations for inclusion and monitoring racial disproportionality in segregated placements. SEAs can also offer grants and incentives for developing effective inclusive schools and provide opportunities via conferences and webinars to share effective practices and how practices have been adapted to meet local contexts.

Several case studies described how district administrators could serve as either advocate (e.g., Mayrowetz & Weinstein, 1999) or barriers to inclusion (e.g., DeMatthews & Mawhinney, 2014; Hoppey et al., 2018). Researchers suggest that districts can play an important role in school reform efforts or act as "implementation curbs" that fail to provide adequate resources or revise policies to support new initiatives (Honig & Venkateswaran, 2012). District administrators should audit their special education policies and initiatives and seek feedback from professionals in schools who are engaged in this work to ensure that principals and schools are well supported in their efforts to create or sustain inclusive schools. Policies or practices that make inclusion more difficult, such as maintaining self-contained classrooms and continuous out-of-boundary enrollment of students with disabilities into these self-contained classrooms, may require revision. Districts can also organize principal learning communities focused on inclusive practices and provide additional resources and support to schools, teachers, and families. In addition, superintendents and other central office administrators can be vocal advocates of inclusion, which has been found as critical support to inclusive reforms on local campuses (Huberman et al., 2012).

These cases also suggest possibilities for actions by others, including policymakers, district administrators, principals, teachers, parents, and university faculty. University faculty and PD providers should consider incorporating these cases into PD and preparation programs. Students in leadership preparation programs might compare and contrast two case studies, identify contextual factors that influenced inclusion and facilitators and barriers to effective change. Table 2.3 provides a list and description of resources of relevance to leadership preparation.

General and Special Education Teachers

Principals across the case studies worked to facilitate teachers' acceptance of inclusion, listening to their concerns, sharing data about students with disabilities' progress in the school, and suggesting alternative ways of thinking about educating students with disabilities. Although general and special educators are expected to address the needs of students with disabilities in inclusive schools, recent evidence suggests that they are not well-prepared for this work. In a recent study of U.S. schools, Stelitano et al. (2019), using a nationally representative study, found that teachers have both limited preservice preparation and PD related to teaching students with disabilities and that general educators have less access to students with disabilities' records and tools for using the data than special educators. In addition, special educators often lack systematic support for "meaningful collaboration" (Fowler et al., 2019, p. 10); thus, even well-prepared teachers may not have opportunities to engage in this work. Thus, teachers need both an understanding of the rationale for inclusion, the role of collaborative teaching in supporting students with disabilities, as well as the specific knowledge, skills, tools (e.g., progress monitoring), and school structures (e.g., time, schedules) to support this work.

Ideally, teacher education programs will consider elements of collaborative teacher education programs in preparing all teachers to address the needs of students with disabilities. University faculty should also provide special and general educators with opportunities to collaborate about the needs of students during both coursework and field experiences. Merged and/or dual certification programs typically provide such opportunities (for examples, see Anderson et al., 2019; Kent & Giles, 2016; Pugach & Blanton, 2012). Faculty interested in developing such programs should consider Pugach and Blanton's (2012) analysis of three elementary/middle preservice teacher preparation programs and what they sought to achieve (e.g., support inclusive education, teach collaborative teaching models, learn to teach with students with disabilities) and the presence or absence of inclusive goals, language, content, and materials, among other elements. Pugach and Blanton also emphasized the need for programs to give greater attention to "diversity of race, class, cultures, or language" (p. 264) if teachers are to be prepared for a diverse population of students. This broader interpretation of inclusion is consistent with Waldron et al.'s (2011) conception of inclusion as meeting all students' needs, not just those with disabilities.

Implications for Research

One of the challenges in studying leadership for inclusive schools is that researchers study varied questions, use different theoretical frameworks, and design their studies with different forms of data collection (see Table 2.1). Although we know some of the general approaches addressed (e.g., teacher teams, PD, differentiation, progress monitoring), we know little about what was occurring in classrooms or with particular students during inclusive change. An exception is Mayrowetz and Weinstein (1999), as they incorporated studies of three elementary students, describing how inclusion influenced their instruction and experiences in schools. Some studies provided student outcome data (e.g., DeMatthews et al., 2015a; McLeskey et al., 2014), but we know little about how inclusion actually changed educators' practices or their students' learning experiences. Inclusion refers to more than the placement of students with disabilities in general education settings, it also includes creating environments in which students with disabilities belong to the class, participate in the class routines and activities that other students participate in, and receive accessible curriculum with supports (Pitonyak, 2017).

Future research might also extend leadership studies to demonstrate how inclusive reform unfolded within a specific classroom and with specific students, documenting key changes. For example, how do educators make sense of information and social interactions with the principal, teacher leaders, families, district administrators, and PD experts to enact inclusive practices within their classrooms and schools? How do students and families experience inclusion? As Kozleski (2020) states, "how educators conceptualize their work, the degree to which they receive support to examine their practices, and the ways in which they grapple with these fundamental challenges place equity in schooling at the heart of what we mean by education" (p. 341). Finally, researchers might consider conducting additional case studies of effective inclusive schools and district-wide inclusive initiatives in diverse contexts.

Conclusion

These case studies provide contextualized descriptions of principals' actions as they supported inclusion or worked toward inclusive reform in a diverse group of elementary schools. These case studies took place in schools serving different populations of students, in urban, suburban, and rural schools, and in high and low-performing schools. Although the school contexts differed, principals were unwavering in their support of inclusion and engaged in similar actions to support inclusion. As Salisbury (2006) stated, "Schools that function inclusively do so for a reason…and the principals in these schools were the reason" (p. 79). Given principals' pivotal roles, their preparation to lead inclusive schools should not be left to chance, rather state education agencies, districts, and universities need to work together to collectively prepare all leaders and educators to address the needs of students with disabilities.

Notes

1 Mayrowetz and Weinstein (1999) included a third case study of a middle school, which we excluded.
2 Response to Intervention (RtI) is a multi-tiered approach to provide high-quality instruction and interventions to address the academic needs of students. Similarly, Positive Behavioral Supports (PBS) provides multi-tiered systems to support the needs of students who struggle with behavior. Today, the term, *Multi-tiered Systems of Support (MTSS)* is typically used, which includes both the academic and non-academic needs of students (e.g., behavior, social, attendance) (see Chapter 6 for more information regarding MTSS, and Chapter 7 for more information regarding PBS).

References

Anderson, K. M., Smith, J., Algozzine, B., & Olsen, J. (2019). An evaluation of contextual-fit and value of clinical placements in a dual licensure program. *Journal of Applied Educational and Policy Research, 4*(1), 50–75. https://journals.uncc.edu/jaepr/issue/view/87

Annamma, S. A., Connor, D., & Ferri, B. (2013). Dis/ability critical race studies (DisCrit): Theorizing at the intersections of race and dis/ability. *Race, Ethnicity and Education, 16*(1), 1–31. doi:10.1080/13613324.2012.730511

Billingsley, B. & Banks, A. (2019). Leadership for inclusive schools (1995–2015). In J. Crockett, B. Billingsley, & M. L. Boscardin (Eds.), *Handbook of leadership & administration for special education* (2nd ed., pp. 196–220). Routledge, Taylor-Francis.

Billingsley, B., McLeskey, J., & Crockett, J. (2019). Success for all students: Leading for effective inclusive schools. In J. Crockett, B. Billingsley, & M. Boscardin (Eds.), *Handbook of leadership and administration for special education* (2nd ed., pp. 306–332). Routledge.

Burstein, N., Sears, S., Wilcoxen, A., Cabello, B., & Spagna, M. (2004). Moving toward inclusive practices. *Remedial and Special Education, 25*(2), 104–116. doi:10.1177/07419325040250020501

Cameron, D. L., & Cook, B. (2013). General education teachers' goals and expectations for their included students with mild and severe disabilities. *Education and Training in Autism and Developmental Disabilities, 48*(1), 18–30.

Causton-Theoharis, J., Theoharis, G., Bull, T., Cosier, M., & Dempf-Aldrich, K. (2011). Schools of promise: A school district-university partnership centered on inclusive school reform. *Remedial and Special Education, 32*(3), 192–205. doi:10.1177/0741932510366163

Council of Chief State School Officers & the Collaboration for Effective Educator Development, Accountability, and Reform Center. (2017). *PSEL 2015 and promoting principal leadership for the success of students with disabilities.* http://www.ccsso.org/Documents/2017/PSELforSWDs01252017.pdf

*DeMatthews, D. E. (2015a). Clearing a path for inclusion: Distributing leadership in a high performing elementary School. *Journal of School Leadership, 25*(6), 1000–1038. doi:10.1177/105268461502500601

DeMatthews, D. (2015b). Making sense of social justice leadership: A case study of a principal's experiences to create a more inclusive school. *Leadership and Policy in Schools*, 1–27. doi:10.1080/15700763.2014.997939

DeMatthews, D., Billingsley, B., McLeskey, J., & Sharma U. (2020). Principal leadership for students with disabilities in effective inclusive schools. *Journal of Educational Administration, 58*(5), 539–554. doi:10.1108/JEA-10-2019-0177

DeMatthews, D. E., & Mawhinney, H. (2013). Addressing the inclusion imperative: An urban school district's responses. *Education Policy Analysis Archives, 21*(61). doi:10.14507/epaa.v21n61.2013

*DeMatthews, D. E., & Mawhinney, H. (2014). Social justice leadership and inclusion: Exploring challenges in an urban district struggling to address inequities. *Educational Administration Quarterly, 50*(5), 844–884.

DeMatthews, D. E., Kotok, S., & Serafini, A. (2019). Leadership preparation for special education and inclusive schools: Beliefs and recommendations from successful principals. *Journal of Research on Leadership Education*, 1–27. doi:10.1177/1942775119838308

Dentith, A., Frattura, E., & Kaylor, M. (2013). Reculturing for equity through integrated services: A case study of one district's reform. *International Journal of Inclusive Education, 17*(3), 223–237. doi:10.1080/13603116.2012.676080

Downing, J. E., Spencer, S., & Cavallaro, C. (2004). The development of an inclusive charter elementary school: Lessons learned. *Research and Practice for Persons with Severe Disabilities, 29*(1), 11–24. doi:10.2511/rpsd.29.1.11

Fisher, D., Caren, S., & Grove, K. A. (2000). The resilience of changes promoting inclusiveness in an urban elementary school. *The Elementary School Journal, 100*(3), l213–227. https://www.jstor.org/stable/1002152

Fox, N. E., & Ysseldyke, J. E. (1997). Implementing inclusion at the middle school level: Lessons from a negative example. *Exceptional Children, 64*(1), 81–98. doi:10.1177/001440299706400106

Fowler, S. A., Coleman, M. R. B., & Bogdan, W. K. (2019). The state of the special education profession survey report. *Teaching Exceptional Children, 52*(1), 8–29. doi:10.1177/0040059919875703

Guzmán, N. (1997). Leadership for successful inclusive schools: A study of principal behaviours, *Journal of Educational Administration, 35*(5), 439–450. doi:10.1108/09578239710184583

Heller, M. F., & Firestone. A. (1995). Who's in charge here? Sources of leadership for change in eight schools. *Elementary School Journal, 96*(1), 65–86. doi:10.1086/461815

Hitt, D. H., & Tucker, P. D. (2016). Systematic review of key leader practices found to influence student achievement: A unified framework. *Review of Educational Research, 86*(2), 531–569. doi:10.3102/0034654315614911

Honig, M. I., & Venkateswaran, N. (2012). School-central office relationships in evidence use: Understanding evidence use as a systems problem. *American Journal of Education, 118*(2), 199–222. doi:10.1086/663282

*Hoppey, D., Black, W. R., & Mickelson, A. M. (2018). The evolution of inclusive practice in two elementary schools: Reforming teacher purpose, instructional capacity, and data-informed practice. *International Journal of Educational Reform, 27*(1), 22–45. doi:10.1177%2F105678791802700102

*Hoppey, D., & McLeskey, J. (2013). A case study of principal leadership in an effective inclusive school. *The Journal of Special Education, 46*(4), 245–256. doi:10.1177%2F0022466910390507

Hoppey, D., & McLeskey, J. (2014). What are qualities of effective inclusive schools? In J. McLeskey, N. L. Waldron, F. Spooner, & B. Algozzine (Eds.), *Handbook of research and practice for effective inclusive schools* (pp. 17–29). Routledge Publishers.

Huberman, M., Navo, M., & Parrish, T. (2012). Effective practices in high performing districts serving students in special education. *Journal of Special Education Leadership, 25*(2), 59–71. https://www.casecec.org/archives/journals.asp

Individuals with Disabilities Education Improvement Act (IDEA) of 2004, P.L. 108-446, 20 U.S.C. $ 1400 et seq.

Katzman, L. (2007). High-stakes testing. In A. Bursztyn (Ed.), *The Praeger handbook of special education* (pp. 127–129). Praeger.

Kent, A., & Giles, A. (2016). Dual certification in general and special education: What is the role of field experience in preservice teacher preparation? *The Professional Educator, 40*(2), 1–14. https://files.eric.ed.gov/fulltext/EJ1120324.pdf

*Keyes, M. W., Hanley-Maxwell, C., & Capper, C. A. (1999). "Spirituality? It's the core of my leadership": Empowering leadership in an inclusive elementary school. *Educational Administration Quarterly, 35*(2), 203–237. doi:10.1177/00131619921968527

Kozleski, E. (2020). Disrupting what passes as inclusive education: Predicating educational equity on schools designed for all. *The Educational Forum, 84*(4), 340–355. doi:10.1080/00131725.2020.1801047

Leithwood, K., Harris, A., & Hopkins, D. (2008). Seven strong claims about successful school leadership, *School Leadership & Management, 28*(1), 27–42. doi:10.1080/13632430701800060

Lynch, J. M. (2012). Responsibilities of today's principal: Implications for principal preparation programs and principal certification policies. *Rural Special Education Quarterly, 31*(2), 40–47. doi:10.1177%2F875687051203100205

MacFarlane, K., & Woolfson, L. M. (2013). Teacher attitudes and behavior toward the inclusion of children with social, emotional and behavioral difficulties in mainstream schools: An application of the theory of planned behavior. *Teaching and Teacher Education, 29*, 46–52. doi:10.1016/j.tate.2012.08.006

Mamlin, N. (1999). Despite best intentions: When inclusion fails. *The Journal of Special Education, 33*(1), 36–49. doi:10.1177/002246699903300104

*Mayrowetz, D., & Weinstein, C. S. (1999). Sources of leadership for inclusive education: Creating schools for all children. *Educational Administration Quarterly, 35*(3), 423–449. doi:10.1177/00131619921968626

McLeskey, J., Barringer, M-D., Billingsley, B., Brownell, M., Jackson, D., & Ziegler, D. (2017, January). High-leverage practices in special education. Council for Exceptional Children & CEEDAR Center. http://ceedar.education.ufl.edu/portfolio/ccsc-2017-high-leverage-prac-tice

McLeskey, J., Landers, E., Williamson, P., & Hoppey, D. (2012). Are we moving toward educating students with disabilities in less restrictive settings? *The Journal of Special Education, 46*(3), 131–140. doi:10.1177/0022466910376670

*McLeskey, J., Waldron, N. L., & Redd, L. (2014). A case study of a highly effective, inclusive elementary school. *Journal of Special Education, 48*(1), 59–70. doi:10.1177%2F0022466912440455

National Policy Board for Educational Administration. (2015). *Professional standards for educational leaders*. National Policy Board for Educational Administration

Olson, A., Leko, M. M., & Roberts, C. A. (2016). Providing students with severe disabilities access to the general education curriculum. *Research and Practice for Persons with Severe Disabilities, 41*(3), 143–157. doi:10.1177/1540796916651975

Osgood, R. (2005). *The history of inclusion in the United States*. Gallaudet University Press.

Patton, M. (2002). *Qualitative research and evaluation methods* (3rd ed.). Sage.

Pazey, B. L., & Cole, H. A. (2013). The role of special education training in the development of socially just leaders: Building an equity consciousness in educational leadership programs. *Educational Administration Quarterly, 49*(2), 243–271. doi:10.1177%2F0013161X12463934

Pazey, B., & Yates, J. (2019). Conceptual and historical foundations of Special Education Administration. In J. Crockett, B. Billingsley, & M. L. Boscardin (Eds.), *Handbook of leadership and administration for special education* (pp. 18–38). Routledge.

Pitonyak, C. (2017). *Inclusion: What does it mean and who is it for?* https://www.youtube.com/watch?v=38IAazlj3Bo&t=22s

Pivik, J., McComas, J., & Laflamme, M. (2002). Barriers and facilitators to inclusive education. *Exceptional Children, 69*(1), 97–107. doi:10.1177%2F001440290206900107

Pugach, M. C., & Blanton, L. P. (2012). Enacting diversity in dual certification programs. *Journal of Teacher Education, 63*(4), 254–267. doi:10.1177%2F0022487112446970

Ryndak, D. L., Reardon, R., Benner, S. R., & Ward, T. (2007). Transitioning to and sustaining district-wide inclusive services: A 7-year study of a district's ongoing journey and its accompanying complexities. *Research and Practice for Persons with Severe Disabilities, 32*(4), 228–246. doi:10.2511/rpsd.32.4.228

Salisbury, C. L. (2006). Principals' perspectives on inclusive elementary schools. *Research & Practice for Persons with Severe Disabilities, 31*(1), 70–82. doi:10.2511%2Frpsd.31.1.70

Sergiovanni, T. J. (1996). *Moral leadership*. Jossey-Bass.

Shogren, K. A., McCart, A. B., Lyon, K. J., & Sailor, W. S. (2015). All means all: Building knowledge for inclusive schoolwide transformation. *Research and Practice for Persons with Severe Disabilities, 40*(3), 173–191. doi:10.1177%2F1540796915586191

Sindelar, P. T., Shearer, D. K., Yendol-Hoppey, D., & Liebert, T. W. (2006). The sustainability of inclusive school reform. *Exceptional Children, 72*(3), 317–331. doi:10.1177/001440290607200304

Sperandio, J., & Klerks, J. (2007). Leadership challenge: Blending inclusive special needs provision and reform of teaching methodology in a Dutch international school. *International Journal of Special Education, 22*(2), 140–149. https://files.eric.ed.gov/fulltext/EJ814497.pdf

Stelitano, L., Perera, R., & Johnston, W. R. (2019). *Supporting students with high-incidence dis-abilities in U.S. schools: National findings from the American educator panels*. RAND Corporation. https://www.rand.org/pubs/research_reports/RR2992.html

Sumbera, M. J., Pazey, B. L., & Lashley, C. (2014). How building principals made sense of free and appropriate public education in the least restrictive environment. *Leadership and Policy in Schools, 13*(3), 297–333. doi:10.1080/15700763.2014.922995

Theoharis, G. (2007). Social justice educational leaders and resistance: Toward a theory of social justice leadership. *Educational Administration Quarterly, 43*(2), 221–258. doi:10.1177%2F0013161X06293717

UNESCO. (2018). Global education monitoring report. https://unesdoc.unesco.org/ark:/48223/pf0000265329

U.S. Department of Education. (2019). *41st Annual Report to Congress on the Implementation of the Individuals with Disabilities Education Act, 2019*. Author. Retrieved from http://www.ed.gov/about/reports/annual/osep.

Wakeman, S. Y., Browder, D. M., Flowers, C., & Ahlgrim-Delzell, L. (2006). Principals' knowledge of fundamental and current issues in special education. *NASSP Bulletin, 90*(2), 153–174. doi:10.1177%2F0192636506288858

*Waldron, N. L., McLeskey, J., & Redd, L. (2011). Setting the direction: The role of the principal in developing an effective, inclusive school. *Journal of Special Education Leadership, 24*(2), 51–60. https://www.casecec.org/resources/jsel.asp

Williams, J. L., Pazey, B., Shelby, L., & Yates, J. R. (2013). The enemy among us: Do school administrators perceive students with disabilities as a threat? *NASSP Bulletin, 97*(2), 139–165. doi:10.1177%2F0192636512473507

Williamson, P., Hoppey, D., McLeskey, J., Bergmann, E., & Moore, H. (2019). Trends in LRE placement rates over the past 25 years. *The Journal of Special Education*. Advance online publication. doi:10.1177%2F0022466919855052

*Met criteria for inclusion in literature review

3

The Roles of Teachers in Effective Inclusive Elementary Schools

Elizabeth Bettini[1], Hannah Morris Mathews[2], Jennifer Lillis[1], Kathryn M. Meyer[1], Tashnuva Shaheen[1], Lindsey Kaler[1], and Nelson C. Brunsting[3]

[1]BOSTON UNIVERSITY BU WHEELOCK COLLEGE OF EDUCATION AND HUMAN DEVELOPMENT, 2 SILBER WAY, BOSTON, MA, 02176

[2]UNIVERSITY OF FLORIDA COLLEGE OF EDUCATION, PO BOX 117042, GAINESVILLE, FL32611-7043

[3]WAKE FOREST UNIVERSITY RAISE CENTER PO BOX 7385, WINSTON-SALEM, NC27109-7385

Setting the Stage: The Importance of Shared Conceptions of Teachers' Roles

Challenges defining special and general educators' roles in inclusive schools date back to the beginning of special education. In 1977, Weatherley and Lipsky traced three MA school districts' responses to Chapter 766, which was passed in 1972 and formed the legal model for the original version of the Individuals with Disabilities Education Act (IDEA). Examining how "street-level bureaucrats" (i.e., local educators responsible for bringing the law to life) enacted Chapter 766, they found that, without adequate resources to fulfill the law's intent fully, educators used their substantial local discretion to make judgments about how to triage their efforts, as a result of which, "a law and its administrative regulations, intended to produce uniform application of procedures, instead yielded wide variations in application" (p. 188). Educators in different contexts conceptualized the law's purposes in different ways, prioritizing different mandates, and thus took up their roles in enacting Chapter 766 in different ways. Subsequent studies of the implementation of the original Education for All Handicapped Children Act (EAHCA, 1975, now IDEA 2004) similarly found wide variability in the enactment of the law across contexts (Singer et al., 1986, 1989).

Though special education law has changed dramatically in the last 40 years, the issues Weatherley and Lipsky identified in 1977 remain. Local educators have substantial discretion to interpret and enact the IDEA (2004) and other legal guidance, without adequate resources to enact all provisions as intended, and they hold varied conceptions of the purposes of special education services, resulting in different applications of the law across contexts (e.g., Bray & Russell, 2018; Gomez-Najarro, 2020). Consequently, despite many attempts to define special and general educators' roles in serving students with disabilities (e.g., Brownell et al., 2010), there is wide variability in how their roles are conceptualized and enacted (Billingsley et al., 2019).

DOI: 10.4324/9781003043874-3

Shared conceptions of special and general educators' roles are essential to effective inclusive elementary schools for several reasons. First, educational systems depend on coordination among multiple institutions (Sykes et al., 2010). State education agencies, teacher education programs, local education agencies, and individual schools depend on one another to foster a special and general educator workforce that can fulfill meaningful roles in serving students with disabilities (Shepherd et al., 2016; Sykes et al., 2010). For example, state education agencies set licensure standards that incentivize prospective teachers to obtain key skills (Sindelar et al., 2019), while teacher education programs prepare future teachers to fulfill their roles (Leko et al., 2015), local education agencies allocate special educators to schools and provide early-career induction and mentoring that fosters their capacity to fulfill those roles (Billingsley et al., 2009), and schools provide them with schedules, curricula, and other resources needed to fulfill those roles (Billingsley et al., 2019). In short, our educational system requires the coordination of multiple institutions in developing the teacher workforce. This coordination depends on a shared vision of special and general educators' roles.

Second, inclusive schools fundamentally depend on the coordination of effort among special educators, general educators, paraprofessionals, related service providers, and administrators, as these personnel all share responsibility for the educational experiences and outcomes of students with disabilities (Brownell et al., 2010; Prewett et al., 2012). Collectively, these personnel must ensure students with disabilities meaningfully participate in inclusive social and academic experiences, with appropriate supports across environments, and ensure students access interventions addressing individual needs. Thus, they must coordinate the times, content, and methods by which students are taught across environments in the school (e.g., across general education settings, resource settings, and so on; Benedict et al., 2020; McLeskey et al., 2014). Effective coordination requires shared understandings of the roles those personnel play in serving students and supporting one another (Bettini, Lillis et al., 2021).

Finally, extant research indicates teachers' conceptions of their roles may shape what they do (e.g., Feiman-Nemser et al., 2014; Grossman et al., 2001; Morris Mathews, 2020; Urbach et al., 2015). For example, in a mixed-methods study of elementary special educators' beliefs about their roles, Urbach et al. (2015) found special educators who obtained lower scores on an evaluation of their reading instruction conceptualized the purpose of their roles as providing a supportive, safe haven where students could "get love" (p. 331). In contrast, those who obtained higher scores emphasized providing intensive instruction, maintaining high expectations, and "teach[ing] regardless" (p. 331) of other factors affecting their work. Other studies have obtained similar findings, indicating that how people conceptualize the purposes of their roles shapes how they use their discretion to enact that role (Morris Mathews, 2020).

In this chapter, we explore stakeholders' conceptions of teachers' roles serving students with disabilities in inclusive elementary schools. We set the stage by defining what we mean by an effective inclusive school and providing a conceptual foundation in role theory. We then discuss how scholars and policy makers have conceptualized teachers' roles in inclusive schools and what research tells us about teachers' roles in inclusive schools. Finally, we propose a path forward, discussing avenues for changing individual and collective beliefs about special and general educators' roles to improve how schools support the inclusion of students with disabilities. Throughout, we contend that, as Weatherley and Lipsky (1977) found, local educators have broad discretion to interpret and enact their roles in special education and that their conceptions of the purposes of their roles shape how they utilize this discretion.

Effective Inclusive Schools

We conceptualize inclusive schools as settings in which students with disabilities are active, valued participants in all aspects of the school and have the supports they need to succeed both academically and socially (McLeskey et al., 2018). We identify with Villa and Thousand's (2016) contention that "Inclusion is both a vision and a practice" (p. 18), as implementing inclusion effectively requires a commitment to both (a) a vision that all students have a right to belong, learn, and achieve high standards in inclusive settings, and also (b) the daily practices that support that vision (e.g., effective instructional methods, collaboration). Effective inclusive schools systematically promote inclusion and employ practices that support it, eliminating barriers to engagement and learning across all contexts in a school (Li & Ruppar, 2020), so all students, including those with disabilities, interact, learn, and play with a diverse group of peers.

Though inclusive schools privilege meeting student needs in general education classes, we recognize that effective inclusive schools include a continuum of placements (e.g., resource, self-contained) to meet the individual needs of students with disabilities. In inclusive schools, restrictive settings should be used only when individual student needs cannot be met in general education settings; these settings should not be a default for any student (e.g., Hoge et al., 2014; Olson et al., 2016), and these settings should be valued and supported, so students make "more than de minimis" progress (Turnbull et al., 2018) toward their goals and toward increasing engagement in general education settings and curricula. Thus, we consider special educators' roles across a full continuum of settings, not only in general education classes.

Conceptual Foundation: Role Theory

Role theory seeks to understand and explain human behavior by considering how a person's position in a complex social system is associated with the expectations for their behavior (Biddle, 1986). Role theory is derived from a theatrical metaphor, comparing the characteristic behavior patterns (roles) in which people engage, in social systems, to roles in a play. Thus, role theory uses three concepts to understand how people act in social contexts: (a) *Roles*, defined as "patterned and characteristic social behaviors" (p. 68); (b) *Parts*, defined as the identities or positions participants take on; and (c) *Scripts*, defined as expectations for someone in a particular part. Just as an actor's part in a play comes with particular expectations (defined by the script) for their behavior, one's position in a social system comes with expectations for what they should do and how they should do it. These expectations can be held by both the individual fulfilling that role and by others interacting with them; moreover, different people may have different expectations for the same role (Biddle, 1986). For example, a special educator might take on a *role* in academic instruction (e.g., teaching foundational skills needed to engage with the general education curriculum) as a function of their *part* or social position (i.e., special educator), which entails particular *scripts* or expectations for their behavior (e.g., planning instruction, using particular instructional materials); and, they and their colleagues may have different expectations for that role—different scripts to which they expect the special educator to adhere (e.g., Antia, 1999; Damore & Murray, 2009). Often, *roles* are defined by their function—the purpose they fulfill in the social system (Biddle, 1986). For example, the special educator in the preceding example could conceptualize the purpose of their role in instruction as teaching foundational skills, or they could conceptualize the purpose as providing accommodations to support learning general education curriculum, or they could have another purpose in mind (e.g., building self-esteem, supporting general educators' efforts).

Role theory has been used in a variety of scholarly traditions, which conceptualize key dimensions of role theory in different ways (Biddle, 1986). For example, they vary in the extent to which they conceptualize individuals as agentically shaping and taking on roles versus the extent to which they conceptualize roles as constrained by social systems (Biddle, 1986). However, they share an assumption that individuals operate from a specific position in complex social systems, and their position comes with particular expectations, both internally held and externally imposed, that can be used to understand patterns in their behavior. In addition, role theory is consistently invested in both

(a) individual's conceptions and enactment of their role, (b) broader organizational conceptions of role and structures for supporting and communicating roles, and (c) interactions between the individual and the organization (Biddle, 1986).

The work of teaching is fundamentally social in nature, based on networks of social interactions between and among teachers, students, administrators, parents, and other personnel (Bryk & Schneider, 2002; Youngs et al., 2012); as such, role theory may offer useful conceptual tools for understanding how teachers engage in and experience their work, especially in inclusive schools, where greater coordination of teachers' work may require shared understandings of teachers' roles (e.g., Bettini, Lillis et al., 2021; McLeskey et al., 2014). In special education, role theory has primarily been used to explore parents' roles in the IEP process (e.g., Hirano & Rowe, 2015); few studies have formally used role theory as a foundation for examining special or general educator's roles (Bettini, Wang et al., 2019 is an exception). However, many studies have sought to understand the roles special and general educators play, exploring their own (e.g., Urbach et al., 2015) and others' (e.g., Ruppar et al., 2017) expectations for their role and the characteristic patterns of behavior that they actually take up (e.g., Mitchell et al., 2012).

What Do We Know from Research and the Wisdom of Practice?

We first examine what policy and scholarship suggest teachers' roles should be. We then consider research on the roles teachers actually take up in the service of students with disabilities.

Conceptions of Role within Policy and Scholarly Guidance

The IDEA (2004) specifies what special education must do for students with disabilities, while the Every Student Succeeds Act (ESSA, 2015) specifies what education must do for all students, including those with disabilities. In some respects, their guidance sets clear parameters around educators' work; for example, The IDEA (2004) requires educators to hold yearly meetings to revise students' Individualized Education Programs (IEPs), as well triennial multidisciplinary evaluation team meetings, working in collaboration with parents, related service providers, and other stakeholders (IDEA 2004); thus, educators must schedule, plan for, and attend these meetings, and demonstrate attempts to engage parents in the process. However, as Weatherley and Lipsky (1977) found, the educators who enact these requirements hold varying conceptions of the purposes of these processes, as well as substantial discretion to determine who does what, when, where, and how; thus, legal provisions may be enacted very differently across contexts.

Moreover, legal guidance includes some potential conflicts that educators must navigate as they choose how to enact their roles in serving students with disabilities, particularly regarding the purposes of their work (McLaughlin, 2010). Policy consistently promotes the long-term aims of minimizing achievement gaps between students with and without disabilities and maximizing students' college/career readiness. However, policy is less consistent regarding the purposes and methods of teachers' daily instruction for students with disabilities (McLaughlin, 2010). Since 1975, IDEA has consistently emphasized that individualization of instructional methods and goals is at the heart of special education services (Yell et al., 2017). Over the past 20–25 years, policy has also consistently mandated that all students with disabilities access the general education curriculum (Yell et al., 2017). This guidance has been codified in the No Child Left Behind Act (NCLB; 2002), the Every Student Succeeds Act (ESSA), and IDEA (1997, 2004; McLaughlin, 2010; Yell & Shriner, 1997; Yell et al., 2017). Consequently, for a generation, special educators have also been consistently expected to play a role in supporting students' learning of general education standards (Brownell et al., 2010).

This imperative is in tension with IDEA's emphasis on addressing individual learning needs (McLaughlin, 2010). As McLaughlin (2010) notes, there is "a fundamental tension between the prevailing K-12 educational policy of universal standards, assessments, and accountability as defined through Title 1 and the entitlement to a Free Appropriate Public Education (FAPE) within IDEA" (p. 265), as "students with disabilities may be treated unjustly in being held to universal standards" (p. 266). This tension can create inadvertent ambiguity regarding the instructional aims teachers' roles should be designed to prioritize for students with disabilities—the purposes toward which they should orient their work (Billingsley et al., 2019; Sayeski et al., 2019). Should educators prioritize individualized instruction in the areas where students struggle, or should they prioritize students' access to and success in general education curricula? Though both are legally mandated and important, and though they may sometimes be meaningfully combined (e.g., Ruppar & Gaffney, 2011), time constraints may limit educators' capacity to fulfill both imperatives, requiring them to set priorities (Sayeski et al., 2019).

Exacerbating this tension, these policies have different accountability mechanisms (Brownell et al., 2010). NCLB and ESSA hold entire systems accountable for students' learning of general education standards through sub-group disaggregation on high stakes tests (Brownell et al., 2010; Shepherd et al., 2016). In contrast, accountability in IDEA emphasizes progress toward individual goals on students' IEPs (Brownell et al., 2010; McLaughlin, 2010). Further, whereas accountability for meeting ESSA's mandates is distributed across an entire system and is enforced by the state (creating a widespread investment, among all personnel in a school, to meet those mandates), accountability in IDEA is intended to be enforced by individual students' caregivers on their behalf, in private interactions between caregivers and schools, thus limiting accountability of the entire system for adherence to the law's provisions and intent, and limiting the potential for this accountability to yield systemic change (Kalyanpur et al., 2000; Skrtic, 2012). Importantly, special educators are expected to meet both sets of imperatives—supporting students' progress on general education curricula while also ensuring progress on individualized goals—whereas general educators are primarily held accountable for the learning of general education curricula (McLaughlin, 2010).

Further, scholars also disagree about what should be educators' core priorities for students with disabilities. Scholars generally agree on the importance of eliminating disparities in educational outcomes between students with and without disabilities and that special and general educators both have a role to play in eliminating these disparities. However, scholars debate the extent to which teachers should prioritize intensive intervention in foundational skills (Fuchs et al., 2010; Sayeski et al., 2019) versus prioritizing access to general education curricula (e.g., Kurth et al., 2020; McLaughlin, 2010). For example, some scholars have expressed deep concern that emphasis on general education access and instruction constitutes "blurring" of special and general education (Fuchs et al., 2010, p. 306), warning of a danger that "special education vanishes in all but name [...] inadvertently weakening the capacity of schools to provide most intensive services to our nation's most instructionally needy children" (p. 309). In contrast, others view inclusion in general education curricula as vital to ensuring equity and raising expectations (McLaughlin, 2010), critiquing the role of special education in replicating low expectations for students with disabilities through an emphasis on individual goals (e.g., Agran et al., 2020; Olson et al., 2016; Siuty, 2019). While scholars have extensively debated these issues, neither those advocating for prioritizing intensive intervention nor those advocating for prioritizing general education curricula have provided a clear answer to the logistical question of how educators should reconcile these competing instructional purposes within the constraints of a 6-hour school day and a 9-month school year.

Response to Intervention (RtI), promoted by IDEA (2004) and adopted by the majority of elementary schools in the U.S. (Bradley et al., 2011), has been proposed as a systematic way to address the needs of all students, while maintaining a focus on standardized core instruction (Brownell et al., 2010; Hoover & Patton, 2008). Often referred to as multi-tiered systems of support (MTSS), which also incorporates positive behavioral interventions and supports (PBIS), RtI provides a structure for situating both general education instruction (i.e., tier 1) and specialized intensive intervention in foundational skills (i.e., tier 3) in the same structure (Hoover & Patton, 2008; Simonsen et al., 2010). Though some have proposed that RtI could resolve debates about special and general educators' roles in serving students with disabilities (Brownell et al., 2010), others have highlighted how differing conceptions of RtI are subject to the same debates (Fuchs et al., 2010), and further, reiterated that the time for addressing foundational skills must come from somewhere, necessitating that students receive intensive intervention at the expense of doing something else in the school day (Sayeski et al., 2019).

These scholarly debates about *what* instructional content educators should prioritize for students with disabilities reflect core differences about the purpose of special education, and thus they are unlikely to be easily resolved (Billingsley et al., 2019). Moreover, these debates echo similar conversations about *where* and *how* educators should be teaching students with disabilities (Billingsley et al., 2019), and they are deeply intertwined with differing conceptions of disability (Anastasiou & Kauffman, 2011; Baglieri et al., 2011; Fuchs et al., 2010). Thus, the answer to the core question (i.e., *What should be special and general educators' roles in inclusive schools?*) remains deeply contested, both in policy guiding special education and among the scholars responsible for preparing special and general educators.

Special and General Educators' Roles in Effective Inclusive Schools

Educators cannot wait for these debates to be resolved. Every day, they must make immediate, consequential decisions about the core purposes they should be fulfilling in teaching students with disabilities and how to organize their work to fulfill these purposes effectively given the particular resources and constraints of their school. In the following sections, we discuss extant research regarding the roles educators fulfill in schools. Note that few studies have explicitly sought to examine teachers' roles in inclusive elementary schools. Rather, most studies examined teachers' roles in RtI (e.g., Gomez-Najarro, 2020) or in schools in general (e.g., Youngs et al., 2011); we discuss studies regardless of the schools on which they focus, but draw particular attention to studies focused on inclusive schools (e.g., Olson et al., 2016).

Special educators' roles in schools are complex, multidimensional, and often less clearly defined than general educators' roles (Billingsley et al., 2019; Youngs et al., 2011). In an observational study of 36 special educators' time, Vannest and Hagan-Burke (2010) described a wide range of activities special educators engaged in, with no single activity taking precedence and non-instructional responsibilities consuming more than half their time; subsequent studies have obtained similar findings (Bettini et al., 2015; Mitchell et al., 2012; Vannest et al., 2010).

General educators' roles are generally more clearly defined than special educators', as they often experience more explicit guidance regarding what to teach, when, how, and to whom (Billingsley et al., 2019; Youngs et al., 2011). However, their roles in serving students with disabilities may be ambiguous, with unclear and sometimes conflicting expectations regarding, for example, the aspects of instruction for which they are primarily responsible and how they should contribute to IEP meetings (Bray & Russell, 2018; Fennick & Liddy, 2001).

For the purposes of this chapter, we describe three roles for which teachers are responsible. Specifically, special and general educators both take on roles as (a) *instructors*, planning and providing instruction; and (b) *collaborators*, coordinating efforts with other educators; and, special educators also take on roles as (c) *IEP case managers*, completing paperwork, working with families, and ensuring legal compliance with IDEA (2004).

These roles are not mutually exclusive, but rather tightly intertwined with one another; for example, collaboration (*collaborator role*) is often focused on designing and providing instruction (*instructor role*) or determining what should be in a student's IEP (*case management role;* Mitchell et al., 2012). As a participant in Ruppar et al.'s (2017) study noted, a special educator's role "switches and morphs depending on the minute" (p. 126). Further, these roles are not comprehensive of all that special and general educators do, as they have other responsibilities beyond these roles (e.g., supervising students during non-instructional time; Vannest et al., 2010). Note also that these roles are relevant regardless of the service delivery model in which students are served. Though special educators' job titles (i.e., their *parts,* from role theory) are often defined by their service delivery model (e.g., co-teacher, resource teacher), their *roles* (i.e., characteristic behavior patterns in service of a purpose) are consistent across instructional settings and have some common expectations (i.e., *scripts,* from role theory). In other words, whether students are in co-taught, resource, or self-contained settings, *instructor, collaborator,* and *IEP case manager* are roles that special and general educators take up in serving them. Using extant research, we first describe what we know about the dimensions of these roles, followed by individual and contextual factors shaping how they conceptualize and enact their roles, as well as the consequences of these roles for burnout, attrition, and instruction.

Instructors

Special Educators

Consistent with how policymakers and scholars conceptualize the work of special education (ESSA, 2015; IDEA 2004), studies of special educators' perspectives underscore that providing academic and behavioral instruction is central to their role (e.g., Jones & Youngs, 2012; Morris Mathews, 2020). As such, one would assume the majority of special educators' days would be comprised of providing instruction. Yet, extant studies indicate otherwise, with estimates ranging from 16% to 46% of their time allocated to providing academic instruction (Mitchell et al., 2012; Vannest & Hagan-Burke, 2010).

However, special educators' time is allocated to many tasks that contribute to instruction (Mitchell et al., 2012). First, special educators gather information about their students to inform their instructional decisions; this may include observing students, reviewing records, collecting data on student progress, or administering standardized measures of academic performance (Bishop et al., 2010; Mitchell et al., 2012; Urbach et al., 2015; Youngs et al., 2011). Second, special educators draw on that information to make decisions about instruction. This includes designing long- and short-term instructional plans; locating, selecting, adapting, and modifying curricula (Bishop et al., 2010; Mitchell et al., 2012; Youngs et al., 2011); and planning instruction to meet student needs (Ruppar et al., 2017; Siuty et al., 2018). Finally, special educators provide instruction, delivering targeted interventions to small groups of students (Mitchell et al., 2012), instructing in co-taught settings (Friend & Cook, 2010; Mitchell et al., 2012), and pushing in to general education classes (Zagona et al., 2020).

General Educators

General educators' roles in instruction are shaped by their expertise in content and their access to curricular materials (Bettini, Lillis et al., 2021; Brownell et al., 2010; Olson et al., 2016). As core content teachers, general educators are responsible for designing and delivering instruction for all students in core curricula (i.e., as defined by state standards), using methods accessible and meaningful to all students (Brownell et al., 2010; McLaughlin, 2010; Soukup et al., 2007). This requires general educators to enact accommodations and modifications that make instruction accessible to students with disabilities (Finnerty et al., 2019; Olson et al., 2016). In some inclusive schools, general educators are responsible for developing accommodations and modifications (Olson et al., 2016). For example, in a case study of how a highly effective, inclusive middle school fostered curricular inclusion of students with severe disabilities, Olson et al. (2016) found general educators' roles included proactively designing instruction that was accessible for students with disabilities and adjusting their instruction, in the moment, to meet student needs. In other schools, special educators may be responsible for designing accommodations and modifications (Mitchell et al., 2012), or special and general educators may collaborate to design them (Finnerty et al., 2019). Regardless of who designs them, general educators are responsible for enacting accommodations and modifications to ensure students access the core curriculum (e.g., Finnerty et al., 2019; Olson et al., 2016). And, because special and general educators' roles are overlapping and interdependent, fulfilling this role requires collaboration.

Collaborators

In inclusive schools, educators' work is interdependent, as multiple educators play unique but complementary roles in serving students with disabilities, and they depend on one another to fulfill their respective roles (Klingner & Vaughn, 2002). Thus, they must collaborate with one another to ensure their work is well-coordinated and mutually reinforces shared goals (Bettini, Lillis et al., 2021; Pratt, 2014). Klingner and Vaughn (2002) highlighted how interdependence represents a change from the past. Over 7 years, they examined how a special educator's role changed as her school gradually became more inclusive. Previously, Joyce, the special educator, checked in with general educators weekly; she said, "I would go before school once a week and say, 'What are you teaching this week?'...and that was about it," because the general educator "had her own agenda... and I had my own" (p. 27). In contrast, when Joyce began providing services in students' classes, collaboration became much more intensive, including such tasks as going over students' goals, interpreting student progress, and setting up instructional objectives and structures that were inclusive and respectful of students with disabilities. More recently, Bettini, Lillis et al. (2021) examined special educators' roles in contexts where students with emotional/behavioral disorders (EBD) were moving from self-contained to inclusive placements. Whereas prior studies of special educators' roles in serving students with EBD highlighted their isolation (O'Brien et al., 2019), Bettini, Lillis et al. (2021) found that, because of students' inclusion, special educators' efforts to meet student needs were interdependent with general educators, paraprofessionals, and administrators. Participants emphasized that effective services depended on all educators coordinating their efforts to meet student needs across contexts.

Special Educators

Special educators report spending substantial portions of their time (8–27%) interacting with other educators (Bettini et al., 2015; Mitchell et al., 2012; Vannest & Hagan-Burke, 2010), and they describe collaboration as a core role in inclusive settings (Bettini, Lillis et al., 2021; Klingner & Vaughn, 2002; Olson et al., 2016; Ruppar et al., 2017). Whereas special educators in separate settings could choose to shut their doors and autonomously provide services independent of other teachers, in inclusive schools, special educators are just one of many educators responsible for serving students with disabilities (Bettini, Lillis et al., 2021).

Special educators collaborate with many other personnel, including general educators, paraprofessionals, related service providers, and administrators (Cole-Lade & Bailey, 2020; Olson et al., 2016). Often, special educators hold primary responsibility for coordinating other educators' work, ensuring all team members understand what they should be doing, why, when, and how (Bettini, Lillis et al., 2021; Pratt, 2014). This is particularly true regarding paraprofessionals, who special educators often train and support (e.g., Brock et al., 2020; French, 2001; Giangreco et al., 2010). However, general educators also report depending on special educators to help them learn about student needs and instructional strategies to meet those needs (e.g., Zagona et al., 2017, 2020), and special educators support general educators to understand how to serve students with disabilities (e.g., Klingner & Vaughn, 2002). Special educators describe their collaborative work with other educators as including a range of tasks, such as discussing lesson plans, collaboratively developing accommodations and modifications, and coordinating schedules to ensure students have support and services when/where needed (Antia, 1999; Bettini, Lillis et al., 2021; Klingner & Vaughn, 2002).

Though these actions may have a short-term aim, special educators also highlight how they often use collaboration as a way to build shared understandings among educators about students' needs and inclusion (Bettini, Lillis et al., 2021; Li & Ruppar, 2020; Miller et al., 2020; Zagona et al., 2017). Special educators often emphasize that shared understandings of the purposes of their work—and a shared commitment to students' inclusion, effective instruction, and success—are essential to effectively coordinating and collaborating with others (Bettini, Lillis et al., 2021; Pratt, 2014; Zagona et al., 2020), though they often report that these conditions are not present (e.g., Fowler et al., 2019). For example, in Pratt's (2014) qualitative study of how co-teachers' relationships evolved over time, teachers emphasized the crucial importance of shared conceptions of their purpose, saying that having "the same goal in mind" (p. 5) was the foundation for symbiotic coordination of effort. Similarly, in Bettini, Lillis et al.'s (2021) study, special educators described depending on other personnel to share their understanding of students' needs and the division of responsibilities for meeting those needs. When they felt they had shared understandings, they felt supported to meet student needs; when they felt others did not share their understandings, this challenged their efforts to serve students effectively.

Because shared understandings are not always present, special educators often describe using collaborative interactions to develop shared understandings (Bettini, Lillis et al., 2021; Li & Ruppar, 2020; Miller et al., 2020). For example, in Bettini, Lillis et al.'s (2021) study, a special educator explained how a general educator did not share the IEP team's belief that a student needed to receive instruction in a separate setting during significant behavioral incidents, and thus did not provide the special educator with instructional materials he had missed; this resulted in the student missing substantial general education content. Because shared understandings were essential to effective collaboration, special educators described using many strategies to build shared understandings, including (a) providing professional development about student needs; (b) collecting and sharing data on student needs and current resource limitations; (c) repeatedly reiterating student needs, despite opposition; and (d) making strategic choices about who to work with (Bettini, Lillis et al., 2021). Similarly, a special educator in Ruppar et al.'s (2015) study described joining a district literacy committee so she could influence decisions that were consequential for her students' literacy instruction, while a special educator in Gomez-Najarro's (2020) study described seeking out informal collaboration with general educators so she could influence decisions about students who they were potentially going to be serving in future. These studies suggest collaboration is not only aimed at directly serving students but is often a means through which special educators try to foster contexts more inclusive of their students.

General Educators

General educators consistently note that collaboration with specialists is important for improving their capacity to teach students with disabilities effectively (e.g., Finnerty et al., 2019; Giangreco et al., 1993). Studies of effective inclusive schools indicate that general and special educators often collaborate in developing accommodations and modifications for students, with the general educator contributing expertise in content and curricula, while the special educator contributes expertise in student learning needs and instructional strategies (Finnerty et al., 2019). General educators report highly valuing the expertise special educators bring to serving students with disabilities and looking to special educators for guidance regarding how to more effectively teach their students (Finnerty et al., 2019; Giangreco et al., 1993; Zagona et al., 2020). For example, in Zagona et al.'s (2020) mixed methods investigation of how general educators fostered the participation of students with complex support needs in the general education curriculum, general educators reported relying on guidance from special educators regarding how to meaningfully include students.

IEP Case Managers

Both special and general educators fulfill instructional and collaborative roles for students with disabilities; in contrast, IEP case management tends to primarily fall to special educators (e.g., Antia, 1999; Bray & Russell, 2018; Fennick & Liddy, 2001). Few studies have examined special educators' roles as IEP case managers, and we know less about variability in the ways special educators conceptualize and enact this role than we do about collaborative and instructional roles (Blackwell & Rossetti, 2014). However, several studies indicate special educators engage in many tasks focused on managing caseloads, including developing IEPs, attending IEP meetings, assessing students' progress toward goals, helping to evaluate students, and more (Bray & Russell, 2016; 2018; Mitchell et al., 2012; Vannest & Hagan-Burke, 2010).

Special educators' case management role often takes up significant portions of their time (Vannest & Hagan-Burke, 2010). In a study of 36 special educators' time use, Vannest and Hagan-Burke reported paperwork accounted for an average of 12.1% of special educators' time; IEPs accounted for an additional 3% and assessments 4.4%. Mitchell et al. (2012) similarly found that paperwork accounted for about 17% of special educators' time, almost one day/week. Special educators often report paperwork is a stressor that creates a discrepancy between what they believe they should be doing (i.e., instruction) and how they are actually spending their time (i.e., paperwork; e.g., Albrecht et al., 2009; Billingsley, 2007; Hagaman & Casey, 2018).

Ideally, IEPs caseload management would be instructionally meaningful, providing substantive guidance to support educators in providing effective services (Bray & Russell, 2016; 2018; Ruppar & Gaffney, 2011). Yet, caseload management is often viewed as an exercise in procedural compliance, rather than a meaningful act of planning for and providing learning opportunities; as such, IEPs may provide limited assistance to special educators regarding the specific supports and services they should provide to students in inclusive settings (Bray & Russell, 2016, 2018; Ruppar & Gaffney, 2011; Russell & Bray, 2013). In their ethnographic examination of IEPs in two inclusive secondary schools, Bray and Russell (2018) noted that only one of the 12 IEPs they examined included "any instructional strategies or interventions, assistive technology, and/or related services to attend to the unique learning needs of students" (p. 254). Instead, IEPs instantiated general education standards-based curriculum and methods with limited accommodations, modifications, or direct services. Caseload management responsibilities were oriented toward "monitor[ing] failure" (p. 255) to ensure students did not fail a class, as course failure could open the school up to liability for failing to meet students' needs. Bray and Russell (2018) further noted that, though IEPs played a limited role in guiding teaching and learning, writing IEPs and convening IEP meetings still took up substantial time.

Other studies have obtained similar findings. Bray and Russell (2016) conducted a qualitative comparative case study of forces structuring IEP team processes for five secondary students with learning disabilities. They found that the IEP acted as a "script" from which IEP teams seldom deviated; though IEP meetings are intended as a forum for generative collaboration, they found these meetings were primarily focused on the special educator mechanically going over what was written in the IEP (Bray & Russell, 2016). Ruppar and Gaffney (2011) obtained similar findings in their instrumental case study of the eligibility determination meetings for an elementary student. The meeting was a site for formalizing decisions that had been made previously and not a site for meaningful collaborative discussion of the student's data, goals, and services (Ruppar & Gaffney,

2011). Further, in an analysis of states' evaluation policies, Gilmour and Wehby (2020) noted that, in many states, special educators' evaluation systems attend to procedural aspects of IEP case management (e.g., timeliness of paperwork), but not more substantive aspects of this role, suggesting institutional pressures may orient educators toward the procedural rather than educational aspects of IEP case management. Because IEP case management roles may often be conceptualized in terms of procedural compliance (e.g., Bray & Russell, 2016, 2018), time spent on this role may feel, to special educators, like a distraction from instructional and collaborative roles that feel more meaningful (Billingsley, 2007; Hagaman & Casey, 2018; Kaff, 2004; Mitchell et al., 2012).

Special educators' roles in managing caseloads may be challenging in other ways as well. Echoing scholarly debates and core tensions embedded within the IDEA (2004) and Title 1 (Fuchs et al., 2010; McLaughlin, 2010), special educators report a conflict between the procedural requirements of IDEA and NCLB as they relate to IEP goals (Russell & Bray, 2013). Ahearn (2006) reported many states were moving toward standards-based IEPs, using the state's grade level content standards to determine students' IEP goals. For some special educators, this pressure to align IEP goals to state standards may conflict with IDEA's focus on individualized service delivery (Ahearn, 2006; Russell & Bray, 2013). Russell and Bray (2013) reported that special educators felt pressured to align to standards in ways that conflicted with their professional judgment regarding priorities for their students. In other words, the IEP document and process may be a site in which conflicting conceptions of the instructional purposes of special education (Fuchs et al., 2010; McLaughlin, 2010) are brought to the fore.

Finally, while SETs often serve as facilitators of IEP meetings, they may not be adequately prepared for this role (Beck & DeSutter 2020). Special educators experience many challenges in facilitating IEP meetings, such as low attendance, poor preparation from other team members, and disagreements between school personnel and family members. Overseeing these diverse teams can be complex, requiring sophisticated skills (e.g., Blackwell & Rossetti, 2014; Rossetti et al., 2017). For example, many special educators struggle to meaningfully involve parents; doing so effectively may require better supporting special educators to run culturally and linguistically responsive IEP meetings, as well as better supporting families to navigate these processes (Blackwell & Rossetti, 2014). Yet, special educators report not having learning opportunities that help them develop these skills (Beck & DeSutter 2020).

Factors Shaping Educators' Conceptions and Enactment of Their Roles

Teachers have broad discretion to enact their roles in a range of different ways, depending on how they conceptualize the purpose of the role; the same actions (e.g., modifying curriculum) could be enacted for different purposes (see, for example, Morris Mathews, 2020; Ruppar et al., 2018; Urbach et al., 2015). For example, in a mixed-methods study of how working conditions shaped special educators' reading instruction for students with EBD in self-contained settings, Morris Mathews et al. (2021) found one special educator and her colleagues conceptualized her instructional role as "flip[ping] a switch" (p. 28) to support general education content when students' behavior prevented them from attending general education classes; thus, her instruction was unscheduled and unproductive, consisting primarily of prompting students to complete work that other students completed in general education. In contrast, other special educators also supported students' access to general education content when behavior prevented them from attending general education classes, but they still viewed themselves as having substantive responsibility for planning and providing instruction in areas where students struggled; thus, they enacted their instructional role in quite different ways. Because educators may conceptualize and enact their roles in quite different ways, it is important to understand what factors may shape how they conceptualize and enact their roles. We thus explore individual (e.g., beliefs) and contextual (e.g., administrators) factors that research suggests may shape how teachers conceptualize and enact their roles.

Individual Factors

Few studies have explored individual factors shaping how teachers conceptualize and enact their roles in serving students with disabilities, but a handful of studies suggest beliefs and knowledge may contribute (Brownell et al., 2014; Kiely et al., 2014).

Beliefs

Extant research indicates several key beliefs may shape how special and general educators take up their roles in serving students with disabilities. First, teachers' expectations for students seem to be crucial (Kiely et al., 2014).

Second, extant research consistently indicates the importance of general educators taking ownership for students with disabilities, viewing instructing students with disabilities as primarily their responsibility (Giangreco et al., 1993). In a foundational study of general educators' experiences including students with severe disabilities in their classes, Giangreco et al. (1993) documented how teachers initially were willing to "host" (p. 7) students with disabilities, yet minimized their role in students' learning. One teacher said, "I don't think of him as one of the children that I educate;" another shared, "The aide will be more or less responsible for seeing to his needs" (p. 367). For most teachers, this changed over the year as they slowly came to recognize their responsibility to the student. At the end of the year, one teacher shared:

> I had always said, "I have 13 students plus Jon," and then I realized: Why am I saying "plus Jon"? He's one of my students [...] I'm the one that got the education, for the certificate for teaching. I'm responsible for every other student. I should be responsible for this student too [...] He's in my class. That's my responsibility (p. 368).

In highly effective, inclusive schools, general educators report feeling ownership for the learning of students with disabilities (Hoppey & McLeskey, 2013; McLeskey et al., 2014; Olson et al., 2016), as this teacher expressed at the end of the year (Giangreco et al., 1993). Further, in these contexts, special educators are more likely to report feeling able to manage their workloads and planning to stay in their jobs (Bettini, Jones et al., 2017; Bettini, Gilmour et al., 2020; Jones et al., 2013), suggesting general educators' sense of ownership for the learning of students with disabilities may facilitate special educators' efforts to fulfill their roles.

Teacher Knowledge and Expertise

Evidence from a handful of studies suggests that expertise, which incorporates multiple types of knowledge, may play a role in how special educators understand the needs of students with disabilities and, consequently, how they conceptualize and enact their roles (e.g., Ruppar et al., 2017; Stough & Palmer, 2003; Urbach et al., 2015). Teachers' expertise incorporates a command of pedagogical content knowledge (as defined by Shulman, 1987) but, importantly in special education, also incorporates a deep knowledge of students' individual learning characteristics, abilities, and histories (Brownell et al., 2010; Lauterbach et al., 2020; Ruppar et al., 2017). Ruppar et al. (2017) highlighted the crucial role of expertise for special educators' conceptions and enactment of their roles in an analysis of interview data from 11 expert special educators teaching students with severe disabilities. They found that, in their instructional roles, expert special educators drew on deep, tacit knowledge of systematic instruction, observation and data collection processes, and individual student needs to design and adapt curricula that were age-appropriate and maintained high expectations. Further, extensive knowledge of their context supported them to collaborate effectively with others to provide learning opportunities that would promote independence and inclusion; they drew on deep situated knowledge of the collaborative and communicative processes in their context to recruit support from others (e.g., paraprofessionals, general educators, families) for students. We previously noted that special educators' collaborative role is not only about fulfilling direct service responsibilities to students but also about improving their school's capacity to meaningfully include students with disabilities; Ruppar et al.'s (2017) findings suggest deep expertise in the school context is necessary to engage in one's collaborative role in this way. Other studies have obtained findings consistent with these, indicating special educators' enactment of their instructional and collaborative roles may be shaped by both (a) their expertise in student learning needs, as well as (b) their expertise in their context (Lauterbach et al., 2020; Stough & Palmer, 2003).

Importantly, these studies find expert teachers' deep knowledge supports them to hold high expectations, such that they conceptualize and enact their instructional and collaborative roles in ways that foster more rigorous and inclusive educational opportunities for students. For example, in Lauterbach et al.'s (2020) study of expert secondary content area teachers of students with learning disabilities, experts' knowledge of the demands of college courses, combined with knowledge of students' learning needs and capacities, led them to design learning opportunities that scaffolded students' development of routines useful for success in college.

Contextual Influences on Roles

Extant studies suggest service delivery models (Embich, 2001), working conditions (Bettini, Wang et al., 2019), and school poverty (Voltz & Fore, 2006) may contribute to how teachers conceptualize and enact their roles.

Service Delivery Model

Special educators' formal titles (i.e., their *parts*, in role theory) are often defined by students' service delivery model—by the places (e.g., general education classroom, resource, self-contained) in which their students receive services (Billingsley & Bettini, 2019; Gilmour et al., 2021). Definitions of service delivery models vary greatly, but these models include (a) co-teaching, when a special and general educator share responsibility for planning and delivering instruction to a single class (e.g., Weiss & Lloyd, 2002); (b) consultant or inclusion specialist, when a special educator consults with general educators to support accommodations and modifications in general education classes and provides services in that setting (e.g., Zagona et al., 2020); (c) resource teacher, when a special educator pulls students out of general education to provide services in another space (e.g., Siuty et al., 2018); and (d) self-contained teacher, when a special educator provides most or all instruction in a separate, special education setting (e.g., Bettini, Wang et al., 2019; O'Brien et al., 2019).

All special educators must act as *instructors*, *collaborators*, and *case managers*, but these roles may be enacted differently depending on where students are primarily taught. In their study of special educators' time use, Vannest and Hagan-Burke (2010) found special educators' time was distributed differently in different service delivery models. Special educators in resource models spent more time directly providing academic instruction compared to special educators in other service delivery models, while those who cotaught spent more time on instructional support (i.e., "providing support to students, with minimal or no direct teaching, during [...] instruction"; p. 141) than other special educators, and those in self-contained settings spent more time on discipline and supervising non-instructional activities than other special educators. These results should be taken with caution as the sample was small (N=36), and they did not test whether the differences were statistically significant. However, results align with other studies, which indicate special educators may enact these roles in different ways in different service delivery models (Bettini, Lillis et al., 2021; Bettini, Wang et al., 2019; Scruggs et al., 2007).

Special educators in co-taught and consultative models often describe the crucial importance of their collaborative roles, as they must work with general educators to co-plan and co-deliver instruction (e.g., Pratt, 2014; Scruggs et al., 2007; Weiss & Lloyd, 2002). Importantly, as the proportion of students with disabilities included in general education classes has increased (Williamson et al., 2019), schools' reliance on coteaching also seems to be increasing; whereas 9% of special educators reported co-teaching in 2000, 17% reported co-teaching in 2012, and 13% reported co-teaching in 2016 (Gilmour et al., 2021). However, extant research indicates special educators often struggle to fulfill meaningful instructional roles in co-taught classes (e.g., Wexler et al., 2018). In a synthesis of research on co-teaching, Scruggs et al. (2007) found special educators were often subordinate to general educators during instruction. They struggled to meaningfully contribute to planning and often spent class time assisting students to complete tasks rather than teaching skills and strategies to support student learning. Findings held across both secondary and elementary settings, but they were more pronounced in secondary (Scruggs et al., 2007). Consistent with this, Jones and Winters (2020) analyzed Massachusetts state data to determine the effects of increasing coteaching on student outcomes. In elementary schools, they found marginal positive effects in math and significant positive effects in English language arts; in secondary schools, they found significant negative effects in both math and English language arts. Thus, in elementary schools, extant evidence indicates special education co-teachers may be able to fulfill productive instructional roles (Jones & Winters, 2020; Scruggs et al., 2007) and that their collaborative roles may be intensified, as they must collaborate to ensure meaningful instructional roles (Klingner & Vaughn, 2002; Scruggs et al., 2007).

In contrast to co-teachers, special educators in self-contained settings report often being relatively isolated, with little to no collaboration except with paraprofessionals (Bettini, Wang et al., 2019; O'Brien et al., 2019). Because these special educators often collaborate primarily with paraprofessionals, their collaborative role may take a different form, requiring more supervisory and training responsibilities and less instructional collaboration than special educators in co-taught settings (Bettini, Cumming et al., 2017; O'Brien et al., 2019). In addition, because they often teach multiple subjects to multiple grades, these special educators may have more intensive instructional responsibilities. For example, in a national survey of special educators serving students with emotional/behavioral disorders in self-contained settings, O'Brien et al. (2019) found special educators averaged more than nine different preparations per week—far more than a typical general educator, who may prepare lessons for four to five different subjects/grades. In Bishop et al.'s (2010) study of novice elementary special educators, a participant in a self-contained class reported having four math groups, five reading groups, and two science groups, which she referred to as a "logistical nightmare" (p. 86). Further, these special educators often report having limited planning time, which they report limits the quality of their instruction (Bettini, Wang et al., 2019; Cumming et al., 2020; Morris Mathews et al., 2020).

Special educators in resource and consultative service delivery models seem to enact their roles in widely varied ways, depending on the distribution of responsibilities among personnel in their school (e.g., Bishop et al., 2010; Mitchell et al., 2012). For example, Mitchell et al. (2012) used mixed methods to examine how seven special educators in resource settings used their time in elementary schools implementing RtI. One special educator spent more than half of their time on IEP case management, while another spent only 15% of their time on this role. Similarly, two teachers spent no time acting as a diagnostician (i.e., evaluating students' skills, progress) because these tasks were assigned to the school psychologist in their school; in contrast, another special educator devoted more than half their time to this role. Though co-taught and self-contained service delivery models may also be enacted in varied ways (e.g., Bettini, Lillis et al., 2021; Morris Mathews et al., 2020), resource and consultative models seem to be especially variable in how they are defined across settings and thus especially varied in their implications for the nature of special educators' roles (Bishop et al., 2010; Mitchell et al., 2012).

Working Conditions

School working conditions –the demands placed on teachers and the resources to meet those demands—may shape how teachers understand and enact their roles (Billingsley et al., 2019; Mathews et al., 2017; Morris Mathews et al., 2020). In Bettini, Lillis et al.'s (2021) qualitative study of special educators serving students with EBD in self-contained settings, special educators described how others often did not share their conceptions of their instructional roles, creating barriers to fulfilling those roles effectively. For example, one participant had no reading curricula because administrators expected her to obtain lesson plans from general educators, but she had no dedicated time to gather those plans; further, she had students who she felt needed foundational skills instruction (e.g., in decoding), but she did not have dedicated time, resources, or collaborative relationships aligned with this need. Thus, she described often fulfilling her instructional role in ad-hoc ways. As this example highlights, several working conditions may shape educators' roles in serving students with disabilities, including administrators, material resources, and time (Bettini, Lillis et al., 2021; Billingsley et al., 2019); in addition, evaluation systems may also contribute (Braun & Youngs, 2020).

Administrators

Because they organize the school's routines and foster the school's culture, administrators may be especially important for shaping educators' roles in inclusive schools (e.g., McLeskey et al., 2014). Administrators who foster a school culture in which all teachers share responsibility for instructing students with disabilities and who align school schedules and resources with that culture may better support teachers to play meaningful roles in serving students with disabilities (Billingsley et al., 2017, 2019; Hoppey & McLeskey, 2013; McLeskey et al., 2014). For example, case studies of effective inclusive schools consistently highlight how administrators in these schools establish clear and high instructional expectations for students with disabilities, orienting the school's schedule and routines to protect students' access to both general education curricula and foundational skills instruction with specialists—and thereby provide crucial supports for teachers' roles in serving students with disabilities (Hoppey & McLeskey, 2013; McLeskey et al., 2014).

In some contexts, key stakeholders, such as administrators, may hold ill-defined conceptions of special educators' roles (e.g., Bays & Crockett, 2007; Garwood et al., 2018; Roberts et al., 2017). For example, some administrators in Bays and Crockett's (2007) study expressed that instruction for students with disabilities is "best left to special educators" (p. 154) and hence did not articulate clear visions of special educators' roles. In such contexts, special educators may expend a considerable time and energy determining and negotiating a meaningful instructional role (Garwood et al., 2018; Mathews, 2018; Youngs et al., 2011), while general educators may hold only ambiguous conceptions of how they should be serving students with disabilities in their classes (Able et al., 2015). In a case study comparing the experiences of novice general and special educators, Youngs et al. (2011) found that novice special educators had to navigate considerable uncertainty about very basic aspects of their instructional roles, such as when, where, and what to teach to whom. Their roles were not clearly defined explicitly (e.g., in communication from administrators) or implicitly (e.g., through schedules and curricula delimiting what they should do when, where, and with whom).

Extant research suggests administrators often have limited knowledge of special education, which could constrain their understanding of special and general educators' roles in serving students with disabilities (Stark et al., 2020). Principals in qualitative studies often describe special educators' instructional roles by highlighting dispositions (e.g., caring about students, patience), but not skills (e.g., providing effective explicit instruction) that they should demonstrate, and by describing special educators' capacity to obtain students' behavioral compliance (Roberts et al, 2017; Steinbrecher et al., 2015). For example, Roberts et al. (2017) conducted a qualitative study of 12 principals' perspectives on high-quality instruction for students with severe disabilities. They found that principals consistently said special educators should be caring and communicate effectively, but principals could not articulate specific instructional practices special educators should use. Further, when describing how they knew a special educator was effective, they did not describe attending to either special educators' instruction or students' academic, social, and behavioral growth; instead, they judged special educators' instruction based on whether special educators were able to obtain student behavioral compliance. In other words, they articulated visions of special educators' instructional roles in which the core purpose was controlling students rather than teaching them. Roberts et al. (2017) concluded that the traits principals identified (e.g., obtaining compliance) are valuable, but "become problematic when they represent *all* a teacher does and *all* an administrator values [...] This limited understanding [...] reproduces low expectations for students with severe disabilities and their teachers" (p. 13). Importantly, if administrators do not have clear, meaningful conceptions of special and general educators' instructional roles in serving students with disabilities, they are unlikely to support these roles effectively (Stark et al., 2020).

Curricula

A handful of studies suggest teachers use their instructional curricula to help them conceptualize the purposes of their instructional role for students with disabilities (e.g., Siuty et al., 2018). In particular, the content in teachers' curricular resources may set implicit expectations about what should be the focus of their instructional efforts. For example, Siuty et al. (2018) examined how 11 middle school special educators' curricular materials related to how they enacted their instructional role. Special educators who had standardized reading curricula, with a focus on basic skills, oriented their instruction toward building basic skills (e.g., fluency, decoding) in areas where the assessments (from their curricula) indicated a need for support; in contrast, those without standardized reading curricula oriented reading instruction toward a wide range of topics, which one teacher referred to as "mashed together" and "disjointed" (Siuty et al., 2018, p. 47). More research is needed to better understand how curricula may shape teachers' conceptions and enactment of their roles in serving students with disabilities, but Siuty et al.'s (2018) results are consistent with a robust body of research in general education, which indicates that teachers often adopt instructional approaches embedded in curricular materials, especially early in their careers (Grossman & Thompson, 2008), and that curricula can promote the use of more effective practices (Jackson & Makarin, 2016; Jimenez et al., 2014).

Schedules

Teachers' schedules determine the time they have available for each of their roles and thus have the potential to constrain how teachers enact their roles (Billingsley et al., 2019). For example, a number of studies have highlighted how limited scheduled time for collaboration may constrain teachers' ability to fulfill their collaborative roles (e.g., Fennick & Liddy, 2001; Morris Mathews et al., 2020; Scruggs et al., 2007) as a result of which teachers then often report only collaborating "on the fly" (Bettini, Wang et al. 2019, p. 11). Without adequate time dedicated to working with colleagues, special educators report struggling to build shared understandings among various stakeholders (e.g., paraprofessionals, general educators, administrators) about how best to meet student needs (Bettini, Lillis et al., 2021).

Schedules can also constrain or facilitate teachers' instructional roles (Billingsley et al., 2019). For example, in McLeskey et al.'s (2014) case study of an effective inclusive elementary school, the principal highlighted the importance of schedules for ensuring specialists could efficiently coordinate the times when they would serve students. A consistent school-wide instructional schedule made it possible for special educators to fulfill their instructional role for all of their students (McLeskey et al., 2014). In contrast, special educators in some studies report that time limitations sometimes push them to constrain their instructional role. For example, in Bettini et al.'s (2015) study, special educators reported that, without scheduled time for planning and paperwork, they sometimes planned other activities (e.g., movies, independent seatwork) for students so that they could complete urgent planning and paperwork responsibilities.

Evaluation Instruments and Procedures

In a qualitative study in one middle school, Braun and Youngs (2020) examined how two special and two general educators perceived and experienced new evaluation procedures in their state. They found that the special educators reported the evaluation criteria were misaligned with core aspects of their role, not evaluating, for example, their very significant and time-consuming IEP case management role. Further, because the evaluation system held them accountable for students' learning on state assessments, special educators reported reevaluating their instructional roles, increasing the priority they placed on standardized curricula while decreasing the priority they placed on individual skill instruction. More research is needed to better understand how evaluation procedures and tools may shape roles, but this study provides some indication that they could contribute to how special educators conceptualize their roles (Braun & Youngs, 2020).

School Poverty

High poverty schools serve students whose communities have often been subject to systematic social disinvestment, which has consequences for schools' financial resources (e.g., Baker et al., 2020), recruitment and retention of leaders able to support long-term school improvement (e.g., Béteille et al., 2012), expectations for student achievement (e.g., Rubie-Davies et al., 2011), teacher recruitment (e.g., Boyd et al., 2003; Early & Shagoury, 2010), teacher working conditions (e.g., Fall & Billingsley, 2011), and teacher retention (e.g., Bettini, Gilmour et al., 2020; Johnson et al., 2012). Due to these differences, policies are often enacted differently in high-poverty schools than in low-poverty schools, as local decision makers use their discretion to comply with policy mandates within tighter constraints than low-poverty schools encounter (e.g., Diamond, 2007, 2012; Diamond & Spillane, 2004). No studies have explored if or how special educators' roles vary in high vs. low poverty schools, but there are some indications that special educators who serve in high-poverty schools may experience substantially different role expectations and supports for fulfilling their roles than special educators in low-poverty schools (Voltz & Fore, 2006).

First, extant research indicates students with disabilities who attend high-poverty schools are significantly less likely to be included in general education settings than students with disabilities who attend low-poverty schools (e.g., Bettini et al., in press; Grindal et al., 2019, 2020; Hehir et al., 2014). For example, analyzing a national dataset, Green et al. (2020) found that, among adolescents with mental health disorders, Black and Latino students—who are disproportionately served in high-poverty schools—are significantly more likely to receive services in separate placements and significantly less likely to have received school counseling (a less restrictive service) as their first form of school-based support for their mental health disorder. Extant research does not indicate why this is the case, but possible explanations include reduced school financial resources (Baker et al., 2020), high administrative turnover (Béteille et al., 2012), and expectations for parent advocacy that are misaligned with parents' other commitments and cultural expectations (Kalyanpur et al., 2000; Skrtic, 2012). Thus, because students in high-poverty schools may be less likely to be placed in inclusive settings, special educators in these schools may be less likely to teach in co-taught or resource service delivery models and may be more likely to teach in self-contained settings.

Second, extant research indicates special educators in high-poverty schools and districts experience significantly more demanding roles, with less support to meet demands, than special educators in low-poverty schools (Fall & Billingsley, 2011). Analyzing a nationally representative survey of special educators from 1999 to 2000, Fall and Billingsley (2011) found that special educators in high poverty districts reported significantly larger caseloads than special educators in low-poverty schools and that they were significantly more likely to report that routine duties and paperwork interfered with their teaching. Despite increased demands, they were significantly less likely to report having collegial support, principal support, or materials. No recent studies have updated Fall and Billingsley's (2011) analysis, and it is unclear whether those patterns remain consistent to the present, though recent studies of general educators do confirm that, in general, teachers experience more challenging workloads and fewer supports in high-poverty schools (Simon & Johnson, 2015). Thus, special educators in high-poverty schools may be more likely to experience role overload, when one has too much to do in the time allotted.

Potential Outcomes of Special Educators' Roles

A number of studies examined how aspects of teachers' roles are associated with their affective outcomes, such as burnout, and their attrition or intent to leave teaching (e.g., Billingsley & Bettini, 2019; Brunsting et al., 2014). In addition, a handful of studies have examined how special educators' conceptions of their roles are associated with their instruction for students with disabilities (e.g., Urbach et al., 2015).

Burnout and Attrition

Extant research indicates that problems with teachers' roles are associated with burnout and intent to leave their jobs (e.g., Brunsting et al., 2014; Embich, 2001; Garwood et al., 2018). Burnout is a condition characterized by emotional exhaustion, cynicism (also termed depersonalization), and a reduced sense of personal accomplishment; this constellation of symptoms occurs when prolonged stress exhausts one's resources to cope (Brunsting et al., 2014; Garwood et al., 2018). Burnout is of great concern, as it is associated with educational processes, including implementation fidelity of interventions and teacher-student interactions (Irvin et al., 2013; Oakes et al., 2020; Wehby et al., 2012; Wong et al., 2017). Further, teachers who are more burned out are more likely to intend to leave (Bettini, Cumming et al., 2020; Bettini, Jones et al., 2017), which is of particular concern for special educators, given the chronic national special educator shortage (Mason-Williams et al., 2020).

Importantly, teachers' role problems are associated with negative affective outcomes such as stress and burnout (Brunsting et al., 2014; Park & Shin, 2020). Role problems include role overload (i.e., feeling one has too many demands within the allotted time), role ambiguity (i.e., uncertainty about core aspects of one's role), and role conflict (i.e., conflicting expectations for one's role due to incompatible or inconsistent demands; Embich, 2001). A full discussion of role problems is beyond the scope of this chapter, but we briefly discuss evidence that role problems may be associated with burnout and attrition among special and general educators.

Special Educators

The many demands on special educators, without adequate time and resources to meet those demands (i.e., role overload), can leave special educators feeling burned out and intending to leave (Bettini, Cumming et al., 2020; Embich, 2001). For example, in a survey of 300 secondary special educators, Embich (2001) found that workload was a significant predictor of the emotional exhaustion component of burnout. Similarly, in a survey of novice elementary and middle school teachers, Bettini, Jones, et al. (2017) found that special educators rated their workloads less manageable than novice general educators, and those who felt their workloads were less manageable were significantly more likely to feel emotionally exhausted and to plan to leave. Some aspects of special educators' roles may be especially important for these outcomes. In particular, extant research indicates special educators are more likely to experience these outcomes when they (a) perceive students have greater behavior challenges (e.g., Bettini, Gilmour et al., 2020; Billingsley, 2007; Conley & You, 2017); (b) report having a larger and/or more complex caseloads (Berry, 2012; Billingsley, 2007; Carver-Thomas & Darling-Hammond, 2017); and (c) report higher paperwork demands and/or insufficient time for paperwork (Albrecht et al., 2009; Berry et al., 2011; Billingsley, 2007). Resources that ameliorate these demands, such as administrative support for managing challenging behavior, may be important for relieving the experience of role overload and sustaining their commitment to stay (Bettini, Cumming et al., 2020; Bettini, Gilmour et al., 2020; Billingsley & Bettini, 2019; Cancio et al., 2013; Garwood et al., 2018). Note, however, that much of this research has focused on special educators in self-contained settings; to our knowledge, no studies have examined factors associated with role overload within inclusive schools (Billingsley & Bettini, 2019).

Role conflict may also contribute to special educators' burnout and attrition (Embich, 2001; Garwood et al., 2018). In a mixed-methods study of 64 rural special educators, Garwood et al. (2018) found role conflict predicted the emotional exhaustion and depersonalization aspects of burnout. Embich (2001) also identified role conflict as a significant predictor of burnout among secondary special educators. Notably, in Embich's (2001) study, role conflict was the most significant predictor of emotional exhaustion for special educators who team-taught with general educators. This aligns with other research that has identified collaborating with general educators as a major stressor due to issues such as conflicting perspectives about inclusion, how to best meet students' needs, and the nature of the special educators' instructional role in a co-taught setting (e.g., Bettini, Lillis et al., 2021; Mathews et al., 2017; Scruggs et al., 2007).

Role ambiguity, or lack of clarity regarding some aspect of one's role, is also associated with burnout (Embich, 2001; Garwood et al., 2018). In Garwood et al.'s (2018) study, role ambiguity explained a significant portion of the variance in rural special educators' sense of personal accomplishment. In their analysis of follow-up interviews, Garwood et al. (2018) found, "Without clear guidelines, even teachers who may be performing well had no idea if they were doing what was expected because most administrators were not offering feedback" (p. 37). Similarly, in Embich's (2001) study, role ambiguity was associated with a reduced sense of personal accomplishment and emotional exhaustion for special educators who team-taught. This finding is also supported by qualitative studies that describe how lack of clear responsibilities, such as ambiguous curricular expectations, can leave special educators feeling confused about what they should be doing (e.g., Youngs et al., 2011).

In a synthesis of research on special educator burnout, Brunsting et al. (2014) corroborated strong support for relationships between role problems and burnout. However, note that most studies on special educators' role problems have not focused on special educators in elementary schools, and, to our knowledge, none have focused exclusively on inclusive schools.

General Educators

Though many studies have examined factors associated with general educators' burnout and attrition (e.g., Borman & Dowling, 2008; Guarino et al., 2006), few studies have examined how general educators' roles in serving students with disabilities may be associated with their burnout and attrition. Gilmour and Wehby (2019) analyzed North Carolina's state administrative dataset to examine how serving students with disabilities were related to general educators' attrition. They found that general education certified teachers who taught more students with disabilities were significantly more likely to leave in the following year, suggesting that their responsibility for teaching more students with disabilities may present general educators with greater demands and that they may often not have adequate resources to meet this demand. However, much more extensive research is needed to understand the potential implications of general educators' roles in inclusive schools for their burnout and attrition.

Instruction

A small body of work indicates a potential relationship between special educators' role beliefs and their instructional quality (Morris Mathews, 2018; Urbach et al., 2015). Urbach et al. (2015) used observation scores from a validated measure of explicit, intensive, and individualized reading instruction (Reading in Special Education [RISE]; Brownell et al., 2009) and interview data to examine distinctions between more and less accomplished special educators' conceptions of their roles. The authors found that special educators who scored higher on RISE (n = 23) believed their roles required providing intensive instruction and maintaining high expectations for students. In contrast, those who scored lower (n = 18) emphasized making learning fun and building relationships. Though both groups emphasized systematic, explicit instructional methods, they differed in terms of the purposes for which they designed explicit instruction. Similarly, Morris Mathews (2018) examined the relationship between three beginning special educators' role beliefs and their instructional quality. Though instructional quality was generally low across these beginning special educators (with the exception of their classroom environment scores), their beliefs about their instructional role provided a signal regarding the quality of their instruction. Whereas two special educators emphasized building confidence, helping students to become a "better person," and accessing the general education curriculum, the one participant whose conception of the role included delivering targeted interventions provided instruction that was more purposeful, scaffolded, and explicit.

These studies both drew from small, purposive samples, and they are not generalizable; thus, extant research supports hypotheses but not substantiated conclusions regarding how role conceptions may relate to instruction. Further, to date, no studies have examined relationships between conceptions of role and outcomes among students with disabilities.

Setting the Course for Effective Inclusion

Local leaders and educators have substantial discretion to determine how they conceptualize teachers' roles in serving students with disabilities (Weatherley & Lipsky, 1977). And, as we have discussed throughout this chapter, extant research indicates that they do, indeed, conceptualize educators' roles in widely different ways, and special and general educators' roles in serving students with disabilities vary greatly across schools (e.g., Bray & Russell, 2018). Though *instructional, collaborative*, and *IEP case management* roles are common across settings, the responsibilities embedded in each of these roles, and the core purposes for which educators enact these roles, differ across schools (e.g., Mitchell et al., 2012).

However, we have argued that effective inclusive schools fundamentally depend on shared conceptions of educators' roles because educators in inclusive schools are interdependent with one another (Bettini 2021 in review), and schools are interdependent with other institutions in their efforts to cultivate and retain a teacher workforce capable of effectively teaching students with disabilities (Brownell et al., 2010; Sykes et al., 2010). Shared conceptions of special and general educators' roles in serving students with disabilities are essential to ensure educators can coordinate their work with one another and crucial to the development of a teacher workforce with the skills and supports needed to enact their roles.

In the following sections, we discuss avenues for first, better understanding what should be special and general educators' roles in inclusive elementary schools, and second, changing individual and collective beliefs about their roles, to improve how schools support inclusion of students with disabilities. We specifically describe (a) research needed to better understand what roles educators should fulfill in effective inclusive schools; (b) how leaders can foster meaningful roles for special and general educators in inclusive elementary schools; (c) how teacher educators can support these efforts; and (d) what teachers themselves can do. Throughout, our aim is not to prescribe roles or limit local discretion, but rather to consider how we might collectively build greater consensus about what special and general educators' roles in serving students with disabilities should be and how we should support those roles in practice.

Future Research

Future research has a crucial role to play in helping build consensus about what should be educators' roles in effective inclusive schools. We particularly recommend that future research systematically examine (a) if students with disabilities are better served when special and general educators' roles are conceptualized and enacted in particular ways; and (b) what factors shape their conceptions and enactment of their roles. We also describe considerations regarding the research methods needed to fulfill these recommendations.

Conceptions and Enactment of Roles

Future research is urgently needed to better understand whether students with disabilities are better served when teachers' roles are conceptualized and enacted in particular ways. We reviewed a handful of studies indicating students with disabilities may experience stronger instruction when teachers conceptualize disability in particular ways (e.g., Jordan et al., 2010) and orient their work toward promoting strong academic skills (e.g., Mathews, 2018; Urbach et al., 2015). However, these were all small studies, using methods that preclude strong inferences; further, none examined the impacts of role conceptions on students' outcomes (e.g., achievement, engagement, inclusion). More extensive research is needed to understand (a) key dimensions of stakeholders' conceptions of special and general educators' roles; (b) how these conceptions shape teachers' enactment of their roles; and (c) effects of different role conceptions/enactment on students' experiences and outcomes. Such research would help our field determine, empirically, what roles special and general educators should be prepared and supported to fulfill.

For example, scholars could replicate Urbach et al.'s (2015) study, with other populations and in other contexts, to determine what aspects of teachers' conceptions and enactment of their roles may be shaping their instructional methods and content for students with disabilities. Scholars could also conduct survey studies, similar to Jordan et al.'s (2010) work, to determine whether teachers who conceptualize their roles in particular ways have students who feel more engaged in school, who are more meaningfully included, and who experience stronger outcomes. Likewise, studies could examine whether students experience stronger outcomes when their special educators orient their instructional roles toward promoting foundational skills instruction (e.g., Sayeski et al., 2019) or general education curricular content (e.g., McLaughlin, 2010), and thus help respond to this persistent debate among scholars.

Such research would be especially beneficial if it attended to multiple stakeholders' conceptions of teachers' roles. Understanding how administrators' conceptions of teachers' roles relate to teachers' enactment of their roles and their students' outcomes would be especially valuable for determining what role beliefs leader educators should be trying to promote among leaders; we found only a few studies that examined administrators' conceptions of teachers' roles in serving students with disabilities (e.g., Roberts et al., 2017; Steinbrecher et al., 2015), despite robust evidence that administrators play a crucial role in supporting teachers to fulfill meaningful roles in serving students with disabilities (e.g., McLeskey et al., 2014). Similarly, we found few studies that examined general educators' conceptions or enactment of their roles in serving students with disabilities; some studies included general educators if the school was the unit of analysis (e.g., Bray & Russell, 2018; Olson et al., 2016), but few studies focused on general educators, even though general educators are the main teacher for most students with disabilities.

Factors Shaping Teachers' Conceptions and Enactment of Their Roles

To develop shared conceptions among stakeholders of special and general educators' roles, the field needs scholarship examining what factors lead teachers to develop certain conceptions of their roles and what leads them to enact their roles in more or less productive ways. For example, are there aspects of curricula that lead teachers to adopt particular approaches to their instructional roles for students with disabilities? How do interactions with administrators shape teachers' conceptions of their roles? How do teachers' conceptions of their roles change when they encounter conditions (e.g., schedules, time constraints) that facilitate or constrain some aspects of their roles? Scholars could investigate these questions using descriptive, correlational, or intervention research. For example, scholars could descriptively use mixed methods to examine how working conditions facilitate or constrain a special educators' enactment of their role; they could use survey research to test hypotheses generated in that mixed methods investigation; and they could test an intervention to determine whether changing working conditions lead to changes in the enactment of their roles.

Research Methods

A focus on role is distinct from how much special education research has examined teachers' work. Most special education scholarship has focused on observable, discrete practices (e.g., behavior-specific praise; Royer et al., 2019). This work has been tremendously productive for identifying instructional methods that benefit students with disabilities, but it is quite different from the research we are proposing. Discrete practices, such as behavior-specific praise, may be part of enacting a role; however, when we focus on role, we conceptualize teachers' work at a broader grain size, asking how discrete practices collectively work together and for what purposes teachers take up these practices. As we have highlighted elsewhere, a special educator may take up a discrete practice (e.g., behavior-specific praise) for a variety of different purposes (e.g., teaching foundational skills, teaching general education curricula, building relationships), depending on how they conceptualize the purpose of their role; and they may use the same discrete practice to promote different student behaviors.

This focus on role thus has implications for the methods scholars use. Some research on role adopts behaviorist measures that are epistemologically aligned with measures used in research on discrete instructional practices. For example, Vannest and Hagan-Burke's (2010) study used operational definitions of observable activities to examine special educators' time use. This was a useful study, and a larger-scale replication of it would be of great value.

However, understanding conceptions and enactment of role will also require research from cognitive and social constructivist orientations, as conceptions of role may be internally held or shared among a community and thus may not objectively observable in the ways that discrete instructional practices are. Understanding how educators use their discretion to orient their work toward a purpose requires researchers to invest in more deeply understanding how teachers think about their work, using methods that take their individual and collective sense-making about their roles seriously (e.g., Youngs et al., 2011). Such work would likely benefit from rich qualitative and mixed methods investigations. Latent measures that quantitatively evaluate key dimensions of teachers' role beliefs, as identified within qualitative and mixed methods research, would be useful for scaling up this research.

Strong theoretical and conceptual foundations are essential for conducting research in robust ways. We found role theory (Biddle, 1986) useful in this chapter and in other investigations (Bettini, Wang et al., 2019). Other potentially useful theories used in some of the stronger studies we reviewed include activity theory (e.g., Gomez-Najarro, 2020), institutional theory (e.g., Bray & Russell, 2018), and sense-making theory (e.g., Youngs et al., 2011). These theories differ in their core tenets and how they orient researchers to data collection and analysis, but they share a focus on individual and collective conceptions of social phenomena, and thus, they may each have utility for supporting the kind of research we are recommending.

Implications for School and District Leaders

School and district leaders bear primary responsibility for structuring schools in which all stakeholders collaborate in service of effective inclusion (Billingsley et al., 2017; DeMatthews et al., 2020; Hoppey & McLeskey, 2013; McLeskey et al., 2014). Fostering meaningful roles for special and general educators is central to fulfilling this charge.

First, leaders should carefully reflect on their own knowledge and beliefs relevant to special education. Though school leaders seldom receive adequate preparation regarding instruction in special education (Stelitano et al., 2020), resources developed by the Council of Chief State School Officers describe practices that are crucial for the success of students with disabilities across settings (Council of Chief State School Officers & Collaboration for Effective Educator Development, Accountability, and Reform, 2017). Leaders should consult these crucial guidance documents and reach out to district special education personnel, to address gaps in their knowledge. We also recommend that school leaders reflect on the beliefs they hold about students with disabilities, critiquing deficit beliefs that could lead them to hold and communicate low expectations for teachers' instructional roles with students with disabilities (e.g., Roberts et al., 2017; Ruppar et al., 2018; Stanovich & Jordan, 1998). Leaders should be mindful that teachers (especially new teachers) look to them for signals on what is expected of students with disabilities, and high expectations are essential to ensure equitable learning opportunities.

Second, we recommend that leaders collaborate with special and general educators, parents, and other stakeholders (e.g., district special education personnel) to craft a vision for their school that is inclusive of and equitable for students with disabilities (Billingsley et al., 2017). This work should be done collaboratively, engaging other stakeholders in the process, ensuring their perspectives are valued, and increasing buy-in (Stark et al., 2020). Leaders can then take responsibility for communicating this collective vision explicitly (e.g., in mission statements), and implicitly, for example, through the ways they support decisions to invest time and money in training and materials for teaching students with disabilities (e.g., Bettini, Benedict et al., 2017; Hoppey & McLeskey, 2013; McLeskey et al., 2014).

Third, leaders should facilitate conversations regarding the distribution of roles and responsibilities among educators in their school, cultivate buy-in for this division of roles, and communicate this vision clearly to all teachers so that teachers can coordinate their efforts efficiently. While doing so, they should consider whether this distribution reflects the efficient utilization of their expert personnel resources. For example, does the distribution of responsibilities capitalize on special educators' expertise in instructional strategies and student learning needs (McLeskey et al., 2014)? They should also consider whether school resources and structures appropriately support this distribution of responsibilities. For example, if special and general educators co-teach, do they have time to co-plan (Scruggs et al., 2007)? If special educators modify and accommodate general education curricular content, do they have all relevant curricular materials, such as teacher's guides and student workbooks (Bettini, Lillis et al., 2021)? If special educators train paraprofessionals, do they have regularly scheduled and dedicated time during paraprofessionals' workdays and while students are not present to plan for and provide training (Morris Mathews et al., 2021)?

Finally, we recognize that most school leaders do not receive adequate preparation for leading special education (e.g., Petzko, 2008; Stelitano et al., 2020) and may struggle with some aspects of this role. We recommend that leaders look to district special education administrators as resources for learning, as these leaders are likely to understand both the constraints in which school leaders are operating and the needs of the students and teachers who school leaders are responsible for supporting. Leaders should also consider special educators as an important resource; by deeply engaging with special educators, getting to know the nuts and bolts of their daily work with students, leaders may come to better understand how to effectively support all educators in fulfilling meaningful roles for students with disabilities.

Implications for Teacher Education

Experiences in teacher preparation foster educators' visions for their professional roles, supporting future teachers to develop normative understandings of good teaching and values that shape how they enact their roles (Darling-Hammond et al., 2006; Feiman-Nemser, 2001; Kennedy, 2006; Morris Mathews, 2020). To do this in a way that supports effective inclusive schools, we recommend teacher educators make explicit: (1) the purpose of special education, (2) special and general educators' roles in fulfilling that purpose, and (3) the ways their roles should be coordinated. These three concepts should be presented in consistent ways across preparation (i.e., in course content, assignments, field placements, supervisory relationships) so future teachers can anchor new learning in a clear, practical understanding of their future roles. These three concepts should also be presented in ways that support future teachers to make connections between what is espoused in teacher preparation and the practical realities of their roles in schools (Hammerness & Klette, 2015), including both limiting field placements misaligned with these concepts, and helping future teachers make sense of and respond to placements misaligned with these concepts (Morris-Mathews, 2020). For example, teacher educators should avoid field placements in which special educators do not play a meaningful instructional role; and, if a future teacher is placed in such a setting, teacher educators should help them make sense of why this happens and how to respond. Ensuring consistency in the ways these three concepts are presented is not easy work and likely requires joint efforts to identify and improve courses, field placements, and other experiences. For example, faculty could review syllabi to determine the extent to which courses promote both a clear, consistent vision of inclusive education, as well as competence in the practices necessary to include students with disabilities successfully.

The structure of teacher preparation could contribute to how well special and general educators are prepared for their interdependent roles (Blanton et al., 2018). However, extant research has not explored which models most effectively support future teachers in developing productive conceptions of their roles or fulfilling those roles effectively. In fact, few studies have traced special or general educators from preparation into their in-service roles to determine how preparation relates to in-service enactment of their roles in serving students with disabilities.

In addition to considering internal program structures, teacher educators must also consider their relationships with local school districts (Billingsley et al., 2020). Teacher education is an interdependent endeavor shared by teacher educators and local districts (Leko & Brownell, 2011). Thus, preparation programs cannot merely inform candidates about their future roles; they must also work with local schools to support the development of field placements and in-service contexts that foster meaningful roles for special and general educators (Babione & Shea, 2005; Dieker et al., 2003; Youngs et al., 2011). Grow Your Own (GYO) programs represent a particularly promising approach to coordinating with local districts (Bianco & Marin-Paris, 2019). GYO programs recruit individuals already rooted in a community (e.g., paraprofessionals, parents) into teaching (Podolsky et al., 2016) and have the advantage of providing a pathway for more teachers of color to enter the profession (e.g., Quiñones, 2018; Wall et al., 2005). For example, in Project CREATE, university and district personnel worked together to improve schools' capacities to implement evidence-based practices for culturally and linguistically diverse learners while also ameliorating the shortage of special educators in local schools (Peterson et al., 2020). This cross-institutional coordination could be a way to facilitate special and general educators' efforts to make sense of and fulfill meaningful roles in inclusive schools.

Recommendations for Teachers

Teachers should not, on their own, be charged with settling long-standing debates about the nature of special education, defining their jobs, or advocating for conditions that facilitate their work. Creating clearly defined, well-differentiated, and manageable roles should be the collaborative work of school leaders, policymakers, and teachers. At the same time, teachers are "active decision makers and school change contributors" (Li & Ruppar, 2020, p. 2) with agentic roles in schools. Thus, we provide recommendations for how teachers can foster more meaningful, supported roles for themselves in effective inclusive schools.

First, we encourage teachers to reflect on their beliefs about students and instruction and to consider how these beliefs may be influencing how they conceptualize and enact their roles in serving students with disabilities. As described earlier, how educators conceptualize disability (e.g., Jordan et al., 2010) and the purpose of their roles (e.g., Ruppar et al., 2017; Urbach et al., 2015) may have important implications for the services they provide to students with disabilities. There are many potential dimensions of educators' beliefs that are worth reflecting on. For example, Ruppar et al. (2018) contrast two perspectives: (1) a deficit vision, in which special educators' primary role is to "care for the students, maintain safety, and control challenging behavior" and (2) a strengths-based vision in which special educators' roles are to "build on competencies and raise the expectations of others." (p. 326). In this chapter, we described other key related beliefs, such as beliefs about whether a disability is inherent to the student or a result of an interaction between students and the environment. We recommend educators reflect on what beliefs may be shaping how they conceptualize and enact their roles, considering whether these beliefs help them foster high expectations, strong learning, and inclusion for their students.

Second, we encourage educators in inclusive schools to take time to develop shared understandings of roles and responsibilities with other professionals in their schools. Shared understandings of roles may help to reduce tension and foster stronger collaboration. When developing shared understandings, educators should consider the strengths and expertise of each professional and how these strengths can be maximized to support student learning.

Finally, teachers should consider any contextual barriers that may be limiting their capacity to fulfill their role consistent with high expectations. In these cases, rather than lowering their expectations (as some teachers have reported doing; Bettini, Wang et al., 2019), they should consider what advocacy efforts might remove these barriers (Brownell, 2020; Cornelius & Gustafson, 2020). For example, in Bettini, Lillis et al.'s (2021) study, a special educator described collecting data to demonstrate, to administrators, that some students were often missing instruction when a peer had significant behavior challenges, using these data to advocate for more personnel resources for her program. A recent special issue of *Teaching Exceptional Children* provides guidelines for self-advocacy that teachers can use to remove barriers to high expectations (e.g., Cornelius & Gustafson, 2020). Though educators should not have to fight for manageable workloads or adequate resources, the reality is that they may sometimes need to educate others about the nature of their work and how they experience their role.

Conclusions

Educational systems for students with disabilities are fundamentally interdependent; multiple institutions are interdependent with one another in cultivating the special and general education teacher workforce, while special and general educators are interdependent with one another (and with other stakeholders) in serving students with disabilities in inclusive schools. Interdependence necessitates shared understandings of the roles special and general education teachers should be prepared and supported to fulfill. Yet, despite general consensus on the long-term aims of special education services, extant scholarship and policy reflect deep divides regarding core aspects of special and general educators' roles in serving students with disabilities, while special and general educators' experiences in schools often reflect limited support and guidance for fulfilling meaningful roles in serving students with disabilities. We contend that addressing these issues should be an urgent priority for our field, which will likely require more extensive research on special and general educators' roles, as well as open conversations among varied stakeholders about how their roles should be constructed to most meaningfully support equitable, inclusive educational opportunities and outcomes for students with disabilities.

References

Able, H., Sreckovic, M. A., Sreckovic, T. R., Garwood, J. D., & Sherman, J. (2015). Views from the teachers: Teacher and student supports needed for full inclusion of students with ASD. *Teacher Education and Special Education, 38*(1), 44–57.

Agran, M., Jackson, L., Kurth, J. A., Ryndak, D., Burnette, K., Jameson, M., Zagona, A., Fitzpatrick, H., & Wehmeyer, M. (2020). Why aren't students with severe disabilities being placed in general education classrooms: Examining relations among classroom placement, learner outcomes, and other factors. *Research and Practice for Persons with Severe Disabilities, 45*(1), 4–13. doi:10.1177/1540796919878134

Ahearn, E. (2006). Standards-based IEPs: Implementation in selected states. *Forum*, http://www.projectforum.org

Albrecht, S. F., Johns, B. H., Mounstevens, J., & Olorunda, O. (2009). Working conditions as risk or resiliency factors for teachers of students with emotional and behavioral disabilities, *Psychology in the Schools, 46*, 1006. doi:10.1002/pits.20440

Anastasiou, D., & Kauffman, J. M. (2011). A social constructionist approach to disability: Implications for special education. *Exceptional Children, 77*, 367–384. doi:10.1177/001440291107700307

Antia, S. D. (1999). The roles of special educators and classroom teachers in an inclusive school. *Journal of Deaf Studies and Deaf Education, 4*(3), 203–214. doi:10.1093/deafed/4.3.203

Babione, C., & Shea, C. (2005). Special education mentoring within the context of rural schools. *Rural Special Education Quarterly, 24*(2), 3–10. doi:10.1177/875687050502400202

Baker, B. D., Srikanth, A., Cotto Jr, R., & Green III, P. C. (2020). School funding disparities and the plight of Latinx children. *Education Policy Analysis Archives, 28*(135). doi:10.14507/epaa.28.5282

Baglieri, S., Bejoian, L. M., Broderick, A. A., Connor, D. J., & Valle, J. (2011). [Re]Claiming "inclusive education" toward cohesion in educational reform: Disability studies unravels the myth of the normal child. *Teachers College Record, 113*, 2122–2154.

Bays, D. A., & Crockett, J. B. (2007). Investigating instructional leadership for special education. *Exceptionality, 15*, 143–161. doi:10.1080/09362830701503495

Beck, S. J., & DeSutter, K. (2020). An examination of group facilitator challenges and problem-solving techniques during IEP team meetings. *Teacher Education and Special Education, 43*, 127–143. doi:10.1177/0888406419839766

Benedict, A. E., Brownell, M. T., Bettini, E., & Sohn, H. (2020). Learning together: General and special education teachers' evolving understandings of word study content during ongoing collaborative professional development. *Teacher Education and Special Education.*

Berry, A. B. (2012). The relationship of perceived support to satisfaction and commitment for special education teachers in rural areas. *Rural Special Education Quarterly, 31*(1), 3–14. doi:10.1177/875687051203100102

Berry, A. B., Petrin, R. A., Gravelle, M. L., & Farmer, T. W. (2011). Issues in special education teacher recruitment, retention, and professional development: Considerations in supporting rural teachers. *Rural Special Education Quarterly, 30*(4), 3–11. doi:10.1177/875687051103000402

Béteille T., Kalogrides, D., & Loeb, S. (2012). Stepping stones: Principal career paths and school outcomes. *Social Science Research, 41*, 904–919. doi:10.1016/j.ssresearch.2012.03.003

Bettini, E., Nguyen, T., Gilmour, A., & Redding, C. (in Press). Disparities in access to well-qualified, well-supported special educators across higher versus lower poverty schools over time. *Exceptional Children.*

Bettini, E., Benedict, A., Thomas, R., Kimerling, J., Choi, N., & McLeskey, J. (2017). Cultivating a community of effective special educators: Local special education administrators' roles. *Remedial and Special Education, 38*, 111–126. doi:10.1177/0741932516664790

Bettini, E., Cumming, M., Merrill, K., Brunsting, N., & Liaupsin, C. J. (2017). Working conditions in self-contained settings for students with emotional disorders. *Journal of Special Education, 51*, 83–94. doi:10.1177/0022466916674195

Bettini, E., Cumming, M., O'Brien, K. M., Brunsting, N., Ragunanthan, M., Sutton, R., & Chopra, A. (2020). Predicting special educators' intent to continue teaching students with emotional/behavioral disorders in self-contained classes. *Exceptional Children, 86*, 209–228. doi:10.1177/0014402919873556

Bettini, E., Gilmour, A. F., Williams, T. O., & Billingsley, B. S. (2020). Predicting special and general educators' intent to continue teaching using conservation of resources theory. *Exceptional Children, 86*, 310–329. doi:10.1177/0014402919870464

Bettini, E., Jones, N. D., Brownell, M. T., Conroy, M., Park, Y., Leite, W., Crockett, J., & Benedict, A. E. (2017). Workload manageability among novice special and general educators: Relationships with emotional exhaustion and career intentions. *Remedial and Special Education, 38*, 246–256. doi:10.1177/074193251 7708327

Bettini, E., Kimerling, J., Park, Y., & Murphy, K. (2015). Responsibilities and instructional time: Relationships identified by special educators in self-contained classes for students with emotional and behavioral disabilities. *Preventing School Failure, 59*, 121–128. doi:10.1080/1045988X.2013.859561

Bettini, E., Lillis, J., Stark, K., Brunsting, N., & Morris-Mathews, H., (2021). Special educators' experiences of interpersonal interactions in self-contained settings for students with emotional/behavioral disorders. Remedial and Special Education. In press.

Bettini, E., Wang, J., Cumming, M., Kimerling, J., & Schutz, S. (2019). Special educators' experiences of roles and responsibilities in self-contained classes for students with emotional/behavioral disorders. *Remedial and Special Education, 31*, 126–142.

Bianco, M., & Marin-Paris, D. (2019). Pathways2Teaching: Addressing the teacher diversity gap through a grow your own program. *Teaching Exceptional Children, 52*(1), 38–40. doi:10.1177/0040059919875704

Biddle, B. J. (1986). Recent developments in role theory. *Annual Review of Sociology, 12*, 67–92. doi:10.1146/annurev.so.12.080186.000435

Billingsley, B. (2007). A case study of special education teacher attrition in an urban district. *Journal of Special Education Leadership, 10*, 11–20.

Billingsley, B., & Bettini, E. (2019). Special education teacher attrition and retention: A review of the literature. *Review of Educational Research, 89*, 697–744. doi:10.3102/0034654319862495

Billingsley, B., Bettini, E., & Jones, N. D. (2019). Supporting special education teacher induction through high-leverage practices. *Remedial and Special Education, 40*, 365–379. doi:10.1177/0741932518816826

Billingsley, B., Bettini, E., Morris-Mathews, H., & McLeskey, J. (2020). Improving working conditions to support special educators' effectiveness: A call for leadership. Invited article for special issue of *Teacher Education and Special Education, 43*, 7–27. doi:10.1177/0888406419880353

Billingsley, B., Griffin, C., Smith, S. J., Kamman, M., & Israel, M. (2009). *A review of teacher induction in special education: Research, practice, and technology solutions. Monograph prepared for the National Center to Inform Policy and Practice in Special Education Professional Development (NCIPP)*, The University of Florida. Retrieved from http://ncipp.education.ufl.edu/files_6/NCIPP_Induc_ES_010310.pdf

Billingsley, B., McLeskey, J., & Crockett, J. B. (2017). *Principal leadership: Moving toward inclusive and high-achieving schools for students with disabilities (Document No. IC-8)*. University of Florida, Collaboration for Effective Educator Development, Accountability, and Reform Center. http://ceedar.education.ufl.edu/tools/innovation-configurations/

Bishop, A. G., Brownell, M. T., Klingner, J. K., Leko, M. M., & Galman, S. A. (2010). Differences in beginning special education teachers: The influence of personal attributes, preparation, and school environment on classroom reading practices. *Learning Disability Quarterly, 33*. doi:10.1177/0731948710033 00202

Blackwell, W. H., & Rossetti, Z. S. (2014). The development of individualized education programs: Where have we been and where should we go now?. *SAGE Open*, 1–15. doi:10.1177/2158244014530411

Blanton, L. P., Pugach, M. C., & Boveda, M. (2018). Interrogating the intersections between general and special education in the history of teacher education reform. *Journal of Teacher Education, 69*(4), 354–366. doi:10.1177/0022487118778539

Borman, J. D., & Dowling, N. M. (2008). Teacher attrition and retention: A metanalytic and narrative review of the research. *Review of Educational Research, 78*, 367–409. doi:10.3102/0034654308321455

Boyd, D., Lankford, H., Loeb, S., & Wyckoff, J. (2003). The draw of home: How teachers' preferences for proximity disadvantage urban schools. *NBER Working Paper Series, 9953*. https://www.nber.org/papers/w9953

Bradley, M. C., Daley, T., Levin, M., O'Reilly, F., Parsad, A., Robertson, A., & Werner, A. (2011). *IDEA National Assessment Implementation Study*. NCEE 2011-4027. https://ies.ed.gov/ncee/pubs/20114026/pdf/20114027.pdf

Braun, A. M. B., & Youngs, P. (2020). How middle school special and general educators make sense of and respond to changes in teacher evaluation policy. *Education Policy Analysis Archives, 28*(59), 1–22. doi:10.14507/epaa.28.5013

Bray, L. E., & Russell, J. L. (2018). The dynamic interaction between institutional pressures and activity: An examination of the implementation of IEPs in secondary inclusive settings. *Educational Evaluation and Policy Analysis, 40*(2), 243–266. doi:10.3102/0162373718756189

Bray, L. E., & Russell, J. L. (2016). Going off script: Structure and agency in individualized education program meetings. *American Journal of Education, 122*, 367–398. doi:10.1086/685845

Brock, M. E., Barczak, M. A., & Dueker, S. A. (2020). A randomized evaluation of group training for paraprofessionals to implement systematic instruction strategies with students with severe disabilities. *Teacher Education and Special Education*. doi:10.1177/0888406420923769

Brownell, M. T. (2020). Advocating for lifelong learning, professional development, and support. *Teaching Exceptional Children*. doi:10.1177/0040059920976067

Brownell, M. T., Dimino, J., Bishop, A. G., Haager, D., Gersten, R., Menon, S., Klingner, J. K., Sindelar, P. T., & Penfield, R. D. (2009). The role of domain expertise in beginning special education teacher quality. *Exceptional Children, 75*(4), 391–411. doi:10.1177/001440290907500401

Brownell, M. T., Sindelar, P. T., Kiely, M. T., & Danielson, L. C. (2010). Special education teacher quality and preparation: Exposing foundations and constructing a new model. *Exceptional Children, 76*, 357–377. doi:10.1177/001440291007600307

Brownell, M. T., Steinbrecher, T., Kimerling, J., Park, Y., Bae, J., & Benedict, A. (2014). Dimensions of teacher quality in general and special education. In P. T. Sindelar, E. D. McCray, M. T. Brownell, & B. Lignugaris Kraft (Eds.), *Handbook of research on special education teacher preparation* (pp. 423–444). Routledge.

Brunsting, N. C., Sreckovic, M. A., & Lane, K. L. (2014). Special education teacher burnout: A synthesis of research from 1979 to 2013. *Education and Treatment of Children, 37*, 681–711. doi:10.1353/etc.2014.0032

Bryk, A., & Schneider, B. (2002). *Trust in schools: A core resource for improvement*. Russell Sage Foundation.

Cancio, E. J., Albrecht, S. F., & Johns, B. H. (2013). Defining administrative support and its relationship to the attrition of teachers of students with emotional and behavioral disorders. *Education and Treatment of Children, 36*, 71–94. doi:10.1353/etc.2013.0035

Carver-Thomas, D., & Darling-Hammond, L. (2017). *Teacher turnover: Why it matters and what we can do about it*. Learning Policy Institute.

Cole-Lade, G. M., & Bailey, L. E. (2020). Examining the role of paraeducators when supporting children with complex communication needs: A multiple case study. *Teacher Education and Special Education, 43*, 144–161. doi:10.1177/0888406419852778

Conley, S., & You, S. (2017). Key influences on special education teachers' intention to leave: The effects of administrative support and teacher team efficacy in a mediational model. *Educational Management Administration, & Leadership, 45*, 521–540. doi:10.1177/1741143215608859

Cornelius, K. E., & Gustafson, J. A. (2020). Relationships with school administrators: Leveraging knowledge and data to self-advocate. *Teaching Exceptional Children*. doi:10.1177/0040059920972438

Council of Chief State School Officers & Collaboration for Effective Educator Development, Accountability, and Reform. (2017). *PSEL 2015 and promoting principal leadership for the success of students with disabilities*. Washington, DC. Retrieved from https://www.ccsso.org/sites/default/files/2017-10/PSELforSWDs01252017_0.pdf

Cumming, M., O'Brien, K. M., Brunsting, N., & Bettini, E. (2020). Special educators' working conditions, self-efficacy, and practices use with students with emotional/ behavioral disorders. *Remedial and Special Education*. doi:10.1177/0741932520924121

Damore, S. J., & Murray, C. (2009). Urban elementary school teachers' perspectives regarding collaborative teaching practices. *Remedial and Special Education, 30*(4), 234–244. Doi: doi:10.1177/0741932508321007

Darling-Hammond, L., Fickel, L., Koppich, J., Macdonald, M., Merseth, K., Miller, L., Ruscoe, G., Silvernail, D., Snyder, J., Whitford, B. L., & Zicchner, K. (2006). *Powerful teacher education: Lessons from exemplary programs*. Jossey-Bass.

Davidson, D. N., & Algozzine, B. (2002). Administrators' perceptions of special education law. *Journal of Special Education Leadership, 15*(2), 43–48.

DeMatthews, D., Billingsley, B. S., McLeskey, J., & Sharma, U. (2020). Principal leadership for students with disabilities in effective inclusive schools. *Journal of Educational Administration, 58*(5), 329–554. doi:10.1108/JEA-10-2019-0177

Diamond, J. B., & Spillane, J. P. (2004). High-stakes accountability in urban elementary schools: Challenging or reproducing inequality? *Teachers College Record, 106*, 1145–1176. doi:10.1111/j.1467-9620.2004.00375.x

Diamond, J. B. (2007). Where the rubber meets the road: Rethinking the connection between high-stakes testing policy and classroom instruction. *Sociology of Education, 80*, 285–313. doi:10.1177/003804070708000401

Diamond, J. B. (2012). Accountability policy, school organization, and classroom practice: Partial recoupling and educational opportunity. *Education and Urban Society, 44*(2), 151–182. doi:10.1177/0013124511431569

Dieker, L. A., McTigue, A., Campbell, G., Rodriquez, J., Savage, M., & Jackson- Thomas, A. (2003). Voices from the field: Teachers from culturally and linguistically diverse backgrounds entering the profession through alternative certification. *Teacher Education and Special Education, 26*, 328–340. doi:10.1177/088840640302600408.

Early, J. S., & Shagoury, R. (2010). Learning from the lived experiences of new language arts teachers working in diverse urban schools. *Teaching and Teacher Education, 26*, 1049–1058. doi:10.1016/j.tate.2009.10.048

Embich, J. L. (2001). The relationship of secondary special education teachers' roles and factors that lead to professional burnout. *Teacher Education and Special Education, 24*, 58–69. doi:10.1177/088840640102400109

Every Student Succeed Act. 2015, Pub. L. No. 114-95.

Fall, A.-M., & Billingsley, B. S. (2011). Disparities in work conditions among early career special educators in high- and low-poverty districts. *Remedial and Special Education, 32*(1), 64–78. doi:10.1177/0741932510361264

Feiman-Nemser, S. (2001). From preparation to practice: Designing a continuum to strengthen and sustain teaching. *Teachers College Record, 103*, 1013–1055. doi:10.1111/0161-4681.00141

Feiman-Nemser, S., Tamir, E., & Hammerness, K. (Eds). (2014). *Inspiring teaching: Preparing teachers to succeed in mission-driven schools.* Harvard Education Press.

Fennick, E., & Liddy, D. (2001). Responsibilities and preparation for collaborative teaching: Co-teachers' perspectives. *Teacher Education and Special Education, 24*, 229–240. doi:10.1177/088840640102400307

Finnerty, M. S., Jackson, L. B., & Ostergren, R. (2019). Adaptations in general education classrooms for students with severe disabilities: Access, progress assessment, and sustained use. *Research and Practice for Persons with Severe Disabilities, 44*, 87–102. doi:10.1177/1540796919846424

Fowler, S. A., Coleman, M. R. B., & Bogdan, W. K.(2019).The State of the Special Education Profession survey report. Arlington, VA: Council for Exceptional Children.

French, N. K. (2001). Supervising paraprofessionals: A survey of teacher practices. *Journal of Special Education, 35*, 41–53. doi:10.1177/002246690103500105

Friend, M., & Cook, L. (2010). *Interactions: Collaboration skills for school professionals* (6th ed.). Merrill.

Fuchs, D., Fuchs, L. S., & Stecker, P. M. (2010). The "blurring" of special education in a new continuum of general education placements and services. *Exceptional Children, 76*, 301–323. doi:10.1177/001440291007600304

Garwood, J. D., Werts, M. G., Varghese, C., & Gosey, L. (2018). Mixed methods analysis of rural special educators' role stressors, behavior management, and burnout. *Rural Special Education Quarterly, 37*(1), 30–43. doi:10.1177/8756870517745270

Giangreco, M. F., Dennis, R., Cloninger, C., Edelman, S., & Schattman, R. (1993). "I've counted Jon": Transformational experiences of teachers educating students with disabilities. *Exceptional Children, 59*(4), 359–372. doi:10.1177/001440299305900408

Giangreco, M. F., Suter, J. C., & Doyle, M. B. (2010). Paraprofessionals in inclusive schools: A review of recent research. *Journal of Educational and Psychological Consultation, 20*, 41–57. doi:10.1080/10474410903535356

Gilmour, A., Nguyen, T., Redding, C., & Bettini, E. (in review). The shifting context of special education teachers' work and its relationship with retention. *Journal of Teacher Education.*

Gilmour, A. F., & Wehby, J. H. (2020).The association between teaching students with disabilities and teacher turnover. *Journal of Educational Psychology, 112*(5), 1042–1060.

Gilmour, A. F., & Jones, N. D.(2020). Policies that define instruction: A systematic review of states' and districts' recommendations for evaluating special educators.Educational Researcher, Advanced online publication.

Gilmour, A., Nguyen, T., Redding, C., & Bettini, E. (2021). The shifting context of special education teachers' work and its relationship with retention. Working paper.

Gomez-Najarro, J. (2020). An empty seat at the table: Examining general and special education teacher collaboration in response to intervention. *Teacher Education and Special Education, 43*(2), 109–126. doi:10.1177/0888406419850894

Green, J. G., McLaughlin, K. A., Alegria, M., Bettini, E., Gruber, M., Hoagwood, K., Le Tai, L., Sampson, N., Zaslavsky, A. M., Xuan, Z., & Kessler, R. C. (2020). Associations of sociodemographic factors and psychiatric disorders with type of school-based mental health services received by youth. *Journal of Adolescent Health*. doi:10.1016/j.jadohealth.2020.02.016

Grindal, T., Schifter, L. A., Schwartz, G., & Hehir, T. (2019). Racial differences in special education identification and placement: Evidence across three states. *Harvard Educational Review, 89*(4), 525–553. doi:10.17763/1943-5045-89.4.525

Grossman, P. L., Valencia, S. W., Evans, K., Thompson, C., Martin, S., & Place, N. (2001). Transitions into teaching: Learning to teach writing in teacher education and beyond. *Journal of Literacy Research, 32*, 631–662. doi:10.1080/10862960009548098

Grossman, P., & Thompson, C. (2008). Learning from curriculum materials: Scaffolds for new teachers? *Teaching and Teacher Education, 24*, 2014–2026. doi:10.1016/j.tate.2008.05.002

Guarino, G. M., Santibañez, L., & Daley, G. A. (2006). Teacher recruitment and retention: A review of the recent empirical literature. *Review of Educational Research, 76*, 173–208. doi:10.3102/00346543076002173

Hagaman, J. L., & Casey, K. J. (2018). Teacher attrition in special education: Perspectives from the field. *Teacher Education and Special Education, 41*(4), 277–291. doi:10.1177/0888406417725797

Hammerness, K., & Klette, K. (2015). Indicators of quality in teacher education: Looking at features of teacher education from an international erspective. In G. K. LeTendre & A. W. Wiseman (Eds.), *International perspectives on education and society* (Vol. 27, pp. 239–277). Emerald Group Publishing Limited. doi:10.1108/S1479-367920140000027013

Hehir, R., Schifter, L., Grindal, T., Ng, M., & Eidelman, H. (2014). Review of special education in the Commonwealth of Massachusetts: A synthesis report. *MA Department of Elementary and Secondary Education Report*. http://www.doe.mass.edu/sped/hehir/

Hirano, K. A., & Rowe, D. A. (2015). A conceptual model for parent involvement in secondary special education. *Journal of Disability Policy Studies, 27*(1), 43–53. doi:10.1177/1044207315583901

Hoge, M. R., Liaupsin, C. J., Umbreit, J., & Ferro, J. B. (2014). Examining placement considerations for students with emotional disturbance across three alternative schools. *Journal of Disability Policy Studies, 24*, 218–226. doi:10.1177/1044207312461672

Hoover, J. J., & Patton, J. R. (2008). The role of special educators in a multitiered instructional system. *Intervention in School and Clinic, 43*, 195–202. doi:10.1177/1053451207310345

Hoppey, D., & McLeskey, J. (2013). A case study of principal leadership in an effective inclusive school. *Journal of Special Education, 45*, 245–256. doi:10.1177/0022466910390507

Individuals with Disabilities Education Improvement Act 2004, Pub. L. No. 108-446.

Irvin, D. W., Hume, K., Boyd, B. A., McBee, M. T., & Odom, S. L. (2013). Child and classroom characteristics associated with the adult language provided to preschoolers with autism spectrum disorder. *Research in Autism Spectrum Disorders, 7*, 947–955. doi:10.1016/j.rasd.2013.04.004

Jackson, K., & Makarin, A. (2016). *Simplifying teaching: A field experiment with online "off-the-shelf" lessons*. National Bureau of Economic Research. Retrieved from www.nber.org/papers/w22398

Jimenez, B. A., Lo, Y., & Saunders, A. F. (2014). The additive effects of scripted lessons plus guided notes on science quiz scores of students with intellectual disability and autism. *The Journal of Special Education, 47*, 231–244. doi:10.1177/0022466912437937

Johnson, S. M., Kraft, M. A., & Papay, J. P. (2012). How context matters in high-need schools: The effects of teachers' working conditions on their professional satisfaction and their students' achievement. *Teachers College Record, 114*(10), 1–39.

Jones, N. D., & Youngs, P. (2012). Attitudes and affect: Daily emotions and their association with the commitment and burnout of beginning teachers. *Teachers College Record, 114*, 1–36.

Jones, N. D., Youngs, P., & Frank, K. A. (2013). The role of school-based colleagues in shaping the commitment of novice special and general educations. *Exceptional Children, 79*, 1–19. doi:10.1177/001440291307900303

Jones, N., & Winters, M. (2020). Are two teachers better than one? The effect of co-teaching on students with and without disabilities. Working paper.

Jordan, A., Glenn, C., & McGhie-Richmond, D. (2010). Supporting effective teaching (SET) project: The relationship of inclusive teaching practices to teachers' beliefs about disability and ability, and about their roles as teachers. *Teaching and Teacher Education, 26*, 259–266. doi:10.1016/j.tate.2009.03.005

Jordan, A., Lindsay, L., & Stanovich, P. J. (1997). Classroom teachers' instructional interactions with students who are exceptional, at risk, and normally achieving. *Remedial and Special Education, 18*, 82–93. doi:10.1177/074193259701800202

Kaff, M. (2004). Multitasking is multitaxing: Why special educators are leaving the field. *Preventing School Failure, 48*, 10–17.

Kalyanpur, M., Harry, B., & Skrtic, T. (2000). Equity and advocacy expectations of culturally diverse families' participation in special education. *International Journal of Disability, Development and Education, 47*(2), 119–136. doi:10.1080/713671106

Kennedy, M. M. (2006). Knowledge and vision in teaching. *Journal of Teacher Education, 57*, 205–211. doi:10.1177/0022487105285639

Kiely, M. T., Brownell, M. T., Lauterbach, A. A., & Benedict, A. (2014). Teachers' beliefs about students with special needs and inclusion. In H. Fives & M. G. Gill (Eds.), *Handbook of research on teacher beliefs* (pp. 475–491). Routledge.

Klingner, J. K., & Vaughn, S. (2002). The changing roles and responsibilities of an LD specialist. *Learning Disability Quarterly, 25*, 19–31. doi:10.2307/1511188

Kurth, J. A., Allcock, H., Walker, V., Olson, A., & Taub, D. (2020). Faculty perceptions of expertise for inclusive education for students with significant disabilities. *Teacher Education and Special Education*. doi:10.1177/0888406420921582

Lauterbach, A. A., Brownell, M. T., & Bettini, E. (2020). Expert secondary content-area teachers' pedagogical schemas for teaching literacy to students with learning disabilities. *Learning Disability Quarterly*. doi:10.1177/0731948719864417

Leko, M. M., & Brownell, M. T. (2011). Special education preservice teachers' appropriation of pedagogical tools for teaching reading. *Exceptional Children*, 77(2), 229–251. doi:10.1177/001440291107700205

Leko, M. M., Brownell, M. T., Sindelar, P. T., & Kiely, M. T. (2015). Envisioning the future of special education personnel preparation in a standards-based era. *Exceptional Children, 82*, 25–43. doi:10.1177/0014402915598782

Li, L., & Ruppar, A. (2020). Conceptualizing teacher agency for inclusive education: A systematic and international review. *Teacher Education and Special Education*. doi:10.1177/0888406420926976

Mason-Williams, L., Bettini, E., Peyton, D., Harvey, A., Rosenberg, M. S., & Sindelar, P. T. (2020). Rethinking shortages in special education: Making good on the promise of an equal opportunity for students with disabilities. *Teacher Education and Special Education, 43*, 45–62. doi:10.1177/0888406419880352

Mathews, H. M., Rodgers, J. D., & Youngs, P. Y. (2017). Sensemaking for beginning special educators: A systematic mixed studies review. *Teaching and Teacher Education, 67*, 23–36. doi:10.1016/j.tate.2017.05.007

Mathews, H. M. (2018, November). *Examining the influence of social context on novice special educators' instructional practice*. Presentation at the Teacher Education Division of the Council for Exceptional Children. Las Vegas, NV.

McLaughlin, M. J. (2010). Evolving interpretations of educational equity and students with disabilities. *Exceptional Children, 76*, 265–278. doi:10.1177/001440291007600302

McLeskey, J., Rosenberg, M., & Westling, D. (2018). *Inclusion: Effective practices for all students* (3rd ed.). Pearson Education.

McLeskey, J., Waldron, N., & Redd, L. (2014). A case study of a highly effective inclusive elementary school. *Journal of Special Education, 48*(1), 59–70. doi:10.1177/0022466912440455

Miller, A. L., Wilt, C. L., Allcock, H. C., Kurth, J. A., Morningstar, M. E., & Ruppar, A. L. (2020). Teacher agency for inclusive education: An international scoping review. *International Journal of Inclusive Education*. doi:10.1080/13603116.2020.1789766

Mitchell, B. B., Deshler, D. D., & Lenz, B. K. B. H. (2012). Examining the role of the special educator in a response to intervention model. *Learning Disabilities: A Contemporary Journal, 10*, 53–74.

Morris Mathews, H., Lillis, J., Bettini, E., Peyton, D., Pua, D., Oblath, R., Jones, N. D., Smith, S. W., & Sutton, R. (2020). Working conditions related to special educators' reading instruction for students with emotional/behavioral disorders: A mixed methods investigation. [Manuscript submitted for publication].

Morris Mathews, H. (2020). Developing a theory of program vision as professional socialization in special education teacher preparation [Manuscript submitted for publication].

No Child Left Behind Act of 2001, 20 U.S.C. 70 §6301 *et seq.* (2002).

O'Brien, K. M., Brunsting, N. C., Bettini, E., Cumming, M. M., Ragunathan, M., & Sutton, R. (2019). Special educators' working conditions in self-contained settings for students with emotional or behavioral disorders: A descriptive analysis. *Exceptional Children, 86*, 40–57. doi:10.1177/0014402919868946.

Oakes, W. P., Lane, K. L., Royer, D. J., Menzies, H. M., Buckman, M. M., Brunsting, N., Cantwell, E. D., Schatschneider, C., & Lane, N. A. (2020). Elementary teachers' self-efficacy during initial implementation of comprehensive, integrated, three-tiered models of prevention. *Journal of Positive Behavior Interventions*. doi:10.1177/1098300720916718

Olson, A., Leko, M. M., & Roberts, C. A. (2016). Providing students with severe disabilities access to the general education curriculum. *Research and Practice for Persons with Severe Disabilities*, *41*(3), 143–157. doi:10.1177/1540796916651975

Park, E.-Y., & Shin, M. (2020). A meta-analysis of special education teachers' burnout. *SAGE Open*. 1–18. doi:10.1177/2158244020918297

Peterson, P. J., Sandigo, A. M., Stoddard, S. E., Abou-Rjaily, K., & Ulrich, J. (2020). Changing lives on the border: Preparing rural, culturally responsive special educators. *Rural Special Education Quarterly*, *39*(1), 71–81. doi:10.1177/8756870519879066

Petzko, V. (2008). The perceptions of new principals regarding the knowledge and skills important to their initial success. *NASSP Bulletin*, *92*(3), 224–250. doi:10.1177/0192636508322824

Podolsky, A., Kini, T., Bishop, J., & Darling-Hammond, L. (2016). *Solving the teacher shortage: How to attract and retain excellent educators*. Learning Policy Institute.

Pratt, S. (2014). Achieving symbiosis: Working through challenges found in co-teaching to achieve effective co-teaching relationships. *Teaching and Teacher Education*, *41*, 1–12. doi:10.1016/j.tate.2014.02.006

Prewett, S., Mellard, D. F., Deshler, D. D., Allen, J., Alexander, R., & Stern, A. (2012). Response to intervention in middle schools: Practices and outcomes. *Learning Disabilities Research & Practice*, *27*(3), 136–147. doi:10.1111/j.1540-5826.2012.00359.x

Quiñones, S. (2018). "I get to give back to the community that put me where I am": Examining the experiences and perspectives of Puerto Rican teachers in Western New York. *Urban Education*, *53*(1), 621–639. doi:10.1177/0042085915623336

Roberts, C. A., Ruppar, A. L., & Olson, A. J. (2017). Perceptions matter: Administrators' vision of instruction for students with severe disabilities. *Research and Practice for Persons with Severe Disabilities*, *43*(1), 3–19. doi:10.1177/1540796917743931

Rossetti, A., Sauer, J. S., Bui, O., & Ou, S. (2017). Developing collaborative partnerships with culturally and linguistically diverse families during the IEP process. *Teaching Exceptional Children*, *49*, 328–338. doi:10.1177/0040059916680103

Royer, D. J., Lane, K. L., Dunlap, K. D., & Parks Ennis, R. (2019). A systematic review of teacher-delivered behavior-specific praise on K-12 student performance. *Remedial and Special Education*, *40*(2), 112–128. doi:10.1177/0741932517751054

Rubie-Davies, C. M., Flint, A., & McDonald, L. G. (2011). Teacher beliefs, teacher characteristics, and school contextual factors: What are the relationships? *British Journal of Educational Psychology*, 1–19. doi:10.1111/j.2044-8279.2011.02025.x

Ruppar, A. L., Roberts, C. A., & Olson, A. J. (2017). Perceptions about expert teaching for students with severe disabilities among teachers identified as experts. *Research and Practice for Persons with Severe Disabilities*, *42*(2), 121–135. doi:10.1177/1540796917697311

Ruppar, A. L., Dymond, S. K., & Gaffney, J. S. (2011). Teachers' perspectives on literacy instruction for students with severe disabilities who use augmentative and alternative communication. *Research & Practice for Persons with Severe Disabilities*, *36*, 100–111. doi:10.2511/rpsd.36.1-2.11

Ruppar, A. L., Gaffney, J. S., & Dymond, S. K. (2015). Influences on teachers' decisions about literacy for secondary students with severe disabilities. *Exceptional Children*, *81*(2), 209–226. doi:10.1177/0014402914551739

Ruppar, A. L., Knight, V. F., McQueston, J. A., & Jeglum, S. R. (2018). Involvement and progress in the general curriculum: A grounded theory of the process. *Remedial and Special Education*, *41*(3), 152–164. doi:10.1177/0741932518806045

Russell, J. L., & Bray, L. E. (2013). Crafting coherence from complex policy messages: Educators' perceptions of special education and standards-based accountability policies. *Education Policy Analysis Archives*, *21*(12), 1–25. doi:10.14507/epaa.v21n12.2013

Sayeski, K. L., Bateman, D. F., & Yell, M. (2019). Re-envisioning teacher preparation in an era of *Endrew F.*: Instruction over access. *Intervention in School and Clinic*, *54*(5), 264–271. doi:10.1177/1053451218819157

Scruggs, T. E., Mastropieri, M. A., & McDuffie, K. A. (2007). Co-teaching in inclusive classrooms: A metasynthesis of qualitative research. *Exceptional Children*, *73*(4), 392–416. doi:10.1177/001440290707300401

Shepherd, K. G., Fowler, S., McCormick, J., Wilson, C. L., & Morgan, D. (2016). The search for role clarity: Challenges and implications for special education teacher preparation. *Teacher Education and Special Education*, *39*(2), 83–97. doi:10.1177/0888406416637904

Shulman, L. (1987). Knowledge and teaching. *Harvard Educational Review*, *57*, 1–23. doi:10.17763/haer.57.1.j463w79r56455411

Simon, N. S., & Johnson, S. M. (2015). Teacher turnover in high-poverty schools: What we know and can do. *Teachers College Record, 117*, 1–37.

Simonsen, B., Shaw, S. F., Faggella-Luby, M., Sugai, G., Coyne, M. D., Rhein, B., Madaus, J., & Alfano, M. (2010). A schoolwide model for service delivery: Redefining special educators as interventionists. *Remedial and Special Education, 31*(1), 17–23. doi:10.1177/0741932508324396

Sindelar, P. T., Fisher, T. L., & Myers, J. A. (2019). The landscape of special education licensure, 2016. *Teacher Education and Special Education, 42*(2), 101–116. doi:10.1177/0888406418761533

Singer, J. D., Butler, J. A., Palfrey, J. S., & Walker, D. K. (1986). Characteristics of special education placements: Findings from probability samples in five metropolitan school districts. *Journal of Special Education, 20*(3), 319–337. doi:10.1177/002246698602000306

Singer, J. D., Palfrey, J. S., Butler, J. A., & Walker, D. K. (1989). Variation in special education classification across school districts: How does where you live affect what you are labeled?. *American Educational Research Journal, 26*, 261–281. doi:10.3102/00028312026002261

Siuty, M. (2019). Inclusion gatekeepers: The social production of spatial identities in special education. *International Journal of Qualitative Studies in Education, 32*(8), 1032–1047. doi:10.1080/09518398.2019.1635283

Siuty, M. B., Leko, M. M., & Knackstedt, K. M. (2018). Unraveling the role of curriculum in teacher decision making. *Teacher Education and Special Education, 41*, 39–57. doi:10.1177/0888406416683230

Skrtic, T. M. (2012). Disability, difference, and justice: Strong democratic leadership for undemocratic times. In J. Crockett, B. Billingsley, & M. L. Boscardin (Eds.), *Handbook of leadership and administration for special education* (pp. 129–150). Routledge.

Soukup, J. H., Wehmeyer, M. L., Bashinski, S. M., & Boviard, J. A. (2007). Classroom variables and access to the general curriculum for students with disabilities. *Exceptional Children, 74*(1), 101–120. doi:10.1177/001440290707400106

Stanovich, P. J., & Jordan, A. (1998). Canadian teachers' and principals' beliefs about inclusive education as predictors of effective teaching in heterogeneous classrooms. *Elementary School Journal, 98*(3), 221–238. doi: 10.1086/461892

Stark, K., Morris-Mathews, H., Bettini, E., & Jones, N. D. (2020). The urgent need for special education instructional leadership. In P. Youngs & J. Kim (Eds)., *Developing principal leadership in a changing policy landscape.* Routledge.

Steinbrecher, T. D., Fix, R., Mahal, S. A., Serna, L., & McKeown, D. (2015). All you need is patience and flexibility: Administrators' perspectives on special educator knowledge and skills. *Journal of Special Education Leadership, 28*(2), 89–102.

Stelitano, L., Johnston, W. R., & Young, C. J. (2020). *Principals could use more support to help students with disabilities — especially in schools serving mostly students of color.* RAND. https://www.rand.org/pubs/research_reports/RR2575z13.html.

Stough, L. M., & Palmer, D. J. (2003). Special thinking in special settings: A qualitative study of expert special educators. *Journal of Special Education, 36*(4), 206–222. doi:10.1177/002246690303600402

Sykes, G., Bird, T., & Kennedy, M. (2010). Teacher education: Its problems and some prospects. *Journal of Teacher Education, 61*, 464–476. doi:10.1177/0022487110375804

Turnbull, H. R., Turnbull, A. P., & Cooper, D. H. (2018). The Supreme Court, Endrew, and the appropriate education of students with disabilities. *Exceptional Children, 84*, 124–140. doi:10.1177/0014402917734150

Urbach, J., Moore, B. A., Klingner, J. K., Galman, S., Haager, D., Brownell, M. T., & Dingle, M. (2015). "That's My Job:" Comparing the beliefs of more and less accomplished special educators related to their roles and responsibilities. *Teacher Education and Special Education, 38*, 323–336. doi:10.1177/0888406415591220

Vannest, K. J., & Hagan-Burke, S. (2010). Teacher time use in special education. *Remedial and Special Education, 31*, 125–142. doi:10.1177/0741932508327459

Vannest, K. J., Soares, D. A., Harrison, J. R., Brown, L., & Parker, R. I. (2010). Changing teacher time. *Preventing School Failure. 54*, 86–98. doi:10.1080/10459880903217739

Villa, R. A., & Thousand, J. S. (2016). *The inclusive education checklist: A self-assessment of best practices.* Dude Publishing.

Voltz, D. L., & Fore, C. (2006). Urban special education in the context of standards-based reform. *Remedial and Special Education, 27*(6), 329–336. doi:10.1177/07419325060270060201

Wall, S., Davis, K. L., Crowley, A. L. W., & White, L. L. (2005). The urban paraeducator goes to college. *Remedial and Special Education, 26*(3), 183–190. doi:10.1177/07419325050260030601

Weatherley, R., & Lipsky, M. (1977). Street-level bureaucrats and institutional innovation: Implementing special education reform. *Harvard Educational Review, 47*(2), 171–197. doi:10.17763/haer.47.2.v870r1v16786270x

Wehby, J. H., Maggin, D. M., Partin, T. C. M., & Robertson, R. (2012). The impact of working alliance, social validity, and teacher burnout on implementation fidelity of the good behavior game. *School Mental Health*, *4*(1), 22–33. doi:10.1007/s12310-011-9067-4

Weiss, M. P., & Lloyd, J. W. (2002). Congruence between roles and actions of secondary special educators in co-taught and special education settings. *Journal of Special Education*, *36*(2), 58–68. doi:10.1177/00224669020360020101

Wexler, J., Kearns, D. M., Lemons, C. J., Mitchell, M., Clancy, E., Davidson, K. A., Sinclair, A. C., & Wei, Y. (2018). Reading comprehension and co-teaching practices in middle school English language arts classrooms. *Exceptional Children*, *84*(4), 384–402. doi:10.1177/0014402918771543

Williamson, P., Hoppey, D., McLeskey, J., Bergmann, E., & Moore, H. (2019). Trends in LRE placement rates over the past 25 years. *Journal of Special Education*, *53*, 236–244. doi:10.1177/0022466919855052

Wong, V. W., Ruble, L. A., Yu, Y., & McGrew, J. H. (2017). Too stressed to teach?: Teaching quality, student engagement, and IEP outcomes. *Exceptional Children*, *83*(4), 412–427. doi:10.1177/0014402917690729

Yell, M. L., & Shriner, J. G. (1997). The IDEA amendments of 1997: Implications for special and general education teachers, administrators, and teacher trainers. *Focus on Exceptional Children*, *30*(1), 1–19. doi:10.17161/fec.v30i1.6756

Yell, M. L., Katsiyannis, A., & Bradley, M. R. (2017). The Individuals with Disabilities Education Act: The evolution of special education law. In J. Kauffman, D. Hallahan, & P. Pullen (Eds.), *Handbook of special education*. Routledge. doi:10.4324/9781315517698-7

Youngs, N., Jones, P., & Low, M. (2011). How beginning special and general education elementary teachers negotiate role expectations and access professional resources. *Teachers College Record*, *113*, 1506–1540.

Youngs, P., Frank, K., Thum, Y., & Low, M. (2012). The motivation of teachers to produce human capital and conform to their social contexts. In T. Smith, L. Desimone, & A. Porter (Eds.), *Yearbook of the National Society for the Study of Education: Organization and effectiveness of induction programs for new teachers*(Vol. 110, pp. 248–272). Blackwell.

Zagona, A. L., Kurth, J. A., & MacFarland, S. Z. C. (2017). Teachers' views of their preparation for inclusive education and collaboration. *Teacher Education and Special Education*, *40*(3), 163–178. doi:10.1177/0888406417692969

Zagona, A. L., Lansey, K. R., Kurth, J. A., & Kuhlemeier, A. (2020). Fostering participation during literacy instruction in inclusive classrooms for students with complex support needs: Educators' strategies and perspectives. *Journal of Special Education*. doi:10.1177/0022466920936671

4

The Role of Teacher Education in Effective Inclusive Elementary Schools

Lawrence Maheady[1], Andrew Hashey[1], Pixita del Prado Hill[2], and Keli Garas-York[2]

[1]EXCEPTIONAL EDUCATION DEPARTMENT

[2]DEPARTMENT OF ELEMENTARY EDUCATION, LITERACY, AND EDUCATIONAL LEADERSHIP, SUNY BUFFALO STATE

Setting the Stage

These are challenging times for classroom teachers, school leaders, and those responsible for their preparation. Teachers and school leaders face higher academic standards for students, more calls for equitable access to general education curricula, and recently a global pandemic (Leko et al., 2015; Sailor et al., 2020). Teacher educators try to prepare professionals to perform effectively in these challenging settings while collecting evidence to support program efficacy for accreditors and dealing with escalating teacher shortages (Boe, 2014; deBettencourt et al., 2016; Shepherd et al., 2016). Within this context, we ask, how can teacher education programs better prepare *all* teachers for effective inclusive elementary schools?

To address this question, we initially examine "traditional" efforts to prepare general and special education teachers for inclusion, highlight important historical themes and trends, and discuss implications for preparing future teachers for inclusive settings. Research on teacher preparation practices for inclusion is then summarized and explored through the lens of educators' professional wisdom and instructional decision-making. A course for reform is set based on principles and practices of practice-based teacher education (PBTE) and a case study is used to illustrate how one institution is working with school partners to better prepare preservice teachers for inclusive classrooms.

Caveats

There are other important aspects of effective teacher preparation that are beyond the scope of this chapter (e.g., recruitment and retention of a diverse teaching force, local context and history of physical and conceptual separation between GE and SE, and the extent of institutional support for inclusive preparation and practice on campus and in public schools). The chapter also focuses on

DOI: 10.4324/9781003043874-4

inclusion in elementary not secondary schools, students with mild and moderate not intensive disabilities, and preservice preparation not professional development (PD) for practitioners.

Third, the chapter adopts an equity- rather than place-based perspective on inclusion (e.g., Kozleski & Proffitt, 2020; Sailor et al., 2020). Equity-based inclusion shifts policy issues away from *where* services are provided and "toward concerns of how all available educational supports and services are equitably matched to measured student needs, regardless of reasons for the specialized support (e.g., special education, English Language Learning, gifted education)" (Sailor et al., p. 6). An equity definition applies to all students and enables a fairer distribution of specialized supports and services at the school level (Waitoller & Kozleski, 2013).

Preparation of General and Special Education Teachers for Inclusion

For over 50 years, educators and researchers world-wide questioned the utility and appropriateness of *segregated* special education classes for students with disabilities (SWDs) and advocated for more inclusive learning environments for all (e. g., Dunn, 1968; Kraska & Boyle, 2014; Pinter et al., 2020; UNESCO, 1994). These efforts paid off in that the percentage of students with disabilities being educated in inclusive classrooms for most of the school day has increased steadily from about 34% in 1990 to 63% in 2016 (U.S. Department of Education, Office of Special Education and Rehabilitative Services, and Office of Special Education Programs, 2016). Yet, teacher preparation programs in general education (GE) and special education (SE) – despite repeated reform efforts - have remained relatively unchanged; characterized more by separation than integration - comprising separate "silos" of content, settings, and practices (Allday et al., 2013; Crispel & Kasperski, 2019).

An extensive historical review of general and special education teacher preparation is beyond the scope of this chapter. Readers are referred to additional sources for more extensive discussion (Blanton et al., 2018; Brownell et al., 2010; Pugach et al., 2011). Here, we describe changes in general and special education teacher preparation practices for inclusion, highlight major controversies and trends, and discuss implications for future research and practice.

Historical Perspectives on Special Education Teacher Preparation

Brownell et al. (2010) noted that special education service delivery, classroom practice, and teacher preparation efforts have evolved in response to changes in educational policy, research, and school practice. They described how teacher preparation in SE moved from disability-specific (i.e., *categorical*) programming - to *non-categorical* approaches that emphasized the use of generic academic and behavioral skill sets (i.e., competencies) - to *integrated* (i.e., general and special education) programs that ran the gamut from requiring GE teachers to take one or two SE courses to making *all* teachers earn multiple licenses (e.g., dual certification).

During the categorical era (i.e., approximately 1950 to 1979), SE teachers were prepared to work with students with *specific* disabilities (e.g., learning disabilities, emotional/behavioral disorders, and hearing impairments), often in segregated settings (e.g., self-contained, special classes or schools). Conceptualizations of disability and treatment were rooted in medicine and psychology, categorical service delivery (e.g., self-contained classes for students with learning disabilities) was prevalent in public schools, and there was explosive growth in SE teacher preparation spawned by federal mandates (e.g., P.L. 94-142; Education of All Handicapped Children's Act, 1975). It is important to note that GE and SE programs were housed typically in separate departments and/or colleges on campus.

By 1980, non-categorical approaches to SE teacher preparation emerged. Proponents viewed disabilities on a continuum of severity (i.e., mild, moderate, and severe) and rejected category-based teaching practices (e.g., aptitude X treatment interventions). Educational researchers (e.g., Brophy, 1979; Stallings, 1980) identified generic teaching practices and/or skill sets that were linked consistently to higher academic achievement, irrespective of student disability status. Effective SE teachers played active teaching roles, directed instruction, and infused it with frequent opportunities for students to respond. The primary focus of teacher preparation was to ensure that preservice teachers mastered identified generic skill sets or competencies (i.e., Competency Based Teacher Education) (e.g., Houston & Howsam, 1972).

From 1990 through 2009 (i.e., integrated preparation era), there were increased efforts to educate SWDs in GE classrooms (i.e., mainstreaming). The movement had its roots in Madeleine Will's (1986) seminal call for *shared responsibility* in educating SWDs, insufficient empirical support for separate special education classes, and educational policies that promoted increased access to GE classrooms. Teacher preparation programs in general and special education became more integrated, although great variability existed in the extensiveness of curricular re-design (e.g., adding one SE course to GE curriculum versus transformative changes to GE and SE programs). Integrated programming in public schools and teacher education required more collaboration between GE and SE and a clearer delineation of professional roles and responsibilities for inclusive classrooms.

Brownell and her colleagues concluded by encouraging policy makers and educators to address two longstanding issues in SE preparation (a) shortages of qualified SE teachers and (b) inadequate preparation of GE teachers to teach SWDs. They recommended using a response-to-intervention (RTI) framework (Sugai et al., 2010) to guide the redesign of integrated programs arguing that this framework would (a) clarify general and special educators' roles and responsibilities, (b) foster collaboration, (c) strengthen SE teachers' understanding of the GE curriculum, and (d) promote GE's understanding and use of effective teaching practices for SWDs.

Role of Collaboration in Teacher Preparation for Inclusion

Pugach and her colleagues (2011) provided an insightful historical analysis on the role of collaboration in teacher education. Collaboration was defined as, "the purposeful integration of general and special education at the preservice level" (p.184), and a common "product" of this integration was that graduates earned two (or more) teaching certificates/licenses, concurrently or sequentially. Efforts to integrate teacher preparation led to noticeable growth in collaborative teacher education programs that emerged over three stages from 1975 through 2010.

The initial stage (1975 to 1982) was marked by the first formal attempts to connect GE and SE teacher preparation. The federal government funded what became known as Deans' Grants Projects (DGPs) whose primary purpose was to integrate preservice curricula across general and special education (Kleinhammer-Tramill, 2003). Although DGPs were conceived as models for transformative change, their primary impact was a narrow focus on adding SE content and experiences to existing GE curricula (i.e., additive model) (Pugach & Blanton, 2009). This was done typically by requiring GE majors to take one or two SE courses (e.g., Introduction to Special Education) or infusing SE content and competencies across the GE curriculum. Additional courses were usually taught by SE faculty often with little input from or collaboration with GE counterparts. The relationship between GE and SE teacher preparation maintained the status quo of *structural segregation*.

From 1983 to 2001, small pockets of general and special education collaborations emerged. Individual preparation programs, for example, reported large-scale reforms (e.g., using different collaboration models to prepare GE and SE teachers together) (Blanton et al., 1997; Bondy & Ross, 2005), while other programs examined the impact of smaller-scale program components (e.g., collaborative planning strategies, team teaching, and/or changing content and experiences in required SE courses) on preservice teachers' knowledge, skills, and/or dispositions.

Overall, progress toward collaboration was described as slow and inconsistent and impeded by special educators arguing among themselves about how best to deliver instruction to SWDs (i.e., full inclusion versus continuum of services). The dominant practice continued to be separate GE and SE programs, connected by one or two required SE courses for preservice GE teachers. General and special educators also engaged in parallel and often competing reform agendas that maintained their historic divisions in theory and practice.

The third stage (2002 to 2010) was characterized by a focus on preservice GE and SE teachers' *content knowledge* and the increased testing of their understandings. The number of collaborative preparation programs grew rapidly, due in part to federally funded 325T grant programs. These grants were designed to foster dialogue, collaboration, and partnership among state education agencies and GE and SE preparation programs. Most newly integrated programs awarded multiple certifications/licenses (e.g., elementary education & special education) to preservice teachers.

Collaborative preservice programs continued to explore the impact of smaller scale program components (e.g., co-teaching preservice classes, combining seminars and fieldwork, and/or creating new, collaboration courses) on preservice teachers' abilities to work more effectively with SWDs. Pugach et al concluded that while collaborative teacher education had moved steadily ahead as a national trend, it had failed to address deep-rooted questions about the structural separation between GE and SE.

Intersections between General and Special Education in Teacher Education Teform

Blanton et al. (2018) suggested that one way to bridge the long-standing structural divide between general and special education was to examine important *intersections* in teacher reform movements. Intersections were defined as, "timely opportunities to address common concerns in teacher preparation" (p. 354). Educational reforms over the past 50 years have provided many occasions for GE and SE to work together and build capacity to improve the preparation of all teachers. The authors' historical analysis described several opportunities for joint action by general and special educators (e.g., joint standards development, student progress monitoring, and school-university partnerships), but identified four factors - *policy, funding, timing*, and *norms of separation* – that seemed to constrain their abilities to respond constructively. The result was missed opportunities to build capacity and improve the preparation of all preservice teachers.

The 1970s, for example, gave GE and SE opportunities to articulate a common knowledge base on teaching and learning that could be codified in the form of professional teaching competencies (i.e., Competency Based Teacher Education). However, special educators were *not* included in early CBTE reform efforts, presumably because historically they were separate from those charged with preparing GE teachers. Special educators proceeded by developing their own knowledge and skill sets - often in the form of competencies – thereby creating separate and parallel knowledge bases on teaching and learning for preservice GE and SE teachers.

Two broad-based, reform movements (i.e., Professional Development Schools (PDS) and multicultural education) emerged during the 1980s that provided additional opportunities for GE and SE collaboration. The Professional Development Schools (PDS) movement, for example, provided GE and SE with opportunities to collaborate on professional teaching standards, more comprehensive ways to define diversity, and the development of school-university partnerships. General and special educators also had opportunities to create shared curricula, clinical experiences, and/or co-teaching opportunities to better prepare preservice teachers to work effectively with SWDs (Bauwens et al., 1989). Ironically, GE teaching standards regularly referenced the importance of "an ability to work with diverse students" yet explicit connections were rarely made to SE programs. Yssel et al (2002) noted as well that PDS roles in SE teacher preparation were not well defined and there were few signs of a desire to participate in collaborative relationships.

Multicultural education provided more opportunities for GE and SE to develop common understandings of the impact of race, culture, language, and class on student development and learning. However, most states responded to the multicultural education movement in the same way they did to special education – adding a separate course(s) to the existing GE curriculum. Special education was rarely seen as a marker of diversity and there were few attempts by multicultural and/or special educators to forge comprehensive and integrated curricula around common priorities (e.g., equity and social justice in education) (Blanton et al., 2018).

The 1990s offered more intersections for joint action to reduce structural segregation. Shared professional teaching standards, advances in educational technologies, student progress monitoring, and collaborative teacher preparation provided more chances for GE and SE collaboration. Again, norms of separation prevailed, and GE and SE proceeded, for the most part on parallel reform tracks. Over the past two decades, Blanton et al identified more occasions for GE and SE to work together to rethink pre-service teacher preparation (e.g., developing and/or refining dual licensure programs, creating common performance-based teacher assessments, and leveraging federal policy to support closer GE and SE relationships). Poorly timed federal initiatives and separate and occasionally competing funding streams again impeded collaboration and joint action.

Blanton et al. offered two overarching concluding recommendations. First, they urged general and special educators to organize themselves into active *Communities for Pre-service Learning* that mirror the way P-6 teachers are expected to work in inclusive schools. These learning communities would address common questions of preparation and practice and hopefully change the organizational culture of teacher education. Second, they encouraged learning community members to develop new tools and protocols that provide structure for shared discussions on a common equity agenda and the preparation of all teachers for inclusive classrooms. The development, refinement, and evaluation of these tools and protocols provide more occasions for joint action between GE and SE.

Other Lessons Learned

Teacher educators have learned through experience that separate, siloed preservice programming does not prepare general or special educators for the realities of inclusive elementary classrooms (Pugach et al., 2014). Moreover, changes in policy, research, and practice have dramatically increased the complexity of special educators' professional work and blurred the lines between GE and SE roles and responsibilities in inclusive settings (Shepherd et al., 2016). As such, general and special education preparation must become more *integrated* and *aligned* in purpose, curricula, and clinical practice and applied teaching experiences must be well-structured, linked to P-6 student needs whenever possible, and evaluated for impact on teacher practice and student learning (Maheady et al., 2007).

History has taught us at least three important lessons about preparing preservice GE and SE teachers for inclusion. First, teacher preparation programs in GE and SE have been characterized by structural segregation since inception despite numerous policy changes and educational reforms. Second, while there have been many occasions for joint action by GE and SE to improve preparation, most have resulted in missed opportunities. Finally, collaborative teacher education programs vary substantially in coursework, clinical experiences, and curricula and as such, cannot be viewed as a common form of intervention. Blanton et al (2018) suggested that the challenge for contemporary GE and SE is not a lack of opportunity to work together, but rather an ability to capitalize on those occasions that do arise.

The next few decades will provide more opportunities for joint action by general and special educators to improve preservice preparation for inclusive educational settings. Blanton and Pugach (2020) recently suggested that dual certification programs may be useful vehicles for re-thinking and refining programs to be more responsive to the broader needs of all students who struggle in school. Moreover, dual certification programs are appealing to major stakeholders (e.g., preservice GE and SE teachers, school leaders, and college administrators) and may be useful in addressing dire shortages of SE teachers.

What We Know from Research and Professional Wisdom

The teacher education research literature in general and special education is broad and complex, and an extensive review is beyond the scope of this chapter. (For more extensive discussion see for example, Cochran-Smith & Zeichner, 2005; Mayer et al., 2017). Here, we begin by summarizing major findings from an extensive quantitative analysis conducted on the impact of preservice preparation practices on teacher quality (Dunst et al., 2020). We then narrow the focus to inclusion-related teacher education inquiry in SE, and further to findings derived from research related to the implementation of practice-based teacher education (PBTE). The chapter then sets a course for effective elementary inclusion by highlighting promising features of PBTE and showcasing changes made by one institution to improve its preservice, elementary dual certification program.

Which Preservice Teacher Preparation Practices Make a Difference?

Dunst and colleagues (2020) synthesized findings from 118 meta-analyses and 12 related reports on teacher preparation variables and novice teacher outcomes that included over 5,000 studies and between 2.5 and 3 million participants. These researchers examined the impact of 14 different types of preparation practices (e.g., methods of course delivery, teaching method of instruction, and clinical experiences) on two different measures of teacher quality (i.e., teacher behavior and performance appraisals). They aggregated findings and classified practices by effect sizes as (a) very high impact, (b) high impact, (c) medium impact, (d) low impact, and (e) no impact.

Dunst et al. reported that three of four preparation practices with the *largest* effect sizes (i.e., > 1.50), "involved active preservice student engagement in learning to use different types of teaching and clinical practices" (p.34). Effect sizes for *extended student teaching* (10+ weeks) were particularly important because they were associated with both better classroom quality and improved teaching practice. These findings highlighted the importance of providing candidates with ongoing and extended opportunities to acquire the skills to perform specific classroom practices and the powerful impact of performance-based feedback.

Dunst et al. also reported that 12 preparation practices produced *large* effect sizes (i.e., > .60). These factors included critical thinking instruction, teaching practices instruction, peer-instruction, microteaching, and inquiry-based learning. These practices were deemed important because they represented deliberate efforts to promote preservice teacher acquisition of core teaching practices. Seven preparation variables were associated with *medium* effect sizes (i.e., > .40). Among these activities were clinical supervision, modeling, and school-based mentoring. Moderator analyses indicated that performance feedback was most effective when it focused on what preservice teachers did well when using specific instructional practices.

It is also important to describe preparation factors that had little or no impact on preservice teacher outcomes. Low impact variables were teacher degrees (e. g, MA/BA versus CDA/AA/HS), number of education classes, and course-based learning methods (e.g., explanation-based versus visually or practice-based learning). Practices with no impact included (a) teacher certification (e. g., in field versus alternative certification), (b) type of preservice program (e. g., tradition versus extended), (c) preparatory practices (e. g., first year seminars), and (d) school-based traditional induction programs (e. g., group seminars and group collaborative planning sessions).

Dunst and colleagues concluded that findings were consistent with clinical- or practice-based approaches to teacher education (e.g., Darling-Hammond, 2014; Hauser & Kavanagh, 2019) that emphasized active and extended preservice teacher learning opportunities, faculty and supervisor coaching with performance feedback, and repeated opportunities to refine core teaching practices.

Research Priorities in Special Education

In 2010 Sindelar and colleagues were invited to assess the status of research on SE teacher preparation and outline a future agenda for improving the quality of the SE workforce. They suggested, among other things, that SE preparation and practice can be improved by (a) clarifying and assessing intended preservice teacher outcomes (e.g., pedagogical content knowledge); (b) validating teaching practices that increased SE understanding and use of evidence-based practices (EBPs) across broad domains (e.g., classroom management & reading); (c) assessing the impact of clinical experiences on student learning and exploring how programs might be structured for success; (d) identifying teaching practices and clinical experiences that improve SE abilities to work effectively with other professionals and families; and (e) delineating strategies and structures to scale up the use of EBPs on campus and in inclusive classrooms. History would suggest that each topic provided opportunities for collaboration and joint action between GE and SE.

Brownell and colleagues (2020) followed-up on this earlier report by conducting a comprehensive review of research articles published in *Teacher Education and Special Education* (TESE) over the past decade. They assessed progress made toward SE research priorities, identified persistent gaps in the knowledge base, and proposed future research directions. They noted that researchers had made important strides in addressing some research priorities, particularly the identification of effective pedagogical practices. The three most prominent practices for improving teachers' knowledge and practice were coaching, multi-component innovations, and content acquisition podcasts (CAPs) (e.g., Kennedy et al., 2018; Sayeski et al., 2019). Brownell et al. found no studies, however, on scaling up innovative practices and/or strategies to improve GE and SE abilities to co-teach or work effectively in inclusive classrooms.

Coaching (i.e., mainly performance feedback) was the most-studied pedagogical practice. It was delivered face-to-face and via bug-in-ear technology (Scheeler & Lee, 2018) and used in combination with modeling (e.g., Shepley et al., 2018) and/or opportunities to practice with feedback in simulated, mixed reality arrangements such as TLE TeachLivE (e.g., Vince Garland et al., 2016). Findings indicated that coaching produced meaningful increases in SE teachers' use of discrete teaching behaviors (e.g., behavior-specific praise) and some improvements generalized to classroom settings (Dawson & Lignugaris Kraft, 2017).

Multi-component interventions were the second most often used strategy for improving teachers' knowledge, skills, and/or student outcomes. Intervention packages included some combinations of explicit instruction, active learning opportunities, modeling, and practice in simulated and/or live learning environments. Findings indicated that multi-component interventions increased SE teachers' use of discrete teaching behaviors (e.g., Horrocks & Morgan, 2011) as well as more complex instructional routines (e.g., Kennedy et al., 2018). There was less evidence, however, that interventions impacted preservice teachers' knowledge and beliefs and/or student academic and behavioral performance.

Content acquisition podcasts (CAPs) were used in at least five empirical studies to improve teacher retention of important knowledge around a specific target (e.g., phonemic awareness). CAPs are brief informational presentations augmented with visual information designed to facilitate teacher understanding and retention of information. CAPs were also used in combination with modeling to help preservice teachers apply acquired knowledge in simulated settings (Alves et al., 2018).

Brownell et al proposed a research agenda grounded in robust theories of teaching, programmatic approaches to teacher development, and more rigorous assessment of teaching quality (i.e., knowledge, teaching practices, and dispositions). They highlighted the need for more studies to help (a) GE and SE teachers develop schemas about when and how to use newly acquired teaching skills in different content areas; (b) teacher educators better understand how preservice teachers integrate practices across content areas and what resources are needed to support integration; and (c) researchers assess GE and SE teacher knowledge, skills, and dispositions more consistently and accurately. Recommendations were directed toward making large-scale revisions to GE and SE preparation programs.

Dynamic Research Model to Address Educational Marginalization.

Blanton and Pugach (2017) noted that there was a, "fragmented research agenda on teacher education for inclusion" (p. 216). They characterized extant research as focused on relatively narrow program components (e.g., the effects of explicit instruction on preservice teacher practice during clinical experiences or the impact of GE and SE co-teaching on preservice teacher knowledge and skills), overrepresented by some topics (e.g., teacher attitudes and/or dispositions & co-teaching), and underrepresented by others (e.g., impact of preservice teacher practice on student learning during clinical experiences).

Moving forward, they proposed a dynamic research model to address broader issues of educational marginalization among all students who struggle in school while maintaining concern and support for SWDs. The dynamic model depicts teacher education programs as comprised of two primary components – *structure* and *content* – nested within layered proximal and distal features (e.g., local context, conceptualizations of practice, understandings of diversity, and meanings of inclusion). They argued that components and features within the model interact in ways that can impact preparation programs and research that is conducted on inclusion.

The authors describe a dynamic and reciprocal relationship between teacher education practice for inclusion and research on teacher education for inclusion. Advances in preparation and practice around inclusion, for example, would inform research by providing new understandings, insights, and questions - grounded in the daily practice of GE and SE teachers and teacher educators – and teacher education for inclusion would design and implement research responsive to these new understandings. (A similar reciprocal relationship is posited later regarding relationships between evidence-based practice and practice-based evidence).

Other Important Research Findings

There are other important research findings relevant to GE and SE teacher preparation and practice for inclusion that cannot be explored in detail here. Instead, we highlight a few themes derived from more substantive research lines that can inform the reform of GE and SE preparation and practice for inclusion.

Some Teaching Practices are More Effective than Others

There is considerable evidence to indicate that some teaching practices are more effective than others in improving academic and behavioral outcomes for students with and without disabilities (e.g., Hattie, 2012). Hattie described *visible* teaching and learning practices that included explicit and challenging goals, deliberate practice geared to student mastery, ongoing positive and constructive feedback, and active student engagement with high levels of student success. Practices with the largest effect sizes included (a) formative assessment, (b) performance-based feedback, (c) cognitive and metacognitive strategies, and (d) spaced versus massed practice opportunities. One implication of these findings is that GE and SE teachers should be taught to use practices with the highest probability of success – whenever possible - particularly with SWDs.

Dunst et al (2020) identified similar sets of preparation practices that were associated with improved teacher quality. They stressed the importance of using practices that produced the largest effect sizes in improving preservice teacher practice such as faculty coaching, simulated instruction with deliberate practice, extended student teaching, and critical thinking instruction. They recommended that teacher preparation programs focus more on the enactment of *specific* teaching practices (i.e., those with empirical support), provide clinically rich coaching and performance-based feedback, and encourage active preservice teacher engagement in knowledge and skill acquisition activities.

A Research-to-Practice Gap Exists in Teacher Education

One persistent and discouraging research finding – not restricted to teacher education - is that even when strong empirical support exists for specific practices, they are *not* used routinely by practitioners. This phenomenon is known as the "research-to-practice gap" (Carnine, 1997), and it is problematic because the most effective teaching strategies available will be of little value to students (or preservice teachers) if they are not used (Cook & Odom, 2013). There is evidence to suggest that this may be the case in teacher preparation and practice for inclusion and that teacher educators may be contributing to the gap. McLeskey et al (2018) suggested, for example, that one reason GE and SE teachers are not using EBPs in inclusive classrooms is because they were not taught to use them in teacher preparation programs.

Begeny and Martens (2006) found that preservice teachers received little direct instruction on EBPs in their preparation programs and the instruction they did receive was devoid of opportunities to apply knowledge and skills. Burns and Ysseldyke (2009) noted that practicing GE and SE teachers reported using teaching strategies with *both* large and small effect sizes regularly with SWDs. Jones (2009) described a general disconnect between what pre-service teachers said and did instructionally. That is, they said they used specific EBPs in their classrooms but were not observed doing so and vice versa.

Finally, Reschly and colleagues (Oliver & Reschly, 2007; Reschly et al., 2008) reported that primary elements of EBPs in beginning reading and classroom management were not present in most teacher education course syllabi and few opportunities were provided for using them in applied settings. An obvious implication of these findings is the need to bridge the research-to-practice gap and increase the use of the most powerful teaching practices, especially when working with students who struggle in school.

Professional Wisdom Plays an Important Role in Implementation

Cook et al (2008) noted that although researchers identify EBPs, practitioners (e.g., teachers and teacher educators) ultimately determine if those practices are used, how they are implemented, and what impact, if any they have on students (and preservice teachers). Practitioner decision-making around implementation is guided, in part, by the *professional wisdom* or the knowledge and understanding teachers have acquired through professional experience. Cook et al. suggested that professional wisdom serves as a filter for making important educational decisions and that teacher educators and researchers must learn how to influence practitioner decision-making, particularly around the selection and use of EBPs.

Cook and Cook (2016) posited that professional wisdom sits squarely at the interplay between (a) empirical (i.e., external) evidence that informs what we know works and (b) teacher use (and adaptation) of those practices to improve student outcomes. One way to foster professional wisdom, therefore, is to teach preservice teachers to use specific EBPs in preparation programs, provide them ample opportunities to practice these skills in multiple applied settings, require them to collect data to assess impact on student performance, and use these data to make instructional decisions (e.g., continue to use, adapt, and/or abandon selected practices). Elliott et al (1998) noted as well that teachers were more likely to implement instructional practices if they had prior experiences using them. Conversely, they were less likely to adopt or use practices with which they were unfamiliar (Telzrow & Beebe, 2002).

Evidence-based Practice and Practice-based Evidence are Important

Evidence-based practice (EBP) has at least two meanings in education: (a) a set of teaching practices validated by rigorous research methods and (b) a decision-making process informed by the best available evidence, professional wisdom, and student needs (for a complete discussion of this topic see Detrich et al., 2008). The decision-making process begins by identifying relevant EBPs that are linked to important student outcomes; practitioners then use their professional wisdom to decide when, where, and how to implement and/or adapt practices. (For research purposes, it is important to ensure that EBPs were implemented with fidelity).

After EBPs are implemented, data are collected to assess intervention effects on student performance. Using student performance under baseline (i.e., existing teaching practices) for comparison, practitioners examine data and determine if student performance improved, deteriorated, and/or stayed the same when using the EBPs. Fink Chorzempa and colleagues (2019) labeled the process of collecting and analyzing classroom-based data to see if relationships existed between instructional practices and student outcomes as *practice-based evidence*. Cook and Cook (2016) posited a reciprocal relationship between practice-based evidence and evidence-based practice; a *bidirectionality* of influence between evidence generated from practice settings and that gleaned through empirical research: each informs the other.

Collecting practice-based evidence (PBE) provides information critical to improving professional decision-making. For example, practitioners can determine if (a) selected practices are working, (b) they are effective with all students, and/or (c) they can be adapted if individuals are not responsive. Cook (2011) suggested that insights derived from PBE provide important external validation data for researchers, reveal nuances or conditional information about the effectiveness of practices, and in turn, contribute to theory.

Including PBE as part of teacher preparation can help novice teachers understand how this kind of evidence is essential in translating EBPs to localized contexts and adapting or abandoning practices when students are non-responsive (Cook & Cook, 2016). Clear demonstrations that preservice teachers can use EBPs effectively in natural settings should also improve student learning, strengthen the external validity of selected practices, and accelerate the generation of evidence developed and refined in practice settings (Walker & Bruns, 2006). Practice-based evidence might also serve as a complement to evidence-based practice in ways that produce mutual benefits for theory, research, and practice (e.g., Barkham & Margison, 2007; Cook, 2011).

A Proposed Model of Research and Professional Wisdom Interplay

Building on the prior discussion, we offer a model for teaching preservice teachers to use EBPs (see Figure 4.1). The model represents (a) possible relationships among research findings, professional wisdom, and practice-based evidence, and (b) how their dynamic interplay might impact the use, adaptation, and/or sustainability of EBPs (i.e., denoted in figure by lightbulbs). Evidence based practices that teachers know about or have used are depicted with arrows falling within the magnifying glass, which represents practitioners use of professional wisdom to make important instructional decisions (e.g., which practices to select, adapt, and apply).

Data generated when practices are implemented (i.e., PBE) then provides feedback on the impact of teacher decision-making. If student performance improves, for instance, selected practices are retained; if most students succeed but some are not responsive, practices are adjusted; and/or if

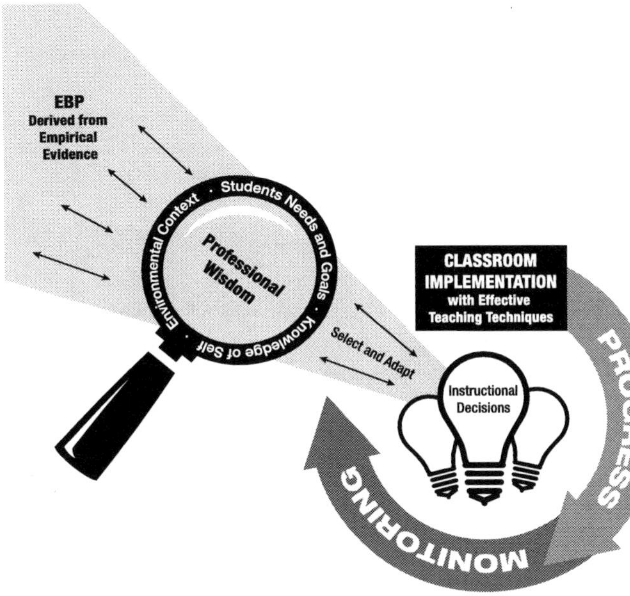

Figure 4.1 A proposed model of the interplay between research, professional wisdom, and teaching practice.

student performance deteriorates, practices are abandoned. The use of double-ended arrows represents the bidirectional flow of information that should inform what we know works in typical classrooms, thereby (a) improving student outcomes (Fink Chorzempa et al., 2019), (b) positioning teachers to make better instructional decisions (Cook, 2011); and (c) enhancing the coherence of teacher preparation by merging knowledge from both research and practice (Cook & Cook, 2016).

Research Summary

Teacher education research provided some important lessons about the effective preparation and practice of preservice GE and SE teachers for inclusive classrooms. Dunst et al (2020) showed that there were several preparation practices associated with improved teacher quality (i.e., very large & large effect sizes) and many were *alterable* variables (i.e., under teacher and/or teacher educator "control" to some extent). General and SE teacher educators, for example, can redesign preparation programs to include active and extended teaching opportunities, coaching with performance-based feedback, and/or repeated opportunities to refine core teaching practices. Similarly, they can add formative data collection responsibilities to clinical experiences and require preservice teachers to use those data for making important instructional decisions.

Brownell et al. (2010) outlined a comprehensive research agenda for SE teacher preparation focused on clarifying and assessing important teacher outcomes, identifying strategies to increase the use of EBPs, and improving SE teachers' abilities to work effectively with professionals and families. Brownell et al. (2020) highlighted important advances in SE research over the past decade, particularly in the use of pedagogical practices, and proposed a research agenda to make transformative changes in GE and SE programs.

Blanton et al. (2018) proposed a dynamic research model to rectify the fragmented research agenda on teacher education for inclusion. The proposed model described a reciprocal relationship between teacher education practice for inclusion and research on teacher education for inclusion.

Other research lines indicated that (a) some teaching and preparation practices were more effective than others; (b) a research-to-practice gap persists in preparation and practice for inclusion; (c) professional wisdom mediates teacher decision-making and it may be leveraged to increase the use of EBP; and (d) the collection and use of practice-based evidence may be a promising way to improve preparation and practice. A model was offered as a heuristic for examining the interplay of EBPs, professional wisdom, and PBE and exploring potential reciprocal and bidirectional relationships.

Setting the Course for Effective Elementary Inclusion

There are multiple ways to proceed in developing and/or refining GE and SE teacher preparation and practice for inclusion. Options range from making broad, multi-institutional programmatic changes aligned around common desired outcomes (e.g., addressing educational marginalization of all students who struggle in school) (Blanton & Pugach, 2020) to modifying specific program components (e.g., co-teaching courses for GE and SE and/or pairing GE and SE for clinical experiences) and assessing the impact on important preservice teacher or student outcomes (Brownell et al. 2020). Ultimately, decisions about how to proceed will be made based on factors in the local context (e.g., skill sets, availability, and interest of faculty; levels of institutional support, and/or history of structural segregation and/or past experiences with inclusive programming).

In this section we describe a practice-based approach to teacher preparation for inclusion and provide a rationale to support its use. We then describe how GE and SE teacher educators at one institution worked collaboratively with PDS partners to infuse specific practice-based elements (e.g., common high leverage practices, co-teaching, and preservice teacher pairings) into a preservice, dual certification program. We conclude by sharing lessons learned and possible directions for future research and practice.

Practice-based Teacher Education

Practice-based teacher education (PBTE) refers to an approach to teacher preparation that makes teaching practice – what teachers *do* instructionally – the central element of the curriculum (Zeichner, 2012). Programs focus on preparing preservice teachers to enact core instructional practices and are characterized by clinically rich, field experiences and strong school-university partnerships (Hauser and Kavanagh, 2019). The rise of PBTE represented a conceptual shift from focusing on what preservice teachers *know* to what they can *do* instructionally (Maheady & Patti, 2020).

Darling-Hammond (2014) noted an escalating trend in adoption of PBTE and suggested this was likely to continue as institutions responded to accreditation demands. The Council for the Accreditation of Educator Preparation (CAEP) Standard 2, for example, requires education programs to ensure that, "effective partnerships and high-quality clinical practice are central to preparation so that candidates develop the knowledge, skills, and dispositions necessary to demonstrate positive impact on all P-12 students' learning and development" (CAEP, 2013, p. 6).

Pugach et al (2014) and Pugach and Blanton (2009) suggested that PBTE has changed the nature, structure, and functions of teacher preparation. PBTE has prompted greater curricular and pedagogical alignment on campuses and in P-6 schools (Pugach et al., 2014); promoted the creation and/or expansion of school-university partnerships with increased emphases on clinical placement, teaching practice, and student learning (CAEP, 2013); and produced calls for more rigorous, classroom-based research to address problems of practice (Maheady et al., 2013).

Improving teacher practice has become a major focus of policymakers and teacher educators for several reasons. First, research has suggested that the most *direct* way to improve outcomes for lower performing students is by increasing the quality of instruction they receive (Hanushek & Rivkin, 2010). Second, there are several teaching practices (e.g., explicit instruction, response cards, & cooperative learning) that have robust evidence bases and are feasible to implement and socially acceptable to teachers and students; characteristics that make them more attractive to users and increase the likelihood of adoption (see for example, Cook & Odom, 2013; Hattie, 2009; Lignugaris-Kraft et al., 2014).

Third, coaching, multicomponent interventions, and performance-based feedback have emerged as effective and practical ways to change teacher practice, specifically in the use of EBPs (Kretlow & Bartholomew, 2010). Finally, States et al. (2012) have argued that modern measures of teacher practice (e.g., fidelity assessments) and student learning (e.g., effect sizes, value-added modeling, and randomized control trials) are more rigorous and technically adequate (i.e., reliable and valid) than their predecessors, thereby making them more trustworthy to use.

Darling-Hammond (2020) described PBTE programs as characterized by core sets of instructional practices around which programs are aligned, long and in-depth clinical experiences, and strong school-university partnerships. These structural characteristics are aligned with high impact practices identified by Dunst et al (2020) and suggest that PBTE programs already include some important components for improving preparation.

To develop fluency in using selected practices, preservice GE and SE teachers need multiple opportunities to practice and receive constructive, performance-based feedback. These teaching/learning opportunities can occur across university and P-6 inclusive classrooms and vary in instructional complexity and level of scaffolded supports. Ericsson (2014) described this as *deliberate practice* with performance feedback. Candidates are given carefully designed practice opportunities that gradually increase in complexity and decrease in levels of support. Deliberate practice opportunities should be driven by P-6 student needs, monitored for implementation fidelity, and examined for impact on student learning.

The Collaboration for Effective Educator Development, Accountability, and Reform (CEEDAR) Center has developed important tools and resources to assist teacher educators in pedagogical redesign for PBTE (Benedict et al., 2016a; Benedict et al., 2016b). Practice guides describe how university faculty can work with school partners to define and plan comprehensive clinical experiences. Specific tools include observation/coaching guides for school-based practitioners and clinical planning templates. Clinical experience templates: (a) map applied experiences by program and candidate, (b) locate them in program and course sequences, (c) delineate participant roles and responsibilities, and (d) outline the scope and sequence of clinical experiences with school partners.

In the section that follows, we provide an illustrative example of the development of a PBTE program at our institution. We used the previously described CEEDAR tools and resources, employed high leverage practices (HLPs) developed for preservice general (U. of Michigan, n.d.) and special education (McLeskey et al., 2017) teachers, and our best collaboration skills to redesign teacher preparation for inclusion in an undergraduate, dual certification program.

We begin the illustrative example with general background information regarding our institution's dual certification preparation program prior to the redesign, and factors that served to precipitate the change for GE and SE faculty. We then describe how we collaboratively planned broad curriculum revisions in the program using selected general and special education HLPs as a framework to guide these changes. Finally, we describe a pilot project that we used to field test and critically examine the feasibility of three new components of our elementary dual certification program: (a) co-teaching between GE and SE university faculty members, (b) shared clinical experiences among GE and SE preservice teachers, and (c) using school partner input to guide changes in coursework and clinical experiences.

An Illustrative Example

Given issues of structural segregation within our existing dual certification program voiced by preservice GE and SE teachers and faculty, accreditation changes, and impetus from a new dean, special and general education faculty began to collaborate (i.e., border crossings) as part of our Professional Development School (PDS) consortium (http://pds.buffalostate.edu). The PDS consortium faculty from GE and SE engaged in board discussions and attended PDS events as an opportunity to collaborate regarding program changes and/or redesign. These faculty eventually proposed that high leverage practices (HLPs) might be used to link PDS needs to improved preparation of preservice teachers for inclusive classrooms. The PDS consortium subsequently adopted *High Leverage Practices* as a major theme, and during an annual conference and school-based meetings centered discussions around using HLPs as the core curriculum that would guide program redesign. The result was a two-pronged approach that institutionalized broad curriculum revisions and used a mini-grant pilot project with PDS partners to infuse HLPs into clinical practice.

Broad Curriculum Revisions

During conversations within the PDS consortium, teacher education faculty agreed that the disjointed nature of the dual certification program did not match the realities of contemporary inclusive classrooms. HLPs then became a catalyst for conversations around how to address these issues while including PDS consortium members and colleagues from across departments.

Curricular Alignment Around High Leverage Practices

Based on these discussions among faculty and partners from the PDS consortium, an organizational decision was made to revise the undergraduate, dual certification program so that it would maintain clinically rich practice but be centered around a core set of mutually agreed upon HLPs. Program revisions then began that would include: (a) better content alignment across three departments—elementary education, special education, and educational foundations, (b) curriculum compacting across similar courses, (c) infusion of HLPs as "core" content, (d) increased modeling of preferred instructional practices and co-teaching, (e) blocked methods courses for teaching students with, without, and at-risk for disabilities, and (f) integrated clinical experiences. Figure 4.2 provides an overview of eight basic phases involved in these curriculum revisions. For the purpose of this chapter, we limit our discussion to a description of critical components of program development related to PBTE, including the development of a framework using selected HLPs from general and special education to guide this work.

Developing a Framework

Initially, a collaborative faculty work group was formed with members from the three education departments. Group members reviewed 19 HLPs developed by the University of Michigan, Teaching Works (Ball & Forzani, 2011; University of Michigan, n. d.) that were applicable to the daily work of elementary education teachers and 25 "draft" HLPs for special education teachers. (The latter set was later reduced to 22 HLPs and adopted formally by the Council for Exceptional Children; McLeskey et al., 2017).

The workgroup discussed how both HLP sets were related to program vision (i.e., common, integrated curriculum, shared clinical experiences, and collaborative working relationships) and created a crosswalk to examine HLP similarities and differences. Members agreed that adopting separate sets of HLPs for GE and SE was inconsistent with program vision and would be impossible to implement. They concurred that the total number of HLPs should be: (a) limited (i.e., under 20), (b) linked to PDS partners' instructional needs, and (c) teachable on and off campus. Following deliberation, they developed a draft set of 17 mutually agreed upon HLPs to serve potentially as a core curriculum for the revised dual certification program.

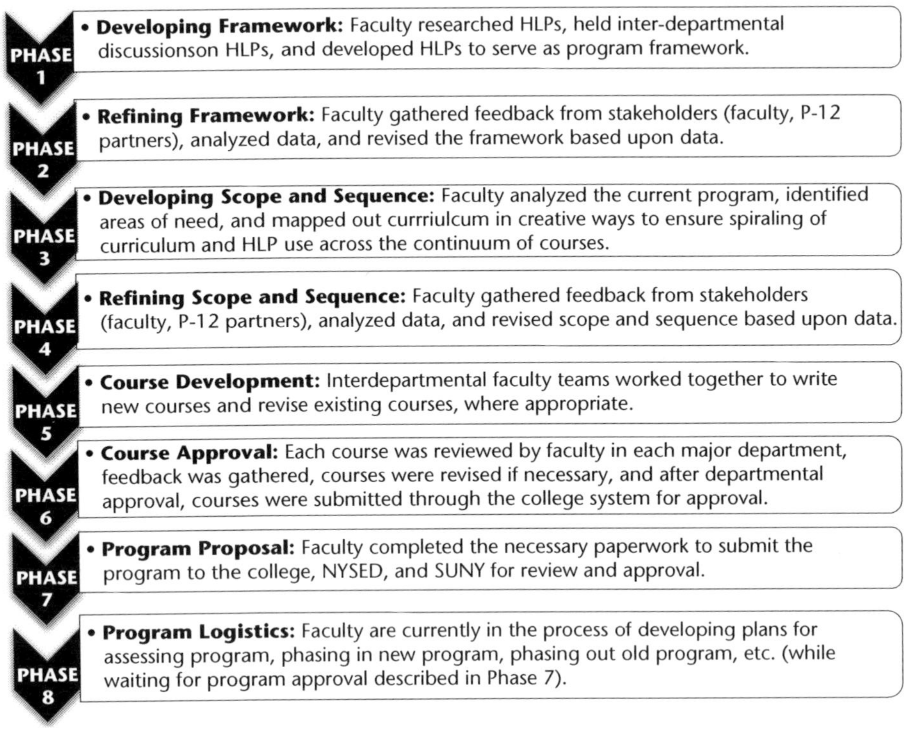

Figure 4.2 Revision process of dual-certification program in special and general education, Grades 1 to 6.

Note. HLPs = high-leverage practices.

To better understand school partner needs, the workgroup shared the draft HLPs with faculty and administrators, presented and took notes at advisory board meetings, conducted workshops at PDS consortium sessions, and developed and sent surveys to PDS consortium teachers and leaders. The goals were to: (a) gather feedback on draft HLPs, (b) determine which HLPs were most *important* and *relevant* to individual PDS, and (c) use this information to align course content and clinical experiences with these prioritized practices.

No substantive modifications were made to the 17 HLPs; however, there was much discussion around language usage which subsequently led to agreement on a shared vocabulary. Additional feedback and support were gathered from faculty in the three education departments and 17 HLPs were formally adopted for the revised, dual-certification program (see Figure 4.3). While consensus building led to the adoption of 17 HLPs, critical questions about *how* to prepare candidates to use them remained to be addressed. A pilot study was designed to begin to address this concern.

PDS Pilot Project

The revised dual-certification program included three new components: (a) co-teaching between university faculty members, (b) shared clinical experiences among candidates, and (c) the use of school needs to guide program implementation. Patti and del Prado Hill (2017) conducted a pilot study to examine the feasibility of implementing these components into coursework and clinical experiences.

One faculty member from GE and SE co-taught a blocked section of courses (i.e., foundations of special education, advanced literacy instruction for students with and without disabilities, and

Communication and Collaboration
HLP 1: Communicate and collaborate effectively with colleagues, parents/guardians, school leaders, and other professionals.
HLP 2: Advocate for students and families to secure needed services and promote social justice.
Instructional Design
HLP 3: Use knowledge about the curriculum and students' present levels of performance to identify short-and long-term goals.
HLP 4: Design a sequence of lessons towards a specific learning outcome.
HLP 5: Choose and adapt curriculum materials and tasks specific to learning goals.
Instructional Delivery
HLP 6: Make learning explicit through modeling, guided practice, and independent practice.
HLP 7: Use strategies to promote active student engagement in whole class and small group instruction.
HLP 8: Scaffold instruction during lessons.
HLP 9: Teach students to work independently.
HLP 10: Select, implement, and evaluate instructional and assistive technologies to support student learning.
HLP 11: Identify and implement an instructional strategy or intervention in response to common patterns of student performance or individual need.
HLP 12: Self-analyze teaching for the purpose of improving instruction and learning.
Classroom Management
HLP 13: Establish and implement effective classroom and individual student management plans to increase student social and academic outcomes.
HLP 14: Provide high rates of specific feedback.
HLP 15: Create and facilitate a safe, respectful, productive, and positive learning environment.
Assessment
HLP 16: Develop/select and implement specific assessment measures to determine relevant information about students' present levels of performance.
HLP 17: Interpret and communicate assessment data to make important educational decisions.

Figure 4.3 List of HLPs used as a framework in the dual-certification, undergraduate program at our institution.

Note: The development of these HLPs was based upon: (a) the combined professional knowledge of SUNY Buffalo State School of Education faculty and partners, (b) HLPs from the University of Michigan, and (c) HLPs from the Council for Exceptional Children.

classroom management) to a cohort of preservice teachers enrolled in the dual certification program across two semesters. Instruction took place at the PDS where candidates completed clinical experiences. University faculty participated in each other's instruction daily by (a) observing to learn one another's content, (b) co-teaching lessons to model collaborative practices and discuss relevant advantages and disadvantages, and (c) interjecting in one another's lessons to make connections between content across two disciplines (i.e., elementary and special education).

Teacher candidates also shared clinical placements. They were assigned in pairs to one co-taught classroom, completed course-related projects (e.g., developing behavioral intervention plans and conducting formal reading assessments), and co-designed, co-taught, and co-evaluated multiple lessons. Each classroom had some combination of GE, SE, and English as a New Language (ENL) mentor teachers and occasionally other specialists. Preservice GE and SE teachers observed and engaged in co-teaching and collaboration activities that mirrored the roles and responsibilities of their mentor teachers in these inclusive settings.

Clinical placements were supervised by GE and SE faculty who co-taught the blocked courses. Preservice teachers received guidance on class projects and feedback on lesson design and implementation from both instructors. Teachers and school leaders had extensive input into the nature of the clinical experience. They delineated preservice teachers' roles and responsibilities and identified important and relevant HLPs for their schools.

The pilot project was conducted in an inclusive, bilingual PDS with large numbers of SWDs, English language learners, and students from high poverty backgrounds. The school had a state-mandated improvement plan with clearly delineated instructional priorities. A liaison committee, consisting of the two university instructors, a representative PDS mentor teacher, and school principal met regularly. Through discussion, two school-wide priorities were established for the pilot project, increasing (a) student talk time and (b) active student engagement during large and small group lessons.

Both targets aligned well with the program's HLP #7, "use strategies to promote active student engagement." During university class time, faculty modeled a variety of empirically supported strategies for increasing active student engagement (e.g., response cards; Heward & Wood, 2015; Randolph, 2007), engaged preservice teachers in role-playing activities, and provided feedback on their use of selected practices. Preservice GE and SE teachers then implemented specific strategies in clinical placements and received performance-based feedback from mentor teachers, university faculty, and peers. The liaison committee also prioritized CEC's HLP #1, "collaborate with professionals to increase student success" and HLP #17, "use flexible grouping" for implementation. University faculty taught related strategies in class and mentor teachers provided opportunities for preservice GE and SE teachers to practice using the skill sets in their clinical placements.

The pilot program was well-received and viewed favorably by university faculty, school partners, and teacher candidates. Two keys to success were mutual benefits and clear and ongoing communication. PDS partners were instrumental in identifying a limited number of important and relevant HLPs that brought focus and coherence to the curriculum and provided meaningful practice-based opportunities for preservice GE and SE teachers.

One persistent challenge was the amount of time required to sustain everyone's efforts. Ongoing communication was required between university faculty, respective department chairs, the Dean of the School of Education, and PDS consortium partners. Most planning was front-loaded, but ongoing communication was necessary throughout the year. This included weekly co-planning sessions between university faculty, weekly in-person "check-ins" with mentor teachers, monthly liaison committee meetings, and regular program updates via email to maintain program focus and logistics.

Conclusion

Teacher education can play a significant role in effective inclusive elementary schools by preparing high quality preservice teachers, forging and maintaining strong school-university partnerships, and engaging in collaborative research to improve teacher practice and student learning. To do this, general and special educators must align and integrate programs in purpose, curricula, and clinical experiences. Some promising themes and directions for reform include practice-based teacher education, equity-based perspectives on inclusion, learning communities of teaching practice, and dual certification programs. The challenge now is for general and special educators to capitalize on local opportunities for collaboration and joint action.

References

Allday, A. R., Neilsen-Gatti, S., & Hudson, T. M. (2013). Preparation for inclusion in teacher education pre-service curriculum. *Teacher Education and Special Education, 36*(4), 298–311.

Alves, K. D., Kennedy, M. J., Kellems, R. O., Wexler, J., Rodgers, W. J., Romig, J. E., & Peeples, K. N. (2018). Improving preservice teacher vocabulary instruction: A randomized controlled trial. *Teacher Education and Special Education, 41*, 340–356

Ball, D. & Forzani, F. M. (2011). Building a common core for learning to teach: And connecting professional learning to practice. *American Educator, 35*(2), 17–21, 38-39.

Barkham, M., & Margison, F. (2007). Practice-based evidence as a complement to evidence-based practice: From dichotomy to chiasmus. In C. Freeman & M. Power (Eds.), *Handbook of evidence-based psychotherapies: A guide for research and practice* (pp. 443–476). West Sussex, England: Wiley & Sons.

Bauwens, J., Hourcade, J. J., & Friend, M. (1989). Cooperative teaching: A model for general and special education integration. *Remedial and Special Education, 10*(2), 17–22.

Begeny, J. C., & Martens, B. K. (2006). Assessing pre-service teachers' training in empirically validated behavioral instruction practices. *School Psychology Quarterly, 21*, 262–285.

Benedict, A., Foley, A., Holdheide, L., Brownell, M., & Kamman, M. (2016a). *Learning to teach: A framework for crafting high-quality, practice-based opportunities.* Washington, DC: American Institutes for Research, Center on Great Teachers and Leaders, and Gainesville, FL: University of Florida, Collaboration for Effective Educator Development, Accountability, and Reform Center. Retrieved from http://cedar.education.ufl.edu/wp-content/uploads/2016/06/Learning-to-TeachRubric.pdf

Benedict, A., Holdheide, L., Brownell, M., & Foley, A. (2016b). *Learning to teach practice-based preparation in teacher education.* Washington, DC: American Institutes for Research, Center on Great Teachers and Leaders, and Gainesville, FL: University of Florida, Collaboration for Effective Educator Development, Accountability, and Reform Center. Retrieved from http://cedar.education.ufl.edu/wpcontent/uploads/2016/07/Learning-to-Teach Rubric.pdf

Blanton, L. P., Griffin, C. C., Winn, J. A., & Pugach, M. C. (Eds.). (1997). *Teacher education in transition: Collaborative programs to prepare general and special educators.* Denver: Love.

Blanton, L. P., & Pugach, M. C. (2020). Dual certification programs. *Oxford Research Encyclopedias.* London, UK: Oxford Press.

Blanton, L. P., & Pugach, M. C. (2017). A dynamic model for the next generation of research on teacher education for inclusion. In L. Florian & N. Pantic (Eds), *Teacher education for the changing demographics of schooling* (pp. 215–228), Inclusive Learning and Educational Equity, 2. Springer International Publishing.

Blanton, L. P., Pugach, M. C., & Boveda, M. (2018). Interrogating the intersections between general and special education in the history of teacher education reform. *Journal of Teacher Education, 69*(4), 354–366.

Boe, E., (2014). Teacher demand, supply, and shortage in special education: A national perspective. In P. Sindelar, E. McCray, M. T. Brownell, & B. Lignugaris Kraft (Eds.), *Handbook of research on special education teacher preparation* (pp. 67–93). New York: Routledge.

Bondy, E., & Ross, D. D. (Eds.). (2005). *Preparing for inclusive teaching: Meeting the challenges of teacher education reform.* Albany: State University of New York Press.

Brophy, J. E. (1979). Teacher behavior and its effects. *Journal of Educational Psychology, 71*, 733–750.

Brownell, M. T., Jones, N. D., Sohn, H., & Stark, K. (2020). Improving teaching quality for students with disabilities: Establishing a warrant for teacher education practice. *Teacher Education and Special Education, 43*(1), 28–44.

Brownell, M. T., Sindelar, P. T., Kiely, M. T., & Danielson, L. C. (2010). Special education teacher quality and preparation: Exposing foundations, constructing a new model. *Exceptional Children, 76*(3), 357–377.

Burns, M. K., & Ysseldyke, J. E. (2009). Reported prevalence of evidence-based instructional practices in special education. *Journal of Special Education, 43*, 3–11.

CAEP (2013). *CAEP Accreditation Standards.* Washington, DC: Council for the Accreditation of Educator Preparation.

Carnine, D. (1997). Bridging the research-to-practice gap. *Exceptional Children, 63*(4), 513–521.

Cochran-Smith, M., & Zeichner, K. M. (2005). *Studying teacher education: The Report of the AERA panel on research and teacher education*. Mahwah, NJ: Lawrence Erlbaum Associates.

Cook, B. G. (2011). Evidence-based practices and practice-based evidence: A union of insufficiencies. *Focus on Research, 24*(4), 1–2.

Cook, B. G., & Cook, L. (2016). Leveraging evidence-based practice through partnerships based on practice-based evidence. *Learning Disabilities: A Contemporary Journal, 14*, 143–157.

Cook, B. G., & Odom, S. L. (2013). Evidence-based practices and implementation science in special education. *Exceptional Children, 79*(2), 135–144.

Cook, B. G., Tankersley, M., & Harjusola-Webb, S. (2008). Evidence-based special education and professional wisdom: Putting it all together. *Intervention in School and Clinic, 44*(2), 105–111.

Crispel, O., & Kasperski, R. (2019). The impact of teacher training in special education on the implementation of inclusion in mainstream classrooms, *International Journal of Inclusive Education*, DOI: 10.1080/13603116.2019.1600590

Darling-Hammond, L. (2020). *Evaluating teacher effectiveness: How teacher performance assessments can measure and improve teaching*. Center for American Progress.

Darling-Hammond, L. (2014). Strengthening clinical preparation: The holy grail of teacher education. *Peabody Journal of Education, 89*(4), 547–561.

Dawson, M. R., & Lignugaris Kraft, B. (2017). Meaningful practice: Generalizing foundation teaching skills from TLE TeachLivETM to the classroom. *Teacher Education and Special Education, 40*, 26–50.

deBettencourt, L. U., Hoover, J. J., Rude, H. A., & Taylor, S. S. (2016). Preparing special education higher education faculty: The influences of contemporary education issues and policy recommendations. *Teacher Education and Special Education, 39*(2), 121–131.

Detrich, R., Keyworth, R., & States, J. (2008). A roadmap to evidence-based education: Building an evidence-based culture. In R. Detrich, R. Keyworth, & J. States (Eds.), *Advances in evidence-based education (Vol. 1): A roadmap to evidence-based education* (pp. 3–19). Oakland, CA: The Wing Institute.

Dunn, L. M. (1968). Special education for the mildly retarded – Is much of it justified? *Exceptional Children, 35*(1), 5–22.

Dunst, C. J., Hamby, D. W., Howse, R. B., Wilkie, H., & Annas, K. (2020). Research synthesis of meta-analyses of preservice teacher preparation practices in higher education. *Higher Education Studies, 10*(1), 29–47. 10.5539/hes.v10n1p29

Elliott, S. N., Kratochwill, T. R., & Schulte, A. G. (1998). The Assessment Accommodation Checklist: Who, what, where, when, why, and how. *Teaching Exceptional Children, 31*(2), 10–14.

Ericsson, K. A. (2014). *The road to excellence: The acquisition of expert performance in the arts and sciences, sports, and games*. Florence, KY: Psychology Press.

Fink Chorzempa, B., Smith, M. D., & Sileo, J. M. (2019). Practice based evidence: A model for helping educators make evidence-based decisions. *Teacher Education and Special Education, 42*(1), 82–92.

Hanushek, E. A., & Rivkin, S. G. (2010). Generalizations about using value-added measures of teacher quality. *American Economic Review, 100*(2), 267–271.

Hattie, J. (2009). *Visible learning: A synthesis of over 800 meta-analyses relating to achievement*. New York: Taylor & Francis.

Hattie, J. (2012). *Visible learning for teachers: Maximizing impact on learning*. New York: Routledge.

Hauser, M., & Kavanagh, S. S. (2019). Practice-based teacher education. *Oxford Research Encyclopedia of Education*. Epub ahead of print March 2019.

Heward, W. L., & Wood, C. L., (2015, April). *Improving educational outcomes in America: Can a low tech, generic teaching practice make a difference?* Retrieved from http://www.winginstitute.org/uploadedFiles/News_And_Events/Summits/2013WingSummitWH.pdf

Horrocks, E. L., & Morgan, R. L. (2011). Effects of inservice teacher training on correct implementation of assessment and instructional procedures for teachers of students with profound multiple disabilities. *Teacher Education and Special Education, 34*, 283–319.

Houston, R. W., & Howsam, R. B. (1972). *Competency-based teacher education: Progress, problems, and prospects*. ERIC Number: ED074017

Jones, M. L. (2009). A study of novice special educators' views of evidence-based practices. *Teacher Education and Special Education, 32*, 121–136.

Kennedy, M. J., Rodgers, W. J., Romig, J. E., Mathews, H. M., & Peeples, K. N. (2018). Introducing the content acquisition podcast professional development process: Supporting vocabulary instruction for inclusive middle school science teachers. *Teacher Education and Special Education, 41*, 140–157.

Kleinhammer-Tramill, J. (2003). An analysis of federal initiatives to prepare regular educators to serve students with disabilities: Dean's Grants, REGI, and beyond. *Teacher Education and Special Education, 26*, 230–245.

Kozleski, E. B., & Proffitt, W. A. (2020). A journey toward equity and diversity in the educator workforce. *Teacher Education and Special Education, 43*(1), 63–84.

Kraska, J., & Boyle, C. (2014). Attitudes of pre-school and primary school pre-service teachers towards inclusive education. *Asia-Pacific Journal of Teacher Education, 42*(3), 228–246.

Kretlow, A. G.& Bartholomew, C. C. (2010). Using coaching to improve the fidelity of evidence-based practices: A review of studies. *Teacher Education and Special Education, 33*(4), 279–299.

Leko, M. M., Brownell, M. T., Sindelar, P. T., & Kiely, M. T. (2015). Envisioning the future of special education personnel preparation in a standards-based era. *Exceptional Children, 82*(1), 25–43.

Lignugaris-Kraft, B., Sindelar, P. T., McCray, E. D., & Kimerling, J. (2014). The "wicked question" of teacher education effects and what to do about it. In P. T. Sindelar, E. D. McCray, M. T., & B. Lignugaris-Kraft (Eds.), *Handbook of research on special education teacher preparation* (pp. 461–471). New York: Routledge.

Maheady, L., Jabot, M., Rey, J., & Michielli-Pendl, J. (2007). An early field based experience and its effects on pre-service teachers' practice and student learning. *Teacher Education and Special Education 30*, 24–33.

Maheady, L., & Patti, A., (2020). High leverage practices for inclusive educational settings. *Oxford Research Encyclopedias*. London, UK: Oxford Press.

Maheady, L., Smith, C., & Jabot, M. (2013). Utilizing evidence-based practice in teacher preparation. *Advances in Learning and Behavioral Disabilities, 26*, 121–147.

Mayer, D., Dixon, M., Kline, J., Kostogriz, A., Moss, J., Rowan, L., Walker-Gibbs, B., & White, S. (2017). *Studying the effectiveness of teacher education.* In: Studying the effectiveness of teacher education. Springer, Singapore. 10.1007/978-981-10-3929-4_2

McLeskey, J., Barringer, M.-D., Billingsley, B., Brownell, M., Jackson, D., Kennedy, M., Lewis, T., Maheady, L., Rodriguez, J., Scheeler, M. C., Winn, J., & Ziegler, D. (2017). *High-leverage practices in special education.* Arlington, VA: Council for Exceptional Children and CEEDAR Center.

McLeskey, J., Billingsley, B., & Ziegler, D. (2018). Using high-leverage practices in teacher preparation to reduce the research-to-practice gap in inclusive settings. *Australasian Journal of Special and Inclusive Education, 42*(1), 3–16. 10.1017/jsi.2018

NCATE (2010, November). *Transforming teacher education through clinical practice: A national strategy to prepare effective teachers.* Washington, D.C. www.ncate.org/publications.

No Child Left Behind Act of 2001 (2002), Pub. L. No. 107-110.

Oliver, R. M., & Reschly, D. J. (2007, December). *Effective classroom management: Teacher preparation and professional development.* Washington, DC: National Comprehensive Center for Teacher Quality. Retrieved from www.tqsource.org.

Patti, A. L., & del Prado Hill, P. (2017). Co-teaching in a co-PDS: Outcomes of a year- long pilot program. *PDS Partners, 13*(1), 10–12.

Pinter, H. H., Bloom, L. A., Rush, C. B., & Sastre, C. (2020). Best practices in teacher preparation for inclusive education. In the *Handbook of research on innovative pedagogies and best practices in teacher education*(pp. 52–68). IGI Global Publishers.

Pugach, M. C., & Blanton, L. P. (2009). A framework for conducting research on collaborative teacher education. *Teaching and Teacher Education, 25*, 575–582.

Pugach, M. C., Blanton, L. P., & Boveda, M. (2014). Working together research on the preparation of general education and special education teachers for inclusion and collaboration. In P. T. Sindelar, E. D. McCray, M. T. Brownell, & B. Lignugaris-Kraft (Eds.), *Handbook of research on special education teacher preparation* (pp. 143–160). New York: Routledge.

Pugach, M. C., Blanton, L. P., & Correa, V. I. (2011). A historical perspective on the role of collaboration in teacher education reform: Making good on the promises to teach all students. *Teacher Education and Special Education, 34*(3), 183–200.

Randolph, J. J. (2007). Meta-analysis of the research on response cards: Effects on test achievement, quiz achievement, participation, and off-task behavior, *Journal of Positive Behavioral Interventions, 9*, 113–128.

Reschly, D. J., Holdheide, L. R., & Smartt, S. M. (2008, December). *Innovation Configuration Tools: Implementing evidence-based practices in teacher preparation.* Washington, DC: National Comprehensive Center for Teacher Quality. Retrieved from www.tqsource.org.

Sailor, W., Skrtic, T. M., Conn, M., & Olmstead, C. (2020). Preparing teacher educators for statewide scale-up of Multi-Tiered Systems of Support (MTSS). *Teacher Education and Special Education, 43*(1), 1–18.

Sayeski, K. L., Hamilton-Jones, B., Cutler, G., Earle, G. A., & Husney, L. (2019). The role of practice and feedback for developing teacher candidate's opportunities to respond expertise. *Teacher Education and Special Education, 42*, 18–35.

Scheeler, M. C., & Lee, D. L. (2018). Effects of immediate feedback using bug-in-ear with paraeducators working with students with autism. *Teacher Education and Special Education, 41*, 24–38.

Shepherd, K. G., Fowler, S., McCormick, J., Wilson, C. L., & Morgan, D. (2016). The search for role clarity: Challenges and implications for special education teacher preparation. *Teacher Education and Special Education, 39*(2), 83–97.

Shepley, C., Lane, J. D., Grisham-Brown, J., Spriggs, A. D., & Winstead, O. (2018). Effects of a training package to increase teachers' fidelity of naturalistic instructional procedures in inclusive preschool classrooms. *Teacher Education and Special Education, 41*, 321339.

Sindelar, P. T., Brownell, M. T., & Billingsley, B. (2010). Special education teacher education research: Current status and future directions. *Teacher Education and Special Education, 33*, 8–24.

Stallings, J. A. (1980). Allocated academic learning time revisited, or beyond time on task. *Educational Researcher, 9*, 11–16.

States, J., Detrich, R., & Keyworth, R. (2012). Effective teachers make a difference. In R. Detrich, R. Keyworth, J. States (Eds.), *Advances in evidence-based education Vol. 2, Education at the Crossroads: The state of teacher preparation* (pp. 1–5). Oakland, CA: The Wing Institute.

Sugai, G., Horner, R. H., Fixsen, D., & Blase, K. (2010). Developing systems-level capacity for RTI implementation: Current efforts and future directions. In T. A. Glover & S. Vaughn (Eds.), *The promise of response to intervention: Evaluating current science and practice* (pp. 286–309). Guilford Press.

Telzrow, C. F., & Beebe, J. J. (2002). *Best practices in facilitating intervention adherence and integrity*. In A. Thomas & J. Grimes (Eds.), Best practices in school psychology IV (p. 503–516). National Association of School Psychologists.

UNESCO (1994). *Final report – World conference on special needs education: Access and quality*. Paris: UNESCO.

University of Michigan. (n. d.) *Teachingworks: High leverage practices*. Retrieved from: http://www.teachingworks.org/work-of-teaching/high-leverage-practices.

U.S. Department of Education, Office of Special Education and Rehabilitative Services, and Office of Special Education Programs. (2016). *40th annual report to Congress on the implementation of the Individuals with Disabilities Education Act, 2018*. Retrieved from https://www2.ed.gov/about/reports/annual/osep/2018/parts-b-c/40th-arc-foridea.pdf

Vince Garland, K. M., Holden, K., & Garland, D. P. (2016). Individualized clinical coaching in the TLE TeachLivE Lab. *Teacher Education and Special Education, 39*, 47–59.

Waitoller, F. R., & Kozleski, E. B. (2013). Working in boundary practices: Identity development and learning in partnerships for inclusive education. *Teaching and Teacher Education, 31*, 35–45. 10.1016/j.tate.2012.11.006

Walker, J. S., & Bruns, E. J. (2006). Building on practice-based evidence: Using expert perspectives to define the wraparound process. *Psychiatric Services, 57*, 1579–1585.

Will, M. C. (1986). Educating children with learning problems: A shared responsibility. *Exceptional Children, 52*, 411–415.

Yssel, N., Koch, K., & Merbler, J. B. (2002). Professional development schools and special education: A promising partnership. *The Teacher Educator, 38*(2), 141–150.

Zeichner, K. (2012). The turn once again toward practice-based teacher education. *Journal of Teacher Education, 63*(5), 376–382.

5

The Role of Professional Development in Effective Inclusive Elementary Schools

Melinda Leko[1], Carly Roberts[2], Lauren Zepp[1], Shweta Chandrashekhar[1], and Malinda Forsberg[1]

[1]UNIVERSITY OF WISCONSIN-MADISON

[2]UNIVERSITY OF WASHINGTON-SEATTLE

Setting the Stage

Effective inclusion in elementary schools is predicated upon teachers having the requisite knowledge, beliefs, and skills to perform their jobs well. In this chapter, we discuss the role effective professional development (PD) plays in preparing teachers to include elementary students with disabilities effectively. Professional development is differentiated from teacher education (discussed in Chapter 4 of this Handbook) in that PD is learning that occurs once teachers have completed educator preparation programs and assume the role of teachers of record within local education agencies. PD is the continual learning that occurs from the time teachers enter the profession until they exit the field. In other words, PD is "on-the-job" learning that takes place after preservice or initial teacher preparation. In this way, PD is also referred to as staff development or in-service teacher education.

Defining Professional Development (PD)

Drawing on the National Staff Development Council's (2012) definition, we refer to PD as a set of coordinated, comprehensive, and intensive activities designed to enhance educators' knowledge, beliefs, skills, and practices for the purpose of improving student outcomes. Similarly, Darling-Hammond et al. (2017) define effective PD as "structured professional learning that results in changes in teacher practices and improvements in student learning outcomes" (Darling-Hammond et al., 2017, p. v). The opportunity for ongoing professional development is of critical importance, as this is how teachers stay attuned to the newest innovations in the field, improve their practice, and prepare for changing roles (Guskey, 2000). Professional development is especially important because of the proliferation of abbreviated or truncated alternative routes to the classroom. Teachers who complete fast-track preparation programs that are limited in length and amount of support will be

DOI: 10.4324/9781003043874-5

particularly dependent on PD because their brief initial teacher preparation experiences may not have prepared them to support students with disabilities in inclusive classrooms (Rosenberg et al., 2007).

Effective Features of PD

Research in general and special education indicates several critical features of PD that are effective and result in changes to teachers' knowledge, beliefs, attitudes, and practices (proximal outcomes) and student achievement (distal outcomes). Effective PD is:

- Coherent—the content, goals, and activities meet teacher needs, are consistent with district goals and the needs of the school, and align with mandated assessments and curricula (Desimone & Garet, 2015; Garet et al., 2001; Penuel et al., 2007; Yoon et al., 2007)
- Content-focused—strategies are associated with specific curriculum content and how students learn it, and teachers have opportunities to blend theory, content knowledge, general teaching principles, and knowledge of students as learners (Benedict et al., 2016; Darling-Hammond et al., 2017; Desimone & Garet, 2015; Yoon et al., 2007)
- Active and situated in classroom settings—teachers are engaged in practicing and personalizing strategies instead of passively "sitting and getting" (Darling-Hammond et al., 2017; Desimone & Garet, 2015; McCutchen et al., 2002)
- Collaborative—teachers are naturally grouped (e.g., by grade level, subject area, or school) and job-embedded contexts are used so that they may engage in critical, reflective discourse about their teaching (Darling-Hammond et al., 2017; Desimone & Garet, 2015; Loucks-Horsley et al., 1996)
- Incorporate and analyze student data—so teachers can make informed data-based decisions about their students' learning needs (Garet et al., 2001; Loucks-Horsley et al., 2003; Penuel et al., 2007)
- Extended in duration—rather than a one-time workshop, there is adequate time for teachers to learn, practice, implement, and reflect on new strategies (Brownell et al., 2011; Darling-Hammond et al., 2017; Desimone & Garet, 2015; Pugach et al., 2009). For example, Benedict et al. (2016) suggest at least 49 hours of PD over an extended period of time to learn to use a complex practice in the classroom.
- Multifaceted—two or more instructional practices are used, including coaching and teacher discussion groups, so practitioners have time to receive, reflect on, and collaborate around feedback (Benedict et al., 2016; Brownell et al., 2017; Darling-Hammond et al., 2017; McCutchen et al., 2002; McLeskey & Waldron 2002)

In a literature review of 28 experimental studies of PD conducted in K-12 core general education classrooms in the United States, Kennedy (2016) concluded that quality PD is greater than the sum of its parts. Individuals providing PD must intellectually engage teachers with content, anchor it to a broader goal (e.g., exposing student thinking), determine what motivates teachers to grow, and coach them in a collaborative rather than an evaluative way (Kennedy, 2016). Furthermore, experts posit PD should be learner-centered rather than expert-centered (Foster et al., 2017; Pugach et al., 2009). Expert-centered PD assumes a one-way transmission of knowledge approach wherein individuals providing PD impart knowledge with little to no long-term follow-up. In this approach, teachers are often trained in new curricula and instructional strategies on a broad level, with the goal being to increase teachers' knowledge (Hawley, 2006). Learner-centered PD, on the other hand, emphasizes PD that is needed to address specific student needs successfully. In this approach, the focus shifts to how teachers can make changes to their practice to increase student achievement

(Foster et al., 2017). Such an approach is often characterized by greater collaboration, modeling, reflection, and coaching (Pugach et al., 2009) and is a critical element in creating effective inclusive schools (McLeskey et al., 2014).

Professional development is a necessary support for teachers throughout the lifespan of their careers. Brief, unidimensional models of PD have not amassed strong research support in effecting change in teachers' knowledge, beliefs, and practice. Instead, experts call for PD that is extended, collaborative, active, and focused on meeting the specific needs of students. In the next sections, we examine research on PD intended to advance the inclusion of elementary students with disabilities. First, we focus on changes to teachers' beliefs and attitudes and then move to teachers' knowledge and instructional skills.

What Do We Know Based on Research and the Wisdom of Practice?

Professional Development and Teacher's Beliefs and Attitudes

Beliefs and attitudes are critical to understanding and supporting teacher learning, change, cognition, and practice (Richardson, 1996). Attitudes towards inclusion are a critical part of inclusive education. Teachers need to believe students with disabilities belong in the general education setting and can contribute to the learning environment in meaningful ways. Moreover, teachers must possess a desire to use a repertoire of skills to ensure the curriculum is accessible to *all* students (Gregory, 2018). Unfortunately, recent studies indicate many teachers, particularly those in general education, have low self-efficacy when it comes to successfully including students with disabilities in general education classrooms (Barnes & Gaines, 2015). In moving the needle in a positive direction when it comes to effecting change in teachers' beliefs and attitudes about inclusion, there is substantial support for the idea that changes in practice that lead to positive outcomes lead to subsequent changes in beliefs (e.g., Fullan, 2015; McLeskey et al., 2001; Waldron, 2007). In other words, when teachers are put into situations that cause them to alter their practices to be more supportive of inclusion (i.e., school-wide reform or insufficient progress toward academic achievement standards), their beliefs often change to be more supportive of inclusion as well (McLeskey et al., 2001; Mulvey et al., 2016; Richardson & Placier, 2001). Professional development plays a significant role in this change process.

One way to influence teachers' beliefs about students with disabilities and inclusion is by focusing on the characteristics of disabilities and how they affect students' participation in the general education setting. Male (2011) studied teachers enrolled in a Master's degree program centered on inclusive education. The teachers participated in a 10-week PD course and completed a survey measuring their attitudes towards inclusion at the beginning and end of the course. The PD was introductory, included basic knowledge on various disabilities, and featured a variety of learning formats (e.g., face-to-face instruction, one-on-one tutoring, and independent study). Results signified a shift in teachers' attitudes towards more positive perceptions of inclusion by the end of the study. In a different study, researchers created a film documenting the experiences and perspectives of a student with Autism Spectrum Disorder (ASD) in the general education classroom (Kelleher, 2015). Five hundred teachers, administrators, and related service providers viewed the film and answered discussion questions that challenged their assumptions about inclusion and deficit-based thinking about students with ASD. Post-test survey results indicated that embedding perspective-taking into PD through instructional media can help teachers better understand how the presence and absence of supports in the general education setting impact students' learning. This study corroborates prior research on the importance of incorporating critical discussions that challenge deficit-oriented beliefs about students with disabilities within PD (Avramidis & Kalyva, 2007).

In addition to understanding how PD on general characteristics of disabilities influence teachers' beliefs about inclusion, some researchers have taken a more focused approach within particular content areas. In one study, teachers participated in *Prime Online,* a year-long PD for teaching mathematics to students with disabilities in general education classrooms (Griffin et al., 2018). The PD consisted of 35 learning modules premised on an inquiry cycle in which teachers collaboratively problem solved problems of practice they encountered in their classrooms. Participating in the PD resulted in a statistically significant change (effect size = 0.47) in teachers adopting more positive beliefs about teaching mathematics and teaching students with disabilities.

Mulvey et al. (2016) investigated the effects of a semester-long PD experience focused on the nature of science and inquiry-based instruction for students with disabilities. The PD was 42 hours and included opportunities for special educators to apply inquiry-based science lessons in classrooms. Teachers also completed reflective logs and received coaching. Results indicated participating in the PD helped teachers adopt more positive views of students with disabilities' abilities, particularly in the area of science. This study makes important contributions to the PD literature because it is situated in science instruction for students with disabilities—an understudied area of research.

Research has also focused on how PD can affect schoolwide change. In a qualitative case study, Hoppey et al. (2018), followed two elementary schools and their evolution of inclusive reform. In both schools, a key to developing a shared vision of inclusion and the necessary beliefs to support inclusion was ongoing job-embedded PD on data literacy. Academic coaches provided PD and supported teachers in examining student data. By becoming data-literate about students with disabilities and their needs, teachers were able to see the progress students were making in general education classrooms, thereby reinforcing pro-inclusion beliefs.

Katz (2015) studied how learning about Universal Design for Learning (UDL) impacted teachers' and administrators' beliefs and practices related to diverse learners and inclusion. The PD taught 58 general educators, special educators, and administrators across 10 schools the elements of a UDL framework for planning and instruction. PD included co-planning and implementing an integrated unit that could be differentiated in an inclusive classroom. Teachers described how implementing the UDL framework resulted in greater student engagement, thereby reducing their job stress. Additionally, following the PD, teachers' beliefs shifted to place more value on inclusion and UDL, and they reported an increased willingness to change their practices to be more inclusive.

Other findings from the literature point to specific guidance in terms of PD duration and the value of attitudinal surveys and measures. Kosko and Wilkins (2009) analyzed data from the Study of Personnel Needs in Special Education (SPeNSE) to learn more about the relationship between PD and general education teachers' self-efficacy for adapting instruction for students with disabilities. Findings indicated that PD significantly predicted teachers' perceived ability to adapt instruction and that "8 hours or more of professional development was twice as effective as less than 8 hours of PD" (Kosko & Wilkins, 2009, p. 7). More recently, Benedict et al. (2016) reviewed a range of studies and concluded that teachers who engaged in 49 hours of PD or more experienced greater proximal and distal outcomes. Additionally, PD that includes surveys about teacher attitudes or self-efficacy, such as the *Multidimensional Attitudes Toward Inclusive Education Scale (MATIES)* (Mahat, 2008) or the *Teachers' Self-Efficacy Scale (TSES)* (Tschannen-Moran & Woolfolk Hoy, 2001), can ensure PD on inclusion is targeted to the areas in which teachers express negative feelings (Gaines & Barnes, 2017).

Taken together, the studies on teachers' attitudes and beliefs about inclusion suggest that positive experiences with inclusion, whether working in inclusive settings or participating in PD on inclusion, help teachers adopt positive beliefs about inclusion and its effects on students (Avramidis & Kalyva, 2007; Griffin et al., 2018; Kelleher, 2015; Kosko & Wilkins, 2009; McLeskey et al., 2001; Male, 2011). PD that is extended in duration, focused on understanding students with disabilities, and tailored to meet the needs of the participating teachers can help them develop a strong sense of self-efficacy for supporting students' instructional needs in inclusive classrooms (Gaines & Barnes, 2017; Griffin et al., 2018; Kelleher, 2015; Kosko & Wilkins, 2009; Yoo, 2016).

Professional Development and Teachers' Knowledge and Instructional Practices

In addition to offering PD that positively influences teachers' beliefs and attitudes about inclusion, there is a need to prepare teachers to implement instructional practices and strategies necessary for successful inclusion. Such practices and strategies pertain to academic content areas (e.g., reading, mathematics), collaboration and co-teaching, and classroom and behavior management. In addition, significant technological advancements illustrate the innovations in PD that are available through digital tools.

Academic Content Areas

Literacy

In a comprehensive review, McMaster and colleagues (2020) identified 26 studies on PD for the implementation of intensive reading interventions. All but one of these studies focused on students in grades K-5, and most included students with and without disabilities. This review found that PD for intensive reading interventions was most frequently delivered through workshops, which were typically 1–2 days in length. Additionally, many studies (n = 20) combined workshops with follow-up support in the form of coaching and consultation. These PD offerings were most frequently led by a researcher (n = 15) or teachers trained to use intensive reading interventions (n = 2). Implementation fidelity measures suggest teachers were able to implement intensive reading interventions with fidelity following training, and teachers rated PD on intensive reading interventions positively (McMaster et al., 2020).

Brownell et al. (2017) evaluated the efficacy of Literacy Learning Cohorts (LLC) on special education teachers' ability to implement reading instruction for elementary students with learning disabilities. The researchers utilized a randomized, group comparison approach to investigate the impact of LLC training versus an initial PD session only. Although no significant difference was found between groups on the quality of teachers' word-level fluency instruction, LLC participants had significantly higher quality instruction in fluency with connected text and word study. Teachers who participated in LLC training spent significantly more instruction time implementing evidence-based fluency strategies at the word level and with connected text. Student achievement measures indicated that students benefited more from receiving instruction with a teacher trained in LLC. This study highlights the potential benefits of extended content-focused PD (Brownell et al., 2017).

McKeown et al. (2019) studied the efficacy of practice-based PD on self-regulated strategy development (SRSD), a persuasive writing approach for 3rd, 4th, and 5th grade students with and without disabilities, across two elementary schools. The PD included expert modeling of SRSD lessons, practice teaching opportunities with feedback, and small group discussions about students' strengths and needs in the area of writing. The researchers found implementation fidelity was lower than expected, particularly for one school. They attributed this variation to levels of teacher buy-in across the schools. At one school, the administration worked to build teachers' investment in the PD, while at the other school, teachers had little understanding of why they were being required to participate or what the potential benefits of the PD were. Although the variation in implementation fidelity resulted in disparities in student learning outcomes, the PD on SRSD was effective at improving students' ability to write persuasively overall (McKeown et al., 2019).

Multi-component approaches to PD also have demonstrated efficacy for improving outcomes in literacy (Benedict et al., 2016; Brownell et al., 2019). Hoover and Soltero-González (2018) utilized a model demonstration project to combine PD on culturally and linguistically responsive (CLR) literacy practices with a CLR referral process for special education identification in a rural elementary school. This study sought to address the gap in teacher knowledge that results in the inappropriate referral of English learners for special education services in literacy. Professional development in this study provided 30 hours of annual PD in a rural school district, along with coaching, mentoring, and observations with an emphasis on active engagement with teachers. Through this collaborative PD process, the participating school district improved the implementation of Multi-Tiered Systems of Support (MTSS) and demonstrated district-wide improvements in reading instruction for linguistically diverse students. The district also adopted a CLR referral process to reduce the disproportionate representation of English learners in special education. As a result of their findings, the researchers called for collaborative partnerships with teachers in the PD process.

Lembke et al. (2017) explored the use of another multi-component approach to support elementary teachers in delivering effective writing instruction. The researchers employed Data-Based Instruction-Tools, Learning, and Collaborative Support (DBI-TLC), which included training on curriculum-based measures, workshops on implementing DBI with fidelity, and follow-up coaching. DBI-TLC improved teachers' knowledge and skills for evidence-based writing instruction, and teachers in the treatment group implemented more pedagogical changes than those in the control group (Lembke et al., 2017).

Mathematics

As reviewed earlier, *Prime Online* is a PD program with a mathematics content focus (Dana et al., 2016; Griffin et al., 2018). In addition to examining changes in teacher beliefs, the research team investigated changes in teacher knowledge and practice. Data were collected using Content Knowledge for Teaching-Mathematics (CKT-M) with subtests for knowledge of content (CK) and knowledge of students (KS). The researchers noted significant linear growth on the CK subtest and an increase in the KS subtest at the mid-year assessment, followed by a decline to pre-test levels at the year-end assessment (Griffin et al., 2018). Teachers responded positively to *Prime Online* throughout the year-long PD process. A major contribution of this study of PD is that it was delivered entirely online, thereby providing implications for delivering PD across large geographic regions.

Collectively, these studies highlight the importance of collaborative, content-focused PD to build teachers' knowledge and skills for inclusive education. When educators participated in multi-component approaches to PD that centered on specific academic content areas, they demonstrated improvements in inclusive pedagogical skills and increased content knowledge.

Collaboration and Co-Teaching

Collaboration is recognized as a critical component of effective teacher PD and inclusive education (Friend & Bursuck, 2018). Using discourse analysis, Leko, Kiely et al. (2015) considered the patterns that emerged during collaborative PD and the impact of those patterns on teachers' learning about reading instruction for elementary students with disabilities. A researcher-created PD focused on content knowledge and pedagogical content knowledge for reading instruction through a 2-day initial training and monthly cohort meetings over a 2-year period. Teachers who asked questions reflected on specific pedagogical practices and demonstrated knowledge of content yielded the most positive learning experiences for their colleagues. However, most teachers' contributions remained superficial, often referencing specific classroom activities, games, or resources rather than addressing deep changes in content knowledge or pedagogical content knowledge. The implications of this research point to the pivotal role of PD providers, as they should play an active role in highlighting and structuring effective discussions amongst teachers (Leko, Kiely et al., 2015).

Although the response to intervention (RTI) framework has a significant research base, few studies have focused on PD to support elementary teachers in implementing RTI through a collaborative context (Benedict et al., 2020). Using a grounded theory approach, Benedict et al. (2020) examined the impacts of combining content-focused PD with lesson study. Further, this study examined how elementary teachers' collective knowledge of word study instruction evolved through a year-long collaborative PD process. The lesson study process involves cycles of collaborative planning, lesson implementation, and collaborative debriefing among a cohort of teachers. The results of this PD included increased connections between content, pedagogy, and the needs of learners among teachers. In addition, teachers developed a more effective approach to coordinated reading instruction across tiers in the RTI model.

In a study of teaming to support the inclusion of students with moderate to severe levels of Intellectual Disability (ID), Jimenez and Barron (2019) used a single-subject multiple probe design across three inclusive classrooms. The participants in each inclusive classroom included the general educator, special educator, and paraprofessional, all of whom played a role in supporting the academic progress of a student with ID. Interestingly, prior to developing the content and structure of the PD, the researchers conducted a formative phase in which they collected qualitative focus group and questionnaire data to assess participants' incoming knowledge of inclusion for students with ID. The finalized PD package included content on Embedded Instruction (EI), a video providing a sample of EI in a mathematics lesson, and a guided planning time for the team to identify learning goals for an upcoming inclusive lesson. Following the initial PD, the teams were instructed to continue joint planning to identify future learning goals and ways to incorporate EI trials within lessons. The researchers conducted classroom observations to record the number of EI trials present in a lesson and which team member(s) provided them. Following the intervention phase, all three teams increased the number of EI trials in instruction, with general educators and paraeducators providing the most number of trials.

When teacher teams participate in PD with a collaborative focus, they are able to improve their individual and collective skills for inclusive pedagogy. PD that emphasizes such collaboration builds bonds between educators through discussions and reflections. These studies highlight the importance of effective collaboration for the implementation of tiered instruction and including students with extensive support needs alongside their peers without disabilities.

Classroom and Behavior Management

Classroom management has been cited as one of the most significant challenges for new educators (Baker et al., 2016). Hirsch et al. (2019) evaluated the impact of Practice-Based Professional Development (PBPD) on universal classroom management using a multiple baseline design across participants. Universal classroom management practices were operationally defined as the use of precorrections, opportunities to respond, praise, and reprimands. This study also specifically considered the impact of PBPD on teachers' interactions with students at risk of identification for emotional and behavioral disabilities. PBPD focused on increasing teachers' knowledge and integration of skills into their classroom practice. Six general education teachers from elementary schools in a small urban district participated in this study. Data collection was comprised of direct observation, Teacher Knowledge of Practices, Teacher Survey of Practices, Teacher Sense of Efficacy Scale, Student Risk Screening Scale, and a social validity measure. PBPD included an initial 3-hour training with embedded Content Acquisition Podcasts for Teachers with video modeling (CAP-TVs). Weekly follow-up sessions occurred for the three weeks immediately following the initial training. The researchers found there was not a functional relationship between PBPD and precorrections, opportunities to respond, and praise. Reprimands, however, significantly decreased through the intervention phase and remained lower than baseline levels during the maintenance phase. Teacher knowledge and self-reporting of teacher practices significantly increased following PBPD training. In addition, teacher self-efficacy increased, and all participants reported a higher sense of control over their learning environments. Social validity measures indicated that teachers were satisfied with the training and would use the universal classroom management practices they learned through PBPD. Finally, there was a statistically significant decrease in risk levels for identified students. The researchers attributed this change to altered teacher perceptions of student behavior, which may reduce the likelihood that students are identified as having emotional and behavioral disabilities.

Owens and colleagues (2020) implemented tiered coaching with video and bug-in-ear technology to increase the implementation fidelity among general education elementary teachers working with students with frequent off-task behaviors. Participants were selected based on principal recommendation and need for coaching based on less than 60% implementation fidelity during the baseline condition. Following an initial PD training on implementing self-monitoring strategies, teachers received individual coaching using video recordings of their use of the self-monitoring strategy. Next, bug-in-ear technology was used to provide teachers with immediate feedback during instruction. Teachers also received a 25-step implementation fidelity checklist and MotivAider® devices were provided to students and teachers to aid in self-monitoring. The researchers used visual analysis to conclude there was a functional relationship between tiered coaching and improved teacher implementation fidelity. There was no clear functional relationship between improved teacher implementation fidelity and student on-task behavior, though students showed higher percentages of on-task behavior following tiered coaching. Social validity measures showed teacher preference for immediate feedback and debriefing following coaching sessions but also noted concerns regarding long-term sustainability and the generalizability of the self-monitoring strategy. This study emphasized the use of a multi-tiered approach to coaching and acknowledged that some teachers, like some students, benefit from more intensive interventions and supports in the learning process.

The Incredible Years Teacher Classroom Management (IY TCM) program was implemented to support teachers of students who exhibited disruptive behaviors (Reinke et al., 2014). The researchers employed a group-randomized trial with 68 teachers and their students (N = 1,148). The intervention group received the IY TCM training and weekly coaching. Data were collected using both teacher reporting and direct observation. The researchers found coaches spent more time with teachers on individual students' behavior support plans than on universal classroom management strategies. Students in the intervention group demonstrated a reduction in disruptive behavior and an increase in prosocial behavior. Teachers in the intervention group displayed a significant reduction in the frequency of reprimands toward students previously identified as exhibiting challenging behaviors. The authors concluded this approach supported teachers in implementing universal and student-specific behavioral supports simultaneously in inclusive elementary settings.

In one of the few studies that included students with more significant disabilities, Bethune and Wood (2013) used a delayed multiple-baseline across participants to examine the effects of coaching on special educators' implementation of function-based interventions for students with ID and ASD. Researchers measured (a) teachers' scores on an implementation fidelity checklist that listed the components of the function-based intervention, (b) the frequency of student problem behaviors, and (c) the frequency of student replacement behaviors. Teachers received upfront training in the basics of applied behavior analysis and then a guided workshop session in which they completed a Function-based Assessment and determined appropriate interventions. Following a baseline phase, teachers received coaching in the form of a pre-observation meeting, side-by-side coaching during instruction, and post-observation meeting. Results indicated a functional relationship between the coaching and the teachers' accuracy of implementation of function-based interventions as well as with increases in students' replacement behaviors.

Social validity measures indicate that teachers value PD on classroom and behavior management strategies, especially when combined with coaching and immediate feedback. The positive outcomes of these studies demonstrate improvements in teacher self-efficacy, increased knowledge of universal classroom management tools, and the corresponding positive impact on students in inclusive classrooms.

Technological Advancements

Significant growth in PD has occurred using technological innovations to increase teacher knowledge and skills (Brownell et al., 2019; Rodgers et al., 2019). Researchers and practitioners increasingly support asynchronous multimedia PD for its efficacy, flexibility, and lower cost than traditional face-to-face PD (Kennedy et al., 2017; VanUitert et al., 2019). Multimedia PD includes Content Acquisition Podcasts for Teachers (CAP-Ts), eCoaching, virtual classroom simulations, and video analysis (Kennedy et al., 2017; Rodgers et al., 2019).

Content Acquisition Podcasts

Content Acquisition Podcasts Professional Development (CAP-PD) has been shown to increase the implementation and efficacy of vocabulary instruction of inclusive teachers (Kennedy et al., 2017, 2018; VanUitert et al., 2019). CAP-PD utilizes a cognitive apprenticeship framework to assist teachers in acquiring new pedagogical skills (Kennedy et al., 2018). This process includes CAPs for Teachers with Embedded Modeling Videos (CAP-TV), CAPs Teacher Slides with instructional content and implementation coaching for teachers. A series of studies have shown teachers who participated in this PD increased their time spent on vocabulary instruction in an inclusive setting from 10% to 46% of class time (Kennedy et al., 2017; Kennedy et al., 2018). Social validity measures indicated that teachers felt positively about the use of multimedia PD packages (Kennedy et al., 2017). The positive effects of CAP-PD are promising, and the relatively small investment makes them a feasible source for ongoing PD (Kennedy et al., 2018).

eCoaching and Bug-in-Ear Technology

Coaching or performance feedback is accepted as fundamental to effective PD (Brownell et al., 2019), and recent innovations afford greater opportunities for immediate feedback through technology (Schaefer & Ottley, 2018). In a literature review, Schaefer and Ottley (2018) found that 89% of studies on Bug-In-Ear (BIE) coaching included evidence that immediate feedback through BIE altered teachers' practices in positive ways. The authors also found consistently high social validity ratings, indicating that teachers perceived BIE coaching to be useful in their learning (Schaefer & Ottley, 2018).

Bug-in-Ear (BIE) eCoaching was found to have a moderate effect on teachers' use of modeling behaviors with students with disabilities across settings (Coogle et al., 2016). In this type of PD, a coach uses video conference software to provide immediate feedback to a teacher using a Bluetooth™ headset (Coogle et al., 2016). eCoaching has also been proven effective for co-teaching training in an inclusive elementary setting (Ploessl & Rock, 2014). When co-teaching dyads utilized bug-in-ear eCoaching, they increased the number of co-teaching models implemented in the classroom, improved the fidelity with which they implemented co-teaching models, and provided a higher number of student-specific accommodations or modifications (Ploessl & Rock, 2014). Throughout the use of bug-in-ear coaching, student engagement increased. Following eCoaching,

80% of teachers reported enjoying the experience and all participants felt the experience was beneficial for inclusive elementary teachers (Ploessl & Rock, 2014).

Virtual Classroom Simulations

Virtual classroom simulations like Mursion TeachLivE™ allow educators to practice pedagogical skills and receive feedback without being in live classrooms. TeachLivE™ provides novice teachers with realistic opportunities for repeated practice and structured feedback (Dawson & Lignugaris Kraft, 2017). Research indicated teachers increased their use of specific praise and error correction through TeachLivE™, and they were able to generalize those skills to their elementary classrooms (Dawson & Lignugaris Kraft, 2017). Another study demonstrated improved fidelity of implementation of a system-of-least prompts among novice teachers of students with Autism following the use of the TeachLivE ™ simulation (Garland et al., 2015).

Video Analysis

Video analysis is another technological innovation that allows educators to reflect on their teaching practices and engage in self-evaluation (Gaudin & Chaliès, 2015; McVee et al., 2015; Morin et al., 2019). This process involves recording a teacher during instruction, viewing the recording, and focusing on specific areas for growth (Morin et al., 2019). Video analysis can be used to improve a variety of teacher behaviors and is flexible enough to be incorporated into many existing PD programs (Morin et al., 2019). Morin et al. (2019) reviewed 30 manuscripts that utilized single-case design to evaluate the impact of video analysis on teacher practices. Through this meta-analysis, the researchers concluded that video analysis might be an effective component of teacher PD, though further study is needed.

Combined, these studies on the use of technology for PD represent innovations in the field with significant potential. Social validity measures in studies utilizing technological advancements were high, indicating that teachers respond positively to this type of PD. In addition, teachers who received PD with embedded technology improved their use of high-leverage practices and demonstrated improved implementation fidelity for co-teaching.

Research on the impacts of PD on teachers' knowledge and instructional practices to support inclusion mirrors findings from the broader PD literature base. In the studies we reviewed, PD was dynamic, involving participating teachers as active learners, and in many cases, linked to the performance of specific students with disabilities. The PD approaches varied and included multiple components, including upfront workshops, discussion groups, coaching, modeling, and analyzing student data. In addition to general principles of classroom and behavior management, researchers examined inclusion within specific content areas, including literacy, science, and mathematics. Increasingly, technology applications and innovations have been incorporated in long-term PD as a way to scale efforts and reduce costs.

Setting the Course for Effective Inclusion

Advancing Research

Since the publication of the first edition of this Handbook, research on PD to support inclusive education has expanded. Current studies focus on a broader array of topical areas, including writing, mathematics, and science instruction. Multiple studies have examined how to support teachers' classroom and behavior management—a persistent concern among novice teachers and those who are including students with challenging behaviors in the general education classroom. Finally, new technologies that have been found to be efficacious in supporting teacher learning and practice provide opportunities to imagine PD in innovative and potentially cost-effective ways. Despite such advances, our review points to multiple gaps in the literature—gaps that we believe must be addressed for inclusion to become a reality for *all* students.

First, we recommend more studies taking place across diverse settings. The majority of studies we reviewed were in mid-size cities and suburban areas. The Hoover and Soltero-González (2018) study was the only one to include schools located in rural areas and few studies took place in densely populated, large urban settings. The needs of students served across rural, urban, and suburban settings can vary, with rural and urban settings often consisting of more resource-poor schools, students living in poverty, and families from culturally, linguistically, and racially diverse backgrounds. PD for these settings will need a strong emphasis on culturally responsive pedagogy in addition to best practices for inclusion; yet we have few models from the research to guide practice.

Second, there is a dire need for more studies of PD that supports the inclusion of students with more intensive support needs (i.e., severe disabilities). The two studies we included (CITE) were exceptional in that PD was provided to teachers who supported students with intensive support needs in the general education classroom; the majority of other studies we found, but did not include, took place in self-contained settings. When studying inclusion for students with more intensive support needs, the idea of teaming and instructional teams comprised of general educators, special educators, paraeducators, and other related service providers (e.g., Occupational Therapists, Speech and Language Therapists) being the unit of analysis is particularly germane. The Jimenez and Barron (2019) study serves as a good model for conceptualizing teams as needing PD rather than individual educators. In our minds, a true vision of inclusion cannot include some students and exclude others; thus, we view the need for more research in this area to be one of the most important directions for advancing research on inclusion.

Finally, more research is needed on developing and implementing PD in cost-effective, feasible ways. Research has consistently shown that multi-component, extended, learner-centered models of PD are most effective in affecting teachers' knowledge, beliefs, and practices. This approach to PD, though effective, may be too cost-prohibitive or time-intensive for many schools and districts (Pugach et al., 2009). The studies we reviewed that incorporate new technologies may be the key to reducing costs and time spent on logistics. For example, the studies by Kennedy et al. (2017, 2018) illustrate how podcasts can be created and used to deliver content over and over again rather than relying on a facilitator. Similarly, the use of BIE and Ecoaching means an expert can provide feedback to teachers from a distance, thereby eliminating travel time and costs to conduct in-person observation and coaching sessions. The studies of *Prime Online* (Dana et al., 2016; Griffin et al., 2018) are particularly informative in understanding how PD can be created entirely online, so it can be delivered to a large number of participants who may live far away from one another. Cost-effectiveness studies would help researchers determine the cost of various PD models relative to the number of participants served; thus helping to answer questions about how to make PD more affordable while not compromising effectiveness. This line of inquiry would create opportunities for special education researchers to forge new partnerships with collaborators within the larger discipline of social sciences, including economists and policy analysts.

Related to cost-effectiveness is feasibility. PD studies most often rely on experts, oftentimes researchers, to create, deliver, and evaluate PD (McMaster et al., 2020), and the studies we reviewed were no exception. However, many schools and districts do not have this type of human capital; thus, PD that is contingent upon particular expertise may not be feasible in local schools and districts. Furthermore, once researchers have concluded a study, we have little knowledge of whether the outcomes of the PD are sustained. Additional research on models that can empower educators, rather than researchers, to lead PD would be useful. One such model is referred to as train-the-trainer and has preliminary support in the literature (Abbott et al., 2006; Vaughn & Coleman, 2004). Studies on the long-term outcomes of various PD efforts are also needed.

Advancing Practice

In this section, we provide implications for advancing practice and providing PD that promotes effective inclusion in elementary schools. School and district administrators, as well as local and state policy makers, play critical roles in supporting effective PD.

Implications for School and District Administrators

Administrators play a central role in supporting PD. Most importantly, administrators can eliminate barriers to teachers' learning and the adoption of new practices. For example, teachers need time to participate in multifaceted PD efforts. This includes time to attend initial PD sessions, follow-up meetings, and collaborative planning or coaching sessions (Leithwood & Jantzi, 2000). This may entail rearranging school schedules, securing substitute teachers, or working to reduce special educators' caseloads and paperwork demands so they are relieved of their instructional and administrative responsibilities and can participate fully in the PD (Leko & Brownell, 2009).

An abundance of research indicates administrators need not wait until teachers "believe" in inclusion or have positive attitudes about it before embarking on schoolwide reform or PD. Upon engaging in high-quality PD and inclusive practices, teachers' beliefs often shift to be more supportive. However, what is important is that administrators attempt to obtain teacher buy-in that the PD is important and that it will better support teachers and students. Administrators can explicitly convey the PD's importance by requiring teachers to implement inclusive practices presented in PD and implicitly convey the importance by participating in the PD themselves. In fact, in their synthesis of school leadership and student outcomes, Robinson et al. (2009) found that leaders' promotion of and participation in teacher learning had the largest effect on student outcomes.

As school and district administrators plan and deliver PD that is learner-centered, it is necessary to consider the local context, as well as individual teacher and student needs (McLeskey & Waldron, 2002); therefore, presenting generic, broad-based PD will not be effective. Schools operate in individualized ways and may be at varying levels in their implementation of inclusion (McLeskey & Waldron, 2002). Likewise, teachers will enter PD with various types and amounts of prior knowledge and experience. The study by Jimenez and Barron (2019) illustrates how a research team collected focus group and questionnaire data to better understand the specific needs of teachers prior to developing PD. Often this is referred to as conducting a needs assessment (McLeskey & Waldron, 2002) and can help ensure resulting PD is individualized and coherent. Pre-existing surveys that can assess teachers' incoming attitudes and self-efficacy include the *Multidimensional Attitudes Toward Inclusive Education Scale (MATIES)* (Mahat, 2008) or the *Teachers' Self-Efficacy Scale (TSES)* (Tschannen-Moran & Woolfolk Hoy, 2001).

Professional development that advances inclusion by influencing teachers' beliefs, knowledge, and practices is multi-faceted and extended in duration. From the studies we reviewed, optimal results were achieved when teachers participated in 40 hours of PD (Benedict et al., 2016). Teachers who received 40 hours of PD integrated complex instructional practices with greater fidelity. Moreover, a key element to effective PD was including opportunities for collaborative communities of practice wherein teachers were supported to analyze student data (Hoppey et al., 2018), reflect on problems of practice (Griffin et al., 2018), and engage in critical discussions that challenge deficit-oriented assumptions about students with disabilities (Kelleher, 2015). PD that included various combinations of these elements led to positive teacher and student-level outcomes in reading, writing, mathematics, science, and behavior management. Long-term support in the form of coaching was also found to be an effective mechanism of supporting teachers' implementation of new inclusive practices (Bethune & Wood, 2013). Such an approach to PD rejects the "one-shot" workshop model, which has been found to be ineffective (Brownell et al., 2017). PD should also be collaborative and include teams of teachers who work together to support students with disabilities in inclusive classrooms, particularly when schools implement schoolwide models such as RTI (Benedict et al., 2020) and UDL (Katz, 2015). This means general educators, special educators, paraeducators, and other related service providers should all learn effective instructional practices and how to collaboratively plan and evaluate instruction (Jimenez & Barron, 2019).

Technology-based PD efforts hold immense potential for supporting the learning of teachers in a variety of ways, including providing (a) content knowledge via podcasts, (b) video-based models of instruction, (c) remote synchronous coaching, and (d) entirely virtual platforms for teachers to acquire pedagogical content knowledge and reflect on pressing problems of practice. Such technology-based PD means teachers from across wide geographic regions may participate without undue costs or time— a factor that could prove particularly beneficial for teachers working in rural settings who may not have access to a wide array of high-quality PD options.

Implications for Policy-makers

Policies that reinforce PD efforts are key levers in advancing inclusion. First and foremost, policy-makers should support funding for high-quality PD. The type of PD that leads to significant changes in teachers' knowledge, beliefs, and practices (i.e., extended, multi-faceted, collaborative) is not cheap but is worth the investment. Such funding may be necessary at the local and state level. Furthermore, policies are needed that incentivize administrators and teachers to participate in PD that promotes inclusion. We envision two potential avenues: one is establishing PD as an important component of ongoing licensure renewal; the other is to endorse evaluation systems that align with PD.

Advancing Professional Development Coherence and Capacity

Despite the identification of evidence-based practices (EBPs) known to promote positive student outcomes and the promise of PD as a way to support effective teacher practice, the longstanding "research-to-practice gap" remains (Cook et al., 2013; McLeskey et al., 2019). In essence, practices that support inclusion are not being implemented broadly or consistently within and across elementary classrooms. Scholars have hypothesized one possible explanation: initial teacher preparation is too short and too scattered in focus for teachers to develop the expertise needed to successfully meet the demands of current PK-12 school contexts (Leko, Brownell et al., 2015). In response, leaders within the fields of general (Ball & Forzani, 2009) and special education (McLeskey et al., 2019) have posited the need to identify and concentrate educator preparation efforts on a small set of core practices that have high impact and utility across a variety of educational contexts. Termed high-leverage practices (HLPs), these core practices are a way to foster *coherence* and *capacity* in terms of initial teacher preparation and PD. Within special education, the Council for Exceptional Children (CEC) has identified 22 HLPs for special education teachers (McLeskey et al., 2017). For more information on how the HLPs can promote inclusive classrooms, we refer readers to *High Leverage Practices for Inclusive Classrooms* by McLeskey et al. (2018).

With a focus on HLPs, PD is no longer a series of scattered and isolated efforts; rather, it can be crafted and delivered in coherent ways that build upon one another, promoting professional expertise and sustainable implementation. The HLPs espouse a common nomenclature that can be shared across pre- and in-service teacher preparation, as well as across general and special education. In terms of building capacity, the HLPs enable PD providers and educational administrators to allocate resources in more strategic ways because PD efforts are centered around a more precise and finite set of instructional practices. If PD were crafted in the high-quality ways reviewed throughout this chapter *and* centered on HLPs, the path to effective inclusion would be more sure-footed and attainable.

Conclusions

Professional development is considered an effective and necessary mechanism through which teachers can be prepared to support students in inclusive schools. By employing learner-centered PD that incorporates individualization, active learning opportunities, and collaboration, teachers can acquire knowledge, beliefs, and practices necessary to implement inclusion in elementary schools. In addition, technological innovations hold promise for structuring and delivering PD in ways that are cost-effective and accessible to large numbers of teachers. With the support of administrators and policy makers and a focus on high-leverage practices, PD will help ensure all students with disabilities receive an equitable and inclusive education.

References

Abbott, M., Greenwood, C. R., Buzhardt, J., & Tapia, Y. (2006). Using technology-based teacher support tools to scale up the classwide peer tutoring program. *Reading & Writing Quarterly, 22*(1), 47–64. doi:10.1080/10573560500203525

Avramidis, E., & Kalyva, E. (2007). The influence of teaching experience and professional development on Greek teachers' attitudes towards inclusion. *European Journal of Special Needs Education, 22*, 367–389. doi:10.1080/08856250701649989

Baker, C., Gentry, J., & Larmer, W. (2016). A model for online support in classroom management: Perceptions of beginning teachers. *Administrative Issues Journal: Education, Practice, and Research, 6*(1), 22–37.

Ball, D. L., Forzani, F. (2009). The work of teaching and the challenge of teacher education. *Journal of Teacher Education, 60* (5), 497–511. DOI: doi:10.1177/0022487109348479

Barnes, M., & Gaines, T. (2015). Teachers' attitudes and perceptions of inclusion in relation to grade level and years of experience. *Electronic Journal of Inclusive Education, 3*(3), 1–19.

Benedict, A. E., Griffin, C. C., Brownell, M. T., Wang, J., & Myers, J. A. (2016). Leveraging professional development to prepare general and special education teachers to teach within response to intervention frameworks. In T. Petty, A. Good, & S. M. Putman (Eds.), *Handbook of research on professional development for quality teaching and learning* (pp. 42–61). IGI Global.

Benedict, A. E., Brownell, M., Bettini, E. & Sohn, H. (2020). Learning together: Teachers' evolving understanding of coordinated word study instruction within an RTI framework. *Teacher Education and Special Education*, 1–26. doi:10.1177/0888406420930686

Bethune, K. S., & Wood, C. L. (2013). Effects of coaching on teachers' use of function-based interventions for students with severe disabilities. *Teacher Education and Special Education, 36*(2), 97–114. doi:10.1177/1098300716680095

Brownell, M. T., Benedict, A. E., Leko, M. M., Peyton, D., Pua, D., & Richards-Tutor, C. (2019). A continuum of pedagogies for preparing teachers to use high-leverage practices. *Remedial and Special Education, 40*(6), 338–355. doi:10.1177/0741932518824990

Brownell, M. T., Kiely, M. T., Haager, D., Boardman, A., Corbett, N., Algina, J., Dingle, M. P., & Urbach, J. (2017). Literacy learning cohorts: Content-focused approach to improving special education teachers' reading instruction. *Exceptional Children, 83*(2), 143–164. doi:10.1177/0014402916671517

Brownell, M. T., Griffin, C., Leko, M. M., Stephens, J. (2011). Improving collaborative teacher education research: Creating tighter linkages. *Teacher Education and Special Education, 34*(3), 235–249. doi:10.1177/0888406411404570

Coogle, C. G., Rahn, N. L., Ottley, J. R., & Storie, S. (2016). eCoaching across routines to enhance teachers' use of modeling. *Teacher Education and Special Education, 39*(4), 227–245. doi:10.1177/0888406415621959

Cook, B. G., Cook, L., & Landrum, T. J. (2013). Moving research into practice: Can we make dissemination stick? *Exceptional Children, 79*(2), 163–180.

Darling-Hammond, L., Hyler, M. E., & Gardner, M. (2017). *Effective teacher professional development.* Learning Policy Institute.

Dana, N. F., Pape, S. J., Griffin, C. C., & Prosser, S. K. (2016). Incorporating practitioner inquiry into an online professional development program: The Prime Online experience. *Professional Development in Education, 43*(2), 212–231. doi:10.1080/19415257.2016.1152592

Dawson, M. R., & Lignugaris Kraft, B. (2017). Meaningful practice: Generalizing foundation teaching skills from TLE TeachLivE™ to the classroom. *Teacher Education and Special Education, 40*(1), 26–50. doi:10.1177/0888406416664184

Desimone, L. M., Garet, M. S. (2015). Best practices in teachers' professional development in the United States. *Psychology, Society, & Education*, 7, 252. doi:10.25115/psye.v7i3.515

Foster, A., Lambert, J., & Kim, J. H. (2017). An exploration of learner-centered professional development for reluctant math teachers. In J. Keengwe & G. Onchwari (Eds.), *Handbook of research on learner-centered pedagogy in teacher education and professional development*. (pp. 181–205). IGI Global.

Friend, M. & Bursuck, W. (2018). *Including students with special needs: A practical guide for classroom teachers* (8th ed.). Pearson Education, Inc. http://docshare04.docshare.tips/files/20511/205115861.pdf

Fullan, M. (2015). *The new meaning of education change*. Teachers College Press.

Garet, M. S., Porter, A. C., Desimone, L., Birman, B. F., & Yoon, K. S. (2001). What makes professional development effective? Results from a national sample of teachers. *American Educational Research Journal*, *38*(4), 915–945. doi:10.3102/00028312038004915

Gaines, T., & Barnes, M. (2017). Perceptions and attitudes about inclusion: Findings across all grade levels and years of teaching experience. *Cogent Education*, *4*, 1–11. doi:10.1080/2331186X.2017.1313561

Garland, K. M., Holden, K., & Garland, D. P. (2015). Individualized clinical coaching in the TLE TeachLivE Lab: Enhancing fidelity of implementation of system of least prompts among novice teachers of students with Autism. *Teacher Education and Special Education*, *39*(1), 47–59. doi:10.1177/0888406415600769

Gaudin, C., & Chaliès, S. (2015). Video viewing in teacher education and professional development: A literature review. *Educational Research Review*, *16*, 41–67. doi:10.1016/j.edurev.2015.06.001

Gregory, J. (2018). Not my responsibility: The impact of separate special education systems on educators' attitudes toward inclusion. *Educational Policy Analysis and Strategic Research*, *13*(1), 127–148. doi:10.29329/epasr.2018.137.8

Griffin, C. C., Dana, N. F., Pape, S. J., Algina, J., Bae, J., Prosser, S. K., & League, M. B. (2018). "Prime online": Exploring teacher professional development for creating inclusive elementary mathematics classrooms. *Teacher Education and Special Education*, *41*(2), 121–139. doi:10.1177/0888406417740702

Guskey, T. R. (2000). *Evaluating professional development*. Corwin Press, Inc.

Hawley, W. D. (Ed.). (2006). *The keys to effective schools: Educational reform as continuous improvement*. Corwin Press, Inc.

Hirsch, S. E., Lloyd, J. W., & Kennedy, M. J. (2019). Professional development in practice: Improving novice teachers' use of universal classroom management. *The Elementary School Journal*, *120*(1), 61–87. doi:10.1086/704492

Hoppey, D., Black, W. R., & Mickelson, A. M. (2018). The evolution of inclusive practice in two elementary schools: Reforming teacher purpose, instructional capacity, and data-informed practice. *International Journal of Educational Reform*, *27*, 22–45. doi:10.1177/105678791802700102

Hoover, J. J., & Soltero-González, L. (2018). Educator preparation for developing culturally and linguistically responsive MTSS in rural community elementary schools. *Teacher Education and Special Education*, *41*(3), 188–202. doi:10.1177/0888406417753689

Jimenez, B. A., & Barron, T. (2019). Learner-centered professional development: A model to increase inclusion for students with moderate intellectual disability. *Inclusion*, 7(2), 125–139. doi:10.1352/2326-6988-7.2.125

Katz, J. (2015). Implementing the three block model of universal design for learning: Effects on teachers' self-efficacy, stress, and job satisfaction in inclusive classrooms K-12. *International Journal of Inclusive Education*, *19*(1), 1–20. doi:10.1080/13603116.2014.881569

Kelleher, J. P. (2015). Perspective taking through film: Educating pre-service and in-service teachers about autism. *Journal of the American Academy of Special Education Professionals*, 83–98.

Kennedy, M. M. (2016). How does professional development improve teaching? *Review of Educational Research*, 86, 945–980. doi:10.3102/0034654315626800

Kennedy, M. J., Rodgers, W. J., Romig, J. E., Lloyd, J. W., & Brownell, M. T. (2017). Effects of a multimedia professional development package on inclusive science teachers' vocabulary instruction. *Journal of Teacher Education*, *68*(2), 213–230. doi:10.1177/0022487116687554

Kennedy, M. J., Rodgers, W. J., Romig, J. E., Mathews, H. M., & Peeples, K. N. (2018). Introducing the content acquisition podcast professional development process: Supporting vocabulary instruction for inclusive middle school science teachers. *Teacher Education and Special Education*, *41*(2), 140–157. doi:10.1177/0888406417745655

Kosko, K. W., & Wilkins, J. L. (2009). General educators' in-service training and their self-perceived ability to adapt instruction for students with IEPs. *The Professional Educator*, *33*(2), 1–10.

Leithwood, K., & Jantzi, D. (2000). The effects of transformational leadership on organizational conditions and student engagement with school. *Journal of Educational Administration*, *38*, 112–129. doi:10.1108/09578230010320064

Leko, M. M., & Brownell, M. T. (2009). Crafting quality professional development for special educators: What school leaders should know. *TEACHING Exceptional Children*, *42*(1), 64–70. doi:10.1177/004005990904200106

Leko, M. M., Brownell, M. T., Sindelar, P. T., & Kiely, M. T. (2015). Envisioning the future of special education personnel preparation in a standards-based era. *Exceptional Children*, *82*(1), 25–43. doi:10.1177/0014402915598782

Leko, M. M., Kiely, M. T., Brownell, M. T., Osipova, A., Dingle, M. P., & Mundy, C. A. (2015). Understanding special educators' learning opportunities in collaborative groups: The role of discourse. *Teacher Education and Special Education*, *38*(2), 138–157. doi:10.1177/0888406414557283

Lembke, E. S., McMaster, K. L., Smith, R. A., Allen, A., Brandes, D., & Wagner, K. (2017). Professional development for data-based instruction in early writing: Tools, learning, and collaborative support. *Teacher Education and Special Education*, *41*(2), 106–120. doi:10.1177/0888406417730112

Loucks-Horsley, S., Love, N., Stiles, K., Mundry, S., & Hewson, P. W. (2003). *Designing professional development for teachers of science and mathematics*. Corwin Press.

Loucks-Horsley, S., Stiles, K., & Hewson, P. (1996). Principles of effective professional development for mathematics and science teachers: A synthesis of standards. *National Institute for Science Education*, *1*(1), 1–6. https://www.rb.gy/bkt9ij

Mahat, M. (2008). The development of a psychometrically-sound instrument to measure teachers' multi-dimensional attitudes toward inclusive education. *International Journal of Special Education*, *23*(1), 82–92.

Male, D. B. (2011). The impact of a professional development program on teachers' attitudes towards inclusion. *Support for Learning*, *26*(4), 183–186. doi:10.1111/j.1467-9604.2011.01500.x

McCutchen, D., Abbott, R. D., Green, L. B., Beretvas, S. N., Cox, S., Potter N. S., Quiroga, T., & Gray, A. L. (2002). Beginning literacy: Links among teacher knowledge, teacher practice, and student learning. *Journal of Learning Disabilities*, *35*(1), 69–86. doi:10.1177/002221940203500106

McKeown, D., FitzPatrick, E., Brown, M., Brindle, M., Owens, J., & Hendrick, R. (2019). Urban teachers' implementation of SRSD for persuasive writing following practice-based professional development: Positive effects mediated by compromised fidelity. *Reading and Writing*, *32*(6), 1483–1506. doi:10.1007/s11145-018-9864-3

McLeskey, J., Barringer, M., Billingsley, B., Brownell, M., Jackson, D., Kennedy, M., Lewis, T., Maheady, L., Rodriguez, J., Scheeler, M. C., Winn, J., & Ziegler, D. (2017). *High-leverage practices in special education*. Council for Exceptional Children.

McLeskey, J., Billingsley, B., Brownell, M. T., Maheady, L., & Lewis, T. J. (2019). What are high-leverage practices for special education teachers and why are they important? *Remedial and Special Education*, *40*(6), 331–337. doi:10.1177/0741932518773477

McLeskey, J., Maheady, L., Billingsley, B., Brownell, M., & Lewis, T. (Eds.). (2018). *High leverage practices for inclusive classrooms*. Routledge.

McLeskey, J., & Waldron, N. L. (2002). Professional development and inclusive schools: Reflections on effective practice. *The Teacher Educator*, *37*, 159–172. doi:10.1080/08878730209555291

McLeskey, J., Waldron, N. L., & Redd, L. (2014). A case study of a highly effective, inclusive elementary school. *The Journal of Special Education*, *48*, 59–70. doi:10.1177/0022466912440455

McLeskey, J., Waldron, N. L., So, T. K., Swanson, K., & Loveland, T. (2001). Perspectives of teachers toward inclusive programs. *Teacher Education and Special Education*, *24*, 108–115. doi:10.1177/088840640102400205

McMaster, K. L., Baker, K., Donegan, R., Hugh, M., & Sargent, K. (2020). Professional development to support teachers' implementation of intensive reading intervention: A systematic review. *Remedial and Special Education*, 1–14. doi:10.1177/0741932520934099

McVee, M. B., Shanahan, L. E., Pearson, P. D., & Rinker, T. W. (2015). Using the gradual release of responsibility model to support video reflection with preservice and inservice teachers. In E. Ortlieb, M. B. McVee, & L. E. Shanahan (Eds.), *Video reflection in literacy teacher education and development: Lessons from research and practice* (pp. 59–80). Emerald.

Morin, K. L., Ganz, J. B., Vannest, K. J., Haas, A. N., Nagro, S. A., Peltier, C. J., Fuller, M. C., & Ura, S. K. (2019). A systematic review of single-case research on video analysis as professional development for special educators. *The Journal of Special Education*, *53*(1), 3–14. doi:10.1177/0022466918798361

Mulvey, B. K., Chiu, J. L., Ghosh, R., & Bell, R. L. (2016). Special education teachers' nature of science instructional experiences. *Journal of Research in Science Teaching*, *53*(4), 554–578. doi:10.1002/tea.21311

National Staff Development Council. (2012). *NSDC Definition of Professional Development*. Author. http://qrisnetwork.org/sites/all/files/session/resources/NSDC%20Definition%20of%20Professional%20Development.pdf

Owens, T. L., Lo, Y., & Collins, B. C. (2020). Using tiered coaching and bug-in-ear technology to promote teacher implementation fidelity. *The Journal of Special Education, 54*(2), 67–79. doi:10.1177/0022466919852706

Penuel, W. R., Fishman, B. J., Yamaguchi, R., & Gallagher, L. P. (2007). What makes professional development effective? Strategies that foster curriculum implementation. *American Educational Research Journal, 44*(4), 921–958. doi:10.3102/0002831207308221

Ploessl, D. M., & Rock, M. L. (2014). eCoaching: The effects on co-teachers' planning and instruction. *Teacher Education and Special Education, 37*(3), 191–215. 10.1177/0888406414525049

Pugach, M. C., Blanton, L. P., Correa, V. I., McLeskey, J., & Langley, L. K. (2009). *The role of collaboration in supporting the induction and retention of new special education teachers.* (NCIPP Doc. No. RS-2ES). National Center to Inform Policy and Practice in Special Education Professional Development. http://www.ncipp.org/reports/rs_2.pdf

Reinke, W. M., Stormont, M. Herman, K. C., Newcomer, L., & King, K. (2014). Use of coaching and behavior support planning for students with disruptive behavior within a universal classroom management program. *Journal of Emotional and Behavioral Disorders, 22*(2), 74–82. doi:10.1177/1063426613519820

Richardson, V. (1996). The role of attitudes and beliefs in learning to teach. In J. Sikula, T. J. Buttery, & E. Guyton (Eds.), *Handbook of research on teacher education* (pp.102–119). Macmillan.

Richardson, V., & Placier, P. (2001). Teacher change. In V. Richardson (Ed.), *Handbook for research on teaching* (pp. 905–947). American Educational Research Association.

Robinson, V., Hohepa, M. K., & Lloyd, C. (2009). *School leadership and student outcomes: Identifying what works and why best evidence synthesis.* Ministry of Education.

Rodgers, W. J., Kennedy, M. J., VanUitert, V. J., & Myers, A. M. (2019). Delivering performance feedback to teachers using technology-based observation and coaching tools. *Intervention in School and Clinic, 55*(2), 103–112. doi:10.1177/1053451219837640

Rosenberg, M. S., Boyer, K. L., Sindelar, P. T., & Misra, S. K. (2007). Alternative route programs for certification in special education: Program infrastructure, instructional delivery, and participant characteristics. *Exceptional Children, 73*, 224–241. doi:10.1177/001440290707300206

Schaefer, J. M., & Ottley, J. R. (2018). Evaluating immediate feedback via bug-in-ear as an evidence-based practice for professional development. *Journal of Special Education Technology, 33*(4), 247–258. doi:10.1177/0162643418766870

Tschannen-Moran, M., & Woolfolk Hoy, A. (2001). Teacher efficacy: Capturing an elusive construct. *Teaching and Teacher Education, 17*(7), 783–805. doi:10.1016/S0742-051X(01)00036-1

VanUitert, V. J., Kennedy, M. J., Rodgers, W. J., Romig, J. E., & Alves, K. D. (2019). A multimedia professional 0 education and professional development. In D. Polly, C. Martin, & K. Dikilitas (Eds.), *Handbook of research on educator preparation and professional learning* (pp. 1–13). Gediz University Press.

Vaughn, S., & Coleman, M. (2004). The role of mentoring in promoting use of research-based practices in reading. *Remedial and Special Education, 25*(1), 25–38. doi:10.1177/07419325040250010401

Waldron, N. L. (2007). Teacher attitudes toward inclusion. In J. McLeskey (Ed.), *Reflections on inclusion: Classic articles that shaped our thinking* (pp. 163–187). Council for Exceptional Children.

Yoo, J. H. (2016). The effect of professional development on teacher efficacy and teachers' self-analysis of their efficacy change. *Journal of Teacher Education for Sustainability, 18*(1), 84–94. doi:10.1515/jtes-2016-0007

Yoon, K. S., Duncan, T., Lee, S. W., Scarloss, B., & Shapley, K. L. (2007). *Reviewing the evidence on how professional development affects student achievement* (Report No. 033.) Institute for Education Sciences: National Center for Evaluation and Regional Assistance. https://ies.ed.gov/ncee/edlabs/regions/southwest/pdf/rel_2007033_sum.pdf

Section II

Effective District, School, and Classroom Frameworks and Interventions

Bob Algozzine

The less things change, the more they stay the same. When researchers asked teachers why they aren't implementing interventions related to educating students with disabilities in general education classrooms, they typically indicate that they need support in areas related to time, training, personnel, materials, class size, and consideration of the severity of disability (Scruggs & Mastropieri, 1996). When researchers review "critical incidents associated with changes in practice," they find that leadership, professional development, and consultation and collaboration are facilitators, that competing perspectives, staff turnover, and varying levels of readiness are inhibitors, and that "access to more effective interventions" is a prominent "wish list" item (Charlton et al., 2018, p. 191). When researchers ask teachers to rate the social validity of practices, they typically document "consumer satisfaction" or how pleased practitioners were with an intervention (McNeil, 2019, p. 4586) rather than more important dependent variables like time and cost-effectiveness that are better associated with implementation and use (Callahan et al., 2017). Not overestimating the worth of using "satisfaction" ratings as validation of evidence-based practices, a common finding in much intervention research is that even when district and school personnel achieve "a measure of ownership of an effective practice," the level of implementation in years following support by external research projects is minimal (cf. Fuchs et al., 1996, p. 244).

In the Presidential Address to the Educational Research Association in 1923, the Assistant Superintendent of Milwaukee Schools W. W. Theisen noted that the "findings of research must be translated into simple lessons for the teacher", but the primary contribution of much of the then-contemporary work was in "pointing out problems" (pp. 307, 314). More recently, the inability to bridge the gap between research and practice has been lamented in writing focused on implementation science in general (Fixsen et al., 2005; Wallace et al., 2008) and reviews focused on inclusion specifically (Grima-Farrell et al., 2011, p. 118) as well as in articles addressing "…key considerations essential to successfully implementing and sustaining validated practices to support teachers in addressing the needs of [all] students within our school systems (Grima-Farrell, 2018, p. 89). In this chapter, our colleagues set the context for inclusion in descriptions of tiered academic and behavior instruction driven by high functioning data teams supported by high-leverage practices that can be used to focus on improving instruction and monitoring relentlessly until fidelity and/or outcome data illustrate that it is time to change.

DOI: 10.4324/9781003043874-102

References

Callahan, K., Hughes, H. L., Mehta, S., Toussaint, K. A., Nichols, S. M., Ma, P. S., et al. (2017). Social validity of evidence-based practices and emerging interventions in autism. *Focus on Autism and Other Developmental Disabilities*, 32(3), 188–197.

Charlton, C. T., Sabey, C. V., Dawson, M. R., Pyle, D., Lund, E. M., & Ross, S. W. (2018). Critical incidents in the scale-up of state multitiered systems of supports. *Journal of Positive Behavior Interventions*, 20(4), 191–202.

Fixsen, D., Naoom, S., Blase, K., Friedman, R., Wallace, F. (2005). *Implementation research: A synthesis of the literature*. University of South Florida, Louis de la Parte Florida Mental Health Institute, National Implementation Research Network.

Fuchs, D., Fuchs, L. S., Harris, A. H., & Roberts, P. H. (1996). Bridging the research-to-practice gap with mainstream assistance teams: A cautionary tale. *School Psychology Quarterly*, 11(3), 244–266.

Grima-Farrell, C. (2018). Bridging the research-to-practice gap: Implementing the research-to-practice model. *Australasian Journal of Special and Inclusive Education*, 42(1), 82–91.

Grima-Farrell, C., Bain, A., & McDonagh, S. (2011). Bridging the research-to-practice gap: A review of the literature focusing on inclusive education. *Australasian Journal of Special Education*, 35(2), 117–136.

McNeil, J. (2019). Social validity and teachers' use of evidence-based practices for autism. *Journal of Autism and Developmental Disorders*, 49(11), 4585–4594.

Scruggs, T. E., & Mastropieri, M. A. (1996). Teacher perceptions of mainstreaming/inclusion, 1958–1995: A research synthesis. *Exceptional Children*, 63(1), 59–74.

Theisen, W. (1923). Recent progress in educational research. *Journal of Educational Research*, 8(4), 301–314.

Wallace, F., Blase, K., Fixsen, D., & Naoom, S. (2008). *Implementing the findings of research: Bridging the gap between knowledge and practice*. Education Research Service.

6

Supporting Inclusive Practices with Multi-Tiered System of Supports

Dale Lynn Cusumano[1] *and Angela I. Preston*[2]

[1]NATIONAL IMPLEMENTATION RESEARCH NETWORK AT UNIVERSITY OF NORTH CAROLINA AT CHAPEL HILL

[2]NORTH CAROLINA DEPARTMENT OF PUBLIC INSTRUCTION

Setting the Stage

Overview of Multi-tiered System of Supports (MTSS)

Multi-tiered System of Supports (MTSS) is a framework of supports with benefits for all students. With the goal of improved academic and behavior outcomes for each and every student, MTSS components include coordinating the delivery of evidence-based interventions across a continuum of increasing support and prevention, monitoring implementation, and evaluating progress and outcomes to inform continuous improvement and ongoing decision making (Batsche et al., 2005; Gersten et al., 2008; Lane et al., 2015; National Center on Response to Intervention, 2010; PBIS, n.d.).

Over time, the term MTSS evolved from Response to Intervention (RtI or RTI), which focused on improving academic outcomes, and Positive Behavior and Intervention Support (PBIS), which focused on improving behavior outcomes. Originally, academics and behavior were viewed as separate processes through RtI and PBIS, but eventually, the two were synthesized into MTSS. As we proceed through this chapter, some of the research occurred prior to the use of the term MTSS and focused specifically on RtI or PBIS. Regardless of the term used, the results are applicable to the MTSS framework.

Based on the results of a national evaluation of RtI (Balu et al., 2015), the need for strengthened implementation support for RtI became apparent. Despite 86% of MTSS sample schools self-reporting full implementation of RtI, a deeper analysis found that not all schools were following the recommended components of RtI implementation (e.g., interventions provided to students performing at or above grade level, interventions replacing core instruction instead of in addition to core instruction), therefore not fully implementing RtI (Fuchs & Fuchs, 2017). This chapter explores implementation practices from research and their application to districts implementing MTSS. We aim to move in a positive direction by connecting research with voices from the field doing the work of implementing MTSS.

Defining the Intervention

As co-authors, we often joke that education loves a triangle diagram. While the MTSS triangle is one of the more recognizable diagrams, the layered triangle assists with visualizing the MTSS

DOI: 10.4324/9781003043874-6

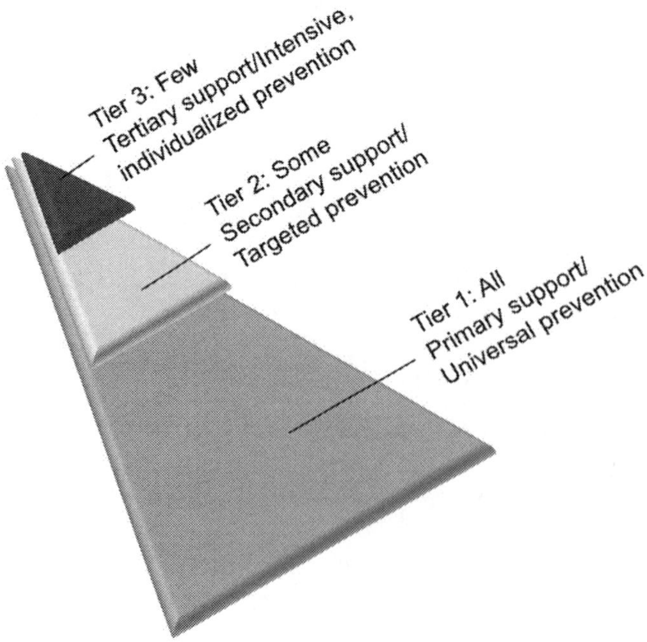

Figure 6.1 Layered tiered model of support and prevention

framework in application to a school population. As depicted in Figure 6.1, the bottom layer represents Tier 1 instruction: Primary support and universal prevention. This visualization is important because this tier reflects what all students receive or their core academic instruction and school-wide behavior instruction. The second layer represents Tier 2: Secondary support and targeted prevention when core instruction is not enough for some students to reach their academic and behavior goals and targets. Tier 2 supports including targeted academic or behavioral interventions are provided in addition to Tier 1 core instruction when such a gap or problem is identified. The third layer represents Tier 3: Tertiary support and intensive, individualized prevention. When solid core instruction and effective allocation of Tier 2 supports are provided to students in need, data-based decision making will identify the smallest number of students who need Tier 3 supports or individualized academic instruction or intensive behavior prevention strategies. As depicted in the model, each new tier is layered on top of the previous tier to indicate that all three levels are integrated and not standalone. Of critical importance is that all students, including students receiving Tiers 2 and 3 supports, must continue to receive core instruction and follow school-wide behavioral expectations (Batsche et al., 2005; Gersten et al., 2008; Lane et al., 2015; National Center on Response to Intervention, 2010; PBIS, n.d.).

To determine the supports a student needs, universal screeners are administered several times a year to identify students who may need more support to reach their academic or behavior goals or targets. After universal screening data are collected, school teams use a problem-solving model to identify students who may need targeted interventions or prevention supports. During this problem-solving process, students' needs are identified and matched to supports and interventions that have a high probability of positively impacting their progress. To monitor the impact of the intervention on student learning or targeted behavioral need, frequent progress monitoring and fidelity of implementation data are collected. Progress monitoring and fidelity data are analyzed regarding the level of change and decisions about intervention supports are made (e.g., continue, modify, increase, or decrease supports). In essence, these data answer questions of "Is the system of support for a student having the desired effect" and "Was the strategy able to be used as intended?" When data indicate that a student is not making adequate progress with Tier 2 supports, avenues to increase the intensity, duration, explicitness, or frequency of a system of support that can accelerate the student's rate of improvement toward his or her academic or behavioral goals are identified. This subsequent modification in a student's system of support is often referred to as Tier 3 interventions. Fidelity (adherence to the expectation) is an ongoing, important feature of MTSS as the impact of change is only as strong as the decisions made, quality of interventions used, and follow-through of implementation (Batsche et al., 2005; Gersten et al., 2008; Lane et al., 2015; National Center on Response to Intervention, 2010; PBIS, n.d.). Later in this chapter, we will dive deeper to unpack the essential components of MTSS, highlighting experiences of voices in the field. But first, we will follow the path that led to the beginning of MTSS.

A Continuing Problem in Need of Solving

Shortly after the passing of PL 94-142, Education of All Handicapped Children law, issues arose on how to identify students with learning disabilities (LD). One commonly used method was the discrepancy model that identified a discrepancy between ability and achievement (although a formula was not identified through law). Other methods included identifying a deficit in academic achievement and using scatter analysis (Bradley et al., 2002; Ysseldyke et al., 1983). For the next few decades, research highlighted issues with the discrepancy model, including: the inconsistencies with qualification for LD (Fletcher et al. 1994, Ysseldyke et al., 1983), increases in students receiving special education (especially students identified with LD), overrepresentation of students with minority background in special education (Hosp & Reschly, 2004), and a lack in early identification (Torgesen et al., 2001; Vellutino et al., 1996). This final issue resulted in the discrepancy model commonly being referred to as the "wait to fail" model. Students needed to show enough of a deficit to qualify for special education supports, essentially waiting until they failed before receiving specialized instruction to "catch up."

A Continuing Search for Solutions

Nearing the turn of the century, research groups and parent groups aspired to change how students with LD were identified and evaluated for special education services. The Office of Special Education Programs (OSEP) developed the LD Initiative to generate positive solutions to identify students with LD (Bradley & Danielson, 2004). Out of their work emerged the beginnings of Response to Intervention (RtI), a framework for allocating delivery of supports for students based on public health tiered prevention models (Averill et al., 2011; Schulte, 2016). In 2004, the Individuals with Disabilities Education Improvement Act (IDEIA) was reauthorized, shifting evaluation for LD to include a process for responding to research-based interventions as opposed to using the discrepancy model (Bradley et al., 2002; Preston et al., 2016). This shift to a proactive approach focused on early intervention and moved away from the reactive approach of waiting for students to fail.

During the same time frame and legislation (IDEA 1997, 2004), another system of supports emerged that focused on using research-based strategies to address problem behaviors in school. Research on Positive Behavior Intervention Support (PBIS) was funded by OSEP through the Technical Assistance Center of PBIS (https://RtI.pbis.org/about/about). Similar to RtI, PBIS (see Chapter 7) uses a tiered framework, universal screenings, continuum of supports, data-based decision making, fidelity of implementation, and evaluation of student performance (Sugai & Horner, 2009). The focus of PBIS was to address the needs of students with serious problem behaviors and address the prevention of problem behaviors (Sugai & Horner, 2009). By developing a set of schoolwide expectations for universal prevention (Tier 1), all students are taught common expectations and classroom expectations that are aligned with school-wide expectations. Teachers follow a continuum of procedures to encourage positive behavior while discouraging problem behavior. For students needing more individualization, targeted prevention (Tier 2) is provided, followed by intensive prevention (Tier 3) for students with the most needs (Sugai & Horner, 2009).

Using both RtI and PBIS, school teams (see Chapter 8) often met to discuss academic concerns and met another time to review behavioral concerns. To address the "whole child," calls for combining RtI and PBIS transpired (Sugai & Horner, 2009). Given the similar practices of RtI and PBIS, MTSS emerged as an encompassing framework (or umbrella) for improving all outcomes for all students (Lane et al., 2015; Utley and Obiakor, 2012). The framework remained constant, but the focus area (academic or behavior problem) shifted based on individual student needs.

Continuing Areas in Need of Change

Despite the original intention of RtI as an alternative means for identifying students with learning disabilities, the scope of impact broadened over time (Horner & Sugai, 2000; Schulte, 2016). As a framework, the value of applying MTSS to support all students in schools was realized and the shift was made from a special education focus to a general education focus. By broadening the focus of MTSS beyond special education identification, all students benefited from receiving academic and behavioral supports at their levels. The MTSS framework also lends itself beyond academics and behavior to other educational initiatives (e.g., counseling, social-emotional learning; Bohanon et al., 2016; National Association of School Psychologists, 2009). Many states currently support districts to use MTSS as a framework allocating supports for academics, behavior, and social-emotional learning (e.g., KS, NY, NC, ND, TN; Arden et al., 2017; CASEL, n.d.; Lane et al., 2015).

In 2015, Balu and colleagues conducted a national evaluation of RtI (detailed later in the chapter). A key takeaway from this study emphasized the importance of multiple tiers with increasing levels of intensity of instruction and supports allocated across its framework. Another point that emerged from their work addressed an urgency to empower and support teachers providing interventions. Finally, the need to empower educators to use data to make instructional decisions surfaced as a critical point in facilitating effective and efficient use of RtI practices. More specifically, Balu's team identified how universal screenings should be administered to identify students at risk, progress monitoring data used to make instructional decisions, and finally, as needed, data could be used to identify students with disabilities.

MTSS as an Inclusive Practice

Restructuring how special education and general education interact is possible through an MTSS framework. Considering students with significant cognitive disabilities and students who are academically and intellectually gifted, the versatile MTSS framework can be applied as a means for allocating supports for students across the ability spectrum by providing tailored instruction to support their needs (Bianco, 2010; Hughes & Rollins, 2009; Thurlow et al., 2020). The tiered model's structure lends itself to promoting inclusive practices through a continuum of services within the general education classroom (Thurlow et al., 2020). By focusing on how special education services can be integrated within each tier, students with significant cognitive disabilities can participate in general education settings (Thurlow et al., 2020). With the evidence base of Universal Design for Learning (UDL), applying UDL practices to core instruction provides stronger access to content standards for all students. This shifts the focus of special education support from a continuum of placements to a continuum of services regardless of placement for all students with disabilities, including those with significant cognitive disabilities (Thurlow et al., 2020). When instruction is tailored to student needs, instruction becomes the key point, with the location of services receiving less attention.

Concurrently, the use of the MTSS framework and related practices can serve as an effective and efficient means to allocate resources and support across the continuum of student needs. Along with identifying students who are struggling, universal screenings have the ability to identify students who are academically and intellectually gifted (Bianco, 2010; Hughes & Rollins, 2009). The multi-tiered framework follows the same structure for students who are achieving beyond their peers. In the primary tier, core instruction consists of evidence-based practices aligned to content standards with differentiated instruction (Hughes & Rollins, 2009). Based on progress monitoring data, students who are achieving at or above grade level in Tier 1 would be provided differentiated instruction, enrichment, or accelerated learning in the secondary tier. Continuing with progress monitoring practices, students for whom Tier 2 supports are still not meeting their advanced needs would be considered for intensive accelerated instruction, or Tier 3 supports that may also be tied to a referral to consider eligibility to gifted programming where they could receive supports that represent the highest rate of advanced content that meets their accelerated learning needs (e.g., grade skipping) or complete advanced placement classes (Bianco, 2010; Hughes & Rollins, 2009). Notably, a collaboration between general educators and gifted teachers holds the potential to fully support and include students who are identified as gifted and students who are identified as twice-exceptional (gifted in one content area and identified with a disability in another content area) in the general education classroom (Hughes & Rollins, 2009). As a system, MTSS provides a versatile framework for the inclusion of each and every student.

Moving On

This brief overview of MTSS, history of origins, and potential for MTSS to support fully inclusive practices are necessary introduction to deepen the understanding of why this shift is essential before diving into implementation of this framework. The justification for the implementation of MTSS is strong enough to shift expectations, but for shifting practices and beliefs, as the old saying goes, *It's easier said than done.* Therefore, we will direct our focus to implement practices that support MTSS adoption. As such, we see the future collaboration between research and practice as not only critical but invigorating. In light of this, we share voices from the field capturing successes and challenges from hands-on work at implementing MTSS at the district and school levels to guide and shape the next steps for research.

What We Know Based on Research

As noted earlier, MTSS coordinates the delivery and monitoring of evidence-based interventions across a continuum of support to inform continuous improvement. In order to accomplish this, common features of MTSS as a tiered service delivery model include universal screening (to identify strengths/weaknesses), progress monitoring student data, data-based decision making, tiered interventions and supports, and fidelity of implementation (Batsche et al., 2005; Gersten et al., 2008; Lane et al., 2015). Essential features of a tiered service delivery model will be explored in depth later in this chapter. This section will explore MTSS as a tiered service delivery model, identify impacts on students, systems, and practices, and conclude with the next steps for effective and inclusive MTSS.

MTSS as a Tiered Service Delivery Model

Over the last 20 years, as MTSS has become more widely implemented, the percentage of students with disabilities identified with a specific learning disability has consistently declined from 45.4% in 2000, to 36.7% in 2010, to 33.2% in 2018 (National Center for Education Statistics, 2019). In theory, it was believed if student needs were supported and monitored early, they would develop necessary skills (e.g., to read, to manage behavior). This would prevent students who needed differentiated instruction from being (mis)-identified with an LD. That is, prior to MTSS, students whose gaps in learning were due to instructional delivery or gaps in core curriculum would often be identified as having a disability rather than an externally driven "curriculum casualty." As mentioned earlier, at the early stages of the adoption of MTSS, one of the goals was to intervene early and prevent students from failing. Based on national data, the general impact of prevention is moving in the right direction, as demonstrated through a consistent decrease in the percentage of students identified with a specific learning disability.

Implementation of MTSS has received national support since its appearance in the Individuals with Disabilities Education Act (2004). Multiple national technical assistance (TA) centers have supported the work of MTSS practitioners throughout the decades (Arden et al., 2017). From 2003 to 2009, the National Center on Student Progress Monitoring was funded to provide states and districts TA support for progress monitoring elementary students (kindergarten to fifth grade). Subsequently, in 2007-2012, the National Center on Response to Intervention was funded to provide TA support for states and districts implementing and evaluating RtI models. Finally, from 2011-2021, the National Center on Intensive Intervention was funded to provide TA support to states, districts, and schools, implementing data-based individualization (DBI) as part of MTSS. While the academic side of MTSS (RtI) has had multiple national TA centers over the years, the behavior side of MTSS (PBIS) has been supported through one TA center. Initially funded by OSEP in 1998, the National Technical Assistance Center on Positive Behavioral Interventions and Supports (PBIS) has supported states, districts, and schools to implement PBIS with fidelity and learn lessons from broad-scale implementation (pbis.org).

Impact on Students, Systems, and Practices

MTSS functions as a vehicle driven to improve outcomes for students. One intriguing finding of a four-year longitudinal cohort comparison study examining the impact of RtI (O'Connor et al., 2013) was that students identified with a learning disability and provided RtI support with Tier 2 interventions (cohort 2) scored lower on reading measures than students with a learning disability who were referred through the traditional discrepancy model (cohort 1). One implication of this finding is that as RtI becomes more widely used, students who qualify for special education services under a learning disability may have more persistent reading difficulties that are challenging to address. This potential shift may require special educators to receive further training to address these challenges (O'Connor et al., 2013).

Another study on the impact of MTSS on LD identification (VanDerHeyden et al., 2007) evaluated the effects of training school psychologists to follow an LD identification decision model on LD placement rates. Results found an increase in accuracy of referrals (the percentage of referrals that resulted in special education placement increased) and a decrease in the proportion of students identified with LD by almost half (6% to 3.5%).

Muscott et al. (2008) found by year two of school-wide PBIS implementation across 22 elementary, middle, and high schools, office discipline referrals (ODRs) decreased by 6,010 referrals (28%). Other findings included the majority of elementary (11 out of 12), high schools (1 out of 1), and multi-level schools (3 out of 4) reported an increase in math achievement, while only one out of five middle schools demonstrated an improvement in math achievement. An implication for this finding is that as ODRs decrease, students remain in class and are provided more opportunities to learn academic content.

In 2015, the Institute of Educational Sciences (IES) conducted a national evaluation on RtI (Balu et al., 2015). A sample of 146 elementary schools was selected as the impact sample because they reported full implementation of RtI for at least three years. A comparison group of 100 elementary schools was selected as the reference sample. The panel focused on three main questions: (a) How did the prevalence of RtI practices differ between impact and reference schools? (b) How did reading services differ between reading groups at different skill levels? and (c) What is the effect of RtI on reading achievement of students just above and below the cut-score on the fall universal screening assessment? Results indicated 86% of impact schools and 56% of reference schools reported full implementation of RtI. More impact schools (97% and 68% respectively) self-reported providing tier 2 interventions three times a week and tier 3 interventions five times a week than reference schools (80% and 47% respectively). Further analysis indicated that not all schools followed RtI recommendations, with 61% of schools meeting the requirement of having at least one student in Tier 1, 2, and 3, despite self-reporting full implementation of RtI (Fuchs & Fuchs, 2017). Schools reported services differed between reading groups because data were used to determine tier placement. It was noted that in first grade, a quarter of students moved tiers between fall and spring. This quarter of students moving across tiers came from Tier 2 (half of the students in Tier 2) and moved to Tier 1 or Tier 3. Finally, the most shocking finding was when comparing first-grade students who scored just below the cut score to students who scored just above the cut score, assignment to Tier 2 or 3 had a negative impact on students who scored just below the cut score. The national evaluation team provided plausible reasons for this final result: a) students were misidentified for the intervention, b) there was a mismatch between instruction and skill deficit, and c) there was poor alignment between Tier 1 (core) and Tier 2 interventions. Balu et al. cautioned that interpreting this finding was only to be used for decisions around identifying cut score levels and not the effectiveness of RtI. No data were collected on whether students received interventions. Results of this evaluation pointed to the importance of implementation fidelity and practical application of MTSS.

In support of the practical application of MTSS, Arden et al. (2017) outlined four recommendations to consider when initiating implementation of MTSS: (a) assess for readiness and capacity to implement MTSS, (b) design professional development (PD) to include both content on MTSS and coaching support, (c) collect and use evaluation (fidelity) data to strengthen support, and (d) include access to MTSS to students with disabilities. Initially, before starting implementation of MTSS, a district should interview stakeholders to determine "readiness" (e.g., buy-in, commitment, perception; Fixsen et al., 2005) and develop implementation support based on the levels of readiness. Subsequently, best practices of PD include more than a one-day training. Teachers need ongoing professional support with embedded coaching to result in adult behavior changes (Arden et al., 2017; Joyce & Showers, 2002). Following this, we cannot say an intervention did not work if we do not know the extent to which an intervention was implemented. Collecting and using fidelity data to ensure MTSS interventions were implemented as intended are necessary to determine quality implementation. Finally, students with disabilities were originally considered the main beneficiaries of MTSS, but as time progressed, more focus was placed on school-wide improvement through MTSS. This resulted in special educators serving in consultation and support roles instead of providing direct services to students with disabilities. Unquestionably, students with disabilities should have access to the same supports within an MTSS framework as their nondisabled peers. By providing support to students with disabilities across the MTSS continuum of supports, general educators and special educators are given the opportunity to collaborate, share knowledge, and support each other as professionals (Arden et al., 2017). Targeting these four areas within the MTSS framework provides a starting point for ensuring that high-leverage MTSS practices are implemented with fidelity.

Without support from legislation, educational change may lack the necessary momentum. One of the deepest impacts of MTSS on systems is the reference of MTSS across decades of federal legislation. Originally, IDEA (1997, 2004) called attention to the prevention of problem behaviors using scientifically based behavioral interventions. PBIS was funded to support this mandate (Sugai & Horner, 2009). The reauthorization of the Individuals with Disabilities Education Act (2004) intentionally aligned areas with No Child Left Behind (No Child Left Behind NCLB Act of 2001) by referencing scientifically-based research and including changes to the identification of students with LD. These changes supported the implementation of RtI and eventually MTSS. Then in 2015, support for implementing SW-PBIS was written into law through the *Every Student Succeeds Act* (von Ravensburg & Blakely, 2017). By mandating the MTSS framework for behavior and supporting its use for the identification of students with learning disabilities, the deep impact on the system was initiated and the push for an integrated framework for both academics and behavior strengthened (Lane et al., 2015).

The impact of MTSS on practices rests on the need for evidence-based practices that have demonstrated effectiveness. Primary support and universal prevention, secondary support and targeted prevention, and tertiary support and intensive individualized prevention require evidence-based instructional practices and behavioral interventions that are used as intended. At first glance, this seems to only impact teachers and staff delivering the evidence-based practices, but the implementation of practices is supported through leadership teams, strong professional development, and coaching supports.

Next Steps for Effective and Inclusive MTSS

A partnership between research and practice would benefit from collaborative (bi-directional) learning around high leverage factors that impact outcomes. One vision of not only key ingredients leading to successful outcomes but also the interplay of these factors is depicted most eloquently by Fixsen and colleagues' (Fixsen et al., 2015) *Active Implementation Formula.* This formula uses the structure of a multiplication problem that includes not only effective practices but also effective implementation and an enabling environment as factors that result in a product of socially significant outcomes.

At first thought, the simplicity of their equation seems to ignore complexities of systems change; however, a deeper examination of the operationalization of each factor reveals not only the depth of each domain but also the interdependency of each factor as housed within a multiplication problem. For example, the first variable, **effective practices**, expands beyond universal assertions that practices must be informed by evidence to proclaim that they also must be *usable.* That is, effective practices also must be defined to the extent that they are teachable, learnable, doable, and observable; thus, increasing the probability that individuals will employ behaviors of the practice with fidelity (Blase & Fixsen, 2013; Blase et al., 2012; Fixsen et al., 2013; Metz & Bartley, 2012; Michie et al., 2009). The next factor, **effective implementation**, underscores the importance of focusing on how competence is developed, maintained, and supported amid varying contextual demands. More specifically, effective implementation brings to light how competence is developed across staff, leaders, and related personnel. Included here are direct users of the practice as well as the personnel who may not deliver the practice itself but, instead, are charged with maintaining a responsive environment. Finally, the last factor in the equation, **enabling context**, acknowledges the importance of ongoing refinement and improvement of systems and ways of work (Blase et al., 2015; Coggins et al., 2003; Metz, & Bartley, 2017). From a larger perspective, Fixsen and colleagues' conceptualization depicts that high-quality implementation requires purposeful attention to all three pieces of the formula; that is, each factor is necessary but insufficient by itself to produce its product of optimal outcomes.

Setting the Course for Effective Inclusion

Effective implementation requires attention to high leverage factors that rise out of the formula components (Blase et al., 2012, 2015; Fixsen et al., 2015, 2010; Metz & Bartley, 2012). In light of this, we have organized this part of the chapter and its solicitation for feedback from the field around three functionally driven actions: (1) **supporting the practice** (e.g., MTSS) or ensuring the effective *practice* is *usable;* (2) **supporting people** by carefully sequencing activities (*implementation stages*) and developing competencies and proactive leadership that supports the use of innovations (*implementation drivers*); and

Table 6.1 Alignment of Formula for Success[1], Operationalization[2], and Agenda Items for Chapter

Formula Component[1]	*Operationalization*[2]	*Agenda Item in Chapter*
Effective Practice	*Usable Innovation*: Effective practices must be defined to the extent that they are teachable, learnable, doable, and observable so that individuals can employ the practice with fidelity.	Defining the Practice
Effective Implementation	*Implementation Drivers*: Mechanisms that develop competency of individuals to use practices with fidelity and leadership that navigates through change within the local and broader context. *Implementation Stages*: Purposeful stage-based sequencing of learning and activities aligned with needs of the system and ongoing learning.	Supporting People
Enabling Context	*Implementation Teams*: Interconnected groups of individuals (teams) who are accountable for managing and improving the health of the system in service to facilitating reliable and consistent use of effective practices. *Improvement Cycles*: Iterative cycles of learning that draw information about the impact of change to inform full and effective use of the practice (usable innovation).	Supporting the System

Notes
1 Fixsen et al. (2015).
2 Blase et al. (2009) and Fixsen et al. (2005).

(3) **supporting systems** of interconnected *teams* that use ongoing learning to *continually improve* infrastructure to support fidelity of MTSS (see Table 6.1). As we captured feedback from the field, we documented challenges, but we also gained an understanding of and learned from their moments of greatness. Our goal was to capture these experiences as fodder for a collaborative partnership between research and sustainable improvement of practice.

Supporting the Practice

Ensuring a practice is usable—or defined to the degree that crucial components can be taught and supported in use—is critical. Coupled with this is the awareness that practices must also be inclusive in their reach and impact. As such, "Is this practice usable" refers not only to the degree to which a practice can be defined but the degree to which a practice supports the equity and inclusion of all students. Therefore, "Is this practice inclusive of students who may benefit from its delivery?" must be pondered when effective practices are examined in the light of also being usable.

Essential Components of MTSS

When used as intended, effective (evidence-based) practices (e.g., including practices allocated within MTSS) result in positive outcomes for students. Unfortunately, many are poorly operationalized and defined, making them difficult to transfer through training and coaching. Evidence of this is cited by Crosse et al. (2011), who found that only 3.5% of practices are used with any level of fidelity over time. Not only does this result in a waste of teachers' and students' time, but it also perpetuates the cycle of failure. To change this outcome, essential components or the key enabling ingredients of the practice must be identified and then fully operationalized. Once these key behaviors are defined, a system to support their use (training and coaching) can be developed to facilitate reliable application and use of the practice that leads to optimal outcomes. In short, to be usable, effective practices must be teachable, learnable, doable, and observable if they are to be sustained and scaled with fidelity (Fixsen et al., 2013).

In light of this assertion, MTSS itself must be defined and operationalized or made "usable." The first step includes identifying the essential components that empower MTSS. Not surprisingly, MTSS has been defined and refined in multiple ways. Indeed, a cursory *Google-driven* sampling of web-based MTSS resources from state and district websites located 18 relevant descriptions for review. Two findings emerged from this activity. First, accessing publicly available, unique electronic resources related to MTSS was somewhat sparse. That is, only 18 local or state agencies had easily accessible information related to MTSS that emerged on this quick survey of websites. Of these, only 10 included published documents that profiled key components driving their vision of MTSS. Second, and perhaps a more positive finding, when this limited sample was reviewed, consistency across the key constructs of MTSS emerged. Overall, eight general themes (high-level constructs) were identified. Table 6.2 presents a summary of the common components found across

Table 6.2 Essential Components in Order of Most Frequently Endorsed

Common Essential Components	*General Definition*
Leadership	Individuals empowered to facilitate, support, and navigate change that includes allocation of resources at the system and local levels that include systems to collaborate across entities.
Multi-Tiered Instruction and Support	System of layered instructional supports that intensifies in duration, focus, frequency, or narrowness as it increases in levels. Supports are allocated equitably based on data, including responsiveness of students' acquisition of skills.
Data Systems	A comprehensive and integrated system of reliable and valid data that are captured to answer questions about student learning and the health and well-being of the MTSS system.
Data-based Problem Solving	A consistent, systematic, and efficient system is used by relevant teams to analyze needs and align them with effective practices leading to sustainable problem resolutions.
Systems for Sustainability	Development of knowledge (competencies), resources, and infrastructure that are driven by data derived from continuous improvement cycles at all levels of the system. Functionally, this systemic approach aims to create consistency, efficiency, and sustainability across people, practices, and resources.
Evidence-based Instruction	Practices to deliver content that are drawn from evidence that documents positive student impact.
Communication and Collaboration	Bi-directional communication facilitates collaboration and communication of status, next steps, and learning across the system. Includes involving external stakeholders in planning and feedback.
Family, Schools, and Community Partnerships	Collaboration of schools, parents, and external stakeholders in identifying needs, feasibility of solutions, and impact.

Source. American Institutes for Research Southeastern Comprehensive Center, California Department of Education (DOE), Colorado DOE, Florida MTSS, Georgia DOE, Massachusetts DOE, Michigan DOE, North Dakota DOE, South Carolina DOE, and Wake County (NC) Public Schools.

these profiles, including leadership, multi-tiered instruction, data systems, data-based problem solving, systems for sustainability, evidence-based instruction, communication and collaboration, and family, schools, and community partnerships.

Although variations in semantics describing the essential components of MTSS were noted, all included references to a tiered system for delivery of instruction and leadership as a key driver of accountability and systems change. Recognition of the importance of a comprehensive and integrated data system that includes measures of student outcomes, system capacity, and fidelity were noted, although elements of the system varied. Most often, data that provided a snapshot of student performance was included, while data that assessed the capacity of the system to support MTSS and related practices were absent. Present across all products was a notation of data as a key driver in problem-solving. On the other hand, several profiles of the key components of MTSS identified systems and infrastructure as a crucial element, with descriptions identifying these as vital for communication, sustainability, and ongoing improvement. Perhaps not surprisingly, evidence-based instruction was identified in many profiles as a stand-alone component. When not acknowledged as their own component, communication, collaboration, and partnerships between home, school, and the community was embed in the philosophical underpinning or vision of MTSS. Although not plentiful in this cursory search, finding any evidence of work operationalizing the essential components that support effective MTSS and related practices is promising. However, what remains to be defined is if these bodies of work were completed as a means to drive and refine training and coaching or as an activity with no further purpose.

Feedback from the Field

As discussed, essential components must be identified and operationalized so that effective training can be developed and data systems to monitor the fit and feasibility of its application be monitored. A glimpse into one district-based team who worked through this phase is offered. This district MTSS leadership team benefited from a flow of communication from MTSS leadership at the state level, who had identified the essential components of MTSS. As such, they started with already identified components and were able to move into the work of operationalizing them within their context during a leadership team meeting. This activity served as a critical step in developing a common understanding across the team of the key components of MTSS. Of most importance, however, it also sets the state for the next and most consequential work of reviewing and, if needed, modifying training and coaching efforts so that they aligned with these components. Tied to this is the work on ensuring those data systems that capture the use of these components from a multi-level perspective be ready to capture content that monitors implementation and scaling and serves as an indicator of the sustainability of MTSS and related practices.

Challenges

A common trend identified across state, district, and building educators were constraints in time (allocated and applied). Many individuals shared that the initial barrier was in allocating the time needed to do this work effectively. Although many shared that there is a better understanding among leaders that time dedicated upfront pays off in the long run; the urgency to "do something" was an underlying and often hard to ignore force pushing steps to be skipped or lack of empowerment across teams. The next barrier was in sharing critical learning needed to facilitate teams to calibrate their thinking and arrive at clear ideas of the essential components of practices. With this proactive work, teams could ensure that training needed to enhance the knowledge, skills, and abilities of key players addressed all aspects needed to support use with fidelity. A second common challenge faced when designing effective training is recognition that a one-size-fits-all approach is an inefficient use of time. In addition, many shared that although they use pre- and posttest training data; few have aligned these metrics with the essential components as they are defined. Finally, resistance or lack of openness to review and revise training plans and data systems so that they drive ongoing improvement of training approaches is common. More specifically, several voices shared that the development and use of training materials often preceded broader systems efforts. That is, training building teams often was one of the first steps in implementing an inclusive multitiered system of support, which often was not based on a collaborative understanding of the essential components of the MTSS framework. As a result, later efforts at reviewing and refining these "finalized" training plans and materials often presented an adaptive challenge.

Another aspect that could hinder defining essential components is called out in Fuchs and Fuchs's (2017) commentary on the national evaluation of RtI. Notable from their questioning of the capacity for schools to define MTSS given its complexities that were hypothesized to muddy the exploratory view of its impact on students. Joining this was their assertion that all RtI (and MTSS) systems should reflect a balance between what is effective and what is doable that is contextualized at the local level. They argued against an "all or nothing" approach to RtI (and MTSS), tempering the understanding that the more adherence to the full MTSS framework, the better the outcomes, with the realization that focusing on strengthening core instruction alone is better than not attempting to implement RtI at all. Keeping this perspective in mind, the need to define the essential components (behavioral characteristics of what it is and what it is not) of a practice rises to the forefront as such clarity serves as the vehicle specifying degrees of freedom for contextualization within the bounds of adherence to basic principles of practice.

What is Working

Prioritizing focused attention to the essential components as they were embedded with the school improvement model emerged as a robust approach to counter teams being overwhelmed. Coupled with this, it allowed teams to leverage already present resources that circumvented the "another new initiative" feeling that often permeates education settings. When district leadership teams held a strong understanding of what an inclusive approach to MTSS looked like and the rationale for including these components, prioritizing and scaling an implementation plan became easier. For example, setting up teaming structures and communication pathways were identified in one district as needed before additional layers of capacity development were needed.

How Research Can Help

Although several voices shared awareness of the importance of identifying and arriving at a common understanding of the essential components of MTSS as an initial step in implementation, many did not or shared resistance they encountered when they pressed teams to take that step. A common question that arose was how to do this in the most effective but efficient manner so that it was not perceived as a step backward but, instead, a step toward continuous improvement of implementation efforts. Similarly, questions arose about how best to facilitate this process and then refine what is learned in a manner that does not reinforce the common response from educators that we are changing things again. In short, research that identified effective and efficient facilitative processes and soundbites that reinforced iterative reviews and refinements as a sign of responsiveness would be meaningful to all.

Supporting People

Implementing any practice has an impact not only on those who deliver the innovation but also across the broader system as it generalizes to those who support, advocate for, and deliver other initiatives. More specifically, people deliver practices, navigate systems to support those practices, and align and then allocate resources to facilitate the use of effective practices and initiatives (e.g., MTSS). To address these needs, attention must be directed at "how" competencies to use practices with fidelity are developed that are informed by a carefully sequenced plan for learning and leadership. All cannot be accomplished at one moment. Purposeful implementation also calls for careful sequencing and distribution of learning and efforts at engineering a system to support the continued use of practice with fidelity. As such, supporting people also takes purposefully and carefully sequenced development of skills and application of learnings.

It Takes Skills

Consistent attention must focus on developing the capacity for individuals to use practices as they were intended. Specifically, support is defined as developing and maintaining the knowledge, skills, and abilities or competence and confidence of individuals to use practices with fidelity. This premise is drawn from a body of work highlighting the need to develop a capacity to use practices (e.g., Fox et al., 2011; Horner & Sugai, 2000; Massar, 2017; Neufeld & Roper, 2003;) is articulated by Fixsen and colleagues' (2005) reference to implementation drivers. Most succinctly, implementation drivers operationalize mechanisms needed to develop and sustain individuals' competencies to support reliable use of practices (Blase et al., 2012, 2015; Fixsen et al., 2010, 2015; Metz & Bartley, 2012).

Developing competency of individuals includes a *selection* of individuals with required skills, abilities and other prerequisite characteristics who will use the practices, *training* to ensure individuals have the knowledge and skills related to the essential components of the practice, and on-the-job *coaching* and performance feedback that provide ongoing support for the use of the practices with fidelity. Critical here is that training is aligned with the needs of participants that can be prepared based on the identification of selection criteria. Training itself—even when embedded with hands-on learning and opportunities for error correction—is not enough to embed skills (Buston et al., 2002; Joyce & Showers, 2002; Putnam & Borko, 2000). Instead, training reflects the foundation upon which job-embedded coaching driven by data about observable use of essential components serves to refine practices used in authentic settings (Cusumano et al., 2018). Importantly, robust training and coaching are not enough as it neglects the contextual complexities that application of practices in real-world settings presents (Fuchs & Fuchs, 2017). Knowledge of organization drivers and leadership to navigate an always-changing landscape to support competency drivers is necessary.

Organizational drivers focus on developing mechanisms to navigate the local context and the greater system to facilitate and support the use of practice with fidelity (e.g., MTSS). For example, a data system (as captured in Decision Support Data System) can generate information at the individual, group, and system levels that, when integrated, describe the health and well-being of practices and processes in place. These data highlight needs and strengths and assist administrators in their work of supporting teachers and staff as they navigate local or site-based challenges (e.g., practices or policies) that hinder the use of effective practices (*Facilitative Leadership*). Similarly, it is necessary that practices or policies that enable the use of the practice to be recognized so that they can be reinforced and maintained. When challenges or enabling conditions are not within the control of the local context (e.g., administrators at a building), a bi-directional pathway along which these findings can be shared (for problem-solving or reinforcement) from one level to the next (e.g., building to district) must be created (*Systems Intervention*). Regardless of the level at which authority exists, for this to thrive, it will be necessary for individuals with effective skills at addressing adaptive and technical challenges to detour barriers or create the context to maintain positive practices and share outcomes of this work along the pathway of communication.

An additional characteristic of implementation drivers speaks to their integrated and compensatory nature. That is, less well-developed supports can be compensated for by more robust drivers. For example, if teachers selected to use data to align student needs with tiered instruction possess limited knowledge of data-based decision making, training and coaching will need to target these skills more intensively than if teachers with strongly related backgrounds are chosen. Overall, people need ongoing support to adopt and sustain their skills to use practices with fidelity and navigate effectively through challenges that may hinder the use of these practices.

Of crucial importance is that implementation drivers be seen as encompassing rather than restrictive in thinking. That is, how do we ensure that competency of staff using and supporting effective practices is developed with a lens that includes the use of these practices with all students. With that in mind, training and coaching must focus on reinforcing skills to meet all students' needs in an effective manner. As such, the fidelity with which practices are used must be closely monitored with an eye on divergence from standardization of practices. These deviations must not only be followed but also explored in their relation to impact on student outcomes.

Purposeful Development

Developing competencies, infrastructure, and support systems take time and awareness of the critical pathway for enabling change. Guidance for individuals supporting the work of implementing MTSS can be drawn from a stage-based process that highlights an activity-based and data-driven approach (Fixsen et al., 2010). Four dynamic and carefully sequenced stages are shared. *Exploration* is the first stage that represents the time where decisions about fit, timing, capacity, and commitment for a school or district to use a practice such as MTSS will be determined. To guide this decision, exploration focuses on identifying and planning what roles, structures, and functions would be needed and housed. When commitment to move forward is reached, transition to *Installation* stage activities where attention focuses on developing infrastructure that supports systemic change (e.g., Implementation Drivers) takes place. For example, essential components of the practice informed development of training and coaching plans, training is facilitated, and resources such as data systems are secured. The initial implementation, the next stage, represents a very fragile time where preliminary changes and probes into the system will occur when practices are infused into educators' interactions with students. It is during initial implementation when coaching systems are first put in place with high-density supports provided to the practices and systems that are designed to support their use. Constant communication and problem-solving are needed as a new practice is established in a previous operating system. When new practices or, for example, MTSS becomes "the way of work," the transition into *Full Implementation* (at least 50% of the practitioners meet fidelity standards for using MTSS) begins. Although linear in presentation, movement from one stage to the next in either direction is not unusual as, for example, challenges (e.g., staff turnover) emerge or new areas of need (new practices) arise. As noted in Fuchs and Fuchs's (2017) review of the national evaluation of Response to Intervention, many of the "impact schools" studied did not follow data decision rules to identify students in need of intervention support. In fact, their review identified that the majority of sites considered as in full implementation were missing the most rudimentary components of MTSS. For example, an essential practice of "test-teach-test" that uses data to identify, provide intensive instruction, and then monitor the impact on the learning of students at risk of failure was absent.

Feedback From the Field

A "train and pray" approach is now commonly understood as an inefficient means to develop skills and competencies to use practices with fidelity. What we have learned, however, is that many districts keep to this mode of professional development. That is, Professional Development days are often identified on district calendars with educators participating in one-stop learning sessions. Although some of these training now includes learning assessments and engagement activities, they often are designed as breaks from learning rather than to provide authentic interactions with content.

Finally, a new venue that has risen out of the COVID-19 era is a reliance on virtual learning. Although this new medium for training offers greater flexibility, particularly when asynchronous options are available, it carries with it a greater risk of disengagement and lower levels of performance feedback. With these thoughts in mind, current challenges and levers for capacity development were drawn from feedback from districts actively engaged in this work.

Challenges

Common trends again emerged across educators leading the work of developing knowledge, skills, and capacity to use inclusive practices of MTSS with fidelity—funding. Developing capacity requires financial resources to fund the training and coaching of staff. When done well, training could be provided in-house; however, it often required trainers themselves to be trained by outside experts, sending teams to training outside the district, and/or bringing in outside experts. Beyond the fees to register, attend, or pay outside consultants, funding to pay subs also had to be included. As research has documented, one-time training events in and of themselves are not effective in facilitating lasting change. Instead, frequent, purposefully distributed sessions that offer opportunities for practice and performance feedback are needed. Job embedded coaching following the acquisition of skills also must be tied to training. The need for coaching highlights the human resources and time allocation aspect as well, with districts needing individuals trained to provide coaching supports (often additional positions needed) and additional time needed to allow for coaching to take place.

An additional challenge was noted across two larger districts that carefully scaled implementation efforts. Regardless of whether building sites were chosen through carefully defined selection criteria or administration volunteering for participation in a stage cohort, inequities in how buildings were empowered to move from exploration to installation to initial implementation occurred. Side effects of this included dissonance and negative feelings associated with a perception of receiving lower levels of attention from district staff were noted.

What is Working

Receiving external funding as seed money was a critical piece projecting the work of implementing inclusive practices of MTSS with fidelity. Not only was the funding itself identified as a key activator for the work but also the accountability pieces tied to the receipt of the money. That is, timely reporting requirements, collection of indicators of progress, and additional resources included as part of the funding were frequently noted as the pivotal pieces that helped leaders maintain momentum in implementation efforts. As has become key points across the work of implementation of MTSS, highlighting and sharing with users the impact that practices have on student outcomes, focusing on identifying the critical aspects of the work that guide optimal findings, and using formative and summative data to drive ongoing improvement and efficiency are critical aspects to sustaining motivation to use effective practices (Andreou et al., 2015; McIntosh & Goodman, 2016).

An additional activity that fueled progress in implementation efforts was developing and consistently reviewing training and coaching plans. Developing a consistent approach to ask questions about effectiveness and efficiency and the ability to course correct when needed was identified as a significant contributor to district progress in securing capacity to use MTSS with fidelity. As has been a recurring theme, keeping learning and the mindset of continuous improvement in the forefront is of critical importance.

How Research Can Help

The greatest contribution that research could make to the field's work developing the capacity to adopt, scale, and sustain MTSS as an inclusive practice would be to identify the high leverage functions that are needed to support MTSS across all stages of implementation: What does it look like, how does it fit best, and what are the degrees of freedom or boundaries for best practices based on contextual factors? Entering implementation with the scope of critical factors identified could serve as guides to state, regional, and local education agencies to lay the foundation for future success or, if using funding to seed the work, set the foundation upon which effective practices can be scaled and sustained.

An additional line of research that would benefit exploration work would be to identify characteristics of scaling units (regions, districts, buildings) that hold the highest probability of serving as effective learning units or as first, second, and later cohorts. That is, what can leaders "look for" when identifying pathways for scaling implementation that hold the greatest potential for supporting inclusive practices? Another way to consider this question is to explore the functioning of the broad system and identify where change happens and who navigates and guides that change. *Is change driven by need at the local (school or district) level, by policy at the state level, or by funding through intermediate or regional entities that are situated between the state and local education (district) agencies?* When that level has been identified, the point for strategic training and capacity development is focused there, with upper agencies receiving knowledge and guidance in facilitating and supporting work at the point where change emanates. For example, state agencies may need primers in knowledge and awareness in how to support (and not hinder) change at the district level where effective practices are embedded in a cycle of ongoing competency development (training and coaching) and improvement (formative and summative planning and review of feasibility and impact).

A final and omnipresent challenge consistently shared across the field was attrition. The ongoing challenge of training and coaching individuals and teams to levels where they were proficient and functioning at high caliber only to have those individuals leave that position presents as a constant barrier to implementation. Developing capacity across the system rather than in only a handful of staff is one approach that has been successful. Identifying best practices to think proactively ahead of staff turnover is another much-needed area for attention.

Supporting Systems

Implementing any practice as intended that leads to desired outcomes requires focused attention not only on the users (e.g., educators) and recipients (e.g., students) but also on infrastructure to support its use. Infrastructure in the form of processes and procedures are not new to many in the field of education; however, what is often lacking is the focus on an iterative review of data that defines the health and well-being of practice in use. Multiple pieces are required to support this systemic view, including those who collect and use data collected, those who develop and refine systems (practice and procedures) to titrate use of the practice so that it achieves the highest levels of efficiency and impact, and those who provide feedback on how the context is responding to the implemented practice. Voids in any part of this cycle can hinder the use of practice and result in challenges to sustainability. This next section will look more closely at these pieces with an eye to the dynamic relation between context and practice. Readers are also directed to chapter 20 for more discussion on the systems in adopting, scaling, and sustaining effective practices such as MTSS.

Developing a Network

Dynamic and responsive systems should be driven by informed decisions made by an organized group of individuals. This group, often referred to as implementation or leadership teams, is accountable for navigating through successes and challenges of systemic change with an eye on empowering mechanisms that support and sustain positive change (Blase, 2010; Greenhalgh et al., 2004; Higgins et al., 2012). Within education, this team of three to five individuals often includes executive leaders and individuals with skills and knowledge about the context, best practices in implementation, decision-making authority, and hands-on experience with implementing effective practices in districts and/or schools. This team functions by using data to allocate resources for ongoing capacity development and problem-solving across the system. In use, teaming structures are most powerful when dispersed in a stepwise and interconnected relationship across the context (Blase, 2010). For example, strategic placement at the state, regional (if available), local (i.e., district), and building levels provides a network of cascading teaming structures across which information, data, and feedback can facilitate learning about contextual responses to change. In essence, the cascading system of implementation teams creates a symbiotic accountability structure across the entire education agency supporting sustainable use of practices in buildings and classrooms (Blase, 2010; Metz & Bartley 2012).

Learning from Doing

Teams are also responsible for being responsive to contextual needs and, as a result, must operate in continuous cycles of improvement. This iterative process requires ongoing data-driven analysis of facilitators and barriers examining usability, alignment with other initiatives, feasibility, and use of practices with fidelity (Bryk et al., 2015; Daniels & Sandler, 2008; Fixsen et al., 2005; Kubiak & Benbow, 2009; Reosekar & Pohekar, 2014; Sanders, 2009). Improvement science provides the backbone to accomplish this task using data that highlights demands of the system and practices as stage-based work in implementation continues.

A common element across improvement science is the PDSA cycle (see Figure 6.2). Specifically, a PDSA cycle is a "complex intervention made up of series of interdependent steps and key principles that inform its application" (Taylor et al., 2014; p. 291). The PLAN phase identifies possible barriers or challenges to efficiency and feasibility. The DO phase uses the "planned" process and collects answers (data) to questions developed in planning. The STUDY phase analyzes data about processes and outcomes. The ACT phase applies learning to improve processes and outcomes. Finally, CYCLE reflects ongoing processing through PDSA phases until learning diminishes and outcomes are attained at sustainable levels across all contexts and settings. Not surprisingly, PDSA cycles are used widely across human services, including education (Cohen-Vogel et al., 2015; Daniels & Sandler, 2008; Varkey et al., 2007) as they learn about expected and unexpected changes

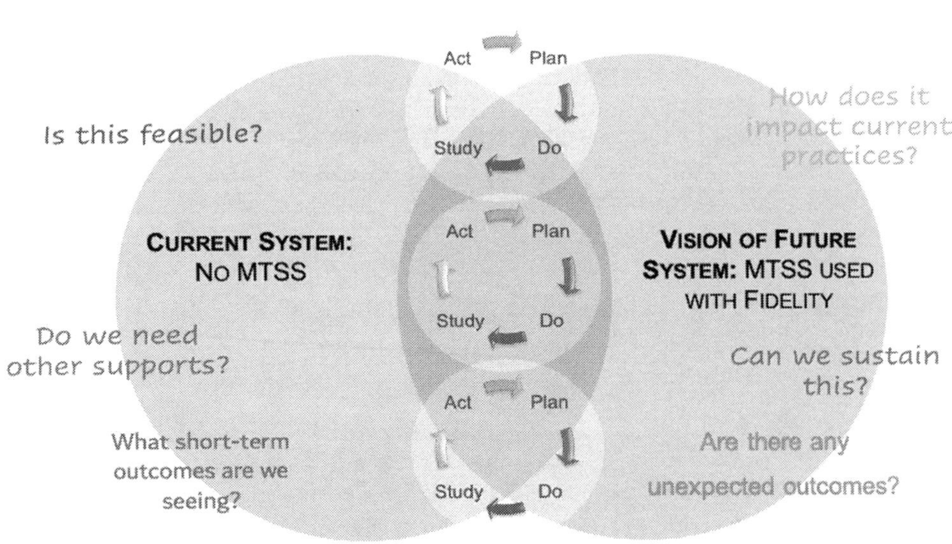

Figure 6.2 Iterative cycles of learning

that result from new practices being put in place as they transition from their current to ideal vision of the future (Bolt, 2005; Griffiths et al., 2007; Vaughn & Fuchs, 2003).

Feedback from the Field

The use of an improvement mindset has highlighted the idea of plasticity in practice and acknowledges the importance of understanding the role that context plays in supporting or hindering the full and effective use of practices such as MTSS. That is, as is noted by Blase et al. (2015), the implementation that leads to optimal outcomes requires careful attention to the characteristics of the context in which the practices will be used with respect to those that may enable (strong support for purposeful planning and use to data to guide implementation) or hinder (an atmosphere that does not have leadership support for change) use of practices. This next section looks at features of the improvement mindset that challenge and support systems level work.

Challenges

A frequent challenge shared reflected the use of data outside the building level. On the positive side, great support and emerging strong skillsets for using data to inform decisions and guide planning is taking hold in school-based teams. Beyond that, however, initial push back or resistance to using data to explore functioning and capacity development at the district, regional, and state levels is often encountered. Often this barrier is due to a lack of knowledge about the measures available and how they fit into a continuous improvement and action planning model.

What is Working

Structuring teams based on the functions they serve emerged as a key strategy that increased efficiency not only in meeting the needs of the system but also in developing fluency in skills and practices. As shared by one district, when responsibilities were clearly defined, not duplicated across teams, and linked by bi-directional communication pathways, collaboration became more efficient and powerful than when grouped as one entity. Notably, a consistent and open flow of communication, including data, decisions, and feedback, is needed across all teaming structures, including the School Improvement Team, for example. Also of importance is the understanding and acceptance that ownership of the system and student enhancement goals was central to all teaming structures.

How Research Can Help

Identifying and providing models for how data are used to guide action planning within a continuous improvement model would benefit the field. Examples of questions to consider, how data could be used to identify facilitators and barriers to implementation, and high leverage responses would serve as strong mediators for the field to consider. As such next steps include examining fidelity of both general (implementation) and specific (inclusive MTSS) practices. In practice, when teams are offered strong models for decision-making, their attention can be directed at moving forward. Research that focused on refining key characteristics, processes, and procedures for continuous improvement of inclusive practices for MTSS is in high demand.

Make it Happen

A key learning from the field is that improvement must be seen as a dynamic process rather than a one-and-done approach. More specifically, the endeavor such as the implementation of MTSS must be undertaken with an eye on continuous regeneration and improvement as the system responds to new practices, new skills, and new ways of work. Although guided by prior learning and best practices, one cannot know how each system will respond to change. Adoption of a new data system to monitor students' progress in response to changes in instruction offers new sources of data for teams to review, for example; however, this also adds an additional data source to a student information system, a new task on an educator's plate, and a new—albeit brief—pull away from students' engagement with learning content. Although these data, when collected with fidelity—make instruction more effective, it also adds a new component to the system. As such, this data collection practice and its interaction with the current context must be followed and studied to ensure that the capacity required to collect and interpret data are adequate.

From another perspective, accountability and leadership to weather the growing pains of implementation of systemic practices such as MTSS are critical. That is leadership that facilitates an ongoing growth mindset that pauses for redesign when data indicate as needed is pivotal to sustaining MTSS, particularly during challenging times such as funding cuts, re-organization, turnover, etc. Instant success is not promised and should not be expected. Instead, awareness that the first steps include changes at the adult level (infrastructure development, fidelity of practice) must happen well before changes at the student level can be seen. Leadership with purpose, patience, and an eye on data are fundamental to the full and effective use of MTSS.

Final Thoughts

We define full implementation as "50% of practitioners meeting fidelity of MTSS." It is at this tipping point that MTSS becomes the "norm," the "way of work," or "how we support students in this school." This same concept applies to MTSS as a framework for other initiatives (e.g., academics, behavior, SEL, counseling, inclusion of students with disabilities). The chasm between the first step in the direction of an MTSS framework and improved student outcomes shrinks with each new addition. As 50% of practitioners meet the fidelity of MTSS in academics, the rest of the school adopts MTSS as its new way of work. In practice, new teachers now learn about MTSS practices and expectations during orientation, teachers embed improvement cycles in MTSS begin embedding improvement cycles to their own classroom lessons or staff professional development sessions, and staff begins asking, "how will we measure that" when considering school improvement goals.

As MTSS teams work to include all students' needs or address behavior or inclusion of students with disabilities, the work of implementation becomes "easier." As new initiatives arise, teaming infrastructure and procedures for decision making and feedback loops coupled with a focus on continuous improvement exist to support the full and effective use of the practice or new way of work (e.g., MTSS). Change (though still difficult) is infused as "what is possible" rather than "what is forced." With this underpinning, each new initiative takes a little less effort and time because infrastructure is in place, alignment a goal and efforts to leverage current resources as a unified effort to meet the needs of all students emerge. Of most importance, the target of improving outcomes for all students never waivers. The outcome—optimizing educational resources and contexts for student success.

References

Andreou, T.E., McIntosh, K., Ross, S. RtI., & Kahn, J. D. (2015). Critical incidents in the sustainability of school-wide positive behavioral interventions and supports. *Journal of Special Education*, 49, 157–167.

Arden, S. V., Gandhi, A. G., Edmonds, R. Z., & Danielson, L. (2017). Toward more effective tiered systems: Lessons from national implementation efforts. *Exceptional Children*, 83, 269–280. doi:1177/0014402917693565

Averill, O., RtI., & Rinaldi, C. (2011). *Research brief: Multi-Tier System of Support (MTSS).* Urban Special Education Leadership Collaborative.

Balu, R., Zhu, P., Doolittle, F., Schiller, E., Jenkins, J., Gersten, R. (2015). Evaluation of response to intervention practices for elementary school reading. Retrieved from http://ies.ed.gov/ncee/pubs/20164000/pdf/20164000.pdf

Batsche, G., Elliott, J., Graden, J., Grimes, J., Kovaleski, J., Prasse, D., et al. (2005). *Response to intervention: Policy considerations and implementation.* National Association of State Directors of Special Education.

Bianco, M. (2010). Strength-based RTI: Conceptualizing a multitiered system for developing gifted potential, *Theory Into Practice*, 49(4), 323–330. doi:10.1080/00405841.2010.510763

Blase, K. (2010). *Cascading logic model.* National Implementation Research Network.

Blase, K. A., & Fixsen, D. L. (February 2013). *Core intervention components: Identifying and operationalizing what makes programs work.* (ASPE Research Brief). https://aspe.hhs.gov/report/core-intervention-components-identifying-and-operationalizing-what-makes-programs-work

Blase, K. A., Fixsen, D. L., Sims, B. J., & Ward, C. S. (2015). *Implementation science: Changing hearts, minds, behavior, and systems to improve educational outcomes.* The Wing Institute.

Blase, K., Van Dyke, M., Fixsen, D., & Wallace Bailey, F., (2012). Implementation science: Key concepts, themes, and evidence for practitioners in educational psychology. In B. Kelly & D. Perkins (Eds.), *Handbook of implementation science for psychology in education* (pp.13–34). Cambridge University Press.

Bohanon, RtI., Gilman, C., Parker, B., Amell, C., & Sortino, G. (2016). Using school improvement and implementation science to integrate multi-tiered systems of support in secondary schools. *Australasian Journal of Special Education*, 40, 99–116. doi:1017/jse.2016.8

Bolt, S. E. (2005). Reflections on practice within the Heartland problem-solving model: The perceived value of direct assessment of students. *The California School Psychologist*, 10, 65–79.

Bradley, R., & Danielson, L. (2004). The office of special education program's LD initiative: A context for inquiry and consensus. *Learning Disability Quarterly*, 27(4), 186–188. doi:2307/1593671

Bradley, R., Danielson, L., & Hallahan, D. P. (2002). *Identification of learning disabilities: Research to practice.* Erlbaum.

Bryk, A. S., Gomez, L. M., Grunow, A., & LeMahieu, P. (2015). *Learning to improve: How America's schools can get better at getting better.* Harvard Education Press.

Buston, K., Wight, D., Hart, G. & Scott, S. (2002). Implementation of a teacher-delivered sex education programme: Obstacles and facilitating factors. *Health Education Research*, 17, (1), 59–72. doi:1093/her/17.1.59

Coggins, C., Stoddard, P., & Cutler, E. (2003). *Improving instructional capacity through field-based reform coaches.* Paper presented at the American Educational Research Association annual meeting, Chicago.

Cohen-Vogel, L., Tichnor-Wagner, A., Allen, D., Harrison, C., Kainz, K., Rose Socol, A., & Xing, Q. (2015). Implementing educational innovations at scale: Remaking researchers into improvement scientists. *Educational Policy*, 29 (1), 257–277.

Collaborative for Academic, Social, and Emotional Learning CASEL. (n.d.). *Multitiered systems of support.* https://casel.org/sp_faq/multitiered-systems-of-support/

Crosse, S., Williams, B., Harmon, H. Liam, M., Liam, R., DiGaetano, R., Broene, P., Alexander, D., Tseng, M., & Derzon, J. (2011). Prevalence and Implementation Fidelity of Research-Based Prevention Programs in Public Schools: Final Report. U.S. Department of Education Office of Planning, Evaluation and Policy Development Policy and Program Studies Service. Rockville.

Cusumano, D.L., Preston, A.I., & Ward, C. (2018). Coaching for Competence and Confidence. *Global Implementation Society*, 1(1). https://globalimplementation.org/app/uploads/2018/03/Coaching-for-Competence-and-Confidence-V9.pdf

Daniels, V. S., & Sandler, I. (2008). Use of quality management methods in the transition from efficacious prevention programs to effective prevention services. *American Journal of Community Psychology*, 41(3-4), 250–261. doi:1007/s10464-008-9170-3

Fixsen, D. L., Blase, K. A., Duda, M. A., Naoom, S. F., & Van Dyke, M. (2010). Sustainability of evidence-based programs in education. *Journal of Evidence-Based Practices*, 11(1), 30–46.

Fixsen, D., Blase, K., Metz, A., & Van Dyke, M., (2015). Implementation science. In J. D. Wright (editor-in-chief), *International encyclopedia of the social & behavioral sciences* (2nd ed., Vol. 11). Oxford: Elsevier. pp. 695–702.

Fixsen, D., Blase, K., Metz, A., & Van Dyke, M., (2013). Statewide implementation of evidence-based programs. *Exceptional Children,* 79(2), 213–230 (Special Issue).

Fixsen, D. L., Naoom, S. F., Blase, K. A., Friedman, R. M., & Wallace, F. (2005). *Implementation research: A synthesis of the literature.* University of South Florida, Louis de la Parte Florida Mental Health Institute, National Implementation Research Network. nirn.fmhi.usf.edu/resources/publications/Monograph/index.cfm

Fletcher, J. M., Shaywitz, S. E., Shankweiler, D. P., Katz, L., Liberman, I. RtI., Stuebing, K. K., Francis, D. J., Fowler, A. E., & Shaywitz, B. A. (1994). Cognitive profiles of reading disability: Comparisons of discrepancy and low achievement definitions. *Journal of Educational Psychology*, 86, 6–23. doi:1037/0022-0663.86.1.6

Fox, L., Hemmeter, M. L., Snyder, P. S., Binder, D. P., & Clarke, S. (2011). Coaching early childhood special educators to implement a comprehensive model for promoting young children's social competence. *Topics in Early Childhood Special Education*, 31, 178–192.

Fuchs, D., & Fuchs, L. S. (2017). Critique of the national evaluation of Response to Intervention: A case for simpler frameworks. *Exceptional Children*, 83, 255–268. doi:1177/0014402917693580

Gersten, R., Compton, D., Connor, C. M., Dimino, J., Santoro, L., Linan-Thompson, S., & Tilly, RtI. D. (2008). *Assisting students struggling with reading: Response to Intervention and multi-tier intervention for reading in the primary grades. A practice guide.* (NCEE 2009-4045). National Center for Education Evaluation and Regional Assistance, Institute of Education Sciences, U.S. Department of Education. Retrieved from https://ies.ed.gov/ncee/wwc/Docs/PracticeGuide/rti_reading_pg_021809.pdf.

Greenhalgh, T., Robert, G., Macfarlane, F., Bate, P., & Kyriakidou, O. (2004) Diffusion of innovations in service organizations: Systematic review and recommendations. *Milbank Quarterly*, 82, 581–629.

Griffiths, A. J., Parson, L. B., Burns, M. K., VanDerHeyden, A., & Tilly, RtI. D. (2007). *Response to intervention: Research for practice*. National Association of State Directors of Special Education.

Higgins, M. C., Weiner, J., & Young, L. (2012). Implementation teams: A new lever for organizational change. *Journal of Organizational Behavior*, 33, 366–388.

Horner, R., & Sugai, G. (2000). School-wide behavior support: An emerging initiative. *Journal of Positive Behavior Interventions*, 2(4), 231–232.

Hosp, J. L., & Reschly, D. J. (2004). Disproportionate representation of minority students in special education: Academic, demographic, and economic predictors. *Exceptional Children*, 70(2), 185–199. doi:4324/9781315231839-13

Hughes, C. E., & Rollins, K. (2009). RtI for nuturing giftedness: Implications for the RtI school-based team. *Gifted Child Today*, 32(3), 31–39.

Individuals with Disabilities Education Act, 20 U.S.C. § 1400 (2004).

Joyce, B. R., & Showers, B. (2002). *Student achievement through staff development* (3rd ed.). Association for Supervision & Curriculum Development (ASCD).

Kubiak, T. M. & Benbow, D. RtI. (2009). *The certified six sigma black belt handbook* (2nd ed.) ASQ Quality Press.

Lane, K. L., Carter, E. RtI., Jenkins, A., Dwiggins, L., & Germer, K. (2015). Supporting comprehensive, integrated, three-tiered models of prevention in schools: Administrators' perspectives. *Journal of Positive Behavior Interventions*, 17(4), 209–222. doi:1177/1098300715578916

Massar, M. M. (2017). *Effects of coach-delivered prompting and performance feedback on teacher use of evidence-based classroom management practices and student behavior outcomes* (Unpublished doctoral dissertation). University of Oregon.

McIntosh, K., & Goodman, S. (2016). *Integrated multi-tiered systems of support.* Guilford Press.

Metz, A., & Bartley, L. (2012). Active Implementation Frameworks for program success: How to use implementation science to improve outcomes for children. *Zero to Three Journal*, 32(4), 11–18.

Metz, A., & Bartley, L. (2017). Co-creating the conditions to sustain the use of research evidence in public child welfare. *Child Welfare*, 94(2), 115–139.

Michie, S., Fixsen, D., Grimshaw, J. M., & Eccles, M. P. (2009). Specifying and reporting complex behaviour change interventions: The need for a scientific method. *Implementation Science*, 4, 40. doi:1186/1748-5908-4-40

Muscott, RtI. S., Mann, E. L., & LeBrun, M. R. (2008). Positive behavioral interventions and supports in New Hampshire: Effects of large-scale implementation of schoolwide positive behavior support on student discipline and academic achievement. *Journal of Positive Behavior Interventions*, 10(3), 190–205. doi:1177/1098300708316258

National Association of School Psychologists. (2009). *Appropriate academic supports to meet the needs of all students.* [Position Statement]. Author.

National Center for Education Statistics.. (2019). *Digest of education statistics.* https://nces.ed.gov/programs/digest/d19/tables/dt19_204.30.asp

National Center on Response to Intervention. (March 2010). *Essential components of RTI—A closer look at response to intervention.* U.S. Department of Education, Office of Special Education Programs, National Center on Response to Intervention.

Neufeld, B., & Roper, D. (2003). *Coaching: A strategy for developing instructional capacity.* Annenberg Institute for School Reform.

No Child Left Behind (NCLB) Act of 2001, Pub. L. No. 107-110, § 101, Stat. 1425 (2002).

O'Connor, R. E., Bocian, K. M., Beach, K. D., Sanchez, V., & Flynn, L. J. (2013). Special education in a 4-year response to intervention (RtI) environment: Characteristics of students with learning disability and grade of identification. *Learning Disabilities Research & Practice*. 28, 98–112.

Positive Behavioral Interventions & Supports. (n.d.). *About the TA center*. https://RtI.pbis.org/about/about

Positive Behavioral Interventions & Supports. (n.d.). *Getting started*. https://RtI.pbis.org/pbis/getting-started

Preston, A. I., Wood, C. L., & Stecker, P. M. (2016). Response to intervention: Where it came from and where it's going. *Preventing School Failure*, 60(3), 173–182. doi:1080/1045988X.2015.1065399

Putnam, R. T. & Borko, RtI. (2000). What do new views of knowledge and thinking have to say about research learning? *American Educational Research Association*, 29, 4–15.

Reosekar, R. S., & Pohekar, S. D. (2014). Six Sigma methodology: A structured review. *International Journal of Lean Six Sigma, 5*(4), 392–422, doi:1108/IJLSS-12-2013-0059.

Sanders, M. (2009). Collaborating for change: How an urban school district and a community-based organization support and sustain school, family, and community partnerships. *Teachers College Record*, 111(7), 1693–1712.

Schulte, A. C. (2016) Prevention and response to intervention: Past, present, and future. In S. R. Jimerson, M. K. Burns, & A. M. Vanderhayden (Eds.), *Handbook of response to intervention: The science and practice of multi-tiered systems of support* (2nd ed., pp. 59–71), Springer.

Sugai, G., & Horner, R. RtI. (2009). Responsiveness-to-intervention and school-wide positive behavior supports: Integration of multi-tiered system approaches. *Exceptionality*, 17(4), 223–237. doi:1080/0936283 0903235375

Taylor, M. J., McNicholas, C., Nicolay, C., Darzi, A., Bel, D., & Reed, J. E. (2014). Systematic review of the application of the plan-do-study-act method to improve quality in healthcare. *British Medical Journal of Quality and Safety*, 23, 290–298.

Thurlow, M. L., Ghere, G., Lazarus, S. S., & Liu, K. K. (2020, January). *MTSS for all: Including students with the most significant cognitive disabilities*. University of Minnesota, National Center on Educational Outcomes/ TIES Center.

Torgesen, J. K., Alexander, A., Wagner, R., Rashotte, G., Voeller, K.,& Gonway, T. (2001). Intensive remedial instruction for children with severe reading disabilities: Immediate and long-term outcomes from two instructional approaches. *Journal of Learning Disabilities*, 34, 33–58.

Utley, C. A. & Obiakor, F. E. (2012). Response to intervention and positive behavior interventions and supports: Merging models to improve academic and behavioral outcomes of culturally and linguistically diverse children with learning disabilities. *Insights on Learning Disabilities*, 9, 37–67.

VanDerHeyden, A. M., Witt, J. C., & Gilbertson, D. (2007). A multi-year evaluation of the effects of a Response to intervention (RTI) model on identification of children for special education. *Journal of School Psychology*, 45, 225–256.

Varkey, P., Reller, M. K., & Resar, R. K. (2007). Basics of quality improvement in health care, *Mayo Clinic Proceedings*, 82, 735–739.

Vaughn, S., & Fuchs, L. S. (2003). Redefining learning disabilities as inadequate response to instruction: The promise and potential problems. *Learning Disabilities Research & Practice*, 18, 137–146.

Vellutino, F. R., Sganlon, D. M., Sipay, E. R., Small, S., Ghen, R., Pratt, A., & Dengkla, M. B. (1996). Cognitive profiles of difficult-to-remediate and readily remediated poor readers: Early intervention as a vehicle for distinguishing between cognitive and experiential deficits as basic causes of specific reading disability. *Journal of Educational Psychology*, 88, 601–638.

Von Ravensberg, H., & Blakely, A. (2017). *Guidance for states on ESSA state plans: Aligning the school climate indicator and SW-PBIS*. U.S. Department of Education, Office of Special Education Programs Technical Assistance Center on Positive Behavioral Interventions and Supports, www.pbis.org

Ysseldyke, J. E., Algozzine, B., & Epps, S. (1983). A logical and empirical analysis of current practices in classifying students as learning disabled. *Exceptional Children*, 50, 160–166.

7

Supporting Inclusive Practices With Positive Behavioral Interventions and Supports

Brandi Simonsen[1] *and Heather Peshak George*[2]

[1]UNIVERSITY OF CONNECTICUT

[2]UNIVERSITY OF SOUTH FLORIDA

Setting the Stage

Schools and educators face a progressively complex landscape that includes diverse student needs and abilities, continued pressures for accountability to ensure "every student succeeds," and unrelenting social, environmental, and most recently, public health challenges. Specifically, approximately 20% of the school-age population currently experiences a mental, emotional, social, or behavioral disorder with a majority of conditions emerging during the early years of learning (e.g., median age of onset age 6 for anxiety, 11 for behavior disorder, 13 for mood, and 15 for substance abuse disorders; Merikangas et al., 2010). Yet less than 1% of all students receive support for an Emotional or Behavioral Disorder (EBD; U.S. Department of Education, 2019).

Children and adolescents with EBD are at greatest risk for a multitude of increasingly negative outcomes (Bradley et al., 2008), and educators consistently state student problemand social behavior success (Algozzine behavior as one of their top concerns (Gable et al., 2012). Problem behavior interferes with instruction and learning, with suspensions and expulsions occurring as early as preschool (Gilliam & Shabar, 2006). Both administrators and teachers report school discipline as one of the greatest demands on their time (Miller-Richter et al., 2012) and a major factor affecting their decision to leave education (Smith & Ingersoll, 2004).

Despite these persistent difficulties, ensuring school safety and establishing a positive and productive educational environment remains critically important for students to achieve maximum benefit from the learning experience. Inclusive schools need a comprehensive, data-driven framework to organize supports for educators and students that maximizes the social, emotional, behavioral, and academic outcomes for all. Positive Behavioral Interventions and Supports (PBIS) is focused on these important outcomes of students, invests in the adoption of evidence-based practices matched to student needs across a continuum of supports, commits to data-based problem-solving to guide instruction, and provides a multi-tiered framework organizing support to educators and families through high-quality implementation (Sugai et al., 2000).

DOI: 10.4324/9781003043874-7

More than 29,000 schools across the United States implement PBIS, and educational leaders have established efforts to support PBIS in 35 countries worldwide (Center for PBIS, 2020). The immense and growing interest in PBIS may be due, in part, to the work of the National Center on PBIS that has sustained continuous funding since 1998 (Center on PBIS, 2020). Over two decades of research and resources have significantly expanded the field from a set of intervention practices and organizational systems to a clearly defined multi-tiered system of supports (MTSS) that articulates core features essential within and across whole school settings to realize positive student outcomes. In this chapter, we present a rationale for and describe critical features of PBIS, highlight empirical support, and provide practical suggestions for establishing positive school-wide and classroom cultures to maximize the impact of effective academic and behavior instruction for all students across all settings.

Why PBIS?

Safety and connection to the school environment can be attributed to dynamic teaching, relationship building, and positive social behavior (Goodman & George, 2020). PBIS enables schools to (a) create positive, predictable, and safe school environments and (b) improve the quality of life for students, families, and educators. In this section, we describe the logic of PBIS and explore the (a) relationship between academic and social-emotional-behavioral success, (b) limitations of traditional volatile approaches to school discipline and behavior management that are often reactive and consequence-based, (c) characteristics and features of a positive, proactive and thus, preventive approach to school-wide discipline and classroom management, and (d) application of multi-tiered support systems.

Relationship Between Academic and Behavioral Success

Most educators agree that good behavior and classroom management enhance good academic teaching and learning and vice versa (Algozzine et al., 2011). However, in practice, behavior management too often tends to be informal, reactive and provided on an "as-needed" basis. While academic instruction is scheduled, direct, and formalized, social skills instruction is provided for only a few students and only after documented social failures. In PBIS, the importance of teaching, monitoring, and recognizing social behavior has equal priority as teaching reading, math, science, a foreign language, or any other academic subject.

The association between academic and social behavior success is well documented. Good teaching promotes good student behavior, and good classroom management enhances student academic engagement. However, care is needed to understand the complexity of this relationship, and "causality" should not be inferred. Teaching students to read or compute math problems, for example, does not teach them how to behave more appropriately. Similarly, teaching social skills does not teach students how to read or do math. Yet, a growing body of evidence supports a strong association between academic and social behavior success (Algozzine et al., 2011, 2012; McIntosh et al., 2006, 2008; Wang & Algozzine, 2011). Students who experience preventive behavior support (social skills instruction) are more likely to be comfortable in school, academically engaged, and benefit from academic instruction. Similarly, by experiencing academic success, students are more likely to learn and display appropriate social behaviors.

Algozzine et al. (2011, p. 13) described this mutually supportive relationship between academic and social behavior success as follows:

> Viewed as outcomes, achievement and behavior are related; viewed as causes of each other, achievement and behavior are unrelated. In this context, teaching behavior as relentlessly as we

teach reading or other academic content is the ultimate act of prevention, promise, and power underlying PBS and other preventive interventions in America's schools.

The goal of PBIS is to establish positive classroom and school-wide social cultures that maximize the impact of effective academic instruction for all students across all classroom and school settings. As such, PBIS formally and directly emphasizes the teaching of individual, classroom, and school-wide behavior expectations and skills to all students across all school contexts by all school staff members. This PBIS rationale shapes the inclusive school perspective in conjunction with the academic mission.

Limitations of Other Approaches

Nearly all schools are required to have disciplinary policies and handbooks that define minor and major rule violations (e.g., disruptions, noncompliance, inappropriate language, physical fighting) and delineate assigned consequences (e.g., verbal reprimands, in-school detention, out-of-school suspensions) with the intent to "punish" occurrences and inhibit future violations. If student behavior is extreme, expulsion may be recommended. These approaches have become the primary tools in the educators' disciplinary toolbox. Some students respond to these approaches because they have the experience and skills to anticipate the potential consequences (inhibiting). In some cases, one experience of the consequence may be enough to stop future displays of the problem behavior.

Most professionals agree that this reactive ("wait to fail" or "respond after a problem") approach has limitations. First, the behavior of a proportion of the school population is not responsive to traditional discipline systems. Instead of exploring alternatives, schools typically deliver more frequent or intense versions of the same punitive disciplinary consequences to try to "punish harder." The result is students with high numbers of office discipline referrals, suspensions, and exclusionary consequences who continue to engage in rule-violating behavior. Second, when schools rely on reactive, consequence-oriented practices, they create a negative school climate, which can encourage lower behavioral expectations, higher rates of problem behavior, and more pessimistic teacher perceptions (Mitchell & Bradshaw, 2013). Third, when adults have high rates of reactive and aversive interactions with students, the quality of student—adult relationships is lessened. Fourth, relying on reactive systems results in less attention on preventive approaches, in which students are taught or re-taught what to do and recognized for what they do correctly. Finally, the more time students spend within the disciplinary system, the less time they have access to and are engaged in successful academic activities. In contrast, PBIS strives to promote high rates of preventive and positive interactions between students such that positive relationships are established, the impact of corrective procedures is increased, and the academic mission of the school is supported.

Shifting Focus to Positive, Preventative, and Proactive Support

PBIS provides a framework for shifting emphasis from a reactive to proactive approach to school discipline and classroom management. Generally, "proactive" refers to practices that are positive and preventive—that is, catching students before they display problem behavior by recognizing what they are doing appropriately. PBIS adopts the definitions and characteristics of prevention science that originated from the early public health and disease control communities (Biglan, 1995; Caplan, 1964; Lewis & Sugai, 1999; Mayer, 1995; Sugai & Horner, 2008, 2002; Walker et al., 1996). Preventative practices and systems are intended to accomplish two important objectives: (a) reduce the occurrence of new cases of a problem (incidence) and (b) reduce the frequency, intensity, and complexity of existing problems (prevalence).

PBIS employs a behavior analytic perspective that focuses on four actions. First, staff members teach social skills to high levels of accuracy and fluency, emphasize multiple examples, provide opportunities to practice, and provide feedback across the many contexts in which these skills are required for academic and social success. Second, staff members explicitly teach all students the same prosocial behavior expectations, such that students are more likely to expect, prompt, and recognize expected social behavior from each other. Third, staff members arrange teaching and learning environments to remove triggers for problem behavior and add prompts for prosocial behaviors (antecedent manipulations). Finally, staff members remove activities that maintain problem behavior and add activities that promote prosocial behavior.

What is PBIS?

PBIS is a multi-tiered prevention framework grounded in the principles and practices of behavioral (Cooper et al., 2020; Skinner, 1953), prevention (Biglan, 1995, 2015), and implementation (Fixsen et al., 2005) sciences. This section defines PBIS and its critical features.

Multi-Tiered Prevention Framework

Based on decades of research in public health (Caplan, 1964), multi-tiered prevention frameworks emphasize a continuum of preventative supports designed to reduce and mitigate risk. Typically, this continuum is operationalized in three tiers of prevention: primary, secondary, and tertiary.

1. **Tier 1: Primary prevention.** All members of a population receive universal intervention to reduce the likelihood of individuals developing challenges. For example, universal handwashing and annual vaccination are universal interventions to decrease the number of people who contract influenza.
2. **Tier 2: Secondary prevention.** Individuals who are at elevated risk or beginning to experience challenges receive targeted intervention to prevent developing and worsening of challenges. For example, individuals over 65 may receive high-dose vaccines, and individuals exposed to influenza may receive anti-viral medications to prevent complications.
3. **Tier 3: Tertiary prevention.** Individuals at high risk or already experiencing chronic or significant challenges receive intensive intervention to reduce severity and impact. For example, individuals experiencing complications from influenza may receive more intensive and/or individualized medical interventions.

In recent decades, educators have adopted prevention frameworks to organize social, emotional, behavioral, and academic supports into multiple tiers of intervention (Walker et al., 1996). Like other multi-tiered systems of supports (MTSS) frameworks (see Chapter 6), PBIS emphasizes systems of evidence-based and culturally-responsive practices that are adapted and aligned with students' needs and responsiveness-to-intervention (Bradley et al., 2002, 2007; Fairbanks et al., 2007; Sugai & Horner, 2002, 2009). The MTSS approach is reflected in PBIS through seven key implementation principles.

1. **Emphasize cultural relevance and equity.** Educators consider cultural relevance when making instructional and intervention decisions. PBIS schools strive to collect and monitor culturally valid data, implement culturally relevant evidence-based practices, and invest in culturally knowledgeable systems to promote culturally equitable student outcomes.
2. **Universally screen.** In PBIS schools, educators screen students for social, emotional, behavioral, and/or academic risk and strengths. Educators may administer standardized or locally

developed screening procedures on a monthly, quarterly, or semesterly basis to identify students who might require additional supports to benefit from core academic instruction and school-wide positive behavior support practices.

3. **Monitor progress.** Educators monitor fidelity and outcome data to assess implementation outcomes and identify necessary adjustments in implementation. For example, educators may administer daily, weekly, or monthly curriculum-based academic and/or social behavior measures to assess student benefit and responsiveness to a lesson or intervention (e.g., quiz, rating scale, probe).
4. **Implement evidence-based and culturally responsive practices with fidelity.** Schools implementing PBIS select, implement, monitor, adjust, and enhance the implementation of evidence-based and culturally responsive practices. Thus, in addition to monitoring student responsiveness to interventions, PBIS schools formally examine the accuracy and fluency of the intervention implementation.
5. **Organize a continuum of practices.** PBIS schools invest in the smallest number of evidence-based and culturally responsive practices that can be integrated into a continuum or tiered system. This continuum is based on the three-tiered public health prevention logic in which (a) Tier 1 provides universal support for all students and staff across all settings, (b) Tier 2 delivers more targeted support for students whose behaviors are unresponsive to Tier 1 practices, and (c) Tier 3 specifies intensive support for students whose behaviors are unresponsive to Tier 1 and 2 practices.
6. **Use data-based decision making.** In PBIS schools, educators use data to make instructional and intervention decisions, including whether (a) goals and outcomes are relevant, equitable, and challenging; (b) practices are evidence-based, culturally relevant, aligned with goals and outcomes, and implemented with fidelity; (c) students are responding to practices or require additional support to be successful; and (d) systems are in place to maximize implementation fidelity and relevance.
7. **Engage in team-based problem-solving.** In PBIS schools, representative leadership teams review data, identify implementation challenges or elevated needs, precisely document the identified challenges, and develop an action plan to improve implementation and outcomes. Thus, leadership team members have the capacity and opportunity to guide the implementation of the PBIS framework.

Critical Features of PBIS

Schools implementing PBIS center their work in equity, identify locally meaningful outcomes, collect and use data to drive decisions, implement evidence-based and culturally relevant practices, and invest in systems to support sustained high-fidelity, equitable implementation. Together, these four critical features (outcomes, data, practices, and systems), centered in equity, operationally define the PBIS framework.

Outcomes

School leadership teams determine the outcomes they plan to achieve through the implementation of PBIS (e.g., decreased rates of office referrals or suspensions, increased percentage of students meeting or exceeding benchmarks on state-wide tests, decreased disproportionately in disciplinary consequences) based on available school data and identified need. PBIS schools strive to ensure outcomes are relevant to all (equitable), written objectively (observable), and based on data (measurable). Then, schools (a) use data to monitor progress toward outcomes, (b) install and implement practices that align with selected outcomes, and (c) invest in systems to support educators in implementing practices with fidelity to maximize the likelihood of achieving outcomes for all students.

Data

As a prevention framework, PBIS emphasizes the importance of data in establishing outcomes; selecting, monitoring, and adjusting practice implementation; ensuring equitable access and benefit; and monitoring systems fidelity and capacity to support sustainability and scalability. Thus, PBIS schools collect relevant data, use data to drive decisions, focus on implementation fidelity, and communicate data.

Collect Relevant Student Data

In PBIS schools, educators collect data on (a) students' social, emotional, behavioral, academic, and other relevant outcomes and (b) implementation fidelity of key practices and systems. For example, schools may collect data to screen using a universal social, emotional, or behavioral screener (see Lane et al., 2020), or schools may use an informal process to review extant data (e.g., attendance, behavioral referrals, grades, nurse visits, credits earned in secondary schools) and/or teacher nominations to identify students who may benefit from additional support. Schools may also use similar formal or informal data sources to monitor progress throughout the year. In addition to identifying and collecting relevant data, it is critical that schools invest in routines that enable them to use data to inform decisions effectively.

Focus on Implementation Fidelity

Fidelity is an essential system requirement of PBIS. Implementation fidelity refers to the accuracy and fluency with which educators implement PBIS practices and systems. School leadership teams may assess fidelity in several ways. First, PBIS school leadership teams develop action plans to guide implementation, and they may use action plans to self-monitor features of their plan (e.g., what activities were completed, by whom, by when, using what resources). Second, leadership teams may use standardized tools, such as the Team Implementation Checklist (Sugai et al., 2014), to self-assess their progress toward implementation. In addition, leadership teams may gather the perspectives of all staff members using the Self-Assessment Survey (Sugai et al., 2009). Third, school leadership teams should also monitor fidelity using a validated fidelity tool, like the Tiered Fidelity Inventory (Algozzine et al., 2014) or Benchmarks of Quality (Kincaid et al., 2010). Taken together, information from these fidelity tools provides school leadership team members with actionable information to modify and enhance their implementation of the PBIS framework.

Use Data to Drive Decisions

PBIS implementation relies on data-driven decision making (see Chapter 8) to improve the processes of selecting, implementing, and evaluating practices; monitoring student progress and responsiveness; assessing implementation fidelity; and integrating other related practices and initiatives (e.g., incorporating evidence-based social skills program within a PBIS framework). An important consideration is establishing the capacity for efficient and effective data management (Algozzine et al., 2010; Irvin et al., 2004, 2006; Simonsen & Sugai, 2007). The development and use of PBIS data management systems emphasize (a) specification of the smallest number of most important questions; (b) measurable, mutually exclusive, and comprehensive definition of data to be collected; (c) tools for easy input, analysis, output, and display of data; (d) schedule for regular data review and decision making; (e) formal teaming organization and process for data utilization and decision making; and (f) more specialized data supports for Tier 2 and 3 practices and systems. PBISApps (www.pbisapps.org) is one example of a data management system that allows schools to enter, monitor, and evaluate their fidelity and outcome data. This free application provides easy access to entering fidelity data and conducting school climate surveys. For a small licensing fee, schools can also use the School Wide Information System (within PBISApps) to enter and manage office discipline referrals (Tier 1), check-in/check-out point card data (Tier 2), and individualized student data (Tier 3).

As a critical component of an efficient and effective data management system, school leadership teams build effective routines to review data regularly, use data to identify and define problems of practice, develop data-informed action plans, and monitor implementation fidelity and outcomes of the plan. One potentially effective approach is Team Initiated Problem Solving (TIPS; Horner et al., 2015), which provides school leadership teams with a structure for effective team meetings and a data-driven problem-solving process (see Chapter 8).

Communicate Data

Educators need relevant, timely, and meaningful information for ongoing problem-solving and to improve the decision making of PBIS implementation, evaluation, progress monitoring, continuous improvement, and sustainability (McIntosh & Goodman, 2016). While it is important for a school team to have an evaluation plan with timelines identified for collecting, reviewing, and disseminating data, it is equally important that a communication plan is established to maintain stakeholder engagement. Stakeholders such as the individuals supporting the implementation practices (e.g., administrators, teachers) as well as the recipients of those practices (e.g., students, family) need to be informed of the impact these practices are making to gain and sustain buy-in.

There are many methods of communication that can build the visibility necessary to sustain implementation, such as sharing announcements at faculty meetings, posting information in the staff lounge, weekly e-mail updates, newsletters, and presentations, and distributing resources on a school website. Using and regularly sharing data assists a team in building and sustaining active involvement across all identified stakeholders while creating an effective, inclusive, and equitable learning environment for all students.

Practices

PBIS emphasizes the careful selection and integration of evidence-based practices into a continuum of effective behavior support. Practices are the interventions, instructional activities, programs, curricula, and other resources provided to support students (Horner et al., 2009). Within a PBIS framework, educators prioritize selecting and implementing practices that have the following important characteristics to enhance outcomes for all students (Sugai et al., 2010).

Evidence-Based

Once school leadership team members select a potential practice, they evaluate relevant information to determine whether a practice will deliver the intended outcome. They give priority to empirically derived quantitative evidence to determine the strength of the relationship between the practice and the intended outcome. They may also consider other sources of evidence, including quasi-experimental research, descriptive studies, qualitative examinations, implementer testimonials and case studies, etc. In addition to examining the available evidence, school teams should develop a plan to collect local data to monitor the effectiveness of the practice in order to achieve the desired outcome.

Culturally Relevant

Practices are designed for specific purposes and tested under controlled conditions. PBIS teams examine the extent to which the practice aligns with the characteristics of their classrooms and schools, including students (e.g., developmental levels, language, disabilities, prior learning history), settings (e.g., classroom vs. non-classroom, elementary vs. high school, large group vs. small group), school staff (e.g., experience, language, prior learning history, specializations), community (e.g., urban vs. rural, language, SES, culture), and family (e.g., SES, race/ethnicity, learning history; Fallon et al., 2012; Sugai et al., 2012;

Vincent et al., 2011). School leadership teams may use the Cultural Responsiveness Field Guide (Leverson et al., 2019) to consider and improve the cultural responsiveness of their school's practices.

Adaptable

The degree and ease with which a practice can be adapted are important for maximizing its relevance and effectiveness: (a) relevance with respect to the factors described above (student, settings, school staff, community, and family) and (b) effectiveness with respect to maintaining and/or increasing the likelihood of achieving desired outcomes. For example, the core features of specific praise (describing the behavior, providing positive feedback) can be implemented with whole groups, small groups, or individual students; said in simple or complex language; delivered publicly, privately, or in writing; provided during in-person, hybrid, or remote learning modes; and delivered in isolation or paired with a variety of other acknowledgment approaches (e.g., token systems). Thus, the practice "specific praise" is highly adaptable and can be relevant and effective with a variety of learners in a variety of contexts.

Feasible

Successful implementation of evidence-based practice is linked to the ease with which the practice can be (a) obtained (availability, cost, etc.), (b) installed where it will be used, (c) implemented with accuracy and fluency by typical implementers, (d) adapted based on local characteristics, (d) implemented in a sustained manner with accuracy, (e) supported by developers and trainers of the practice, and (f) evaluated so that progress can be determined. Thus, team members consider existing resources and supports when considering the feasibility of practices for their contexts.

Inclusive

An essential feature of an integrated continuum of support is that practices are considered from an inclusive perspective in which selection of more specialized supports is cumulative—intensive supports are added to supplement, rather than replace, existing supports. For example, students whose behavior is not responsive to the school-wide teaching of social skill expectations may participate in additional small group social skills practice and extra performance feedback but would continue to participate in whole-school instruction, practice, recognition, and booster activities.

Relevant

Rather than prioritizing packages or programs, schools focus on practices that appropriate and that highlight core features of establishing a positive and preventative approach to school-wide behavior support. Specifically, in Tier 1, educators establish a common approach to discipline; develop predictable routines for common settings (e.g., classroom, cafeteria, hallway); select, define, and explicitly teach a small number of positively stated expectations within those routines; prompt, model, and monitor expected behavior; actively engage students in learning and other school activities, develop a school-wide approach to acknowledge student behavior; implement a consistent, equitable, and instructionally-focused approach to respond to behavioral errors; and use data to monitor and adjust implementation.

In Tier 2, educators are more targeted with the implementation of these core features based on common student needs. For example, educators may use a check-in/check-out (CICO) approach to increase the frequency with which students receive reminders, feedback, and acknowledgment for behavior throughout the day (Crone et al., 2010). In addition, educators may use smaller groups to teach critical social, emotional, and behavioral skills for students who need targeted instruction (Crone et al., 2015). Finally, in Tier 3, educators individualize and intensify supports by conducting a functional-behavioral assessment, developing an individualized positive behavior support plan, and coordinating more complex supports with a wraparound or person-centered approach (https://nwi.pdx.edu/wraparound-basics/). Within each tier, implementation of core practice features is team driven, data-driven, and supported by systems.

Systems

To move evidence-based practices from research to practice settings, implementers need supports that enable effective, efficient, and relevant implementation. The PBIS framework formalizes implementation by adopting system-level working structures, developed from the science of implementation and technical assistance (Fixsen et al., 2005, 2013; McIntosh et al., 2009, 2010; Simonsen et al., 2012; Sugai & Horner, 2006; Sugai et al., 2000, 2008, 2010). These structures, or system features, are critical to effective, sustained, and scaled PBIS implementation.

Critical Features

The PBIS Implementation Blueprint (Center on PBIS, 2015) defines critical systems features for state, district, and school-level implementation. Chapter 20 describes key systems features, sometimes described as implementation drivers (Fixsen et al., 2005), at the district level. This section highlights relevant systems features for school-wide implementation, including school leadership teams, training, coaching, evaluation, local implementation demonstrations, and coordination with district-level organizational supports.

Establish School Leadership Teams

A key system structure of SWPBIS is coordinated implementation through a team approach (Mathews et al., 2014). School leadership team members are representative of the implementation community (e.g., students, families, grade-level or departmental teachers, school administrators, specialists, paraprofessionals, non-classified staff; Sugai et al., 2012; 2010). To ensure the PBIS team prioritizes equity and considers cultural and contextual relevance, it is critical to include multiple family members and active student voices that represent the broader school community. In addition, active administrator participation is important to ensure leadership teams have the authority to make decisions, including those that require resources (e.g., professional development time, administrative support for data management).

The school leadership team organizes implementation at the school-wide (Tier 1) level to support all students. Overall, teams are intended to ensure student success with PBIS as well as support the educators in implementing the PBIS practices reliably. Depending on the size of the school, specific needs, and resources available, these teams are typically comprised of five to seven members (Goodman & George, 2020). Contextual fit is critical, so the function of the team, the types of data reviewed, and the resources available determine the number of PBIS teams formed in a school. For example, schools may have both a school-wide leadership team that coordinates Tier 1 PBIS and additional student support team(s) that coordinate targeted (Tier 2) and intensive (Tier 3) supports. However, some schools with limited personnel may have only one PBIS team that includes all the tiers of support. Other schools may be fluent in the PBIS process, including data-based decision-making and have found one team to be more efficient in problem-solving both school-wide and individual student data as described in Chapter 8. Regardless of team structure within a district or school level, key individuals with the knowledge, experience and skills needed to implement planned PBIS activities share unique responsibilities (as described in Chapter 20; McIntosh et al., 2020) and are essential in (a) organizing school-wide supports; (b) identifying, prioritizing, delivering, and monitoring intervention effectiveness; and (c) providing ongoing communication to all relevant stakeholders (e.g., administrators, educators, students, families, community members).

Provide District-Supported Training

The school leadership team members participate in training and receive ongoing support from district-level PBIS trainers and coordinators. To install school-level behavioral capacity and ownership of PBIS implementation, district teams provide professional development supports directly to school leadership teams (Lewis et al., 2010). If the district has not developed sufficient training capacity, school teams may participate in training alongside a district team. In this case, both school and district teams may engage state-level trainers or outside experts to build district and school capacity simultaneously. Team training occurs regularly during the first 2 to 3 years of PBIS adoption and initial implementation. During this time, trainers focus on helping school leadership teams (a) establish effective teaming routines, (b) invest in data systems, and (c) develop and implement plans addressing the improvement of whole-school social culture (universal Tier 1). Subsequently, trainers support school teams during their initial implementation and help them prioritize systems that will enable them to sustain implementation after training.

Support School-Based Coaching

To build the link between training and implementation, coaching support accompanies school leadership team training. School leadership teams identify two or more members of the team to act as school-based coaches. In selecting coaches, the leadership team should consider individuals who have opportunities to engage in coaching, have established an effective relationship with administrators and school staff, have good communication and problem-solving skills, and have an interest and background in social behavior content. By sharing the coaching role, members of the school leadership team build local capacity. Because two or more members develop coaching expertise, the team is better able to sustain their implementation efforts if one coach shifts roles or leaves the school. When schools initially install PBIS, the district PBIS team also provides training and support to school-based coaches and maintains active relationships by conducting regular district-wide coaching meetings.

Coaching is not a stand-alone job. Instead, school-based coaching is a set of functions typically performed within the context of other school-based roles (e.g., school psychologist, specialist). Coaching functions include (a) providing reminders about team responsibilities (e.g., regular meeting, data review), (b) connecting with district trainers when questions or issues arise, (c) facilitating communications between school and district teams, (d) assisting school administrators in coordinating team activities, and (e) encouraging and reinforcing progress and accomplishments.

Thus, with district support and school-based coaching, school leadership teams develop data-based action plans that guide selection and facilitate the implementation of PBIS systems and practices. In addition, school leadership teams consider how to integrate all evidence-based and culturally relevant social, emotional, and behavioral initiatives, programs, and interventions within the PBIS framework. Because of the close association between academic and behavioral success, PBIS leadership teams work closely with academic teams. Alternately, PBIS and academic leadership teams may merge within an integrated-MTSS leadership team (www.mtss.org).

Support Local Implementation Demonstrations

District leadership teams support and recognize schools that demonstrate successful student outcomes and implementation fidelity as local demonstrations for other schools. These schools have data across multiple years documenting improved student outcomes, high implementation accuracy and fluency at school and classroom levels, school leadership teaming, administrative participation, and school-based behavioral expertise. Similarly, school leadership teams may recognize exemplary classroom implementation to celebrate and share successes with other educators.

Exemplar schools and classrooms also demonstrate the capacity to adapt to new conditions over time. This capacity, called "continuous regeneration," refers to the school's ability to (a) adjust a practice to enhance outcomes, (b) streamline support components when successful outcomes are achieved and sustainability is targeted, (c) eliminate and/or combine practices that have similar outcome objectives, (d) use local data to determine if new issues or needs require attention, and (e) enhance supports if implementation accuracy and/or fluency are not satisfactory (Sugai et al., 2010). For example, during the global pandemic in 2020, exemplary schools leveraged established systems to pivot practices into the new contexts of remote or hybrid learning modes. Educators taught expectations in the context of remote platforms (Center on PBIS, March 2020); implemented targeted interventions, like check-in/check-out, remotely (Center on PBIS, May 2020); and partnered with families to support student behavior at home (Center on PBIS & Center for Parent Information and Resources, March 2020).

Provide District Organizational Supports

School leadership teams benefit when districts invest in executive teaming functions or organizational supports, such as stakeholder engagement, funding and alignment, policy, and workforce capacity, which promote sustained implementation at the school level. Stakeholder engagement refers to the extent to which district leadership and other key stakeholder groups (e.g., parents, community mental health, local business associations) are engaging in bi-directional communication to shape the PBIS implementation effort at the district and school levels. Superintendents, assistant and associate superintendents, division and department heads, school board members, parent support groups, and city government officials should have regular opportunities to receive information and provide feedback on implementation efforts and outcomes and for comment. These informational and advisement opportunities occur formally through reports during meetings, regularly distributed newsletters and news flashes, the invitation to leadership meetings and school events, and informally through occasional communications and meetings. Having an informed and involved leadership provides additional support for the efforts of district and school PBIS implementation teams.

When schools or districts initiate PBIS, they often secure funding from multiple, short-term sources, such as grants (Horner et al., 2014). However, in order to support sustained and high-quality PBIS implementation within and across schools, successful districts invest in funding sources that are stable line items in district and school budgets and likely to be recurring and refunded over a 3 to 5-year interval. This commitment brings a high return on investment: for every $1 spent on PBIS, Swain-Bradway et al. (2017) estimated that schools save approximately $105 by preventing suspensions, expulsions, and dropouts. Further, districts can braid funding streams and/or align initiatives with common objectives to increase their capacity to support all students' social, emotional, behavioral, and academic performance and continuous improvement and growth.

Policy supports emphasize institutionalizing effective and relevant practices, programs, and systems, which in turn enhance decision making when personnel make transitions, consider new initiatives and priorities, and introduce new practices. In addition, successful and sustained PBIS implementation at the school level is dependent on the presence of expert behavioral capacity at the district level. This capacity is shared across individuals to minimize the impact of staff turnover and transition and is located across disciplines, departments, and programs to avoid "silo-ing" expertise, personnel, and practices. Beyond district expertise, schools develop workforce capacity by (a) engaging in training and coaching activities and (b) incorporating PBIS into their hiring practices, such that all educators have the skills to effectively support all students.

Considerations for Systems to Support Implementation

Systems enable educators to sustain and scale evidence-based and culturally relevant practices within a PBIS framework. Implementation is a dynamic, multi-stage process (Fixsen et al., 2005; McIntosh et al., 2010; Sugai et al., 2010). Though the implementation is not linear, school teams typically move through the following phases.

- Exploration: specification of the need and search for possible solutions;
- Installation: preparation of implementation personnel and setting;

- Initial implementation: pilot or trial implementation with supports to determine if full implementation is indicated and possible; and,
- Full implementation: accurate and fluent implementation with supports across the setting or context in which the need exists.

These phases are important for guiding decisions about coordination, resources, training, and other implementation focus areas.

The main message is that school implementers need systems (structures, routines, and tools) that maximize the impact of evidence-based practices. One-time, didactic professional development activities may be useful for initial awareness and knowledge; however, they are insufficient to achieve maximum practice uptake, sustained use, continuous regeneration, and student outcomes.

What Do We Know Based on Research?

These critical features of PBIS are grounded in an extensive literature base across the continuum of support (Tier 1, Tier 2, Tier 3). This next section describes (a) the evidence base of PBIS within the multi-tiered framework and (b) specific factors that support schools in maximizing and sustaining outcomes that lead to effective inclusive practices.

What Is the Evidence-Base Supporting PBIS?

Spanning over two decades, substantial research has demonstrated the positive effects of PBIS implementation on critical student, staff, and school outcomes to improve social, emotional, behavioral, and academic outcomes when implemented with fidelity. These effects have ranged from larger systems (e.g., school-wide teaching of expectations, whole school positive reinforcement, district teaming practices) to classrooms (e.g., providing explicit instruction in classroom routines and expectations) to the individual student level (e.g., function-based support, continuous progress monitoring, social skills instruction).

Evidence Supporting Tier 1

Tier 1 (Universal) supports are systematically and proactively delivered to all students and emphasize defining prosocial skills and behavior expectations, teaching, and steadily acknowledging appropriate student behavior across classroom and school settings (Simonsen et al., 2012). Providing Tier 1 supports paves the way to invest in the prevention of future problem behavior and includes the following key practices: (a) identifying behavior expectations, (b) teaching behavior expectations, (c) monitoring student behavior, (d) reinforcing behavior expectations, and (e) correcting behavior errors (Goodman & George, 2020). When implemented with fidelity, Tier 1 PBIS effectively meets the needs of 80% or more of the students within a school and thereby allows time and resources to address students with more intensive support needs (George et al., 2009).

Researchers have demonstrated that when educators implement Tier 1 PBIS practices school-wide and with fidelity, student and teacher outcomes improve. This compelling body of research documents the effectiveness of PBIS in reducing reactive and exclusionary discipline practices, including (a) office discipline referrals (Bradshaw et al., 2010, 2012; Horner et al., 2009) and (b) suspensions (Bradshaw et al., 2010; Gage et al., 2018, 2019). In addition, students report fewer instances of (c) bullying behaviors and peer rejection (Ross & Horner, 2009; Waasdorp et al., 2012) and (d) drug and alcohol abuse (Bradshaw et al., 2012, 2015). Further, when PBIS is implemented with fidelity, students increase: (e) academic achievement (Algozzine et al., 2012;

Bradshaw et al., 2010; Freeman et al., 2016; Gage et al., 2017, 2019; Horner et al., 2009; McIntosh et al., 2011) and (f) attendance (Freeman et al., 2016). Effective implementation of SWPBIS has also led to improvements in (g) school organizational health (Bradshaw et al., 2008; Bradshaw, Koth et al., 2009; Flannery et al., 2014), (h) perceptions of school safety (Horner et al., 2009), (i) perception of teacher efficacy and reported well-being (Kelm & McIntosh, 2012; Ross et al., 2012), and (j) social-emotional skills of students (Bradshaw et al., 2012).

Evidence Supporting Tier 2

Educators implement tier 2 (targeted) practices to support students who have not been responsive to Tier 1 and/or demonstrate at-risk behaviors (e.g., frequent classroom disruptions). Tier 2 practices are delivered quickly with minimal resources to increase the fluency of demonstrating expected, pro-social behaviors. Providing Tier 2 PBIS supports involves the following key steps: identify students, implement targeted evidence-based and culturally relevant practices, and monitor progress (Goodman & George, 2020). Tier 2 practices typically include an increase in: (a) instruction and practice with self-regulation and social skills, (b) adult supervision, (c) opportunity for positive re-inforcement, (d) pre-corrections, (e) focus on the possible function of problem behavior, and (f) access to academic supports (Center on PBIS, 2020). When implemented with fidelity, Tier 2 PBIS effectively meets the needs of 5–15% of students and requires additional teaching and practice opportunities to increase their likelihood of success (Crone et al., 2015; Fairbanks et al., 2007; Yong & Cheney, 2013).

Research has demonstrated that when Tier 2 practices are anchored in the universal Tier 1 practices (e.g., school-wide expectations), they can be readily modified to meet individual student needs with efficiency (McDaniel et al., 2015; Mitchell et al., 2011). Using data from a randomized controlled effectiveness trial, Bradshaw et al. (2015) found the effects of SWPBIS on student outcomes tend to be greatest among at-risk and high-risk children. Specific empirical studies have supported a variety of Tier 2 practices with *Check-in/Check-out* (CICO; Crone et al., 2010) as being one of the most widely implemented Tier 2 interventions derived from single-case research documenting functional relations between the implementation of CICO and reduced problem behavior (Campbell & Anderson, 2008; Hawken et al., 2014; Maggin et al., 2015; Mitchell et al., 2017; Simonsen et al., 2011; Wolfe et al., 2016). Similarly, when implemented with fidelity, *First Step to Success* demonstrated a functional relationship to reducing problem behavior (e.g., Golly et al., 1998; Walker et al., 2009; Sprague & Perkins, 2009) and *Check and Connect* has been shown to reduce student dropout (Anderson et al., 2004; Lehr et al., 2003; Sinclair et al., 1998). While this list is not exhaustive, other Tier 2 evidence-based practices include practices such as social skills instruction (e.g., Elliott & Gresham, 2013; Lane et al., 2003; Miller et al., 2011); *Check, Connect, and Expect* (Cheney et al., 2009); and self-management (Bruhn et al., 2015).

Evidence Supporting Tier 3

Tier 3 (Intensive) supports focus on the development of comprehensive, individualized, function-based student support plans to address intensive and challenging student unwanted behaviors (Strickland-Cohen & Horner, 2015). These interventions integrate an extensive history that is well articulated in ABA (e.g., Cooper et al., 2020; Dunlap, 2006; Horner & Sugai, 2015) and are designed to target the 3–5% of students with the highest support needs. Similar to the previous tiers described, both Tier 3 systems and practices depend on strong foundational Tier 1 and 2 systems, which can lessen the number of students actually requiring more intensive supports and interventions can be delivered efficiently and effectively to enhance a full continuum of supports (McIntosh et al., 2009). Key practices in Tier 3 include: (a) function-based assessments (Dunlap et al., 2010; O'Neill, et al., 2015), (b) wraparound systems of supports (Eber et al., 2011; Scott & Eber, 2003), including person-centered planning (Kincaid & Fox, 2002; Smith-Bird & Turnbull, 2005) with (c) consideration of the cultural and contextual fit (Center on PBIS, 2020) to design a behavior support plan.

The research supporting the effectiveness of functional behavioral assessment (FBA), the design of individualized behavioral interventions, and the active use of data in the implementation of behavior support is well documented in the literature (e.g., Carr et al., 1999) and research has demonstrated that interventions guided by FBAs and implemented with fidelity result directly in reducing problem behavior and improving desired outcomes (e.g., Burke et al., 2003; Crone et al., 2007; Ervin et al., 2000; Fairbanks et al., 2007; Ingram et al., 2005; Kern et al., 2004; Lucyshyn et al., 2007; Newcomer & Lewis, 2004; Preciado et al., 2009). Building upon the integration of the three tiers within a continuum of supports, Lewis (2009) demonstrated that implementing Tier 1 with fidelity improved academic, behavioral, and social-emotional outcomes for students needing Tier 2 and Tier 3 supports.

What Specific Factors Support Schools in Maximizing and Sustaining Outcomes?

Schools invest a tremendous amount of time, personnel, and money in evidence-based practices in order to achieve intended outcomes. Thus, investing in supports to maximize and sustain these outcomes is in the best interest of schools. Sustainability is the durable implementation of a practice at a level of fidelity that continues to produce valued outcomes (McIntosh et al., 2009). In other words, to maintain positive outcomes, the goal is implementing PBIS (or any large-scale framework for reform or change) with a high degree of fidelity over time (McIntosh et al., 2018). This section explores critical factors that promote and maximize sustained positive outcomes: district-wide support, an active school leadership team that shares data with faculty, implementation fidelity, and classroom-level implementation (see Chapter 20).

District-Wide Support

McIntosh et al. (2013) identified factors related to the sustainability of school-wide PBIS implementation, including two district-level factors: district priority and capacity building. Expanding on this finding from a national sample of over 860 schools implementing PBIS, McIntosh et al. (2014) found that to support the sustained implementation of PBIS at the school level, districts (a) built PBIS into written policy, (b) included PBIS competencies into hiring criteria, and (c) developed district coaching capacity. Recent research has demonstrated that district variables are significant predictors of the implementation and sustainability of school practices (George et al., 2018; McIntosh et al., 2018) and specific coaching activities have been most related to sustained implementation (Bastable et al., 2020). High-quality PBIS implementation within and across schools is coordinated by a district leadership team, comprised of district-level coordinators, supervisors, and leaders of projects and programs related to supporting positive and preventive school cultures for all students (Bradshaw et al., 2012; George & Kincaid, 2008; George et al., 2018; Sugai et al., 2012). Further, leadership teams with identified roles and the authority to make decisions have been successful in securing political and fiscal support that aid sustainability critical for large scale-up of PBIS (Horner et al., 2014).

Active School Leadership Team that Shares Data with Faculty

In addition to district supports, McIntosh et al. (2014) found that school team actions, especially the frequency of communicating and sharing data school-wide, were statistically related to sustainability. The school team's use of data included activities such as (a) school team/staff skill, (b) regular team meetings, (c) data collection, (d) use of data for decision making, and (e) presenting data to the staff and community. Further explorations found that school teams that successfully sustained PBIS through administrator turnover engaged in practices at both the school and district levels. Specifically, sustaining schools (a) maintained their PBIS handbook, (b) documented support among stakeholders, (c) collected and shared data, and (d) oriented the new administrator.

Importance of Implementation Fidelity

Schools are complex systems with many moving parts that impact outcomes. Intentional focus on implementation is critical to achieving desired outcomes (e.g., reducing time-intensive discipline incidents to gain instructional time and improved academic scores). According to Merriam-Webster (n.d.), *fidelity* is "strict observance of promises, loyalty, adherence to fact or detail, accuracy, and exactness." Therefore, *implementing with fidelity* involves actively adhering to the specific components (i.e., critical elements) identified as essential practices within PBIS (George & Childs, 2012). Schools that implement with fidelity experience greater improvements in student outcomes than schools that have not met fidelity criteria (e.g., Simonsen et al., 2012). Further, the evidence base supporting PBIS implementation, described in the previous section, has documented the relationship between PBIS when implemented with fidelity and improved outcomes.

Emphasis on Classroom-Level Implementation

One of the key findings of large-scale research is the importance of classroom-level implementation. Specifically, implementation fidelity of classroom PBIS practices is related to (a) improved student outcomes (Childs et al., 2016) and (b) enhanced sustainability (Mathews et al., 2014). Therefore, supporting educators' implementation of PBIS practices in the classroom is critical. The Office of Special Education Programs (2015) provided specific guidance for supporting and responding to student behavior in the classroom, including foundational practices (effective classroom design, predictable routines, positive expectations), prevention practices (active supervision, prompting, engaging instruction, specific praise, and other acknowledgment strategies), and response practices (specific error corrections and additional response strategies). By implementing these critical PBIS practices in the classroom, educators increase the likelihood that all students will succeed.

Setting the Course for Effective Inclusion

Although PBIS provides a framework that sets all students and educators up for success, an intentional focus on inclusive practice is critical. Preliminary evidence suggests that students with disabilities benefit when schools implement Tier 1 support to create effective, supportive, proactive, positive, and inclusive school cultures. Specifically, when schools implement Tier 1 PBIS, students with disabilities may be (a) more likely to engage in appropriate, prosocial behavior and emotional regulation; (b) less likely to demonstrate clinical symptoms, aggressive or challenging behavior, concentration problems; and (c) experience less reactive and exclusionary discipline, including office referrals, suspensions, physical restraint, and referrals to alternative schools (Benner et al., 2010; Bradshaw et al., 2012; Farkas et al., 2012; Gage et al., 2019; Grasley-Boy et al., 2019; Loman et al., 2018; Simonsen et al., 2010, 2020; Vincent et al., 2011). Unfortunately, special educators report that not all students with disabilities participate in and benefit from Tier 1 PBIS practices (Shuster et al., 2017). Thus, it is critical to consider key lessons for practice and the need for further research to maximize the impact of PBIS on students with disabilities.

Key Lessons for Practice

Across decades of research, there have been many lessons learned to support practice. Among the most important lessons is the importance of leveraging the PBIS framework to develop inclusive environments that support all students, including students with disabilities. When educators differentiate Tier 1 support, coordinate supports within the continuum, and adopt a person-centered and strengths-based approach, they increase the likelihood that students with intensive needs will experience positive outcomes.

Differentiate Tier 1 Support

Tier 1 support is for everyone. As described, core features of Tier 1 practices include creating effective environmental design, developing predictable routines, explicitly teaching positive expectations, prompting and monitoring expected behavior, actively engaging students in learning and other school activities, providing specific praise and other acknowledgment of student behavior, and responding to student behavioral errors in an equitable and instructionally-focused way. Effective educators implement and differentiate Tier 1 supports such that a majority of students benefit from Tier 1. Therefore, Tier 1 supports should match the intensity of student need within each setting, such that at least 80% of students are successful with Tier 1 support. For example, in alternative educational settings that serve students with intensive needs, educators may increase how often they explicitly teach, prompt, and reinforce expected behavior.

To differentiate Tier 1, educators consider students' unique needs, focus on core features of each practice, and determine the best approach to modifying, adapting, or intensifying core features of that practice (Meyer et al., 2020). For example, in organizing the physical environment, it may be necessary to modify the layout to accommodate students with diverse visual or physical abilities. When prompting students to engage in expected behavior, educators may consider the frequency of prompting (e.g., before every transition vs. new transitions), specificity of prompting (e.g., indirect reminder vs. direct verbal instructions), or mode of prompting (e.g., verbal, gestural, picture, written) to ensure prompts work for all students. These simple strategies to differentiate implementation will increase all students' access to and benefit from Tier 1.

Coordinate Supports within the Continuum

Although Tier 1 is for everyone, some students will need additional support, layered on top of differentiated Tier 1 support to be successful. For these students, it is critical that targeted (Tier 2) and intensive (Tier 3) supports are aligned with Tier 1. For example, all students may receive social skills instruction and acknowledgment linked to school-wide expectations. For students participating in check-in/check-out (CICO) as part of Tier 2, the increased prompts, targeted social skills instruction, and frequent feedback are linked to the school-wide expectations. Thus, students on CICO receive an increased "dose" of support, but educators align the supports with what all students receive in Tier 1.

Similarly, a student may have Tier 3 support documented in a function-based, individualized positive behavior support plan (BSP). Their BSP may include strategies for prompting, teaching, and reinforcing a replacement behavior (e.g., ask for a break in lieu of hitting to escape an aversive situation) and preventing contextually inappropriate behavior (e.g., hitting). Rather than teaching that skill in isolation, educators teach the replacement behavior in the context of school-wide expectations (e.g., asking for a break is an example of being safe) and provide function-based reinforcement (e.g., brief break) alongside school-wide recognition (e.g., specific praise ticket for appropriately requesting a break). Thus, all students receive and have an opportunity to benefit from Tier 1 and experience a connected continuum of support.

In addition to connecting tiers of support, a key component of developing an effective continuum is fluid, team-driven, and data-informed movement between tiers. Thus, teams regularly review data to identify students who (a) are being successful with their current level of support, (b) need additional layers of support to be successful, or (c) have met targeted or individualized goals for Tier 2 or 3 support, respectively, and are ready to have those supports faded. Thus, educators do not "place" students in a tier of intervention; educators provide support to promote students' fluency, maintenance, and ultimately generalized and independent use of social, emotional, behavioral, and/or academic skills such that most students can be successful with Tier 1 support.

Adopt a Strengths-Based, Person-Centered Approach

In contrast to traditional "wait to fail" models of special education, a multi-tiered approach facilitates a proactive approach to matching supports to student needs in an effort to ensure all students experience success. To ensure this approach is inclusive and equitable, school leadership teams adopt a strengths-based and person-centered approach (Shogren et al., 2017a, 2017b). As the name suggests, strengths-based approaches focus on students' skills and areas for growth and enhancement, as opposed to deficits and remediation. Person-centered approaches engage students and their family members as active partners and leaders in designing the goals, selecting the methods, and contextualizing support. Consistent with these approaches, school leadership teams (a) prioritize strong family and student voice, (b) emphasize inclusivity and equity, and (c) use data to guide team-based decisions that build on student strengths in ways that students, families, and educators see as contextually appropriate and culturally relevant.

Additional Research is Needed

Although preliminary research supports the potential for PBIS to establish inclusive environments that support all students, including students with disabilities, additional research is needed in three key areas. First, research documenting the effects of Tier 1 PBIS for students is preliminary and based on either small-scale studies (e.g., Loman et al., 2018), larger research projects that focus on all students (e.g., Bradshaw et al., 2012), or existing state or national datasets (e.g., Grasley-Boy et al., 2019). A rigorous study of the effects of high-fidelity implementation and differentiation of Tier 1 supports for students with disabilities is needed to better understand the potential for PBIS to create inclusive environments and document outcomes for all students, including those with disabilities. Second, in addition to documenting the effects of differentiated Tier 1 support, some students will require additional layers of targeted (Tier 2) and/or intensive (Tier 3) support. Although evidence supports specific Tier 2 and Tier 3 practices, additional research is needed to understand the effects of a full continuum of support within the PBIS framework for all students, including students with disabilities. Third, though carefully controlled and rigorous studies are critical, it is also important for researchers to document the supports needed (e.g., amount of training and coaching), feasibility, and cost-effectiveness of schools and districts implementing advanced tiers with sufficient fidelity to support students with or at-risk for disabilities in inclusive schools.

Final Thoughts

Effective inclusive schools provide a full range of academic and behavioral supports for all students. Traditional reactive management practices are not effective with many students and can lead to a variety of negative outcomes. Instead, PBIS organizes social, emotional, and behavioral supports into an effective and efficient prevention continuum that gives all students and staff access to evidence-based and culturally relevant practices across all settings. Employing a multi-tiered approach, PBIS implementation emphasizes cultural relevance and equity, universal screening, progress monitoring, evidence-based and culturally responsive practices, a continuum of practices, data-based decision making, and team-based problem solving and action planning. School leadership teams center their work in equity and identify meaningful outcomes, collect relevant data, prioritize implementation fidelity, and use data to drive implementation decisions. Further, school teams give priority to PBIS practices that are evidence-based, culturally relevant, adaptable, feasible, inclusive, and have clearly articulated core features.

PBIS systems enhance the impact of evidence-based behavioral practices by considering implementation as dynamic and multi-staged. School leadership teams emphasize core systems features, including a representative school leadership team, district-supported training, school-based coaching, local implementation demonstrations, and coordinated organizational functions (i.e., stakeholder engagement, funding and alignment, policy, and workforce capacity) at the district level. The empirical support for PBIS implementation is increasing, especially in relation to schools that implement it with high fidelity and experience important achievement and social behavior outcomes. Rigorous, randomized trials of the PBIS framework have demonstrated significant, sustained effects of PBIS on a range of student behavioral, mental health, and educational outcomes. In addition, the PBIS framework appears to be a useful means for considering a number of educational issues (e.g., bullying behavior, equity in discipline, school climate, school violence). Although further research is necessary to demonstrate the full potential of PBIS to create inclusive environments that support all students, including students with disabilities, preliminary evidence supports the potential for PBIS to improve supports and decrease reactive and exclusionary discipline for students with disabilities.

References

Algozzine, B., Horner, R. H., Sugai, G., Barrett, S., Dickey, S. R., Eber, L., Kincaid, D., Lewis, T., & Tobin, T. (2010). *Evaluation blueprint for school-wide positive behavior support*. Center on PBIS. www.pbis.org

Algozzine, B., Wang, C., & Violette, A. S. (2011). Reexamining the relationship between academic achievement and social behavior. *Journal of Positive Behavioral Interventions, 13*, 3–16. doi:10.1177/1098300709359084

Algozzine, B., Putnam, R., & Horner, R. H. (2012). Support for teaching students with learning disabilities academic skills and social behaviors within a response-to-intervention model: Why it doesn't matter what comes first. *Insights on Learning Disabilities, 9*(1), 7–36.

Algozzine, B., Wang, C., White, R., Cooke, N., Marr, M. B., Algozzine, K., Helf, S. S., & Duran, G. Z. (2012). Effects of multi-tier academic and behavior instruction on difficult-to-teach students. *Exceptional Children, 79*, 45–64. doi:10.1177/001440291207900103

Algozzine, B., Barrett, S., Eber, L., George, H., Horner, R., Lewis, T., Putnam, B., Swain-Bradway, J., McIntosh, K., & Sugai, G. (2014). *School-wide PBIS Tiered Fidelity Inventory*. Center on Positive Behavioral Interventions and Supports. www.pbis.org

Anderson, A. R., Christenson, S. L., Sinclair, M. F., & Lehr, C. A. (2004). Check & Connect: The importance of relationships for promoting engagement with school. *Journal of School Psychology, 42*(2), 95–113. doi:10.1016/j.jsp.2004.01.002

Bastable, E., Kittelman, A., McIntosh, K., & Hoselton, R. (March 2015). *Do high schools implementing SWPBIS have lower rates of illegal drug and alcohol use?* Center on PBIS. www.pbis.org

Bastable, E., Massar, M. M., & McIntosh, K. (2020). A survey of team members' perceptions of coaching activities related to Tier 1 SWPBIS implementation. *Journal of Positive Behavior Interventions, 22*(1), 51–61. doi:10.1177/1098300719861566

Benner, G. J., Beaudoin, K. M., Chen, P.-Y., Davis, C., & Ralston, N. C. (2010). The impact of intensive positive behavioral supports on the behavioral functioning of students with emotional disturbance: How much does fidelity matter? *Journal of Behavior Assessment and Intervention in Children, 1*, 85–100. doi:10.1037/h0100361

Biglan, A. (1995). Translating what we know about the context of antisocial behavior into a lower prevalence of such behavior. *Journal of Applied Behavior Analysis, 28*, 479–492. https://onlinelibrary.wiley.com/doi/abs/10.1901/jaba.1995.28-479

Biglan, A. (2015). *The nurture effect: How the science of human behavior can improve our lives and our world.* New Harbinger Publications.

Bradley, R., Danielson, L., & Hallahan, D. P. (Eds.) (2002). *Identification of learning disabilities: Research to practice.* Erlbaum. doi:10.4324/9781410606297

Bradley, R., Danielson, L., & Doolittle, J. (2007). Response to intervention: 1997 to 2007. *Teaching Exceptional Children, 39*(5), 8–12. doi:10.1177/004005990703900502

Bradley, R., Doolittle, J., & Bartolotta, R. (2008). Building on the data and adding to the discussion: The experiences and outcomes of students with emotional disturbance. *Journal of Behavioral Education, 17*, 4–23. doi:10.1007/s10864-007-9058-6

Bradshaw, C. P., Koth, C. W., Bevans, K. B., Ialongo, N., & Leaf, P. J. (2008). The impact of school-wide positive behavioral interventions and supports (PBIS) on the organizational health of elementary schools. *School Psychology Quarterly, 23(4)*, 462–473. doi:10.1037/a0012883

Bradshaw, C. P., Koth, C. W., Thornton, L. A., & Leaf, P. J. (2009). Altering school climate through school-wide Positive Behavioral Interventions and Supports: Findings from a group-randomized effectiveness trial. *Prevention Science, 10*(2), 100–115. doi:10.1007/s11121-008-0114-9

Bradshaw, C. P., Mitchell, M. M., & Leaf, P. J. (2010). Examining the effects of schoolwide positive behavioral interventions and supports on student outcomes: Results from a randomized controlled effectiveness trial in elementary schools. *Journal of Positive Behavioral Interventions*, 12(3), 133-148. https://doi.org/10.1177/1098300709334798

Bradshaw, C., Waasdorp, T., & Leaf, P. (2012). Effects of school-wide positive behavioral interventions and supports on child behavior problems. *Pediatrics, 130*, 1136–1145. doi:10.1542/peds.2012-0243

Bradshaw, C. P., Pas, E. T., Debnam, K. J., & Johnson, S. L. (2015). A focus on implementation of positive behavioral interventions and supports (PBIS) in high schools: Associations with bullying and other indicators of school disorder. *School Psychology Review, 44*, 480–498. https://doi.org/10.17105/spr-15-0105.1

Bruhn, A., McDaniel, S., & Kreigh, C. (2015). Self-monitoring interventions for students with behavior problems: A systematic review of current research. *Behavioral Disorders, 40*, 102–121. doi:10.17988/BD-13-45.1

Burke, M. D., Hagan-Burke, S., & Sugai, G. (2003). The efficacy of function-based interventions for students with learning disabilities who exhibit escape-maintained problem behavior: Preliminary results from a single case study. *Learning Disabilities Quarterly, 26*, 15–25. doi:10.2307/1593681

Caplan, G. (1964). *Principles of preventive psychiatry.* Basic Books.

Campbell, A., & Anderson, C. M. (2008). Enhancing effects of Check-In/Check-Out with function-based support. *Behavioral Disorders, 33*(4), 233–245. doi:10.1177%2F019874290803300404

Carr, E. G., Horner, R. H., Turnbull, A. P., Marquis, J., Magito-McLaughlin, D., McAtee, M. L., Smith, C. E., Anderson-Ryan, K., Ruef, M. B., & Doolabh, A. (1999). *Positive behavior support for people with developmental disabilities: A research synthesis.* American Association on Mental Retardation.

Center on Positive Behavioral Interventions and Supports. (2020). *Website.* www.pbis.org

Center on PBIS. (2015). *Positive behavioral interventions and supports (PBIS) implementation blueprint.* Center on Positive Behavioral Interventions and Supports. www.pbis.org

Center on PBIS & Center for Parent Information & Resources. (2020, March). *Supporting families with PBIS at home.* Center on PBIS. www.pbis.org

Center on PBIS. (2020, March). *Creating a PBIS behavior teaching matrix for remote instruction.* Center on Positive Behavioral Interventions and Supports. www.pbis.org

Center on PBIS. (2020, May). *Guidance on adapting Check-in Check-out (CICO) for distance learning.* Center on Positive Behavioral Interventions and Supports. www.pbis.org

Cheney, D. A., Stage, S. A., Hawken, L. S., Lynass, L., Mielenz, C., & Waugh, M. (2009). A 2-year outcome study of the Check, Connect, and Expect intervention for students at risk for severe behavior problems. *Journal of Emotional and Behavioral Disorders, 17*(4), 226–243. doi:10.1177/1063426609339186

Childs, K. E., Kincaid, D., George, H. P., & Gage, N. A. (2016). The relationship between school-wide implementation of positive behavior intervention and supports and student discipline outcomes. *Journal of Positive Behavior Interventions, 18*(2), 89–99. doi:10.1177/1098300715590398

Cooper, J., Heron, T., & Heward, W. (2020). *Applied behavior analysis* (3rd ed.). Merrill Publishing Company.

Crone, D. A., Hawken, L. S., & Bergstrom, M. K. (2007). A demonstration of training, implementing, and using Functional Behavioral Assessment in 10 elementary and middle school settings. *Journal of Positive Behavior Interventions, 9*(1), 15–29. doi:10.1177/10983007070090010301

Crone, D. A., Hawken, L. S., & Horner, R. H. (2010). *Responding to problem behavior in schools: The Behavior Education Program* (2nd ed.). Guilford Press.

Crone, D. A., Hawken, L. S., & Horner, R. H. (2015). *Building positive behavior support systems in schools: Functional Behavioral Assessment*, (2nd ed.). Guilford Press.

Dunlap, G. (2006). The applied behavior analytic heritage of PBS: A dynamic model of action-oriented research. *Journal of Positive Behavior Interventions, 8*(1), 58–60. doi:10.1177/10983007060080010701

Dunlap, G., Iovannone, R., Wilson, K. J., Kincaid, D. K., & Strain, P. (2010). Prevent-Teach-Reinforce: A standardized model of school-based behavioral intervention. *Journal of Positive Behavior Interventions, 12*(1), 9–22. doi:10.1177/1098300708330880

Eber, L., Hyde, K. & Suter, J. C. (2011). Integrating wraparound into a schoolwide system of positive behavior supports. *Journal of Child and Family Studies, 20,* 782–790. doi:10.1007/s10826-010-9424-1

Elliott S. N., Gresham F. M. (2013). Social Skills Improvement System. In F. R. Volkmar (Ed.), *Encyclopedia of autism spectrum disorders*. Springer. doi:10.1007/978-1-4419-1698-3_509

Ervin, R. A., Kern, L., Clarke, S., Dupaul, G. J., Dunlap, G., & Friman, P. C. (2000). Evaluating assessment-based intervention strategies for students with ADHD and comorbid disorders within the natural classroom context. *Behavioral Disorders, 25*(4), 344–358. doi:10.1177/019874290002500403

Fairbanks, S., Sugai, G., Guardino, D., & Lathrop, M. (2007). Response to intervention: Examining classroom behavior support in second grade. *Exceptional Children, 73,* 288–310. doi:10.1177/001440290707300302

Farkas, M. S., Simonsen, B., Migdole, S., Donovan, M. E., Clemens, K., & Cicchese, V. (2012). Schoolwide positive behavior support in an alternative school setting: An evaluation of fidelity, outcomes, and social validity of tier 1 implementation. *Journal of Emotional and Behavioral Disorders, 20*(4), 275–288. doi:10.1177/1063426610389615

Fallon, L. M., O'Keeffe, B. V., & Sugai, G. (2012). Consideration of culture and context in School-wide Positive Behavior Support: A review of current literature. *Journal of Positive Behavior Interventions, 14,* 209–219. doi:10.1177/1098300712442242

Fixsen, D. L., Naoom, S. F., Blase, K. A., Friedman, R. M., & Wallace, F. (2005). *Implementation research: Synthesis of the literature.* University of South Florida, Louis de la Parte Florida Mental Health Institute, The National Implementation Research Network (FMHI Publication #231).

Fixsen, D., Blase, K., Metz, A., & Van Dyke, M. (2013). Statewide implementation of evidenced-based programs. *Exceptional Children, 79,* 213–220. doi:10.1177/001440291307900206

Flannery, K. B., Fenning, P., Kato, M. M., & McIntosh, K. (2014). Effects of school-wide positive behavioral interventions and supports and fidelity of implementation on problem behavior in high schools. *School Psychology Quarterly, 29*(2), 111–124. doi:10.1037/spq0000039

Freeman, J., Simonsen, B., McCoach, D. B., Sugai, G., Lombardi, A., & Horner, R. (2016). Relationship between school-wide positive behavior interventions and supports and academic, attendance, and behavior outcomes in high schools. *Journal of Positive Behavior Interventions, 18*(1), 41–51. doi:10.1177/1098300715580992

Gable, R. A., Tonelson, S. W., Sheth, M., Wilson, C., & Park, K. L. (2012). Importance, usage, and preparedness to implement evidence-based practices for students with emotional disabilities: A comparison of knowledge and skills of special education and general education teachers. *Education and Treatment of Children, 35*(4), 499–519. doi:10.1353/etc.2012.0030

Gage, N. A., Adamson, R., MacSuga-Gage, A. S., & Lewis, T. J. (2017). The relation between the academic achievement of students with emotional and behavioral disorders and teacher characteristics. *Behavioral Disorders, 43*(1), 213–222. doi:10.1177/0198742917713211

Gage, N. A., Lee, A., Grasley-Boy, N., & George, H. P. (2018). The impact of school-wide positive behavior interventions and supports on school suspensions: A statewide quasi-experimental analysis. *Journal of Positive Behavior Interventions, 20*(4), 217–226. doi:10.1177/1098300718768204

Gage, N. A., Grasley-Boy, N., George, H. P., Cox, K. E., & Kincaid, D. (2019). A quasi-experimental design analysis of the effects of school-wide positive behavior interventions and supports on discipline in Florida. *Journal of Positive Behavior Interventions, 21*(1), 50–61. doi:10.1177%2F1098300718768208

George, H. P. & Kincaid, D. (2008). Building district-level capacity for positive behavior support. *Journal of Positive Behavior Interventions, 10*(1), 20–32. doi:10.1177%2F1098300707311367

George, H. P., Kincaid, D. & Pollard-Sage, J. (2009). Primary tier interventions and supports. In W. Sailor, G. Dunlap, G. Sugai, & R. Horner (Eds.), *Handbook of positive behavior support. Issues in clinical child psychology* (pp. 375–394). Springer https://link.springer.com/chapter/10.1007%2F978-0-387-09632-2_16

George, H. P. & Childs, K. E. (2012). Evaluating implementation of schoolwide behavior support: Are we doing it well? *Preventing School Failure, 56*(4), 197–206. doi:10.1080/1045988X.2011.645909

George, H. P., Cox, K. E., Minch, D., & Sandomierski, T. (2018). District practices associated with successful SWPBIS implementation. *Behavioral Disorders, 43*(3), 393–406. doi:10.1177%2F0198742917753612

Gilliam, W., & Shabar, G. (2006). Preschool and child care expulsion and suspension rates and predictors in one state. *Infants and Young Children, 19*(3), 228–245. https://journals.lww.com/iycjournal/Abstract/2006/07000/Preschool_and_Child_Care_Expulsion_and_Suspension_.7.aspx

Golly, A. M., Stiller, B., & Walker, H. M. (1998). First step to success: Replication and social validation of an early intervention program. *Journal of Emotional and Behavioral Disorders, 6*(4), 243–250. doi:10.1177/106342669800600406

Goodman, S., & George, H. P. (2020). School-wide positive behavioral interventions and supports. In *Oxford Research Encyclopedia of Education.* Oxford University Press. doi:10.1093/acrefore/9780190264093.013.1203

Grasley-Boy, N. M., Gage, N. A., & Lombardo, M. (2019). Effect of SWPBIS on disciplinary exclusions for students with and without disabilities. *Exceptional Children, 86*, 25–39. doi:10.1177/0014402919854196

Hawken, L. S., Bundock, K., Kladis, K., O'Keeffe, B., & Barrett, C. A. (2014). Systematic review of the check-in, check-out intervention for students at risk for emotional and behavioral disorders. *Education & Treatment of Children, 37*(4), 635–658. doi:10.1353/etc.2014.0030

Horner, R., Sugai, G., Smolkowski, K., Eber, L., Nakasato, J., Todd, A., & Esperanza, J., (2009). A randomized, wait-list controlled effectiveness trial assessing school-wide positive behavior support in elementary schools. *Journal of Positive Behavior Interventions, 11*(3), 133–145. doi:10.1177/1098300709332067

Horner, R. H., Kincaid, D., Sugai, G., Lewis, T., Eber, L., Barrett, S., Dickey, C. R., Richter, M., Sullivan, E., Boezio, C., Algozzine, B., Reynolds, H., & Johnson, N. (2014). Scaling up school-wide positive behavioral interventions and supports: Experiences of *Seven States With Documented Success. Journal of Positive Behavior Interventions, 16*(4), 197–208. doi:10.1177/1098300713503685

Horner, R. H., Newton, J. S., Todd, A. W., Algozzine, B., Algozzine, K., Cusumano, D. L., & Preston, A. I. (2015). *The Team-Initiated Problem Solving (TIPS II) training materials.* Center on PBIS. www.pbis.org

Horner, R. H., & Sugai, G. (2015). School-wide PBIS: An example of applied behavior analysis implemented at a scale of social importance. *Behavior Analysis in Practice, 8*(1), 80–85. doi:10.1007/s40617-015-0045-4

Ingram, K., Lewis-Palmer, T., & Sugai, G. (2005). Function-based intervention planning: Comparing the effectiveness of FBA indicated and contra-indicated intervention plans. *Journal of Positive Behavior Interventions,* 7(4), 224–236. doi:10.1177/10983007050070040401

Irvin, L. K., Tobin, T. J., Sprague, J. R., Sugai, G., & Vincent, C. G. (2004). Validity of office discipline referral measures as indices of school-wide behavioral status and effects of school-wide behavioral interventions. *Journal of Positive Behavior Interventions, 6*(3), 131–147. doi:10.1177/10983007040060030201

Irvin, L. K., Horner, R. H., Ingram, K., Todd, A. W., Sugai, G., Sampson, N. K., & Boland, J. B. (2006). Using office discipline referral data for decision making about student behavior in elementary and middle schools: An empirical evaluation of validity. *Journal of Positive Behavior Interventions, 8*(1), 10–23. doi:10.1177/10983007060080010301

Kelm, J. L., & McIntosh, K. (2012). Effects of school-wide positive behavior support on teacher self-efficacy. *Psychology in the Schools, 49*(2), 137–147. doi:10.1002/pits.20624

Kern, L., Hilt, A. M., & Gresham, F. (2004). An evaluation of the functional behavioral assessment process used with students with or at risk for emotional and behavioral disorders. *Education & Treatment of Children, 27*(4), 440–452. https://www.jstor.org/stable/42899816

Kincaid, D., & Fox, L. (2002). Person-centered planning and positive behavior support. In S. Holburn & P. Vietze (Eds.), *Research and practice in person-centered planning* (pp. 29- 50). Paul H. Brookes.

Kincaid, D., Childs, K. E., & George, H. (2010). *School-wide benchmarks of quality* (Revised) (Unpublished instrument). University of South Florida. www.flpbis.org

Lane, K. L., Wehby, J., Menzies, H. M., Doukas, G. L., Munton, S. M., & Gregg, R. M. (2003). Social skills instruction for students at risk for antisocial behavior: The effects of small-group instruction. *Behavioral Disorders, 28*(3), 229–248. doi:10.1177/019874290302800308

Lane, K. L., Oakes, W. P., Buckman, M. M., Sherod, R., & Lane, K. S., (November, 2020). *Systematic screening for behavior in current K-12 Settings.* Center on PBIS, University of Oregon. www.pbis.org.

LeBlanc, L. A., Raetz, P. B., Sellers, T. P., & Carr, J. E. (2016). A proposed model for selecting measurement procedures for the assessment and treatment of problem behavior. *Behavior Analysis in Practice, 9*(1), 77–83. doi:10.1007/s40617-015-0063-2

Lehr, C. A., Hansen, A., Sinclair, M. F., & Christenson, S. L. (2003). Moving beyond dropout towards school completion: An integrative review of data-based interventions. *School Psychology Review, 32*(3), 342–364. doi:10.1080/02796015.2003.12086205

Leverson, M., Smith, K., McIntosh, K., Rose, J., & Pinkelman, S. (2019). *PBIS cultural responsiveness field guide: Resources for trainers and coaches.* Center on PBIS. www.pbis.org.

Lewis, T. J., & Sugai, G. (1999). Effective behavior support: A systems approach to proactive school-wide management. *Focus on Exceptional Children, 31*(6), 1–24. doi:10.17161/foec.v31i6.6767

Lewis, T. J. (2009). Connecting school-wide positive behavior supports to the academic curriculum in PBIS high schools. In B. Flannery & G. Sugai (Eds.), *SWPBS implementation in high schools: Current practice and future directions* (pp. 57–80). Center for Positive Behavioral Interventions and Supports.

Lewis, T. J., Barrett, S., Sugai, G., & Horner, R. H. (2010). *Blueprint for school-wide positive behavior support training and professional development*. Center on PBIS. www.pbis.org.

Loman, S. L., Strickland-Cohen, M. K., & Walker, V. L. (2018). Promoting the accessibility of SWPBIS for students with severe disabilities. *Journal of Positive Behavior Interventions, 20*(2), 113–123. doi:10.1177/10983 00717733976

Lucyshyn, J. M., Albin, R. W., Horner, R. H., Mann, J. C., Mann, J. A., & Wadsworth, G. (2007). Family implementation of positive behavior support for a child with autism: longitudinal, single-case, experimental, and descriptive replication and extension. *Journal of Positive Behavior Interventions, 9*(3), 131–150. doi:10.11 77/10983007070090030201

Maggin, D. M., Zurheide, J., Pickett, K. C., & Baillie, S. J. (2015). A systematic evidence review of the check-in/checkout program for reducing student challenging behaviors. *Journal of Positive Behavior Interventions, 17*(4), 197–208. doi:10.1177/1098300715573630

Mathews, S., McIntosh, K., Frank, J. L., May, S. (2014). Critical features predicting sustained implementation of school-wide positive behavioral interventions and supports. *Journal of Positive Behavior Interventions, 16*(3), 168–178. doi:10.1177/1098300713484065

Mayer, G. R. (1995). Preventing antisocial behavior in the schools. *Journal of Applied Behavior Analysis, 28*(4), 467–478. doi:10.1901/jaba.1995.28-467

McDaniel, S. C., Bruhn, A. L., & Mitchell, B. S. (2015). A Tier 2 framework for behavior identification and intervention. *The Counseling Psychologist, 24*(1), 6–38. doi:10.1177/0011000010378402

McIntosh, K., Chard, D. J., Boland, J. B., & Horner, R. H. (2006). Demonstration of combined efforts in school-wide academic and behavioral systems and incidence of reading and behavior challenges in early elementary grades. *Journal of Positive Behavioral Interventions, 8*(3), 146–154. doi:10.1177/10983007060080030301

McIntosh, K., Horner, R. H., Chard, D. J., Dickey, C. R., and Braun, D. H. (2008). Reading skills and function of problem behavior in typical school settings. *Journal of Special Education, 42*(3), 131–147. doi:1 0.1177/0022466907313253

McIntosh, K., Horner, R. H., Sugai, G. (2009). Sustainability of systems-level evidence-based practices in schools: Current knowledge and future directions. In W. Sailor, G. Dunlap, G. Sugai, & R. Horner (Eds.), *Handbook of positive behavior support. Issues in clinical child psychology* (pp. 327–352). Springer. doi:10.1007/ 978-0-387-09632-2_14

McIntosh, K., Campbell, A. L., Carter, D. R., & Rossetto Dickey, C. (2009). Differential effects of a tier two behavior intervention based on function of problem behavior. *Journal of Positive Behavior Interventions, 11*(2), 82–93. doi:10.1177/1098300708319127

McIntosh, K., Filter, K. J., Bennett, J., Ryan, C., & Sugai, G. (2010). Principles of sustainable prevention: Designing scale-up of school-wide positive behavior support to promote durable systems. *Psychology in the Schools, 47*(1), 5–21. doi:10.1002/pits.20448

McIntosh, K., Bennett, J. L., & Price, K. (2011). Evaluation of social and academic effects of school-wide positive behavior support in a Canadian school district. *Exceptionality Education International, 21*(1), 46–60. doi:10.5206/eei.v21i1.7669

McIntosh, K., Mercer, S. H., Hume, A. E., Frank, J. L., Turri, M. G., & Mathews, S. (2013). Factors related to sustained implementation of schoolwide positive behavior support. *Exceptional Children, 79*, 293–311.

McIntosh, K., Predy, L. K., Upreti, G., Hume, A. E., Turri, M. G., & Mathews, S. (2014). Perceptions of contextual features related to implementation and sustainability of school-wide positive behavior support. *Journal of Positive Behavior Interventions, 16*(1), 31–43. doi:10.1177/1098300712470723

McIntosh, K., & Goodman, S. (2016). *Integrated multi-tiered systems of support: Blending RTI and PBIS*. Guilford Press.

McIntosh, K., Mercer, S. H., Nese, R. N. T., Strickland-Cohen, M. K., Kittelman, A., Hoselton, R., & Horner, R. H. (2018). Factors predicting sustained implementation of a universal behavior support framework. *Educational Researcher, 47*(5), 307–316. doi:10.3102/0013189X18776975

McIntosh, K., Kittleman, A., Morris, K., George, H. P., Simonsen, B., & Lewis, T. (2020). Support for district change. In J. McLeskey, F. Spooner, B. Algozzine, & N. L. Waldron (Eds.), *Handbook of effective inclusive elementary schools: Research and practice* (2nd ed.). Routledge.

Merikangas, K. R., He, J., Burstein, M., Swanson, S. A., Avenevoli, S., Cui, L., Benjet, C., Georgiades, K., & Swendsen, J. (2010). Lifetime prevalence of mental disorders in U. S. adolescents: Results from the national comorbidity survey replication – adolescent supplement (NCS-A). *Journal of the American Academy of Child and Adolescent Psychiatry, 49*(10), 980–989. doi:10.1016/j.jaac.2010.05.017

Meyer, K., Sears, S., Putnam, R., Phelan, C., Burnett, A., Warden, S., & Simonsen, B. (2020). Supporting students with disabilities with universal positive behavioral interventions and supports (PBIS): Lessons learned from research and practice. Manuscript under review.

Miller, M. A., Fenty, N., Scott, T. M., & Park, K. L. (2011). An examination of social skills instruction in the context of small-group reading. *Remedial and Special Education, 32*(5), 371–381. doi:10.1177/0741932510362240

Mitchell, B. S., Stormont, M., & Gage, N. A. (2011). Tier two interventions implemented within the context of a tiered prevention framework. *Behavioral Disorders, 36*(4), 241–261. doi:10.1177/019874291103600404

Mitchell, B. S., Adamson, R., & McKenna, J. W. (2017). Curbing our enthusiasm: An analysis of the check-in/check-out literature using the Council for Exceptional Children's evidence-based practice standards. *Behavior Modification, 41*(3), 343–367. doi:10.1177/0145445516675273

Mitchell, M. M., & Bradshaw, C. P. (2013). Examining classroom influences on student perceptions of school climate: The role of classroom management and exclusionary discipline strategies. *Journal of School Psychology, 51*(5), 599–610. doi:10.1016/j.jsp.2013.05.005

Newcomer, L. L., & Lewis, T. J. (2004). Functional behavioral assessment: An investigation of assessment reliability and effectiveness of function-based interventions. *Journal of Emotional and Behavioral Disorders, 12*(3), 168–181. doi:10.1177/10634266040120030401

O'Neill, R. E., Albin, R. W., Storey, K., Horner, R. H., & Sprague, J. R. (2015). *Functional assessment and program development for problem behavior: A practical handbook* (3rd ed.). Cengage Learning.

Preciado, J. A., Horner, R. H., & Baker, S. K. (2009). Using a function-based approach to decrease problem behaviors and increase academic engagement for Latino English language learners. *The Journal of Special Education, 42*(4), 227–240. doi:10.1177/0022466907313350

Richter, M. M., Lewis, T. J., & Hagar, J. (2012). The relationship between principal leadership skills and school-wide positive behavior support: An exploratory study. *Journal of Positive Behavior Interventions, 14*(2), 69–77. doi:10.1177/1098300711399097

Ross, S., & Horner, R. (2009). Bully prevention in positive behavior support. *Journal of Applied Behavior Analysis, 42*(4), 747–759. doi:10.1901/jaba.2009.42-747

Ross, S. W., Romer, N., & Horner, R. H. (2012). Teacher well-being and the implementation of school-wide positive behavior interventions and supports. *Journal of Positive Behavior Interventions, 14*(2), 118–128. doi:10.1177/1098300711413820

Scott, T. M., & Eber, L. (2003). Functional assessment and wraparound as systemic school processes: Primary, secondary, and tertiary systems examples. *Journal of Positive Behavior Interventions, 5*(3), 131–143. doi:10.1177/10983007030050030201

Shogren, K. A., Wehmeyer, M. L., Lane, K. L., & Quirk, C. (2017a). Multitiered systems of supports. In M. L. Wehmeyer & K. A. Shogren (Eds.), *Handbook of research-based practices for educating students with intellectual disability* (pp. 185–198). Routledge/Taylor & Francis Group.

Shogren, K. A., Wehmeyer, M. L., & Thompson, J. R. (2017b). Person-centered and student-directed planning. In M. L. Wehmeyer & K. A. Shogren (Eds.), *Handbook of research-based practices for educating students with intellectual disability* (pp. 167–182). Routledge/Taylor & Francis Group.

Shuster, B. C., Gustafson, J. R., Jenkins, A. B., Lloyd, B. P., Carter, E. W., & Bernstein, C. F. (2017). Including students with disabilities in positive behavioral interventions and supports: Experiences and perspectives of special educators. *Journal of Positive Behavior Interventions, 19*(3), 143–157. doi:10.1177/1098300716675734

Simonsen, B., & Sugai, G. (2007). Using school-wide data systems to make decisions efficiently and effectively. *School Psychology Forum, 1*(2), 46–58. https://www.nasponline.org/publications/periodicals/spf/volume-1/volume-1-issue-2/using-school-wide-data-systems-to-make-decisions-efficiently-and-effectively

Simonsen, B., Britton, L., & Young, D. (2010). School-wide positive behavior support in an alternative school setting: A case study. *Journal of Positive Behavior Interventions, 12*(3), 180–191. doi:10.1177/1098300708330495

Simonsen, B., Myers, D., & Briere, D. E. (2011). Comparing a behavioral check-in/check-out (CICO) intervention with standard practice in an urban middle school using an experimental group design. *Journal of Positive Behavior Interventions, 13*(1), 31–48. doi:10.1177/1098300709359026

Simonsen, B., Eber, L., Black, A. C., Sugai, G., Lewandowski, H., Sims, B., & Myers, D. (2012). Illinois statewide positive behavioral interventions and supports: Evolution and impact on student outcomes across years. *Journal of Positive Behavior Interventions, 14*(1), 5–16. doi:10.1177/1098300711412601

Simonsen, B., Freeman, J., Myers, D., Dooley, K., Maddock, E., Kern, L., & Byun, S. (2020). Effects of targeted professional development on teachers' implementation of key classroom management skills. *Journal of Positive Behavior Interventions, 22*(1), 3–14. doi:10.1177/1098300719859615

Sinclair, M. F., Christenson, S. L., Evelo, D. L., & Hurley, C. M. (1998). Dropout prevention for youth with disabilities: Efficacy of a sustained school engagement procedure. *Exceptional Children, 65*(1), 7–21. doi:10.1177/001440299806500101

Skinner, B. F. (1953). *Science and human behavior.* MacMillan.

Smith, T. M., & Ingersoll, R. M. (2004). What are the effects of induction and mentoring on beginning teacher turnover? *American Educational Research Journal, 41*(3), 681–714. doi:10.3102/00028312041003681

Smith-Bird, E., & Turnbull, A. P. (2005). Linking positive behavior support to family quality-of-life outcomes. *Journal of Positive Behavior Interventions,* 7(3), 174–180. doi:10.1177/10983007050070030601

Sprague, J., & Perkins, K. (2009). Direct and collateral effects of the First Step to Success program. *Journal of Positive Behavior Interventions, 11*(4), 208–221. doi:10.1177/1098300708330935

Strickland-Cohen, M. K., & Horner, R. H. (2015). Typical school personnel developing and implementing basic behavior support plans. *Journal of Positive Behavior Interventions, 17*(2), 83–94. doi:10.1177/1098300714554714

Sugai, G., Horner, R. H., Dunlap, G., Hieneman, M., Lewis, T. J., Nelson, Scott, T., Liaupsin, C., Sailor, W.,Turnbull, A. P., Turnbull, H. R., Wickham, D., Wilcox, B., & Reuf, M. (2000). Applying positive behavior support and functional behavioral assessment in schools. *Journal of Positive Behavior Interventions, 2*(3), 131–143. doi:10.1177/109830070000200302

Sugai, G., & Horner, R. H. (2002). The evolution of discipline practices: School-wide positive behavior supports. *Child and Family Behavior Therapy, 24*(1-2), 23–50. doi:10.1300/J019v24n01_03

Sugai, G., & Horner, R. (2006). A promising approach for expanding and sustaining the implementation of school-wide positive behavior support. *School Psychology Review, 35*(2), 245–259. doi:10.1080/02796015.2006.12087989

Sugai, G., & Horner, R. H. (2008). What we know and need to know about preventing problem behavior in schools. *Exceptionality, 16*(2), 67–77. doi:10.1080/09362830801981138

Sugai, G., Horner, R. H., & McIntosh, K. (2008). Best practices in developing a broad-scale system of support for school-wide positive behavior support. In A. Thomas & J. P. Grimes (Eds.), *Best practices in school psychology V* (Vol. 3, pp. 765–780). National Association of School Psychologists.

Sugai, G., Horner, R., & Todd, A. (2009). *PBIS Self-Assessment Survey (SAS) Assessing and Planning Behavior Support in Schools* (Version 3.0). Center on PBIS. www.pbis.org

Sugai, G., & Horner, R. H. (2009). Responsiveness-to-intervention and school-wide positive behavior supports: Integration of multi-tiered approaches. *Exceptionality, 17*(4), 223–237. doi:10.1080/09362830903235375

Sugai, G., Horner, R. H., Algozzine, R., Barrett, S., Lewis, T., Anderson, C., Bradley, R., Choi, J. H., Dunlap, G., Eber, L., George, H., Kincaid, D., McCart, A., Nelson, M., Newcomer, L., Putnam, R., Riffel, L., Rovins, M., Sailor, W., Simonsen, B. (2010). *School-wide positive behavior support: Implementers' blueprint and self-assessment.* Center on PBIS. www.pbis.org

Sugai, G., & Horner, R. H., Fixsen, D., & Blase, K. (2010). Developing systems-level capacity for response to intervention implementation: Current efforts and future directions. In T. A. Glover & S. Vaughn (Eds.), *Response to intervention: Empowering all students to learn – A critical account of the science and practice* (pp. 286–309). Guilford.

Sugai, G., O'Keeffe, B. V., & Fallon, L. M. (2012). A contextual consideration of culture and school-wide positive behavior support. *Journal of Positive Behavior Interventions, 14*(4), 197–208. doi:10.1177/1098300711426334

Sugai, G., O'Keeffe, B. V., Horner, R. H., & Lewis, T. (2012). Leadership and school-wide positive behavior support. In J. B. Crockett, B. S. Billingsley, & M. L. Boscardin (Eds.), *Handbook of leadership in special education* (pp. 297–314). Taylor & Francis/Routledge.

Sugai, G., Horner, R., Lewis-Palmer, T., & Rossetto-Dickey, C. (2014). *PBIS Team Implementation Checklist (TIC 3.1).* Center on PBIS. www.pbis.org

Swain-Bradway, J., Johnson, S. L., Bradshaw, C., & McIntosh, K. (November, 2017). *What are the economic costs of implementing SWPBIS in comparison to the benefits from reducing suspensions?* Center on PBIS. www.pbis.org

Todd, A. W., Horner, R. H., Sugai, G., & Sprague, J. R. (1999). Effective behavior support: Strengthening school-wide systems through a team-based approach. *Effective School Practices, 17*(4), 23–27.

U. S. Department of Education. (2019). *41stannual report to Congress on the implementation of the Individuals with Disabilities Education Act, 2019.* U.S. Department of Education, Office of Special Education Programs. https://www2.ed.gov/about/reports/annual/osep/2019/parts-b-c/41st-arc-for-idea.pdf

Vincent, C. G., Swain-Bradway, J., Tobin, T. J., & May, S. (2011). Disciplinary referrals for culturally and linguistically diverse students with and without disabilities: Patterns resulting from school-wide positive behavior support. *Exceptionality, 19*(3), 175–190. doi:10.1080/09362835.2011.579936

Waasdorp, T. E., Bradshaw, C. P., & Leaf, P. J. (2012). The impact of school-wide positive behavioral interventions and supports on bullying and peer rejection: A randomized control effectiveness trial. *Archives of Pediatrics and Adolescent Medicine, 166*(2), 149–156. doi:10.1001/archpediatrics.2011.755

Walker, H. M., Horner, R. H., Sugai, G., Bullis, M., Sprague, J. R., Bricker, D., & Kaufman, M. J. (1996). Integrated approaches to preventing antisocial behavior patterns among school-age children and youth. *Journal of Emotional and Behavioral Disorders, 4*(4), 193–256. doi:10.1177/106342669600400401

Walker, H. M., Seeley, J. R., Small, J., Severson, H. H., Graham, B. A., Feil, E. G., Serna, L., Golly, A. M., & Forness, S. R. (2009). A randomized controlled trial of the First Step to Success early intervention: Demonstration of program efficacy outcomes in a diverse, urban school district. *Journal of Emotional and Behavioral Disorders, 17*(4), 197–212. doi:10.1177/1063426609341645

Wang, C., & Algozzine, B. (2011). Rethinking the relationship between reading and behavior in early elementary school. *Journal of Educational Research, 104*(2), 100–109. doi:10.1080/00220670903567380

Wolfe, K., Pyle, D., Charlton, C., Sabey, C., Lund, E., & Ross, S. (2016). A systematic review of the empirical support for Check-In Check-Out. *Journal of Positive Behavior Interventions, 18*(2), 74–88. doi:10.1177/1098300715595957

Yong, M., & Cheney, D. A. (2013). Essential features of Tier 2 social-behavioral interventions. *Psychology in the Schools, 50*(8), 844–861. doi:10.1002/pits.21710

8

The Form and Function of Data Teams in Inclusive Schools

Erin A. Chaparro[1], Robert H. Horner[1], Rhonda N. T. Nese[1], Bob Algozzine[2], and Anne Todd[1]

[1]UNIVERSITY OF OREGON

[2]UNIVERSITY OF NORTH CAROLINA AT CHARLOTTE

Setting the Stage

An under-appreciated feature of inclusive education is the need for rapid and iterative decision-making. Students arrive with a wide range of academic, mental health, and behavior support needs. Academic and behavior instructional supports must be tailored to the student, community, and faculty, and some students may need more intensive, individualized support (Tier 3) to benefit from Tier 1 (Universal) and Tier 2 (Targeted) opportunities (McIntosh & Goodman, 2016). Information about student needs and school strengths guide initial support decisions, while ongoing decision making and adaptations to school practices are dependent on the frequent assessment of the success of student supports. The net result is that inclusive education is effective only when schools use an efficient and effective process for decision-making. The assumptions underlying this chapter are that *effective* decision-making (a) is more likely done by a team than by individuals, (b) is more likely when the team has access to relevant and easy-to-interpret data and (c) is more likely when the team has a formal process for problem solving and decision-making. In this chapter, we discuss the promise of data teams in inclusive schools and how they have evolved. We focus especially on what is known about the features of effective data teams, describe a validated decision-making framework, and discuss the role of data teams in integrating evidence-based practices in inclusive schools.

The Promise of Data Teams

A unifying characteristic of schools in America is the reliance on teams to organize educational reform and improvement. This is especially true for schools working to improve inclusive education where teams of administrators, faculty, staff, students, and families are focused on improving the ability to succeed across a wider range of educational challenges (Newton et al., 2014). These teams constantly search for new practices that will make efforts more effective, equitable, and easier to implement. Successful teams typically combine their values, organizational context, and vision with regular review and discussion of data. Thus, school teams that consistently use data for decision

DOI: 10.4324/9781003043874-8

making (e.g., identifying problems, monitoring progress, evaluating status and outcomes) are considered "data teams."

The promise of data teams, however, is realized not just when a team has access to data but when the team is well organized and clear about the problem-solving protocol that will be used to achieve practical outcomes (Todd et al., 2012). Effective teams meet to identify and solve problems. Meetings are organized to improve instructional outcomes for all students. A familiar routine includes meeting regularly to review pertinent data, make plans to bring about change, and check to ensure that the plans are being implemented as intended and having desired effects. The outcomes to determine the successful implementation of the plan may or may not be easy to track. All teams begin with good intentions, but sometimes team members leave the meeting unclear about what decisions were made, what was planned, and if the plan is going to support the student. When teams meet as a data team or problem-solving team, they are planning to be:

a. organized to maximize efficiencies and resources,
b. fluent with gathering appropriate data and interpreting the data to make decisions,
c. knowledgeable in action plan development and implementation, and
d. communicative with multiple stakeholders (Newton et al., 2014).

In addition to those characteristics, an effective data team must also have skills in areas that are less frequently emphasized. Although not all team members need expertise in data interpretation, it is helpful to have a team composed of individuals with complementary and overlapping competencies. For example, effective teams should include some members who are knowledgeable about a range of evidence-based academic and behavioral interventions. Other team members need more fluency in using data to enable adaptations of interventions. In addition, team members need to bring the authority and resources needed for the team to be effective. When these skills and resources come together to support an effective problem-solving process, the impacts can be powerful and positive (Todd et al., 2012).

The Evolution of Data Teams

Foundational research on data teams used the problem-solving approach to identify students at risk for academic and behavioral difficulties (McIntosh & Goodman, 2016). Little focus was on who was on the data team, how the data team operated, and what the function of the team was beyond solving problems at the individual student level. In more modern contexts, and with the contribution of areas of research on implementation, we know that teams play an important role in making problem-solving decisions for individual students, groups of students, and sometimes the entire school building (Fixsen et al., 2013). Although we know that data teams are important, challenges remain determining the number of data sources and the best methods for using those data to improve outcomes (Hamilton et al., 2009; Kekahio & Baker, 2013; Marsh et al., 2006).

The steps in a problem-solving process have remained consistent. The framework discussed in this chapter, Team-Initiated Problem Solving (TIPS; Newton et al., 2012), uses both Bransford and Stein's (1984) and Deno's (2005) problem-solving approach as foundations. Bransford and Stein's work integrated research findings into a simple, easy-to-understand framework referred to as the "IDEAL" model; **i**dentify the problem, **d**efine the problem, **e**xplore strategies, **a**ct on the strategies, **l**ook back and evaluate the outcome. Deno (2005) translated the IDEAL model into a format specifically designed for school-based problem solvers, emphasizing the usefulness of the model's problem-solving steps for assessment (measurement) procedures and associated evaluation decisions. Deno's framework has been adapted to fit the procedural and content expectations of school data teams in the TIPS model. The core steps have been retained and specific procedures for using data to fulfill functions at each step have been developed (Newton, Todd et al., 2009). In this context, the focus for data teams in schools is (a) identifying problems and goals for change with precision and (b) selecting, implementing, monitoring, and adapting solutions to achieve outcomes that benefit students.

Data teams to Support Individual Students

Without a frequent and consistent review of data, the needs of students may go unidentified and a lack of progress may go unnoticed (Newton, Horner et al., 2009). Similarly, students who have been identified with a disability may receive ineffective supports if data are not reviewed and a team does not monitor the implementation of plans. The importance of data use for inclusive schools is of heightened importance given the key role of team decision-making for children with disabilities. Since 2011, the number of students aged 3-21 years who receive special education services has increased from 6.3 to 7 million. In the 2017-2018 academic year, students with disabilities made up 14% of the student population. Of those students, 34% had a specific learning disability, and 5% had the disability category emotional disturbance. Most students with disabilities performed at the "below basic" level (McFarland et al., 2019). Research shows that a student's academic and behavior skills are strongly related (Madigan et al., 2016). Discipline disparities experienced by students with disabilities compared to those without disabilities have been recognized extensively in research and national reports. For example, students with disabilities are overrepresented by 13.2% among students suspended from schools (U.S. Department of Education, 2018). The higher likelihood of negative outcomes for students with disabilities is disheartening, especially as we have several strategies known to be effective with all students, including students with disabilities. Minority students, including African American, Latinx, and Native Indigenous students, are overrepresented as having a disability (McFarland et al., 2019). An estimated 60% of students eligible for special education instruction receive about 20% of their instruction in special education classrooms (McFarland et al., 2019), with the remaining receiving their instruction in inclusive settings. When data teams have access to accurate and appropriate data, they can be sure to monitor action plans closely.

In the remainder of this chapter, we discuss what we know about data teams from research and steps schools can take to use these principles to enhance data teams and problem solving with the end goal of enhancing inclusive settings for students. We focus on the TIPS framework, which can support the form of what data teams do as well as improve their overall functioning in inclusive schools.

What Do We Know Based on Research?

Impressive literature provides guidance and recommendations about the need for and the process of team-based problem solving (Bransford & Stein, 1984; Carroll & Johnson, 1990; D'Zurilla et al., 2004; Gilbert, 1978; Huber, 1980; Jorgensen et al., 1981; Newton, Horner et al., 2009; Tropman, 1996; Ysseldyke et al., 2006). There are evidence-based environmental supports that can encourage efficient team meetings (Newton, Horner et al., 2009). For example, having a regular schedule for meetings with team members that hold specific roles and having agreed upon team mission has been found to support the efficiency of the teaming. In the remainder of this section, we introduce one scientifically based framework for data teaming called TIPS, which stands for Team-Initiated Problem Solving.

TIPS is a six-stage model of data-based decision making that has been used within the implementation of multi-tiered systems of academic and behavior support and validated in one multiple baseline single case study and two randomized waitlist-controlled trials (Horner et al., 2018;

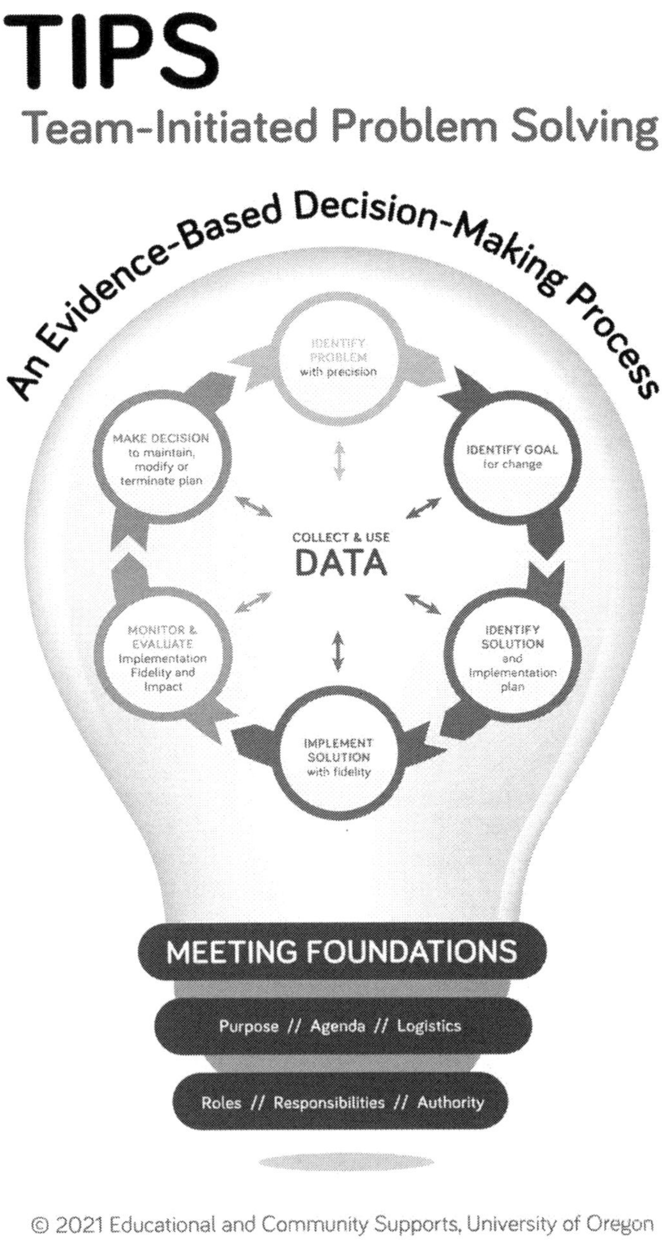

Figure 8.1 The TIPS Framework (Copyright 2021 Educational and Community Supports, University of Oregon. Reprinted with permission from author.)

Newton et al., 2012). The TIPS framework is comprised of two major components (a) meeting foundations and (b) an evidence-based problem-solving process. These two components can be broken down into sub-features and are named in Figure 8.1, which will be discussed in greater detail in later sections of this chapter. First, it is important to understand that the TIPS framework, both meeting foundations and the problem-solving process, have been validated through multiple studies. Next, we will highlight three empirical studies.

Todd et al. (2011) used a multiple baseline design with four elementary data teams. Using a multiple baseline design allowed researchers to observe and document a functional relation between training on TIPS and the problem solving behaviors of the data team. In this study (Todd et al., 2011), behavior support teams focused on individual student problem solving were made up of 3 to 10 educators, including a building administrator, a school psychologist, classroom teachers and other representatives as needed (i.e., caregiver or school social worker). Each of the four schools who participated was already implementing MTSS for behavior (i.e., PBIS) and had received a score of 80% or higher on a fidelity measure indicating strong systems-level implementation of universal or Tier 1 systems. Direct observation data were collected at team meetings before the TIPS training (baseline) and after the 6-hour in-person training. After the TIPS training, the first two meetings were facilitated by a district coach to model and ensure that the team was able to initially demonstrate the defining features of the TIPS framework. After the first two coached meetings, the teams continued independently to determine if the teams could sustain and apply their learning from the training and coached meetings. Results from this study indicate that after the training, teams did, in fact, make an immediate and sustained improvement (e.g., averaging 86% fidelity) on both meeting foundations and problem-solving practices. With a one-day training and two coached meetings, typical behavior support teams were able to implement and sustain research-recommended practices for effective problem solving and data teaming.

Newton et al. (2012) report on an experimental study that randomly assigned 34 Tier 1 PBIS teams to receive the TIPS training in the first cohort or to a wait-list condition that required the teams to receive the training in the second cohort. These teams were responsible for the oversight of PBIS implementation by ensuring that the overall systems were running smoothly. For example, the responsibilities of a Tier 1 PBIS team can include training teachers, providing lesson plans for teachers, creating and sharing the school-based incentive systems, and looking at data to problem-solve any areas where groups of students are struggling (e.g., 4th graders being disrespectful at recess). Teams in this study had 10 members on average. Teams were mostly made up of classroom teachers with perhaps a special education teacher and an administrator. The team who received the five-hour training and two coached meetings first had statistically significant improvements in the areas of meeting foundations and, more importantly, in the areas of using data to make decisions, establishing solutions, implementing action plans, and defining problems with precision. In short, teams that received the training plus two coach-facilitated meetings demonstrated greater implementation integrity in the key features of the TIPS framework. The schools in the wait-list condition, or second cohort, were included in a replication study. Once again, the training plus coaching formula was successful in leading to increased implementation of the meeting foundations and components of the data-based decision-making process (Newton et al., 2012). While it is critical to establish this direct connection between professional development, coaching, and data team behaviors, it is imperative to know if these practices can positively impact student outcomes.

With the goal of once again experimentally evaluating the TIPS professional development and coaching but with the added goal of impacting student outcomes, the same team of researchers conducted another randomized controlled trial with teams assigned to receiving the treatment in the first cohort or the second waitlist cohort (Horner et al., 2018). Thirty-eight Tier 1 PBIS teams were observed monthly and data was gathered before they received treatment and after they received the treatment. Significant differences were not observed in the meeting foundations growth largely because the teams started the study with well-organized roles, responsibilities, and practices. The more complicated aspects of the TIPS framework (e.g., problem-solving procedures and decision-making processes) demonstrated improvement only with direct training and coaching. This study demonstrates that teams using TIPS can improve quickly and that the use of data is critical for both initial problem-solving and ongoing adaptations and modifications to interventions. So, what about the improved student outcomes questions? We already knew adult behavior could be changed. The question remained; can data teams positively improve student outcomes by improving their data-based decision-making skills as a team? This study reports that when teams improved their problem solving and decision-making practices, they were statistically more likely to document a reduction in office discipline referrals per 100 students than waitlist teams. In addition, TIPS treatment teams had statistically significant reduced numbers of Out-of-School Suspensions (OSS) after participating in the training/coaching and had a greater reduction of OSS than schools in the waitlist condition (Horner et al., 2018). Now we have confirmation that teams using the TIPS framework are:

a. more likely to use academic and behavioral data to identify problems,
b. more likely to select practical and functional solutions,
c. more likely to implement those solutions, and most importantly,
d. more likely to document academic and behavioral gains for students (Horner et al., 2018).

A strong research base now exists indicating that the TIPS framework is effective at improving the effectiveness and efficiency of school-based data teams and delivering valued change in student outcomes. In the following sections, we describe in greater detail the function of data teams (i.e., the data-based decision-making) and the form of data teams (i.e., the meeting foundations).

The Function of Data Teams

There are many teams in every school, and it seems that all teams have some source of data they are asked to review and use. Any emphasis on building data teams needs to recognize the danger of data overload. Too often, educators are given too much data in the wrong format and with limited ability, time or structure for productive problem solving. Successful data teams have the right data, in the right format, at the right time, and with an agreed upon protocol for decision making. The first step in effective problem-solving, however, is not the data but the structure, function, and purpose of the team. A critical discussion for any group of gathered professionals is to determine the purpose of the time spent together. Is the team's purpose to identify students who need supports and to refer those students to other teams? Is the team's purpose to monitor intervention effectiveness? Or is the team's purpose to use data to develop an intervention plan for a student or small group of students? Essentially, each data team must decide how they will function to support individual students or to support the school systems that allow teachers and specialists to support students. Data teams make decisions about how to allocate the limited resources in schools (time, people, materials) to best meet the needs of their students. Successful teams focus first on clarifying their purpose and their decision-making authority, and once these are defined, they focus on the type and format of data needed to make good decisions. Data teams help to make action plans and decisions for individual students and for the overall system. The teams also facilitate communication between these supports systems. Let us take a closer look at individual student support, systems-level support, and communication and coordination between the two levels.

Individual Student Support

The literature examining data teams has often been targeted on teams building support for individual students and how those students may be included successfully in typical school settings and activities. At the individual student level, we can use data to assist the team with the goal of authentic inclusion while maximizing student learning. A positive result does not automatically occur because we have placed a student in an inclusive setting for part of their school day. In the placement and scheduling process, teams can use data to answer questions about student progress within each setting and content area. Those questions might ask if the student is growing on measurable academic or behavioral outcomes and how much progress the student is making within a specific period of time. In addition to student performance goal questions, a data team can also ask questions about the fidelity with which a support plan is being delivered. For example, if a student is scheduled to be in a 3rd grade classroom for reading instruction every day of the school week, but the speech therapist pulls the student out from that period regularly, we know the fidelity of the plan is less than intended. Both student performance data and fidelity data should be easy to collect, monitor, and interpret so that teams can make decisions and be responsive in a timely manner.

Systems Level Support

Data teams also play a critical role at the whole-school level. Few schools today are delivering the most effective academic and behavior supports needed to make schools safe and effective learning environments (Gershoff & Font, 2016; Hussar et al., 2020; Lacoe & Steinberg, 2019; U.S. Department of Education, 2017; Wagner et al., 2009). It can be the role of a data team to help the school and district decide which evidence-based strategies to select, train, coach, and support. This is an example of a system that supports inclusion practices in schools. Systems-level decisions can determine how many teachers need training in effective behavior support strategies for inclusive classroom environments or determine what percentage of students in inclusive settings are making desired levels of progress. These data are going to be gathered across multiple students, grade levels, and teachers. A data team making systems-level decisions can answer questions about a building's capacity for serving students with different needs, how many staff are needed to provide various services, and if the desired outcomes are being met. While student-level data are being reviewed weekly, systems-level data teams usually answer these types of questions on a monthly, quarterly, or longer basis.

Communication and Coordination

Whether teams are established at the student-level or systems-level data team, it is important for all teams to build formal strategies to share information (with each other, with the faculty, and with families). For example, if an intervention data team knows they have room to serve 25 students in the school (systems-level), but they are only serving 20, then they can communicate to all staff and to the student study team (student level) to identify individual students who might benefit from an intervention applied proactively. Conversely, if an individual student study team has an action plan for an individual student but does not have the needed resources, they may need to make a request to the building leadership team (systems-level) for additional resources like personnel time or materials. Data teams at all levels are gathering, interpreting, and using data from multiple sources, and they should also be sharing and communicating the results of their process with various stakeholders, including other teachers, administrators, and district boards. Data teams making decisions for individual students and systems can use the TIPS framework to facilitate both the structure or form of their data team and the function or the process by which data are interpreted and used.

The Form of Data Teams

There are teams for everything in school buildings, so when we think of data teams, we sometimes assume that we are all on the same page about who is on a data team and how the data team should function. Through the TIPS framework, we have carefully defined the form of data teams to take the guesswork out of that awkward moment when you are looking for someone to take notes or find the data that is needed for the team. In the next section, we will describe just that—the form of data teams.

Meeting Foundations

Within the TIPS framework, we define the meeting foundations as the context within which effective decision making occurs. There are six components to the meeting foundations: (1) specified roles and (2) responsibilities for each member of the team, (3) a person of authority as a member, (4) a clear purpose for the team, (5) an agenda for each meeting, and (6) clear logistical expectations. Descriptions of components 1 through 3 are provided below. Although components 4–6 may seem more common, they can help to set the tone for a functional meeting. As we stated earlier, it is important for every team to know the primary purpose and the scope and reach of their efforts (Component 4). It can be disheartening if one group is replicating the efforts of another instead of completing new and complementary work. Component 5 is having an agenda. The agenda should match the purpose of the meeting, which will help to reinforce the focus of the decision-making and goal-setting procedures to come. Finally, you may ask which logistical expectations (Component 6) should be set. The TIPS framework emphasizes starting and ending the meeting on time, having the meeting scheduled in advance, and reserving meeting spaces or computer equipment in advance so that these logistical issues do not take valuable meeting time away from the agenda. TIPS meetings are designed to be efficient, beginning and ending within 10 minutes of the scheduled times and prompting the team to review the most critical information for rendering and evaluating decisions in a time-sensitive manner. The three features of the meeting foundations—purpose, agenda, and logistics—are carried out by the various members of the team. The other aspects of meeting foundations define and describe the roles and responsibilities of data team members using the TIPS framework.

Roles and Responsibilities

A team has a clear purpose, has data gathered data, and has logistics organized from where the meeting will be located to how often the meeting will occur. Too often, when a team member arrives for a meeting, it is unclear who is going to do the various task needed for an effective meeting. Time is then spent figuring out who is going to take notes and present the data and communicate with others about what needs to be done with the gathered data. To avoid those unproductive moments that cost the team valuable time, the other essential features of the TIPS meeting foundations are to identify the roles and responsibilities of all team members and to ensure that one team member has administrative authority. All team members have general responsibilities, and specific members have additional responsibilities depending on their assigned role (see Table 8.1).

Within a TIPS data meeting, there are five clearly defined roles: Facilitator, Minute Taker, Data Analyst, Administrator, and Team Member. The Facilitator guides the team through the agenda. The Minute Taker records critical information from the team's decision making and data analysis discussions into the TIPS Meeting Minutes form (or similar) for future tracking and follow-up. The Data Analyst summarizes and interprets data for the team during the meeting and ensures all relevant data will be available for the meeting. The administrator is available to make resource allocation decisions needed to move forward with action plans. Finally, all personnel on the team are referred to as Team Members and these other roles of Data Analyst, Facilitator, Minute Taker, and Administrator are layered onto the role and responsibility of the Team Member. Because it's important to have various voices from your school building fulfill these roles, you may find that from year-to-year people may shift in their roles and thereby increase their depth of knowledge of the decision-making process.

Each team can assign one person to each role, and ideally, a second person can also be assigned as a back-up. Having a back-up person ensures there is rarely a reason for the meeting to be delayed or canceled because a critical team member is absent or has duties that require their presence elsewhere.

Table 8.1 TIPS Team Responsibilities

Participant	*Expectation*
All	Before meeting: • Inform facilitator of potential or planned absence/prepare backup • Complete assigned tasksDuring meeting: • Practice focused & active participation • Ask questions of inquiry & clarification • Acknowledge ideasAfter meeting: • Review tasks and timelines • Take appropriate actions
Facilitator	Before meeting: • Remind team members about upcoming meeting and related tasks • Prepare meeting agendaStart meeting: • Call to order • Review roles for meeting • Review and adapt meeting agendaDuring meeting: • Manage time & flow of meeting • Ensure implementation fidelity of TIPS • Confirm next meeting date, roles, location
Data Analyst	Before meeting: • Prepare data summaries from previous meeting minutes • Review data for students of concernDuring meeting: • Generate data summaries/reports as needed
Minute Taker	Before meeting: • Prepare meeting minutesDuring meeting: • Record decisions in meeting minutesAfter meeting: • Clean up meeting minutes to ensure accuracy • Post meeting minutes
Administrator	During meeting: • Make authoritative decisions as needed

With the meeting foundations in place, a team is ready to move on to the critical work of using data to make decisions. In the next section, we will introduce the phases of the process at the heart of every data team. Using Figure 8.1 as a reference, note that the base of the lightbulb includes the meeting foundations, and the light bulb itself is illuminated through the successful execution of the decision-making process.

Decision-Making Process

The TIPS decision-making process includes six stages: (a) identifying a problem with precision, (b) identifying a goal for change, (c) identifying a solution and implementation plan, (d) implementing the solution with fidelity, (e) monitoring and evaluating implementation fidelity and impact, and (f) making a decision to maintain, modify, or terminate the plan. In the following section, we will generally describe the decision-making process so that it could be applied to either the student level or the systems level.

In our experience, the three most common difficulties encountered in team meeting processes are (a) spending the meeting time in discussion but without making decisions, (b) making decisions about solving a problem without first defining the problem with precision, and (c) failing to use data to guide decision-making. Each of these becomes less likely when a team agrees to a formal process for presenting and reviewing data and a clear protocol for decision-making. Among the most helpful elements of an effective decision making protocol is to agree that problems will be defined with operational precision before the team moves to a discussion about the selection of solutions. Precision problem identification involves the specification of six key elements related to the problem being observed: (a) what is the problem (e.g., the behavior that is different from desired patterns), (b) when is the problem most likely to occur, (c) who is engaging in or affected by the problem, (d) where is the problem most (and least) likely to occur, (e) how often is the problem occurring, and (f) why does the problem keep happening (e.g., what reinforcers maintain the unwanted behavior). By clearly identifying each of these elements based on available data, teams can select a reasonable and ambitious goal (e.g., how would the team like the behavior to change) that is logically related to both the magnitude of the problem and the hypothesized maintaining function of the problem. Within the TIPS framework, a goal must specify what change will occur on a given indicator of performance (e.g., oral reading fluency will increase to 120 words correct per minute, or name-calling on the playground will decrease to no more than two events per week), and by what date the change will occur. Once an appropriate goal has been identified, the team moves on to selecting a solution that it anticipates will meet the specified goal for those involved. At this point, it is important for teams to utilize a clear and systematized protocol for identifying and selecting solutions that address the function of the academic and/or social behavior that is in need of improvement, build on prosocial and adaptive skills, and have evidence to suggest that they are effective at reaching the desired outcome that the students are working to achieve.

Solutions emphasize environmental changes and malleable factors associated with instruction (e.g., the actual intervention). Effective teams discuss solution options and identify practices that are both evidence-based and consistent with the cultural needs of the context. A plan is then articulated for how the identified solution will be implemented in practice for those affected. The plan is developed by the team collaboratively. Specifically, the team will determine who will be responsible for implementing the proposed changes/intervention, when the changes will occur, with what frequency it will be implemented, and when it will be delivered during the school day (matched to the "when" of the problem statement for problems involving social behavior). Following the specification of the solution implementation plan, the team decides how and by whom implementation will be monitored for fidelity.

For problems that have been well addressed (e.g., precisely defined, a goal set, a solution with contextual fit selected and implemented, and fidelity monitored), the team will review student progress and fidelity of implementation data at subsequent meetings. The implementation of the solution will be monitored using fidelity data collected according to the implementation plan. The impact of this implementation on relevant student performance (individual students or groups of students) will be evaluated. Once this has occurred, a summative evaluation decision will be made regarding the effectiveness of a particular intervention for a particular student or group of students. After confirming that the implementation of the intervention or instruction was carried out with fidelity, the team can make decisions about continuing, modifying, or terminating the plan with confidence. During the evaluation of intervention impact on student performance, the team may determine that the intervention had no effect, it had a detrimental effect, performance improved but not to criterion, performance improved to criterion (goal is met), or that the data are unclear.

Based upon this evaluation, the team will then make a summative evaluation decision. If improvement occurred but not to criterion, the team will either identify a malleable factor (e.g., number of students in small group instruction) to adjust or decide to defer further action and see if the impact increases during the next data collection cycle. If the goal has been met, the intervention will likely be reduced in intensity or potentially discontinued altogether. If performance has not improved, the intensity will be increased, or another malleable factor will be altered (e.g., repeat the directions for appropriate requests for help before each instructional session rather before every other instructional session). An intervention modification can potentially include the trial of a completely different intervention better matched to the precision problem statement. This decision-making process can be used at the student level for individualized inclusion planning or at the systems level to understand the functioning of overall efforts to increase inclusion outcomes for selected groups of students.

In summary, nearly every team in a school is a data team and those teams can only be effective in their efforts if they have the data they need to make important decisions and a protocol for using those data for decision-making. The TIPS framework is an evidence-based strategy that data teams can use to help structure a team meeting by using the meeting foundations through assigned roles and responsibilities for all team members and by having a plan for important logistics such as the what, when, and why of the meeting. With the meeting foundations in place, the team is well-poised to focus on the important work described in their purpose and agenda. A data team using the TIPS framework can follow the phases of the decision-making process to guide them through the six steps detailed above. The team moves through the process of identifying a problem with precision, identifying a goal for change, and identifying a solution as well as an implementation plan. When the team regroups, they can focus on the next steps of the decision-making process. This requires the team to follow up on the implementation of their plan by monitoring and evaluating the outcomes of the plan as well as the fidelity of the implementation if needed. Finally, the team will arrive at the decision-making crossroads whereby the data can guide the decision to maintain, modify or terminate the plan. All of these pieces work together to help teams feel that their work is impactful and their time is being used efficiently. The TIPS Framework and data teaming for the purpose of inclusion do not get implemented overnight, and to set the course for effective inclusion, school teams require support and resources, which we will discuss in the next section.

Setting the Course for Effective Inclusion

Research demonstrates that implementing integrated systems of tiered academic and support is associated with positive student outcomes, including an increase in literacy performance and a reduction in student unwanted behaviors (McIntosh et al., 2006); however, effectively implementing multiple initiatives like tiered systems as well as intricate systems such as inclusive classrooms can be challenging for schools to manage without district-wide support. For example, it is important to have high-quality professional development, and it is also critical to have ongoing coaching for teams to ensure that newly learned practices are realized in the daily school-wide activities. The role of school-level data teams can be strengthened by district-level assistance and guidelines. District leadership teams or district implementation teams (Chaparro et al., 2019) are often well-equipped to provide training and coaching to support data teams as they navigate the complex work of collecting, analyzing, and using data to improve school outcomes for all students.

Rationale for District-Wide Support

The heart of effective education is the quality of interaction between individual teachers and students. The likelihood of successful teacher-student interactions, especially in inclusive contexts, increases, however, when attention is focused not just within the classrooms, hallways, and playgrounds of individual schools but at the capacity of supporting districts. Our experience with schools that both implement the TIPS approach and experience strong student gains is that these schools are likely to receive strong district support. Districts that rely on data teams to guide the adoption and ongoing improvement of inclusive education have several common features that build unity, efficiency, and effectiveness. Effective districts start by being clear about the district-wide values, outcomes and expectations that will guide all education in the district. If "inclusion" is an approach used to benefit all children, including those with disabilities, it should be an approach overtly adopted in policy at the district level. It is from this commitment to values and policy that districts grow the systems to (a) select personnel with demonstrated competence and experience with multi-tiered, inclusive practices, (b) invest in annual professional development focused on the most current practices that benefit students, families and faculty, (c) invest in the coaching of these practices to ensure that professional development efforts change school practices and benefit children, (d) invest in district-wide data systems that make it easy and practical for school personnel to monitor both fidelity of intervention implementation and highly valued academic, behavioral and mental health outcomes for students, (e) allocate the time for multi-tiered teams to meet, review data and make decisions that guide best practice in their school, and (f) organize multiple paths of communication to ensure that families, students, staff and faculty are informed about efforts to support and enhance effective inclusion and successful education. Installing data teaming requires a coordinated effort from the district office to each school.

Integrating District Support

District leadership teams take responsibility for the use of evidence-based practices and the ongoing measurement and monitoring of the district's capacity, fidelity, training, and coaching that will lead to positive impacts for students—in this case, for students with disabilities who would benefit from instruction in inclusive settings. District leadership teams are thus well positioned to support school-level data teams and their effective installation and use of inclusive practices. The district leadership team communicates district-wide goals, distributes district resources to support evidence-based inclusive practice implementation across the district, and includes stakeholder views from caregivers to community members.

There are several key features that any district leadership team can emphasize to support school data teams. Key drivers of implementation that the district office can initiate are systematic coaching and the use of district-wide adopted procedures that directly name and outline effective data teaming practices and are commonly held across the district. In school-based initiatives, it has been found that training supported by coaching is a more effective solution than training or professional development alone (Chaparro et al., 2019; Joyce & Showers, 2002; Kraft et al., 2018; Newton et al., 2009). District leadership teams can direct a coordinated approach to coaching and data teaming procedures while having district-level goals for inclusion as a guide.

Integrating Coaching Support

Nearly all schools invest in annual professional development for teachers and staff, yet a small proportion makes the additional investment to provide coaching following the initial professional development events. "Coaching" includes the delivery of prompts, instruction, and feedback to increase the likelihood that newly learned skills are performed under natural school conditions (Massar, 2017).

Coaching is an important process that supports the durable implementation of evidence-based practices like data teaming (Fixsen et al., 2015). Coaching can also serve as the bridge between initial training and implementation (Reinke et al., 2014). Within school systems, coaching is linked with valued outcomes such as increasing teachers' fidelity of implementation and use of evidence-based instructional and behavior management practices (Kretlow et al., 2012). Coaching can be provided by administrators, specialists, or designated district coaching personnel. The most common format is coaches who work at the district level and support school sites in the implementation of a new program, initiative, or framework (Glasgow & Farrell, 2007; Knight, 2005; Marsh et al., 2010; Swinnerton, 2007). Effective coaching can improve not just school-level performance but also district-level capacity by supporting the development of a coherent infrastructure of complicated systems (Adelman & Taylor, 2007). The broad message for district decision makers is that investing in on-site coaching is a key component needed to make major professional development efforts produce a practical change in schools.

A key feature of effective data teams is the ability to rapidly solve problems to support students. Similarly, a key feature of effective district leadership teams is to rapidly solve the problems of practice in schools. One way that district leadership teams can gather data is through coaching and the collection of fidelity measures (Chaparro et al., 2019). With coaches in buildings supporting data teams, the coaches can share information back to the district leadership team so that the inclusive practices and data used in the school buildings inform the development of supportive policy. This builds confidence that the policy developed will support and sustain the efforts of their data teams.

Integrating Coaching with Training and Professional Development

Coaching can support the integrity of data teams and the decision-making process, but districts also benefit from investing in training to set a solid foundation for the coaching. Coaching follows effective training and is integral to the success of the district and schools' TIPS framework implementation (Todd et al., 2011). Schools have data teams made up of personnel with a variety of experiences that can necessitate different professional development content according to teachers' experiences or roles in the school. For example, a seasoned special education teacher will have different professional development needs from a first-year special education teacher. In addition, data teams focused on inclusion will have members representing both general and special education and will have team members who change year to year. Just as we use differentiation strategies in an inclusive classroom, we can benefit from a similar strategy by implementing differentiated and targeted training for the various team members according to their role, experience, and familiarity with the content (Simonsen et al., 2019; Sumsion et al., 2015).

The TIPS framework training employs differentiation. The scope of training moves systematically across each TIPS framework component and process (e.g., meeting foundations, identifying a problem with precision, identifying a goal). Initial efforts to train TIPS to data teams included two days of in-person training: one day for coaches and one day for data teams joined by their coach. Embedded within the TIPS training model are opportunities for active, collaborative, and effective decision making that can be delivered in content-specific modules of effective practices. During the single full-day workshop format, with all members of a given team present and participating, teams apply what they have learned in a mock team meeting near the end of the day. Additionally, follow-up coaching for the next two team meetings is an integrated component of TIPS professional development (Newton et al., 2009; Todd et al., 2011). The in-person training covers the TIPS framework, including the meeting foundations as well as the decision-making process, which is the primary function of the data teams at all service delivery levels, Tier 1 through Tier 3.

Because schools often lack adequate time and resources to provide training, most professional development is delivered after school or in the summer before, both of which are also needed for planning and addressing issues during the school year (Wei et al., 2010; Yoon et al., 2007). Teacher frustration due to time conflicts, irrelevance of content, and little choice in what professional development they receive has been repeatedly documented (Dede et al., 2005, 2008). Online learning provides one avenue to mitigate some of these challenges by having more flexibility around where and when data team members can engage as well as by increasing the accessibility of content to more schools.

To accommodate the increased focus on online learning and the decreased funding for professional development, we have developed a hybrid model of online training with in-person coaching called TIPS for Tier 2 Online Training (Todd et al., 2019). Instead of full-day training for data teams, the online modules are differentiated by the role of the team member because of feedback we received from school-based educators (Nese et al., 2020). In our TIPS for Tier 2 Online Training, each member takes online modules that are only relevant to their role on the team (i.e., Team Member, Data Analyst, Facilitator, Minute Taker, or Administrator). These online learning modules can be assigned by the coach, with team members watching the videos and participating in the modules as a group or individually as an alternative to the full-day group workshop. In the future, our research will examine the impact of online training versus in-person training. Our intention is that districts can deploy relevant, differentiated, and efficient online training modules for data teams that will cut down on the overall cost of training and help to meet training challenges for new staff who join existing data teams or help to extend the knowledge of experienced team members taking on new data team roles.

Conclusion

The promise of fully inclusive schools and classrooms can be elusive or, at the very least, confusing when teachers and specialists do not have the proper tools needed to make rapid decisions about student growth and resource allocation to meet the needs of students. Inclusion can be promoted by using TIPS across the service-delivery model and not just for student study teams, student intervention teams, or Tier 3 teams. Every classroom teacher, special education, and administrator find themselves with an abundance of data. The challenge comes in making sure that those individuals, when gathered as a decision-making team, have the right data in the right format, at the right time, with a process for decision-making that leads to improved educational practices. Schools can benefit from implementing data teams that incorporate both an effective teaming form and function.

The TIPS framework is a scientifically based model that can support schools in their goals to provide an inclusive environment based on appropriate data that ensures effective action-plan development and adaptation. Technology tools such as online training can possibly save time but also increase district capacity for training and facilitate successful and targeted coaching. Given recent developments in information technology, the opportunity for school teams to have current information about student performance is both feasible and practical. Information systems focused on social behavior (e.g., the School-wide Information System: SWIS: May et al., 2003) or academic performance (e.g., Fuchs & Fuchs, 2006) are available, inexpensive, and effective. The TIPS framework offers the organizational structure for using these data for efficient problem solving by school teams and embedding coach-delivered performance feedback to enhance the fidelity of implementation (Burns et al., 2008). The TIPS approach fits well with the rising emphasis on multi-tiered models of support and creating inclusive environments at all Tiers. Implementing the TIPS framework with integrity can lead to instructional plans that may be more effective over time, which will facilitate effective inclusion for students with disabilities. District leadership teams can support school data teams at all Tiers through mutually beneficial communication loops that can create shared ownership and collective accountability for the implementation of the practices that support all their students.

References

Adelman, H. S., & Taylor, L. (2007). Systemic change for school improvement. *Journal of Educational and Psychological Consultation, 17*, 55–77.

Bransford, J. D., & Stein, B. S. (1984). *The IDEAL problem solver: A guide for improving thinking, learning, and creativity*. W. H. Freeman and Company.

Burns, M. K., Peters, R., & Noell, G. H. (2008). Using performance feedback to enhance implementation fidelity of the problem-solving team process. *Journal of School Psychology, 46*, 537–550.

Carroll, J. S., & Johnson, E. J. (1990). *Decision research: A field guide*. Sage Publications.

Chaparro, E. A., Smolkowski, K., & Jackson, K. R. (2019). Scaling up and integrating effective behavioral and instructional support systems (EBISS): A study of one state's professional development efforts. *Learning Disability Quarterly*, *43*(1), 4–17. doi:10.1177/0731948719851750

Dede, C., Breit, L., Ketelhut, D. J., McCloskey, E., & Whitehouse, P. (2005). *An overview of current findings from empirical research on online teacher professional development*. Harvard Graduate School of Education.

Dede, C., Jass Ketelhut, D., Whitehouse, P., Breit, L., & McCloskey, E. M. (2008). A research agenda for online teacher professional development. *Journal of Teacher Education*, *60*, 8–19. doi:10.1177/0022487108327554

Deno, S. L. (2005). Problem-solving assessment. In R. Brown-Chidsey (Ed.), *Assessment for intervention: A problem-solving approach* (pp. 10–40). Guilford.

D'Zurilla, T. J., Nezu, A. M., & Maydeu-Olivares, A. (2004). Social problem solving: Theory and assessment. In E. C. Chang, T. J. D'Zurilla, & L. J. Sanna (Eds.), *Social problem solving: Theory, research and training* (pp. 11–27). American Psychological Association.

Fixsen, D. L., Blase, K. A., Horner, R., Sims, B., & Sugai, G. (2013, September). Readiness for change. *Scaling-up Brief*, *3*. Retrieved from the University of North Carolina, Frank Porter Graham Child Development Institute, State Implementation & Scaling up of Evidence Based Practices Center website: http://fpg.unc.edu/resources/scaling-brief-3-readiness-change-0

Fixsen, D. L., Blase, K. A., Naoom, S. F., & Duda, M. (2015). *Implementation drivers: Assessing best practices*. National Implementation Science Network, FPG Child Development Center, University of North Carolina at Chapel Hill.

Fuchs,, D., & Fuchs, L. (2006). Introduction to response to intervention: What, why, and how valid is it? *Reading Research Quarterly*, *41*, 93–99. doi:10.1598/RRQ.41.1.4

Gershoff, E. T. & Font, S. A. (2016). Corporal punishment in US public schools: Prevalence, disparities in use, and status in state and federal policy. *Social policy report*, *30*.

Gilbert, T. F. (1978). *Human competence: Engineering worthy performance*. McGraw-Hill.

Glasgow, N. A., & Farrell, T. S. C. (Eds.) (2007). *What successful literacy teachers do: 70 research-based strategies for teachers, reading coaches, and instructional planners*. Corwin Press.

Hamilton, L., Halverson, R., Jackson, S., Mandinach, E., Supovitz, J., & Wayman, J. (2009). *Using student achievement data to support instructional decision making (NCEE 2009-4067)*. National Center for Education Evaluqation and Regional Assistance, Institute of Education Sciences, U. S. Department of Education. Retrieved from http://ies.ed.gov/ncee/wwc/publications/practiceguides

Horner, R., Newton, J. S., Todd, A., Algozzine, B., Algozzine, K., Cusumano, D., & Preston, A. I. (2018). A randomized wait-list controlled analysis of team-initiated problem solving professional development and use. *Behavioral Disorders*, *43*(4), 444–456. doi: 10.1177/0198742917745638

Huber, G. P. (1980). *Managerial decision making*. Scott Foresman, and Company.

Hussar, B., Zhang, J., Hein, S., Wang, K., Roberts, A., Cui, J., Smith, M., Bullock Mann, F., Barmer, A., and Dilig, R. (2020). *The condition of education 2020 (NCES 2020-144)*. U.S. Department of Education. National Center for Education Statistics. Retrieved [8-12-20] from https://nces.ed.gov/pubs2020/2020144.pdf.

Jorgensen, J. D., Scheier, I. H., & Fautsko, T. F. (1981). *Solving problems in meetings*. Nelson-Hall.

Joyce, B., & Showers, B. (2002). *Student achievement through staff development* (3rd ed.). Association for Supervision and Curriculum Development.

Kekahio, W., & Baker, M. (2013). *Five steps for structuring data-informed conversations and action in education (REL 2013-001)*. U.S. Department of Education, Institute of Education Sciences, National Center for Education Evaluation and Regional Assistance, Regional Educational Laboratory Pacific. Retrieved from http://ies.ed.gov/ncee/edlabs

Knight, J. (2005). A primer on instructional coaches. *Principal Leadership*, *5*, 16–21.

Kraft, M. A., Blazar, D., & Hogan, D. (2018). The effect of teacher coaching on instruction and achievement: a meta-analysis of the casual evidence. *Review of Educational Research*, *88*, 547–588.

Kretlow, A. G., Cooke, N. L., & Wood, C. L. (2012). Using in-service and coaching to increase teachers' accurate use of research-based strategies. *Remedial and Special Education*, *33*, 348–361.

Lacoe, J. & Steinberg, M. P. (2019). Do suspensions affect student outcomes? *Educational Evaluation and Policy Analysis*, *41*, 34–62.

Madigan, K., Cross, R. W., Smolkowski, K., & Strycker, L. A. (2016). Association between schoolwide positive behavioral interventions and supports and academic achievement: A nine-year evaluation. *Educational Research and Evaluation*, *22*, 402–421. doi:10.1080/13803611.2016.1256783

Marsh, J. A., McCombs, J. S., & Martorell, F. (2010). How instructional coaches support data-driven decision making policy implementation and effects in Florida middle schools. *Educational Policy*, *24*, 872–907.

Marsh, J. A., Pane, J. F., & Hamilton, L. S. (2006). *Making sense of data-driven decision making in education: Evidence from recent RAND research*. RAND Education Occasional Paper.

Massar, M. (2017). *Effects of coach-delivered prompting and performance feedback on teacher use of evidence-based classroom management practices and student behavior outcomes* (Doctoral dissertation). University of Oregon, Eugene.

May, S., Ard Jr., W., Todd, A. W., Horner, R. H., Glasgow, A., & Sugai, G. (2003). *Schoolwide information system*. University of Oregon, Educational and Community Supports.

McFarland, J., Hussar, B., Zhang, J., Wang, X., Wang, K., Hein, S., Diliberti, M., Forrest Cataldi, E., Bullock Mann, F., & Barmer, A. (2019). *The condition of education 2019 (NCES 2019-144)*. U.S. Department of Education. National Center for Education Statistics. Retrieved [date] from https://nces.ed.gov/pubsearch/pubsinfo.asp?pubid=2019144.

McIntosh, K., Horner, R. H., Chard, D. J., Boland, J. B., & Good, R. H. (2006). The use of reading and behavior screening measures to predict non-response to school-wide positive behavior support: A longitudinal analysis. *School Psychology Review, 35*, 275–291.

McIntosh, K., & Goodman, S. (2016). *Integrated multi-tiered systems of support: Blending RTI and PBIS*. Guilford Publications.

Nese, R. N. T., Meng, P., Breiner, S., Chaparro, E. A., & Algozzine, B. (2020). Using stakeholder feedback to improve online professional development opportunities. *Journal of Research on Technology in Education, 52*(2), 148–162. 10.1080/15391523.2020.1726233

Newton, J. S., Horner, R. H., Algozzine, R. R., & Todd, A. W., & Algozzine, K. M. (2009). Using a problem-solving model to enhance data-based decision making in schools. In W. Sailor, G. Dunlap, G. Sugai, & R. Horner (Eds.), *Handbook of positive behavior support* (pp. 551–580), a volume in the *Issues in Clinical Child Psychology* series. Springer.

Newton, J. S., Horner, R. H., Algozzine, B., Todd, A. W., & Algozzine, K. M. (2012). A randomized wait-list controlled analysis of team-initiated problem solving. *Journal of School Psychology, 50*, 421–441.

Newton, J. S., Todd, A. W., Algozzine, B., Algozzine, K., Horner, R. H., & Cusumano, D. L. (2014). Supporting team problem solving in inclusive schools. In J. McLeskey, N. L. Waldron, F. Spooner, & Algozzine, B. (Eds.), *Handbook on research and practice for effective inclusive schools*. Routledge.

Newton, J. S., Todd, A., Algozzine, K. M., Horner, R. H., & Algozzine, B. (2009). *Team initiated problem solving training manual*. Educational and Community Supports, University of Oregon. Unpublished manuscript.

Reinke, W. M., Stormont, M., Herman, K. C., & Newcomer, L. (2014). Using coaching to support teacher implementation of classroom-based interventions. *Journal of Behavioral Education, 23*, 150–167.

Simonsen, B., Freeman, J., Myers, D., Dooley, K., Maddock, E., Kern, L., & Byun, S. (2019). The effects of targeted professional development on teachers' use of empirically supported classroom management practices. *Journal of Positive Behavior Interventions*. doi:10.1177/1098300719859615

Sumsion, J., Lunn Brownlee, J., Ryan, S., Walsh, K., Farrell, A., Irvine, S., Mulhearn, G., & Berthelsen, D. (2015). Evaluative decision-making for high-quality professional development: cultivating an evaluative stance. *Professional Development in Education, 41*, 419–432. doi:10.1080/19415257.2014.989257

Swinnerton, J. (2007). Brokers and boundary crossers in an urban school district: Understanding central office coaches as instructional leaders. *Journal of School Leadership, 17*, 195–221.

Todd, A., Horner, R., Algozzine, B., Chaparro, E. A., Nese, R., Ramshaw, D., Cameron, R., & Daily, J. (2019). *TIPS for Tier 2 teams training*. [Online Course]. Educational and Community Supports.

Todd, A. W., Horner, R. H., Berry, D., Sanders, C., Bugni, M., Currier, A., Potts, N., Newton, J. S., Algozzine, B., &Algozzine, K. (2012). A case study of team-initiated problem solving addressing student behavior in one elementary school. *Journal of Special Education Leadership, 25*, 81–89.

Todd, A. W., Horner, R. H., Newton, J. S., Algozzine, R. F., Algozzine, K. M., & Frank, J. L. (2011). Effects of team-initiated problem solving on decision making by schoolwide behavior support teams. *Journal of Applied School Psychology, 27*, 42–59.

Tropman, J. E. (1996). *Making meetings work: Achieving high quality group discussions*. Sage.

U.S. Department of Education. (2017).*39th annual report to Congress on the implementation of the Individuals with Disabilities Education Act, 2017*. https://www2.ed.gov/about/reports/annual/osep/2017/parts-b-c/39th-arc-for-idea.pef

U.S. Department of Education, National Center for Education Statistics. (2018). *Digest of Education Statistics, 2016* (NCES 2014-015).

Wagner, M., Sumi, C., Woodbridge, M., Javitz, H., & Thornton, S. P. (2009). Coordinating research implementation of evidence-based school interventions for children with serious behavior problems. *Journal of Emotional and Behavioral Disorders, 17*, 244–249.

Wei, R. C., Darling-Hammond, L., & Adamson, F. (2010). *Professional development in the United States: Trends and challenges*. National Staff Development Council.

Yoon, K. S., Duncan, T., Lee, S. W.-Y., Scarloss, B., & Shapley, K. (2007). *Reviewing the evidence on how teacher professional development affects student achievement* (Issues & Answers Report, REL 2007–No. 033). Institute of Education Sciences, National Center for Education Evaluation and Regional Assistance, Regional Educational Laboratory Southwest.

Ysseldyke, J. E., Burns, M. K., Dawson, M., Kelly, B., Morrison, D., Ortiz, S., Rosenfield, S., & Telzrow, C. (2006). School psychology: A blueprint for training and practice III. In J. Grimes & A. Thomas (Eds.), *Best Practices in School Psychology V*. National Association of School Psychologists.

9

The Role of High Leverage Practices in Effective Inclusive Elementary Schools

Angela L. Patti, Lisa A. Rafferty, Shannon Budin, and Lawrence Maheady

Setting the Stage

There have been many legislative efforts to ensure that individuals with diverse learning needs and backgrounds have equitable and integrated access to public schools and classroom settings (e.g., American with Disabilities Act of 1990; Boroson, 2017; Brown v. the Board of Education, 1954; Education for All Handicapped Children Act, 1975). As a result of these combined efforts, today's classrooms are more diverse and inclusive than at any other time in the history of the United States. However, access to inclusive school and classroom settings does not lead to proficient student learning without effective teacher practice.

Today, although the educational system is making headway on the social justice issue of access to inclusive classrooms, an unacceptably low percentage of students in the U.S. from all backgrounds are performing at or above levels of proficiency in core subject areas (Keyworth, 2020; National Center for Education Statistics [NCES], 2019). Those from culturally and linguistically diverse backgrounds (Murphey, 2014; NCES, 2019) and students with disabilities (SWD) are faring the worst on standardized outcomes (Hurwitz et al., 2020; NCES, 2019). One of the most troubling trends is that these gaps in achievement have gone relatively unchanged since at least the early 1990s (Keyworth, 2020). Reports in achievement such as these have prompted some scholars to label their performance as "abysmal" particularly for those educated in inclusive educational settings (Fuchs et al., 2018).

Despite common and deeply entrenched concerns that inclusion of students with diverse learning needs, particularly those with disabilities, will detract from the educational environment (Boroson, 2017; Henninger & Gupta, 2014; Vaz et al., 2015), research suggests that *appropriate* inclusion of SWD in general education classrooms can have a positive impact on all students in the classroom (Henninger & Gupta, 2014). For example, SWD often fare better over time academically and socially when included versus when educated in self-contained settings (e.g., Cosier et al., 2013; Sermier Dessemontet et al., 2012). Additionally, students without disabilities are not academically disadvantaged when educated in classes with peers who have disabilities, and research results suggest these students make social-behavioral gains in inclusive classrooms (Henninger & Gupta, 2014; Salend & Garrick Duhaney, 1999).

So, what factors related to teaching contribute to *effective* inclusion, ensuring the best outcomes for *all* students? While many out-of-school and in-school factors can be considered, research

DOI: 10.4324/9781003043874-9

indicates that the one in-school factor that has the greatest impact on student learning is teacher quality (Darling-Hammond, 2000; National Council for Accreditation of Teacher Education [NCATE], 2010; Stronge et al., 2011). While there may be some factors that cannot be controlled in the classroom (e.g., factors related to students' backgrounds, access to resources, etc.), teacher quality is one important factor that *can* be influenced.

Research also suggests that teacher attitudes and expectations are contributors to successful inclusive classrooms where there is equitable participation of all students (Henninger & Gupta, 2014; Salend & Garrick Duhaney, 1999; Vaz et al., 2015). Although attempts to identify factors associated with teachers' attitudes towards inclusion have been mixed (e.g., Salend & Garrick Duhaney, 1999), trends suggest that limited training and self-efficacy in teaching and meeting all students' needs in diverse classrooms are two notable factors that impact teachers' attitudes (Scruggs & Mastropieri, 1996; Vaz et al., 2015). If teachers are not adequately prepared for inclusive settings and/or do not feel adequately prepared, they will be less successful. Thus, it is important to consider the impact of teacher development both in terms of: (a) good, quality teacher preparation programming for pre-service teachers and (b) effective professional development (PD) for in-service teachers.

Teacher Development

Good, quality teacher preparation programming must involve opportunities to not only learn about academic content and pedagogy but to practice it. Teacher preparation programs have traditionally emphasized coursework focusing mostly on content and other professional aspects of teaching, culminating in opportunities to practice using evidence-based knowledge and practices in classroom settings for a short period of time (NCATE, 2010). This was judged to be insufficient and led to transformative efforts in making more clinical-based preparation the norm through new standards and expectations across the field (i.e., Council for the Accreditation of Educator Preparation [CAEP], 2013; Darling-Hammond, 2010; NCATE, 2010). As pre-service teachers are afforded more deliberate, frequent opportunities to use and practice vital teaching skills, they enter the field more prepared and, thus, can be more effective in meeting the needs of all learners.

To address quality at the in-service teacher level, effective PD is key. At the in-service level, teachers are usually provided with training outside of the classroom with limited or no support and limited follow-up opportunities linked to classroom implementation (Darling-Hammond et al., 2017; NCATE, 2010). Indeed, faulty implementation is often cited as a cause for little or no impact on student learning outcomes (Fixsen et al., 2019).

Whether preparing beginning teachers or developing in-service teachers, there has been a push towards restructuring teacher development efforts (i.e., Darling-Hammond et al., 2017; NCATE, 2010). For example, some shifts emerged around the time of NCATE's Blue-Ribbon Panel Report that outlined 10 reform principles to turn teacher preparation in the United States "upside down" (p. ii). In their report, members of the Blue-Ribbon Panel recommended a movement away from emphasizing what teacher candidates should *know* (i.e., content and pedagogical knowledge) to what they must *do* (i.e., teacher practices; NCATE, 2010). Indeed, the first principle was that P-12 student learning should serve as the focal point for the design and implementation of clinically-based teacher education and assessment of novice educators and the programs responsible for their preparation. Systemic changes were proposed in school-based experiences to make them more "fully grounded in clinical practice and interwoven with academic content and professional courses" (p. ii). The panel also recommended transitioning from an intuitive- to deliberate-based approach for developing candidates' instructional competence.

Similarly, at the in-service teacher level, Desimone and Garet (2015) dissect a common framework for effective PD for teachers that prioritizes the importance of not just a change in content knowledge but actual teaching practice. They report that the success of PD is facilitated when it is linked to practice in the teacher's classroom lessons and routines, particularly when feedback is part of this active learning approach. Additionally, PD can be enhanced via the concept of "collective participation" (Desimone & Garet, 2015), whereby professionals from the same subject, grade, or school come together and engage in PD in a sort of interactive learning community; this practice may make particular sense for inclusive environments.

The belief of "collective participation" could also be applied to bridge the gap between teacher education programs and P-12 settings, particularly as it relates to clinical preparation. Collaborations such as those found in Professional Development Schools (see Brindley et al., 2008) are undoubtedly aligned to the principles in areas such as comprehensive clinical preparation that are found in the Blue-Ribbon Panel Report (Van Scoy & Eldridge, 2012). These planned partnerships emphasize the importance of teaching *practice* and the value of high-quality PD to enhance the skills needed to be effective teachers. Collectively, these general recommendations spawned what has become known as practice-based teacher education.

Practice-Based Teacher Education

Practice-based teacher education aims to make instruction the central element of educator preparation and many programs have increasingly embraced the movement (e.g., Maheady et al., 2019). There is reason to believe that this trend will continue as educational institutions respond to federal mandates and accreditation demands. The Individuals with Disabilities Education Act (IDEA, 2004), No Child Left Behind (NCLB, 2002), and Every Student Succeeds Act (ESSA, 2015) required: (a) greater access to general education curricula for SWDs and those at-risk for identification, (b) increased use of scientific- and evidence-based teaching practices, and (c) greater accountability for teachers, school leaders, and teacher educators.

The 10 reform principles in the Blue-Ribbon Panel Report also shaped subsequent professional teaching standards and institutional accreditation requirements. CAEP Standard 2, for example, requires education programs to ensure that "effective partnerships and high-quality clinical practice are central to preparation so that candidates develop the knowledge, skills, and dispositions necessary to demonstrate a positive impact on all P-12 students' learning and development" (CAEP, 2013, p. 6). The practice-based teacher education movement has changed the nature, structure, and functions of teacher preparation. It has prompted greater curricular and pedagogical alignment both on campus and in P-12 schools (Blanton et al., 2014; Pugach & Blanton, 2012); promoted the creation and/or expansion of school-university partnerships with increased emphases on clinical placement, teaching practice, and student learning (CAEP, 2013); and, produced calls for more rigorous, classroom-based research to address problems of "practice" (Belfiore & Lee, 2014; Maheady et al., 2013). It was within the context of practice-based teacher education that the notion of "high leverage practices" emerged as a possible "core curriculum" in teacher education (e.g., Maheady et al., 2019).

Ball and Forzani (2011) argued that teacher education "must establish a common core of fundamental professional knowledge and skills that can be taught to aspiring teachers, across all types of programs and pathways" (p. 19). This shared content must focus directly on the development of teaching practice, lend itself to reliable and formative assessment, and provide a foundation for ongoing PD.

HLPs are fundamental teaching procedures that, based on research, are used often across various classroom contexts and have an important effect on student outcomes (McLeskey et al., 2019). While experienced teachers can and do use HLPs, they are procedures that beginning teachers can learn and use upon entering the field, thus making them appropriate for integration into teacher preparation programs. In addition, HLPs might also serve as an instructional framework to use in partnership with P-12 schools to provide PD to facilitate effective inclusion in elementary schools (Billingsley et al., 2019).

Moving On

Our goal is to introduce and examine HLPs in relation to improving outcomes in inclusive elementary classrooms. After consideration of a few caveats, we: (a) provide an overview of HLPs and what is known about them, (b) examine potential benefits and models for using HLPs as a framework for teacher preparation programs and P-12 PD, and (c) provide several specific case examples.

Caveats

First, there are other important aspects of practice-based teacher education and HLPs beyond the scope of this chapter. These include diverse and opposing conceptualizations of teaching and learning and implementation-related issues (e.g., how to support HLP usage on campus and in P-12 schools; Maheady & Patti, 2020). Second, HLPs have been developed for multiple educational disciplines (e.g., mathematics, science, and modern languages; Hlas & Hlas, 2012; Windschitl et al., 2012). However, this chapter focuses exclusively on applications in elementary and special education, with a focus on inclusive settings. Third, HLPs are not promoted as the sole source of effective teaching practice. Rather, they are a foundational set of teaching practices that must be broadened, refined, and augmented with conditional knowledge to know when and where to apply them (McLeskey et al., 2017). There are other, well-established sources of validated instructional practices (e.g., Best Evidence Encyclopedia; Center for Evidence-based Policy; Promising Practices Network; What Works Clearinghouse) that should also be considered to supplement HLP sets as an instructional framework. Finally, although this chapter focuses on instructional *practice*, it does not diminish the important roles that cognitive, affective, cultural, and contextual factors play in teacher development and student learning. As other chapters point out, race, class, and linguistic and experiential background exert powerful influences over student access, performance, and success in our public schools; only some influences are addressed in current HLPs.

What Do We Know About HLPs Based on Research?

In recent years, HLPs have emerged as an important framework for teacher preparation and PD in the field of education. Before we can describe how HLPs can be used to improve teacher practice and enhance student outcomes in inclusive settings, however, it is important to explore their definition and placement in general, special, and inclusive education as well as research and professional wisdom that support their generalized use.

HLPs Defined

HLPs were defined formally as "a set of practices that are fundamental to support student learning, and that can be taught, learned, and implemented by those entering the profession" (Windschitl et al., 2012, p. 880). They were described further as limited in number, research-based, often used by teachers during the school day, and applied broadly across age and grade levels, as well as diverse subject areas (see Figure 9.1 for a list of key components of HLPs).

By definition, HLPs should be practices that are widely used across educational contexts. While there is a fair amount of commonality between practices deemed most critical across educational disciplines, distinct sets of HLPs have been developed for specific content areas (e.g., mathematics, foreign languages, science; Hlas & Hlas, 2012; Windschitl et al., 2012). In this chapter, we will focus primarily on HLPs developed for general and special education (McLeskey et al., 2017; Teaching Works, 2015), as well as how those sets can be considered together in the context of the complexity

HLPs are a set of practices that are:

- Fundamental to support student learning
- Able to be taught, learned, and implemented by those entering the profession
- Limited in number
- Research-based
- Used often by teachers during the school day
- Applied broadly across age-and grade-levels, as well as diverse subject areas

Figure 9.1 Key components of definition of HLPs

Note: Adapted from "Proposing a Core Set of Instructional Practices and Tools for Teachers of Science," by Windschitl, Thompson, Braaten, and Stroupe 2012, *Science Education, 96*(5), 878–903 (https://doi.org/10.1002/sce.21027). Copyright by Wiley Periodicals, Inc.

of inclusive, elementary classrooms. While a full explanation of all general and special education HLPs is beyond the scope of this chapter, a few examples of each have been provided for illustrative purposes.

HLPs in General Education

In the field of general education, Ball and Forzani (2011) advocated for better preparation of teachers through the development of a common set of fundamental knowledge and skills that could be taught to pre-service teachers and serve as a foundation for PD for practicing teachers. Thus, faculty members in the University of Michigan's School of Education worked to develop a core set of practices to be taught to beginning elementary educators (Teaching Works, 2015). Through a multi-step process, they ultimately developed a set of 19 HLPs (see Figure 9.2).

The set of 19 HLPs represent the skills deemed fundamental and essential for general education teachers. For example, these teachers need to be able to set up and manage both whole group (HLP #1) and small group (HLP #9) instruction. They need to develop and teach classroom routines and procedures to minimize behavioral difficulties and maximize instructional time (HLP #8), as well as effectively respond to both appropriate and inappropriate student behavior (HLP #7). They need to develop short- and long-term goals for students (HLP #13) and carefully design lessons and instructional units to meet those goals (HLP #14). They also need to be skilled in both formal and informal assessment practices and know how to use assessment data to provide feedback to students and guide future instruction (HLPs #15-18).

HLPs in Special Education

Following the University of Michigan's general education work, the Council for Exceptional Children (CEC) appointed a writing team in 2014 to work on developing a set of HLPs for novice special education teachers. The team reviewed the general education HLPs, considered the distinct role of special education teachers, and ultimately developed a set of 22 HLPs across four domains: collaboration, assessment, social/emotional/behavioral, and instruction (McLeskey et al., 2017; see Figure 9.3).

As per the first domain, special educators must be skilled in collaborating and communicating with other professionals (HLP #1), as well as families (HLP #3), to meet the needs of SWD. The

HLP 1: Leading a group discussion.

HLP 2: Explaining and modeling content, practices, and strategies.

HLP 3: Eliciting and interpreting student thinking.

HLP 4: Diagnosing particular common patterns of student thinking and development in a subject matter domain.

HLP 5: Implementing norms and routines for classroom discourse and work.

HLP 6: Coordinating and adjusting instruction during a lesson.

HLP 7: Specifying and reinforcing productive student work behavior.

HLP 8: Implementing organizational routines.

HLP 9: Setting up and managing small group work.

HLP 10: Building respectful relationships with students.

HLP 11: Talking about a student with a parents or other caregivers.

HLP 12: Learning about students' cultural, religious, family, intellectual, and personal experiences and resources for use in instruction.

HLP 13: Setting long-and short-term learning goals for students.

HLP 14: Designing single lessons and sequences of lessons.

HLP 15: Checking student understanding during and at the conclusion of lessons.

HLP 16: Selecting and designing formal assessments of student learning.

HLP 17: Interpreting the results of student work, including routine assignments, quizzes, tests, projects, and standardized assessments.

HLP 18: Providing oral and written feedback to students.

HLP 19: Analyzing instruction for the purpose of improving it.

Figure 9.2 Set of 19 HLPs developed for general educators

Note: Adapted from "High Leverage Practices" by Teaching Works, 2015 (http://www.teachingworks.org/work-of-teaching/high-leverage-practices). In the public domain.

second domain includes a variety of assessment practices, such as using multiple data sources to understand a student's strengths and needs (HLP #4) and using student data to make needed adjustments to instruction (HLP #6). In the social/emotional/behavioral domain, special educators need to be able to establish a positive and productive learning environment (HLP #7) and deal with ongoing, challenging behaviors by conducting a functional behavior assessment (FBA) to inform the development of a behavior intervention plan (BIP) (HLP #10). Finally, the largest domain, instruction, comprises 12 of the 22 special education HLPs. This domain includes skills such as using explicit instruction (HLP #16), using strategies to promote active student engagement (HLP #18), and teaching students to maintain and generalize learning (HLP #21).

HLPs for Inclusive Classrooms

While there is not a formally published set of HLPs for inclusive classrooms, it could be argued that practices from both the general education and special education sets are critical for meeting the needs of all learners in inclusive settings. Further, there is a great deal of overlap between the two sets of

Collaboration

HLP 1: Collaborate with professionals to increase student success.

HLP 2: Organize and facilitate effective meetings with professionals and families.

HLP 3: Collaborate with families to support student learning and secure needed services.

Assessment

HLP 4: Use multiple sources of information to develop a comprehensive understanding of a student's strengths and needs.

HLP 5: Interpret and communicate assessment information with stakeholders to collaboratively design and implement educational programs.

HLP 6: Use student assessment data, analyze instructional practices, and make necessary adjustments that improve student outcomes.

Social/Emotional/Behavioral

HLP 7: Establish a consistent, organized, and respectful learning environment.

HLP 8: Provide positive and constructive feedback to guide students™ learning and behavior.

HLP 9: Teach social behaviors.

HLP 10: Conduct functional behavioral assessments to develop individual student behavior support plans.

Instruction

HLP 11: Identify and prioritize long-and short-term learning goals.

HLP 12: Systematically design instruction toward a specific learning goal.

HLP 13: Adapt curriculum tasks and materials for specific learning goals.

HLP 14: Teach cognitive and metacognitive strategies to support learning and independence.

HLP 15: Provide scaffolded supports.

HLP 16: Use explicit instruction.

HLP 17: Use flexible grouping.

HLP 18: Use strategies to promote active student engagement.

HLP 19: Use assistive and instructional technologies.

HLP 20: Provide intensive instruction.

HLP 21: Teach students to maintain and generalize new learning across time and settings.

HLP 22: Provide positive and constructive feedback to guide students' learning and behavior.

Figure 9.3 Set of 22 HLPs developed for special educators

Note: Adapted from "High Leverage Practices in Special Education," by J. McLeskey, M.-D. Barringer, B. Billingsley, M. Brownell, D. Jackson, M. Kennedy, D. Ziegler, 2017 Council for Exceptional Children & CEEDAR Center. In the public domain.

practices; many practices appear in both sets, albeit they are often discussed using different terminology or context. Later in this chapter, we will provide examples of how HLPs from both sets can be utilized in improving instruction in inclusive elementary classrooms.

Nature of Research on HLPs

Reporting on the research base for HLPs is complex. Between the two published HLP sets discussed in this chapter (general education and special education), there are over 40 practices included. Describing research support for each of these practices is beyond the scope of this chapter. Further, the HLPs vary in grain size, with some HLPs being very specific in nature, with a well-established research base of their own, and other HLPs being more general. The more general or broad HLPs are composed of component practices that each have their own research base. For example, there is an extensive research base (Hughes et al., 2019) to support the use of explicit instruction (special education HLP #16), which is a practice with very specific procedures and guidelines. On the other hand, checking for understanding throughout a lesson (general education HLP #15) is a more general practice, with other research-based practices (e.g., response cards; Randolph, 2007) falling underneath this heading. While it could be argued that all published HLPs have a research base to support them, the nature of that research base varies greatly in focus, depth, and content.

Further, little is known at this point about the use of HLPs as a framework to guide teacher preparation and PD. Some authors have begun to share their work in this area. For example, Maheady et al. (2019) describe how teacher education faculty revised a dual certification (elementary and special education) teacher education program. The goals of their work included: (a) shifting from a focus on what teacher candidates *know* to what teacher candidates can *do*, (b) developing common language and understanding between the fields of general education and special education, and (c) preparing candidates to meet the needs of *all* learners in inclusive settings. Drawing from the published general education and special education HLP sets, Maheady et al. developed their own set of HLPs that reflect a combined set of practices understood by both general and special educators that are now being used as a foundation for their inclusive program. Moving forward, they plan to measure the effects of this program change on their teacher candidates' development, as well as the P-12 students with whom those candidates work.

Nature of Professional Wisdom Regarding HLPs

In addition to the range of research evidence to support individual HLPs, practices that fall under individual HLPs, and the use of HLP sets to guide teacher development, it is also important to recognize the role of practicing teacher input in establishing the face validity of HLPs. Strain et al. (2012) reinforce the notion that when teachers recognize the effectiveness and social validity of an intervention or practice, they are willing to implement it and sustain its use over time, even in cases where they originally viewed the strategies as "complex and radically different" (p. 197). Strain et al. recognized the potential influence of a teacher "liking" an intervention on the fidelity of its implementation. In other words, teachers are more likely to carry out a practice the way it is intended to be carried out if they see value in the practice in their teaching/learning context. Thus, having teachers "on board" and engaged with HLPs is a great first step in acquiring their buy-in when using HLPs for pre-service or in-service teacher training.

The workgroups that developed both the general education and special education HLP sets discussed in this chapter sought input from practicing teachers. For example, the School of Education faculty at the University of Michigan initially developed a list of over 100 teaching tasks deemed important for novice general education teachers (Teaching Works, 2015). They then elicited feedback on this work from practicing teachers across the United States; this feedback was used in the process of whittling down the list to the agreed-upon set of 19 practices that have since been published. Similarly, CEC's workgroup initially started out with a draft of 26 HLPs for special educators. After conducting focus groups that included teacher educators, practicing teachers, and teacher leaders, the draft was revised to result in the 22 HLPs which were published for beginning special educators (McLeskey et al., 2017). In both cases, gaining input from practicing teachers has given credibility to HLPs; these are practices that teachers *really do* and that *really matter* in terms of student outcomes.

Setting the Course for Effective Inclusion

Considering the practice-based teacher education movement and the need to improve outcomes in inclusive elementary schools, HLPs offer a potential solution. To set the course for using HLPs to promote and support effective inclusion, we will explore benefits, models, and tips related to using HLPs as a framework for improving teacher practice. We will also illustrate this content with case studies.

Benefits of Using HLPs for Improving Teacher Practice

Although research is necessary to systematically evaluate the long-term benefits of using HLP sets as a framework for improving teacher practice, it can be assumed that since HLP sets were developed based upon the best available evidence that there are inherent benefits of doing so. Below are some potential benefits of using teacher practices—specifically HLPs—to frame teacher education programs and PD opportunities that are focused on inclusive programming:

- Inclusive classrooms are comprised of students who have a variety of strengths and needs. HLPs are focused on teacher actions that can capitalize on the strengths and meet the needs of *all* learners.
- Teachers' attitudes and expectations are often significant barriers to successfully implementing inclusive programming (Vaz et al., 2015). Often, their attitudes are based upon practical concerns about how to implement inclusive education. f pre- and in-service training opportunities are focused on teacher practices and include structured opportunities to engage with and receive feedback on the use of practices, these practical concerns may be limited or eliminated.
- Since HLPs are based upon teacher actions (i.e., practices), they are observable. Therefore, it is easier to link student outcomes back to teacher actions, which makes progress monitoring and potential adjustments to instruction easier to implement, especially in a diverse learning environment where students' strengths and needs vary to a greater degree than in more segregated settings.
- The use of HLPs can also help professionals with various areas of expertise by understanding and using common language, especially in circumstances where experts agree on one set of HLPs to use, particularly between general education and special education both at the higher education and P-12 levels.
- Since HLPs are based upon evidence-based practices, they also have the potential to decrease the research-to-practice gap, especially when they are used as the core curriculum (McLeskey et al., 2018).
- Using HLPs as a framework for teacher preparation programs can provide teacher educators and partner school personnel with a shared understanding of desired outcomes for teacher candidates. With clear expectations, it is more likely that the candidates will be provided with strong mentoring that focuses on the development of these practices (Maheady et al., 2019).

Models for Using HLPs for Improving Teacher Practice

There are at least three ways to use HLPs to improve teacher practice. Each targets an important area in initial and continuing PD.

First, HLPs can be used to reframe an entire teacher education program (Maheady et al., 2019). Traditional models of teacher preparation may emphasize professional standards and knowledge of content while offering limited opportunities to demonstrate and assess candidate skills. Reframing candidate learning outcomes to reflect HLPs emphasizes a candidate's ability to not only demonstrate effective practices but evaluate the impact of those practices on student learning. This is where a "continuum of pedagogies" can be used whereby candidates "approximate authenticity" (Brownell et al., 2019). This model of program design provides teacher educators with a more realistic view of their candidates' preparedness to meet the demands of the classroom on day 1.

Second, HLPs can be infused into an existing teacher preparation program on a smaller scale, without a complete overhaul. In this case, more concrete opportunities to learn about and practice HLPs can be offered. A few relevant HLPs can be identified and targeted with various learning opportunities. For example, when teaching about the concept of collaboration in inclusive settings, an instructor could assign roles of general education teacher, paraprofessional, or other support staff with whom the special educator must engage. The team could be required to develop and adjust a class-wide behavioral intervention for the general education classroom, which would involve sharing ideas, active listening, questioning, planning, problem solving, and negotiating with one another (Special Education HLP 1: Collaborate with professionals to increase student success). Although it may not be feasible to ensure mastery of all HLPs within a set, it is possible to identify a few that may have the biggest impact in an inclusive environment.

Third, HLPs can be used as a foundation for PD in P-12 settings. Billingsley 2019 suggest that HLPs offer coherence across many domains and roles often required of special education teachers. They suggest using HLPs as an instructional framework for induction to provide content as well as a shared language. The HLPs can offer insight into both *what* and *how* to teach for a beginning special educator and perhaps, their general education colleagues in inclusive settings.

Tips for Using HLPs for Improving Teacher Practice

Regardless of the model selected for using HLPs to improve teacher practice, by their very nature, HLPs must be *practiced*. Both pre-service and in-service teachers require a range of planned and structured opportunities to ensure the use of HLPs in P-12 settings. Inclusive classrooms provide an ideal environment to use and refine HLPs, given the need for a variety of these skills—from collaboration to specialized instruction to establishing a consistent, organized, and respectful learning environment.

The Blue-Ribbon Panel on Clinical Preparation and Partnerships for Improved Student Learning (NCATE, 2010) suggests that pre-service teachers must be afforded "robust opportunities to develop as practitioners via expertly mentored experiences in the field and through pedagogically designed approximations of practices such as case studies and simulations..." (p. 27). Brownell et al. (2019) describe a "continuum of pedagogies for preparing teachers to use high-leverage practices" that "approximate authenticity" (p. 338). These approximations provide increasingly realistic teaching experiences and allow frequent, distributed, and scaffolded practice-based opportunities. Examples of this approach might start with case learning, progress to peer teaching simulations, and then virtual, computer-simulated teaching experiences (Brownell et al., 2019). Next, a pre-service teacher may conduct a formal lesson, emphasizing a specific teaching practice where a bug-in-the-ear feedback tool is used for coaching, before finally applying their knowledge and skills in a structured field experience where they move from tutoring to small group instruction to whole group teaching (Brownell et al., 2019).

Similarly, in-service teachers may enter the field with an awareness of HLPs, but additional support is often needed to ensure teachers can effectively use and apply these core instructional practices (i.e., Billingsley et al., 2019). This can take the form of high-quality PD sessions followed by coaching. Wood et al. (2016) talk about the role of coaching when it comes to developing teacher practice. When teachers receive individualized coaching, they can focus on elements of their own practice that can be improved in response to the needs of the students in their own classrooms. In the case of HLPs, not all teachers will need to improve the same practices. Further, teachers will vary in the elements within a practice that they need to improve and/or that will have the greatest potential to benefit their students. Thus, individualized and ongoing coaching on HLPs can maximize the impact of PD.

Although HLPs can provide a framework for teacher development opportunities, these practices alone do not magically lead to improved student outcomes by virtue of simply being on a curated list. Although HLPs are indeed "practices," they do not capture the entire notion of professional teaching practice—that is, "all professional activities of an educator" (Spencer et al., 2012, p. 129). Rather, the human element holds the key to the potential success of HLPs. The practitioners themselves can ignite the power of HLPs when they: (a) view a teaching practice as acceptable and (b) use their experience and individual judgment in instructional decision making. Spencer et al. (2012) provide a framework that includes these elements in the process of evidence-based practice. In their framework, practice extends beyond a list of empirically validated tools or strategies and involves a complete problem-solving process, leading to positive student outcomes. Similarly, Cook et al. (2008) describe the importance of "professional wisdom" when it comes to selecting, using, and continuing to use empirically-supported practices that meet the diverse and individualized learning needs of their students.

Thus, when developing teachers' skills related to HLPs, consideration must be given to the components of decision-making needed to effectively employ HLPs. Teachers need to be able to identify instructional problems clearly; select appropriate HLPs and research-validated practices that can address those problems; and implement and monitor the effectiveness of those practices. Teachers need to use available evidence, combined with their experience and individual judgment throughout this process. For example, a teacher may know and be able to demonstrate the steps of explicit instruction, but if that teacher fails to understand in which situations to employ this practice or how to determine if the practice is effective, then the HLP does not stand to benefit students.

A final consideration is the role of school-university partnerships in developing teachers' use of HLPs. This chapter includes examples of HLPs being used as a framework in teacher preparation programs, as well as in PD in P-12 schools. However, ideally, these two efforts would occur in tandem through strong school-university partnerships. Maheady et al. (2019) provide an example of university faculty, teacher candidates, practicing mentor teachers, and school administrators all working together to utilize HLPs to improve pre-service and in-service teacher practice. This type of partnership can result in: (a) shared language and understanding about teaching practice between all parties, and (b) improved teaching practice for both pre-service and in-service teachers. The benefits can perpetuate as teachers who have improved practice can ultimately serve as strong mentors for other teachers by modeling and supporting effective HLP implementation.

Case Examples of Using HLPs for Improving Teacher Practice

As previously stated, there are various ways that HLPs can be systematically used to improve teacher practice at the pre- and in-service levels. Different institutions will be at various points in developing or revising teacher preparation or PD programs. Further, some institutions will have more resources (e.g., financial, human, material) than others to undertake this work. Therefore, while it may make sense for one institution to reimagine and revamp their entire program using HLPs as a framework, other institutions, individuals, or workgroups may start small by integrating a focus on just one or two HLPs into the work they are already doing. In this section, we provide case examples illustrating the use of HLPs to improve teacher practice for a range of potential scenarios: (a) overhauling a teacher preparation program, (b) infusing HLPs into an existing teacher preparation program, and (c) using HLPs to frame PD in P-12 schools.

Case A: Overhauling a Teacher Preparation Program

At Josephine's university, the special education faculty experts are in a separate department from her colleague experts in elementary education. Although they have a combined program that results in teacher candidates who are eligible for both special education certification and elementary education certification, the program is not truly integrated; the special education faculty teach the special education courses, and the elementary education faculty teach the elementary education courses, resulting in a "siloed" approach.

Although the program "worked" when it was first developed 15 years ago, over time, it became apparent that it is not serving the candidates or the local school agencies as well as it could. For example, Josephine and her colleagues in both departments have: (a) noted that students have difficulty with the different jargon that can be used within each specialty area; (b) periodically realized that there is some overlap in content and/or conflicting information taught; and (c) heard from teachers and administrators that the current program is not preparing the candidates well for collaborative teaching situations, such as co-taught classrooms.

Given that the program had not been revised in many years, Josephine and a small group of her colleagues set out to revise their program. Given the deep history of practice-based opportunities at their institution, using HLPs to frame their program made a lot of sense. What they needed to decide upon was whether to use the general education HLPs or the special education HLPs to frame the program. To help guide the discussion, Josephine set up a document that included both sets of HLPs side-by-side.

During the small group discussion, the group agreed that it would not be feasible to focus on two combined sets of HLPs. They also agreed that it did not align with their vision of a truly integrated program where faculty from special education and elementary education worked collaboratively to train the teacher candidates. After much discussion, the group realized that there were many overlapping ideas between the two sets and wondered if developing a combined, smaller set of HLPs would be appropriate for their program that led to a dual certification versus choosing one over the other or using both sets. The group diligently worked to identify the most important practices that a candidate graduating with expertise in both areas would need in order to be a successful teacher of all students in a variety of classroom settings, including a co-taught classroom.

After developing a smaller set of HLPs for their programs, they knew that they needed to vet them at various levels with stakeholders in the college and local educational agencies. The group gathered feedback using small focus groups, surveys, presentations with feedback, and hands-on, collaborative workshops. Throughout the process, the team made modifications to the set. Once the set was finalized, each department discussed the set and voted upon whether faculty agreed that they should be used to frame the new dual certification program.

At that point, Josephine and her colleagues invited individuals who taught courses in the unrevised program to be a part of workgroups to help overhaul the current program and courses. The group used the HLP set to frame the program, develop new courses, and revise others where appropriate. They also worked together to map out and systematically integrate scaffolded practice opportunities for the HLPs into the program development; they discussed where HLPs would be introduced and acquired by the candidates and where they would expect the candidates to master each practice at a novice level. Finally, they developed a plan to assess candidate progress and a system to evaluate and reevaluate the program as it was being implemented.

After the draft program was completed, Josephine and her colleagues shared the plan with local educational agencies and their faculty colleagues at the university for feedback before the program was finalized and submitted to the state for review and approval. Josephine and her colleagues believed that it was important to get feedback from various stakeholders for the program to be successful and to have the intended impact on developing truly versatile teachers who could effectively implement HLPs that would result in positive outcomes for students with, at-risk for, and without disabilities.

Case B: Infusing HLPs into an Existing Teacher Preparation Program

David is a faculty member in a small teacher preparation program that prepares candidates for elementary-level certification in both general education and special education. At a recent professional conference, he attended several sessions focused on HLPs. He had heard of HLPs, but at his institution, HLPs were not yet being used in their programs. After returning to his campus, he spent some time examining resources that had been suggested at his conference, including the University of Michigan's Teaching Works and the CEEDAR Center. Meanwhile, he learned that several of his colleagues had been investigating HLPs over the past semester. A group of interested faculty met to discuss how they might use their knowledge about HLPs to enhance their existing preparation program.

While the group members believed it would be beneficial to infuse HLPs throughout their program, they realized that with limited resources, it would make sense to start small. So, they decided to each identify one HLP that could be highlighted in an existing course they would be teaching in the upcoming semester. They examined both the general education and special education published HLPs sets. They noticed a great deal of overlap between the two sets (as evidenced by the HLPs crosswalk document available on the CEEDAR website) and agreed that they could choose from either set as they were both relevant for their candidates. In his introduction to assessment and instruction course, David decided to focus on HLP #15 from the general education set: "checking student understanding during and at the conclusion of lessons" (Teaching Works, 2015). He noted that this HLP aligns very closely to HLP #6 from the special education set: "use student assessment data, analyze instructional practices, and make necessary adjustments that improve student outcomes." While David had always taught the topic of formative assessment within his course, he felt he could be much more explicit and thorough about it, rather than having it simply be a topic covered in a lesson. Prior to the new semester, he planned how he would introduce the HLP, explicitly teach it, and provide his candidates with practice opportunities.

David met with his candidates once per week for this course. In the first class session, David briefly introduced the concept of HLPs and shared the HLP that would be a focus within their course. He provided a rationale for choosing this HLP, articulating the benefits for both students and teachers of using formative assessment.

Throughout each of his weekly class sessions, David modeled at least one method of formative assessment that could be used during a lesson (e.g., response boards) or at the end of a lesson (e.g., exit tickets). When he utilized these methods in class, he explicitly pointed out that he was doing so to his candidates. For example, he would say, "Today, I am going to check for your understanding by utilizing a method called Numbered Heads Together. I'll explain how this works and then we'll try it out." David would then: (a) explain the strategy, (b) provide a written list of steps to be used, (c) engage his candidates in the strategy in relation to whatever course content they were learning that day, and (d) hold a debriefing conversation about the strategy to discuss how it went and possible applications in the P-12 classroom. David would also periodically point out to his students how he was using data from these assessment methods to inform his instruction. For example, he would say, "Last class, I had you complete an exit ticket before leaving. After reviewing your responses, I want to explain to you how I am going to use that information to inform today's lesson..." Using this model, throughout the semester, candidates were able to learn about many strategies that can be used to check students' understanding and participate in them from a student perspective.

Further, David wanted to give his candidates the opportunity to practice the strategies from a teacher's perspective. While his introductory course did not include a field component, he did utilize micro-teaching to have each of his candidates develop and deliver a brief lesson towards the end of the semester to practice the various elements of assessment and instruction taught in the course. To integrate the HLP related to checking for student understanding, David modified the lesson plan template he typically had candidates use to include a requirement that they use at least one method of checking for student understanding during the lesson and at least one method at the end of the lesson. Candidates were to choose from the list of strategies David had modeled throughout the semester. In their planning, they had to indicate which methods they would use, provide a brief rationale, and describe how they would use the data to inform their instruction. While the candidates delivered their lessons in class, David used the list of steps for each strategy he had provided when he taught them throughout the semester to check off the steps used by the candidates and provide feedback.

After the semester, David met back up with his group of colleagues, who all discussed how the integration of HLPs went in their courses. They shared successes, lessons learned, and suggestions for improvement. They also discussed ideas for how they might work with other faculty outside their group to expand the integration of HLPs into more courses across the program.

Case C: Using HLPs to Frame PD in P-12 Schools

Yvette is a new elementary principal in a challenging school. Coming into the position, Yvette learned that literacy assessment results at the school have been below acceptable levels for several years in a row, and teachers are discouraged about the lack of progress. Yvette met with small groups of general and special education teachers, as well as the school literacy specialist, to gather more information about their concerns. She learned the teachers feel students have not been responding well to the literacy program selected by the district; the teachers indicated many students seem tuned out and not interested. Further, with large class sizes, teachers are aware they are simply not able to provide enough practice opportunities for each of their students, particularly the students with and at-risk for disabilities in their inclusive classrooms.

While the decisions for curriculum, materials and class size are made at the district level, Yvette knows that she and her teachers can still make a difference when considering how instruction is delivered in the classroom. Having recently completed her graduate work at a local university, Yvette had learned about HLPs and their role in effective teaching. Using the CEC HLP set (e.g., McLeskey et al., 2017), she worked with a small group of interested teachers to identify two HLPs that could serve as the foundation of the school's PD for the first few months of the upcoming school year; this group became the school's PD team. The two HLPs selected were HLP #17, "use flexible grouping," and HLP #18, "use strategies to promote active student engagement." Both seemed very relevant to the concerns identified by the teachers in relation to literacy and could also have potential benefits across content areas.

In a faculty meeting, Yvette and the PD team introduced the two HLPs, provided an overview of them, and drew connections to the problems previously identified by teachers in relation to literacy. Teachers were then given the opportunity to self-select which HLP they wanted to focus on for PD in the upcoming months. They were encouraged to select the HLP they believed they had the most to learn about and/or that would have the greatest impact on the issues they had seen in their own classrooms.

On the first PD day of the year, teachers went to a morning session based on which HLP they selected. In each session, a couple of members of the PD team shared additional research on the HLP along with specific strategies/techniques that could be used. For example, in the group exploring flexible grouping, the session included topics related to grouping, such as selecting grouping arrangements (e.g., homogenous vs. heterogenous, teacher-led vs. independent), designing instructional activities, setting expectations, and monitoring student progress.

In the afternoon session, teachers had independent time to complete an action plan identifying how they could integrate what they learned about their selected HLP in their classroom. Each teacher had one-on-one time with a PD team member to ask questions, review their plan, and set up times in their schedule for follow-up coaching.

Throughout the first few months of the school year, teachers implemented their plans and received guidance and feedback from PD team members in the form of email communication, consultation sessions, and non-evaluative observations of teaching with feedback. At a PD day in late fall, teachers were brought together in small groups to share with colleagues who had addressed the same HLP as them, and then also in groups of colleagues who had addressed the other HLP. Successes and challenges were discussed, and many teachers informally decided to continue working on improving the HLP they had been addressing and/or begin to explore the other HLP.

Yvette surveyed teachers to solicit feedback on the PD model they had used throughout the fall. For the most part, teachers responded favorably. Teachers appreciated many aspects of the model, including: (a) having PD directly related to an authentic problem they had identified within their school, (b) being given the autonomy to select which HLP they wanted to explore and develop an individualized plan of how to do so in their classroom, and (c) having the process be ongoing, with communication and coaching by the PD team for guidance and support. While Yvette was unsure how these results would translate to the school's literacy assessment results in spring, she was pleased that her school had focused its efforts on improving relevant teacher practices known to have an impact on student performance.

Getting Started Where You Are

The three previous case studies demonstrate examples of how HLPs can be used as a framework for teacher development. Whether starting big or small, when setting out to use HLPs in your own context, resources are available to explore the "reimagining" of teacher education programs and P-12 PD delivery options. For example, the Collaboration for Effective Educator Development, Accountability, and Reform (CEEDAR) Center offers a Roadmap for Educator Preparation Reform that can help educator preparation programs in their quest to integrate HLPs and other evidence-based practices within and across coursework and field experiences (CEEDAR, nd). In whatever way you choose to utilize HLPs in your own context, the focus is ultimately on improving teacher practice and, in turn, student outcomes. Teachers will be well poised to meet the needs of all learners in inclusive settings when they are skilled in the main HLP areas of: (a) engaging in effective collaboration; (b) identifying needs and strengths through assessment; (c) meeting the social/emotional/behavioral needs of students; and (d) planning and conducting well-designed, strategic, and adaptable instruction.

Conclusion

In this chapter, we described HLP sets developed for novice elementary and special education teachers, suggested potential benefits of using HLPs to frame teacher education programs and PD opportunities, and provided three ways that HLPs can be used to improve teacher practice (i.e., complete program redesign; thoughtful program addition; framework for PD in P-12 schools). We presented case studies aligned with each vision. What is needed now is collective action among those who prepare teachers and provide for their continuing PD (McLeskey et al., 2019). As Windschitl et al. (2019) commented, "…even modest shifts toward HLPs in teacher education programs can begin to address some perennial problems" (p. 389).

How we proceed to enact this new vision of teacher preparation and PD will determine whether teacher practice and student learning are improved. We recommend that we proceed with caution and not underestimate the enormous challenges inherent in the implementation and sustainability of innovative practices (Fixsen et al., 2019). Perhaps harnessing the strength of collaborative teacher preparation and the P-12 system is the first step. A professional development school model has the potential to enhance the practice of both pre-service and in-service teachers leading to improved teacher and student outcomes (Voltz, 2001). Other creative approaches to help with implementation and sustainability might involve coaching models (Knight, 2007), *Networked Improvement Communities* (NICs; Bryk et al., 2015), or innovative PD methods, such as multimedia PD (i.e., Kennedy et al., 2017; Schumaker et al., 2020).

As more students with wide-ranging abilities and needs continue to be included in general education settings, HLPs have considerable potential as a vehicle for improved outcomes. Their all-encompassing nature can not only help address the social, behavioral, and academic needs of students, but help teachers collaborate to meet those needs. As educators, we must continue to explore the best ways to facilitate student success—improving teacher practice is one critical way and must not be overlooked.

References

Americans with Disabilities Act of 1990, 42 U.S.C. § 12101 *et seq.* (1990). http://www.ada.gov/pubs/adastatute08.htm

Ball, D., & Forzani, F. (2011). Building a common core for learning to teach: And connecting professional learning to practice. *American Educator, 35*(2), 17–21, 38-39.

Belfiore, P. J., & Lee, D. L. (2014). Shaping the field of general and special education: The role of evidence in practice, and practice in dissemination. *Journal of Evidence-Based Practices for Schools, 15*(2), 138–150.

Billingsley, B., Bettini, E., & Jones, N. (2019). Supporting special education teacher induction through high leverage practices. *Remedial and Special Education, 40*(6), 365–379. doi:10.1177/0741932518816826

Blanton, L. P., Pugach, M. C., & Boveda, M. (2014). *Teacher education reform initiatives and special education: Convergence, divergence, and missed opportunities.* (Document No. LS-3). Collaboration for Effective Educator, Development, Accountability, and Reform Center. http://ceedar.education.ufl.edu/tools/literature-syntheses/

Boroson, B. (2017). Inclusive education: Lessons from history. *Differences, Not Disabilities, 74*(7), 18–23. http://www.ascd.org/publications/educational-leadership/apr17/vol74/num07/Inclusive-Education@-Lessons-From-History.aspx

Brindley, R., Field, B. E., & Lessen, E. (2008). *What it means to be a professional development school.* National Association for Professional Development Schools. Brown v. Board of Education, 347 U.S. 483 (1954). http://www.oyez.org/cases/1940-1955/347us483

Brownell, M. T., Benedict, A. E., Leko, M. M., Peyton, D., Pua, D., & Richards-Tutor, C. (2019). A continuum of pedagogies for preparing teachers to use high leverage practices. *Remedial and Special Education, 40*(6), 338–355. doi:10.1177/0741932518824990

Bryk, A. S., Gomez, L. M., Grunow, A., & LeMahieu, P. G. (2015). *Learning to improve: How America's schools can get better at getting better.* Harvard Education Publishing.

Council for Accreditation of Educator Preparation. (2013). *CAEP accreditation standards.* Author. https://Users/admin/Downloads/caep-2013- accreditation-standards.pdf

Collaboration for Effective Educator, Development, Accountability, and Reform Center. (n.d.). *Roadmap for educator preparation reform.* https://ceedar.education.ufl.edu/roadmap/

Cook, B. G., Tankersley, M., & Harjusola-Webb, S. (2008). Evidence-based special education and professional wisdom: Putting it all together. *Intervention in School and Clinic, 44*(2), 105–111. doi:10.1177/1053451208321566

Cosier, M., Causton-Theoharis, J., & Theoharis, G. (2013). Does access matter? Time in general education and achievement for students with disabilities. *Remedial and Special Education, 34*(6), 323–332. doi:10.1177/0741932513485448

Darling-Hammond, L. (2000). Teacher quality and student achievement: A review of state policy evidence. *Education Policy Analysis Archives*, *8*(1), 1–44. doi:10.14507/epaa.v8n1.2000

Darling-Hammond, L. (2010). Teacher education and the American future. *Journal of Teacher Education*, *61*(1-2), 35–47. doi:10.1177/0022487109348024

Darling-Hammond, L., Hyler, M. E., & Gardner, M. (2017). *Effective teacher professional development*. Learning Policy Institute. https://learningpolicyinstitute.org/sites/default/files/product-files/Effective_Teacher_Professional_Development_REPORT.pdf

Desimone, L. M., & Garet, M. S. (2015). Best practices in teachers' professional development in the United States. *Psychology, Society, & Education*, 7(3), 252–263. doi:10.25115/psye.v7i3.515

Every Student Succeeds Act, 20 U.S.C. § 6301 (2015). https://www.congress.gov/114/plaws/publ95/PLAW-114publ95.pdf

Fixsen, D. L., Van Dyke, M., & Blase, K. A. (2019). *Implementation science: Fidelity predictions and outcomes*. Active Implementation Research Network. www.activeimplementation.org/resources

Fuchs, D., Fuchs, L. S., McMaster, K. L., & Lemons, C. J. (2018). Students with disabilities' abysmal school performance: An introduction to the special issue. *Learning Disabilities Research & Practice*, *33*, 127–130. doi:10.1111/ldrp.12180

Henninger, W., & Gupta, S. (2014). How do children benefit from inclusion? In first steps to preschool inclusion: How to jumpstart your program wide plan. In S. Gupta, W. R. Henninger, & M. E. Vihn (Eds.), *First steps to preschool inclusion: How to jumpstart your programwide plan* (pp. 33–57). Brookes Publishing. http://archive.brookespublishing.com/documents/gupta-how-children-benefit-from-inclusion.pdf

Hlas, A., & Hlas, C. (2012). A review of high-leverage teaching practices: Making connections between mathematics and foreign languages. *Foreign Language Annals*, *45*(51), S76–S97. doi:10.1111/j.1944-9720.2012.01180.x

Hughes, C. A., Riccomini, P. J., & Morris, J. R. (2019). Use explicit instruction. In J. McLeskey, L. Maheady, B. Billingsley,M. T. Brownell, & T. J. Lewis (Eds.), *High leverage practices for inclusive classrooms* (pp. 215–236). Routledge.

Hurwitz, S., Perry, B., Cohen, E. D., & Skiba, R. (2020). Special education and individualized student growth: A longitudinal assessment of outcomes for students with disabilities. *American Educational Research Journal*, *57*(2), 576–611. doi:10.3102/0002831219857054

Individuals with Disabilities Education Act, 20 U.S.C. § 1400. (2004). https://sites.ed.gov/idea/statuteregulations/

Kennedy, M. J., Rodgers, W. J., Romig, J. E., Lloyd, J. W., & Brownell, M. T. (2017). Effects of a multimedia professional development package on inclusive science teachers' vocabulary instruction. *Journal of Teacher Education*, *68*(2), 130–213. doi:10.1177/0022487116687554.

Keyworth, R. (2020). *Overview of national achievement tests*. The Wing Institute. https://www.winginstitute.org/student-national-standardized-tests.

Knight, J. (2007). *Instructional coaching: A partnership approach to improving instruction*. Corwin Press.

Maheady, L., & Patti, A., (2020). High leverage practices for inclusive educational settings. *Oxford research encyclopedias*. Oxford Press. doi:10.1093/acrefore/9780190264093.013.1180

Maheady, L. J., Patti, A. L., Rafferty, L. A., del Prado Hill, P. (2019). School–university partnerships: One institution's efforts to integrate and support teacher use of high-leverage practices. *Remedial & Special Education*, *40*(6), 356–364. doi:10.1177/0741932518812689

Maheady, L., Smith, C., & Jabot, M. (2013). Utilizing evidence-based practice in teacher preparation. *Advances in Learning and Behavioral Disabilities*, *26*, 121–147. doi:10.1108/S0735-004X(2013)0000026008

McLeskey, J., Barringer, M-D., Billingsley, B., Brownell, M., Jackson, D., Kennedy, M., Lewis, T., Maheady, L., Rodriguez, J., Scheeler, M. C., Winn, J., & Ziegler, D. (2017). *High leverage practices in special education*. Council for Exceptional Children & CEEDAR Center. https://ceedar.education.ufl.edu/wp-content/uploads/2017/07/CEC-HLP-Web.pdf

McLeskey, J., Billingsley, B., & Ziegler, D. (2018). Using high-leverage practices in teacher preparation to reduce the research-to-practice gap in inclusive settings. *Australasian Journal of Special and Inclusive Education*, *42*(1), 3–16. doi:10.1017/jsi.2018.3

McLeskey, J., Maheady, L., Billingsley, B., Brownell, M. T., & Lewis, T. J. (2019). Some final thoughts regarding high leverage practices. In J. McLesky, L. Maheady, B. Billingsely, M. T. Brownell, & T. J. Lewis (Eds.), *High leverage practices for inclusive classrooms* (pp. 327–333). Routledge.

Murphey, D. (2014). The academic achievement of English language learners: Data for the U. S. and each of the states. *Child Trends*. doi:10.13140/RG.2.2.33510.63041.

National Center for Education Statistics. (2009). *National assessment of educational progress*. Author. https://catalog.data.gov/dataset/2009-national-assessment-of-educational-progress

National Council for Accreditation of Teacher Education. (2010). *Transforming teaching education through clinical practice: A national strategy to prepare effective educators*. A report of the Blue-Ribbon Panel on Clinical Preparation and Partnership for Improved Student Learning. NCATE. http://caepnet.org/~/media/Files/caep/accreditation-resources/blue-ribbon-panel.pdf

No Child Left Behind Act, 20 U.S.C. § 6319. (2002). https://www.congress.gov/107/plaws/publ110/PLAW-107publ110.htm

Pugach, M. C., & Blanton, L. P. (2012). Enacting diversity in dual certification programs. *Journal of Teacher Education, 63*, 254–267. doi:10.1177/0022487112446970

Randolph, J. J. (2007). Meta-analysis of the research on response cards: Effects on test achievement, quiz achievement, participation, and off-task behavior. *Journal of Positive Behavioral Interventions, 9*, 113–128. doi:10.1177/10983007070090020201

Salend, S. J., & Garrick Duhaney, L. M. (1999). The impact of inclusion on students with and without disabilities and their educators. *Remedial and Special Education, 20*(2), 114–126. doi:10.1177/074193259902000209

Schumaker, J., Fisher, J., Walsh, L., & Lancaster, P. (2020). Effects of multimedia versus live professional development on teachers' and students' performance related to the question exploration routine. *Learning Disabilities Research and Practice, 35*, 180–200.

Scruggs, T. E., & Mastropieri, M. A. (1996). Teacher perceptions of mainstreaming/inclusion, 1958-1995. *Exceptional Children, 63*, 59–74. doi:10.1177/001440299606300106

Sermier Dessemontet, R., Bless, G., & Morin, D. (2012). Effects of inclusion on the academic achievement and adaptive behavior of children with intellectual disabilities. *Journal of Intellect Disability Research, 56*(6), 579–587. doi:10.1111/j.1365-2788.2011.01497.x

Spencer, T. D., Detrich, R., & Slocum, T. A. (2012). Evidence-based practice: A framework for making effective decisions. *Education and Treatment of Children, 35*(2), 127–151. doi:10.1353/etc.2012.0013

Strain, P. S., Barton, E. E., & Dunlap, G. (2012). Lessons learned about the utility of social validity. *Education and Treatment of Children, 35*(2), 183–200. doi:10.1353/etc.2012.0007

Stronge, J. H., Ward, T. J., & Grant, L. W. (2011). What makes good teachers good? A cross-case analysis of the connection between teacher effectiveness and student achievement. *Journal of Teacher Education, 62*(4), 339–355. doi:10.1177/0022487111404241

Teaching Works. (2015). High leverage practices. Retrieved from http://www.teachingworks.org/work -of-teaching/high-leverage-practices.

U.S. Congress, Public Law 94-142, Education for All Handicapped Children Act. (November 29, 1975).

Van Scoy, I. J., & Eldridge, D. B. (2012). NCATE's Blue Ribbon Panel Report and NAPDS: Working together. *School-University Partnerships, 5*(1), 7–12. https://files.eric.ed.gov/fulltext/EJ974363.pdf

Vaz S., Wilson, N., Falkmer, M., Sim A., Scott, M., Cordier R., & Falkmer, T. (2015). Factors associated with primary school teachers' attitudes towards the inclusion of students with disabilities. *PLoS ONE 10*(8): e0137002. doi:10.1371/journal.pone.0137002

Voltz, D. L. (2001). Preparing general education teachers for inclusive settings: The role of special education teachers in the professional development school context. *Learning Disability Quarterly, 24*(4), 288–296. doi:10.2307/1511117

Windschitl, M., Thompson, J., Braaten, M., & Stroupe, D. (2012). Proposing a core set of instructional practices and tools for teachers of science. *Science Education, 96*(5), 878- 903. doi:10.1002/sce.21027

Windschitl, M., Thompson, J., Braaten, M., & Stroupe, D. (2019). Sharing a vision, sharing practices: How communities of educators improve teaching. *Remedial and Special Education, 40*(6), 380–390. doi:10.1177/0741932518810796

Wood, C. L., Goodnight, C. I., Bethune, K. S., Preston, A. I., & Cleaver, S. L. (2016). Role of professional development and multi-level coaching in promoting evidence-based practice in education. *Learning Disabilities: A Contemporary Journal, 14*(2), 159–170.

10

Effective Literacy Instruction in Inclusive Schools

Ronda Fritz[1] *and Beth Harn*[2]

[1]EASTERN OREGON UNIVERSITY

[2]UNIVERSITY OF OREGON

Setting the Stage

Despite significant federal investments to improve reading outcomes, according to the National Assessment of Education Progress (NAEP), only one-third of fourth and eighth grade students are reading at or above grade level (National Center on Education Statistics, 2019). As Foorman (2016) wrote, we have made surface-level improvements through our Response to Intervention/Multi-tiered Systems of Support efforts but have achieved a negligible impact on improving learning outcomes.

Professionals are in a unique situation in the field of literacy instruction. Currently, there exists a stockpile of reading methods and programs that have been found effective in rigorous research studies. However, these same programs have had an unpredictable impact when taken to scale or when deployed in schools (Harn, 2017). Dr. Mark Schneider, Director of the Institute on Education Sciences, validated this point when he explicitly stated that we need to do more to get research-based practices into the classroom and hands of teachers (Schneider, 2018). If inclusive classrooms are to meet the needs of all students, teachers and administrators must be informed of effective practices for improving outcomes for students with disabilities in their classrooms and be provided with the right tools, assessments, and curricula. Thes practices supported by research include both instructional methods and collaboration between special and general education.

One avenue for bridging the research-to-practice gap is through teacher preparation. Teacher preparation programs must take responsibility for ensuring that new teachers begin their careers as prepared as possible to provide literacy instruction to all students. To begin, teacher preparation programs must educate pre-service teachers regarding scientifically-based reading instruction. The National Council for Teacher Quality (NCTQ), in their 2020 Teacher Prep Review (Drake & Walsh, 2020), found that the number of elementary education teacher preparation programs teaching scientifically-based reading instruction has increased since their 2013 review. However, almost half of teacher preparation programs are still not including adequate coverage of scientifically-based reading research. If inclusive classrooms are to meet the needs of all children effectively, it is imperative that teacher preparation programs strive to include scientifically-based literacy instruction in their programs. General education teachers need to have these foundational instructional practices

DOI: 10.4324/9781003043874-10

established so that the special education teachers can collaborate with them in a meaningful manner to better meet the needs of students with disabilities.

Teacher preparation programs should encourage collaboration between special education and general education to ensure that students with disabilities are provided with instruction designed for their individual needs (see Chapter 4). It cannot be assumed that teachers, both general and special education, will know how to collaborate to improve outcomes for students (Kloo & Zigmond, 2008). The skills required for collaboration should be developed in teacher preparation programs through both coursework and clinical experiences, preferably with colleges of education modeling collaborative relationships between general and special education departments (Harvey et al., 2010). Providing resources to allow for courses taught by faculty from both departments, as well as specific courses in collaboration, could enhance collaboration skills for teacher candidates (Harvey et al., 2010; Weiss et al., 2017). Having both the content expertise of the general education teacher, as well as the instructional design expertise of the special educator working together, has the potential to bring about powerful learning outcomes for students with disabilities. But, without specific training on how to co-teach effectively, outcomes may be less than optimal (Bateman & Cline, 2016; Kloo & Zigmond, 2008).

For teachers who are already practicing, enhancing classroom practices is dependent on targeted professional development opportunities and leadership that can provide resources and support for developing collaborative relationships (see Chapter 5). Despite inclusion being the most common special education delivery model (Kloo & Zigmond, 2008), very few teachers have received specific training in this area (Wang & Fitch, 2010). Professional development opportunities must involve both general and special education teachers and focus on enhancing the areas of expertise of both parties. Leadership is instrumental in helping all parties determine roles and responsibilities that will affect the best outcomes (see Chapter 2). This also requires administrative support in overtly designating co-planning time, resources (e.g., materials, training, etc.), and progress monitoring, as well as regular evaluation of inclusionary practices (Dagen & Bean, 2020).

For inclusive literacy instruction to be effective, both general and special education teachers need to have the skills and knowledge related to effective literacy instruction, in addition to training regarding co-teaching and data-based decision making (see Chapter 8). It is also imperative that schools provide leadership that has the capacity and knowledge to guide and monitor the implementation of effective practices. In the remainder of this chapter, we will explore the research regarding inclusive literacy practices, as well as specific knowledge and practices that all teachers and administrators must accept for literacy instruction in the inclusive classroom to be successful.

What Do We Know Based on Research and the Wisdom of Practice?

This section will outline the research base related to inclusionary literacy practices. This will include evidence for the need for a systems-level approach to literacy instruction that includes coordination of services between general and special education, strong leadership, and decisions made based on data. In addition, this section will highlight the evidence for differentiated literacy instruction that is aligned with the core curriculum and delivered by staff that is well-trained and carefully allocated to best support all students through small-group instruction and individualization based on students' needs. With staff allocation in mind, this section will also address the evidence for professional development that is targeted and ensures that all staff is informed and supported in providing effective instruction for students with disabilities in an inclusive classroom.

Importance of Planning and Coordination

Effective inclusionary practices cannot occur without adequate planning and collaboration. In schools demonstrating the most impressive outcomes in literacy achievement, inclusion occurs as part of a comprehensive, coordinated, school-wide model designed to meet the needs of all students and prevent reading difficulties from occurring. This model is commonly implemented as Response to Intervention (RtI).

RtI can be an effective system for ensuring prevention, early identification, and intervention for students at-risk for reading disabilities. For students with reading disabilities, an RtI instructional framework is essential to plan and regularly evaluate for effective inclusionary experiences using a multi-tiered system of support (Harn et al., 2011; Honig et al., 2018). The critical components of a school-wide RtI reading model include:

- coordinated, multi-tiered systems of support,
- use of evidence-based instructional materials for each level of support,
- data-based decision-making systems, and
- targeted professional development.

Teaming and collaboration are necessary to coordinate systems of support adequately. Active leadership and instructional teams are a crucial underlying component for improving literacy outcomes within a school (Dagen & Bean, 2020; Jones et al., 2010). These teams provides the structure necessary for general education, special education, and intervention staff to work together to identify and solve problems, make academic and behavioral instructional decisions, and evaluate the effectiveness of schoolwide systems (Denton et al., 2006). Ideally, administrators are part of this leadership team so that resources can be most effectively allocated. Without administrator support, these elements can be difficult to manipulate (Dagen & Bean, 2020). An administrator often has to make decisions regarding curriculum, staffing, schedules, and time allowed for professional development. More importantly, however, research has shown that effective school leaders focus on tasks related to improving instruction in addition to the managerial aspects of their jobs (Leithwood et al., 2004). One aspect of improving instruction that school leaders can strongly influence is insisting on the use of evidence-based practices (EBPs). Employing EBPs in general education, typically discussed as a Tier 1 core reading program, is likely to decrease the number of students struggling to learn to read, as well as decrease the number of students qualifying for special education services (Chard et al., 2008).

Helman and Pekel (2020) overtly addressed the crucial need for the principal to be involved in the literacy leadership team (e.g., RtI team). They emphasized that the principal should facilitate the collective efforts by creating a culture of collaboration and a goal of continuous improvement. This requires that the school have structures in place, including common planning time, quality materials as well as regular data-based decision-making efforts examining both school and student level improvement. Schools where adults learn together with strong literacy leadership teams become schools where students learn together (Walpole & Vitale, 2020).

As Heller et al. (1982) emphasized when establishing the need to use an RtI approach for LD identification, the effectiveness of RtI is predicated on the quality of instruction provided in both general education and intervention supports. Most schools now have access to evidence-based programs (EBPs) for use in general education, as well as intervention settings (e.g., Tier 2 or Tier 3); however, many schools still struggle to deliver universal/core (i.e., Tier 1) instruction with sufficient quality and intensity to accelerate learning for students who are not achieving as expected (Foorman et al., 2016; Simmons, 2015).

There is also evidence that the coordination of supports with the core program may be a more effective means of meeting the needs of learners needing support beyond the core reading curriculum (Chard & Harn, 2008; Harn et al., 2011). Harn et al. (2011) documented that interventions (e.g., Tiers 2 or 3) that are selected or designed to specifically align with the content and instructional practices taught in the core reading program were differentially more effective at accelerating reading development for the most at-risk first grade readers than non-aligned intervention efforts.

Creating this coordinated instructional support system requires the teaming of all instructional support staff with the knowledge of the grade-level expectations and the nature of the instructional materials, as well as the skills for determining how to effectively differentiate for the range of learners and/or collaborative skills in working with special education personnel to make the general education material accessible to all students (Dagen & Bean, 2020). This level of understanding requires that the school or district provide adequate training to all personnel who will be delivering instruction. Not only do teachers need to be fully trained on evidence-based practices for teaching reading (Chard et al., 2008), but paraprofessionals who also may be delivering instruction must be well-trained. Having these extra individuals in the classroom can mean that more students will have the opportunity to receive more targeted instruction more frequently, but without proper training, the results of their assistance may not be maximized (Causton-Theoharis et al., 2007; Giangreco et al., 2010).

Schools that systematically align their instructional supports (i.e., content/program and personnel) by carefully scheduling sufficient instructional time (i.e., general education and intervention) and personnel (i.e., general and special education, Title 1) that maximizes the school day get better outcomes than schools that do not (Baker et al., 2011; Coyne et al 2016; Simmons, 2015). As discussed in Dougherty Stahl (2016), Tier 2 and Tier 3 interventions need to be substantial enough to bolster or go beyond and augment what is provided as part of Tier 1 primary/universal instruction. However, as noted in Balu et al. (2015), approximately one-third of schools in their study reported that Tier 2 interventions were provided by the general education teacher, which begs the question of whether these were actual interventions or differentiated instruction (Dougherty Stahl, 2016). For inclusive schools to successfully deliver literacy instruction to meet the needs of all students, both differentiated instruction and interventions must be deployed (Dagen & Bean, 2020).

Differentiated instruction typically retains the same objectives and content as the core instruction but may vary in how teachers present and students learn the material (e.g., in small groups, using manipulatives, with more time) and how they demonstrate what they know (e.g., dictation, performance, graphics). Whereas interventions may focus on different content and skills delivered in a more explicit manner than Tier 1 instruction that is intended to meet the needs of the majority of students. So, Tier 1 instruction would include the teacher providing differentiated instruction within the allocated core instructional time. If this is done well, then the school can plan and deliver truly supplemental instruction/intervention: explicit and systematic instruction that is targeted toward the specific needs of the student that can be delivered by varied personnel to accelerate learning (Dougherty Stahl, 2016; Simmons, 2015).

Allocation of Staff Resources

An important component of coordinating supports is allocating staff in a more effective way during the literacy or reading block. 90-minute reading blocks are a common practice within successful schoolwide reading systems (Chard, 2013) but are subject to a school's master schedule that allocates staffing to support classroom teachers for differentiation and individualization for students with disabilities. An ideal schedule is designed to ensure adequate reading time within classrooms, as well as to coordinate staff to provide optimal support for differentiation and individualization within each classroom (Helman & Pekel, 2020). Within that block, students might participate in whole-group reading instruction led by the classroom teacher, as well as small-group instruction focusing on specific skills led by the classroom teacher, special education or Title I teacher, or paraprofessionals. It is important to consider that inclusion cannot mean a lack of differentiation and individualization through the delivery of interventions specifically tailored to the needs of the student with disabilities. This targeted individualization is critical to the reading development of students with disabilities (Batemen & Cline, 2016; Obiakor et al., 2012).

Using Small Group Instruction for Differentiation and Individualization

To provide targeted differentiation and individualization to students with or at-risk for a reading disability, resources must be allocated to provide small group instruction. For years, research has suggested that small groups of three to four students have better outcomes than larger groups of eight to ten students (Lou et al., 1996; Vaughn et al., 2003, 2012; Wanzek & Vaughn, 2007) and that the use of small groups in the general education classroom is related to much better reading outcomes (Hong & Hong, 2009; Taylor et al., 1999). Students with reading disabilities who receive intervention in small groups or one-on-one will show more growth in reading achievement than those who are provided instruction in larger groups (Vaughn et al., 2003; Wanzek & Vaughn, 2007); and groups of two to four students, or one-on-one, will provide the most intensive interventions for students with the greatest needs (Vaughn et al., 2012). Providing small group differentiated instruction will require a classroom structure that includes teacher- and paraprofessional-led small groups as well as centers that provide additional independent or minimally-guided practice opportunities (Kosanovich et al., 2007).

Varying Size, Time, and Content in Small Groups According to Need

Not all children will receive equal amounts of time in teacher- or paraprofessional-directed small groups. Those students who are below or far below grade level expectations should receive the most time in teacher-led instruction while those who are at or above grade level would spend less time in teacher-directed instruction and more time in independent practice opportunities through centers (Gersten et al., 2009; Harn et al., 2008; Kosanovich et al., 2007). For instance, the groups with the most intensive needs may receive teacher-led, small group instruction for 30 minutes daily, while a group with more strategic needs may only receive instruction three times per week for 20 minutes (Kosanovich et al., 2007). Another important factor is how the time is spent within the instructional groups. For students with the most intensive needs, it is important to adjust the time spent on each instructional area (e.g., phonemic awareness, phonics) depending on the response of the students in the group and their changing needs (Harn et al., 2008). The needs of each student should also determine the size of the group. For struggling readers, groups of 3-5 are optimal, while groups of 5-7 can be used effectively with other students (Kosanovich et al., 2007).

Importance of Data-Based Decision Making

Data-based decision-making (see Chapter 8) is the underlying mechanism that drives the coordinated supports in the schoolwide literacy model and helps to determine grouping and instructional needs. This decision-making process begins with screening measures designed to be used with all students, including students with disabilities, in order to determine the typical performance of most students and to provide a gauge of how discrepant some students are from the 'expected' performance range (Riley-Tilman et al., 2013).

The difference between typical peer performance and the included student should inform how intensive the instructional supports need to be to support that student adequately to ensure growth (Harn et al., 2008). After students are screened and instruction is being provided, regular progress monitoring determines whether students are receiving services that are accelerating their learning or whether additional or different supports need to be implemented (Chard & Harn, 2008). Additionally, the school should regularly (e.g., beginning, middle, and end of year) review grade-level performance and evaluate it in comparison to prior year performance in order to determine whether more system changes (e.g., change of program, modification of intervention supports, more professional development in comprehension, etc.) are needed (Jones et al., 2010; Riley-Tilman et al., 2013).

Importance of Professional Development for Optimal Reading Outcomes

The first goal of a school professional development plan should be to maximize the core literacy program. While many EBPs address critical skills in literacy development, targeted professional development can ensure increased fidelity of implementation and higher outcomes when coupled with effective instructional practices. Teachers and paraprofessionals providing instruction need to be taught and supported to use principles of effective instruction such as:

- optimizing engaged time/time on task,
- promoting high levels of success,
- increased content coverage,
- increased time in smaller, homogenous groups, and
- scaffolded instruction (Archer & Hughes, 2011)

These explicit instruction practices are necessary for supporting the learning of all students and essential for effective individualization for students with disabilities. For students at risk for reading difficulties, increasing the explicitness of the instruction can be one way to differentiate and intensify lessons (Wanzek et al., 2020). Another important way to intensify instruction for students who are at-risk in the inclusive classroom is to be more systematic, ensuring that complex practices are taught in small, manageable steps in an order that progresses from easier to more difficult (NRP, 2000; Wanzek et al., 2020). Studies have shown that explicit, systematic instruction is an effective and efficient approach to delivering reading instruction for all learners, but that it is critical for learners with disabilities (Gersten et al., 2009). To ensure all learners' needs are met, explicit, systematic instruction must be the norm in inclusive classrooms.

Professional development will also need to have components to teach staff to use data to inform and support differentiated instruction. Data should drive decisions regarding grouping for effective skill instruction as well as levels of support required for different topographies of learners in evaluating response to interventions. Using data can also identify the instructional areas needing differentiation and individualization. By identifying these areas, schools and teachers can choose appropriate methods for providing targeted intervention that is optimally intensified for each student's needs.

Informed Professional Development

Data should also inform the professional development needs of the school staff. High-quality, evidence-based reading programs must be paired with high-quality professional development and support to improve instructional practices (Chard, 2004).

Data can and should be collected to determine the instructional competency of all staff delivering instruction in the general education classroom and drive the professional development to improve instructional delivery as needed (Goe & Croft, 2009; Semmelroth & Johnson, 2014). Historically, general education classroom teachers have been observed and provided feedback on their performance through school or district evaluation procedures (Brophy & Good, 1986; Chomat-Mooney et al., 2008). Observation tools designed for general education classrooms can provide important data regarding whole class instruction (e.g., Danielson, 2013; La Paro et al., 2004), but tools designed to measure instructional quality in small groups and intervention are not as common but are needed (Fritz et al., 2019; Semmelroth & Johnson, 2014).

The field of implementation science provides evidence that the quality of instructional delivery of interventions is directly related to student outcomes (Gersten et al., 2005), and the use of frequent observation and feedback is important for improving instructional quality (Fixsen et al., 2013).

Therefore, finding tools that can facilitate frequent and efficient observation and feedback data are critical to identifying areas of support needed to improve instruction and, therefore, student outcomes (Chomat-Mooney et al., 2008; Fixsen et al., 2013; Fritz et al., 2019). Some researchers have begun to develop tools for this purpose (Harn et al., 2012; Johnson & Semmelroth, 2012) and studies have found one tool, *The Quality of Intervention Delivery and Receipt* (Harn et al., 2012), to be reliable and valid when conducting short, 10-minute observations to collect data that can be used to provide feedback and coaching (Brafford et al., 2019; Fritz et al., 2019).

Examination of the data can determine the intensity, frequency, and duration of necessary professional development to provide the staff with support in implementing research-based practices with levels of quality and fidelity that will improve student achievement (Honig et al., 2018). Collaboration and school-based literacy coaching have been shown to be effective components of professional development, with evidence suggesting that a literacy coach can provide support for teachers' professional learning, self-efficacy, and engagement while improving instruction (Nielsen et al., 2008). This may be particularly important for teachers who are including students with a wider range of skills and disabilities and/or who have limited skills and knowledge on how to effectively differentiate and individualize (Denton, 2012; Zigmond & Kloo, 2011).

Setting a Course for Effective Inclusion

Research supports the key elements of a system-wide approach as outlined in the above section. The content of the literacy instruction, however, as related to the need for evidence-based practices, is a critical element of inclusive literacy education. Without both general and special educators sharing a common understanding of effective evidence-based literacy practices, including students with disabilities in the general education classroom is unlikely to ensure achievement for those with disabilities or those who are at-risk for disabilities in literacy. The following section will outline the necessary components of instruction necessary for an effective inclusive elementary literacy classroom.

The content of literacy instruction is vital to ensuring all children become proficient readers and writers. If all students are going to reach proficiency in literacy, the instruction that is provided in the inclusive classroom must include evidence-based practices incorporated into everyday instruction, not just reserved for intervention (Dagen & Bean 2020; Jones et al., 2012). This requires that teachers have a solid foundation in literacy development, including the importance of the specific components necessary for successful development (Moats, 2009). The next section will focus on the specific content necessary for the successful literacy development of all elementary students.

Two decades ago, the National Reading Panel (2000) outlined the necessary components of reading instruction: phonological and phonemic awareness, phonics and word recognition, fluency, vocabulary, and comprehension. In the sections that follow, each component is explained and suggestions for explicitly and systematically incorporating the component in an inclusive classroom are provided. Without this multi-component approach to literacy instruction, many students are not likely to become proficient readers, regardless of the presence of a disability.

Phonological and Phonemic Awareness

Instruction in phonological awareness is critical to supporting students' understanding of the structure of spoken language. It is the ability to hear sounds in language and manipulate the parts of language from the largest element of language, words, to the smallest element, phonemes (Wanzek et al., 2020). Phonological awareness at the phoneme level (phonemic awareness) has been found to be predictive of reading development in young children and is a foundational skill that supports all aspects of reading and writing (Ehri, 1998, 2020). For older, typically-developing readers, phonological awareness training is not necessary; however, for older students who are not demonstrating skill in decoding, targeted phonological and phonemic awareness instruction may make a big difference in improving decoding skills (Ehri, 2020; Mercer & Mercer, 2004).

Elements of Effective Phonological Awareness Instruction

Fortunately, phonological and phonemic awareness include skills that teachers can significantly influence through explicit, systematic instruction (Pullen & Lane, 2014). In addition to ensuring instructional delivery is explicit and systematic, there are additional characteristics that must be present:

- Teacher knowledge of the structure of language, including the correct pronunciation of phonemes (Ehri, 2020; Lane & Pullen, 2004; Washburn et al., 2011)
- Systematic instruction that progresses from easiest to most difficult skills (Honig et al., 2018)
- Explicit instruction that includes teacher modeling and multiple practice opportunities (Honig et al., 2018)
- Instruction in small groups (optimally 3-5 students) to allow frequent practice opportunities and teacher feedback (Foorman & Torgesen, 2001; Wanzek et al., 2020)
- Lessons targeting only one or two phonological awareness skills at a time for 10-15 minutes per session (Honig et al., 2018)
- Use of manipulatives, games, and interactive activities to keep instruction engaging and interesting (Honig et al., 2018)

There are specific curricula that target phonemic awareness (e.g., Adams et al., 1998; Heggerty & VanHekken, 2020), but there are also multiple additional online resources that can aid in providing engaging phonemic awareness activities to supplement core reading programs that may lack sufficient instruction and practice in phonemic awareness. For instance, the Florida Center for Reading Research provides multiple center games and activities that can be used to introduce or reinforce phonological and phonemic awareness skills: https://fcrr.org/student-center-activities. Another resource that provides multiple engaging activities related to phonemic awareness comes from the University of Florida Literacy Institute: https://education.ufl.edu/ufli/virtual-teaching/main/instructional-activities/phonemic-awareness/. In addition, the Reading Rockets website provides various classroom strategies for improving phonological and phonemic awareness: https://www.readingrockets.org/strategies#skill1038.

Assessing Phonological Awareness to Target Instruction

As with other literacy skills, assessment is important for determining the needs of a whole class and individual students. Screening assessments for phonological awareness can quickly and efficiently get an overview of class performance and indicate which students may need additional intervention. Screening measures for phonological awareness are crucial for children in early primary grades (Honig et al., 2018) to ensure they have the skills to benefit from decoding instruction. Children who have low decoding skills in first grade and later may also need to be assessed in phonological awareness to determine instructional needs (Honig et al., 2018). Students who have been identified as at-risk should also receive frequent progress monitoring to ensure that the interventions being provided are effective and to identify continuing specific needs. Curriculum-based measures (CBMs) are effective and practical for use in progress monitoring (Wanzek et al., 2020). Diagnostic assessments may also be important for older students to ensure interventions are targeting specific areas of weakness, so instructional time is not wasted on skills already mastered (Mercer & Mercer, 2004).

Phonics and Word Recognition

According to the simple view of reading (SVR; Hoover & Gough, 1990), fluent and accurate word recognition, along with language comprehension, are the two cognitive capacities critical to comprehension (Hoover & Tunmer, 2018). Word recognition is defined as the ability to decode and read words without a dependency on context (Wanzek et al., 2020). Recognizing words accurately and fluently is critical to ensure that the reader has adequate cognitive resources to understand the text being read (Perfetti, 2011).

Characteristics of Effective Phonics Instruction

Initial instructional effort in phonics should be focused on developing word recognition skills in young readers through explicit and systematic instruction (Dehaene, 2009; Ehri, 2020; National Reading Panel, 2000). According to the findings of the National Reading Panel and more recent research, children who received systematic and explicit phonics instruction had better reading outcomes than those who received either nonsystematic instruction or no phonics instruction at all (Brady, 2011; Ehri, 2020; National Reading Panel, 2000). The National Reading Panel (2000) found that systematic and explicit phonics instruction significantly improves reading and spelling in kindergarten and first grade, as well as students' ability to comprehend. It has also been found that the benefits of systematic and explicit phonics instruction were true for all students regardless of socioeconomic status, and were not harmful to any child (Snow & Juel, 2005). Because of its utility and effectiveness with all students, explicit and systematic instruction in phonics seems logical and necessary for use in the inclusive classroom.

Systematic and explicit phonics instruction is the most efficient and effective method for improving phonics and word recognition skills (Honig et al., 2018). Systematic instruction in phonics involves presenting letter-sound correspondences in a logical sequence, beginning with those that are most common and useful to allow young readers to begin decoding words early in the process of learning and moving to more difficult skills as instruction progresses (Armbruster et al., 2001; Murray, 2016). In addition, the order in which letter-sound correspondences are presented can aid in maximizing learning, such as spreading out the presentation of b, d, p, and q to minimize visual confusion and separating letters that have similar sounds such as /e/ and /i/ (Wanzek et al., 2020). When phonics instruction is presented systematically, it greatly increases the likelihood that children will be ready for new learning of letter-sound correspondences because they already have the prior knowledge necessary to learn the new skill efficiently (Adams, 2017). There are additional phonics instruction characteristics that are found to be important for effective phonics instruction within the explicit and systematic framework:

- Phonemic awareness instruction should be incorporated into phonics instruction because the two skills have a reciprocal relationship and the combination provides better outcomes than separate instruction of the two skills (Henbest & Apel, 2017; Pullen & Lane, 2014, 2016; Weiser & Mathes, 2011)
- Encoding (spelling) regularly spelled words reinforces phonics concepts (Wanzek et al., 2020)
- Automaticity is critical to allow the reader to utilize cognitive load for understanding, so instruction should provide multiple practice opportunities for reading words in isolation and connected text (Honig et al., 2018; Perfetti, 2011)

Practice opportunities can be provided in whole group, small group, and peer coaching situations. Peer-assisted learning strategies for kindergarten and 1st grade students (PALS K-1; Fuchs & Fuchs, 2005) have been found to be effective for increasing reading outcomes for young children, including English learners (Calhoon et al., 2006; Fuchs & Fuchs, 2005). The kindergarten version focuses primarily on phonological awareness and decoding and word recognition, whereas the first-grade iteration also incorporates partner reading activities after approximately 10 weeks of partner work on phonological awareness and decoding work at the word level (The IRIS Center, 2008a). The IRIS Center provides a training module that includes printable materials that can be used to implement PALS K-1 in the classroom. This module can be found at https://iris.peabody.vanderbilt.edu/module/palsk1/#content.

Irregular Word Reading Instruction

Because not all words are regular and can be sounded out using phonics skills, children must also be taught to read irregular words (Wanzek et al., 2020). Words are considered irregular if they contain one or more letter-sound correspondences that a student does not know, making it necessary for the child to memorize the whole word rather than applying phonics skills (Honig et al., 2018). Some words are permanently irregular, meaning that they have letter-sound correspondences that are not pronounced conventionally. Temporarily irregular words are words that may be irregular as a child first begins to read using phonics but may eventually become regular once the child has learned that phonics skill (Carnine et al., 2006). These guidelines should be followed when providing instruction on irregular words:

- Choose words from an upcoming passage that the child will be reading (Honig et al., 2018).
- Teach words systematically and explicitly (Wanzek et al., 2020).
- Introduce new irregular words at least one lesson prior to encountering the word in the connected text (Honig et al., 2018).
- When introducing an irregular word, help students make connections between the letter sequence and/or sounds in the word by modeling, students repeating, spelling the word (orally or on paper), and repeating again (Wanzek et al., 2020).

Advanced Decoding and Word Analysis Skills in Upper Elementary

Even children who have mastered reading one-syllable words using phonics skills and strategies are likely to have difficulty reading multisyllabic words without explicit instruction in the skills required to decode such words (Duncan & Seymour, 2003; Toste et al., 2017). Explicit instruction in recognizing syllables and morphemes within words can give students the necessary skills to be successful readers of longer words (Honig et al., 2018). This becomes particularly important for struggling readers in upper elementary grades (i.e., fourth grade and beyond) as the instructional focus moves away from basic decoding and word reading to reading for comprehension and learning (Toste et al., 2017). Within an inclusive upper elementary classroom, it is necessary to provide opportunities for learning and practicing multisyllabic word reading skills, especially for those students with disabilities in reading (Toste et al., 2017). Online resources for teaching more advanced word reading skills, including multi-syllabic words and morphology, can be found at https://education.ufl.edu/ufli/virtual-teaching/main/instructional-activities/decoding-and-encoding/big-words/ and https://fcrr.org/student-center-activities/second-and-third-grade.

Importance of Using Decodable Text

Reading connected, decodable text daily is especially important for beginning readers as they acquire decoding skills (Wanzek et al., 2020). They need to be able to explicitly connect the phonics and word recognition skills they are acquiring with the text that they are being asked to read so that they are using letter-sound knowledge to decode unknown words and reinforcing skills they are learning. Whatever text is chosen for daily reading must be text that is decodable for that reader. It is important not to present words to them that are outside their word recognition skills at that point in time (Wanzek et al., 2020). These controlled texts can allow children to read more independently and feel a higher level of success very early in reading instruction (Castles et al., 2018).

Assessment of Phonics and Word Recognition

Teachers can use formal, commercially available letter-sound knowledge measures to determine mastery of each specific letter-sound relationship, but informal measures can also be used to plan lessons (Wanzek et al., 2020). Informal measures can simply be a list of letters in which the student says the letter name and its sound. This can help a teacher make decisions about which letters need to be taught or reviewed to ensure mastery (Wanzek et al., 2020). In addition to assessing the child's knowledge of individual letter sounds, it is important to measure the child's ability to decode words, beginning with simple consonant vowel consonant (CVC) words (Honig et al., 2018). The best way to measure this skill is to use a nonsense word measure. By using nonsense words to assess, you are ensuring that the child hasn't simply memorized the word being presented and must rely on phonemic decoding to do so (Fien et al., 2008). To measure irregular word reading automaticity, it is recommended that students be asked to read aloud from a set of previously introduced irregular words (Honig et al., 2018).

Fluency

The goal of reading is comprehension, but the bridge from decoding and word recognition to comprehension is formed through fluency (Pikulski & Chard, 2005). Fluency refers to decoding accurately and with automaticity but expands to reading expressively to increase understanding of the text (Rasinski, 2004). When children reach a level of fluency and automaticity with decoding, they can free up attention to allow for better comprehension (LaBerge & Samuels, 1974). Fluency includes three elements that lead to comprehension: accuracy, rate, and prosody (Hudson et al., 2005).

Within an inclusive classroom, common fluency activities appropriate for typically developing and struggling readers include such activities as modeling fluent reading through read-aloud or providing time for silent reading (Honig et al., 2018; Rasinski, 2004). While these are important elements of classroom instruction to encourage fluency and may provide adequate modeling and practice for good readers, those who are struggling readers or have learning disabilities in reading will require more structured supports and specific interventions (Hairrell et al., 2010; Wanzek et al., 2020).

Explicit Fluency Instruction and Practice

Multiple methods can be used to ensure that struggling readers receive adequate explicit instruction and practice time focused on all elements of fluency:

- Teacher-assisted reading involves the teacher reading aloud using appropriate rate and prosody to model how a fluent reader sounds as students follow along with the text (Honig et al., 2018).
- Peer-assisted reading in which a more fluent reader is paired with a less fluent reader to serve as a model in a motivating and socially supportive environment shows evidence for improving accuracy and rate (Calhoon et al., 2006; The IRIS Center, 2008b).
- Repeated reading of a passage at a student's appropriate level multiple times until a fluent level is reached has been found to improve accuracy and rate for elementary students (Hammerschmidt-Snidarich et al., 2019; Honig et al., 2018; Lee & Yoon, 2017).

- Readers theatre can give an authentic, motivating opportunity for multiple readings and has been found to be effective for increasing fluency, including prosody, in elementary school readers (Mraz et al., 2013; Young & Rasinski, 2018).

Assessment of Fluency

Oral reading fluency (ORF) measures combine rate and accuracy to derive a measure of fluency that can provide data to guide instruction (Honig et al., 2018). Curriculum-based measurement (CBM) is reliable and valid and is commonly used to obtain information regarding the risk of reading failure, progress with current instruction, and which students may need additional diagnostic assessments (Ardoin et al., 2013). Prosody has proven to be more difficult to measure reliably and is typically measured through observation of oral reading of a connected text using a checklist or a more quantifiable rating scale (Daane et al., 2005; Honig et al., 2018; Hudson et al., 2005; Rasinski, 2004).

Vocabulary

Developing vocabulary is another critical element of literacy instruction in the inclusive classroom because of the strong relationship between vocabulary and comprehension (Biemiller, 2001). Vocabulary is the knowledge of word and word meanings, and it is a skill that continues to expand across a person's lifetime (Honig et al., 2018). Inclusive classrooms have large variations in learner skills and knowledge, but they can be especially divergent in levels of vocabulary development. There is often a gap in vocabulary knowledge before children ever enter school that can stem from language or hearing impairments, reading disability, learning English as a second language, or lack of exposure to language experiences (Fernald & Weisleder, 2015; Hart & Risley, 1995). Despite the importance of vocabulary knowledge and the need to close the vocabulary gap, evidence suggests that little emphasis is placed on vocabulary acquisition in schools, particularly in the primary grades (Biemiller, 2001; Wanzek, 2014).

Language and Vocabulary Development through Read-Aloud

One approach to vocabulary development, particularly for young children, is through read-aloud. Read-aloud is a common practice in most elementary classrooms, but careful planning and strategic use of that time can maximize vocabulary development for children (Beck & McKeown, 2001; Coyne et al., 2007). Researchers have found that including explicit vocabulary instruction during read-aloud provides greater improvements in vocabulary knowledge than simply reading the text or using incidental opportunities for vocabulary development (Baker et al., 2013; Coyne et al., 2007).

One specific read-aloud technique that has been shown to be effective in improving vocabulary and language development in young children is the practice of dialogic reading (DR; Carlisle et al., 2013; Towson et al., 2017). DR enhances read-aloud by providing a specific, systematic framework for engaging children in interactive reading and has shown promise in improving language development for elementary students with disabilities and those at-risk for reading difficulties (Swanson et al., 2011; Towson et al., 2017). DR accelerates language development by providing practice, feedback, and scaffolded interactions that ensure that the children, not the teacher, do most of the talking (Arnold et al., 1994; Urbani, 2020).

Another explicit instruction read-aloud method that has been shown to be effective in improving language and vocabulary achievement in children is *Text Talk* (Beck & McKeown, 2001, 2007). In this approach, the teacher poses questions that will encourage children to talk about and connect with a story. *Text Talk* is designed to enhance comprehension while also attending to language development by explicitly teaching and encouraging the use of sophisticated language found in children's trade books (Beck & McKeown, 2001, 2007). Specific vocabulary instruction of these words is then completed after reading and discussing the book (Beck & McKeown, 2007). Instruction after the reading gives the children a familiar context on which to draw to enhance their understanding of the new word while also avoiding interruption of the process of building an understanding of the story (Beck & McKeown, 2007).

Explicit Vocabulary Instruction

Corresponding with the findings of the importance of explicit attention to vocabulary and language development within a read-aloud context, it has been found that explicit vocabulary instruction with or without a story context is beneficial for improving vocabulary knowledge for elementary students, including English learners and learners with disabilities (Beck & McKeown, 2007; Coyne et al., 2007, 2019; McKeown, 2019; Puhalla, 2011). It is impossible for teachers to explicitly teach every vocabulary word. Therefore, it is important for teachers to focus instruction on words that are most likely seen in print and that will help students to build connections to other words while also teaching word-learning strategies (Beck & McKeown, 2007). For very young children, Beck et al., (2013) recommend obtaining words from familiar stories, then developing a definition that is accessible to children, providing an example, and then giving the children time to practice interacting with the words. They also recommend introducing no more than 10 new words in a week to young children. For older children, the authors recommend providing multiple exposures within various contexts for each word that is being learned. This will allow students to begin to understand the nuances, subtleties, and various uses of each targeted word (Beck et al., 2013).

Explicit Morphology Instruction

Research suggests that instruction in morphology, the study of how the smallest units of meaning in language (morphemes) combine to create words (Templeton, 2012), is effective for increasing vocabulary and reading comprehension outcomes across elementary and middle school learners and is particularly beneficial for struggling readers (McKeown, 2019). Teaching morphology helps children to recognize patterns in language that can help them to identify and define unknown words (McKeown, 2019). Effectively teaching morphology involves bringing children's attention to not just word meanings but also how words work and how to use word knowledge to enhance understanding of the text (McKeown, 2019). In two meta-analyses, evidence indicated that morphological instruction enhances spelling and vocabulary learning and helped students to understand the meanings of new words (Bowers et al., 2010; Goodwin & Ahn, 2013). Manyak et al. (2018) provide guidance on morphological analysis instruction and which morphemes should be introduced in the upper elementary grades (i.e., 3rd through 5th grade):

- The 92 suggested morphemes include the most common affixes, organized into affix families
- Affixes are then organized into their appropriate grade level for instruction and practice
- Selected affixes enable students to infer the meaning of as many novel words containing the target affix as possible
- Some Latin and Greek word roots, appropriate for instruction in the upper elementary, are included and recommended for use with fourth and fifth grade students

Assessment of Vocabulary

The National Reading Panel (2000) suggested that multiple points of data should be used to assess students' vocabulary knowledge. Standardized tests can provide baseline data that can be useful in determining students who may need more support. As with other aspects of literacy instruction, it is important to monitor the progress of students, especially those who are at-risk or have reading difficulties, so that instruction can be intensified as needed. Some CBMs have components to measure (e.g., easyCBM Vocabulary; Alonzo et al., 2006). Assessments that are matched to the instructional context can also give the teacher a good idea of a student's learning, so informal, teacher-created checklists reflecting words already taught may be appropriate (Honig et al., 2018).

Comprehension

Most literacy educators can agree that the final component, as outlined by the National Reading Panel (2000), comprehension, is the goal and culmination of all of the five processes working together. The RAND Reading Study Group (RRSG, 2002) defined comprehension as "the process of simultaneously extracting and constructing meaning through interaction and involvement with written language" (p. 11). The group agreed that reading comprehension involves three elements that must work together for understanding to occur. The elements include the text that is to be understood, the reader, and the activity or task variables. These task variables include the purpose, processes, and outcomes of performing the activity or task. All these elements are said to be shaped by the larger social and cultural context in which the reading occurs (RRSG, 2002).

Considering the three elements of comprehension helps to frame how instruction must occur in an inclusive classroom. In order for a child to understand a given text, they must already have the skills to accurately and fluently decode the words and the language and vocabulary skills to understand the meanings of each word within the context of the passage. If one of these component pieces is missing, the child is not likely to successfully comprehend the text (Wanzek et al., 2020). With this idea in mind, comprehension instruction in an inclusive classroom must attend to all of the elements and use assessment to determine exactly where the breakdown in comprehension may have occurred for a struggling reader and tailor instruction to meet those specific needs.

Comprehension and Language Development

Even if a child is able to decode a particular passage fluently and accurately, if they are unable to attach meaning to the words through understanding the language, they will not be able to comprehend the passage (Wanzek et al., 2020). Providing opportunities to build background knowledge and language skills is critical to ensuring that students can understand what they are reading. As discussed in the previous section, explicit instruction in vocabulary can contribute to a child's language comprehension. Prior knowledge can also contribute to a child's understanding of new words when they can connect a known word to a new word in some conceptual way (Wanzek et al., 2020).

Building and activating background knowledge is critical to language development, and therefore, reading comprehension. Increasingly diverse student populations in inclusive classrooms ensure that students will come to classrooms with highly variable background knowledge (Fisher et al., 2012). Reading comprehension has been found to correlate with the amount of knowledge a reader has about the topic of the text being read (Pearson et al., 1979). Fortunately, the building of background knowledge can compensate for weak initial background knowledge and allow for increased comprehension (Fisher et al., 2012). Building or activating background knowledge prior to reading can be accomplished through direct instruction of essential concepts, previewing the text, asking questions of students' experiences related to the text, and asking students to make predictions or ask questions that may be answered through the reading of the text (Wanzek et al., 2020).

Comprehension Strategy Instruction

Decades of research have provided evidence that an effective approach to improving comprehension for all students, including English learners and those with disabilities, is through explicit comprehension strategy instruction (Gersten et al., 2001; Pilonieta et al., 2019; Wanzek et al.., 2010). The National Reading Panel (NRP; 2000) found that explicit teaching of such strategies as summarizing, self-questioning, story structure instruction (e.g., story maps), graphic and semantic organizers, and comprehension monitoring is effective for improving comprehension.

Peer-Assisted Learning Strategies (PALS; Fuchs et al., 1997) for students in 2nd grade and older can be an effective method for improving comprehension strategies and skills within an inclusive classroom. In the 2nd–6th grade version of PALS, partners engage in three main activities: partner reading with retelling, paragraph shrinking, and prediction relay (The IRIS Center, 2008b). The goal of these activities is to practice reading strategies, increase fluency, and improve comprehension (Sáenz et al., 2005). PALS is a reciprocal peer tutoring model meaning that each partner takes a turn at acting as the coach. Students are systematically paired by ranking all of their students by reading performance, dividing the list in half, and pairing the top high-performing student with the top low-performing student and repeating until all pairs are established. Peer pairing in this manner has been found to be beneficial for both partners, whether or not one child and/or the other has a learning disability or mild intellectual and developmental disability (The IRIS Center, 2008b). A module for PALS for grades 2–6, including materials for implementation, can be found at https://iris.peabody.vanderbilt.edu/module/pals26/.

Collaborative Strategic Reading (CSR) is another approach to comprehension strategy instruction that utilizes cooperative learning groups to improve reading comprehension while maximizing student engagement in upper elementary grades and above (Vaughn & Klingner, 1999). CSR explicitly teaches reading comprehension strategies and, through cooperative peer groups, provides scaffolding to maximize comprehension of expository text. Peer groups are trained to incorporate before, during, and after reading strategies to enhance comprehension. (The IRIS Center, 2008c). CSR has a strong research base that provides evidence that it is an effective approach for improving comprehension within inclusive classrooms and shows especially promising results for students with learning disabilities and English learners (Boardman et al., 2016; Klingner et al., 2004). An instructional module, as well as materials, can be found at https://iris.peabody.vanderbilt.edu/module/csr/.

Assessment of Comprehension

Assessment of comprehension using measures that are closely tied to the curriculum is necessary so that teachers can identify students who may need additional support within an inclusive classroom (Kirby, 2003). There are some issues with measures of reading comprehension that teachers and administrators will need to keep in mind as they choose assessments to guide their decisions about instruction and supports. No single assessment can capture the nuances and complexities of comprehension (RRSG, 2002; Spear-Swerling, 2006). Most comprehension assessments are targeting only a few tasks such as immediate recall, reading for main idea, or reading for inferences (RRSG, 2002). For this reason, it is recommended that teachers employ various comprehension assessments to ensure that they get a more accurate picture of a student's comprehension abilities (Honig et al., 2018; Spear-Swerling, 2006).

Some examples of formats that can be used for comprehension assessment include: (1) Cloze, which asks students to fill in the blank by choosing from a word bank; (2) Maze CBM, in which students choose from three possible words to complete a sentence; (3) Open-ended, which asks students to provide an oral or written response to questions about a passage; (4) Multiple-choice questions, in which students choose the best answer from a selection of several possible answers; (5) Oral retelling of a passage; (6) Think aloud, in which students discuss their thinking as they read a passage, following periodic teacher prompts (Honig et al., 2018). Assessing comprehension strategies and processes is also an important aspect of comprehension assessment (RSRG, 2002; Honig et al., 2018). This can help teachers to determine which strategies need more instruction and support. In general, it is recommended that teachers combine traditional assessments (e.g., Cloze, Maze CBM, standardized multiple-choice tests) with ongoing, informal assessments (e.g., oral retelling, think-aloud, open-ended questions) to get a complete picture of students' comprehension skills and strategies (Honig et al., 2018).

Final Thoughts

Including students with disabilities in the general education classroom is a controversial topic (Connor & Ferri, 2007; Obiakor et al., 2012). Some question the practicality of meeting the needs of all students in an inclusive classroom (Mock & Kauffman, 2002) and others purport that inclusion is a path to social justice for students with disabilities (Causton-Theoharis & Theoharis, 2008; Polat, 2011). Achieving positive social outcomes and social justice for all while also meeting the academic needs of all students is the goal of inclusive education (Obiakor et al., 2012). Meeting this goal in the context of literacy will require the right systems and structures to ensure that teachers are well-trained so that students with disabilities have the instructional and emotional supports to be successful readers and writers in inclusive elementary school classrooms.

Multi-tiered Systems of Support (see Chapter 6) can provide a frame for this system but requires a focused leadership team who can guide the implementation in a way that achieves the best results. Administrators must be well-informed regarding effective elementary literacy systems and instruction and prioritize resources to ensure that the best results can be obtained (Dagen & Bean, 2020; Klingner et al., 2013). This begins with ensuring that Tier 1 instruction is of the highest quality. If all students are going to reach proficiency in literacy, the instruction that is provided in the inclusive classroom must include evidence-based practices incorporated into everyday instruction, not just reserved for intervention in Tiers 2 and 3 (Jones et al., 2012). This means using methods that are shown to be effective for all students, such as delivering comprehensive literacy instruction that includes all five elements outlined by the National Reading Panel (2000) in an explicit and systematic way (Archer & Hughes, 2011) and providing targeted small group instruction for differentiation and individualization (Kosanovich et al., 2007). Furthermore, the instruction must be delivered by personnel that are supported by a system that prioritizes training and ongoing coaching and professional development to ensure students are receiving the highest quality instruction regardless of the level of supports they are receiving (Dagen & Bean, 2020; Klingner et al., 2013).

References

Adams, M. J. (2017). Alphabetic anxiety and explicit, systematic phonics instruction: A cognitive science perspective. *Handbook of Early Literacy Research, 1*, 66–80.

Adams, M. J., Foorman, B. R., Lundberg, I., & Beeler, T. (1998). *Phonemic awareness in young children: A classroom curriculum*. Brookes Publishing.

Alonzo, J., Tindal, G., Ulmer, K., & Glasgow, A. (2006). easyCBM online progress monitoring assessment system. Center for Educational Assessment Accountability. Available at http://easycbm.com.

Archer, A. L., & Hughes, C. A. (2011). *Explicit instruction: Effective and efficient teaching*. Guilford Press.

Ardoin, S. P., Christ, T. J., Morena, L. S., Cormier, D. C., & Klingbeil, D. A. (2013). A systematic review and summarization of the recommendations and research surrounding curriculum-based measurement of oral reading fluency (CBM-R) decision rules. *Journal of School Psychology, 51*(1), 1–18.

Armbruster, B. B., Lehr, F., Osborn, J., O'Rourke, R., Beck, I., Carnine, D., & Simmons, D. (2001). *Put reading first.* National Institute for Literacy.

Arnold, D. H., Lonigan, C. J., Whitehurst, G. J., & Epstein, J. N. (1994). Accelerating language development through picture book reading: Replication and extension to a videotape training format. *Journal of Educational Psychology, 86*(2), 235.

Baker, S. K., Santoro, L. E., Chard, D. J., Fien, H., Park, Y., & Otterstedt, J. (2013). An evaluation of an explicit read aloud intervention taught in whole-classroom formats in first grade. *The Elementary School Journal, 113*(3), 331–358.

Baker, S. K., Smolkowski, K., Smith, J. M., Fien, H., Kame'enui, E. J., & Thomas Beck, C. (2011). The impact of Oregon Reading First on student reading outcomes. *The Elementary School Journal, 112*(2), 307–331.

Balu, R., Zhu, P., Doolittle, F., Schiller, E., Jenkins, J., & Gersten, R. (2015). *Evaluation of response to intervention practices for elementary school reading.* NCEE 2016-4000. National Center for Education Evaluation and Regional Assistance.

Batemen, D. & Cline, J. (2016). *A teacher's guide to special education.* Association for Supervision & Curriculum Development.

Beck, I. L., & McKeown, M. G. (2001). Text talk: Capturing the benefits of read-aloud experiences for young children. *The Reading Teacher, 55*(1), 10–20.

Beck, I. L., & McKeown, M. G. (2007). Increasing young low-income children's oral vocabulary repertoires through rich and focused instruction. *The Elementary School Journal, 107*(3), 251–271.

Beck, I. L., McKeown, M. G., & Kucan, L. (2013). *Bringing words to life: Robust vocabulary instruction.* Guilford Press.

Biemiller, A. (2001). Teaching vocabulary: Early, direct, and sequential. *American Educator, 25*, 24–29

Boardman, A. G., Vaughn, S., Buckley, P., Reutebuch, C., Roberts, G., & Klingner, J. (2016). Collaborative strategic reading for students with learning disabilities in upper elementary classrooms. *Exceptional Children, 82*(4), 409–427.

Bowers, P. N., Kirby, J. R. & Deacon, S. H. (2010). The effects of morphological instruction on literacy skills: A systematic review of the literature. *Review of Educational Research, 80*(2), 144–179.

Brady, S. A. (2011). Efficacy of phonics teaching for reading outcomes: Indications from post-NRP research. In S. A. Brady, D. Braze, & C. A. Fowler (Eds.), *Individual differences in reading: Theory and evidence* (pp. 69–96). Psychology Press.

Brafford, T., Fritz, R. & Harn, B. A. (2019, Oct. 3). *Examining instructional quality of small group intervention across time: A replication study.* Council for Learning Disabilities.

Brophy, J., & Good, T. L. (1986). Teacher behavior and student achievement In M. C. Witrock (Ed.), *Handbook of research on teaching* (3rd ed., pp. 328–375). MacMillan Publishing Company.

Calhoon, M., Al Otaiba, S., Greenberg, D., King, A., & Avalos, A. (2006). Improving reading skills in predominantly Hispanic Title 1 first grade classrooms: The promise of Peer-Assisted Learning Strategies. *Learning Disabilities Research & Practice, 21*(4), 261–272.

Carlisle, J. F., Kenney, C. K., & Vereb, A. (2013). Vocabulary instruction for students at risk for reading disabilities: Promising approaches for learning from texts. In *Research-based strategies for improving outcomes in academics* (pp. 47–60). Penguin Books.

Carnine, D., Silbert, J., Kame'enui, E., Tarver, S., & Jungjohann, K. (2006). *Teaching struggling and at-risk readers: A direct instruction approach.* Prentice Hall.

Castles, A., Rastle, K., & Nation, K. (2018). Ending the reading wars: Reading acquisition from novice to expert. *Psychological Science in the Public Interest, 19*(1), 5–51.

Causton-Theoharis, J. N., Giangreco, M. F., Doyle, M. B., & Vadasy, P. F. (2007). The "sous-chefs" of literacy instruction. *Teaching Exceptional Children, 40*(1), 56–62.

Causton-Theoharis, J., & Theoharis, G. (2008). Creating inclusive schools for all students. *School Administrator, 65*(8), 24–25.

Chard, D. J. (2013). Systems impact: Issues and trends in improving school outcomes for all learners through multitier instructional models. *Intervention in School and Clinic, 48*(4), 198–202.

Chard, D. J. (2004). Toward a science of professional development in early reading instruction. *Exceptionality, 12*(3), 175–191.

Chard, D., & Harn, B. (2008). Project CIRCUITS: Center for improving reading competence using intensive treatments schoolwide. In *Schoolwide prevention models: Lessons learned in elementary schools* (pp. 70–83). Guilford Press.

Chard, D. J., Harn, B. A., Sugai, G., Horner, R. H., Simmons, D. C., & Kame'enui, E. J. (2008). Core features of multi-tiered systems of reading and behavioral support. In C. R. Greenwood, T. R. Kratochwill, & M. Clements (Eds.), *Schoolwide prevention models: Lessons learned in elementary schools* (pp. 31–60). Guilford Press.

Chomat-Mooney, L. I., Pianta, R. C., Hamre, B. K., Mashburn, A. J., Luckner, A. E., Grimm, K. J., & Downer, J. T. (2008). A practical guide for conducting classroom observations: A summary of issues and evidence for researchers Unpublished report to the WT Grant Foundation.

Connor, D. J., & Ferri, B. A. (2007). The conflict within: Resistance to inclusion and other paradoxes in special education. *Disability & Society*, *22*(1), 63–77.

Coyne, M. D., McCoach, D. B., & Kapp, S. (2007). Vocabulary intervention for kindergarten students: Comparing extended instruction to embedded instruction and incidental exposure. *Learning Disability Quarterly*, *30*(2), 74–88.

Coyne, M. D., McCoach, D. B., Ware, S., Austin, C. R., Loftus-Rattan, S. M., & Baker, D. L. (2019). Racing against the vocabulary gap: Matthew effects in early vocabulary instruction and intervention. *Exceptional Children*, *85*(2), 163–179.

Coyne, M. D., Oldham, A., Leonard, K., Burns, D., & Gage, N. (2016). Delving into the details: Implementing multitiered K-3 reading supports in high-priority schools. In B. Foorman (Ed.), *Challenges to implementing effective reading intervention in schools* (Vol. 154, pp. 67–85). New Directions for Child and Adolescent Development,

Daane, M. C., Campbell, J. R., Grigg, W. S., Goodman, M. J., & Oranje, A. (2005). *Fourth-grade students reading aloud: NAEP 2002 special study of oral reading*. The Nation's Report Card. NCES 2006-469. *National Center for Education Statistics*.

Dagen, A. S., and Bean, R. M. (2020). *Best practices of literacy leaders* (2nd ed.). The Guilford Press.

Danielson, C. (2013). *The Framework for Teaching evaluation instrument, 2013 edition: The newest rubric enhancing the links to the Common Core State Standards, with clarity of language for ease of use and scoring*. Association for Supervision and Curriculum Development.

Dehaene, S. (2009). *Reading in the brain: The new science of how we read*. Penguin.

Denton, C. A. (2012). Response to intervention for reading difficulties in the primary grades: Some answers and lingering questions. *Journal of Learning Disabilities*, *45*(3), 232–243.

Denton, C. A., Fletcher, J. M., Anthony, J. L., & Francis, D. J. (2006). An evaluation of intensive intervention for students with persistent reading difficulties. *Journal of Learning Disabilities*, *39*(5), 447–466.

Dougherty Stahl, K. A. (2016). Response to intervention: Is the sky falling?. *The Reading Teacher*, *69*(6), 659–663.

Drake, G., & Walsh, K. (2020). 2020 *Teacher prep review: Program performance in early reading instruction*. National Council on Teacher Quality.

Duncan, L. G., & Seymour, P. H. (2003). How do children read multisyllabic words? Some preliminary observations. *Journal of Research in Reading*, *26*(2), 101–120.

Ehri, L. C. (2020). The science of learning to read words: A case for systematic phonics instruction *Reading Research Quarterly*, *55*(S1), S45–S60.

Ehri, L. C. (1998). Grapheme—phoneme knowledge is essential for learning to read words in English. *Word Recognition in Beginning Literacy*, *3*, 40.

Fernald, A., & Weisleder, A. (2015). Twenty years after "meaningful differences," it's time to reframe the "deficit" debate about the importance of children's early language experience. *Human Development*, *58*(1), 1–4.

Fien, H., Baker, S. K., Smolkowski, K., Smith, J. L. M., Kame'enui, E. J., & Beck, C. T. (2008). Using nonsense word fluency to predict reading proficiency in kindergarten through second grade for English learners and native English speakers. *School Psychology Review*, *37*(3), 391–408.

Fisher, D., Frey, N., & Lapp, D. (2012). Building and activating students' background knowledge: It's what they already know that counts: Teachers must assess and build on the background knowledge students possess. *Middle School Journal*, *43*(3), 22–31.

Fixsen, D., Blase, K., Metz, A., & Van Dyke, M. (2013). Statewide implementation of evidence-based programs. *Exceptional Children*, *79*(2), 213–230.

Foorman, B. (Ed.). (2016). *Challenges to implementing effective reading intervention in schools: New directions for child and adolescent development* (Vol. 154). John Wiley & Sons.

Foorman, B., Dombek, J., & Smith, K. (2016). Seven elements important to successful implementation of early literacy intervention. *New Directions for Child and Adolescent Development*, *2016*(154), 49–65.

Foorman, B. R., & Torgesen, J. (2001). Critical elements of classroom and small-group instruction promote reading success in all children. *Learning Disabilities Research & Practice*, *16*(4), 203–212.

Fritz, R., Harn, B., Biancarosa, G., Lucero, A., & Flannery, K. B. (2019). How much Is enough? Evaluating intervention implementation efficiently. *Assessment for Effective Intervention*, *44*(2), 135–144.

Fuchs, D., & Fuchs, L. (2005). Peer-assisted learning strategies: Promoting word recognition, fluency, and reading comprehension in young children. *The Journal of Special Education*, *39*(1), 34–44.

Fuchs, D., Fuchs, L. S., Mathes, P. G., & Simmons, D. C. (1997). Peer-assisted learning strategies: Making classrooms more responsive to diversity. *American Educational Research Journal, 34*(1), 174–206.

Gersten, R., Baker, S. K., Haager, D., & Graves, A. W. (2005). Exploring the role of teacher quality in predicting reading outcomes for first-grade English learners: An observational study. *Remedial and Special Education, 26*(4), 197–206.

Gersten, R., Compton, D., Connor, C. M., Dimino, J., Santoro, L., Linan-Thompson, S., & Tilly, W. D. (2009). *Assisting students struggling with reading: Response to Intervention and multi-tier intervention for reading in the primary grades. A practice guide (NCEE 2009-4045).* National Center for Education Evaluation and Regional Assistance, Institute of Education Sciences. http://ies.ed.gov/ncee/wwc/publications/practiceguides.

Gersten, R., Fuchs, L. S., Williams, J. P., & Baker, S. (2001). Teaching reading comprehension strategies to students with learning disabilities: A review of research. *Review of Educational Research, 71*(2), 279–320. 10.3102/00346543071002279

Giangreco, M. F., Suter, J. C., & Doyle, M. B. (2010). Paraprofessionals in inclusive schools: A review of recent research. *Journal of Educational and Psychological Consultation, 20*(1), 41–57.

Goe, L., & Croft, A. (2009). *Methods of evaluating teacher effectiveness. Research-to-Practice Brief.* National Comprehensive Center for Teacher Quality.

Goodwin, A. P., & Ahn, S. (2013). A meta-analysis of morphological interventions in English: Effects on literacy outcomes for school-age children. *Scientific Studies of Reading, 17*(4), 257–285.

Hairrell, A., Edmonds, M., Vaughn, S., & Simmons, D. (2010). Independent silent reading for struggling readers: Pitfalls and potential. In *Revisiting silent reading: New directions for teachers and researchers* (pp. 3–23). International Reading Association.

Hammerschmidt-Snidarich, S. M., Maki, K. E., & Adams, S. R. (2019). Evaluating the effects of repeated reading and continuous reading using a standardized dosage of words read. *Psychology in the Schools, 56*(5), 635–651.

Harn, B. A. (2017). Making RTI effective by coordinating the system of instructional supports. *Perspectives on Language and Literacy, 43*(4), 15–18. https://mydigitalpublication.com/publication/?i=445106&article_id=2908443&view=articleBrowser&ver=html5

Harn, B. A., Chard, D. J., & Kame'enui, E. J. (2011). Meeting societies' increased expectations through responsive instruction: The power and potential of systemwide approaches. *Preventing School Failure: Alternative Education for Children and Youth, 55*(4), 232–239.

Harn, B. A., Forbes-Spear, C., Fritz, R., & Berg, T. (2012). *Quality of Intervention Delivery and Receipt (QIDR) observation tool.* University of Oregon.

Harn, B. A., Linan-Thompson, S., & Roberts, G. (2008). Intensifying instruction: Does additional instructional time make a difference for the most at-risk first graders? *Journal of Learning Disabilities, 41*(2), 115–125.

Hart, B., & Risley, T. R. (1995). *Meaningful differences in the everyday experience of young American children.* Paul H Brookes Publishing.

Harvey, M. W., Yssel, N., Bauserman, A. D., & Merbler, J. B. (2010). Preservice teacher preparation for inclusion: An exploration of higher education teacher-training institutions. *Remedial and Special Education, 31*(1), 24–33.

Heggerty, M., & VanHekken, A. (2020). *Phonemic awareness: the skills that they need to help them succeed.* Literacy Resources, Inc.

Heller, K., Holtzman, W., & Messick, S. (1982). *National Research Council special task force report.* National Academy Press.

Helman, L. & Pekel. K. (2020). The principal's role in literacy leadership. In A. S. Dagen & R. M. Bean (Eds.), *Literacy leadership best practices of literacy leaders* (2nd ed., pp. 92–110). The Guilford Press.

Henbest, V. S., & Apel, K. (2017). Effective word reading instruction: What does the evidence tell us?. *Communication Disorders Quarterly, 39*(1), 303–311.

Hong, G., & Hong, Y. (2009). Reading instruction time and homogeneous grouping in kindergarten: An application of marginal mean weighting through stratification. *Educational Evaluation and Policy Analysis, 31*(1), 54–81.

Honig, B., Diamond, L., & Gutlohn, L. (2018). *Teaching reading sourcebook* (3rd ed.). Consortium on Reading Excellence in Education, Inc.

Hoover, W. A., & Gough, P. B. (1990). The simple view of reading. *Reading and Writing, 2*(2), 127–160.

Hoover, W. A., & Tunmer, W. E. (2018). The simple view of reading: Three assessments of its adequacy. *Remedial and Special Education, 39*(5), 304–312.

Hudson, R. F., Lane, H. B., & Pullen, P. C. (2005). Reading fluency assessment and instruction: What, why, and how?. *The Reading Teacher, 58*(8), 702–714.

Johnson, E. S., & Semmelroth, C. L. (2012). Examining interrater agreement analyses of a pilot special education observation tool. *Journal of Special Education Apprenticeship, 1*(2), n2.

Jones, S., Burns, D., & Pirri, C. (2010). *Leading literacy change: Strategies and tools for administrators, teachers, and coaches*. Cambium Learning.

Jones, R. E., Yssel, N., & Grant, C. (2012). Reading instruction in tier 1: Bridging the gaps by nesting evidence-based interventions within differentiated instruction. *Psychology in the Schools, 49*(3), 210–218.

Kirby, S. N. (2003). *Developing an R & D program to improve reading comprehension*. RAND Corporation. https://www.rand.org/pubs/research_briefs/RB8024.html.

Klingner, J. K., Boardman, A. G., & McMaster, K. L. (2013). What does it take to scale up and sustain evidence-based practices?. *Exceptional Children, 79*(2), 195–211.

Klingner, J. K., Vaughn, S., Arguelles, M. E., Tejero Hughes, M., & Ahwee Leftwich, S. (2004). Collaborative strategic reading: "Real-world" lessons from classroom teachers. *Remedial and Special Education, 25*(5), 291–302.

Kloo, A., & Zigmond, N. (2008). Coteaching revisited: Redrawing the blueprint. *Preventing School Failure: Alternative Education for Children and Youth, 52*(2), 12–20.

Kosanovich, M., Ladinsky, K., Nelson, L., & Torgesen, J. (2007). *Differentiated reading instruction: Small group alternative lesson structures for all students*. Guidance Document for Florida" Reading First" Schools. Florida Center for Reading Research.

LaBerge, D., & Samuels, S. J. (1974). Toward a theory of automatic information processing in reading. *Cognitive Psychology 6*(2), 293–323.

Lane, H. B., & Pullen, P. C. (2004). *A sound beginning: Phonological awareness assessment and instruction*. Allyn & Bacon.

La Paro, K., Pianta, R. C., & Stuhlman, M. (2004). Classroom assessment scoring system (CLASS): Findings from the pre-k year. *The Elementary School Journal, 104*, 409–426.

Lee, J., & Yoon, S. Y. (2017). The effects of repeated reading on reading fluency for students with reading disabilities: A meta-analysis. *Journal of Learning Disabilities, 50*(2), 213–224.

Leithwood, K., Louis, K. S., Anderson, S., & Wahlstrom, K. (2004). *How leadership influences student learning. Review of research*. The Wallace Foundation.

Lou, Y., Abrami, P. C., Spence, J. C., Poulsen, C., Chambers, B., & d'Apollonia, S. (1996). Within-class grouping: A meta-analysis. *Review of Educational Research, 66*(4), 423–458.

Manyak, P. C., Baumann, J. F., & Manyak, A. M. (2018). Morphological analysis instruction in the elementary grades: Which morphemes to teach and how to teach them. *The Reading Teacher, 72*(3), 289–300.

McKeown, M. G. (2019). Effective vocabulary instruction fosters knowing words, using words, and understanding how words work. *Language, Speech, and Hearing Services in Schools, 50*(4), 466–476.

Mercer, C. D., & Mercer, A. R. (2004). *Teaching students with learning problems* (7th ed.). Merrill Publishing Co.

Mock, D. R., & Kauffman, J. M. (2002). Preparing teachers for full inclusion: Is it possible?. *The Teacher Educator, 37*(3), 202–215.

Moats, L. (2009). Knowledge foundations for teaching reading and spelling. *Reading and Writing, 22*(4), 379–399.

Mraz, M., Nichols, W., Caldwell, S., Beisley, R., Sargent, S., & Rupley, W. (2013). Improving oral reading fluency through readers theatre. *Reading Horizons: A Journal of Literacy and Language Arts, 52*(2), 5.

Murray, M. S. (2016). Word recognition skills: One of two essential components of reading comprehension. In *Steps to success: Crossing the bridge between literacy research and practice*. Pressbooks.

National Center on Education Statistics (2019). *The nation's report card: Reading*. National Center for Education Statistics, Office of Educational Research and Improvement, U.S. Dept. of Education.

National Reading Panel (2000). *Report of the National Reading Panel: Teaching children to read: An evidence-based assessment of the scientific research literature on reading and its implications for reading instruction*. National Institute of Child Health and Human Development, National Institutes of Health.

Nielsen, D. C., Barry, A. L., & Staab, P. T. (2008). Teachers' reflections of professional change during a literacy-reform initiative. *Teaching and Teacher Education, 24*(5), 1288–1303.

Obiakor, F. E., Harris, M., Mutua, K., Rotatori, A., & Algozzine, B. (2012). Making inclusion work in general education classrooms. *Education and Treatment of Children, 35*(3), 477–490.

Pearson, P. D., Hansen, J., & Gordon, C. (1979). The effect of background knowledge on young children's comprehension of explicit and implicit information. *Journal of Reading Behavior, 11*(3), 201–209.

Perfetti, C. A. (2011). Phonology is critical in reading-but a phonological deficit is not the only source of low reading skill. In S. A. Brady, D. Braze, & C. A. Fowler (Eds.), *Explaining individual differences in reading* (pp.153–171). Taylor and Francis.

Pilonieta, P., Hathaway, J., Medina, A., & Casto, A. (2019). The impact of explicit comprehension strategy instruction on first-and second-grade at-risk students. *Journal of Education, 199*(3), 128–141.

Pikulski, J. J., & Chard, D. J. (2005). Fluency: Bridge between decoding and reading comprehension. *The Reading Teacher, 58*(6), 510–519.

Polat, F. (2011). Inclusion in education: A step towards social justice. *International Journal of Educational Development, 31*(1), 50–58.

Puhalla, E. M. (2011). Enhancing the vocabulary knowledge of first-grade children with supplemental booster instruction. *Remedial and Special Education, 32*(6), 471–481.

Pullen, P. C., & Lane, H. B. (2016). Hands-on decoding: guidelines for using manipulative letters. *Learning Disabilities: A Multidisciplinary Journal, 21*(1), 27–37.

Pullen, P. C., & Lane, H. B. (2014). Teacher-directed decoding practice with manipulative letters and word reading skill development of struggling first grade students. *Exceptionality, 22*(1), 1–16.

RAND Reading Study Group. (2002). *Reading for understanding. Toward an R&D program in reading comprehension.* RAND Reading Study Group.

Rasinski, T. (2004). Creating fluent readers. *Educational Leadership, 61*(6), 46–51.

Riley-Tilman, C., Burns, M. & Gibbons, K. (2013). *RTI applications, Volume 2: Assessment, analysis, and decision making*. Guilford Press.

Sáenz, L. M., Fuchs, L. S., & Fuchs, D. (2005). Peer-assisted learning strategies for English language learners with learning disabilities. *Exceptional Children, 71*(3), 231–247.

Schneider, M. (2018, November 14). *Institute of Education Sciences (IES): How to make education research relevant to teachers.* https://ies.ed.gov/director/remarks/11-14-2018.asp

Semmelroth, C. L., & Johnson, E. (2014). Measuring rater reliability on a special education observation tool. *Assessment for Effective Intervention, 39*(3), 131–145.

Simmons, D. (2015). Instructional engineering principles to frame the future of reading intervention research and practice. *Remedial and Special Education, 36*(1), 45–51.

Snow, C. E., and Juel, C. (2005). Teaching children to read: What do we know about how to do it? In M. J. Snowling, C. Hulme, & C. J. Hulme (Eds.), *The science of reading: A handbook* (pp. 501–520). Blackwell.

Spear-Swerling, L. (2006). Assessment of reading comprehension. *LDOnline*. Retrieved from http://www.ldonline.org/spearswerling/Assessment_of_Reading_Comprehension

Swanson, E., Vaughn, S., Wanzek, J., Petscher, Y., Heckert, J., Cavanaugh, C., & Tackett, K. (2011). A synthesis of read-aloud interventions on early reading outcomes among preschool through third graders at risk for reading difficulties. *Journal of Learning Disabilities, 44*(3), 258–275.

Taylor, B. M., Pearson, P. D., Clark, K. F., & Walpole, S. (1999). Center for the improvement of early reading achievement: effective schools/accomplished teachers. *The Reading Teacher, 53*(2), 156–159.

Templeton, S. (2012). Teaching and learning morphology: A reflection on generative vocabulary instruction. *Journal of Education, 192*(2–3), 101–107. 10.1177/0022057412192002-312

The IRIS Center (2008a). *PALS: A reading strategy for grades K-1.* https://iris.peabody.vanderbilt.edu/module/palsk1/#content

The IRIS Center (2008b). *PALS: A reading strategy for grades 2-6.* https://iris.peabody.vanderbilt.edu/module/pals26/

The IRIS Center (2008c). *CSR: A reading comprehension strategy.* https://iris.peabody.vanderbilt.edu/module/csr/#content

Toste, J. R., Williams, K. J., & Capin, P. (2017). Reading big words: Instructional practices to promote multisyllabic word reading fluency. *Intervention in School and Clinic, 52*(5), 270–278.

Towson, J. A., Fettig, A., Fleury, V. P., & Abarca, D. L. (2017). Dialogic reading in early childhood settings: A summary of the evidence base. *Topics in Early Childhood Special Education, 37*(3), 132–146.

Urbani, J. M. (2020). Dialogic reading: Implementing an evidence-based practice in complex classrooms. *TEACHING Exceptional Children, 52*(6), 392–402.

Vaughn, S., & Klingner, J. (1999). Teaching reading comprehension through collaborative strategic reading. *Intervention in School and Clinic, 34*(5), 284–292.

Vaughn, S., Linan-Thompson, S., Kouzekanani, K., Pedrotty Bryant, D., Dickson, S., & Blozis, S. A. (2003). Reading instruction grouping for students with reading difficulties. *Remedial and Special Education, 24*(5), 301–315.

Vaughn, S., Wexler, J., Leroux, A., Roberts, G., Denton, C., Barth, A., & Fletcher, J. (2012). Effects of intensive reading intervention for eighth-grade students with persistently inadequate response to intervention. *Journal of Learning Disabilities, 45*(6), 515–525.

Walpole, S., & Vitale, M. N. (2020). PreK-12 literacy programs: Moving from curriculum to collaboration to collective efficacy. In A. S. Dagen & R. M. Bean (Eds.), *Best practices of literacy leaders: Keys to school improvement* (2nd ed., pp. 113–132). The Guilford Press.

Wang, M., & Fitch, P. (2010). Preparing pre-service teachers for effective co-teaching in inclusive classrooms. In C. Forlin (Ed.), *Teacher education for inclusion: Changing paradigms and innovative approaches* (pp. 112–119). Routledge.

Wanzek, J. (2014). Building word knowledge: Opportunities for direct vocabulary instruction in general education for students with reading difficulties. *Reading & Writing Quarterly, 30*, 139–164. doi:10.1080/10573569.2013.789786

Wanzek, J., Al Otaiba, S., & McMaster, K. L. (2020). *Intensive reading interventions for the elementary grades*. Guilford Publications.

Wanzek, J., & Vaughn, S. (2007). Research-based implications from extensive early reading interventions. *School Psychology Review, 36*(4), 541–561.

Wanzek, J., Wexler, J., Vaughn, S., & Ciullo, S. (2010). Reading interventions for struggling readers in the upper elementary grades: A synthesis of 20 years of research. *Reading and Writing, 23*(8), 889–912.

Washburn, E. K., Joshi, R. M., & Cantrell, E. B. (2011). Are preservice teachers prepared to teach struggling readers?. *Annals of Dyslexia, 61*(1), 21–43.

Weiser, B., & Mathes, P. (2011). Using encoding instruction to improve the reading and spelling performances of elementary students at risk for literacy difficulties: A best-evidence synthesis. *Review of Educational Research, 81*(2), 170–200.

Weiss, M. P., Pellegrino, A., & Brigham, F. J. (2017). Practicing collaboration in teacher preparation: Effects of learning by doing together. *Teacher Education and Special Education, 40*(1), 65–76.

Young, C., & Rasinski, T. (2018). Readers Theatre: effects on word recognition automaticity and reading prosody. *Journal of Research in Reading, 41*(3), 475–485.

Zigmond, N., & Kloo, A. (2011). General and special education are (and should be) different. In J. M. Kauffman (Ed.), *Handbook of special education*(pp. 160–172). Routledge.

11

Creating Opportunities for Struggling Mathematics Learners in Inclusive Schools

Cynthia C. Griffin[1], Jemma Bae Kwon[2], Kristen Apraiz[1], and Lauren N. Wong[1]

[1]UNIVERSITY OF FLORIDA

[2]CALIFORNIA STATE UNIVERSITY, SACRAMENTO

Setting the Stage

Enhancing the academic performance of *all* students continues to be a national priority (Every Student Succeeds Act [ESSA], 2015; Individuals with Disabilities Education Act [IDEA], 2004; National Council of Teachers of Mathematics [NCTM], 2000, 2007, 2014). However, data from The National Assessment of Educational Progress (NAEP; National Center for Education Statistics [NCES], 2019) reveal persistent shortfalls in mathematics learning for students with disabilities (SWD). While 86% of all 4th grade students without identified disabilities fell at or above the *Basic* achievement level on the NAEP, only 50% of SWD reached this rudimentary target in 2019. For 8th graders, the difference was even greater. About one-third (32%) of SWD scored at or above *Basic*, compared to three-fourths (75%) of eighth-grade students without identified disabilities. These differences require thoughtful attention if attaining widespread mathematical preparedness is to become a reality in mathematics classrooms that include both students with and without disabilities.

Factors Affecting Students' Mathematics Learning

Differences in students' mathematics achievement have been attributed to imbalances in learning opportunities between students who are perceived to be more capable or have a higher aptitude and those who are low performing (NCTM, 2014). For example, students tracked in low-level math groups and classes lack (or are completely denied) access to challenging mathematics content (Ellis, 2008; Stiff et al., 2011), thereby hindering them from gaining knowledge and skills necessary to improve mathematics achievement over time. Other factors external to students that may also impact their mathematics achievement include teachers' self-efficacy beliefs for teaching mathematics (Holzberger et al., 2013) and teachers' weak mathematical content knowledge for teaching (Hill et al., 2005).

DOI: 10.4324/9781003043874-11

Research has also identified factors specific to students with learning disabilities in mathematics (MLD) to explain differences in mathematics achievement between students with and without disabilities. Younger students with MLD and other struggling mathematics learners typically possess a poor conceptual understanding of counting, use less mature and inefficient counting strategies, and experience persistent difficulties retrieving basic math facts from memory (Geary, 1993, 2004; Jordan et al., 2003). Older students have been shown to exhibit poor conceptual knowledge of rational numbers (Mazzocco & Devlin, 2008) with persistent difficulties in fraction knowledge (Hansen et al., 2017) due in part to troubles with estimating numerical magnitudes on a number line, long division, calculation fluency, working memory, and attentive behavior (e.g., Hansen et al., 2015; Jordan et al., 2013, 2017). Early difficulties in learning fractions are a significant concern because this knowledge is strongly related to high school mathematics achievement (Siegler et al., 2012) and predicts performance in gateway classes such as algebra (Booth & Newton, 2012).

Collaboration Between Mathematics Education and Special Education

The Individuals with Disabilities Education Act (IDEA, 2004) has supported interdisciplinary collaboration since its inception. Therefore contributions by both mathematics education and special education to policy, research, and practice are relevant for addressing the progress of SWD and other struggling mathematics learners. The National Council of Teachers of Mathematics (NCTM) has called for partnerships between special educators and mathematics teachers to work together to achieve equitable practices in mathematics classrooms, where teachers assume a "growth mindset [that] values all students' thinking and uses pedagogical practices such as differentiated tasks, mixed-ability groupings, and public praise for contributions and perseverance to cultivate mathematical participation and achievement" (NCTM, 2014, p.65). This collaborative approach to practice is necessary given that 68% of students with specific learning disabilities spend 80% or more of the school day in general education classrooms (NCES, 2016). Because responsibility for teaching all students is to be shared between general and special education (IDEA, 2004), teachers must be able to work together to identify struggling mathematics learners and students with MLD and effectively address their learning needs with the goal of improving outcomes.

Strong collaborative skills are essential when teachers work together and also when they interact with parents of SWDs, related service providers, and school leaders to ensure that the individualized needs of each SWD are met (Friend & Cook, 2017). According to the Council for Exceptional Children's High-Leverage Practices in Special Education (McLeskey et al., 2017), skills for fostering professional collaboration involve "sharing ideas, active listening, questioning, planning, problem solving [and] negotiating" (p. 28). Teachers must also know how to "organize and facilitate effective meetings" (p. 30) for building consensus around issues such as instructional design, student response to instruction, and student outcomes. Professional collaboration that promotes both student *and* teacher learning (Benedict et al., 2020) has the potential to be more successful.

Support Systems, EBPs, and HLPs

Multi-Tiered Systems of Support (MTSS) is one way that school-wide collaboration, including the joint responsibility among general and special educators for teaching all students, can be initiated and supported. MTSS is often used as an umbrella term for "a comprehensive continuum of evidence-based, systemic practices to support a rapid response to students' needs with regular observation to facilitate data-based instructional decision making" (ESSA, 2015; 20 U.S.C. § 7801(33)). Response-To-Intervention (RTI) and Positive Behavior Interventions and Supports (PBIS) are specified tiered systems of support, the latter focused on student behavior and the former, academic learning. We use the term RTI in this chapter due to our focus on mathematics content learning. In *Assisting*

Students Struggling with Mathematics: Response to Intervention (RtI) for Elementary and Middle Schools, RTI is described as "an early detection, prevention, and support system that identifies struggling students and assists them before they fall behind academically" (Gersten et al., 2009, p. 4). Schools are expected to prevent significant difficulties by identifying struggling learners early and implementing highly impactful instructional interventions that are supported by research evidence, including evidence-based practices (EBPs; Cook et al., 2012). EBPs are "instructional approaches supported by trustworthy bodies of research that meet standards regarding quantity, quality, research design, and effect on student outcomes" (p. 22) and a central aspect of an RTI system. EBPs can be appropriate for teaching all students but are particularly critical for teaching SWD and other struggling mathematics learners because EBPs are more likely to improve student learning.

To address teacher knowledge and skills, *high-leverage practices* (HLPs; Ball & Forzani, 2011; see Chapter 9) have been developed to ensure that teachers are capable of promoting the school success of all students (McDonald et al., 2013; McLeskey et al., 2017). Building on results from earlier studies (e.g., Ball & Forzani, 2009) and the Teacher Education Initiative projects (TeachingWorks, n.d.), researchers, teacher educators, and school professionals worked together to research, develop, and broadly disseminate HLPs for improving teacher preparation programs, with a particular focus on beginning and early career teachers. HLPs and related materials resulting from these efforts are found on the TeachingWorks website (http://www.teachingworks.org/). Because special education teachers must be able to teach students with the most complex learning and behavioral difficulties, the Council for Exceptional Children (CEC) and the CEEDAR Center, in conjunction with other professional organizations and stakeholders, created a set of HLPs referred to as CEC's High-Leverage Practices in Special Education (McLeskey et al., 2017). Further information about CEC's HLPs can be found at https://highleveragepractices.org/.

Given this context, we now expand our discussion to explore research for strengthening educator knowledge for teaching effectively in inclusive elementary mathematics classrooms with examples for teacher preparation and professional development programs. We then summarize literature from both mathematics education and special education that address ways teachers can strengthen their students' mathematics learning in inclusive contexts.

What Do We Know Based on Research?

We begin this subsection with an overview of research on RTI. The RTI framework addresses both prevention and intervention in mathematics learning. It is a flexible, proactive, personalized model for identifying students' learning needs before their struggles significantly impede learning and referrals for special education services are made. RTI is widely used across the United States (Zirkel & Thomas, 2010) and can play a role in structuring instructional supports in mathematics for helping students make progress toward grade-level expectations.

RTI Implementation

Although the purpose and impact of multilevel prevention systems have been debated (e.g., Fuchs et al., 2010, 2012; Gersten et al., 2017), the RTI framework has been endorsed and applied as a framework for helping schools address the needs of struggling mathematics learners in the elementary and middle grades (e.g., Gersten et al., 2009). The Office of Special Education and Rehabilitative Services (OSERS) recommends five primary characteristics of RTI models: (a) high-quality, research-based instruction in general education, (b) universal screening for academic and behavior problems, (c) continuous progress monitoring, (d) multiple tiers of progressively more intense instruction/interventions, and (e) fidelity measures (OSERS, 2007), however, no formally agreed upon RTI model is used across states. Though much is left to the states' discretion in regard to the number of tiers, duration of interventions, rate of progress, and professional qualifications to provide interventions, RTI typically comprises three tiers of instruction: (1) standards-based, core instruction used with all students (Tier 1), (2) supplementary instruction for students who have not met important learning benchmarks (Tier 2), and (3) intensive instruction for the lowest performing students (Tier 3).

To evaluate the strengths and limitations of RTI implementation on mathematics learning, Fuchs et al. (2012) examined findings from four efficacy studies of small-group tutoring interventions with first and third grade struggling mathematics learners (i.e., Fuchs et al., 2005, 2008, 2009, 2012). From these four sets of results, the researchers considered the (1) percentage of students who were unresponsive or failed to respond to the intervention, (2) post-intervention achievement gap between intervention and control students, and (3) extent of intervention transfer across components of the mathematics curriculum. Their findings suggest the following general conclusions. First, struggling mathematics learners at-risk for poor mathematics development achieve substantially less well when they remain in the core mathematics program (Tier 1) and do not receive the kind of small group tutoring interventions over 15-20 weeks (Tier 2) used in the four studies. These tutoring sessions were characterized by explicit and systematic instruction used to teach effective and efficient strategies with the frequent and cumulative practice for building both conceptual and procedural foundational mathematics knowledge and skills in students. With a rate of unresponsiveness at around 4% across the four studies, findings also suggest that prevention services in either Tier 2 or 3 that are perceived as short-term will not supplant the ongoing and intensive services needed by the most challenging mathematics learners, such as some students with MLD, and provided with special education resources. Second, the gap between struggling learners' mathematics performance and that of their typically performing peers grows when struggling learners do not receive small group tutoring. And, third, tutoring focused on knowledge of numbers (i.e., "number sense"; Berch, 2005) during sessions promoted stronger performance on math computation problems and word problem solving performance, but the transfer did not extend to word problems when math facts were the focus of tutoring.

Despite documented benefits of RTI reported by teachers, such as the early identification of struggling students, opportunities to problem-solve and review student data with colleagues, small group instruction, and meeting students' needs (Swanson et al., 2012) and well-intentioned attempts by schools to implement RTI, teachers continue to lack comprehensive knowledge about MTSS/RTI and find the collaborative demands of implementing it challenging (Fuchs & Fuchs, 2017). Teachers' have reported uncertainties about the content and nature of Tier 3 supports, how to use data to make instructional decisions, and EBPs and where to find them (Al Otaiba et al., 2019; Barrio & Combes, 2015; Castillo et al., 2016; Castro-Villarreal et al., 2014; Nagro et al., 2019).

Educators have also reported alignment issues between core curriculum and instruction (Tier 1) and interventions and instruction intended for low-performing students (Tiers 2 and 3), such as differences in the mathematics topics covered, the depth at which topics are covered, and the vocabulary used to teach similar concepts and skills (Fuchs et al., 2016; Gersten, 2016). Recently, Nelson et al. (2019) systematically examined the alignment of instructional practices and mathematics vocabulary across a widely implemented, daily core curriculum (i.e., *Math Expressions*) and two intervention programs designed for struggling mathematics learners (i.e., SRA *Connecting Math Concepts* and *Early Numeracy Interventions*). After coding both mathematics practices and mathematics vocabulary used within all three programs across kindergarten through grade 6 materials, the researchers found very little overlap among programs for both practices and vocabulary. This finding suggests that students receiving Tier 1 and intervention supports (Tiers 2 and/or 3) may experience difficulties maintaining and generalizing what they have learned when the supports they receive across tiers are incongruent and do not complement and reinforce students' learning goals. Alternatively, curricular programs alone cannot be expected to meet all students' instructional needs, and core and intervention programs may justifiably include different language, practices, and strategies based on distinct instructional purposes. Nelson and colleagues offer several recommendations for reducing the differences that separate core and intervention mathematics instruction, examples include the use of:

- systematic and explicit instruction in core programs, such as: pre-teaching new concepts, skills and mathematics vocabulary; modeling concepts and skills using a range of multiple examples; making connections to prior knowledge, and using think-aloud;
- teacher modeling of *concrete and pictorial representations* of mathematics with several opportunities for students to demonstrate their mathematical understandings through representations;
- explicit teaching to help students discuss and justify their mathematical thinking that includes immediate feedback and error correction to prevent misconceptions; and,
- teaching of mathematics vocabulary across core and intervention programs through communication and coordination among teachers.

Moving forward, Fuchs and Fuchs (2017) recommend that MTSS systems be designed locally and reflect a balance between what is effective and what is doable. Others suggest that teachers will need collaborative and sustained opportunities to improve their knowledge of and skills for implementing, RTI such as time to plan, observe, and debrief with others about their instruction (Benedict et al., 2020; Gomez-Najarro, 2020).

Strengthening Teachers' Mathematics Knowledge for Teaching

In the next section, we focus on the learning of teachers of mathematics by highlighting essential, research-based teaching practices. Teachers should know and be able to use these "high-leverage practices" (Ball & Forzani, 2011) as they have been found to be most important for student learning.

High Leverage Practices in Mathematics

According to the National Mathematics Advisory Panel (NMAP, 2008) report, a substantial portion of the variability in students' mathematics achievement gains is due to the *teacher*, and "the effects of teachers on student achievement compound dramatically if students receive a series of effective or ineffective teachers" (p. 35). Research suggests that teachers' mathematics content knowledge for teaching, instructional practices and curriculum used, and ability to identify individual differences in mathematics learning can impact student outcomes (Hill et al., 2005; Mazzocco et al., 2013; NMAP, 2008; Siegler et al., 2010). A number of studies have documented specific difficulties teachers experience teaching mathematics content, such as articulating the mathematical logic behind an answer, suggesting that teachers understand mathematics as they were taught—through procedures only (e.g., Ball, 1990, 1992; Knuth, 2002; Ma, 2010). Other studies have demonstrated the challenges that both general and special education teachers experience teaching in inclusive mathematics classrooms, such as a lack of (1) understanding the learning characteristics of, and teaching approaches effective for, students with mathematics difficulties and disabilities, (2) awareness of legislative requirements and content standards, (3) knowledge of assessment practices, including progress monitoring, and (4) opportunities for teachers to collaborate around these issues (Bottge et al., 2015).

Certainly, teacher knowledge and use of EBPs and research-informed pedagogical approaches to mathematics learning are important, including mathematics activities using visual representation with manipulative materials and other models of mathematical concepts. Yet, student engagement is often low during these tasks and activities (Hill et al., 2008) and low levels of thinking are emphasized during lessons, such as a focus on only procedural skills (Stein et al., 2000). Furthermore, language, examples, and representations used during lessons and discussed by students can distort the meaning of mathematics concepts and, in turn, lead to student misconceptions (Heaton, 1992, 2000; Ma, 2010), especially when teachers do not know how to recognize or respond effectively to these misconceptions.

TeachingWorks HLPs

Because teachers clearly matter to students' mathematics learning, the nineteen HLPs (Ball & Forzani, 2011) from TeachingWorks and 22 HLPs in Special Education from CEC (McLeskey et al., 2017) offer significant and sustained support for improving pre-service teacher knowledge of and skill at implementing, fundamental practices for promoting the success of all students—across subject areas, grade levels, and teaching contexts. In particular, both TeachingWorks HLPs and HLPs in Special Education have direct implications for mathematics teaching that is central to all students' mathematics learning, but especially SWDs and other struggling mathematics learners in inclusive settings.

For example, the TeachingWorks HLP, ***Explaining and Modeling Content, Practices, and Strategies,*** addresses teachers' competence at modeling in a way that makes conceptual understanding and procedural fluency in mathematics explicit by making thinking visible to students. To do so, teachers carry out core practices that are intended to: (a) emphasize what the class is working on and why they are doing it (***Annotating)***; (b) rule out what may be distracting to the key aspects of the work or lead to misconceptions (***Backgrounding)***; (c) send clear signals to key points that need special attention, and the most complex or confusing aspects of the content that require further explanation and elaboration (***Foregrounding***); (d) address key elements in a logical fashion with verbal, tone, or visual markers (***Marking***); (e) provide verbal explanations to make thinking visible (***Thinking Aloud***) and indicate these moments as think-alouds (***Marking Metacognition***); (f) define terms (***Defining Content Terminology***); (g) provide a public report (e.g., using whiteboard) after translating verbal ideas and thinking processes that were used in the work (***Recording and Representing***); (h) explicitly connect linguistic (e.g., explanations), visual (e.g., drawings), and mathematically conventional (e.g., equations) representations of concepts (***Connecting Representations***); and (i) continue to use terms and representations that are precise, concise, developmentally appropriate, and accessible to all students ***(Consistent Verbal and Visual Representations).*** Although this list is not exhaustive, it reflects major areas of skillful teaching for modeling mathematics concepts and procedures (TeachingWorks, 2019).

Another example TeachingWorks HLP that would be important for successfully including SWDs in general education mathematics classrooms is ***Eliciting and Interpreting Individual Students' Thinking (EIST)***. Research conducted in reform-oriented, or standards-based, mathematics classrooms (e.g., Baxter et al., 2001; Baxter et al., 2002) indicates that students with learning difficulties assume passive roles, encounter difficulties with the cognitive load of the activities and curricular materials, are more likely to report using limited and ineffective strategies, and their progress is substantially below that of their more competent peers. When struggling mathematics learners interact with more competent peers, they typically allow the more skilled learners to do most of the thinking and the work (Bottge et al., 2002). Consequently, EIST is foundational to changing this situation for struggling learners by ensuring that pre-service teachers know how to (1) pose questions that allow students to reveal their thinking about mathematics, (2) respond appropriately, and (3) adapt their instruction to address student misunderstandings and encourage student participation.

Each TeachingWorks HLP is broken down, or "decomposed", into elements that are manageable and achievable for the pedagogical purpose of teacher learning (Ball & Forzani, 2009; Sleep, 2012). Decomposition of an HLP enables teacher educators to design and implement learning activities based on the notion of *approximation of practice*. That is, learning activities can be developed and enacted on a continuum from a facet of an HLP to a core practice encompassing all constituent parts and underlying principles (Janssen et al., 2015).

According to TeachingWorks' decomposition of EIST, ambitious mathematics teaching requires that teachers carefully select mathematics tasks and questions that are open to students' active engagement in sharing their point of view, thinking, and new ideas. The crux of EIST actions and interactions is not having students understand the target mathematics but seeking to understand how students are making sense of the mathematics they are learning. So, the EIST consists of three phases: (a) *Formulating and Presenting Tasks and Questions*; (b) *Listening to and Interpreting Student Ideas*; and (c) *Developing Additional Questions, Prompts, and Tasks* (TeachingWorks, 2019). The decomposition of EIST by the three phases follows:

Formulating and Presenting Tasks and Questions

- Formulate linguistically and culturally responsive tasks and questions
- Design tasks that are conducive to EIST
- Develop hypotheses about how the student may hear and respond to the question
- Pose initial open-ended questions with the design task
- Give students leveled prompts and enough time to understand and process the posed task and question
- Offer multiple means of communication (e.g., drawing, speaking, writing)

Listening to and Interpreting Student Ideas

- Allow supportive thinking time for students to prepare for verbal responses and mathematical representations to communicate their thinking (e.g., talk with a partner first, drawing, writing)
- Allow enough time for students to communicate their thinking without unnecessary interruptions
- Listen for ideas using non-academic language
- Interpret student responses building on what students know as competent learners by first noticing common patterns, strengths, new ideas, engaged mathematical points, and then weaknesses and errors
- Use funds of knowledge (e.g., student experience, background knowledge) to make sense of student responses and to articulate student thinking

Developing Additional Questions, Prompts, and Tasks

- Identify particular features of students' thinking to be probed further
- Identify particular strategies highlighted in students' thinking to be probed further
- Develop tasks, prompts, and probing questions to address both foci above

Other TeachingWorks HLPs, such as ***Leading a Group Discussion*** and ***Providing Oral and Written Feedback to Students,*** can be implemented to transform common classroom practices typically based on sorting and labeling students to those that honor all students as sense-makers and active contributors to mathematics learning regardless of their social-economic, racial/ethnicity, or gender identity (Aguirre et al., 2013) and mathematical proficiency levels (Shaughnesssy et al., 2020). Collectively, the TeachingWorks HLPs of EIST, Leading Group Discussions, and Providing Feedback can help to create inclusive learning opportunities for SWD and other students from marginalized learner populations who have been excluded from aspects of mathematics learning deemed too difficult for them, such as mathematical reasoning and justification (Lampert et al., 2013), and instead create frequent opportunities for all students to engage in these more rigorous activities because teachers are prepared to teach in ways that meet diverse students' needs.

HLPs in Special Education

CEC's HLPs in Special Education (McLeskey et al., 2017) were recently developed and published as essential practices for special education teachers and teacher candidates to learn with mastery. Teacher education in special education has a history of putting forth knowledge specifications and/or expected learning outcomes for prospective and practicing teachers in the form of standards (e.g., Council for Exceptional Children, CEC Professional Standards, n.d.-a, n.d.-b). A distinguishing feature of the HLPs in Special Education is urging teacher educators to focus on both teacher learning outcomes—knowing foundational teaching practices that are impactful on student learning—and being able to enact them in classrooms. This can be fulfilled by bridging coursework and field experiences. Teacher candidates' learning experiences have often been siloed into unrelated activities, applications, and experiences across coursework and fieldwork. This disconnected approach to learning may influence graduates' preparedness for impacting student outcomes (Leko et al., 2015). Systematically aligned coursework and fieldwork afford multiple opportunities for teacher candidates to practice teaching fundamentals that are constantly used by effective special education teachers and critical to impacting students' academic and social-emotional outcomes (McLeskey et al., 2019). Implementing HLPs into mathematics methods courses must occur within an integrated approach that attends to both the general learning activities and practice-based learning activities in these courses, as well as experiences teacher candidates will have in field-based classrooms (see Figure 11.1).

Knowledge

Most, if not all, mathematics methods courses or professional development programs expect participating teacher-learners to acquire knowledge about the mathematics topics they teach, how students interact with the mathematics content (e.g., common challenges and misconceptions in student learning), and effective pedagogical strategies, including EBPs. Moving forward, the ultimate goal of gaining these forms of knowledge is to develop *adaptive expertise* (i.e., efficiency in problem solving and ability to adapt to various situations and contexts; Bransford et al., 2000; Schwartz et al., 2005). Through the lens of adaptive expertise, pre-service and in-service special education teachers' (SETs) knowledge should extend beyond the mathematics content, learner characteristics, and principles and procedures of teaching to a better understanding of the complexities of teaching. As experts, teachers are able to recognize problems and identify multiple perspectives beneath an emerging situation, case, or scenario, and then put into practice a myriad of observable and unobservable behaviors (Bransford et al., 2000; Fairbanks et al., 2010).

It is imperative, therefore, to allow SETs to actively engage in deliberately designed opportunities in which they explore behaviors expected of SETs with adaptive expertise. Since classroom discourse and communication have been placed at the heart of developing students' mathematical competencies and identities (NCTM, 2000), how members in the mathematics community (i.e., teacher and students) communicate is crucial to quality mathematics teaching (Walshaw & Anthony, 2008). Viewed in this light, SET learning opportunities often rely on targeted teacher utterances, or "talk moves", that adaptive experts are more likely to demonstrate during their interactions with mathematics and students. Although it is developmentally difficult for SETs to practice the behaviors of adaptive experts, teacher educators must help novice teachers understand the importance of building expert behaviors in themselves, especially the skill of facilitating mathematical discussions or talk moves.

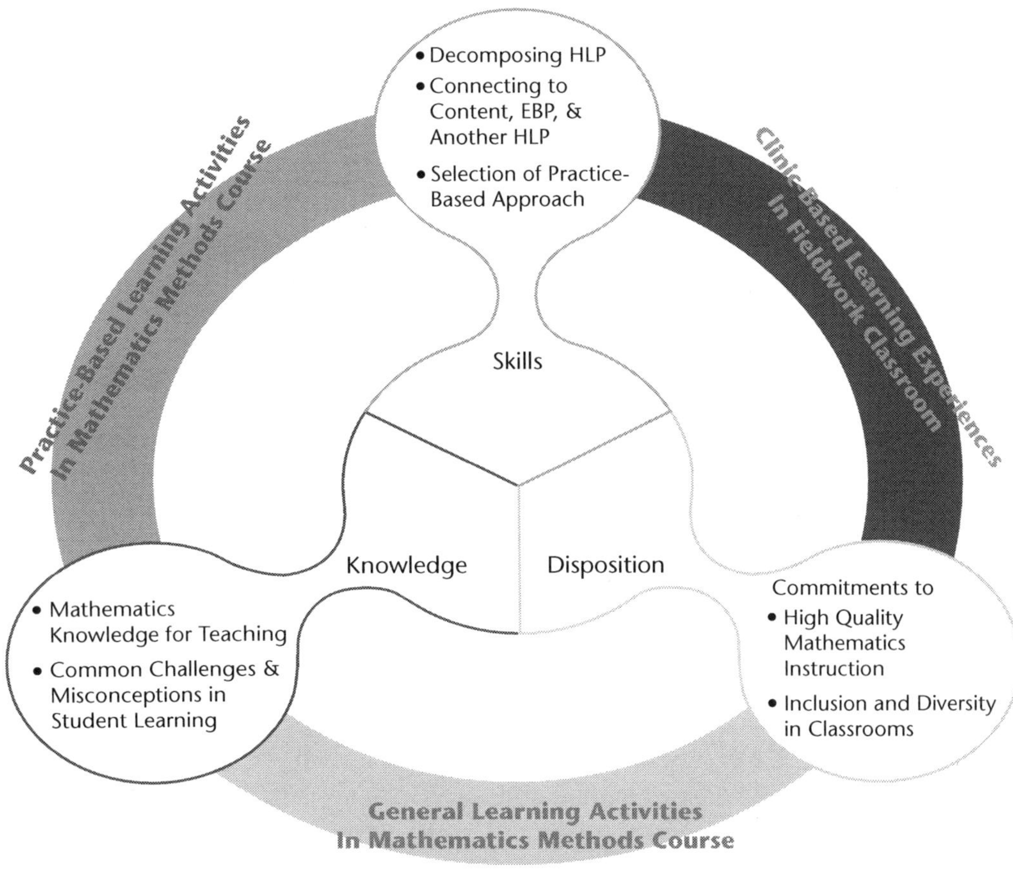

Figure 11.1 An integrated model of mathematics course development

Skills

Having a set of HLPs is merely a starting point (McLeskey et al., 2019), and using them in teacher learning requires a great deal of attention to the utility of an HLP and the effectiveness of each HLP. In terms of *utility*, the decomposition of HLPs takes different forms depending on the nature of a particular HLP, the context of the teacher preparation program, and its teacher candidates' learning needs. For example, a core HLP in Special Education that is also important for teaching mathematics to struggling learners (e.g., Swanson et al., 2015) is to *Teach Cognitive and Metacognitive Strategies* (CMS) *to Support Learning and Independence*. This HLP could be decomposed into a list of sequenced components as follows:

Formulating Target CMS

- Identify learning objectives and challenges
- Identify cognitive strategies
- Identify metacognitive strategies
- Incorporate metacognitive strategies into cognitive strategies (e.g., incorporate a way to monitor one's own performance into a cognitive routine)

Explicitly Teaching CMS Use

- Orchestrate discussions that motivate students to use CMS
- Orchestrate an Explicit Instruction Lesson for the target CMS

Maintaining and Generalizing the Use of Learned CMS

- Orchestrate evaluation discussion of CMS use
- Plan distributed practice opportunities

Another aspect of the refinement process is connecting the target HLP to mathematics content and content-specific EBPs. Since HLPs were developed to be applicable across subject areas, learning to teach mathematics requires further refinement of them by connecting decomposed elements with mathematics topics and EBPs that enhance mathematics instruction (Billingsley et al., 2019). For instance, teaching fractions using visual representation is effective for developing students' fraction concepts (Siegler et al., 2010), including area (e.g., fraction rectangle), length (e.g., number lines), and set models (e.g., counters). For students who struggle to learn fraction concepts, the concrete-representational-abstract (CRA) sequence is one effective approach for visually representing fractions. Results of research synthesis (Shin & Bryant, 2015) suggest that concrete and visual representations, such as CRA, lead to improved performance on measures of fractions concepts and skills. The CRA sequence involves visual representations by representing fractions in physical (e.g., Cuisenaire Rods) and graphical models (e.g., drawings). Given the CMS HLP decomposed above, a teacher would be expected to know how to represent fractions across the area, length, and set models when the learning objective is to explain why two fractions with different denominators are equivalent. This HLP would also require teachers to know (1) which model may be most effective to their students' learning, (2) how to connect the visual model with the specific language and notations associated with fractions, and (3) how to incorporate those mathematics models and language into the CRA sequence instruction. Building on the knowledge, the teacher should be able to plan the lesson and orchestrate instructional moves and talk moves.

Once teacher-learners are able to select and use appropriate mathematical representations (e.g., virtual manipulatives of Cuisenaire Rods for teaching equivalent fractions; Shin et al., 2017), they are at a stage of learning where instructional moves can be incorporated, in particular, "talk moves" that have the potential to impact students' mathematics learning (Griffin et al., 2009). Examples of this type of teacher talk follow:

- Use of higher-order questions eliciting student thinking, not simply soliciting a fact (e.g., "You placed one brown rod showing the unit. What can you do to show the whole using different color rods?")
- Encourage student-to-teacher exchanges, including inviting questions (e.g., "Can you tell me why you chose white rods and what you are going to do with them to show a unit?"); and asking students to revoice their responses (e.g., "Alex, please tell the class what Drew just talked about related to his model with the white rods?")
- Use wait time after both teacher questions and student responses (e.g., "Think for one minute about how many red rods you need. I am starting the timer now.")
- Probe a student's thinking with a request for deeper thinking (e.g., "So, how do you know that purple rods show the unit too?")
- Encourage student-to-student exchanges (e.g., "Let's do Think-Pair-Share about your models using different color rods.")

It is worth noting that the decomposition of CMS HLP clearly presents spaces where other HLPs can be interwoven, such as, *Use Explicit Instruction* and *Teach Students to Maintain and Generalize New Learning Across Time and Settings*. Moreover, learning experiences designed for the CMS HLP turn out to set up practice opportunities for other HLPs. Specifically, teacher-learners will be naturally exposed to activities to explore and practice such elements of explicit instruction as *Use clear and concise language* and *Provide an adequate range of examples and non-examples*. Going back to the fraction example, in addition to all instructional talk moves described above for teaching equivalent fractions using virtual Cuisenaire Rods, teacher-learners can explore how other colored rods, such as green (partitioned into 3 parts), yellow (5 parts), and black rods (7 parts) compare to the brown rods (8 parts) as the unit or the whole.

The creators of TeachingWorks HLPs and HLPs in Special Education also underscore the importance of developing practice-based teacher education programs characterized by the close alignment between learning that occurs in coursework and in field-based experiences. In a study conducted by Sayeski et al. (2019), greater learning outcomes were demonstrated by special education teacher candidates who were assigned to a practice-based methods course as opposed to candidates who were in the business-as-usual course. The target HLP used in this study was *Use Strategies to Promote Active Student Engagement*, operationalized as opportunities to respond (OtR). The research team unpacked the core practice, OtR, into more specific, fine-grained techniques, such as cold call, response cards, choral response, whiteboards, guided notes, and worksheets. These individual techniques were practiced during distributed practice opportunities. The research team also developed an observation tool to evaluate teacher learning and teacher use of the decomposed elements noted above.

Strengthening Students' Mathematics Knowledge

In this next section of the chapter, we target students' learning in inclusive mathematics classrooms. The research is drawn from both the mathematics education and special education literature. This section also includes a return to the RTI framework and specific examples for Tier 1, Tier 2, and Tier 3 mathematics instruction.

Inclusive Education from a Mathematics Education Perspective

The *Principles and Standards for School Mathematics* (National Council of Teachers of Mathematics, 2000) and the *Common Core State Standards* (CCSS; National Governors Association Center for Best Practices, 2010) challenge the traditional view of what it means to learn and succeed within the mathematics domain. The principles and standards reveal that learning mathematics involves a way of thinking that engages students in reasoning and justifying their mathematical solutions. Students must (1) develop well-connected conceptual knowledge as a foundation underlying mathematical procedures, (2) acquire productive dispositions toward learning and behaving mathematically, and (3) learn and carry out a variety of strategies while continuing to develop more efficient retrieval and reasoning strategies over time (Carpenter et al., 1999; Siegler, 2005). Although long-established goals of mathematics learning (e.g., procedural fluency) remain important, an instructional focus on math facts and mathematical algorithms is no longer sufficient as end goals of mathematics learning if students are to attain mathematical preparedness for employment and/or post-secondary education (Every Student Succeeds Act of 2015, 2015).

Because "standards alone...will not realize the goal of high levels of mathematical understanding by all students", the NCTM further developed and articulated their vision for mathematics education in, *Principles to Actions: Ensuring Mathematical Success for All* (National Council of Teachers of Mathematics, 2014, p. vii). *Principles to Actions* discusses current realities in classrooms, schools, and districts that impede the goal of high levels of mathematical understanding for all students, including low expectations of students, an emphasis on high-stakes assessments, an instructional focus on procedures rather than mathematical understanding, and professionally isolated teachers with limited access to effective instructional materials and supports. More recently, the NCTM published, *Catalyzing Change in Early Childhood and Elementary Mathematics* (2020), intended to initiate critical conversations about topics brought to light in *Principles to Actions*, such as deep mathematical understanding for every student, equitable learning structures, and equitable teaching practices. To develop the knowledge, skills, strategies, and dispositions necessary for achieving rigorous mathematics standards for success in school and later in life, NCTM recommends that a broad range of stakeholders (e.g., teachers, mathematics specialists, administrators, educational leaders and policy makers) support and implement "strongly recommended, research-informed actions" (p. 4) for strengthening teaching and learning. In short, students must have access to impactful instruction, curriculum, technology, learning supports and enrichment opportunities (National Council of Teachers of Mathematics, 2014). Moreover, when students struggle to learn mathematics well, even when emersed in high-quality learning environments, teachers must also be able to skillfully identify student misunderstandings and effectively and efficiently address them. All students' mathematical preparedness for employment and/or post-secondary education, and especially struggling learners and SWDs, depends on a fundamentally different way of teaching and learning mathematics.

NCTM's perspective on teaching and learning is grounded in the National Research Council's (NRC, 2001) publication titled, *Adding It Up: Helping Children Learn Mathematics*. This seminal document offers a synthesis of research from cognitive psychology and mathematics education for defining *mathematical proficiency,* or the mathematical knowledge, skills, and dispositions needed by all pre-kindergarten through eighth grade students for successfully learning mathematics. Mathematical proficiency involves the development of five interdependent strands: (1) *conceptual understanding* ("integrated and functional grasp of mathematical ideas"), (2) *procedural fluency* ("knowledge of procedures…when and how to use them appropriately…flexibly, accurately, and efficiently"), (3) *strategic competence* ("ability to formulate mathematical problems, represent them, and solve them"), (4) *adaptive reasoning* ("capacity to think logically about relationships among concepts and situations"), and (5) *productive disposition* ("to see sense in mathematics, to perceive it as both useful and worthwhile, to believe that steady effort in learning mathematics pays off, and to see oneself as an effective learner and doer of mathematics") (NRC, 2001, pp. 118, 121, 124, 129, 131). Achieving the lofty goal of mathematical proficiency for all students demands that teachers develop deep understandings of the mathematical content they are expected to teach (Ball et al., 2008) and at the same time aware of all five strands of proficiency as they plan and teach math to students.

The "strongly recommended, research-informed…high-leverage practices" in *Principles to Actions* (National Council of Teachers of Mathematics, 2014, p. 4, 9) for strengthening students' mathematics knowledge have been articulated in eight Mathematics Teaching Practices. These practices are listed in Table 11.1, along with brief explanations of each practice.

For SWD and other struggling mathematics learners in inclusive mathematics classrooms, *Principles to Actions* advocates "high-quality mathematics curriculum, effective teaching and learning, high expectations, and the support and resources needed to maximize their learning potential." (NCTM, 2014, p. 59). Specifically, the support and resources recommended include monitoring student progress with both formative and summative assessment data for designing interventions based on specific learning difficulties and achieving learning goals. Special education teachers and mathematics resource teachers, or math coaches (Ellington et al., 2017), are viewed as sources of support. For example, mathematics educators and special educators are encouraged to co-teach classes with a smaller than average class size, using the Mathematics Teaching Practices described above along with various tools (e.g., manipulative materials) and technology (e.g., tablet computers, whiteboards). Teachers should also be supported through professional development opportunities and online resources.

Table 11.1 NCTM Mathematics Teaching Practices with Brief Explanations

Mathematics Teaching Practice	*Brief Explanation*
Establish mathematics goals to focus learning	Goals inform instruction, address Standards, reflect learning progressions, and are understood by students.
Implement tasks that promote reasoning and problem solving	High-level student thinking improves learning. Teachers and students use various mathematical representations and strategies to support reasoning and problem solving.
Use and connect mathematical representations	Mathematics can be represented in several ways (e.g., visually, verbally, physically, contextually, symbolically). Students need to make connections among various representations to enhance understanding.
Facilitate meaningful mathematical discourse	Instructional opportunities are provided for students to learn the language of mathematics and how to speak and write about their mathematical understandings.
Pose purposeful questions	Teachers ask questions for several reasons (e.g., to gather information about student understanding for modifying lessons, to probe student thinking about how they arrived at a problem solution, to encourage students to justify their answers).
Build procedural fluency from conceptual understanding	Both conceptual understanding of mathematics and procedural fluency are essential for mathematical proficiency, with fluency being built on students' mathematical understandings.
Support productive struggle in learning mathematics	Opportunities are provided for students to fully engage in challenging mathematics problems with support when needed to persevere without removing all challenging aspects of the problem.
Elicit and use evidence of student thinking	Teachers regularly assess their students' mathematical thinking for making better instructional decisions.

RTI and Research-Based Practices in Mathematics

Beginning in 2010, Karen Karp, Russell Gersten, and representatives from the NCTM and CEC organized and hosted working conferences on RTI and related strategies for teaching and assessment in mathematics with funding from the National Science Foundation. The goals of this effort were to: (a) build a core community of researchers and practitioners from mathematics education and special education to identify, expand, and sustain research needs; (b) identify and improve the research available for teaching mathematics within an RTI model; and (c) develop professional development resources to support teachers' understanding and application of research-based RTI strategies in mathematics. Although a detailing of outcomes of this collaborative effort is beyond the scope of this chapter, early results were presented at both the NCTM and CEC national conferences in 2012, and professional relationships between mathematics education and special education researchers and practitioners developed and have sustained over time. One pivotal outcome of this collaborative effort is that many special education researchers with interest in mathematics embraced the stance that it is important to consider mathematics instruction for struggling learners and SWDs through a mathematics education lens while simultaneously integrating evidence-based practices generated from special education research.

Not unlike the effort described above, the Institute of Education Sciences (IES) practice guides in mathematics represent a collaborative venture among special education and mathematics education researchers and practitioners, as evidenced in the lists of review panelists who served as judges of the best available evidence for teaching math. Of the six current IES Practice Guides for mathematics available on the What Works Clearinghouse (WWC) website (see https://ies.ed.gov/ncee/wwc/Math/), three guides offer recommendations with direct implications for teaching mathematics in inclusive elementary classrooms. The recommendations in these three practice guides are provided below. However, elementary school educators may benefit from the recommendations provided across all six practice guides because they give these teachers a sense of the important experiences with mathematics recommended for young children (e.g., building number sense) and what may be expected of their students in the future in middle school and high school (e.g., facility with algebra). Elementary mathematics instruction may need to reflect the absence of important early experiences and anticipate the demands to come in secondary school for some students. The three highlighted practice guides are presented below, beginning with a purpose statement and followed by a list of recommendations. A brief discussion of supplemental resources found on the WWC website is also provided.

Assisting Students Struggling with Mathematics: Response to Intervention (RtI) for Elementary and Middle Schools was written to "help teachers, principals, and school administrators use Response to Intervention (RtI) to identify students who need assistance in mathematics and to address the needs of those students through focused interventions" (Gersten et al., 2009, p. 1). Eight recommendations addressing the early detection, prevention, and support of struggling mathematics learners follow:

1. Screen all students to identify those at risk for potential mathematics difficulties and provide interventions to students identified as at risk.
2. Instructional materials for students receiving interventions should focus intensely on in-depth treatment of whole numbers in kindergarten through grade 5 and on rational numbers in grades 4 through 8.
3. Instruction during the intervention should be explicit and systematic.
4. Interventions should include instruction on solving word problems that are based on common underlying structures.
5. Intervention materials should include opportunities for students to work with visual representations of mathematical ideas and interventionists should be proficient in the use of visual representations of mathematical ideas.
6. Interventions at all grade levels should devote about 10 minutes in each session to building fluent retrieval of basic arithmetic facts.
7. Monitor the progress of students receiving supplemental instruction and other students who are at risk.
8. Include motivational strategies in tier 2 and tier 3 interventions.

Developing Effective Fractions Instruction for Kindergarten Through 8th Grade is "intended to help educators improve students' understanding of, and problem-solving success with, fractions" (Siegler et al., 2010, p. 7). Because SWD and other struggling learners experience persistent difficulties acquiring fraction knowledge (Hansen et al., 2017) and this knowledge is a strong predictor of achievement in algebra (Siegler et al., 2012), it is essential that teachers develop students' understanding of fractions concepts and ideas to better prepare them to successfully solve computations and word problems involving fractions. Of the five recommendations found below, four address ways teachers can help students better understand and solve fractions problems. The final recommendation targets teachers and building their own understanding of fractions:

1. Build on students' informal understanding of sharing and proportionality to develop initial fraction concepts.
2. Help students recognize that fractions are numbers and that they expand the number system beyond whole numbers.

3. Help students understand why procedures for computations with fractions make sense.
4. Develop students' conceptual understanding of strategies for solving ratio, rate, and proportion problems before exposing them to cross-multiplication as a procedure to use to solve such problems.
5. Professional development programs should place a high priority on improving teachers' understanding of fractions and how to teach them.

Improving Mathematical Problem Solving in Grades 4 Through 8 offers "...recommendations for improving mathematical problem-solving skills, regardless of which curriculum is used" (Woodward et al., 2012, p. 6). Word problem solving is difficult for most students because of the complex solution processes needed to solve these problems (e.g., Jonassen, 2003). For SWDs and other struggling mathematics learners, problem solving becomes an even more difficult task if reading and/or attention problems exist. Five recommendations follow for improving students' word problem solving in mathematics:

1. Prepare problems and use them in whole-class instruction.
2. Assist students in monitoring and reflecting on the problem-solving process.
3. Teach students how to use visual representations.
4. Expose students to multiple problem-solving strategies.
5. Help students recognize and articulate mathematical concepts and notation.

Each recommendation found on the WWC website links noted above are accompanied by a brief video-recorded explanation, with most featuring one of the review panel members. Supplemental resources also provide summary documents and related videos of webinars and interviews.

RTI and Research-Based Intensive Interventions in Mathematics

In addition to the practice guides, we also present several interventions for Tier 2 and Tier 3 mathematics instruction from recently published studies. We begin with an overview of the Taxonomy of Intervention Intensity (Fuchs et al., 2017) as a guide for evaluating interventions that claim to be intensive. The Taxonomy includes the following dimensions: *strength* (evidence of effectiveness for struggling learners); *dosage* (opportunities to respond and receive feedback); *alignment* (aligns with academic skills and grade-appropriate standards); *attention to transfer* (intervention is designed to teach in multiple contexts, environments, and with multiple examples); *comprehensiveness* (incorporates a comprehensive array of explicit instruction principles); and, *behavioral support* (academic intervention incorporates behavioral strategies such as self-regulation and motivation).

Tier 2 instruction typically takes place in homogeneous small groups and provides additional frequency and duration of instruction that is supplemental to Tier 1 (Berkeley et al., 2009). The amount of time suggested for this type of instruction should be at least 30 minutes a day, 4 times a week, and last for a minimum of 8-10 weeks (Fuchs et al., 2010); a total of about 960 to 1,200 minutes of instruction. Within the small groups, teachers or tutors use research-based interventions coupled with systematic and explicit instructional procedures (Bryant et al., 2008). Bryant and colleagues also state the need for "ongoing progress monitoring to assess response to treatment" (p. 48). Students who are still not showing adequate progress after receiving Tier 1 and Tier 2 instruction should then receive more intensive instruction in Tier 3.

Tier 3 instruction is usually delivered as one-on-one tutoring that employs a mix of instructional interventions and is very individualized to the needs of each child (Gersten et al., 2009). Fuchs et al. (2010) suggest that this one-on-one instruction takes place 5 times a week for 60 minutes each day. Additionally, the achievement goals for a student's progress should be set and then activities and instruction should address the student's individual strengths and needs for attaining goals. A rate of progress should be calculated, which allows the teacher to determine the amount of progress the student should make each week or month in order to meet the end goal in a specified amount of time. The student's current progress should then be frequently compared to the targeted rate of progress using weekly progress monitoring. If adequate progress is not being met, the intensity of the instructional program should be increased or revised as needed. Researchers have studied Tier 2 and Tier 3 interventions designed in similar ways to these earlier recommendations. The following interventions were all conducted with struggling mathematics learners in the early elementary years to prevent more significant learning difficulties in the future.

ROOTS

The ROOTS (Clarke et al., 2016) intervention targets the development of young children's number sense and their procedural fluency and conceptual understanding of whole numbers. Number sense "permits a child to flexibly manipulate numbers, use computation methods, and understand strategies for solving real-world and mathematical problems". Children with a developed sense of numbers are able to "use efficient counting strategies, compose and decompose numbers, make magnitude comparisons, and understand mathematical relationships" (Berch, 2005; Clarke et al., 2016, p. 154). ROOTS is a Tier 2 program targeting kindergarten students and delivered during small group instruction within the context of Tier 1, research-based, Early Learning in Mathematics (ELM) core program (Clarke et al., 2011). ROOTS students received all of the ELM instruction plus the ROOTS intervention 3 times per week for 16 to 20 weeks. The ROOTS program consists of 50 lessons, 20 minutes in duration, and involves 4 to 5 brief math activities in each lesson, which translates into the same number of minutes of instruction recommended by Fuchs et al. (2010). The whole number standards in the CCSS (2010) are addressed in ROOTS including: counting and cardinality, number operations, and base 10 place value. Systematic and explicit instruction undergirds the program and lessons are characterized by modeling, guided practice, use of visual representations of mathematics, sequenced examples and non-examples, and academic feedback. The program also provides students with frequent practice opportunities such as verbalizing what they know and are learning about math. These verbalizations allow the teacher to engage all students and individuals and allows for differentiation (e.g., asking for different responses from students aligned with their individual misunderstandings).

Ninety-one percent of the students in the Clarke et al., 2016 study scored below the 10th percentile on the Test of Early Mathematics Ability (TEMA; Ginsburg & Baroody, 2007) with 95% of students in the ROOTS group and 88% of students in the control group, below the 10th percentile. Findings revealed statistically significant differences between students who received ROOTS compared to students in control groups on the TEMA but not on a curriculum-based measure (Early Numeracy Curriculum-Based Measurement; Clarke et al., 2008), both distal measures. However, students in the ROOTS intervention made positive improvements on both measures and the achievement gap was reduced between them and their typically developing peers. Follow-up replication studies of the ROOTS intervention (Clarke et al., 2017; Doabler et al., 2019) reveal positive effects for small groups of both 2:1 and 5:1 ratios of students to teacher, and for the comparable intensive instruction in both groups, thereby supporting conventionally sized groups of five students when using ROOTS.

Fusion

Clarke and his colleagues (Clarke et al., 2014; Cary et al., 2017) have also studied the Tier 2 Fusion intervention designed for first grade struggling mathematics learners, for which they also achieved positive effects on math learning. Fusion is a 60-lesson intervention designed to promote first grade students' proficiency with whole number concepts and skills in two mathematical domains the CCSS (2010) standards: Operations and Algebraic Thinking and Number and Operations in Base Ten for first grade. Within these domains, Fusion focuses on basic number combinations, place value concepts, multi-digit computation without regrouping, and word problem solving. As in the ROOTS intervention, the 60 Fusion lessons include the design principles of systematic and explicit instruction (e.g., Baker et al., 2002) and are delivered 3 times per week for 30 minutes in small groups of 4 to 5 students. The duration of this intervention is about 600 minutes longer than ROOTS and the recommendations from Fuchs et al. (2010), which may be due to the more comprehensive selection of mathematics topics covered in Fusion.

Precision Mathematics Level 1

PM-L1 (Doabler et al., 2019) is a Tier 2 mathematics intervention to teach struggling mathematics learners the foundational concepts and problem-solving skills associated with the CCSS Measurement and Data domain for mathematics in first grade. PM-L1 is composed of eight first grade life science-based units aligned with the Next Generation Science Standards (NGSS; National Research Council, 2013), in which students learn to solve grade-level problems involving measurement and data analysis. This intervention also includes two other features: (a) the teaching of mathematical language and vocabulary, and (b) word problem solving taught by priming the underlying structure of the word problems (Jitendra & Lein, 2015). PM-L1 also incorporates technology activities, guided by the teacher's iPad, and offers individualized instruction on the students' iPads. The program also includes opportunities for mathematical discourse with the teacher and peers. Each unit is taught in small groups of students (4 to 5 per teacher), spans 4 consecutive days, 30 min per session, for 8 weeks (i.e., 32 lessons and about 960 instructional hours). In the Doabler et al. (2019) study, all treatment effects were positive with effect sizes at or greater than 0.19, although findings for most of the measures were not statistically significant. However, PM-L1 students made statistically significant greater gains on a set of researcher-developed CBMs focused on measurement skills (g=0.45). The study also revealed a differential response to PM-L1 for students with number proficiency and early literacy risk factors in favor of PM-L1. That is, gains were greater for treatment students with more intensive needs.

A Tier 3 Intervention

Bryant et al. (2008, 2011) conducted two studies demonstrating the effectiveness of Tier 2 supplemental intervention for first grade students. In the Bryant et al. (2016) study, this Tier 2 intervention was adapted and implemented with 12 second graders who had already received two rounds of the Tier 2 intervention the previous school year but continued to fall at or below the 10th percentile on a proximal measure and below the 16th percentile on a distal measure.

Several adaptations were made to the Tier 2 intervention aligned with the Taxonomy of Intervention Intensity (Fuchs et al., 2017) noted above. First, lesson content on early numeracy concepts and procedures was added, including: (a) counting activities, (b) activities involving magnitude comparisons of numbers and quantities and sequencing of numbers, (c) activities to build an understanding of the base 10 system (e.g., partitioning and grouping of hundreds, tens, and ones; composing and decomposing numbers), (d) activities to build an understanding of addition and related subtraction facts and properties, and (e) fluency building activities. Compared to the Tier 2 intervention dosage, the Tier 3 intervention increased lesson time for 20 to 30 min, and from 4 days a week to 5. In addition, ratios within small groups were reduced from 1 teacher to 5 students in Tier 2, to 1:2 and 1:3 in Tier 3. The Tier 2 lessons were also modified to include a review of previous material, increased checks for understanding, immediate error correction, and both individual and choral responding. Teacher talk was greatly reduced in the Tier 3 lessons to simple questions after modeling. To reduce the cognitive load of the lessons, emphasis was placed on number concepts that were identified as most difficult for students, and a restricted range of numbers was used. For example, instead of using the number range expected in second grade (i.e., 0 to 999), a number range of 1-50 was used for the first two weeks of the 10-week intervention. The concrete-semi-concrete-abstract sequence (Butler et al., 2003) was used in the Tier 2 intervention, but more time was spent on the concrete and semi-concrete stages in Tier 3. Supports were added to the lesson and gradually faded, such as using tallies or dots next to numbers in problems. Also, progress monitoring used once or twice a week in Tier 2 was used daily in Tier 3. On the last day of each week, additional practice was added to the Tier 3 intervention in the form of a game to reinforce concepts taught that week. All students involved in the study also received core (Tier 1) mathematics instruction. Results revealed that most of the students experienced significant improvement, scoring at or above the 25th percentile, which allowed them to exit the Tier 3 intervention.

Setting the Course for Effective Inclusion

As research evolves to further enhance inclusive elementary mathematics teaching and learning, RTI offers an important framework for continuing to explore issues that require careful consideration today and in the future. In this chapter, we reviewed literature broadly across areas related to RTI, including professional collaboration, professional preparation and teacher development, instructional research, and school and classroom practice, from the perspectives of two professional fields in education (i.e., mathematics education and special education). Reflecting on the literature presented and insights revealed in this chapter, we conclude with several recommendations for future research, policy, and practice.

In regard to **professional collaboration**, efforts have been made to enhance relationships and encourage knowledge-sharing between special educators and mathematics educators at both the national level and through individual efforts (e.g., one of the authors of this chapter is a mathematics educator). Although important progress has been made over the past decade, more can be done in this area. Successful examples of collaboration between special educators and mathematics educators are rare in the literature. A couple of articles that we mention here (Hord et al., 2016; Lynch et al., 2018) offer descriptions of the end products of collaboration (i.e., helping struggling mathematics students in difficult learning situations), but these examples tell us little about how the professionals arrived at their solutions. Knowing more about the process of collaboration across special education and mathematics education may help initiate and enhance working relationships in the future. NCTM and CEC may provide leadership and guidance for how professionals with potentially different knowledge and views about teaching and learning can come together to impact student learning in significant ways.

In the area of **teacher preparation and teacher professional development**, the recent development of HLPs is a critically important step to ensuring that teachers know and can implement essential practices for promoting school success for all students. However, the literature suggests that teachers, particularly elementary school teachers, lack a deep understanding of the mathematics content they teach. Mathematics knowledge for teaching, or the lack thereof, has the potential to impact students' mathematics performance in either positive or deleterious ways. Moreover, teacher knowledge of how individuals and diverse groups of students learn is equally important. Coupling HLPs with the mathematics content taught and what is known about students with learning disabilities in mathematics are important associations to explore in teacher education and professional development programs. Griffin et al. (2018) offer an example of how this might be accomplished in an online, teacher professional development program focused on teacher content knowledge for teaching mathematics and the needs of SWDs and other struggling learners in inclusive classrooms. Elementary school teachers should know and be able to effectively teach the mathematics content they are responsible for and address students' various learning needs. If they are unable to do so, resource teachers, such as math coaches and/or learning support specialists, must be readily available to assist. Additional research addressing all of these areas is sorely needed.

Recent advances in **research involving RTI and mathematics** have been encouraging, with researchers learning more about the impact of Tier 2 and Tier 3 interventions with low-performing students and students with the most persistent learning difficulties in math. However, few studies have examined the impact of Tier 1 research-based core mathematics programs and Tier 2 or Tier 3 intervention programs in combination. More studies that examine how intensive intervention supports generalize to core instruction are needed. In addition, most Tier 2 and Tier 3 intervention studies have focused on Number and Operations in Base Ten (CCSS, 2010). We identified only one study that addressed another mathematics domain (i.e., Measurement and Data; Doabler et al., 2019). Further research on Tier 2 and Tier 3 interventions in mathematics are needed across all domains, but also in areas less well researched (e.g., Geometry, Operations & Algebraic Thinking). It is also important to mention that all of Tier 2 and Tier 3 interventions reviewed in this chapter were grounded in the CCSS, an essential connection for achieving access and progress in the general education curriculum for SWD. Finally, future research on Tier 2 and Tier 3 interventions might also apply a treatment intensity framework, such as the Fuchs et al. 2017 Taxonomy, evidenced in the Bryant et al. (2016) study. In general, longitudinal studies of the effects of intensive interventions are also indicated.

As research is translated into **schools and classrooms,** improving treatment fidelity for both instructional programs, specific interventions, and HLPs is recommended. Schools may also benefit from more specific guidelines for implementing RTI in mathematics, given results of recent studies suggesting that teachers need this information, especially in the areas of EBPs and data decision making. As noted earlier, Fuchs and Fuchs (2017) recommend that systems be designed locally and reflect a balance between what is effective and what is doable. This suggestion may allow districts to make decisions about RTI implementation and selection of intervention programs that are better aligned with the learning needs of their students and the priorities of their communities as they work to promote the success of all their mathematics learners.

References

Aguirre, J., Mayfeld-Ingram, K., & Martin, D. B. (2013). *The impact of identity in K-8 mathematics.* National Council of Teachers of Mathematics.

Al Otaiba, S., Baker, K., Lan, P., Allor, J., Rivas, B., Yovanoff, P., & Kamata, A. (2019). Elementary teacher's knowledge of response to intervention implementation: A preliminary factor analysis. *Annals of Dyslexia, 69*(1), 34–53. doi:10.1007/s11881-018-00171-5

Ball, D. L. (1990). The mathematical understandings that prospective teachers bring to teacher education. *Elementary School Journal, 90*(4), 449–466.

Ball, D. L. (1992). Magical hopes: Manipulatives and the reform of mathematics education. *American Educator, 16*(2), 14–18, 46-47.

Ball, D. L. & Forzani, F. M. (2009). The work of teaching and the challenge for teacher education. *Journal of Teacher Education, 60*(5), 497–511. doi:10.1177/0022487109348479

Ball, D. L. & Forzani, F. M. (2011). Building a common core for learning to teach: And connecting professional learning to practice. *American Educator, 35*(2), 17–21.

Ball, D. L., Thames, M. H., & Phelps, G. (2008). Content knowledge for teaching: What makes it special? *Journal of Teacher Education, 59*(5). doi:10.1177%2F0022487108324554.

Baker, S. K., Gersten, R. M., & Lee, D.S. (2002). A synthesis of empirical research on teaching mathematics to low-achieving students. *The Elementary School Journal, 103*, 51–73.

Barrio, B. L. & Combes, B. H. (2015). General education pre-service teachers' levels of concern on response to intervention (RTI) implementation. *Teacher Education and Special Education, 38*(2), 121–137. doi:10.1177/0888406414546874

Baxter, J. A., Woodward, J. & Olson, D. (2001). Effects of reform-based mathematics instruction on low achievers in five third-grade classrooms. *The Elementary School Journal, 101*(5), 529–547.

Baxter, J. A., Woodward, J., Voorhies, J., & Wong, J. (2002). We talk about it, but do they get it? *Learning Disabilities Research & Practice, 17*(3), 173–185. doi:10.1111/1540-5826.00043

Benedict, A.E., Brownell, M., Bettini, E., & Sohn, H. (2020). Learning together: Teachers' evolving understanding of coordinated word study instruction within an RTI framework. *Teacher Education and Special Education*. doi:10.1177/0888406420930686.

Berch, D.B. (2005). Making sense of number sense. *Journal of Learning Disabilities, 38*, 333–339.

Berkeley, S., Bender, W.N., Peaster, L.G., & Saunders, L. (2009). Implementation of Response to Intervention: A snapshot of progress. *Journal of Learning Disabilities, 42*(1), 85–95.

Billingsley, B., Bettini, E., & Jones, N. D. (2019). Supporting special education teacher induction through high-leverage practices. *Remedial and Special Education, 40*(6), 365–379. doi:10.1177/0741932518816826

Booth, J. L., & Newton, K. J. (2012). Fractions: Could they really be the gatekeeper's doorman? *Contemporary Educational Psychology, 37*, 247–253.

Bottge, B., Heinrichs, M., Mehta, Z. D., & Hung, Y. (2002). Weighing the benefits of anchored math instruction for students with disabilities in the general education classes. *The Journal of Special Education, 35*(4), 186–200. doi:10.1177/002246690203500401

Bottge, B. A., Toland, M. D., Gassaway, L., Butler, M., Choo, S., Griffen, A. K., Ma, X. (2015). Impact of enhanced anchored instruction in inclusive math classrooms. *Exceptional Children, 81*(2), 158–175. doi:10.1177/0014402914551742

Bransford, J. D., Brown, A. L., & Cocking R. R. (2000). *How people learn: Brain, mind, experience, and school*. National Academy Press.

Bryant, B. R., Bryant, D. P., Porterfield, J., Dennis, M. S., Falcomata, T., Valentine, C., Brewer, C., & Bell, K. (2016). The effects of a tier 3 intervention on the mathematics performance of second grade students with severe mathematics difficulties. *Journal of Learning Disabilities, 49*(2), 176–188. doi:10.1177/0022219414538516

Bryant, D. P., Bryant, B. R., Gersten, R. M., Scammacca, N. N., Funk, C., Winter, A., Shih, M., & Pool, C. (2008). The effects of Tier 2 intervention on the mathematics performance of first-grade students who are at risk for mathematics difficulties. *Learning Disability Quarterly, 31*(2), 47–63. doi:10.2307/20528817

Bryant, D. P., Bryant, B. R., Roberts, G., Vaughn, S., Pfannenstiel, K. H., Porterfield, J., & Gersten, R. M. (2011). Early numeracy intervention program for first-grade students with mathematics difficulties. *Exceptional Children, 78*, 7–23. doi:10.1177/F001440291107800101

Butler, F. M., Miller, S. P., Crehan, K., Babbit, B., & Pierce, T. (2003). Fraction instruction for students with mathematics disabilities: Comparing two teaching sequences. *Learning Disabilities Research & Practice, 18*, 99–111.

Carpenter, T.P., Fennema, E., Franke, M.L., Levi, L. & Empson, S.B. (1999). *Children's mathematics: Cognitively guided instruction*. Heinemann.

Cary, M. G., Clarke, B., Doabler, C. T., Smolkowski, K., Fien, H., & Baker, S. K., (2017). A practitioner implementation of a tier 2 first-grade mathematics intervention. *Learning Disability Quarterly, 40*(4), 211–224. doi:10.1177/0731948717714715

Castillo, J. M., March, A. L., Tan, S. Y., Stockslager, K. M., & Brundage, A. (2016). Relationships between ongoing professional development and educators' beliefs relative to response to intervention. *Journal of Applied School Psychology, 32*(4), 287–312. doi:10.1080/15377903.2016.1207736

Castro-Villarreal, F., Rodriguez, B. J., & Moore, S. (2014). Teachers' perceptions and attitudes about response to intervention (RTI) in their schools: A qualitative analysis. *Teaching and Teacher Education, 40*, 104–112. doi:10.1016/j.tate.2014.02.004

Clarke, B., Baker, S., Smolkowski, K., & Chard, D.J. (2008). An analysis of early numeracy curriculu7m-based measurement: Examining the role of growth in student outcomes. *Remedial and Special Education, 29(1)*, 46–57. doi:10.1177/0741932507309694

Clarke, B., Doabler, C., Smolkowski, K., Baker, S. K., Fien, H., Doabler, C.T., & Chard, D.J. (2011). The impact of a comprehensive Tier 1 core kindergarten program on the achievement of students at risk in mathematics. *The Elementary School Journal, 111*(4), 561–584. doi:10.1086/659033

Clarke, B., Doabler, C., Cary, M.S., Kosty, D., Baker, S. K., Fien, H., & Smolkowski, K. (2014). Preliminary evaluation of a Tier 2 mathematics intervention for first-grade students: Using a theory of change to guide formative evaluation activities. *School Psychology Reviewl, 43*(2), 160–178. doi:10.1080/02796015.2014.12087442

Clarke, B., Doabler, C. T., Smolkowski, K., Baker, S. K., Fien, H., & Cary, M. S. (2016). Examining the efficacy of a tier 2 kindergarten mathematics intervention. *Journal of Learning Disabilities*, *49*(2), 152–165. doi:10.1177/0022219414538514

Clarke, B., Doabler, C.T., Kosty, D., Kurtz-Nelson, E., Smolkowski, K., Fien, H., & Baker, S.K. (2017). Testing the efficacy of a kindergarten mathematics intervention by small group size. *AERA Open*, *3*(2), 1–16.

Cook, B. G., Smith, G. J., Tankersley, M. (2012). Evidence-based practices in education. In Harris, K. R., Graham, S., Urdan, T. (Eds.), *APA educational psychology handbook*, (Vol. 1, pp. 495–528). American Psychological Association.

Council for Exceptional Children. (n.d.-a). *CEC Advanced Level Special Educator Preparation Standards*. Retrieved from https://exceptionalchildren.org/standards/advanced-special-education-preparation-standards.

Council for Exceptional Children. (n.d.-b). *CEC Initial Level Special Educator Preparation Standards*. Retrieved from https://exceptionalchildren.org/standards/initial-special-education-preparation-standards.

Doabler, C. T., Clarke, B., Kosty, D., Kurtz-Nelson, E., Fien, H., Smolkowski, K., & Baker, S. K. (2019). Examining the impact of group size on the treatment intensity of a tier 2 mathematics intervention within a systematic framework of replication. *Journal of Learning Disabilities*, *52*(2), 168–180. doi:10.1177/0022219418789376

Doabler, C. T., Clarke, B., Kosty, D., Turtura, J. E., Firestone, A. R., Smolkowski, K., Jungjohann, K., Brafford, T. L., Nelson, N. J., Sutherland, M., Fien, H., & Maddox, S. A. (2019). Efficacy of a first-grade mathematics intervention on measurement and data analysis. *Exceptional Children*, *86*(1), 77–94. doi:10.1177/001440291 9857993

Ellington, A., Whitenack, J., Trinter,C., & Fennell, F.S. (2017). Preparing and implementing successful mathematics coaches and teacher leaders, *Journal of Mathematical Behavior*, *46*, 146–151.

Ellis, M. (2008). Leaving no child behind yet allowing none too far ahead: Ensuring (in)equity in mathematics education through the science of measurement and instruction. *Teachers College Record*, *110*(6), 1330–1356.

Every Student Succeeds Act of 2015, Pub. L. No. 114-95 § 114 Stat. 1177 (2015-2016).

Fairbanks, C. M., Duffy, G. G., Faircloth, B. S., He, Y., Levin, B., Rohr, J., & Stein, C. (2010). Beyond knowledge: Exploring why some teachers are more thoughtfully adaptive than others. *Journal of Teacher Education*, *61*, 161–171. doi:10.1177/0022487109347874

Friend, M. & Cook, L. (2017). *Interactions: Collaboration skills for school professionals* (8th ed.). Pearson.

Fuchs, D. & Fuchs, L. S. (2017). Critique of the national evaluation of response to intervention: A case for simpler frameworks. *Exceptional Children*, *83*(3), 255–268. doi:10.1177/0014402917693580

Fuchs, D., Fuchs, L. S., & Compton, D. L. (2012). Smart RTI: A next-generation approach to multilevel prevention. *Exceptional Children*, *78*(3), 263–279. doi:10.1177/001440291207800301

Fuchs, D., Fuchs, L. S., & Stecker, P. M. (2010). The "blurring" of special education in a new continuum of general education placements and services. *Exceptional Children*, *76*(3). doi:10.1177/001440291007600304.

Fuchs, L. S., Compton, D. L., Fuchs, D., Paulsen, K., Bryant, J. D., Hamlett, C. L. (2005). The prevention, identification, and cognitive determinants of math difficulty. *Journal of Educational Psychology*, *97*, 493–513.

Fuchs, L. S., Fuchs, D., Craddock, C., Hollenbeck, K. N., Hamlett, C. L., Schatschneider, C. (2008). Effects of small-group tutoring with and without validated classroom instruction on at-risk students' math problem solving: Are two tiers of prevention better than one? *Journal of Educational Psychology*, *100*, 491–509.

Fuchs, L. S., Fuchs, D., & Malone A. S. (2017). The taxonomy of intervention intensity. *Teaching Exceptional Children*, *50*(1), 35–43.

Fuchs, L. S., Powell, S. R., Seethaler, P. M., Cirino, P. T., Fletcher, J. M., Fuchs, D., Hamlett, C. L., & Zumeta, R. O. (2009). Remediating number combination and word problem deficits among students with mathematics difficulties: A randomized control trial. *Journal of Educational Psychology*, *101*, 561–576. doi:10.1 037/a0014701

Fuchs, L. S., Sterba, S. K., Fuchs, D., & Malone, A. S. (2016). Does evidence-based fractions intervention address the needs of very low-performing students? *Journal of Research on Educational Effectiveness*, *9*, 662–677.

Geary, D. C. (1993). Mathematical disabilities: Cognitive, neuropsychological, and genetic components. *Psychological Bulletin*, *114*(2), 345–362. doi:10.1037/0033-2909.114.2.345

Geary, D. C. (2004). Mathematics and learning disabilities. *Journal of Learning Disabilities*, *37*(1). doi:10.1177%2 F00222194040370010201.

Gersten, R. (2016). What we are learning about mathematics interventions and conducting research on mathematics interventions. *Journal of Research on Educational Effectiveness*, *9*, 684–688.

Gersten, R., Beckmann, S., Clarke, B., Foegen, A., Marsh, L., Star, J. R., & Witzel, B. (2009). *Assisting students struggling with mathematics: Response to Intervention (RtI) for elementary and middle schools* (NCEE 2009-4060). National Center for Education Evaluation and Regional Assistance, Institute of Education Sciences, U.S. Department of Education. http://ies.ed.gov/ncee/wwc/publications/practiceguides/

Gersten, R., Jayanthi, M., & Dimino, J. (2017). Too much, too soon? Unanswered questions from national response to intervention evaluation. *Exceptional Children, 83*(3), 244–254.

Ginsburg, H. P., & Baroody, A. J. (2007). *TEMA-3: Test of Early Mathematics Ability-Third Edition.* PRO-ED.

Griffin, C. C., Jitendra, A. K., & League, M. B. (2009). Special educators' instructional practices, communication patterns, and content knowledge for teaching mathematics. *Teacher Education and Special Education, 32*(4), 319–336.

Griffin, C. C., Dana, N. F., Pape, S. J., Algina, J., Bae, J., Prosser, S. K., & League, M. B. (2018). *Prime Online*: Exploring teacher professional development for creating inclusive elementary mathematics classrooms. *Teacher Education and Special Education, 41*(2), 121–139. doi:10.1177/0888406417740702

Gomez-Najarro, J. (2020). An empty seat at the table: Examining general and special education teacher collaboration in response to intervention. *Teacher Education and Special Education, 43*(2), 109–126. doi:10.1177/0888406419850894

Hansen, N., Jordan, N. C., & Rodrigues, J. (2017). Identifying learning difficulties with fractions: A longitudinal study of student growth from third through sixth grade. *Contemporary Educational Psychology, 50*, 45–59. doi:10.1016/j.cedpsych.2015.11.002

Hansen, N., Jordan, N. C., Fernandez, E., Siegler, R. S., Fuchs, L., Gersten, R., & Micklos, D. (2015). General and math-specific predictors of sixth-graders' knowledge of fractions. *Cognitive Development, 35*, 34–49. doi:10.1016/j.cogdev.2015.02.001

Heaton, R. M. (1992). Who is minding the mathematics content? A case study of a fifth-grade teacher. *The Elementary School Journal, 93*(2), 153–162.

Heaton, R. M. (2000). *Teaching mathematics to the new standard: Relearning the dance* (Vol. 15). Teachers College Press.

Hill, H. C., Rowan, B., & Ball, D. L. (2005). Effects of teachers' mathematical knowledge for teaching on student achievement. *American Educational Research Journal, 42*(2), 371–406.

Hill, H. C., Blunk, M. L., Charalambous, C. Y., & Lewis, J. M. (2008). Mathematical knowledge for teaching and the mathematical quality of instruction: An exploratory study. *Cognition and Instruction, 26*(4), 430–511.

Holzberger, D., Philipp, A., & Kunter, M. (2013). How teachers' self-efficacy is related to instructional quality: A longitudinal analysis. *Journal of Educational Psychology, 105*(3), 774–786. doi:10.1037/a0032198

Hord, C., Marita, S., Walsh, J. B., Tomaro, T. M., & Gordon, K. (2016). Encouraging students with learning disabilities. *Mathematics Teacher, 109*(8), 612–617.

Individuals with Disabilities Education Act (2004), 20 U.S.C. §§ 1400-1487.

Janssen, F., Grossman, P., & Westbrook, H. (2015). Facilitating decomposition and recomposition in practice-based teacher education: The power of modularity. *Teaching and Teacher Education, 51*, 137–146. doi:10.1016/j.tate.2015.06.009.

Jitendra, A.K., & Lein, A. (2015). Strategy instruction that primes the problem structure. *Current Practice Alerts, 22*, 1–5.

Jonassen, D.H. (2003). Designing research-based instruction for story problems. Educational *Psychology Review, 15*, 267–296.

Jordan, N. C., Hanich, L. B., & Kaplan, D. (2003). A longitudinal study of mathematical competencies in children with specific mathematics difficulties verses children with comorbid mathematics and reading difficulties. *Child Development, 74*(3), 834–850.

Jordan, N. C., Hansen, N., Fuchs, L. S., Siegler, R. S., Gersten, R., & Micklos, D. (2013). Developmental predictors of fraction concepts and procedures. *Journal of Experimental Child Psychology, 116*(1), 45–58. doi:10.1016/j.jecp.2013.02.001

Jordan, N. C., Resnick, I., Rodrigues, J., Hansen, N., Dyson, N. (2017). Delaware longitudinal study of fraction learning: Implications for helping children with mathematics difficulties. *Journal of Learning Disabilities, 50*, 621–630.

Knuth, E. J. (2002). Secondary school mathematics teachers' conceptions of proof. *Journal for Research in Mathematics Education, 33*(5), 379–405.

Lampert, M., Franke, M. L., Kazemi, E., Ghousseini, H., Turrou, A. C., Beasley, H., Cunard, A., & Crowe, K. (2013). Keeping it complex: Using rehearsals to support novice teacher learning of ambitious teaching. *Journal of Teacher Education, 64*(3), 226–243. doi:10.1177/0022487112473837

Leko, M. M., Brownell, M. T., Sindelar, P. T., & Kiely, M. T. (2015). Envisioning the future of special education personnel preparation in a standards-based era. *Exceptional Children, 82*(1), 25–43. doi:10.1177/0014402915598782

Lynch, S. D., Hunt, J. H., & Lewis, K. E. (2018). Productive struggle for all: Differentiated instruction. *Mathematics Teaching in the Middle School, 23*(4), 194–201.

Ma, L. (2010). *Knowing and teaching elementary mathematics: Teachers' understanding of fundamental mathematics in China and the United States* (2nd ed.). Routledge.

Mazzocco, M. M. M., & Devlin, K. T. (2008). Parts and 'holes': Gaps in rational number sense among children with vs. without mathematical learning disabilities. *Developmental Science, 11*, 681–691. doi:10.1111/j.1467-7687.2008.00717.x

Mazzocco, M. M. M., Murphy, M. M., Brown, E. C., Rinne, L., & Herold, K. H. (2013). Persistent consequences of atypical early number concepts. *Frontiers in Psychology, 4*, 486. doi:10.3389/fpsyg.2013.00486

McDonald, M., Kazemi, E., & Kavanagh, S. S. (2013). Core practices and pedagogies of teacher education: A call for a common language and collective activity. *Journal of Teacher Education, 64*(5). doi:10.1177%2F00224 87113493807.

McLeskey, J., Barringer, M-D., Billingsley, B., Brownell, M., Jackson, D., Kennedy, M., Lewis, T., Maheady, L., Rodriguez, J., Scheeler, M. C., Winn, J., & Ziegler, D. (2017, January). *High-leverage practices in special education.* Council for Exceptional Children & CEEDAR Center.

McLeskey, J., Billingsley, B., Brownell, M. T., Maheady, L., & Lewis, T. J. (2019). What are high-leverage practices for special education teachers and why are they important? *Remedial and Special Education, 40*(6), 331–337. doi:10.1177/0741932518773477

Nagro, S. A., Hooks, S. D., & Fraser, D. W. (2019). Over a decade of practice: Are educators correctly using tertiary interventions? *Preventing School Failure: Alternative Education for Children and Youth, 63*(1), 52–61. doi:10.1080/1045988X.2018.1491021

National Council of Teachers of Mathematics. (2000). *Principles and standards for school mathematics.* Author.

National Council of Teachers of Mathematics. (2007). *Curriculum focal points.* Author.

National Council of Teachers of Mathematics. (2014). *Principles to actions.* Author.

National Council of Teachers of Mathematics. (2020). *Catalyzing change in early childhood and elementary mathematics.* Author.

National Governors Association Center for Best Practices, Council of Chief State School Officers (2010). *Common core state standards—mathematics.* National Governors Association Center for Best Practices, Council of Chief State School Officers: Authors.

National Mathematics Advisory Panel. (2008). *Foundations for success: The final report of the National Mathematics Advisory Panel.* U.S. Department of Education. http://www.ed.gov/about/bdscomm/list/mathpanel/report/final-report.pdf

National Research Council. (2001). Adding it up: Helping children learn mathematics. J Kilpatrick, J. Swafford, and B. Findell (Eds.), *Math learning study committee, center for education, division of behavioral and social sciences and education.* National Academy Press.

Nelson, G., Pfannenstiel, K. H., and Edmonds, R. Z. (2019). Examining the alignment of mathematics instructional practices and mathematics vocabulary between core and intervention materials. *Learning Disabilities Research & Practice, 35*(1). doi:10.1111/ldrp.12210

Office of Special Education and Rehabilitative Services. (2007). *Questions and answers on response to intervention (RTI) and early intervening services (EIS)* [USDOE publication]. https://sites.ed.gov/idea/files/07-0021.RTI_.pdf

Sayeski, K. L., Hamilton-Jones, B., Cutler, G., Earle, G. A., & Husney, L. (2019). The role of practice and feedback for developing teacher candidate's opportunities to respond to expertise. *Teacher Education and Special Education, 42*(1), 18–35. doi:10.1177/0888406417735876

Schwartz, D. L., Bransford, J. D. & Sears, D. (2005). Efficiency and innovation in transfer. In *Transfer of Learning from a modern multidisciplinary perspective.* Information Age Publishing.

Shaughnessy, M., DeFino, R., Pfaff, E., & Blunk, M. (2020). I think I made a mistake: How do prospective teachers elicit the thinking of a student who has made a mistake? *Journal of Mathematics Teacher Education,* doi:10.1007/s10857-020-09461-5.

Shin, M. & Bryant, D. P. (2015). Fraction interventions for students struggling to learn mathematics: A research synthesis. *Remedial and Special Education, 36*(6), 374–387. doi:10.1177/0741932515572910

Shin, M., Bryant, D. P., Bryant, B. R., & McKenna, J. W. (2017). Virtual manipulatives: Tools for teaching mathematics to students with learning disabilities. *Intervention in School and Clinic, 52*(3), 148–153.

Siegler, R. S. (2005). Children's learning. *American Psychologist, 60*(8), 769–778. doi:10.1037/0003-066X.60.8.769

Siegler, R. S., Carpenter, T., Fennell, F., Geary, D., Lewis, J., Okamoto, Y., Thompson, L., & Wray, J. (2010). *Developing effective fractions instruction for kindergarten through 8th grade: A practice guide* (NCEE #2010-4039). National Center for Education Evaluation and Regional Assistance, Institute of Education Sciences, U.S. Department of Education. http://whatworks.ed.gov/%20publications/practiceguides.

Siegler, R. S., Duncan, G. J., Davis-Kean, P. E., Duckworth, K., Claessens, A., Engel, M., Susperreguy, M. I., & Chen, M. (2012). Early predictors of high school mathematics achievement. *Psychological Science, 23*(7), 691–697. doi:10.1177/0956797612440101

Sleep, L. (2012). The work of steering instruction toward the mathematical point: A decomposition of teaching practice. *American Educational Research Journal, 49*(5), 935–970. doi:10.3102/0002831212448095

Stein, M. K., Smith, M. S., Henningsen, M. A., & Silver, E. A. (2000). *Implementing standards-based mathematics instruction: A casebook for professional development.* Teacher College.

Stiff, L. V., Johnson, J. L., & Akos, P. (2011). Examining what we know for sure: tracking in middle grades mathematics. InW. Tate, K. King, & C. R. Anderson (Eds.), *Disrupting tradition: research and practice pathways in mathematics education* (pp. 63–75). National Council of Teachers of Mathematics.

Swanson, E., Solis, M., Ciullo, S., & McKenna, J.W. (2012). Special education teachers' perceptions and instructional practices in response to intervention implementation. *Learning Disability Quarterly, 35*(2), 115–126.

Swanson, H. L., Lussier, C. M., & Orosco, M. J. (2015). Cognitive strategies, working memory, and growth in word problem solving in children with math difficulties. *Journal of Learning Disabilities, 48*(4), 339–358. doi:10.1177/0022219413498771

TeachingWorks. (n.d.) *Teaching works grew out of the Teacher Education Initiative (TEI) at the University of Michigan.* TeachingWorks. Retrieved September 27, 2020 from http://www.teachingworks.org/about/history

TeachingWorks. (2019, August). *High-leverage practices.* TeachingWorks Resource Library. Retrieved September 29, 2020 from https://library.teachingworks.org/curriculum-resources/high-leverage-practices/

Walshaw, M., & Anthony, G. (2008). The teacher's role in classroom discourse: A review of recent research into mathematics classrooms. *Review of Educational Research, 78*(3), 516–551. doi:10.3102/0034654308320292

Woodward, J., Beckmann, S., Driscoll, M., Franke, M., Herzig, P., Jitendra, A., Koedinger, K. R., & Ogbuehi, P. (2012). *Improving mathematical problem solving in grades 4 through 8: A practice guide* (NCEE 2012-4055). National Center for Education Evaluation and Regional Assistance, Institute of Education Sciences, U.S. Department of Education. http://ies.ed.gov/ncee/wwc/publications_reviews.aspx#pubsearch/

Zirkel, P. A., & Thomas, L. B. (2010). State laws and guidelines for implementing RTI. *Teaching Exceptional Children, 43*(1), 60–73. doi:10.1177/004005991004300107

12

Writing in Inclusive Elementary Schools: To Be a Writer or Not to Be a Writer

Linda H. Mason[1], *Shawn Datchuk*[2], *and Stacie Brady*[1]

[1]GEORGE MASON UNIVERSITY

[2]UNIVERSITY OF IOWA

Setting the Stage

Few would argue the importance of elementary school instruction for establishing the foundational knowledge and skills needed for future academic success. Students who develop strong writing skills in elementary school gain a tool that will support learning, communication, and self-expression throughout their schooling (Graham, Bollinger et al., 2012). In point of fact, learning to write is critical to students' future success (Graham, 2019).

For students with disabilities, writing is challenging. Writing requires the coordination of multiple metacognitive and self-regulatory skills to learn and apply basic skills to produce a written product (Graham & Harris, 1996). Students with learning disabilities, for example, often have difficulties in basic transcription skills such as handwriting and spelling, in writing effective sentences, and in brainstorming ideas and organizing those ideas for written expression (Taft & Mason, 2011). Students with attention and behavioral disabilities, in addition to having the difficulties noted above, may lack goal setting and the self-monitoring skills needed to complete a writing task. Students with cognitive, memory, or language disabilities may lack the required vocabulary and grammar skills for writing. Many students with autism, who often think in literal terms, may struggle with writing creatively by using their imagination (Asaro-Saddler & Saddler, 2010). Given the potential difficulties students with disabilities may have when writing, teachers should deliver evidence-based instruction in inclusive classrooms with increasing levels of intensity and continuous progress monitoring.

All That Glitters is Not Gold

National data compels a change in how writing instruction is provided in the United States. The National Assessment of Educational Progress (NAEP) writing assessment, using the comparable scores for writing on a laptop in 2017, indicated lower results when compared to 2011 (National Center for Education Statistics, 2017). Furthermore, NAEP writing results have indicated no statistically significant improvement in closing score gaps for students with disabilities. Poor writing

DOI: 10.4324/9781003043874-12

outcomes for students with disabilities indicate a need for remediating basic skill deficits and for improving students' skills and use of strategies for writing sentences and for planning, composing, revision, and editing written compositions (Graham & Harris, 2003). With intensive intervention, students have the potential to reduce the risk of academic failure (Johnson et al., 2006).

Instructional Context

How is writing instruction provided in the inclusive elementary school classroom? In early grades, handwriting and spelling instruction is often included in early reading instruction. Although 169 surveyed teachers reported having little training for teaching handwriting, 90% noted spending approximately 70 minutes a week on handwriting instruction (Graham et al., 2005). When looking across elementary grades, 168 surveyed teachers reported spending approximately 90 minutes a week for spelling instruction (Graham et al., 2008). The majority of these teachers note using a commercial program, 42% reported making few or no adaptations for weak spellers. In Cutler and Graham (2008), the majority of the 177 teachers surveyed noted teaching sentence construction skills several times a week.

Most teachers support some variation of instruction within the writing process (Brindle et al., 2016; Cutler & Graham, 2008) that includes four overlapping processes—planning, composing, revision, and editing. When planning, a conceptual plan is completed by generating and organizing ideas and by setting goals for the writing task. The plan is then translated into written words, phrases, clauses, and sentences. During revision, the written text is read and modifications are made to content, syntax, and vocabulary. A teacher's use of evidence-based practices for teaching the writing process and for adapting instruction for weak writers is often determined by their beliefs and teacher training (Brindle et al., 2016)

Of the 92% of teachers survey with teacher certification through a teacher education program in Cutler and Graham (2008), only 28% noted that their preparation was either very good or outstanding; 42% noted that their preparation was adequate and 28% noted that their preparation was poor or inadequate. Furthermore, despite the importance of instructional time needed for in-school writing (Graham, Bollinger et al., 2012), teachers report spending only 15 minutes a day teaching writing, with students spending only 25 minutes a day at school writing (Brindle et al., 2016). Poor outcomes for students with disabilities are not surprising, given that teacher preparation in writing instruction and instructional time devoted to this is often insufficient (Ciullo & Mason, 2017).

Instructional Content

Instruction for developing writing skills should be aligned with a student's developmental level for the given task. The relationship of oral language processing, transcription, and short- and long-term memory skills at the sentence level should be considered (Berninger & Amtmann, 2003). What Work Clearinghouse (WWC) recommendations (*Teaching Elementary School Students to Be Effective Writers: A Practice Guide*: Graham, Bollinger et al., 2012) and initiatives in state standards (e.g., National Governors Association Center for Best Practices & Council of Chief State School Officers: NGA & CCSSO, 2010), have provided guidelines for students' writing across grade levels. Handwriting instruction for upper and lower case letters is specific; for example, it should begin by kindergarten and be completed by the end of first grade.

Spelling, sentence writing, and written expression, on the other hand, is graduated across the elementary years. In early elementary years, students learn how to write simple and compound sentence structures with the goal of constructing diverse sentence structures by the end of fourth grade. For written expression, across the elementary grades, students should learn how (1) write to tell a story, persuade, and inform; (2) write with clarity and cohesion, (3) write to meet the task, purpose, and audience; (4) plan their writing; (5) revise and edit; (6) use technology for writing; (7) write short and long responses to demonstrate understanding of subject matter; (8) gather evidence and integrate multiple sources in writing; and (9) write in both short and extended time frames.

In the rest of the chapter, we examine the research base for core areas of writing instruction in the United States. We then set a course for the future by describing research and promising interventions for improving students with disabilities' success in the general education classroom. Technology, ever more important in 2020 when this chapter was written, is also addressed. In each section, we begin by looking at basic skills, many taught at the beginning of elementary school and connect them to instruction that transitions students for middle school and beyond.

What Do We Know Based on Research? What is Past is Prologue

Historically, when compared to published empirical research in reading and mathematics instruction, research for writing instruction is negligible. This phenomenon has set the stage for writing instruction research in elementary and secondary general education classrooms (Slavin et al., 2019). However, in setting the stage for change, writing researchers have established strong lines of empirical research by focusing on improving writing outcomes for students with and at-risk for disabilities. We review this foundational research and describe the instructional approaches for teaching transcription skills, sentence construction, written expression, and writing from text sources.

Transcription Skills

Transcription skills—handwriting, spelling, and word processing—provide a foundation for continued writing development. Research suggests that proficiency in these skills promotes both writing quantity and quality (Kim et al., 2011; Kim & Schatschneider, 2017). Some elementary students have persistent difficulty in acquiring transcription skills (Abbott et al., 2010), and students with disabilities tend to struggle the most. A recent meta-analysis (Graham et al., 2017) reported that students with disabilities significantly underperform their typically-developing peers on measures of handwriting (effect size: ES = −0.78, confidence interval: CI = −1.17, −0.38) and spelling (ES = −1.50, CI = −1.78, −1.22). Recent findings suggest a similar gap may exist for word processing (Foxworth et al., 2019).

Transcription skills of handwriting, spelling, and word processing are interrelated. Handwriting, the production of legible alphabetic letters, is used to produce correctly spelled words. Word processing is an alternative mode of transcription in which letters and words are typed and edited with word-processing tools. There are a variety of word-processing tools; for instance, the computer-administered writing subtest of the National Assessment of Education Progress (NAEP; White et al., 2015) includes tools for editing (i.e., cut/copy/paste, delete, and backspace), formatting (i.e., underline, bold, italicize, highlight, and indent), and word choice (i.e., spell/grammar checker, dictionary, and thesaurus).

Given the interrelated nature of transcription skills, elementary students are expected to make concurrent and gradual progress (Graham, Bollinger et al., 2012; NGA & CCSSO, 2010). By the end of kindergarten and first grade, it is recommended that all students, regardless of disability status, learn how to handwrite upper- and lower-case letters, spell words that follow phonetic rules as well as common irregular words (i.e., do not follow phonetic rules), and begin typing. In later elementary grades, students are expected to develop a more sophisticated knowledge of spelling (e.g., generalize spelling patterns to unknown words and learn new morphemes), to type as fast as they can handwrite, and to type and edit at least a single page of text in a single sitting by the end of fourth grade.

Instructional Approaches for Transcription Skills

Despite debate about the merits of directly addressing transcription skills and the suggestion that passive or incidental approaches are adequate (for a discussion, see Graham & Santangelo, 2014), there is compelling evidence that transcription skills should be explicitly taught through formal instruction and practice. Two recent meta-analyses (Graham & Santangelo, 2014; Santangelo & Graham, 2016) found formal instruction was superior to no instruction on handwriting legibility (ES = 0.59, CI = 0.33-0.85), handwriting fluency, (ES = 0.63, CI = 0.27-0.99), and spelling (ES = 0.54, CI = 0.39-0.70). Some evidence suggests word processing without formal instruction can improve the writing of students with writing difficulties; however, formal instruction is likely needed for students who lack adequate typing fluency or use a limited range of word-processing tools (Foxworth et al., 2019). Compared to their peers, low-performing writers may be less likely to use potentially helpful word-processing tools, such as spell check, or accept suggested automated corrections (White et al., 2015).

Sentence Construction

In addition to transcription skills, sentence construction—writing sentences of different structures, such as simple or compound—is a foundational aspect of written expression that contributes to overall writing quality (Allen et al., 2018). Some elementary students struggle to develop sentence construction, and an achievement gap exists between students with and without disabilities. Two recent meta-analyses (Graham et al., 2016, 2017) found students with high-incidence disabilities—learning disabilities (ES = −0.81, CI = −1.34, −0.29) and those with attention deficit hyperactivity disorder (ES = −0.81, CI = −0.96, −0.46)—tend to produce significantly fewer sentences than their typically-developing peers.

Sentence construction is broadly comprised of two types of skills: text writing and sentence structure. Text writing refers to the transcription of multiple words that follow conventions of semantics, spelling, syntax, and usage (Ritchey et al., 2016). Text writing is used within different sentence structures, ranging from simple sentences to more complicated sentence structures (e.g., compound or complex). Simple sentence structures are comprised of at least one subject and one verb (i.e., an independent clause). More complicated sentence structures feature additional parts of speech, such as multiple subjects or verbs, and sophisticated academic language (e.g., logical connectives, pronoun reference, and verb tense) that can improve the coherence of a text and contribute to high-quality composition (Truckenmiller & Petscher, 2020).

As recommended by state academic standards and researchers (Graham, Bollinger et al., 2012; NGA & CCSSO, 2010), the multiple skills involved in sentence construction (i.e., text writing and sentence structure) are gradually acquired across elementary grades. During kindergarten and first grade, it is expected that elementary students acquire multiple text-writing skills, such as grammar (e.g., singular and plural nouns, adjectives, and verb tense) and usage (e.g., capitalization of beginning sentences and proper nouns), and practice writing simple and compound sentence structures. These skills are further developed in later elementary grades. By the end of third and fourth grade, students are expected to be facile and fluent in constructing diverse sentence structures (i.e., simple, compound, and complex) and to use increasingly sophisticated usage (e.g., quotation marks) and academic language (e.g., pronoun reference and prepositional phrases).

Instructional Approaches for Sentence Construction

To help students learn how to construct different sentence structures, three complementary approaches may prove beneficial (Datchuk & Kubina, 2013; Datchuk et al., 2020): (a) explicit instruction with fluency practice, (b) strategy instruction, and (c) sentence combining with peer-assisted learning strategies. The first approach, explicit instruction and fluency practice, is a promising instructional procedure used to teach simple sentence structure and related text-writing skills of syntax (i.e., nouns, verbs, and subject-verb agreement) and usage (i.e., capitalization and punctuation). In prior studies, students have shown gradual increases in their number of correct writing sequences (CWS) on timed writing tasks (Datchuk, 2017; Datchuk et al., 2015)—CWS is a measure of the number of words within a sentence that correctly uses semantics, syntax, and usage. Of importance, younger, elementary-aged students have shown greater gains from explicit instruction with fluency practice compared to adolescents (Datchuk et al., 2020).

The second approach, strategy instruction or, more specifically, the strategic instructional model (SIM; Schumaker & Deshler, 2003), is used to teach both simple and more complicated sentence structures. The majority of prior research has been conducted with older adolescents (Rogers & Graham, 2008), but some research suggests SIM may be effective for younger, elementary-aged students (Bui et al., 2006). In this approach, students learn a strategy to identify the parts of a complete sentence, then use the strategy to write their own complete sentences. Strategy instruction follows several recursive steps of modeling, guided practice, and independent application.

The third approach, sentence combining with peer-assisted learning strategies, is used to teach more complicated sentence structures, such as simple sentences with multiple nouns and adjectives or compound sentences. In this approach, student dyads are taught how to collaborate with each other and combine kernels (i.e., sentences, phrases, or words) into complicated sentence structures (Saddler & Graham, 2005). As a result of sentence combining, elementary-aged students have not only increased their number of taught sentence structures but also their compositional writing quality (Saddler et al., 2018). Increases in writing quality stem may stem from the fact that students can use sentence combining to edit their compositions, and it prompts students to self-monitor their writing process.

Written Expression

Writing in the early grades can be used to tell a story, give an opinion, or provide information. Writing helps students to communicate their thoughts and ideas, persuade others, organize information, and express themselves creatively. WWC (Graham, Bollinger et al., 2012) provides specific recommendations to help educators teach elementary students to be effective writers. These include develop a supportive writing environment and teach strategies for the writing process.

A supportive writing environment for elementary students includes providing additional daily writing time, providing collaborative writing routines and peer assistance, and contingence praise. In a study with 90 students in fourth grade, for example, Berninger et al. (2006) compared business-as-usual classroom instruction with classroom instruction plus additional instruction through after-school writing clubs. Results (*Fisher statistic* = 4.436, p =.02) demonstrated a significant effect indicating that more children in the writing club group met the state standard in writing on the high stakes test in writing than those in the control group.

In collaborative writing routines, students work together to brainstorm ideas and edit each other's work (Graham, Bollinger et al., 2012). For example, Yarrow and Topping (2001) completed a study comparing paired writing and individual writing. The paired writing group used a writing flow chart that noted the steps to generate ideas, draft, read, edit, best copy, and evaluate. The effect size of the overall writing quality of the experimental group, when compared to the control group, was 0.58. Graham, McKeown's et al. (2012) meta-analysis identified four studies with elementary students that used peer assistance to support writing. The results indicated that students working with peers displayed an increase in writing quality (weighted ES = 0.89).

Graham et al. (2015), in a meta-analysis and a meta-synthesis of research-based writing practices, examined previous writing reviews. Findings from the synthesis noted four single-subject design writing studies that used contingent praise to support writing performance with students in the elementary grades. The researchers noted a large positive effect. The final recommendation, noted by the WWC (Graham, Bollinger et al., 2012), is to teach elementary students to understand the various processes in the writing process as well as understand how to use the strategies in a variety of ways with different genres. Students should be explicitly taught about different genres and should be taught how to write effectively to convey their intended meaning to the proposed audience. According to state academic standards (e.g., NGA & CCSSO, 2010), story writing, opinion writing, and informative writing are types of genres that students are expected to write in elementary school. A specific purpose defines genres (e.g., tell a story, persuade an audience, share information), and each has a different text structure. Students need to understand how to adapt their writing for the intended purpose and for the specific audience. Being able to include these elements requires the writer to plan the composition process effectively and use the self-regulation strategies that are described in the social-cognitive model of writing.

Instructional Approaches for Written Expression

The social-cognitive model of writing requires environmental, behavioral, and personal self-regulation. Self-regulatory environmental processes include manipulating and organizing the environment to create and maintain an effective writing atmosphere. Self-talk and progress monitoring are included with behavioral self-regulation processing. Personal self-regulatory processes involve cognitive processes such as planning, goal setting, outlining, and mental imagery (Mason & Reid, 2018). The social-cognitive model of writing emphasizes that writers must be aware of the readers' expectations and be willing to devote time and energy to compose a text that communicates effectively. In the 1990s, Karen R. Harris developed the self-regulated strategy development (SRSD) instructional model for teaching students with learning disabilities strategies and self-regulation procedures for planning and organizing their writing (Graham & Harris, 1996).

A meta-analysis of writing instruction for students in elementary grades (Graham, McKeown et al., 2012) examined the effectiveness of strategy instruction across 20 studies. Findings indicated all of the strategy instruction studies enhanced the quality of students' writing and produced a positive effect, yielding a statistically significant average weighted ES of 1.02. Fourteen of the twenty studies used SRSD. The average weighted ES for SRSD was 1.17.

Self-Regulated Strategy Development

SRSD (Graham & Harris, 1996) combines explicit instruction for strategy acquisition with self-regulated learning. Theoretical components in students' cognitive development and learning, student behavior, and the role of affect are all utilized in SRSD. SRSD instruction is recursive, instructional stages and lessons can be repeated and revisited (Harris et al., 2008). In SRSD, students are taught to criterion performance, generally noted to be when students have learned to independently apply strategy steps and self-regulation to complete a written task. Six stages for strategy acquisition are included in SRSD lessons:

- *Develop background knowledge.* Prior to introducing a strategy, students' background knowledge and pre-skills for the writing task should be evaluated. The teacher discusses vocabulary (e.g., transition words) and concepts (e.g., components in a good story) and describes how good writers support the writing process by self-regulating their writing.

- *Discuss it.* While discussing each strategy step, the teacher describes and how and when to use the strategy. Anchor or example papers are read, evaluated, and the strategy elements are related to each step are identified. During this early stage, students set goals and commit to learning and using the strategy. Students' current performance can be reviewed and charted at this time or after the next stage, *Model it.*
- *Model it.* A teacher or a peer models how to apply each step of the strategy and how to use self-regulation procedures by "thinking aloud" while writing an authentic story or essay. Modeling includes specific self-instruction for setting goals, planning and organizing notes, composing the written response, evaluating and self-monitoring performance, and using self-reinforcement.
- *Memorize it.* Students begin to memorize the strategy and how to apply it when it is introduced in *Discuss it.* Initially, mnemonic charts are used to support memorization, but these visual supports should be faded over time to support students' independence. Lessons can begin or end with memorization practice by asking students to recite steps.
- *Support it.* Scaffolding students' application of strategies and self-regulation by gradually fading teacher and/or peer support is critical. Revisiting prior lesson and instructional stages by providing booster sessions to reinforce learning is often needed during this stage.
- *Independent performance.* The teacher should provide students with opportunities for independent practice across time and settings. Independent practice supports maintenance and generalization. To check that the student has not lapsed into ineffective writing habits, students' application of writing strategies and self-regulation should be monitored.

Procedures for self-regulation—self-instruction, goal-setting, self-monitoring, and self-reinforcement—are embedded throughout into SRSD (Mason & Reid, 2018). Teachers assist students in setting appropriate individualized goals (i.e., specific, proximal, and appropriately challenging). Goal setting begins prior to writing and is revisited and revised as the students learn the strategy. Students are also taught to reflect on and evaluate their progress in meeting goals by self-monitoring writing performance. Graphing progress towards meeting goals provides the student and the teacher with information about specific areas in need of remediation and is especially effective for students with disabilities. An often ignored but important self-regulation procedure is self-instruction (i.e., the things said in one's head). Students should develop personalized self-instruction for problem definition (e.g., *What is the first step of the strategy?*; focus of attention and planning (e.g., *I need to reread the prompt if I did not understand*; strategy use (e.g., *The first step tells me to write a topic sentence*); self-evaluation and error-correcting (e.g., *The second step tells me to write three reasons. I have only two. I need to write one more.*); and coping and self-control (e.g., *I am tired of writing but I see that I have only two steps left to go. I can do this!*). Self-reinforcement, an ongoing self-regulatory procedure, is supported by positive self-instruction (e.g., *I did it!*) and by graphing progress in meeting goals.

Story Writing

There are four interrelated language systems: speaking, listening, reading, and writing (Shanahan, 2006). Each supports story development. Using language to tell stories is an innate part of being human (Bruner, 1991). Initially, children begin to tell stories orally, assisting them with making sense of their lived experiences. As children are exposed to literacy, they begin to construct oral monologues that have features of storytelling such as intonation, syntax, and lexical structure appropriate for writing (Sulzby, 1996). When writing stories, the student author should include story elements such as characters, settings, problems, ordering temporal events, and solutions.

In an early study, Troia and Graham (2002) used explicit teacher-directed strategy instruction to teach story writing to 20 fourth and fifth grade students with learning disabilities (LD). Troia and Graham compared two groups: a process writing instruction group (comparison group) and an experimental treatment planning strategies group. The experimental group of students was taught planning strategies which included identifying the purpose of the story writing activity, setting appropriate goals, brainstorming ideas, and organizing the ideas using the acronym STOP & LIST (Stop, Think of Purposes, and List Ideas, Sequence Them). Students that were taught explicit teacher-directed strategy instruction spent more time planning and produced stories that were qualitatively better. The posttest scores for the planning strategy treatment group for story quality [$t(18) = 2.11$, $p = 0.05$] demonstrated a significant difference (ES = 1.00) when compared to the process writing instruction group.

Two studies provided the foundation for SRSD story writing research (Graham et al., 2005; Harris et al., 2008). In 2009, Tracy et al. (2009) replicated SRSD strategy instruction for story writing with 127 third grade students. The researchers compared the use of SRSD ($n = 64$) with an experimental group to a control group ($n = 63$) that provided instruction in basic writing skills such as spelling, grammar, and punctuation. The groups were asked to write a story about the picture line-drawn prompts (e.g., a girl looking at a giant egg that is cracking open). The SRSD group was taught a general planning strategy using the mnemonic POW (*Pick* my idea, *Organize* my notes, and *Write* and say more). They were also taught a specific strategy for writing in the story genre using the WWW, What=2, How=2 mnemonic (*Who* are the main characters? *When* does the story take place? *Where* does the story take place? *What* do the main characters do or want to do? *What* happens next? *How* do the main characters feel? *How* does that story end?). Students generated notes to use for each question. Findings, comparing the two groups, indicated the SRSD experimental group wrote stories that were longer ($d = 0.55$), had more parts ($d = 0.71$), and of better quality than the control group ($d = 0.35$).

Opinion Writing

According to state academic standards (e.g., NGA & CCSSO, 2010), students should learn to write an opinion paper supported with reasons beginning in the primary grades. As students advance to the later elementary years, their opinion papers should also use evidence and explanations to support their reasons. WWC (Graham, Bollinger et al., 2012) recommends that educators teach student writers to expand their concept of audience. It is important to design an opinion paper with reasons that the target audience might find persuasive (Philippakos & MacArthur, 2020). Students should set writing goals and provide reasons that support their view of an argument.

SRSD instruction for the POW+TREE opinion writing strategy was first examined with 73 third-grade struggling writers (Graham et al., 2005). TREE includes eight elements or essay parts—*Topic* sentence, *Reasons* (3 or more), *Explanations* (1 for each reason), and *Ending*. Students were assigned to one of three groups—SRSD instruction, SRSD plus peer support to foster generalization and maintenance, or a writing workshop business-as-usual comparison group. Results indicated students who received SRSD or SRSD with peer support instruction spent more time writing opinion papers (ES = 1.88 and 2.34 respectively) than the comparison group; quality was also significantly better (ES = 2.80 and 2.14 respectively). The Harris et al. (2008) study with 66 second-grade struggling writers had similar results. TREE was adapted for the younger writers to five parts—*Topic* sentence, *Reasons* (3 or more), *Ending*, *Examine* parts. Students in the two SRSD groups, when compared to the comparison group, spent more time writing opinions (ES = 1.10 and 1.21 respectively) and wrote better opinions (ES = 1.31 and 1.63 respectively).

Informative Writing

Informative writing focuses on telling how or why. Informative writing may include information regarding explaining a process, developing a concept, or providing new knowledge (Mason et al., 2006). To develop skills required to compose informational text, students need to be taught about the writing process and organizational structures of informative writing (Englert et al., 1988). Knowledge about the writing process includes strategies for planning, drafting, editing, and revising.

In addition to understanding the writing process, the writer must also understand text structure. There are several types of text structures for informative text—description, sequence, problem/solution, compare/contrast, and cause/effect. Teaching students to understand different types of text structure results in higher writing composition quality. Graham, McKeown et al. (2012) found an average weighted ES = 0.59 for improving writing quality with text structure instruction in nine second through sixth grade studies. A meta-analysis and meta-synthesis (Graham et al., 2015) on research-based writing practices, and the common core, and determined students' use of pre-writing activities (e.g., graphic organizers, brainstorming, drawing, or reading) to gain knowledge improved writing quality (average weighted ES = 0.54).

In order for students to compose informative text, they need to be familiar with their subject. Importantly in inclusive classroom instruction, prior to writing about text, students must be able to read a text and determine the important information from that text (Graham & Hebert, 2011; Graham et al., 2018). Given this, it is critical that students are explicitly taught how to write from the text.

Writing from Text Sources

The relationship between reading and writing and the literacy challenges between the two domains are well documented (Graham & Hebert, 2011; Kang et al., 2016). In actuality, state academic standards (NGA & CCSSO, 2010) for informational text reading and informational/explanatory writing in elementary school are closely aligned. In reading, for example, students are expected to (a) refer to details and examples in a text when explaining what has been read, (b) identify the main idea of a text, (c) determine the overall text structure (e.g., classification, temporal sequence of events), and (d) explain how the author uses reasons and evidence. Informative/explanatory writing addresses standards such as (a) introduce a topic clearly and group related information in paragraphs and sections; (b) develop the topic with details, facts, information, and examples; (c) link ideas and information categories using words and phrases (e.g., for example, because); and (d) use precise language and domain-specific vocabulary to explain the topic. Graham and Hebert's (2011) meta-analytic findings indicated multi-component interventions that target both domains (e.g., reading text plus summary writing or written recall) improve students' comprehension on standardized tests (ES = 0.40) and researcher-developed (ES = 0.51) assessments.

Students with disabilities who already experience difficulties in comprehending text may also struggle with the processes needed for writing about the content learned through reading (Toste et al., 2020). Intensive interventions focused on remediated reading and writing deficits have the potential to reduce the risk of academic failure across the curriculum (Clemens et al., 2020).

Instructional Approaches for Writing from Text

By improving students' ability to write effectively about a text that has been read, learning is facilitated by improving understanding of complex texts, by helping students relate topics to personal experiences, and by supporting the reformulation and extension of ideas (Afflerbach et al., 2020). One instructional approach is SRSD for TWA (*Think* before reading, think *While* reading, think *After* reading: Mason, 2004)+ PLANS (*Pick* goals, *List* ways to meet goals, *And* make *Notes*, *Sequence* notes: Graham et al., 1992). In SRSD for TWA+PLANS, students are taught to self-regulate their use of reading strategies throughout all reading phases, self-regulate writing notes from text, and then taught to set goals to self-regulated writing an informative essay. Two SRSD for TWA+PLANS instructional studies with fourth grade students (Mason et al., 2006, 2013) were evaluated and noted to have met expected design standards (Kang et al., 2016). In both studies, TWA was taught first, followed by instruction in writing notes on a TWA graphic organizer, and ending with informative writing instruction with PLANS.

In the first TWA phase, *Think* before reading, students are taught to think about the author's reasons for writing and the structure of the text "think about the author's purpose." The next two steps—"think about what you know" and "think about what you want to know"- are adapted from Ogle's (1989) What I *K*now, What do I *W*ant to Learn, What I *L*earned (KWL) strategy. Three steps are taught in the think *While* reading phase: "think about reading speed," "think about linking knowledge," and "think about rereading parts." The linking knowledge step, an extension of KWL, prompts students to make connections between what they know and what is being read. In the think *After* reading phase, students are asked to think about the information in the passage and apply research-based strategies for main idea development (Graves & Levin, 1989), summarization (Brown & Day, 1983), and then retell what was learned.

SRSD for PLANS informative writing provides students with steps for developing personal writing goals (*Pick* goals) and structure for monitoring and evaluating (*List* ways to meet goals) their own performance (Graham et al., 1992). Goal setting is a critical component of the writing process. Goals that are specific, proximal, and challenging help writers understand the specific tasks to be completed and foster effort and motivation (Harris et al., 2011). Goals in PLANS instruction are individualized with student involvement and commitment, and when needed, can be revised. In addition, students are encouraged to attribute improvement in writing to achieving goals.

The first TWA+PLANS study, a multiple baseline single case study, included nine low-achieving fourth-grade students with and without disabilities (Mason et al., 2006). Results indicated that students' reading comprehension, measured through oral retelling and informative writing, improved to criterion (i.e., main idea and evidence for each text paragraph orally stated and written) after instruction. Findings from the second study, a randomized controlled trial study with 72 low-achieving fourth-grade students (Mason et al., 2013), indicated that students in TWA+PLANS treatment, compared to a business-as-usual control, had positive large effect differences in oral retell (main ideas + evidence: Posttest ES =.61–.93, Maintenance ES =.93–1.17), writing measures (main ideas + evidence: Posttest ES =.73–1.37, Maintenance ES =.93–1.55), and a vocabulary measure (number of different words written: Posttest ES =1.29, Maintenance ES =1.37). Importantly, in both studies, students reported that instruction helped them write about what they learned.

Setting the Course for Effective Inclusion

If students are to succeed in school, they must learn to write (Graham, 2019). The poor writing instruction in inclusive classrooms noted earlier in this chapter has done little to address the increasing accountability for positive outcomes and the increasing expectations for all learners, including those with disabilities, for success in middle school and beyond. Highlights of research that can bridge the gap between elementary and middle school grades are presented next.

Transcription Skills

Transcription skills include handwriting alphabetic letters and spelling complete words. In addition, alphabetic letters and words can be typed and edited with keyboarding tools for additional practice and engagement.

Handwriting

There are several recommendations to improve the handwriting of elementary students with and without disabilities, including content, instructional practices, and curriculum (Datchuk & Kubina, 2013; Santangelo & Graham, 2016). Regarding content, early-elementary students should be taught the shape, name, and order of all upper- and lower-case letters. All three of these aspects are involved in how handwriting is measured across time, and it highlights the fact that handwriting is not simply a physical action but it involves cognitive processes and language (Berninger & Amtmann, 2003). In fact, intervening on motor processes alone (i.e., in isolation from handwriting letters and alphabetic knowledge) has produced mixed results (Santangelo & Graham, 2016). It is recommended that all aspects of handwriting content are taught through explicit, scaffolded instruction.

Instructional practices for handwriting include scaffolded instruction, visual cues, activities for memory retrieval and orthographic coding, fluency practice, and technology integration (Datchuk & Kubina, 2013; Santangelo & Graham, 2016). Scaffolded instruction involves teacher-led modeling, followed by guided practice with frequent opportunities for students to respond and receive feedback, and independent practice without additional assistance. Visual cues of (a) arrows to show direction and (b) numbers to show the order of letter strokes are used to assist students in handwriting letters. Initially, students trace over faintly written examples (i.e., letters written with dashed lines or dots), using visual cues for order and direction, then they write their own letters from memory.

Activities for memory retrieval and orthographic coding are done to commit letter shape, letter name, and alphabetic order to memory. These activities include cover-copy-compare steps: Students view a letter, cover it, copy it from memory, then uncover it and compare their response. In addition, students can write and say letters presented in order (e.g., d e f g), then letters are gradually removed (e.g., d _ f _) and students write and say the missing letters from memory. Fluency practice is done to help students build upon legible letter formation with increased speed. During fluency practice, students quickly copy letters or handwrite them from memory within a specified time (e.g., 2 minutes). Following practice, students receive feedback on their performance. In addition to practice, preliminary research has found possible benefits from integrating technology into handwriting instruction by having students handwrite with their fingers or a stylus on a tablet device (Berninger et al., 2015).

Many of these instructional practices are found in the CASL Handwriting Program (Graham & Harris, 1999). It is a supplemental, paper-based curriculum that includes teacher and student materials for 27 lessons. Prior studies have found that as little as 15 minutes of instruction per day can improve student handwriting (Graham et al., 2000).

Spelling

Even though spelling describes the production of whole words, there are multiple sub-linguistic aspects that need to be addressed (Graham, Bollinger et al., 2012; Squires & Wolter, 2016; Williams et al., 2017). These aspects include phonological awareness, phonics, morphemes, and orthography. Phonological awareness is the detection and manipulation of speech sounds, and phonics is the relation of these sounds to printed letters. Morphemes are the smallest units of words with meaning (e.g., prefixes and suffixes). Orthography refers to the rules and conventions governing written language, such as spelling rules (e.g., i before e except after c) and whole-word spelling of irregular words that do not follow phonetic rules. Given its overlap with early reading skills, it is no surprise that spelling instruction can also improve student reading (Graham & Santangelo, 2014).

Research suggests that multiple aspects of spelling should be addressed with a combination of teacher-led explicit instruction and student-led word study (Wanzek et al., 2006; Williams et al., 2017). For teacher-led explicit instruction, students receive scaffolded assistance (i.e., modeling, guided practice, and independent practice), multiple practice opportunities, and immediate feedback and error correction. *Spelling Mastery* (Dixon, 2007) is one commercially available curriculum with evidence that it improves student spelling performance. It uses an explicit, direct instruction approach to teach multiple aspects of spelling, including phonological awareness, phonics, morphemes, spelling rules, and whole-word memorization of irregular (i.e., non-phonetic) words.

For student-led word study, students are taught a procedure to memorize whole-word spelling: They self-monitor their use of procedure steps as well as their performance. A common word study procedure is cover, copy and compare. Students first view a word, then cover it up. After a time delay, they attempt to copy the word from memory. Then, the original word is uncovered, and students compare their responses to it. If the word is misspelled, students repeat the cover, copy, and compare steps.

Word Processing

Compared to the other two transcription skills of handwriting and spelling, less is known about effective instructional approaches to teach typing and word-processing tools. Touch typing is the skill of producing text via a keyboard without having to locate individual letters visually. Preliminary evidence suggests that touch-typing instruction may improve student typing fluency and writing quantity (Donica et al., 2018; Weerdenburg et al., 2018); however, more research is needed to determine the benefits of specific curriculum materials or online software and other applications.

Besides touch typing, brief, explicit instruction on word-processing tools may prove beneficial. In several studies, students were taught how to use word-processing tools (e.g., cut/copy/paste, delete, and use of backspace) prior to learning strategies to plan, compose, and revise extended composition (Evmenova et al., 2016; Regan et al., 2017). More research is needed on how to efficiently teach a variety of word-processing tools (e.g., font selection and formatting), but these results suggest that students can be briefly taught word-processing skills that are relevant to a specific writing task. For instance, in one study, students were taught how to cut/copy/paste text when using a computer-based graphic organizer to plan their writing (Evmenova et al., 2016).

Sentence Construction

Students develop complementary sentence structures across elementary grades. Sentence structures include simple sentences and more complicated structures, such as compound or complex sentences.

Simple Sentence Structure

Explicit instruction with fluency practice is a promising approach to teach simple sentence structure and related text-writing skills (Datchuk et al., 2020). During instruction and practice, simple sentences are defined in student-friendly terms. Specifically, simple sentences are defined as having two parts: a part that names someone/something or something and a part that tells more. Text-writing skills related to syntax (i.e., nouns, verbs, and subject-verb agreement) and usage (i.e., capitalization and punctuation) are taught using this student-friendly definition. For example, to teach subject-verb agreement (e.g., *was* for singular nouns or *were* for plural nouns), students are told that when a sentence names more than one someone/something (e.g., Bob and Daveed), then *were* is used to tell more (e.g., Bob and Daveed were at their school).

Explicit instruction is delivered first to establish sentence writing accuracy, then fluency practice is delivered to increase sentence writing speed. During explicit instruction, the multiple skills addressed (i.e., sentence structure and text writing) are segmented into small instructional units to control for task difficulty, and scaffolded support (i.e., modeling, guided practice, and independent practice) is provided. Students follow a standard sequence of activities: They identify correct and incorrect instances of simple sentence structure and text-writing skills, complete fill-in-the-blank items, and generate their own responses. In addition, picture-word prompts are used to reduce cognitive demands (e.g., idea generation) associated with sentence writing. As an example, a picture-word prompt may depict a small child building a sandcastle with the words *child* and *castle.*

Following explicit instruction, students engage in fluency practice writing simple sentences. During fluency practice, students complete multiple practice timings (e.g., three, 1-minute practice timings), writing simple sentences to a variety of picture-word prompts. Following each practice timing, students are provided performance feedback (i.e., number of CWS), praise for complete sentences and text writing skills, and error correction. At the end of each fluency practice session, students record their best performance on a table or graph and are encouraged to increase their performance.

Simple and Complicated Sentence Structures

Strategy instruction or SIM is another approach to teach simple and more complicated sentence structures (Schumaker & Deshler, 2003; Schumaker & Sheldon, 1998). Like explicit instruction, SIM involves segmenting multiple skills into small instructional units and providing scaffolded instruction. Sentence structures are segmented into two broad categories: (a) parts of a complete sentence and (b) sentence formulas. Students are taught there are five parts to a complete sentence: a capital letter at the beginning, end punctuation, a subject, a verb, and it makes sense. Sentence formulas are shorthand for a variety of simple and complicated sentence structures, such as SV (subject and verb), SSV (subject, subject, and verb), and SVV (subject, verb, and verb). Both of these broad categories—parts of a complete sentence and sentence formulas—are then taught in a highly structured, scaffolded manner: Students identify examples and non-examples (e.g., beginning capitalization of a sentence), complete fill-in-the-blank sentence frames (e.g., write a verb for an SV formula), and generate their own sentences.

As part of SIM, several strategy instruction steps are used in a recursive process. Prior to formal instruction, students make a commitment to learn the PENS MARK strategy. The first word, PENS, stands for Pick a formula, Explore words to fit the formula, Note the word, and Search and check. The second word, MARK, further explains the search and check steps: Mark out the infinitives, Ask is there a verb, Root out the subject, and Key in on the beginning (i.e., capitalization), ending (i.e., punctuation), and meaning. During strategy instruction, the PENS MARK strategy is modeled. Then, students engage in the controlled practice of identifying or completing sentences in isolation and advanced practice generating their own sentences that follow a sentence formula. Towards the end of strategy instruction, students make a commitment to generalize the use of PENS MARK to other classes and writing tasks and practice applying it to new writing tasks.

In addition to SIM, sentence combining is another approach to teach more complicated sentence structures, such as simple sentences with adjectives or compound sentences (Saddler & Graham, 2005; Saddler et al., 2018). With sentence combining, students are taught how to combine sentence kernels and cues into a single sentence. Sentence kernels are words, phrases, or sentences. Cues are underlined words, punctuation marks, or conjunctions. As an example, two sentence kernels with an underlined cue can be combined into a simple sentence with an adjective: *Lanqi went to the store* + *The store was large* = *Lanqi went to the large store.* As another example, two sentence kernels with a conjunction cue can be combined into a compound sentence: *Jamil closed the jar lid slowly* + *The fireflies flew away* + *and* = *Jamil closed the jar lid slowly, and the fireflies flew away.* Students are taught how to use sentence combining to construct and edit their own sentences, paragraphs, and extended compositions.

Sentence combining has typically been taught through a combination of teacher-led instruction and peer-assisted learning strategy (Saddler et al., 2008). Teachers model how to construct sentences through sentence combining, then lead students through guided and independent practice. Students are paired into dyads, and they engage in oral and written practice. Specifically, one student reads aloud sentence combinations while the other student provides feedback regarding the structure and overall quality. Following oral practice, students collaborate on writing sentence combinations, editing paragraphs, and composing and editing extended compositions.

Written Expression

Writing expression instruction provided to elementary students has received considerable research, including multiple meta-analyses and synthesis, establishing the quality of the research and the strong effects of the intervention. (e.g., Graham, Bollinger et al., 2012). The acquisition of effective writing skills in the early years is crucial to achieving the literacy demands of the middle and high school years. In order to prepare students to meet the rigorous writing standards in later grades, educators should use evidence-based writing strategies and instructional approaches. Standards, such as state academic standards (e.g., NGA & CCSSO, 2010), require that upper elementary school students be able to use writing for a variety of purposes, revise and edit, and acquire note-taking skills (Ciullo & Mason, 2017). Acquisition of these skills is often challenging for students with disabilities. To support students with diverse writing needs in the inclusion classroom and to prepare these students for successful writing in middle school and beyond, strategies for writing in content classrooms, for increasing expectations, for improving writing quality through revision and editing, and for note-taking should be part of their instruction.

Writing in the Content Classroom

Students often demonstrate their understanding of content in social studies and science through writing. Quick writes (short extended written responses), for example, are often used to support students in synthesizing content learned (Frey & Fisher, 2008). The POW (Pick my idea, Organize my notes, Write and say more) + TIDE (Topic, Important Evidence, Details to Support Evidence, and Ending) strategy (Mason et al., 2012) can be used to support an informative writing task in content (e.g., for science, *Select one simple machine and clearly explain how it works;* for social studies, *Describe the process for becoming a Supreme Court judge*). Students respond to the prompt by writing for 10 minutes using the mnemonic POW+ TIDE to plan and write. When teaching quick writing, students are introduced to transitional words, a graphic organizer, and a mnemonic chart to support strategy use during writing. Gradually, the supports are removed to demonstrate independent use of the POW+TIDE strategy (Mason et al., 2009). Benedek-Wood et al. (2014) demonstrated that SRSD for informative, quick writes in four inclusive sixth-grade science classrooms improved writing quality and quantity for both students with and without disabilities. Using an evidence-based teaching approach, such as SRSD, is most effective in supporting students with disabilities' quick writing performance in the inclusive classroom.

Argumentative Writing

Scaffolding students writing from persuasive writing (i.e., writing that includes emotions and personal opinions) to writing arguments (i.e., writing that includes logic and reasoning) is critical in upper grades. Writing arguments helps students interpret and organize historical and scientific information (De La Paz, 2005). One evidence-based argumentative writing strategy, STOP (Suspend judgment, Take a side, Organize ideas, and Plan) and DARE (Develop a topic sentence, Add supporting ideas, Reject an argument for the other side, End with a conclusion), can be used assist students in organizing reasons for supporting an argument. Prior to composing, students list all the argumentative reasons/ideas for the topic (e.g., reasons for eating snacks in column one and reasons for not eating snacks in column two). The mnemonic STOP reminds students to consider one side of the argument to support their essay. The second mnemonic, DARE, is used to add essay elements and consider the reader's perspective (Harris et al., 2008). In 2005, De La Paz tested the effects of SRSD for STOP and DARE with 70 eighth grade students with varying abilities, including students with disabilities. Students in the experimental group used the STOP and DARE strategy to plan argumentative essays and wrote historically more accurate essays (ES ranged from 1.17 to 1.23 for essay length, persuasiveness, and number of arguments). In two studies, Ennis et al. (2013) and Ennis and Jolivette (2014) evaluated the effects of SRSD for STOP and DARE with elementary students with emotional and behavioral disabilities in residential settings. After instruction, students' writing improved in quality, number of essay elements, and written words, supporting the premise that this strategy can be effective for elementary-aged students.

Revising and Editing

Students are required to plan, compose, revise, and edit during the writing process. Teaching upper elementary students to understand this writing process prepares them for writing in the middle grades (Ciullo & Mason, 2017). And, the WWC recommends that students learn and use the writing process, including revising and editing (Graham, Bollinger et al., 2012). Most low-achieving writers recognize the need for good handwriting and spelling in writing; however, they are less aware of the importance of revising for content (Harris et al., 2011; Zimmerman & Risemberg, 1997). It is important that revision, specifically for addressing the content and meaning of what has been written, be taught and implemented prior to focusing on editing for mechanical errors.

In 1988, Graham and MacArthur taught fifth and sixth grade students the six-step SCAN revising and editing strategy for improving composition clarity and cohesiveness and for detecting and correcting mechanics. The SCAN strategy prompts students to: "(a) Read your essay; (b) Find the sentence that tells what you believe-is it clear?; (c)Add two reasons why you believe it; (d) SCAN each sentence (Does it make sense? Is it connected to my belief? Can I add more? Note errors.); (e) Make changes on the computer; (f) Re-read the essay and make final changes" (p.138). Using the SCAN strategy, students in the Graham and MacArthur study made more revisions following instruction as well as increased the quantity of words written.

One WWC (Graham, Bollinger et al., 2012) recommended strategy students can use to edit an essay is COPS (Capitalization, Organization, Punctuation, and Spelling). It is critical that students' authentic writing is used when learning to edit and for COPS to be explicitly taught (Ciullo & Mason, 2017). During instruction, for example, teachers should model editing questions such as, *Have I capitalized?* or *Is my punctuation correct?* Students can ask themselves editing questions such as, *Did I spell words correctly?* or *How is the overall appearance of my paper?*

Note-Taking

Note-taking is considered a writing standard (NGA & CCSSO, 2010) that needs to be addressed in elementary classrooms to prepare students for middle school. Students are required to listen and take notes on the critical content information. Students with diverse writing needs may require scaffolding to support the complex and cognitively demanding task of notetaking in the classroom (Ciullo & Mason, 2017). Ciullo and Mason recommend the use of guided notes to scaffold note-taking, especially for writing in content area classrooms such as science and social studies. A basic template can be used for creating guided notes by leaving blank lines and spaces in text for students to write in the missing information (e.g., *A ________ is a type of simple machine.*). In Patterson's (2005) study with eight students with disabilities in a fourth-grade inclusion classroom, students used teacher-created guided notes to record information presented during a lesson. Overall, the mean scores of the students' quizzes increased from 33% to 91% when using guided notes to study.

Alternative Modes of Composing

State academic standards (e.g., NGA & CCSSO, 2010) recommend that writing digital text should be a priority for middle school students. Being competent in digital writing prepares students to complete academic, personal, and career-related skills (Martin & Lambert, 2015). Williams and

Beam's (2019) research review of 29 technology and writing studies found that students using technology for writing demonstrated improvements in the composition process, motivation, and collaboration with peers. Technology was particularly supportive for reluctant writers, with demonstrated improved enthusiasm and increased writing time. Martin and Lambert (2015) determined that students using technology have different digital writing levels and suggested that instruction should be differentiated depending on the level of technology experiences and exposure. Many students with disabilities benefit from additional instruction, guidance, and exposure in using digital tools and features.

The WEGO (Writing Efficiently with Graphic Organizer) is a digital graphic organizing tool that students can use to support writing persuasive, argumentative and narrative essays. The self-regulation strategies in WEGO assist students with goal-setting, self-monitoring, and self-evaluation (Evmenova et al., 2020). Students are asked to (a) pick a goal for their writing, (b) complete an organizing table, (c) edit and revise their work, and (e) evaluate their writing and receive feedback. Results in Evmenova and colleagues' (2016) study found the use of the digital organizer increased students with disabilities writing quality as well as improved perceptions and attitudes.

Speech-to-text dictation tools have also demonstrated writing improvements for students with disabilities. When students with learning disabilities, for example, wrote without the demands of transcription skills (e.g., handwriting, spelling), the quality of writing improved (Gillespie & Graham, 2014). Speech-to-text technology can remove transcription barriers and allow the writer to focus on content development. Gillespie and Graham found that dictation resulted in statistically significant improvements in writing quality (average weighted ES = 0.55, $p<.01$).

We Know What We Are, But Know Not What We May Be And When I Am Forgotten…Say, I Taught Thee

As substantiated by national writing assessment data, a significant number of students with disabilities are failing to meet standards in transcription skills, sentence writing, and written expression. Although benchmarks have been established to address this problem (e.g., NGA & CCSSO, 2010), teachers have noted being ill-prepared in using evidence-based practices for writing (e.g., Graham et al., 2007; 2008). Teachers note-making few or little adaptations to their writing instruction for low-achieving writers (e.g., Cutler & Graham, 2008), directly impacting students with disabilities who may have writing deficits. As noted throughout this chapter, a number of interventions have been evaluated and found effective for students with disabilities; however, writing instruction is often neglected (Graham, 2019). Graham notes four factors that need attention for change—increase teachers' classroom time for teaching writing; improve teachers' preparation, training, and beliefs about writing; include writing instruction in national, state, district, and school policies. And, most importantly for the inclusive classroom, address the historical, social, cultural, and political influences that place writing as less important when compared to other academic domains.

References

Abbott, R. D., Berninger, V. W., & Fayol, M. (2010). Longitudinal relationships of levels of language in writing and between writing and reading in grades 1 to 7. *Journal of Educational Psychology*, *102*(2), 281–298. doi:10.1037/a0019318

Afflerbach, P., Biancarosa, G., Hurt, M., & Pearson, P. D. (2020). *Teaching reading for understanding: Synthesis and reflections on the curriculum and instruction.* Portfolio. In P. D. Pearson, A. S. Palincsar, G. Biancarosa, & A. Berman (Eds.), *Reaping the rewards of the reading for understanding initiative* (pp. 215–250). National Academy of Education. https://naeducation.org/wp-content/uploads/2020/06/Reaping-the-Rewards-of-the-Reading-for-Understanding-Initiative.pdf

Allen, A. A., Poch, A. L., & Lembke, E. S. (2018). An exploration of alternative scoring methods using curriculum-based measurement in early writing. *Learning Disability Quarterly, 42*(2), 85–99. doi:10.1177-0731 9487177725490

Asaro-Saddler, K., & Saddler, B. (2010). Planning instruction and self-regulation training: Effects on writers with autism spectrum disorders. *Exceptional Children*, 77(1), 107–124. doi:10.1177/001440291007700105

Benedek-Wood, E., Mason, L. H., Wood, P. H., Hoffman, K. E., & McGuire, A. (2014). An experimental examination of quick writing in the middle school science classroom. *Learning Disabilities: A Contemporary Journal, 12*(1), 69–92. http://search.ebscohost.com.mutex.gmu.edu/login.aspx?direct=true&db=ehh&AN=97606363&site=ehost-live

Berninger, V. W., & Amtmann, D. (2003). *Preventing written expression disabilities through early and continuing assessment and intervention for handwriting and/or spelling problems: Research into practice.* In H. L. Swanson, K. R. Harris, & S. Graham (Eds.), *Handbook of learning disabilities* (pp. 345–363). Guilford Press. https://www.guilford.com/books/Handbook-of-Learning-Disabilities/Swanson-Harris-Graham/9781462518685

Berninger, V. W., Nagy, W., Tanimoto, S., Thompson, R., & Abbott, R. D. (2015). *Computers & Education, 81*, 154–168. doi:10.1016/j.compedu.2014.10.005

Berninger, V. W., Rutberg, J. E., Abbott, R. D., Garcia, N., Anderson-Youngstrom, M., Brooks, A., & Fulton, C. (2006). Tier 1 and Tier 2 early intervention for handwriting and composing. *Journal of School Psychology, 44*(1), 3–30. doi:10.1016/j.jsp.2005.12.003

Brindle, M., Graham, S., Harris, K. R., & Hebert, M. (2016). Third and fourth grade teacher's classroom practices in writing: A national survey. *Reading and Writing, 29*(5), 929–954. doi:10.1007/s11145-015-9604-x

Brown, A. L., & Day, J. D. (1983). Macrorules for summarizing texts: The development of expertise. *Journal of Verbal Learning and Verbal Behavior, 22*(1), 1–14. doi:10.1016/S0022-5371(83)80002-4

Bruner, J. (1991). The narrative construction of reality. *Critical Inquiry 18*(15), 1–21. https://www-jstor-org.mutex.gmu.edu/stable/1343711

Bui, Y. N., Schumaker, J. B., & Deshler, D. D. (2006). The effects of a strategic writing program for students with and without learning disabilities in inclusive fifth-grade classes. *Learning Disabilities Research & Practice, 21*(4), 244–260. doi:10.1111/j.1540-5826.2006.00221.x

Ciullo, S., & Mason, L. (2017). Prioritizing elementary school writing instruction: Cultivating middle school readiness for students with learning disabilities. *Intervention in School and Clinic, 52*(5), 287–294. doi:10.11 77/1053451216676801

Clemens, N. H., Hsiao, Y. Y., Lee, K., Martinez-Lincoln, A., Moore, C., Toste, J., & Simmons, L. (2020). The differential importance of component skills on reading comprehension test performance among struggling adolescent readers. *Journal of Learning Disabilities.* doi:10.1177/0022219420932139.

Cutler, L., & Graham, S. (2008). Primary grade writing instruction: A national survey. *Journal of Educational Psychology, 100*(4), 907–919. doi:10.1037/a0012656

Datchuk, S. M., & Kubina, R. M. (2013). A review of teaching sentence-level writing skills to students with writing difficulties and learning disabilities. *Remedial and Special Education, 34*(3), 180–192. doi:10.1177/0741932512448254

Datchuk, S. M., Wagner, K., & Hier, B. O. (2020). Level and trend of writing sequences: A review and meta-analysis of writing interventions for students with disabilities. *Exceptional Children, 86*(2), 174–192. doi:10.11 77/0014402919873311

De La Paz, S. (2005). Effects of historical reasoning instruction and writing strategy mastery in culturally and academically diverse middle school classrooms. *Journal of Educational Psychology, 97*(2), 139–156. doi:10.103 7/0022-0663.97.2.139

Dixon, R. (2007). *Spelling mastery.* McGraw-Hill. https://www.mheducation.com/prek-12/program/spelling-mastery/MKTSP-UTC03M0.html?page=1&sortby=title&order=asc&bu=seg

Donica, D. K., Giroux, P., & Faust, A. (2018). Keyboarding instruction: Comparison of techniques for improved keyboarding skills in elementary students. *Journal of Occupational Therapy, Schools, & Early Intervention, 11*(4), 396–410. doi:10.1080/19411243.2018.1512067

Englert, C. S., Raphael, T. E., Fear, K. L., & Anderson, L. M. (1988). Students' metacognitive knowledge about how to write informational texts. *Learning Disability Quarterly, 11*(1), 18–46. doi:10.2307/1511035

Ennis, R. P., & Jolivette, K. (2014). Existing research and future directions for self-regulated strategy development with students with and at risk for emotional and behavioral disorders. *The Journal of Special Education, 48*(1), 32–45. doi:10.1177/0022466912454682

Ennis, R. P., Jolivette, K., & Boden, L. J. (2013). STOP and DARE: Self-regulated strategy development for persuasive writing with elementary students with E/BD in a residential facility. *Education and Treatment of Children, 36*(3), 81–99. doi:10.1353/etc.2013.0026

Evmenova, A. S., Regan, K., Boyokin, A., Good, K., Hughes, M., MacVittie, N., Sacco, N., Ahn, S. Y., & Chirinos, D. (2016). Emphasizing planning for essay writing with a computer-based graphic organizer. *Exceptional Children*, *82*(2), 170–191. doi:10.1177/0014402915591697

Evmenova, A. S., Regan, K., & Hutchison, A. (2020). AT for writing: Technology-based graphic organizers with embedded supports. *TEACHING Exceptional Children*, *52*(4), 266–269. doi:10.1177/0040059920907571

Foxworth, L. L., Hashey, A., & Sukhram, D. P. (2019). Writing in the digital age: An investigation of digital writing proficiency among students with and without LD. *Reading & Writing Quarterly*, *35*(5), 445–457. doi:10.1080/10573569.2019.1579011

Frey, N., & Fisher, D. (2008). *Improving adolescent literacy: Content area strategies at work*. Pearson Prentice Hall. https://www.pearson.com/us/higher-education/program/Fisher-Improving-Adolescent-Literacy-Content-Area-Strategies-at-Work-4th-Edition/PGM240947.html

Gillespie, A., & Graham, S. (2014). A meta-analysis of writing interventions for students with learning disabilities. *Exceptional Children*, *80*(4) 454–473. doi:10.1177/0014402914527238

Graham, S. (2019). Changing how writing is taught. *Review of Research in Education*, *43*(1), 277–303. doi:10.3102/0091732X18821125

Graham, S., Bollinger, A., Booth Olson, C., D'Aoust, C., MacArthur, C., McCutchen, D., & Olinghouse, N. (2012). *Teaching elementary school students to be effective writers: A practice guide (NCEE 2012-4058)*. National Center for Education Evaluation and Regional Assistance, Institute of Education Sciences, U.S. Department of Education. https://ies.ed.gov/ncee/wwc/Docs/PracticeGuide/WWC_Elem_Writing_PG_Dec182018.pdf

Graham, S., Collins, A. A., & Rigby-Wills, H. (2017). Writing characteristics of students with learning disabilities and typically achieving peers: A meta-analysis. *Exceptional Children*, *83*(2), 199–218. doi:10.1177/0014402916664070

Graham, S., Fishman, E. J., Reid, R., & Hebert, M. (2016). Writing characteristics of students with attention deficit hyperactive disorder: A meta-analysis. *Learning Disabilities Research & Practice*, *31*(2), 75–89. doi:10.1111/ldrp.12099

Graham, S., & Harris, K. R. (1996). *Self-regulation and strategy instruction for students who find writing and learning challenging*. In C. M. Levy & S. Ransdell (Eds.). *The science of writing: Theories, methods, individual differences, and applications* (pp. 347–360). Lawrence Erlbaum Associates, Inc. https://www.taylorfrancis.com/books/9780203811122

Graham, S., & Harris, K. (1999). *The CASL handwriting program*. http://peabody.vanderbilt.edu/docs/pdf/sped/CASL%20Handwriting%20Program.pdf

Graham, S., & Harris, K. R. (2003). *Students with learning disabilities and the process of writing: A meta-analysis of SRSD studies*. In H. L. Swanson, K. R. Harris, & S. Graham (Eds.), *Handbook of learning disabilities* (pp. 323–344). The Guilford Press. https://www.guilford.com/books/Handbook-of-Learning-Disabilities/Swanson-Harris-Graham/9781462518685

Graham, S., Harris, K. R., & Fink, B. (2000). Is handwriting causally related to learning to write? Treatment of handwriting problems in beginning writers. *Journal of Educational Psychology*, *92*(4), 620–633. doi:10.1037/0022-0663.92.4.620

Graham S., Harris K.R., & Mason L. H. (2005). Improving the writing performance, knowledge, and self-efficacy of struggling young writers: The effects of self-regulated strategy development. *Contemporary Educational Psychology*, *30*(2), 207–241. doi:10.3102/00028312043002295

Graham, S., Harris, K.R., Mason, L.H., Fink, B., Moran, S., & Saddler, B. (2008). Teaching handwriting in the primary grades: A national survey. *Reading and Writing: An Interdisciplinary Journal*, *21*(1-2), 49–69. doi:10.1007/s11145-007-9064-z

Graham, S., Harris, K.R., Morphy, P., Fink, B., Saddler, S., Moran, S., & Mason, L.H. (2008). Primary grade teachers' adaptation for poor spellers: A national survey. *American Education Research Journal*, *45*(3), 796–825. doi:10.3102/0002831208319722

Graham, S., & Hebert, M. (2011). Writing to read: A meta-analysis of the impact of writing and writing instruction on reading. *Harvard Educational Review*, *81*(4), 710–744. doi:10.17763/haer.81.4.t2k0m13756113566

Graham, S., Liu, X., Aitken, A., Ng, C., Bartlett, B., Harris, K. R., & Holzapfel, J. (2018). Effectiveness of literacy programs balancing reading and writing instruction: A meta-analysis. *Reading Research Quarterly*, *53*(3), 279–304. doi:10.1002/rrq.194

Graham, S., & MacArthur, C. (1988). Improving learning disabled students' skills at revising essays produced on a word processor: Self-instructional strategy training. *The Journal of Special Education*, *22*(2), 133–152. doi:10.1177/002246698802200202

Graham, S., Macarthur, C., Schwartz, S., & Page-Voth, V. (1992). Improving compositions of students with learning disabilities using a strategy involving product and process goal-setting. *Exceptional Children, 58*(4), 322–334. doi:10.1177/001440299205800405

Graham, S., McKeown, D., Kiuhara, S., & Harris, K. R. (2012). A meta-analysis of writing instruction for students in the elementary grades. *Journal of Educational Psychology, 104*(4), 879–896. doi:10.1037/a0029185

Graham, S., & Santangelo, T. (2014). Does spelling instruction make students better spellers, readers, and writers? A meta-analytic review. *Reading and Writing, 27*(9), 1703–1743. doi:10.1007s11145-014-9517-0

Graves, A. W., & Levin, J. R. (1989). Comparison of monitoring and mnemonic text-processing strategies in learning disabled students. *Learning Disabilities Quarterly, 12*(3), 232–236. doi:10.2307/1510693

Harris, K. R., Graham, S., MacArthur, C., Reid, R., & Mason, L. H. (2011). Self-regulated learning processes and children's writing. In B. Zimmerman & D. Schunk (Eds.), *Handbook of self-regulation of learning and performance* (pp. 187–2010). Routledge. https://psycnet.apa.org/record/2011-12365-001

Harris, K. R., Graham, S., Mason, L. H., & Friedlander, B. (2008). *Powerful writing strategies for all students.* Brooks Publishing Co. Inc. https://products.brookespublishing.com/Powerful-Writing-Strategies-for-All-Students-P186.aspx

Johnson, E., Mellard, D. F., Fuchs, D., & McKnight, M. A. (2006). *Responsiveness to Intervention (RTI): How to do it. [RTI Manual].* National Research Center on Learning Disabilities. https://eric.ed.gov/?id=ED496979

Kang, E. Y., McKenna, J. W., Arden, S., & Ciullo, S. (2016). Integrated reading and writing interventions for students with learning disabilities: A review of the literature. *Learning Disabilities Research & Practice, 31*(1), 22–33. doi:10.1111/ldrp.12091

Kim, Y. S. G., Al Otaiba, S., Puranik, C., Folsom, J. S., Greulich, L., & Wagner, R. K. (2011). Componential skills of beginning writing: An exploratory study. *Learning and Individual Differences, 21*(5), 517–525. doi:10.1016/j.lindif.2011.06.004

Kim, Y. S. G., & Schatschneider, C. (2017). Expanding the developmental models of writing: A direct and indirect effects model of developmental writing (DIEW). *Journal of Educational Psychology, 109*(1), 35–50. doi:10.1037/edu0000129

Laframboise, K. L., & Klesius, J. (1993). A survey of writing instruction in elementary language arts classrooms. *Reading Psychology: An International Quarterly, 14*(4), 265–284. doi:10.1080/027027193140401

Martin, N. M., & Lambert, C. S. (2015). Differentiating digital writing instruction. The intersection of technology, writing, instruction and digital genre knowledge. *Journal of Adolescent & Adult Literacy, 59*(2), 217–227. doi:10.1002/jaal.435

Mason, L. H. (2004). Explicit self-regulated strategy development versus reciprocal questioning: Effects on expository reading comprehension among struggling readers. *Journal of Educational Psychology, 96*(2), 283–296. doi:10.1037/0022-0663.96.2.283

Mason, L. H., Benedek-Wood, E., & Valasa, L. (2009). Quick writing for students who struggle with writing. *Journal of Adolescent and Adult Literacy, 53*(4), 313–322. doi:10.1598/JAAL.53.4.4

Mason, L. H., Dunn Davison, M., Hammer, C. S., Miller, C. A., & Glutting, J. (2013). Knowledge, writing, and language outcomes for a reading comprehension and writing intervention. *Reading and Writing: An Interdisciplinary Journal, 26*(7), 1135–1158. doi:10.1007/s11145-012-9409-0

Mason, L. H., Hickey Snyder, K., Sukhram, D. P., & Kedem, Y. (2006). Self-regulated strategy development for expository reading comprehension and informative writing: Effects for nine 4th-grade students who struggle with learning. *Exceptional Children, 73*(1), 69–89. doi:10.1177/001440290607300104

Mason, L. H., & Reid, R. (2018). Individual and group differences in self-regulation of learning and performance self-regulation: Implications for individuals with special needs. In D. Schunk & J. Greene (Eds.), *Handbook of self-regulation of learning and performance* (2nd ed.). Routledge. https://www.routledge.com/Handbook-of-Self-Regulation-of-Learning-and-Performance/Schunk-Greene/p/book/9781138903197

Mason, L. H., Reid, R., & Hagaman, J. (2012). *Building comprehension in adolescents: Powerful strategies for improving reading and writing in content areas.* Brooks Publishing Co. Inc. https://products.brookespublishing.com/Building-Comprehension-in-Adolescents-P261.aspx

National Governors Association (NGA) Center for Best Practices & Council of Chief State School Officers (CCSSO). (2010). *Common core state standards: English language arts.* NGA & CCSO. http://www.corestandards.org/ELA-Literacy/

National Center for Education Statistics (2017). *Technical Summary of Preliminary Analyses of NAEP 2017 Writing Assessments.* https://nces.ed.gov/nationsreportcard/subject/writing/pdf/2017_writing_technical_summary.pdf

Ogle, D. M. (1989). The know, want to know, learn strategy. In K. D. Muth (Ed.), *Children's comprehension of text* (pp. 205–223). International Reading Association. https://eric.ed.gov/?id=ED304672

Patterson, K. (2005). Increasing positive outcomes for African American males in special education with the use of guided notes. *The Journal of Negro Education*, *74*(4), 311–320. https://www-jstor-org.mutex.gmu.edu/stable/40026731

Philippakos, Z. A., & MacArthur, C. A. (2020). Integrating collaborative reasoning and strategy instruction to improve second graders' opinion writing, *Reading & Writing Quarterly*, *36*(4), 379–395. doi:10.1080/10573569.2019.1650315

Regan, K., Evmenova, A. S., Boykin, A., Sacco, D., Good, K., Ahn, S. Y., MacVittie, N., & Hughes, M. D. (2017). Supporting struggling writers with class-wide teacher implementation of a computer-based graphic organizer. *Reading & Writing Quarterly*, *33*(5), 428–448. doi:10.1080/10573569.2016.1221781

Ritchey, K. D., McMaster, K. L., Al Otaiba, S., Puranik, C. S., Grace Kim, Y. S., Parker, D. C., & Ortiz, M. (2016). Indicators of fluent writing in beginning writers. In. K. D. Cummings & Y. Petscher (Eds.), *The fluency construct* (pp. 21–66). Springer. https://www.springer.com/gp/book/9781493928026

Rogers, L. A., & Graham, S. (2008). A meta-analysis of single subject design writing intervention research. *Journal of Educational Psychology*, *100*(4), 879–906. doi:10.1037/0022-0663.100.4.879

Saddler, B., Behforooz, B., & Asaro-Saddler, K. (2008). The effects of sentence-combining instruction on the writing of fourth-grade students with writing difficulties. *The Journal of Special Education*, *42*(2), 79–90. doi:10.1177/0022466907310371

Saddler, B., Ellis-Robinson, T., & Asaro-Saddler, K. (2018). Using sentence combining instruction to enhance the writing skills of children with learning disabilities. *Learning Disabilities: A Contemporary Journal*, *16*(2), 191–202. https://psycnet.apa.org/record/2018-54384-005

Saddler, B., & Graham, S. (2005). The effects of peer-assisted sentence-combining instruction on the writing performance of more or less skilled young writers. *Journal of Educational Psychology*, *97*(2), 43–54. doi:10.1037/0022-0663.97.1.43

Santangelo, T., & Graham, S. (2016). A comprehensive meta-analysis of handwriting instruction. *Educational Psychology Review*, *28*, 225–265. doi:10.1007/s10648-015-9335-1

Schumaker, J. B., & Deshler, D. D. (2003). Can students with LD become competent writers? *Learning Disability Quarterly*, *26*(2), 129–141. doi:10.2307/1593595

Schumaker, J. B., & Sheldon, J. B. (1998). *Fundamentals in the sentence writing strategy*. University of Kansas Center for Research on Learning. https://sim.drupal.ku.edu/fundamental-sentence-writing

Shanahan, T. (2006). Relations among oral language, reading, and writing development. In C. A. MacArthur, S. Graham, & J. Fitzgerald (Eds.). *Handbook of writing research* (pp. 171–183). The Guilford Press. doi:10.1111/j.1467-873X.2008.00423.x

Slavin, R. E., Lake, C., Inns, A., Baye, A., Dachet, D., & Haslam, J. (2019). *A quantitative synthesis of research on writing approaches in grades 2 to 12*. Best Evidence Encyclopedia. https://www.semanticscholar.org/paper/A-Quantitative-Synthesis-of-Research-on-Writing-in-Slavin-Lake/429c023671 6e0f28c61fa66e3aec9d2571dfef2c

Squires, K. E., & Wolter, J. A. (2016). The effects of orthographic pattern intervention on spelling performance of students with reading disabilities: A best evidence synthesis. *Remedial and Special Education*, *37*(6), 357–369. doi:10.1177/0741932516631115

Sulzby, E. (1996). *Roles of oral and written language as children approach conventional literacy*. In C. Pontecorvo, M. Orsolini, B. Burge, & L. B. Resnick (Eds.), *Children's early text construction* (pp. 25–46). Lawrence Erlbaum Associates, Inc. https://psycnet.apa.org/record/1996-97345-002

Taft, R., & Mason, L.H. (2011). Examining effects of writing interventions: Spotlighting results for students with primary disabilities other than learning disabilities. *Remedial and Special Education*, *32*(5), 359–370. doi:10.1177/0741932510362242

Toste, J. R., Didion, L., Peng, P., Filderman, M. J., & McClelland, A. M. (2020). A meta-analytic review of the relations between motivation and reading achievement for K-12 students. *Review of Educational Research*, *90*(3), 420–456. doi:10.3102/0034654320919352

Tracy, B., Reid, R., & Graham, S. (2009). Teaching young students strategies for planning and drafting stories: The impact of self-regulated strategy development, *The Journal of Educational Research*, *102*(5), 323–332. doi:10.3200/JOER.102.5.323-332

Troia, G., & Graham, S. (2002). The effectiveness of a highly explicit, teacher-directed strategy instruction routine: Changing the writing performance of students with learning disabilities. *Journal of Learning Disabilities*, *35*(4), 290–305. doi:10.1177/00222194020350040101

Truckenmiller, A. J., & Petscher, Y. (2020). The role of academic language in written composition in elementary and middle school. *Reading and Writing*, *33*(1), 45–66. doi:10.1007/s11145-019-09938-7

Wanzek, J., Vaughn, S., Wexler, J., Swanson, E. A., Edmonds, M., & Kim, A. H. (2006). A synthesis of reading interventions and their effects on the spelling outcomes of students with LD. *Journal of Learning Disabilities*, *39*(6), 528–543. doi:10.1177/00222194060390060501

Weerdenburg, M. V., Tesselhof, M., & Meijden, H. V. (2018). Touch-typing for better spelling and narrative-writing skills on the computer. *Journal of Computer Assisted Learning, 35*(1), 143–152. doi:10.1111/jcal.12323

White, S., Kim, Y., Chen, J., & Liu, F. (2015). *Performance of fourth-grade students in the 2012 NAEP computer-based writing pilot assessment: Scores, text length, and use of editing tools* (NCES 2015-119). National Center for Education Statistics, Institute of Education Sciences, U.S. Department of Education. https://nces.ed.gov/nationsreportcard/subject/writing/pdf/2015119.pdf

Williams, C., & Beam, S. (2019). Technology and writing: Review of research. *Computers & Education, 128*, 227–242. doi:10.1016/j.compedu.2018.09.024

Williams, K. J., Walker, M. A., Vaughn, S., & Wanzek, J. (2017). A synthesis of reading and spelling interventions and their effects on spelling outcomes for students with learning disabilities. *Journal of Learning Disabilities, 50*(3), 286–297. doi:10.1177/0022219415619753

Yarrow, F., & Topping, K. J. (2001). Collaborative writing: The effects of metacognitive prompting and structured peer interaction. *British Journal of Educational Psychology, 71*(2), 261–282. doi:10.1348/000709901158514

Zimmerman, B. J., & Risemberg, R. (1997). Becoming a self-regulated writer: A social cognitive perspective. *Contemporary Educational Psychology, 22*(1), 73–101. doi:10.1006/ceps.1997.0919

Section III

Effective Frameworks and Interventions for Students with Severe Disabilities

Fred Spooner

The term severe disabilities refers to students with low incidence disabilities that impact intellectual/cognitive functioning (e.g., autism, developmental disabilities, multiple disabilities, significant cognitive disabilities, intellectual disability, Browder et al., 2020). Over the years, the term has changed, but the people included in it have remained largely the same. For example, when the Education for All Handicapped Children Act was enacted in 1975, the phrasing of "severely and profoundly handicapped" was used and a few years later, it shifted to the phrasing of "severely handicapped". In the mid-1980s, the field changed to "person first" language and used phrasing like "people with severe handicaps". Next, the language to referring to persons with severe disabilities moved to use phrasing like "people with moderate and/or severe disabilities". Most recently, the shift has been in the direction of individuals with "extensive support needs" (ESN), putting the emphasis on the type of support and off of the type of disability. Authors in this section interchangeably have used students with severe disabilities and students with extensive support needs.

The chapters in this section reflect the continued interest and recent updates in critical areas of support for students with severe disabilities, including access to the general education curriculum, teaching academic skills (literacy, mathematics, and writing), and alternate assessment via alternate achievement standards. Additional important components to inclusion and to the success of these students in inclusive environments are the collaboration and teaming that is essential between and among professionals who teach and support students with severe disabilities, the use of peer support strategies to assist in imparting rigorous systematic instruction, and the intensive behavior support that is sometimes necessary to improve their overall functioning (academic, social, activities of daily living), and the use and extension of self-determination to younger students. As with other chapters in this book, evidence-based practices define and drive the presentations of this content.

Reference

Browder, D. M., Spooner, F., & Courtade, G. (2020). *Teaching students with moderate and severe disabilities* (2nd ed.). Guilford.

DOI: 10.4324/9781003043874-13

13

Access to the General Education Curriculum

Melissa E. Hudson[1], Leah Wood[2], Jenny Root[3], and Addie McConomy[4]

[1]EAST CAROLINA UNIVERSITY

[2]CALIFORNIA POLYTECHNIC STATE UNIVERSITY

[3]FLORIDA STATE UNIVERSITY

[4]ADDIE MCCONOMY

Setting the Stage

Students with extensive support needs (ESN) are finally receiving the opportunity to learn what all students their age learn. Since the passage of the Individuals with Disabilities Education Act amendments (IDEA, 1997), all students are required to receive access to the general curriculum and schools must assess students' achievement of state standards. Even alternate assessments based on alternate achievement standards for students with significant cognitive disabilities must align with the state's academic content standards (U.S. Department of Education, 2005). States continue to adopt and revise state standards, many based on the Common Core State Standards (CCSS) in English/Language Arts and Mathematics (Common Core State Standards Initiative, 2010) and, as a result, many states have recently revised their alternate assessment to reflect these changes.

A challenge is for educators to find meaningful ways to teach state standards to students with ESN while also providing enough instruction in nonacademic life skills to meet individual student needs. When considering ways to ensure access to the general curriculum, it is important to consider the relationship of the context (the physical space), the content (curricular choices), and student learning (Jackson et al., 2008). Both context and content are important and have a direct impact on student learning outcomes. In this chapter, we aim to focus specifically on the content, or curricular priorities, and the research and evidence-based academic interventions for teaching the general curriculum to elementary students with ESN.

Curricular priorities for students with ESN have shifted to include the knowledge, practices (or skills), and processes that comprise the general curriculum. This means that in addition to foundational knowledge acquisition, students with ESN are expected to learn higher-order thinking routines through opportunities to apply the knowledge they learn. Academic practices are the component parts of academic processes. A practice is a behavior that requires both content

DOI: 10.4324/9781003043874-103

knowledge and procedural knowledge. A student who has learned information about ecosystems and has learned how to ask a question can then ask a question about animal habitats. Academic processes include the combination of practices to achieve a goal or outcome. Endeavoring to answer a question through inquiry or solve a problem using an engineering design process are examples of engaging in academic processes. Additionally, students with ESN can and should be taught in ways that promote acquisition, fluency, maintenance, and generalization of grade-aligned knowledge, practices, and processes (Wood, Root et al., 2019).

Specific curricular priorities vary across content areas. For English/Language Arts instruction, students with ESN should have opportunities to access and comprehend text. Recent research shows us students with ESN can learn to independently decode and read connected text (Ahlgrim-Delzell et al., 2016). Students should access a wide range of text (e.g., fictional, expository) across grade levels (Browder et al., 2009). In mathematics, curricular priorities include foundational math (early numeracy skills), grade-level domains (e.g., Counting and Cardinality, Measurement and Data, Geometry) and mathematical practices (e.g., problem-solving skills). Saunders et al. (2019) recommended a curricular shift for students with ESN from early numeracy to real-world applications as students move from elementary to secondary grades. Problem-solving instruction (and an emphasis on all mathematical practices) can be taught alongside basic early numeracy skills (Saunders et al.).

Science, engineering, and social studies should be accessible for students with ESN. Curricular priorities for science include foundational knowledge of scientific vocabulary and concepts to build an understanding of science content (or the domains of science). Students can apply this knowledge while learning science or engineering practices (e.g., asking questions, identifying problems, interpreting data) and complex processes, like inquiry or problem-solving (Knight et al., 2019). Social studies have similar priorities. Students with ESN will benefit from learning conceptual knowledge about different disciplines of social studies (i.e., civics, economics, geography, history). Further, students can develop as engaged citizens by applying their conceptual knowledge to practices and processes (Scruggs et al., 2008). Historical inquiry, for example, is the process of developing questions, examining data from historical artifacts, text, or other primary sources, and drawing conclusions. Across all academic content areas, there is a need and benefit to learning factual information, core concepts, and related vocabulary. Additionally, students should receive instruction in how to develop the academic skills and practices necessary to engage in higher-order thinking processes (like inquiry or problem-solving). An important consideration is that addressing these curricular priorities should not be at the expense of meeting the individualized needs of students with ESN (Spooner et al., 2017). Educators have the ambitious task of prioritizing and simplifying academic content so that students make meaningful gains that will maintain and generalize across contexts.

In addition to content, context matters. Students placed in general curriculum classrooms often have more opportunities to access the general curriculum, benefit from the content area expertise of their teachers, and use materials that are age and grade-appropriate when compared to peers in self-contained placements (Agran et al., 2020). For example, Ruppar et al. (2018) examined the exposure to literacy for students eligible to take the alternate assessment. The team found that participants who engaged in literacy activities in general education settings alongside peers without disabilities were *10 times more likely* to encounter academic literacy and a wide variety of text types when compared to students in self-contained settings. Context alone, however, is not enough. The integration of research and evidence-based practices for students to fully access general curriculum content is needed.

Planning instruction that aligns with state or national standards (e.g., Next Generation Science Standards, 2013) can be especially daunting given the lack of emphasis on academic learning in many published resources. Historically, research for students with ESN has focused on nonacademic activities, even when addressing academic content. Until recently, research in reading was primarily focused on functional sight word instruction (Browder et al., 2006), in mathematics on money and simple computation (Browder, Spooner et al., 2008), and in science primarily on daily living tasks (Spooner et al., 2011). Next, we will briefly review recent research that has provided models for teaching state standards to students with ESN, including the acquisition of academic knowledge, practices, and processes.

In a comprehensive review of 128 studies that included reading instruction for students with ESN, Browder et al. (2006) determined there was strong support for using systematic instruction to teach sight word and picture recognition. In a follow up review, Browder et al. (2009) identified constant time delay, specifically, as an evidence-based practice for teaching literacy skills to students with ESN. As curricular priorities have shifted to include higher-order thinking and access to wide ranges of text, researchers have examined practices for teaching comprehension. Hudson and Test (2011) evaluated the use of task-analyzed shared stories and determined there was moderate, promising support for this practice. Additionally, studies have continued to examine strategies for promoting comprehension. For example, Wood, Browder et al. (2020) taught elementary-aged students with moderate intellectual disability to generate questions about expository e-text. Students were taught to develop questions using systematic instruction and an iPad template. Students learned to access and play science e-texts with text-to-speech capabilities and then searched for answers to their questions in the text. Finally, Ahlgrim-Delzell et al. (2016) taught students to decode using time delay and a system of least prompts. Students with intellectual disability, autism spectrum disorder, and complex communication needs engaged in scripted, systematic lessons and used a phoneme grid on an iPad to blend and segment sounds in words. Research in ELA continues to demonstrate that students with ESN can learn to read and comprehend.

Second to English/Language Arts, mathematics is the most researched academic content area for students with ESN (Spooner et al., 2017). Browder, Spooner et al. (2008) conducted a meta-analysis in which they identified 68 studies in which mathematics was taught to students with severe disabilities. Most of the studies included numbers (e.g., number identification), basic computation, or measurement. In a follow up review, Spooner et al. (2019) identified an additional 36 studies in which mathematics was taught to students with ESN. The team determined that in addition to systematic instruction, instructional procedures of technology-aided instruction, graphic organizers, manipulatives, and explicit instruction were found to be EBPs for teaching mathematics to this population. Recent research has examined interventions for teaching mathematical practices and processes, like problem solving. Browder et al. (2018) taught students with moderate intellectual disability to solve addition and subtraction word problems using modified schema-based instruction. Brosh et al. (2018) extended these findings and embedded literacy instruction and outcomes in mathematics problem solving lessons.

While science instruction for students with ESN is not as well researched as English/Language Arts and mathematics, there is a growing body of studies that suggest systematic instruction can be used to teach disciplinary core ideas, science and engineering practice, and processes like inquiry or problem solving. Spooner et al. (2011) identified 17 studies in which science was taught to students with ESN. Most studies, which were identified between 1985 and 2009, included instruction in health, safety, and nutrition. Knight et al. (2019) extended the findings of the Spooner et al. review and identified 15 studies, 12 of which met the criteria for analysis. The authors evaluated the evidence base for teaching both science content and practices. The authors determined multiple exemplar training, task analytic instruction, and time delay were EBPs for teaching science content and practices to students with ESN. Additionally, the authors determined the practices of model-lead-test, examples and non-example training, and graphic organizers (e.g., KWHL charts) were "potentially EBPs", meaning there were studies with positive effects, but more data is needed to consider these EBPs.

In contrast to other academic content areas, social studies are the least researched for students with ESN. There are currently no comprehensive social studies content reviews and only a small number of experimental research studies in this content area. Even within broad academic reviews, the research on social studies has been non-existent or scant. Knight and Sartini (2015) conducted a broad review of comprehension strategies across academic content areas and did not identify any research for social studies that met the authors' criteria for inclusion in their analysis. Hudson et al. (2013) reviewed literature in which students with ESN were taught academic skills in inclusive settings. The authors identified four studies in which social studies vocabulary was taught to students with ESN in general education settings using systematic instruction (i.e., embedded time delay, simultaneous prompting). Recent research includes a handful of studies that promote social studies text comprehension (e.g., Courtade et al., 2017; McKissick et al., 2013; Zakas et al., 2013). Finally, two additional studies have investigated methods for teaching higher-order thinking skills, like procedural or investigative learning, for students with ESN. These methods included teaching students to ask and answer questions about grade-level social studies texts that were read aloud (Wood et al., 2015) and the use of structured inquiry and graphic organizers on social studies comprehension for students with autism spectrum disorder (Schenning et al., 2013).

What Do We Know Based on Research?

In a comprehensive review of the research literature, Spooner et al. (2012) identified methods for teaching academic content to students with severe disabilities. In nearly all this research, principles of applied behavior analysis were used and systematic prompting with feedback was found to have a strong evidence base. While most studies in this review were conducted in self-contained special education settings, the importance of systematic instruction was reconfirmed in a comprehensive review of interventions provided in general education classrooms to teach academic skills conducted by Hudson et al. (2013). Hudson et al. found 17 experimental studies that focused on academic learning in general education settings by students with moderate or severe intellectual disability. The studies varied across instructional strategies (e.g., embedded trial instruction, system of least prompts, multiple exemplars, graphic organizers); modes of delivery (e.g., peer tutors, paraprofessionals, general educators); and content (e.g., science, math, literacy). The results indicated that students with ESN could learn academic content in general education settings.

In a recent study conducted by Afacan et al. (2018), the researchers found that multicomponent instruction for teaching reading was important for learners with intellectual disabilities. In the past, reading instruction for students with ESN, including students with intellectual disability, was often limited to one dimension of reading, such as sight word recognition (Browder et al., 2006) which is contrary to the recommendations of the National Reading Panel (2000) who recommended five components of reading instruction be addressed (i.e., phonemic awareness, phonics, vocabulary, comprehension, fluency). Afacan et al. evaluated seven studies that used a multicomponent instruction approach for elementary-aged learners with intellectual disability (mean age ranged from 7.5 to 9.4 years). The researchers found that students with intellectual disabilities who were exposed to multicomponent reading programs significantly improved their reading skills compared to their peers with intellectual disabilities who received traditional sight word instruction or to their previous reading performance. The researchers also noted the importance of instruction on phonemic awareness skills in the early grades for learners with intellectual disability because phonemic awareness skills are necessary for reading development and are often difficult for students with intellectual disability to learn. Allor et al. (2014) found that students with lower IQs may need high-quality reading instruction at greater frequency and duration (i.e., dosage) to learn foundational reading skills such as phonemic awareness.

Instructional Strategies

Embedded Time Delay Instruction

The first strategy Hudson et al. (2013) found to be evidence-based involved embedding a systematic instructional trial in the ongoing milieu of a general education lesson. An instructional trial is an opportunity for a student to make a discrete response (e.g., read a word, identify a number) or a chained response such as reading a passage or solving a problem (Collins, 2012). An instructional session may be comprised of a single trial or multiple trials, depending on how many trials the student needs to practice the skill adequately. These trials can be massed together by offering several opportunities in succession in which the student makes the same or similar responses (e.g., reading a list of words or identifying the same word several times in a row). The trials also can be distributed across an activity (e.g., identifying the number 5 whenever it shows up during a lesson). When these distributed trials are embedded within a naturally occurring lesson or routine, it is called embedded instruction. Embedding instructional trials may promote the generalization of skills due to the natural fluctuation of materials, settings, and teachers throughout typical instruction.

When an opportunity to respond is given, students may need a prompt such as a model of touching or saying the correct answer. Once a prompt is used, the challenge then becomes fading this prompt so that the student provides the response without assistance. Time delay procedure (Snell & Gast, 1981; Touchette, 1971) is an errorless learning procedure that employs delay procedures as a means of shifting stimulus control. When applied to classroom instruction, the time delay procedure can reduce the number of errors students make, which, in turn, promotes the acquisition of new skills. Time delay is an evidence-based practice that has been used widely in research on literacy for students with severe disabilities to fade prompting (Browder et al., 2009). When using time delay, the prompt is first presented along with the discriminative stimulus that starts the instructional trial. For example, the teacher says the word "friends" while holding up a flashcard with the word printed on it. This first trial is conducted at a 0-s delay to promote errorless responding. Over teaching trials, the instructor inserts small increments of time (e.g., 2 s) between presenting the target stimulus and giving the prompt. In this example, the teacher shows the flashcard, waits 2 s for the student to anticipate the correct response, and, if the student does not answer, models the correct response by saying "friends". The student then repeats the answer "friends". Over time, the student begins to anticipate the correct response before the prompt. Researchers have used a constant time delay method in which a preset number of 0-s delay trials are given and then the prompt is delayed by a constant amount of time (e.g., 4 s). Another form of time delay used in research is a progressive time delay in which the prompt is delayed gradually across trials (e.g., 2 s, 4 s, 6 s, 8 s). As the student anticipates the correct response before the prompt, stimulus control is transferred from the prompt to the target stimulus. Time delay can be an efficient and effective method of instruction by promoting near errorless learning.

Research on embedded trial instruction has primarily used time delay methodology (Jimenez & Kamei, 2015). These applications have been successful across grade levels and content areas. For example, Johnson et al. (2004) used embedded trials and constant time delay to teach sight words (e.g., police, stop, danger) from a first grade reading curriculum to a 7-year-old student with developmental disabilities. The special education teacher, general education teacher, and a member of the research team worked collaboratively to select words for instruction that were part of the standard curriculum being taught in the general education classroom before the words were taught to general education students. The general education teacher delivered embedded trial instruction during opening or closing activities, transitions, or breaks. Since sight word instruction was completed before the words were introduced to other students, the student with disabilities was often the first to identify a sight word when it was introduced to the class.

Similarly, Jameson et al. (2012) examined the effects of embedding English/Language Arts instruction to teach pre-reading skills to an elementary-aged student with developmental disabilities and autism spectrum disorder. Teachers and researchers derived target pre-reading skills from the state's standards for phonological and phonemic awareness. The special education teacher taught the student to recognize similar and dissimilar word sounds. For instance, given a list of CVC words, the student learned to identify words with similar or dissimilar beginning or ending sounds. Embedded trial instruction has also been used to teach mathematics to elementary aged students. Polychronis et al. (2004) conducted a study in which general education teachers delivered instruction to students with moderate intellectual disability in the second and fifth grades. One teacher taught a student to identify the numerals 0–9, while another teacher taught tell timing at 15 min and 30 min past the hour, consistent with the second grade state mathematics standard of telling time.

System of Least Prompts

A second prompting strategy that can be used to teach academic content to elementary students with ESN is the system of least prompts (also call least intrusive prompts). While most applications of time delay use one prompt, the system of least prompts include two or more prompts given in sequence, beginning with the least intrusive level of assistance and ending with a prompt that ensures the student makes the correct response (called the controlling prompt). To illustrate how the system of least prompts works, in the next example, the system of least prompts is used to teach a student the steps needed to use a calculator to add two numbers and the prompt hierarchy consists of a verbal prompt, a model prompt, and a physical prompt. After giving the student the opportunity to use a calculator on his own, the teacher gives a verbal prompt to tell the student what to do in the first step (e.g., teacher says, "enter the first number"). If the student is successful, the teacher provides praise and moves on to the next step. If the student does not respond or begins to make an error, the teacher uses a model prompt that shows the student what to do (e.g., teacher says, "enter 5 like this" and demonstrates how to enter 5) and provides another opportunity. The student may imitate this model and be ready to move on to the next step. If not, the teacher uses the third and controlling prompt by guiding the student to respond (e.g., teacher says, "let me help you press the 5" and physically guides the student to press the number). While this example uses three common prompts in the prompt hierarchy (i.e., verbal, model, physical), it is important for teachers to understand that prompts can be anything that provides additional information to the student to come up with the correct response.

Courtade et al. (2013) taught three general education teachers to use the system of least prompts during story-based lessons to promote academic engagement for elementary students with intellectual disabilities and autism aged 6–8 years who were included in their classrooms. Three teacher pairs that consisted of a special education teacher and a general education teacher developed and implemented the story-based lessons. Special education teachers adapted grade-level stories, reading series passages, and informational text following a 12-step task analysis adapted from Browder et al. (2009). Then general education teachers used the adapted text and a 10-step tasks analysis for teaching story-based lessons adapted by Browder et al. (2009) to engage learners with disabilities during the lesson in the general education classroom. General education teachers were taught to use the system of least prompts to provide help to students if needed for several steps of the task-analyzed story-based lessons, including identifying target vocabulary words and answering comprehension questions about the adapted text. The study's results indicated that five of six teachers consistently used the task analysis to either adapt the story or to implement a story-based lesson and all students improved their academic engagement during story-based lessons.

Another option for using the system of least prompts strategy was developed by Hudson et al. (2014) for listening comprehension of adapted grade-level text. During a fourth grade general education science class, trained peer tutors used the system of least prompts to support listening comprehension for three learners with moderate intellectual disability. The peer tutors read aloud adapted science passages and asked factual recall and inferential comprehension questions about the adapted science text. When students needed help to answer a factual recall comprehension question, peer tutors delivered four levels of prompts including: (a) rereading selected text such as the paragraph containing the target response, (b) rereading the sentence containing the target response, (c) telling the target response, and (d) showing the target response. For inferential comprehension questions, the first and last prompts were the same as for answering factual recall questions, but the second and third prompts involved a think aloud. For the think-aloud, peer tutors asked participants to think about their experience as the second level prompt (e.g., *How do you feel when you haven't eaten since breakfast?*). When the student did not make the correct response, the peer tutors delivered the third prompt by modeling how they related to the experience (e.g., *I feel hungry when I haven't eaten since breakfast.)*

In a similar study, Hudson and Browder (2014) used a peer-delivered system of least prompts intervention and read-aloud of an adapted grade-level story (i.e., The Watson's Go to Birmingham—1963) to teach listening comprehension to elementary students with moderate intellectual disability aged 9–11 years during fifth-grade reading class. Trained peer tutors delivered the system of least prompts intervention during their reading class. In this application of the system of least prompts, peer tutors also included three instructional scaffolds in the first prompt. First, students were told the type of wh—word question that was going to be asked (e.g., The next question is a *who* question.) Second, a rule for the wh—word question was given (e.g., When you hear *who*, listen for a *person's name*). Third, students were told to listen for relevant information as the text was read again (e.g., Listen for *who* was hurt as the text is read again). All students with disabilities improved their listening comprehension with this approach.

Multiple Exemplars

In addition to the prompting strategies, another effective instructional strategy for teaching academic content to elementary students with ESN is to use multiple exemplars of the target material to promote the generalization of the academic concept. Through exposure to multiple representations of a single concept, students can learn the essential component of a concept rather than fixate on an irrelevant attribute of the presentations of the concept (Collins, 2012). Researchers have shown how elementary students with ESN can acquire science concepts when materials are varied. For example, Root (2019) used explicit instruction with four categories of stimuli (i.e., far distractor objects, near distractor objects, near distractor pictures, and environmental objects) to teach acquisition and generalization of mathematical concepts (more, different, long) to an elementary student with autism and intellectual disability. In another study, Knight et al. (2012) used examples and non-examples with the explicit instruction to teach 15 science descriptors (e.g., different, wet, on, change) to three elementary students with autism spectrum disorder and mild or moderate intellectual disability. During the model-lead-test intervention, five objects were displayed (i.e., three examples and two non-examples). The interventionist provided a model of the objects (e.g., "this is *wet*" or "this is *not wet*.") During the lead phase, students said or pointed to the objects with the interventionist and during the test phase, the objects were shuffled, and participants were given an opportunity to name each object. All three participants increased the number of science descriptors they acquired, and some generalized use of the science descriptors to novel objects, pictures, and an inquiry science lesson in general education.

Graphic Organizers

A fourth strategy to consider when planning academic instruction in the general education setting for elementary students with ESN is the use of graphic organizers. Graphic organizers provide a visual representation of content that is enhanced by organizational tools for categorizing or describing important content. The National Reading Panel (2000) identified the use of graphic organizers as one of the eight successful methods for teaching comprehension in general education settings. While the use of graphic organizers in special education is not uncommon, until recently, most of the research on the effects of graphic organizers on learning has been conducted with students with learning disabilities (see the meta-analysis by Dexter & Hughes, 2011).

The use of graphic organizers, however, is beginning to appear in the literature for teaching academics to students with ESN (Browder et al., 2012; Jimenez et al., 2012; Zakas et al., 2013). While these next three examples illustrate how graphic organizers can be used to teach academics with middle school students, the procedures described could apply to elementary-aged students learning academic content. Jimenez et al. taught peers without disabilities to embed constant time delay to teach the use of a KWHL chart for middle school students with moderate intellectual disability. The general education teacher provided inquiry science instruction to all students, including daily use of the KWHL chart, and peer tutors taught their student partners to follow components of the KWHL chart using constant time delay instructional trials embedded in the general education science lesson. Students with disabilities also received embedded instruction from their peer tutors on the science concepts addressed in the inquiry lesson. The number of correct science responses increased for all five participants across all science units taught throughout the study.

Browder et al. (2012) used task-analytic instruction, read-aloud of math word problems, and a graphic organizer to teach four middle school students with moderate intellectual disability to solve math problems derived from state middle school math standards. Four units of instruction were created that included eight word problems for each math standard (i.e., algebra, data analysis, geometry, measurement) and an adapted math story for each problem based on activities (e.g., shopping, voting) and numbers (i.e., 1–10) familiar to students. Adapted math stories were created by pairing key vocabulary with picture symbols using picture symbol software. A graphic organizer was created for each unit that students used to interact with the math content (e.g., department store site map in the geometry unit) during instruction. Task-analytic instruction included the steps needed to solve the math problem (e.g., identify a point on a map, draw a line from point to point). The special education teacher used the system of least prompts as needed and prompts included non-specific verbal direction, specific verbal direction, model, and physical guidance. Although the Browder et al. study was conducted in a self-contained classroom, these math graphic organizers could be embedded in general education with peer support like that used by Jimenez et al. (2012).

Zakas (2013) also used a graphic organizer in a self-contained setting to improve comprehension of self-read history passages for three middle school students with autism spectrum disorder and intellectual disability. She adapted grade-level social studies text by summarizing story passages and adding picture symbols for main ideas and key vocabulary. Students first learned definitions for the words used in the graphic organizer (i.e., *event, people, location, time, detail, sequence, and outcome*) and demonstrated comprehension by matching each vocabulary word to its definition. Next, students completed a graphic organizer using scripted lessons in which the student read the passage and answered questions to complete the graphic organizer (e.g., What was the event?) If needed, prompts were provided (e.g., stating the definition of the vocabulary word, rereading the text). When completed, the graphic organizer contained (a) the *event*, (b) the *people* involved in the event, (c) the *location* of the event, (d) three *details* from the passage, and (e) the *outcome* of the event. Generalization was measured using new passages not used for instruction.

Task-Analytic Instruction

In a recent review of mathematics instruction for students with severe disabilities, Hudson et al. (2018) found task analytic to be an evidence-based practice for teaching mathematics and an earlier literature review by Hudson and Test (2011) found a moderate level of evidence to support the use of a task-analysis to promote comprehension during a read-aloud lesson for students with severe disabilities. A task analysis is often used with a graphic organizer and systematic prompting and feedback to promote academic learning for students with ESN. A task analysis is used to break a complex task (or lesson) into discrete steps that can be used for teaching and data collection. These steps can then be taught using forward chaining, backward chaining, or total task presentation. The use of task analytic instruction has been used to teach many academic skills for elementary learners with ESN, including participating in an early science lesson (Smith et al., 2013), increasing task independence (Cohen & Demchak, 2018), solving a math problem (Knight et al., 2018), engaging in a read-aloud lesson (Courtade et al., 2013), and asking questions during a social studies lesson (Wood et al., 2015).

Technology

Increasingly, technology is being used along with task-analytic instruction and graphic organizers to teach elementary learners with ESN in inclusive settings. For example, Knight et al. (2018) used video prompting and task-analytic instruction to teach three elementary students with autism spectrum disorder and intellectual disability to complete a multi-step task in the general education classroom. The researchers created a video prompt using first-person perspective (i.e., the adults' hands), demonstrating the steps for solving double-digit addition problems, generating fractions, determining habitats, spelling own name, identifying numbers, and determining geographic locations (e.g., cities). These grade-aligned core content tasks were selected because they were included in the students' IEPs and were currently being taught in the general education classroom. The task analyses ranged in a number of steps from 10–14 steps, and the video prompts averaged 3:48 minutes (range of 1 min 2 s–7:00 min). The video prompting intervention was delivered by trained paraprofessionals during academic periods in the general education classroom. Results from the study indicated that all students performed all skills at higher levels in the intervention condition than in the baseline conditions. Social validity data from paraprofessionals and general education teachers also indicated that the intervention was well received.

Likewise, Wood et al. (2020) used technology-based supports (i.e., electronic graphic organizer), systematic instruction, and a student-friendly task-analysis to teach comprehension of science e-text to elementary-aged students with moderate intellectual disability. While this study was conducted in a separate special education classroom in a public school, embedded probes during general education science class were conducted four times throughout the study. The researcher developed a two-page question generating template using a commercially available software app and a 12-step student-friendly task-analysis for accessing an e-text through a website. Students used the template to generate literal recall questions about the e-text. On the first page of the template, students selected the type of question they wanted to ask (e.g., who, where, what) and then followed a four-step process for developing the question using the second page of the template. Students could voice their complete questions using text-to-speech capabilities. All students increased the number of questions generated using the template and the number of independent correct responses to comprehension questions about the e-text with the intervention.

Delivery of Instruction

Although systematic prompting and feedback is an effective strategy for students with ESN, finding ways to deliver this instruction in a general education class can be challenging. The research in inclusive settings offers several models for who might be effective in providing systematic instruction.

Peer Tutors

Peers are a natural and effective means for providing support for students with disabilities in the school environment (Heinrich et al., 2016). Daily interactions with peers provide students with models for various academic and functional activities and skills. Although opportunities for peers and students with disabilities to interact is often a typical component of a school day, the literature supports the practice of explicitly teaching peers skills and strategies for providing instruction to others. Within this robust body of research exists a growing subset of studies specifically showing peers can be effective instructors for students with ESN (e.g., Godsey et al., 2008; Hudson & Browder, 2014; Hudson et al., 2014; Jameson et al., 2012; Jimenez et al., 2012). Before peers can be asked to provide systematic instruction like time delay, some method is needed to build the peers' capacity for delivering this instruction. Consideration also needs to be given to how the peers will maintain their own academic learning.

One option is to provide the peers with a manual and some training. Using a detailed manual and specific verbal feedback, Jameson et al. (2008) trained peer tutors to teach health and art concepts to students with significant cognitive disabilities. Jameson et al. developed a three-page training manual that specifically described procedures for embedding constant time delay trials in typical classroom routines. Peers may be able to learn the procedures without a manual if sample materials are provided. Jimenez et al. (2012) trained peers to embed a minimum of nine trials each session in the science classroom using a constant time delay. Additionally, peers learned to embed self-monitoring trials using a KWHL chart. A third option is to provide the peer tutor with a script to read while delivering instruction (e.g., Hudson & Browder, 2014; Hudson et al., 2014; Jameson et al., 2012; Wolery et al., 1997). For example, Jameson et al. gave middle school peer tutors an example of an instructional script to use in providing embedded constant time delay instruction during general education class. For younger peer tutors, Wolery et al. (1997) placed target stimuli on the front of 10 cm x 15 cm white cards and a script for delivering time delay instructional trials on the back. The cards were bound together into a book using a black comb and could be rebound as needed.

Researchers using peer tutors to deliver academic instruction in general education classrooms have also evaluated the impact of peer tutoring on the peer tutors (e.g., Hudson & Browder, 2014; Jameson et al., 2012; Jimenez et al., 2012). Results from these studies are consistent with previous research (e.g., Carter et al., 2016; McDonnell et al., 2000) that found benefits for both students with and without disabilities.

Paraprofessionals

Often paraprofessionals deliver instruction and provide support to students with disabilities across all domains of a school environment (Heinrich et al., 2016; Knight et al., 2018; Ryan et al., 2019). Paraprofessionals are an essential element of the services provided to students with severe disabilities due to the varied and intricate needs of this population. Careful and consistent collaboration between the special education teacher and the paraprofessional can help ensure the likelihood that paraprofessionals are delivering supports and instruction with fidelity and to the appropriate extent. There is a need for caution in relying on paraprofessionals. For instance, one-on-one peer assistance in a general education setting may be less stigmatizing than one-on-one adult assistance. Another caveat is paraprofessionals, like peer tutors, are not typically trained in delivering instruction to students with severe disabilities in a general education classroom. As students with ESN are increasingly educated alongside their peers, consideration should be applied to methods used to train paraprofessionals to promote such learning. Like peers, paraprofessionals may benefit from having scripts, manuals, and special training sessions (Jameson et al., 2012).

General Education Teachers

General education teachers need to teach academic content to many students and may not have either the training or time to provide one-to-one or small group systematic instruction. However, with explicit training on embedding instruction into naturalistic classroom routines, general education teachers may have the potential to promote the learning of students with severe disabilities during whole class instruction (Courtade et al., 2013; Hudson & Browder, 2014; Wolery et al., 1997). Wolery et al. provided general education teachers with detailed training, which included explicit instruction for how to integrate these procedures into their regular teaching. Wolery et al. taught three general education teachers to embed instructional trials using a constant time delay. A less intensive role for the general education teacher might be to provide opportunities for the student with severe disabilities to generalize learned content. Hudson and Browder (2014) taught a fifth grade general education teacher to implement the system of least prompts during generalization probes of listening comprehension during literacy class. Another option is for the special education teacher to provide these embedded trials in a coteaching context. Additionally, Courtade et al. trained three elementary general education teachers to use the system of least prompts procedure to support the students during task-analyzed steps of the story-based lesson and to answer comprehension questions. Using the adapted book created by the special education teachers, the general education teachers planned for the inclusion of the steps of the story-based lesson within the general education read-aloud lesson.

Setting the Course for Effective Inclusion

Universal Design for Learning

Planning for the effective inclusion of students with disabilities in the general education classroom should be guided by the Universal Design for Learning (UDL) framework. Instruction is proactively designed to anticipate variability in the learning needs of all students in the classroom by identifying barriers in the learning environment and curriculum that prevent meaningful access and increase opportunities for learning through multiple options to reach and measure goals (Meyer et al., 2014). The inclusion of UDL in federal legislation (i.e., Every Student Succeeds Act of 2015; Individual with Disabilities Education Improvement Act of 2004) reflects the magnitude of importance that has been placed on UDL for providing access to the general curriculum. In fact, when a panel of leaders met at the 2015 National Goals conference, UDL was identified as a topic they believed to be most critical to improving the education of learners with intellectual and developmental disabilities (Thoma et al., 2015).

The UDL framework has nine guidelines and 31 checkpoints that center around three main principles: (a) representation, (b) action and expression, and (c) engagement. That is, lessons and assessments are provided in more than one format so that learners can benefit from the representation that best suits their learning strengths. Relatedly, students have choices regarding how they interact with material and show what they know. All the while, structures and supports are in place to maximize engagement and motivation through choice making, self-regulation, and goal setting. The guidelines and checkpoints surrounding these three principles are intended to be implemented flexibly and benefit a variety of learners within the general education setting, not only those with identified disabilities (Meyer et al., 2014). It is important to note that these principles provide an overarching and intertwined structure for curriculum, materials, instruction, and assessment (Jimenez & Hudson, 2019).

While the promise of UDL to provide access to general curriculum content and contexts has been widely discussed (Copeland & Cosbey, 2008; Jimenez et al., 2007), there is limited empirical evidence of this for students with ESN (Smith & Lowrey, 2017; Rao et al., 2017). Most publications on UDL specific to this population relate to training pre-service and in-service teachers or use qualitative methods to describe implementation and perceptions of UDL in classrooms (e.g., McDonnell et al., 2001; Spooner et al., 2007). There are challenges to the implementation and identification of experimental studies of UDL, including variability in description and measurement of impact on student outcomes (Cook & Rao, 2018; Lowrey & Smith, 2018). Kennedy et al. (2014) argue this variability contributes to the paradox of UDL being flexible and broad enough to meet the needs of all learners in all content areas within this era of evidence-based practice. As such, Kennedy and colleagues call for instructional design and practice that is grounded in strong theory and valid measurement. Rao et al. echo these recommendations, urging researchers to consider how ULD can be used in conjunction with existing effective practices to support skill acquisition.

Examples of using the UDL framework to design instruction that incorporates research-based practices can be seen in the work of Browder, Mims et al. (2008) and Root et al. (2020). Browder, Mims et al. used the UDL framework to adapt books in a shared-story intervention to increase engagement of elementary students with complex multiple disabilities. Baseline data indicate simply providing accessible materials, an opportunity to select a text, reading the text aloud, and providing opportunities for engagement did not increase independence or engagement. Prior to intervention, researchers and the teacher worked together to individualize the task analysis using the UDL framework in order to improve student responding. Intervention data show that student independence and engagement increased only after participants were provided with systematic instruction on how to engage in each step of a shared story. The findings of Root et al. (2020) provide additional evidence to the efficacy of using systematic instruction in combination with a universally designed intervention in the area of mathematical problem solving for middle school students with ESN. During baseline, students were provided with choices of themes for their problems (e.g., school basketball game, barbershop), videos explaining how the math skill could be used in the selected community theme, graphic organizers, and task analysis while they solved problems related to calculating tips and discounts. It was not until after students received explicit instruction on vocabulary and the problem solving process, with multiple opportunities to practice and receive feedback, that students made progress and gained independence in problem solving.

Guidelines for Choosing an Instructional Strategy

While knowing the instructional strategies available is important, it is also helpful to know when to apply a specific strategy. Teachers should first remind themselves that instruction should be "no more different than necessary" (Browder et al., 2013). Instruction should begin with layering evidence-based practices for students with ESN on top of existing general education practices. For example, all students in the class may be learning to follow a mnemonic to use schematic diagrams (i.e., graphic organizers) to model mathematical word problems. Students who demonstrate difficulty with following the mnemonic due to their level of literacy or executive functioning skills may be given a task analysis instead and be provided with color-coded schematic diagrams if they have difficulty with drawing the diagrams themselves.

Decisions to increase or decrease support should be driven by data (Jimenez, Mims et al., 2012) and instructional approaches or strategies will vary across the four stages of learning: acquisition, fluency, maintenance, and generalization (Shurr et al., 2019). When students are in the initial acquisition phase of learning, errorless learning procedures such as constant time delay and simultaneous prompting are efficient and effective because they promote only learning the correct skill, preventing mistakes and the need to "unlearn" (Collins, 2012; Wood et al., 2020). For students to

Table 13.1 Research-Supported Strategies Aligned to Academic Tasks for Instructional Planning

Type of Content	*Examples*	*Strategy*	*Research Example*
Vocabulary-Definitions and identification	Science definitions Geometric figures Numbers	-Simultaneous prompting -Constant time delay -Explicit instruction delivered via Computer-assisted Instruction	-Heinrich et al. (2016) -Smith et al. (2013) -Hawkins-Lear and Grisham-Brown (2019)
Inquiry-based lessons	Social studies concepts Science concepts	-embedded trials with system of least prompts and constant time delay	-Ryan et al. (2019) -Jimenez, Browder et al. (2012)
Multistep Process	Double-digit addition, spelling	Video prompting	-Knight et al. (2018)
Comprehension of Text	Grade-aligned adapted literature Content-area text	-System of Least Prompts -Graphic Organizers	-Hudson and Browder (2014) -Hudson et al. (2014) -Wood et al. (2015)
Higher Order Thinking Skills	Question generating Writing	System of least prompts Task analysis	-Wood et al. (2015) -Lim & Lee (2019)
Self-determination skills	Goal attainment	Peer support arrangements	Carter et al. (2016)
Engagement and participation	Social participation Peer connections Group responding	Peer support arrangements Response cards	Carter et al. (2016)Clarke et al. (2016)

develop higher-order thinking skills and engage in practices expected in general education settings, instruction will need to adjust and promote automaticity (automatic retrieval) and fluency (accurate and fast retrieval). This will allow students to dedicate more of their working memory to complex tasks (e.g., constructing explanations) instead of foundational tasks (e.g., sounding out words). Teachers can support fluency by fading reinforcement and prompts while giving opportunities to practice across time and materials. Finally, it is important that skills are maintained over time and can generalize to untrained contexts. This can be supported by periodically reviewing and reusing previously learned content.

Even when planning with UDL and applying the rule of "no more different than necessary", there will be times a student with ESN needs the individualized strategies described in this chapter. Table 13.1 below gives some research-supported strategies aligned to common academic tasks that can serve as a starting point for instructional planning.

Summary

Providing access to the general curriculum in inclusive settings should begin with UDL and incorporate evidence-based and research-based practices for students with ESN. This chapter offers some starting points for teachers to build capacity to include all students in learning state standards in general education classrooms. Creating lessons that anticipate the variability in learning needs for all participants may save time and maximize learning. When individual supports for learning are needed, systematic prompting strategies, multiple exemplars, and graphic organizers can support students with ESN to master the content. These supports can be delivered by peers, paraprofessionals, or teachers.

References

Afacan, K., Wilkerson, K. L., & Ruppar, A. L. (2018). Multicomponent reading interventions for students with intellectual disability. *Remedial and Special Education, 39*(4), 229–242. doi:10.1177/0741932517702444

Agran, M., Jackson, L., Kurth, J. A., Ryndak, D., Burnette, K., Jameson, M., Zagona, A., Fitzpatrick, H., & Wehmeyer, M. (2020). Why aren't students with severe disabilities being placed in general education classrooms: Examining the relations among classroom placement, learner outcomes, and other factors. *Research and Practice for Persons with Severe Disabilities, 45*(1), 4–13. doi:10.1177/1540796919878134

Ahlgrim-Delzell, L., Browder, D. M., Wood, L., Stanger, C., Preston, A. I., & Kemp-Inman, A. (2016). Systematic instruction of phonics skills using an iPad for students with developmental disabilities who are AAC users. *Journal of Special Education, 50*(2), 86–97. doi:10.1177/0022466915622140

Allor, J. H., Mathes, P. G., Roberts, J. K., Cheatham, J. P., & Al Otaiba, S. (2014). Is scientifically based reading instruction effective for students with below-average IQs? *Exceptional Children, 80*(3), 287–306. doi:10.1177/0014402914522208

Brosh, C. R., Root, J. R., Saunders, A. F., Spooner, F., & Fisher, L. B. (2018). Embedding literacy in mathematics problem solving instruction for learners with intellectual and developmental disability: Problem solving. *Inclusion, 6*(2), 81–96. doi:10.1352/2326-6988-6.2.81

Browder, D. M., Jimenez, B. A., & Trela, K. (2012). Grade-aligned math instruction for secondary students with moderate intellectual disability. *Education and Training in Autism and Developmental Disabilities, 47*(3), 373–388. http://daddcec.org/Publications/ETADDJournal.aspx

Browder, D. M., Mims, P. J., Spooner, F., Ahlgrim-Delzell, L., & Lee, A. (2008). Teaching elementary students with multiple disabilities to participate in shared stories. *Research and Practice for Persons with Severe Disabilities, 33*(1-2), 3–12. doi:10.2511/rpsd.33.1-2.3

Browder, D. M., Hudson, M. E., & Wood, L. (2013). Using principles of high quality instruction in the general education classroom to provide access to the general education curriculum. In J. McLeskey, N. L., Waldron, F. Spooner, & B. Algozzine (Eds.), *Handbook of effective inclusive schools: Research and practice*. Routledge.

Browder, D. M., Spooner, F., Ahlgrim-Delzell, L., Harris, A. A., & Wakeman, S. (2008). A meta-analysis on teaching mathematics to students with significant cognitive disabilities. *Exceptional Children, 74*(4), 407–432. doi:10.1177/001440290807400401

Browder, D. M., Spooner, F., Lo, Y., Saunders, A. F., Root, J. R., Ley Davis, L., & Brosh, C. R. (2018). Teaching students with moderate intellectual disability to solve word problems. *Journal of Special Education, 51*(4), 222–235. doi:10.1177/0022466917721236

Browder, D. M., Wakeman, S. Y., Spooner, F., Ahlgrim-Delzell, L., & Algozzine, B. (2006). Research on reading instruction for individuals with significant cognitive disabilities. *Exceptional Children, 72*(4), 392–408. doi:10.1177/001440290607200401

Browder, D. M., Ahlgrim-Delzell, L., Spooner, F., Mims, P. J., & Baker, J. N. (2009). Using time delay to teach literacy to students with severe developmental disabilities. *Exceptional Children, 75*(3), 343–364. doi:10.1177/001440290907500305

Carter, E. W., Asmus, J., Moss, C. K., Biggs, E. E., Bolt, D. M., Born, T. L., Brock, M. E., Cattey, G. N., Chen, R., Cooney, M., Fesperman, E., Hochman, J. M., Huber, H. B., Lequia, J. L., Lyons, G., Moyseenko, K. A., Riesch, L. M., Shalev, R. A., Vincent, L. B., & Weir, K. (2016). Randomized evaluation of peer support arrangements to support the inclusion of high school students with severe disabilities. *Exceptional Children, 82*(2), 209–233. doi:10.1177/0014402915598780

Common Core State Standards Initiative. (2010). *Common core state standards*. http://www.corestandards.org/read-the-standards/

Clarke, L. S., Haydon, T., Bauer, A., & Epperly, A. C. (2016). Inclusion of students with an intellectual disability in the general education classroom with the use of response cards. *Preventing School Failure, 60*(1), 35–42. doi:10.1080/1045988X.2014.966801

Cohen, A., & Demchak, M. (2018). Use of visual supports to increase task independence in students with severe disabilities in inclusive educational settings. *Education and Training in Autism and Developmental Disabilities, 53*(1), 84 –99. https://scholarworks.unr.edu/handle/11714/4215

Collins, B. C. (2012). *Systematic instruction for students with moderate and severe disabilities*. Brookes.

Cook, S. C., & Rao, K. (2018). Systematically applying UDL to effective practices for students with learning disabilities. *Learning Disability Quarterly, 41*(3), 179–191. doi:10.1177/0731948717749936

Copeland, S. R., & Cosbey, J. (2008). Making progress in the general curriculum: Rethinking effective instructional practices. *Research and Practice for Persons with Severe Disabilities, 33*(4), 214–227. doi:10.2511/rpsd.33.4.214

Courtade, G. R., Lingo, A. S., & Whitney, T. (2013). Using story-based lessons to increase academic engaged time in general education classes for students with moderate intellectual disability and autism. *Rural Special Education Quarterly, 32*(4), 3–14.

Courtade, G. R., Gurney, B. N., & Carden, R. (2017). Using read-alouds of grade-level social studies text and systematic prompting to promote comprehension for students with severe disabilities. *Journal of Social Studies Research, 41*(4), 291–301. doi:10.1016/j.jssr.2017.05.002

Dexter, D. D., & Hughes, C. A. (2011). Graphic organizers and students with learning disabilities: A meta-analysis. *Learning Disabilities, 34*(1), 51–72. doi:10.1177/073194871103400104

ESSA (2015). Every Student Succeeds Act of 2015, Pub. L. No. 114-95 § 114 Stat. 1177 (2015–2016).

Godsey, J. R., Schuster, J. W., Lingo, A. S., Collins, B. C., & Kleinert, H. L. (2008). Peer-implemented time delay procedures on the acquisition of chained tasks by students with moderate and severe disabilities. *Education and Training in Developmental Disabilities, 43*(1), 111–122. https://www.jstor.org/stable/23879748

Hawkins-Lear, S., & Grisham-Brown, J. (2019). Teaching early math skills to young children with disabilities in rural blended early childhood settings. *Rural Special Education Quarterly, 38*(1), 15–25. doi:10.1177/8756870518792907

Heinrich, S., Collins, B. C., Knight, V., & Spriggs, A. D. (2016). Embedded simultaneous prompting procedure to teach STEM content to high school students with moderate disabilities in an inclusive setting. *Education and Training in Autism and Developmental Disabilities, 51*(1), 41–54. https://search.proquest.com/docview/1764709235/fulltextPDF/66243D18ACB149A0PQ/1?accountid=10639

Hudson, M. E., & Browder, D. M. (2014). Improving listening comprehension responses for students with moderate intellectual disability during literacy class. *Research and Practice for Persons with Severe Disabilities, 39*(1), 11–29. doi:10.1177/1540796914534634

Hudson, M. E., Browder, D. M., & Jimenez, B. A. (2014). Effects of a peer-delivered system of least prompts intervention and adapted science read-alouds on listening comprehension for participants with moderate intellectual disability. *Education and Training in Autism and Developmental Disabilities, 49*(1), 60–77. https://www.jstor.org/stable/23880655

Hudson, M. E., Browder, D. M., & Wood, L. A. (2013). Review of experimental research on academic learning by students with moderate and severe intellectual disability in general education. *Research and Practice for Persons with Severe Disabilities, 38*(1), 17–29. doi:10.2511/027494813807046926

Hudson, M. E., Rivera, C. J., & Grady, M. M. (2018). Research on mathematics instruction with students with significant cognitive disabilities—has anything changed? *Research and Practice for Persons with Severe Disabilities, 43*(1), 38–53. doi:10.1177/1540796918756601

Hudson, M. E., & Test, D. W. (2011). Evaluating the evidence base of shared story reading to promote literacy for students with extensive support needs. *Research and Practice for Persons with Severe Disabilities, 36*(1/2), 34–45. doi:10.2511/rpsd.36.1-2.34

Individuals with Disability Education Act Amendments of 1997 [IDEA]. (1997). https://www.congress.gov/105/plaws/publ17/PLAW-105publ17.pdf

Individuals with Disabilities Education Act, 20 U.S.C. § 1400 (2004).

Jackson, L. B., Ryndak, D. L., & Wehmeyer, M. L. (2008). The dynamic relationship between context, curriculum, and student learning: A case for inclusive education as a research-based practice. *Research and Practice for Persons with Severe Disabilities, 33–34*, 175–195. doi:10.2511/rpsd.33.4.175

Jameson, J. M., Walker, R., Utley, K., & Maughan, R. (2012). A comparison of embedded total task instruction in teaching behavior chains to massed one-to-one instruction for students with ID: Accessing general education settings and core academic content. *Behavior Modification, 36*(3), 320–340. https://pubmed.ncbi.nlm.nih.gov/22584370/

Jimenez, B. A. Mims, P. J., & Browder, D. M. (2012). Data-based decisions guidelines for teachers of students with severe intellectual and developmental disabilities. *Education and Training in Autism and Developmental Disabilities, 47*(4), 407–413. https://www.jstor.org/stable/23879634

Jimenez, B. A., Browder, D. M. & Spooner, F., & DiBiase, W. (2012). Inclusive inquiry science using peer-mediated embedded instruction for students with moderate intellectual disability. *Exceptional Children, 78*(3), 301–317. doi:10.1177/001440291207800303

Jimenez, B. A., & Hudson, M. E. (2019). Including students with severe disabilities in general education and the potential of universal design for learning for all children. *Handbook of inclusion and diversity in education*. Sage. doi:10.4135/9781526470430.n25

Jimenez, B. A., & Kamei, A. (2015). Embedded instruction: An evaluation of evidence to inform inclusive practice. *Inclusion, 3*(3), 132–144. doi:10.1352/2326-6988-3.3.132

Jimenez, T. C., Graf, V. L., & Rose, E. (2007). The promise of universal design for learning gaining access to general education. *Issues in Teacher Education, 16*, 41–54. https://pdfs.semanticscholar.org/a887/fb8aab6e5396e8410f3f8118cb64a6e40271.pdf?_ga=2.75461467.895449907.1599509020-1586645662.1599509020

Johnson, J. W., McDonnell, J., Holzwarth, V. N., & Hunter, K. (2004). The efficacy of embedded instruction for students with developmental disabilities enrolled in general education classes. *Journal of Positive Behavior Interventions, 6*(4), 214–227. doi:10.1177/10983007040060040301

Kennedy, M. J., Thomas, C. N., Meyer, J. P., Alves, K. D., & Lloyd, J. W. (2014). Using evidence-based multimedia to improve vocabulary performance of adolescents with LD: A UDL approach. *Learning Disability Quarterly, 37*(2), 71–86. doi:10.1177/0731948713507262

Knight, V. F., Kuntz, E. M., & Brown, M. (2018). Paraprofessional-delivered video prompting to teach academics to students with severe disabilities in inclusive settings. *Journal of Autism and Developmental Disorders, 48*(6), 2203–2216. doi:10.1007/s10803-018-3476-2

Knight, V. F., & Sartini, E. (2015). A comprehensive literature review of comprehension strategies in core content areas for students with autism spectrum disorder. *Journal of Autism and Developmental Disorders, 45*(5), 1213–1229. doi:10.1007/s10803-014-2280-x

Knight, V. F., Smith, B. R., Spooner, F., & Browder, D. M. (2012). Using explicit instruction to teach science descriptors to students with autism spectrum disorders. *Journal of Autism and Developmental Disorders, 42*(3), 378–389. https://pubmed.ncbi.nlm.nih.gov/21503795/

Knight, V. F., Wood, L., McKissick, B. R., & Kuntz, E. M. (2019). Teaching science content and practices to students with intellectual disability and autism. *Remedial and Special Education*. Advance online publication. doi:10.1177/0741932519843998

Lim, Z., & Lee, S. H. (2019). Effects of an interview article writing intervention using class-wide SNS on writing abilities and self-esteem of students with intellectual disabilities and peers' attitudes. *Journal of Special Education Technology, 34*(1), 27–40. doi:10.1177/0162643418780496

Lowrey, K. A., & Smith, S. J. (2018). Including individuals with disabilities in UDL framework implementation: Insights from administrators. *Inclusion, 6*(2), 127–142. doi:10.1352/2326-6988-6.2.127

McDonnell, J., Mathot-Buckner, C., Thorson, N., & Fister, S. (2001). Supporting the inclusion of students with moderate and severe disabilities in junior high school general education classes: The effects of classwide peer tutoring, multi-element curriculum, and accommodations. *Education and Treatment of Children, 24*(2), 141–160. https://www.jstor.org/stable/42899651

McDonnell, J., Thorson, N., Allen, C., & Mathot-Buckner, C. (2000). The effects of partner learning during spelling for students with severe disabilities and their peers. *Journal of Behavioral Education, 10*, 107–121. doi: 10.1023/A:1016684029389

McKissick, B. R., Spooner, F., Wood, C. L., & Diegelmann, K. M. (2013). Effects of computer-assisted explicit instruction on map-reading skills for students with autism. *Research in Autism Spectrum Disorders,* 7(12), 1653–1662. doi:10.1016/j.rasd.2013.09.013

Meyer, A., Rose, D., & Gordon, D. (2014). *Universal design for learning: Theory and practice*. CAST.

National Reading Panel. (2000). *Teaching children to read: An evidence-based assessment of the scientific research literature on reading and its implications for reading instruction*. (NIH Publication No. 00-4754). US Department of Health and Human Services. https://www.nichd.nih.gov/sites/default/files/publications/pubs/nrp/Documents/report.pdf

Next Generation State Standards (NGSS) Lead States. (2013). *Next generation science standards: For states, by states.* The National Academies Press.

Polychronis, S. C., McDonnell, J., Johnson, J. W., Riesen, T., & Jameson, M. (2004). A comparison of two trial distribution schedules in embedded instruction. *Focus on Autism and Other Developmental Disabilities, 19*(3), 140–151. doi:10.1177/10883576040190030201

Rao, K., Smith, S. J., & Lowrey, K. A. (2017). UDL and intellectual disability: What do we know and where do we go? *Intellectual and Developmental disabilities, 55*(1), 37–47. doi:10.1352/1934-9556-55.1.37

Root, J. R. (2019). Effects of explicit instruction on acquisition and generalization of mathematical concepts for a student with autism spectrum disorder. *Research in Autism Spectrum Disorders, 57*, 1–6. doi:10.1016/j.rasd.2 018.09.005

Root, J., Cox, S. K., Saunders, A. F., & Gilley, D. (2020). Applying the universal design for learning framework to mathematics for learners with extensive support needs. *Remedial and Special Education, 40*(4), 194–206. doi:10.1177/0741932519887235

Ruppar, A., Fisher, K. W., Olson, A. J., & Orlando, A.-M. (2018). Exposure to literacy for students eligible for the alternate assessment. *Education and Training in Autism and Developmental Disabilities, 53*(2), 192–208. https://search.proquest.com/docview/2042209772/fulltextPDF/529139FC682D4710PQ/1?accountid=10639

Ryan, J., Jameson, J. M., Coleman, O. F., Eichelberger, C., Bowman, J. A., Conradi, L. A., Johnston, S. S., & McDonnell, J. (2019). Inclusive social studies content instruction for students with significant intellectual disability using structured inquiry-based instruction. *Education and Training in Autism and Developmental Disabilities, 54*(4), 420–436. https://search.proquest.com/docview/2315014086/fulltextPDF/D1498F9C27514F57PQ/1?accountid=10639

Saunders, A. F., Root, J. R., & Jimenez, B. A. (2019). Inclusive mathematics education practices involving students with severe disabilities. *Inclusion*, 7(2), 75–91. doi:10.1352/2326-6988-7.2.75

Schenning, H., Knight, V. F., & Spooner, F. (2013). Effects of structured inquiry and graphic organizers on social studies comprehension by students with autism spectrum disorders. *Research in Autism Spectrum Disorders*, 7(4), 526–540. doi:10.1016/j.rasd.2012.12.007

Scruggs, T. E., Mastropieri, M. A., & Okolo, C. M. (2008). Science and social studies for students with disabilities. *Focus on Exceptional Children*, *41*(2), 1–24. http://web.b.ebscohost.com/ehost/pdfviewer/pdfviewer?vid=2&sid=8dd53846-e6cc-4dd2-a194-14135b8de8ea%40pdc-v-sessmgr03

Shurr, J. C., Jimenez, B. A., & Bouck, E. C. (Eds.). (2019). Book 1: Research-based practices and education science. In *Educating students with Intellectual Disability and Autism Spectrum Disorder*. Council for Exceptional Children.

Smith, S. J., & Lowrey, K. A. (2017). Making the UDL framework universal: Implications for individuals with intellectual disability. *Intellectual and Developmental Disabilities*, *55*(1), 2–3. doi:10.1352/1934-9556-55.1.2

Smith, B. R., Spooner, F., Jimenez, B. A., & Browder, D. M. (2013). Using an early science curriculum to teach science vocabulary and concepts to students with severe developmental disabilities. *Education & Treatment of Children*, *36*(1), 1–31. http://www.educationandtreatmentofchildren.net/

Smith, B. R., Spooner, F., & Wood, C. L. (2013). Using embedded computer-assisted explicit instruction to teach science to students with autism spectrum disorder. *Research in Autism Spectrum Disorders*, 7(3), 433–443. doi:10.1016/j.rasd.2012.10.010

Snell, M. E., & Gast, D. L. (1981). Applying time delay procedure to the instruction of the severely handicapped. *The Journal of the Association for the Severely Handicapped*, *6*(3), 3–14. doi:10.1177/154079698100600301

Spooner, F., Baker, J. N., Harris, A. A., Ahlgrim-Delzell, L., & Browder, D. M. (2007). Effects of training in universal design for learning on lesson plan development. *Remedial and Special Education*, *28*(2), 108–116. doi:10.1177/07419325070280020101

Spooner, F., Knight, V. F., Browder, D. M., Jimenez, B., & DiBiase, W. (2011). Evaluating evidence-based practice in teaching science content to students with severe developmental disabilities. *Research and Practice for Persons with Severe Disabilities*, *36*(1-2), 62–75. doi:10.2511/rpsd.36.1-2.62

Spooner, F., Knight, V. F., Browder, D. M., & Smith, B. R. (2012). Evidence-based practices for teaching academic skills to students with severe developmental disabilities. *Remedial and Special Education*, *33*(6), 374–387. doi:10.1177/0741932511421634

Spooner, F., McKissick, B. R., & Knight, V. F. (2017). Establishing the state of affairs for evidence-based practices in students with severe disabilities. *Research and Practice for Persons with Severe Disabilities*, *42*(1), 8–18. doi:10.1177/1540796916684896

Spooner, F., Root, J. R., Saunders, A. F., & Browder, D. M. (2019). An updated evidence-based practice review on teaching mathematics to students with moderate and severe developmental disabilities. *Remedial and Special Education*, *40*(3), 150–165. doi:10.1177/0741932517751055

Thoma, C. A., Cain, I., & Walther-Thomas, C. (2015). National goals for the education of children and youth with intellectual and developmental disabilities: Honoring the past while moving forward. *Inclusion*, *3*(4), 219–226. doi:10.1352/2326-6988-3.4.219

Touchette, P. (1971). Transfer of stimulus control: Measuring the moment of transfer. *Journal of the Experimental Analysis of Behavior*, *15*(3), 347–354.

U.S. Department of Education. (2005). *Alternate achievement standards for students with the most significant cognitive disabilities: Non regulatory guidance*. U.S. Department of Education Office of Elementary and Secondary Education.

Wolery, M., Anthony, L., Snyder, E. D., Werts, M. G., & Katzenmeyer, J. (1997). Training elementary teachers to embed instruction during classroom activities. *Education & Treatment of Children*, *20*(1), 40–58. https://www.jstor.org/stable/42940550

Wood, L. Browder, D. M., & Flynn L. (2015). Teaching students with intellectual disability to use a self-questioning strategy to comprehend social studies text for an inclusive setting. *Research and Practice for Persons with Severe Disabilities*, *40*(4), 275–293. doi:10.1177/1540796915592155

Wood, L., Browder, D. M., & Spooner, F. (2020). Teaching students with moderate intellectual disability to use a self-questioning strategy and iPad to comprehend science e-text. *Journal of Special Education Technology*, *35*(4), 272–285. 10.1177/0162643419882421

Wood, L., Root, J. R., & Thompson, J. (2019). *Academics*. In E. Bouck, B. A. Jimenez, & J. Shurr (Eds.), *Evidence-based practices and instructional information for students with intellectual disability and autism spectrum disorders*. Council for Exceptional Children.

Zakas, T.-L., Browder, D. M., Ahlgrim-Delzell, L., & Heafner, T. (2013). Teaching social studies content to students with autism using a graphic organizer intervention. *Research in Autism Spectrum Disorders*, 7(9), 1075–1086. doi:10.1016/j.rasd.2013.06.001

14

Planning for Effective Inclusive Instruction in Core Content

Ginevra Courtade[1], Bree Jimenez[2], Jenny Root[3], and Robert Pennington[4]

[1]UNIVERSITY OF LOUISVILLE

[2]UNIVERSITY OF TEXAS-ARLINGTON

[3]FLORIDA STATE UNIVERSITY

[4]UNIVERSITY OF NORTH CAROLINA AT CHARLOTTE

Setting the Stage

Since the early 2000s, there has been a clear, sometimes controversial, emphasis on teaching core content to students with severe disabilities (Ayres et al., 2011; Courtade et al., 2012). Federal mandates requiring access to the general curriculum for all students (e.g., Individuals with Disabilities Education Act [IDEA], 1997, 2004) and professional conversations around high expectations for students with severe disabilities led to an expanse of research focused on academic instruction for this population of students. Researchers completed studies and literature reviews on the teaching and learning of core content as well as offer research- and evidence-based instructional strategies effective in literacy, mathematics, and science for students with severe disabilities (e.g., Browder et al., 2006, 2008; Pennington & Delano, 2012; Spooner et al., 2011, 2012). Additionally, as noted in Chapter 13, the principles of high-quality instruction that are effective for students with severe disabilities across all curricular areas (i.e., areas other than academics) are being used to support students in general education classrooms (Hudson et al., 2013).

This chapter begins by outlining the current research on teaching core content skills to students with severe disabilities. Major literature reviews are described, and more importantly, the evidence-based practices that were gleaned from these reviews will be explicated. Research in specific topic areas of core content will be discussed. The remainder of the chapter combines effective practices for teaching core content and effective inclusive practices to outline curricular supports for the successful inclusion of students with severe disabilities in general education content and classrooms. The authors suggest and give examples of instructional supports that can be used across all content areas to support all students.

 DOI: 10.4324/9781003043874-14

What Do We Know Based on Research?

Current federal education legislation (Individuals with Disabilities Education Improvement Act [IDEA], 2004; Every Student Succeeds Act [ESSA], 2015) requires the use of evidence-based or research-based practices for the instruction of students with disabilities. Individual research groups developed quality indicators for different research designs and criteria for evidence-based practices using research that met the quality indicators (e.g., single-case design; Horner et al., 2005; group design; Gersten et al., 2005). Subsequently, the Council for Exceptional Children (CEC) used these works and others to guide the development of *Standards for Evidence-Based Practices in Special Education* (CEC, 2014). In a discussion of evidence-based practices, Cook et al. (2008) emphasize the importance of educators using these practices shown to improve student learning and behavior over time. To date, there have been seven reviews that have used the proposed quality indicators and criteria for evidence-based practices to discern strategies that educators can use to instruct students with severe disabilities in the core content curriculum.

In 2006, Browder et al. conducted a review of 128 studies (published between 1975 and 2003) on teaching reading to students with significant cognitive disabilities. The authors categorized the studies by the five components the National Reading Panel has determined critical for learning to read: phonics, phonemics awareness, fluency, vocabulary, and comprehension (NRP, 2000). Browder et al. then applied the Horner et al. (2005) and Gersten et al. (2005) criteria for quality indicators and finally reviewed the quality studies to determine if evidence-based practices could be defined. The results of the review not only delineated evidence-based practices by specific reading component area but also brought to light the lack of research in areas critical to reading success. The results indicated the use of massed trial training as an evidence-based practice for teaching vocabulary (sight words and pictures) and comprehension; time delay to teach vocabulary (sight words) and fluency; varied systematic prompting to teach vocabulary (sight words and pictures) and comprehension; and the use of pictures and functional activities to teach comprehension. The authors also noted that there were too few studies in the categories of phonics and phonemic awareness that met quality indicators and would support the determination of evidence-based practices.

Browder et al. (2009) built off of the results of the Browder et al. (2006) reading review and focused a review on the use of time delay as an evidence-based practice to teach picture and word recognition skills to individuals with severe disabilities. The authors reviewed 30 experiments published between 1975 and 2007 that explicitly stated that time delay was at least part of the intervention, picture or word recognition was a dependent variable, and that a single-case design that demonstrates experimental control was used. The Horner et al. (2005) quality indicators were applied to the 30 experiments and 22 were found to meet all indicators. Within these 22 studies, the criteria for evidence-based practice were also met. The authors suggest that because of the strong evidence of the success of using time delay in teach sight words, the practice should be used to teach other types of symbols in core content areas (e.g., mathematics symbols).

Similar to the Browder et al. (2006) reading review, Browder et al. (2008) conducted a literature review on teaching mathematics to individuals with severe disabilities. The authors reviewed 68 experiments published between 1975 and 2005 and categorized the experiments by strands of the National Council of Teachers of Mathematics Standards (NCTM, 2000; i.e., numbers and operations, measurement, data analysis and probability, geometry, algebra). The authors applied the Horner et al. (2005) quality indicators criteria to the 54 single-case studies. Nineteen of the studies met all of the quality indicators. Three evidence-based practices emerged from this review: in vivo instruction (teaching a real-life application of the principle; teaching in real-life settings); systematic instruction (see Chapter 13); and opportunities to respond (giving the student multiple opportunities to learn and practice the skills). Similar results to the reading review were found as the specific components/ strands of mathematics being taught were examined. The 19 studies that met the criteria for quality fell into only two of the five strands (13 in measurement, six in numbers and operations). Although evidence-based practices have been defined for teaching mathematics to students with severe disabilities, these practices are not still being thoroughly researched across all areas of the mathematics curriculum.

Research in the area of science instruction for students with severe disabilities is more limited than literacy or mathematics. In 2007, Courtade et al. published a literature review of studies that addressed science content for students in this population. The review encompasses research published from 1985-2005. Only 11 studies were found that investigated content that aligned with the National Science Content Standards (NRC, 1996). More recently, Spooner et al. (2011) conducted a literature review of science content taught to students with severe disabilities and were able to apply the Horner et al. (2005) criteria to determine evidence-based practices. This review included research published between 1985 and 2009. Seventeen studies were located and 14 met the criteria for high or adequate quality. Using the Horner et al. criteria, the authors determined that a systematic instructional package is an evidence-based practice for teaching science to students with severe disabilities. Specifically, task analytic instruction was strongly supported. Similar to the reading and mathematics reviews, not all science content areas were addressed. Spooner et al. found no studies that addressed content in science and technology or history and nature standards.

Writing instruction for students with severe disabilities is another area with limited research. Pennington and Delano (2012) conducted a review of the literature on writing instruction for children with autism spectrum disorder (ASD). The authors found 15 studies that met inclusion criteria for the review (i.e., published between 1994 and 2011; experimental, quasi-experimental, or single-case research; participants with ASD between the ages of 3 to 21; writing instruction involving the composition of text). Although the authors were not able to identify any evidence-based interventions based on the Horner et al. (2005) or Gersten et al. (2005) criteria, they concluded that students with ASD benefit from explicit writing instruction (e.g., self-regulated strategy development, computer-assisted instruction, modeling, selections from a visual array of possible responses, and reinforcement to engage participants in instruction).

A current review related to evidence-based practices for teaching core content to students with severe disabilities was completed by Spooner et al. (2012). Although the results of the review were discussed in the previous chapter (Chapter 13), it is important to note that the authors specifically examined the context of the instruction. Of the 18 studies that met the Horner et al. (2005) quality criteria, seven studies were implemented in general education classrooms. Finally, Hudson et al. (2013) conducted a review of literature on academic learning in general education settings for students with severe disabilities. The researchers found a total of 17 studies that fit the inclusion criteria and evaluated those studies using Horner et al.'s criteria. Twelve studies met the criteria for quality research; five studies met the criteria for quality research with reservation. Results of the review indicated that embedded instruction trials using constant time delay is an evidence-based practice for teaching academic content to students with severe disabilities in general education. Further, the use of the system of least prompts was identified as a promising practice.

The recent Supreme Court decision in *Endrew F. v. Douglas County School District* (2017) further emphasized an educational benefit standard that requires schools to offer an individualized education program (IEP) reasonably calculated to enable a student to make appropriate progress in light of the child's circumstances. IEPs must be designed to provide measurable benefits given a student's capabilities (Yell & Bateman, 2017). This decision continues to push the field toward higher expectations for students with severe disabilities. Until there is more quality research on the core content instruction of students with severe disabilities in inclusive settings, we must rely on the evidence-based practices that exist and the promising practices that are evolving. "EBPs [evidence-based practices] should interface with the professional wisdom of teachers to maximize the outcomes of students with disabilities" (Cook et al., 2008). The following section is meant to guide researchers and practitioners to improve the instruction of core content for students with severe disabilities by using both evidence-based practices and promising instructional supports.

Setting the Course for Effective Inclusion

A clear implication of the previous section is that the research base for teaching core content skills to students with severe disabilities has vastly grown. The evidence of social and academic student outcomes aligned to core content instruction has provided the field with greatly needed strategies to support such instruction. While the research is growing in each specific content area (e.g., science, writing), a series of common strategies and supports have begun to emerge that resonates among all academic instruction (e.g., systematic instruction, the use of graphic organizers). As this chapter has previously outlined, the most recent literature reviews in the field are providing both "promising" and "evidence-based" practices that should outline strategies and supports used in the inclusive classroom to teach students with severe disabilities. While many of these strategies are not new to the field (e.g., systematic instruction, first likely defined by Snell in 1978), they may be new to teachers providing core content instruction to students with severe disabilities.

When planning core content instruction for this population of students, it is critical to consider instructional methods and context. First, it is important to ground instruction in those methods that have been proven to be effective for students with severe disabilities while taking into consideration the unique goals and characteristics of the content itself (e.g., science *v* American literature). Much of the current research on teaching academic content to students with severe disabilities have incorporated the use of the previously mentioned evidence-based practice and five instructional supports (see Figure 14.1). While these supports can be used to develop instruction specific to students' needs to gain access to and make progress in the curriculum, the fact still remains that much of the research supporting these practices and has been conducted in special education settings. In practice, educators need to apply evidence-based practices in general education contexts to enable students to have access to and make progress in the curriculum by prioritizing learning goals and anticipating and supporting student learning variability. This requires practitioners to negotiate a variety of complex issues related to areas such as instructional planning, collaboration, pacing, grouping, adaptations, and progress monitoring. Administrators can support teachers in providing effective core content instruction in inclusive contexts by scheduling regular co-planning opportunities, limiting the number of grade levels per caseload, and providing the professional development necessary to develop a culture of inclusion. The five supports provide a strong foundation to guide the collaborative planning of general educators and special educators. In the remainder of this

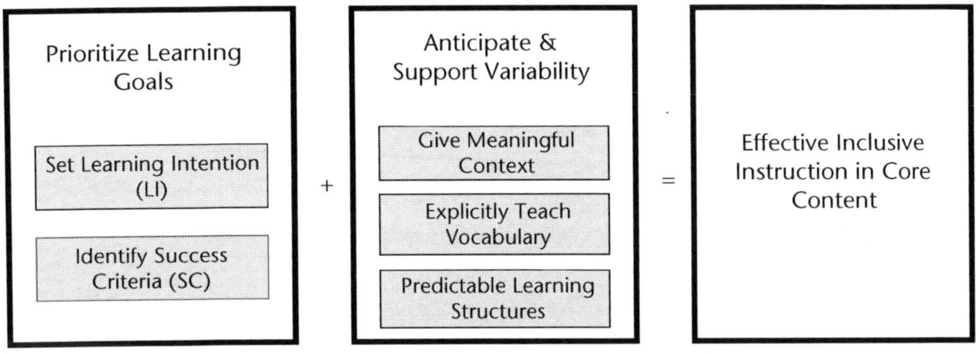

Figure 14.1 Supporting effective inclusive instruction in core content

section, the authors give examples of incorporating learning intentions, success criteria, meaningful context, explicitly taught vocabulary and predictable learning structures into core content curricula.

Planning for Effective Inclusive Instruction in Core Content

Learning Intentions

Prioritized learning goals are a necessary element of planning for effective instruction. Well-designed inclusive education incorporates features of Universal Design for Learning (UDL; see Chapter 13). An essential element of UDL is the teacher providing ownership of learning to students through flexibility and choice by creating multiple means to access information and materials and giving students a variety of opportunities to show what they know. The use of learning intentions (LIs) and success criteria (SC) are important when developing instruction (Crichton & McDaid, 2016; Hattie, 2012; Sharratt, 2019), especially within the inclusive classroom.

LIs are goals developed directly from state standards or curriculum expectations, stemming from the notion of big ideas and essential questions (Sharratt, 2019). LIs are not a list of what the student will do, rather what they will learn and why the content they are learning is important. Personal relevance to the learner is key in the development of LIs. LIs are written in student-friendly language and in a manner that is meaningful to students.

LIs support the idea of making learning visible to both the teacher and students, allowing teachers to design instruction that is challenging yet attainable (Hattie, 2012; McLeskey et al., 2017). LIs can be written as short-term (for a lesson) or longer-term (across multiple lessons or a unit) goals and should be used to provide feedback to students through ongoing formative assessments. If teachers are not clear about what they want students to learn and what that learning looks like, the creation of quality assessments of learning will be difficult.

LIs should be explicitly taught throughout the lessons (i.e., not only at the beginning), helping students see what they are supposed to learn (see Figure 14.2 for examples across content areas). While lessons may include other content, LIs help to focus the lesson, supporting systematically designed instruction and assessment with focus and intentionality. This approach to planning for instruction allows teachers the clarity of what they should be planning for and how to use their time efficiently during instruction. Because not all students work at the same rate or begin instruction

Content Area	Example
ELA	We are learning to describe feelings of characters in a story.
Writing	We are learning to write simple sentences about a picture.
Mathematics	We are learning to solve multiplicative comparison word problems.
Science	We are learning to identify how plants use sunlight to create energy.

Figure 14.2 Examples of learning intentions across content areas

with the same level of skills, content, and concepts, LIs should be developed to include all learners (Hattie, 2012).

Success Criteria

Assessment of learning involves teacher identification of students' current knowledge and goal setting for students based on that knowledge and the curriculum. In order to determine how to make learning accessible for all students within the inclusive classroom, educators must clearly articulate the learning that should occur. Based upon LIs, success criteria (SC) define what the student needs to do to show what they know. LIs focus on the big ideas of the unit; however, they do not tell the student what they need to do or show for learning when they are assessed. When SC are well defined, students are able to become reflective of their own learning and engage in self-regulation and self-monitoring of their own progress (Hattie, 2012).

SC are not the completion of activities or engagement in an activity; rather, they promote student engagement by providing clear guidelines for success. SC should be visible in the classroom and can be used to guide student agency throughout a lesson. When presented as "I can" statements SC allow students to self-assess and determine their own level of independence as they work towards the LIs.

Through the development of LIs and SC, inclusive educators take all students into account as they plan. As priority learning goals and assessment criteria are determined within the unit or lesson, educators have a clear goal in mind of what is most important for students to learn and how students can reach that goal (Sharratt, 2019). Within the heterogeneous classroom, teachers use SC as they consider learners' prior and current depth of knowledge. Teachers then are able to proactively plan their lessons based upon their knowledge of their students' strengths and needs, taking into consideration barriers to learning. It is not feasible for inclusive educators to foresee all barriers that may be present for all students across all lessons and content areas; however, planning SC that are Essential (necessary to know or perform), Ideal (helps the learner perform the task or gain depth of knowledge), and Possible (increased depth of performance or knowledge that allows learners to exceed beyond what is expected) can support planning, instruction, and assessment (Root et al., 2021).

When educators begin planning for the non-negotiable learning that all students will achieve, those essential skills or knowledge become the focus of the lesson driving the content, materials, and activities. Essential SC describe the learning that should occur by the end of the lesson/series of lessons. In addition, the Ideal SC is content/skills that build upon the Essential SC; and offers breadth and depth within the content/skill. Educators may ask themselves: "What else could students know or be able to do?" Finally, the Possible SC allows educators to provide students with learning goals at an even deeper level of application or problem-solving. SC should allow for all students to demonstrate their learning in multiple ways and provide varying degrees of performance (breadth and depth; Jimenez & Humphreys, 2018). See Figure 14.3 for examples of SC that are essential, ideal, and possible.

Through clearly articulated SC, teachers can focus their universally designed planning upon these key learning goals. Prioritized learning allows inclusive educators to meet the diverse needs of all students in the classroom, not only those with disabilities or already identified as having barriers to learning (Brookhart & Lazarus, 2017). By planning with the end in mind, students know what to expect and teachers can proactively support learning for all without losing focus of the big idea and essential questions as they try to make every component of every lesson fully accessible to each diverse student. See Figure 14.4 for a science example of how Big Ideas, LIs and SC work together to guide learning goals and outcomes.

Content Area	Example
Reading	**Essential:** I can name a feeling that describes a character in a story. **Ideal:** I can explain why I chose that feeling. **Possible:** I can compare the feelings of two different characters.
Writing	**Essential:** I can write a sentence about a picture that names a person or thing and tells more about it. **Ideal:** I can write varied sentences about a picture that names a person or thing and tells more about it. **Possible:** I can write a sentence that names a person or thing and tells more about it.
Mathematics	**Essential:** I can follow a heuristic to find the answer to multiplicative comparison problems **Ideal:** I can use manipulatives to model multiplicative comparison problems **Possible:** I can explain why my answer makes sense
Science	**Essential:** I can identify what living things need to survive **Ideal:** I can identify the source of energy for plants **Possible:** I can identity and outline the process where plants use sunlight to create energy

Figure 14.3 Example of success criteria across content areas

Provide Meaningful Context

Providing a meaningful context for content area instruction is emphasized in the UDL framework in terms of both engagement and representation (CAST, 2018). Engagement may be enhanced when instruction optimizes relevance, value, and authenticity. In contrast to a traditional task-driven "functional" approach to academics (Saunders et al. 2017), contextualized instruction begins the planning process with academic standards and then moves into identifying real-life activities that present an opportunity to apply the standard (Root et al., 2020). All instruction does not have to be equivalent to real life, but it does need to be personally, culturally, and socially relevant. Student funds of knowledge are valued when understandings students bring into the classroom from their home community and out-of-school experiences are incorporated into school learning tasks (Driver & Powell, 2017). This provides opportunities for teachers to use a culturally sustaining approach to instruction that addresses multiple priorities within academic instruction (e.g., self-determination, social skills, vocational skills). Heinrich et al. (2016) prioritized STEM content and skills based on how they could be applied within high school students with severe disabilities' current and future

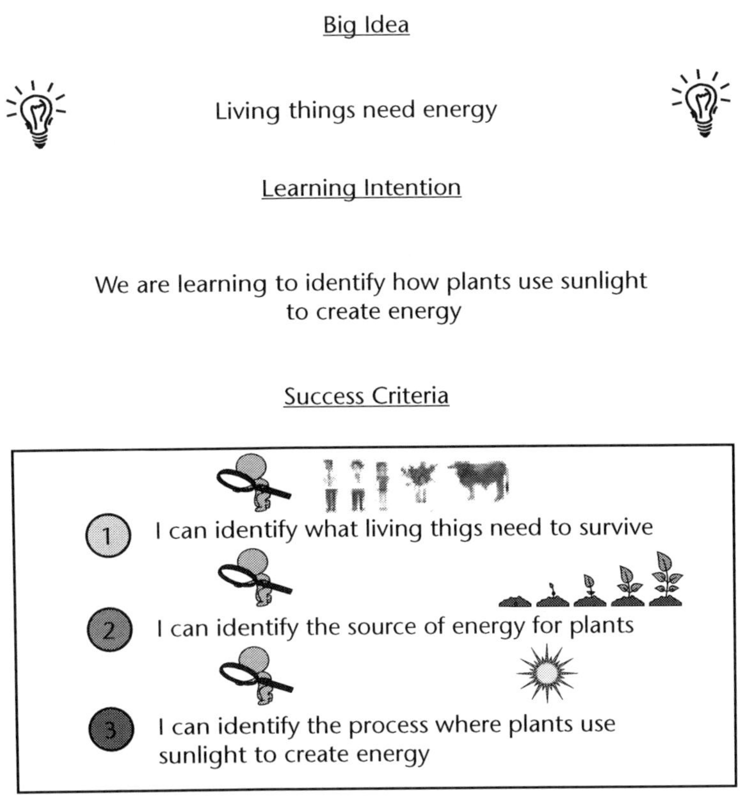

Figure 14.4 Science example of LIs and SC

environments. For example, one student was taught to solve linear equations within the context of determining how much money she would make at the end of the week at her part-time job at a restaurant. Driver and Powell taught elementary students with mathematics disabilities who were English language learners to solve word problems that made references to student's daily lives, pop culture interests, and cultural heritage. Students were asked information about their personal lives (e.g., if they had siblings, about their favorite TV shows, what they did over the weekend) that was then used to create problems using both English and their native languages.

An additional benefit of giving context to core content standards is that the context programs for generalization as students are exposed to multiple situations, exemplars, and stimuli that they may encounter outside of their current classroom setting. Root et al. (2020) taught middle school students with severe disabilities to solve and discriminate between percent of change problems involving calculating a tip as a percent of the bill and calculating a discount as a percent of the total cost using modified schema-based instruction. Students had the opportunity to select a community location from a menu (e.g., barbershop, nail salon, food truck), which served as the context for all of their word problems that day. In a related study, Root et al. (2018) found that not only were students able to acquire the targeted mathematics skill (solving percent of change problems), but they were able to generalize when presented with real-world stimuli (e.g., receipts, coupons, menus).

As described in the examples above, contextualized instruction is not synonymous with community-based instruction (Root et al., 2018). Context can be provided by the instructional materials and how targeted skills and concepts are practiced. Videos and stories can be used to provide a context for instruction to increase the personal relevance of prioritized skills (Saunders et al., 2018).

Content Area	Example
Reading	Given the context of a similar situation, students learn to compare their own feelings to the feelings of the characters in the book.
Writing	Students learn to write simple sentences to make requests (e.g., I want________), to describe real life experiences, (I saw_____, I went to_________), or describe how they feel (e.g., I feel_______________).
Mathematics	Daily themes for word problems representing real life contexts for using multiplicative comparison problems (e.g., scaling up ingredients in a recipe, making supply list for class party, comparing scores of sports teams)
Science	Wonder stories are short stories developed and presented to students to help control for prior knowledge, linking everyday occurrences with the science concepts. Stories are written from first person perspective, 'wondering' how plants grow and eat; debunking misconceptions (e.g., I know the plant my sister put in her dark bedroom died, even though she watered it, I wonder why!).

Figure 14.5 Examples of contextualizing instruction across content areas

Students with severe disabilities will likely need systematic instruction with repeated opportunities to respond at greater dosage or intensity than their typically developing peers (Collins, 2012). Varying the context and instructional materials can help maintain engagement in the task by varying the product while maintaining the instructional process. Wood et al. (2015) taught elementary students with severe disabilities to use a self-questioning strategy to develop and respond to literal WH questions about US History during inclusive social studies lessons. Students practiced the self-questioning strategy using a different passage from the social studies textbook in each session, giving them a meaningful purpose that aligned with what their peers were also working on. When contextualized instruction aligns to the LIs and SC of a lesson, students are poised to engage in meaningful, rigorous instruction with purpose (see Figure 14.5 for examples across the content areas).

Explicit Instruction of Key Vocabulary

Academic and domain-specific vocabulary is emphasized in state standards across content areas and grade levels as the understanding of academic language are directly related to academic achievement (Townsend et al., 2012). While some students may acquire specialized language through embedded or incidental teaching, for many students in inclusive classrooms, this is not sufficient (Riccomini et al., 2015). The UDL framework emphasizes building knowledge of language and symbols through clarifying vocabulary, syntax and structure, and promoting understanding across languages to address barriers students may have in perceiving and comprehending information presented to them (CAST, 2018). Vocabulary knowledge could be a gatekeeper for students demonstrating higher-order thinking skills. For example, reciprocal understanding that the equal sign means "same as" not "is" or "equals" is essential for conceptual understanding of algebraic equations. Research on teaching vocabulary to students with severe disabilities has historically focused on basic sight words (Riggs et al., 2013), which would be classified by Beck et al. (2013) as tier one words that are used in everyday life in a variety of contexts and settings. Alternatively, tier two vocabulary words are those that are used with high frequency across multiple domains. Academic language, especially in general education settings, is made up primarily of tier two vocabulary words (e.g., calculate, analyze, sequence, predict). Academic vocabulary words are often unfamiliar to students with and without disabilities, and therefore need to be explicitly taught in order for students to have meaningful access to and make progress in the general curriculum.

Explicitly teaching vocabulary prevents student errors in the use or understanding of key vocabulary and concepts, making instructional time-efficient and focus on correct usage and application (Riccomini et al., 2015). Explicit vocabulary instruction involves teachers introducing and teaching words and their meanings in a systematic and purposeful way (Archer & Hughes, 2011). An example sequence provided by Archer and Hughes includes: (a) introduce the word, (b) provide a student-friendly explanation of the word, (c) illustrate with examples, and (d) check students' understanding. Students with severe disabilities may benefit from the teacher's use of constant time delay (CTD) within this explicit instruction framework, as it is one evidence-based practice for teaching vocabulary to students with severe disabilities (Browder et al., 2009) and has been used in recent research to teach tier two academic vocabulary words.

Acquiring this academic language then enables students to access and make progress in higher-order thinking processes such as reading comprehension and mathematical problem solving. Story grammar terms assist students in comprehending both grade level texts and task directions. For example, Zakas et al. (2013) taught middle school students with severe disabilities story grammar terms related to social studies informational texts (e.g., sequence, detail, event) using constant time delay before they used the terms to complete graphic organizers and answer comprehension questions about the text. Browder et al. (2017) taught elementary students with severe disabilities story grammar terms related to narrative stories (e.g., character, setting, main idea) using constant time delay before they used the terms to complete story maps and answer comprehension questions. In the area of mathematics, Root and Browder (2019) used constant time delay to teach vocabulary related to algebraic equations (e.g., equation, equals, variable) before teaching students to solve algebraic word problems. Figure 14.6 provides examples of tier 2 vocabulary instruction embedded across content areas. Figure 14.7 provides an illustration of examples and non-examples of what is a plant and what is not a plant in an I do, we do, and you do format.

Predictable Learning Structures

Academic curricula, learning processes, and the language we use to describe them often are framed within organizational structures that facilitate their understanding and application across contexts. These predictable learning structures are initially formed and refined through repeated exposure to environmental contingencies (e.g., successfully solving a problem, receiving feedback from others) and, ultimately, are established as formal properties within a given learning context. These predictable structures provide the learner two powerful benefits. First, they help the learner to more quickly and accurately identify relevant information within the academic content. For example, once elementary students learn basic story elements, they may be more

Content Area	Example
Reading	Use constant time delay in teaching story grammar related to expository text (e.g., compare/ contrast; description/ categorization) prior to asking students to determine characters' feelings in a biography.
Writing	Teacher provides a review of key vocabulary in a picture book by prompting students to match key words to pictures in the text, prior to asking them to write about what they have read.
Mathematics	Use constant time delay and multiple exemplar training to teach components multiplicative comparison word problem: referent, scalar, and comparative value.
Science	Use direct instruction (I do, we do, you do) and multiple exemplars to teach the concepts of energy, plants, and living. Images are used to show students many examples and non-examples, controlling for overgeneralization or lack of generalization of new concepts (e.g., vocabulary); See Figure 14.7.

Figure 14.6 Examples of key vocabulary across content areas

likely to locate the problem and its solution within a given story. Second, as learners become familiar with these structures, they are able to use them to form their responses in ways that are more effective and easily recognizable by those around them. For example, using their knowledge of story elements, elementary students can compose a variety of cohesive stories that different readers can easily understand. The research literature is replete with references to these structures (schema [Jitendra & Hoff, 1996; Root et al., 2018], autoclitic frames [Pennington et al., 2018; Skinner, 1957], patterns [Rivera & Becker, 2009]) and they are ubiquitous across academic content areas often serving as essential curricular items (e.g., scientific method, story grammar, solving for X, grammatical conventions).

Some students with severe disabilities may have difficulty in recognizing and applying these structures during academic instruction and may require additional support to promote their effective use. Recently, several research teams have evaluated interventions using predictable learning structures to improve academic outcomes for students with severe disabilities, and their collective work outlines a general process in teaching these structures. First, teachers should select a particular structure or set of structures around which instruction will be focused (e.g., sentence-type, story structure, problem type, repeated storyline). This often will be dictated by the academic standard around which the student's goal is designed. For example, when addressing a first-grade writing standard (i.e., write informative/explanatory texts in which they name a topic, supply some facts about the topic, and provide some sense of closure; CCSSI, 2021), a teacher might develop the frame, *I read about (subject). A (subject) is a (descriptive word), The end.* Second, teachers must identify a range of instructional stimuli that will be presented within that structure. For example, when applying a mathematical problem-solving structure (i.e., strategy), the teacher must present multiple

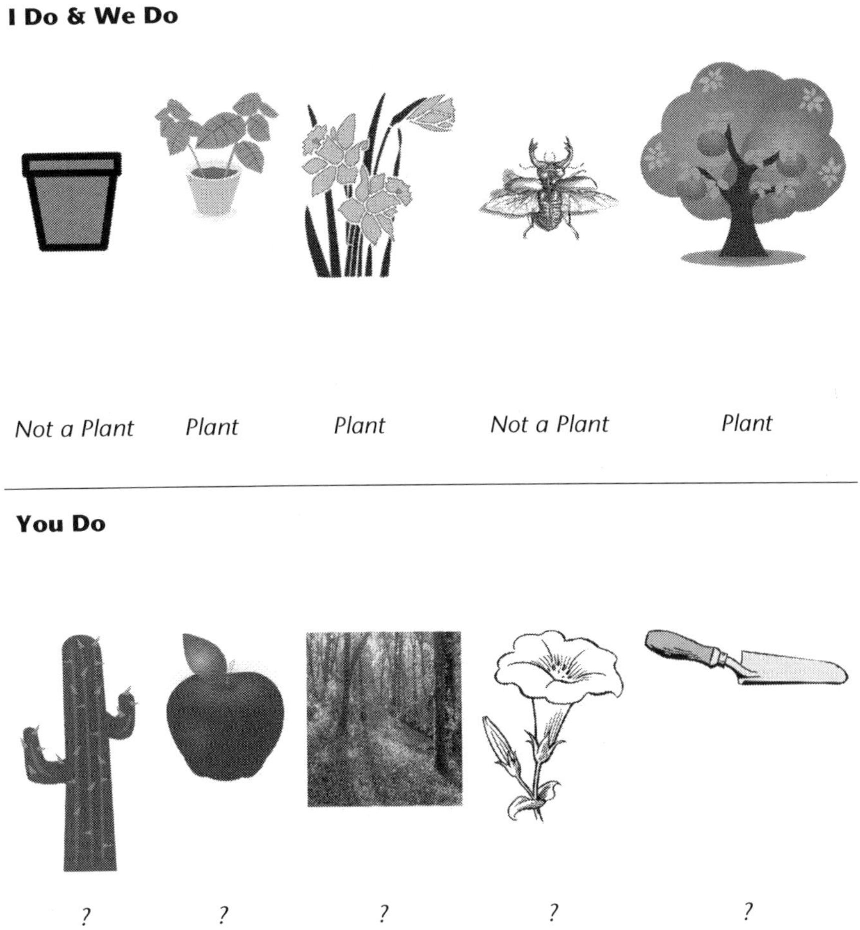

Figure 14.7 Example and non examples of science concept of plant

problems with which to apply the structure or when teaching students to apply a sentence format (e.g., *I see a [noun]*), the teacher must teach the students to apply that format to multiple writing prompts using different vocabulary (e.g., *I see a dog, I see a tree.*). This step is essential, as the focus of this instruction is to teach the accurate application of the structure and not any single response. Finally, teachers must decide whether additional supports will be needed to highlight the targeted learning structure for their students. In some cases, repeated and explicit instruction of a particular pattern may be sufficient to facilitate students' use of structures. Pennington and colleagues (2014, 2017, 2019) used response prompting to teach writing structures (i.e., story structure, simple sentences, opinion texts) to students with severe disabilities. During instruction, teachers prompted students to construct different texts within a predetermined structure until students were able to generate written products without prompting. Some students may require the use of additional cues for identifying and using learning structures. Most often, these are in the form of graphic organizers or visual stimulus prompts. When using stimulus prompts, the teacher uses additional stimuli to highlight the structure (e.g., highlighted repeated storyline) or to signal a particular response to that structure (e.g., picture symbols representing steps of an experiment). Spencer and Petersen (2018)

Content Area	Example
Reading	Provide students response board that contain *Wh*-word rules to support generalization of comprehension questions (e.g., "When" tells us about a time or date).
Writing	Provide students with fill in the blank templates for constructing informational texts. Teach students to describe the main idea in multiple pictures by teaching them to select words from a digital bank to construct sentences in the pattern (The ______is _______).
Mathematics	Provide student-friendly task analysis with space for students to self-monitor completion by marking whether steps were completed independently (e.g., "by myself") or if prompting was needed (e.g., "with help")
Science	Display a KWHL chart for all students to use, guiding them to identify what they Know, Want to know, How they may find out, and finally what they Learned. Throughout the lesson(s) students complete the chart with words and images. The chart is used to guide the lesson, using predictable patterns from one lesson to the next. I wonder communication (sentence) stems are used to promote initiation and problem solving (I know ________,I wonder ________), students can generate ideas, or choose from a word/picture bank.

Figure 14.8 Examples of incorporating predictable learning structures across content areas

used picture symbols representing story grammar elements as a part of an instructional package to support students' comprehension and story retelling skills. When using graphic organizers, teachers provide a written or visual depiction of the structure in which they can insert information related to the particular instructional task. For example, Cox and Root (2020) used graphic organizers to guide students with ASD in applying strategies to solve proportional word problems. Similarly, Lee et al. (2016) presented students with ID with a graphic organizer to collect and display important information from a text. Subsequently, they provided a narrative template (i.e., frame) in which to insert information from the organizer. Refer to Figure 14.8 for examples of predictable learning structures across content areas.

Conclusion

The incorporation of evidence-based practices to teach core content and instructional supports that sustain successful inclusive education for students with severe disabilities is a must for current and future special education teachers. Future research in these areas should provide teachers with additional evidence-based practices and provide clear guidance for promoting achievement in core content in inclusive settings.

References

Archer, A., & Hughes, C. A. (2011). *Explicit instruction: Efficient and effective teaching*. Guilford.

Ayres, K. M., Lowrey, K. A., Douglas, K. H., & Sievers, C. (2011). I can identify Saturn but I can't brush my teeth: What happens when the curricular focus for students with severe disabilities shifts. *Education and Training in Autism and Developmental Disabilities*, *46*(1), 11–21.

Beck, I. L., McKeown, M. G., & Kucan, L. (2013). *Bringing words to life: Robust vocabulary instruction*. Guilford.

Brookhart, S., & Lazarus, S. (2017). *Formative assessment for students with disabilities*. Commissioned by the Council of Chief State School Officers State Collaboratives on Assessing. Special Education Students and Formative Assessment.

Browder, D. M., Ahlgrim-Delzell, L., Spooner, F., Mims, P. J., & Baker, J. N. (2009). Using time delay to teach literacy to students with severe developmental disabilities. *Exceptional Children*, *75*(3), 343–364.

Browder, D. M., Root, J. R., Wood, L., & Allison, C. (2017). Effects of a story-mapping procedure using the iPad on the comprehension of narrative texts by students with autism spectrum disorder. *Focus on Autism and Other Developmental Disabilities*, *32*(4), 243–255. doi:10.1177/1088357615611387

Browder, D. M., Spooner, F., Ahlgrim-Delzell, L., Wakeman, S. Y., & Harris, A. (2008). A meta-analysis on teaching mathematics to students with significant cognitive disabilities. *Exceptional Children*, *74*(4), 407–432. doi:10.1177/001440290807400401

Browder, D. M., Wakeman, S. Y., Spooner, F., Ahlgrim-Delzell, L., & Algozzine, B. (2006). Research on reading instruction for individuals with significant cognitive disabilities. *Exceptional Children*, *72*(4), 392–408. doi:10.1177/001440290607200401

CAST (2018). Universal design for learning guidelines (version 2.2). http://udlguidelines.cast.org

Council for Exceptional Children. (2014). Standards for evidence-based practices in special education. *TEACHING Exceptional Children*, *46*(6), 206–212. doi:10.1177/0040059914531389

Collins, B. C. (2012). *Systematic instruction for students with moderate and severe disabilities*. Paul H. Brookes Publishing Company.

Cook, B. G., Tankersley, M., Cook, L., & Landrum, T. J. (2008). Evidence-based practices in special education: Some practical considerations. *Intervention in School and Clinic*, *44*(2), 69–75. doi:10.1177/0022466911420877

Courtade, G., Spooner, F., & Browder, D. M. (2007). Review of studies with students with significant cognitive disabilities which link to science standards. *Research and Practice for Persons with Severe Disabilities*, *32*(1), 43–49.

Courtade, G., Spooner, F., & Browder, D. M., & Jimenez, B. (2012). Seven reasons to promote standards-based instruction for students with severe disabilities: A reply to Ayres, Lowrey, Douglas, & Sievers (2011). *Education and Training in Autism and Developmental Disabilities*, *47*(1), 3–13.

Crichton, H., & McDaid, A. (2016) Learning intentions and success criteria: learners' and teachers' views. *Curriculum Journal*, *27*(2), 190–203. doi:10.1080/09585176.2015.1103278

Driver, M. K., & Powell, S. R. (2017). Culturally and linguistically responsive schema intervention: Improving word problem solving for English language learners with mathematics difficulty. *Learning Disability Quarterly*, *40*(1), 41–53.

Endrew F. v. (2017). Douglas County School District, 580 U.S. ____.

Every Student Succeeds Act of 2015, Pub. L. 114-95. 20 U. S. C. § 6301 *et seq.*

Gersten, R., Fuchs, L. S., Compton, D., Coyne, M., Greenwood, C., & Innocenti, M. S. (2005). Quality indicators for group experimental and quasi-experimental research in special education.*Exceptional Children*, *71*(2), 149–164 . doi.org/10.1177/001440290507100202.

Hattie, J. (2012). *Visible learning for teachers: Maximizing impact on learning*. Routledge.

Heinrich, S., Collins, B. C., Knight, V., & Spriggs, A. D. (2016). Embedded simultaneous prompting procedure to teach STEM content to high school students with moderate disabilities in an inclusive setting. *Education and Training in Autism and Developmental Disabilities*, *51*(1), 41–54.

Horner, R., Carr, E., Halle, J., McGee, G., Odom, S. L., & Wolery, M. (2005). The use of single-subject research to identify evidence-based practice in special education. *Exceptional Children, 71*(2), 165–179. doi:10.1177/001440290507100203.

Hudson, M. E., Browder, D. M., & Wood, L. A. (2013). Review of experimental research on academic learning by students with moderate and severe intellectual disability in general education. *Research and Practice for Persons with Severe Disabilities, 38*(1), 17–29. doi:10.2511/027494813805046926

Individuals with Disabilities Education Act Amendments of 1997, Pub. L. No. 10.5-17. 20 U. S. C. §§ 1400 *et seq.*

Individuals with Disabilities Education Improvement Act of 2004, Pub. L. 108-466, 20 U. S. C. §1400, H. R. 1350.

Jimenez, B., & Humphreys, S. (2018). *Big ideas planner* [Unpublished infographic]. https://inclusiveschools.com.au

Jimenez, B., & Warren, S. H. (2021). *Building self-determination via student engaged formative assessments for students with intellectual disability* [Manuscript submitted for publication]. Department of Curriculum and Instruction, University of Texas at Arlington.

Jitendra, A. K., & Hoff, K. (1996). The effects of schema-based instruction on the mathematical word-problem-solving performance of students with learning disabilities. *Journal of Learning Disabilities, 29*(4), 422–431. doi:10.1177/002221949602900410

McLeskey, J., Barringer, M-D., Billingsley, B., Brownell, M., Jackson, D., Kennedy, M., Lewis, T., Maheady, L., Rodriguez, J., Scheeler, M. C., Winn, J., & Ziegler, D. (2017). *High-leverage practices in special education.* Council for Exceptional Children & CEEDAR Center.

National Council of Teachers of Mathematics. (2000). *Principles and standards for school mathematics.* Author.

National Reading Panel. (2000). *Report of the National Reading Panel: Teaching children to read: An evidence-based assessment of the scientific research literature on reading and its implications for reading instruction.* National Institute for Literacy.

National Research Council. (1996). *National science education standards.* National Academy Press.

Pennington, R. C., Collins, B. C., Stenhoff, D. M., Turner, K, & Gunselman, K. (2014). Using simultaneous prompting to teach generative writing to students with autism. *Education and Training in Autism and Developmental Disabilities, 49*(3), 396–414

Pennington, R. C., & Delano, M. D. (2012). Writing instruction for students with autism spectrum disorders: A review of literature. *Focus on Autism and Other Disabilities, 27*(3), 158–167. doi:10.1177/1088357612451318

Pennington, R. C., Flick, A., & Smith-Wehr, K. (2018). The use of response prompting and frames for teaching sentence writing to students with moderate intellectual disability. *Focus on Autism and Other Developmental Disabilities, 33*(3), 142–149. doi:10.1177/1088357616673568

Pennington, R. C., Stanger, C. Mims, P. J., Kirkman, C., Aldridge, S., Stanley, M., & Chapman, S. (2019). A pilot investigation of an autonomous technology-based instructional program for teaching sentence construction to students with extensive support needs. *Journal of Special Education Technology.* doi:10.1177/0162643419879767

Pennington, R. C., & Koehler, M. (2017). The effects of modeling, story templates, and self-graphing in the use of story elements by students with moderate intellectual disability, *Education and Training in Autism and Developmental Disabilities, 52*(3), 280–290.

Riccomini, P. J., Smith, G. W., Hughes, E. M., & Fries, K. M. (2015). The language of mathematics: The importance of teaching and learning mathematical vocabulary. *Reading & Writing Quarterly, 31*(3), 235–252. doi:10.1080/10573569.2015.1030995

Riggs, L., Collins, B. C., Kleinert, H., & Knight, V. F. (2013). Teaching principles of heredity to high school students with moderate and severe disabilities. *Research and Practice for Persons with Severe Disabilities, 38*(1), 30–43. doi:10.2511/027494813807046971

Rivera, F. D., & Becker, J. R. (2009). Algebraic reasoning through patterns. *Mathematics Teaching in the Middle School, 15*(4), 212–221.

Root, J. R., Cox, S. K., Hammons, N., Saunders, A. F., & Gilley, D. (2018). Contextualizing mathematics: Teaching problem solving to secondary students with intellectual and developmental disabilities. *Intellectual and Developmental Disabilities, 56*(6), 442–457. doi:10.1352/1934-9556-56.6.442

Root, J. R., & Browder, D. M. (2019). Algebraic problem solving for middle school students with autism and intellectual disability. *Exceptionality, 27*(2), 118–132. doi:10.1080/09362835.2017.1394304

Root, J. R., Cox, S. K., Saunders, A., & Gilley, D. (2020). Applying the universal design for learning framework to mathematics instruction for learners with extensive support needs. *Remedial and Special Education, 41*(4), 194–206. doi:10.1177/0741932519887235

Root, J., Jimenez, B., & Saunders, A. (2021). *Leveraging the UDL framework to plan grade-aligned mathematics in inclusive settings* Inclusive Practices. Advance online publication. doi.org/2732474521990028.

Saunders, A. F., Browder, D. M., & Root, J. R. (2017). Standards-based mathematics and science instruction for students with developmental disabilities. In M. Wehmeyer & K. Shogren (Eds.), *Research-based practices for educating students with intellectual disability*. Routledge.

Saunders, A. F., Spooner, F., & Ley Davis, L. (2018). Using video prompting to teach mathematical problem solving of real-world video-simulation problems. *Remedial and Special Education, 39*(1), 53–64. doi:10.1177/0741932517717042

Sharratt, L. (2019). *Clarity: What matters most in learning, teaching, and leading*. Corwin.

Skinner, B. F. (1957). *Verbal behavior*. Copley.

Snell, M. E. (Ed.). (1978). *Systematic instruction of the moderately and severely handicapped*. Merrill Press.

Spencer, T. D., & Petersen, D. B. (2018). Bridging oral and written language: An oral narrative language intervention study with writing outcomes. *Language, speech, and hearing services in schools, 49*(3), 569–581. doi:10.1044/2018_LSHSS-17-0030

Spooner, F., Knight, V., Browder, D. M., Jimenez, B., & DiBiase, W. (2011). Evaluating evidence-based practices in teaching science content to students with severe developmental disabilities. *Research and Practice for Persons with Severe Disabilities, 36*(1-2), 62–75. doi:10.2511/rpsd.36.1-2.62

Spooner, F., Knight, V., Browder, D. M., & Smith, B. (2012). Evidence-based practice for teaching academics to students with severe developmental disabilities. *Remedial and Special Education, 33*(6), 374–387. doi:10.1177/0741932511421634

Townsend, D., Filippini, A., Collins, P., & Biancarosa, G. (2012). Evidence for the importance of academic word knowledge for the academic achievement of diverse middle school students. *The Elementary School Journal, 112*(3), 497–518.

Wood, L., Browder, D. M., & Flynn, L. (2015). Teaching students with intellectual disability to use a self-questioning strategy to comprehend social studies text for an inclusive setting. *Research and Practice for Persons with Severe Disabilities, 40*(4), 275–293.

Yell, M. L., & Bateman, D. F. (2017). Endrew F. v. Douglas County School District (2017): FAPE and the U.S. Supreme Court. *TEACHING Exceptional Children, 50*(1), 7–15. doi:10.1177/0040059917721116

Zakas, T. L., Browder, D. M., Ahlgrim-Delzell, L., & Heafner, T. (2013). Teaching social studies content to students with autism using a graphic organizer intervention. *Research in Autism Spectrum Disorders*, 7(9), 1075–1086. doi:10.1016/j.rasd.2013.06.001

15

Alternate Assessments and Monitoring Student Progress in Inclusive Classrooms

Shawnee Y. Wakeman[1], Meagan Karvonen[2], Claudia Flowers[1], and Lindsay Ruhter[2]

[1]UNIVERSITY OF NORTH CAROLINA AT CHARLOTTE

[2]UNIVERSITY OF KANSAS

Setting the Stage

Academic expectations for students with extensive support needs (ESN) have increased substantially since 2000. Prior to the Individuals with Disabilities Education Act of 1997 (IDEA), students with significant disabilities were often excluded from the general curriculum and their exposure to academics was limited to functional applications (Browder et al., 2007). IDEA 1997 introduced the requirement that states include all students with disabilities in the general curriculum and provide alternate assessments for students who could not participate in large-scale (statewide) assessments, even with appropriate accommodations.

Under the most recent ESEA reauthorization (ESSA, 2015), alternate assessments are intended for students with "the most significant cognitive disabilities."[1] IEP teams determine each student's appropriate participation in alternate assessments using state-developed definitions of the student population, eligibility guidelines, and factors that should not lead to alternate assessment participation. In 2018-19 the most common characteristics of states' eligibility criteria included cognitive and adaptive function, the student's need for individualized instruction and supports, and the student's academic instruction being grounded in alternate content standards (Thurlow et al., 2019). Educational service model and educational setting are among the factors that states caution against using to make these decisions. In other words, being eligible for an alternate assessment based on alternate academic achievement standards does not mean a student should automatically be served in a separate setting (Sabia & Thurlow, 2019). Students with ESN can receive appropriate academic instruction and assessment in inclusive settings so they can make progress in the general curriculum.

Helping students with ESN meet high academic expectations requires effective methods for assessing, monitoring progress, and using data to inform inclusive instruction. The TIES Center (www.tiescenter.org) explains that inclusive instruction is accessible, engaging instruction that includes accommodations and modifications so that students with ESN work alongside their peers.

 DOI: 10.4324/9781003043874-15

We define inclusive instruction as rigorous and grade-level aligned, using strategies that promote attainment of contemporary alternate achievement expectations in inclusive settings. The remainder of this section discusses academic expectations and the history of academic assessments for students with ESN. We then describe the need for information about academic progress for students with ESN.

High Expectations for Academic Instruction and Assessment in the Classroom

Alternate assessments have been a key driver of decisions about how academic content standards are interpreted for students with ESN, which content is prioritized for instruction and the amount of academic achievement that should be expected by the end of the year. Wakeman, Browder et al. (2011) identified two specific challenges in setting targets for educational outcomes for this population of students: (a) selecting the content to be assessed and (b) setting the appropriate performance expectations.

States were first required to implement alternate assessments by 2001. Early alternate assessments were often based on functional curricula (e.g., leisure, daily living, vocational, and self-help skills), including functional academics (Wakeman, Browder et al., 2011). The No Child Left Behind (NCLB Act, 2002) required that alternate assessments are aligned to grade-level content standards for a student's chronologically appropriate grade in English language arts (ELA) and mathematics by 2004 and in science by 2007. In this era, states often create extended content standards or curriculum frameworks that reduce the state's academic content standards in depth, breadth, and complexity to create appropriate expectations for students with ESN. Around 2010, states began adopting more rigorous ELA and mathematics content standards to promote college and career readiness by the end of high school (for example, http://www.corestandards.org/). Science followed with the release of the Next Generation Science Standards (NGSS, https://www.nextgenscience.org/) in 2013. The NGSS define science as three-dimensional; students are expected to demonstrate what they know and can do by integrating the dimensions, for example, by using the science and engineering practice (SEP) to explore a science concept or disciplinary core idea (DCI), linked to different science domains and content areas through a crosscutting concept (CCC).

The newer college and career-ready content standards led to higher expectations for students with significant cognitive disabilities as well. For example, two multi-state consortia (National Center and State Collaborative [NCSC] and Dynamic Learning Maps [DLM]) developed grade-level academic expectations to be used in next-generation alternate assessments. Table 15.1 illustrates the contrast between old and new expectations for what students with ESN should know and be able to do by the end of fifth grade. In all three subjects, students with ESN are expected to do more complex things with academic content.

Table 15.1 Academic Expectations for Students with ESN Under NCLB-era Standards and College and Career Ready Standards

NCLB Era Expectation	*College and Career Ready Expectation*
Identify descriptive words.	Identify words in the text to answer a question about explicit information.
Identify one side of a non-square rectangle as longer than another side using manipulatives.	Sort two-dimensional figures and identify the attributes (angles, number of sides, corners, color) they have in common.
Describe and compare observable characteristics of water, air, rocks, and soil.	Make observations and measurements to identify materials based on their properties (e.g., weight, shape, texture, buoyancy, color, or magnetism).

Both NCSC and DLM used organized learning models (learning progressions and learning map models, respectively) to identify content along the pathway toward the standard and provide access points for the range of students with ESN as they work toward grade-level expectations. These access points served as the targets for assessment items and were made available to teachers to guide instruction.

While content standards define the content for instruction, achievement standards indicate how much a student is expected to demonstrate at the end of the year. Alternate assessments measure what students know and can do in each academic subject, and results are reported in terms of alternate academic achievement standards. Those achievement standards are set through rigorous procedures, with panels of educators and other key stakeholders making judgments about appropriate standards and performance expectations.

Achievement standards for NCLB-era alternate assessments were not always differentiated across grades (Flowers et al., 2009), so that students were expected to know more in upper grades. Those assessments also tended to have low achievement standards and high proficiency rates (Karvonen et al., 2013). In contrast, newer alternate assessments have higher achievement standards and fewer students are proficient. For example, more than 90,000 students with significant cognitive disabilities take DLM assessments. In 2015 fewer than 50% of students scored proficient or above in ELA and fewer than 25% scored proficient or above in mathematics (DLM Consortium, 2016).

There are several challenges to helping students meet higher academic expectations. Special educators, who often lack academic coursework in their degree programs (Leko et al., 2015), feel unprepared to teach academics (Lee et al., 2016) or perceive academics as competing with other curricular priorities (Hunt et al., 2012). Ten years after the IDEA requirement for general curriculum access, a survey conducted in several states revealed that teachers still prioritized a narrow range of academic content, best aligned with functional academics, as the academic curriculum for students with significant cognitive disabilities (Karvonen et al., 2013). The literature on effective academic instruction for students with severe disabilities (e.g., Hudson et al., 2018; Spooner et al., 2011, 2012, 2019) is grounded in earlier generations of academic expectations and instructional methods that treat academics as isolated skills. Promising practices for teaching to higher expectations on more complex standards are only recently emerging (e.g., Erickson & Koppenhaver, 2020; Jimenez, 2020). However, since few students with ESN are served in inclusive settings (Burnes & Clark, 2020), there is still limited evidence of effective strategies for academic instruction in inclusive settings that promote student attainment of high expectations (Saunders et al., 2020). In addition to placement in inclusive settings, aligned educational systems, instruction based on Universal Design for Learning (UDL) principles, teacher use of data-based decision-making, and self-determination are strategies that have a direct relationship with academic outcomes for students with ESN (Karvonen et al., 2017).

Rigorous academic content standards and challenging academic achievement standards support student preparation for post-secondary opportunities in college, career, and community life (Kearns et al., 2010), including opportunities for competitive integrated employment (Workforce Innovation and Opportunity Act, 2014). Nonregulatory guidance and legal decisions stress the goal for educational programs to help students with ESN meet higher expectations. For example, guidance from the Office of Special Education and Rehabilitative Services (U. S. Department of Education, 2005) indicated that IEPs must be aligned with the state's academic content standards for a student's enrolled grade and that IEP goals should be "sufficiently ambitious to help close the gap" (p. 5) between content standards and the student's present level of performance. In the 2017 Endrew F. decision, the US Supreme Court ruled that students receiving special education services must make progress in their learning objectives, and IEPs must provide measurable benefit to a student (Yell & Bateman, 2017). Collectively, this guidance reinforces the importance of holding students to high expectations each year with increasing expectations across grade levels (Karvonen et al., 2017).

The History of Academic Assessment for Students with Extensive Support Needs

Much of the history of academic assessment for students with ESN is grounded in large-scale alternate assessments. Teachers also use teacher-developed data collection systems or curriculum-based measures to track progress on academic skills, discussed later in this chapter.

Assessment Methods

In response to the IDEA 1997 mandate to provide alternate assessment, many states used a portfolio assessment to gather evidence of student performance for the prioritized content from functional curricula (Wakeman, Browder et al., 2011). Since then, most states have changed the format of their assessment. By 2004, only 12 states reported using a portfolio, while 13 states reported using a body of evidence format with a standardized set of performance-based items, and 7 states reported using a rating scale or checklist format (Thompson et al., 2005). In a 2009 survey, Altman et al. (2010) found that 12 regular states reported using only a portfolio or body of evidence, 18 used performance tasks, 8 used a portfolio with performance tasks, 8 used multiple-choice responses, and 2 used other methods.

Each alternate assessment design has benefits and drawbacks (Hess et al., 2011) that reflect the tension between standardization and flexibility (Marion & Pellegrino, 2006). Performance tasks support standardized administration and gather more evidence across a broader range of academic content, but the design of the tasks may leave some students with no way of demonstrating what they know. Portfolios with teacher-selected academic targets are flexible and allow students to demonstrate what they know much like they would during daily instruction. Yet portfolios risk losing their connection to academic content standards and repeating the same skills across grades, limiting the student's ability to demonstrate growth across years. Checklists can be efficient and reduce administrative burden, but without supporting evidence, checklist ratings can be subjective and difficult to corroborate.

The newest generation of alternate assessments, developed between 2010 and 2015, tend to balance standardization and flexibility. They tend to consist of selected response items or performance tasks with embedded options for flexible assessment. More than past generations, these assessments are managed and administered online, bringing benefits including the reduced burden on teachers, more efficient assessment (i.e., more items administered in less time), and faster scoring. These assessments were also designed using UDL and evidence-centered design principles to ensure fidelity to the intended academic content and that student responses would elicit the intended cognitive process (Bechard et al., 2019).

Alternate assessments developed by the NCSC and DLM consortia provide examples of these new designs. Multi-State Alternate Assessments (MSAA; developed by NCSC) are individually administered and computer-based with an option for paper-pencil administration (MSAA, 2019). MSAA items contain built-in supports that allow students to use materials they are most familiar with and communicate what they know and can do as independently as possible. The assessments are stage adaptive, so each student is routed to one of three forms at different levels of difficulty for the second stage based on their performance on the first stage. MSAA uses selected response items in all three subjects and an open-ended prompt to create a writing product on the writing portion of the assessment. Items are available at four levels of complexity.

DLM assessments are administered as a series of testlets, each with 3-10 items at one of five complexity levels called linkage levels (DLM Consortium, 2016). Testlets are either teacher-administered or computer-delivered. For teacher-administered testlets, the testlet is administered outside the system, often using provided teacher response cards or common classroom objects as manipulatives, and the test administrator records the student's response into the system. Students able to interact independently with the testlet content, with or without accessibility supports, take computer-administered testlets. Test administrators and students may use the same accessibility supports on DLM assessments as they use during daily instruction, including, but not limited to, read-aloud, alternate keyboards, or switches. Testlets are aligned to one linkage level within one EE, and testlets are adaptive across EEs. If a student demonstrates mastery at one linkage level, the DLM system will assign the next testlet at a higher linkage level.

As of the 2020-21 school year, more than half of states use either MSAA or DLM alternate assessments. Based on the trajectory of alternate assessment design over the past 20 years, future alternate assessments are likely to be standardized with options for flexibility. Portfolios are likely to be eliminated or used only in combination with models that meet standards for technical adequacy (Samuels, 2018).

Assessment Results

Along with changes in academic achievement standards and assessment design, alternate assessments also have changed in terms of what counts in scoring and what results are communicated. Early alternate assessments incorporated indicators of student responses (e.g., skill, progress) and system indicators (e.g., appropriateness, participation in general education settings) in their scoring model (Quenemoen, 2008). By 2009 most states still scored based on the student's demonstrated skill and level of support, and fewer than 10 states retained program-related or non-academic factors (e.g., parent satisfaction, self-determination) in their scoring models (Altman et al., 2010). Six states counted students' participation in general education settings in their scoring models.

With the newest generation of alternate assessments, there has been more of a shift to produce results that only indicate the student's demonstrated academic achievement. MSAA individual student score reports include an overall scale score for the subject and the associated performance level (levels 1-4; Multi-State Alternate Assessment, 2019). DLM individual student score reports provide an overall performance level, performance within smaller clusters of related standards, and the student's demonstrated mastery of each linkage level for each tested Essential Element (DLM Consortium, 2016).

Current Issues and Needs for Academic Assessment Information

Assessment results are used for many different purposes. For example, alternate assessments were created to ensure information about students with disabilities was included in accountability systems that drive decisions about educational programs (Thurlow et al., 2001). However, when results are reported as an overall achievement level for an entire subject, alternate assessment results have limited value in designing individualized curricula or making classroom decisions (Karvonen et al., 2017). For example, when describing a student's present level of academic performance, an IEP team might note that a student was "proficient" on the previous year's alternate assessment. But that label does not indicate the student's strengths and needs in specific, grade-level aligned academic content.

In recent years, states have shifted from a focus solely on large-scale summative assessments that indicate what students know and can do at the end of a year to more balanced or comprehensive systems (CCSSO, 2015). Recognizing different types of assessments have different purposes, states and districts are now supporting formative assessment practices and interim or benchmark assessments to provide actionable information for teachers ahead of summative assessments.

Unfortunately, there are few parallel options available for students who take alternate assessments. Most commercially available benchmark assessments are not designed for students with ESN. Packaged curricula (some of which include assessments) may not be fully aligned to academic content standards (Taub et al., 2020). The DLM assessment system includes instructionally embedded assessments that teachers can use flexibly to assess students after instruction. Teachers can generate score reports on demand, review information about student mastery of specific academic content, and use the information to plan instruction. Instructionally embedded assessments are neither benchmark nor formative assessments. Reports show results based on cumulative assessments since the beginning of the year so teachers can see changes in skill mastery over time. However, the system does not have a score-based indicator of "progress." More options are needed for monitoring the academic progress of students with ESN.

Research-based Progress Monitoring Methods of Student Performance

While alternate assessments produce summative data regarding student performance, these assessments were not originally designed to measure within-year student growth. Herman (2010) discussed a developmental coherence within an assessment system as "the extent to which learning goals, instruction, and assessment are continually intertwined over time to promote student progress" (p. 6). While the alternate assessment allows the opportunity for all students to participate in a more inclusive education system for all students, it alone is not sufficient to ensure that a quality education based upon data will occur. High-quality assessment data is essential if changes in instructional practices are to be effective (Crawford, 2014; Popham, 2006). Much of the research literature documents student progress for this population through data collection efforts that represent formative information. These methods may be better measures of student growth that represent valid and reliable performance.

Progress Monitoring

Progress monitoring efforts within a classroom, as well as more standardized assessment efforts at designated points in time during a school year, allow teachers and students to understand the progress being made and the work that remains to be done to reach academic outcomes successfully. Progress monitoring occurs in different ways (e.g., formative assessments such as curriculum-based measures [CBM], discrete skill data collection), with most resulting in some form of data-based decision making (DBDM) process. As instructional planning is based upon student performance in relation to content standards, it is necessary to discuss progress monitoring in the form of formative assessment.

Multi-Tiered System of Supports (MTSS) and Response to Intervention (RTI).

Teachers in an inclusive classroom are typically familiar with a system for RTI. RTI is designed to be a multi-level prevention system with increasing intensiveness within instruction to support students in the general education classroom (www.rti4success.org) and is a typical practice for students who are considered at risk as well as those with learning disabilities. RTI has four essential components, which include progress monitoring and interventions to inform teachers about how to best decide how to support students during instruction for success. Deno (2016) purported that DBDM is the core within the RTI process and outlined how the practices within DBDM are relevant within an RTI system. It is important to note that while RTI focuses on instructional interventions, MTSS encompasses not only RTI but also includes the behavioral, social, and emotional needs of students. MTSS is more comprehensive (see https://blog.edgenuity.com/rti-mtss/ for more information on the distinctions between RTI and MTSS).

Ongoing progress monitoring is a hallmark of the MTSS framework, highlighted in the Every Student Succeeds Act (ESSA) as an approach that improves student achievement, including students with disabilities. MTSS is a framework in which a three-tiered system with data-based decisions at its core (National Center for Response to Intervention, 2010; See Chapter 8 for in-depth information about MTSS). Agran et al. (2020) identified the use of MTSS as a way to "counteract entrenched policies of separating and segregating students from general education" (p. 9). Educators in an MTSS system continuously make data-based decisions for the benefit of all students academically and behaviorally, including those students with ESN in inclusive classrooms. As assessments provide ongoing student-level data, frequent adjustments in instruction and interventions can be made that are specific to the needs of individual students. This system is designed to support students to keep them in the general education classroom rather than move them to a more restrictive placement because of their learning needs (Sailor & McCart, 2014). Unfortunately, the application of MTSS with all students, including those with ESN, has yet to be realized in many states (Thurlow et al., 2020).

Formative Assessment

The Council of Chief State School Officers (CCSSO) defined formative assessment as follows:

> Formative assessment is a planned, ongoing process used by all students and teachers during learning and teaching to elicit and use evidence of student learning to improve student understanding of intended disciplinary learning outcomes and support students to become self-directed learners. (CCSSO, 2018, p. 2).

There are several important elements within this definition. First, formative assessment is a planned process that is purposefully designed to allow for the ongoing review of student performance or preference data. Teachers design formative assessment efforts that align with the purpose of the assessment (e.g., student thinking and learning, preferences, self-assessment, peer reviews). The teacher plans formative assessments to be responsive to student needs and responses rather than one size fits all. Formative assessments are not a point in time assessment but allow the teacher to consistently review data *during* student learning. Second, while formative assessment requires some form of evidence, the form does not necessarily have to be in a typical assessment format (i.e., test, quiz). It does, however, need to serve as a guide for the next steps within the teaching and learning process. Third, the definition highlights the connection between the characteristics of students and the content the students engage with. Assessments that are designed to recognize the relationship between the learner and the content provide greater opportunity for identification of where student understanding is on a continuum rather than at an isolated point. Finally, student self-direction is important if students are to actively engage with teachers as part of the teaching and learning process. The transition from teacher to student to direct and guide the learning is a necessary step for learners that formative assessment supports.

Seminal research by Black and Wiliam (1998) indicated that focused efforts to improve formative assessment practices produced significant gains in student learning, and these practices were generally more effective than one-on-one tutoring, intensive reading instruction, or other instructional interventions. While there continues to be some debate about the magnitude of the effectiveness of formative assessment (Bennett, 2011; Kingston & Nash, 2011), almost all educators agree that to support student learning, teachers must engage learners within the process to evaluate their students' understanding.

The crux of formative assessment is the development of student learning during the learning process rather than after the fact (Heritage, 2011). Formative assessment is likely not a graded product but serves as a quick form of communication between teachers and students about what has and has not occurred as a result of instruction (CCSSO, 2018; Heritage, 2010). With an understanding of the wide variety of ways this type of data can be collected from students, teachers are better equipped to plan future lessons and students are recognized for what they do and do not understand or prefer. For example, by simply asking students about what they perceive to be the most difficult and successful part of a lesson, teachers gather information about the instructional strategies they used and specific aspects of the content that may require re-teaching using other approaches. This technique also sends the message to each student that their voice counts and is important in the classroom, as well as help the student identify what works best for them instructionally during self-directed learning. Done correctly, formative assessment can yield a wealth of information for teachers, including information about (a) effective instructional practices and materials, (b) the realistic nature of the objectives covered in a lesson, (c) how well students understand the content within the current lesson, (d) the degree to which student understanding from previous lessons is maintained and utilized, and (e) the appropriateness of the sequence of the lessons taught.

Curriculum-Based Measures (CBM)

The most well-researched form of student progress monitoring is Curriculum-Based Measurement (CBM). CBM now has more than 200 empirical studies published in peer-reviewed journals supporting both its technical quality and capacity to help teachers improve student outcomes in the elementary grades (Deno, 2003). Some of the standard tasks used for CBM are reading aloud from text and selection of words deleted from the text (maze) in reading, writing word sequences when given a story starter or picture in writing, writing letter sequences from dictation in spelling and writing correct answers/digits in solving problems in arithmetic (Deno). In contrast, CBM has rarely been applied with students with ESN who participate in AA-AAS and is usually limited to mastery measures. Typical mastery measures for students with ESN provide information on isolated knowledge or skills or on a collection of skills in a chained task performed independently or with prompts (e.g., Browder et al., 2011). To some extent, this has been due to the nature of the curriculum taught to students in this population. While historically, the curriculum for this population has focused more on skills of daily living than academic content, the curriculum in the past 15 years has shifted to include, if not now predominately focus on, academic content standards. Even as students who participate in alternate assessments receive instruction on more academic content, research using CBMs has been slow to keep pace. One trend for the use of CBMs is the evaluation of the progress of students with disabilities participating in intensive interventions in inclusive classrooms (Deno). While most applications of CBMs are not with students with ESN, the potential of their use in an inclusive setting is intriguing. While learning targets or goals within instruction may be different between students with ESN and peers in the general education classroom, the same or similar CBM may be utilized. However, if the prioritized content for students with ESN is different than that of their peers in the inclusive class, teachers would need to design and validated additional CBMs that match the instructional content for both sets of students.

While some literature identifies three basic types of CBMs, including general-outcome measures, skills-based measures, and mastery measures (Hosp et al., 2016), other literature describes general-outcome and skill-based measures as CBM, separating mastery measures out from CBM (Austin & Filderman, 2020). The IRIS Center (2020) outlined a mastery measure as one that evaluates student understanding and proficiency of the individual-specific skill to determine if the student is able to learn the skill in a timely fashion and move forward to another skill. In contrast, a general-outcomes measure allows for the frequent measurement of a variety of skills at the same time. One of the most common forms of a general outcome measure is oral reading fluency. When reading aloud, the student applies a variety of skills to decode, recognize vocabulary, and use context clues. The advantage of a general-outcome measure is that it reduces the number of CBMs a teacher needs to use, but the disadvantage is that it may not pinpoint what skills the student lacks (e.g., ecoding is underdeveloped). In a skills-based measure, a group of skills is assessed together but with distinct items for each. A common example is a CBM in mathematics that includes different types of computation (e.g., problems in subtraction and addition with and without regrouping).

Data-Based Decisions

A critical component within the formative assessment is the use of data to inform changes to teaching and learning. Regardless of the form taken to monitor student progress, it is expected that a data review will occur to shape the next steps. While there is an established research base of teachers using DBDM during the instruction of students with ESN, it is very limited in the context of an inclusive classroom. This base substantially exists of incorporating a behavioral approach to data collection (e.g., discrete trials and task analysis) teaching to mastery in a special education classroom. The data-based decision guidelines in Jimenez et al. (2012) focused on interpreting the graphed number of occurrences of a discrete skill (such as number of sight words), rather than the seven steps common to DBDM data collection models used in targeting academic constructs (Filderman et al., 2018). Jimenez et al. (2016) found that training on DBDM alone was not sufficient for special educators to carry over to the measurement of progress for their own students.

Much of the research on progress monitoring with this population shows that providing teachers with a specific system for measuring student progress, summarizing ongoing data, and making instructional decisions based on data patterns promotes student progress on a discrete skill or chained task (e.g., Wood et al., 2015). While research has emerged that students with ESN can make academic gains in inclusive settings on grade-aligned instruction (Hudson et al., 2013; Jimenez & Kamei, 2015; Saunders et al., 2020), much of this research follows a single-case design that collects data typically on single skills or steps in a task. For example, several studies conducted in inclusive classrooms used embedded instruction, which typically includes the review of specific skills or content during natural breaks within instruction in a general education classroom.

While much of the literature on embedded instruction in inclusive settings focuses on teaching discrete skills, there are ways to adapt and modify such an approach that is more representative of the daily practice in general education classrooms. For example, Jameson et al. (2012) used embedded task analytic instruction and constant time delay to teach phonemic awareness skills in a kindergarten classroom. The instruction was distributed over the class period and occurred naturally during the instructional opportunities on specific content for individual students who needed support, much like all teachers do as they monitor student performance in a classroom. The academic gains for students with ESN in inclusive classrooms identified in the research literature will not continue to be realized if teachers do not use a system that includes making instructional changes based on the data (e.g., Hager & Slocum, 2011; Quenemoen et al., 2004).

Standards-Based Grading

One area that continues to be of great concern and serves as a barrier is the grading of students with ESN in inclusive classrooms. Data-based decision models designed to collect progress data and have been the basis of student performance for students with ESN in the past do not typically translate into grades, or maybe, more importantly, do not communicate the same thing that grades in an inclusive classroom communicate, which traditionally is student performance or mastery of content taught at a rapid pace. Research overall is lacking on grading practices for students with disabilities (Jung, 2009; Jung & Guskey, 2010), with no research regarding grading practices for students with ESN in inclusive settings. Welsh et al. (2013) described standards-based grading as reporting student performance levels on specific educational goals rather than traditional grading methods that describe performance in broad terms. Beatty (2013) described three principles within standards-based grading. First, the grades should have meaning and provide information directly connected to the student's performance in relation to the content standards. Second, students should have multiple opportunities with accompanying feedback to practice the content within the standards that directly inform the grade. Third, grades should not include outside influences such as extra credit and completion. The use of student performance data that is directly tied to individual standards allows students to showcase what they know and can do with specificity. For example, instead of a student earning a grade of C in the third quarter in math class, proficiency levels for the individual standards are reported. This type of approach allows teachers to use and identify patterns within student performance data to inform instructional strategy and support decisions that are directly tied to the content standards.

While general education teachers alone may not be able to consistently collect valid and reliable data from students with ESN using measures designed for their general education peers, collaborative discussions and co-teaching can occur to adapt assessments to promote accessibility for students with ESN. Reyes et al. (2020) highlighted that collaborations are necessary so that decisions regarding what exactly is being graded and how that grading is to occur are an essential part of standards-based grading in an inclusive classroom.

Influence of Technology on Assessment Practices

Technology and its fast-paced advances have capitalized on the flexibility to embed accessibility and address the needs of individuals with disabilities (Russell, 2018). Assistive technology (AT), augmentative and alternative communication (AAC), and digitally delivered assessments continue to change instructional and assessment practices in the K-12 school system. These technologies can eliminate barriers and provide access to academic content, which is necessary for effective instruction and fair testing (Kettler et al., 2018). These technologies can also support students with ESN who receive instruction in inclusive classrooms.

AT includes any equipment, product system, or service that is used to increase, maintain, or improve the functional capabilities of individuals with disabilities (IDEA, 2004). Current advancements in AT range in sophistication from low to high technology (Cook et al., 2020). Lower-end AT are usually simple adaptive tools that do not require much training and are often inexpensive. Examples of low technology tools include graphic organizers, response cards, and mathematics manipulatives. Higher-end AT are devices that have some electronic components. Examples of these tools include classroom response systems (e.g., clickers and computer applications), text-to-speech applications, virtual reality, and online progress monitoring. AT provides flexible ways for students to express themselves, which is especially important when teachers use formative assessment in inclusive classrooms. While there is research that examines the effectiveness of many AT tools (e.g., Fisher & Frey, 2015; Monem et al., 2018; Schulz et al., 2020), much more research is needed to better understand how to optimize accessibility for all students.

A positive change in the educational field is consideration of accessibility in the early stages of designing instruction and tests. UDL provides a framework that can guide educators and test designers to create more equitable and effective assessments for all students (Meyer et al., 2014). UDL has become prominent in educational practices and policies (Rose et al., 2018), including in the National Educational Technology Plan (U.S. Department of Education, Office of Educational Technology, 2016), in the Educational Technology Developer's Guide (U.S. Department of Education, Office of Educational Technology, 2015), and in ESSA (2015).

As Stone and Cook (2018) noted, "We are heartened by the gains that have been made in the awareness of the importance of administering fair and accessible tests to individuals, particularly those with disabilities recently" (p. 71). Many of the issues of providing access to academic content for all students seemed impossible just 20 years ago. While there is still a lot of work to do, there are positive movements to increase educational opportunities for all students and technology will be a key driver for providing access for all students.

Setting the Course for Effective Instruction

Supporting students with ESN as they make progress in the general curriculum requires starting with the least dangerous assumption criterion, first proposed by Donnellan (1984): "in the absence of conclusive data, educational decisions ought to be based on assumptions that, if incorrect, will have the least dangerous effect on the likelihood that students will be able to function independently as adults" (p. 141). For students with ESN, this criterion is important for decisions about instruction, assessment, and placement (Taub et al., 2019). Unfortunately, IEP team decisions about assessment participation and placement have historically been intertwined (Agran et al., 2020). IEP teams should review student data using a least dangerous assumption approach when making these crucial decisions.

The IEP team's decision about assessment participation is whether a student with ESN should take the state's general or alternate academic assessment. This decision requires teams to be familiar with the state's eligibility guidelines, which typically include a criterion regarding whether the student is receiving instruction in grade-level content standards or extended, grade-aligned content standards. Teams should be familiar with the general and alternate academic achievement standards (Kearns et al., 2020) and consider the student's long-term goals, including the pursuit of post-secondary opportunities, before making a decision about which statewide assessment the student should take. The least dangerous assumption is that the student should have the opportunity to receive instruction that prepares them to take the general assessment based on grade-level content and achievement standards.

The IEP team also should make the least dangerous assumption when making placement decisions. The least restrictive requirement in IDEA was designed to ensure that every child is educated with non-disabled peers to the greatest extent possible. Even if a student with ESN works on a prioritized set of content standards and works toward alternate achievement standards, the foundation for the content of the instruction and assessment for that student should remain grade aligned or grade-level content standards. With this foundation, students with ESN should receive services in inclusive classrooms to the maximum extent possible. IEP teams must be aware of the options for service and should not equate an alternate assessment with a separate placement (Agran et al., 2020; Sabia & Thurlow, 2019). Regardless of the setting, IEP teams must have appropriate, adequate, and reliable data regarding a student's performance for decision making purposes.

Assessment and Data Collection in Inclusive Classrooms

Assessment of students with ESN in inclusive classrooms requires thoughtful consideration of the purpose of the assessment and the intended use of the data. Regardless of whether the assessment is one with a formative purpose to inform instruction in the next minute during a lesson, in the next lesson, or in the next unit; or one with a summative purpose to provide evidence of student performance at a point in time; determination of the use of that data—the purpose of the assessment—should be the starting point. What will teachers, students, schools, families, states do with the results? How will the data be used for determinations within IEPs?

Teachers can use formative and summative assessment results to plan and evaluate instruction. Results from alternate assessments may be useful if the results are reported at a level that can inform instruction (e.g., groups of content standards or individual content standards). Formative approaches described earlier in this chapter provide information more closely tied to instruction and more immediately actionable. Formative and some summative assessments can be used to generate grades and report cards.

Assessments vary for the methodology of how data is collected. Datasheets are a common tool used to collect multiple responses of students with ESN. Kurth et al. (2020), for example, proposed a data collection tool for prioritized content for use within an inclusion classroom designed to capture multiple student responses on IEP goals. Data collection of academic content tied to lesson objectives in an inclusive classroom, however, will likely be in a different format and at a different rate than what is possible in more segregated settings. While the collection of student performance on lesson objectives is recommended at a daily rate (the same as the general education peers), one assessment measure may not provide enough data to determine a pattern of student progress. Data collection on a priority objective may require regular adaptions to the daily objective measure to include items related to the student's priority. For example, while children in an inclusive classroom all work on partitioning shapes into parts with equal areas, students with ESN may also be working on labeling the equal areas numerically (the student's priority content).

Formative Assessment Examples with Students with ESN

There are a number of formative assessment strategies that can be utilized with students with ESN. Wakeman, Hudson et al. (2011) discussed several types, including 5-minute strategies, rubrics, and response cards. An example of a 5-minute strategy would be to have the students write/select/state the learning objective or main concept of a lesson. Students could select the objective or concept written in words, picture symbols, photographs, or objects (e.g., "What do you think this symbol means [÷]?" or "What do you think was the most significant outcome of the American Revolution?"). Teachers could also have students provide a demonstration. The assessment could be completed at the end of a step in a lesson, at the very end of a lesson or as the warm-up before the next lesson.

Response cards are another simple approach to gathering information about student understanding and progress. There is a research base about the use of response cards with students with and with disabilities (Schnorr et al., 2016). This concept can easily be adapted for students with ESN and used in an inclusive classroom. For example, students can be provided two pictures on popsicle sticks—one of the Earth rotating or spinning on its axis and another of the Earth revolving around the sun in its orbit. Students can be asked a series of questions to distinguish between the revolving and rotating of the Earth and what happens as a result of both. Students can easily indicate an answer by raising or eye gazing at a popsicle stick, thus allowing all students to participate. Additionally, the teacher can quickly scan the room and see the students' responses in a matter of seconds. This information provides the teachers with information to make instructional decisions immediately within the same lesson or in future lessons.

A rubric is a guideline that both clearly defines the expectations for learning (i.e., formative assessment) and the system for evaluation and grading (i.e., summative assessment; Wakeman, Hudson et al., 2011). There are several benefits of using rubrics for students with disabilities (Jackson & Larkin, 2002). It allows teachers to communicate student performance expectations clearly. The rubric allows students the opportunity to monitor their own progress toward the learning objective or outcome. Additionally, the rubric can be used by the student as a final checklist to ensure they have met the requirements before turning in work. Of particular importance is the fact that rubrics can be designed to fit individual student needs. Wakeman, Hudson et al. include an example of how to adapt a developed rubric for use with students with ESN.

Other formative techniques that are well-established for other students with disabilities, such as CBM, could be useful as well. For students with ESN in inclusive classrooms, CBMs need to expand beyond the mastery models often used with this population. A mastery model may not lend itself to the instructional methods or academic expectations typically utilized in a general education classroom. While mastery measures provide the most diagnostic information, they do not inform a broader picture for long-term instruction. For example, a mastery measure on addition facts does not give the teacher a year-long method to monitor progress towards the achievement of first grade mathematics. If instruction and assessment target isolated content, it is possible that students develop splinter skills which may cause breaks in the expected progression for learning. Educators should design and use multiple sources of evidence, including other types of CBM, other formative approaches, and the alternate assessment when possible, to guide instructional decisions.

Using Assessment Data

Teachers, both general and special educators, need to learn more than how to collect and summarize data. Changes in student performance require making modifications in instruction based on data patterns (Burney & Shores, 1979). While teachers routinely collect data in classrooms, it is meaningless unless there is the explicit use of that data to inform instructional efforts. Fahsl and McAndrews (2012) describe a diagnostic teaching cycle in which the teacher establishes learning outcomes, plans assessment, plans instruction, implements instruction, and analyzes individual student learning. Planning formative measures prior to instruction helps facilitate specific feedback within instruction and allows for the systematic analysis of student performance data and learning.

One important step in evaluating and using data to support inclusive instruction is a collaboration between general and special educators. In most elementary settings, teachers meet in professional learning communities (PLC) to regularly review assessment data to inform instruction. These PLCs are designed to allow teachers to reflect upon student performance data as well as their own instructional practices and subsequently plan as a collective. By creating ways to promote a reflective cycle for planning, teachers together can produce lesson plans and valid student progress measures resulting in greater accessibility and growth for students. Historically, it has been difficult for special educators to join PLCs with their general education peers (Blanton & Perez, 2011), which may be due to large and diverse caseloads across grade levels and the lack of common planning time. Designing opportunities for special educators to regularly participate in a PLC with general educators throughout the year is essential.

Another opportunity for general and special educators to collaborate and meet the needs of students with ESN in general education classrooms is including these students in schoolwide tiered support models: RTI for instruction and MTSS for behavioral needs. Many states have adopted or plan to adopt this framework in schools. However, students with ESN have typically been excluded from tiered support models (Thurlow et al., 2020). While they may be excluded because they are already identified as needing intensive, individualized instruction (i.e., tier III supports), excluding them from schoolwide tiered supports means they may not fully access or have the opportunity to make progress in the general curriculum. While evidence-based strategies have been identified for students with extensive support needs in inclusive classrooms (e.g., Saunders et al., 2020), their use within an MTSS system has been untested. But, as Rowe (2020) suggests, when there are gaps in the research literature, it is possible to adapt those processes that have been proven effective in other contexts or with other populations before published research catches up to provide evidence of the effectiveness of those strategies for students with ESN. As such, Thurlow et al. suggested how students with ESN could be included in an MTSS system at all three tiers.

Standards-Based Grading

Teachers must consider how to grade equitably in inclusive classrooms, which is no small task. Teachers have to make decisions about what is formally graded, including what is factored into that grade and what that grade is intended to communicate to students and families. The William & Mary Training & Technical Assistance Center (2015) outlined four quality considerations for grading within the inclusive classroom. These included (a) grades are accurate, (b) grades are meaningful, (c) grades are consistent, and (d) grades are supportive of learning. The authors went further to compare eight methods of grading through a lens of the four conditions and made recommendations for grading practices for students with disabilities—rubrics and categorical grading, mastery grading, and standards-based grading. Jung and Guskey (2010) also recommended standards-based grading as the grading practice for students with disabilities in inclusive classes. Standards-based grading is more commonly found as a practice in elementary schools than in secondary environments. As such, it is necessary to consider how students with ESN in all grades can participate equitably in such a grading system.

While not specific to students with ESN, Jung and Guskey (2007) described the need to separate three types of learning criteria (product—a summative assessment measuring accuracy; process—effort, behavior and work habits; and progress-growth from the beginning) prior to utilizing a five-step inclusive grading model which fits in a standards-based grading system and is fair for students with disabilities. Standards-based grading untangles the layers within a grade and allows the meaning of the grade to be clearly communicated. Work habits and behaviors (e.g., turning work in on time) is not convoluted with performance on a task or progress made since the last assessment.

One benefit for the use of standards-based grading in inclusive classrooms is the ability to create common language and priorities for students with ESN that addresses the grade-level standards as well as the individual needs of students. Report cards can identify those areas in which the student is and is not making progress by content standard rather than by broad content domains. Clarity about learning targets, instruction and grading are provided by the specificity and separation of learning criteria, which reduces barriers for students with ESN to participate fully in inclusive classrooms and shares ownership of all students with the general education teachers.

Using Universal Design for Learning to Design Formative and Summative Assessments

One area that educators can continue to apply in both assessment and instruction is the use of the principles of UDL. UDL is a framework that all educators can use to promote flexibility and access as they plan instruction and assessments (Meyer et al., 2014). Rao et al. (2017) described the application of the guidelines within UDL within the methods, materials, and assessments for lessons to promote accessibility for all students. Kurth et al. (2015) outlined best practices for supporting students with severe disabilities in general education classrooms, including the use of adaptations to support individual students. Finnerty et al. (2019) found that greater access for students with severe disabilities can be created when (a) class materials were made tangible to meet the strengths and needs of the individual students, (b) materials were blended with the classroom materials that the general education students used, (c) assessments were adapted to allow all students to show what they know, and (d) assessment the patterns of learning for all learning when the assessments were immersed in the activities versus in isolation. As Finnerty et al.'s work indicates, evidence of the use of UDL in the planning for instruction and assessment for the entire class creates a more inclusive educational experience for all students.

While UDL should be applied in teacher-designed assessments, it is also a necessary consideration during the design of summative assessments such as the alternate assessment. For example, within assessment design, it is necessary to ensure there aren't construct-irrelevant features interfering with presentation and response options while allowing for some flexibility. For example, some students require response options in pictorial form to make a valid response. If these options are not available to students and the assessment item requires students to read written text, the item assesses the child's ability to read, which may not be the construct being assessed.

There are several ways that technology can facilitate greater access for students with ESN during assessments and subsequently yield more valid student performance data. Determining ways to improve access can be complex (Stone & Cook, 2018). Simply providing a new digital tool does not ensure students will have greater access. What might work for one student may have a detrimental impact on another student. Considerations must be given to the individual student's communication, access skills, and assessment needs. Important considerations include (a) how the student takes in information, (b) what mode (or multiple modes) provide the student with the greatest opportunity to receive information (e.g., auditory, visual, tactile), and (c) how the student best demonstrates what they know and can do. A tool for helping educators determine their students' communication and assessment needs is the Learner Characteristics Inventory (LCI: Kearns et al., 2006). Information from LCI could help educators select appropriate AT by evaluating the student's expressive communication, receptive language, vision, hearing, motor, and engagement level.

UDL includes providing flexibility in the ways students are given information, their response or demonstration of knowledge and skills, and their engagement in the environment (CAST, 2011). Examples of different presentation modes include large print, AT, use of manipulatives, braille, and text-to-speech. Examples of response mechanisms could include dictation, typing rather than writing, eye-gaze technology, and speech-to-text applications. Examples of multiple means of engagement include topics of personal interest, token economy, and self-monitoring systems. Using information about a student's accessibility needs, digital delivery of instruction and assessments are able to customize the content presented to students and select the method of student's engagement with the materials, which makes the learning environment optimal for each student. With the introduction of technology-enhanced items, students can now use their tablets, which allows them to interact with the test in a more tactile sense (Stone & Cook, 2018).

One way that computer testing creates flexibility based upon student needs within testing administration is the incorporation of testing accommodations. Computer testing allows accommodations to be embedded in the platform, which may include an array of accessibility tools and testing supports. For example, text-to-speech tools allow students to listen to all or a portion of the content without depending on an adult reader. It is important to ensure that these accommodations are used not only in testing but consistently in day-to-day instruction.

Final Thoughts

Much has changed in the past 20 years about academic expectations, instruction, assessment, and inclusive opportunities for students with ESN. Unfortunately, there is still much improvement to be made. Since the onset of the expectations for student assessment of academic performance, which included students with ESN and the subsequent development of alternate assessments, much has been learned about the expectations for this population and the documentation of their ability to regularly demonstrate learning once not thought possible. Policy related to assessment forever changed the landscape of education for students with ESN. We can expect even more positive changes for students in this population in the next 20 years as a movement toward equity becomes engrained as a societal value.

Until there is a stronger research base demonstrating evidence of the benefit of inclusion regardless of the severity of a child's disability, we must continue to proceed following the least dangerous assumption. We can continue to borrow strategies tested elsewhere that result in student learning and adapt them for use with students with ESN that include effective assessment methods. Research for all students is built upon a foundation of valid data sources. These data collection methods must continue to grow and adapt to reflect the accurate performance of students with ESN in inclusive classrooms.

Note

1 When not referring to the legislative definition, we refer to the population of students who take alternate assessments as "students with extensive support needs" throughout this chapter.

References

Agran, M., Jackson, L., Kurth, J., Ryndak, D., Burnette, K., Jameson, M., Zagona, A., Fitzpatrick, H., & Wehmeyer, M. (2020). Why aren't students with severe disabilities being placed in general education classrooms: Examining the relations among classroom placement, learner outcomes, and other factors. *Research and Practice for Persons with Severe Disabilities, 45*(1), 4–13. doi:10.1177/1540796919878134

Altman, J. R., Lazarus, S. S., Quenemoen, R. F., Kearns, J., Quenemoen, M., & Thurlow, M. L. (2010). *2009 survey of states: Accomplishments and new issues at the end of a decade of change.* University of Minnesota, National Center on Educational Outcomes. https://nceo.umn.edu/docs/OnlinePubs/2009StateSurvey.pdf

Austin, C. R., & Filderman, M. J. (2020). Selecting and designing measurements to track the reading progress of students with disabilities. *Intervention in School and Clinic, 56*(1), 13–21. doi:10.1177/1053451220910736

Beatty, I. D. (2013). Standards-based grading in introductory university physics. *Journal of the Scholarship of Teaching and Learning, 13*(2), 1–22. https://scholarworks.iu.edu/journals/index.php/josotl/article/view/3264

Bechard, S., Clark, A., Swinburne Romine, R., Karvonen, M., Kingston, N., & Erickson, K. (2019). Use of evidence-centered design to develop learning maps-based assessments. *International Journal of Testing, 19*(2), 188–205. doi:10.1080/15305058.2018.1543310

Bennett, R. E. (2011). Formative assessment: A critical review. *Assessment in Education: Principles, Policy & Practice, 18*(1), 5–25. doi:10.1080/0969594X.2010.513678

Black, P., & Wiliam, D. (1998). Inside the black box: Raising standards through classroom assessment. *Phi Delta Kappan, 80*, 139–148. doi:10.1177/003172171009200119

Blanton, L. P., & Perez, Y. (2011). Exploring the relationship between special education teachers and professional learning communities: Implications of research for administrators. *Journal of Special Education Leadership, 24*(1), 6–16.

Browder, D. M., Spooner, F., & Jimenez, B. (2011). Standards-based IEPs and progress monitoring. In D. M. Browder & F. Spooner (Eds.), *Teaching students with moderate and severe disabilities* (pp. 42–91). Guilford Press.

Browder, D. M., Wakeman, S. Y., Flowers, C., Rickelman, R., Pugalee, D., & Karvonen, M. (2007). Creating access to the general curriculum with links to grade level content for students with significant cognitive disabilities: An explication of the concept. *The Journal of Special Education, 41*(1), 2–16. doi:10.1177/00224669070410010101

Burnes, J. J., & Clark, A. K. (2020). *Characteristics of students who take Dynamic Learning Maps® alternate assessments* (Technical Report No. 20-01). University of Kansas, Accessible Teaching, Learning, and Assessment Systems. https://dynamiclearningmaps.org/sites/default/files/documents/publication/Characteristics_of_Students_Who_Take_DLM_AAs.pdf

Burney, J. D., & Shores, R. E. (1979). A study of relationships between instructional planning and pupil behavior. *Journal of Special Education Technology, 2*(3), 16-25. doi.org/10.1177/016264347900200303.

CAST (Center for Applied Special Technology). (2011). *Universal design for learning guidelines version 2.0.* Author.

Council of Chief State School Officers. (2018). *Revising the definition of formative assessment.* https://ccsso.org/sites/default/files/2018-06/Revising%20the%20Definition%20of%20Formative%20Assessment.pdf

Cook, A. M., Polgar, J. M., & Encarnacao, P. (2020). *Assistive technologies: Principles and practice*(5th ed.). Mosby.

Crawford, L. (2014). The role of assessment in a response to intervention model. *Preventing School Failure: Alternative Education for Children and Youth, 58*(4), 230–236. doi:10.1080/1045988X.2013.805711

Deno, S. L. (2003). Developments in curriculum-based measurement. *The Journal of Special Education, 37*(3), 184–192. doi:10.1177/00224669030370030801

Deno S. (2016) Data-based decision-making. In S. Jimerson S., M. Burns, & A. VanDerHeyden (Eds.), *Handbook of Response to Intervention* (pp. 9–28). Springer. doi:10.1007/978-1-4899-7568-3_2

Donnellan, A. M. (1984). The criterion of the least dangerous assumption. *Behavioral Disorders, 9*(2), 141-150. doi.org/10.1177/019874298400900201.

Every Student Succeeds Act, 20 U.S.C. § 6301. (2015). https://www.congress.gov/114/plaws/publ95/PLAW-114publ95.pdf

Fahsl, A. J., & McAndrews, S. L. (2012). Journal writing: Support for students with learning disabilities. *Intervention in School and Clinic, 47*(4), 234–244. doi:10.1177/1053451211424602

Filderman, M. J., Toste, J. R., Didion, L. A., Peng, P., & Clemens, N. H. (2018). Data-based decision making in reading interventions: A synthesis and meta-analysis of the effects for struggling readers. *The Journal of Special Education, 52*(3), 174–187. doi:10.1177/0022466918790001

Finnerty, M., Jackson, L., & Ostergren, R. (2019). Adaptations in general education classrooms for students with severe disabilities: Access, progress assessment, and sustained use. *Research and Practice for Persons with Severe Disabilities, 44*(2), 87–102. doi:10.1177/1540796919846424

Fisher, D., & Frey, N. (2015). Show & tell: A video column/don't just gather data—Use it. *Educational Leadership, 73*(3), 80–81. http://www.ascd.org/publications/educational-leadership/nov15/vol73/num03/Don't-Just-Gather-Data%E2%80%94Use-It.aspx

Flowers, C., Wakeman, S., Browder, D. M., & Karvonen, M. (2009). Links for academic learning (LAL): A conceptual model for investigating alignment of alternate assessments based on alternate achievement standards. *Educational Measurement: Issues and Practice, 28*(1), 25–37. doi:10.1111/j.1745-3992.2009.01134.x

Hager, K. D., & Slocum, T. A. (2011). Using alternate assessment to improve educational outcomes. *Rural Special Education Quarterly, 30*(1), 24–29. doi:10.1177/875687051103000105

Heritage, M. (2010). *Formative assessment: Making it happen in the classroom*. Corwin.

Heritage, M. (2011). Formative assessment: An enabler of learning. *Better: Evidence-based Education, 3*(3), 18–19. http://www.betterevidence.org/us-edition/issue-7/formative-assessment-an-enabler-of-learning/

Herman, J. L. (2010). *Coherence: Key to next generation assessment success* (AACC Report) (ED524221). University of California; ERIC. https://files.eric.ed.gov/fulltext/ED524221.pdf

Hess, K., Burdge, M., & Clayton, J. (2011).Challenges to developing and implementing alternate assessments based upon alternate achievement standards (AA-AAS). InM. Russell & M. Kavanaugh (Eds.), *Assessing students in the margins: challenges, strategies and techniques* (pp. 171–214). Information Age.

Hosp, M. K., Hosp, J. L., & Howell, K. W. (2016). *The ABCs of CBM: A practical guide to curriculum-based measurement* (2nd ed.). Guilford Press.

Hudson, M. E., Browder, D. M., & Wood, L. A. (2013). Review of experimental research on academic learning by students with moderate and severe intellectual disability in general education. *Research and Practice for Persons with Severe Disabilities, 38*(1), 17–29. doi:10.2511/027494813807046926

Hudson, M. E., Rivera, C. J., & Grady, M. M. (2018). Research on mathematics instruction with students with significant cognitive disabilities: Has anything changed? *Research and Practice for Persons with Severe Disabilities, 43*(1), 38–53. doi:10.1177/1540796918756601

Hunt, P., McDonnell, J., & Crockett, M. A.(2012). Reconciling an ecological curricular framework focusing on quality of life outcomes with the development and instruction of standards-based academic goals. *Research and Practice for Persons with Severe Disabilities*, 37(3), 139–152.. https://doi.org/10.2511/027494812804153471.

Individuals with Disabilities Education Act of 1990, 20 U.S.C. § 1400 *et seq.* (1990). (amended 1997). https://www2.ed.gov/policy/speced/leg/idea/idea.pdf

IRIS Center (2020). *Progress monitoring: Mastery measurement versus general-outcome measurement*. https://iris.peabody.vanderbilt.edu/wp-content/uploads/modules/pmr/pdf/IRIS_PM_InfoBrief_011420.pdf#content

Jackson, C. W., & Larkin, M. J. (2002). Teaching students to use grading rubrics. *Teaching Exceptional Children, 35*(1), 40–45. doi:10.1177/004005990203500106

Jameson, J. M., Walker, R., Utley, K., & Maughan, R. (2012). A comparison of embedded total task instruction in teaching behavior chains to massed one-to-one instruction for students with intellectual disabilities: Accessing general education settings and core academic content. *Behavior Modification, 36*(3), 320–340. doi:10.1177/0145445512440574

Jimenez, B., Mims, P., & Browder, D. (2012). Data-based decisions guidelines for teachers of students with severe intellectual and developmental disabilities. *Education and Training in Autism and Developmental Disabilities*, 47(4), 407–413. Retrieved June 18, 2021, from http://www.jstor.org/stable/23879634

Jimenez, B. A., & Kamei, A. (2015). Embedded instruction: An evaluation of evidence to inform inclusive practice. *Inclusion*, 3, 132–144. doi:10.1352/2326-6988-3.3.132.

Jung, L. A. (2009). The challenges of grading and reporting in special education: An inclusive grading model. In T. R. Guskey (Ed.), *Practical solutions to serious problems in standards-based grading* (pp. 27–40). Corwin.

Jung, L. A., & Guskey, T. R. (2007). Standards-based grading and reporting: A model for special education. *TEACHING Exceptional Children, 40*(2), 48–53. doi:10.1177/004005990704000206

Jung, L. A., & Guskey, T. R. (2010). Grading exceptional learners. *Educational Leadership, 67*, 31–35.

Karvonen, M., Flowers, C., & Wakeman, S. (2013, April 27–May 1). *An exploration of methods for measuring academic growth for students with significant cognitive disabilities* [Paper presentation]. American Educational Research Association Annual Meeting.

Karvonen, M., Wakeman, S., & Kingston, N. (2017). Alternate assessment. In M. L. Wehmeyer & K. A. Shogren (Eds.), *Handbook of research-based practices for educating students with intellectual disability* (pp. 102–118). Routledge.

Kearns, J., Kleinert, H., Harrison, B., Sheppard Jones, K., Hall, M., & Jones, M. (2010). *What does 'college and career ready' mean for students with significant cognitive disabilities?* National Alternate Assessment Center. http://www.naacpartners.org/publications/CareerCollegeReadiness.pdf

Kearns, J., Kleinert, H., Kleinert, J., & Towles-Reeves, E. (2006). *Learner characteristics inventory*. University of Kentucky, National Alternate Assessment Center.

Kearns, J., Thurlow, M., Wakeman, S., & Reyes, E. N. (2020, November). Academic standards for students with significant cognitive disabilities in inclusive classrooms: Same content standards, alternate achievement standards (TIPS Series: Tip #14). University of Minnesota, TIES Center.

Kettler, R. J., Elliott, S. N., Beddow, P. A., & Kurz, A. (2018). Accessible instruction and testing today. In S. N. Elliott, R. J. Kettler, P. A. Beddow, & A. Kurz (Eds.), *Handbook of accessible instruction and testing practices: issues, innovations, and applications* (2nd ed., pp. 1–16). Springer International Publishing.

Kingston, N., & Nash, B. (2011). Formative assessment: A meta-analysis and a call for research. *Educational Measurement: Issues and Practice, 30*(4), 28–37. doi:10.1111/j.1745-3992.2011.00220

Kurth, J., Lyon, K., & Shogren, K. (2015). Supporting students with severe disabilities in inclusive schools: A descriptive account from schools implementing inclusive practices. *Research and Practice for Persons with Severe Disabilities, 40*(4), 261–274. doi:10.1177/1540796915594160

Kurth, J. A., Miller, A. L., & Toews, S. G. (2020). Preparing for and implementing effective inclusive education with participation plans. *Teaching Exceptional Children*. doi:10.1177/0040059920927433

Lee, A., Browder, D. M., Flowers, C., & Wakeman, S. (2016). Teacher evaluation of resources designed for adapting mathematics for students with significant cognitive disabilities. *Research and Practice for Persons with Severe Disabilities, 41*(2), 132–137. doi:10.1177/1540796916634099

Leko, M. M., Brownell, M. T., Sindelar, P. T., & Kiely, M. T. (2015). Envisioning the future of special education personnel preparation in a standards-based era. *Exceptional Children, 82*(1), 25–43. doi:10.1177/0014402915598782

Marion, S. F., & Pellegrino, J. W. (2006). A validity framework for evaluating the technical quality of alternate assessments. *Educational Measurement: Issues and Practice, 25*(4), 47–57. doi:10.1111/j.1745-3992.2006.00078.x

Meyer, A., Rose, D. H., & Gordon, D. (2014). *Universal design for learning: Theory and practice*. Center for Applied Special Technology.

Monem, R., Bennett, K. D., & Barbetta, P. M. (2018). The effects of low-tech and high-tech active student responding strategies during history instruction for students with SLD. *Learning Disabilities: A Contemporary Journal, 16*(1), 87–106.

Multi-State Alternate Assessment. (2019). *Multi-state alternate assessment: 2019 guide for score report interpretation*. https://cms.azed.gov/home/GetDocumentFile?id=5baa4f811dcb2503b8980679

No Child Left Behind Act of 2001, Public Law 107-110, 107th Cong. Codified as U.S. Code 20. (2002) (reauthorized 2006).

Office of Educational Technology. (2015). *Ed tech developer's guide: A primer for software developers, startups, and entrepreneurs*. U.S. Department of Education. https://tech.ed.gov/files/2015/04/Developer-Toolkit.pdf

Office of Educational Technology. (2016). *Future ready learning: Reimagining the role of technology in education*. U.S. Department of Education. https://tech.ed.gov/files/2015/12/NETP16.pdf

Office of Special Education and Rehabilitative Services. (2005). *Twenty-sixth annual report to Congress on the implementation of the Individuals with Disabilities Education Act, 2004, Vol. 1*. U.S. Department of Education. https://www2.ed.gov/about/reports/annual/osep/2004/26th-vol-1.pdf

Popham, W. J. (2006). *Classroom assessment: What teachers need to know* (3rd ed.). Allyn and Bacon.

Quenemoen, R. (2008). *A brief history of alternate assessments based on alternate achievement standards* (Synthesis Report 68). University of Minnesota, National Center on Educational Outcomes. https://nceo.umn.edu/docs/OnlinePubs/Synthesis68/Synthesis68.pdf

Quenemoen, R., Thurlow, M., Moen, R., Thompson, S., & Morse, A. B. (2004). *Progress monitoring in an inclusive standards-based assessment and accountability system* (Synthesis Report 53). University of Minnesota, National Center on Educational Outcomes. https://nceo.umn.edu/docs/OnlinePubs/Synth53report.pdf

Rao, K., Smith, S., & Lowrey, K. (2017). UDL and intellectual disability: What do we know and where do we go? *Intellectual and Developmental Disabilities, 55*(1), 37–47. doi:10.1352/1934-9556-55.1.37

Reyes, E. N., Wakeman, S., & Thurlow, M. (2020). *Grading for students with significant cognitive disabilities in inclusive classrooms (TIPS Series: Tip 11)*. University of Minnesota, TIES Center. https://publications.ici.umn.edu/ties/foundations-of-inclusion-tips/grading-for-students-with-significant-cognitive-disabilities-in-inclusive-classrooms

Rose, D. H., Robinson, K. H., Hall, T. E., Coyne, P., Jackson, R. M., Stahl, W. M., & Wilcauskas, S. L. (2018). Accurate and informative for all: Universal design for learning (UDL) and the future of assessment. In S. N. Elliott, R. J. Kettler, P. A. Beddow, & A. Kurz (Eds.), *Handbook of accessible instruction and testing practices: Issues, innovations, and applications* (2nd ed., pp. 167–180). Springer International Publishing.

Rowe, D. A. (2020). Succeeding in the classroom when research is limited. *Teaching Exceptional Children, 52*(3), 124–125. doi:10.1177/0040059919895134

Russell, M. (2018). Recent advances in the accessibility of digitally delivered educational assessments. In S. N. Elliott, R. J. Kettler, P. A. Beddow, & A. Kurz (Eds.), *Handbook of accessible instruction and testing practices: issues, innovations, and applications* (2nd ed., pp. 247–262). Springer International Publishing.

Sabia, R., & Thurlow, M. L. (2019, May). Taking the alternate assessment does NOT mean education in a separate setting! (Brief #2). University of Minnesota, TIES Center. https://files.tiescenter.org/files/Mdg9JhH6n-/ties-brief-2.pdf

Sailor, W. S., & McCart, A. B. (2014). Stars in alignment. *Research and Practice for Persons with Severe Disabilities*, 39(1), 55–64. https://doi.org/10.1177/1540796914534622.

Samuels, C. (2018, April 18). Ed. Dept. policing ESSA rules on portfolio assessments for students with disabilities. *Education Week*. http://blogs.edweek.org/edweek/speced/2018/04/essa_places_restrictions_on_portfolio_tests.html

Saunders, A., Wakeman, S. Y., & Reyes, E. (2020). *An updated review of experimental research on academic interventions for students with significant cognitive disabilities in inclusive settings* [Manuscript in preparation]. The TIES Center, University of North Carolina at Charlotte.

Schnorr, C., Freeman-Green, S., & Test, D. (2016). Response cards as a strategy for increasing opportunities to respond: An examination of the evidence. *Remedial and Special Education*, *37*(1), 41–54. doi:10.1177/0741932515575614

Schulz, T., Cividini-Motta, C., Blair, K.-S. C., & MacNaul, H. (2020). A comparison of high-tech and low-tech response modalities to improve student classroom behavior. *Journal of Behavioral Education*. doi:10.1007/s10864-020-09393-3

Spooner, F., Knight, V., Browder, D. M., Jimenez, B., & DiBiase, W. (2011). Evaluating evidence-based practice in teaching science content to students with severe developmental disabilities. *Research and Practice for Persons with Severe Disabilities*, *36*(1-2), 62–75. doi:10.2511/rpsd.36.1-2.62

Spooner, F., Knight, V. F., Browder, D. M., & Smith, B. R. (2012). Evidence-based practice for teaching academics to students with severe developmental disabilities. *Remedial and Special Education*, *33*(6), 374–387. doi:10.1177/0741932511421634

Spooner, F., Root, J. R., Saunders, A. F., & Browder, D. M. (2019). An updated evidence-based practice review on teaching mathematics to students with moderate and severe developmental disabilities. *Remedial and Special Education*, *40*(3), 150–165. doi:10.1177/0741932517751055

Stone, E. A., & Cook, L. L. (2018). Fair testing and the role of accessibility. In S. N. Elliott, R. J. Kettler, P. A. Beddow, & A. Kurz (Eds.), *Handbook of accessible instruction and testing practices: issues, innovations, and applications* (2nd ed., pp. 59–73). Springer International Publishing.

Taub, D., Apgar, J., Foster, M., Ryndak, D. L., Burdge, M. D., & Letson, S. (2020). Investigating the alignment between English language arts curricula developed for students with significant intellectual disability and the CCSS. *Remedial and Special Education*, *41*(5), 284–295. doi:10.1177/0741932519843184

Taub, D., Wakeman, S., Saunders, A., Thurlow, M. L., & Lazarus, S. S. (2019). *Using the least dangerous assumption in educational decisions (TIPS Series: Tip #6)*. University of Minnesota, TIES Center. https://publications.ici.umn.edu/ties/foundations-of-inclusion-tips/using-the-least-dangerous-assumption-in-educational-decisions

Thompson, S. J., Johnstone, C. J., Thurlow, M. L., & Altman, J. R. (2005). *2005 state special education outcomes: Steps forward in a decade of change*. University of Minnesota, National Center on Educational Outcomes. https://nceo.umn.edu/docs/OnlinePubs/2005StateReport.pdf

Thurlow, M. L., Ghere, G., Lazarus, S. S., & Liu, K. K. (2020, January). MTSS for all: Including students with the most significant cognitive disabilities. University of Minnesota, National Center on Educational Outcomes/TIES Center. https://nceo.umn.edu/docs/OnlinePubs/NCEOBriefMTSS.pdf

Thurlow, M. L., Lazarus, S. S., Albus, D. A., Larson, E. D., & Liu, K. K. (2019). 2018-19 participation guidelines and definitions for alternate assessments based on alternate academic achievement standards (NCEO Report 415). University of Minnesota, National Center on Educational Outcomes. https://nceo.umn.edu/docs/OnlinePubs/NCEOReport415.pdf

Thurlow, M., Quenemoen, R., Thompson, S., & Lehr, C. (2001). *Principles and characteristics of inclusive assessment and accountability systems (Synthesis Report 40)*. University of Minnesota, National Center on Educational Outcomes. http://hdl.handle.net/11299/173953

Wakeman, S. Y., Browder, D. M., & Flowers, C. (2011). Alternate achievement standards for alternate assessments: Considerations for policy and practice. In M. Russell & M. Kavanaugh (Eds.), *Assessing students in the margins: Challenges, strategies, and techniques*. Information Age.

Wakeman, S. Y., Hudson, M., & Ahlgrim-Delzell, L. (2011, April 25–28). *How to conduct formative assessments with students with severe intellectual disabilities [Paper presentation]*. Council for Exceptional Children Convention and Expo, National Harbor.

Welsh, M. E., D'Agostino, J. V., & Kaniskan, B. (2013). Grading as a reform effort: Do standards-based grades converge with test scores? *Educational Measurement: Issues and Practice*, *32*(2), 26–36. doi:10.1111/emip.12009

William & Mary Training & Technical Assistance Center. (2015). *Inclusive grading and progress-monitoring practices.* Retrieved from https://education.wm.edu/centers/ttac/documents/packets/inclusivegrading.pdf

Wood, L., Browder, D. M., & Flynn, L. (2015). Teaching students with intellectual disability to use a self-questioning strategy to comprehend social studies text for an inclusive setting. *Research and Practice for Persons with Severe Disabilities*, *40*(4), 275–293. doi:10.1177/1540796915592155

16

Supporting Inclusion Through Peer Support

Elizabeth E. Biggs and Elizabeth Burnett Rossi

VANDERBILT UNIVERSITY

Setting the Stage

Inclusive elementary schools give students with disabilities the opportunity to experience the plentiful benefits of social interactions and relationships with peers, including reciprocal friendships. Meaningful interactions and relationships with peers have crucial roles in promoting development and well-being for all students, including students with disabilities (Bukowski & Sippola, 2005; Rubin et al., 2009). But what exactly is meant by the term peer interaction? Rubin et al. (2015) define it as being dyadic and reciprocal in nature, focusing on the fact that in social interaction, "participants' actions are interdependent such that each actor's behavior is both a response to, and stimulus for, the other's behavior" (p. 331). Learning to navigate these social exchanges is a crucial part of what children learn in school, such that social interactions and relationships with peers should be thought of as an integral part of the informal curriculum (Thompson et al., 2017) and part of the very 'stuff of school' itself.

A tremendous amount of study of peer interaction and relationships over decades of research has all led to an important conclusion: when it comes to thinking about what is important for children to learn both in and outside of school, learning to relate well with peers is one of the most important undertakings (Rubin et al., 2015; Shonkoff & Phillips, 2000). For children with and without disabilities, peer interactions support development across a number of different areas, including language and communication, cognitive skills, social skills, and emotional regulation (Rubin et al.). Other positive outcomes include increased personal adjustment, self-esteem, and overall well-being (Berndt, 2002; Bukowski & Sippola, 2005). Social interactions with peers, particularly around shared interests and experiences, also provide fertile soil for the development of friendships, which are best thought of as relationships that are reciprocal in nature, marked by commitment and stability across time, and that serve functions such as mutual companionship, emotional support, and affection (Parker et al., 2006; Rossetti & Keenan, 2018; Webster & Carter, 2007). High-quality friendships are associated with higher achievement and positive attitudes about school, and they have been shown to provide a protective effect against peer rejection and being victimized by peers (Osterman, 2000; Parker et al., 2006). Research has also documented that reciprocal friendships play an important role in promoting belonging, happiness, and well-being for children with and without disabilities (Holder & Coleman, 2009; Williams & Downing, 1998).

DOI: 10.4324/9781003043874-16

This chapter focuses on the ways in which peer support can have a powerful role in improving social, academic, and developmental outcomes for students with severe disabilities, including students with limited verbal speech who use different forms of augmentative and alternative communication (AAC), such as gestures, vocalizations or sounds, signs, picture symbols, or speech-generating devices to communicate. We will first set the stage for thinking about peer support by discussing *supports* and *belonging* as being critical dimensions of inclusion, outlining the varied social experiences of students with severe disabilities in schools today, and discussing the negative impact of over-reliance on adult support. Then, we will review existing research on peer support to highlight the power of peers in promoting what it means for students to be truly included in their schools and classrooms. Finally, we will provide practical guidance for how future research and practice can be improved to support effective inclusive education through peer support.

Supports and Belonging as Critical Dimensions of Inclusion

Over the last several decades, educational policy and practice changes have increased inclusive placements for students with disabilities, but the picture for students with severe disabilities and more intensive support needs is more complicated. McLeskey et al. (2012) analyzed national placement data between the years 1990 and 2008 and found that educational placements in elementary schools changed substantially during this 18-year period, with more students with disabilities placed in increasingly less restrictive settings. Specifically, elementary-level placement rates in general education settings for 80% or more of the school day rose approximately 60% between the 1990–1991 and the 2007–2008 school year, while placement in pull-out classrooms decreased by 41%, and placement in self-contained classes or separate schools decreased by approximately 27%. Williamson et al. (2020) extended this analysis and found the same general trend, noting, though, that changes in general education placement have slowed considerably since 2007. Even when taking into account this slowing, these general trends demonstrate an expansion of placement in general education settings for students with disabilities. However, this expansion has not included all students with disabilities. For example, both McLeskey et al. and Williamson et al. found that the proportion of students with intellectual disability who were placed in segregated settings such as special schools and classrooms remained high, even with the increases in the proportion of students served in general education settings. Despite the growing body of research indicating that students with severe disabilities can access the general education curriculum and learn both academic and functional skills in general education settings when given appropriate support, students with severe disabilities continue to be disproportionately placed in restrictive and segregated settings (Morningstar et al., 2017).

Thus far, the focus of this section has been about placement and access to general settings. But, *placement* in general education settings is clearly not the same as *inclusion* in these settings. What, then, does it mean for students with severe disabilities to be included? Defining inclusion is a difficult task and one that researchers and school leaders have attempted to clarify numerous times over the years (Palmer & Williams-Diehm, 2020; Ryndak et al., 2000). What remains clear even as policies and practices have evolved is that inclusion cannot simply mean the location of services. Further, this means that students with severe disabilities cannot simply leave their separate special education classrooms to "go to inclusion," as some well-meaning educators might say. Conceptualizations of inclusion that focus on placement alone will always fall short of reaching desired outcomes. Instead, inclusion means that all students—including students with severe disabilities—have access to and make progress in the general education curriculum alongside and with their peers, are valued members of their classroom and school, and receive appropriate supports at both universal (e.g., school, classroom) and individual levels to make these goals possible (Rodriguez et al., 2020; Ryndak et al. 2020; Wehmeyer & Shogren, 2017).

This notion of effective systems of support is important to a conceptualization of inclusion. Within the intellectual disability field, increasing use of strengths- and support-based approaches have led to a growing emphasis on the critical role of *supports* for students with severe disabilities in schools today (Thompson et al., 2009). Based on social-ecological models of disability, support- and strengths-based approaches emphasize the need to understand the demands of students' environments and identify and utilize supports that will maximize growth, participation, and flourishing in these different environments, rather than focusing on areas of deficit (Wehmeyer & Shogren, 2017). This way of thinking about students with disabilities recognizes that "all people have support needs" (Shogren et al., 2017, p. 185) while also recognizing that students with severe disabilities will have more intensive support needs related to learning and participating in general education settings than their peers without disabilities. The emphasis of supports can also be seen in the introduction of tiered intervention models, or Multitiered Systems of Supports (MTSS), and school reform that systematically applies integrated and increasingly individualized methods for supporting the learning and well-being of students as needed (Sailor et al., 2018; Shogren et al. 2017). Thinking about supports as being crucial to effective inclusive education also highlights how peers can play a central role in supporting students' participation and learning. Peer supports can be utilized in ways to help ensure that students with severe disabilities access the general education curriculum and are truly included in their classrooms and schools.

Another important aspect of a strong conceptualization of inclusion is the notion of belonging. Ryndak and her colleagues (2000) analyzed statements from experts who had published about inclusive education for students with severe disabilities, proposing a five-part definition of inclusion that focused on: (a) placement in general education classrooms, (b) shared instruction and learning opportunities, (c) effective supports, (d) belongingness, and (e) effective collaboration and integrated services by educational teams. Ryndak explained belonging as students with severe disabilities being accepted and "being valued, contributing, and equal members of the class and school they would naturally attend" (p. 110). Belongingness, though, is not a need just for students with disabilities, but rather a fundamental psychological need for all people (Mahar et al., 2013; Osterman, 2000). This means that students with and without disabilities need schools and classrooms where true communities are built and sustained—in which students feel committed to one another, cared for and supported, that they each matter to one another and the school and classroom as a whole, and in which they build meaningful personal relationships with one another (Osterman).

Further, children with disabilities themselves have talked about the importance of the notion of belongingness. Foley et al. (2012) conducted focus groups with 20 children with disabilities, including cerebral palsy, autism, Down syndrome, intellectual disability, and visual impairment. When asked about what makes a good life, these children talked about making friends, spending time with friends during shared activities, being a part of the life of the school, and having personally meaningful things to do. The findings from these focus groups highlighted the importance that children themselves place on social relationships and fully participating in different activities and settings, described by one child in the study as being the things that helped her "to feel belonged" (Foley et al., p. 380).

The Social Lives of Students with Severe Disabilities

Although social interactions and relationships with peers are clearly important, the social experiences of elementary-aged students with severe disabilities can vary quite widely within and across schools. Existing research demonstrates that some children with severe disabilities do experience rich social lives at school, including through close, meaningful friendships (Rossetti & Keenan, 2018). For example, Anderson et al. (2011) conducted semi-structured interviews with peers without disabilities about their friendships with children who had cerebral palsy and used speech-generating devices to communicate. Although these peers did describe differences in the friendship relative to other relationships (e.g., physical access barriers for their friend, navigating being a friend and providing care), they also described these relationships as being close and offering rewarding companionship. Similarly, Biggs and Snodgrass (2020) interviewed elementary-aged children who were friends with students with severe disabilities who were learning to use aided AAC. The interviews focused on understanding how children experienced different friendships, both with a friend with a disability and another friend without a disability. Children discussed their friendships as being positive and rewarding, regardless of the disability status of the friend they were talking about. Findings also indicated that the nature of how these children talked about the depth of their friendship ranged fairly widely from relationships that were primarily characterized by affinity (e.g., positive perceptions of the friend, having fun, shared interests and characteristics) to relationships that were marked by deeper intimacy (e.g., understanding, trust, commitment). However, this variation seemed to be evident within and across children regardless of the disability status of their friend.

Together, this research highlights that there is potential for all children, including children with severe disabilities, to form close, meaningful, and reciprocal friendships with peers. However, many relationships between children with and without disabilities in schools may fall short of this, looking more like *helping* relationships than reciprocal friendships (Rossetti & Keenan, 2018). For example, peers without disabilities may wrestle with the tension between being a friend and taking on caring roles, such as helping during transitions or classroom activities (Anderson et al., 2011). Offering support and care is a natural and important part of healthy social relationships for children and adults alike. However, relationships built solely on unilateral support from a peer are not the same as friendships because "friendships include more than help" (Rosetti & Keenan, p. 205). Whether peer relationships have the potential to develop into reciprocal friendships may depend on peers' attitudes about disability, including the ways that experience, talk about, and make meaning of disability (Anderson et al. 2011; Biggs & Snodgrass, 2020). For example, reciprocal friendships rather than 'helping' relationships may require that peers see their classmate with a disability as an individual with unique strengths, interests, and personality, rather than primarily seeing their areas of difference or need (Biggs & Snodgrass).

Given this, an important question to ask is: If there is this potential for strong, reciprocal relationships between students with and without disabilities, are relationships among children with and without disabilities regularly occurring? Despite this potential, the experiences of many students with significant support needs are far less positive, and even social interactions between peers with and without disabilities have been found to be infrequent or even altogether absent in schools today. For example, Chung and Carter (2013) observed elementary and middle school students with disabilities who used various forms of AAC and found that although these students were present in general education classrooms and in proximity to peers, they almost never interacted with peers, and instead interacted almost exclusively with adults such as a paraprofessional. Similarly, Andzik et al. (2016) observed 23 students for over 117 hours of observation, finding that communication occurred primarily with adults and that students had few opportunities to communicate with peers without disabilities. Other research focusing on recess has shown that although this is a time that is ripe for socialization centered around play, students with disabilities such as autism spectrum disorder spend more time alone and less time jointly engaged than their peers (Locke et al., 2016). Finally, children with significant disabilities have been found to have less quality, reciprocal friendships and be on the periphery of social networks in their classroom as compared to peers without disabilities (Kasari et al., 2011; Raghavendra et al., 2012), a challenge that appears to become increasingly complex and prevalent as children move into the later elementary grades (Rotheram-Fuller et al., 2010).

What is clear from this overview of the literature is that although positive interactions and reciprocal relationships between students with and without disabilities may be possible, they are unlikely to occur without careful planning and support. Therefore, as educators work to support develop strong, inclusive schools and classrooms, it is important to understand how peer support might be a pathway for promoting children's skill development and functioning in different school environments, as well as to support children's social flourishing and belonging.

Over-Reliance on Individually Assigned Paraprofessional Support

Educational teams often assign paraprofessionals to support students with severe disabilities, believing that high levels of adult support will promote positive outcomes. In reality, though, over-reliance on adult support brings a number of unintended negative effects, impeding both social and academic outcomes (Giangreco et al., 2005). When paraprofessionals are used as the sole or primary support, this can result in students with disabilities being isolated from peers, interacting less frequently with general educators, and developing a dependence on the paraprofessional (Carter et al., 2007; Giangreco et al., 2005). Concern about heavy reliance on paraprofessionals as individually assigned supports has been increasingly raised for some time (Giangreco et al., 2005, 2012), and yet this practice continues to persist in schools without any convincing empirical support. Although adults do have critical roles in supporting students with disabilities in inclusive classrooms and other settings, many other strategies are more effective supports than relying primarily on individually assigned paraprofessionals. These other strategies might include technology supports, using paraprofessionals to provide support to all students with and without disabilities in a classroom (rather than assigning as individual support), curricular adaptations, and—the focus of this chapter—peer supports. The over-reliance on paraprofessional support is a call for educators to identify ways to utilize adult support more effectively to support desired outcomes for students in inclusive settings.

The Power of Peer Support

Thus far, we have highlighted the importance of *supports* and *belonging* to defining and enacting inclusive education, described the varied social experiences of students with severe disabilities in elementary schools, and highlighted the unintended negative consequences of over-reliance on adult support. Therefore, it is crucial that education teams look beyond simply where students with severe disabilities will spend their day to determine the supports needed for students to access and make progress in the general curriculum at school and to belong to their school and classroom communities. Positive interactions and relationships with peers are central to effective inclusive education, and there is a strong and growing body of evidence on the effectiveness of peer support interventions to promote the aspects of what it means to be truly included in classrooms and schools.

What Do We Know Based on Research?

Intervention Models involving Peers

The field has had a longstanding history of involving peers without disabilities in interventions to improve social and academic outcomes for students with disabilities. Early research in our field highlighting the unique and powerful place of peers in the lives of children with disabilities dates back to nearly 50 years ago (see Odom & Strain, 1984 for an early review). There is now abounding evidence on the utilization and effectiveness of peer-mediated or peer support interventions for children with disabilities, including children with autism, intellectual disability, and other developmental disabilities (Chang & Locke, 2016; Watkins et al., 2015). Although early applications tended to be within the context of self-contained classrooms or non-instructional settings, an increasing focus has been on how peer support can be utilized within general education classrooms and other general education settings (e.g., playgrounds, lunchrooms) to promote both social inclusion and greater access to general education curriculum (Biggs & Carter, 2017). Peer support may be aimed toward a number of different outcomes, such as increasing social interactions and engagement, fostering integration into different school environments, or promoting the development of new skills (e.g., communication, social, academic).

Additionally, ongoing research has led to greater sophistication with how peer support interventions are designed, implemented, and evaluated, including the development of a number of different intervention models. All of these different types of peer support interventions have a shared aim of using intentional, supported opportunities for students with and without disabilities to work together to improve outcomes for children with disabilities, as well as outcomes for peers without disabilities. This intentionality means that peer support interventions are different than simply ensuring students with and without disabilities have indirect contact with one another by being in the same classrooms, passing in the hallway, or eating in the same lunchroom. Instead, peer support interventions involve formal and sustained experiences in which an adult supports peers without disabilities to provide social, academic, communication, or other types of supports to a classmate with a disability (Chan et al., 2009).

Though all peer support interventions share these features in common, intervention models also vary in numerous ways, such as the ways peers and students are grouped together, the roles peers assume, the training peers receive, the location of the intervention, and the roles of adults. For example, peer support arrangements involve equipping and supporting one or more peers to provide ongoing social, communication, and/or academic support to a student with a disability who is in the same general education class as the peers (Biggs et al., 2017; Brock & Huber, 2017). Peer network interventions, on the other hand, involve establishing a cohesive social group with a student with a disability and a small group of peers (generally 2–6), focusing on facilitating opportunities for students to play and interact through shared activities in non-academic contexts (Biggs et al., 2018; Kamps et al., 2015). Given that peer support can take so many forms, it is helpful for educators to have a way to understand the similarities and differences of all of these interventions. In this chapter, we will review research focused on three broad categories of interventions that involve elementary-aged peers without disabilities: (a) class-wide approaches, (b) peer network interventions and recess-based interventions, and (c) peer-mediated instruction and peer support arrangements in classroom settings.

Peer-mediated instruction, peer support arrangements, and peer network interventions all involve matching peers without disabilities with children with disabilities, either to form dyads or groups. However, as evident by their name, class-wide approaches actually involve the majority or entirety of students in a class. Though some types of class-wide approaches may not strictly be a form of peer-mediated intervention, they form an important foundation for positive interactions among children with and without disabilities. Class-wide approaches can help foster positive attitudes about people with disabilities, emphasize strengths-based approaches for thinking about disability, and ensure regular classroom instruction involves supported opportunities for students with and without disabilities to learn from and with one another.

Several different researchers have talked about the importance of classroom-wide approaches as the foundation to a multi-tiered approach to promoting positive interactions and friendships among children with and without disabilities (Brown et al., 2001; Meyer & Ostrosky, 2016). A multi-tiered approach means that educators first employ class-wide interventions before moving on to increasingly more intensive and individualized interventions. More intensive interventions (e.g., peer-mediated instruction, social skills instruction) may be more complex, demand more resources or time, or be less natural for students with disabilities and their peers, and these can build on class-wide approaches that are aimed toward promoting acceptance of classmates with disabilities and arranging opportunities for all children in an inclusive classroom to interact, get to know one another, and learn from one another. This framework can be quite helpful for educators in making decisions among the many different peer support interventions that are research-based. Further, a multi-tiered approach highlights the benefits—both in terms of effectiveness and acceptability or feasibility—of employing a combination of class-wide and more individualized approaches to peer support when students have more intensive support needs.

Class-wide Approaches

Class-wide approaches themselves also can take many different forms. The list of studies in Table 16.1 highlights a number of different classroom-wide intervention approaches, including affective-focused interventions, class-wide peer tutoring, cooperative learning groups, and strategy-focused classroom interventions. Table 16.1 is not intended to be a comprehensive list of all class-wide peer support interventions, but it is intended to illustrate the breadth of research-based interventions, and the similarities and differences in both peer and adult roles across studies. Affective-focused interventions are designed to nurture positive attitudes about disability and classmates who have d disabilities, creating a classroom culture of inclusion, acceptance, and belonging (Brown et al., 2001; Favazza & Odom, 1997). Class-wide peer tutoring and cooperative learning groups—including class-wide peer buddies and structured play groups—focus on arranging the instructional design so that students in the inclusive classroom have supported opportunities to learn from and with one another (Hunt et al., 1994; Piercy et al., 2002). Finally, class-wide approaches can also involve teaching all students in the classroom specific types of supports or strategies to use when interacting with a classmate with a disability (e.g., Cosbey & Johnston, 2006).

Research findings across several decades suggest that class-wide affective interventions can increase peer acceptance of people with disabilities but are by themselves not likely to lead to close friendships among children with and without disabilities (Favazza & Odom, 1997; Meyer & Ostrosky, 2016). For example, Meyer and Ostrosky investigated whether a class-wide disability awareness curriculum would lead to increased friendships for Kindergarten-aged children with disabilities who were enrolled in inclusive classrooms. The primary intervention, called *Special Friends,* involved educators leading class-wide read-aloud discussions using children's books about disabilities, facilitating mixed-ability cooperative learning or play groups, and sending home a copy of the book with a reading guide to promote positive conversations about disability at home. The intervention was compared to a *Science* program that was structured to mirror the components of the *Special Friends* intervention (i.e., class-wide read-aloud discussions about science, mixed-ability cooperative learning groups about science, supporting science discussions and book reading at home). The *Special Friends* intervention resulted in an increase in peer acceptance that—though statistically not significant—may have signaled the intervention had a protective factor against worsening peer attitudes toward their classmates with disabilities (Dorsey et al., 2016). However, contrary to the expectations of the researchers, participating in the class-wide affective intervention did not increase the number of close or 'best' friendships for students with disabilities, but close friendships did increase for students participating in the *Science* intervention (Meyer & Ostrosky, 2016).

What might explain these findings? The researchers suggested that the nature of the difference between the cooperative learning and play groups in the two conditions is important to consider. In the *Science* intervention, the cooperative learning groups were structured with clearly defined goals and activities, while the groups in the *Special Friends* intervention participated in open-ended play themes (e.g., restaurant-themed play). Without adult facilitation as a part of these groups, the researchers suggested that the children with disabilities in the *Special Friends* program may not have had play skills to support engagement in extended open play-based interactions. Similarly, peers were not taught to know how to support and scaffold play-based interactions with their classmates with disabilities. These findings suggest that mixed-ability cooperative learning groups may be a powerful

Table 16.1 Example Studies of Class-Wide Interventions Involving Peers

Article	Intervention	Participants	Peer roles	Roles of adults	Outcomes
Cosbey and Johnston (2006)	Strategy-focused classroom intervention	3 students with multiple disabilities and their peers *(3–6 years)*	Respond to their classmate's use of a single-switch AAC device which was programmed with the phrases "That looks fun. Can I play?"	Set up AAC access, identify preferred activities and toys, train and coach peers to respond to communication attempts, create opportunities for social interaction, prompt AAC use	Increased requests to access play and for students with disabilities and responses from peers
Dugan et al. (1995)	Cooperative learning groups with peer tutoring	2 students with autism and their peers *(9–10 years)*	Participate in cooperative learning groups that involved reciprocal peer tutoring and a cooperative activity	Establish the cooperative learning groups, teach new material prior to the group, teach about group social skills, monitor and provide feedback to the groups, provide reinforcement to groups	Increased scores on weekly quizzes, academic engagement, and peer interaction for students with autism and peers
Favazza and Odom (1997)	Affective-focused intervention with play groups	15 students with intellectual disability or multiple disabilities and their peers *(5–6 years)*	Participate in discussions about books, structured play groups	Lead read-aloud and discussions with books about children with disabilities, set up structured play groups, send home a copy of the book each week with a reading guide for parents	Increased peer acceptance
Hunt et al. (1994)	Cooperative learning groups	3 students with multiple disabilities *(7–9 years)*	Participate in cooperative learning groups, provide communication supports to the classmate with a disability	Establish the cooperative learning groups, teach peers about how the student with a disability communicates and how to provide communication supports, provide support to cooperative groups	Increased performance on quizzes for peers without disabilities, acquisition of a targeted communication behavior for the students with disabilities
Jacques et al. (1998)	Cooperative learning groups	24 students with intellectual disability and their peers *(9–11 years)*	Participate in cooperative learning groups	Establish cooperative learning groups, adapt social studies texts, provide support to cooperative groups	Increased peer acceptance
Kamps et al. (1994)	Class-wide peer tutoring	3 students with autism and their peers *(8–9 years)*	Participate in a reciprocal tutoring arrangement to provide and receive feedback on oral reading and ask and answer questions about the passage	Arrange tutoring pairs, teach students about the tutoring arrangement, monitor students in the tutoring groups, provide reinforcement to dyads	Increased oral reading fluency rates and performance on reading comprehension questions for students with autism and peers; Increased peer interaction

(*Continued*)

Table 16.1 (Continued)

Article	Intervention	Participants	Peer roles	Roles of adults	Outcomes
					during free time in the classroom for the students with autism
Kamps et al. (1995)	Cooperative learning groups with peer tutoring	3 students with autism and their peers *(8–13 years)*	Participate in cooperative learning groups that involve reciprocal peer tutoring and a team learning activity	Establish the cooperative learning groups, provide instruction on social skills for cooperative groups, monitor and provide feedback to the group, provide reinforcement to groups	Increased scores on weekly quizzes, academic engagement, and peer interaction for the students with autism and peers
Laushey and Heflin (2000)	Class-wide peer buddies	2 students with autism and their peers *(5 years)*	Participate in "buddy time" as a part of free play center time, which involved staying with, playing with, and talking with the buddy	Establish the buddy system, lead a brief discussion to teach the buddy system and discuss that all people being alike and different in many ways, rotate buddies each day, provide reinforcement to dyads	Increased social skills performance for the two students with autism
Meyer and Ostrosky (2016)	Affective-focused intervention and cooperative learning groups	26 students with disabilities and their peers *(5–6 years)*	Participate in discussions about read-aloud and in cooperative learning groups with classmates	Lead read-aloud and discussions with books about disabilities, facilitate mixed-ability cooperative learning groups, send home a copy of the book with a reading guide for parents	Participating in the class-wide affective intervention did not increase the number of best friendships for students with disabilities; but the intervention with mixed-ability science cooperative learning groups did
Mortweet et al. (1999)	Class-wide peer tutoring	4 children with intellectual disability and their peers *(8–10 years)*	Participate in a reciprocal tutoring arrangement to practice spelling words while providing and receiving positive and corrective feedback	Arrange tutoring pairs, teach students about the tutoring arrangement, monitor students, provide reinforcement to dyads	Increased performance on spelling tests and academic engagement for students with and without disabilities
Piercy et al. (2002)	Cooperative learning groups	6 children with intellectual disability and their peers *(6–7 years)*	Participate in cooperative learning groups	Establish the cooperative learning groups, teach children to work cooperatively, provide social praise to reinforce collective effort and products	Increased peer acceptance and social interaction with peers for the students with disabilities

Note. AAC, augmentative or alternative communication.

way to promote peer acceptance, interaction, and even friendship, but that students may need adults to take a role in clearly defining goals and ensuring equal-status roles for students with and without disabilities in order to benefit socially from these groups.

Other research has focused more specifically on understanding the effects of these types of mixed-ability cooperative learning groups (e.g., 3–7 students with varying skills, including a student with a more severe disability). Strategies within cooperative learning groups may include working together to accomplish a specific task or goal, practicing skills, sharing in reinforcement contingencies that apply to the whole group, and engaging in social interactions (Hunt et al., 1994; Piercy et al., 2002). Although different researchers trace the origins of cooperative learning in inclusive classrooms differently (Slavin, 2011), many trace the theoretical foundation to Allport (1954), who argued that when negative or ambivalent attitudes and behaviors might be expected in heterogeneous groups, positive relations depend on group members having equal status, being in pursuit of a common goal, and having tasks and roles structured so that all group members can (a) make a significant contribution to the group and (b) engage socially to get to know the other members of the group as individuals. This foundational understanding provides helpful insight for educators to know how to use cooperative learning groups to support social and learning outcomes for students with and without severe disabilities in inclusive classrooms.

For example, Piercy et al. (2002) conducted cooperative learning sessions with small groups of 3 to 4 students, which each included a student with an intellectual disability. The teacher began instruction by clearly explaining that each group included children with different strengths and that all members had something to offer the group, and then the learning activities were designed so that students needed to work together and so that students with intellectual disability could fully participate in the activity. At the completion of each session, the teacher offered social praise for collective efforts and products. Results indicated that the cooperative learning groups resulted in positive changes across several different measures of social acceptance of the children with intellectual disabilities, including increased social interactions outside the cooperative learning groups.

A related strategy is class-wide tutoring arrangements with reciprocal tutoring, in which both students in a dyad alternate between the roles of being the tutor and the learner (Delquadri et al., 1986). Though class-wide peer tutoring has been more researched for students with disabilities such as reading or math disabilities (e.g., Fuchs et al., 2020), it also has been utilized with students with autism and/or intellectual disability (Kamps et al., 1994, 1995; Mortweet et al., 1999), and variations of the strategy have been used during play-based interactions with young elementary-aged students, such as in the form of class-wide peer "buddies" during centers in the classroom (Laushey & Heflin, 2000). For example, Kamps et al. employed classroom-wide peer tutoring during which all students in inclusive classrooms—including three students with autism—worked together in tutor-learner pairs. Results demonstrated increased oral reading fluency rates and performance on reading comprehension questions for students with and without disabilities in the classroom. Further, social interactions during unstructured free time in the classroom (immediately following the class-wide peer tutoring) also increased for the three students with autism. Components of effective classroom-wide peer tutoring tend to include alternating tutor-learner roles, having the dyads practice academic or other skills and provide specific types of feedback, providing adult monitoring and support, and providing reinforcement for all students (Kamps et al.; Mortweet et al.).

Across all of these different class-wide approaches, the role of educators in facilitating the intervention is important. There is little evidence that proximity or brief training alone will be sufficient for leading to sustained increases in positive social interaction between students with and without disabilities (Biggs & Carter, 2017). Instead, educators will need to continue to play important roles in facilitating classroom-wide interventions after they are arranged. For example, in Cosbey and Johnston (2006), Kindergarten-aged classroom peers were taught to respond to a classmate's single-switch AAC device that was programmed with the phrases, "That looks fun. Can I play?" Adults had many roles in the intervention, including setting-up AAC access for each child based on their individual capabilities, identifying preferred activities and toys, prompting AAC use by the student with a disability (i.e., naturalistic constant time delay), and training and coaching peers to respond to the AAC requests. Results of the study indicated that the classroom-wide intervention increased students' unprompted requests to peers to play. However, an important finding was that classroom peers responded independently to their classmate with a disability in only about half of the opportunities, requiring something like an indirect or direct verbal prompt in the other half. This finding illustrates the importance of sustained adult facilitation, including the need for systematic approaches built to decrease the level of prompting and involvement of adults over time.

Additionally, it is important to note that not all group-based interventions aimed at increasing peer acceptance of classmates with disabilities are effective. Some interventions that are designed to raise disability awareness may be ineffective or even increase disability stigma in the classroom or school. For example, disability simulations (e.g., using wheelchairs to mimic physical disabilities or blindfolds to simulate visual impairment) may present inaccurate representations or information about people with disabilities, sometimes leading to worsened attitudes toward individuals with disabilities (Salinger, 2020). Similarly, education-focused interventions that primarily present information about differences between individuals with and without disabilities may reinforce negative stereotypes and have no impact or even negative impact on peer acceptance, interaction, and friendship (Salinger, 2020). These approaches may be ineffective because they propagate and reinforce deficit-based ways of thinking about disability and people with disabilities. Instead, peer support interventions both at a class-wide and more individualized level should help children without disabilities see the individuality and strengths of their classmates with disabilities and come to understand disability as a natural part of human diversity, defined by the need for supports to flourish in different environments rather than defined by deficits (Shogren et al., 2017).

Peer Network Interventions and Recess-Based Interventions

A number of different peer support interventions are socially focused, designed to improve interaction and relationships for students with severe disabilities and their peers by supporting greater integration into different social environments at schools, such as lunch, recess, or free time in the classroom (see Table 16.2 for a list of example studies). The earliest peer network interventions in schools reported in the literature date back approximately three decades ago (Gaylord-Ross et al., 1984; Haring & Breen, 1992), and since then, this intervention model has been implemented and tested fairly widely in elementary and secondary levels (Asmus et al., 2017; Biggs et al., 2018; Kamps et al., 2015). A peer network involves establishing a small group comprised of the student with a disability and approximately 2–6 peers without disabilities. The group meets together regularly, which provides repeated opportunities for social interaction and the development of social relationships. Peers provide social or other types of supports (e.g., communication support), and an adult such as a paraprofessional or teacher provides ongoing facilitation for the network. Although the primary focus of peer network interventions tends to be on enhancing social opportunities rather than on instruction, some peer network interventions involve embedding instruction on social or communication skills, either through naturalistic (Biggs et al.) or direct, behavioral approaches (Kamps et al., 2015). Another source of variation within peer network interventions is that the focus can be on establishing a cohesive group in which the same peers participate throughout the duration of the intervention (Biggs et al., 2018; McFadden et al., 2014) or on rotating peers across different intervention sessions (Kamps et al., 1997, 2014, 2015). Establishing a cohesive group of peers can provide students more sustained opportunities to build close friendships, while rotating peers can keep group numbers small with the aim of facilitating generalization across peers.

For example, Kamps and colleagues conducted a series of studies to develop and test the effects of a peer network intervention that involved direct instruction on social skills for students with autism

Table 16.2 Example Studies of Peer Network Interventions and Recess-Based Interventions

Article	Participants	Peers	Intervention components	Roles of adults	Outcomes
Biggs et al. (2018)	4 students with intellectual disability and/or autism *(9–10 years)*	3–4 peers with each student with a disability	Met regularly to play or participate in a shared social activity; peers learned strategies to support social interaction (e.g., wait time, modeling use of AAC)	Select peers, plan collaboratively for the networks, orient students to the network, prepare materials, provide support to all students in the network, train and coach peers on social interaction strategies	Increased peer interaction and communication skills for the students with disabilities
Brock et al. (2018)	11 students with autism *(8–12 years)*	3–4 peers with each student with autism	Peers were trained to use strategies based on pivotal response treatment to use at recess (e.g., ask a buddy to play, show and talk about how to play, social praise, take turns)	Select peers, train peers on interaction strategies, provide ongoing support to peers during recess	Increased peer interaction and appropriate play with peers for the students with autism during recess
Harper et al. (2008)	2 students with autism *(8–9 years)*	2 peers with each student with autism	Peers were trained to use strategies based on pivotal response treatment to use at recess (e.g., ask a buddy to play, show and talk about how to play, social praise, take turns)	Select peers, train peers on interaction strategies, provide ongoing support to peers during recess	Increased social initiations and turn-taking of the students with autism during recess
Kamps et al. (1997)	3 students with autism *(6–8 years)*	7–11 peers for each student with autism; rotated 2–5 peers at a time in each session	Met regularly across settings to interact socially and learn and practice social skills	Select peers, establish each peer network, provide instruction on social skills, monitor the group and provide feedback and support, provide reinforcement	Increased interaction time with peers across settings for the student with autism
Kamps et al. (2014)	4 students with autism *(6–7 years)*	4–6 peers for each student with autism; rotated 2 peers at a time in each session	Met regularly to play games with direct social skills instruction embedded within the group; peers provided prompting on social skills	Select peers, provide direct social skills instruction, monitor the group and provide feedback and support, provide reinforcement	Increased peer interaction for the students with autism
Kamps et al. (2015)	95 students with autism *(5–7 years)*	4–6 peers for each student with autism; rotated 2 peers at a time in each session	Met regularly to play games with direct social skills instruction embedded within the group; peers provided	Select peers, provide direct social skills instruction, monitor the group and provide feedback and support, provide reinforcement	Increased initiations to peers, language skills, and adaptive communication skills for the students with autism

(*Continued*)

Table 16.2 (Continued)

Article	Participants	Peers	Intervention components	Roles of adults	Outcomes
			prompting on the social skills		
Kasari et al. (2012)	60 students with autism *(6–11 years)*	3 peers from each classroom of each student with autism	Peers were taught how to support interactions with any children with social challenges on the playground, including by identifying children who were alone, asking them to play, and providing social support	Select peers, provide peer training and support	Increased social network salience, number of friendship nominations, teacher-reported social skills, and decreased isolation on the playground for students with autism
Mason et al. (2014)	3 students with autism *(6–8 years)*	4–6 peers for each student with autism; rotated 2 peers at a time in each session	Met regularly during recess to interact socially and learn and practice social skill	Select peers, provide direct social skills instruction, monitor the group and provide feedback and support, provide reinforcement	Increased peer interaction for the three students with autism
McFadden et al. (2014)	4 students with autism *(5–8 years)*	4–5 peers for each student with autism	Role-played social skills with the student with autism; met regularly during recess where peers would model social skills and initiate play with the student with autism	Select peers, provide class-wide social skills instruction, lead pre-recess huddle, monitor play, prompt peers to initiate during recess play, check-in with peers and the student about the use of social skills, provide reinforcement	Increased peer interaction for the students with autism
Owen-DeSchryver et al. (2008)	3 students with autism *(7–10 years)*	3–4 peers for each student with autism	Peers were encouraged to interact and become friends with the student with autism and taught strategies to support interaction	Select peers, provide peer training	Increased peer initiations with the students with autism by trained and untrained peers

Note. AAC = augmentative or alternative communication

(Kamps et al., 1997, 2014, 2015; Mason et al., 2014; McFadden et al., 2014). In a randomized control trial, educators provided the intervention to 56 kindergarten and first-grade children, comparing the effects with 39 children who did not participate in the intervention. During each peer network meeting, a small group comprised of the student and two peers met to participate in direct social skills instruction and then practice these skills by playing games. Results of the study indicated that students in the peer networks showed more growth in social initiations to peers during play-based sessions with trained peers and with untrained peers, compared to the control group students who did not participate in a peer network intervention. Teacher reports of language skills and pragmatic communication skills were also greater for students who participated in the peer network intervention.

The vast majority of the literature on peer network interventions has focused on students with autism and students who use verbal speech to communicate. However, researchers more recently have begun to investigate the effects of peer network interventions for a broader, more diverse group of students with disabilities, including students with complex communication needs (Biggs et al., 2018; Herbert et al., 2020). Biggs et al. investigated the effects of a peer network intervention for four elementary-aged students with intellectual disability or autism who had limited verbal speech and communicated primarily through prelinguistic modes (e.g., gestures, vocalizations or sound) but were learning to use different forms of aided AAC. Teams consisting of each student's special education teacher, paraprofessional, speech-language pathologist, parents, and general education teacher collaboratively planned for the intervention by discussing intervention goals, selecting peers (3–4), using student interests to plan activities for the network, and identifying target vocabulary. During the intervention, all peer network members met regularly during lunch or free time in the classroom to engage in a shared activity related to students' interests (e.g., animal crafts, making jewelry, space station set). A paraprofessional supported the network, and peers learned simple social interaction strategies, which included initiating interaction, using wait time, and modeling the use of aided AAC during natural interactions (i.e., the peer would not prompt the student to use the aided AAC device but would use it as part of their own communication, such as by point to *MY TURN* in a communication book or speech-generating device while saying "It's my turn now.") Results indicated that the peer network increased peer interaction for the students with disabilities and that students began using symbolic communication more in their interactions with peers when peers also used the aided AAC device as a shared means of communication.

Closely related to peer network interventions are recess-focused interventions that involve peer support (Brock et al., 2018; Harper et al., 2008; Kasari et al., 2012; Mason et al., 2014). For example, Brock et al. and Harper et al. found that peer interaction and play increased for students with autism when 2–4 peers were trained to use social support strategies based on pivotal response treatment (PRT), including asking a buddy to play, modeling and talking about how to play, providing social praise, and taking turns. Kasari et al. developed an intervention that—instead of specifically identifying the student with ASD as being the recipient of peer support—taught 3 peers from each classroom about how to support positive interactions with children who were alone or unengaged on the playground. This included teaching peers to identify children who were alone, ask them to play, and provide social support, such as by modeling or facilitating engagement in games and play. In a group design study with 60 children with autism spectrum disorder (ASD) and their classroom peers, the researchers found that the peer support intervention decreased isolation on the playground and improved students' social network salience (i.e., the prominence or centrality of a child within a classroom social network), friendship nominations, and teacher-report of social skills in the classroom. The study design compared the peer support intervention with a child-focused intervention that involved direct instruction on social skills through didactic instruction and practice with an adult. Although the child-focused intervention also improved social network salience, the changes were smaller and more temporary than for the peer support intervention. Taken together, this research emphasizes the powerful role that peers can have in improving social outcomes for students with severe disabilities.

Peer-Mediated Instruction and Peer Support in Classroom Settings

Another broad category of peer support interventions involves peer-mediated instruction or peer support in classroom settings. These interventions typically involve researchers or educational practitioners (e.g., teachers, paraprofessionals), selecting peers to provide support, arranging the classroom environment to facilitate opportunities for students and peers to work together (e.g., adjusting seating

Table 16.3 Example Studies of Peer-Mediated Instruction and Peer Support in Classroom Settings

Article	Participants	Peers	Peer Roles	Roles of adults	Outcomes
Chung and Douglas (2015)	3 students with autism *(10–12 years)*	2 peers for each student with autism	Initiate and respond to social interaction with support from the paraprofessional	Select peers, arrange seating to sit with peer partners, program vocabulary on SGDs, train paraprofessionals to facilitate interaction by prompting initiations	Increased SGD use and reciprocal peer interaction for the students with autism
Hudson et al. (2014)	3 students with intellectual disability *(Upper elementary)*	3 peers who worked in a one-to-one format with the students with disabilities	Read an adapted text and ask questions about the text, provide prompting (least-to-most prompting) when asked for help	Select peers, adapt grade-level science lessons and texts, create response boards, write scripts for peer tutors, train peer tutors	Increased correct responses to comprehension questions about grade-aligned science texts
Hunt et al. (2002)	3 students with severe and multiple disabilities *(Grades K-5)*	Multiple peers for each student	Provide individualized social, communication, and academic supports	Meet collaboratively to develop individualized support plans, implement and review identified supports	Decreased non-engagement and increased reciprocal peer interaction, communicative initiations, and AAC use for the students with disabilities
Hunt et al. (2003)	3 students with severe disabilities and 3 other struggling learners *(4th Grade)*	Multiple peers for each student	Provide individualized social, communication, and academic supports	Meet collaboratively to develop individualized support plans, implement and review identified supports	Decreased non-engagement and increased reciprocal peer interaction and communicative initiations for the students with disabilities and who were struggling learners
McCurdy and Cole (2014)	3 students with autism *(7–11 years)*	1 peer for each student with autism	Provide behavioral supports by reminding about desired behaviors, providing encouragement, providing prompting if off-task, provide praise	Select and train the peer supporter, arrange seating for the student and peer to sit next to each other, monitor the peer supporter	Decreased minor off-task behaviors of the students with autism
Wu et al. (2020)	3 students with autism and/or intellectual disability *(8–9 years)*	3 peers for each student with a disability	Teach science concepts through individual tasks (e.g., model-lead-test, model the SGD, provide reinforcement)	Select peers, write scripts for peer tutors, orient and train peers for their roles, teach peers how to use the SGD, teach science concepts to peers	Increased demonstrated knowledge of science concepts for the students with disabilities

Note. SGD = Speech-generating device

arrangements), and encouraging peers to use different strategies to provide social, academic, communication, or other types of supports to a student with a disability. Table 16.3 provides examples of studies that have focused on peer-mediated instruction or peer support in classroom settings, outlining the various roles of adults in each intervention.

Although peer support arrangements in inclusive classrooms have been more widely investigated at secondary levels (Biggs et al., 2017; Brock & Huber, 2017; Carter et al., 2016), there also are a number of studies that have addressed this type of support at elementary levels. For example, Hunt and colleagues conducted a series of studies focused on the effectiveness of a collaborative teaming process that involved general and special education staff on the academic and social participation of students with disabilities in general education classrooms (Hunt et al., 2002, 2003). Individualized supports and adaptions were selected for each student using a method of planning called a *Unified Plan of Support*. An integral part of the plans included various forms of peer support, such as having students work with peers in small groups or pairs, having peers provide assistance when asked by the student, and teaching peers to provide social and communication support (e.g., initiating interaction, modeling manual signs). Results indicated that the collaborative teaming process supported the consistent implementation of the *Unified Plans of Support* and was effective at increasing students' engagement in classroom activities, social interactions with peers, and academic skills.

Several studies investigating peer support in instructional settings have focused specifically on students with complex communication needs who use various forms of AAC, such as speech-generating devices (Chung & Douglas, 2015; Hunt et al., 2002; Wu et al., 2020). For example, Chung and Douglas evaluated the impact of an intervention package that involved training paraprofessionals to encourage peers to initiate interaction and respond to communication attempts from students who used speech-generating devices during related arts classes (e.g., art, library). The results indicated that the intervention was effective in increasing communication and reciprocal peer interaction within these classroom settings. Wu et al. examined the effects of peer support to promote general education access for students who used speech-generating devices, focusing on peer-mediated instruction on science concepts. The intervention involved peers working in specific roles (i.e., leading instruction through a model-lead-test procedure, modeling science-related vocabulary on the speech-generating device, and providing reinforcement), and was found to be effective in increasing knowledge of grade-aligned science concepts, as measured by performance on multiple-choice science quizzes. However, it is important to note that the intervention was delivered in a separate setting and further research is needed to extend this research to inclusive classroom settings.

Outcomes of Peer Support Interventions

Social-Related Benefits for Students with Disabilities

When used effectively, peer support interventions can help children with disabilities develop social and communicative competence (Biggs et al., 2018; Chung & Douglas, 2015; Kamps et al., 2015; Kasari et al., 2012), can facilitate friendship development among students with and without disabilities, and help students experience a sense of belonging in their classroom and school communities (Biggs & Carter, 2017; Meyer & Ostrosky, 2016). It is important to recognize that these benefits can come from peer support interventions designed to be socially focused, but also those that have an academic focus. For example, cooperative learning groups and classroom-wide peer tutoring have a strong academic focus, but these interventions also can lead to improved social outcomes because they provide structured opportunities for students with and without disabilities to interact with one another, build social and communication skills, and establish a classroom community within meaningful shared learning experiences with one another (Kamps et al., 1994; Mortweet et al., 1999).

Academic-Related Benefits for Students with Disabilities

Collectively, research indicates that peer support interventions not only offer advantages related to fostering social interactions and peer relationships, but that these interventions also promote academic engagementequally well, as if not better than, individually assigned paraprofessional supports (Brock & Huber, 2017; Carter et al., 2007). Further, peer support at class-wide and individual levels can be used to promote the acquisition of academic knowledge and skills, promoting meaningful access to and progress in general education curriculum for students with disabilities (Dugan et al., 1995; Hudson et al., 2014; Hunt et al., 2003; Wu et al., 2020).

Benefits for Peers without Disabilities, Teachers, and Classrooms

The benefits of peer support interventions are not exclusive to students with disabilities. For example, Cushing and Kennedy (1997) demonstrated that peers without disabilities also experienced benefits from participating in peer support interventions in classroom settings, such as increased academic engagement, assignment completion, and classroom participation. Similarly, peers without disabilities have been shown to make more academic progress and be more engaged in their learning when they participate in class-wide cooperative learning groups and reciprocal tutoring arrangements with classmates with disabilities, as compared with adult-led instruction alone (Dugan et al., 1995; Kamps et al., 1994, 1995; Mortweet et al., 1999). For peers, shared learning experiences and challenges with their classmates with disabilities may be particularly powerful in shaping perceptions of being "similar" to their classmates with disabilities. As described by Jackson et al. (2008), feelings of similarity occur not necessarily because peers perceive their sets of abilities as being the same but because they have shared experiences and face shared learning challenges. Thus, benefits for peers participating in well-designed peer support interventions can include increased acceptance of classmates with disabilities and friendships with these classmates (Biggs et al., 2018; Biggs & Snodgrass, 2020; Meyer & Ostrosky, 2016; Piercy et al., 2002).

At times, teachers, administrators, or parents may be concerned that peer support interventions could negatively impact the peers without disabilities, either socially or academically. In contrast to these concerns, there is no evidence that participating in peer support interventions negatively impacts peers. For example, Schaefer et al. (2016) reviewed peer support literature to examine the impact on peers, concluding that educators can pursue implementing these interventions with "confidence that the interventions will not negatively affect peers" (p. 352). Looking more specifically at social impact, other research found that peers who participated in a social skills intervention with children with autism maintained a high, positive social status over the duration and following the intervention (Locke et al., 2015).

Finally, other studies also indicate that peers without disabilities who participate in peer support interventions rate their experiences in the intervention positively, saying they would want to continue serving in these roles and would recommend these types of roles to other students in the future (e.g., Biggs et al., 2018; Brock et al., 2018).

Educators themselves, such as general education teachers and paraprofessionals, also can benefit from implementing peer support interventions. For example, as a follow-up to the *Special Friends* class-wide intervention, Kindergarten teachers participated in an interview about their perceptions and experiences. Teachers reported that they benefited from the intervention because they felt more comfortable and confident discussing disability-related topics, whereas they felt uncomfortable and uncertain about how to do this before (Dorsey et al., 2016). Implementing peer support interventions with support and supervision from licensed special education teachers can also help paraprofessionals better understand their roles and move from being exclusive or primary supports for students with disabilities to more facilitative roles. In several studies, paraprofessionals have shared they enjoy their roles facilitating peer support interventions, found them rewarding, and wanted to continue them or implement them with other students (e.g., Biggs et al., 2017; Chung & Douglas, 2015).

Setting the Course for Effective Inclusion

Important Components of Interventions Involving Peers

The different peer support approaches that have been reviewed are diverse, but each also has a number of different components in common. Identifying these components can help educators understand key considerations in the utilization of peer support interventions to support outcomes in inclusive schools and classrooms. These components include: a strengths-based approach to disability, collaboration among educators and service providers, meaningful and motivating shared activities for students with and without disabilities, communication support for students with disabilities, and high-quality adult support.

Strengths-Based Approach to Disability

Although the history of special education has been shaped primarily by deficit-based views of disability, there are ongoing efforts to shift educational practices so they are driven by strengths-based approaches and a social-ecological model of disability (Shogren et al., 2017). This approach means that educators seek to enhance students' functioning in natural settings by identifying and arranging supports to effectively address any mismatches between students' areas of personal competence and their environmental demands (Shogren et al., 2017). This can include identifying the supports needed to meet environmental demands in general education classrooms and related to accessing the general education curriculum, but also across inherently social settings at schools such as hallways, at recess, in the lunchroom, and before and after school. Peer support interventions are particularly promising to support effective inclusive education when educators see the focus of peer support as being a means of providing natural supports that can maximize students' functioning across these different natural settings at school. Therefore, important components to successful peer support interventions include positive peer and educator attitudes about the capabilities of students with disabilities and a focus on identifying, arranging, and encouraging supports that peers can provide that will promote students' participation, membership, and belonging in natural settings at school.

Collaborative Planning and Implementation Among Educators

Supporting students with disabilities in inclusive settings requires careful planning and support, which necessitates strong collaborative teaming across educational team members, such as special education teachers, general education teachers, and paraprofessionals. For many students, the involvement of other related service providers may also be crucial to the success of peer support interventions, such as involving speech-language pathologists in intervention planning and implementation for students with complex communication needs who are learning to use AAC. Peer support interventions should be planned carefully and collaboratively, not implemented haphazardly. In most cases, planning will need to involve individualizing certain aspects of the intervention, such as identifying specific goals, ensuring access to effective communication response modes through AAC, adjusting peer support strategies to meet specific expectations or activities in the classroom or other environment, and building on student interests and strengths in the design of interventions.

The literature is replete with examples of how to carefully and collaboratively plan for supports in inclusive settings, which can be leveraged to support this important aspect of peer support interventions (Biggs et al., 2017, 2018; Hunt et al., 2002, 2003). For example, Cushing et al. (2005) outlined a general framework for planning that is useful for classroom settings. This planning process involves consideration of (a) grade-level academic standards and learning objectives, (b) the expectations of general education teachers for students in their classrooms, (c) specific Individualized Education Program (IEP) goals that a student is working toward, and (d) the supports that students need to be able to participate in the social and learning opportunities in that classroom. Carter et al. (2011) outlined a planning worksheet that is specifically focused more specifically on identifying peer support strategies across different segments of a class, such as at the start of class, during whole-class instruction, during small group or partner activities, during independent work, and during transitions in the classroom. This planning worksheet has since been further developed and applied multiple times, including for students with complex communication needs (Biggs et al., 2017; Brock et al., 2020; Carter et al., 2016). Functioning similarly to an ecological assessment, the team can use the planning worksheet to focus on each of these segments of the class and: (a) identify what all peers are doing, (b) evaluate how the student with a disability can participate, (c) list specific ways the peers can support the student during each activity, and (d) identify strategies for how adults—such as paraprofessionals—can facilitate the student and peers in working and learning together (Brock et al., 2020; Carter et al., 2011). Kurth et al. (2020) offer another similar planning tool that involves ecological assessments to identify universal and individualized supports for including students in general education classrooms, which can easily be used to identify ways include peer support as a means for improving participation, membership and learning in inclusive settings.

Written plans are important because they can help everyone on a team have common expectations and understandings about the intervention, including paraprofessionals. Paraprofessionals can be a tremendous asset in implementing peer support interventions in both classroom and social settings at school (Biggs & Carter, 2017), and they will likely have valuable input to share when planning for peer support arrangements about strategies that will be effective and feasible. However, it is important to remember that paraprofessionals should not be left to assume the role of making primary instructional decisions for students with disabilities. Beyond this, it is also important to remember that planning should ultimately support a successful implementation, should not be overburdensome, and should be approached in a dynamic way that allows for adjustment based on input from team members, peers, and students with disabilities themselves. For example, in the model of using *Unified Plans of Support,* the collaborative teams reviewed and revised plans over time by using the planning worksheet to guide regular monthly discussion about the extent to which supports were being implemented and their effects (Hunt et al., 2003). Peer supports that are perceived by team members as being ineffective or not practical to implement can then be revised or removed from the plan.

Meaningful and Motivating Shared Activities

One of the core ingredients in peer support interventions is ensuring students with and without disabilities have opportunities to spend meaningful time learning and socializing together. Unfortunately, many students with severe disabilities still spend much or most of their day in segregated settings such as special classes, and one of the most prominent barriers to interaction among students with and without severe disabilities is that these students are not spending time in the same places, doing the same things (Brock et al., 2020; Kurth et al., 2020). However, more than simply shared environments, it is shared learning and social activities that are critical to the success of peer support interventions. Further, the types of activities that form the context for peer support, and the roles that peers are asked to assume, are important to consider. Although some peer support interventions adopt unilateral support roles for peers, reciprocal interactions and relationships among children with and without disabilities are not likely to come from peer support interventions unless these interventions ensure reciprocal, valued roles for all students (Allport, 1954; Biggs & Snodgrass, 2020; Brock et al., 2020). Thus, when planning and implementing peer support interventions, educators should consider whether the activities and roles for peers emphasize predominantly 'helping' relationships or provide a context out of which reciprocal interactions and relationships might be more likely to develop.

Communication Support for Students with Disabilities

A sizeable number of students with severe disabilities have not established a reliable mode of communication (Kearns et al., 2011). Such students may communicate pre-intentionally, use idiosyncratic means of communication that are not readily understood by others, or be still learning to use conventional or symbolic forms of communication, such as having a small number of single words, signs, gestures, or symbols on a speech-generating device that they use for restricted purposes or in restricted types of settings. Thus, successful communication support, such as access to and integration of different forms of aided AAC (e.g., picture symbols, speech-generating devices), is an important part of effective interventions involving peers. When planning for and implementing peer support interventions, educational teams should ask themselves: Do students have a reliable means of communicating with their peers? What communication supports do students need to ensure this is possible? Peers themselves can actually be quite effective at providing communication support when they are shown how to do this well. For example, with training and support, peers can learn to incorporate AAC, such as the use of speech-generating devices in their interactions, which then provides natural models of language when they talk, play, and learn with their classmates with disabilities (Biggs et al., 2018; Wu et al., 2020). Teaching peers to use AAC as a shared means of communication with a classmate with a disability can demonstrate the AAC device is a valuable and encouraged means of communication and help students build connections between spoken words, graphic symbols on the AAC system, and the things or ideas that these symbols represent. (Biggs et al., 2019).

High-Quality Adult Support

Over time, this burgeoning body of literature has made it clear that the roles of adults in peer support interventions are crucial. Simply putting children with and without disabilities in physical proximity without further guidance or support is not very effective. Instead, the roles of educators such as special and general educators, paraprofessionals, and other school staff are crucial to the effectiveness of peer support interventions. Prior research has shown that intrusive adult support can hinder social interactions among students with and without disabilities (Carter et al., 2007; Giangreco et al., 2005), yet it also is clear that the facilitative roles of adults in peer support interventions are crucial, such as selecting and inviting peers, arranging the environment and designing instruction to support students in learning and socializing with one another, orienting peers and students to working together, equipping peers with specific support strategies, and providing ongoing feedback and support (Biggs & Carter, 2017). Thus, it is important that educators find the right balance between providing just enough adult support to ensure the success of the intervention but not too much or too intrusive support that it hinders social interactions and relationships among children with and without disabilities. Biggs and Snodgrass (2020) used interviews with peers without disabilities to learn about their views about developing friendships with other children with and without disabilities, and the findings are helpful for illustrating these points about adult roles in peer support interventions. In the interviews, children talked about how they became friends with classmates with disabilities in ways that clearly signaled important roles of adults (e.g., facilitating opportunities for shared learning and social activities, promoting ways for children to get to know one another, providing communication support for students with disabilities); however, the children themselves had very little to say about the roles of adults in their friendships. This finding reinforces the idea that although educators need to play active roles in peer support intervention, it is important to do so in a way that is minimally intrusive to the interactions themselves between students. Gifford-Smith and Brownell (2003) talked about this as being the "separate social world" (p. 236) of children who are friends. Learning how to find the right balance can be difficult for educators and will require intentional effort, as well as training and support. For example, some teachers have discussed that stepping back and directly intervening less can be one of the more challenging aspects of implementing peer support interventions (Dorsey et al., 2016).

Supporting Implementation of Peer Support Interventions

Peer support interventions offer incredible promise for supporting what it truly means for students with disabilities to be included and belong to their schools and communities. The literature reviewed in this chapter underscores that well-designed peer support interventions can offer numerous benefits to students with disabilities, their peers, their educators, and their broader classroom and school communities. However, these interventions cannot fulfill this promise unless they are consistently implemented well in everyday schools. It has long been recognized that there is a persistent and growing gap between the identification and use of effective interventions in practice (Cook & Odom, 2013) and that a number of different contextual determinants impact the extent to which and quality with which effective interventions are implemented (Domitrovich et al., 2008). Contextual determinants can be thought of as facilitators or barriers to successful implementation—the numerous factors at intersecting levels (e.g., students, educators, schools) that push and pull on how well research-based interventions such as peer support interventions can be implemented.

In the broader literature, research has helped to generate knowledge about these contextual determinants, as well as possible resources and strategies to address the problems and complexities of implementation in real-world schools and classrooms (Cook & Odom, 2013; Locke et al., 2016). Much of this literature has signaled that an important determinant to effective intervention implementation and outcomes is the social validity of an intervention, a term that refers to the extent to which key stakeholders such as educators, peers, and students with disabilities themselves think an intervention is important, has acceptable procedures, and produces valuable outcomes (Wolf, 1978). Researchers have assessed the social validity of peer support interventions using a number of different methods, including interviews, questionnaires, focus groups, rating scales, and even analysis of journal entries of educators implementing the intervention. Generally speaking, this research has affirmed the social validity of peer support interventions. Students with disabilities, peers, and educators have indicated that they enjoy participating in these interventions, find the outcomes beneficial and meaningful, would want to continue participating in the future and would recommend peer support interventions to other students or educators (e.g., Biggs et al., 2018; Brock et al., 2018; Chung & Douglas, 2015; Dorsey et al., 2016; McCurdy & Cole, 2014)

Moving forward, though, there are still many important and unanswered questions about what factors influence the effective implementation of peer support interventions as an effective strategy for inclusive education and the extent to which these different factors might be malleable. There is an important need for research focused on understanding how individual (e.g., teacher), organizational (e.g., school), and macro-level factors (e.g., district) influences the implementation of effective peer support interventions in practice (Domitrovich et al., 2008), as there has been little empirical research focused on this area. Doing this may require that researchers build on work and theories that have been generated in related fields. For example, Locke et al. (2015) expanded prior work about barriers to implementation of mental health interventions in school settings to learn that many of the same determinants impacted the implementation of a recess-focused intervention for students with autism. Factors that acted as barriers included policies that limited recess time, staffing shortages, limited foundational training and knowledge about students with disabilities, competing demands and priorities, the level of respect and support for paraprofessionals, and availability of resources. More intently pursuing answers to these types of questions will be a crucial pathway for future research related to peer support interventions, as will finding strategies and resources to support implementation in real-world schools. Doing this will ensure that the promise of peer support can become a reality in everyday schools, supporting participation, membership, and learning for all students, including students with severe disabilities.

References

Allport, G. (1954). *The nature of prejudice*. Addison-Wesley.

Anderson, K., Balandin, S., & Clendon, S. (2011). "He cares about me and I care about him." Children's experiences of friendship with peers who use AAC. *Augmentative and Alternative Communication*, *27*(2), 77–90. doi:10.3109/07434618.2011.577449

Andzik, N. R., Chung, Y. C., & Kranak, M. P. (2016). Communication opportunities for elementary school students who use augmentative and alternative communication. *Augmentative and Alternative Communication*, *32*(4), 272–281. doi:10.1080/07434618.2016.1241299

Asmus, J. M., Carter, E. W., Moss, C. K., Biggs, E. E., Bolt, D. M., Born, T. L., Bottema-Buetel, Brock, M. E., Cattey, G. N., Cooney, M., Fesperman, E. S., Hockman, J. M., Huber, H. B., Lequia, J., Lyons, G. L., Vincent, L. B., & Weir, K. (2017). Efficacy and social validity of peer network interventions for high school students with severe disabilities. *American Journal on Intellectual and Developmental Disabilities*, *122*(2), 118–137. doi:10.1352/1944-7558-122.2.118

Berndt, T. J. (2002). Friendship quality and social development. *Current directions in psychological science*, *11*(1), 7–10. doi:10.1111/1467-8721.00157

Biggs, E. E., & Carter, E. W. (2017). Supporting the social lives of students with intellectual disability. In M. L. Wehmeyer & K. A. Shogren (Eds.), *Handbook of research-based practices for educating students with intellectual disability* (pp. 235–254). Routledge.

Biggs, E. E., Carter, E. W., & Gilson, C. B. (2019). A scoping review of the involvement of children's communication partners in aided augmentative and alternative communication modeling interventions. *American Journal of Speech-Language Pathology*, *28*(2), 743–758. doi:10.1044/2018_AJSLP-18-0024

Biggs, E. E., Carter, E. W., & Gustafson, J. (2017). Efficacy of peer support arrangements to increase peer interaction and AAC use. *American Journal on Intellectual and Developmental Disabilities*, *122*(1), 25–48. doi:1 0.1352/1944-7558-122.1.25

Biggs, E. E., Carter, E. W., Bumble, J. L., Barnes, K., & Mazur, E. L. (2018). Enhancing peer network interventions for students with complex communication needs. *Exceptional Children*, *85*(1), 66–85. doi:10.11 77/0014402918792899

Biggs, E., & Snodgrass, M. (2020). Children's perspectives on their relationships with friends with and without complex communication needs. *Research and Practice for Persons with Severe Disabilities*, *45*(2), 81–97. doi:1 0.1177/1540796919901271

Brock, M. E., Carter, E. W., & Biggs, E. E. (2020). Supporting peer interactions, relationships, and belonging. In F. Brown, J. McDonnell, & M. E. Snell (Eds.), *Instruction of students with severe disabilities* (9th ed., pp. 384–417). Pearson.

Brock, M. E., Dueker, S. A., & Barczak, M. A. (2018). Brief report: Improving social outcomes for students with autism at recess through peer-mediated pivotal response training. *Journal of Autism and Developmental Disorders*, *48*(6), 2224–2230. doi:10.1007/s10803-017-3435-3

Brock, M. E., & Huber, H. B. (2017). Are peer support arrangements an evidence-based practice? A systematic review. *The Journal of Special Education*, *51*(3), 150–163. doi:10.1177/0022466917708184

Brown, W. H., Odom, S. L., & Conroy, M. A. (2001). An intervention hierarchy for promoting young children's peer interactions in natural environments. *Topics in Early Childhood Special Education*, *21*(3), 162–175. doi:10.1177/027112140102100304

Bukowski, W. M., & Sippola, L. K. (2005). Friendship and development: Putting the most human relationship in its place. In L. A. Jensen & R. W. Larson (Eds.), *New horizons in developmental theory and research: New directions for child and adolescent development* (Vol. 109, pp. 91–98). Jossey-Bass.

Carter, E. W., Asmus, J., Moss, C. K., Biggs, E. E., Bolt, D. M., Born, T. L., Brock, M. E., Gillian, N., Cattey, G. N., Chen, R., Cooney, M., Fesperman, E., Hochman, J. M., Huber, H. B., Lequia, J. L., Lyons, G., Moyseenko, K. E., Riesch, L. M., Shalev, R. A., Vincent, L. B., & Weir, K. (2016). Randomized evaluation of peer support arrangements to support the inclusion of high school students with severe disabilities. *Exceptional Children, 82*(2), 209–233. doi:10.1177/0014402915598780

Carter, E. W., Sisco, L. G., Melekoglu, M., & Kurkowski, C. (2007). Peer supports as an alternative to individually assigned paraprofessionals in inclusive high school classrooms. *Research and Practice for Persons with Severe Disabilities, 32*(4): 213–227.

Carter, E. W., Moss, C. K., Hoffman, A., Chung, Y., & Sisco, L. G. (2011). Efficacy and social validity of peer support arrangements for adolescents with disabilities. *Exceptional Children, 78*(1), 107–125. doi:10.1177/001440291107800107

Chan, J. M., Lang, R., Rispoli, M., O'Reilly, M., Sigafoos, J., & Cole, H. (2009). Use of peer-mediated interventions in the treatment of autism spectrum disorders: A systematic review. *Research in Autism Spectrum Disorders, 3*(4), 876–889. doi:10.1016/j.rasd.2009.04.003

Chang, Y. C., & Locke, J. (2016). A systematic review of peer-mediated interventions for children with autism spectrum disorder. *Research in Autism Spectrum Disorders, 27*, 1–10. doi:10.1016/j.rasd.2016.03.010

Chung, Y. C., & Carter, E. (2013). Promoting peer interactions in inclusive classrooms for students who use speech-generating devices. *Research and Practice for Persons with Severe Disabilities, 38*(2), 94–109. doi:10.2511/027494813807714492

Chung, Y. C., & Douglas, K. H. (2015). A peer interaction package for students with autism spectrum disorders who use speech-generating devices. *Journal of Developmental and Physical Disabilities, 27*(6), 831–849. doi:10.1007/s10882-015-9461-1

Cook, B. G., & Odom, S. L. (2013). Evidence-based practices and implementation science in special education. *Exceptional Children, 79*(3), 135–144. doi:10.1177%2F001440291307900201

Cosbey, J. E., & Johnston, S. (2006). Using a single-switch voice output communication aid to increase social access for children with severe disabilities in inclusive classrooms. *Research and Practice for Persons with Severe Disabilities, 31*(2), 144–156. doi:10.1177/154079690603100207

Cushing, L. S., & Kennedy, C. H. (1997). Academic effects of providing peer support in general education classrooms on students without disabilities. *Journal of Applied Behavior Analysis, 30*(1), 139–151. doi:10.1901/jaba.1997.30-139

Cushing, L. S., Clark, N. M., Carter, E. W., & Kennedy, C. H. (2005). Access to the general education curriculum for students with severe disabilities: What it means and how to accomplish it. *TEACHING Exceptional Children, 38*(2), 6–13. doi:10.1177/004005990503800201

Delquadri, J. Greenwood, C. R., Whorton, D., Carta, J. J., & Hall, R. V. (1986). Classwide peer tutoring. *Exceptional Children, 52*(4), 535–542. doi:10.1177%2F001440298605200606

Domitrovich, C. E., Bradshaw, C. P., Poduska, J. M., Hoagwood, K., Buckley, J. A., Olin, S., Romanelli, L. H., Leaf, P. J., Greenberg, M. T., & Ialongo, N. S. (2008). Maximizing the implementation quality of evidence-based preventative interventions in schools: A conceptual framework. *Advances in School Mental Health Promotion, 1*(3), 6–28. doi:10.1080/1754730X.2008.9715730

Dorsey, E. A., Mouzourou, C., Park, H., Ostrosky, M. M., & Favazza, P. C. (2016). Teacher perceptions of two multi-component interventions: Disability awareness and science. *Topics in Early Childhood Special Education, 36*(2), 103–114. doi:10.1177/0271121415626711

Dugan, E., Kamps, D., Leonard, B., Watkins, N., Rheinberger, A., & Stackhaus, J. (1995). Effects of cooperative learning groups during social studies for students with autism and fourth-grade peers. *Journal of Applied Behavior Analysis, 28*(2), 175–188. doi:10.1901/jaba.1995.28-175

Favazza, P. C., & Odom, S. L. (1997). Promoting positive attitudes of kindergarten-age children toward people with disabilities. *Exceptional Children, 63*(3), 405–418. doi:10.1177/001440299706300308

Foley, K. R., Blackmore, A. M., Girdler, S., O'Donnell, M., Glauert, R., Llewellyn, G., & Leonard, H. (2012). To feel belonged: The voices of children and youth with disabilities on the meaning of wellbeing. *Child Indicators Research, 5*(2), 375–391. doi:10.1007/s12187-011-9134-2

Fuchs, D., Cho, E., Toste, J. R., Fuchs, L. S., Gilbert, J. K., McMaster, K., Svenson, E., & Thompson, A. (2020). A quasiexperimental evaluation of two versions of first-grade PALS: One with and one without repeated reading. *Exceptional Children*. Advance online publication. doi:10.1177/0014402920921828

Gaylord-Ross, R. J., Haring, T. G., Breen, C., & Pitts-Conway, V. (1984). The training and generalization of social interaction skills with autistic youth. *Journal of Applied Behavior Analysis, 17*(2), 229–247. doi:10.1901/jaba.1984.17-229

Giangreco, M. F., Doyle, M. B., & Suter, J. C. (2012). Constructively responding to requests for paraprofessionals: We keep asking the wrong questions. *Remedial and Special Education, 33*(6), 362–373. doi:10.1177/0741932511413472

Giangreco, M. F., Yuan, S., McKenzie, B., Cameron, P., & Fialka, J. (2005). "Be careful what you wish for...": Five reasons to be concerned about the assignment of individual paraprofessionals. *TEACHING Exceptional Children, 37*(5), 28–34. doi:10.1177/004005990503700504

Gifford-Smith, M. E., & Brownell, C. A. (2003). Childhood peer relationships: Social acceptance, friendships, and peer networks. *Journal of School Psychology, 41*(4), 235- 284. doi:10.1016/S0022-4405(03)00048-7

Harper, C. B., Symon, J. B., & Frea, W. D. (2008). Recess is time-in: Using peers to improve social skills of children with autism. *Journal of Autism and Developmental Disorders, 38*(5), 815–826. doi:10.1007/s10803-007-0449-2

Haring, T. G., & Breen, C. G. (1992). A peer-mediated social network intervention to enhance the social integration of persons with moderate and severe disabilities. *Journal of Applied Behavior Analysis, 25*(2), 319–333. doi:10.1901/jaba.1992.25-319

Herbert, M. E., Brock, M. E., Barczak, M. A., & Anderson, E. J. (2020). Efficacy of peer network interventions for high school students with severe disabilities and complex communication needs. *Research and Practice for Persons with Severe Disabilities, 45*(2), 98–114.

Holder, M. D., & Coleman, B. (2009). The contribution of social relationships to children's happiness. *Journal of Happiness Studies, 10*(3), 329–349. doi:10.1007/s10902-007-9083-0

Hudson, M. E., Browder, D. M., & Jimenez, B. A. (2014). Effects of a peer-delivered system of least prompts intervention and adapted science read-alouds on listening comprehension for participants with moderate intellectual disability. *Education and Training in Autism and Developmental Disabilities, 49*(1), 60–77. doi:10.2307/23880655

Hunt, P., Soto, G., Maier, J., & Doering, K. (2003). Collaborative teaming to support students at risk and students with severe disabilities in general education classrooms. *Exceptional Children, 69*(3), 315–332. doi:10.1177/001440290306900304

Hunt, P., Soto, G., Maier, J., Müller, E., & Goetz, L. (2002). Collaborative teaming to support students with augmentative and alternative communication needs in general education classrooms. *Augmentative and Alternative Communication, 18*(1), 20–35. doi:10.1080/aac.18.1.20.35

Hunt, P., Staub, D., Alwell, M., & Goetz, L. (1994). Achievement by all students within the context of cooperative learning groups. *Journal of the Association for Persons with Severe Handicaps, 19*(4), 290–301. doi:10.1177/154079699401900405

Jackson, L. B., Ryndak, D. L., & Wehmeyer, M. L. (2008). The dynamic relationship between context, curriculum, and student learning: A case for inclusive education as a research-based practice. *Research and Practice for Persons with Severe Disabilities, 34*(1), 175–195. doi:10.2511/rpsd.33.4.175

Jacques, N., Wilton, K., & Townsend, M. (1998). Cooperative learning and social acceptance of children with mild intellectual disability. *Journal of Intellectual Disability Research, 42*(1), 29–36. doi:10.1046/j.1365-2788.1998.00098.x

Kamps, D. M., Barbetta, P. M., Leonard, B. R., & Delquadri, J. (1994). Classwide peer tutoring: An integration strategy to improve reading skills and promote peer interactions among students with autism and general education peers. *Journal of Applied Behavior Analysis, 27*(1), 49–61. doi:10.1901/jaba.1994.27-49

Kamps, D. M., Leonard, B., Potucek, J., & Garrison-Harrell, L. (1995). Cooperative learning groups in reading: An integration strategy for students with autism and general classroom peers. *Behavioral Disorders, 21*(1), 89–109. doi:10.1177/019874299502100103

Kamps, D. M., Mason, R., Thiemann-Bourque, K., Feldmiller, S., Turcotte, A., & Miller, T. (2014). The use of peer networks to increase communicative acts of first grade students with autism spectrum disorders. *Focus on Autism and Other Developmental Disabilities, 29*(4), 230–245. doi:10.1177/1088357614539832

Kamps, D. M., Potucek, J., Lopez, A. G., Kravits, T., & Kemmerer, K. (1997). The use of peer networks across multiple settings to improve social interaction for students with autism. *Journal of Behavioral Education, 7*(3), 335–357. doi:10.1023/A:1022879607019

Kamps, D., Thiemann-Bourque, K., Heitzman-Powell, L., Schwartz, I., Rosenberg, N., Mason, R., & Cox, S. (2015). A comprehensive peer network intervention to improve social communication of children with autism spectrum disorders: A randomized trial in kindergarten and first grade. *Journal of Autism and Developmental Disorders, 45*(6), 1809–1824. doi:10.1007/s10803-014-2340-2

Kasari, C., Locke, J., Gulsrud, A., & Rotheram-Fuller, E. (2011). Social networks and friendships at school: Comparing children with and without ASD. *Journal of Autism and Developmental Disorders, 41*(5), 533–544. doi:10.1007/s10803-010-1076-x

Kasari, C., Rotheram-Fuller, E., Locke, J., & Gulsrud, A. (2012). Making the connection: Randomized controlled trial of social skills at school for children with autism spectrum disorders. *Journal of Child Psychology and Psychiatry*, *53*(4), 431–439. doi:10.1111/j.1469-7610.2011.02493.x

Kearns, J. F., Towles-Reeves, E., Kleinert, H. L., Kleinert, J. O., & Thomas, M. K. (2011). Characteristics of and implications for students participating in alternate assessments based on alternate academic achievement standards. *The Journal of Special Education*, *45*(1), 3–14. doi:10.1177/0022466909344223

Kurth, J. A., Miller, A. L., & Toews, S. G. (2020). Preparing for and implementing effective inclusive education with participation plans. *TEACHING Exceptional Children*. doi:10.1177/0014402903069003O4

Laushey, K. M., & Heflin, L. J. (2000). Enhancing social skills of kindergarten children with autism through the training of multiple peers as tutors. *Journal of Autism and Developmental Disorders*, *30*(3), 183–193. doi:10.1 023/A:1005558101038

Locke, J., Shih, W., Kretzmann, M., & Kasari, C. (2016). Examining playground engagement between elementary school children with and without autism spectrum disorder. *Autism*, *20*(6), 653–662. doi:10.11 77/1362361315599468

Locke, J., Olsen, A., Wideman, R., Downey, M. M., Kretzmann, M., Kasari, C., & Mandell, D. S. (2015). A tangled web: the challenges of implementing an evidence-based social engagement intervention for children with autism in urban public school settings. *Behavior Therapy*, *46*(1), 54–67. doi:10.1016/j.beth.2014.05.001

Mahar, A., Cobigo, V., & Stuart, H. (2013). Conceptualizing belonging. *Disability and Rehabilitation*, *35*(12), 1026–1032. doi:10.3109/09638288.2012.717584

Mason, R., Kamps, D., Turcotte, A., Cox, S., Feldmiller, S., & Miller, T. (2014). Peer mediation to increase communication and interaction at recess for students with autism spectrum disorders. *Research in Autism Spectrum Disorders*, *8*(3), 334–344. doi:10.1016/j.rasd.2013.12.014

McCurdy, E. E., & Cole, C. L. (2014). Use of a peer support intervention for promoting academic engagement of students with autism in general education settings. *Journal of Autism and Developmental Disorders*, *44*, 883–893. doi:10.1007/s10803-013-1941-5

McFadden, B., Kamps, D., & Heitzman-Powell, L. (2014). Social communication effects of peer-mediated recess intervention for children with autism. *Research in Autism Spectrum Disorders*, *8*(12), 1699–1712. doi:1 0.1016/j.rasd.2014.08.015

McLeskey, J., Landers, E., Williamson, P., & Hoppey, D. (2012). Are we moving toward educating students with disabilities in less restrictive settings? *The Journal of Special Education*, *46*(3), 131–140. doi:10.1177/ 0022466910376670

Meyer, L. E., & Ostrosky, M. M. (2016). Impact of an affective intervention on the friendships of kindergarteners with disabilities. *Topics in Early Childhood Special Education*, *35*(4), 200–210. doi:10.1177/02 71121415571419

Morningstar, M. E., Kurth, J. A., & Johnson, P. E. (2017). Examining national trends in educational placements for students with significant disabilities. *Remedial and Special Education*, *38*(1), 3–12. doi:10.1177/074193251 6678327

Mortweet, S. L., Utley, C. A., Walker, D., Dawson, H. L., Delquadri, J. C., Reddy, S. S., Greenwood, C. R., Hamilton, S., & Ledford, D. (1999). Classwide peer tutoring: Teaching students with mild mental retardation in inclusive classrooms. *Exceptional Children*, *65*(4), 524–536. doi:10.1177/001440299906500407

Odom, S. L., & Strain, P. S. (1984). Peer-mediated approaches to promoting children's social interaction: A review. *American Journal of Orthopsychiatry*, *54*(4), 544–557.

Osterman, K. F. (2000). Students' need for belonging in the school community. *Review of educational research*, *70*(3), 323–367. doi:10.3102/00346543070003323

Owen-DeSchryver, J. S., Carr, E. G., Cale, S. I., & Blakeley-Smith, A. (2008). Promoting social interactions between students with autism spectrum disorders and their peers in inclusive school settings. *Focus on Autism and Other Developmental Disabilities*, *23*(1), 15–28. doi:10.1177/1088357608314370

Palmer, S., & Williams-Diehm, K. (2020). The importance of elements of inclusive education. *Inclusion*, *8*(1), 2–5. doi:10.1352/2326-6988-8.1.2

Parker, J. G., Rubin, K. H., Erath, S. A., Wojslawowicz, J. C., & Buskirk, A. A. (2006). Peer relationships, child development, and adjustment: A developmental psychopathology perspective. In D. Cicchetti & D. J. Cohen (Eds.), *Developmental psychopathology: Theory and method* (pp. 419–493). John Wiley & Sons, Inc.

Piercy, M., Wilton, K., & Townsend, M. (2002). Promoting the social acceptance of young children with moderate—severe intellectual disabilities using cooperative-learning techniques. *American Journal on Mental Retardation*, *107*(5), 352–360. doi:10.1352/0895-8017(2002)107<0352:PTSAOY>2.0.CO;2

Raghavendra, P., Olsson, C., Sampson, J., McInerney, R., & Connell, T. (2012). School participation and social networks of children with complex communication needs, physical disabilities, and typically developing peers. *Augmentative and Alternative Communication*, *28*(1), 33–43. doi:10.3109/07434618.2011.653604

Rodriguez, A. M., Taub, D., Scott, L., Copeland, S. R., Williams-Diehm, K., Landmark, L. J., Sinclair, T. E., Black, R. S., Palmer, S. B., & Thoma, C. A. (2020). Reflecting on the education position statement of AAIDD and the Arc. *Inclusion*, *8*(1), 6–26. doi:10.1352/2326-6988-8.1.6

Rossetti, Z., & Keenan, J. (2018). The nature of friendship between students with and without severe disabilities. *Remedial and Special Education*, 39(4), 195–210. doi:10.1177/074193251770371

Rotheram-Fuller, E., Kasari, C., Chamberlain, B., & Locke, J. (2010). Social involvement of children with autism spectrum disorders in elementary school classrooms. *Journal of Child Psychology and Psychiatry*, *51*(11), 1227–1234. doi:10.1111/j.1469-7610.2010.02289.x

Rubin, K. H., Bukowski, W. M., & Bowker, J. C. (2015). Children in peer groups. In R. M. Lerner, W. F. Overton, & P. C. M. Molenaar (Eds.), *Handbook of child psychology and developmental science* (7th ed., pp. 1–48). John Wiley & Sons. doi:10.1002/9781118963418.childpsy405

Rubin, K. H., Bukowski, W. M., & Laursen, B. P. (Eds.). (2009). *Handbook of peer interactions, relationships, and groups*. Guilford Press.

Ryndak, D., Jackson, L., & Billingsley, F. (2000). Defining school inclusion for students with moderate to severe disabilities: What do experts say? *Exceptionality*, *8*(2), 101–116. doi:10.1207/S15327035EX0802_2

Sailor, W., McCart, A., & Choi, J. (2018). Reconceptualizing inclusive education through multi-tiered system of support. *Inclusion*, *6*(1), 3–18. doi:10.1352/2326-6988-6.1.3

Salinger, R. (2020). Empirically based practices to address disability stigma in the classroom. *Journal of Applied School Psychology*. doi:10.1080/15377903.2020.1749203

Schaefer, J. W., Cannella-Malone, H. I., & Carter, E. W. (2016). The place of peers in peer-mediated interventions for students with intellectual disability. *Remedial and Special Education*, *37*(6), 345–356. doi:10.11 77%2F0741932516629220

Shogren, K. A., Wehmeyer, M. L., Lane, K. L., & Quirk, C. (2017). Multitiered systems of supports. In M. L. Wehmeyer & K. A. Shogren (Eds.), *Handbook of research-based practices for educating students with intellectual disability* (pp. 185–198). Routledge.

Shonkoff, J. P., & Phillips, D. A. (Eds.). (2000). *From neurons to neighborhoods: The science of early childhood development*. National Academies Press.

Slavin, R. E. (2011). Cooperative learning. In V. Aukrust (Ed.), *Learning and cognition in education* (pp. 160–166). Academic press.

Thompson, J. R., Bradley, V., Buntinx, W. H. E., Schalock, R. L., Shogren, K. A., Snell, M. E., & Yeager, M. H. (2009). Conceptualizing supports and the support needs of people with intellectual disability. *Intellectual and Developmental Disabilities*, *47*(2), 135–147. doi:10.1352/1934-9556-47.2.135

Thompson, J. R., Shogren, K. A., & Wehmeyer, M. L. (2017). Supports and support needs in strengths-based models of intellectual disability. In M. L. Wehmeyer & K. A. Shogren (Eds.), *Handbook of research-based practices for educating students with intellectual disability* (pp. 31–49). Routledge.

Watkins, L., O'Reilly, M., Kuhn, M., Gevarter, C., Lancioni, G. E., Sigafoos, J., & Lang, R. (2015). A review of peer-mediated social interaction interventions for students with autism in inclusive settings. *Journal of Autism and Developmental Disorders*, *45*(4), 1070–1083. doi:10.1007/s10803-014-2264-x

Webster, A. A., & Carter, M. (2007). Social relationships and friendships of children with developmental disabilities: Implications for inclusive settings. A systematic review. *Journal of Intellectual and Developmental Disability*, *32*(3), 200–213. doi:10.1080/13668250701549443

Wehmeyer, M. L., & Shogren, K. A. (2017). Implications of strengths-based models of disability for the education of students with intellectual disability. In M. L. Wehmeyer & K. A. Shogren (Eds.), *Handbook of research-based practices for educating students with intellectual disability* (pp. 50–59). Routledge.

Williams, L. J., & Downing, J. E. (1998). Membership and belonging in inclusive classrooms: What do middle school students have to say? *Research and Practice for Persons with Severe Disabilities*, *23*(2), 98–110. doi:1 0.2511/rpsd.23.2.98

Williamson, P., Hoppey, D., McLeskey, J., Bergmann, E., & Moore, H. (2020). Trends in LRE placement rates over the past 25 years. *The Journal of Special Education*, *53*(4), 236–244. doi:10.1177/0022466919855052

Wolf, M. M. (1978). Social validity: The case for subjective measurement or how applied behavior analysis is finding its heart. *Journal of Applied Behavior Analysis*, *11*(2), 203–214. doi:10.1901/jaba.1978.11-203

Wu, Y. P., Chen, M. C., Lo, Y., & Chiang, C. H. (2020). Effects of peer-mediated instruction with AAC on science learning and communitive responses of students with significant cognitive disabilities in Taiwan. *Research and Practice for Persons with Severe Disabilities*, *45*(3), 178–195. doi:10.1177/154079691990099

17

Collaborative Teaming for Effective Inclusive Education for Students with Severe Disabilities

Diane Lea Ryndak[1], *Donna Lehr*[2], *Nancy Harayama*[2], *and Megan H. Foster*[3]

[1]UNIVERSITY OF NORTH CAROLINA GREENSBORO

[2]BOSTON UNIVERSITY

[3]UTICA COLLEGE

Setting the Stage

Shortly after the education of all students with disabilities was guaranteed by the Education for All Handicapped Children Act (EAHCA, 1975), information on education for students with severe disabilities began to be published (Sontag et al., 1977). The term severe disabilities, however, is not one of the 13 disability categories defined in EAHCA or its current reauthorization, the Individuals with Disabilities Education Improvement Act (IDEA, 2004). Instead the term severe disabilities has been used in the literature to refer to a subset of students identified as having a primary disability within one of several of the disability categories defined in the legislation, including intellectual disability, deaf-blindness, autism spectrum disorders, traumatic brain injury, physical disability, and other health impairments. In addition, students with severe disabilities often have a combination of two or more intellectual, physical, or sensory disabilities and might be identified as having either multiple disabilities or extensive and pervasive support needs (Thompson et al., 2014). Because of their multiple needs and intensity of their disabilities, this group of students is described as heterogeneous and individual students are described as having complex learning needs (Westling et al., 2015). Today these students are at least as complex and heterogeneous as when the EAHCA was passed, as young children with even more extensive medical needs are surviving and entering the early intervention, early childhood, and education systems (Lehr & Harayama, 2020).

To meet their complex and unique learning needs, knowledge and skills are required from multiple individuals who represent various perspectives. In addition to professionals in general education, special education and related services, relevant individuals include the students' parents, guardians, and/or caregivers. This set of knowledge and skills can exist only within a collection of individuals who: (a) focus on meeting the unique learning needs of the whole student; (b) bring sets

DOI: 10.4324/9781003043874-17

of specialized knowledge to all aspects of the educational experience for each student; (c) engage in a collaborative teaming model comprising a consistent and on-going approach to identifying and meeting a student's learning needs; and (d) develop, implement and evaluate collaborative instruction that is embedded in general education classes and other inclusive contexts. This type of model is proactive and contrasts with early models in which teachers and related services personnel each provided services in isolation, with very little interaction occurring among service providers and with very little input from families.

Today, many students with severe disabilities are receiving instruction in general education classes (U.S. Department of Education, 2019). Planning, implementing and evaluating the impact of instruction requires proactive, collaborative teams to provide instruction that actively engages the student with severe disabilities with their grade-level general education classmates within general education instruction in meaningful ways, resulting in progress on the general curriculum (Root et al., 2017), embedded essential skills (e.g., communication, mobility; Gee, 2020a), and relationship building (Dukes & Darling, 2017).

While the learning needs of students with severe disabilities necessitate collaboration, not all teachers nor related service personnel have sufficient knowledge and skills to teach these students (Agran et al., 2020; Gee, 2020b), nor have the knowledge and skills necessary to collaborate effectively (Da Fonte & Barton-Arwood, 2017; Gomez-Najarro, 2020). While many states require general education teachers to complete at least one higher education course in special education, few such courses focus on preparing educators to meet the needs of students with severe disabilities. Consequently, general educators most frequently lack specialized expertise to meet the needs of students with severe disabilities enrolled in their classes (Pugach et al., 2012; Zagona et al., 2017). In addition, many states require special education teachers to obtain initial licensure in high incidence disabilities (e.g., learning disabilities) and provide the option of completing requirements in one or more low incidence disability areas to fulfill licensure requirements is an optional add on. This frequently results in special educators completing only the initial licensure requirements and, therefore, having limited or no specialized expertise in meeting the learning needs of students with severe disabilities. This reality necessitates collaboration among general educators and other educational personnel to bring together the requisite specialized knowledge and skills (McDonnell et al., 2020). For a student with severe disabilities, therefore, collaborative team members minimally should include their elementary general education teacher(s), a special education teacher *with expertise in severe disabilities*, the student's parents or guardians, and their related service providers. To meet each student's learning needs, additional team members might include a school nurse, guidance counselor, instructors for specials (e.g., art, library, music), general education classmates, and paraeducators as appropriate.

As students with severe disabilities increasingly are being placed with grade-level classmates in general education classes (U.S. Department of Education, 2019), there has been a concomitant shift in the knowledge and skills needed to meet the learning needs not just of students with varying abilities (e.g., severe disabilities; gifted and talented), but also students with other learning challenges associated with poverty, homelessness, and racial, ethnic, and linguistic diversity. In these complex and heterogeneous general education contexts, teachers, related service providers, parents, paraeducators, and other educational personnel must navigate a complicated system of legislated accountability for student learning and teacher performance, for the use of evidence-based instructional strategies and interventions, and for access to general education content standards for all of their students, including those with severe disabilities. The importance of planning, implementing, and evaluating rigorous instructional plans has higher stakes than in the past for: (a) the students, especially those in states where graduation is dependent on passing a state test; (b) teachers and administrators, when their performance scores, professional development plans, and merit salary increases are based on student progress; and (c) schools, districts, and states, which are rated based on annual yearly progress (No Child Left Behind Act, 2001). Few single teachers would be able to acquire the depth and breadth of expertise and skills required to meet the accountability expectations for all their students.

All of these variables have led to a more widespread need for, and acceptance of, the development of collaborative teams whose members bring their own specialized knowledge to discussions about curriculum, instruction, supports and other accommodations to meet the learning needs of students with varying instructional needs in the same class and instructional session. Therefore, in addition to team members who collaboratively can meet the learning needs of a student with severe disabilities, the composition of collaborative teams may vary. For example, s a teacher of English language learners (Kangas, 2018) or a social worker may be appropriate additions based on the needs of the students.

Student and Collaborative Team Vignettes

What follows are vignettes of three students with severe disabilities, with each student demonstrating various learning and instructional needs. These vignettes are designed to illustrate the needs of a small sample of students with severe disabilities for whom collaborative teaming would serve to maximize their learning. These students will be referenced in other sections of the chapter.

First, let us consider Ava, an energetic first grader with Down syndrome. She is fully included in a classroom in which a general and a special educator co-teach full time with the support of a para-educator. In addition, she receives speech and language therapy, as well as occupational therapy. She identifies several sight words and is beginning to answer 'what' and 'who' questions by selecting from an array of picture communication symbols after listening to a classmate read with her. She imitates strokes of the letters in her name when given adapted, raised line paper and pencil grip, and writes by sequencing picture symbols. She counts ≤5 objects with one-to-one correspondence, identifies numerals 1-3, rote counts ≤10, identifies what comes next in an ABAB pattern, counts blocks to measure length, etc. Her parents would like to see her continue to make progress in the general education curriculum. (Team members: parents, general education teacher, special education teacher, para-professional, speech/language pathologist, occupational therapist, general education classmates, etc.).

Second, let us discuss Santiago, who is in third grade, immigrated to the U.S. two years ago and was diagnosed with Autism Spectrum Disorder (ASD) upon arrival. Prior to his immigration, he intermittently attended a special program for children with disabilities in Guatemala. Upon immigration, he exhibited echolalic speech and did not have a functional communication method. Therefore, he relied on nonverbal communication acts and behaviors, such as biting and spitting. He now relies on object cues to support literacy skills and is beginning to imitate key words in stories. He attempts to count up to five in both English and Spanish. Given his needs in both daily living skills and behavioral support, he is receiving occupational therapy and in-home ABA services. His mother has a lot of questions about the diagnosis and placement and benefits from a cultural liaison. (Team members: parent, general education teacher, special education teacher, speech/language pathologist, occupational therapy, ABA therapist, general education classmates, etc. Needs translator/cultural liaison.)

Finally, let us consider Malik, who is a fifth grader with multiple disabilities. He uses a Dynavox with Tobii mounted on his wheelchair to communicate and participate in all classroom activities. During literacy activities, he reads a modified text that is augmented with picture symbols and writes up to three sentences using Tobii with word prediction for rate enhancement. He adds/subtracts 2-digit numbers with regrouping, identifies largest/smallest values on graphs, and measures length to the nearest quarter-inch when the ruler is positioned for him. In other curricular areas, he can identify some of the original 13 colonies, name key historical figures, and write a paragraph about them with the support of a graphic organizer. His parents want him to continue to participate in all general education curriculum areas and have instruction on essential skills embedded into the daily routines of his general education class. (Team members: parents, general education teacher, special education teacher, speech/language pathologist, physical therapist, occupational therapy, assistive technology specialist, general education classmates.)

As we proceed through the chapter, references will be made to the learning needs of Ava, Santiago, and Malik. In addition, examples will be provided related to the role of collaborative teams and teaming in meeting their learning needs within general education classes and other inclusive settings.

Legal Mandates Relevant for Collaboration

The overriding goal of IDEA (2004) is assisting each student to achieve educational benefit through the provision of a free and appropriate public education (FAPE) in the least restrictive environment (LRE). To achieve this goal, IDEA mandates the use of education teams and provides some guidance in relation to the responsibilities of team members in descriptions of key functions that require collaboration. Three of these key functions include the:

a. determination of a child's eligibility for special education and related services through either early intervention, early childhood, or K-12 education systems (Part B Section 1414 (b) (4) (A);
b. development of an annual IEP that recognizes a student's current performance level identifies relevant grade- and age-appropriate annual goals on both the general curriculum and embedded essential skills that cumulatively lead to desired long-term outcomes for an enviable life, and determines the supports and services the student will need to make progress on those annual goals (Section 1414 (d) (1) (A) (i) (I)); and
c. ongoing formative and summative monitoring of the student's progress on their IEP goals and objectives, as well as the determination of whether the student is making sufficient progress annually to ensure their long-term goals might be realized. (Section 1414 (d) (1) (A) (i) (III))

Bateman and Yell (2019) stated that the intent of the team process mandated within the IDEA (2004) is that the team is composed of members

> ...because of his or her particular expertise. The general education teacher is there because of his or her expertise in the curriculum. The special education teacher is there because of his or her expertise and knowledge of how to work with students in special education and understanding of the special education process. (p. 192)

IDEA regulations define the role, criteria or qualifications of various team members. Some of this information is brief; for example, in 34 CFR section 300.34(c)(9), we learn, "Physical therapy means services provided by a qualified physical therapist" (IDEA). Information for other team members is more detailed. In 34 CFR section 300.34 (c)(6), we learn,

> Occupational therapy—(i) means services provided by a qualified occupational therapist, and (ii) includes—(A) improving, developing, or restoring functions impaired or lost through illness, injury, or deprivation; (B) improving ability to perform tasks for independent functioning if functions are impaired or lost; and (C) preventing, through early intervention, initial, or further impairments or loss of function. (IDEA)

Information on the roles and responsibilities of parents is primarily included in the definition of a free and appropriate public education (FAPE). Additionally, IDEA requires schools to provide services for any student with disabilities in the least restrictive environment, starting with the premise that the student belongs in general education classes, with the provision of supports and services that meet the student's learning needs. Many argue that such placement in general education classes with support and services constitutes the least restrictive environment and describe such services as inclusive education.

For the purpose of this chapter, inclusive education for a student with severe disabilities is defined as comprising three indicators:

1. The student is *engaged with and making progress in the general education content standards and individually identified essential skills to participate in grade-level general education classes and other contexts.*
2. The student *interacts and develops relationships with their grade-level classmates.*
3. The student is *engaged in activities within their general education class, school, and home communities.*

Teams must consistently monitor the degree to which these key indicators are evident as they co-plan, co-implement, and co-evaluate the effectiveness of each individual student's educational and related services.

For these indicators to be actualized, collaborative teams must address four aspects of a student's education, including instructional (a) content, (b) context, (c) instruction, and (d) accountability (Ryndak et al., 2013). For instance, it is critical for teams to collaboratively identify and prioritize the most relevant *instructional content* from both the grade-level general education content standards and individually identified essential skills needed to engage in the general education instruction on those standards. While there are numerous approaches to identify content to include on a student's IEP or to match instructional outcomes for a general education instructional unit, each approach could result in different conclusions; thus, the process used by a collaborative team will impact the content that ultimately is prioritized for a student.

For *context*, it is critical for collaborative teams to focus first on the general education contexts in which instruction is delivered for the student's grade-level classmates, as well as other general education contexts in which the student reasonably could use the content being taught (e.g., other general education classes, inclusive school settings, inclusive non-school settings). In addition to these contexts with grade-level classmates, teams can focus on other contexts which are part of the student's life (e.g., home dinner table, scouts) into which the student could generalize the use of the content (Ryndak et al., 2020). Context, however, is broader than a specific setting. Context includes every aspect of each setting, such as instructional activities and materials, the person leading or supporting instruction, other persons in the setting, and expectations related to engagement and performance levels. As with instructional content, there are different approaches for identifying the contexts in which a student will receive instruction, and the process used by a collaborative team to identify contexts will reflect their values, beliefs, and biases about students with severe disabilities and the educational services they deserve, as well as their expectations for each student's growth (Lansey et al., 2020).

For *instruction*, it is critical collaborative teams learn about research-, evidence-, and practice-based instructional methods that meet the complex learning needs of students with severe disabilities and strategize on how to embed those methods in grade-level general education contexts (McDonnell et al., 2020). As with content and context, there are numerous approaches to identifying inclusive education practices to be used. To ensure continuity of instruction across contexts and instructors, the process a collaborative team uses to identify inclusive education practices must result in approaches that match both a student's learning needs and the grade-level contexts in which they receive instruction.

For *accountability*, collaborative teams must develop and implement a system for collecting formative and summative data that are meaningful to all team members and that measure progress on both general education content standards and individually identified essential skills prioritized for a student. In addition, the accountability system must reflect the student's progress on both short- and long-term desired outcomes and the social validity of those outcomes. While each state and school district has requirements and specific tools for measuring student progress (e.g., alternate assessment; alternate achievement standards), collaborative teams frequently have difficulty obtaining detailed information that meaningfully reflects a student's progress on the prioritized content by using these formalized measures. Thus, to address accountability, effective collaborative teams supplement such measures required by their state and district systems with individualized data collection systems that match the student's learning needs, content, contexts, and instruction.

Foci for Additional Chapter Sections

The remainder of this chapter will focus on four main areas, including (a) the current state of both research and the wisdom of practice related to collaborative teaming for students with severe disabilities, (b) challenges to effective implementation of collaborative teaming, (c) use of collaborative teaming when identifying instructional content for students with severe disabilities, and (d) collaborative teaming practices for the provision of effective instruction for students with severe disabilities. Throughout these sections, we will refer to the student vignettes to provide an illustration of some key points.

Research on Collaborative Teaming and the Wisdom of Practice

While much is written about the benefits of collaborative teaming, there is not an extensive body of research demonstrating its effectiveness as related to student outcomes. A systematic review of the literature conducted by Vangrieken et al. (2015) revealed that most of the extant research has focused on teacher and organizational outcomes, with limited research focused on student outcomes. Further, she described difficulty with summarizing that research due to the lack of uniform definitions of collaboration. Vangrieken and her colleagues noted:

> A considerable amount of different terms is used to describe this phenomenon: teacher teams, teacher collaboration, professional (learning) communities, (teacher) learning communities, (teacher) learning teams, etc. These terms were often used interchangeably, and different researchers tended to allot different interpretations to the same term. (p. 23)

The authors summarized what was described in the articles as occurring on a continuum, "ranging from mere aggregates of individuals to strong team collaboration" (p. 17). This lack of clarity regarding terms makes it difficult to interpret the research, but never-the-less many continue to advocate for teams to go beyond being cooperative and focus on instructional teams collaboratively improving upon existing processes, exploring complex problems, developing deeper understandings of challenges, and developing thoughtful solutions (Herrmann, 2019). Included in the following sections of this chapter is a discussion of models of collaboration in schools and the evidence of its effectiveness in general education, special education overall, and special education for students with severe disabilities. Also presented is a primary driver for implementing a collaborative teaming approach: logic codified as legal requirements.

Models of Teaching: Isolative and Collaborative

Teaching was once described as an isolative practice by Lortie (2002) in a sociological study of general education teachers. He depicted the traditional model of schools existing since the 19th century in which teachers were assigned to their individual classrooms with the responsibility of teaching the students within them—a so-called egg-crate model. He noted that both physical barriers of the separate room and psychological barriers of teachers trying to figure out their roles independently contributed to teachers' isolation. At that time, teachers had considerable autonomy regarding what and how to teach their students and they were expected to work independently. He argued that this autonomy and expectation, along with little time to interact with other teachers, contributed to the lack of collaboration among teachers. Most general education teachers still primarily teach in isolation (Scholastic and the Bill & Melinda Gates Foundation, 2012).

The literature includes some emphasis on collaboration as related to professional development (McLeskey et al., 2017, 2019). Called communities of practice (Trust & Horrocks, 2017), lesson study (Fujii, 2016), and professional learning communities (Stoll et al., 2006), these professional development approaches are designed to bring together general education teachers to improve their practice (Scholastic and the Bill & Melinda Gates Foundation, 2012). A comprehensive survey of general education teachers (Scholastic and the Bill & Melinda Gates Foundation, 2012), however, revealed that they spent only 15 minutes a day collaborating with other teachers. Despite this limited time, some studies have demonstrated improved outcomes for students with the collaboration of this nature (Hargreaves, 2019), though most of the research has focused on teacher satisfaction with collaboration and self-efficacy.

While the same egg-crate model of teaching exists within special education, there are some peculiarities of the field that prevent special education teachers from being completely isolated. Earlier in this chapter, we noted the complexity of learning needs for students with severe disabilities. No one teacher can be an expert across these areas of learning needs; have sufficient content knowledge across academic subjects (e.g., science, history, mathematics); have expertise in specialized instructional approaches for students with sensory impairments and severe behavioral challenges; and have specialized knowledge of the provision of health care services. This precisely is the reason that special education law dictates that educational teams collaborate to co-plan, co-implement, and co-evaluate students' educational programs.

In one of the first texts focused on the education of students with severe disabilities, Hart (1977) noted:

> The need for professionals from many disciplines to work with the handicapped [sic] has been advocated for years, but never has this need been as critical as it is in educating the severely and profoundly handicapped [sic]. Because of the complexities of these children, their heterogeneity, their multiple handicaps, and their age ranges, effective programming for them must be based on a cooperative effort by a variety of experts. (p.6)

Shortly after the passage of EAHCA, Bricker (1976) conceptualized an approach to teaming that focused on the role of the special education teacher. She proposed that the teacher should be the educational synthesizer "…who can draw relevant information from a variety of sources and then incorporate it into daily intervention procedures for children." She stated that "The educational synthesizer becomes the pivotal force in the overall educational program by seeking and coordinating the necessary resources to produce growth and change in the severely impaired [sic] child" (p. 88).

This model of a sole teacher gathering and integrating information from multiple disciplines, however, was seen by some as being insufficient to meet the needs of students with severe disabilities. Others (United Cerebral Palsy National Collaborative Infant Project, 1976) proposed alternative models for bringing together the necessary expertise to support the development and learning of these students. One such model is the *multidisciplinary model*, composed of specialists who apply their specialized knowledge and skills directly and independently with students. By contrast, the *interdisciplinary model* includes a team of specialists that work directly with students, but they also interact with other team members regarding shared goals for the students. The *transdisciplinary model* was described by York et al. (1990) as follows:

> Two features that distinguish transdisciplinary teamwork from traditional more isolated team approaches are (a) a high degree of collaboration and joint decision-making among team members (including parents) in conducting assessments, establishing program priorities, and designing and implementing individualized educational programs; and (b) teaching the skills traditionally associated with one discipline to other team members who function in direct service capacities and work directly with learners throughout each day across a variety of environments and activities (role release). (p. 73)

In his early textbook, Sontag (1977) described the predominant model of educational service delivery as that of one special educator, one or more paraeducators, and, frequently, volunteers, providing educational services for students with severe disabilities in self-contained special education classes. Related services personnel provided services (e.g., occupational therapy) in pull-out models that removed students from those classrooms. In 1986, as students with severe disabilities increasingly were being educated in general education classes, the then Assistant Secretary for the Office of Special Education, Madeline Will (1986), emphasized the need for general and special educators to share responsibility for assessment and intervention to meet the needs of students with disabilities, and a more collaborative approach to teaming. Since then, several other approaches to collaborative teaming have emerged and a research base has begun to be developed related to those approaches. On the other hand, much of that work has focused on students with high incidence disabilities. What is known is described in the following sections.

Collaborative Teaming Practices in the Research

Though it is limited, there is some existing research that supports the overall use of collaborative teams, as well as their use of specific practices, when serving students with severe disabilities in inclusive general education classes. The research supports the overall use of education teams, individualized instruction within teaming models, and the role of team members. For instance, Fisher and Frey (2001) found that collaboration among education team members was critical for ensuring access to the general curriculum and participation in general education instructional activities for one student with severe disabilities in elementary school, one in middle school, and one in high school. Similarly, Hunt et al. (2003) found that collaborative teams designing Unified Plans of Supports for students with severe disabilities in general education classes and implementing those plans consistently resulted in increases in the students' (a) acquisition of academic skills, (b) participation in-class activities, (c) interactions with peers, and (d) student-initiated interactions. Finnerty et al. (2019) found that collaboration between general and special educators was associated with sustained use of adaptations for students with severe disabilities.

Embedding Instruction

Research also supports the use of specific practices by collaborative teams. For instance, it supports various team members embedding individualized instruction for students with severe disabilities within general education instructional instruction and routines. In a series of studies, McDonnell and his colleagues (Jameson et al., 2008, 2012; Johnson et al., 2004; McDonnell et al., 2002) found that: (a) embedding individualized interventions for students with severe disabilities into general education instructional activities led to improved student outcomes on general education content standards, functional content, and the use of communication devices; and (b) peers, paraeducators, and general and special educators were effective at embedding individualized instruction with fidelity. In addition, Johnson et al. found that general educators "viewed embedded instruction as a practical, effective, and efficient strategy for teaching students with developmental disabilities in general education settings" (p. 214).

Communication Across Providers of Instruction

Research also exists on the roles of special education teachers and paraeducators in the delivery of services for students with severe disabilities in general education classes. This research describes various models in which paraeducators are used and raises questions about appropriate roles for paraeducators and special education teachers related to specific responsibilities (Giangreco, 2001; Suter & Giangreco, 2009). While research does not reveal officially identified evidence-based practices, experts point to the critical role of communication among special educators and paraprofessionals to ensure that students are receiving high-quality instruction that includes consistency of instruction across providers (Biggs et al., 2016, 2017).

General Education Classmates on Collaborative Teams

The existing research also supports general education classmates having a role in collaborative teams. For instance, Fisher and Frey (2001) found that the involvement of classmates on a student's collaborative team was critical to ensuring access to and participation in the general curriculum. The role of classmates also has been studied related to the effectiveness of individualized instruction when provided by various team members. Jameson et al. (2008) found that classmates were effective implementers of embedded instruction that used constant time delay. Carter et al. (2005) found not only that classmates were critical members of collaborative teams, but also that having two classmates, instead of one, supporting the student with severe disabilities in general education contexts led to "higher levels of social interaction and contact with the general curriculum" (p. 15).

Co-Teaching

Co-teaching is one model of collaboration, one that focuses on two teachers, one in general and one in special education, working together (Friend, 2021). In co-teaching arrangements, students with disabilities receive supports and services in general education classrooms to which both general and special education teachers are assigned. This model most often is used when students with high incidence disabilities are in general education classes; however, in some schools, it is a general approach used for all students (e.g., The Henderson School in Boston Public Schools). Six models of co-teaching are prevalent in the literature and are described by Friend as follows. In the *one teach and one observe model*, one teacher observes to collect information for joint analysis at a later time. In the *one teach and one assist model*, one teacher teaches while a second teacher plays a supporting role for individual students. In the *station teaching model*, each teacher is assigned to various learning stations through which their students rotate. In the *parallel teaching model*, teachers share the responsibility for teaching the same content but for different groups of students. In the *alternative teaching model*, one teacher provides specialized instruction to a small group of students, while the second teacher provides instruction to the rest of the class at the same time. In the *team teaching model*, teachers share equally the responsibilities for teaching all the students.

Friend and Cook (1990) pointed out that co-teaching was intended to go far beyond the presence of two teachers during the same class. They suggested that "…collaboration is a style for interaction between at least two co-equal parties voluntarily engaged in shared decision making as they work toward a common goal" (p. 72). They described six characteristics that must be present for collaborative efforts to be effective: (a) mutual goals, (b) parity, (c) shared participation, (d) shared resources, (e) shared accountability, and (f) voluntariness (i.e., members voluntarily participate in collaborative efforts). It is when decision making is shared as teachers work toward common goals that students with severe disabilities have the greatest likelihood of receiving effective inclusive education services and instruction on the general education content standards within general education contexts.

Several features are critical for a co-teaching model to be effective. After completing a meta-analysis of studies on co-teaching, Scruggs et al. (2007) stated that some of these variables included: (a) administrative support, as reflected in the availability of space and time to collaborate, as well as professional development related to collaborative teaming; (b) voluntary participation in co-teaching models; and (c) choice of and compatibility among co-teaching partners. While it might be desirable to allow teachers to volunteer to participate in co-teaching models and choose the colleague with whom they co-teach, these features might not be possible or even be compatible with including several students with severe disabilities across a grade level or school. Often only one teacher with specialized expertise in severe disabilities is employed in a school building; therefore, that teacher must be on each collaborative team, and choices of co-teachers are no longer an option (Ryndak et al., 2007). Additionally, allowing general education teachers to volunteer to teach a class that includes one or two students with severe disabilities or other extensive support needs enables other teachers to avoid responsibility for collaborating and limits the extent to which a grade level or school is inclusive for all students (Ryndak et al., 2007).

Friend et al. (2010) pointed out:

> Despite considerable enthusiasm expressed by those who write about co-teaching and those who implement it, co-teaching illustrates the complexity of conceptualizing and studying collaboration in special education. Most inquiry on co-teaching has emphasized co-teachers' roles and relationships or program logistics rather than demonstrating its impact on student achievement and other key outcomes, and far more literature exists describing co-teaching and offering advice about it than carefully studying it. (p. 9)

Teaming Processes

Some research exists on the processes used by teams to collaborate in co-planning, co-implementing, and co-evaluating the effectiveness of instruction. For instance, Giangreco (1993) adapted and field-tested variations of the Osborn-Parnes Creative Problem-Solving process for use by collaborative teams to meet the needs of students with severe disabilities in general education classes. Snell and Janney (2000) found that team members used several methods for collaborating to resolve concerns related to the effectiveness of services for students with severe disabilities included in general education classes. These included steps that were similar to those reported by other researchers and were described as follows: (a) identify the problem; (b) collect information; (c) generate possible solutions; (d) evaluate those possibilities; (e) implement solutions; and (f) evaluate by watching, thinking and talking.

Multiple Collaborative Teams

Researchers also have begun to study the impact one effective collaborative team can have on other teams. For instance, Hunt et al. (2001) found that an effective collaborative team from one school could "visit" a "home" team at a second school and teach the "home" team to use a collaborative problem-solving process to more effectively co-plan, co-implement, and co-evaluate the effectiveness of their services for students with severe disabilities in general education classes.

Key Factors for Collaborative Teams for Students with Severe Disabilities

Beyond the existing research related to collaborative teaming, the literature consistently recommends several variables as critical to meeting the needs of students in inclusive general education classes. Some of these variables and examples of their relevance for meeting the learning needs of students with severe disabilities, such as Ava, Santiago and Malik, are presented in the following sections.

Members with Relevant Expertise

Collaborative teams are considered effective when they comprise members with expertise across areas relevant to the needs of the students with severe disabilities they serve. It is critical, however, that these areas include specific knowledge related to the education of students with severe disabilities, such as:

1. use of evidence-based interventions, instructional strategies, and inclusive education practices (Brown et al., 2020; Downing, 2010);
2. methods for embedding evidence-based interventions, instructional strategies, and practices across general education contexts and activities (Kennedy & Horn, 2004);
3. use of Universal Design for Learning (UDL) principles to design, implement, and evaluate instruction for all students (Meyer et al., 2014; Rose & Meyer, 2002);
4. use of accommodations and modifications to curriculum, instruction, materials, and contexts (Copeland & Keefe, 2007; Downing, 2010; Kluth, 2003);
5. adherence to guidelines for selecting, teaching the use of and evaluating students' use of assistive technology (AT) and augmentative and alternative communication (AAC) systems (QIAT Leadership Team, 2015); and
6. methods for embedding instruction on, and the use of, AT and AAC in inclusive general education classes and activities (Kleinert et al., 2019).

When considering Malik and his multiple disabilities, general and special education teachers must work together to ensure lessons are universally designed and Malik is receiving necessary accommodations. During co-planning, his teachers look at the general education content standards addressed within each lesson and the instruction that Malik will receive to ensure he has access to that content and is engaged with and making progress in the general education content standards. His speech/language pathologist works closely with his teachers to program his communication device to support his upcoming lessons and provides services to Malik in the classroom by embedding instruction on his use of the communication device in natural settings. This provides opportunities for Malik to learn how to use his device to engage in the lessons with his peers. Additionally, the therapist models for his teachers how to engage Malik through the use of his device. The skills learned by the teachers are then routinely used and integrated as an ongoing part of daily classroom activities.

A Common Vision of Services for All Students

To be collaborative, team members share the overall goals of the services they provide for all of their students. This requires that they have a common vision of services and a keen understanding of how their respective roles support the design, implementation, and evaluation of those services (Fisher & Frey, 2001).

For instance, Santiago's collaborative team members all recognize the importance of addressing his challenging behaviors through positive behavior interventions and supports while also working on his communication and ESL needs. Their common vision reflects the expectation that he interacts and develops relationships with his general education classmates and engages with them during activities within their general education classes, school, and community.

Shared Ownership and Responsibility

Members of collaborative teams have equal ownership of and responsibility for planning, implementing and evaluating the effectiveness of their combined services for the students with severe disabilities they serve in general education classes. This shared ownership and responsibility for the learning of all students, as well as the measurement of that learning, lead to shared accountability and acknowledgment for the student outcomes they achieve through their collaborative efforts (Ryndak et al., 2007).

Shared ownership and responsibility are evident when Ava's collaborative team discuss, agree upon, implement across members and contexts, and evaluate the effectiveness of practices related to her general education content standard goals, communication, and fine motor needs. Each team member works to support all of Ava's needs instead of focusing solely on one area. For example, Ava's occupational therapist provides services to her during general education classes when she addresses fine motor challenges while also supporting instruction on the content of the general education lesson and encouraging increased communication.

Role Release

To use resources wisely, members of collaborative teams share their diverse expertise so that specialized uses of that expertise (e.g., positioning students with physical needs; embedding instruction; using evidence-based interventions) are implemented with fidelity by all team members across the school day. In this way, team members also develop expertise from each other and implement with fidelity the specialized interventions they learn. As team members engage in role release, they learn specialized knowledge and implement specialized interventions that are supervised by the team member with the relevant licensure for each aspect of services (Orelove et al., 2017).

The collaborative team for Santiago demonstrates role release when they provide instruction on content that does not match their specific expertise. Since the language used in Santiago's home is Spanish, his instruction may be provided by various members of the team who have learned evidence-based language support strategies by those who have expertise in bilingual education, as well as in augmentative and alternative communication. For example, the general education teacher may use key vocabulary in Spanish and provide object cues during a literacy activity. The special education teacher might model these communication strategies for his grade-level classmates so that Santiago can interact and communicate meaningfully during group activities in class, during recess, and during lunch. Finally, the occupational therapist may learn key phrases in Spanish in teaching individually identified essential embedded skills for use during routines.

Ground Rules for Team Functioning

To function efficiently, collaborative teams develop and adhere to ground rules for team functioning. Some recommended ground rules include (a) demonstration of mutual respect among team members, (b) establishment of team goals, (c) assignment of clear roles, (d) individual accountability, (e) measurement of effectiveness, (f) reflective evaluation of the team's functioning, (g) problem-solving processes and action planning, and (h) receipt of mutual benefits from their collaboration (Jorgensen et al., 2010; Pugach et al., 2012).

The effective use of ground rules for collaborative team functioning is evident in the way that Malik's team operates. The parents, general education teacher, special education teacher, speech/language pathologist, physical therapist, occupational therapy, and assistive technology specialist actively listen to each member's perspectives and collaboratively set goals based on Malik as a 'whole' child, rather than from a discipline-specific view, and set expectations for responsibilities as a collective group, as well as individuals. For example, if there are different perspectives about an adaptation for teaching multiplication, the team can listen to the advantages and disadvantages of each method and then determine which to use. Once a decision is made, the assistive technology specialist may make the necessary adjustments to Dynavox and Tobii, and the special education teacher may collect data on its effectiveness. Then, the team can reflect upon their problem-solving process and co-evaluate the impact of their decisions.

Only as Special as Necessary

Rather than automatically adding an adult with specialized expertise to an instructional context, collaborative teams use role release to determine how services that require specialized expertise can be implemented by team members who have less or different expertise (e.g., classmate, para-educator, math teacher). In this way, instruction that requires specialized expertise can be implemented across the school day by team members with less professional development, but with preparation and supervision to implement services provided by team members with the specialized expertise. In this way, team members whose services are most expensive are present for a student's instruction only when their presence is necessary (i.e., when they have not been able to teach other team members to use specific expertise to meet a student's learning needs). In this way, the expertise of the team member implementing services is only as special as necessary, allowing flexibility in the use of the more specialized team members while allowing specialized instruction to occur across each school day, rather than only when a team member with specialized expertise is available (Carter et al., 2009; Giangreco, 2001).

This concept of 'only as special as necessary' can be seen in how supports for Ava are co-planned and co-implemented by her team. For example, during the literacy block, a peer-assisted learning strategy might be used. The general education teacher introduces a phonemic awareness activity to a small group and pairs Ava with a general education classmate who has been taught to support her so they can continue to work on the activity. The effectiveness of peer-assisted learning is then evaluated by the special education teacher, who examines the data collected by a trained para-professional. Additionally, the occupational therapist may train the paraeducator to teach Ava to open snack packages in the cafeteria, and the speech and language therapist may provide training to the peers to ask Ava open-ended questions about favorite cartoons to increase the number of communication exchanges.

Challenges to Effective Collaborative Teaming

The idea of collaborative teaming is widely accepted. At the same time, however, implementing collaborative practices is perceived as challenging because of how personnel are prepared, differing mindsets and beliefs they might hold, administrative infrastructures and processes within which they practice, and how teams function.

Differences in Professional Development

Teams comprising individuals from different disciplines sometimes experience challenges caused by individual members' various points of view that reflect the perspectives of their professional development programs. Varying programs frequently focus on discipline-specific content within different theoretical and conceptual models (e.g., medical, clinical, inclusive, disability-based). While individual team members should have different discipline-specific expertise, the use of different terminology, different goals for services, and different visions of what constitutes effective practices can be problematic for team functioning. For example, consider this difference: Central to special education practice is the concept of individualized instruction; however, central to general education practice is group instruction. These different practices, and their underlying differences in beliefs about teaching and instruction, can result in team members holding different opinions about "fairness," especially related to the use of accommodations and modifications to meet the learning needs of individual students. Consider, too, the challenges related to the different professional vocabulary used by various team members. Occupational and physical therapists typically use terminology related to the medical field, while general or special educators use terminology related to pedagogy and learning. A lack of understanding of the terminology used by team members can be challenging to a team's communication, shared vision, and effectiveness.

Team members with specialized expertise often are challenged by the concept of role release; that is, the practice of sharing specialized expertise so all team members can use that knowledge and skills in their own practice with individual students. Some professionals believe that their knowledge and skills are so specialized that others would not be able to understand or apply specific practices. Others are concerned that if they release their roles to team members, their expertise might not be needed in the future. Conversely, team members might be challenged by the concept of learning new knowledge and skills from other team members, believing that this could emphasize the importance of the expertise of other team members while diminishing the importance of their own expertise and their ability to use it with individual students.

Finally, personality differences among team members also can result in challenges to team functioning and collaboration (Hamilton-Jones & Vail, 2014). For example, the critical variables of equal membership, shared responsibility and shared accountability can be threatened by dominant personalities and by perceptions of unequal power or rewards.

Mindsets and Beliefs

As mentioned previously, one of the six characteristics needed for effective collaboration is voluntariness (Friend & Cook, 1990). Team members must be willing to work collaboratively with each other to support inclusive education practices for all students. Specifically, research indicates that the more positively a teacher feels about inclusive education, the more open they are to make adaptations to meet the needs of all students and work collaboratively to design and implement inclusive education for all students (Cullen et al., 2010). Cullen et al. found that general educators frequently hold negative beliefs about inclusive education, fearing that including all students would take too much time for co-planning, co-implementing, and co-evaluating instruction. In addition, some special and general educators cite general educators' lack of knowledge and skills as reasons not to provide inclusive education for students with severe disabilities.

Similar to educators and administrators, parents also hold beliefs about inclusive education and inclusive instructional practices that can shape both the educational placement of their child and collaborative teaming practices. Palmer and his colleagues (2001) found that while some parents supported inclusive education and believed it would benefit their child academically, many parents of children with severe disabilities feared that the severity of their child's disability was too great for their child to benefit from being with general education classmates in general education settings. In addition, Palmer et al. found that parents feared their child would not be welcomed in general education classes. School districts have a responsibility to work with parents to alleviate these concerns and share information on inclusive education practices associated with improved student outcomes.

Team Functioning

Teams can function well only if there is time to co-plan, co-implement, and co-evaluate instruction; however, a challenge to collaborative teaming often identified by general educators is the lack of sufficient time for these activities (Foster, 2013). The factors that potentially inhibit time to collaborate are numerous. For instance, paraeducators might be paid only for the time they spend interacting directly with students; related service providers might travel between schools on tight schedules; general and special educators might not have planning time scheduled in common. Each of these factors makes it difficult to schedule meetings, yet meetings are essential for effective collaboration. To address, research indicates that administrative support is essential to ensuring sufficient common planning time is built into schedules for effective collaborative teaming (Harding, 2009; Smith & Leonard, 2005). To function well, teams require the use of practices that facilitate efficient and effective use of the limited time allocated for meeting. Time available can be optimized by the utilization of practices to increase efficiency. Commonly recommended practices include the assignment of roles of timekeeper, note-taker, and facilitator for each meeting.

A final challenge to effective collaborative teaming is how to embed teams within existing school-wide structures, so they enhance those school-wide structures, rather than functioning separately from, or in conflict with, those structures. For example, collaborative teamwork should be embedded within multi-tiered systems of support (Sailor, 2015), which provide a continuum of support that enhances learning for all students. While models for multi-tiered systems of support vary across schools, common elements include "multiple tiers of intervention service delivery, a problem-solving method, and an integrated data collection and assessment system to inform decisions at each tier of service delivery" (Averill & Rinaldi, 2011, p. 91). Collaborative teams also should be embedded within grade-level teams and subject area teams.

Multi-level Administrative Support and Infrastructures for Collaborative Teaming

Since one of the main characteristics of effective collaboration is voluntariness, it is critical for administrators to provide the necessary infrastructures and support that assist all educators to be invested in collaborative processes. Federal mandates (IDEA, 2004) ensure that certain provisions are in place for all students with disabilities, including education in the least restrictive environment, access to the general education content standards, and active parental participation. In addition to federal policy, state and district policies might add regulations regarding services that local education agencies must provide to students with disabilities, as well as procedures that must be followed. Beyond federal, state and district policies and procedures, numerous federally-funded projects and state departments of education have developed tools that summarize research- and evidence-based practices that comprise effective collaborative services for students with severe disabilities. For example, one set of tools used for systems at different levels (i.e., state, district, school, education team) are known as RISE tools (Reflecting on Inclusive Systems of Education; TIES National Technical Assistance Center on Inclusive Practices and Policies, 2021). Teams of stakeholders use these tools first to reflect on the extent to which their services reflect evidence-based practices, including those that support collaborative teaming, and then to strategize how to increase and improve their use of evidence-based practices across their education system.

The RISE tools reflect an understanding that the vision and mission statements of a district and each school have a powerful influence over the acceptance of and willingness to implement inclusive education policies and practices, including collaborative teaming. Foster (2013) found that both general and special educators were more supportive of inclusive education and collaborative teaming practices when the practices were clearly embedded in their district's mission statement and had their administrators' support. In contrast, Foster found that teachers who worked under administrators that were not supportive of inclusive education practices did not believe these practices to be in the best interest of all students. In addition, they were more likely to refer students with disabilities to segregated settings. Roberts et al. (2018) found that administrators working in inclusive schools welcomed students with severe disabilities, worked collaboratively with team members and made changes to general education services to best support all learners. The beliefs and actions of administrators surrounding inclusive education and collaborative practices were paramount in the philosophy of the school and all its members. Thus, the extent to which effective collaborative teams can develop and function with and across schools is directly impacted by the vision and mission explicitly stated and supported by the leaders of those systems.

An additional barrier to collaborative teaming described by general educators is a lack of expertise and relevant professional development that teaches and models collaborative practices. In response, administrators must develop infrastructures that support collaborative teaming, and provide effective professional development activities, technical assistance, and coaching that teach and model collaborative teaming practices so all team members (e.g., general and special educators, related services personnel, paraeducators) can develop and practice them.

An additional barrier to collaborative teaming is the trend of administrators hiring dual- or triple-licensed educators and expecting them to be responsible for multiple roles (i.e., the role of both the general educator and the special educator). While this sounds positive in theory, in practice, it is less positive. In situations where one individual is responsible for multiple roles, there are not team members with whom that individual can collaborate to co-plan, co-implement, and co-evaluate instruction. If a general educator is hired with certification in both elementary and special education, and that teacher is solely responsible for the education of all students in the classroom, this person loses the benefit of brainstorming, receiving feedback, sharing expertise, and gaining the perspective of another team member. In addition, they lose the support for completing tasks such as developing materials, teaching groups of students, and sharing supervision of students during instruction. Administrators can alleviate such losses by ensuring that even dually-licensed educators are part of a collaborative team and that no educator is teaching in isolation.

Collaborative Teaming and Identifying Instructional Content

A key area in which collaboration is essential is planning instructional content for students with severe disabilities. With the advent of a focus on access to the general education content standards, access to grade-level general education classmates, accountability for progress on the general curriculum, and specially-designed instruction on standards-based content for students with severe disabilities, new attention is being given to the students' instruction on general education content standards. While evidence-based practices support the use of processes through which collaborative teams can identify relevant instructional content for a student with severe disabilities, prepackaged curricula have begun to be developed specifically stating their purpose as providing access to the general education content standards for students with severe disabilities. Some curriculum packages, such as *Early Literacy Skills Builder* (Browder et al., 2010), *Promoting Awareness of Sounds in Speech* (Roth et al., 2012), and *Early Numeracy* (Jimenez et al., 2013), are noted as having been developed with the consideration for the diverse adaptation needs of students with severe disabilities. On the other hand, researchers are beginning to question the extent to which such curricula are aligned with grade-level general education content standards and, therefore, questioning their effectiveness in assisting students with severe disabilities in making progress on the general education content standards as they are taught to their grade-level classmates (Taub et al., 2019, 2020). If used, most commercially available prepackaged curricula rarely can be used directly off-the-shelf without individualization to meet some of the heterogeneous needs of the students. In addition, teams must also collaborate to ensure that instructional content for any student with severe disabilities is aligned with content and instruction delivered in general education classes.

For students like Malik, it is critical for the team to collaborate to make adaptations that allow true access to the general curriculum and instruction, providing real opportunities to learn (Taub et al., 2017). The general and special educators will need to collaborate to determine the level of complexity at which he will access grade-level general education content standards. The two educators and related service providers will need to collaborate to identify, develop, and use adaptations and supports for both presenting instruction and student responding. Finally, while prepackaged curricula might be treated as sources for concrete or reproducible materials (e.g., worksheets), ultimately, the content on which instruction is provided, as well as 'how' that instruction is provided, will have to be decided by each student's collaborative team after initiating collaboration around the general education class content and instruction. These decisions would include the appropriate level of prompting and the use of instructional strategies like time delay, error correction, and reinforcement.

Various curricular access models have been presented to inform the selection of high-priority grade-level academic standards for instruction (Browder et al., 2007; Hunt et al., 2012; Ryndak et al., 2009). Several of these models have components in common. For instance, first and foremost, these models begin with collaborating with the student's family to ensure that the selected standards are consistent with their priorities. For example, Hunt et al. (2012) described an ecological model of providing access to the general curriculum that begins with the identification of goal areas using a family-centered approach. Tools such as *Choosing Outcomes and Accommodations for Children* (*COACH*; Giangreco et al., 2011) can be used to facilitate the process of identifying family priorities in a systematic manner. Santiago's family would benefit from this process with the addition of an interpreter and cultural liaison for a culturally- and linguistically-responsive approach to the selection of priority goals.

These models also describe a student's collaborative team as considering various criteria when selecting relevant high-priority grade-level content standards. Among these are: (a) identification of grade-level content standards based on chronological age, (b) examination of the representativeness of the key strand areas within the subject area, (c) alignment to grade-level expectations with consideration for scope, (d) differentiation over the years, and (e) preservation of the integrity of the content area standards (Browder et al., 2007). The use of these criteria requires deep content-area knowledge and collaboration with general education teachers. As Ryndak et al. (2009) pointed out, the underlying assumptions and perspectives of team members about context and content, as well as what it means to provide access to the general education content standards and opportunities to learn, impact this process. This highlights the importance of shared responsibility; development of collaboration skills; and accountability systems that support collaborative teaming for co-planning, co-implementing, and co-evaluating the effectiveness of instruction.

The process of identifying high-priority grade-level content standards also must be based on longitudinal planning. This means that instruction should be provided to target standards that are critical for growth within specific strand areas. For example, Collins et al. (2006) described how a high-priority math skill of telling time could be developed by targeting telling time to the hour, to the half-hour, increments of 15-minutes, etc., and having students apply it to their class and daily schedules. Similarly, money handling can be addressed by targeting coin identification, value of combinations of bills and coins, comparison of prices, calculation of tips and taxes, budgeting, etc. This requires collaboration with general education teachers to ensure that students are being taught content based on a logical progression of more sophisticated skills and concepts within meaningful contexts. For a student like Ava who has emerging academic skills, it is critical that instructional planning consider long-term growth.

In addition, horizontal integration of targeted academic skills is critical in ensuring that core academic skills are addressed across content areas. For example, if a priority academic standard for a student is to answer 'w' questions, then the team would collaborate to ensure that 'w' questions are addressed across content areas in social studies with 'w' questions about historical events (e.g., who the historical figure was, what happened during the event, when the event occurred, where it occurred); in earth and space science with 'w' questions about the weather phenomena (e.g., what the weather event is, when it occurs, where it occurs, how it occurs, etc.); and in English language arts with 'w' questions after reading narrative and expository text. This again requires collaborative teaming to ensure that these high-priority academic skills are addressed across content areas and related services. In addition, the format of the presentation of the questions and response modalities would be determined collaboratively.

Collaborative teams also decide the level of complexity at which the selected high-priority grade-level standards would be addressed. As stated earlier, it is important to preserve the integrity of the grade-level content standards and avoid reverting to lower grade-level content. Some states (e.g., Massachusetts) have provided resource guides for teachers of students with severe disabilities that show a continuum of complexity for each grade-level standard to facilitate this team process (Massachusetts Department of Elementary and Secondary Education, 2020). The expertise of general education teachers is critical to maintain focus on the selected grade-level content standards and prevent overstretching (e.g., having a student draw an animal when the life science standard is about habitats) or mismatching (e.g., naming animals when the life science standard is about the differences and similarities of plants and animals) (Courtade & Flowers, 2007). Similarly, the expertise of special education teachers is critical for identifying, developing and ensuring the effectiveness of instructional supports provided to afford students opportunities to learn and make progress on the general education content standards.

Collaborative Teaming and Providing Effective Instruction

Collaborative teaming is necessary for effective instruction in an inclusive setting. Considering the heterogeneity of students with severe disabilities, systematic adaptations require the expertise of each member of the team. In addition, the students' need to have essential skills embedded meaningfully into daily routines makes coordination paramount. The co-planning and co-implementing of evidence-based practices, as well as co-evaluating, are discussed below.

Systematic Adaptations for Instruction on Grade-Level Content Standards

Related service providers are critical in determining the appropriate presentation of materials and student response. For instance, for the presentation of materials, the speech/language pathologist could provide input about the level of symbolic representation (e.g., text, picture symbols, photos, tactile materials, concrete objects) and level of vocabulary that match a student's learning needs; the physical therapist could make recommendations about the placement of the materials (e.g., plane of presentation or positioning for the inhibition of primitive reflexes such as the asymmetrical tonic neck reflex [ATNR]); the occupational therapist could make recommendations regarding placement of materials regarding hand dominance, size of manipulatives for ease of grasp, adaptations for turning pages of a book, etc.; the teacher of students with visual impairments could suggest materials that provide enlargement/color contrast of materials, tactile materials, etc. For a student like Malik, input from team members with differing expertise is critical to assure appropriate individualization.

For student response, various considerations such as the format of response (e.g., open-ended, multiple-choice), modality of response (e.g., verbal, written by handwriting or assistive technology, a selection from an array of picture symbols using pointing, eye gaze, augmentative and alternative communication device, etc.), and complexity of the response need to be taken into account. This process will require the collaboration of speech/language pathologists, physical and occupational therapists, and assistive technologist specialists.

Some students, such as Santiago, might require behavioral supports during academic instruction. In collaboration with other team members, a behavior specialist can conduct a functional behavioral assessment to identify antecedents and consequences associated with challenging behaviors and recommend preventative and instructional strategies for appropriate replacement behaviors. Considering that the academic task itself might serve as an antecedent and trigger the behavior, collaboration with the entire team could be critical to prevent any mismatch between the difficulty level of the academic tasks and the student's current level of performance and to ensure that there are appropriate adaptations and supports in place.

Embedded Essential Skills

Students with severe disabilities have additional needs that require instruction across various domains of life (e.g., daily living skills, community, etc.). Rather than perceiving the mandate to provide access to the general education content standards as competing against the need for instruction on embedded essential skills or classifying skills into mutually exclusive categories of academic or functional, there are ways to reconcile them and to consider overlaps. For example, Hunt et al. (2012) presented the ecological model that teams can use to determine outcomes that are standards-aligned within priority goal areas identified by the family and to provide instruction across meaningful contexts, rather than just in the classroom. Essential skills of socializing with peers (e.g., turn-taking) and communicating (e.g., staying on topic) can be embedded within academic contexts, and academic skills can be embedded in daily routines. This again requires collaboration with the entire team to ensure that all the students' goals are addressed in meaningful contexts to the maximum extent possible.

Planning and Implementing Effective Instruction with Evidence-based Practices

Instructional planning in an inclusive setting should begin with the general education teacher adhering to the principles of Universal Design for Learning (UDL; Rose & Meyer, 2002). The extent to which the general education teacher plans with the needs of all students, including those with severe disabilities, in mind by providing multiple means of engagement, representation, and action and expression will have an inverse relationship to the need to add-on adaptations as an afterthought. While the need for all individualized adaptations cannot be completely eliminated even with UDL, the team can collaborate to identify appropriate assistive technology for reading (e.g., digital texts with text-to-speech, electronic picture dictionaries for key words, age-appropriate online books at accessible readability level), composition (e.g., electronic picture-based graphic organizers, word prediction), motor aspects of writing (e.g., adapted keyboard and mouse, speech-to-text, eye gaze input), and math (e.g., adapted calculator, virtual math manipulatives). The team can select augmentative and alternative communication methods (e.g., object/miniature objects, picture symbols on academic topic boards or pragmatic organization dynamic display, voice-output devices with a static display, or app-based systems with dynamic display) by considering expressive/receptive language, physical abilities, and levels of symbolic representation and literacy levels, as well as ensuring that the key academic vocabulary for each lesson is readily accessible for the student's use.

The use of *systematic instruction* was identified as an evidence-based practice to teach academic skills (Browder et al., 2006; Orlando & Ruppar, 2016; Saunders et al., 2020; Spooner et al., 2011, 2019). Systematic instruction, which incorporates the use of task analysis, appropriate prompting procedures and error correction, requires careful planning. The steps of the academic task will need to be systematically identified, the level within the prompt hierarchy (i.e., visual, verbal, modeling, physical) and prompt latency (e.g., 5-second constant time delay or 0-, 2-, 4-, 6-second progressive time delay) will need to be identified, and specific procedures for error correction will need to be pre-planned. Selection of the appropriate level of prompt requires consideration of the advantages/disadvantages of each (e.g., modeling requires the student to have imitation skills and consideration for the chunking of the model into rememberable steps, verbal prompts may need to be adjusted for vocabulary level and used with caution to minimize prompt dependency, physical prompts may be beneficial for errorless learning, but some may be averse to touch).

These details need to be communicated clearly to all team members. The clarity and specificity of instructional plans become critical considering the number of individuals on the team who work directly with the student. For example, paraprofessionals are frequently used to provide instruction in inclusive settings. If an instructional plan only states that the student is to be provided prompts, the paraprofessional might not know which type of prompts to use. Simply stating "verbal prompt" would not make it clear as to whether to provide a direction to reattempt (e.g., "Try again"), encouragement (e.g., "I know you can do it!"), redirection of attention (e.g., "Look here), or content-related prompt (e.g., "Look at the first word"). Depending on the paraprofessional, there might be a very long wait time or rapid-fire series of prompts. Therefore, for paraprofessionals who work with students like Ava, Santiago, and Malik, the instructional steps to be implemented must be explicitly described and documented.

The strategies used for planning systematic instruction are based on applied behavior analysis (ABA). Unfortunately, there is a misconception of equating ABA with discrete trial training in which students are taught on a one-on-one basis by an ABA technician using massed trials outside of general education classes. This is problematic due to the lack of opportunities to have peer models during skill acquisition, challenges with the generalization of academic skills to meaningful contexts, and lack of maintenance of skills through distributed practice. It is critical to recognize that prompting, reinforcement, and error correction strategies used in systematic instruction are transportable and can be implemented within the contexts of general education classes through collaborative teaming and doing so helps to assure generalization of skills across people, places, and things.

Addressing Differences in Perspectives on Collaborative Teams

As stated earlier, there are various barriers to effective collaboration. General education teachers might follow an inquiry-based, constructivist approach and might perceive the explicit instruction model and systematic instruction used by special education teachers as being diametrically opposed to their theoretical framework. Professional development provided for related service providers might impact their perspectives about the student and their disabilities, service delivery models, instructional contexts, etc. Attitudes about the competence of individuals with severe disabilities might serve as a barrier to inclusive placements (Vandercook et al., 2020). Some parents might even view inclusion with suspicion, as though it may result in a dilution of services. Some team members might perceive trans-disciplinary service delivery as an encroachment on their turf as disciplinary boundaries are blurred. Such challenges can be remedied through school- and district-level leadership, allocation of common planning time and resources for collaboration, team-based professional development, accountability systems, and other variables.

Multi-tiered Systems of Supports

Multi-tiered system of supports (MTSS) was initially designed to address the needs of students at risk and to identify students with suspected specific learning disabilities who fail to respond to the intervention and, thereby, are determined to be in need of special education. Therefore, students with severe disabilities often were excluded from the discussion of the MTSS model. On the other hand, MTSS actually was conceptualized to be inclusive and to address the needs of students with severe disabilities through tiered levels of support (e.g., response to intervention, positive interventions and supports, Thurlow, 2020). In fact, as Thurlow noted, the Every Student Succeeds Act (2021) permits funds to be used for students with the most significant cognitive disabilities so they can meet academic standards (Sec 2103(b)(3)(F)). In this conceptualized of MTSS, collaborative team members can collaborate to provide academic Tier 1 supports (e.g., identification of priority goals, use of AAC systems), Tier 2 supports (e.g., activating background knowledge or pre-teaching key concepts), and Tier 3 supports (e.g., providing targeted instruction). Similarly, behavioral supports at Tier 1 (e.g., accessible presentation of expectations and behavioral rules), Tier 2 (e.g., breaks, explicit instruction of social skills), and Tier 3 (i.e., individualized positive behavior support plan based on the results of a functional behavioral assessment) can be provided through collaborative team planning.

Assessing Progress

Students with severe disabilities are assessed for various purposes (e.g., diagnosis, initial or re-evaluation for special education eligibility, instructional planning, monitoring of progress, participation in the statewide accountability system). Historically, the evaluation of students has been discipline-specific (e.g., the occupational therapist focuses on fine motor skills; the speech therapist focuses on speech and language development). But this approach ignores discipline overlaps and results in fragmented findings written with discipline-specific terminology that might be unfamiliar to family members or other term members. What is needed is a focus on the whole child, considering relevant activities and contexts and findings that are instructionally meaningful. Such focus would be family-friendly and could assist in the development of IEP objectives. For students like Ava, Santiago, and Malik, a collaborative approach to assessment is needed (Brown et al., 2020). In addition to the evaluation for special education eligibility, ongoing data collection for the attainment of IEP objectives for formative purposes is necessary, and team members would share a collective responsibility.

Related to assessment is the matter of assignment of grades for work performance. General education teachers often struggle with how to assign grades for students with severe disabilities on report cards. It is critical for the team to consider and come to an agreement regarding the grading criteria for a standards-aligned report card for students with severe disabilities who might not meet the same grade-level achievement as their classmates. Finally, the social validity of each student's outcomes must be evaluated by asking the student, family members, and even the student's friends if the outcomes are important, meaningful outcomes for the student.

Conclusion

In this chapter, we noted the legal mandate for the provision of effective special education and related services for students with disabilities by education teams and the need for expanded membership on teams charged with meeting the heterogeneous educational needs of students with severe disabilities within general education classes and other inclusive contexts. While many terms have been used to refer to these education teams and how they function, a collaborative teaming approach is supported by the literature as the most relevant for students with severe disabilities. It is not clear in the literature, however, that collaborative teaming practices are being implemented on a large scale.

We identified three indicators that define inclusive education for students with severe disabilities, including the students: (a) engaging with and making progress in the general curriculum and individually identified essential skills to participate in grade-level general education classes and other contexts; (b) interacting and developing relationships with their grade-level classmates; and (c) engaging in activities within their general education classes, school, and home communities. To accomplish this, we described how teams consistently monitor the degree to which these key indicators are evident as they co-plan, co-implement, and co-evaluate the effectiveness of each individual student's special education and related services. We further discussed how, for these indicators to be actualized, collaborative teams must address four aspects of a student's education: content, context, instruction, and accountability.

With this foundational information, we then discussed what the research and collective wisdom of practice tell us about collaborative teaming and meeting the needs of students with severe disabilities in inclusive general education settings. For instance, these tell us that a teaming teaching model is more effective than an isolative teaching model and that collaborative teaming is the most effective model of teaching. They inform us about several practices that support effective collaborative teaming, including the embedding of instruction within general education instruction and routine tasks, communication across all providers of instruction and other services, and the membership of a student's general education classmates on their collaborative team. They tell us that co-teaching models are effective and require support from the school's administrative, teaching and support personnel; and that teaming processes exist that facilitate co-planning, co-implementing, and co-evaluating the effectiveness of instruction. They also support the interaction of members of multiple teams to support the development and implementation of multiple collaborative teams within and across schools. Finally, they inform us that several factors are key to the effective implementation of collaborative teams for students with severe disabilities. These include members contributing the expertise relevant to meeting a student's unique and multiple learning needs, a common vision of services for all students, shared ownership and responsibility, use of role release practices, ground rules for team functioning, and services being provided by personnel with expertise that is only as special as necessary.

We also discussed challenges to effective collaborative teaming that have been identified, including the difference in the professional development of various team members, how that professional development and other experiences frequently result in differing mindsets and beliefs about teams and how they should function, and the need for administrative support and infrastructures that facilitate collaborative teaming and cross multiple levels of a system (e.g., classroom, school, district). Finally, we described how collaborative teaming processes could impact the instructional content identified for a student with severe disabilities and the provision of effective instruction on that content. Through collaborative teaming, students with severe disabilities are more likely to have systematic adaptations for instruction on grade-level curriculum content, instruction on essential skills embedded within grade-level instruction and routines, implementation of evidence-based practices across instructional activities, instruction that reflects the expertise of multiple collaborative team members, engagement in class- and school-wide multi-tiered systems of supports, and valid and reliable assessment of progress.

Though collaborative teaming is the most efficacious approach to meeting the educational needs of students with severe disabilities, we recognize that it is not widely or consistently implemented across schools or districts. Greater efforts must be made to develop and implement collaborative teaming to respond to the intent of our education legislation and provide services informed by research and wisdom of practice. To do so, we argue for the increased use of implementation science approaches by education teams, schools, districts, and states to ensure both initial implementation and scaling up collaborative practices systemically.

References

Averill, O. H., & Rinaldi, C. (2011). Multi-tier system of supports (MTSS). *District Administration*, *48*(8), 91–95. doi:10.1007/s10567-020-00317-1

Agran, M., Jackson, L., Kurth, J. A., Ryndak, D., Burnette, K., Jameson, M., Zagona, A., Fitzpatrick, H., & Wehmeyer, M. (2020). Why aren't students with severe disabilities being placed in general education classrooms: Examining the relations among classroom placement, learner outcomes, and other factors. *Research and Practice for Persons with Severe Disabilities*, *45*(1), 4–13. doi:10.1177/1540796919878134

Bateman, D. F., & Yell, M. L., (Eds.) (2019). *Current trends and legal issues in special education*. Corwin. doi: 10.4135/9781071800539

Biggs, E. E., Gilson, C. B., & Carter, E. W. (2016). Accomplishing more together: Influences to the quality of professional relationships between special educators and paraprofessionals. *Research and Practice for Persons with Severe Disabilities*, *41*(4), 256–272. doi:10.1177/1540796916665604

Biggs, E. E., Carter, E. W., & Gustson, J. (2017). Efficacy of peer support arrangements to increase peer interaction and AAC use. *American Journal on Intellectual and Developmental Disabilities, 122*(1), 25–48. doi:10.1352/1944-7558-122.1.25

Bricker, D. (1976). Educational synthesizer. In M. A. Thomas (Ed.), *Hey! don't forget about me! Education's investment in the severely, profoundly, and multiply handicapped* (pp. 84–97). Council for Exceptional Children.

Browder, D. M., Ahlgrim-Delzell, L., Courtade, G., Gibbs, S., & Flowers, C. (2008). Evaluation of the effectiveness of an early literacy program for students with significant developmental disabilities. *Exceptional Children, 75*(1), 33–52. doi:10.1177/001440290807500102

Browder, D. M., Gibbs, S., Ahlgrim-Delzell, L., Courtade, G., & Lee, A. (2010). *Early literacy skills builder.* Attainment Company.

Browder, D. M., Wakeman, S. Y., Flowers, C., Rickelman, R. J., Pugalee, D., & Karvonen, M. (2007). Creating access to the general curriculum with links to grade-level content for students with significant cognitive disabilities: An explication of the concept. *Journal of Special Education, 41*(2), 2–16. doi:10.1177/00224669070410010101

Browder, D. M., Wakeman, S. W., Spooner, F., Ahlgrim-Delzell, L., & Algozzine, B. (2006). Research on reading for students with significant cognitive disabilities. *Exceptional Children, 72*(4), 392–408. doi:10.1177/001440290607200401

Brown, F., McDonnell, J., & Snell, M.E. (2020). *Instruction of students with severe disabilities.* (9th ed.) Pearson.

Carter, E. W., Cushing, L. S., Clark, N. M., & Kennedy, C. H. (2005). Effects of peer support interventions on students' access to the general curriculum and social interactions. *Research and Practice for Persons with Severe Disabilities, 30*(1), 15–25. doi:10.2511/rpsd.30.1.15

Carter, E. W., Cushing, L. S., & Kennedy, C. H. (2009). *Peer support strategies for improving all students' social lives and learning.* Paul H. Brookes.

Collins, B., Kleinert, H., & Land, L. A. (2006). Addressing math standards and functional math. In D. M. Browder & F. Spooner (Eds.), *Teaching language arts, math, and science to students with significant cognitive disabilities.* Paul H. Brookes.

Copeland, S. R., & Keefe, E. B. (2007). *Effective literacy instruction for students with moderate or severe disabilities.* Paul H. Brookes.

Council for Exceptional Children & CEEDAR Center (2019). *Introducing high-leverage practices in special education: A professional development guide for school leaders.* Council for Exceptional Children & CEEDAR Center. www.highleveragepractices.org

Courtade, G., & Flowers, C. (2007). *Best practice and policy considerations in science teaching and testing for students with significant cognitive disabilities.* https://nceo.info/Resources/publications/Teleconferences/tele14/default.html

Cullen, J. P., Gregory, J. L., & Noto, L. A. (2010). *The teacher attitudes toward inclusion* scale (TATIS) Technical Report. Online Submission.

Da Fonte, M. A., & Barton-Arwood, S. M. (2017). Collaboration of general and special education teachers: Perspectives and strategies. *Intervention in School and Clinic, 53*(2), 99–106. doi:10.1177/1053451217693370

Downing, J. E. (2010). *Academic instruction for students with moderate and severe intellectual disabilities in inclusive classrooms.* Corwin.

Dukes, C., & Darling, S. M. (2017). Common core state standards and students with severe disabilities: An introduction to the special issue. *Research and Practice for Persons with Severe Disabilities, 42*(3), 139–142. doi:10.1177/1540796917715408

Education for All Handicapped Children Act (1975), Pub. L. No. 94-142, (November 29, 1975).

Education of All Handicapped Children Act of 1975, 20 U.S.C. § 1400 et seq. (1975).

Every Student Succeeds Act (ESSA) GovTrack.us (2021. S.1177-114th Congress. https://www.govtrack.us/congress/bills/114/s1177

Finnerty, M. S., Jackson, L. B., & Ostergren, R. (2019). Adaptations in general education classrooms for students with severe disabilities: Access, progress assessment, and sustained use. *Research and Practice for Persons with Severe Disabilities, 44*(2), 87–102. doi:10.1177/1540796919846424

Fisher, D., & Frey, N. (2001). Access to the core curriculum: Critical ingredients for student success. *Remedial and Special Education, 22*(3), 148–157. doi:10.1177/074193250102200303

Foster, M. H. (2013). *The perceived impact of education policy on the inclusion of students with disabilities in two contrasting schools.* [Doctoral dissertation, University of Buffalo]. ProQuest Dissertations & Theses Global.

Friend, M. (2021). *Interactions: Collaboration skills for school professionals.* Pearson.

Friend, M., & Cook, L. (1990). Collaboration as a predictor for success in school reform. *Journal of Educational and Psychological Consultation, 1*(1), 69–86.

Friend, M., Cook, L., Hurley-Chamberlain, D., & Shamberger, C. (2010). Co-teaching: An illustration of the complexity of collaboration in special education. *Journal of Educational and Psychological Consultation, 20*(1), 9–27. doi:10.1080/10474410903535380

Fujii, T. (2016) Designing and adapting tasks in lesson planning: a critical process of Lesson Study. *ZDM Mathematics Education, 48*, 411–423. doi:10.1007/s11858-016-0770-3

Gee, K., Gonzalez, M., & Cooper, C. (2020a). Outcomes of inclusive versus separate placements: A matched pairs comparison study. *Research and Practice for Persons with Severe Disabilities.* doi:10.1177/154079692 0943469.

Gee, K. (2020b). Why indeed? *Research and Practice for Persons with Severe Disabilities, 45*(1), 18–22. doi:10.11 77/1540796919900951

Giangreco, M. F. (1993). Using creative problem-solving methods to include students with severe disabilities in general education classroom activities. *Journal of Educational and Psychological Consultation, 4*(2), 113–135. doi:10.1207/s1532768xjepc0402_1

Giangreco, M. F. (2001). *Guidelines for making decisions about I.E.P. services.* Vermont Department of Education. http://www.uvm.edu/~cdci/iepservices/pdfs/decision.pdf

Giangreco, M. F., Cloninger, C. J., & Iverson, V. S. (2011). *Choosing outcomes and accommodations for children (COACH): A guide to educational planning for students with disabilities* (3rd ed.). Brookes.

Gomez-Najarro, J. (2020). An empty seat at the table: Examining general and special education teacher collaboration in response to intervention. *Teacher Education and Special Education, 43*(20), 109–126. doi:10.11 77/0888406419850894

Hamilton-Jones, B. M., & Vail, C. O. (2014). Preparing special educators for collaboration in the classroom: Pre-service teachers' beliefs and perspectives. *International Journal of Special Education, 29*(1),76–86.

Harding, S. (2009). Successful inclusion models for students with disabilities require strong site leadership: Autism and behavioral disorders create many challenges for the learning environment. *International Journal of Learning, 16*(3), 91–104.

Hargreaves, A. (2019). Teacher collaboration: 30 years of research on its nature, forms, limitations and effects. *Teachers and Teaching, 25*(5), 603–621. doi:10.1080/13540602.2019.1639499

Hart, V. (1977). The use of many disciplines with the severe and profoundly handicapped. In E. Sontag, J., Smith, & N. Certo (Eds.), *Educational programming for the severely and profoundly handicapped* (pp. 391–396).Council for Exceptional Children.

Herrmann, Z. (2019). Cooperate or collaborate: Your team's purpose could determine its process. *Educational Leadership, 76*, 68–72.

Hunt, P., Doering, K., Hirose-Hatae, A., Maier, J., & Goetz, L. (2001). Across-program collaboration to support students with and without disabilities in a general education classroom. *Journal for the Association for Persons with Severe Handicaps, 26*(4), 240- 256. doi:10.2511/rpsd.26.4.240

Hunt, P., McDonnell, J., & Crockett, M. A. (2012). Reconciling an ecological framework focusing on quality of life outcomes with the development and instruction of standards-based academic goals. *Research and Practice for Persons with Severe Disabilities, 37*(3), 139–152. doi:10.2511/027494812804153516

Hunt, P., Soto, G., Maier, J., & Doering, K. (2003). Collaborative teaming to support students at risk and students with severe disabilities in general education classrooms. *Exceptional Children, 69*(3), 315–332. doi:1 0.1177/001440290306900304

Individuals with Disabilities Education Improvement Act of 2004, PL 108-446, 20 U.S.C. § 1400 et seq. (2004).

Jameson, J. M., McDonnell, J., Polychronis, S., Riesen, T., & Taylor, S. J. (2008). Embedded, constant time delay instruction by peers without disabilities in general education classrooms. *American Journal on Intellectual and Developmental Disabilities, 46*(5), 346–363. doi:10.1352/2008.46:346-363

Jameson, J. M., Walker, R., Utley, K., & Maughan, R. (2012). A comparison of embedded total task instruction in teaching behavioral chains to massed one-on-one instruction for students with intellectual disabilities: Accessing general education settings and core academic content. *Behavior Modification, 36*(3), 320–340. doi:10.1177/0145445512440574

Jimenez, B. A., Browder, D. M., & Saunders, A. F. (2013). *Early numeracy.* Attainment Company.

Jimenez, B. A., & Staples, K. (2015). Access to the common core state standards in mathematics through early numeracy skill building for students with significant intellectual disability. *Education and Training in Autism and Developmental Disabilities, 50*(1), 17–30.

Johnson, J. W., McDonnell, J., Holzwarth, V. N., & Hunter, K. (2004). The efficacy of embedded instruction for students with developmental disabilities enrolled in general education classes. *Journal of Positive Behavior Interventions, 6*(4), 214–227. doi:10.1177/10983007040060040301

Jorgensen, C. M., McSheehan, M., & Sonnenmeier, R. M. (2010). *The beyond access model: Promoting membership, participation, and learning for students with disabilities in the general education classroom.* Paul H. Brookes.

Kangas, S. (2018). Why working apart doesn't work at all: Special education and English learner teacher collaborations. *Intervention in School and Clinic, 54*(1), 31–39. doi:10.1177/1053451218762469

Kennedy, C. H., & Horn, E. M. (2004). *Including students with severe disabilities.* Pearson Education.

Kleinert, J., Kearns, J., Liu, K. K., Thurlow, M. L., & Lazarus, S. S. (2019). *Communication competence in the inclusive setting: A review of the literature* (TIES Center Report 103). University of Minnesota, The TIES Center.

Kluth, P. (2003). *"You're going to love this kid!" Teaching students with autism in the inclusive classroom.* Paul H. Brookes.

Lansey, K. R., Burnette, K. K., & Ryndak, D. L. *Disrupting the system: How social systems perpetuate the educational segregation of students with extensive support needs across place and time.* [Manuscript submitted for publication]. College of Education, University of Arizona.

Lehr, D., & Harayama, N. (2020). Understanding and meeting the health care needs of students with severe disabilities. In F. Brown, J. McDonnell, & M. Snell (Eds.), *Instruction of students with severe disabilities* (9th ed., p. 275–303). Pearson Education.

Lortie, D. C. (2002). *Schoolteacher: A sociological study 1975.* University of Chicago.

Massachusetts Department of Elementary and Secondary Education. (2020). *Resource guide to the 2017 Massachusetts Curriculum Frameworks or Students with Disabilities: English Language Arts and Literacy PreK-Grade 12. Pre-Kindergarten–Grade 12.* https://www.doe.mass.edu/mcas/alt/resources.html.

McDonnell, J., Johnson, J. W., Polychronis, S., & Riesin, T. (2002). Effects of embedded instruction on students with moderate disabilities enrolled in general education classes. *Education and Training in Mental Retardation and Developmental Disabilities, 37*(4), 363–377.

McDonnell, J., Snell, M. E., Brown, F., Coleman, O., & Eichelbergfer, C. (2020). Individualized instructional strategies. In F. Brown, J. McDonnell, & M. Snell (Eds.), *Instruction of students with severe disabilities* (9th ed., pp. 156–206). Pearson Education.

McLeskey, J., Barringer, M-D., Billingsley, B., Brownell, M., Jackson, D., Kennedy, M., Lewis, T., Maheady, L., Rodriguez, J., Scheeler, M. C., Winn, J., & Ziegler, D. (2017, January). *High-leverage practices in special education.* Arlington, VA: Council for Exceptional Children & CEEDAR Center.

McLeskey, J., Maheady, L., Billingsley, B., Brownell, M. T., & Lewis, T. J. (2019). *High leverage practices for inclusive classrooms.* Routledge.

Meyer, A., Rose, D. H., & Gordon, D. (2014). *Universal design for learning: Theory and practice.* CAST, Inc.

No Child Left Behind Act of 2001, 20 U.S.C. § 6319 (2008).

Orelove, F. P., Sobsey, D., & Giles, D. (2017). *Education children with multiple disabilities: A collaborative approach.* Paul H. Brookes.

Orlando, A., & Ruppar, A. (2016). *Literacy instruction for students with multiple and severe disabilities who use augmentative/alternative communication* (Document No. IC-16). http://ceedar.education.ufl.edu/tools/innovation-configurations/

Palmer, D. S., Fuller, K., Arora, T., & Nelson, M. (2001). Taking sides: Parent views on inclusion for their children with severe disabilities. *Exceptional children, 67*(4), 467–484. doi:10.1177/001440290106700403

Pugach, M. C., Johnson, L. J., Drame, E. R., & Williamson, P. (2012). *Collaborative practitioners/Collaborative schools* (3rd ed.). Love Publishing Co.

QIAT Leadership Team (2015). *Quality indicators for assistive technology: A comprehensive guide to assistive technology services.* CAST Professional Publishing.

Roberts, C. A., Ruppar, A. L., & Olson, A. J. (2018). Perceptions matter: Administrators' vision of instruction for students with severe disabilities. *Research and Practice for Persons with Severe Disabilities, 43*(1), 3–19. doi:10.1177/1540796917743931

Reflecting on Inclusive Systems of Education. (2021). TIES National Technical Assistance Center on Inclusive Practices and Policies. University of Minnesota.

Root, J. R., Knight, V. F., & Mims, P. J. (2017). A guide to addressing multiple priorities in core curriculum instruction for student with severe disabilities. *Career Development and Transition for Exceptional Individuals, 40*(1), 56–61. doi:10.1177/2165143416680997

Rose, D. H., & Meyer, A. (2002). *Teaching every student in the digital age: Universal design for learning.* Association for Supervision and Curriculum Development.

Roth, F., Worthington, C., & Troia, G. (2012). *Promoting awareness of speech sounds.* Attainment Company.

Ryndak, D. L., Jackson, L. B., & White, J. M. (2013). Involvement and progress in the general curriculum for students with extensive support needs: K-12 inclusive-education research and implications for the future. *Inclusion, 1*(1), 28–49. doi:10.1352/236-6988-1.1.028

Ryndak, D. L., Moore, M. A., Orlando, A. M., & Delano, M. (2009). Access to the general curriculum: The mandate and the role of context in research-based practice for students with extensive support needs. *Research and Practice for Persons with Severe Disabilities, 34*(1), 199–213. doi:10.2511/rpsd.33.4.199

Ryndak, D. L., Orlando, A., & Burnette, K. K. (2020). Creating and implementing inclusive education. In F. Brown, J. McDonnell, & M. Snell (Eds.), *Instruction of students with severe disabilities* (9th ed., pp. 207–231). Pearson Education.

Ryndak, D. L., Reardon, R., Benner, S., & Ward, T. (2007). Transitioning to district-wide inclusive services: The ongoing journey and its accompanying complexities. *Research and Practices for Persons with Severe Disabilities, 32*(4), 228–246. doi:10.2511/rpsd.32.4.228

Sailor, W. (2015). Advances in schoolwide inclusive school reform. *Remedial and Special Education, 36*(2), 94–99.

Saunders, A., Wakeman, S., Reyes, E., Thurlow, M., & Vandercook, T. (2020). *Instructional practices for students with the most significant cognitive disabilities in inclusive settings: A review of the literature.* TIES Center. https://tiescenter.org/resource/8j/b6pdFjSmKSVg6x4oGRGw

Scholastic and the Bill & Melinda Gates Foundation (2012), *Primary sources: America's teachers on the teaching profession.* Scholastic Inc.

Scruggs, T. E., Mastropieri, M. A., & McDuffie, K. A. (2007). Co-teaching in inclusive classrooms: A metasynthesis of qualitative research. *Exceptional Children, 73*(4), 392–416. doi:10.1177/001440290707300401

Smith, R., & Leonard, P. (2005). Collaboration for inclusion: Practitioner perspectives. *Equity & Excellence in Education, 38*(4), 269–279. doi:10.1080/10665680500299650

Snell, M. E., & Janney, R. E. (2000). Teachers' problem-solving about children with moderate and severe disabilities in elementary classrooms. *Exceptional Children, 66*(4), 472–490. doi:10.1177/001440290006600403

Sontag, E., Smith, J., & Certo, N. (Eds.). (1977). *Educational programming for the severely and profoundly handicapped.* Council for Exceptional Children.

Spooner, F., Knight, V., Browder, D. M., Jimenez, B., & DiBiase, W. (2011). Evaluating evidence-based practice in teaching science content to students with severe disabilities. *Research and Practice for Persons with Severe Disabilities, 36*(1-2), 62–75. doi:10.2511/rpsd.36.1-2.62

Spooner, F., Root, J. R., Saunders, A. F., & Browder, D. M. (2019). An updated evidence-based practice review on teaching mathematics to students with moderate and severe developmental disabilities. *Remedial and Special Education, 40*(3), 150–165. doi:10.1177/0741932517751055

Stoll, L., Bolam, R., McMahon, A., Wallace, M., & Thomas, S. (2006). Professional learning communities: A review of the literature. *Journal of Educational Change,* 7(4), 221–258. doi:10.1007/s10833-006-0001-8

Suter, J. C., & Giangreco, M. F. (2009). Numbers that count: Exploring special education and paraprofessional service delivery in inclusion-oriented schools. *Journal of Special Education, 43*(2), 81–93. doi:10.1177/0022466907313353

Taub, D., Apgar, J., Foster, M., Ryndak, D. L., Burdge, M. D., & Letson, S. (2020). *Investigating the alignment of math curricula developed for students with significant intellectual disabilities and the CCSS.* Department of Specialized Education Services, UNC Greensboro.

Taub, D., Apgar, J., Rudka, M., Ryndak, D. L., Burdge, M., & Letson, S. (2019). Investigating the alignment between English Language Arts curricula developed for students with significant intellectual disabilities and the CCSS. *Remedial and Special Education, 41*(5), 284–295). doi:10.1177/0741932519843184

Taub, D., McCord, J., & Ryndak, D. (2017). Opportunities to learn for students with extensive support needs: A context of evidence-based practices for all in general education classes. *Journal of Special Education, 51*(3), 127–137. doi:10.1177/0022466917696263.

Thompson, J. R., Wehmeyer, M. L., Hughes, C., Shogren, K. A., Palmer, S. B., & Seo, H. (2014). The supports intensity scale–Children's version: Preliminary reliability and validity. *Inclusion,* 2(2), 140–149. doi:10.1352/2326-6988-2.2.140

Thurlow, M. L., Ghere, G., Lazarus, S. S., & Liu, K. K. (2020, January). *MTSS for all: Including students with the most significant cognitive disabilities.* University of Minnesota, National Center on Educational Outcomes/TIES Center.

TIES National Technical Assistance Center on Inclusiove Practices and Policies (2019). *Reflecting on opportunities for excellence in inclusive education.* University of Minnesota.

Trust, T., & Horrocks, B. (2017). 'I never feel alone in my classroom': teacher professional growth within a blended community of practice. *Professional Development in Education, 43*(4), 645–665. doi:10.1080/19415257.2016.1233507

United Cerebral Palsy National Collaborative Infant Project. (1976). *Staff development handbook: A resource for the transdisciplinary process.* Author.

U.S. Department of Education (2019). Office of Special Education and Rehabilitative Services, Office of Special Education Programs, *41st Annual Report to Congress on the Implementation of the Individuals with Disabilities Education Act*, Washington, D.C. 2020.

Vandercook, T., Taub, D., Loiselle, T., & Shopa, A. (2020). Why students with severe disabilities are not being placed in general education classrooms: Using the frame of a basic change model to expand the discussion. *Research and Practice for Persons with Severe Disabilities*, *45*(1), 63–68. doi:10.1177/1540796919895970

Vangrieken, K., Dochy, F., Raes, E., & Kyndt, E. (2015). Teacher collaboration: A systematic review. *Educational Research Review*, *15*, 17–40. doi:10.1016/j.edurev.2015.04.002

York, J., Rainforth, B., & Giangreco, M. F. (1990). Transdisciplinary teamwork and integrated therapy: Clarifying the misconceptions. *Pediatric Physical Therapy*, *2*(2), 73–79. doi:10.1097/00001577-199002020-00003

Westling, D. L., Fox, L., & Carter, E. W. (2015). *Teaching students with severe disabilities* (5th ed.). Pearson Education.

Will, M. C. (1986). Educating children with learning problems: A shared responsibility. *Exceptional children*, *52*(5), 411–415.

Zagona, A. L., Kurth, J. A., & MacFarland, S. Z. C. (2017). Teachers' views of their preparation for inclusive education and collaboration. *Teacher Education and Special Education*, *40*(3), 163–178. doi:10.1177/0888406417692969

18

Intensive Behavioral Support

Craig H. Kennedy

UNIVERSITY OF CONNECTICUT

Setting the Stage

Challenging behavior is frequently cited as one of the greatest barriers to effective inclusion for students with disabilities (Crosland & Dunlap, 2012; Simpson, 2004). The impact of these behaviors includes decreased academic achievement, poorer socialization, and increased likelihood of being placed in a more restrictive setting. Both the effects of problematic behaviors themselves and the resources to adequately address student needs stand as major challenges for educational systems (Lloyd et al., 2019). Without adequate behavioral support programs, many students with disabilities are precluded from placement in the least restrictive environment and, particularly, general education settings (Division for Early Childhood, 2017; National Research Council and Institute of Medicine, 2009). The development, implementation, and monitoring of such support programs typically rest with special educators under the provisions of the Individuals with Disabilities Education Act (IDEA, 2004; see also Public Law 114-95, the Every Student Succeeds Act, 2015).

Some types of challenging behavior are mild forms that cause disruptions in the classroom and/or school routines. Such behaviors can include talking out in class, tardiness, and being out of their seat. Other forms of behavior are more harmful and potentially dangerous to the student or others. These actions can include physical aggression, self-injury, and property destruction (Carr et al., 1999). Although this broad range of responses qualifies as challenging behavior, in general, the more severe the behavior, the more likely the student is to receive special education services and is at greater risk for more restrictive educational placements (Lane et al., 2006).

As educational systems have evolved, there has been an increasing focus on educating all students in general education settings and integrating their learning needs within the general curriculum (Browder & Spooner, 2014; Gilmour et al., 2019). Concurrent with the greater emphasis on inclusion for students with disabilities has been the development of schoolwide systems delivering multiple levels of support depending on students' behavioral and academic needs (Horner & Sugai, 2015; Simonsen et al., Chapter 7 of this book). Typically referred to as multi-tiered support systems, schoolwide supports are conceptualized at three levels of intensity. Tier 1 strategies provide universal supports for all students that include classroom management, promoting academic success, and preventing the development of challenging behaviors. Tier 2 strategies increase levels of support for academic and social functioning with the aim of

DOI: 10.4324/9781003043874-18

minimizing the impact and intensity of behavior challenges. Tier 3 strategies incorporate function-based support and an interdisciplinary team to manage the most severe and persistent challenging behaviors.

In this chapter, we will focus on the support needs of students requiring Tier 3 levels of behavioral support—also referred to as *intensive behavioral support*. This level of support is intended for students who emit the most dangerous forms of challenging behavior: Physical aggression, self-injury and/or property destruction. Students who engage in these severe challenging behaviors can include individuals with emotional/behavioral disorders, conduct disorders, autism spectrum disorders, intellectual disability and traumatic brain injury. A defining feature of supports for challenging behavior at this intensity level is to link assessment outcomes with behavioral interventions. In particular, assessments focus on the operant functions of challenging behavior, a process referred to as Functional Behavioral Assessment (FBA). This information is then used to design individualized behavioral support plans. The remainder of the chapter will discuss FBA approaches, how to develop and implement individualized support plans, and how these interventions are integrated into interdisciplinary support systems.

Emergence of Functional Behavioral Assessment

In the late 1970s, researchers began to identify environmental events that seemed linked to the occurrence of challenging behaviors (Baer et al., 1987). Prior to these insights, challenging behavior was often viewed as caused by a person's psychological or psychiatric diagnosis. The result being that interventions were likely pharmacological in nature and sought to remediate symptoms of the diagnosis (e.g., neuroleptic medications to treat psychosis symptoms). When behavioral interventions were used, they had an arbitrary relationship with behavior and either punished responding (e.g., contingent electric shock) or used contrived reinforcers (e.g., providing candy for "good" behaviors). In either case, interventions were selected based on clinical intuition rather than objective and replicable assessment results.

The seminal shift in conceptualizing the causes of challenging behavior occurred with the publication of an article outlining the possible reinforcement-based functions of problematic behavior. Carr (1977) noted that behaviors of concern tended to produce changes in a child's environment that could be described as positive or negative reinforcement processes. For example, when a child screamed, teachers attempted to comfort the child with hugs and praise. Such as a description of events parallels the behavior-analytic definition of *positive reinforcement*. Or a child might scream when asked to do academic work, with the result being that teachers stop making instructional demands to quiet the child. This set of events parallels the behavior-analytic definition of *negative reinforcement*. Carr's (1977) article showed how positive and negative reinforcement could account for the causes of challenging behavior, aligning them with external events and the actions of other people in the child's environment.

The idea of linking the behavioral reinforcement causing challenging behavior with an objective and replicable assessment process was made by Iwata and colleagues in 1982. In their assessment approach, Iwata et al. (1982, 1994) tested specific reinforcement contingencies in relation to challenging behavior to see if these behaviors were sensitive to various types of reinforcement. The researchers were able to show that different individual's behaviors could be maintained by specific forms of reinforcement and insensitive to other reinforcement processes, showing specific behavioral processes causing the challenging behaviors. The innovations of Carr (1977) and Iwata et al. (1982, 1994) were followed by numerous replications and extensions by other researchers focusing both on the operant functions of behavior and approaches for conducting FBAs (O'Neill et al., 1997).

Linking Assessment and Intervention

FBAs are designed to link environmental events and the occurrence of challenging behavior. Environmental events are sometimes types of social interaction and, at other times, can be events or objects. Common types of social interactions that can function as reinforcers include positive attention from adults or peers (e.g., praise or hugs), instructional demands made by others (e.g., being taught math problems), and negative social interactions (e.g., reprimands or scolding). Common forms of events or objects that function as reinforcers can include preferred toys or objects (e.g., videogames), engaging in preferred activities (e.g., playing basketball), or leaving noisy or distressing situations (e.g., a loud school lunchroom). A wide range of interactions, events, and objects can function as reinforcers and may be idiosyncratic to a particular student. It is the role of FBAs to identify these stimuli and suggest the reinforcing function they serve (Hanley et al., 2003).

Social interactions involving praise, demands, hugs, or reprimands can all function as various types of reinforcers. The same observation is true for objects and events. We will talk about three types of reinforcement processes in the remainder of this chapter. In the previous section, we mentioned two: *positive reinforcement* and *negative reinforcement*. We will add to these reinforcement processes a third type: *automatic reinforcement*. Positive reinforcement occurs when a behavior increases in likelihood when the occurrence of a stimulus follows the behavior. For example, a child might bite himself if an adult provides him with a preferred toy to "calm him down." Or a student might destroy instructional materials because it results in attention from a preferred teacher. Negative reinforcement occurs when a behavior increases in likelihood when a stimulus is removed or decreased following the behavior (Catania, 2013; Cooper et al., 2020). An example might include a child biting himself to be removed from a noisy hallway during classroom transitions. Or a student might destroy instructional materials because it causes the teacher to withdraw instructional demands. Automatic reinforcement occurs when a behavior causes some form of sensory stimulation produced directly by the response. For example, a child with autism might engage in hand waiving because of the visual stimulation it produces.

It is important when assessing possible reinforcer functions to keep in mind that the form or topography of the potential reinforcer (e.g., praise or reprimands) *does not* specify its reinforcing function. Form and function are distinct, and it is the role of the FBA to identify both the forms of stimuli and their reinforcing functions. For example, for one student, adult praise may function as a positive reinforcer, but for another student, it is something to be avoided (i.e., a negative reinforcer). Another role of FBAs is to identify *antecedent events* that might predict challenging behavior. For example, the presence of a particular teacher might be associated with attention being a positive reinforcer, but for another teacher, attention might be a neutral event. Or, a looming math test might increase the probability that a student will lash out at her peers.

All of these variables—challenging behaviors, reinforcing stimuli, reinforcer functions, and antecedent events—influence the occurrence of behaviors severe enough to warrant a Tier 3 intervention. It is the role of assessment, in the form of FBA, to identify the relevant behaviors, reinforcers, and precursors associated with severe behavioral challenges. However, with Tier 3 interventions, a comprehensive assessment is only the start. The next step is to develop an intervention that is linked to the reinforcers and associated events causing challenging behavior (see the section below on "Using FBAs to Develop Intensive Behavioral Supports"). One of the first studies to make the FBA-to-intervention link was conducted by Carr and Durand (1985). These authors identified the reinforcers maintaining the challenging behavior of students with autism and taught the students alternative, appropriate communication strategies matched to the same reinforcers maintaining their problematic behaviors. For example, a student who scratched teachers resulting in negative reinforcement in the form of removing math instruction might be taught to request assistance from the teacher in solving difficult problems. In this instance, the student learned to communicate appropriately as an alternative to challenging behavior when math instruction was difficult. Although only an example, this type of assessment-to-intervention link is the hallmark of successfully treating severe challenging behaviors.

Educational and Social Inclusion as Primary Outcomes

We will focus more intently on FBAs and the linking of intervention programs in Tier 3 support systems later in this chapter (see "What Do We Know Based on Research"). However, the behavioral support plans we develop are intended to do much more than to reduce the occurrence of challenging behaviors. Our goal as educators of students with a range of disabilities is to increase their academic and social success in schools and elsewhere. At the beginning of this chapter, it was noted that students with challenging behaviors have significantly poorer outcomes relating to academic performance (e.g., reading and mathematics), social development (e.g., social skills), and participation in the least restrictive environment (e.g., general education classrooms; Lane et al., 2006). As the intensity of challenging behavior increases, not surprisingly, educational outcomes decline in direct proportion to the status of problem behaviors (Lamport et al., 2012).

Although many people think of intensive behavioral supports as focusing on decreasing challenging behavior, these team-based support systems exist within a broader set of educational outcomes. While it is important to reduce challenging behaviors because they place the student and/or others at risk for harm, the broader goals of academic success and social inclusion stand as the overarching goals of intensive behavioral support efforts (Dunlap et al., 2006; Horner & Sugai, 2015; see Table 18.1). Such goals often are reflected at multiple levels within behavioral support interventions. The first level is facilitating students' access to the general curriculum with its focus on mathematics, reading, and science as curricular objectives. This academic access is reflected as instructional goals that specify levels of academic performance and measurable goals that students are expected to achieve. The second level involves the social development of students that is reflected in educational goals focusing on communication, social skills, and social relationship facilitation. The third level of outcomes focuses on maximizing the amount of educational time spent in regular education and other less restrictive settings at school and in the community.

When developing and implementing intensive behavioral support plans, it is important to contextualize behavior deceleration goals within the broader set of academic and social goals that are the foundation of special education (McLeskey et al., 2014). These goals exist in parallel and are often closely linked to each other. For example, the goal of replacing a student's aggressive verbalizations with appropriate social skills should not only result in decreased aggressive statements but also increased social communication, social participation with peers without disabilities, and greater access to the general education curriculum and settings. Keeping these broader goals in mind as we delve into the technical aspects of FBAs and intensive support interventions in the next section of this chapter will help remind everyone involved in these support systems that the educational goals for a student are greater than a sole focus on reducing behaviors of concern.

Table 18.1 Primary Outcomes of Intensive Behavioral Support

Facilitate Student's Access to the General Education Curriculum
Increase Student's Social Development
Maximize Student's Time Spent in General Education Settings

What Do We Know Based on Research

Conducting FBAs is warranted in cases where a student's challenging behavior is not responsive to Tier 2 support strategies following several months of intervention, and such efforts are considered an evidence-based practice (Horner & Sugai, 2015). FBAs are a core component of Tier 3 support strategies and are the foundation for intervention efforts (Anderson & Scott, 2009). In addition, IDEA (2004) specifies that when special education services for a student are being changed to more restrictive placements because of challenging behavior, that FBAs be included in the development of support plans.

How to Conduct Functional Behavioral Assessments

It is important to understand that there is a range of FBA approaches and even a cursory search for assessment strategies will yield a variety of approaches. We will review the primary evidence-based approaches, when their use is warranted, and what types of information each provides for framing intervention strategies. While different methods are employed in various FBA approaches, all share the common goal of *identifying the reinforcers maintaining challenging behavior*. In general, the approaches used in FBAs can be summarized as (a) indirect, (b) descriptive, and (c) experimental (Lloyd & Kennedy, 2014; O'Neill et al., 1997).

Indirect FBA methods use questionnaires, rating scales, and/or interviews that draw information from people who know the student well—educators and family members. These methods use people's familiarity with the student and their challenging behavior to identify antecedents that might predict the occurrence of behavior and possible maintaining reinforcers. Commonly used indirect instruments include the *Functional Analysis Interview* (O'Neill et al., 1997), *Functional Analysis Screening Tool* (Iwata et al., 2013), *Motivation Assessment Scale* (Durand & Crimmins, 1992), *Problem Behavior Questionnaire* (Lewis et al., 1994), *Questions About Behavioral Functioning Scale* (Vollmer & Matson, 1999), and *Student-Assisted Functional Assessment Interview* (Kern et al., 1994). Indirect methods are typically considered a starting point for identifying variables associated with challenging behaviors and developing testable hypotheses regarding their operant function. These methods are time and cost-efficient but rely on subjective impressions of a student's challenging behavior rather than more objective sources of information.

FBA approaches using *descriptive methods* directly observe challenging behavior in the settings where the behavior occurs. These methods typically assess the antecedents and consequences temporally surrounding challenging behavior to identify "triggers" and reinforcers associated with problem behavior. Typical descriptive assessments include antecedent-behavior-consequent (ABC) narrative or checklist recording (Bijou et al., 1968), scatter plots (Touchette et al., 1985), structural analyses (Borrero & Borrero, 2008; Wehby et al., 1995), or sequential analysis methods (Lloyd et al., 2013; Yoder & Symons, 2010). ABC and scatter plot techniques document when behaviors of concern occur, time of occurrence and events that preceded and followed the problem behaviors. Structural analyses present a student with an arranged situation (e.g., nonpreferred academic tasks) and assess whether it evokes challenging behavior. Sequential analyses are statistical techniques using observational data to identify statistically significant associations from ABC events.

FBA data collected using descriptive assessments allow for estimating the baseline levels of challenging behavior, assess associations between ABC events, and provide evidence for formulating hypotheses regarding variables maintaining behavior (i.e., consequences) and antecedents that predict the occurrence of a behavior. These methods are more objective than indirect assessments but require greater time and training on the part of educational staff. However, the information gained from these techniques is often needed to develop a substantive hypothesis regarding what reinforcers are maintaining challenging behavior. The information is often more reliable and valid than indirect approaches and also can be used to assess consistency between indirect and descriptive assessment results.

If the results of the indirect and/or descriptive FBAs are inconclusive, contradictory, or suggest multiple types of reinforcers associated with challenging behavior, *experimental analyses* are the next step. Experimental analyses allow direct, empirical identification of behavior-consequence functional relations and provide the most definitive FBA results (Carr & Durand, 1985; Iwata et al., 1982, 1994). This approach, in essence, conducts a series of discrete experiments to test response-reinforcer relations. Individual tests of reinforcement contingencies for hypothesized reinforcers are tested with the student to assess possible roles for adult or peer attention, escaping instructional demands, accessing preferred activities, and potentially any other type of reinforcer for challenging behavior (Hanley et al., 2003). The benefits of experimental analyses are the opportunity to directly test hypotheses about maintaining reinforcers and potentially clarifying unambiguous results. Limitations include the technical skills needed to arrange and conduct the assessments and the time and logistical arrangements associated with this approach (Lloyd & Kennedy, 2014).

Ultimately the goal of FBAs is to identify situations that predict challenging behaviors and identify the reinforcer(s) to maintain responding. Whether a single approach or multiple levels of assessments are necessary is ultimately determined by how clear and well justified the resulting hypotheses regarding the causes of challenging behavior. This information is critical for the development of effective behavioral interventions (Maggin et al., 2016; O'Neill et al., 1997).

Using FBAs to Develop Intensive Behavioral Supports

The findings from FBAs lead directly to the selection of intervention approaches. As an overview, intensive behavioral support strategies contain the following elements: (a) Target behaviors are selected to be decreased and others to be increased; (b) Interventions are based on the response-consequence (i.e., reinforcers) identified as maintaining challenging behavior; (c) Antecedent strategies are incorporated into the intervention package; (d) Behavioral support strategies are often packages that include multiple intervention components. Each of these elements will be discussed below in turn.

Intervention strategies should focus on both decreasing challenging behavior and increasing more socially desirable behavior (Didden et al., 2006). Although the former seems obvious, it is important to appreciate that effective interventions do not only decrease behavior but interventions also should build skills that replace challenging behaviors with more socially desirable responses. Whether the alternative behaviors are new forms of communication (e.g., requesting assistance) or improved academic performance (e.g., reading comprehension), the goal is to improve a student's ability to act in socially desirable ways. It also is important to make sure there is a link between the replacement responses and the reinforcers maintaining challenging behavior (e.g., requesting assistance with difficult tasks, rather than aggressing toward others to escape the task).

The foundation of intensive behavioral supports is linking the reinforcers maintaining challenging behavior to an alternative course of action for the student to achieve a similar means or obviate the need to engage in challenging behaviors in the first place (Carr et al., 1999). For example, if a student with behavioral disorders acting out in class is positively reinforced by teacher attention, then the teacher can (a) ignore the student's acting out, (b) prompt the student to engage in more appropriate behavior (e.g., raising her hand to ask a question), and (c) provide teacher attention for the appropriate behavior. Carr and Durand (1985) referred to this as *functional communication training* (FCT). FCT matches an appropriate response serving the same reinforcer function as the challenging behavior and places the problematic behavior on *extinction*. Extinction is an important element in reinforcement-based interventions because it eliminates the positive or negative reinforcer maintaining challenging behavior, so it is no longer "rewarded" (Lerman & Iwata, 1996).

Typically, extinction is used simultaneously with a *differential reinforcement* contingency to decrease challenging behavior and increase desirable behaviors (Catania, 2013). Differential reinforcement and extinction are a fundamental approach for FBA-derived interventions and are frequently embedded within intensive behavioral support strategies. For example, in an instance where a student with ASD screams when asked to solve mathematics problems, instructors might teach the student to request assistance making the task less difficult while ignoring screaming if it occurs. In this instance, a negatively reinforced behavior (i.e., screaming) is placed on extinction and asking for assistance is differentially negatively reinforced. A broad range of differential reinforcement and extinction programs can be developed based on the findings of an FBA (Trump et al., 2020).

Another form of reinforcement-based intervention is referred to as *noncontingent reinforcement* (NCR, Vollmer et al., 1993). With NCR, the reinforcer identified via the FBA is provided (in the case of positive reinforcers) or withdrawn (in the case of negative reinforcers) on a fixed- or variable-time interval in the absence of the challenging behavior (Phillips et al., 2017). For example, if a child's challenging behavior is occasionally positively reinforced by peer attention, providing that social attention more frequently can effectively reduce or eliminate the challenging behavior. NCR also is frequently used for automatically reinforced behaviors where alternative sources of stimulation matched to the hypothesized stimulation maintaining the stereotypical behavior are provided. For example, Kennedy and Souza (1995) provided a videogame to a young adult with multiple disabilities who would otherwise poke his eye for visual stimulation when he was "bored" (i.e., low levels of environmental stimulation were present). The videogame, but not music via headphones, when provided in an NCR intervention, reduced his self-injurious behavior.

Most intensive behavioral support strategies also include *antecedent interventions* (Kern et al., 2006). Antecedent strategies look at the environmental factors associated with challenging behavior during FBAs to identify contextual conditions that can be altered to reduce or eliminate challenging behaviors. These interventions typically fall into three categories: (a) *curricular revisions*, (b) *providing choices*, or (c) *building social competence*. Curricular revision includes strategies that reduce the difficulty of instructional tasks, focusing on instructional tasks that are preferred by the student, or reduce the duration of instructional sessions (Dunlap et al., 1991). In general, these approaches reduce the aspects of instruction that negatively reinforce challenging behavior. Choice-making entails allowing a student to select from a fixed menu of activities or tasks (Reutebuch et al., 2015). Such approaches may increase access to positively reinforced activities or tasks and allow the student to avoid those events that serve as negative reinforcers. Building social competence focuses on developing *social skills* that enable students to access social reinforcers from peers and adults that they might not otherwise be able to obtain (Kamps et al., 2017; Odom, 2019). In antecedent interventions, the emphasis is on changing environmental contexts before challenging behavior would otherwise occur.

Many interventions for severe challenging behavior are combined into a comprehensive support package (Bambara et al., 1994; Lewis et al., 2017). Sometimes FBAs identify a single, very clear instance that occasions severe challenging behaviors. For example, a particular type of loud noise or a specific type of instructional task elicits behavioral challenges and may only require the elimination of that event (e.g., as an antecedent intervention). In most cases, however, antecedent interventions, differential reinforcement in the form of FCT or NCR, and the teaching of alternative behaviors are used as a comprehensive intervention package. In addition, these packages are typically implemented in multiple locations, by multiple people, and at various times of the school day. Therefore, most intensive behavioral support plans require a clear explication of what interventions are used when, where, and by whom so that they comprehensively address a student's behavior support needs (O'Neill et al., 1997).

Setting the Course for Effective Inclusion

Intensive behavioral interventions have a strong evidence base of research demonstrating their efficacy (Lloyd & Kennedy, 2014). FBAs and the identification of the reinforcers maintaining challenging behavior and the antecedents that can occasion behavioral episodes drive the intervention approach. Effective interventions are tailored to the behavioral outcomes of an FBA and can be very specific (e.g., reading instruction or a noisy lunchroom) or contain multiple components and contexts based on the student's support needs. However, whatever form the behavioral support plan takes, it is implemented in the context of schoolwide support systems in multiple school and classroom settings requires a team of support personnel, is sustained with fidelity over time, and produces meaningful learning and social outcomes (Shuster et al., 2017; Horner & Sugai, 2015). In the final section of this chapter, we will discuss how to address these various support needs to effectively deliver intensive behavioral supports to students with severe challenging behavior.

Professional Development and Consultation

Ongoing professional development is critical for all educators. Training in current and emerging findings and techniques for educating students is part of professional licensure/certification requirements and required by federal legislation (ESSA, 2015; IDEA, 2004). As with other professional disciplines (e.g., nursing, psychology, or physical therapy), the continuous updating of practitioner's expertise is a central element in post-degree education (see Leko, Chapter 5 of this book). In regard to individuals who develop and/or implement intensive behavioral support plans, ongoing professional development in evidence-based practices includes behavioral assessment and intervention, but also instructional innovations (e.g., academic and social skills).

Although ongoing professional development is important for educators supporting students with severe challenging behaviors, the technical complexity of the assessment and intervention approaches needed in many cases require *consultation* (Anderson et al., 2013; Benazzi et al., 2006). Such consultation may come from personnel in the school building, school district, or an external expert hired to deliver specialized assistance. Depending on a school system's enrollment, internal resources may exist to provide FBA assistance and long-term support to those implementing the support plan, or, in some instances, the school system may need to contract with external experts in FBA and intensive behavioral supports. Increasingly, the most knowledgeable experts regarding FBA and associated support approaches hold graduate degrees in behavior analysis and are certified by the Behavior Analysis Certification Board (BAC Board, 2014; Shook & Favell, 2008). These individuals may have backgrounds in educational psychology, psychology, special education or social work, but all are trained in the specifics of FBAs and behavioral support plans.

Ultimately, *intensive behavioral supports require a range of professional expertise and a team-based approach* for effective and sustainable intervention delivery (see below). When an individual is providing behavior-analytic support, it is critical that they have demonstrated expertise in a range of FBA approaches, conceptual knowledge of behavioral mechanisms, and experience in developing complex intervention plans. It also is important that the person have training and experience in working with interdisciplinary teams. Although the technical knowledge relating to conducting and interpreting FBAs is highly specialized, the more professional development that educators have in behavioral supports, the more likely there will be to contribute to the assessment process and deliver effective interventions (Anderson et al., 2013; Benazzi et al., 2006).

Databased Decision Making

Just as the outcomes of FBAs drive the content and development of interventions, databased decision making is the foundation for effective and sustained intervention success. Objective systems for assessment of salient behavioral outcomes allow support team members to make informed judgments regarding the effectiveness of intensive interventions and to plan for future behavioral support efforts (Lindsley, 1990). These systems are based on direct measurement of challenging behavior, academic performance, and social competence. Not only do data allow for better-informed planning, but they also help team members have a consistent reference point for how a student is succeeding.

Databased decision making has five core features that are continuous and iterative in their use: (a) goals, (b) measurement systems, (c) data collection, (d) data analysis, and (e) planning (see Table 18.2). First, team members need to identify the goals of intensive intervention. The criterion for intervention needs to be specified in an objective, measurable way that can be used as an index of success. Similarly, academic and social outcomes need to be identified and goals created. Goals are typically specified as a quantitative index of student performance that can be directly measured (e.g., frequency per unit time, percentage correct, or duration of occurrence; see Cook et al., 2007). For example, a student's goals may include a reduction in aggression to one occurrence per week, 90% of sight words read correctly, or 45 min of social interaction per day with peers without disabilities. For each goal identified in the behavioral support plan, a systematic measurement system needs to be identified. Such systems need to directly record observed behavior (e.g., occurrence of aggression) or byproducts of behavior (e.g., software-generated reading scores). The measures also need to be reliable and valid assessments of student performance. A wide range of measurement approaches are available and include paper-and-pencil or tablet/smartphone apps that can measure the duration, frequency, and other relevant aspects of student performance (Kennedy, 2005).

The third feature of databased decision-making is data collection. Using the goals and measurement systems just noted, team members need to identify when, where, how often, and by whom data will

Table 18.2 Core Features of Databased Decision Making

Core Feature	*Purpose*
Goals	*Identify the outcomes to be changed by the intervention.* What challenging behaviors will be decreased? What forms of communication will be increased? What types of academic gains will be realized? What forms of social skills will be increased? What level of physical and social inclusion will be increased?
Measurement Systems	*Identify how the goals will be quantified and documented.* What type of measurement system will be used for each goal? What dimensional quantities of performance will be selected to capture behavior change? How will observers document that the measurement system is reliable?
Data Collection	*Identify how data will be obtained for analysis.* When will data be collected? How often will the information be obtained? How long will observations or data collection last? Who will be responsible for obtaining the information?
Data Analysis	*Identify how the data will be summarized and interpreted.* Which outcomes will be included in the analysis? Will the data be summarized in tables and/or graphic displays? What approaches will be taken to interpret the data? Who will be responsible for conducting and sharing the results of the data analysis?
Planning	*Identify how decisions will be made regarding intervention effectiveness.* Who will be involved in the decision-making process? How often will the data be reviewed and changes considered? When the data are reviewed, will the intervention be maintained, modified, or terminated?

be collected on student performance. The focus should be on sampling enough of the student's behavior in relevant settings to provide a meaningful picture of the person's behavior (Cooper et al., 2020). Once the goals, measures, and data collection schedules are defined and information collected, team members need to follow a process for analyzing the data. Typically, in behavior-analytic interventions, educators graph the data so they can visually inspect student outcomes and assess trends and patterns in the student's behavior (Alberto & Troutman, 2013). There are three decision choices that need to be made when performance data are evaluated: Should the intervention be maintained (e.g., it is continuing to have the intended effect on a particular behavior), modified (e.g., changes in the intervention are necessary to adapt to changing circumstances or student performance), or terminated (e.g., the intervention has met its goal and new goals need to be developed)? The results of this process, which the support team needs to agree upon, lead to decisions about support system planning. Is there reasonable progress across the goals? Are some goals improving more than others? Have some goals been accomplished and new objectives identified?

An example of this process can be illustrated with an FBA for a student with behavioral disorders noted earlier in this chapter. The student's acting out (i.e., rudely commenting on other students) was positively reinforced by the teacher's attention it occasioned (e.g., "Shawna, please be quiet"). The classroom situations in which this happened could be identified and an FCT intervention developed. In this case, the primary intervention was reminding the student to engage in appropriate behaviors (e.g., raising her hand to ask a question), ignoring outbursts, and positively engaging the student when she acted appropriately. As data are collected on the frequency of outbursts and appropriate engagement, the support team can assess the effectiveness of the intervention. In this instance, because challenging behavior is being placed on extinction (i.e., no teacher attention), educators should expect a short period in which the outbursts will increase and then subside as the appropriate behavior increases and is positively reinforced by teacher praise. If this pattern is reflected in the data, then the team should continue the intervention and assess whether the outbursts continue to decrease and appropriate behaviors increase. If this is, indeed, the case, team members may choose to continue the intervention or expand it to focus on increasing the student's social competence in group contexts.

In some instances, behavioral support plans may need to be modified to meet unexpected effects on student performance. We previously examined a student with ASD whose behavior was negatively reinforced by having mathematics instruction stopped when he screamed. In this instance, the screaming was placed on extinction (i.e., ignored) and asking for assistance was prompted. When the intervention was implemented, the screaming increased, as did asking for assistance. Initially, the team members agreed to persist with the intervention to see if the screaming would decrease and asking for help would replace the challenging behavior. However, after several weeks the screaming and asking for assistance continued. In consultation with a behavior analyst working with the school district, the team arrived at the conclusion that the mathematics problems were too difficult for the student and even when he was asking for assistance, the problems were beyond his developmental level and so he continued to try to escape by screaming. The decision was then arrived at to modify the intervention by re-assessing the student's mathematics performance and adjust his lessons to focus on problems he knew how to solve. Once implemented, he stopped screaming and solved the easier mathematics problems. The team, following the data, then decided to gradually increase the difficulty of the mathematics problems and actively prompt the student to request assistance. This modified intervention was implemented and met with continued success for the student (and his teachers).

The use of data provides objective information for support providers to assess and make team decisions about the continuation, changing, or termination of the components of those programs. The process is ongoing and iterative and adjusts for both the occurrence of challenging behavior and the developing academic and social needs of the student. Importantly, in addition to the dynamic and ongoing nature of support plans, the process, its implementation, and evaluation is a team-based effort. Therefore, in the next section, we will discuss support teams and how they manage intensive behavioral support programs.

Support as a Team-Based Effort

Supporting a student with severe challenging behavior should never be the responsibility of a single individual. The needs of students receiving intensive behavioral supports, the technical complexity of best-practices, and multiple intervention settings require a school-wide system of support (Eber et al., 2002). Typically, a support team is comprised of a school administrator, special education personnel, general education personnel, behavior specialist, student advocate, and possibly other areas of expertise (e.g., health professionals). From this group, a team leader should be identified as the coordinator of the team-based efforts. Support teams include the perspective of multiple individuals from various school settings and various curricular and instructional foci. Together they can provide a comprehensive intervention context and share professional expertise and perspectives.

Coordination among team members is an essential part of delivering an effective behavioral support program (Bradshaw, 2013; Dowd-Eagle & Eagle, 2014). The team leader takes the lead in coordinating team activities and ensures that (a) all members are aware of the current support plan elements, (b) it is being implemented across settings as identified by the support plan, and (c) the elements of the plan are being delivered with fidelity (Sanetti & Kratochwill, 2007). Regularly scheduled meetings and sharing of data collected to evaluate challenging behavior, academic performance, and social development are key to delivering support plans with integrity and adjusting those plans as a student's support needs change.

As an example, consider the FCT intervention for Shawna noted previously in this chapter. The intervention was implemented in three different classroom contexts (English, mathematics, and special education resource room). After several weeks of support delivery, the data indicated challenging behavior had increased and then decreased in two classrooms (mathematics and special education resource room) but had remained at consistent levels in the English class. At a regularly scheduled team meeting, it was decided that the team leader and an assistant principal would observe the English and mathematics classes to assess how the intervention was being implemented. Observations using a fidelity intervention checklist (e.g., Anderson et al., 2013) suggested that the intervention was not correctly implemented in the English class but was implemented with high fidelity in the mathematics class. As a follow-up, the assistant principal and mathematics teachers agreed to assist and mentor the English teacher in the implementation of the FCT intervention components. With changes in the intervention delivery, Shawna's challenging behavior in the English class was reduced to levels similar to the other two intervention contexts.

Following evidence-based practices, as noted earlier in this chapter, intensive behavioral supports (i.e., Tier 3 interventions) occur within a larger sphere of school-wide behavioral supports. In the case of Tier 3 interventions, the support team helps identify the need for intensive behavioral supports, oversees the conduct of FBAs and other diagnostic assessments, implements the intervention, and monitors its effectiveness (Anderson et al., 2013). While Tier 3 interventions are the most intensive level of a school's multi-tiered intervention systems, the movement to less intensive supports (i.e., Tier 1 or 2) is the underlying goal of intensive behavioral supports.

Outcomes Drive Intervention Goals

As just noted, ultimately, it is the lessening of behavioral support intensity that is a focal goal of Tier 3 interventions. However, the outcomes support teams seek to achieve, as noted previously in this chapter, are broader than reductions in challenging behaviors. Intervention outcomes should also focus on improved academic performance, greater inclusion in school and community settings, and building a student's social competence. The results of an FBA provide multiple opportunities for focusing on skill-building as a means of achieving reductions in challenging behavior (e.g., FCT; Carr et al., 1999). The functions of behavior, whether they are driven by social interaction, changes in curricular design, or reducing/avoiding specific contexts, should emphasize the broader outcomes of receiving special education supports. Thus, all intensive support interventions should include clear benchmarks for accessing the general education curriculum and building social competence for a student (Dunlap et al., 2006; Horner & Sugai, 2015).

Summary

Intensive behavioral supports are designed for students with the most severe challenging behavior. Key elements in this type of behavioral technology include the use of FBAs to identify the reason(s) a student engages in challenging behavior. This information is then used to develop a comprehensive support system that focuses on increasing a student's inclusion at school and community and academic skills while simultaneously decreasing their challenging behaviors. These support systems are developed by an interdisciplinary team working across a range of settings and are focused on data-based decision making and achieving a range of positive outcomes for the student. These key elements have proven very successful and can help educators enable the success of students with even the most severe challenging behavior in school and community contexts.

References

Alberto, P., & Troutman, A. C. (2013). *Applied behavior analysis for teachers* (9th ed.). Pearson.

Anderson, C. M., Horner, R. H., Rodriguez, B. J., & Stiller, B. (2013). Building systems for successful implementation of function-based support in schools. *International Journal of School and Educational Psychology, 1*(3), 141–153. doi.10.1080/21683603.2013.804798

Anderson, C. M., Lewis-Palmer, T., Todd, A., Horner, R., Sugai, G., & Sampson, N. (2008). *Individual student systems evaluation tool.* Educational and Community Supports, University of Oregon.

Anderson, C. M., & Scott, T. M. (2009). Implementing function-based support within schoolwide positive behavior support. In W. Sailor, G. Dunlap, G. Sugai, & R. H. Horner (Eds.), *Handbook of positive behavior support.* (pp. 705–728). Springer Publishing Co.

Behavior Analyst Certification Board. (2014). *Professional and ethical compliance code for behavior analysts.* Author.

Baer, D. M., Wolf, M. M., & Risley, T. R. (1987). Some still-current dimensions of applied behavior analysis. *Journal of Applied Behavior Analysis, 20*(4), 3123–3327. doi.10.1901/jaba.1987.20-313

Bambara, L. M., Mitchell-Kvacky, N. A., & Iacobelli, S. (1994). Positive behavioral support for students with severe disabilities: An emerging multicomponent approach for addressing challenging behaviors. *School Psychology Review, 23*(2), 263–278.

Benazzi, L., Horner, R. H., & Good, R. H. (2006). Effects of behavior support team composition on the technical adequacy and contextual fit of behavior support plans. *Journal of Special Education, 40*(3), 160–170. doi.10.1177/00224669060400030401

Bijou, S. W., Peterson, R. F., & Ault, M. H. (1968). A method to integrate descriptive and experimental field studies at the level of data and empirical concepts. *Journal of Applied Behavior Analysis, 1*(2), 175–191. doi: 10.1901/jaba.1968.1-175

Borrero, C. S. W., & Borrero, J. C. (2008). Descriptive and experimental analyses of potential precursors to problem behavior. *Journal of Applied Behavior Analysis, 41*(1), 83–96. doi.10.1901/jaba.2008.41-83

Bradshaw, C. P. (2013). Preventing bullying through positive behavioral interventions and supports (PBIS): A multitiered approach to prevention and integration. *Theory Into Practice, 52*(4), 288–295. doi.10.1080/00405841.2013.829732

Browder, D. M., & Spooner, F. (2014). *More language arts, math, and science for students with severe disabilities.* Paul H. Brookes Publishing Co.

Carr, E. G. (1977). The motivation of self-injurious behavior: A review of some hypotheses. *Psychological Bulletin, 84*(4), 800–816. doi.10.1037/0033-2909.84.4.800

Carr, E. G., & Durand, V. M. (1985). Reducing behavior problems through functional communication training. *Journal of Applied Behavior Analysis, 18*(2), 111–126. doi.10.1901/jaba.1985.18-111

Carr, E. G., Horner R. H., Turnbull A. P., Marquis J. G., Magito-McLaughlin D., McAtee M. L. & Doolabh A. (1999). *Positive behavior support for people with developmental disabilities: A research synthesis.* American Association on Mental Retardation Monograph Series.

Catania, A. C. (2013). *Learning* (5th ed.). Sloan Publishing.

Cook, C. R., Crews, S. D., Wright, D. B., Mayer, G. R., Gale, B., Kraemer, B., & Gresham, F. M. (2007). Establishing and evaluating the substantive adequacy of positive behavioral support plans. *Journal of Behavioral Education, 16*(2), 191–206. doi.10.1007/s10864-006-9024-8

Cooper, J. O., Heron, T. E., & Heward, W. L. (2020). *Applied behavior analysis* (3rd ed.). Pearson Publishing.

Crosland, K., & Dunlap, G. (2012). Effective strategies for the inclusion of children with autism in general education classrooms. *Behavior Modification, 36*(30), 251–269. doi.10.1177/0145445512442682

Didden R., Korzilius H., van Oorsouw W., & Sturmey P. (2006). Behavioral treatment of challenging behaviors in individuals with mild mental retardation: Meta-analysis of single-subject research. *American Journal of Mental Retardation, 111*(4), 290–298. doi.10.1352/0895-8017(2006)111[290:BTOCBI]2.0.CO;2

Division for Early Childhood. (2017). *Position statement on challenging behavior and young children.* Council for Exceptional Children.

Dowd-Eagle, S., & Eagle, J. (2014). Team-based school consultation. In W. P. Erchul & S. M. Sheridan (Eds.), *Handbook of research in school consultation* (2nd ed., pp. 450–472). Routledge.

Dunlap, G., Kern-Dunlap, L., Clarke, S., & Robbins, F. R. (1991). Functional assessment, curricular revision, and severe behavior problems. *Journal of Applied Behavior Analysis, 24*(2), 387–397. doi.10.1901/jaba.1991.24-387

Dunlap, G., Strain, P. S., Fox, L., Carta, J. J., Conroy, M., Smith, B. J., Kern, L., Hemmeter, M. L., Timm, M. A., Mccart, A., Sailor, W., Markey, U., Markey, D. J., Lardieri, S., & Sowell, C. (2006). Prevention and intervention with young children's challenging behavior: Perspectives regarding current knowledge. *Behavioral Disorders, 32*(1), 29–45. doi.10.1177/019874290603200103

Durand, V. M., & Crimmins, D. B. (1992). *The motivation assessment scale administrative guide.* Monaco & Associates.

Eber, L., Sugai, G., Smith, C. R., & Scott, T. M. (2002). Wraparound and positive behavioral interventions and supports in the schools. *Journal of Emotional and Behavioral Disorders, 10*(3), 171–180. doi.10.1177/106342 66020100030501

Every Student Succeeds Act of 2015. 20 U.S.C.A. § 6301.

Gilmour, A. F., Fuchs, D., & Wehby, J. H. (2019). Are students with disabilities accessing the curriculum? A meta-analysis of the reading achievement gap between students with and without disabilities. *Exceptional Children, 85*(3), 329–346. doi.10.1177/0014402918795830c

Hanley, G. P., Iwata, B. A., & McCord, B. E. (2003). Functional analysis of behavior problem: A review. *Journal of Applied Behavior Analysis, 36*(2), 147–185. doi.10.1901/jaba.2003.36-147

Horner, R. H., & Sugai, G. (2015). School-wide PBIS: An example of applied behavior analysis implemented at a scale of social importance. *Behavior Analysis in Practice, 8*(1), 80–85. doi.10.1007/s40617-015-0045-4

Individuals with Disabilities Education Improvement Act of 2004, PL 108-466, 20 U. S. C. §1400, H. R. 1350.

Iwata, B. A., DeLeon, I. G., & Roscoe, E. M. (2013). Reliability and validity of the functional analysis screening tool. *Journal of Applied Behavior Analysis, 46*(1), 271–284. doi.10.1002/jaba.31

Iwata, B. A., Dorsey, M. F., Slifer, K. J., Bauman, K. E., & Richman, G. S. (1982, 1994). Toward a functional analysis of self-injury. *Analysis and Intervention in Developmental Disabilities, 2*(1), 3–20. Reprinted in the *Journal of Applied Behavior Analysis, 27*(1), 197-209. doi.10.1016/0270-4684(82)90003-9

Kamps, D. M., Mason, R., & Heitzman-Powell, L. (2017). Peer mediation interventions to improve social and communication skills for children and youth with autism spectrum disorders. In J. Leaf (Ed.), *Handbook of social skills and autism spectrum disorder.* Autism and Child Psychopathology Series. Springer.

Kennedy, C. H. (2005). *Single-case designs for educational research.* Prentice Hall.

Kennedy, C. H., & Souza, G. (1995). Functional analysis and treatment of eye-poking. *Journal of Applied Behavior Analysis, 28*(1), 27–37. doi.10.1901/jaba.1995.28-27

Kern, L., Dunlap, G., Clarke, S., & Childs, K. E. (1994). Student-assisted functional assessment interview. *Diagnostique, 19*, 29–39. doi.10.1177/073724779401900203

Kern, L., Sokol, N. G., & Dunlap, G. (2006). Assessment of antecedent influences on challenging behavior. In J. K. Luiselli (Ed.), *Antecedent intervention: Recent developments in community focused behavior support* (pp. 53–71). Paul H. Brookes Publishing.

Lamport, M. A., Graves, L., & Ward, A. (2012). Special needs students in inclusive classrooms: The impact of social interaction on educational outcomes for learners with emotional and behavioral disabilities. *European Journal of Business and Social Sciences, 1*(1), 54–69.

Lane, K. L., Carter, E. W., Pierson, M. R., & Glaeser, B. C. (2006). Academic, social, and behavioral characteristics of high school students with emotional disturbances or learning disabilities. *Journal of Emotional and Behavioral Disorders, 14*(2), 108–117. doi.10.1177/10634266060140020101

Lerman, D. C., & Iwata, B. A. (1996). Developing a technology for the use of operant extinction in clinical settings: An examination of basic and applied research. *Journal of Applied Behavior Analysis, 29*(3), 345–382. doi.10.1901/jaba.1996.29-345

Lewis, T. J., McIntosh, K., Simonsen, B., Mitchell, B. S., & Hatton, H. L. (2017). Schoolwide systems of positive behavior support: Implications for students at risk and with emotional/behavioral disorders. *AERA Open*. doi.10.1177/2332858417711428

Lewis, T. J., Scott, T., & Sugai, G. (1994). The problem behavior questionnaire: A teacher-based assessment instrument to develop functional hypotheses of problem behavior in general education classrooms. *Diagnostique, 19*(2-3), 103–115. doi.10.1177/073724779401900207

Lindsley, O. R. (1990). Precision teaching: By teachers for children. *TEACHING Exceptional Children, 22*(1), 10–15.

Lloyd, B. P., Bruhn, A. L., Sutherland, K. S., & Bradshaw, C. P. (2019). Progress and priorities in research to improve outcomes for students with or at risk for emotional and behavioral disorders. *Behavior Disorders, 44*(1), 85–96. doi.10.1177/019874291808485

Lloyd, B. P., & Kennedy, C. H. (2014). Assessment and treatment of challenging behavior in individuals with intellectual disabilities: A research review. *Journal of Applied Research in Intellectual Disabilities, 27*(3), 187–199. doi.10.1111/jar.12089

Lloyd, B. P., Kennedy, C. H., & Yoder, P. J. (2013). Quantifying contingent relations from observation data: Transitional probability comparisons vs. Yule's Q. *Journal of Applied Behavior Analysis, 46*(2), 479–497. doi.10.1002/jaba.45

Maggin, D. M., Wehby, J. H., Farmer, T. W., & Brooks, D. S. (2016). Intensive interventions for students with emotional and behavioral disorders: Issues, theory, and future directions. *Journal of Emotional and Behavioral Disorders, 24*(3), 127–137. doi.10.1177/1063426616661498

McLeskey, J., Waldron, N. L., Spooner, F., & Algozzine, B. (2014). What are effective inclusive schools and why are they important? In J. McLeskey, N. L. Waldron, F. Spooner, & B. Algozzine. (Eds.), *Handbook of effective inclusive schools* (pp. 13–26). Routledge.

National Research Council and Institute of Medicine (2009). Preventing mental, emotional, and behavioral disorders among young people: Progress and possibilities. In M. E. O'Connell, T. Boat, & K. E. Warner (Eds.), *Committee on the prevention of mental disorders and substance abuse among children, youth, and young adults: Research advances and promising interventions*. The National Academics Press.

Odom, S. L. (2019). Peer-based Interventions for children and youth with autism spectrum disorder: History and effects. *School Psychology Review, 48*(2), 170–176.

O'Neill, R. E., Horner, R. H., Albin, R. W., Sprague, J. R., Storey, K., & Newton, J. S. (1997). *Functional assessment and program development for problem behavior* (2nd ed.). Brooks/Cole.

Phillips, C. L., Iannaccone, J. A., Rooker, G. W., & Hagopian, L. P. (2017). Noncontingent reinforcement for the treatment of severe problem behavior: An analysis of 27 consecutive applications. *Journal of Applied Behavior Analysis, 50*(2), 357–376. doi.10.1002/jaba.376

Reutebuch, C. K., El Zein, F., & Roberts, G. J. (2015). A systematic review of the effects of choice on academic outcomes for students with autism spectrum disorder. *Research in Autism Spectrum Disorders, 20*(4), 1–16. doi.10.1016/j.rasd.2015.08.002

Sanetti, L. M. H., & Kratochwill, T. R. (2007). Treatment integrity in behavioral consultation: Measurement, promotion, and outcomes. *International Journal of Behavioral Consultation and Therapy, 4*(1), 95. doi.10.1037/h0100835

Shuster, B. C., Gustafson, J. R., Jenkins, A. B., Lloyd, B. P., Carter, E. W., & Bernstein, C. F. (2017). Including students with disabilities in positive behavioral interventions and supports: Experiences and perspectives of special educators. *Journal of Positive Behavior Interventions, 19*(3), 143–157. doi.10.1177/1098300716675734

Shook, G. L., & Favell, J. E. (2008). The Behavior Analyst Certification Board and the profession of behavior analysis. *Behavior Analysis in Practice, 1*(1), 44–48. doi.10.1007/BF03391720

Simpson, R. L. (2004). Inclusion of students with behavior disorders in general education settings: Research and measurement issues. *Behavioral Disorders, 30*(2), 19–31. doi.10.1177/001440290407000201

Touchette, P. E., MacDonald, R. F., & Langer, S. N. (1985). A scatter plot for identifying stimulus control of problem behavior. *Journal of Applied Behavior Analysis, 18*(4), 343–351. doi.10.1901/jaba.1985.18-343

Trump, C. E., Ayres, K. M., Quinland, K. K., & Zabala, K. A. (2020). Differential reinforcement without extinction: A review of the literature. *Behavior Analysis: Research and Practice, 20*(2), 94–107. doi.10.1037/bar0000169

Vollmer, T. R., Iwata, B. A., Zarcone, J. R., Smith, R. G., & Mazaleski, J. L. (1993). The role of attention in the treatment of attention-maintained self-injurious behavior: Noncontingent reinforcement and differential reinforcement of other behavior. *Journal of Applied Behavior Analysis, 26*(1), 9–21. doi.10.1901/jaba.1993.26-143

Vollmer, T. R., & Matson, J. L. (1999). *Questions about behavioral functioning manual.* Scientific Publishers.

Wehby, J., Symons, F. J., & Shores, R. E. (1995). A descriptive analysis of aggressive behavior in classrooms for children with emotional and behavioral disorders. *Behavioral Disorders, 20*(2), 87–105. doi.10.1177/019874299502000207

Yoder, P., & Symons, F. (2010). *Observational measurement of behavior.* Springer.

19

The Potential for Developing and Supporting Self-Determination in Early Childhood and Elementary Classrooms

Karrie A. Shogren[1], Kathleen N. Zimmerman[1], and Jessica R. Toste[2]

UNIVERSITY OF KANSAS

THE UNIVERSITY OF TEXAS AT AUSTIN

Setting the Stage: What is Self-Determination and Why is it Important

What is Self-Determination?

In early childhood and elementary education, researchers and practitioners target specific skills and abilities that are associated with self-determination (e.g., choice-making, self-monitoring/management, self-regulation, self-awareness); however, these skills and abilities are typically targeted in isolation, without a clear focus on how they fit together and relate to the development of self-determination across the life course. This differs from secondary education, where a focus on promoting self-determination is often used to integrate instruction in these skills and abilities across academic, social-emotional, and transition domains (Shogren et al., 2016). While researchers have emphasized the importance of promoting the development of self-determination across the life course, beginning in early childhood and elementary education (Wehmeyer et al., 2017), the primary focus in assessment and intervention research has been secondary education. For these reasons, there is a need for the expansion of self-determination assessment and instruction to create a unified approach to promoting self-determination across the life course (Shogren & Wittenburg, in press). This has the potential to enhance not only early childhood and elementary outcomes but also secondary and post-school outcomes by linking instruction and supports throughout early childhood, elementary, and secondary education. This chapter will bring together terminology in early childhood, elementary, and secondary education related to promoting motivation and self-determination, creating a framework for practice that emphasizes a life course perspective on building self-determination.

The term self-determination is used across disciplines and fields. In education, self-determination is understood to be a set of skills and abilities that can be fostered across the life course, from early childhood throughout adulthood, with meaningful opportunities coupled with effective supports and

DOI: 10.4324/9781003043874-19

instruction in inclusive environments. Causal Agency Theory, a widely adopted theory of self-determination in the disability field, defines self-determination as a "dispositional characteristic manifested as acting as the causal agent in one's life" (Shogren et al., 2015, p. 258). Causal agents are people who have the skills, abilities, and supports to set and work towards goals that they value in their lives, using goal setting, problem solving, and self-regulatory skills. Promoting self-determination through interventions and supports is recognized as best practice, particularly in secondary education and transition services (National Technical Assistance Center on Transition, 2017). This is because of the documented association between self-determination and in-school and post-school outcomes for young adults with disabilities (Shogren & Shaw, 2016; Shogren et al., 2012, 2015, 2019). Although not as widely researched but often acknowledged by researchers in the field, building the foundation for self-determination begins in early childhood and elementary education and there is a critical need for attention during this developmental period to enhancing self-determination (Wehmeyer et al., 2017).

Self-determination first received attention in the disability field in the 1990s (Shogren & Ward, 2018), largely because of the disability rights movement and the push by advocates with disabilities for "nothing about us without us" (Charlton, 2000). This led to the recognition that education and other disability support systems often failed to promote self-determination and that people with disabilities were entitled to supports that empowered them to act as casual agents who set and went after goals aligned with their visions and values for their lives (Wehmeyer, Bersani et al., 2000). Between 1990 and 1994, the U.S. Department of Education's Office of Special Education Programs funded 26 model demonstration projects to develop methods, materials, and strategies to promote the self-determination of youth and young adults with disabilities during the transition from school to post-school environments (Sands & Wehmeyer, 1996; Ward, 1996). These efforts led to an array of effective practices for use in secondary education and transition, including some that are still used today. However, there is a critical and compelling need to begin efforts to promote self-determination in early childhood and elementary environments. That is the focus of this chapter.

Causal Agency Theory

Given the emphasis on self-determination across research, policy, and practice in the disability and education fields, there has not always been consistency in the adoption of a clear theoretical framework to guide self-determination assessment and intervention. To address these issues and ensure that there was a clear theoretical framework to guide assessment and intervention across the life course, Causal Agency Theory was introduced (Shogren et al., 2015).

Causal Agency Theory defines self-determination as a psychological construct within the organizing structure of theories of human agentic behavior (Shogren et al., 2017). Agentic theories view humans as active contributors to, or agents of, their behavior. An agentic person engages in self-regulated and goal-directed action using a continually evolving and actively monitored self-system that gives rise to a sense of personal agency, or the agentic self. Unlike stimulus–response accounts of behavior, agentic action is directed toward self-regulated goals and triggered by contexts that provide supports and opportunities across the life course (Little et al., 2002). Causal Agency Theory emphasizes the role of identifying goals, developing plans to achieve goals, self-regulating behavior to progress towards goals, and flexibly adjusting behavior using self-advocacy skills in response to changing environmental demands. These processes develop over the life course, and the demands of early childhood environments will be different from secondary and post-school environments. However, skills and abilities associated with self-determination can be fostered in each of these environments, with individualized supports.

Causal Agency Theory recognizes the critical role of supportive environments in fostering these abilities. To promote self-determined learning, a critical step for educators, regardless of the age of students there are teaching, is to first consider how the environment can enhance the development of self-determination skills (Shogren et al., 2014). Creating autonomy-supportive learning

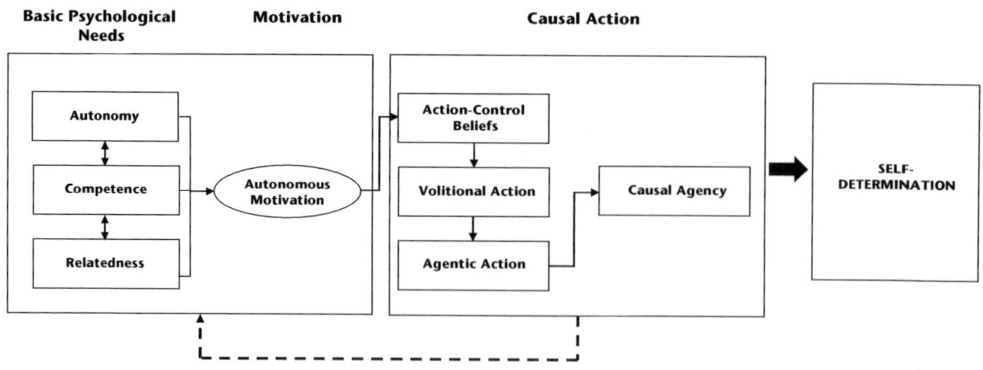

Figure 19.1 The Development of Self-Determination (reprinted with permission from Shogren, 2018)

environments can maximize student involvement and self-direction and minimize teacher-controlled actions. Autonomy-supportive learning environments can foster motivation and address student's basic psychological needs for autonomy, relatedness and competence (Ryan, 2012), creating contexts that enable growth in self-determination abilities, as shown in Figure 19.1.

Causal Agency Theory emphasizes that self-determination skills can be fostered in all people with instruction, opportunities, and supports. However, the development of self-determination will be influenced by the supports available for its development across the life course. It also is important to note, especially when considering the application of self-determination in early childhood and for students with complex support needs, that self-determination is not equivalent to other terms or outcomes such as independence. A causal agent acts or causes things to happen in their lives; they may not necessarily make these things happen independently (e.g., delegating a decision or activities to someone else can still be self-determined, so long as the person is fully engaged in making that choice). Further, supports for self-determination must be provided in ways that are meaningful for students, based on their communication preferences and needs. Causal agency, therefore, emphasizes that self-determined people engage in actions to *cause* an effect to *accomplish* a *specific goal*. Self-determined actions enable a person to move toward personally valued goals, but people do not need to independently perform each of the actions necessary to achieve that goal and instead can and should recruit and utilize supports so long as they are self-directing the process. This may look different across the life course, but engaging elementary students in this process is possible with appropriate supports and interventions in supportive contexts.

Essential Characteristics of Self-determined Actions

Causal Agency Theory elaborates on the characteristics that define self-determined actions, as well as the skills and attitudes that contribute to the development of self-determination. This framework can guide instruction and support across the life course. Table 19.1 provides an overview of the relationship between the three essential characteristics defined by Causal Agency Theory—volitional action, agentic action, and action-control beliefs—and associated component constructs and skills that all have application and foundations in early childhood and elementary school settings.

Volitional Action

Self-determined people act volitionally, which means that they use choice-making, decision-making, goal-setting, problem-solving, and planning skills to identify what they want in their life

Table 19.1 Component Elements of Causal Agency Theory (reprinted with permission from Shogren, 2018)

Essential Characteristics	*Component Constructs*	*Component Elements*
Volitional Action	AutonomySelf-Initiation	• Choice-making skills • Decision-making skills • Goal-setting skills • Problem solving skills • Planning skills
Agentic Action	Self-RegulationSelf-DirectionPathways Thinking	• Self-regulation • Goal attainment skills • Problem solving skills • Self-advocacy skills
Action-Control Beliefs	Psychological EmpowermentSelf-RealizationControl expectancy	• Self-awareness • Self-knowledge

(i.e., set goals based on personal interests, preferences, and values). As such, acting volitionally involves making conscious choices that reflect one's preferences and interests. Conscious choices are intentionally conceived, deliberate acts that occur without direct external influence, although one's choices and preferences are influenced by previous opportunities and experiences and cultural values. Volitional actions are therefore defined in Causal Agency Theory as being self-initiated and contributing to greater autonomy (component constructs associated with volitional action, as shown in Table 19.1). Essentially, volitional actions involve the initiation and activation of a person's ability to identify personally meaningful goals based on interests, preferences, and options—initiating the process of making things happen in one's life.

Agentic Action

Self-determined people also act agentically, meaning that they have the skills and abilities to identify and use pathways to self-regulated actions toward their goals. When acting agentically, people use self-regulation, goal attainment, problem-solving, and self-advocacy skills. The use of these skills leads to the use of self-direction and pathways thinking. People who use pathways thinking can identify multiple ways to achieve their goals, and when they encounter barriers, use problem-solving and decision-making skills to find other pathways to attain their goal. In doing so, people self-regulate their behavior, directing actions that guide them to a specific end. The identification of pathways, or pathways thinking, is a proactive, purposive process and leads to the capacity to sustain action toward a goal.

Action-Control Beliefs

Self-determined people, in applying volitional and agentic actions over the lifespan, develop action-control beliefs. Action control beliefs contribute to a person feeling that they have what it takes to attain their goals. People with adaptive action control beliefs have self-awareness and self-knowledge that they use to inform their selection of goals and the actions that they take to achieve their goals. They perceive a link between their actions and the outcomes they experience and develop a sense of control expectancy (i.e., that their environment will be responsive to their actions) and psychological empowerment (i.e., feeling empowered to take steps toward their goals). People with adaptive action control beliefs also experience self-realization. They recognize the value of understanding themselves and their support needs and aligning their actions toward that understanding.

Development of and Supports for Self-Determination across the Life Course

Evidence from a variety of perspectives converges to support the notion that fostering human agentic behavior is associated with positive outcomes (Geldhof et al., 2017; Reeve et al., 2008). Causal Agency Theory provides clear connections to classroom practices that can promote and enhance students' potential to become self-determined. For example, the Causal Agency Theory has led to assessment and intervention practices that can be used across the life course, like the *Self-Determined Learning Model of Instruction* (SDLMI; Shogren et al., 2018; Wehmeyer, Palmer et al., 2000), which will be described in later sections. Further, Causal Agency Theory highlights the importance of structuring classrooms to be autonomy-supportive, fostering motivation, engaging, and the drive for autonomy, relatedness and competence (Ryan, 2012), which builds to volitional and agentic action as well as action control beliefs, ultimately leading to greater self-determination (see Figure 19.1).

There is much that can be done throughout early childhood, ranging from creating autonomy-supportive classrooms to creating opportunities for the development of the essential characteristics of self-determination. However, more work is needed that addresses how to plan throughout early childhood to build to later self-determination and incorporate developmental considerations into supports and instructional opportunities. Educators planning for self-determination across the life course can focus on how to: (a) teach self-determination skills, (b) create opportunities for students to use these skills across contexts, and (c) provide individualized supports necessary to enable all students to express and use self-determination abilities. Having opportunities to respond to challenges in one's environment in developmentally appropriate ways creates a natural opportunity for the use of volitional and agentic actions, supporting the development of action control beliefs throughout childhood and into adolescence.

What Do We Know Based on Research?

Why Self-Determination?

Prior to describing what is known about self-determination in early childhood and elementary education, it is necessary to reiterate why a life course perspective on self-determination is so critical. Accumulating evidence indicates that self-determination develops across the lifespan and supporting self-determination in children can positively impact longer-term outcomes (Wehmeyer et al., 2017). There is substantial correlational and causal evidence that teaching self-determination skills and abilities result in enhanced self-determination and more positive in-school and postschool outcomes for adolescents and young adults with disabilities (Algozzine et al., 2001; Burke et al., 2020; Hagiwara et al., 2017; Powers et al., 2012; Shogren et al., 2015; Test, Fowler et al., 2009; Test, Mazzotti et al., 2009)

Wehmeyer and Palmer (2000) argued, "Because young children are not yet developmentally or emotionally capable of being autonomous and self-regulating does not abrogate the need to enable all children, including children with disabilities, to learn and develop the attitudes and abilities they will need to achieve this outcome" (p. 66).

Elementary school is the time students are meant to learn how to work with less directed support from their teachers (Day & Connor, 2017). With increased opportunities in the early elementary years to apply self-determination skills, students are building a foundation for engaging in self-directed learning in later years. Both educators and researchers agree that an early foundation of self-determination is important for improved quality of life, particularly for students with disabilities in inclusive settings (Palmer et al., 2013; Stang et al., 2009). Additionally, research on motivation highlights the importance of a greater focus on providing supports for self-determination in elementary education. Motivation to engage in self-determination actions is influenced by development and research suggests a need to differentiate interventions and supports for elementary versus secondary students (Geldhof & Little, 2011; Gottfried et al., 2001; Muenks et al., 2018). Research on the development of intrinsic motivation consistently reveals a marked decrease as students enter upper elementary and middle school, suggesting the necessity of a focus on building intrinsic motivation in early childhood classrooms. Second, evidence suggests that children's understanding of factors such as effort, ability, and luck—and their influence on performance—change dramatically with age, particularly between elementary and secondary school (Nicholls, 1979; Nicholls & Miller, 1984). Supporting positive action-control beliefs to enable the use of volitional and agentic actions as described by Causal Agency Theory is critical in elementary school. Third, it has been argued that children are able to engage in self-regulated learning when contexts, materials, and instruction explicitly support this action (Butler, 2005). Establishing self-regulated and self-directed learning expectations in elementary school can impact trajectories of self-determination and engagement in secondary education and post-school environments. However, most interventions designed to promote self-determination have exclusively been conducted with adolescents and young adults (Burke et al., 2020).

Despite limited evaluations of comprehensive self-determination interventions in elementary schools, both elementary general and special educators generally report self-determination as an important domain to teach in classrooms (Stang et al., 2009). However, elementary teachers differentially rank the importance of specific skills associated with self-determination. For example, elementary teachers rank problem-solving as the most important component of self-determination to teach in their classrooms (82.7% of 563 surveyed teachers) but also the skill they report teaching most often. Over half of surveyed teachers reported self-management (65.1%), decision making (57%), and choice-making (51.2%) as important skills to teach elementary students (Stang et al., 2009). However, less than half of teachers (37.9%-48.4%) reported currently delivering instruction in any of the aforementioned domains. And, less than half of teachers rated goal setting, self-awareness, and self-advocacy as important skills to teach (Stang et al., 2009). Teacher implementation of instruction, as well as their priorities for teaching self-determination skills, are likely influenced by the lack of existing research on self-determination in elementary classrooms. Although the overall concept of self-determination has not been robustly evaluated in elementary classrooms, components of self-determination (e.g., choice-making, problem-solving) do have evidentiary support for use in elementary settings.

In the sections that follow, we elaborate on what is known about the relevance of these skills and abilities in early childhood and elementary settings, including how they can be taught and supported to lead to more positive outcomes throughout K-12 education. We conclude with information on a multi-component intervention (i.e., targets multiple self-determination skills concurrently), the *Self-Determined Learning Model of Instruction* (SDLMI; Shogren et al., 2018; Wehmeyer, Palmer et al., 2000). While primarily evaluated in secondary settings, it does have preliminary data in elementary settings and has been identified as a potential practice that could be adopted in inclusive elementary settings and target multiple skills and abilities associated with self-determination simultaneously, providing elementary teachers with the means to teach a range of skills they rank as important and meaningful for their students (Palmer & Wehmeyer, 2003).

Creating Autonomy-Supportive Environments

As noted previously, foundational to teaching self-determination skills are creating environments that are supportive of intrinsic motivation and engagement, enabling students to feel empowered to use self-determination skills. Researchers have identified practices that can be effectively used by educators, including elementary educators, to promote autonomy-supportive learning environments. These practices include providing students' substantial opportunities to respond, encouraging students' efforts, offering strategies when student progress is slow, and acknowledging improvement or mastery of skills (Reeve & Jang, 2006; Ryan & Deci, 2017). Reeve (2002) summarized several studies of autonomy-supportive teaching and concluded that, among instructional behaviors, "autonomy-supportive teachers distinguished themselves by listening more, spending less time holding instructional materials such as notes or books, giving students time for independent work, and giving fewer answers to the problems students face" (p. 186). Vansteenkiste et al. (2012) found that when teachers build choice-making opportunities, clearly explain expectations, and solicit student opinions, students feel more volitional in their learning. These instructional behaviors create opportunities for students to engage in goal-directed actions and pre-emptively act to fulfill their own needs.

Teaching and Creating Opportunities for Self-Determination Skills

Choice-Making

In autonomy-supportive classrooms, young children can learn and use an array of self-determination skills. A skill for which there are frequent opportunities in early childhood and elementary education is choice-making. Choice-making occurs when a "student is provided with two or more options, is allowed to select an option independently, and is provided with the selected option" (Jolivette et al., 2002, p. 28). Providing instructional choices supports students' development by increasing students' self-direction (Rispoli et al., 2013), motivation (Cordova & Lepper, 1996), engagement (Shogren et al., 2004; Walker et al., 2014), and self-determination (Kern et al., 2002; Shogren et al., 2004). As student engagement in instruction increases, challenging or disruptive behaviors also decrease (Rispoli et al., 2013). Providing choices can personalize learning to increase student motivation (Cordova & Lepper, 1996) or increase opportunities to embed student preferences to increase "buy in" during instructional activities. Simply the act of introducing an opportunity for students to control how, what, or with whom they are learning may be sufficient to improve student performance (Kern & State, 2009). Providing choice-making opportunities has effectively improved the performance of students with (Walker et al., 2014) and without (Carson & Eckert, 2003; Dunlap et al., 1994; Lannie & Martens, 2008) disabilities in inclusive classroom settings.

Choices can be provided between-tasks (e.g., ordering literacy tasks [word work, writing, read to self, listening center]) or within-tasks (e.g., materials [writing with a pencil or typing]) (Dibley & Lim, 1999). Offering choices of materials (Powell & Nelson, 1997), reinforcers to access after completing work (Skerbetz & Kostewicz, 2015), and peer partners or group members (Bicard et al., 2012; Cole & Levinson, 2002) for work completion are also ways in which choice can be offered in classrooms. Choice-making can be embedded during group or individual content instruction, including literacy (Lane et al., 2015) or math (Hua et al., 2014).

Problem Solving

Problem solving is often initially associated with students learning to make choices (Palmer et al., 2013). However, problem-solving moves beyond students selecting between forced or presented choices and instead presents opportunities for students to generate solutions or ideas beyond those presented by adults in their environment. Steps for problem-solving for young students include (1) identifying the problem, (2) generating and selecting solutions to the problem, (3) identifying and analyzing how to resolve any barriers to the problem, and (4) enacting the solution (Agran et al., 2002). Young students can be presented with solutions to problems through visuals depicting possible solutions (e.g., the solution suitcase; Hemmeter et al., 2006), facilitated problem-solving with adult conversation and coaching (Wehmeyer & Palmer, 2000), and explicit instruction (Joseph & Strain, 2010). Elementary students can also be taught problem-solving to complete academic tasks (Peltier & Vannest, 2017; Powell, 2011). Connecting choice making and problem-solving can begin to build self-determination abilities by linking more complex self-determination skills.

Self-Management and Self-regulation

Self-management includes self-monitoring, self-assessment, self-instruction, and self-reinforcement-
(Cooper et al., 2020). As students develop self-management skills, they acquire the abilities to assess and monitor their performance or progress and adjust their behavior accordingly to reach goals they may have set across academic, social, behavioral, and adaptive domains (Briesch et al., 2019; Bruhn et al., 2015; Carter et al., 2011; Konrad et al., 2007; Lee et al., 2007). Self-management results in improvements in on-task and disruptive behaviors as well as increases in social interactions (Briesch et al., 2019). Self-management interventions in elementary classrooms occur most frequently as self-monitoring interventions (Briesch et al., 2019; Bruhn et al., 2015). In fact, self-monitoring is the most frequently taught self-determination skill in elementary classrooms (Carter et al., 2011), although it is not always linked with other self-determination skills, such as goal setting or problem-solving. Self-monitoring interventions include paper-pencil checklists (Bruhn et al., 2015) and technology-based tools (Bruhn & Wills, 2018) that identify targeted behavior(s) for students to display, frequent time-based intervals to assess and record if they are engaging in the behavior, and goal setting to engage in the targeted behavior(s) at specific levels to improve performance. Most self-monitoring interventions also include the provision of adult feedback on performance (Briesch et al., 2019). The most effective self-monitoring interventions also include contingent reinforcement of the targeted behaviors (e.g., on-task behaviors named in the interventions) rather than reinforcement delivered for any prosocial or positive behaviors. Student performance further improves when accurate use of the self-monitoring tool also results in the delivery of reinforcement. Finally, self-monitoring interventions can be further enhanced by matching the delivery of reinforcement to the identified function of the student's challenging behavior (Bruhn et al., 2015).

Self-regulation includes controlling emotions, behavior, thinking processes, and social interactions (Bronson, 2000). In young students, self-regulation may develop in the context of relationships with other children, families, or meaningful adults in their lives (Center on the Social and Emotional Foundations for Early Learning, n.d.). Self-regulation also may develop as young students respond to stimuli in their environment such as loud noises or crowded locations and adjust their behavior to novel contexts (Dunn, 2010). Self-regulation strategies are often included in self-monitoring interventions in elementary classrooms and are targeted far more often than the other self-determination components (Didion et al., in press).

Goal Setting and Attainment

Goal setting in elementary classrooms often occurs alongside self-management and self-regulation interventions (Didion et al., in press; Konrad et al., 2007). Literacy, math, and behavior domains are frequently targeted as goals set and selected by educators for elementary students. However, elementary students can successfully set meaningful goals in literacy, mathematics, behavioral, and social domains with explicit instruction as they become self-determined learners (Kleinert et al., 2010; Palmer & Wehmeyer, 2003). Although limited explicit research on teaching elementary students to set their own goals and create plans to evaluate their progress and attainment of the goals has occurred, unlike in secondary settings where this is a major focus, inclusion of goal setting in the aforementioned self-monitoring and regulation studies provide supports for considering a focus on goal setting in inclusive elementary classrooms.

Decision-making and Self-advocacy

Evaluations of interventions designed to improve elementary students' decision-making and self-advocacy skills are limited. Kleinert 2010 Researchers have examined how elementary learners make decisions about goals (Kleinert et al., 2010; Palmer & Wehmeyer, 2003) and how they make decisions about reinforcers for self-management interventions (see Bruhn et al., 2015 for a review) . Teaching decision-making in elementary classrooms moves beyond students simply being provided choices from which to select and moves to actively including elementary students in decisions regarding their instructional foci, arrangements, materials, and priorities. Decision-making can be centered on the elementary student with adults in their environment, providing scaffolded and developmentally appropriate support (Kleinert et al., 2010).

Self-advocacy training in upper elementary grades has included advocating for effective learning strategies (Merlone & Moran, 2008), communication preferences (Schoffstall et al., 2015), and participation in individualized education programs (IEPs; Neale & Test, 2010). A recent review of studies to promote self-advocacy skills in students with disabilities found one study conducted with elementary students (Roberts et al., 2016). Upper elementary students' improved the quantity and quality of their contributions to their IEP meetings after engaging in explicit instruction in advocating for their strengths and needs (Neale & Test, 2010). Transitioning from families leading advocacy efforts for young children to the elementary student as a self-determined agent in their life requires strategic planning and structure in elementary schools (Kleinert et al., 2010). However, models or instructional strategies for teaching young elementary students to begin to advocate for themselves as self-determined learners have not been evaluated in the empirical literature.

Self-Determined Learning Model of Instruction (SDLMI)

In the previous sections, we highlight research on ways to structure classroom environments and teach specific skills associated with self-determination. However, researchers have suggested that rather than targeting a skill in isolation, multi-component interventions that concurrently build multiple skills can be more effective, particularly in relation to building self-determination (Cobb et al., 2009). For these reasons, the SDLMI (Shogren et al., 2018; Wehmeyer, Palmer et al., 2000) was developed. The SDLMI provides a model of instruction that educators can use across settings and ages to engagestudents in a self-regulated, problem solving process where they learn and apply—over time—multiple skills associated with self-determination, with increased opportunities to direct these skills toward personally meaningful and culturally relevant goals. While primarily evaluated in secondary settings, it does have preliminary data in elementary settings and has been identified as a potential practice that could be adopted in inclusive elementary settings and target multiple skills and abilities associated with self-determination simultaneously (Palmer & Wehmeyer, 2003).

Grounded in Causal Agency Theory, the SDLMI is not a specific curriculum to teach self-determination but a model of instruction to facilitate self-directed learning that can be integrated within a range of contexts. The SDLMI is an evidence-based practice in transition (National Technical Assistance Center on Transition, 2017) and has been examined in over 21 single-case design, quasi-experimental, and randomized controlled trial studies (Hagiwara et al., 2017). The SDLMI has been implemented in one-on-one, small group, and class-wide contexts with students with and without disabilities. It also has been applied to instruction across multiple domains, including transition planning and secondary mathematics and English courses. With secondary students, researchers have found that the SDLMI leads to changes (in comparison to a control group) in self-determination (Wehmeyer et al., 2012) as well as changes in academic goal attainment and access to the general education curriculum (Shogren et al., 2012). Further, Shogren et al. (2014) found that implementing the SDLMI positively impacted teachers' views of student capacity and opportunity for self-determination (versus teachers in a control group). This finding suggests that the use of the SDLMI not only enhances student outcomes but also changes classroom conditions that are linked to motivation processes. In recent work in secondary inclusive, secondary general education mathematics classes with students with and without disabilities, researchers have found enhanced overall self-determination and mathematics-related goal attainment (Raley et al., 2018b). Researchers have also highlighted the potential of the SDLMI in early childhood settings, with modified supports for the instructional process. For example, one empirical evaluation of the SDLMI was conducted with 50 kindergarten to third grade students with disabilities in elementary schools (Palmer & Wehmeyer, 2003). Teachers reported the SDLMI was feasibly implemented with young elementary students. Students in early elementary grades could set goals, and students rated their progress in goal attainment similarly to their teachers (Palmer & Wehmeyer, 2003). Students set goals across math, literacy, and behavioral domains (e.g., counting to 20, reading sight words, writing paragraphs, checking work before submission, and following directions; Palmer & Wehmeyer, 2003). Teachers also offered suggestions for incorporating goal setting in elementary classrooms: (1) organizing students in small groups for peer check-ins about goal progress, (2) introducing the concepts at the beginning of the year and scheduling progress monitoring in similar ways to academic content domains, and (3) setting goals in content domains for each student to easily incorporate the components of the SDLMI in multiple aspects of the school day.

Setting the Course for Effective Inclusion

In the previous sections, we highlighted the importance of an integrated approach to promoting self-determination across the life course, inclusive of early childhood and elementary education. We introduced a theoretical framework, Causal Agency Theory, that emphasizes the role of creating supportive environments and delivering effective instruction and supports leading to enhanced self-determination (see Figure 19.1). We also highlighted existing research on building supportive environments and teaching specific self-determination skills in early childhood and elementary education while noting that more limited work has focused on the implementation of multi-component interventions like the SDLMI. Research has suggested potential benefits for younger students as well as ways to modify strategies used at the secondary level to support implementation in inclusive elementary settings.

Overall, there is a critical need to further develop an integrated approach to self-determination in early childhood and elementary education that targets multiple skills that lead to the development of causal agency and its application in developmentally and culturally valued ways throughout the life course. In the sections that follow, we highlight ways that educators, administrators, researchers, policy makers, and families and students can begin to take steps to integrate a more comprehensive focus on self-determination across early childhood and elementary education, emphasizing how to support all students in inclusive settings to begin the life-long process of developing self-determination abilities. We note that in considering the application of these concepts, it will be critical to focus on ways to foster family-student-professional partnerships in addressing the changing demands of school and home environments and to build culturally sustaining practices through culturally responsive self-determination interventions that emphasize the goals and supports that are valued by young people, their families, and their communities.

Creating Autonomy-Supportive Classrooms and Teaching Self-Determination Skills

Early childhood and elementary classrooms provide the opportunity for students to build abilities and skills that lead to volitional and agentic action and action control beliefs. Young students begin to develop their interests and preferences as they develop their volitional self and engage in new experiences in school. Students can begin to identify their own interests and preferences in elementary school through supportive classroom environments. Providing students with opportunities to experience multiple strategies or tools to engage in their learning (e.g., hundreds chart, number line, manipulatives to solve math problems) can support them in identifying preferences in the instructional environment. Supporting student development and identification of their own interests can be fostered by engaging students in supportive conversations about topics, activities, or ideas that interest them. Providing texts, learning activities, and opportunities for students to apply instructional skills in their areas of interest can foster the development of volitional action. For example, when teaching first grade students about non-fiction text features, the non-fiction content can be selected based on student interest and preference. Modeling and allowing opportunities for students to classify if they preferred a strategy or activity through self-reports and conversations can make opportunities for the incorporation of preference and interest in ongoing instruction more salient for children.

Rather than structuring classrooms with only adult-directed choices, teachers who want to develop children's ability to engage in agentic action can create learning environments that foster opportunities for student decision-making and choices. Purposefully planning opportunities for decisions and choice-making in classrooms shows young students these opportunities can and should exist in their learning environment. By first making opportunities explicit and salient, students are provided opportunities to identify when they can act as causal agents in their learning. As students identify more opportunities to make decisions and choices, teachers can support the incorporation of interests and preferences in decision-making and choices through guided questions such as asking students about their preferences in materials, activities, learning strategies, and social partners. For example, a kindergarten teacher may provide three ways for children to learn about Martin Luther King, Jr: watch a BrainpopJr© video, listen to a podcast, or read facts in a text. To support children in deciding how to select their method of learning, teachers can engage students in supportive questions to identify how their preferences and interests may influence their selection, building action control beliefs. A young student with language support needs may prefer the video because it provides visual and auditory information, or they may prefer the video because they like to watch videos online. Supporting language and communication preferences and needs is essential to supporting self-determination. The teacher supporting the student in noting how both their instructional support needs and personal interests can influence their decision-making will engage the student in developing abilities to make decisions in their environment based on their personal interests, strengths, and needs (volitional and agentic action).

Implementation of the SDLMI

These foundational activities can also enable teachers to work toward integrating and using intervention approaches, like the Self-Determined Learning Model of Instruction in their classroom. As mentioned, the SDLMI can and has been implemented in inclusive elementary classrooms with students with disabilities. Guided by a facilitator, the SDLMI consists of a three-phase instructional process that is repeated over time to enable students to set and work towards multiple goals and build their self-determination abilities. Educational supports can be individualized learning for each student based on needs. Figure 19.2 shows the three phases of the SDLMI, including the Student Questions, Facilitator Objectives, and Educational Supports used to guide instruction. Facilitators are often teachers but may be other professionals or interventionists in the school building.

Each of the three phases of the SDLMI presents a problem to be solved by the student. The student solves this problem by posing and answering a series of four *Student Questions* per phase, building self-regulation skills by learning to use, modify to make their own, and apply questions to reach self-selected goals. The *Student Questions* in the model are constructed to direct the student

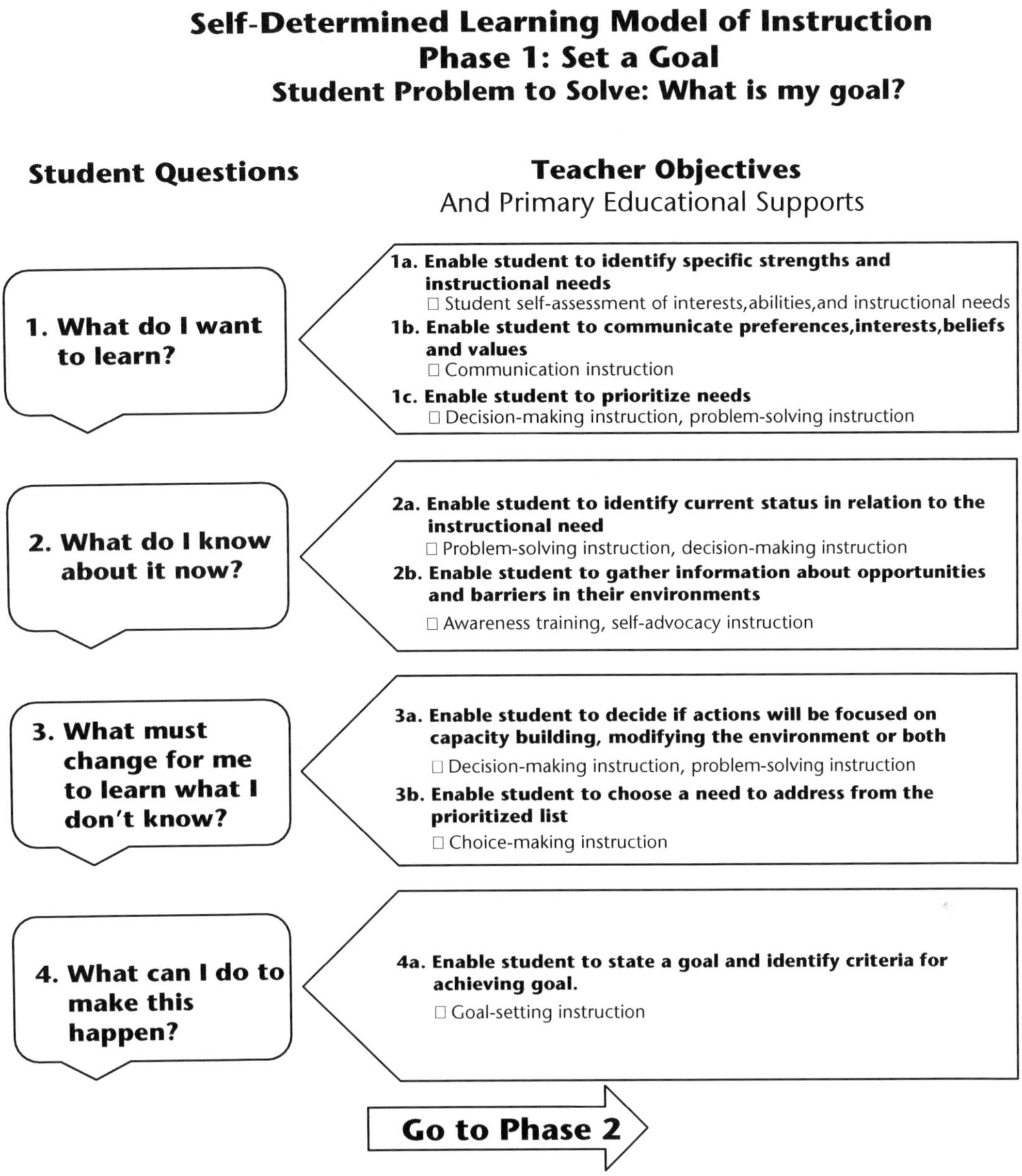

Figure 19.2 SDLMI Phases 1–3 Reprinted With Permission from the SDLMI Teacher's Guide (Shogren et al., 2018)

Self-Determined Learning Model of Instruction
Phase 2: Take Action
Student Problem to Solve: What is my plan?

Student Questions	Teacher Objectives And Primary Educational Supports
5. What can I do to learn what I don't already know?	**5a. Enable student to self-evaluate current status and self-identified goal status** ☐ Goal attainment instruction
6. What could keep me from taking action?	**6a. Enable student to determine plan of action to bridge gap between self-evaluated current status and self-identified goal status** ☐ Goal attainment instruction, self-management instruction
7. What can I do to remove these barriers?	**7a. Collaborate with student to identify appropriate instructional strategies** ☐ Communication instruction **7b. Teach student needed student-directed learning strategies** ☐ Antecedent cue regulation instruction **7c. Support student to implement student-directed learning strategies** ☐ Self-instruction, self-scheduling instruction **7d. Provide mutually agreed upon teacher-directed instruction**
8. When will I take action?	**8a. Enable student to determine schedule for action plan** ☐ Self-scheduling instruction **8b. Enable student to implement action plan** ☐ Self-instruction **8c. Enable student to self-monitor progress** ☐ Self-monitoring instruction

Go to Phase 3

Figure 19.2 (*continued*)

Self-Determined Learning Model of Instruction
Phase 3: Adjust Goal or Plan
Student Problem to Solve: What have I learned?

Student Questions	Teacher Objectives And Primary Educational Supports
9. What actions have I taken?	**9a. Enable student to self-evaluate progress toward goal achievement** □ Self-evaluation instruction, self-recording instruction
10. What barriers have been removed?	**10a. Collaborate with student to compare progress with desired outcomes** □ Self-monitoring instruction, self-evaluation instruction
11. What has changed about what I don't know?	**11a. Support student to re-evaluate goal if progress is insufficient** □ Goal-attainment instruction **11b. Assist student to decide if goal should remain the same or change** □ Decision-making instruction **11c. Collaborate with student to identify if action plan is adequate or inadequate given revised or retained goal** □ Self-evaluation instruction **11d. Enable student to choose a need to address from the prioritized list** □ Choice-making instruction
12. Do I know what I want to know?	**12a. Enable student to decide if progress is adequate, inadequate, or if goal has been achieved** □ Self-evaluation instruction, self-reinforcement instruction

Figure 19.2 (*continued*)

through a problem-solving sequence and to be repeatedly used over time. The solution to the problem in each phase leads to the problem-solving sequence in the next phase (e.g., "What do I want to learn?" in Phase 1 leads to "What is my plan?" in Phase 2). Development of the *Student Questions* was based on theory in the problem-solving and self-regulation literature that suggests there is a sequence of thoughts and actions, a means-end problem-solving sequence, which must be followed for any person's actions to produce results that satisfy their needs and interests (Wehmeyer et al., 2000). Each *Student Question* is linked to a set of *Facilitator Objectives*. The *Facilitator Objectives* provide a road map for facilitators to support students in solving the problem of the *Student Question*. For example, with the first *Student Question* ("What do I want to learn?"), the *Facilitator Objectives* are to enable the student to identify specific strengths and instructional needs; identify and communicate preferences, interests, and beliefs; and prioritize needs. These objectives are met by facilitators using specific strategies or *Educational Supports*.

It is not assumed that every student will have the same skills, abilities, and experiences that enable them to answer each question. The *Student Questions* are written in a relatively simple format and meant to be a starting point for discussion between the facilitator (e.g., teacher) and the student. Some students will be able to engage with and respond to all questions, while others may need the questions stated differently to be more understandable. The ability to engage with these questions will also change over the life course. And students with more intense instructional needs may require the facilitator to scaffold interaction with the questions through more explicit instructional language or supporting materials (e.g., activity to think through how we prioritize and make a choice). Figure 19.3 from the SDLMI Teacher's Guide (Shogren et al., 2018) provides suggestions for how each of the *Student Questions* can be adapted or scaffolded to support a range of learner needs.

Educators in inclusive elementary classrooms can use the SDLMI with students in the context of academic instruction as well as to promote social-emotional learning. For example, educators can use the approach to help students set goals and develop action plans individually or as a class for what books to read, what targets to set for learning new vocabulary, or for completing activities at home (e.g., sharing books with family members). Educators also can use the SDLMI process to target social-emotional skills by having students set goals and develop action plans for engaging with friends, collaborating with peers in class activities, at recess, or in the community or for managing feelings that may emerge in the classroom or when interacting with peers. To ensure that an educators' supports are aligned with the intent of the SDLMI, it is important to engage in ongoing reflection and self-assessment to consider students' continued growth as a self-directed learner. Table 19.2 provides a series of questions adapted from the SDLMI Fidelity Measure (Shogren et al., in press) that educators might use to guide such self-assessment.

Building Tiered Supports

We previously noted that the SDLMI and the Educational Supports built into the model could be used to intensify instruction for students based on learning needs. It is important to reiterate that all students, irrespective of their support needs, can develop self-determination so long as supports are individualized to student needs and enable the student to act as an agent over their goals and decisions, even if they do not do each step independently. This creates an opportunity to think about integrating the SDLMI and self-determination instruction into other efforts to promote multi-tiered systems of support (MTSS) to promote academic, behavioral, and social outcomes in elementary education. For example, skills associated with self-determined action are critical for all students, a finding acknowledged in both the general and special education literature. Researchers frequently suggest the critical nature of problem-solving skills to succeed in core academic subjects, particularly mathematics (Miller, 2013; Wenrick et al., 2013). For example, the National Council of Teachers of Mathematics (2000) states that "contexts that promote problem solving, reasoning,

Alternate Phrasing for Student Questions

Phase 1 Student Questions	Alternate Phrasing
1. What do I want to learn?	What do I want to do? What do I want to know about? What goal do I want to work on?
2. What do I know about it now?	What can I tell someone about it?
3. What must change for me to learn what I don't know?	Do I need to change? Should I try to change something else?
4. What can I do to make this happen?	What can I do to make these changes?

Phase 2 Student Questions	Alternate Phrasing
5. What can I do to learn what I don't know?	Where do I start? What is the first step?
6. What could keep me from taking action?	What is in my way? What is stopping me?
7. What can I do to remove these barriers?	How can I get these things out of my way? How can I fix the problem? What can I do to remove these problems? How can I fix it?
8. When will I take action?	When do I start? When will I begin?

Phase 3 Student Questions	Alternate Phrasing
9. What actions have I taken?	What have I done? What is the result? Is my plan working?
10. What barriers have been removed?	What problem has been removed? What problem have I solved?
11. What has changed about what I don't know?	What have I learned? What progress have I made? What has changed about my situation?
12. Do I know what I want to know?	Did I learn what I wanted to learn? Did I reach my goal?

Figure 19.3 Alternate Phrasing for Student questions, Reprinted With Permission from the SDLMI Teacher's Guide (Shogren et al., 2018)

communication, making connections…" are fundamental to learning mathematics. Integrating efforts to promote self-determination appears to be a natural fit given the emphasis in MTSS on enabling youth to become self-regulated, goal-directed learners, skills and attitudes directly linked to self-determination (Shogren et al., 2016, 2017). Although only recently conceptualized as a tiered system, researchers have noted that people with and without disabilities need opportunities to develop and express self-determination in inclusive settings (universal supports), but that some students will need more intense supports to develop specific skills (e.g., increasingly explicit instruction in problem-solving, goal setting, self-advocacy).

Promoting self-determination with all students in inclusive environments can provide a means to motivate students and raise expectations, creating opportunities for students to learn skills and begin to perceive themselves as self-regulated, goal-oriented learners from elementary school throughout

Table 19.2 Guiding Questions for Teachers in Implementing the SDLMI (reprinted with permission from Shogren, 2018)

SDLMI Implementation	• Overall, has your use of the SDLMI led to students...
	  • setting goals?
	  • making action plans?
	  • adjusting their goal or plan?
	• Overall, has your use of the SDLMI been more student-directed compared to teacher-directed?
	• If so, how might you introduce additional educational supports to increase student-directed learning?

Educational Supports	• What *Educational Supports* did you provide? • How did you provide these supports (e.g., what did your support "look like")? • How did the provided *Educational Supports* meet students' individual needs? • What evidence do you have that students benefitted from these supports?
Generalizing Skills	• During instruction, did you reference students' goals, action plans, and evaluation strategies? • In what areas would your students benefit most from increasing their self-directed actions (e.g., reading, mathematics, classroom behavior)? Which *Educational Support(s)* can be integrated into this area of instruction?

secondary education. Educators have highlighted the positive impacts on student goal attainment and developed ways to feasibility implement the SDLMI in inclusive secondary classrooms (Raley et al., 2018a, 2018b). This can translate to inclusive elementary contexts as well (Palmer & Wehmeyer, 2003). By focusing on self-determination skills in inclusive elementary settings, educators can focus on identifying students who may need more targeted or individualized supports to build their self-regulated, goal-directed actions. Existing research in early childhood and elementary education targeting self-determination skills can be used to guide more targeted Tier 2 and 3 supports. For example, some students may need more explicit instruction in one or more key skills promoting self-determination: solving problems, setting goals, making decisions, self-advocating, for example. Explicitly teaching steps in skill areas that students are struggling with in Tier 1 instruction could provide a meaningful Tier 2 intervention for targeted groups of students based on the assessment of self-determination and progress monitoring information.

Engaging Families and Promoting Culturally Sustaining Practices

In early childhood and elementary education, partnerships with families and integration of cultural values in instruction are critical to support the development of self-determination. Families play a key role in providing a foundation for self-determination development through modeling self-determination in familial and cultural contexts and providing opportunities for students to practice their self-determination skills at home and in the community. Turnbull and Turnbull (1996) noted the importance of educators recognizing the diverse ways that families promote and support self-determination.

> Having a prototypical "ideal family" in mind and judging all families against that prototype is a strategy that brings only frustration and failure. A key for success is not only recognizing family diversity, but indeed honoring it and taking it fully into account (p. 216).

When designing self-determination instruction and supports, different approaches to identify goals and building self-determination skills may need to be considered to honor a student and family's culture. Educators can integrate questions into a family survey or parent conferences at the start of the year to better understand the norms and expectations of the family around self-determination. It also is important to recognize that families will have varying capacities to engage with the school around self-determination. Communicating with families about their preferred methods of engagement with their student's education can support educators' understanding of how collaborative partnerships to promote self-determination can be developed. Communication methods should be varied (e.g., in-person after hours, via phone or text, via email, via written communication) to ensure families can effectively collaborate with school personnel in decision-making processes (Fox et al., 2002; Soutullo et al., 2016). Continuous access to translation services across all communication modalities (Carreón et al., 2005) and awareness of potential microaggressions (e.g., race-based comments about types of parental involvement; Posey-Maddox, 2017) are two ways to support the engagement of all families. Additionally, some families may not be able to participate in classroom activities during the school day but may engage in a range of activities during other times, activities that educators can learn about and integrate into school-based activities. Understanding the diversity that exists in our classrooms—and, by association, in our students' families—will allow us to foster skills that students will have the opportunity to practice and generalize in their home environments.

Work with families, particularly from diverse backgrounds (Shogren, 2011), suggests that the construct of self-determination has relevance and is valued across cultures, but that conflicts often emerge when school's approaches not flexible and supportive of diverse operationalizations of self-determination and how to promote it (Goff et al., 2007; Shogren, 2012; Trainor, 2005). Some families will want deep and ingrained family connections and decision-making processes to be valued, particularly in school-based services and supports (Palmer et al., 2013; Valenzuela & Martin, 2005). Thus, efforts to support the development of self-determination must adopt a flexible self-determination perspective (Shogren, 2011) that recognizes the need to understand and embed cultural considerations in efforts to support the development of self-determination to enable children to begin to initiate and direct their action toward goals aligned with their personal cultural identities. Thus, the actions and outcomes of self-determined action can and will look different and will vary across contexts and cultures and over the life course. Acknowledging the "inclusive and interacting nature" (Trainor et al., 2008, p. 57) of multiple factors in shaping cultural identities will be critical and can enable educators across the life span to support all students to become self-determining and address oppression, exclusion, and discrepant education and postsecondary opportunities.

Conclusion

Self-determination develops across the life course and can be fostered in early childhood and elementary inclusive classrooms to promote student outcomes. Creating autonomy-supportive classrooms and infusing self-determination instruction into classroom activities can lay the foundation for young students to develop skills and abilities that will enable them to self-determine their personal and family priorities as well as educational goals. We close with the following recommendations for educators supporting students with and without disabilities in inclusive early childhood and elementary settings.

- Recognize that young children have the capacity to develop into autonomous, self-directed learners when autonomy-supportive classrooms and instruction are provided throughout their early school years.
- Infuse opportunities for and instruction in self-determination in a wide range of classroom activities. Integrating self-determination instruction does not take away from other instructional

activities (e.g., teaching reading, building social skills); instead, it enhances this instruction and contributes to enhanced goal attainment and academic and social-emotional outcomes.

- Collaborate with students and families to identify and incorporate each student's cultural and familial priorities alongside instructional opportunities to practice self-determination skills.
- Recognize that all students, irrespective of the intensity of their support needs, can develop in their self-determination abilities when appropriate communication and instructional supports are provided. Consider ways to align communication supports and explicit instruction with the needs of all students to grow in their self-determination abilities.
- Adopt a life course perspective. Promoting the development of self-determination in early childhood and elementary classrooms will not only benefit young children but set them up for greater success in secondary and post-school environments.

References

Agran, M., Alper, S., & Wehmeyer, M. (2002). Access to the general curriculum for students with significant disabilities: What it means to teachers. *Education and Training in Mental Retardation and Developmental Disabilities*, *37*(2), 123–133.

Algozzine, B., Browder, D., Karvonen, M., Test, D. W., & Wood, W. M. (2001). Effects of interventions to promote self-determination for individuals with disabilities. *Review of Educational Research*, *71*, 219–277. doi.10.3102/00346543071002219

Bicard, D. F., Ervin, A., Bicard, S. C., & Baylot-Casey, L. (2012). Differential effects of seating arrangements on disruptive behavior of fifth grade students during independent seatwork. *Journal of Applied Behavior Analysis*, *45*(2), 407–411. doi.10.1901/jaba.2012.45-407

Briesch, A. M., Daniels, B., & Beneville, M. (2019). Unpacking the term "self-management": Understanding intervention applications within the school-based literature. *Journal of Behavioral Education*, *28*(1), 54–77. doi.10.1007/s10864-018-9303-1

Bronson, M. B. (2000). *Self-regulation in early childhood: Nature and nurture*. Guilford Press.

Bruhn, A., Mcdaniel, S., & Kreigh, C. (2015). Self-monitoring interventions for students with behavior problems: A systematic review of current research. *Behavioral Disorders*, *40*(2), 102–121. doi.10.17988/bd-13-45.1

Bruhn, A., & Wills, H. P. (2018). Emerging research and development in technology-based self-monitoring. In *Emerging Research and Issues in Behavioral Disabilities*. Emerald Publishing Limited.

Burke, K. M., Raley, S. K., Shogren, K. A., Hagiwara, M., Mumbardó-Adam, C., Uyanik, H., & Behrens, S. (2020). A meta-analysis of interventions to promote self-determination for students with disabilities. *Remedial and Special Education*, *41*(3), 176–188. doi.10.1177/0741932518802274

Butler, R. A. (2005). Competence assessment, competence, and motivation between early and middle childhood. In A. J. Elliot & C. S. Dweck (Eds.), *Handbook of competence and motivation* (pp. 202–221). Guilford Press.

Carreón, G. P., Drake, C., & Barton, A. C. (2005). The importance of presence: Immigrant parents' school engagement experiences. *American Educational Research Journal*, *42*(3), 465–498. doi.10.3102/00028312042003465

Carson, P. M., & Eckert, T. L. (2003). An experimental analysis of mathematics instructional components: Examining the effects of student-selected versus empirically-selected interventions. *Journal of Behavioral Education*, *12*(1), 35–54. doi.10.1023/A:1022370305486

Carter, E. W., Lane, K. L., Crnobori, M., Bruhn, A. L., & Oakes, W. P. (2011). Self-determination interventions for students with and at risk for emotional and behavioral disorders: Mapping the knowledge base. *Behavioral Disorders*, *36*(2), 100–116. doi.10.1177/019874291103600202

Center on the Social and Emotional Foundations for Early Learning. (n.d.). Self-Management What Works Brief. http://csefel.vanderbilt.edu/resources/wwb/wwb7.html

Charlton, J. I. (2000). *Nothing about us without us: Disability oppression and empowerment*. University of California Press.

Cobb, R. B., Lehmann, J., Newman-Gonchar, R., & Alwell, M. (2009). Self-determination for students with disabilities: A narrative metasynthesis. *Career Development for Exceptional Individuals*, *32*, 108–114. doi.10.1177/0885728809336654

Cole, C. L., & Levinson, T. R. (2002). Effects of within-activity choices on the challenging behavior of children with severe developmental disabilities. *Journal of Positive Behavior Interventions*, *4*(1), 29–37, 52.

Cooper, J. O., Heron, T. E., & Heward, W. L. (2020). *Applied behavior analysis* (3rd ed.). Pearson.

Cordova, D. I., & Lepper, M. R. (1996). Intrinsic motivation and the process of learning: Beneficial effects of contextualization, personalization, and choice. *Journal of Educational Psychology*, *88*(4), 715–730. doi.10.1037/0022-0663.88.4.715

Day, S. L., & Connor, C. M. (2017). Examining the relations between self-regulation and achievement in third-grade students. *Assessment for Effective Intervention*, *42*(2), 97–109. doi.10.1177/1534508416670367

Dibley, S., & Lim, L. (1999). Providing choice making opportunities within and between daily school routines. *Journal of Behavioral Education*, *9*(2), 117–132. doi.10.1023/A:1022888917128

Didion, L. A., Toste, J. R., Benz, S., & Shogren, K. A. (in press). How are self-determination components taught to improve reading outcomes for elementary students with or at risk for learning disabilities?. Learning Disability Quarterly. doi:10.1177/0731948721989328.

Dunlap, G., dePerczel, M., Clarke, S., Wilson, D., Wright, S., White, R., & Gomez, A. (1994). Choice making to promote adaptive behavior for students with emotional and behavioral challenges. *Journal of Applied Behavior Analysis*, *27*(3), 505–518.

Dunn, W. (2010). Sensory processing: Tools for supporting young children in everyday life. In C. J. Groark & S. P. Maude (Eds.), *Early childhood intervention: Shaping the future for children with special needs and their families: Proven and promising practices in EI/ECSE* (Vol. 2, pp. 137–165). ABC-CLIO/Praeger.

Fox, L., Dunlap, G., & Cushing, L. (2002). Early intervention, positive behavior support, and transition to school. *Journal of Emotional and Behavioral Disorders*, *10*(3), 149–157. doi.10.1177/10634266020100030301

Geldhof, G. J., Fenn, M. L., & Finders, J. K. (2017). A self-determination perspective on self-regulation across the life span. In M. L. Wehmeyer, K. A. Shogren, T. D. Little, & S. J. Lopez (Eds.), *Development of self-determination through the life-course* (pp. 221–235). Springer.

Geldhof, G. J., & Little, T. D. (2011). Influences of children's and adolescents' action-control processes on school achievement, peer relationships, and coping with challenging life events. *New Directions for Child and Adolescent Dvelopment*, *133*, 45–59.

Goff, C., Martin, J. E., & Thomas, M. K. (2007, December 1, 2007). The burden of acting white: Implications for transition. *Career Development for Exceptional Individuals*, *30*, 134–146. doi.10.1177/08857288070300030301

Gottfried, A. E., Fleming, J. S., & Gottfried, A. W. (2001, 2015-02-24). Continuity of academic intrinsic motivation from childhood through late adolescence: A longitudinal study. *Journal of Educational Psychology*, *93*(1), 3–13. doi.10.1037/0022-0663.93.1.3

Hagiwara, M., Shogren, K., & Leko, M. (2017). Reviewing research on the Self-Determined Learning Model of Instruction: Mapping the terrain and charting a course to promote adoption and use. *Advances in Neurodevelopmental Disorders*, *1*, 3–13. doi.10.1007/s41252-017-0007-7

Hemmeter, M. L., Ostrosky, M., & Fox, L. (2006). Social and emotional foundations for early learning: A conceptual model for intervention. *School Psychology Review*, *35*(4), 583–601.

Hua, Y., Lee, D., Stansbery, S., & McAfee, J. (2014). The effects of assignment format and choice on task completion. *Journal of Education and Learning*, *3*, 101–110.

Jolivette, K., Stichter, J. P., & McCormick, K. M. (2002). Making choices—Improving behavior—Engaging in learning. *Teaching Exceptional Children*, *34*(3), 24–29. doi.10.1177/004005990203400303

Joseph, G. E., & Strain, P. S. (2010). Teaching young children interpersonal problem-solving skills. *Young Exceptional Children*, *13*(3), 28–40. doi.10.1177/1096250610365144

Kern, L., Choutka, C. M., & Sokol, N. G. (2002). Assessment -based antecedent interventions used in natural settings to reduce challenging behavior: An analysis of the literature. *Education and Treatment of Children*, *25*(1), 113–130.

Kern, L., & State, T. M. (2009). Incorporating choice and preferred activities into classwide instruction. *Beyond Behavior*, *18*(2), 3–11.

Kleinert, J. O. R., Harrison, E. M., Fisher, T. L., & Kleinert, H. L. (2010). "I can" and "I did"—Self-advocacy for young students with developmental disabilities. *Teaching Exceptional Children*, *43*(2), 16–26.

Konrad, M., Fowler, C. H., Walker, A. R., Test, D. W., & Wood, W. M. (2007). Effects of self-determination interventions on the academic skills of students with learning disabilities. *Learning Disability Quarterly*, *30*, 89–113. doi.10.2307/30035545

Lane, K. L., Royer, D. J., Messenger, M. L., Common, E. A., Ennis, R. P., & Swogger, E. D. (2015). Empowering teachers with low-intensity strategies to support academic engagement: Implementation and effects of instructional choice for elementary students in inclusive settings. *Education & Treatment of Children, 38*(4), 473–504. doi.10.1353/etc.2015.0013

Lannie, A. L., & Martens, B. K. (2008). Targeting performance dimensions in sequence according to the instructional hierarchy: Effects on children' math work within a self-monitoring program. *Journal of Behavioral Education, 17*(4), 356–375. doi.10.1007/s10864-008-9073-2

Lee, S. H., Simpson, R. L., & Shogren, K. A. (2007). Effects and implications of self-management for students with autism: A meta-analysis. *Focus on Autism and Other Developmental Disabilities, 22*, 2–13.

Little, T. D., Hawley, P. H., Henrich, C. C., & Marsland, K. W. (2002). Three views of the agentic self: A developmental synthesis. In E. L. Deci & R. M. Ryan (Eds.), *Handbook of self-determination research* (pp. 389–404). University of Rochester Press.

Merlone, L., & Moran, D. (2008). Transition works: Self-awareness and self-advocacy skills for students in the elementary learning center. *Teaching Exceptional Children Plus, 4*(4), 1–10.

Miller, D. L. (2013). Got it wrong? Think again. And again. *Phi Delta Kappan, 94*(5), 50–52.

Muenks, K., Wigfield, A., & Eccles, J. S. (2018). I can do this! The development and calibration of children's expectations for success and competence beliefs. *Developmental Review, 48*, 24–39.

National Council of Teachers of Mathematics. (2000). *Principles and standards for school mathematics*. NCTM.

National Technical Assistance Center on Transition. (2017). *Evidence-based practices and predictors in secondary transition: What we know and what we still need to know*. Author.

Neale, M. H., & Test, D. W. (2010). Effects of the "I Can Use Effort" strategy on quality of student verbal contributions and Individualized Education Program participation with third- and fourth-grade students with disabilities. *Remedial and Special Education, 31*(3), 184–194. doi.10.1177/0741932508327462

Nicholls, J. G. (1979). Development of perception of own attainment and causal attributions for success and failure in reading. *Journal of Educational Psychology, 71*, 94–99.

Nicholls, J. G., & Miller, A. T. (1984). Development and its discontents: The differentiation of the concept of ability. *Advances in Motivation and Achievement, 3*, 185–218.

Palmer, S. B., Summers, J. A., Brotherson, M. J., Erwin, E. J., Maude, S. P., Haines, S. J., Stroup-Rentier, V. L., & Chu, S. Y. (2013). Foundations for Self-Determination in early childhood intervention: Fidelity, feasibility, and outcomes. *Journal of Early Intervention, 33*, 38–47.

Palmer, S. B., Summers, J. A., Brotherson, M. J., Erwin, E. J., Maude, S. P., Stroup-Rentier, V., Wu, H.-Y., Peck, N. F., Zheng, Y., Weigel, C. J., Chu, S.-Y., McGrath, G. S., & Haines, S. J. (2013). Foundations for self-determination in early childhood: An inclusive model for children with disabilities. *Topics in Early Childhood Special Education, 33*(1), 38–47. doi.10.1177/0271121412445288

Palmer, S. B., & Wehmeyer, M. L. (2003). Promoting self-determination in early elementary school: Teaching self-regulated problem-solving and goal-setting skills. *Remedial and Special Education, 24*, 115–126.

Peltier, C., & Vannest, K. J. (2017). A meta-analysis of schema instruction on the problem-solving performance of elementary school students. *Review of Educational Research, 87*(5), 899–920. doi.10.3102/003465431772 0163

Posey-Maddox, L. (2017). Schooling in suburbia: the intersections of race, class, gender, and place in black fathers' engagement and family–school relationships. *Gender and Education, 29*(5), 577–593. doi.10.1080/ 09540253.2016.1274389

Powell, S., & Nelson, B. (1997). Effects of choosing academic assignments on a student with attention deficit hyperactivity disorder. *Journal of Applied Behavior Analysis, 30*(1), 181–183. doi.10.1901/jaba.1997.30-181

Powell, S. R. (2011). Solving word problems using schemas: A review of the literature. *Learning Disabilities Research & Practice, 26*(2), 94–108. doi.10.1111/j.1540-5826.2011.00329.x

Powers, L. E., Geenen, S., Powers, J., Pommier-Satya, S., Turner, A., Dalton, L., Drummond, D., & Swand, P. (2012). My Life: Effects of a longitudinal, randomized study of self-determination enhancement on the transition outcomes of youth in foster care and special education. *Children and Youth Services Review, 34*, 2179–2187.

Raley, S. K., Shogren, K. A., & McDonald, A. (2018a). How to implement the self-determined learning model of instruction in inclusive general education classrooms. *Teaching Exceptional Children, 51*(1), 62–71. doi.1 0.1177/0040059918790236

Raley, S. K., Shogren, K. A., & McDonald, A. (2018b). Whole-class implementation of the Self-Determined Learning Model of Instruction in inclusive high school mathematics classes. *Inclusion, 6*(3):164–174

Reeve, J. (2002). Self-determination theory applied to educational settings. In E. L. Deci & R. M. Ryan (Eds.), *Handbook of self-determination research* (pp. 183–203). University of Rochester Press.

Reeve, J., & Jang, H. (2006). What teachers say and do to support students' autonomy during a learning activity. *Journal of Educational Psychology, 98*(1), 209–218.

Reeve, J., Ryan, R. M., Deci, E. L., & Jang, H. (2008). Understanding and promoting autonomous self-regulation: A self-determination theory perspective. In D. H. Schunk & B. J. Zimmerman (Eds.), *Motivation and self-regulated learning: Theory research and applications* (pp. 223–244). Lawrence Erlbaum.

Rispoli, M., Lang, R., Neely, L., Camargo, S., Hutchins, N., Davenport, K., & Goodwyn, F. (2013). A comparison of within-and across-activity choices for reducing challenging behavior in children with autism spectrum disorders. *Journal of Behavioral Education, 22*(1), 66–83. http://www.jstor.org/stable/41824597

Roberts, E. L., Ju, S., & Zhang, D. (2016). Review of practices that promote self-advocacy for students with disabilities. *Journal of Disability Policy Studies, 26*(4), 209–220. doi.10.1177/1044207314540213

Ryan, R. M. (Ed.). (2012). *The Oxford handbook of human motivation*. Oxford University Press.

Ryan, R. M., & Deci, E. L. (Eds.). (2017). *Self-determination theory: Basic psychological needs in motivation development and wellness*. Guilford.

Sands, D. J., & Wehmeyer, M. L. (Eds.). (1996). *Self-determination across the life span: Independence and choice for people with disabilities*. Paul H. Brookes.

Schoffstall, S., Cawthon, S. W., Tarantolo-Leppo, R. H., & Wendel, E. (2015). Developing consumer and system-level readiness for effective self-advocacy: Perspectives from vocational rehabilitation counselors working with deaf and hard of hearing individuals in post-secondary settings. *Journal of Development and Physical Disabilities, 27*(4), 533–555.

Shogren, K. A. (2011). Culture and self-determination: A synthesis of the literature and directions for future research and practice. *Career Development for Exceptional Individuals, 34*, 115–127. doi.10.1177/0885728811398271

Shogren, K. A. (2012). Hispanic mothers' perceptions of self-determination. *Research and Practice for Persons with Severe Disabilities, 37*, 170–184.

Shogren, K. A. (2018). *Self-determination theoretical framework*. Kansas University Center on Developmental Disabilities.

Shogren, K. A., Burke, K. M., Antosh, A. A., Wehmeyer, M. L., LaPlante, T., Shaw, L. A., & Raley, S. K. (2019). Impact of the Self-Determined Learning Model of Instruction on self-determination and goal attainment in adolescents with intellectual disability. *Journal of Disability Policy Studies, 30*(1), 22–34. doi.10.1177/1044207318792178

Shogren, K. A., Faggella-Luby, M., Bae, S. J., & Wehmeyer, M. L. (2004). The effect of choice-making as an intervention for problem behavior: A meta-analysis. *Journal of Positive Behavior Interventions, 6*(4), 228–237.

Shogren, K. A., Palmer, S. B., Wehmeyer, M. L., Williams-Diehm, K., & Little, T. D. (2012). Effect of intervention with the Self-Determined Learning Model of Instruction on access and goal attainment. *Remedial and Special Education, 33*(5), 320–330. doi.10.1177/0741932511410072

Shogren, K. A., Plotner, A. J., Palmer, S. B., Wehmeyer, M. L., & Paek, Y. (2014). Impact of the Self-Determined Learning Model of Instruction on teacher perceptions of student capacity and opportunity for self-determination. *Education and Training in Autism and Developmental Disabilities, 49*(3), 440–448.

Shogren, K. A., Raley, S. K., Burke, K. M., & Wehmeyer, M. L. (2018). *The Self-Determined Learning Model of Instruction: Teacher's Guide*. Kansas University Center on Developmental Disabilities.

Shogren, K. A., Raley, S. K., Rifenbark, G. G., Lane, K. L., Bojanek, E. K., Karpur, A., & Quirk, C. (in press). The Self-Determined Learning Model of Instruction: Promoting implementation fidelity. *Inclusion*.

Shogren, K. A., & Shaw, L. A. (2016). The role of autonomy, self-realization, and psychological empowerment in predicting early adulthood outcomes for youth with disabilities. *Remedial and Special Education, 37*, 55–62. doi.10.1177/0741932515585003

Shogren, K. A., & Ward, M. J. (2018). Promoting and enhancing self-determination to improve the post-school outcomes of people with disabilities. *Journal of Vocational Rehabilitation, 48*, 187–196.

Shogren, K. A., Wehmeyer, M. L., & Lane, K. L. (2016). Embedding interventions to promote self-determination within multi-tiered systems of supports. *Exceptionality, 24*(4), 213–224. doi.10.1080/09362835.2015.1064421

Shogren, K. A., Wehmeyer, M. L., Lane, K. L., & Quirk, C. (2017). Multi-tiered systems of supports. In M. L. Wehmeyer & K. A. Shogren (Eds.), *Handbook of research-based practices for educating students with intellectual disability* (pp. 185–198). Routledge.

Shogren, K. A., Wehmeyer, M. L., & Palmer, S. B. (2017). Causal agency theory. In M. L. Wehmeyer, K. A. Shogren, T. D. Little, & S. J. Lopez (Eds.), *Handbook on the development of self-determination* (pp. 55–70). Springer.

Shogren, K. A., Wehmeyer, M. L., Palmer, S. B., Forber-Pratt, A. J., Little, T. J., & Lopez, S. (2015). Causal agency theory: Reconceptualizing a functional model of self-determination. *Education and Training in Autism and Developmental Disabilities, 50*(3), 251. doi.10.1007/978-94-024-1042-6_5

Shogren, K. A., Wehmeyer, M. L., Palmer, S. B., Rifenbark, G. G., & Little, T. D. (2015). Relationships between self-determination and postschool outcomes for youth with disabilities. *Journal of Special Education, 53*, 30–41. doi.10.1177/0022466913489733

Shogren, K. A., & Wittenburg, D. (in press). Improving outcomes of transition age youth with disabilities: A life course perspective. *Career Development and Transition for Exceptional Individuals*.

Skerbetz, M. D., & Kostewicz, D. E. (2015). Consequence choice and students with emotional and behavioral disabilities: Effects on academic engagement. *Exceptionality, 23*(1), 14–33. doi.10.1080/09362835.2014.986603

Soutullo, O. R., Smith-Bonahue, T. M., Sanders-Smith, S. C., & Navia, L. E. (2016). Discouraging partnerships? Teachers' perspectives on immigration-related barriers to family-school collaboration. *School Psychology Quarterly, 31*(2), 226–240. doi.10.1037/spq0000148

Stang, K. K., Carter, E. W., Lane, K. L., & Pierson, M. R. (2009). Perspectives of general and special educators on fostering self-determination in elementary and middle schools. *The Journal of Special Education, 43*, 94–106. doi.10.1177/0022466907313452

Test, D. W., Fowler, C. H., Richter, S. M., White, J., Mazzotti, V., Walker, A. R., Kohler, P., & Kortering, L. (2009). Evidence-based practices in secondary transition. *Career Development for Exceptional Individuals, 32*, 115–128. doi.10.1177/0885728809336859

Test, D. W., Mazzotti, V. L., Mustian, A. L., Fowler, C. H., Kortering, L., & Kohler, P. (2009). Evidence-based secondary transition predictors for improving postschool outcomes for students with disabilities. *Career Development for Exceptional Individuals, 32*, 160–181. doi.10.1177/0885728809346960

Trainor, A. A. (2005). Self-determination perceptions and behaviors of diverse students with LD during the transition planning process. *Journal of Learning Disabilities, 38*, 233–248. doi.10.1177/00222194050380030501

Trainor, A. A., Lindstrom, L., Simon-Burroughs, M., Martin, J. E., & Sorrells, A. M. (2008). From marginalized to maximized opportunities for diverse youths with disabilities: A position paper of the Division on Career Development and Transition. *Career Development for Exceptional Individuals, 31*, 56–64. doi.10.1177/0885728807313777

Turnbull, A. P., & Turnbull, H. R. (1996). Self-determination within a culturally responsive family systems perspective. In L. E. Powers, G. H. S. Singer, & J. Sowers (Eds.), *On the road to autonomy: Promoting self-competence in children and youth with disabilities* (pp. 195–220). Brookes.

Valenzuela, R. L., & Martin, J. E. (2005). Self-directed IEP: Bridging values of diverse cultures and secondary education. *Career Development for Exceptional Individuals, 28*, 4–14.

Vansteenkiste, M., Sierens, E., Goossens, L., Soenens, B., Dochy, F., Mouratidis, A., Aelterman, N., Haerens, L., & Beyers, W. (2012). Identifying configurations of perceived teacher autonomy support and structure: Associations with self-regulated learning, motivation and problem behavior. *Learning and Instruction, 22*, 431–439. doi.10.1016/j.learninstruc.2012.04.002

Walker, H. M., Forness, S. R., & Lane, K. L. (2014). Design and management of scientific research in applied school settings. In B. Cook, M. Tankersley, & T. J. Landrum (Eds.), *Advances in learning and behavioral disabilities: Special education past present and future* (Vol. 27, pp. 141–169). Emerald.

Ward, M. J. (1996). Coming of age in the age of self-determination: A historical and personal perspective. In D. J. Sands & M. L. Wehmeyer (Eds.), *Self-determination across the life span: Independence and choice for people with disabilities*. Paul H. Brookes.

Wehmeyer, M. L., Bersani, H., Jr., & Gagne, R. (2000). Riding the third wave: Self-determination and self-advocacy in the 21st century. *Focus on Autism and Other Developmental Disabilities, 15*, 106–115.

Wehmeyer, M. L., & Palmer, S. B. (2000). Promoting the acquisition and development of self-determination in young children with disabilities. *Early Education and Development, 11*(4), 465–481.

Wehmeyer, M. L., Palmer, S. B., Agran, M., Mithaug, D. E., & Martin, J. E. (2000). Promoting causal agency: The Self-Determined Learning Model of Instruction. *Exceptional Children, 66*(4), 439–453. doi.10.1177/001440290006600401

Wehmeyer, M. L., Shogren, K. A., Little, T. D., & Lopez, S. J. (Eds.). (2017). *Handbook on the development of self-determination*. Springer.

Wehmeyer, M. L., Shogren, K. A., Palmer, S. B., Williams-Diehm, K. L., Little, T. D., & Boulton, A. (2012). The impact of the Self-Determined Learning Model of Instruction on student self-determination. *Exceptional Children, 78*(2), 135–153. doi.10.1177/001440291207800201

Wenrick, M., Behrend, J. L., & Mohs, L. C. (2013). A pathway for mathematical practices. *Teaching Children Mathematics, 19*, 354–362.

Section IV

Systematically Developing Effective Inclusive Schools Now and in the Future

James McLeskey and Nancy L. Waldron

The chapters in the previous sections reveal that there are many reasons for optimism regarding schooling for students with disabilities and the potential for improved outcomes in school and in life for these individuals. In the US, students with a full range of disabilities are currently included in general education settings more than ever before. To better support these students in effective inclusive schools, we have gained a better understanding of the critical role that principals play in developing and supporting improved outcomes for students with disabilities and how to better prepare teachers through teacher education and continuing professional development for their varied roles in these settings. Advances have also been made in the use of effective instructional and behavioral interventions that have resulted in improved outcomes for many students with disabilities. Furthermore, substantial changes are occurring in schools, as major initiatives are underway to alter the structures in which services are delivered to students with disabilities and others who struggle academically and/or behaviorally (e.g., multi-tiered systems of support, Positive Behavioral Interventions and Supports (PBIS)), and how accountability is monitored to ensure the effectiveness of interventions and the progress that students make academically and behaviorally.

In this final section, we address topics that are critical to providing schools with the systemic support needed for the development of schools that are both effective and inclusive. Chapter 20 describes the role of district-level leadership teams in supporting the implementation of school-wide initiatives while using PBIS as an illustrative example. Critical functions of district leadership teams for building the systems to implement, sustain, and scale up tiered behavior supports in schools to improve outcomes for all student groups are described. This chapter also offers recommendations for practice regarding how to increase district capacity to support schools in developing systems of support that improve student outcomes. Then in Chapter 21, the components and use of implementation science at a school level are described. A case illustration of school change is then employed to demonstrate how the components of implementation science are used to support schools as they implement effective practices (e.g., high-leverage practices and evidence-based practices) to improve outcomes for all students.

Chapter 22 addresses the importance of providing an equitable educational experience for students with an array of backgrounds and needs. The chapter initially provides a description of the

DOI: 10.4324/9781003043874-104

diversity of students who rely on schools to serve them well and then provides examples of the importance of inclusive schools for improved long-term outcomes. Finally, approaches that minimize or eliminate difficulties experienced by minoritized learners are described, including engaging families and tapping their funds of knowledge; providing culturally responsive instruction, intervention, and assessment; facilitating culturally and contextually appropriate referral and evaluation; and individualizing support.

Information in Chapter 23 provides a review of established and emerging technologies that may be used to promote inclusion and effective instruction in schools and classrooms. It includes strategies that elementary teachers can use to approach technology-mediated learning, specifically through high leverage practices and Universal Design for Learning. The chapter ends with practical considerations and examples for how elementary teachers may use technology to promote increased learning and engagement for all students.

In the final chapter, the editors of this Handbook provide considerations for supporting effective inclusive schools now and in the future. Initially, the chapter addresses the limited progress that has been made related to school improvement and student outcomes, despite considerable effort. Then the chapter describes what is known about why goals are sometimes not achieved and why school improvement efforts often fail. Finally, perspectives are provided regarding what can be done to promote conditions that support school improvement that is sustained over time.

20

Support for District Change and Improvement

Kent McIntosh[1], Angus Kittelman[1], Kelsey Morris[2], Heather Peshak George[3], Brandi Simonsen[4], and Timothy J. Lewis[2]

[1]UNIVERSITY OF OREGON

[2]UNIVERSITY OF MISSOURI

[3]UNIVERSITY OF SOUTH FLORIDA

[4]UNIVERSITY OF CONNECTICUT

AUTHOR NOTE: THE RESEARCH REPORTED HERE WAS SUPPORTED BY THE INSTITUTE OF EDUCATION SCIENCES AND OFFICE OF SPECIAL EDUCATION PROGRAMS, U.S. DEPARTMENT OF EDUCATION, THROUGH GRANTS R324A1800027 AND H326S180001 TO THE UNIVERSITY OF OREGON. THE OPINIONS EXPRESSED ARE THOSE OF THE AUTHORS AND DO NOT REPRESENT VIEWS OF THE INSTITUTE, OFFICE, OR THE U.S. DEPARTMENT OF EDUCATION.

Setting the Stage

In an archaic view of education, the blame for an individual student's lack of success was attributed to the student. Likewise, in a traditional view of educational systems change, any blame for the failure to implement effective school practices has been attributed to the individual teacher. Fortunately, behavioral science has demonstrated the factors (e.g., environmental context, empirically-supported practices) that promote success for students and adults, and implementation science has demonstrated factors (e.g., context, implementation drivers) that promote successful educational systems change. As the responsibility for implementing effective school practices has shifted from the individual educator to the school, there is increasing consensus that the responsibility for building capacity and sustainability is at the district level (McIntosh & Goodman, 2016).

District systems are often neglected because they are more removed from student learning than school systems, but they are vitally important (Fixsen et al., 2010; George & Kincaid, 2008; Strickland-Cohen et al., 2014). Recent research has shown that district variables are significant predictors of implementation and sustainability of school interventions (George et al., 2018; McIntosh et al., 2013; McIntosh et al., 2018). This chapter describes these variables, with attention to how district and state leaders can arrange their district initiatives to optimize effectiveness, efficiency, equity, and sustainability.

DOI: 10.4324/9781003043874-20

What Do We Know Based on Research and the Wisdom of Practice?

Key District Functions for Supporting School Implementation

We know much about key variables supporting the implementation of school practices from nearly three decades of researchers and technical assistance providers working with district and school leadership teams to support their implementation efforts of Positive Behavioral Intervention and Supports (PBIS; (Barrett et al., 2008; George et al., 2018; George & Kincaid, 2008; Horner et al., 2010; Newton et al., 2012). In the early years of PBIS implementation, many of these key variables were identified by working directly with school leadership teams to establish successful model demonstration schools (i.e., positive exemplars; Netzel & Eber, 2003; Sugai & Horner, 2006). Since these early demonstrations, research has shown implementation of PBIS with fidelity impacts a host of important academic and social outcomes for children and youth (Horner et al., 2010; Mitchell et al., 2016, 2018). The majority of research conducted to date has been conducted at the elementary level. For example, Bradshaw and colleagues have documented improvements in social and academic engagement and reductions in overall levels of problem behavior (Bradshaw et al., 2008, 2010, 2012). Reductions of aggressive and anti-social behavior have also been empirically demonstrated (Benedict et al., 2007; Farkas et al., 2012), along with reductions in bully behavior with increases in prosocial behavior and emotional regulation (Waasdorp et al., 2012). Embedding differentiated academic supports within a PBIS framework also has demonstrated an additive impact on both academics and behavior (Chaparro et al., 2012; Gage et al., 2013).

Given the core elements of PBIS focus on explicitly teaching and practicing expected social, emotional, and behavioral expectations across all classroom and non-classroom settings, the logic of school-wide PBIS fits in well in the overall mission of elementary schools (Horner et al., 2010). As implementation efforts shifted to scaling-up (i.e., broadening the delivery of PBIS; Hagermoser Sanetti & Collier-Meek, 2019) and sustaining PBIS within districts (i.e., implementing with high fidelity of implementation over time; McIntosh et al., 2018), some key district variables have been found to facilitate implementation in schools (Barrett et al., 2008; George et al., 2018; Kittelman et al., 2020; McIntosh et al., 2018). Many of these lessons learned have been distilled into a single document, the PBIS Implementation Blueprint (Center on Positive Behavioral Interventions and Supports, 2015), which describes PBIS in particular but can be applicable to a wide range of complex school practices (Fixsen et al., 2005).

Figure 20.1 provides a graphic of key functions of organizational implementation of educational initiatives, which are applicable to agencies at the state, region, and district. In the center of the figure is leadership teaming. The functions above the team are the executive functions, and the functions below the team are implementation functions. This section will begin by describing teaming, followed by descriptions of each of the related functions in turn.

District Leadership Teaming

Although district leadership teams have a larger scope and reach than school leadership teams, both have some similar roles and functions. Table 20.1 provides a summary of these similarities between the district and school leadership teams. Similar to school leadership teams, district teams include key individuals with the authority, knowledge, experience, and skills to carry out specific implementation activities. Key individuals include district and school personnel (e.g., administrators, general and special education teachers, school psychologists, counselors, district coaches/coordinators) and community stakeholders (e.g., parents, business partners, healthcare providers, community mental health providers).

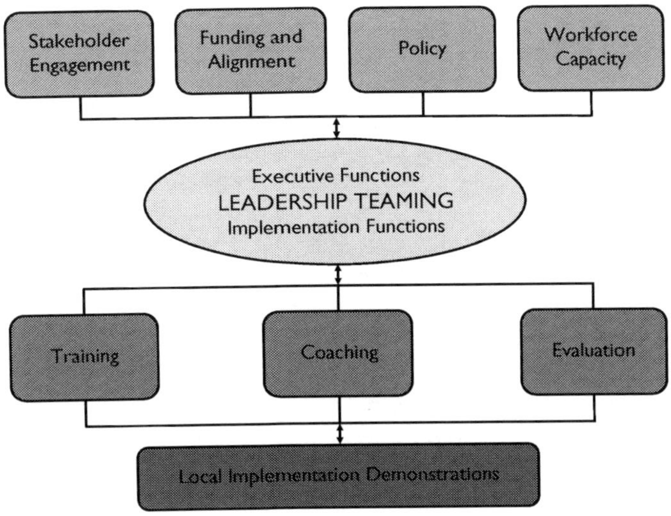

Figure 20.1 Key Functions of Organizational Implementation of Educational Initiatives (Reprinted With Permission from the Center on PBIS)

As described in Table 20.1, district leadership teams have unique responsibilities related to providing the vision, resources (e.g., funding, technical assistance), and coordination to support school leadership teams in their implementation efforts. For example, district and school administrators assist in providing visibility, political support, and funding for PBIS implementation efforts. Administrators showing public support and enthusiasm for implementation efforts is important for school personnel and community stakeholder buy-in and perceived to be critical for successful implementation of large-scale initiatives (Forman et al., 2009; George et al., 2018; Langley et al., 2010). General and special education teachers are integral for ensuring that district leadership teams have representation from those implementing practices in the classroom (Strickland-Cohen et al., 2014). This representation is especially important because stronger implementation of Tier 1 classroom practices is associated with sustained implementation of PBIS in schools, improved student outcomes, and improved racial/ethnic equity in student outcomes (Childs et al., 2016; Mathews et al., 2014; Tobin & Vincent, 2011). Classroom teachers help to contextualize implementation efforts (e.g., embed evidence-based practices into classroom routines) and address potential barriers during implementation.

Other district and school personnel include those with content expertise and experience implementing PBIS systems and social-emotional-behavioral practices (Goodman-Scott, 2013). These individuals often include school psychologists, counselors, and behavior specialists, who may hold dual roles as coordinators and district coaches (George & Kincaid, 2008). Depending on the size of the school district and resources for district implementation, larger districts may have multiple coordinators and coaches on district leadership teams (George et al., 2018). These individuals typically work directly with school leadership teams to: (a) conduct annual external evaluations of fidelity of implementation, (b) help guide action planning activities, and (c) provide training and coaching on implementing evidence-based practices, systems, and assessment tools (Bastable et al., 2020; Center on Positive Behavioral Interventions and Supports, 2020a; George et al., 2018).

In addition, community stakeholders (e.g., parents, school board members, social workers, business leaders, healthcare providers, community mental health providers) provide valuable input and external resources for implementation as active members of district leadership teams (e.g., ensuring practices are culturally responsive, engaging families in implementation activities; Center

Table 20.1 Activities and Functions of District and School Leadership Teams

District Leadership Teams	*School Leadership Teams*
• Define a unified vision for the district with measures used to assess the success of efforts to reach that vision.	• Align school vision and policies (i.e., school personnel and student handbooks) with district vision.
• Obtain and allocate funding to support school implementation efforts (i.e., training, coaching, buy-out of school personnel time for professional development activities).	• Allocate funding for school implementation activities (e.g., professional development, materials for implementation, incentive systems).
• Develop policies and strategies for engaging and communicating with stakeholders (i.e., family and community members) on implementation efforts and student outcomes.	• Engage and communicate with stakeholders on implementation efforts and student outcomes using district strategies.
• Develop and apply human resources policies to select, train, coach, and evaluate school and district personnel who will implement evidence-based practices.	• Use district human resource guidelines to select, coach, and evaluate school personnel who will implement evidence-based practices.
• Identify and promote the use of a standard set of evidence-based, multi-tiered practices, systems, and assessment tools.	• Implement district-recommended evidence-based practices, systems, and assessment tools.
• Develop 3-5 year evaluation plan to assess implementation progress and student outcomes.	• At least annually assess and evaluate implementation progress and student outcomes.
• Coordinate and assist school teams in developing action plans to improve implementation efforts.	• Regularly assess, evaluate, and develop action plans to improve implementation efforts.
• Provide differentiated training and ongoing coaching to support school leadership teams. Allocate FTE for coaching of trained skills and implementing evidence-based practices.	• Provide training to incoming and returning school personnel on PBIS implementation.
• Identify model demonstration exemplars.	• Contextualize implementation efforts to align with staff, student, and stakeholder community values.
• Increase district capacity to support schools implementing evidence-based practices.	• Increase school capacity to support students on evidence-based practices across tiers.
• Scale-up PBIS within districts.	

on Positive Behavioral Interventions and Supports, 2020a; Horner et al., 2017; Langley et al., 2010). Their participation can be especially helpful for preventing known barriers to student participation in evidence-based practices. For example, Langley et al. (2010) conducted structured interviews with district and school mental health clinicians and program directors to identify variables perceived to have facilitated or inhibited the implementation of a manualized evidence-based Tier 2 social-emotional-behavioral practice (Cognitive Behavioral Intervention for Trauma in Schools; Jaycox, 2004). The authors found that a lack of family engagement was the highest-rated barrier among successful implementers and the second highest-rated barrier among non-successful implementers. In addition, Kittelman et al. (2019) found that the percentage of students within districts receiving free or reduced lunch was a significant predictor for the rate of schools within districts adopting PBIS. As many students living in poverty are likely to need additional social and mental health services (Cappella et al., 2008), broadening the team to include community stakeholders can increase the district capacity to support students needing social and mental health services (e.g., identify additional resources within the community, obtaining external grant funding for resources).

Executive Functions

Some of the key activities of district leadership teams are to define, provide resources for, and engage district and school personnel and stakeholders in PBIS implementation efforts. These activities can be organized into four executive functions: stakeholder engagement, funding and alignment, policy, and workforce capacity.

Stakeholder Engagement

A key executive function of the district leadership team is to establish an array of strategies for engaging stakeholders in district implementation efforts. These strategies include gathering stakeholder input on district goal setting and policy development, disseminating information on PBIS implementation and district outcomes, and encouraging district leaders to participate in implementation activities and events with stakeholders (Center on Positive Behavioral Interventions and Supports, 2020a; Garbacz et al., 2017; Minch et al., 2017). Including stakeholders in district goal setting and policy development activities is useful for ensuring that community stakeholders value district improvement goals. Input can be gathered through surveys sent to families, organizing public meetings, and gathering feedback from stakeholders serving on district leadership teams. In addition to goal identification, district leadership teams can assist school leadership teams by creating clear policies and guidelines for how to actively engage stakeholders in PBIS implementation activities beyond only school-sponsored PBIS events (Garbacz et al., 2017). For example, these policies may provide incentives for encouraging school personnel to identify creative strategies to strengthen home-to-school communications when students are receiving Tier 2 and 3 support (Minch et al., 2017).

In addition, district leadership teams can identify and promote a range of strategies for disseminating information to stakeholders related to PBIS implementation and student outcomes (Center on Positive Behavioral Interventions and Supports, 2020a). These strategies may include dedicating a portion of district and school websites to sharing information about PBIS implementation activities and student data associated with district improvement goals, sending letters to new families describing PBIS efforts and activities, and sharing brief evaluation reports to stakeholders on PBIS implementation and student improvement goals. Finally, teams can cultivate stakeholder partnerships by ensuring that district leaders, such as school board members and superintendents, attend school-sponsored activities and events related to the initiative. District leaders play important roles in providing visible support of PBIS implementation and can help articulate to stakeholders how PBIS efforts are aligned with district improvement goals (Minch et al., 2017).

Funding and Alignment

Another executive function of the district leadership team is to obtain and allocate funding for implementation efforts (Center on Positive Behavioral Interventions and Supports, 2020a). Strategies helpful for securing funding for district implementation activities include demonstrating to district and state leaders (e.g., school board members) how investing in PBIS leads to improved district outcomes and partnering with state and district-level practitioners and university researchers to seek external funding from state and federal grants (Goodman-Scott, 2013; Strickland-Cohen et al., 2014). District budget plans are useful for dedicating funding to support school leadership teams for their implementation efforts. For example, it is unlikely that school leadership teams have the funding needed to hire internal PBIS coaches. Therefore, district leadership teams are more likely to hire a small number of district coaches to assist schools with their implementation efforts (e.g., provide coaching on implementing Tier 3 practices, assisting school teams with progress monitoring; Bastable et al., 2020; George & Kincaid, 2008). From George and Kincaid's experiences supporting district leadership teams in Florida (George & Kincaid, 2008), they suggested that leadership teams consider allocating as much as 50% of a district coach or coordinator's time to supporting up to six schools in a district and

100% of their salary for supporting up to 10 schools. Additional funding is also often allocated for other professional development activities, such as buying out school personnel time for professional development (e.g., summer training) and sending district and school leadership teams to receive external professional development through attending state or regional practitioner-orientated conferences (George & Kincaid, 2008; Strickland-Cohen et al., 2014).

Scarcity of funding for PBIS implementation is a reoccurring barrier faced by many district and school leadership teams (Coffey & Horner, 2012; Netzel & Eber, 2003; Pinkelman et al., 2015). As an example, Pinkelman et al. (2015) interviewed school personnel from over 800 schools implementing PBIS and found that a lack of funding was one of the top three perceived barriers affecting sustained PBIS implementation in schools. Additionally, one school member noted that their school did not have a required budget for PBIS implementation and was implemented with minimal funding (Pinkelman et al., 2015). District budget plans can also be useful in aligning funding allocated for separate, often competing for initiatives under one integrated PBIS budget (Kittelman et al., 2020; Pinkelman et al., 2015). If multiple initiatives are being implemented to address a similar outcome (e.g., improve equity in school discipline), it may present an opportunity for district leadership teams to save on funding by combining siloed work. For example, a district leadership team may decide to implement equity-focused behavior support as part of their Tier 1 preventative practices rather than continue funding a separate and standalone attendance intervention that may be costly in terms of personnel time, materials, and space. Such efforts have been shown to be successful, even with the pernicious problems of inequity (McIntosh et al., in press; McIntosh et al., 2020).

Policy

Numerous policies exist in school districts (e.g., school board policies, district and school administrative policies). Horner (2020) described that effective policies should serve to (a) create a shared vision or mission that aligns the implementation of evidence-based practices with core district beliefs and values (e.g., educational equity for all students, improve social-emotional competency), (b) provides motivation and incentives to engage in using these practices, and (c) defines the resources (i.e., funding, organizational systems) needed to implement the practices. Strong alignment is achieved when policies at different levels (school board, district, and school) are consistent and include these key features. Ensuring that these policies are in place is an important and early implementation step for district leadership teams, as it provides direction to school leadership teams on how to align their policies (as found in district discipline policies and school handbooks) with the values and mission of the district (Pinkelman & Horner, 2019). Additionally, these policies help to build district priority for improving student outcomes (Green et al., 2015; Horner, 2020), which has been found to be a significant predictor of sustained implementation of Tier 1 PBIS systems and practices in schools (McIntosh et al., 2013).

Workforce Capacity

Turnover among district and school personnel is a well-documented barrier to implementing evidence-based practices in schools (Coffey & Horner, 2012; Flannery et al., 2009; Forman et al., 2009; Kittelman et al., 2020; McIntosh et al., 2014; Pinkelman et al., 2015; Turri et al., 2016). As an example, turnover among school leadership team members has been perceived as a powerful barrier to PBIS implementation (Kittelman et al., 2020). Although some degree of turnover is inevitable, several strategies can be helpful for ensuring that district leadership teams maintain the capacity to support PBIS implementation over time. First, it is critical to recruit and hire district and school personnel that have knowledge and skills in implementing PBIS (Blase et al., 2013). Hiring school personnel with experience working in schools implementing PBIS is likely to reduce professional development costs (already trained on PBIS practices and systems) and increase the likelihood they buy into PBIS (Bambara et al., 2009; George et al., 2018). Additionally, hiring personnel with expertise in developing behavioral supports and interventions is beneficial for implementing evidence-based advanced tiers with fidelity. For example, Bambara et al. (2009) conducted interviews with different stakeholder groups (i.e., administrators, teachers, parents, district coaches) and found that one of the key barriers to implementing Tier 3 behavior supports was school personnel not having the skills to implement these complex practices. Second, those implementing PBIS may not be provided sufficient time for implementation activities (Kittelman et al., 2020; Pinkelman et al., 2015). To address this challenge, time for these activities (e.g., implementing Tier 3 practices, attending training) needs to be included within the job descriptions of the district and school personnel. As an example, for school psychologists also serving as district coaches, time for coaching (e.g., assisting school leadership teams with evaluation and action planning, data collection) needs to be explicitly built into their job descriptions in addition to their responsibilities as the school psychologist (Barrett et al., 2008; Bastable et al., 2020; George & Kincaid, 2008; Sullivan et al., 2011). Third, district leadership teams need to develop and use annual performance evaluations for new and returning district and school personnel to assess their knowledge and skills for initiative implementation. These data will be useful not only for evaluating their performances for the current year but also for informing future professional development activities (e.g., additional training on how to use data collection measures when implementing Tier 3 support plans).

Implementation Functions

The second set of functions of the district leadership team (in the lower section of Figure 20.1) includes support for school leadership teams with implementing the district-selected practices, systems, and tools through training, coaching, and evaluation (Bastable et al., 2020; George & Kincaid, 2008; George et al., 2018; Newton et al., 2011).

Training

Training is the first of several implementation strategies districts and school leadership teams use and is designed to teach new skills and knowledge to personnel (Massar, 2017). It is expected that a certain number of school PBIS trainings, or abbreviated refresher training, will occur each school year because of personnel turnover and implementation of Tier 2 and 3 systems (Turri et al., 2016). In planning and coordinating these training activities, it is helpful for district leadership teams to develop a three-to-five-year professional development calendar (Chaparro et al., 2012). In developing this calendar, it is useful for district team members to collect pre-training (baseline) data from the school sites (fidelity and student outcome) to help inform and tailor what training is needed and how much growth in fidelity can be expected. For example, Nese et al. (2018) found that the length of time from initial training to reaching adequate fidelity for elementary schools ranged from 1.82 to 2.30 years, middle schools ranged from 2.04 to 2.88 years, and for high schools from 2.31 to 3.8 years.

Table 20.2 provides an example of a five-year professional development plan developed by the Sunset School District leadership team (hypothetical school district). The district leadership team plans to implement PBIS in a step-wise pattern across the 12 schools in the district (six elementary, four middle schools, and two high schools), beginning with the elementary schools and one middle school in Year 1 (2022-2023 school year). This decision was made because the elementary school leadership teams were committed to the implementation and were most likely to reach adequate fidelity the quickest and the one middle school already had an established school leadership team and started implementing Tier 1 PBIS the previous year. In Year 2, the three remaining middle schools would begin Tier 1 implementation training, and in Year 3, the two high schools would begin Tier 1 implementation training.

Table 20.2 Five Year District Leadership Team Professional Development Calendar for Sunset School District

	2022-2023	*2023-2024*	*2024-2025*	*2025-2026*	*2026-2027*
Group A:6 Elem,1 Middle	T1 training	T1 refresher T2 training	T1 refresher T2 training T3 training	T1 refresher T2 refresher T3 training	T1 refresher T2 refresher T3 refresher
Group B:3 Middle		T1 training	T1 training	T1 refresher T2 training	T1 refresher T2 training T3 training
Group C:2 High			T1 training	T1 training	T1 refresher T2 training
Coaching	0.6 FTE Coaching	1.0 FTE Coaching	1.5 FTE Coaching	1.5 FTE Coaching	1.5 FTE Coaching
Model Demonstrations		Identify model demonstration school(s)	Identify model demonstration school(s)	Identify model demonstration school(s)	Identify model demonstration school(s)
Communities of Practice		Establish elementary community of practice	Establish secondary (middle/high) community of practice	Maintain community of practice groups	Maintain community of practice groups

Coaching

Coaching is another important (and often underused) function for supporting school leadership teams and personnel with using newly learned skills after the initial training has occurred (Bastable et al., 2020; Freeman et al., 2017; Massar, 2017). It is common for district leadership teams to allocate funding for coaching to assist school leadership teams and personnel with a variety of coaching activities to enhance implementation efforts (Bastable et al., 2020; Freeman et al., 2017; George & Kincaid, 2008). Coaching activities vary depending on each school's stage of implementation and status (Fixsen et al., 2005; McIntosh et al., 2018). For example, a school leadership team in their first year of Tier 1 implementation may need coaching on how to run meetings effectively and efficiently (i.e., defining roles, preparing and reviewing student discipline data, making data-based decisions) compared to a school leadership team in their second year of Tier 2 implementation that needs support developing fading procedures for students receiving Tier 2 practices. Coaching can be conducted through one-on-one activities and facilitating communities of practice peer networks (i.e., assisting school team members with sharing resources and describing when and how to use them; see Table 20.2). Bastable et al., 2020 surveyed 264 school leadership team members to identify different types of coaching activities provided by internal and external coaches, including ones perceived as most important for Tier 1 PBIS and those related to Tier 1 fidelity. The authors found that the three most frequently used coaching activities included attending school leadership team meetings, listening to school personnel concerns, and assisting with team action planning. The top three perceived as being most important for Tier 1 implementation were assisting with team action planning, assisting with data collection, and sharing knowledge of PBIS systems, while those positively and significantly related to Tier 1 fidelity were running data reports for the team and modeling PBIS implementation (Bastable et al., 2020).

Evaluation

The third implementation element includes the use of evaluation systems to monitor fidelity and student outcomes. Similar to the three-to-five-year professional development plan, evaluation systems are useful for district leadership teams to establish a formal companion evaluation plan to document when evaluation activities will occur, what data will be collected (i.e., administering fidelity measures, school walkthroughs by district PBIS coaches), and how data will be shared with district and school personnel and community stakeholders (Center on Positive Behavioral Interventions and Supports, 2015). To complete these evaluation activities, it is the responsibility of the district leadership team to identify, use, and promote highly efficient data evaluation systems that school leadership teams can use to enter data and generate reports for decision making (George et al., 2018; McIntosh et al., 2018). In semi-structured interviews with district leadership team members, George et al. (2018) reported that having strong district data infrastructures (e.g., for collecting discipline, behavior, and fidelity data) was perceived to be a major factor for strong district PBIS implementation among high-performing school districts. Moreover, McIntosh et al. (2018) also found that school leadership teams that regularly used data for decision making to improve implementation and student outcomes were more likely to sustain Tier 1 PBIS implementation with strong fidelity several years later.

Local Implementation Demonstrations

For district leadership teams in the early stages of implementation, it is common to first focus on piloting implementation efforts with a small number of model demonstration schools (Pinkelman & Horner, 2019). These successful demonstration schools help to build political and financial support for the initiative by demonstrating to district leaders in charge of funding (e.g., superintendents, school board members, administrators) that implementation of PBIS with strong fidelity results in improved student and school outcomes (Horner et al., 2019; Pinkelman & Horner, 2019). For example, Netzel and Eber (2003) described one district's PBIS implementation efforts that began by piloting PBIS in one elementary school with high levels of suspensions. After one year of Tier 1 implementation, the leadership team saw a substantial drop in suspensions. Findings from the pilot school were shared with the superintendent and school board, and they expressed a need to expand the implementation of PBIS in the district. The following year, five schools in the district began Tier 1 implementation (Netzel & Eber, 2003).

Model demonstration schools are also highly valuable in helping district leadership teams scale up PBIS efforts within districts (Horner et al., 2019). For example, as the number of schools within districts implementing PBIS expand, additional model demonstration sites are useful for providing schools with successful demonstration across different school types (e.g., grade levels) and tiers of implementation (i.e., Tier 2, Tier 3; see Table 20.2). District leadership teams will also need to identify effective strategies for communicating information about these successful demonstrations to school leadership teams through professional development activities. For example, during a community of practice event facilitated by a district coach (see Table 20.2), the coach may have an elementary school leadership team share out regarding how they developed and implemented their incentive systems so that school leadership teams are able to learn from this exemplar. Finally, as the initiative starts to scale up, research has shown that when more schools in districts are implementing PBIS, they are more likely to continue implementing PBIS with high fidelity (McIntosh et al., 2018). This is evident from research showing that the proportion of schools in the district implementing PBIS is a significant predictor of sustained implementation of PBIS in schools over time (McIntosh et al., 2018).

Increasing District Capacity to Support School Practices

The process of scaling or expanding practices is seldom consistent or linear. Descriptive data summarizing the PBIS implementation process across the country point to an iterative or cyclical sequence of the stages of implementation (Fixsen et al., 2005, 2009), such that organizations may repeat stages as they move from one school to the next or different schools may be at different stages based upon readiness and capacity (Horner et al., 2014). The time necessary for a given stage varies based on many factors (e.g., district support, adequate time for professional development, principal commitment).

Notwithstanding, evaluation and measurement of capacity are present in each stage of implementation. As teams are exploring implementation, they begin by carefully self-assessing their current status (strengths and needs) and capacity to implement change, as well as existing, feasible options for pursuing change (Fixsen et al., 2005). This information can help assess readiness for change and identify initial systems, practices, and data decisions to improve student outcomes (Lewis et al., 2016). As teams progress to initial implementation, they begin to establish the capacity for scaling and expansion by measuring fidelity and outcomes as a means of evaluating the difference between proposed implementation and actual implementation. In light of unforeseen implementation barriers, assessing initial implementation allows organizations to reassess training, coaching, and evaluation needs (Horner et al., 2014). Advancing to full implementation involves operating all systemic components and a range of practices while being responsive to evaluation data by using the data to make decisions. It is this responsiveness to evaluation that propels teams to successful sustained implementation. Achieving sustained scaling requires teams to engage in cycles of continuous quality improvement, in which they are actively adapting systems and practices based upon evaluation to achieve better fidelity and outcomes (Horner et al., 2014).

Measurement of District Capacity

Scaling and expanding implementation requires teams to conduct both baseline and ongoing assessments to identify current areas of strength and areas for continued growth (Horner et al., 2014). There are several measurements and tools teams can use to self-assess what core elements of the framework are already in place and guide the development of planning for the next steps.

District Capacity Assessment

The District Capacity Assessment (DCA; Ward et al., 2015) is designed to help districts measure their capacity to support and advance school-level implementation of any innovation (i.e., intervention or initiative). The goal of the DCA is to provide the district team with information to better align resources with intended outcomes and develop action plans to facilitate meaningful school support. Through the DCA, the capacity of a district is assessed in terms of the necessary systems, activities, and resources for successful adoption and sustained implementation of an effective innovation (Ward et al., 2015). As such, the DCA is completed for one specific innovation (e.g., early literacy, PBIS). The administration is facilitated by a trained, external facilitator who guides the District Implementation Team through assessment of key implementation drivers derived from the implementation science research literature (Fixsen et al., 2005), such as leadership, competency, and organization. The resulting data provides the team with information to both develop an action plan for increasing capacity and monitor progress towards district capacity-building goals.

District Systems Fidelity Inventory

The District Systems Fidelity Inventory (DSFI; Center on Positive Behavioral Interventions and Supports 2020a) is a team-based self-assessment designed to provide an efficient index of implementation capacity and current status for districts exploring or actively implementing multi-tiered systems of support (MTSS) for social-emotional-behavioral efforts (e.g., PBIS). It is intended to serve as an update to and replacement of the PBIS Implementation Blueprint Self-Assessment, an informal capacity measure included in the PBIS Implementation Blueprint (Center on Positive Behavioral Interventions and Supports, 2015). As such, the DSFI guides teams through an assessment of implementation drivers aligned to the elements and functions shown in Figure 20.1: (a) leadership teaming, (b) stakeholder engagement, (c) funding and alignment, (d) policy, (e) workforce capacity, (f) training, (g) coaching, (h) evaluation, and (i) local implementation demonstrations. The resulting data can be used to facilitate action planning to increase district capacity relative to the implementation drivers and also for progress monitoring of short- and long-term district improvement priorities identified to improve fidelity and outcomes. State leadership teams can use the State Systems Fidelity Inventory (Center on Positive Behavioral Interventions and Supports, 2019), a parallel measure for state efforts.

The DSFI is completed by a district leadership team established to lead the implementation of the district-wide multi-tiered system of support for social-emotional-behavioral domains. It is recommended to be completed prior to installation of an MTSS for social-emotional-behavioral efforts and then annually, thereafter, to progress monitor ongoing implementation. Once the DSFI is completed, the team can use the results, along with other district-level data (e.g., implementation phases, levels, and fidelity by building; building-level and district-level student outcomes; evidence of teacher practices), to organize short- and long-term action plans tailored to the district's unique needs and context.

Creating a Comprehensive Evaluation Plan

District capacity is simply one aspect that a district, region, or state can measure to improve outcomes. The PBIS Evaluation Blueprint (Center on Positive Behavioral Interventions and Supports, 2020b) provides a structure for districts to develop, conduct, and use results from a tailored evaluation plan for a district initiative. With evaluation being a key implementation driver, the blueprint serves to increase district capacity for developing evaluation plans, using data to engage in continuous improvement cycles and disseminating evaluation reports. The Evaluation Blueprint proposes an evaluation model to assess initiative reach, process, capacity, fidelity, and outcomes. The blueprint stresses the use of evaluation to make systems more effective, efficient, equitable, and sustainable.

Processes for Increasing Capacity

District leadership teams can use the data from district-level measures (e.g., DCA, DSFI) to identify current strengths and areas for growth, which can be envisioned as short-term goals (e.g., 1 year) and long-term goals (e.g., 3 to 5 years). Identifying strengths and goals facilitates the design of an action plan that is both strategic in nature and comprehensive in scope. The purpose of the action plan is to gain and sustain commitment for implementation, organize and arrange for the supports necessary for large-scale implementation (i.e., training, coaching, evaluation), and monitor implementation progress across sites (George & Kincaid, 2008).

Although the quality and efficacy of the individual interventions or practices are important, the absence of an infrastructure or systems to support good implementation results in poor implementation and, ultimately, poor outcomes and rejection of the practice (Fixsen et al., 2011). To increase capacity across the organization, it is helpful to attend to the necessary functions of implementation (i.e., leadership teaming, stakeholder engagement, funding and alignment, policy, workforce capacity, training, coaching, evaluation, local implementation demonstrations), which can facilitate broad and sustained systems change (George & Kincaid, 2008; Horner et al., 2014).

Setting the Course for District Change

Engaging in successful PBIS implementation requires a systematic and collaborative approach. Researchers and practitioners have identified promising strategies for supporting PBIS implementation in schools and several key variables that lead to positive district change. Extensive professional development is less effective and more likely to be abandoned without a clear vision with articulated and aligned goals derived from regular examination of data. As district leadership teams use this guidance to organize resources to facilitate successful implementation, more research is needed to empirically validate these strategies as a means to determine which are most likely to strengthen school implementation. Findings from research as well as data examined at the local level will provide practitioners guidance in how to successfully execute sustainable change at the district level.

Recommendations for Practice

School-wide PBIS is a widely implemented evidence-based, multi-tiered framework for systematically supporting the social-emotional-behavioral development of students through cohesive and preventative practices. Schools implementing PBIS at fidelity are shown to produce better outcomes for students (e.g., Bradshaw et al., 2010), and districts demonstrating key characteristics have been shown to produce a high proportion of schools implementing PBIS with fidelity. Systematic and collaborative planning are essential to organize the resources and supports necessary to build capacity for implementing and maintaining district change. This section provides guidance for practitioners that supports sustainable change at the district level.

Leadership Teaming

District leadership teams actively coordinate implementation efforts across schools and have the mission of increasing capacity for implementation (Center on Positive Behavioral Interventions and Supports, 2015). Horner et al. (2014) describe how districts can progress through the exploration stage without having a defined leadership team. In this early stage, leadership can be facilitated among strong advocates, subcontracted specialists, in-district collaboratives, as well as other supporters. However, because of their vital role in scaling up, district leadership teams are the most important element to establish prior to moving into the installation phase and initiating implementation (George & Kincaid, 2008; Horner et al., 2014). At this stage, teams must measure readiness for implementation and use the information from the exploration stage to help the organization assess readiness for change and identify the initial systems, practices, and data decisions that will be necessary to implement to the degree that improved student outcomes are evident (Lewis et al., 2016). Establishing a leadership team with roles and decision-making authority aids sustainability and is a necessary precursor for the political and fiscal support necessary for large-scale expansion (Horner et al., 2014).

For effective implementation and expansion, district leadership team members should be collectively committed to the science and framework of PBIS, have a plan for future expansion and sustainability, possess the authority to make key decisions (e.g., budget, implementation, policy, data systems), and have the capacity to allocate resources to implementation and expansion efforts (Center on Positive Behavioral Interventions and Supports, 2015; George & Kincaid, 2008). Because the district leadership team oversees implementation across all district sites, the team should have representation from a wide range of stakeholders including, but not limited to, individuals having (a) capacity to influence district-level professional development, (b) knowledge about the operations of the district across grade levels and programs, (c) access to district-level executive leadership, (d) responsibility for coordinating community and family engagement, (e) special education administrative authority, (f) administrative authority with social-emotional-behavioral support providers (e.g., counselors, social workers, school psychologists), (g) behavioral science expertise across the full continuum of behavior support (Tiers 1, 2, 3), and (h) representing the local community (e.g., community center leader, school board member; Center on Positive Behavioral

Interventions and Supports, 2020a). One suitable process for ensuring that the appropriate personnel and stakeholders have been identified to establish and lead implementation is to create a roster identifying team members and their position/title and compare it to the range of stakeholders previously described (a-h above).

When planning for district-wide expansion, one essential task of the district leadership team is to identify a district-level employee who can both facilitate the district-level team and serve as the PBIS district coordinator (George & Kincaid, 2008). District coordinators play a pivotal role in organizing and supervising professional development, implementation, and evaluation efforts within the district and while planning for scaling (Lewis et al., 2016). Effective coordinators possess adaptive skills ranging from technical (i.e., training and coaching) to management (e.g., hiring personnel, planning distributed training, disseminating evaluation data; Horner et al., 2014) and possess institutional knowledge with established relationships with school administrators (George et al., 2018). George and Kincaid (2008) note that because the amount of time allocated for a PBIS district coordinator correlates with the number of trained schools, as the quantity of PBIS implementation activities and the number of implementing schools increases, so, too, should the time equivalence of the coordinator.

Stakeholder Engagement

As district leadership teams plan for expansion, they should reflect on the visibility of their current and future work. With strategic communication, district leadership teams can increase awareness of implementation efforts which can foster increased levels of stakeholder engagement and also safeguard against scaling efforts being sidelined by competing initiatives.

By engaging stakeholders (internal and external), districts are better able to improve school climate; provide timely supports and services for families; and enhance student success at home and in the community through shared values (Epstein et al., 2009). Additionally, making an effort to engage all stakeholders benefits the district leadership team by enabling implementation in ways that are relevant to the culture, context, and values of the community. By considering stakeholder perspectives, district leadership teams obtain a more robust and clearer understanding of the experiences and values of the very consumers for which their systems, policies, practices, and larger implementation processes are intended.

Districts can bring about meaningful stakeholder engagement through strategic efforts to actively involve stakeholders in goal setting; disseminate information, data, and accomplishments to stakeholders; and interact with stakeholders at implementation events and activities (Center on Positive Behavioral Interventions and Supports, 2020a). One approach for organizing stakeholder engagement is developing and maintaining a stakeholder engagement plan. Such plans help district leadership teams establish systems for open, ongoing two-way communication. The purpose of a stakeholder engagement plan is to guide the district leadership team in the development and execution of action steps that engage multiple and diverse perspectives. Plans are comprehensive and designed to include: (a) an objective statement aligned to a measure of fidelity (e.g., DSFI, Tiered Fidelity Inventory, Self-Assessment Survey), (b) a communication/engagement goal the district seeks to achieve to attain the objective which is aligned to the scoring criteria of the fidelity measure, (c) action steps outlining all items necessary for reaching the goal, (d) progress monitoring of action steps, (e) persons responsible, (f) target audience, (g) type of information to be shared (data, accomplishments, implementation progress), (h) frequency or timeline for engagement, and (i) method of communication (print, electronic, verbal; University of Missouri Center for Schoolwide Positive Behavior Support, 2020).

There are many ways to facilitate information dissemination and district leadership teams should establish multiple systems for communicating information, data, and accomplishments on a regular basis and review them annually for fidelity. Through means such as newsletters, presentations to district and community leaders, district and school websites, recognition of exemplar schools, and pieces in the local media, districts can build the visibility necessary to scale and sustain PBIS. Such efforts not only increase interest in expansion, but they also advance the vision that PBIS implementation is connected to the district's larger and related improvement goals (e.g., reduce behavioral challenges, enhance academic-related behaviors, increase time in instruction) and is more than a momentary fascination (George & Kincaid, 2008).

Beyond espousing a vision, it is important for district leaders to endorse the daily work of implementation on a regular basis. By actively participating in PBIS events and activities (e.g., PBIS conferences, annual PBIS events, implementation site visits, acknowledgment of district/school progress), organizational leaders such as superintendents, board of education members, and department coordinators visibly affirm the PBIS goals and show public support for implementation efforts. Additionally, by participating in PBIS events and activities, district leaders are able to engage stakeholders and solicit feedback on implementation progress and outcomes (University of Missouri Center for Schoolwide Positive Behavior Support, 2020).

Funding and Alignment

A key aspect of district leadership is fiscal planning. During the early phases of an implementation initiative, districts may take advantage of external funding (e.g., grants) to support their PBIS initiatives. Although external funding sources can help stimulate a district's efforts and incentivize engagement, they are short-term in nature and not reliable for developing the infrastructure necessary for long-term implementation and systems change (George & Kincaid, 2008). Short-term funds can create barriers to increasing district capacity as a result of implementation efforts catering to the funding source rather than the design of a larger district infrastructure to support sustainability (George & Kincaid, 2008). To sustain and expand efforts within the district, a primary objective of the district leadership team should be developing a district budget plan with recurring funding and regularly allocated line items (i.e., prioritized funding) to support implementation and continuing support of the PBIS framework.

To enhance capacity to achieve full and sustainable implementation, it is important that the district leadership team inventory and assess what initiatives, programs, and practices are currently being promoted and implemented across the district. It is also important to evaluate the district's current reality and valued outcomes (i.e., goals) to identify the initiatives, programs, and practices that will move the district forward, those which are disconnected from the larger district vision, and how to best align efforts across the district to maximize resource and workforce potential. To this end, district leadership teams should engage in collaboration and coordinate across initiatives, programs, and practices and carefully plan for expansion (George & Kincaid, 2008).

One roadblock to expansion is diluted implementation capacity as a result of juggling multiple initiatives. Districts often have numerous foci which schools and educators are expected to attend to and implement. However, spreading attention across numerous objectives weakens the capacity to implement with integrity and fidelity (Sugai & Horner, 2006). For this reason, it is vitally important for the district to align initiatives. One effective way to achieve greater levels of alignment is to link the PBIS implementation action plan with the larger district improvement (i.e., strategic) plan and related goals. By clearly articulating within the action plan how PBIS activities relate to and address larger, relative district goals, the district leadership team can reduce redundancies, inefficiencies, and conflicting messages (Lewis et al., 2016).

Additionally, the Center on Positive Behavioral Interventions and Supports (2017) has produced a *Technical Guide for Alignment of Initiatives, Programs, and Practices in School Districts,* which teams can use to create an inventory of what is being done and then analyze the information to identify and readjust priorities. By conducting an annual audit of programming, districts can better maintain alignment and integration, problem-solve proactively, and ensure the fit of new initiatives, programs, and practices.

Policy, Systems, and Workforce Support

As districts scale implementation across schools, identifying social-emotional-behavioral health as one of the district's key goals can unify sites and personnel with a common purpose. A vision statement that clearly articulates the significance of positive school climate and student social-emotional-behavioral health in relation to student achievement and the reasoning for district-wide PBIS implementation serves to provide direction for all stakeholders and support for the work.

The district leadership team has the ability to influence policy development and, therefore, the responsibility to make recommendations for policies and procedures that support students' social-emotional-behavioral needs through the use of proactive, instructional, and ethical practices and which support the implementation of PBIS (Center on Positive Behavioral Interventions and Supports, 2020b; University of Missouri Center for Schoolwide Positive Behavior Support, 2020). As well, policies and procedures should encourage and promote equitable outcomes for all students by emphasizing the consistent use of evidence-based strategies for behavior support across student populations and demographics, including students with disabilities.

Relatedly, guidance for disciplinary decisions should be written and distributed to key stakeholders (internal and external) on a regular basis (Center on Positive Behavioral Interventions and Supports, 2020a). By annually auditing discipline policies and systems (e.g., code of conduct, student handbooks, staff handbooks), the district leadership team can refine discipline systems such that they enhance both social-emotional-behavioral and academic outcomes as well as fidelity of implementation.

Guidance on policy and discipline are constructive ways to better support the district's workforce (i.e., faculty and staff) with PBIS implementation. To achieve durable, large-scale implementation of PBIS, districts should also consider how their recruitment, hiring, and evaluation practices support the capacity of their workforce and support sustainability. By explicitly naming PBIS and embedding implementation activities (e.g., training and coaching) with dedicated time into job descriptions, districts are able to recruit and retain personnel with the knowledge, skill, and experience implementing PBIS. Likewise, by providing guidance on hiring criteria and selection for district/school administrators, relevant coaches, teachers, and other staff, district leadership teams can positively influence the selection of personnel who will advance the work. Moreover, district leadership teams can embed PBIS implementation into performance evaluations of administrators, teachers, and related instructional/support personnel to assess knowledge and skills related to PBIS systems implementation. In doing so, districts establish systems and structures for meaningful performance feedback and, in turn, support and retain a high-quality workforce.

Professional Development: Training and Coaching

District leadership teams can establish an effective professional development system by following a multi-step process. First, teams can assess their schools' current levels of PBIS implementation across the district to better understand the depth and breadth of implementation. Utilizing data from established fidelity measures can help district leadership teams better understand the number of sites implementing and at what tier. Second, teams can then self-assess their current professional development capacity. By considering individuals based on their expertise and role rather than their unique position or title, districts can effectively and efficiently establish a cadre of trainers and coaches. For example, schools at the installation or initial implementation stage can be trained by the district PBIS coordinator, district PBIS coaches, or even PBIS team leaders from fully implementing schools. As well, roles such as school counselor, school psychologist, and behavior consultant can be leveraged and used to fulfill PBIS coaching functions (Lewis et al., 2016).

To make adequate determinations about the needs of training and coaching personnel, districts can use the PBIS Trainer/Coach Assessment included in the PBIS Professional Development Blueprint (Lewis et al., 2016) to measure the current level of knowledge and skills of trainers and coaches across all tiers of PBIS (George & Kincaid, 2008; Lewis et al., 2016). In addition to helping district leadership teams identify current levels of in-district behavioral expertise, the results can facilitate the identification of the skill sets current trainers and coaches will need for sustaining implementation, guide the allocation of professional development provided to trainers and coaches, and identify the personnel needed to meet the district's needs (George & Kincaid, 2008; Lewis et al., 2016). When considering the necessary personnel to expand and sustain implementation, district leadership teams can identify the roles and functions required for establishing implementation and sustaining the initiative as a priority by looking across service areas. In doing so, districts can identify district-level personnel who may serve as coaches to provide technical assistance to school-based teams and assist in the regular monitoring of school progress (George & Kincaid, 2008). Local experts such as school psychologists, social workers, and special educators with higher-level behavioral knowledge can aid full implementation at the advanced tiers and support training and coordination needs (Horner et al., 2014).

Once capacity for professional development is assessed and established, districts can use schools' fidelity data to better understand professional development needs across campuses and the district. Professional development needs can be organized into three categories: (a) assistance for sites at the exploration stage with overviews and readiness, (b) ongoing training along all three tiers of the PBIS framework differentiated by team readiness, and (c) readily available technical assistance and coaching. To facilitate this work, districts need the capacity to deliver training that are targeted on pivotal skills, taught with opportunities to see and hear examples, and include dedicated time during and after to apply concepts to the school's context with coaching support (Lewis et al., 2016).

District trainers and coaches, in conjunction with the District PBIS Coordinator, can use school-level self-assessment data to design a professional development action plan to guide school-level teams through the phases of implementation across all tiers of PBIS. The PBIS Professional Development Blueprint (Lewis et al., 2016) provides guiding questions, tools and supports, activities, and desired outcomes to assist district leadership teams with the development of a comprehensive professional development plan. Simultaneously, it is important for the district also to establish a professional development action plan for district trainers and coaches to enhance their expertise and skills. One straightforward, manageable way to support trainers and coaches is by hosting regular (monthly, bimonthly) meetings consisting of data sharing, skill-building activities, success stories, problem-solving, and networking (George et al., 2018; George & Kincaid, 2008).

Evaluation

Scaling, expanding, and increasing capacity for broad-scale implementation requires the evaluation of fidelity of implementation and impact on student outcomes to be more organized, coordinated and disseminated (Horner et al., 2014). Districts can increase their capacity to support school practices by developing an evaluation infrastructure (i.e., adequate evaluation measures, data collection systems, cadres with evaluation expertise) so that school and district implementers can regularly assess whether systems and practices are being implemented with fidelity and if that implementation is benefitting students (Center on Positive Behavioral Interventions and Supports, 2020b).

Using the PBIS Evaluation Blueprint (Center on Positive Behavioral Interventions and Supports, 2020b), district teams can establish comprehensive evaluation plans that measure (a) reach ("Who is participating?"), (b) process ("What is happening with the initiative?"), (c) capacity ("What is the capacity of the organization to implement and sustain?"), (d) fidelity ("Are we implementing as intended?"), and (e) outcomes ("Is the initiative achieving valued outcomes?"). A comprehensive approach to evaluation with data from various instruments aids teams in refining and enhancing the implementation process. By having data systems in place to collect common data which facilitate continuous decision making, districts are better positioned to assess current levels of implementation, determine strengths and weakness of implementation activities, plan for ongoing professional development and coaching to support staff, and refine resource allocation and policies (Childs et al., 2016; McIntosh et al., 2017; Mercer et al., 2017).

Local Implementation Demonstrations

To realize full implementation across all buildings, district leadership teams should plan for local implementation demonstrations and consider how to best use pilot and model schools as part of the strategic plan for scaling up (Center on Positive Behavioral Interventions and Supports, 2020a; George & Kincaid, 2008). Model demonstration sites are recognized as being exemplars of PBIS implementation with fidelity and typically have annual data indicating sustained high levels of fidelity of implementation and visible activities, data (e.g., success in improving student outcomes), and products to serve as local examples of process and outcomes (George & Kincaid, 2008). As districts work to scale up implementation, it is imperative teams plan for a range of demonstrations and models, with sites across tiers and levels (e.g., early childhood, elementary, middle, high; Center on Positive Behavioral Interventions and Supports, 2020b).

The achievements of model demonstration sites can strengthen and promote the reasoning for continued district expansion and ultimately become a training resource as implementation expands to new schools within the district or for teams struggling with implementation (Sugai & Horner, 2006). Additionally, establishing model or exemplar demonstrations can help facilitate support among executive-level leadership within the organization (McIntosh et al., 2016). As the number of demonstration schools increases and exemplar sites document feasibility and beneficial student outcomes, political support for implementation expansion shifts and results in an increased willingness to invest in the organizational systems needed for broad-scale implementation (e.g., training, coaching, evaluating, intervening practices; Horner et al., 2014) at the district level.

Recommendations for Research

In general, research has shown that teaming is an essential component to successful outcomes and has pointed to the importance of collaboration, integration, planning and data-based problem-solving (George et al., 2018; Horner et al., 2018; McIntosh et al., 2018). However, little is known regarding the impact of the engagement of diverse stakeholders in relation to actual outcomes achieved. What function of district team members will likely produce changes in student outcomes? Randomized control trials of PBIS have demonstrated significant effects across a range of student outcomes (e.g., Horner et al., 2010). However, for schools to sustain high fidelity implementation of the full PBIS framework, they need continuous support from their district. Further examination of the leadership team component such as individual team functions, procedures, or overall structures related to improved student outcomes at the district level is needed. This analysis may be of value for establishing more effective leadership teaming as well as the identification of specific team activities that may result in better student outcomes.

Over a decade of research on the critical role that the fidelity of PBIS has on student outcomes is noteworthy. Research should continue to define and better clarify the relation between district leadership teaming practices and student outcomes. District interviews conducted by George et al. (2018) were the first to reveal the distinct contributions of the district coordinator and the integrated teaming structure. Although relationships and enthusiasm are difficult to measure, further research on these critical attributes in relation to student outcomes may assist districts when hiring a coordinator, individuals serving a coaching capacity, or even administrators in leadership roles.

Further, McIntosh et al. (2013) identified factors related to the sustainability of school-wide PBIS implementation, including two district-level factors, district priority and capacity building. Expansion of this finding examined the specific coaching activities most related to sustained implementation (Bastable et al., 2020). Future research could identify how some of these activities and attributes also interact with contextual factors (e.g., demographics, resources) and district leadership teaming actions that improve student outcomes. For example, is there a difference in key variables needed across the phases of implementation at the district level?

Implementing PBIS requires resource allocation that may include funding for personnel, database systems, training, coaching, and other activities. Further examination of how teams can most effectively allocate resources is needed to guide district leadership teams in planning their implementation activities. Although some researchers have assessed the cost of school-wide PBIS at the school, district and state levels (Bradshaw et al., in press; Swain-Bradway et al., 2017), more research is needed to fully examine the actual costs incurred on these specific budgets. Investigating the cost savings of PBIS across both a range of schools (e.g., elementary, middle, high) and geographic area (e.g., rural, suburban, urban) as well as the personnel critical to an effective infrastructure can assist district leadership teams in evidence-based decision making and appropriate allocation of resources (e.g., hiring coaches, identifying training activities, aligning initiatives, preventing attrition). This information can also assist in determining the needs of the workforce capacity, delivering essential training, and integrating performance evaluation aligned with improved outcomes (e.g., school climate, fidelity, consumer satisfaction). Research is also needed on the impact of existing district policies, such as the delivery of intensive interventions by specialized personnel or the engagement of exclusionary practices that may hinder student outcomes and impact higher costs of implementation. Further evidence demonstrating a return on investment may assist teams in leveraging district-wide visibility and political support and thus, directly impact funding.

Conclusion

Districts invest in systems to support, sustain, and scale implementation of the PBIS framework throughout their schools. Following the PBIS Implementation Blueprint (Center on Positive Behavioral Interventions and Supports, 2015), a representative leadership team engages in executive team functions (stakeholder engagement, funding and alignment, policy, and workforce capacity), develops and carries out critical implementation functions (training, coaching, and evaluation), and celebrates local implementation demonstrations. Much like school teams, district teams complete measures to monitor systems fidelity (e.g., DCA, DSFI), design and conduct a comprehensive evaluation plan, and develop and implement an action plan to increase capacity. Thus, districts play a critical role in developing systems to support school-level implementation and ultimately improving outcomes for educators and students. Although current evidence supports a variety of implications for practice, described in detail in this chapter, further research is necessary to uncover and understand relations between key district features (e.g., teaming structures and functions), implementation fidelity, and student outcomes.

References

Bambara, L., Nonnemacher, S., & Kern, L. (2009). Sustaining school-based individualized positive behavior support: Perceived barriers and enablers. *Journal of Positive Behavior Interventions*, *11*, 161–178.

Barrett, S. B., Bradshaw, C. P., & Lewis-Palmer, T. (2008). Maryland statewide PBIS initiative: Systems, evaluation, and next steps. *Journal of Positive Behavior Interventions*, *10*(2), 105–114. doi:10.1177/1098300707312541

Bastable, E., Massar, M. M., & McIntosh, K. (2020). A survey of team members' perceptions of coaching activities related to Tier 1 SWPBIS implementation. *Journal of Positive Behavior Interventions, 22*(1), 51–61. doi:10.1177/1098300719861566

Benedict, E. A., Horner, R. H., & Squires, J. K. (2007). Assessment and implementation of positive behavior support in preschools. *Topics in Early Childhood Special Education, 27*(3), 174–192.

Blase, K. A., Van Dyke, M., & Fixsen, D. L. (2013). *Implementation drivers: Assessing best practices.* The University of North Carolina, FPG, SISEP. http://sisep.fpg.unc.edu/sites/sisep.fpg.unc.edu/files/resources/SISEP-Brief2-Intensive-TA-02-2009.pdf

Bradshaw, C. P., Debnam, K. J., Player, D., Bowden, B., & Lindstrom Johnson, S. (in press). A mixed-methods approach for embedding cost analysis within fidelity assessment in school-based programs. *Behavioral Disorders.* doi:10.1177/0198742920944850

Bradshaw, C. P., Mitchell, M. M., & Leaf, P. J. (2010). Examining the effects of schoolwide positive behavioral interventions and supports on student outcomes: Results from a randomized controlled effectiveness trial in elementary schools. *Journal of Positive Behavior Interventions, 12*(3), 133–148. doi:10.1177/1098300709334798

Bradshaw, C. P., Reinke, W. M., Brown, L. D., Bevans, K. B., & Leaf, P. J. (2008). Implementation of school-wide positive behaivoral interventions and supports (PBIS) in elementary schools: Observations from a randomized trail. *Education and Treatment of Children, 31*(1), 1–26. doi:10.1353/etc.0.0025

Bradshaw, C. P., Waasdorp, T. E., & Leaf, P. (2012). Effects of school-wide positive behavioral interventions and supports on child behavior problems. *Pediatrics, 130*(5), e1136–e1145. doi:10.1542/peds.2012-0243

Cappella, E., Frazier, S. L., Atkins, M. S., Schoenwald, S. K., & Glisson, C. (2008). Enhancing schools' capacity to support children in poverty: an ecological model of school-based mental health services. *Administration and Policy in Mental Health, 35*(5), 395–409. doi:10.1007/s10488-008-0182-y

Center on Positive Behavioral Interventions and Supports. (2015). *Positive Behavioral Interventions and Supports (PBIS) implementation blueprint.* University of Oregon. https://www.pbis.org/resource/pbis-implementation-blueprint

Center on Positive Behavioral Interventions and Supports. (2017). *Technical guide for alignment of initiatives, programs, practices in school districts.* Eugene, OR. www.pbis.org

Center on Positive Behavioral Interventions and Supports. (2020a). *Positive Behavioral Interventions and Supports District Systems Fidelity Inventory (DSFI)—Pilot version 0.2.* University of Oregon.https://www.pbis.org/resource/pbis-district-systems-fidelity-inventory-dsfi-pilot-version-v0-1

Center on Positive Behavioral Interventions and Supports. (2019). *Positive Behavioral Interventions and Supports State Systems Fidelity Inventory (SSFI)—Pilot version 0.1.* University of Oregon. https://www.pbis.org/resource/pbis-state-systems-fidelity-inventory-ssfi-pilot-version-v0-1

Center on Positive Behavioral Interventions and Supports. (2020b). *Positive Behavioral Interventions and Supports (PBIS) evaluation blueprint.* University of Oregon. https://www.pbis.org/resource/pbis-evaluation-blueprint

Chaparro, E. A., Smolkowski, K., Baker, S. K., Hanson, N., & Ryan-Jackson, K. (2012). A model for system-wide collaboration to support integrated social behavior and literacy evidence-based practices. *Psychology in the Schools, 49*(5), 465–482. doi:10.1002/pits.21607

Childs, K. E., Kincaid, D., George, H. P., & Gage, N. A. (2016). The relationship between school-wide implementation of positive behavior intervention and supports and student discipline outcomes. *Journal of Positive Behavior Interventions, 18*(2), 89–99. doi:10.1177/1098300715590398

Coffey, J. H., & Horner, R. H. (2012). the sustainability of schoolwide positive behavior interventions and supports. *Exceptional Children, 78*(4), 407–422. doi:10.1177/001440291207800402

Epstein, J. L., Sanders, M. G., Sheldon, S., Simon, B. S., Salinas, K. C., Jansorn, N. R., Van Voorhis, F. L., Martin, C. S., Thomas, B. G., Greenfield, M. D., Hutchins, D. J., & Williams, K. J. (2009). *School, family, and community partnerships: Your handbook for Action.* (3rd ed.). Corwin Press.

Farkas, M. S., Simonsen, B., Migdole, S., Donovan, M. E., Clemens, K., & Cicchese, V. (2012). Schoolwide positive behavior support in an alternative school setting: An evaluation of fidelity, outcomes, and social validity of Tier 1 implementation. *Journal of Emotional and Behavioral Disorders, 20*(4), 275–288. doi:10.1177/1063426610389615

Fixsen, D. L., Blase, K. A., Duda, M. A., Naoom, S. F., & Van Dyke, M. (2010). Implementation of evidence-based treatments for children and adolescents. In J. R. Weisz & A. E. Kazdin (Eds.), *Evidence-based psychotherapies for children and adolescents* (pp. 435–450). Guilford.

Fixsen, D. L., Blase, K. A., Horner, R. H., & Sugai, G. (2009). Concept paper: Developing the capacity for scaling up the effective use of evidence-based programs in state departments of education. Retrieved from http://ea.niusileadscape.org/docs/FINAL_PRODUCTS/LearningCarousel/DevelopingCapacity.pdf.

Fixsen, D. L., Blase, K. A., & Van Dyke, M. K. (2011). Mobilizing communities for implementing evidence-based youth violence prevention programming: A commentary. *American Journal of Community Psychology, 48*, 133–137. doi:10.1007/s10464-010-9410-1

Fixsen, D. L., Naoom, S. F., Blase, K. A., Friedman, R. M., & Wallace, F. (2005). *Implementation research: Synthesis of the literature*. University of South Florida, Louis de la Parte Florida Mental Health Institute, The National Implementation Research Network (FMHI Publication #231).

Flannery, K. B., Sugai, G., & Anderson, C. M. (2009). School-wide positive behavior support in high school: Early lessons learned. *Journal of Positive Behavior Interventions, 11*(3), 177–185. doi:10.1177/1098300708316257

Forman, S. G., Olin, S. S., Hoagwood, K. E., Crowe, M., & Saka, N. (2009). Evidence-based interventions in schools: Developers' views of implementation barriers and facilitators. *School Mental Health, 1*(1), 26. doi:10.1007/s12310-008-9002-5

Freeman, J., Sugai, G., Simonsen, B., & Everett, S. (2017). MTSS coaching: Bridging knowing to doing. *Theory Into Practice, 56*(1), 29–37. doi:10.1080/00405841.2016.1241946

Gage, N. A., Sugai, G., Lewis, T. J., & Brzozowy, S. (2013). Academic achievement and school-wide positive behavior supports. *Journal of Disability Policy Studies, 25*(4), 199–209. doi:10.1177/1044207313505647

Garbacz, S. A., Witte, A. L., & Houck, S. N. (2017). Family engagement foundations: Supporting children and families. In M. D. Weist, S. A. Garbacz, K. L. Lane, & D. Kincaid (Eds.), *Aligning and integrating family engagement in positive behavioral interventions and supports (PBIS): Concepts and strategies for families and schools in key contexts*. (pp. 9–30). Center for Positive Behavioral Interventions and Supports (funded by the Office of Special Education Programs, U.S. Departement of Education).

George, H. P., Cox, K. E., Minch, D., & Sandomierski, T. (2018). District practices associated with successful SWPBIS implementation. *Behavioral Disorders, 43*(3), 393–406. doi:10.1177/0198742917753612

George, H. P., & Kincaid, D. K. (2008). Building district-level capacity for positive behavior support. *Journal of Positive Behavior Interventions, 10*(1), 20–32. doi:10.1177/1098300707311367

Goodman-Scott, E. (2013). Maximizing school counselors' efforts by implementing school-wide positive behavioral interventions and supports: A case study from the field. *Professional School Counseling, 17*(1), 2156759X0001700106. doi:10.1177/2156759X0001700106

Green, A., Nese, R. N. T., McIntosh, K., Nishioka, V., Eliason, B., & Delabra, A. C. (2015). *Key elements of policies to address discipline disproportionality: A guide for district and school teams*. OSEP Technical Assistance Center on Positive Behavioral Interventions and Supports. Available at http://www.pbis.org.

Hagermoser Sanetti, L. M., & Collier-Meek, M. A. (2019). Increasing implementation science literacy to address the research-to-practice gap in school psychology. *Journal of School Psychology, 76*, 33–47. doi:10.1016/j.jsp.2019.07.008

Horner, R. H. (2020). The marriage of policy, practices and data to achieve educational reform. *American Journal of Intellectual and Developmental Disabilities, 125*(5). doi:10.1352/1944-7558-125.5.340

Horner, R. H., Kincaid, D., Sugai, G., Lewis, T., Eber, L., Barrett, S., Dickey, C. R., Richter, M., Sullivan, E., Boezio, C., Algozzine, B., Reynolds, H., & Johnson, N. (2014). Scaling up school-wide positive behavioral interventions and supports: Experiences of seven states with documented success. *Journal of Positive Behavior Interventions, 16*(4), 197–208. doi:10.1177/1098300713503685

Horner, R. H., Newton, J. S., Todd, A. W., Algozzine, B., Algozzine, K., Cusumano, D., & Preston, A. (2018). A randomized waitlist controlled analysis of team-initiated problem solving professional development and use. *Behavioral Disorders, 43*(4), 444–456. doi:10.1177/0198742917745638

Horner, R. H., Sugai, G., & Anderson, C. M. (2010). Examining the evidence base for School-wide positive behavior support. *Focus on Exceptional Children, 42*(8), 1–14.

Horner, R. H., Sugai, G., & Fixsen, D. L. (2017). Implementing effective educatioanl practices at scales of social importance. *Clinical Child and Family Psychology Review, 20*(1), 25–35. doi:10.1007/s10567-017-0224-7

Horner, R. H., Ward, C. S., Fixsen, D. L., Sugai, G., McIntosh, K., Putnam, R., & Little, H. D. (2019). Resource leveraging to achieve large-scale implementation of effective educational practices. *Journal of Positive Behavior Interventions, 21*(2), 67–76. doi:10.1177/1098300718783754

Jaycox, L. H. (2004). *Cognitative behavioral intervention for trauma in schools*. Sopris West Educational Services.

Kittelman, A., McIntosh, K., & Hoselton, R. (2019). Adoption of PBIS within school districts. *Journal of School Psychology, 76*, 159–167. doi:10.1016/j.jsp.2019.03.007

Kittelman, A., Strickland-Cohen, M. K., Pinkelman, S. E., & McIntosh, K. (2020). Variables contributing to abandonment and readoption of SWPBIS. *Journal of Positive Behavior Interventions, 22*(2), 67–77. doi:10.1177/1098300719888748

Langley, A. K., Nadeem, E., Kataoka, S. H., Stein, B. D., & Jaycox, L. H. (2010, 2010/09/01). Evidence-based mental health programs in schools: barriers and facilitators of successful implementation. *School Mental Health, 2*(3), 105–113. doi:10.1007/s12310-010-9038-1

Lewis, T. J., Barrett, S., Sugai, G., Horner, R. H., Mitchell, B. S., & Starkey, D. (2016). *Training and professional development blueprint for positive behavioral interventions and supports*. National Technical Assistance Center on Positive Behavior Interventions and Support. www.pbis.org

Massar, M. M. (2017). *Effects of coach-delivered prompting and performance feedback on teacher use of evidence-based classroom management practices and student behavior outcomes.* [Dissertation, University of Oregon]. Eugene, OR.

Mathews, S., McIntosh, K., Frank, J. L., & May, S. L. (2014). Critical features predicting sustained implementation of school-wide positive behavior support. *Journal of Positive Behavior Interventions, 16*, 168–178.

McIntosh, K., Girvan, E. J., McDaniel, S. C., Santiago-Rosario, M. R., St. Joseph, S. D., Fairbanks Falcon, S., Izzard, S., & Bastable, E. (in press). Effects of an equity-focused PBIS approach to school improvement on exclusionary discipline and school climate. *Preventing School Failure.* doi:10.1080/1045988X.2021.1937027

McIntosh, K., Girvan, E. J., Smolkowski, K., Falcon, S., Bastable, E., McDaniel, S. C., Santiago-Rosario, M. R., Austin, S. C., Izzard, S., & Nese, R. N. T. (in press). Effects of an equity-focused PBIS approach on equity in school discipline: Results from a randomized controlled trial. *School Psychology.*

McIntosh, K., & Goodman, S. (2016). *Integrated multi-tiered systems of support: Blending RTI and PBIS.* Guilford Press.

McIntosh, K., Kelm, J. L., & Canizal Delabra, A. (2016). In search of how principals change: A qualitative study of events that help and hinder administrator support for school-wide PBIS. *Journal of Positive Behavior Interventions, 18*, 100–110. doi:10.1177/1098300715599960

McIntosh, K., Massar, M. M., Algozzine, R. F., George, H. P., Horner, R. H. J. T. L., & Swain-Bradway, J. (2017). Technical adequacy of the SWPBIS tiered fidelity inventory. *Journal of Positive Behavior Interventions, 19*(1), 3–13. doi:10.1177/1098300716637193

McIntosh, K., Mercer, S. H., Hume, A. E., Frank, J. L., Turri, M. G., & Mathews, S. (2013). Factors related to sustained implementation of schoolwide positive behavior support. *Exceptional Children, 79*(3), 293–311.

McIntosh, K., Mercer, S. H., Nese, R. N. T., Strickland-Cohen, M. K., Kittelman, A., Hoselton, R., & Horner, R. H. (2018). Factors predicting sustained implementation of a universal behavior support framework. *Educational Researcher, 47*(5), 307–316. doi:10.3102/0013189X18776975

McIntosh, K., Predy, L. K., Upreti, G., Hume, A. E., Turri, M. G., & Mathews, S. (2014). Perceptions of contextual features related to implementation and sustainability of school-wide positive behavior support. *Journal of Positive Behavior Interventions, 16*, 29–41. doi:10.1177/1098300712470723

Mercer, S. H., McIntosh, K., & Hoselton, R. (2017). Comparability of fidelity measures for assessing tier I school-wide positive behavioral interventions and supports. *Journal of Positive Behavior Interventions, 19*(4), 195–204. doi:10.1177/1098300717693384

Minch, D., Kincaid, D., Tremaine, V., & Thomas, R. (2017). Translating family engagement strategies to practice in local sites implementing PBIS. In M. D. Weist, S. A. Garbacz, K. L. Lane, & D. Kincaid (Eds.), *Aligning and integrating family engagement in positive behavioral interventions and supports (PBIS): Concepts and strategies for families and schools in key contexts.* (pp. 32–70). Center for Positive Behavioral Interventions and Supports (funded by the Office of Special Education Programs, U.S. Departement of Education).

Mitchell, B. S., Bruhn, A. L., McDaniel, S. C., & Lewis, T. J. (2016). Early intervention and prevention of aggressive and violent behavior through school-wide systems of positive behvior support. In P. Sturmey (Ed.), *The Wiley handbook of violence and agression* (Vol. 3, pp. 539–562). Wiley.

Mitchell, B. S., Hatton, H., & Lewis, T. J. (2018, 2018/10/01). An examination of the evidence-base of school-wide positive behavior interventions and supports through two quality appraisal processes. *Journal of Positive Behavior Interventions, 20*(4), 239–250. doi:10.1177/1098300718768217

Nese, R. N. T., Nese, J. F. T., McIntosh, K., Mercer, S. H., & Kittelman, A. (2018). Predicting latency of reaching adequate implementation of tier i schoolwide positive behavioral interventions and supports. *Journal of Positive Behavior Interventions, 21*(2), 106–116. doi:10.1177/1098300718783755

Netzel, D. M., & Eber, L. (2003). Shifting from reactive to proactive discipline in an urvan school district: A change of focus through pbis implementation. *Journal of Positive Behavior Interventions, 5*(2), 71–79. doi:10.1177/10983007030050020201

Newton, J. S., Algozzine, B., Algozzine, K., Horner, R. H., & Todd, A. W. (2011). Building local capacity for training and coaching data-based problem solving with positive behavior intervention and support teams. *Journal of Applied School Psychology, 27*(3), 228–245. doi:10.1080/15377903.2011.590104

Newton, J. S., Horner, R. H., Algozzine, B., Todd, A. W., & Algozzine, K. (2012). A randomized wait-list controlled analysis of the implementation integrity of team-initiated problem solving processes. *Journal of School Psychology, 50*(4), 421–441. doi:10.1016/j.jsp.2012.04.002

Pinkelman, S. E., & Horner, R. H. (2019). Applying lessons from the teaching-family model: Positive Behavioral Interventions and Supports (PBIS). *Perspectives on Behavior Science, 42*(2), 233–240. doi:10.1007/s40614-019-00199-x

Pinkelman, S. E., McIntosh, K., Rasplica, C. K., Berg, T., & Strickland-Cohen, M. K. (2015). Perceived enablers and barriers related to sustainability of school-wide positive behavioral interventions and supports. *Behavioral Disorders, 40*(3), 171–183. doi:10.17988/0198-7429-40.3.171

Strickland-Cohen, M. K., McIntosh, K., & Horner, R. H. (2014). Sustaining effective practices in the face of principal turnover. *Teaching Exceptional Children*, *46*(3), 18–24.

Sugai, G., & Horner, R. H. (2006). A promising approach for expanding and sustaining the implementation of school-wide positive behavior support. *School Psychology Review*, *35*, 245–259.

Sullivan, A. L., Long, L., & Kucera, M. (2011). A survey of school psychologists' preparation, participation, and perceptions related to positive behavior interventions and supports. *Psychology in the Schools*, *48*(10), 971–985. doi:10.1002/pits.20605

Swain-Bradway, J., Lindstrom Johnson, S., Bradshaw, C., & McIntosh, K. (2017). *What are the economic costs of implementing SWPBIS in comparison to the benefits from reducing suspensions?* OSEP TA Center on Positive Behavioral Interventions and Supports.

Tobin, T. J., & Vincent, C. G. (2011). Strategies for preventing disproportionate exclusions of African American students. *Preventing School Failure*, *55*, 192–201. doi:10.1080/1045988X.2010.532520

Turri, M. G., Mercer, S. H., McIntosh, K., Nese, R. N. T., Strickland-Cohen, M. K., & Hoselton, R. (2016). Examining barriers to sustained implementation of school-wide prevention practices. *Assessment for Effective Interventions*, *42*(1), 6–17. doi:10.1177/1534508416634624

University of Missouri Center for Schoolwide Positive Behavior Support. (2020). *PBIS district leadership team practice guide*. [Unpublished manuscript]. Department of Special Education, University of Missouri-Columbia.

Waasdorp, T. E., Bradshaw, C. P., & Leaf, P. J. (2012). The impact of school-wide positive behavioral interventions and supports on bullying and peer rejection: A randomized controlled effectiveness trial. *Archives of Pediatrics & Adolescent Medicine*, *166*(2), 149–156. doi:10.1001/archpediatrics.2011.755

Ward, C., Martin, S., Horner, R. H., Duda, M., Ingram-West, K., Tedesco, M., Putnam, D., Buenrostro, M., & Chaparro, E. (2015). *District capacity assessment*. University of North Carolina at Chapel Hill. https://fpg.unc.edu/node/7586

21

Support for School Change and Improvement

Caryn S. Ward, Sophia Farmer, Kathleen Ryan Jackson, and Tanya Ihlo

UNIVERSITY OF NORTH CAROLINA AT CHAPEL HILL; DEVELOPMENT OF THIS CHAPTER WAS SUPPORTED BY THE OFFICE OF SPECIAL EDUCATION PROGRAMS U.S. DEPARTMENT OF EDUCATION (H326K120003). OPINIONS EXPRESSED HEREIN ARE THOSE OF THE AUTHORS AND DO NOT NECESSARILY REFLECT THE POSITION OF THE U.S. DEPARTMENT OF EDUCATION, AND SUCH ENDORSEMENTS SHOULD NOT BE INFERRED.

Setting the Stage

To address education disparities for students with disabilities, there is a continued call for the use of practices supported by evidence to improve the quality and effectiveness of services provided. Despite gains in knowing what practices work, educators continue to struggle in adopting and using evidence-based practices and producing impactful change (Burns & Ysseldyke, 2009; Madon et al., 2007). Nationally, students in U.S. schools are not considered proficient in core academic areas (i.e., reading, mathematics). According to the most recent data from the National Center for Education Statistics, only 37% of twelfth grade students performed at or above proficient levels in reading and 25% performed at or above proficient levels in mathematics (National Center for Education Statistics, 2019). For students with disabilities, the proficiency results are even lower and have been referred to as "abysmal" (Fuchs et al., 2018, p. 127). Historically, efforts at school improvement or school reform have not yielded dramatic gains for students, especially for students with disabilities (Dragoset et al., 2017). This gap between what we know works and utilization of those practices in schools and classrooms may deny students with disabilities proven benefits (Dew & Boydell, 2017).

To effect meaningful change in educational outcomes in effective inclusive schools, simultaneous attention is needed to not only what evidence-based and other effective practices are selected but also how they are implemented. Implementation science, the multi-disciplinary study of methods and strategies to promote the use of research findings in practice, seeks to address this by providing frameworks to guide the creation of conditions and activities that facilitate adoption and use of evidence-based and other effective practices such as the high-leverage practices (described in Chapter 9 of this Handbook) (Eccles & Mittman, 2006). Specifically, school leaders and educators can use implementation science methods and tools found to be effective in addressing the research to practice gap so that practices are being effectively used and ultimately outcomes are being improved for students in effective inclusive schools.

DOI: 10.4324/9781003043874-21

Implementation Science Introduction

Within the field of implementation science, previous research reveals common tenets or themes across various implementation frameworks and strategies (Meyers et al., 2012). First is the recognition that systems, such as education systems, are complex, often unpredictable, and must be responsive to changes needed to support effective use of practices. Purposeful selection of effective practices (including evidence-based and high leverage practices) to address needs, use of readiness assessments, meaningful inclusion of stakeholders, a focus on cultivating staff confidence and capacity, and active engagement of leaders to cultivate collaborative cultures also are common across frameworks. In addition, the use of a stage-based approach to guide general and specific capacity development and infrastructure, responsiveness to iterative data cycles, and use of bidirectional feedback loops are common tenets found to be crucial to attaining and sustaining socially significant outcomes (Fixsen et al., 2015, Metz et al., 2015; Saldana et al., 2012).

Implementation science research also identifies the need to strengthen the alignment of policy and practice in education systems. Schools are one part of a larger complex education system comprised of nesting and intersecting organizations in support of successful education for students and families within the community. Specifically, a school is part of the District or Local Education Agency. The District is often part of a regional or county system within the state and part of the State education system. Each of these education organizations within the system has a specific role with responsibilities and functions to be engaged for support of educators in their use of effective practices to create inclusive and impactful settings for the communities they serve.

For example, the State Education agency often sets standards and provides guidance and resources. States in collaboration with regional and county offices provide supports for districts and schools to use as guidance for achieving the standards. Districts allocate resources and set policies and procedures that schools work within. Districts also support schools and teachers in their effective use of practices and ensure that implementation supports such as training, coaching, data, and community relations systems are accessible and of high quality. Districts and schools often share responsibility in the co-design and use of the needed implementation supports. Using the allocated resources, provided guidance, and implementation supports, schools are responsible for the instructional design and delivery of practices or programs and leadership supports as well as engagement with community stakeholders. For successful implementation of effective practices at the school level, alignment and coherence is needed within the education system and amongst its agencies (classroom to state level). It is paramount for schools in collaboration with district leadership to align initiatives and leverage existing resources to accomplish school improvement goals (Coburn et al., 2016; McIntosh et al., 2013).

Overall, the findings from implementation science indicate there are three critical factors necessary for achieving socially significant impact: Effective Practices x Effective Implementation x Enabling Context = Socially Significant Outcomes (Fixsen et al., 2015). Schools need to select practices supported by evidence and matched to student needs and their school improvement goals (effective practices). Infrastructure for training, coaching, use of data, communication and leadership is needed to support educators to implement in a deliberate and adaptive manner (effective implementation). Finally, a hospitable environment with supportive policies and a culture of continuous improvement is needed to ensure educators and effective practices thrive and sustain (enabling context). These three factors summarize what is being implemented (e.g., a high-leverage instructional practice such as explicit instruction), how it is being implemented, and where it is being implemented.

For the purpose of this chapter, we will define and describe the necessary implementation components of these factors for effective school improvement and change. These components are summarized and defined in Table 21.1. We will share the research basis for each component, outline

Table 21.1 Implementation Components

Implementation Component	Description
Usable Innovation	Activities to ensure high-leverage practices are clearly defined so that they are teachable, learnable, doable, and assessable.
Implementation Drivers	Visible infrastructure supports that ensure the development of skilled staff and strong organization and system.
Implementation Stages	Steps matched to intended outcomes needed over time for effective implementation.
Implementation Teams	Group of staff and stakeholders responsible for overseeing implementation and continuous improvement of inclusive practices.
Improvement Cycles	Process for using data systematically and purposefully for making small incremental improvements.

the practices necessary at the school level, and provide a case illustration of school change using these components. Specifically, the case illustration is inclusive of examples and recommendations for practice. Finally, we provide recommendations and potential future directions for research on implementation components needed for the use of effective practices within school change efforts.

What Do We Know Based on Research and the Wisdom of Practice?

To ensure the three factors necessary for achieving socially significant outcomes are present, the implementation components and their relevant methods and tools have been organized into several frameworks, called the Active Implementation Frameworks (Fixsen et al., 2015). The Active Implementation Frameworks synthesize the many common tenets and themes across implementation science theories and research and have been informed by practice-based evidence from the application within numerous health and human service fields, including K-12 education (Fixsen et al., 2013).

Effective Practices

In order to achieve significant impact, effective practices (the what) need to be well specified and matched to the needs of the student population within the school. Specifically, practices are more likely to be implemented well and achieve intended outcomes when (a) stakeholders (teachers, students, and others) find the practices acceptable to meet locally identified needs, (b) the school has the capacity to support sustained training, coaching, and data needs with district support, (c) the practices are operationalized with clearly defined essential components to help teachers and others know what they should be doing and saying, and (d) adaptations to the practices are systematically made based on data (Zaheer et al., 2020). When practices lack specification, it is challenging for teachers, staff, and leaders to figure out the "what" of the practices they should be using so that impediments to using the practice can be identified and removed (Hall & Hord, 2006). Crosse et al. (2011) found that only 3.5% of practices are used with any level of fidelity over time due to practices being poorly defined and therefore difficult to support. This results in a waste of time and resources for teachers and students, impedes replication of the practice in additional classrooms or expanding its use to other schools, and ultimately results in little improvement or change in student outcomes. To ensure effective use, repeated use, and scalability, the effective practices, need to be "teachable, learnable, doable, and assessable" (Fixsen et al., 2013).

Usable Innovation

The Usable Innovation framework outlines four criteria for schools to use in determining whether a practice is usable and provides guidance on how to ensure the practice is. To ensure practices are usable, (a) the underlying philosophy, values, and principles of the practice should be articulated and understood, (b) the essential components, or key ingredients, should be identified to help understand what must be implemented for the practice to be successful, (c) those components need to be fully operationalized so it is clear what teachers and others should be saying and doing, and (d) fidelity assessments should be identified or developed to assess the use of the essential components (Fixsen et al., 2013; Metz, 2016).

In practice, a clear description of the practice is established by a team with diverse perspectives and roles (district, school, community). They use feedback from educators who are not on the team and information gathered from a thorough literature review and district-school document review to establish a clear philosophy, common values, and shared principles (Metz, 2016). This process ensures the practice is a good fit for the district and schools so that it will be used consistently by teachers from school to school and classroom to classroom. It also supports the creation of readiness and buy-in because educators see their voice in the team's decisions through the use of communication loops between the team to their stakeholders. The team also establishes inclusion and exclusion criteria to clearly identify who the practice is for (target population of students to benefit) and who it is not for based on recommendations and findings from the research as well as the school's experience.

Using the information gathered from the review, the team can identify the essential components or key ingredients of the practice that must be present for successful outcomes. The team then operationally defines each function so they know what they would see or observe in the classroom for each component. Finally, they identify or develop a common fidelity assessment that aligns with each essential function and operational definition. Once defined, the school team then refines the practice through the use of iterative Plan, Do, Study, Act cycles. That is, they conduct small tests of change or engage in a trial and learning approach to ensure the practice is, in fact, usable and acceptable to teachers, students, and others.

Implementation science tools to guide a team through this process of ensuring the practice is usable include Innovation Configurations (Hall & Hord, 2006) or Practice Profiles (Metz, 2016). Using these tools, teams can articulate the four criteria of a Usable Innovation for practice through the research-based process described above. Once developed, the tools facilitate the development of effective professional learning plans, coaching strategies, use of fidelity assessments, and refinement of the school procedures and processes (e.g., scheduling, planning time, resource allocation, communications) to enable the use of the practice (Metz, 2016). Schools and their districts should ensure there are team members that have the necessary knowledge of and experience with the practices being defined or have access to the developer or purveyor (i.e., national or state level trainer or technical assistance provider) of the practice.

Effective Implementation

For implementation to be effective, we need to identify needed infrastructure or capacity building supports and when activities for designing, developing, and improving those supports are needed. The factor of effective implementation is operationalized within the two frameworks of Implementation Stages and Drivers. These frameworks provide guidance for school teams on what actions are needed and when within the context of their school improvement or change process for creating inclusive settings.

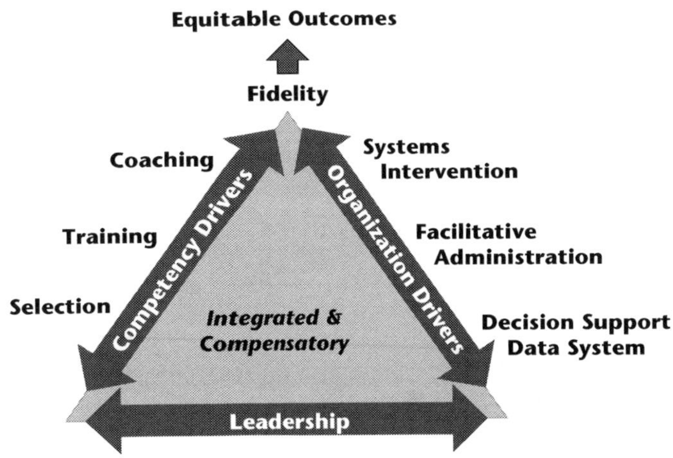

Figure 21.1 Implementation Drivers

Implementation Drivers

It is widely recognized that robust infrastructure supports are required to implement effective practices effectively. Over 90% of 25 published implementation frameworks include capacity-building strategies and infrastructure development as critical components of successful implementation (Meyers et al., 2012). These components comprise the majority of strategies found on compiled menus of implementation strategies (Michie et al., 2013; Powell et al., 2012). Implementation infrastructure includes supports of competent practice, organizational, and systems change (Metz & Bartley, 2012). The field of implementation science has identified several practices to build, improve, and sustain the infrastructure needed for high-quality implementation, often are referred to as strategies and drivers (Fixsen et al., 2005, 2015; Powell et al., 2015).

For the purposes of this chapter, implementation infrastructure is defined through implementation drivers, the mechanisms of the infrastructure needed to support practice, organizational, and systems change (see Figure 21.1). Based on the commonalities among successfully implemented practices, two categories of implementation drivers, Competency and Organizational, supported by effective leadership, emerged (Fixsen et al., 2005, 2009)

Competency drivers are aimed at fully and effectively using effective practices and include the *selection* of educators with required skills and abilities; *training* of educators and others involved at the school to provide knowledge related to the theory and underlying values of the practice; on-the-job *coaching* to rehearse and master the new skills; and use of multiple data sources for feedback for educators to improve *fidelity*. Collectively, the competency drivers ensure the development and improvement of staff confidence and competence to effectively use the effective practices.

Organizational drivers (e.g., *systems intervention, facilitative administration and decision support data system)* are essential to sustainable change. Data systems need to be established to support decision-making, including the collection and use of programmatic, fidelity, and outcome data. In addition, administrators need to facilitate the new practice by (1) providing the necessary leadership to address challenges and create solutions, (2) developing clear communication and feedback loops, (3) adjusting and developing policies and procedures to support the practice, (4) allocating necessary resources, and (5) engaging external stakeholders collaboratively in the implementation process. Collectively, organization drivers create the facilitating processes, procedures, and systems environments needed for the effective practices to be used with fidelity by educators and achieve expected outputs and outcomes.

These drivers are supported by and founded on effective school leadership practices. School leaders are most effective for school change efforts when they are knowledgeable about the practice to be implemented, proactive in problem-solving, support staff, and maintain disciplined attention through the ups and downs of the implementation process (Aarons et al., 2014; Moullin et al., 2017). Implementation also requires different types of leadership strategies to address the different types of challenges and problems encountered in implementation (Heifetz & Laurie, 1997). Adaptive challenges are often referred to as wicked problems in implementation and are characterized by competing perspectives and differing views on whether there is a problem, what the problem is, and the solutions that are not always readily available. Adaptive challenges require the use of specific leadership strategies such as "protecting all voices" where staff are provided safe space to identify conflicts and constructively disagree, or "regulating distress" by managing the pace of the work and setting realistic deadlines for school staff. Adaptive leadership strategies are different from technical leadership strategies that are used for technical problems. Technical problems can still be complex, but they are characterized by having clear agreement on the problem and having available solutions, such as resource allocation, making a plan, and providing accountability (i.e., management leadership). Both types of problems are often encountered in the school change process requiring the use of varied leadership strategies (Blase et al., 2015).

School implementation teams can use a structured problem-solving process to assess the strength of the implementation drivers. The *Drivers Best Practice Assessment* (DBPA; Ward et al., 2018; Ogden et al., 2012) is a tool schools can use to assess and continuously improve their implementation infrastructure. Teams use the items on the assessment to strengthen their hiring practices, including the addition of interview questions, behavioral rehearsals and performance tasks. They ensure ongoing training for staff by aligning school and district goals with funding for professional learning based on the fidelity of implementation data. Effective schools capitalize on the skills and capacity of teacher leaders to become school and district trainers and sometimes peer-to-peer coaches. Having a coaching system and way to measure coaching effectiveness is imperative to improvement (Crosse et al., 2011). With a system for training, coaching, and data use in place, measures of effectiveness for each driver can be developed and used by teams to determine what is effective and what needs improvement. Having an easy-to-use data system (i.e., decision support data system) is imperative to the effective use of data at the school level. Teams must have access to data at least monthly that is current and easily accessed. An important role in fulfilling on each team is a data analyst who ensures that data is ready to use and supports the team in using data for improvement.

Effectively implementing a new practice is dependent on teams' fluent use of multiple forms of implementation data (e.g., fidelity, process, programmatic) and student outcome data. Fidelity assessment data are used to determine the follow-up training or coaching required by teachers to continuously improve the use of a given practice. The fidelity assessment is formative and never used for teacher evaluation purposes (Akin et al., 2013; Darling-Hammond et al., 2017). Rather, the data are used to determine the strength of the implementation infrastructure supporting the use of the practice and what improvements can be made.

In summary, implementation drivers define for schools what key mechanisms are necessary to support the school change efforts and sustain those changes over time. It should be noted that the infrastructure of a school is often supported and shared in terms of decision making with the district within which the school resides. Depending on the district, schools have varying levels of autonomy in decision making. Districts may set policy and guidelines for supports, such as the selection process for staff that schools must abide by and use. Regardless of the level of autonomy, schools should advocate for, collaboratively co-design with districts, and support the use of policies and processes that are enabling the appropriate use of effective practices in classrooms.

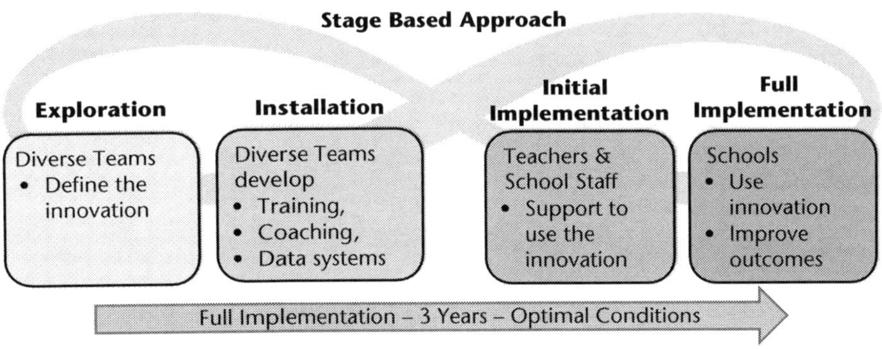

Figure 21.2 Implementation Stages

Implementation Stages

There is consensus in the study of implementation that all efforts should proceed from identification of need and assets and exploration of potential solutions to adoption and sustainability (Aarons et al., 2011; Metz et al., 2015; Meyers et al., 2012). Implementation is a two to four-year process toward a goal with a clear theory of action that involves stakeholders making decisions, taking action, and identifying improvements needed to support the successful use of selected effective practices in schools (Fixsen et al., 2001; Saldana, 2014). Implementation starts when a school begins to consider change and full implementation is reached when the change is fully in place and producing intended outcomes in all classrooms. The process includes four Stages that can lead to the long-term survival (sustainability) and continued effectiveness of any effective practice in a context of constant change. These stages include: Exploration, Installation, Initial Implementation, and Full Implementation (Figure 21.2; Fixsen et al., 2013; Metz & Bartley, 2012). The stages serve as a roadmap for schools by outlining the necessary activities and intended outcomes of implementation work (e.g., acceptability, adoption).

Exploration

The first stage of implementation, Exploration, is a time when schools make decisions about fit, feasibility, capacity, and commitment to using selected effective practices. During this stage, schools develop a team with diverse representation from school administration, district leadership, general and special education staff, other key staff, community, families, and students to schools engage in activities related to identifying needs, assets, and potential root causes to determine needed changes. With support from the district, the school team considers possible options of effective practices to address the needed changes, examines the fit and feasibility of the identified practices to decide if they will move forward with implementation, and communicates with stakeholders throughout the process.

Intentional and purposeful use of exploration activities results in the establishment of readiness and collective commitment of all staff. Through shared understanding and consensus-building, school staff begin to understand the benefits of using an effective practice to meet equitable student outcome goals (Kilbourne et al., 2007; Ingvarson et al., 2005); make a collective commitment to goals, objectives, roles, and responsibilities; and co-create the supports with leadership's active participation and commitment to equitable resources (Metz, 2015; Padua et al. 2014). Attempts to use a new program or practice in schools by proclamation or persuasion of leaders are costly because, without broad-based ownership in the process, schools produce lower rates of implementation at a higher cost (Romney et al., 2014). Conversely, when organizations engage in exploration activities with those who are expected to use a new practice, they produce better outcomes at a lower cost (Nutt, 2001). Exploration matters because with shared commitment to proceed, schools legitimize the process and marshal the human capital willing to design and use an implementation infrastructure for continuous improvement of effective practices (Ryan Jackson et al., 2018).

Installation

Following the decision to implement the selected effective practices, implementation teams develop or refine the necessary infrastructure to support staff and organizational competency during the Installation stage. In this stage, the school team works closely with the district team to ensure the practices are clearly defined and usable for the staff who will be implementing them. The team also develops an implementation plan that outlines (a) protocols for selecting staff needed for implementation, (b) training and coaching supports, (c) data systems including what data will be collected (i.e., outcome, fidelity, and process data), and how and when data will be collected, analyzed, and shared, and (d) decision-making criteria for determining success. In addition, it is during the Installation stage that school teams identify teachers who will participate; provide initial training; ensure access to materials and equipment necessary to support the use of the effective practices; and develop and use feedback loops among staff, leadership, community partners and stakeholders to ensure effective communication (Metz & Bartley, 2012; Saldana et al., 2012).

All too often, districts choose a practice by edict, provide minimal training without an opportunity to rehearse and receive feedback from a coach regarding a new practice and then expect teachers and school staff to use the practice with fidelity and enact policy they have little knowledge of or voice in development (Hattie, 2003; Joyce & Showers, 1995, 2002). By district and school professionals working together to co-create the implementation infrastructure, school staff and other stakeholders are included in the process and their current work is valued. In addition, school staff will have the professional learning, materials, resources, and measures to assess and continuously improve equitable systems of support based on the school's context, capacity, and needs of teachers and their diverse student population (Metz, 2015; Ryan Jackson et al., 2018; Saldana et al., 2012). School staff depends on knowing how they will receive ongoing support to use a new practice to ensure implementation as intended (Groff, 2020). With the infrastructure in place, principals, teachers, and school staff know they will be sufficiently trained before they are expected to use a new practice and they know there is a system for collecting practice data (e.g., walkthrough, fidelity, integrity) and a system to use multiple forms of implementation data for continuous improvement (Bryk et al., 2015; Taylor et al., 2014).

Initial Implementation

During Initial Implementation, the selected effective practices are put into use in the school and classrooms and teachers begin receiving coaching supports. It is critical during this time for the school team to meet regularly to use data to examine the effectiveness of the supports being provided and make improvements to the implementation infrastructure to meet the needs of teachers and maximize success for students. The team also uses data and decision-making criteria for expanding the use of the practice by additional school staff. It is imperative that strong communication protocols are in place from teachers in the classroom to the school's leadership team, which ensures teachers have the support they require, and to the district leadership who can enact procedural changes for sustainability.

Having a district representative with authority to solve implementation barriers as they arise, support or serve on the school leadership team is an effective practice and ensures district commitment and prioritization of the work (George et al., 2018; McIntosh et al., 2013). For example, when a school team encounters a barrier and they cannot keep pushing on, they have to stop and address how to overcome the barrier and see that their needs will be met (Fixsen et al., 2013). A district administrator may be instrumental in providing support to the school team when this occurs. This support legitimizes the process and reinforces staff's collective commitment to improvement and communicates to them that district administration values the work they are doing. As the district's and school's capacity improves, their ability to use implementation data to continuously strengthen training and coaching systems based on fidelity data as well as academic outcomes of a diverse student body is critical in leading the school and district to full implementation (Kentucky Department of Education (KDE), 2019, Kloos et al., 2020).

Full Implementation

When a school has at least fifty percent of their teachers using effective practices with integrity and the desired student outcomes are being achieved, they are in the Full Implementation stage. It is key during this time that teams not get complacent and remove supports or stop meeting, assuming smooth sailing is ahead. To ensure continued success and prevent drift back to previous practice, teams should maintain the provision of needed training and coaching supports, use of feedback loops, and regular use of data for continuous improvement. Schools continue to return to previous stage-based activities as they onboard new staff, apply their implementation infrastructure to other school-wide practices, and continuously develop the capacity of school staff, their community, and local school boards. By engaging in these implementation activities, practice can inform policy and policy can enable effective practice where school funding formulas and finance policies are equitable and lead to closing long-standing disparities in student outcomes.

Key Characteristics of Implementation Stages

Implementation stages have several key characteristics. First, the stages are not linear. Ending one stage to begin another is seldom the case, rather the stages may overlap, and stage-based activities may be applied across multiple stages. For example, a school in full implementation and producing good outcomes in 50% of their classrooms may revisit exploration as they scale to additional classrooms. Secondly, the activities of the stages repeat at each level of the system. That is, a school team will need to go through stage-based activities in addition to the district or central office members going through the activities. A third characteristic is that a school can be in different stages at the same time for different practices. For example, a school may be in initial implementation for their selected literacy practice but are also in exploration as they identify needs for a practice to address social-emotional skills. Fourth, sustainability is attended to throughout the stages, beginning with Exploration. Finally, implementation work is never done. Even when achieving outcomes, work is needed to ensure continued effective use of the practices and avoid "drift" or return to previous ways of work. The Implementation Stages Planning Tool (NIRN, 2020; https://nirn.fpg.unc.edu/resources/stages-implementation-analysis-where-are-we) may be used to guide a team in identifying their current stage of implementation and provides a checklist of activities and outcomes needed to establish or strengthen staff readiness and needed implementation supports. Teams can use the data to assess, monitor, and communicate their current implementation efforts to key stakeholders.

Enabling Context

The use of effective practices in classrooms is much more implementable when done so in collaboration with stakeholders and within a culture of continuous improvement (Rycroft-Malone et al., 2013; Metz,

2016). An enabling context is one in which there is an accountable and representative team with diverse skills and perspectives at the school level to engage stakeholders in the work of implementation and use data for continuous improvement. The Active Implementation Frameworks provide guidance for school leadership teams on the functions and perspectives needed for school change. The use of Improvement Cycles provides processes and guidance for how the team should use data to make decisions. The two implementation components of Implementation Teams and Improvement Cycles for creating and sustaining an enabling context are presented next.

Implementation Teams

In a review of implementation frameworks, 68% of 25 frameworks identified the creation and use of an implementation team as a critical component for ensuring quality implementation (Meyers et al., 2012). An implementation team is a group of staff and stakeholders that oversees, attends to, and is accountable for performing key functions in the selection, use, and continuous improvement of effective practices. As the formal implementation structure, teams purposefully apply stage-based activities to ensure a) school staff, students, and families are engaged in the implementation process, b) the practice is well-defined and a good fit with the school context, c) implementation supports are in place, d) fidelity is measured and improved as needed, and e) student outcomes are achieved and sustained.

Using implementation teams to actively and intentionally make changes produces higher rates of success more quickly than traditional methods of implementation that do not take such an active, team-based approach (Higgins et al., 2012; Metz et al., 2015). Without teams, the implementation effort ends up relying on individual leaders. Reliance on an individual leader for school change or use of top-down leadership solely does not always produce stakeholder buy-in, integration and alignment within the system, and sustainability to achieve equitable outcomes (Lane et al., 2014; Metz et al., 2017; Strunk et al., 2015).

The school implementation team takes responsibility for the appropriate use of effective practices by teachers in the classroom. A school implementation team should be comprised of between six and ten members so that they are representative of perspectives but also "as small as possible," given the work to be accomplished (Wageman et al., 2005, p. 4). The school implementation team may be a subset of a larger school leadership team or be the school leadership team if it is a good fit. The goal of the implementation team is to be nimble and efficient in the work needed. For sustainability purposes, it is recommended that time dedicated to the role of serving on the team be included in job descriptions.

Highly effective school implementation teams have members representing a diversity of experiences, skills, and perspectives. Across the team, members should have knowledge and skill in the selected practice as well as with the needed implementation supports such as professional learning, coaching, and use of data for decision making. Leadership for the team is a key to ensuring effective functioning (Aarons & Palinkas, 2007). Administrators from the school and district are needed on the team so they can allocate required resources when a need is identified as quickly as possible. This helps to create continued buy-in and collective commitment to the process because teachers and school staff realize they will be supported and the onus for improvement no longer rests solely on teachers.

Teachers must also assume leadership roles, so it is imperative that a general and special education teacher leader and other key school staff (e.g., a paraprofessional leader) are members of the implementation team. The representative teachers act as liaisons with colleagues and provide feedback and data to the implementation team from teacher teams (e.g., grade level, content-specific) who also meet monthly to review, for example, fidelity and formative assessment data to set school-wide goals for practice improvement and make requests for needed resources and supports.

Implementation teams engage in several key functions to support the implementation work. The team uses data (i.e., fidelity, process, outcome) and a structured team meeting process at least monthly to identify needs and develop solutions (Horner et al., 2018; King-Sears et al., 2018). This process is iterative and the cycle never ends. There are always new challenges to solve as implementation and teacher teams use data for continuous improvement of supports for teacher and student outcomes.

Communication is another key function of the team. School implementation teams should have clear protocols for communication with key stakeholders (e.g., school leadership team, school staff, district leadership, their families, and other identified stakeholders). Teams should develop and regularly use these bi-directional communication processes at every stage of implementation to share progress about what is or is not working and what is being learned, as well as to solicit feedback and input (Hurlburt et al. 2014). Finally, research demonstrates that effective school teams need professional learning opportunities to further develop their team members' skills and data being generated for them to use (Higgins et al., 2012; Kloos et al., 2020). Without opportunities to further develop skills needed or data for the team to use, the team's progress will be limited or stalled.

Improvement Cycles

The use of implementation and improvement methods and tools is complex, with many moving parts and communication challenges. Often, a lack of readiness for change can create "push back" among staff. An effective approach to introducing change is the use of a trial and learning process of improvement in which school staff are involved in the design and "roll out" of a new practice or process. This is often referred to as a continuous quality improvement (CQI) process (Bryk et al., 2015; Varkey et al, 2007). CQI is the process of identifying, describing, and analyzing key data indicators and challenges, identifying and carrying out potential solutions, monitoring their effectiveness, and revising solutions based on results. Though CQI is a critical aspect of the ongoing improvement of implementation efforts, it is not the only component for achieving equitable outcomes. Effective implementation requires all of the necessary components described in this chapter. Effective CQI processes require the development of a school and district culture and system that fosters continuous learning and growth. In addition, CQI processes should be routinized in the school's mission, vision, and organizational practices (Lee et al., 2012).

The basis of CQI work is the Plan-Do-Study-Act cycle (PDSA). The PDSA cycle is a process derived from industrial quality control research (Deming, 1986; Shewhart, 1931) and is now used widely in human services and education (Bryk et al., 2015; Varkey et al, 2007). The PDSA cycle is used for making incremental improvements as well as significant 'breakthroughs' in performance. The process can be used to conduct a small test of change, help define and refine a new effective practice and implementation supports, be applied to scale-up efforts, and align policies and guidelines to support the use of the effective practices.

Prior research has shown that PDSA cycles are intuitive for educators working in schools and districts, however, they do require considerable time and resources to implement effectively (Taylor et al., 2014; Tichnor-Wagner et al., 2017). To effectively engage in CQI, implementation teams should engage in the following: (1) commit to using PDSA cycles (Higgins et al., 2012); (2) ensure access to reliable and accurate data; (3) receive support as needed to use data for decision making purposes (US DHHS, 2012); (4) build the process into school routines such as regular team meetings (Fullan & Quinn, 2016; Horner et al., 2018); and, (5) share intentional and unintentional lessons from engaging in CQI process with staff and stakeholders.

The district's role in supporting an inclusive school's use of effective instructional and behavioral practices cannot be understated. Qualitative data from principals and school staff suggest districts must provide high-quality data and training to use the data; a structured problem-solving model for all decision making that links classroom practices to outcomes; and ensure sufficient funding and resources to schools for improvement (Bottoms & Fry, 2009). For example, greater impact on student learning was noted when teachers were co-creators of a shared vision and the systems of support and schools were provided with the commitment of long term fiscal resources responsibility by district leadership and the governing board (Hattie, 2003; Ingvarson et al., 2005; KDE, 2019; Sadler & Sugai, 2009). Teachers in a school are expected to improve the outcomes of diverse learners through the use of effective practices, Therefore, school, district, and governing boards must take responsibility for equitably providing resources and ongoing support through training, coaching, and data use. Each level of the system has a role in meeting the needs of teachers in order to improve outcomes for diverse learners (Darling-Hammond, Hyler et al., 2017).

Setting the Course for Effective Inclusion

In recent years, there has been considerable growth in the amount and quality of evidence related to effective practices in the classroom. Research is generating important knowledge to identify, understand and intervene in systemic inequities that result in disparate outcomes for vulnerable populations, including students with disabilities (Baumann & Cabassa, 2020). The adoption, successful implementation, and sustained use of these practices in everyday classrooms, however, has lagged behind, often leading to a disconnect between evidence on effective practices and teaching and learning occurring day to day in classrooms. The following case illustration represents an elementary school in a large suburban district successfully applying tools and practices from implementation science to impact outcomes for students with disabilities in inclusive settings. To fully realize successful outcomes, the school focused their school improvement efforts on applying the research and learnings on effective practices.

Case Illustration

School Demographics

River Run Elementary School serves 1,301 students in preschool through fifth grade and is situated in a large suburban district within the mid-Atlantic United States. The population demographics are as follows: 19.2% Asian, 21.1% Black, 16.2% Hispanic, .2% Native Hawaiian, 36% White, 7.1% two or more races. Sixteen-point five percent of students receive special education services, 22.7% qualify as economically disadvantaged, 15.6% are English language learners, .2% are homeless and 14% are military connected. The population of military connected students is notable in that 3% of these students are also students with disabilities.

Exploration Stage

While River Run Elementary School has met benchmarks for federal and state accountability measures for all students, calculated risk ratios indicate that students with disabilities are 2.5 times more likely to score 'not proficient' on state accountability assessments than same-age peers in math and 1.8 times in reading. These data have remained relatively consistent over the past three years. The school's improvement team met to review data from a variety of sources, including error analyses of items from the state standardized assessment, benchmark data, common formative assessments, attendance, and discipline data in an attempt to identify a clear statement of need.

Initial findings indicated that attendance or time out of class due to disciplinary actions did not appear to be a factor in lower performance. Additionally, 5th grade students with disabilities were significantly more likely than 3rd or 4th grade students with disabilities to score below proficiency benchmarks on standardized testing or fail benchmark and end-of-year math tests. It was also discovered that while students with disabilities in 4th and 5th grades were being provided remediation during classroom times set aside for intervention and enrichment, there were no data to indicate the efficacy of the remediation strategies.

Based on this initial review of the math data, the school improvement team decided to begin with a focus on 5th grade co-taught math classes. Given this focus and the prevalence of this concern, the school leadership encouraged the school improvement team to review their team membership and engage others, with specific expertise in this area, for ongoing support. With this opportunity, the team decided to meet after school to engage a greater diversity of perspectives and expertise as well as employ a user-centered approach. They invited a district-level math coach, the math lead teacher, a 6th grade middle school math co-teaching team, both 5th grade co-teaching teams and a rotating pair of 5th grade student volunteers with identified disabilities (as ad hoc members whose input was solicited at critical decision points) to join the assistant principal, the school counselor, the special education coordinator and the building instructional coach (a subset of the school improvement team). The sixth-grade co-teaching team was included to exemplify vertical articulation as well as to ease transitions for students. This group, now the math implementation team, set a goal to share learning about what works well and what does not when implementing selected math practices to ensure a 20% increase in the number of students passing the 5th grade state-administered standardized assessment by end of the school year.

The team decided to gather data from students, families and colleagues to develop a greater understanding of the need for change and begin to build readiness. They conducted three focus group interviews with 5th grade students and families and 4th and 6th grade teachers to get a better understanding of their perceptions of barriers to success in 5th grade math achievement and what could be contributing to those barriers. The focus groups were representative of the school community and included students with and without disabilities, both currently doing well in 5th grade math and those not doing well. Likewise, parents of both students who were experiencing success and those having challenges with math were interviewed to ensure a balance of perspectives. Parents and students in focus groups reported the following concerns (a) lack of active engagement, characterized by statements such as "too much seatwork and homework worksheets" or "too many math problems to work"; (b) students not remembering all of the steps or "tricks" to solving multistep problems; and (c) word problems. Similarly, teachers reported students not completing assigned work, lack of fluency with basic math facts and difficulty completing multistep algorithms or word problems.

Using this focus group data, error analyses of student math work (e.g., common formative assessments and classwork), and leaderships' reading on effective practices for students with disabilities, the team conducted a root cause analysis using the Fishbone Strategy (Doggett, 2005) for the focus area of improving math achievement for 5th grade students with disabilities. Through the Fishbone analysis, the team prioritized the potential root cause as a need for targeted professional learning for teachers in active engagement techniques and strategies for improving memory for math facts and multi-step problems. The team also discussed a need for teachers to receive professional learning and coaching in deeper math conceptual knowledge and vertical articulation of math concepts. The team believed if teachers were able to engage students in a deeper understanding of number sense and basic math concepts, they would not need to rely on rote memorization tactics, or 'drill and kill' strategies, and repeated practice in the form of worksheets.

Given this information and data review, a team member asked: "What are we, in the Math department, already doing to address the problem of improving math achievement for students with disabilities in any grade?" To answer this question, the team reviewed the district-level initiative inventory (https://nirn.fpg.unc.edu/resources/lesson-10-initiative-inventory), which provided a scan of what programs or practices are already recommended, supported and in place in other schools to address this issue. Using this inventory as the basis for discussion, the school team conducted their own initiative inventory. Through their review, the team learned that 6th grade special education teachers are effectively using several explicit instructional practices. A district Special Education Coordinator provided professional learning and coaching for these teachers as they learned to use additional explicit instruction strategies.

At the same time the initiative inventory was being used, the team reviewed the *What Works Clearing House* website (https://ies.ed.gov/ncee/wwc/) to determine what other evidence-based programs or practices are available to address math achievement. Based on this review, four programs were listed as having some evidence of effectiveness for elementary school students in math achievement. However, the team determined that none were a good fit for their particular needs. The team did find useful information in a practice guide addressing mathematics (Woodward et al., 2012), which indicated strong evidence for the effectiveness of explicit and systematic instruction. The team also found information on explicit instruction from the Council for Exceptional Children (https://highleveragepractices.org/) and the CEEDAR Center websites (https://ceedar.education.ufl.edu/high-leverage-practices/).

Now that the school had ensured a representative team, gathered information from a variety of stakeholders through focus groups, determined the root cause, and identified several options from their current work and clearinghouses, they needed to identify options to assess for fit and feasibility of implementation. The team reviewed their agreed-upon decision making process and the various options generated from the inventory and review of information from the *What Works Clearinghouse.* Given their need to address 5th grade math achievement and the root causes related to the depth of teacher math knowledge across grade spans, student engagement and 'memory' skills, the team identified explicit instruction strategies with a focus on 'retrieval practice' as the practice on which to focus within the classroom. However, prior to making a final decision, the team decided to assess this practice for fit and feasibility using the *Hexagon Tool* (Metz & Louison, 2018; https://nirn.fpg.unc.edu/resources/hexagon-exploration-tool).

Using the Hexagon Tool process, the team analyzed the fit and feasibility of retrieval practice as the appropriate selection for the identified need. The Hexagon Tool is divided into two categories, program indicators and implementing site indicators. Within the two categories, there are six total indicators; evidence, support, usability, need, fit, and capacity. The team discovered this particular practice has strong **evidence** to suggest it is one of the most effective techniques used by educators (Pooja & Bain, 2019). Retrieval practice has available **supports** within the district as both math coaches and special education coordinators have readily available resources, training, and coaching capacity to provide ongoing support to teachers. With limited budgets, there is no fiscal demand and time for learning could be leveraged at existing meetings and training opportunities. Their analysis of the practice revealed that it addressed the stakeholder identified root causes and the **need** to improve learning and retention of information over the long term, increase engagement and attention in class, improve the mental organization of knowledge and increase higher-order thinking and deep conceptual knowledge. The practice **fit** with the stakeholder priority (identified in focus groups) of less homework because with increased, focused opportunities for practice with feedback strategically spaced during class time, there is less need for lengthy practice opportunities for homework. Additionally, the practice fits with the existing curriculum and programs and can easily be incorporated into current lessons and pacing guides. River Run Elementary School determined they had some **capacity** to utilize the practice given that it was currently in use by the 4th grade special educators. The team made the final recommendation to select the practice but needed to ensure that their implementation is focused on **strengthening the capacity** of the staff and the **usability of the program**.

Installation Stage

With the recommendation to explicitly and systematically utilize 'retrieval practice' to address the math disparities for 5th grade students with disabilities, the team was ready to move forward with securing the infrastructure supports needed to implement the practice with fidelity. In a team meeting, one of the 4th grade special educators asked if the district had a clear definition or examples of retrieval practice. He stated that when his team started using the practice, they thought it meant just giving more frequent quizzes or formative assessments. The district did not have such a resource and decided that for the practice to be teachable, learnable, usable and doable, they needed to define the nuances or facets of the practice. The team then defined the philosophy or rationale behind the practice and completed a practice profile (https://nirn.fpg.unc.edu/resources/lesson-3-practice-profiles) to clearly identify the critical components of the practice and provide both examples and non-examples of the practice in use. Within the process of clarifying expectations for the practice, the team developed a fidelity check of the core features of the practice that included not just adherence to the features, but the quality of the implementation, dosage (frequency and duration), and student engagement during instruction. The new practice profile and fidelity assessment were added to the larger district training plan.

To persist in the implementation team's commitment to engage in this work to learn about what works well and what does not when implementing selected math practices, each 5th grade co-teaching pair opted to begin use of the practice in one classroom each across three different lessons. The special education coordinator planned to deliver the initial professional learning and coaching to the teachers during joint planning periods. The district math coach committed to attending the training and learning to use the fidelity tool to provide growth-oriented feedback. The team leveraged an existing district-led system and schedule of coaching provided by instructional coaches after the training but prior to the first fidelity checks. The coaching system included opportunities for both modeling and co-teaching using the practice. Finally, the team developed a plan outlining who, when, and how student data, fidelity data and additional implementation data would be collected and utilized for decision making.

In keeping with the team's user-centered approach, they decided to dive deeper into the implementation data by sending a short survey to the initial student focus group (which included students who were to receive the intervention) and 5th grade co-teaching pairs implementing the practice. The survey consisted of questions to ascertain the acceptability, appropriateness and feasibility of the selected practice in use. The goal was to understand if students were feeling more successful and whether or not the practice supported their learning and teachers felt that the practice was efficient and effective enough to sustain over time. These data would be incorporated into future meetings for ongoing improvement in the use of the practice.

Initial Implementation

Prior to launching the implementation of the new effective practice, the instructional coach assigned by the district to the elementary school met with each co-teaching pair to review the lessons and determine the coaching strategy to be used for mastery of the critical elements of the practice (e.g., observation with feedback, modeling, partner teaching). River Run Elementary school 5th grade co-teaching pairs started the implementation of explicit retrieval practice at the beginning of the second 9 weeks grading period. Data were collected on fidelity, implementation (e.g., surveys to teachers to ascertain feasibility or ease of use and confidence in utilizing new strategies) and student outcomes (e.g., common formative assessment).

The Math Implementation Team met to review the data and make any necessary improvements to the infrastructure. The team identified a few barriers to the ultimate successful adoption of the practice. First, the co-teaching pairs felt that while it was an easy strategy to utilize, they were over-reliant on one particular retrieval practice (exit tickets) and, in at least one instance, they ran out of time to complete the exercise. Second, students did not report feeling more engaged but that they were being given more 'quizzes' at the end of each period. Lastly, the team realized they had not developed a plan for sharing the lessons learned and successes with the faculty to build confidence and skills. As a result, the team generated a chart of additional retrieval practice strategies and when in a lesson it would be beneficial to utilize them. Some examples listed were 'bell ringers' at the beginning of lessons, response cards for any time during a lesson, as well as 'brain dumps', 'two things', and 'retrieval guides.' At the next faculty meeting, they shared the list for other teachers who might be interested in implementing the practice and spent a few minutes creatively generating other ideas for helping students retrieve learning. Additionally, the team had the co-teachers ask students to list or tell all of the ways they like to "show what they know" as a way to generate greater engagement.

The co-teaching pairs continued to implement the practice, incorporating the changes and achieving fidelity in their use of the practice. Data were collected from teachers regarding the acceptability of the program and perceived effectiveness for their students, confidence with use, and satisfaction with the support they were receiving for implementation. These data were reviewed in the monthly implementation team meetings and used to identify implementation issues and celebrate successes.

As implementation issues arose, the team continued to systematically problem solve and plan to address these issues. For example, after two months of implementation, the team noted that achievement for students with disabilities was not improving as anticipated. Rather than abandoning the process, the team examined the quality of implementation more closely versus simply adherence to the practice and dosage. It was discovered that teachers needed to increase rates of task-specific feedback and the variety of questioning from beyond fact-based recall to concept-based and/or more complex questions. As a result, the team revised the implementation plan and the building instructional coach created a series of brief presentations for faculty meetings on task-specific feedback and increased question rigor. The presentations were recorded and stored for future reference and review.

As implementation of this change began, the co-teaching pairs opted to first observe each other and provide feedback, followed by an observation by the instructional coach. The same types of data were collected on the schedule described in the first plan iteration. Within this data collection cycle, students reported feeling more engaged and liked the inclusion of student-driven practice strategies from the list generated. Additionally, teachers reported feeling more confident in the use of the practice and continued to report that the strategies were easy to incorporate into any lesson. While teachers were observed using a greater variety of question stems, they reported wanting the opportunity to generate others with colleagues in future faculty meetings and adding that list with the presentation videos from previous meetings.

Full Implementation

By the fourth 9 weeks grading period, the majority of 5th grade teachers were implementing all retrieval practice strategies consistently and both benchmark and yearly testing data were beginning to trend upwards. Surveys indicated that staff felt supported in implementation and more effective for their students. The implementation team surveyed the original focus group students and families for follow up. Both students and families indicated students were feeling more confident in their math skills and grades were improving. Additionally, the gap between students with disabilities and all other students in math achievement was closing. One parent asked for a list of 'retrieval practice' strategies to be used at home, resulting in a newsletter sent to the 5th grade parents. The team continued to monitor student progress and implementation data on a regular basis and problem solve as issues arose.

Due to the success of this effort, the district-level math coach approached the district Math Director to determine if the capacity built in this school around this set of practices could be leveraged in other schools facing similar challenges. The Math coaches, together with the director, reviewed district and school data and selected a group of 5 additional elementary schools. After engaging in a period of exploration, 4 schools were selected as being ready for participation. With support from the district, the co-teaching pairs at River Run Elementary provided professional learning to the new school teams and made themselves available as peer support throughout the process. A similar implementation process was followed in the additional schools with minor changes to ensure contextual fit. The successful use of this data-informed the decision-making process and supported the development of a culture of support and efficacy in the schools that dedicated the time to this shared learning process.

Recommendations for Research

The expanded body of research on what works in classrooms has provided a good start (Dew & Boydell, 2017). However, if the impact of these practices is to be fully realized for the benefit of students and families, a greater understanding of how to use effective implementation strategies to create hospitable contexts that support the broader use of effective practices is needed. The implementation components that have been reviewed in this chapter are based on effective practices and have been developed, tested, expanded and refined in implementing sites. Improving routine and sustained use of the implementation components depends on having more extensive research. Districts and schools need a greater understanding of *which* features within the components result in the highest level of practitioner use with fidelity, as well as what *effective and efficient* processes are for developing those features in an acceptable timeframe within complex educational systems.

Several recommendations for research on factors critical to successful implementation at the school level are presented. First, researchers need to determine and specify for educators the essential features or program components that define effective practices or programs and how those components can be adapted to address local context needs (Kaplan et al., 2020; Spybrook et al, 2020). Guidance and research are further needed for educators on how to adapt these components to meet the needs of the local context without reducing the practice's potential for impact. The FRAME model (Stirman et al., 2019) provides initial guidance on making adaptations to practices; however, further research is needed to establish its feasibility and utility by educators and leaders. Research also is needed to ascertain which core features are common across practices, programs or interventions and support the development of alignment processes for district and school leaders and educators. Common features alone could then be taught more generally in teacher preparation programs as well as strengthened in professional learning opportunities provided by districts and schools.

Second, further research is needed to determine the effectiveness of adapting implementation components as they are used in schools and classrooms. Similar to the practice/program adaptation, the core features of implementation drivers (e.g., selection, coaching, training, data-informed decision making) need to be carefully operationalized and studied to understand the impact of adapting these implementation strategies or components and when these adaptions should occur in the implementation process. Research on the adaptation of implementation strategies and under which conditions is a relatively new topic of research (Birken et al., 2017).

Third, reliable and valid measures of implementation processes and outcomes need to be developed, tested and studied to allow educational systems to fully understand the operational definitions of building and sustaining the infrastructure needed to implement any practice or program. Ward et al. (2020) pointed out that implementation measures typically are general measures that do not specifically address core implementation components or are measures specific to a given practice or program that may lack generalizability across programs (Elliott & Morrison, 2008; Mihalic & Irwin, 2003). From early efforts to develop these measures, it is clear that, rather than emphasizing the development of narrow measures of implementation tied to each practice (i.e., literacy, math, behavior, mental health), the field needs a reliable and valid tool that could both guide and measure basic capacity elements at the school level. Purveyors and researchers can then begin to understand the range of interaction effects across components over time and establish the empirical relationship between fidelity of implementation of practices and programs and, ultimately, student outcomes. The *Drivers Best Practices Assessment* (Ward et al., 2018) is an example of a capacity assessment tool that has been used by school teams, but research is needed to establish its validity and reliability within k-12 education.

To better understand implementation processes and enable research of the comparative effectiveness of implementation strategies, more knowledge is needed regarding how to conceptualize implementation outcomes within a larger framework of system variables (Proctor et al., 2011). Implementation outcomes support the growth or improvement of an organization by serving as an indicator of implementation success and are the more immediate indicators of progress toward a school's improvement goals. Implementation outcomes are defined as the effects of "the specified set of activities designed to put into practice an activity or program of known dimensions" (Fixsen et al., 2005). These might include such measures as acceptability, adoption, appropriateness, feasibility, fidelity, penetration and sustainability. The Proctor et al. (2009) framework for understanding implementation outcomes proposes that implementation outcomes are needed before student outcomes, with the latter being the most important criterion for determining success. Using this framework, researchers can organize and measure key variables. Measuring and testing implementation outcomes at different stages will help to define the causal relationships within the implementation process and the relationship between implementation outcomes and success. Specifically, when in the stage of Exploration, the acceptability and appropriateness of the effective practice can be measured. In Installation, the level of adoption or the intention or action to support the uptake of the evidence-based practice is assessed. The feasibility, fidelity, cost, and reach or penetration of the intervention are all implementation outcomes to be measured within the initial implementation. Within full implementation, the impact of the practices on expected outcomes and sustainability of the use of the practice can be measured.

Lastly, further research is needed to understand the organizational and socio-political factors that create and define the contexts that enable the successful implementation of effective programs or practices with fidelity. A difficult area to study, the information discovered through this research could help to guide policy development. Understanding the key features of environments hospitable to the implementation of practices with fidelity could reduce organizational barriers in new sites as well as lead to recommendations for facilitative policies and mandates.

Conclusion

Leaders and educators in inclusive elementary schools undertaking school improvement to improve effectiveness need to attend to three factors and their implementation components. These factors include *what* practices, supported by evidence, are selected to support the needs of students with disabilities (e.g., high-leverage practices); *how* districts and schools attend to the deliberate implementation of an infrastructure for training, coaching, use of data, communication, and the necessary leadership; and that practices are implemented in schools with supportive district policies and a culture of continuous improvement *(where)*. Should any of these factors be missing from the equation, socially significant outcomes cannot be realized. Districts and schools must be able to apply the necessary components of each factor for effective and efficient improvement and change. Schools, however, cannot act alone. To allow educators a singular focus on the efficacy of teaching and learning interactions, policy makers and education leaders at every level of the system must come together with their communities to co-create an implementation infrastructure that can be effectively used, tested, scaled and sustained from one teacher to the next, one school to the next, one district to the next, one region to the next, and one state to the next until we have transformed the system.

References

Aarons, G. A., Ehrhart, M. G., & Farahnak, L. R. (2014). The implementation leadership scale (ILS): development of a brief measure of unit level implementation leadership. *Implementation Science, 9*, 45. doi:10.1186/1748-5908-9-45

Aarons, G. A., Cafri, G., Lugo, L., & Sawitzky, A. (2012). Expanding the domains of attitudes towards evidence-based practice: The Evidence Based Attitudes Scale-50. *Administration and Policy in Mental Health and Mental Health Services Research*, 5, 331–340.

Aarons, G. A., Hurlburt, M., & Horwitz, S. M. (2011). Advancing a conceptual model of evidence-based practice implementation in public service sectors. *Administration, Policy and Mental Health*, 38, 4–23. doi:10.1007/s10488-010-0327-7

Aarons, G. A. & Palinkas, L. A. (2007). Implementation of evidence-based practice in child welfare: service provider perspectives. *Administration and Policy in Mental Health and Mental Health Services Research*, 34, 411–419. doi:10.1007/s10488-007-0121-3

Akin, B. A., Bryson, S. A., Testa, M. F., Blase, K. A., McDonald, T., & Melz, H. (2013). Usability testing, initial implementation, and formative evaluation of an evidence-based intervention: Lessons from a demonstration project to reduce long-term foster care. *Evaluation and Program Planning*, 41, 19–30. doi:10.1016/j.evalprogplan.2013.06.003

Archer, A. L. & Hughes, C. A. (2011). *Explicit instruction: Effective and efficient teaching.* Guildford Press.

Baumann, A., & Cabassa, L. (2020). Reframing implementation science to address inequities in healthcare delivery. *BMC Health Services Research*, 20, 190.

Birken, S. A., Powell, B. J., Shea, C. M., Haines, E. R., Kirk, A., Leeman, J., Rohweder, C., Damschroder, L., & Presseau, J. (2017). Criteria for selecting implementation science theories and frameworks: results from an international survey. *Implementation Science*,12, 124. doi:10.1186/s13012-017-0656-y

Blase, K., Fixsen, D., Sims, B., & Ward, C. (2015). *Implementation science—changing hearts, minds, behavior, and systems to improve educational outcomes.* National Implementation Research Network, University of North Carolina at Chapel Hill.

Bottoms, G., & Fry, B. (2009). *The district leadership challenge: Empowering principals to improve teaching and learning.* Southern Regional Education Board (SREB).

Bryk, A. S., Gomez, L., Grunow, A., & LeMahieu, P. (2015). *Learning how to improve: How America's schools can get better at getting bettter.* Harvard Education Publishing.

Burns, M. & Ysseldyke, J. (2009). Reported prevalence of evidence-based instructional practices in special education. *The Journal of Special Education*, 43(1), 3–11.

Coburn, C. E., Hill, H. C., & Spillane, J. P. (2016). Alignment and accountability in policy design and implementation: The Common Core State Standards and implementation research. *Educational Researcher*, 45(4), 243–251. doi:10.3102/0013189X16651080.

Crosse, S., Williams, B., Hagen, C. A., Harmon, M., Ristow, L., DiGaetano, R., Broene, P., Alexander, D., Tseng, M., & Derzon, J. H. (2011). *Prevalence and implementation fidelity of research-based prevention programs in public schools: Final report.* U.S. Department of Education.

Darling-Hammond, L., Burns, D., Campbell, C., Goodwin, A. L., Hammerness, K., Low, E. L., McIntyre, A., Sato, M. & Zeichner, K. (2017). *Empowered educators: How high-performing systems shape teaching quality around the world.* John Wiley & Sons

Darling-Hammond, L. Hyler, M. E., & Gardner, M. (2017). *Effective professional development. Research brief.* Learning Policy Institute. https://learningpolicyinstitute.org/sites/default/files/product-files/Effective_Teacher_Professional_Development_BRIEF.pdf

Deming, W. E. (1986). *Out of the crisis.* MIT Press.

Dew, A. & Boydell, K. M. (2017). Knowledge translation: bridging the disability research-to-practice gap. *Research and Practice in Intellectual and Developmental Disabilities*, 4(2), 142–157. doi:10.1080/23297018.2017.1315610

Doggett, M. A. (2005). Root cause analysis: A framework for tool selection. *The Quality Management Journal*, 12(4), 45.

Dragoset, L., Thomas, J., Herrmann, M., Deke, J., James-Burdumy, S., Graczewski, C., Boyle, A., Upton, R., Tanenbaum, C., & Giffin, J. (2017). School improvement grants: Implementation and effectiveness. Executive summary. National Center for Education Evaluation and Regional Assistance. Retrieved from https://files.eric.ed.gov/fulltext/ED572213.pdf

Eccles, M. P., & Mittman, B. S. (2006). Welcome to implementation science. *Implementation Science*, 1. doi:10.1186/1748-5908-1-1

Elliott, J., & Morrison, D. (2008). *Response to intervention blueprints: District level edition.* National Association of State Directors of Special Education, Inc.

Fixsen, D. L., Blase, K., Duda, M., Naoom, S., & Wallace, F. (2009). Core implementation components. *Research on Social Work Practice*, 19, 531–540.

Fixsen, D., Blase, K., Metz, A., & Van Dyke, M. (2013). Statewide implementation of evidence-based programs. *Exceptional Children*, 79, 213–230.

Fixsen, D. L., Blase, K. A., Metz, A., & Van Dyke, M. (2015). Implementation science. In J. Wright (Ed.), *International encyclopedia of the social & behavioral sciences* (2nd ed., pp. 695–702). Elsevier.

Fixsen, D. L., Blase, K. A., Timbers, G. D., & Wolf, M. M. (2001). In search of program implementation, 792 replications of the teaching-family model. In G. A. Bernfeld, D. P. Farrington, & A. W. Leschield (Eds.), *Offender rehabilitation in practice: Implementation and evaluating effective programs* (pp. 149–166). Wiley.

Fixsen, D. L., Naoom, S. F., Blase, K. A., Friedman, R. M., & Wallace, F. (2005). *Implementation research: A synthesis of the literature* (No. FMHI publication #231). University of South Florida, Louis de la Parte Florida Mental Health Institute, National Implementation Research Network.

Fuchs, D., Fuchs, L., McMaster, K., & Lemons, C. (2018). Students with disabilities' abysmal school performance: An introduction to the special issue. *Learning Disabilities Research and Practice*, 33(*3*), 127–130.

Fullan, M. & Quinn, J. (2016). *Coherence: The right drivers in action for schools, districts, and systems*. Corwin.

Groff, L. R. (2020). *School wide positive behavior interventions and supports tiered fidelity inventory: A predictor of student outcomes* (Doctoral dissertation, University of Oregon).

George, H. P., Cox, K. E., Minch, D., & Sandomierski, T. (2018). District practices associated with successful SWPBIS implementation. *Behavioral Disorders*, 43(3), 393–406.

Hall, G. E., & Hord, S. M. (2006). Implementing change: Patterns, principles, and potholes.

Hattie, J. (2003, October). *Teachers make a difference: What is the research evidence?* Building Teacher Quality: What does the research tell us ACER Research Conference, Melbourne, Australia. http://research.acer.edu.au/research_conference_2003/4/

Heifetz, R. A., & Laurie, D. L. (1997). The work of leadership. *Harvard Business Review*, 75(1), 124–134.

Higgins, M. C., Weiner, J., & Young, L. (2012). Implementation teams: a new lever for organizational change. *Journal of Organizational Behavior*, 33, 366–388. doi:10.1002/job.1773

Horner, R. H., Newton, J. S., Todd, A. W., Algozzine, B., Algozzine, K., Cusumano, D., & Preston, A. (2018). A randomized waitlist controlled analysis of team-initiated problem solving professional development and use. *Behavioral Disorders*, 43(4), 444–456.

Hughes, C. A., Morris, J. R., Therrien, W. J., & Benson, S. K. (2017) Explicit instruction: Historical and contemporary contexts. *Learning Disabilities Research and Practice* 32(3), 143.

Hurlburt, M., Aarons, G. A., Fettes, D., Willging, C., Gunderson, L., & Chaffin, M. (2014). Interagency collaborative team model for capacity building to scale up evidence-based practice. *Children and Youth Services Review*, 39, 160–168.

Ingvarson, L., Meiers, M., & Beavis, A. (2005). Factors affecting the impact of professional development programs on teachers' knowledge, practice, student outcomes & efficacy. *Education Policy Analysis Archives*, 13(10), 1–28.

Joyce, B. R., & Showers, B. (1995). *Student achievement through staff development* (Rev. ed.). Longman.

Joyce, B. R., & Showers, B. (2002). *Student achievement through staff development* (3rd ed.). Association for Supervision and Curriculum Development.

Kaplan, A., Cromley, J., Perez, T., Dai, T., Mara, K., & Balsai, M. (2020). The role of context in educational RCT findings: A call to redefine "evidence-based practice." *Educational Researcher*, 49(4). doi:10.3102/0013189X20921862

Kentucky Department of Education. (2019). *State systemic improvement plan: Phase III.* https://education.ky.gov/specialed/excep/instresources/Documents/Kentucky%20SSIP%20Phase%20III-3%20final.pdf

Kilbourne, A. M., Neumann, M. S., Pincus, H. A., Bauer, M. S., & Stall, R. (2007). Implementing evidence-based interventions in health care: Application of the replicating effective programs framework. *Implementation Science*, 2(42). doi: 10.1186/1748-5908-2-42

King-Sears, M. E., Walker, J. D., & Barry, C. (2018). Measuring teachers' intervention fidelity. *Intervention in School and Clinic*, 54, 89–96.

Kloos, E., Nacik, E. & Ward, C. (2020). *Developing implementation capacity of a state education agency to improve outcomes for students with disabilities* (Manuscript submitted for publication). Minnesota Department of Education.

Lane, B., Unger, C., & Souvanna, P. (2014). *Turnaround practices in action: A practice guide and policy analysis.* Institute for Strategic Leadership and Learning. Retrieved from http://www.instll.com/resources/2014practicesreport.pdf

Lee., S., Bright, C. L., & Berlin, L. J. (2012). Organizational influences on data use among child welfare workers. *Child Welfare*, 92, 97–116.

Madon, T., Hofman, K. J., Kupfer, L., & Glass, R. I. (2007). Public health implementation science. *Science*, 318, 1728–1729.

McIntosh, K., Mercer, S. H., Hume, A. E., Frank, J. L., Turri, M. G., & Mathews, S. (2013). Factors related to sustained implementation of schoolwide positive behavior support. *Exceptional Children*, 79, 293–311.

Metz, A. & Louison, L. (2018) *The Hexagon tool: Exploring context*. National Implementation Research Network, University of North Carolina at Chapel Hill.

Metz, A. (2015). *The potential of co-creation in implementation science* [Brief]. National Implementation Research Network, University of North Carolina at Chapel Hill.

Metz, A. (2016). *Practice profiles: A process for capturing evidence and operationalizing innovations* [White Paper]. National Implementation Research Network, University of North Carolina at Chapel Hill.

Metz, A., & Bartley, L. (2012). Active implementation frameworks for program success: How to use implementation science to improve outcomes for children. *Zero to Three Journal*, 34, 11–18.

Metz, A., Naoom, S., Halle, T., & Bartley, L. (2015). *An integrated stage-based framework for implementation of early childhood programs and systems*. Office of Planning, Research, and Evaluation, U.S. Department of Health and Human Services.

Metz, A., Bartley, L., & Moultry, M. (2017). *Supporting the sustainable use of research evidence in child welfare services*. National Implementation Research Network, University of North Carolina at Chapel Hill.

Meyers, D. C., Durlak, J. A., & Wandersman, A. (2012). The quality implementation framework: A synthesis of critical steps in the implementation process. *American Journal of Community Psychology*, 50, 462–480.

Michie, S., Richardson, M., Johnston, M., Abraham, C., Francis, J., Hardeman, W., Eccles, M. P., Cane, J., & Wood, C. E. (2013). The behavior change technique taxonomy (v1) of 93 hierarchically clustered techniques: Building an international consensus for the reporting of behavior change interventions. *Annuals Behavior Medicine*, 46, 81–95. doi:10.1007/s12160-013-9486-6.

Mihalic, S., & Irwin, K. (2003). From research to real world settings: Factors influencing the successful replication of model programs. *Youth Violence and Juvenile Justice*, 1, 307–329.

Moullin, J. C., Ehrhart, M. G., & Aarons, G. A. (2017). The role of leadership in organizational implementation and sustainment in service agencies. *Research on Social Work Practice*, 28(5), 558–567. doi:10.1177/1049731517718361

National Center for Education Statistics. (2019). The nation's report card, 2019. U.S. Department of Education, Institute of Education Sciences. Retrieved from https://nces.ed.gov/nationsreportcard/studies/statemapping/

National Implementation Research Network. (2020). *Implementation stages planning tool*. National Implementation Research Network, FPG Child Development Institute, University of North Carolina at Chapel Hill.

Nutt, P. C. (2001). Contingency approaches applied to the implementation of strategic decisions. *International Journal of Business*, 6(1), 53–84.

Ogden, T., Bjørnebekk, G., Kjøbli, J., Patras, J., Christiansen, T., Taraldsen, K., & Tollefsen, N. (2012). Measurement of implementation components ten years after a nationwide introduction of empirically supported programs—a pilot study. *Implementation Science*, 7(1), 49.

Padua, D. A., Frank, B., Donaldson, A., Motte, S. D. L., Cameron, K. L., Beutler, A. I., & Marshall, S. W. (2014). Developing and implementing a preventive training program: Lessons learned from JUMP-ACL and beyond. *Clinical Sports Medicine*. doi:10.1016/j.csm.2014.06.012

Pooja, A. & Bain, P. (2019). *Powerful teaching: Unleash the science of learning*. Jossey-Bass.

Powell, B. J., McMillen, J. C., Proctor, E. K., Carpenter, C. R., Griffey, R. T., Bunger, A. C., Glass, J. E., & York, J. L. (2012). A compilation of strategies for implementing clinical innovations in health and mental health. *Medical Care Research and Review*, 69(2), 123–157. doi:10.1177/1077558711430690

Powell, B. J., Waltz, T. J., Chinman, M., Damschroder, L. J., Smith, J. L., Matthieu, M. M., & Kirchemer, J. (2015). A refined compilation of implementation strategies: results from the expert recommendations for implementing change (ERIC) project. *Implementation Science*, 10, 21.

Proctor, E. K., Landsverk, J., Aarons, G., Chambers, D., Glisson, C., & Mittman, B. (2009). Implementation research in mental health services: An emerging science with conceptual, methodological, and training challenges. *Administration and Policy in Mental Health and Mental Health Service Research*, 36(1), 24–34.

Proctor, E. K., Silmere, H., Raghavan, R., Hovmand, P., Aarons, G., Bunger, A., Griffey, R., & Hensley, M. (2011). Outcomes for implementation research: conceptual distinctions, measurement challenges and research agenda. *Administration and Policy in Mental Health and Mental Health Service Research*, 38, 65–76.

Romney, S., Israel, N., & Zlatevski, D. (2014). Effect of exploration-stage implementation variation on the cost- effectiveness of an evidence-based parenting program. *Zeitschrift fur Psychologie*, 222, 37–48.

Ryan Jackson, K., Fixsen, D., Ward, C., Waldroup, A., & Sullivan, V. (2018). *Accomplishing effective and durable change to support improved student outcomes* [White Paper]. National Implementation Research Network, University of North Carolina at Chapel Hill.

Rycroft-Malone, J., Wilkinson, J., Burton, C. R., Harvey, G., McCormack, B., Graham, I., & Staniszewska, S. (2013). Collaborative action around implementation in collaborations for leadership in applied health research and care: Towards a programme theory. *Journal of Health Services Research & Policy*, 18, 3(supplementary): 13–26.

Sadler, C., & Sugai, G. (2009). Effective behavior and instructional support: A district model for early identification and prevention of reading and behavior problems. *Journal of Positive Behavior Interventions*, 11(1), 35–46.

Saldana, L. (2014). The stages of implementation completion for evidence-based practice: Protocol for a mixed methods study. *Implementation Science*, 9, 43. doi:10.1186/1748-5908-9-43

Saldana, L., Chamberlain, P., Wang, W., & Brown, H. C. (2012). Predicting program start-up using the stages of implementation measure. *Administration and Policy in Mental Health*, 39(6), 419–425. doi:10.1007/s10488-011-0363-y.

Shewhart, W. A. (1931). *Economic control of quality of manufactured product*. D. Van Nostrand.

Strunk, K. O., Marsh, J. A., Bush-Mecenas, S. C., & Duque, M. R. (2015). The best laid plans: An examination of school plan quality and implementation in a school improvement initiative. *Educational Administration Quarterly*, 52(2), 259–309.

Stirman, S. Baumann, A., & Miller, C. (2019). The FRAME: an expanded framework for reporting adaptations and modifications to evidence-based interventions. *Implementation Science*, 14, 58. doi:10.1186/s13012-019-0898-y

Spybrook, J., Zhang, Q., Kelcey, B., & Dong, N. (2020). Learning from cluster randomized trials in education: An assessment of the capacity of studies to determine what works, for whom, and under what conditions. *Educational Evaluation and Policy Analysis*. 42(3), 354–374. doi:10.3102/0162373720929018

Taylor, M. J., McNicholas, C., Nicolay, C., Darzi, A., Bell, D., & Reed, J. E. (2014). Systematic review of the application of the plan–do–study–act method to improve quality in healthcare. *BMJ quality & safety*, 23(4), 290–298.

Tichnor-Wagner, A., Wachen, J., Cannata, M., & Cohen-Vogel, L. (2017). Continuous improvement in the public school context: Understanding how educators respond to plan–do–study–act cycles. *Journal of Education Change*, 18, 465–494 doi:10.1007/s10833-017-9301-4

U.S. Department of Health and Human Services (2012). *Continuous quality improvement in Title IV-B and IV-E programs, 8/27/12 (Information Memorandum, ACYF-CB-IM-12-07)*. Administration on Children, Youth, and Families, Administration for Children and Families, Children's Bureau. Retrieved from: http://www.acf.hhs.gov/sites/default/files/cb/im1207.pdf

Varkey, P., Reller, M. K., & Resar, R. K. (2007). Basics of quality improvement in health care. *Mayo Clinical procedures*, 82(6), 735–739. doi:10.4065/82.6.735

Ward, C., Metz, A., Louison, L., Loper, A., & Cusumano, D. (2018). *Drivers best practices assessment*. National Implementation Research Network, University of North Carolina at Chapel Hill.

Ward, C., Harns, A., St. Martin, K., Cusumano, D., Russell, C., & Horner, R. (2020). *Development and technical adequacy of the District Capacity Assessment*. (Manuscript submitted for publication). University of North Carolina-Chapel Hill.

Wageman, R., Hackman, J. R., & Lehman, E. V. (2005). Team diagnostic survey: development of an instrument. *Journal of Applied Behavioral Science*, 41, 1–27.

Woodward, J., Beckmann, S., Driscoll, M., Franke, M., Herzig, P., Jitendra, A., Koedinger, K. R., & Ogbuehi, P. (2012). *Improving mathematical problem solving in grades 4 through 8: A practice guide* (NCEE 2012-4055). National Center for Education Evaluation and Regional Assistance, Institute of Education Sciences, U.S. Department of Education. Retrieved from http://ies.ed.gov/ncee/wwc/publications_reviews.aspx#pubsearch/.

Zaheer, I., Ward, C., McCurdy, B., Ihlo, T., & Farmer, R. (2020). *Implementation science as framework for future of school psychology*. (Manuscript submitted for publication). University of North Carolina-Chapel Hill.

22

Supporting Learners from Culturally and Linguistically Diverse Backgrounds

Erica D. McCray[1], Sylvia Linan-Thompson[2], and Dia A. Jackson[3]

[1]UNIVERSITY OF FLORIDA

[2]UNIVERSITY OF OREGON

[3]AMERICAN INSTITUTES FOR RESEARCH

Setting the Stage

Public schools in the United States continue to enroll increasing numbers of students from culturally (i.e., ethno-racially[1]) and linguistically diverse backgrounds (McFarland et al., 2019). However, these students experience inequitable outcomes and opportunities to learn when compared to their White, monolingual peers. Disability identification further exacerbates the inequities for students with marginalized identities (Artiles, 2019). Researchers have examined school contexts and the dispositions, knowledge, and skills of the professionals responsible for meeting the complex needs of diverse groups of learners (e.g., Harry & Klingner, 2006). There are myriad factors that, if intentionally addressed, can improve outcomes for all learners. These factors interact across multiple levels and actors, including: policies, education agencies (state, district, and school), teachers, leaders, and related services personnel. Policies frame the work of educators in schools and have implications for funding and the services provided to students. This chapter begins by describing the diversity of students relying on schools to serve them well and a description of the teacher workforce, followed by examples from the literature demonstrating the importance of effective inclusive schools for improving long-term outcomes. The chapter concludes with suggestions for practice, research, and policy.

Current Demographics

According to the *41st Annual Report to Congress on the Implementation of IDEA* 2017-18 (U.S. Department of Education, 2019a), 9.2% of the total school-aged population (age 6-21, served under Part B) received special education services and 38.2% were identified with specific learning disabilities. Approximately 64% of students served under IDEA Part B are from culturally and linguistically diverse (CLD) backgrounds. Risk indices–the percentage of an ethno-racial group that

DOI: 10.4324/9781003043874-22

receives special education services–were highest for students identified as American Indian or Alaska Native (15.1), Native Hawaiian or Other Pacific Islander (13.9), and Black or African American (12.2). The Institute of Education Sciences (IES) recently released the 2019 National Assessment of Educational Progress (NAEP) results for math and reading as part of the "Nation's Report Card" (U.S. Department of Education, 2019b). Students with and without disabilities demonstrated little to no improvement in reading and math since the previous assessment in 2017, and the achievement gap between these groups persisted. On the NAEP, eighty-eight percent of students with disabilities performed at "below basic" or "basic" achievement levels in reading; 83% of students with disabilities were rated "below basic" in math. Overall, students from minoritized backgrounds were rated disproportionately below proficiency in reading and math. Similarly, 90% of ELs performed at or "below basic" on the NAEP in reading; 84% of English Learners (ELs) were rated below basic in math.

The National Center on Education Statistics (McFarland et al., 2019) reported that in the fall of 2016, 9.6% of students were identified as ELs. Representation varied from .9% in West Virginia to 20.2% in California, with increasing concentrations in areas across the country (e.g., Texas, North Carolina, Georgia). State-by-state variability creates implications for policies that support learning among ELs. California, as the first state adopting the "Seal of Biliteracy," has been considered a leader in a progressive policy providing a foundation for systems-level support (National Academies of Science, Engineering, & Medicine, 2017). Similarly, New York adopted its Seal of Biliteracy program to promote multilingual learning, including for students with disabilities (New York State Education Department, 2016). The increasing diversity in the United States (U.S.) reflects families migrating from other countries. A recent report indicated that new immigrants represent various regions, primarily from Asian (47%) and Latin American (29%) countries (National Academies of Science, Engineering, & Medicine, 2017). Thus, children of immigrants are rapidly entering schools with an array of needs. Policies such as Deferred Action for Childhood Arrivals (DACA) can provide important safeguards for continuity of schooling and success among ELs. Educators' ability to accurately distinguish between English-language learning needs and special educational needs are essential to students receiving services that are individualized, which might include special education, English language, or both (National Academies of Science, Engineering, & Medicine, 2017).

The U.S. educator workforce is much less diverse than the student population. Teachers and school leaders continue to be overwhelmingly White, middle-class women (McFarland et al., 2019). In general, educators have limited preparation for the range of backgrounds and needs that students present, particularly students who have cultural and linguistic backgrounds different than their teachers (Ford et al., 2014; Reese et al., 2018; Zion & Sobel, 2014). Research has shown the benefits of having a diverse educator workforce. As Kozleski and her colleagues (2014) noted, teacher diversity matters because they not only "draw on rich cultural histories, but also the nuances of their practices (are) mediated by the institutional cultures in which they practice" (p. 120). Moreover, other researchers have found positive effects of race-matched teachers on student performance (Dee & Penner, 2017) as well as the benefits to students of any race having a teacher of Color (Carver-Thomas, 2018). Ultimately, all students deserve opportunities to learn from teachers from diverse backgrounds who are also responsive to their needs (Council of Chief State School Officers, 2019); however, CLD students continue to experience culturally incongruent schools.

Curricula and learning opportunities in schools often lack a cultural filter to ensure that all students' funds of knowledge (Moll et al., 1992) are reflected and tapped. Further, disproportionate discipline results from classroom management approaches that punish and further exclude students who engage in ways that are inconsistent with traditionally monocultural, monolingual classrooms (Brown et al., 2019; Kourea et al., 2016; McIntosh et al., 2014). Disproportionality continues to be a widespread but localized issue (Trent et al., 2014). Yet, some schools and districts are intentional about meeting the needs of their diverse populations of learners yielding positive outcomes (Bal et al., 2014).

In a longitudinal case study of comprehensive school reform (CSR) implementation in 13 culturally and linguistically diverse elementary schools, researchers (Datnow et al., 2003) examined the influence of state and district factors on the implementation and adaptation of reform efforts to meet the needs of students in "multicultural, multilingual contexts" (p. 143), and on student achievement outcomes paying particular attention to bilingual learners. In addition to comprehensive school reform implementation, a state consent decree required that all instructional staff receive professional development to support ELs. The researchers found variability in CSR implementation, with some teachers adapting the models in favor of increased EL instructional approaches. In other instances, Datnow et al. (2003) found that certain reform models embedded culturally relevant practices. For example, staff in one school noted that their particular CSR model's "philosophy promoted inclusion" (p. 157) and emphasized the importance of understanding family backgrounds. In another school, teachers were observed asking higher-order questions and assigning writing activities in English and Spanish. Overall, they found that stronger implementation of the reform models benefited all students, and specific models showed greater effects for students receiving EL supports. Most importantly, the study underscored the importance of examining curriculum, pedagogy, and "social constructions of ability, race, and language in order to provide improved educational opportunities" (p. 165). All of these factors are important to meet the needs of CLD students in inclusive schools.

Students are more likely to transition smoothly into school if their family and community culture are congruent with the school. For some children, elementary school is their first exposure to formal learning experiences with adults and peers outside of their families; this often means interacting with people from different cultural and linguistic backgrounds. Students' ability to meet academic and behavioral expectations is paramount to their success throughout their academic careers (Rabiner et al., 2016). If their identity characteristics are not reflected in the curriculum or context, they are placed at a significant disadvantage. As educators address accountability measures, they are less likely to consider individualized needs unless these needs are reflected in federal, state, or district requirements (Datnow et al., 2003). Schooling has the potential to alter the life outcome trajectories for students based on how schools respond to students' backgrounds. Policy *and* practice must support an inclusive educational ethos.

Inclusion for All

Artiles and his colleagues (2006) cautioned against an either/or approach to meeting the needs of all students in a school, suggesting a shift from individualistic or communitarian models of inclusion to a more transformative approach. They offer a transformative, inclusive education model that includes a focus on ideological and historical assumptions about difference; how programs are conceptualized and operationalized; how groups are represented and engaged; and distribution of resources. This more expansive approach has the potential to responsively meet the needs of all students and families. To illustrate, a Latinx student who is an emergent bilingual, identified with a learning disability, from a family living below the poverty line might qualify for and garner federal funding for a number of services, including: Language Instruction for English Learners and Immigrant Students (*Every Student Succeeds Act*, Title III), special education (*Individuals with Disabilities Education Act* [IDEA] (2004)), and targeted resources for a more equitable, high-quality education (*Every Student Succeeds Act*, Title I). If each of these identified need areas is addressed independently, the student will likely be removed from the classroom to receive support from an EL specialist, a special education teacher, and possibly a content area specialist. Conversely, if the system is universally designed to meet the student's needs, specialists would consult with the core instruction teacher or provide services in the classroom to address learning objectives based on an integrated learning plan (Hatheway et al., 2015). To better address the needs of CLD students, we must acknowledge how systems marginalize and maintain barriers to their learning and identify and enact solutions.

The remainder of the chapter provides an overview of what we know about the needs of CLD learners in U.S. elementary schools and promising practices for meeting their needs. It is important to disambiguate and define some terms used throughout the chapter. Multi-Tiered Systems of Supports (MTSS), Response to Intervention (RTI), and Positive Behavior Interventions and Supports (PBIS) are discussed as frameworks that provide school-level infrastructure to support students' academic and/or behavioral needs with increasing intensity as appropriate. MTSS typically describes integrated academic and behavioral systems, RTI often refers to academic intervention, and PBIS primarily focuses on behavior. We acknowledge that behavior and academic supports are reciprocal and necessary for student success. Inclusion and inclusive education are framed differently in different contexts. We are advancing a notion of inclusion and inclusive education that encompasses and acknowledges: the complexity of identities that each individual possesses, how intersectionality (Artiles et al., 2006; Boveda & Aronson, 2019; Collins, 1990; Crenshaw, 1989) as a lens allows us to understand and serve students holistically, and that all students deserve an equitable educational experience responsive to their needs. In that sense, an equitable education ensures that each student gets what they need to result in positive outcomes regardless of dis/ability, cultural or linguistic background, socioeconomic status, or any other salient identity marker.

Diversity is defined as "a variety." We acknowledge that the student population is diverse in a number of ways, but non-White students are commonly referred to collectively as culturally and linguistically diverse, even as individuals. We use culturally and linguistically diverse as it is commonly used in the literature but hope to impress that ethno-racially and linguistically diverse is a more precise framing. Further, throughout the literature and over time, certain ethno-racial referents have shifted. For clarity and simplicity, we use Black to refer to people of African descent born in the U.S. and abroad; White to denote those who might be referred to in the literature as White, European American, or Caucasian; and Latinx to describe people whose ethnicity or nationality is Hispanic or Latino, understanding that they might also identify as racially White or Black. Additionally, we discuss emergent bilinguals/multilinguals as English Learners (ELs) rather than the various terms used in the literature (e.g., Limited English Proficient, English Language Learners, dual language learners) to emphasize the benefits of gaining fluency in multiple languages rather than the challenges presented by lacking proficiency in the dominant language. Finally, we use the term "minoritized" to highlight "the ongoing social experience of marginalization, even when groups subject to racial-ethnic discrimination achieve a numerical majority in the population" (Chase et al., 2014; p. 671).

In the next section, we review and synthesize common themes in the literature related to inclusion for students with disabilities who are also from a culturally and/or linguistically diverse background. Inclusive schools are organized to support all students well while attending to the individual learning needs of each student.

What Do We Know Based on Research and the Wisdom of Practice?

Extant research suggests that disparities in schooling exist for CLD students as well as for students with disabilities (e.g., Artiles, 2019; Curran, 2016; Smolkowski et al., 2016). Taking an intersectional view of the problem and potential solutions is critical. Many of the prevention and intervention approaches prevalent in special education are viewed as evidence-based broadly but could be further strengthened by providing services through a system that layers on a culturally and linguistically relevant educational[2] (Aronson & Laughter, 2016) lens.

Promising Practices: Build an Evidence-based Case for Improving Practice

Special education researchers and practitioners have identified and implemented frameworks with varying levels of evidence or promise for improving outcomes for students with disabilities. Multi-

Tiered Systems of Support (MTSS), Response to Intervention (RTI), and Positive Behavior Intervention and Supports (PBIS) are commonly employed and are reflected in legislation as supporting improved outcomes for students with and at-risk for disabilities. Over the years, scholars have examined and critiqued the evidence base as lacking a cultural filter (e.g., Artiles et al., 2010; Hartlep & Ellis, 2012; Klingner & Edwards, 2006; Sullivan & Thorius, 2010). When implemented well, these frameworks should support prevention and intervention for students with disabilities and disrupt inequities for children from CLD backgrounds. The involvement of families and communities is essential for effective implementation as students are part of larger ecological systems that influence their success inside and outside of school (Francis, Blue-Banning, Turnbull et al., 2016).

Family Engagement

Parent involvement and family engagement are widely discussed in the general education literature as a strategy to support student development from early learning through graduation (e.g., Epstein & Dauber, 1991; Stefanski et al., 2016). Parents have a significant influence on their children's school readiness; they are most familiar with their strengths and needs and provide learning support before they enter formal schooling. The expectation that parents will facilitate their child's ability to meet developmental milestones is understood. Yet, the Funds of Knowledge (Moll et al., 1992) that families tap into to ensure their children thrive prior to entering school is not always perceived equally when they enter the standardized educational system. Traditional engagement efforts in these systems tend to hold the priorities of schools in higher regard than the priorities of families and communities (Antony & Banks-Joseph, 2010; Ishimaru et al., 2016).

Llopart and Esteban-Guitart (2018) reviewed scholarly papers that applied or extended Funds of Knowledge (FoK) published between 2011-2015. The majority of the included papers focused on FoK application in literacy and language acquisition/multilingualism in US elementary schools. Central findings from their review included: connections to other theoretical frameworks, including Yosso's Community Cultural Wealth model (2005), which identifies forms of capital as "an array of knowledge, skills, abilities, and contacts possessed and utilized by communities of color to survive and resist macro- and micro-forms of oppression" (Yosso, 2005, p. 77); and extensions of the concept such as children's Funds of Knowledge-based interests (e.g., Hedges, 2011). The social and cultural capital that families—particularly those from culturally and linguistically diverse backgrounds—bring to school is often undervalued unless educators intentionally affirm and integrate their various forms of capital (Ishimaru et al., 2016; Trainor, 2010). Education professionals must know their learners, families, and communities well (Llopart & Esteban-Guitart). Strategies such as family response journals (Rowe & Fain, 2013) and digital storytelling and photovoice (Greene et al., 2018) can support this goal.

In some schools, family liaisons or parent advocates serve as a bridge between families and professionals. Ishimaru et al. (2016) conducted comparative case studies in three purposefully selected schools to examine the parent engagement practices of these "cultural brokers." The sites were part of a larger project focused on community-school engagement and meeting educator workforce needs. The study was theoretically guided by equitable collaboration and instructional agency. The authors explained that they employed "this conceptual framework to distinguish cultural brokering work that aims to 'widen the pipeline' (improve access without challenging deficit framings or conventional parent involvement approaches) from potential forms of parent and family agency and power to 'change the world' (transform family-school relations and educational systems)" (p. 858). Ishimaru et al. found that most cultural brokers approached their role conventionally, focusing on acculturating families to the dominant school culture. The researchers identified instances of a more relational, reciprocal approach that helped establish relationships and networks among parents. Interestingly, they noted differences in the approach taken by brokers that were community-based rather than school district-based. For instance, community-based facilitators enacted a broader conception of family engagement focused on community building and interacting with schools as part of the community. Conversely, school district-based facilitators were more likely to serve as liaisons enculturating families into the school milieu. Critical features of successful implementation included leaders who provided access and opportunities to create support for families and cultural brokers' ability to "span boundaries" between the schools and community.

In special education, IDEA mandates meaningful parent participation; this requirement was codified in law and reaffirmed by the U.S. Supreme Court (Winkelman v. Parma City School Dist., 2007). Trainor (2010) conducted focus group interviews to understand teacher perspectives on parent use of cultural and social capital for meaningful participation and collaboration. The researcher purposefully delineated "participation" and "collaboration" to show how the teachers perceived and invited parents as partners in their child's education. Participation was described as "family members' efforts to address educational issues relative to their children with disabilities" (p. 34), both formally and informally. Collaboration, however, required parity in responsibilities between families and professionals. The overarching themes included: (a) Expectations of parental capital; and (b) Educators' roles in facilitating parents' cultural and social capital. The teachers acknowledged that parents face barriers and it was partly their responsibility to help parents work around them. However, they seemed to expect parents to take on the lion's share of responsibility for collaborating despite the barriers. Further, the participants seemed more focused on knowing about certain families' home situations and making referrals rather than on adjusting their practices to engage them effectively.

The literature is replete with parents' concerns about the lack of meaningful collaboration with schools on behalf of their children (Zagona et al., 2019). More commonly, families of students with disabilities are narrowly engaged to support Individualized Education Program (IEP) development and implementation (Rodriguez et al., 2014; Ruppar & Gaffney, 2011); this is even more challenging for families of students with significant needs (Tucker & Schwartz, 2013). However, high-quality IEPs can anchor meaningful participation of families of students with disabilities (Childre & Chambers, 2005) when educators use IEPs as part of a process to engage families equitably in the decision-making process (Fish, 2008).

Sailor and his colleagues (McCart et al., 2014; Sailor & Roger, 2005) examined schools characterized as inclusive for students with disabilities to establish a model that was transferable to other settings. They found that professionals in these schools create a culture of belonging for all students and families (Francis, Blue-Banning, Haines et al., 2016; Francis, Blue-Banning, Turnbull et al., 2016; Haines et al., 2015). The schoolwide approach they developed based on their research emphasizes systems change to equitably support all learners, which includes as a guiding principle: "schools have open boundaries in relation to their families and communities" (Sailor & Roger, 2005, p. 507). Schools enact this principle in context-specific ways that include establishing a school-based family resource center or parent liaison, and inviting family participation in school activities beyond traditional parent organizations with parents ultimately assuming leadership roles.

Similarly, Yoon (2019) documented one school's approach to reimagining inclusion by doing "*bridging* work to connect families from vastly different neighborhoods" (p. 428), ensuring families had specific staff members with whom they could connect, and that caregivers were present as engaged members of the school community. Additional—often different—efforts are necessary for inclusion to be effective. Addressing inequities requires first acknowledging challenging histories such as segregation because of race and/or disability status (Yoon, 2019) and how systems might maintain them. As Artiles (2019) asserted, "systematic attention to context and historical contingencies is imperative…" (p. 326) as educators make judgments about families and determinations for their student's education.

Inequitable Achievement and Opportunities to Learn

Differences in achievement among students from ethno-racially diverse backgrounds, between students from economically advantaged and disadvantaged homes, and between students with and without disabilities (Artiles & Klingner, 2006; Artiles, Kozleski, et al., 2010; Aud et al., 2012; Rueda & Stillman, 2012) begin in elementary school and persist through high school (Suárez-Orozco et al., 2010). As a result, by the time they reach high school, students with disabilities (Impecoven-Lind & Foegen, 2010) and those from CLD backgrounds (Callahan, 2005; Umansky, 2016) are often behind in or do not have access to core subjects.

Systemic factors that contribute to achievement gaps including inequities in funding; the quality of teachers assigned to schools (i.e., teachers who are less experienced, are teaching outside their certification area or have fewer qualifications (García & Weiss, 2019); access to and enrollment in rigorous coursework (Callahan, 2005; Umansky, 2016); and access to high-quality support and up-to-date resources (Benson & Borman, 2010) have been identified and explored (Cramer et al., 2014). Factors that affect ELs include the lack of availability of appropriate language programs, and in the case of ELs with disabilities, lack of interventions that address English language development and the availability of bilingual special educators (Olsen, 2012; Sullivan, 2011). All these factors, individually and combined, impact students' access to high-quality instruction (Benson & Borman, 2010) and appropriate education. This is particularly true for CLD students with disabilities, many of whom attend schools that are under-resourced (Blanchett et al., 2009).

Response to Intervention (RTI), a framework that includes high-quality core instruction, universal screening, increasing levels of intervention, and progress monitoring, is used to identify students in need of academic support and to determine eligibility for special education. Once hailed as a solution to the disproportionate representation of students from CLD backgrounds, RTI has not consistently lived up to that promise (Cavendish et al., 2016). Among the issues identified in the literature are (a) teachers lack training to distinguish between language or cultural acquisition and a learning disability; (b) lack of culturally responsive materials, strategies, and curriculum in core instruction and intervention; (c) the use of standardized screening and progress monitoring assessments that do not include multiple contexts; and (d) the lack of a critical examination of the quality of the instruction provided to students who do not make progress (King et al., 2008; Klingner et al., 2007). A culturally responsive RTI model may improve outcomes for minoritized students and reduce disproportionality if it accounts for the factors that can impact student scores on screening and progress monitoring measures such as inappropriate instruction and lack of English language proficiency (e.g., Artiles, 2015; Artiles, Bal et al., 2010; García and Ortiz, 2008; Harris-Murri et al., 2006, Klingner & Edwards, 2006).

In culturally and linguistically responsive schools, students' education is aligned with their cultural values and they have access to high-quality, dignified, and meaningful education (Jones & Vagle, 2013; Ladson-Billings, 1995). Teachers in these schools are expected to provide culturally competent instruction and assessment to support students' academic learning and to maintain high expectations and affirm students, which is important for their socio-emotional well-being and motivation. In addition to having knowledge of practices that support student learning, teachers have explicit knowledge about cultural diversity, the ability to identify effective pedagogical approaches and adjust content (Villegas & Lucas, 2002). Schools implementing MTSS should embed these values and practices.

Teacher Factors

Teacher dispositions and sense of efficacy influence instructional decision making and the environment in classrooms and schools (McHatton, & McCray, 2013). Teachers must be open to the diversity of their students' experiences and ways of being and feel confident in their ability to build on them to meet their learning needs. Differences related to teachers' perspectives on good teaching and how to support students were noted in a focus group study of Black and White teachers' (Bacon et al., 2007). All teachers similarly described effective instruction, but the White teachers focused on motivating students and providing clear expectations, while the Black teachers focused on relationships beyond school and providing extra support as needed. In fact, the White teachers noted the distinct relationships that Black teachers, women, in particular, had with Black students. They believed that Black students were more accepting of correction from Black women and that Black teachers' communication styles were more congruent and thus more likely to be accepted by students. Conversely, Black teachers perceived White teachers' communication with and about the Black students as pitying rather than supportive and directed (Bacon et al., 2007).

Teachers model their perspectives on inclusivity and community for their students (Berry, 2006; Utley et al., 2011). Therefore, beliefs and resulting behaviors might unintentionally reify stereotypes and further marginalize CLD students (Juvonen et al., 2019). Nishina et al. (2019) posited that experiencing inclusive schools influences later success in a global workplace. To foster a sense of inclusion, the authors suggested promoting ethnic identity development, providing diversity training and cooperative learning, and facilitating social competence and prosocial behaviors (Nishina et al., 2019). Classrooms influence and are influenced by the larger school ethos. MTSS with culturally responsive practices should leverage the instructional assets of a whole school to meet the needs of individual learners.

Evidence-based Culturally Responsive Teaching Practices

Focused, systematic, and long-term implementation of culturally and linguistically responsive MTSS begins with purposeful planning to best organize systems to support all students, coordinate professional development efforts to ensure all educators are prepared to meet the needs of CLD students in each tier of instruction and sustain effective practices over time. At the school level, instructional leaders oversee the implementation of high-quality and responsive delivery of appropriate instruction and systematic evaluation of how students are responding to the instructional experiences that include active reflection on the quality and fidelity of the instruction provided.

Appropriate instruction integrates high-leverage practices *and* culturally and linguistically responsive practices for students with disabilities. For example, there are a number of these practices that can be integrated into explicit instruction, a high-leverage instructional practice, to provide CLD students with effective core instruction and intervention (Aceves & Orozco, 2014; Cartledge & Kourea; 2008; García & Ortiz, 2008; McLeskey et al., 2019; Richards-Tudor et al., 2016). Whether students are learning in their first or second language, initial instruction that includes modeling tasks, maintaining a spirited pace, scaffolding student learning, and providing corrective feedback are key components of explicit instruction that are effective for CLD students (Aceves & Orozco, 2014; Cartledge & Kourea; 2008; Richards-Tudor et al., 2016; Vaughn, Linan-Thompson, et al. 2006; Vaughn, Mathes et al., 2006). Peer-mediated activities are an effective means for providing collaborative practice to CLD students with and without disabilities (Calhoon, et al., 2006; Cartledge & Korea, 2008; García & Ortiz, 2008; Sáenz et al., 2005). Linguistically appropriate instruction for ELs, as well as any student who needs to develop academic language skills, provides students opportunities to develop an academic oral and written language and vocabulary across content areas (Baker et al., 2014; García and Ortiz, 2008; Richards-Tudor et al., 2016). Ongoing progress monitoring should also be used to document, adjust, and support the use of appropriate instruction.

Assessment to Inform Instruction

It is important to identify students' strengths and needs in order to differentiate instruction during core instruction and intervene early if needed. Within an RTI framework, assessment consists of universal screening and progress monitoring. Universal screening is used to determine students' academic skill level, group students, and design data-informed interventions. Progress monitoring is used to establish students' learning trajectories, measure students' progress toward benchmarks, and evaluate the effectiveness of the intervention. When working with ELs in an English as a Second Language program, establishing students' learning trajectory is necessary since a typical growth rate when learning in a second language is unknown.

RTI data collection practices can be enhanced to better serve CLD students by employing a comprehensive approach that includes using a variety of measures, including Curriculum-Based Measures (CBM), ensuring that tools are valid and reliable, and ensuring that teachers have the ability to interpret student data considering students' past experiences. A comprehensive assessment approach can include informal measures of language proficiency and language use and information regarding students' educational history in addition to the language surveys required when students enter school and yearly language proficiency assessments. Rating scales and checklists can be used to track changes in social and academic language skills. The results of informal measures can be used to identify students who need additional opportunities to develop language and to compare student levels relative to annual state-mandated language proficiency benchmarks. Teachers can also become knowledgeable of family literacy practices to help them identify culturally relevant practices and materials.

Curriculum-based measures are valid and reliable tools for identifying students in need of additional instruction and recording their progress (Demie, 2005; Klingner et al., 2005; Vanderwood et al., 2008). However, educators should ensure that the tools they are using have been normed with populations similar to their school population (Al Otaiba et al., 2009; Graves et al. 2005; Richards-Tutor et al., 2012; Wiley & Deno, 2005). It is also important to determine the language of assessment. Student assessment should be conducted in the language of instruction across all tiers in transitional bilingual and ESL programs and in both languages if students are enrolled in dual language programs or begin the transition in bilingual programs (Linan-Thompson & Ortiz, 2009).

Ensuring that school personnel have clear criteria for decision making set by the district or school in each language and for students who are in the process of transitioning will facilitate teachers' ability to interpret data from various sources (Esparza Brown & Sanford, 2011). For example, when examining scores on CBMs of students learning in English, teachers should also consider students' opportunities to learn English before determining how to intervene (Hosp et al., 2011; Linan-Thompson & Ortiz, 2009). This can help teachers more accurately distinguish between ELs who have learning difficulties and those who have had inadequate instruction or opportunity to learn. In addition to considering students' opportunities to learn English, teachers should affirm what students know and can do–regardless of the language–because many early literacy skills transfer across languages.

Referrals for Special Education

The cultural and linguistic bias inherent in the special education referral and evaluation process is well documented. According to IDEA Child Find regulations, educators must refer a student they suspect has a disability. Of all CLD students, Black students are most persistently overrepresented (Artiles, Kozleski, et al., 2010; Skiba et al., 2016; Sullivan & Bal, 2013) and Black students ages 6 -21 are 40% more likely to be referred to special education services than their White peers (U.S. Department of Education, 2016). Nationally, Black students are twice as likely to be identified as having emotional disturbance (U.S. Department of Education, 2016). In a highly controversial study, Morgan and his colleagues (2016) analyzed national data sets and concluded that minoritized students are under-identified for special education. However, a substantive research base built over decades and subsequent critiques (Skiba et al., 2016) suggest that the design and analyses used are simplistic and otherwise problematic (Trent et al., 2014).

Disproportionality is defined as the "overrepresentation" and "under-representation" of a particular population or demographic group in special or gifted education programs relative to the presence of this group in the overall student population (National Association for Bilingual Education, 2002). The overrepresentation of CLD students in special education has been a concern for several decades. As reflected in the risk indices noted earlier, Black, Latinx, and Native American students are referred to special education at much higher rates than White students. Once in special education, these same students are placed in more restrictive settings at higher rates than their White peers (Artiles et al., 2004; Ford, 2012; Klingner et al., 2005; U.S. Department of Education, 2016). Given the long-standing implications of being inappropriately referred to special education coupled with the persistent bias in aspects of the process, this issue is regarded as one of the most "critical and enduring problems in special education" (Skiba et al., 2008, p. 264).

Leading scholars attribute deficit thinking and pathologizing of cultural differences as a root cause for disproportionality (Artiles, 2015; Blanchett, 2006; Skiba et al., 2008), while others emphasize the role of implicit bias (Lhamon, 2016) in responding to student needs (e.g., Artiles, Bal, et al., 2010; Cohen et al., 2015; Skiba et al., 2016). Specific factors in the decision-making process that shape disproportionality include bias in referral, identification, and placement (Skiba et al., 2008; Sullivan et al., 2019); challenges related to living in poverty; the impact of systemic bias and discrimination in society reflected within schools (Skiba et al., 2016; Sullivan & Artiles, 2011); and inequitable educational opportunities and access to high-quality instruction and intervention (Artiles & Trent, 1994; Klingner et al., 2007).

Teacher judgment plays a role in referral, given that the general education teacher most often initiates referrals for special education. Given the widespread educational failure experienced by Black students, particularly boys, a referral may be the result of poor-quality instruction or unwarranted perspectives on learners' abilities (Jordan, 2016). However, the process for documenting and substantiating suspected disabilities varies widely by context. The documented cultural (i.e., ethno-racial) mismatch between teachers and students coupled with the lack of evidence-based, culturally responsive practices at Tier 1 increases the likelihood of disparate outcomes. In addition to the unconscious bias and ambiguity involved in the referral process, there is also a long history of bias in standardized testing (Skiba et al., 2008). Culturally and linguistically biased testing provides fertile ground for the over-identification of minoritized students.

Evaluation and Identification

Researchers agree that disproportionality is a symptom of systemic inequities present in society that impact minoritized communities. Additionally, disproportionality is the result of multiple practices and factors that influence decision making (Skiba et al., 2008). Sullivan and Bal (2013) conducted a study in an urban school district with a sample of 18,000 students across 39 schools. Multilevel analyses showed that the most consistent predictors of disability identification across the categories were students' gender, race, socioeconomic status, and the number of suspensions. Nearly a quarter of Black students were identified for special education and were nearly three times more likely to be identified with a specific learning disability or emotional disorder and were 2.5 times more likely to be identified as cognitively impaired than were White students. Moreover, male students of color were most disproportionately identified with disabilities across seven categories.

Skiba et al. (2008) identified psychometric test bias, poverty-related factors, and bias in the special education referral and eligibility processes as contributors to disproportionality. Test bias has a long and well-documented history as a factor that places Black students at risk for being labeled with a disability and deemed eligible for special education services (Skiba et al., 2008). Researchers argue that standardized assessments are often normed on middle-class White students, which creates a bias toward all other students and diminishes validity (Hosp & Reschly, 2004; Powers et al., 2004;

Warner et al., 2002). Special education evaluation should be culturally relevant and multidimensional (Jones, 2009), comprise a battery of assessments, and be analyzed and interpreted in culturally and linguistically relevant ways (Flanagan et al., 2007; National Association of School Psychologists, 2013). Culturally and linguistically relevant evaluation and identification approaches have shown promise in reducing bias and increasing appropriate educational placement for CLD students with disabilities (Hernandez et al., 2008). Studies continue to document the complexity of the decision-making process, including the role of team members and their interpretation of student data and the broader educational contexts (Ishii-Jordan, 2000; Sciuchetti, 2017; Skiba et al., 2008). Specifically, the role and perspectives of the referring teacher and the evaluation team members, including school psychologists, are important factors (Sullivan et al., 2019). This is especially important in observations and ratings of students with perceived challenging behaviors, particularly Black boys. Research has shown that Black children, especially boys, are perceived as older and not given the "protections of childhood equally to their peers" (Goff et al., 2014, p. 526).

Discipline Disparities

Federal data collection for the 2015–2016 school year indicated that CLD students and those with disabilities were disproportionately disciplined and referred to law enforcement or subjected to school-related arrests (U.S. Department of Education, Office for Civil Rights, 2019c). Black boys' representation among students suspended or expelled was around three times greater than their overall enrollment. Similarly, Latinx boys and Black girls were disproportionately suspended and expelled from school. The data are not reported in ways that pinpoint the intersections of race, gender, and disability status; however, the disproportionate expulsion of students with disabilities includes some of the same CLD students subjected to harsh and exclusionary discipline.

Curran (2016) used deterrence theory to frame quantitative analyses of the National Center for Education Statistics survey and other relevant state policy data to examine the effects of zero-tolerance discipline and expulsion. Consistent with previous scholarship (e.g., Gregory et al., 2010; Skiba et al., 2011; Walker, 2014), Curran found that Black students were disproportionately affected by an increase in suspensions. Further, zero-tolerance laws minimally deterred problem behavior or principals' perceptions of them. This suggests that policy implementation must account for the knowledge, skills, and dispositions of the educators and the contexts where they will be enacted.

Vulnerable Decision Points

McIntosh and his colleagues (2014) established a conceptual model to explain and identify some of the decision-making processes that allow disproportionate discipline to persist for Black students. They draw on education, cognitive, and social psychology to show how implicit racial bias shows up in discretionary decision making about the severity and problematic nature of subjective behaviors. Moreover, they illuminate the link between racial bias and disproportionate discipline, specifically the "decision situation." That is, contextual variables might subtly increase the probability of certain actions. The authors frame these instances as "vulnerable decision points to mean contextual events or elements of the immediate situation that increase the likelihood of bias affecting discipline decision making" (McIntosh et al., 2014, p. 9).

Subsequent tests of this model were conducted to determine opportunities to disrupt disproportionate discipline (Smolkowski et al., 2016). Using data from elementary schools using the School-Wide Information System, they analyzed 424,840 subjective Office Disciplinary Referrals (ODR) and 58,846 objective ODRs representing schools in 45 states. The investigators found that Black students were more likely to receive subjective ODR than White students; this was most acute in the classroom and when the ODR was categorized as major rather than minor.

Additionally, Black students were at greatest risk for referral during the first 90 minutes of the school day. Accounting for race and gender, Black boys were more vulnerable than White boys, and Black girls were most vulnerable. Removing students from class at the beginning of the day can lead to a full-day or longer loss of access to instruction. These findings, consistent with similar studies (Gregory et al., 2010; Wilson et al., 2020), implicated teachers' implicit racial bias in discretionary decision making. The role of the educator is critical, but even more importantly, the systems in place have the potential to perpetuate or disrupt inequities.

PBIS as a Structure

Schoolwide Positive Behavioral Interventions and Supports (SWPBIS) has been adopted as a framework in many schools to provide support for academic and social success for students with a wide range of needs (Bilias-Lolis et al., 2017; Swain-Bradway et al., 2014). When implemented as designed, it supports "both the whole school-culture and additional tiers of behavior support intensity needed to improve educational and social outcomes for all students" (Horner & Sugai, 2015, p. 80).

Beyond structures for primary prevention, secondary and tertiary supports are layered on for students at-risk for behavior considered inconducive to the learning environment, providing increased access to adults and academic engagement and decreased need for more intensive intervention (Ennis & Swoszowski, 2011; Vincent et al., 2012). Vincent et al. (2012) examined access to secondary supports among Black, Latinx, and White students at risk for behavioral difficulties and how ODR affected access. They found that Black students who had high ODR and received secondary supports early saw a decrease in ODR over the course of the year. Latinx students, similar to White peers, were less likely to have high rates of ODR but were more likely to receive secondary supports. This suggests cultural mismatch plays a role in discipline disparities.

Culturally Responsive Behavior Supports

Scholars (Banks & Obiakor, 2015; Swain-Bradway et al., 2014) argue that while SW-PBIS is generally effective in supporting behavior universally, discipline disparities persist for students from CLD backgrounds, particularly Black boys. Swain-Bradway et al. (2014) synthesized related literature to illuminate the potential for culturally relevant pedagogy to improve the effectiveness for all students and reduce discipline disparities for students most affected. Key recommendations for culturally responsive evidence-based behavior support delivered in a multi-tiered system of support include: (a) support structures that allow for variable intensity; (b) ongoing data collection for screening, diagnosis, and progress monitoring; (c) interpretation to determine the appropriateness of intervention; (d) racialized understandings of data interpretations; (e) proactive, culturally-grounded interventions; and (f) family and community involvement (Bal et al., 2016; Robinson-Ervin et al., 2011; Vincent et al., 2012).

Within and across the tiers of SWPBIS, interventions and supports are tailored to target specific needs of groups and/or individual students. Regardless of the framework, the implementers must be committed to culturally relevant pedagogy (Vincent et al., 2011, 2012). The developers of SW-PBIS assert that rebranding to explicitly label cultural responsiveness (e.g., CRPBIS) is unnecessary because "contextual-fit is a core principle of SWPBIS, SWPBIS is not fully implemented until it is culturally responsive" (Leverson et al., 2019, p. 2). Despite this intention, there is a growing literature base focused on highlighting and aligning tenets of SW-PBIS with other lenses such as cultural responsiveness and social-emotional learning (Banks & Obiakor, 2015; Barnes, 2019; Cressey, 2019; Markowitz & Bouffard, 2020; Vincent et al., 2011). Scholars have highlighted potential incongruence between the behavioral underpinnings of PBIS and culturally responsive practices (Bal et al., 2016) and the potential for unintentionally reinforcing dominant cultural norms (Banks & Obiakor, 2015).

The literature documenting the school experiences and outcomes of CLD learners with and at-risk for disabilities show persistent disparities in educational opportunities and achievement. Students who are Black, Latinx, Native American/Alaska Native, Native Hawaiian/Other Pacific Islander are at greatest risk for being identified with disabilities and experience only modest achievement on national assessments. This should not be surprising when many of them attend under-resourced schools that disregard their funds of knowledge, offer monocultural/monolingual curriculum, supply few effective teachers who provide rigorous instruction, and deny access through exclusionary discipline practices. Unintentional bias in the infrastructure of schooling and the special education process begins even before referral.

In order to disrupt the inequities in schools, inclusion must be implemented as a philosophy and in practice. The evidence base and frameworks the field draws on for service delivery are not without reproach. As long as disparities persist, we must continue to critique research, policy, and practice to identify promising instances of positive deviance that meet the diverse and intersecting needs of all students.

Setting the Course for Effective Inclusion

MTSS and RTI have been critiqued and acclaimed as a systematic way to address persistent disproportionality. Based on the findings of their critical race theoretical analysis of RTI, Hartlep and Ellis (2012) offered four recommendations, including: using RTI with an explicit culturally and linguistically responsive lens and conducting regular equity audits in special education. Drawing from García and Ortiz (2008), they noted that systems and frameworks must "take into account the sociopolitical, cultural, and linguistic contexts of schooling" (Hartlep & Ellis, 2012, p. 104). Moreover, they suggested equity audits as an integral component of culturally and linguistically responsive RTI, aimed at illuminating and eliminating patterns of inequities often built into processes and procedures. These disparities should be addressed at different stages, including referral (Sullivan & Thorius, 2010), identification (Harris-Murri et al., 2006; Klingner & Edwards, 2006), and throughout schooling to graduation.

MTSS implemented with an explicit cultural lens has shown promise for supporting positive outcomes. The fluid and layered nature of providing instruction and intervention allow individual students' instructional and behavioral needs to be addressed (Robinson-Ervin et al., 2011; Rodriguez et al., 2014; Swain-Bradway et al., 2014). The professionals implementing any system of support are key to its effectiveness.

In this section, we describe both evidence-based and promising practices for students with disabilities in inclusive elementary schools to provide guidance for sustained and effective inclusion. The research, frameworks, and strategies have implications for inclusive practice, as well as equity-oriented research and policy. There is a clear need for a comprehensive, culturally and linguistically relevant educational system characterized by family engagement, data-based referrals and evaluation, effective instruction and assessment, and intentional behavior support.

Family Engagement

Authentically engaging families requires parity among all who are involved with the growth and development of the learner (Valle, 2011). This begins with establishing shared understanding and priorities for expected outcomes among families, school professionals, and community stakeholders (Sawyer, 2015). Educators, special education teachers, in particular, must ensure that family members understand the student's learning needs, their rights as outlined in IDEA, and the support the school will provide. Ongoing communication using modes amenable to families is key to the timely exchange of information and decision-making in the best interest of the child (Ford et al., 2014).

Ultimately, families should feel empowered through their involvement in and out of school (Francis, Blue-Banning, Haines et al., 2016; Francis, Blue-Banning, Turnbull et al., 2016; Haines et al., 2015; Robertson, 2016).

Families' funds of knowledge and related social and cultural capital should be reflected in the culture and curriculum of a school and classrooms, encompassing different values, beliefs, and perspectives (Llopart & Esteban-Guitart, 2018; Rodriguez et al., 2014; Trainor, 2010). School leaders set the tone in the school building and must support all personnel in developing an asset orientation towards families. This might require school professionals to critically examine–and change–policies and procedures to create opportunities for families to be involved in different ways and contexts, which means accepting different home and community norms (Antony & Banks-Joseph, 2010). District policies should require school leaders and teachers to garner various forms of family feedback. While a climate survey is often used to solicit input, focus groups facilitated by cultural brokers in community settings might provide deeper insights, particularly from minoritized families.

Tapping into community resources and agencies to broker relationships can facilitate seamless systems of support for families. Ishimaru et al. (2016) found that community-based cultural brokers, with roles tightly aligned to expected outcomes, were able to support bridging school and community and establishing networks among parents. Partnerships that involve families, schools, and communities are primed for culturally relevant educational opportunities for all.

Referrals and Identification

RTI consists of core elements that set the stage for more equitable referral and decision-making processes. Through data-based decision making that includes clear decision rules; valid, and reliable data; and a team-based process of collecting and analyzing information, appropriate decisions can be made for students based on their needs. A variety of data should inform decisions about the type and level of instruction or intervention students need and will receive. Based on initial data, the decision-making team should determine how progress with a given intervention will be monitored and on what schedule to ensure the student's success. In this way, RTI has the potential to minimize bias in referrals and support a more individualized, data-based system for instruction, referral, and evaluation. Students should only be referred for special education evaluation after they have been provided culturally appropriate, evidence-based interventions and progress has been monitored to determine responsiveness to the intervention (García & Ortiz, 2008).

Appropriate Evaluation

Culturally and linguistically responsive evaluation is more than simply unbiased testing. The types of data collected and how they are interpreted are key to the resulting decision (Cruz & Rodl, 2018; Sullivan et al., 2019). Gathering multiple types of data to include information about the student's background and strengths are critical to the decision-making process. Culturally responsive assessment and evaluation includes multiple data points and examines systemic factors surrounding the data. For example, when analyzing standardized test scores that are below grade level, schools should determine if the student has been exposed to effective instruction and a high-quality curriculum as part of the comprehensive evaluation process. Schools should also ensure that students have access to culturally responsive instruction and intervention prior to evaluation (Cartledge & Korea, 2008).

Klingner and Edwards (2006) suggested the most effective way to eliminate disproportionality for CLD students is by engaging stakeholders with diverse perspectives to critically examine school practices and cultures. Bal et al. (2016) implemented and studied *Learning Labs* as one approach to improving data-based decision-making processes. In a *Learning Lab*, stakeholders with various perspectives systematically collect and analyze data while critically examining their school context.

The ultimate goal is to reimagine school discipline to better support CLD students. Presumably, this approach would also support academic goals.

Instruction and Assessment

In a comprehensive approach to culturally and linguistically responsive MTSS, school personnel work collaboratively to integrate students' diverse language/linguistic, cultural, and personal experiences into lesson planning and delivery (Cartledge et al., 2016). This approach can increase the relevance of the instruction provided and to the assessment processes used to ensure students receive the support they need prior to referral for special education. A systematic approach requires that all instructional personnel are committed to using culturally and linguistically responsive practices in combination with explicit instruction and other evidence-based practices that have demonstrated effectiveness for students with disabilities. This will empower each teacher to provide instruction that engages and motivates students, increases students' outcomes, and promotes students' English language skills. Equally important are the alignment of high-leverage practices across all levels of instructional supports (i.e., Tier 1-Tier 2; Tier 1-Tier 3) and the use of materials that reflect students funds of knowledge. For Tier 1 to be preventative and effective for CLD students, instruction should include content that is relevant such as topics of social justice and problems that involve critical thinking and learning that are made relevant to the daily lives of students and families.

The purpose of MTSS is to intervene early to prevent school failure and to monitor student progress to determine eligibility for special education. To ensure that CLD students are identified early but not disproportionately identified for tier 2 and 3 interventions requires procedures beyond the administration of CBMs and the use of benchmarks based on the performance of monolingual students from advantaged backgrounds. Although the basic assessment procedures used in RTI are valid to determine if students are mastering basic skills, its use to identify students for Tiers 2 and 3 interventions and eligibility for special education require additional considerations. Many CLD students' cultural and linguistic experiences are not reflected in the school curriculum and their knowledge and skills may not match those assessed in schools. Therefore, to better understand students' strengths and skills, teachers should use a variety of measures and gather information from various sources and across settings, such as opportunities to use English outside of school or home literacy practices (García & Ortiz, 2008). Teachers who are knowledgeable about their students are better able to interpret and contextualize data from various measures. Assessments should be unbiased and consider multiple views of students, including their strengths, not only focused on deficit areas but acknowledging students' intersectionality (Artiles, 2019).

Districts and schools serving ELs and implementing RTI should have a clearly articulated vision and set of procedures for ELs, including how language and literacy support will be provided. Leadership is particularly critical to supporting ELs within MTSS, to ensure a vision that promotes the success of all students and to prevent EL programs from being marginalized (e.g., separate or parallel MTSS practices for ELs, continuing discrepancies in the success of ELs). While the use of English and students' first language varies across programs for bilingual students, data from language measures should be used to capture student trajectories toward English proficiency.

Behavior Support

The culture and climate in schools should be based on shared norms that reflect culturally-grounded perspectives about appropriate individual and social behavior (Brown et al., 2019; Leverson et al., 2019; Sciuchetti, 2017). Bilias-Lolis et al. (2017) compared common inclusion models implemented in schools and communities and highlighted connections among PBIS, trauma-informed schools, and social inclusion. The authors suggested schools aim for "climates of compassion" (p. 1235) and collective responsibility to serve all students equitably. Going further, Joseph and her colleagues (2020) drew from policy, research, and professional practice to outline a multi-tiered system of support centering race, trauma-informed care, and restorative practices. They pointed to explicit mention of trauma-informed care in the Every Student Succeeds Act (2015) and legal precedent, which require educators to employ trauma-informed practices, particularly with students who have a history of adverse childhood experiences–namely children from CLD backgrounds (*Peter P., et al., v. Compton Unified School District et, al.,*2015). By integrating restorative practices, they provide a framework for professionals (e.g., teachers, school counselors, school social workers) to collaborate in support of student inclusion and behavioral success. Specifically, they suggested practitioners ask themselves questions such as: "What identity-based stressors are my students experiencing in society?" and "What opportunities do students have to share their counterstory before, during, and after disciplinary interactions?" (Joseph et al., 2020, p. 7). Ongoing reflective questioning makes it possible to identify and interrupt bias in disciplinary decisions (Dray & Wisneski, 2011), which should lead to more equitable practice and access to instruction.

As McIntosh and his colleagues (McIntosh et al., 2014; Smolkowski et al., 2016) suggested, both prevention and intervention are necessary for identifying and addressing issues in the learning environment and behavior. Effective, culturally responsive instruction and schoolwide behavior supports are foundational to teaching and learning for all students. However, educators must also regularly disaggregate and examine discipline data to determine how they might be harming certain students through unfair and inequitable discipline and punishment. By identifying vulnerable decision points–those instances that place students at greater risk for disciplinary consequences–and employing an explicit discipline decision-making process as suggested by Joseph et al. (2020), schools can become more inclusive and equitable for all students.

While the previously described primary prevention supports to address the social and behavioral needs of many students, some will need additional support to experience success in school. MTSS, when implemented well, flexibly layers on more intensive and individualized behavioral and social instruction. Again, educators designing and delivering secondary and tertiary interventions must consider race and culture and be committed to cultural responsiveness (Garner et al., 2014; Simmons-Reed & Cartledge, 2014). Students–particularly those who have a history of adverse experiences–need explicit instruction on behavioral expectations, accepted peer models, and opportunities to demonstrate with feedback (Lo & Cartledge, 2006; Robinson-Ervin et al., 2011; Utley et al., 2007). Additionally, involving students and families in the development and implementation of behavioral intervention plans increases the appropriateness of the intervention and the likelihood of positive outcomes over time (Robertson, 2016; Serpell et al., 2020).

Progress monitoring efforts must go beyond determining students' behavioral performance trajectory to determine influences on outcomes, including school policies and teacher practices. Inclusive schools benefit from an ongoing review of policies and practices to eliminate those that make certain students more vulnerable. School improvement plans should include equity audits that disaggregate student and personnel data by race, language, gender, and dis/ability to examine and address instances of disproportionality and/or increased risk for failure or exclusion (Hartlep & Ellis, 2012). These progress monitoring activities are enhanced when personnel with varied expertise, families, and community stakeholders engage in critical review from different vantage points (Bal et al., 2014; Harry et al., 2005).

Conclusion

Students from culturally and linguistically diverse backgrounds at risk for or identified with disabilities are best served in inclusive schools that attend to and explicitly integrate their cultural capital and funds of knowledge. Extant research demonstrates that the success of CLD learners is contingent upon policies that address their needs from an asset-based perspective, teacher and leader practices that are informed by an array of data sources, including the perspectives of families and communities. Schools and educators must continuously improve the implementation of high-leverage and evidence-based practices with a critical and cultural lens (Annamma et al., 2018). Existing practices and frameworks such as MTSS show promise, but only when context and history are considered.

Notes

1 Non-White people are often described as culturally diverse and we acknowledge (a) the normativity of Whiteness and (b) the persistent disparities in outcomes for learners who are from specific ethnic/racial (ethno-racially) backgrounds, including: Native American/Alaska Native, Native Hawaiian/Other Pacific Islander, Black, or Latinx

2 Culturally Relevant Education is a systems-level descriptor to include culturally responsive teaching, culturally relevant pedagogy, culturally sustaining pedagogy; we also name language as a critical focus.

References

Aceves, T. C., & Orozco, M. J. (2014). *Culturally responsive teaching* (Document No. IC-2). Retrieved from: ceedar.education.ufl.edu/tools/innovation-configurations/

Al Otaiba, S., Petscher, Y., Pappahihiel, N. E., Williams, R. S., Dyrlund, A. K., & Connor, C. (2009). Modeling oral reading fluency development in Latino students: A longitudinal study across second and third grade. *Journal of Educational Psychology*, 101(2), 315–319. doi: doi:10.1037/a0014698

Annamma, S. A., Ferri, B. A., & Connor, D. J. (2018). Disability critical race theory: Exploring the intersectional lineage, emergence, and potential futures of DisCrit in education. *Review of Research in Education*, 42(1), 46–71. doi:10.3102/0091732X18759041

Antony, P. J., & Banks-Joseph, S. R. (2010). Indian families in the U.S. who have children with disabilities: Implications for inclusive and culturally responsive practices. *Multiple Voices for Ethnically Diverse Exceptional Learners*, 12(2), 21–32. DOI: doi:10.5555/muvo.12.2.0170530458upr732

Aronson, B., & Laughter, J. (2016). The theory and practice of culturally relevant education: A synthesis of research across content areas. *Review of Educational Research*, 86(1), 163–206. doi:10.3102/0034654315582066

Artiles, A. J. (2015). Beyond responsiveness to identity badges: future research on culture in disability and implications for response to intervention. *Educational Review*, 67(1), 1–22. doi:10.1080/00131911.2014.934322

Artiles, A. J. (2019). Fourteenth annual *Brown* lecture in education research: Reenvisioning equity research: Disability identification disparities as a case in point. *Educational Researcher*, 48(6), 325–335. doi:10.3102/0013189X19871949

Artiles, A. J., Bal, A., & Thorius, K. A. K. (2010). Back to the future: A critique of response to intervention's social justice views. *Theory Into Practice*, 49, 250–257. doi:10.1080/00405841.2010.510447

Artiles, A. J., Harris-Murri, N., & Rostenberg, D. (2006). Inclusion as social justice: Critical notes on discourses, assumptions, and the road ahead. *Theory Into Practice*, 45(3), p260–268. doi:10.1207/s15430421tip4503_8

Artiles, A. J. & Klingner, J. K. (2006). Forging a knowledge base on English language learners with special needs: Theoretical, population, and technical issues. *Teachers College Record*, 108, 2187–21994.

Artiles, A. J., Kozleski, E. B., Trent, S. C., Osher, D., & Ortiz, A. (2010). Justifying and explaining disproportionality, 1968–2008: A critique of underlying views of culture. *Exceptional Children*, 76(3), 279–299. doi:10.1177/001440291007600303

Artiles, A. & Trent, S. C. (1994). Overrepresentation of minority students in special education: A continuing debate. *Journal of Special Education*, 27, 410–437. doi:10.1177/002246699402700404.

Artiles, A. J., Trent, S. C., & Palmer, J. (2004). Culturally diverse students in special education: Legacies and prospects. In J. A. Banks & C. M. Banks (Eds.). *Handbook of Research in Multicultural Education* (2nd ed., pp. 716–735). Jossey-Bass.

Aud, S., Husser, W., Johnson, F., Kena, G., & Roth, E. (2012). *The condition of education 2012*. (NCES 2012045). National Center for Educational Statistics.

Bacon, E., Banks, J., Young, K., & Jackson, F. R. (2007). Perceptions of African American and European American teachers on the education of African American boys. *Multiple Voices for Ethnically Diverse Exceptional Learners*, 10(1&2), 160–172. doi:10.5555/muvo.10.1-2.42640877v6646546

Baker, S., Lesaux, N., Jayanthi, M., Dimino, J., Proctor, C. P., Morris, J., Gersten, R., Haymond, K., Kieffer, M. J., Linan-Thompson, S., & Newman-Gonchar, R. (2014). *Teaching academic content and literacy to English learners in elementary and middle school* (NCEE 2014-4012). National Center for Education Evaluation and Regional Assistance (NCEE), Institute of Education Sciences, U.S. Department of Education. Retrieved from: http://ies.ed.gov/ncee/wwc/publications_reviews.aspx.

Bal, A., Kozleski, E. B., Schrader, E. M., & Rodriguez, E. M., & Pelton, S. (2014). Systemic transformation from the ground-up: Using Learning Lab to design culturally responsive schoolwide positive behavioral supports. *Remedial and Special Education*, 35(6), 327–339. doi:10.1177/0741932514536995

Bal, A., Schrader, E. M., Afacan, K. & Mawene, D. (2016). Using learning labs for culturally responsive positive behavioral interventions and supports. *Intervention in School and Clinic*, 52(2),122–128. doi:10.1177/1053451216636057

Banks, T. & Obiakor, F. E. (2015). Culturally responsive positive behavior supports: Considerations for practice. *Journal of Education and Training Studies*, 3(2), 83–90. doi:10.11114/jets.v3i2.636

Barnes, T. N. (2019). Changing the landscape of social emotional learning in urban schools: What are we currently focusing on and where do we go from here? *The Urban Review*, 51, 599–637.

Benson, J. & Borman, G. (2010). Family, neighborhood, and school setting across seasons: When do socio-economic context and racial composition matter for the reading achievement growth of young children? *Teachers College Record*, 112, 1338–1390.

Berry, R. A. W. (2006). Inclusion, power, and community: Teachers and students interpret the language of community in an inclusion classroom. *American Educational Research Journal*, 43(3), 489–529. doi:10.3102/00028312043003489

Bilias-Lolis, E., Gelber, N. W., Rispoli, K. M., Bray, M. A., & Maykel, C. (2017). On promoting understanding and equity through compassionate educational practice: Toward a new inclusion. *Psychology in the Schools*, 54(10), 1229–1237. doi:10.1002/pits.22077

Blanchett, W. J. (2006). Disproportionate representation of African American students in special education: Acknowledging the role of white privilege and racism. *Educational Researcher*, 35(6), 24–28. doi:10.3102/0013189X035006024

Blanchett, W. J., Klingner, J. K., & Harry, B. (2009). The intersection of race, culture, language, and disability: Implications for urban education. *Urban Education*, 44(4), 389–409. doi:10.1177/0042085909338686

Boveda, M., & Aronson, B. A. (2019). Special education preservice teachers, intersectional diversity, and the privileging of emerging professional identities. *Remedial and Special Education*, 40(4), 248–260. doi:10.1177/0741932519838621

Brown, B. A., Boda, P., Lemmi, C., & Monroe, X. (2019). Moving culturally relevant pedagogy from theory to practice: Exploring teachers' application of culturally relevant education in science and mathematics. *Urban Education*, 54, 775–803. doi:10.1177/0042085918794802

Callahan, R. (2005). Tracking and high school English learners: Limiting opportunities to learn. *American Educational Research Journal*, 42, 305–328. doi:10.3102/00028312042002305

Calhoon, B., Al Otaiba, S., Greenberg, D., King, A., & Avalos, A. (2006). Boosting the intensity of reading instruction for culturally diverse first grade students: The promise of Peer-Assisted Learning Strategies.*Learning Disabilities Research and Practice*, 21(4), 261–272.

Cartledge, G. & Korea, L. (2008). Culturally responsive classrooms for culturally diverse students with and at risk for disabilities. *Exceptional Children*, 74, 351–371. doi:10.1177/001440290807400305

Cartledge, G., Kea, C. D., Watson, M., & Oif, A. (2016). Special education disproportionality: A review of response to intervention and culturally relevant pedagogy. *Multiple Voices for Ethnically Diverse Exceptional Learners*, 16(1), 29–49. doi:10.5555/2158-396X.16.1.29

Carver-Thomas, D. (2018). *Diversifying the teaching profession: How to recruit and retain teachers of color*. Learning Policy Institute.

Cavendish, W., Harry, B., Menda, A. M., Espinosa, A., & Mahotiere, M. (2016). Implementing response to intervention: challenges of diversity and system change in a high stakes environment. *Teachers College Record*, 118(5), 1–36.

Chase, M.M., Dowd, A.C., Pazich, L.B., & Bensimon, E.M. (2014). Transfer equity for "minoritized" students: A critical policy analysis of seven states. *Educational Policy*, 28(5), 669–717. doi:10.1177/0895904812468227

Childre, A. & Chambers, C. R. (2005). Family perceptions of student centered planning and IEP meetings. *Education and Training in Developmental Disabilities*, 40, 217–233.

Cohen, D. R., Burns, M. K., Riley-Tillman, C., & Hosp, J. L. (2015). Are minority students under- or overrepresented in special education? *Communique*, 44, 22–23.

Collins, P. H. (1990). *Black feminist thought: Knowledge, consciousness, and the politics of empowerment*. Routledge.

Council of Chief State School Officers. (2019). *A vision and guidance for a diverse and learner-ready teacher workforce.* Author.

Cramer, E. D., Pellegrini-Lafont, C., & Gonzalez, L. (2014). Toward culturally responsive and integrated instruction for all learners: The integrated learning model. *Interdisciplinary Journal of Teaching and Learning*, 4, 110–124.

Crenshaw, K. (1989). Demarginalizing the intersection of race and sex: A Black feminist critique of antidiscrimination doctrine, feminist theory and antiracist politics. *University of Chicago Legal Files*, 139–167.

Cressey, J. (2019). Developing culturally responsive social, emotional, and behavioral supports. *Journal of Research in Innovative Teaching & Learning*, 12(1), 53–67. doi:10.1108/JRIT-01-2019-0015

Cruz, R. A., & Rodl, J. E. (2018). An integrative synthesis of literature on disproportionality in special education. *The Journal of Special Education*, 52(1), 50–63. doi:10.1177/0022466918758707

Curran, F. C. (2016). Estimating the effect of state zero tolerance laws on exclusionary discipline, racial discipline gaps, and student behavior. *Educational Evaluation and Policy Analysis*, 38(4), 647–668.

Datnow, A., Geoffrey, D., Borman, S. S., Overman, L. T., & Castellano, M. (2003). Comprehensive school reform in culturally and linguistically diverse contexts: Implementation and outcomes from a four-year study. *Educational Evaluation and Policy Analysis*, 25, 143–170. doi:10.3102/01623737025002143

Dee, T. S., & Penner, E. K. (2017). The causal effects of cultural relevance: evidence from an ethnic studies curriculum. *American Educational Research Journal*, 54, 127–166. doi:10.3102/0002831216677002

Demie, F. (2005). Achievement of black Caribbean pupils: Good practice in Lambeth schools. *British Educational Research Journal*, 31, 481–508. doi:10.1080/01411920500148705

Dray, B. J., & Wisneski, D. B. (2011). Mindful reflection as a process for developing culturally responsive practices. *TEACHING Exceptional Children*, 44(1), 28–36. doi:10.1177/004005991104400104

Ennis, R. P., & Swoszowski, N. C. (2011). The top 10 things to consider when implementing secondary-tier PBIS interventions. *Beyond Behavior*, 20(1), 42–44.

Epstein, J. L., & Dauber, S. L. (1991). School programs and teacher practices of parent involvement in inner-city elementary and middle schools. *The Elementary School Journal*, 91, 289–305. doi:10.1086/461656

Esparza Brown, J., & Sanford, A. (2011). *RTI for English language learners: Appropriately using screening and progress monitoring tools to improve instructional outcomes.* Retreived from http://www.rti4success.org/images/stories/pdfs/rtiforells.pdf

Every Student Succeeds Act, 20 U.S.C. § 6301 (2015). https://www.congress.gov/bill/114th-congress/senate-bill/1177

Fish, W. W. (2008). The IEP meeting: Perceptions of parents of students who receive special education services. *Preventing School Failure*, 53(1), 8–14. doi:10.3200/PSFL.53.1.8-14

Flanagan, D. P., Ortiz, S. O., & Alfonso, V. C. (2007). Essentials of cross-battery assessment, (2nd ed.). Wiley Press.

Ford, B. A., Stuart, D. H., & Vakil, S. (2014). Culturally responsive teaching in the 21st century inclusive classroom. *Journal of the International Association of Special Education*, 15(2), 56–62.

Ford, D. Y. (2012). Culturally different students in special education: Looking back to move forward. *Exceptional Children*, 78(4), 93–99. doi:10.1177/001440291207800401

Francis, G. L., Blue-Banning, M., Haines, S. J., Turnbull, A. P., & Gross, J. M. S. (2016). Building "our school": Parental perspectives for building trusting family-professional partnerships. *Preventing School Failure*, 60(4), 329–336. doi:10.1080/1045988X.2016.1164115

Francis, G. L., Blue-Banning, M., Turnbull, A. P., Hill, C., Haines, S. J., & Gross, J. M. S. (2016). Culture in inclusive schools: Parental perspectives on trusting family-professional partnerships. *Education and Training in Autism and Developmental Disabilities*, 51(3), 281–293.

García, S. B., & Ortiz, A. A. (2008). A framework for culturally and linguistically responsive design of Response-to-Intervention models. *Multiple Voices for Ethnically Diverse Exceptional Learners*, 11(1), 24–41. doi:10.5555/muvo.11.1.gu04327p723217t0

García, E. & Weiss, E. (2019). *The teacher shortage is real, large and growing, and worse that we thought.* Economic Policy Institute, March 2019.

Garner P. W., Mahatmya, D., Brown, E. L., & Vesely, C. K. (2014). Promoting desirable outcomes among culturally and ethnically diverse children in social emotional learning programs: A multilevel heuristic model. *Educational Psychology Review*, 26(1), 165–189. doi:10.1007/s10648-014-9253-7

Goff, P. A., Jackson, M. C., Allison, B., DiLeone, L., Culotta, C.M., & DiTomasso, N. A. (2014). The essence of innocence: Consequences of dehumanizing Black children. *Journal of Personality and Social Psychology*, 106(4), 526–545. doi:10.1037/a0035663

Graves, A. W., Plasencia-Peinado , J., Deno, S. L., & Johnson, J. R., (2005). Formatively evaluating the reading progress of first-grade English learners in multiple-language classrooms.*Remedial and Special Education, 26*(4), 215–225.

Greene, S., Burke, K. J., & McKenna, M. K. (2018). A Review of research connecting digital storytelling, photovoice, and civic engagement. *Review of Educational Research*, 88(6), 844–878. doi:10.3102/003465431 8794134

Gregory, A. Skiba, R. J., & Noguera, P. A. (2010). The achievement gap and the discipline gap: Two sides of the same coin? *Educational Researcher*, 39(1), 59–68. doi:doi:10.3102/0013189X09357621

Haines, S. J., Gross, J. M. S., Blue-Banning, M., Francis, G. L., & Turnbull, A. P. (2015). Fostering family-school partnerships in inclusive schools: Using practice as a guide. *Research and Practice for Persons with Severe Disabilities*, 40(3), 227–239.

Harris-Murri, N., King, K., & Rostenberg, D. (2006). Reducing disproportionate minority representation in special education programs for students with emotional disturbances: toward a culturally responsive response to intervention model. *Education and Treatment of Children*, 29, 779–799.

Harry, B. & Klingner, J. K. (2006). *Why are so many minority students in special education? Understanding race and disability in schools.* Teachers College Press.

Harry, B., Klingner, J. K., & Hart, J. (2005). African American families under fire: Ethnographic views of family strengths. *Remedial and Special Education*, 26(2), 101–112. doi:10.1177/07419325050260020501

Hartlep, N. D., & Ellis, A. L. (2012). Chapter 6: Just what is Response to Intervention and what's it doing in a nice field like education? A critical race theory examination of Response to Intervention. *Counterpoints*, 425, 87–108.

Hatheway, B., Shea, D., & Winslow, M. (2015). Dual language program meets integrated collaborative teaching. *Journal of Multilingual Education Research*, 6(Article 8), 137–151.

Hedges, H. (2011). Rethinking sponge bob and ninja turtles: Popular culture as funds of knowledge for curriculum co-construction. *Australasian Journal of Early Childhood*, 36, 25–29. doi:10.1177/183693911103 600105

Hernandez, J. E., Ramanathan, A. K., Harr, J., & Socias, M. (2008). Study of the effects of an intervention to reduce disproportionate identification in the category of emotional disturbance in Los Angeles unified school district. *Journal of Special Education Leadership*, 27, 64–73.

Horner, R. H. & Sugai, G. (2015). School-wide PBIS: An example of applied behavior analysis implemented at a scale of social importance. *Behavior Analysis Practice*, 8, 80–85. doi: 10.1007/s40617-015-0045-4

Hosp, J. L., & Reschly, D. J. (2004). Disproportionate representation of minority students in special education: Academic, demographic, and economic predictors. *Exceptional Children*, 70, 185–199. doi:10.1177/0014402 90407000204

Hosp, J. L., Hosp, M. A., & Dole, J. K. (2011). Potential bias in predictive validity of universal screening measures across disaggregation subgroups. *School Psychology Review*, 40, 108–131. doi:10.1080/02796015. 2011.12087731

Impecoven-Lind, L. S. & Foegen, A. (2010). Teaching algebra to students with learning disabilities. *Intervention in School and Clinic*, 46, 31–37. doi:10.1177/1053451210369520

Individuals with Disabilities Education Act, 20 U.S.C. § 1400 (2004).

Ishii-Jordan, S. R. (2000). Behavioral interventions used with diverse students. *Behavioral Disorders*, 25(4), 299–309.

Ishimaru, A. M., Torres, K. E., Salvador, J. E., Lott, II, J., Williams, M. C., & Tran, C. (2016). Reinforcing deficit, journeying toward equity: Cultural brokering in family engagement initiatives. *American Educational Research Journal*, 53(4), 850–882. doi:10.3102/0002831216657178

Jones, J. M. (Ed.). (2009). *The psychology of multiculturalism in schools: A primer for practice, training, and research.* National Association of School Psychologists.

Jones, S. & Vagle, M. D. (2013). Living contradictions and working for change: Toward a theory of social class-sensitive pedagogy. *Educational Researcher*, 42, 129–141. doi:10.3102/0013189X13481381

Jordan, K.-A. (2016). The practice of special education referral: Teachers' discursive assumptions. *International Journal of Learner Diversity & Identities*, 23(3), 33–54. doi:10.18848/2327-0128/cgp/v23i03/33-54

Joseph, A. A., Wilcox, S. M., Hinilca, R. J., & Hansen, M.C. (2020). Keeping race at the center of school discipline practices and trauma-informed care: An interprofessional framework. *Children & Schools*. doi.10.1 093/cs/cdaa013

Juvonen, J., Lessard, L. M., & Rastogi, R. (2019). Promoting social inclusion in educational settings: Challenges and opportunities. *Educational Psychologist*, 54(4), 250–270. doi:10.1080/00461520.2019.1655645

King, K. A., Kozleski, E. B., Artiels, A. J., Sullivan, A. L., Rueb, C., Duran, W., & Herron, B. (2008). *Culturally responsive response to intervention models.* Professional Learning Module Series. National Center for Culturally Responsive Education Systems.

Klingner, J. K., & Edwards, P. A. (2006). Cultural considerations with response to intervention models. *Reading Research Quarterly*, 41(1), 108–117. doi:10.1598/RRQ.41.1.6

Klingner, J. K., Artiles, A. J., Kozleski, E., Harry, B., Zion, S., Tate, W., Durán, G. Z., & Riley, D. (2005). Addressing disproportionate representation of culturally and linguistically diverse students in special education through culturally responsive educational systems. *Education Policy Analysis Archives*, 13(38). Retrieved from http://epaa.asu.edu/epaa/v13n38/

Klingner, J. K., Sorrels, A. M., & Barrera, M. T. (2007). Considerations when implementing response to intervention with culturally and linguistically diverse students. In D. Haager, J. K. Klingner, & S. Vaughn (Eds.), *Evidence-based reading practices for response to intervention* (pp. 223–244). Brookes.

Kourea, L., Lo, Y., & Owens, T. L. (2016). Using parental input from Black families to increase cultural responsiveness for teaching SWPBS expectations. *Behavioral Disorders*, 41(4), 226–240. doi:10.17988/bedi-41-04-226-240.1

Kozleski, E. B., Artiles, A. J., McCray, E. D., & Lacy, L. (2014). Equity challenges in the accountability age: Demographic representation and distribution in the teacher workforce. In P.T. Sindelar, E.D. McCray, M.T. Brownell, & B. Lignugaris Kraft, (Eds.) *Handbook of Research on Special Education Teacher Preparation* (pp. 113–126). Routledge.

Ladson-Billings, G. J. (1995). Toward a theory of culturally relevant pedagogy. *American Educational Research Journal*, 32(3), 465–491. doi:10.3102/00028312032003465

Leverson, M., Smith, K., McIntosh, K., Rose, J., & Pinkelman, S. (2019). *PBIS cultural responsiveness field guide: Resources for trainers and coaches.* Retrieved from: https://www.pbis.org/resource/pbis-cultural-responsiveness-field-guide-resources-for-trainers-and-coaches

Lhamon, C. (2016). *Dear colleague letter: Preventing racial discrimination in special education.* U.S. Department of Education, Office for Civil Rights.

Linan-Thompson, S. & Ortiz, A. A. (2009). Response to intervention and English language learners: Instructional and assessment considerations. *Seminars in Speech and Language*, 30, 105–120. doi:10.1080/02702710500285748

Llopart, M., & Esteban-Guitart, M. (2018). Funds of knowledge in 21st century societies: Inclusive educational practices for under-represented students: A literature review. *Journal of Curriculum Studies*, 50, 145–161. doi:10.1080/00220272.2016.1247913

Lo, Y-Y., & Cartledge, G. (2006). FBA and BIP: Increasing the behavior adjustment of African American boys in schools. *Behavioral Disorders*, 31, 147–161. doi:10.1177/019874290603100204

Markowitz, N. L., & Bouffard, S. M. (2020). *Teaching with a social, emotional, and cultural lens: A framework for educators and teacher educators.* Harvard Education Press.

McCart, A. B., Sailor, W. S., Bezdek, J. M., & Satter, A. L. (2014). A framework for inclusive educational delivery systems. *Inclusion*, 2, 252–264. doi:10.1352/2326-6988-2.4.252

McFarland, J., Hussar, B., Zhang, J., Wang, X., Wang, K., Hein, S., Diliberti, M., Forrest Cataldi, E., Bullock Mann, F., & Barmer, A. (2019). *The condition of education 2019* (NCES 2019-144). U.S. Department of Education. National Center for Education Statistics. Retrieved from https://nces.ed.gov/pubsearch/pubsinfo.asp?pubid=2019144.

McHatton, P. A. & McCray, E. (2013). Diversity: Beyond teachers. In L. Smith, T. Knopp, & D. Skarbeck (Eds.), *Professional teacher dispositions: Additions to the mainstream* (pp. 51–66). Rowman & Littlefield Education.

McIntosh, K., Girvan, E. J., Horner, R. H., & Smolkowski, K. (2014). Education not incarceration: A conceptual model for reducing racial and thenic disproportionality in school discipline. *Journal of Applied Research on Children: Informing Policy for Children at Risk*, 5(2), article 2.

McLeskey, J., Billingsley, B., Brownell, M. T., Maheady, L., & Lewis, T. J. (2019). What are high-leverage practices for special education teachers and why are they important? *Remedial and Special Education*, 40(6), 331–337. doi:10.1177/0741932518773477

Moll, L. C., Amanti, C., Neff, D., & Gonzalez, N. (1992). Funds of knowledge for teaching: Using a qualitative approach to connect homes and classrooms. *Theory Into Practice*, 31, 132–141. doi:10.1080/00405849209543534

Morgan, P. L., Farkas, G., Hillemeier, M. M., Mattison, R., Maczuga, S., Li, H., & Cook, M. (2016). Minorities are disproportionately underrepresented in special education: Longitudinal evidence across five disability conditions. *Educational Researcher*, 44(5), 278–292. doi:10.3102/0013189X15591157

National Academies of Science, Engineering, & Medicine. (2017). *Promoting the educational success of children and youth learning English: Promising futures.* The National Academies Press. doi:10.17226/24677.

National Association for Bilingual Education. (2002). *Determining appropriate referrals of English language learners to special education: A self-assessment guide for principals.* Council for Exceptional Children.

National Association of School Psychologists (2013). *Racial and ethnic disproportionality in education* [Position statement]. Author.

New York State Education Department. (2016). *The New York state seal of biliteracy handbook*. Retrieved from http://www.nysed.gov/common/nysed/files/programs/world-languages/nyssb-handbook.pdf

Nishina, A., Lewis, J. A., Bellmore, A., & Witkow, M. R. (2019). Ethnic diversity and inclusive school environments. *Educational Psychologist*, 54, 306–321. doi:10.1080/00461520.2019.1633923

Olsen, L. (2012). *Ensuring academic success for English learners*. University of California Linguistic Minority Research Institute Newsletter, 15, 1–7.

Peter P., et al., *v. Compton Unified School District et, al.*, (2015).

Powers, K. M., Hagans-Murillo, K., & Restori, A. F. (2004). Twenty-five years after Larry P.: The California response to overrepresentation of African Americans in special education. *California School Psychologist*, 9, 145–158.

Rabiner, D. L., Godwin, J., & Dodge, K. A. (2016). Predicting academic achievement and attainment: the contribution of early academic skills, attention difficulties, and social competence. *School Psychology Review*, 45, 250–267.

Reese, L., Richards-Tutor, C., & Hansuvadha, N. (2018). Teachers for inclusive, diverse urban settings. *Issues in Teacher Education*, 27(1), 17–27.

Richards-Tudor, C., Aceves, T., & Reese, L. (2016). *Evidence-based practices for English learners* (Document No. IC-18). Retrieved from: ceedar.education.ufl.edu/tools/innovation-configurations/

Richards-Tutor, C., Solari, E. J., Leafstedt, J. M., Gerber, M., Filippini, A., & Aceves, T. C. (2012). Response to intervention for English learners: Examining models for determining response and nonresponse. *Assessment for Effective Intervention*, 38(3), 172–184. doi:10.1177/1534508412461522

Robertson, R. (2016). Effectiveness and acceptability of parent-implemented behavior interventions for children with autism in three African-American families. *Education and Training in Autism and Developmental Disabilities*, 51(2), 107–121.

Robinson-Ervin, P., Cartledge, G., & Keyes, S. (2011). Culturally responsive skills instruction for adolescent black males. *Multicultural Learning and Teaching*, 6. doi:10.2202/2161-2412.1075

Rodriguez, R. J., Blatz, E. T., & Elbaum, B. (2014). Parents' views of schools' involvement efforts. *Exceptional Children*, 81, 79–95. doi:10.1177/0014402914532232

Rowe, D., & Fain, J. G. (2013). Family backpack project: Responding to dual-language texts through family journals. *Language Arts*, 90, 402–416.

Rueda, R., & Stillman, J. (2012). The 21st century teacher: A cultural perspective. *Journal of Teacher Education*, 63, 245–253. doi:10.1177/0022487112446511

Ruppar, A. L., & Gaffney, J. S. (2011). Individualized education program team decisions: A preliminary study of conversations, negotiations, and power. *Research & Practice for Persons with Severe Disabilities*, 36(1-2), 11–22. doi:10.2511/rpsd.36.1-2.11

Sáenz, L. M., Fuchs, L. S., & Fuchs, D. (2005). Peer-assisted learning strategies for English language learners with learning disabilities. *Exceptional Children*, 71, 231–247. doi:10.1177/001440290507100302

Sailor, W., & Roger, B. (2005). Rethinking inclusion: Schoolwide applications. *Phi Delta Kappan*, 86, 503–509. doi:10.1177/003172170508600707

Sawyer, M. (2015). BRIDGES: Connecting with families to facilitate and enhance involvement. *TEACHING Exceptional Children*, 47(3), 172–179. doi:10.1177/0040059914558946

Sciuchetti, M. B. (2017). Addressing inequity in special education: An integrated framework for culturally responsive social emotional practice. *Psychology in the Schools*, 54(10), 1245–1251. doi:10.1002/pits.22073

Serpell, Z. N., Wilkerson, T., Evans, S. W., Nortey-Washington, M., Johnson-White, R., & Paternite, C. E. (2020). Developing a framework for curtailing exclusionary discipline for African-American students with disruptive behavior problems: A mixed-methods approach. *School Mental Health*. doi: 10.1007/s12310-020-09380-z

Simmons-Reed, E. A., & Cartledge, G. (2014). School discipline disproportionality: Culturally competent interventions for African American males. *Interdisciplinary Journal of Teaching and Learning*, 4(2), 95–109.

Skiba, R. J., Artiles, A. J., Kozleski, E. B., Losen, D. J., & Harry, E. G. (2016). Risks and consequences of oversimplifying educational inequities: A response to Morgan et al. (2015). *Educational Researcher*, 45(3), 221–225. doi:10.3102/0013189X16644606

Skiba, R., Horner, R. H., Chung, C-G., Rausch, M. K., May, S. L., & Tobin, T. J. (2011). Race is not neutral: A national investigation of African American and Latino disproportionality in school discipline. *School Psychology Review*, 40, 85–107.

Skiba, R. J., Simmons, A. B., Ritter, S., Gibb, A. C., Rausch, M. K., Cuadrado, J., & Chung, C-G. (2008). Achieving equity in special education: History, status, and current challenges. *Exceptional Children*, 74, 264–288. doi:10.1177/001440290807400301

Smolkowski, K., Girvan, E. J., McIntosh, K., Nese R. N. T., & Horner, R. H. (2016). Vulnerable decision points for disproportionate office discipline referrals: Comparisons of African American and white elementary school students. *Behavioral Disorders*, 41(4), 178–195. doi:10.17988/bedi-41-04-178-195.1

Stefanski, A., Valli, L., & Jacobson, R. (2016). Beyond involvement and engagement: The role of the family in school-community partnerships. *School Community Journal*, 2016, 26, 135–160.

Suárez-Orozco, C., Gaytan, F. X., Bang, H. J., Pakes, J., O'Connor, E., & Rhodes, J. (2010). Academic trajectories of newcomer youth. *Developmental Psychology*, 43(3), 602–618. doi:10.1037/a0018201

Sullivan, A. L. (2011). Disproportionality in special education identification and placement of English language learners. *Exceptional Children*, 77(3), 317–334. doi:10.1177/001440291107700304

Sullivan, A. L., & Artiles, A. J. (2011). Theorizing racial inequity in special education: Applying structural inequity theory to disproportionality. *Urban Education*, 46(6), 1526–1552. doi:10.1177/0042085911416014

Sullivan, A. & Bal, A. (2013). Disproportionality in special education: Effects of individual and school variables on disability risk. *Exceptional Children*, 79(4), 475–494. doi:10.1177/001440291307900406

Sullivan, A. L., Sadeh, S., & Houri, A. K. (2019). Are school psychologists' special education eligibility decisions reliable and unbiased? A multi-study experimental investigation. *Educational Psychology*, 77, 90–109. doi:10.1016/j.jsp.2019.10.006

Sullivan, A. L., & Thorius, K. A. K. (2010) Considering intersections of difference among students identified as disabled expanding conceptualizations of multicultural education. *Race, Gender & Class*, 17(1/2), 93–109.

Swain-Bradway, J., Loman, S. L., & Vincent, C. G. (2014). Systematically addressing discipline disproportionality through the application of school-wide framework. *Multiple Voices for Ethnically Diverse Exceptional Learners*, 14(1), 3–17. doi:10.5555/muvo.14.1.jl626n21408t4846

Trainor, A. A. (2010). Reexamining the promise of parent participation in special education: Am analysis of cultural and social capital. *Anthropology & Education Quarterly*, 41, 245–263. doi:10.1111/j.1548-1492.2010.01086.x

Trent, S. C., Driver, M. K., Rodríguez, D., Oh, K., Stewart, S., Kea, C., Artiles, A., & Hull, M. (2014). Beyond Brown: Empirical research on diverse learners with or at-risk for specific learning disabilities from 1994-2012. *Multiple Voices for Ethnically Diverse Exceptional Learners*, 14 (2) 12–29. doi:10.5555/2158-396X.14.2.12

Tucker, V. & Schwartz, I. S. (2013). Parents' perspectives of collaboration with school professionals: Barriers and facilitators to successful partnerships in planning for students with ASD. *School Mental Health*, 5. doi: 10.1007//s12310-012-9102-0

Umansky, I. M. (2016). To be or not to be EL: An examination of the impact of classifying students as English learners. *Educational Evaluation and Policy Analysis*, 38, 714–737. doi:10.3102/0162373716664802

U.S. Department of Education (2016). *FACT SHEET: Equity in IDEA*. Retrieved from https://www.ed.gov/news/press-releases/fact-sheet-

U.S. Department of Education, Institute of Education Sciences, National Center for Education Statistics. (2019b). *National Assessment of Educational Progress* (NAEP). Retrieved from https://www.nationsreportcard.gov

U.S. Department of Education, Office for Civil Rights. (2019c). *2015-2016 Civil Rights data collection: School climate and safety*. Retrieved from: https://www2.ed.gov/about/offices/list/ocr/docs/school-climate-and-safety.pdf

U.S. Department of Education, Office of Special Education and Rehabilitative Services, Office of Special Education Programs. (2019a). *41st Annual Report to Congress on the Implementation of the Individuals with Disabilities Education Act, 2017-18*. Author.

Utley, C. A., Greenwood, C. R., & Douglas, K. (2007). The effects of a social skills strategy on disruptive and problem behaviors in African American students in an urban elementary school: A pilot study. *Multiple Voices for Ethnically Diverse Exceptional Learners*,10(1&2), 173–190. doi:10.5555/muvo.10.1-2.501t712t21604j37

Utley, C. A., Obiakor, F. E., & Bakken, J. P. (2011). Culturally responsive practices for culturally and linguistically diverse students with learning disabilities. *Learning Disabilities: A Contemporary Journal*, 9(1), 5–18.

Valle, J. W. (2011). Down the rabbit hole: A commentary about research on parents and special education. *Learning Disabilities Quarterly*, 34(3), 183–190. doi:10.1177/0731948711417555

Vanderwood, M. L., Linklater, D., & Healy, K. (2008). Predictive accuracy of nonsense word fluency for English language learners. *School Psychology Review*, 37(1), 5–17. doi:10.1080/02796015.2008.12087904

Vaughn, S. R., Linan-Thompson, S., Mathes, P. G., Cirino, P. T., Carlson, C. D., Pollard-Durodola, S. D., Fletcher, J. M., & Francis D. J. (2006). Effectiveness of Spanish intervention for first-grade English language learners at risk for reading difficulties. *Journal of Learning Disabilities*, 39, 56–73. doi:10.1177/00222194060390010601

Vaughn, S. R., Mathes, P. G., Linan-Thompson, S., Cirino, P. T., Carlson, C. D., Pollard-Durodola, S. D., Fletcher, J. M., & Francis, D. J. (2006). Effectiveness of an English intervention for first grade English language learners at risk for reading problems. *The Elementary School Journal*, 107, 153–180. doi: 10.1086/510653

Villegas, A. M. & Lucas, T. (2002). Preparing culturally responsive teachers: Rethinking the curriculum. *Journal of Teacher Education*, 53, 20–132. doi:10.1177/0022487102053001003

Vincent, C. G., Swain-Bradway, J., Tobin, T. J., & May, S. (2011). Disciplinary referrals for culturally and linguistically diverse students with and without disabilities; patterns resulting from school-wide positive behaviour support. *Exceptionality A Special Education Journal*, 19, 175–190. doi:10.1080/09362835.2011.579936

Vincent, C. G., Tobin, T. J., Hawken, L. S., & Frank, J. L. (2012). Discipline referrals and access to secondary level support in elementary and middle schools: Patterns across African-American, Hispanic-American, and white students. *Education and Treatment of Children*, 35(3), 431–458. doi:10.1353/etc.2012.0018

Walker, B.L.T. (2014). Suspended animation: A legal perspective of school discipline and African American learners in the shadows of Brown. *The Journal of Negro Education*, 83(3), 338–351.

Warner, T. D., Dede, D. E., Garvan, C. W., & Conway, T. W. (2002). One size still does not fit all in specific learning disability assessment across ethnic groups. *Journal of Learning Disabilities*, 35(6), 501–509. doi:10.1177/00222194020350060201

Wiley, H. I., & Deno, S. L., (2005). Oral reading and maze measures as predictors of success for English learners on a state standards assessment. *Remedial and Special Education*, 26, 207–214. doi:10.1177/07419325050260040301

Wilson, M. A. F., Yull, D. G., & Massey, S. G. (2020). Race and the politics of educational exclusion: explaining the persistence of disproportionate disciplinary practices in an urban school district. *Race Ethnicity and Education*, 23(1), 134–157, doi:10.1080/13613324.2018.1511535

Winkelman v. Parma City School Dist., 550 U.S. 516. (2007).

Yoon, I. H. (2019). Haunted trauma narratives of inclusion, race, and disability in a school community. *Educational Studies*, 55(4), 420–435. doi:10.1080/00131946.2019.1629926

Yosso, T. J. (2005). Whose culture has capital? A critical race theory discussion of community cultural wealth. *Race Ethnicity and Education*, 8, 69–91. doi:10.1080/1361332052000341006

Zagona, A. L., Miller, A. L., Kurth, J. A., & Love, H. R. (2019). Parent perspectives on special education services: How do schools implement team decisions? *School Community Journal*, 29, 105–128.

Zion, S., & Sobel, D. (2014). Mapping the gaps: Redesigning a teacher education program to prepare teachers for inclusive, urban schools. *Journal of the International Association of Special Education*, 15, 63–73.

23

Using Technology to Support Effective Inclusive Elementary Schools

Maya Israel[1], Matthew T. Marino[2], Wei Yan[1], and John H. Samuels[1]

[1]UNIVERSITY OF FLORIDA

[2]UNIVERSITY OF CENTRAL FLORIDA

Setting the Stage

Context of Technology Integration into Elementary School Instruction

Technological innovations have the potential to positively impact the way elementary teachers teach and the way their students experience the world around them. Emerging technologies are increasingly influencing elementary education as school districts invest resources for young learners. The recognition that technology can play a critical role in teaching and learning has resulted in heavy financial investments in technology-related resources (Koba, 2015). This financial investment has included both class-wide technologies (e.g., interactive whiteboards), general classroom technologies (e.g., tablet and laptop computers), and content-specific technologies (e.g., scientific probes, serious games). However, research points toward mixed findings regarding whether this investment has resulted in increased student learning (e.g., Delgado et al., 2015; Lim et al., 2013; Liu et al., 2017). The differential research findings result from the variability in factors such as how educational technology and tools are used to promote learning, teachers' comfort with technology and school-level infrastructure and access to professional development (e.g., Liu et al., 2017; Ross, 2020).

When integrated effectively, technology is used as a tool to support and enhance effective pedagogy rather than the other way around. The pedagogy must drive technology implementation. At the same time, technology cannot simply be an afterthought to instructional decision-making. The decision to include technology within instruction in inclusive schools should be made during instructional planning (Okojie et al., 2006). Instructional goals, pedagogical decisions and the use of assistive and instructional technologies should be considered together. Technology can increase learning opportunities, improve access, help students monitor learning, and provide critical assessment data to teachers to help inform instructional decision making. At the same time, technology can pose barriers to students' participation if those technologies are not accessible and engaging to all learners.

DOI: 10.4324/9781003043874-23

Definitions of Technologies in Elementary Education

There are many definitions of educational technology in the research literature. However, these technologies can broadly be defined as technologies that are used for teaching and learning. For the purpose of this chapter, when considering inclusive education, elementary teachers broadly use two types of instructional technologies as part of inclusive education, including:

1. *Assistive technologies (AT):* According to Section 1401 of the Individuals with Disabilities Education Act (IDEA), assistive technologies are defined as "any item, piece of equipment or product system, whether acquired commercially, off the shelf, modified, or customized, that is used to increase, maintain, or improve functional capabilities of individuals with disabilities." There are many uses for AT, including for instructional purposes (e.g., reading, writing, mobility, hearing, vision, and communication). The focus of AT is to provide access that allows for the fullest level of participation.
2. *Instructional/educational technologies:* Unlike the term AT, which has a formal definition in the IDEA, the term instructional or educational technology is broader and has multiple definitions, some broader than others. Thus, there is no single "dictionary" definition of instructional technologies. Broadly, these technologies are those tools used to facilitate, enhance, and improve instruction. The Association for Educational Communications and Technology (AECT) added the explicit focus on ethical practice in choosing and using technology to facilitate learning (Molenda & Januszewski, 2008). This focus on ethical use is extremely valuable when considering inclusive practices as one ethical consideration is clearly whether all students have access to learning in the classroom. These technologies include a broad range of tools and media (e.g., video conferencing, digital media, word processing). Educational technologies fall into two broad categories: general educational technologies that can be applied across multiple content areas (e.g., touchscreen devices) and content-specific technologies (e.g., scientific probes, calculators).

Assistive Technologies, Instructional Technologies, and Universal Design for Learning

To understand how assistive and instructional technologies are used in inclusive elementary settings, it is important to understand the different but intersecting rationale and approaches that drive the use of these two types of technologies. As explained below, the innovations and use of assistive technologies have historically been driven by mandates for individual accessibility for students with disabilities, whereas innovations and the use of instructional technologies have primarily been focused on the needs of students with disabilities. The focus on Universal Design for Learning (UDL) has primarily focused on all learners, including students with disabilities, in general education settings.

Assistive Technology

It has been nearly three decades since the first assistive technologies (AT) enabled students with disabilities to actively participate and learn with their peers in inclusive settings (Edyburn, 2015). Early studies (e.g., Scherer, 1996) identified the benefits of AT as often extending beyond the classroom, improving students' performance at home or in other informal settings. The rapid evolution of technology in the classroom has allowed elementary students to take advantage of applications that were previously considered emerging but are now available in most elementary classrooms. An example of such technology is Read & Write (Texthelp, 2020), which highlights text as it is read to students, translates text to other languages, and allows students to use speech-to-text software while completing other tasks. Many of these types of toolsets are cloud-based such as with Microsoft Office 365 suite, which is common in elementary schools across the United States (Microsoft Education Team, 2018).

Universal Design for Learning (UDL)

UDL is a proactive design framework for meeting the needs of neurotypically diverse individuals (Kasch, 2019). The main premise of UDL rests on considering flexible ways of meeting the needs of all learners (i.e., goals, materials, instruction, and the environment). The framework is organized around nine guidelines and 31 checkpoints, organized vertically to provide: (1) multiple means of engagement, (2) multiple means of representation, and (3) multiple means of action and expression (Meyer et al., 2014). The UDL framework recently added clarification about how students could access, build, and internalize learning materials as they strive toward the goal of becoming expert learners who are purposeful, motivated, resourceful, strategic, and goal-directed (CAST, 2018).

King-Sears (2020) pointed out UDL-based interventions must include a flexible and purposeful design in order to engage a maximum number of learners. Vasquez and Marino (2020) added that the proactive identification of barriers across physical, social/emotional, cultural, and cognitive aspects of the lesson were critical during UDL-based lessons. Additionally, a major emphasis of UDL is that its principles, guidelines, and checkpoints should be applied in a contextually appropriate manner. For example, a UDL-based lesson in a 3rd grade literacy lesson will look different than a 5th grade science lesson. Additionally, even within a 3rd grade literacy lesson, UDL will be applied differently with different compositions of students. Thus, the goal of UDL is to alter the instructional environment rather than the learners within it.

Relationship between AT and UDL

While the focus on AT has remained steady as technological advances have resulted in increased accessibility, there has been a broader discussion about how to integrate technology to support learning for all students. Rose et al. (2005), for example, described the relationship between AT and UDL as two sides of the same coin. The function of AT is to provide individualized support to overcome barriers while UDL focuses on the entire classroom environment, including proactively addressing barriers within the curriculum, instructional tools and materials, and assessments. Thus, although AT and UDL have distinct functions, the relationship between the two has continued to blur. Some technologies considered assistive technologies at one time are now available to all learners. For example, digital texts were historically provided as assistive technologies for students with print-based disabilities, but they are now widely available to all learners; the flexibility within these technologies can enhance reading for a broader range of learners who might prefer reading with larger text font, brighter or dimmer backgrounds, or with text-to-speech features.

Advanced Organizer for the Chapter

This chapter provides an overview of research and the wisdom of practice related to both established and emerging technologies used to promote inclusion within elementary classroom settings. It positions technology use in elementary instruction along with Universal Design for Learning (UDL) as a means for making inclusive, accessible instructional decisions for how to utilize technology to support learning. The chapter then provides examples of both content-specific technology use and emerging technologies to promote inclusion and access for elementary students with disabilities. Finally, the chapter ends with practical considerations and examples for how elementary teachers may approach using technology to promote increase learning and engagement for all learners.

What Do We Know Based on Research and the Wisdom of Practice?

This section provides an overview of how technology has been used in elementary education to promote inclusion and access for students with disabilities. It begins with a discussion of how Universal Design for Learning (UDL) can guide the use of technology to support improved instruction for all students. This section provides illustrations of how technology has been used to support learning both in core academic areas (reading, mathematics, and science, technology, engineering, and mathematics—STEM—learning) as well as emerging areas of advanced learning technologies. Finally, this section concludes with barriers that elementary teachers face in using technology for instruction in inclusive classrooms.

Teaching with Technology Through the UDL Framework

Numerous research articles have been written about how UDL can be used to design learning environments that are inclusive and address the needs of all learners, including those with disabilities (e.g., Ok et al., 2017). Many of these articles utilize technology within UDL implementation. For example, several studies examined the use of digital text within literacy-based interventions (e.g., Coyne et al., 2012; Dalton et al., 2011). These studies utilized technology such as universally designed digital books and software to scaffold and support reading. Other studies designed technology-enhanced UDL-based instruction within content areas (e.g., Israel et al., 2020; Marino et al., 2014; Rappolt-Schlichtmann et al., 2013). For example, Israel et al. (2020) studied how teachers taught elementary computer science through the UDL framework and found a wide range of implementation depending on students' instructional needs. Marino et al. (2014) utilized science-based video games in inclusive classrooms to teach scientific concepts such as cellular structures and found increased student engagement with the UDL-aligned curriculum. Other studies have found positive effects associated with a UDL approach when teaching mathematics (Root et al., 2020), chemistry (King-Sears & Johnson, 2020), and in other inclusive classroom settings (Giovanni, 2020).

These studies are contextualized in a specific content area and grade level and point to the fact that implementing UDL in one setting do not generalize to other settings due to how contextualized UDL-based instructional decision making can be. Thus, how UDL is applied and contextualized in different instructional settings to support all learners is still emerging and is quite complex (Ok et al., 2017; Rao et al., 2014). Flexibility is inherent within the framework of UDL, which means there will be a significant amount of variability in its application across different classroom contexts.

Several prominent scholars noted challenges associated with implementing the UDL framework. For example, Edyburn (2010), in a seminal critique of the UDL framework, noted while UDL calls for the instructional designers to proactively plan for diversity, misconceptions arise when publishers claim they are implementing UDL because they are integrating multimedia or web 2.0 tools in curricular materials. Rao et al. (2014) noted difficulty pinpointing the level of UDL application because of its numerous flexible permutations, making it challenging to evaluate its efficacy. Capp (2017) pointed out how specific UDL checkpoints appear similar in practice to differentiated instruction, resulting in ambiguity about whether UDL is just good teaching.

Recent publications have begun to address these issues. For example, in March of 2017, a group of researchers and practitioners gathered to establish consistent reporting criteria (RC) in order to evaluate the efficacy of UDL (Rao et al., 2020). Validation of the UDL RC, which was strategically mapped to the CAST 2.0 framework, occurred by using 20 previously conducted studies (between 2008 and 2016) claiming to incorporate UDL in the instructional design process. The reporting criteria included eight constructs. Of the 20 studies, only two (King-Sears et al., 2015; Marino et al., 2014) met all of the reporting criteria. Additional information about the UDL RC can be found at https://udl-irn.org/udl-reporting-criteria/.

Basham et al. (2020) provided an alternative approach to documenting UDL implementation with the iterative development and testing of the UDL Observation Management Tool (UDL-OMT). The tool was developed using a Delphi process with experts at the Universal Design for Learning Innovation and Research Network annual conference. It was designed to provide a dynamic assessment of classroom-level UDL implementation. The tool contains 42 items, organized into four sections: (1) introduction to new material, (2) content representation and delivery, (3) expression of understanding, and (4) activity and student engagement. These efforts are all still emerging and will hopefully offer additional clarity into how to consider the efficacious implementation of UDL in different content areas and across a range of instructional settings.

In summary, Universal Design for learning has received increased scrutiny as it has evolved. Recent studies have demonstrated the ability to measure its implementation and efficacy. Intentionally planning for learner diversity and providing multiple pathways to achieve learning objectives has been shown to assist students during the learning process.

Technology Applications in Inclusive Elementary Content Areas

Elementary teachers are typically considered generalists, meaning that they teach all subject areas. In order for them to use technology effectively, they must consider how technologies can be used across content areas to meet the needs of all learners. The Common Core State Standards (CCSS, 2010) include expectations for technology and digital literacy skills to be incorporated into the scope and sequence across content areas. There is an expectation that teachers will incorporate technology within the content areas. The CCSS for English Language Arts, for example, includes anchor standards related to digital literacy that can be applied to reading, writing, and speaking and listening grade-level standards. One such ELA standard is: "Integrate and evaluate information presented in diverse media and formats, including visually, quantitatively, and orally" (CCSS, 2010). This anchor standard is applied in second grade as, "Use information gained from the illustrations and words in a print or digital text to demonstrate understanding of characters, setting, or plot." Thus, the role of technology in the elementary grades is not only to include learning that facilitates access in inclusive classrooms but also to incorporate technologies as part of students' disciplinary experiences. The following section outlines some of the common content-specific technology applications with research support used to teach within inclusive elementary classrooms.

Reading Instruction

Increasingly, elementary students are using technology to support reading both in and out of school. Reading instructional technologies include both assistive and instructional technologies and support reading using multiple modes for students to interact with text, including computer-assisted instruction (CAI), e-readers, and text-to-speech functions with digital texts. Multiple studies have been conducted on computer-assisted instruction (CAI) in reading to support decoding, fluency, and reading comprehension (e.g., Kim et al., 2017; Stetter & Hughes, 2010; Weng et al., 2014). Many of these include explicit, scaffolded instruction that provides feedback to learners at a pace that is individualized for the learner (e.g., Hall et al., 2000; Mackiewicz et al., 2011).

Text-to-speech tools have been widely implemented to assist students in improving reading skills. In essence, when students are presented with both text and auditory representations, the cognitive load required to decode the written words decreases. Whereas text-to-speech was formerly used strictly in the realm of assistive technologies, these technologies are now gaining popularity across multiple settings, including elementary classrooms. These technologies vary in features, but many allow students to adjust the reading rates, the type of voice outputs, as well as highlight and tag segments of text. Given the wide variability in features and tools, the wide implementation of different text-to-speech software has outpaced research. Questions remain about the level of technical understanding students must have in order to use such technologies effectively, how much support students and their teachers must have in order to use these technologies to support reading and the extent to which different features within these systems are being used by students. Despite this variability, a meta-analysis by Wood et al. (2018) on the use of text-to-speech indicated positive findings on reading comprehension, indicating that oral presentation of the text (through text-to-speech) to students with disabilities can have a positive effect on their reading comprehension.

Alongside text-to-speech, e-readers have been used to support reading both as an assistive and instructional technology in elementary classrooms. These allow students to customize the display, including font type and size, background brightness, and spacing between lines of text. Several studies have shown the effectiveness of using e-readers on reading comprehension (e.g., Rello et al., 2016). Anderson (2018), in a study of third grade students' use of e-readers during independent reading, found e-readers led to increased engagement, motivation, and a positive attitude across a diverse range of learners. Huang and Liang (2015) noted the ability to track students' reading rate and comprehension during silent reading tasks was enhanced with e-readers as compared to print-based text.

Math Instruction

Technology plays a major role in inclusive elementary mathematics education through technologies such as games, virtual manipulatives, and mathematical simulations that occur either on computers or touchscreen devices. Like with literacy, the pedagogy and instructional goals should inform the technology use. The goals of technology-mediated math (TMM) instruction will result in different technological features and outcomes. Thus, TMM focused on explicit instruction to promote procedural understanding will look different from TMM focused on reinforcement of skills or exploration and conceptual understanding will have different features and outcomes. Additionally, using technology to support mathematical understanding in inclusive elementary classrooms depends on whether the goal is the acquisition of new mathematical understanding as compared to generalizing knowledge that can be applied independently.

Most studies focused on students with disabilities and TMM instruction have focused on the combination of explicit instruction alongside the technologies themselves. In a review of literature (Kiru et al., 2018), TMM studies at the elementary grades demonstrated positive effects on increasing students' fluency with understanding and using basic number combinations, students' understanding of whole numbers concepts and word-problem solving. An example of such technology is KinderTEK (Clarke et al., 2020) which provides young learners with three instructional models for teaching students early math skills. These three models (sequenced, directed, and exploratory) provide teachers with different approaches based on students' needs. Another such technology is Zearn Math, which provides both print- and software-based math instruction to young learners in a self-paced and guided manner (Morrison et al., 2019).

Some TMM use gamification within mathematics instruction. Educational games use game design elements to teach and reinforce mathematical learning (e.g., increasing levels, points, achievement goals; Deterding et al., 2011). Dragon Box Algebra is an app that may be used to teach young learners about operations, addition, multiplication, fractions, and solving expressions and equations. It has 20 levels wherein the learner moves game pieces to solve expressions and level up (Moyer-Packenham & Bolyard, 2016). Other examples of mathematics educational games include Avatar and NumberShire (Kennedy & Boyle, 2017), which can provide students with an immersive learning environment to interact with math knowledge. Additionally, the immediate feedback within such games can correct students' misconceptions in the learning process.

Another technology that has been effectively used to support inclusive mathematics education is the use of virtual manipulatives. Virtual manipulatives are defined as "an interactive, technology-enabled visual representation of a dynamic mathematical object, including all of the programmable features that allow it to be manipulated, that presents opportunities for constructing mathematical knowledge" (Moyer-Packenham & Bolyard, 2016, p. 13). This definition is broad and includes virtual manipulatives that can use a range of technology-mediated environments and on a range of devices. There is a growing body of evidence showcasing that using virtual manipulatives has a positive effect on learning for students both with and without disabilities (e.g., Bouck et al., 2019; Bouck & Park, 2020). The National Library of Virtual Manipulatives (http://nlvm.usu.edu/), for example, includes web-based virtual manipulatives that allow students to engage and practice critical mathematical concepts.

Science, Technology, Engineering, and Mathematics (STEM)

Recently, there has been an increased focus on promoting Science, Technology, Engineering, and Mathematics (STEM) career opportunities for individuals with disabilities (Schreffler et al., 2019). Griffiths et al. (2020) presented a framework for engaging girls with disabilities in STEM. The framework highlights the importance of starting early in the elementary education process with hands-on learning, mentoring, and accessible instructional materials. Promoting STEM in elementary schools can be accomplished through coding classes, engineering experiments, and science investigations (Estapa & Tank, 2017). Students need early exposure to STEM in order to promote interest in STEM careers. Skills translating to STEM career readiness include students' understanding their role during cooperative groups, effective communication strategies, teaching self-advocacy and self-determination skills (Office of Science and Technology Policy, 2019). In addition, students must be able to access and actively participate in STEM clubs. These clubs can include STEM career mentors, who build personal relationships with the students while explaining how the elementary school club is teaching them skills they will need for later employment. The STEM mentors can participate remotely using teleconferencing software.

An emerging STEM area of interest is the use of robotics to engage students with disabilities. Lindsay and Hounsell (2017) adapted the FIRST LEGO League in Canada for elementary and middle school students with disabilities. Participants met for 2 hours, once a week, for six weeks. Each week a different concept was taught (e.g., week 1 pulleys, week 2 gears). The researchers reported the students not only enjoyed the program but would consider working in this area in the future. Samuel et al. (2020) similarly examined technology-mediated STEM learning but did so through makerspace activities (hands-on learning and tinkering with technologies such as 3D printers, laser cutters, and sewing machines) designed through the UDL framework. This study pointed out how technology combined with the UDL framework can lead to increased inclusive educational opportunities for individuals with disabilities in makerspaces. However, this study, like many other technology-mediated educational research, also pointed out the need for extensive teacher professional development related to not only UDL but also related to the disciplinary content (e.g., hands-on STEM activities), the use of technology tools, and supports for individualizing instruction (e.g., accommodations, the role of paraeducators). Thus, although many of these studies point toward encouraging results, findings should be interpreted in light of barriers to implementation.

Barriers to Technology Use in Inclusive Elementary Settings

Although integration of technologies that support inclusive practices in elementary schools has great promise, several barriers to implementation have been noted consistently in the literature (e.g., Francom, 2020). Generally, these barriers are defined as conditions that make it difficult for teachers to implement the use of technology in their classrooms successfully. These barriers are often referred to as "first order" and "second order" barriers (Ertmer, 1999; Ertmer et al., 2012).

First order barriers, or extrinsic barriers, are those that are outside the control of the teacher. These are generally focused on lack of or limited resources that support sustained use of technologies that would promote instruction in inclusive classrooms. Examples of first-order barriers to the use of technologies that promote effective instructional practices in inclusive classrooms include:

- Lack of access to accessible technology
- Lack of professional development opportunities for how to use technologies, both assistive and instructional, in ways that promote learning and inclusion
- Lack of technical support for implementing assistive and instructional technologies
- Limited administrative support for inclusive approaches to technology use
- Limited planning and learning time for teachers to integrate technologies into instruction.

These first order barriers are generally more prevalent in low-income schools (Purcell et al., 2013). In fact, access is often identified by teachers as a financial barrier (e.g., Atanga et al., 2019). Additionally, many low-income schools face multiple first order barriers that, taken together, are difficult to overcome. For example, if a school has technology but limited professional development, teachers can seek professional learning opportunities outside of the school, but if the school lacks the technology and professional learning opportunities, teachers would have to seek funding for technology and then find professional development opportunities to learn how to use those technologies.

Second-order barriers, or intrinsic barriers, are those rooted in teachers' beliefs and experiences. These barriers are less tangible than first-order barriers and may be even more difficult to address as they are more personal (Ertmer, 1999). Examples of second-order barriers to the use of technology to support all learners in inclusive classrooms include:

- Teachers' competence with the use of assistive and instructional technologies. In one study, students' use of AT was predicted by their teachers' competence with those technologies (Connor et al., 2010)
- Teachers' beliefs about the importance of inclusive approaches to technology use
- Teachers' values about the importance of inclusion and the role of students with disabilities as full participants in their classroom environments.

These classifications of barriers are useful in considering ways of improving approaches to supporting elementary teachers' use of technologies in inclusive settings to meet the needs of all learners. However, considering these barriers as a list of tasks that can be checked off to increase technology use in a more inclusive manner is an oversimplification for three reasons.

1. First and second order barriers are often interrelated. This can include inadequate professional learning opportunities that result in a lack of teacher knowledge of both assistive and instructional technologies. Further, lack of professional development can reduce teachers' confidence and self-efficacy in using these technologies in meaningful ways.
2. Although first-order barriers to technology implementation may be addressed by obtaining resources, professional development, and creating school-wide conditions that can encourage technology use, second-order barriers may be more challenging to address. Successfully addressing second-order barriers would require challenging teachers' beliefs about the role of technology in meeting the needs of all learners.
3. Although teachers may not necessarily face all these barriers, any one of the above barriers can significantly reduce the chance that teachers use technology to include all learners meaningfully (Ertmer, 1999).

Emerging Technologies in the Elementary Classroom

Common technologies available in most elementary schools to improve access and participation for all students typically started as emerging technologies. Additionally, there is often a trickle-down effect, wherein technology enhancement is introduced in high school settings, move to middle schools, and finally get introduced in elementary school settings. This introduction of emerging technologies has accelerated since the COVID-19 pandemic began as school districts in many states were forced to move to remote learning (Basham et al., 2020).

The following section provides an overview of a few technologies that are not commonplace in elementary classrooms but hold great promise to become more ubiquitous.

Digital Notetaking Devices

Digital notetaking with stylus devices such as the Livescribe 3 Smartpen has been shown to be beneficial for students at the high school and middle school levels (Harper et al., 2017). However, these devices have the potential for use in elementary classrooms once students have become proficient at handwriting. The pen utilizes Bluetooth technology to sync with mobile-learning devices. It includes an audio recorder, internal speaker and camera. The pen is used with a customized notebook, allowing students to tap record and have everything they hear, write, and draw in the notebook recorded. Playback speed can be adjusted to meet the students' preferences. These styluses look and feel like actual pens, thus reducing the chances of stigmatization. Parents, teachers, and students reported the use of the pen led to increased independence and more time for leisure activities. Harper et al. (2017), in a qualitative study of elementary students with dyslexia, found that using a smart pen was an AT that improved both academics as well as students' lives beyond the school day, including increased independence during homework and consequently reduced frustration at home.

Mobile Learning

The widespread adoption of mobile learning (m-learning) has substantially increased the accessibility of academic content (Crompton et al., 2017). Mobile devices such as iPads, tablets, and smartphones provide portable access to the Internet, allowing students to access content in a personalized manner. Students can access courses at any time, in any location, as many times as they would like. Domingo and Gargante (2016) identified six aspects of m-learning that benefit both teachers and students: (1) interactivity, (2) portability, (3) connectivity, (4) context-sensitivity (i.e., m-learning devices can gather real or simulated data), (5) social media, and (6) individuality. Each of these factors contributes to teachers' ability to collect authentic student data while allowing students to engage with real or simulated content across content areas. Chelkowski et al. (2019), in a literature review of students with disabilities and mobile devices, found that the most important aspect of successful m-learning was teacher and staff training to use the devices. Instructors need to know how, why, and when to use the devices, as well as how to configure them to meet individual student needs.

Chauhan (2017) conducted a meta-analysis of m-learning across formal and informal learning environments. Eighteen studies were included in the analysis. Study findings indicated intervention duration of greater than 6 months produced higher gains on learning than shorter duration studies, suggesting a long-term m-learning implementation plan is more beneficial than ad-hoc or occasional adoption of m-learning. Jingrong et al. (2018), in a review of research on m-learning for individuals with disabilities, concluded the use of mobile devices led to increased student performance across content areas.

Zhang et al. (2015) reported positive evidence supporting the use of m-learning apps in elementary schools. In an exploratory study of 4th graders from traditionally marginalized populations, students were compared across two math groups: struggling learners vs. typical peers. Struggling students (including those with disabilities) made larger gains than their typical peers across three 15–20 item paper and pencil assessments of mathematics knowledge of decimal numbers obtained from the apps. Thus, although both groups made improvements after the use of the math apps, the struggling learners made larger gains across the assessments and the achievement gap between the groups was reduced. Marino et al. (2014) reported similar findings in middle school science classes using both alternative print-based texts and game-enhanced science curriculum aligned with the UDL principles. Students with disabilities made larger learning gains pre- to post-test than their peers without disabilities on post-test measures of knowledge related to cell organelles.

Leaman and Corcoran (2018) reported on an action research project where the authors used iPad apps as a means to enhance social studies inquiry projects for sixth grade students. They reported students' online postings allowed them to highlight strong projects by students who were less likely to participate in whole group instruction. Chmiliar (2016) reported students with learning disabilities benefitted from Simplex spelling apps on m-learning devices. The study included 23 middle school students with reading levels at the third-grade level. Students improved their reading ability by 2–3 years during the study. Spanning across content areas, Leinonen et al. (2016) found mobile apps to be effective because they allow students to use audio and video during the reflection process.

Rodriguez and Cumming (2017) examined the impact of the Language Builder app on expressive and receptive vocabulary as well as sentence formation of second graders. Treatment ($n = 20$) vs control group ($n = 11$) comparisons were made across the three dependent measures. The 30 minutes a day, 8-week iPad intervention did not lead to statistically significant differences in expressive or receptive language. This intervention did, however, lead to statistically significant higher sentence formation scores for the treatment group and as well as significantly higher scores related to using a variety of vocabulary with their teachers. As there are more middle school than elementary school studies examining m-learning for students with disabilities, there is a need for further exploration with elementary students with disabilities.

Augmented Reality

An area of mobile learning that is gaining increasing attention is Augmented Reality (AR). It involves software that allows virtual objects to be overlayed in real-time on physical objects in the environment. Augmented reality is broadly defined as having three characteristics: (1) AR involves the integration of virtual and real objects, (2) students can interact with virtual objects in real-time, and (3) AR is a three-dimensional experience (Azuma, 1997). Wu et al. (2018), in a study of fourth grade students studying science, found AR reduced the cognitive load necessary to develop a conceptual understanding of scientific concepts. However, Cheng and Tsai (2019) noted that elementary students might not be able to independently utilize AR tools. They advocated for reciprocal dialogue with teachers and parents to obtain guidance about how to use the AR tools and develop deep cognitive understandings of the content. Relatively few research studies related to AR have been conducted in the United States, with the majority occurring in southeast Asia and Europe.

A meta-analysis of AR research conducted by Ozdemir et al. (2018) found AR was utilized in European elementary schools, primarily on mobile devices. Students seemed to benefit from the software, but not at a statistically significant level. Outcomes were higher for high school students in natural sciences (e.g., biology) than in social sciences. Results indicated investing in AR at the elementary level offers a limited return on investment. However, additional research is necessary before this conclusion can be substantiated.

Virtual Reality

The use of virtual reality in elementary schools in the United States has been limited because of device warnings indicating children below the age of 13 should not use head-mounted displays. These computer-simulated environments allow students to be fully immersed in virtual reality through a head-mounted display. Recent research by Tychsen and Foeller (2020) in a study of 50 children aged 4–10 (mean = 7.2 years) found 94% of children had no adverse effects (e.g., reduced visuomotor function or motion sickness) following virtual reality experiences. This study indicates virtual reality is a potential instructional tool for use in elementary schools.

Virtual reality allows students to participate in previously inconceivable opportunities. For example, in Mission: ISS, students are transported to the International Space Station, where they experienced what it looks and feels like to be immersed in zero gravity (Oculus, 2019). Research from other countries indicates positive effects from VR at the elementary level. For example, Cheng and Tsai (2019) found head-mounted displays enabled elementary students to actively participate in virtual field trips during social studies classes. The experience increased their motivation while lowering their test anxiety. Other studies in science (e.g., Beyoglu et al., 2020) have drawn similar conclusions. Virtual reality is an area where additional research is clearly needed.

Setting the Course for Effective Inclusion

As noted in the previous sections, elementary teachers can choose from a range of technologies to support inclusive practices, and these assistive and instructional technologies continue to increase. From a practical perspective, then, it is important to consider how elementary teachers should consider integrating technologies into their instruction as technologies continue to evolve. Addressing this consideration is quite complex but can be simplified by focusing on the teachers' instructional aims and the needs of the learners. The next section provides practical considerations and guidance for elementary teachers to help them use technology to successfully support the inclusion of all learners. This section begins by describing ways in which UDL can be used to plan technology-mediated inclusive elementary education. The next section provides information regarding how high-leverage practices (HLPs) can be incorporated into such instruction. Next, an illustrative example is provided for technology-mediated inclusive elementary instruction. Finally, the section ends with suggestions provided by the ISTE standards for developing teaching competence in technology-mediated instruction in inclusive classrooms.

Decision-making Guidance for Technology Use

As stated earlier, designing inclusive technology-mediated elementary instruction relies on sound pedagogy focused on accessibility, engagement, and learning for all students. As stated above, the Universal Design for Learning framework enables teachers to proactively plan for student diversity and provide multiple ways for students to interact with the content. In addition, technology can provide alternative assessments of student learning. The Universal Design for Learning Implementation and Research Network (UDL-IRN) has a set of resources that support teachers in planning and teaching such instruction through the UDL framework. One helpful resource is their Instructional Planning Process guide (UDL-IRN, 2011). This guide includes five steps that teachers can take to implement UDL. Below is a summary of those steps alongside technology integration suggestions. Although UDL and technology-mediated instruction are not synonymous, these steps from the UDL-IRN provide a roadmap for teachers regarding the use of technology-mediated instruction.

"I Can..." statements

- *I can log into my Scratch account.*
- *I can identify the important parts of Scratch.*
- *I can closely observe a Scratch program and find the scripts that caused the actions.*
- *I can remix, save, and share Scratch programs.*
- *I can make changes to a program so that it does what I want it to.*

Figure 23.1 Statements to Support Student Learning

- Step 1: Establish clear outcomes that are specific and related to an essential "big idea". A big idea is the instructional goal of the activity, often tied to standards or instructional objectives. Given that students often do not understand why they are engaging in instructional activities, a major aspect of this step is communicating these goals to the learners. Figure 23.1 provides example "I Can" statements related to helping students learn how to use the Scratch programming environment, which is a free programming environment for young learners developed by MIT Media Lab. Within Scratch, students can create and share interactive stories, animations, and games (see https://scratch.mit.edu/).

- Step 2: Anticipate learner needs, strengths, and curriculum barriers. Once teachers have established the instructional goals, it is important to consider the needs, strengths, and challenges of the students in the classroom. UDL implementation, to be effective, should be closely tied to the needs of the learners. Figure 23.2 provides an example of curricular barriers students may face when learning to use the Scratch programming environment.

- Step 3: Consider how to measure learning. Assessment is a key element of instructional planning and should align with the instructional goals established in step 3. In this step, teachers attempt to find a range of options to help students authentically demonstrate their understanding. In our example, wherein the students are learning to use the Scratch programming environment, we can

Anticipated Barriers

- Logging in to a new program can be challenging for some children. Providing pictorial or video versions of the verbal/written directions would be helpful.
- Children often forget the procedure for remixing, even after being taught.
  - Children often forget to remix.

Figure 23.2 Curricular Barriers to Student Learning

Table 23.1 Example Rubric for Scratch Computational Artifact

	1 (Needs attention)	2 (Mastery)	3 (Exceeds)
Blocks	3 or fewer blocks used	Less than 8 blocks	More than 8 blocks
Background	No background	One background	More than one background with change in scenes
Sprites	No sprites used	1 sprite used	2 or more sprites used
Motion	No motion	1-2 motion blocks	At least 3 motion blocks

assess both the computational artifact that the students create using a flexible rubric (see Table 23.1) or assess their storyboard or project planning document (see Figure 23.3).

- Step 4: Instructional Experience. This is where the teacher develops the instructional plan using the three UDL principles in a way that account for Steps 1-3 using the three UDL principles:

1. Which sprite will you choose?
   A penguin and a yellow monster
2. What will sprite 1 say?
   Do you want to get ice cream?
3. What will sprite 2 say?
   Sure. I love ice cream.
4. Draw or insert a picture of your scene

Figure 23.3 Example Project Plan

Code Blocks	What does this Block Do?
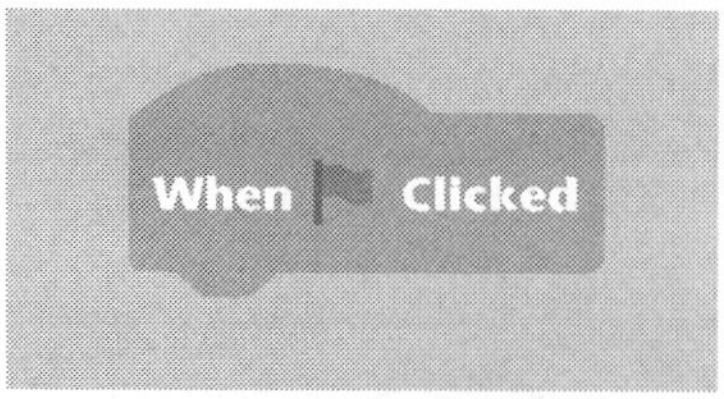	This block starts the animation or program.
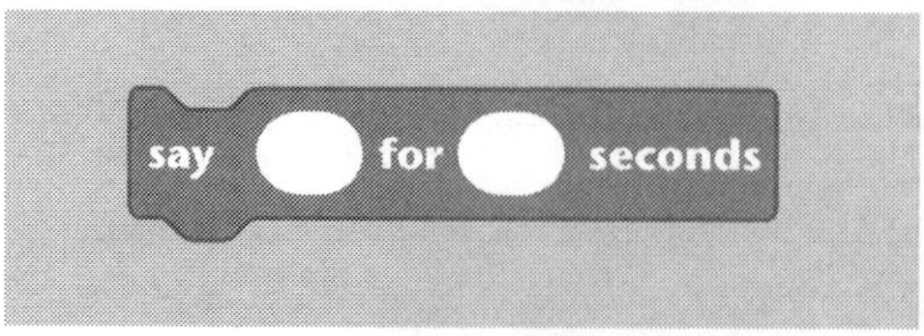	Use this block to make speech bubbles for a sprite for a certain amount of time. For example, you can make a sprite say "Hello!" for 2 seconds.
	This block is used whenever a sprite must wait for another action. For example, you can use the wait block between sprites speaking.
	If your sprite is shown, you can use this blog to hide the sprite.

Figure 23.4 Student Reference Guide

- Multiple means of engagement: How are students going to be engaged in the lesson in a way that is motivating and allows for self-monitoring of learning?
- Multiple means of representation: How can the information presented in the lesson be presented using a range of strategies, tools, and technologies to account for learners' challenges and preferences? For example, Figure 23.4 showcases a reference guide cueing students to applications of different Scratch coding blocks.
- Multiple means of action and expression: How can students demonstrate learning in a way that leverages their strengths and support areas of challenge? Figure 23.5, for example, illustrates how students can demonstrate their understanding through a storyboard activity in addition to a computational artifact.

- Step 5: Reflection. In this final and crucial step, the teacher can look back at how the lesson was implemented and ask questions about what went well and what did not go as anticipated, for whom, and why. In this step, the teacher can also reflect on how the tools and technologies were integrated into instruction and whether the teacher needs additional support in using those technologies in a way that promotes the inclusive practice.

	Scene ___	Scene ___
Sprite 1	**Costume:**	**Costume:**
	Action:	**Action:**
	Duration:	**Duration:**
Sprite 2	**Costume:**	**Costume:**
	Action:	**Action:**
	Duration:	**Duration:**

Figure 23.5 Using a Storyboard Activity to Demonstrate Student Understanding

High Leverage Practices in Planning Technology-rich Instruction in Elementary Education

Technology implementation has outpaced research on the effective use of technology in the classroom. With that said, a high-leverage practices (HLP, McLeskey et al., 2017) approach can be helpful in considering how technology can be used to design experiences that support effective instructional practices for all learners. Of all the HLPs, one specifically addresses the use of technology: HLP 19: Use assistive and instructional technologies. This HLP also calls out the Universal Design for Learning (UDL) framework for selecting, designing, implementing, and evaluating student outcomes. However, when considering the other 11 instructional HLPs, there is a clear role for technology. Table 23.2 provides examples of how technology can be applied within some of the other HLPs. For more information about HLPs, visit https://highleveragepractices.org/.

How Do Teachers Use Technology to Support Inclusive Practices: An Illustrative Case

Elementary teachers can incorporate both well-established technologies and emerging technologies in a UDL-based approach. This illustrative case study shows how elementary teachers can include all learners in a technology-rich educational experience.

Table 23.2 Examples of Technology Applications within HLPs

High Leverage Practice	Technology Applications
HLP 12. Systematically design instruction towards a specific learning goal	Technology can be leveraged to develop new learning that builds on previous experiences with resources that build background knowledge and supports that enhance learning experiences.
HLP 13. Adapt curriculum tasks and materials for specific learning goals	Technology-enhanced materials, as well as assistive and instructional technologies, should be chosen based on addressing students' needs.
HLP 15. Provide scaffolded support	Technology can be a powerful tool for scaffolding learning through personalized learning systems that promote independence.
HLP 18 Use strategies to promote active student engagement	Technology-supported strategies for active engagement include using tools that connect learning to students' lives and help with monitoring learning.
HLP 22: Provide positive and constructive feedback to guide student learning and behavior	Educational technology is often designed with systems to provide immediate feedback to students that can inform students about more effective approaches and strategies for improvement.

Throughout the United States, there has been a push to bring computer science (CS) into K-12 instructional settings. Many school districts have "CS for All" initiatives wherein students receive robust CS instruction, beginning in the elementary grades. Providing inclusive CS instruction at the elementary grades relies heavily on a UDL-based approach to planning, teaching, and assessing learning. During the elementary grades, CS instruction heavily emphasizes teaching basic computational "big ideas" through the use of playful robotics such as Dash Robot, graphically-intuitive block-based programming environments such as Scratch, or even unplugged activities that do not use any technologies (see Table 23.3 for examples).

Elementary teachers often teach foundational CS concepts such as decomposition (i.e., breaking tasks into component tasks that are easier to solve) or debugging (fixing errors in a

Table 23.3 Elementary Computer Science Multiple Access Points

Unplugged Activities (Example: Cup Stacking to teach about algorithms)	Robotics (Example: Dash Robot to teach sequence of steps)	Block-based Programming (Example: Scratch to teach sequencing programming scripts)
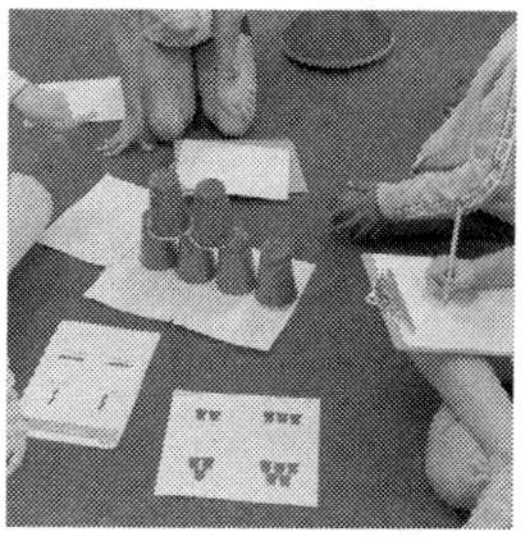		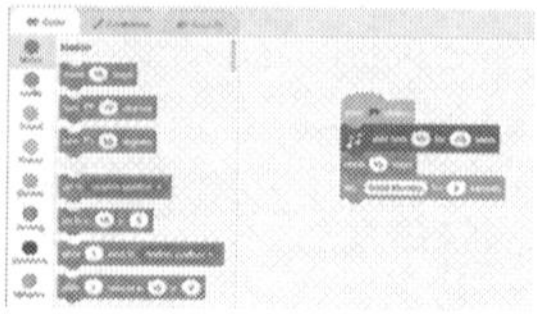

systematic way). Several studies have examined inclusive and UDL-based CS instruction at the elementary level. These studies have found that UDL-based CS instruction looks very different in different teachers' CS classrooms when teachers are responsive to their students' specific needs (e.g., Israel et al., 2020). For example, Israel and colleagues (2020) found notable variability in emphases on the three UDL principles as well as within these principles. For example, some teachers had an equal emphasis on all three principles, while others focused more on engagement or representation. Within each of the principles, the teachers also chose to emphasize different checkpoints, depending on the needs of their students and their instructional goals.

Instructional approaches that support CS instruction often include the use of explicit instruction (e.g., Snodgrass et al., 2016; Taylor, 2018) as well as tangible technologies (such as robots), which allow for active manipulation of physical objects (González-González, 2019). Other studies, however, have indicated that UDL-based inclusive CS instruction can be challenging for teachers to implement and often requires extensive professional development and instructional coaching (e.g., Israel et al., 2018). These findings are consistent with studies in other content areas that suggest that elementary teachers require professional development and support to effectively integrate technology, especially when considering how to include all learners.

Strategies that teachers have used to increase inclusion in elementary CS education may often bring together the High Leverage Practices and UDL. For example:

- Making the learning goals explicit to the students with strategies such as "I can" statements that are revised based on student comprehension levels.
- Balancing explicit instruction within more open-ended activities to allow for more direct instruction and scaffolded activities. For example, complex computational activities such as developing a project in Scratch can be broken down into smaller activities with explicit instruction and modeling within each smaller activity.
- Use of video tutorials alongside teacher modeling so that students can revisit key concepts and procedures.
- Academic language supports including visuals alongside new concepts and anchoring new vocabulary with personally relevant concepts. For example, in teaching the word "algorithm", teachers have often showcased the series of steps that people take to brush their teeth in the morning and reinforce the idea that the order must be followed in an exact manner for the teeth brushing algorithm to be effective. If you brush your teeth prior to putting the toothpaste on the toothbrush, that algorithm would not be nearly as efficient as if the toothpaste was placed on the toothbrush prior to brushing teeth.

Implementing the ISTE Educator Standards: Elementary Teacher as Lead Learner

The International Society for Technology in Education (ISTE) Standards for Educators (https://www.iste.org/standards/for-educators) provide a framework for teachers to deepen their own practice and rethink how their lessons can use technology to foster more inclusive classrooms. As reflective practitioners, elementary school teachers can engage their students through technology-mediated learning that empowers and supports all of their students. The ISTE educator standards provide a practical structure for visions to become a reality. There are seven ISTE educator standards. This section highlights three of these standards (Standard 1, 2, and 5) that describe how teachers can actively choose technology to create inclusive classrooms and guide their instructional practice.

ISTE Educator Standard 1 (Learner)

Technology is always changing, always adapting. If educators are going to commit to using technology, they must commit to continual learning. Standard 1 focuses on collaboration, emphasizing the need for elementary teachers to constantly set goals around their technology use in the classroom, stay up to date with the latest technologies and ideas, and plug into communities across the world that align with their own personal interests and goals. Standard 1 sets the expectation for collaboration to encourage teachers to create their own learning networks and environments. Elementary teachers can attend conferences, workshops, and webinars to engage with new knowledge and learn from other experts who are using technology to make their practice more inclusive. By staying up to date with the latest educational technology research and subscribing to educational technology journals, elementary practitioners can ground their instructional decisions in research-based strategies from reputable sources. The ultimate goal is to have elementary teachers as active participants in professional development to deepen learning for themselves and their students.

ISTE Educator Standard 2 (Leader)

Teachers should be included in decision-making so that they can thrive as school-based leaders. It is in this space where we see teacher leadership thrive. Teacher leadership empowers teachers to become more involved in making important decisions in regard to student learning and honors their intelligence and professionalism in the field (Katzenmeyer & Moller, 2009). The ISTE standards reinforce the need for teacher leadership in education as it relates to technology. Standard 2 encourages teachers to engage with educational stakeholders and their peers about integrating technology into instruction while establishing the need for teacher leaders to use their leadership, activism, and voice to advocate for more equitable student opportunities and resources with technology. Standard 2 gives new teacher leaders a starting point to engage in powerful work that seeks to have a positive effect on student success. As instructional leaders, elementary teachers are critical of the technology they use or plan to use, assessing how inclusive the technology is and how it relates to the instructional goals (ISTE Standards for Educators). They can also serve as mentors to other teachers and lead book clubs or professional development about inclusive technology practices. Being involved in decision-making at the school, district, state, or even national level is another way for elementary teacher leaders to bring standard 2 to life. By participating in the decision-making, teachers can continue to advocate for the inclusion of effective technology practices and advocate for more inclusive elementary schools.

ISTE Educator Standard 5 (Designer)

Teachers are already doing the critical design work of Standard 5 every day. They are:

- Creating, adapting, and personalizing learning experiences that foster independence and accommodates/differentiates
- Designing standards-based authentic learning activities that encourage deep active learning
- Applying instructional design principles to creative, innovative learning environments

Standard 5 extends the work that is already being done in classrooms by integrating technology and reiterating the pedagogical emphasis on the intentionality of the technology. It is not a matter what technology can be used, but how the technology will help reach the goals and objectives of the lesson and support effective inclusive classrooms. As instructional designers, elementary teachers can integrate inclusive technology practices by:

- Experimenting with other forms of technology instruction in the classroom. For example, elementary teachers can attempt to teach with one-to-one devices, blended learning, flipped classroom approaches.
- Building authentic experiences into lessons with technology, integrating real-world issues and actual student interests into their instruction to personalize their learning.

Leveraging Learning Communities to Sustain and Extend Learning and Using Technology

The current educational climate brings attention to the need for community and resiliency. It requires teachers to engage with technology to propel student success and interact with multiple professional learning communities to build their own capacities and shift what they know about integrating technology to support effective inclusive elementary classrooms beyond the brick and mortar setting. School-based, professional organizations and online communities provide elementary educators with opportunities to connect with networks of colleagues who are engaging with technology in ways that help improve their practice and increase student achievement.

Using Social Media Affinity Groups

Social media groups allow teachers to feel less isolated (Reich et al., 2011). Social media platforms like Facebook and Twitter have established networks of educators sharing inclusive technology practices. Using Twitter hashtags like: #UDL, #EdChat, #EdTech, #InclusiveEducation, #ConnectEveryStudent, and #ElementaryTeaching can help teachers connect with others based on specific interests, conversations, and initiatives. Additionally, elementary teachers can connect with others through synchronous Twitter chats. Rather than single posts, a Twitter Chat will engage teachers in facilitated, scheduled, and time-bound conversations. These typically last an hour and are scheduled in the evenings, when teachers may be available. These Twitter chats focus on a broad range of topics relevant to teachers and use hashtags such as the ones above, as well as hashtags focused specifically on the facilitated discussion such as #UDLchat, #EdTechChat, #PBISchat, and #ElemChat.

School-based Community of Practice

Working collaboratively with colleagues on technology use in the classroom and increasing access can support elementary educators as they support the students in their classroom (Ertmer, 1999, p. 55). School-wide collaborative teaming on inclusive technology practices ensures that students in every classroom have equitable and appropriate access to technology that supports their learning and participation. These types of collaborations work best when administrators adapt the organizational structure of the school to allow for elementary teachers to meet both within grade levels and across grade levels so that the instructional staff can learn, plan, and reflect about how instruction can become more inclusive and how technology and UDL can support such efforts.

Conclusion

This chapter provided an overview of how technologies can be utilized to support effective inclusive elementary schools. As can be gleaned from the above sections, both assistive and instructional technologies have shaped the educational experiences of all learners and have created opportunities for greater participation, learning, and inclusion. However, this chapter also highlights the complexity of integrating technology into elementary school settings. Systemic barriers such as lack of resources and teacher-level barriers such as lack of knowledge about technology can prevent effective technology integration. Additionally, because technological innovations are outpacing research, there is not a strong evidence base associated with all the technologies that are entering elementary schools. Therefore, the only way to approach technology integration in a manner that considers access and inclusion is through deliberate pedagogical decision making that considers effective practices (e.g., the HLPs, McLeskey et al., 2017) and UDL (CAST, 2018) as a framework for designing instruction that meets the needs of all students.

References

Ahlfeld, K. (2017). Device-driven research: The impact of Chromebooks in American schools. *International Information & Library Review, 49*(4), 285–289. doi:10.1080/10572317.2017.1383756

Anderson, T. L., (2018). E-readers make a difference for diverse readers. *International Journal of Technology in Education and Science, 2*(1), 40–56. https://www.ijtes.net/index.php/ijtes/article/view/10

Atanga, C., Jones, B. A., Krueger, L. E., & Lu, S. (2019). Teachers of students with learning disabilities: Assistive technology knowledge, perceptions, interests, and barriers. *Journal of Special Education Technology*, 1–13. doi:10.0162643419864858.

Azuma, R. (1997). A survey of augmented *reality presence: Teleoperators and virtual environments, 6*(4), 355–385.

Basham, J. D., Blackorby, J. & Marino, M. T. (2020). Opportunity in crisis: The role of Universal Design for Learning in educational redesign. *Learning Disabilities: A Contemporary Journal, 18*(1), 71–91.

Beyoglu, D., Hursen, C., & Nasiboglu, A. (2020). Use of mixed reality applications in teaching science. *Education and Information Technologies, 25*, 4271–4286. doi:10.1007%2Fs10639-020-10166-8

Bouck, E. C., & Park, J. (2020). App-based manipulatives and the system of least prompts to support acquisition, maintenance, and generalization of adding integers. *Education and Training in Autism and Developmental Disabilities, 55*(2), 158–172.

Bouck, E. C., Park, J., Satsangi, R., Cwiakala, K., & Levy, K. (2019). Using the virtual-abstract instructional sequence to support acquisition of algebra. *Journal of Special Education Technology, 34*(4), 253–268.

Capp, M. J. (2017). The effectiveness of Universal Design for Learning: A meta-analysis of literature between 2013 and 2016. *International Journal of Inclusive Education, 21*, 791– 807. doi:10.1080/13603116.2017.1325074?journalCode=tied20

CAST. (2018). *Universal Design for Learning Guidelines version 2.2.* http://udlguidelines.cast.org

Chauhan, S. (2017). A meta-analysis of the impact of technology on learning effectiveness of elementary students. *Computers and Education, 105*, 14–30. doi:10.1016/j.compedu.2016.11.005

Chelkowski, L., Yan, Z., & Asaro-Saddler, K. (2019). The use of mobile devices with students with disabilities: a literature review. *Preventing School Failure: Alternative Education for Children and Youth. 69*(3), 277–295. doi:10.1080/1045988X.2019.1591336

Cheng, K. H., & Tsai, C. C. (2019). A case study of immersive virtual field trips in an elementary classroom: Students' learning experience and teacher-student interaction behaviors. *Computers and Education, 140*, 103600. doi:10.1016/j.compedu.2019.103600

Chmiliar, L. (2016). Improving the spelling skills of students with learning disabilities using Apps on the iPad. *International Journal of Technology and Inclusive Education (IJTIE), 3*(1). Retrieved from https://infonomics-society.org/wp-content/uploads/ijtie/published-papers/special-issue-volume-3-2016/Improving-the-Spelling-Skills-of-Students-with-Learning-Disabilities-using-Apps-on-the-iPad-1.pdf

Clarke, B., Strand Cary, M. G., Shanley, L., & Sutherland, M. (2020). Exploring the promise of a number line assessment to help identify students at-risk in mathematics. *Assessment for effective intervention, 45*(2), 151–160.

Common Core State Standards Initiative. (2010). Common Core State Standards for English language arts and literacy in history/social studies, science, and technical subjects. Retrieved from http://www.corestandards.org/ELA-Literacy/

Connor, C., Snell, M., Gansneder, B., & Dexter, S. (2010). Special education teachers' use of assistive technology with students who have severe disabilities. *Journal of Technology and Teacher Education, 18*, 369–386.

Coyne, P., Pisha, B., Dalton, B., Zeph, L. A., & Smith, N. C. (2012). Literacy by design: A Universal Design for Learning approach for students with significant intellectual disabilities. *Remedial and Special Education, 33*(3), 162–172.

Crompton, H., Burke, D., & Gregory, K. H. (2017). The use of mobile learning in PK-12 education: A systematic review. *Computers & Education, 110*, 51–63. https://www.sciencedirect.com/science/article/abs/pii/S0360131517300660?via%3Dihub

Dalton, B., Proctor, C. P., Uccelli, P., Mo, E., & Snow, C. E. (2011). Designing for diversity: The role of reading strategies and interactive vocabulary in a digital reading environment for fifth-grade monolingual English and bilingual students. *Journal of Literacy Research, 43*(1), 68–100.

Delgado, A. J., Wardlow, L., McKnight, K., & O'Malley, K. (2015). Educational technology: A review of the integration, resources, and effectiveness of technology in K-12 classrooms. *Journal of Information Technology Education, 14*, 397–416.

Deterding, S., Dixon, D., Khaled, R., & Nacke, L. (2011, September). From game design elements to gamefulness: Defining "gamification". In *Proceedings of the15th International Academic MindTrek Conference: Envisioning future media environments* (pp. 9–15). ACM.

Domingo, M. G. & Gargante, A. B. (2016). Exploring the use of educational technology in primary education: Teachers' perception of mobile technology learning impacts and applications' use in the classroom. *Computers in Human Behavior, 56*, 21–28. https://www.sciencedirect.com/science/article/abs/pii/S0747563215302387?via%3Dihub

Edyburn, D. L. (2010). Would you recognize Universal Design for Learning if you saw it? Ten propositions for new directions for the second decade of UDL. *Learning Disability Quarterly, 33*, 33–41. doi:10.1177/073194871003300103

Edyburn, D. L. (2015). Expanding the use of assistive technology while mindful of the need to understand efficacy. In D. L. Edyburn (Ed.), *Advances in special education technology, Volume 1: Efficacy of assistive technology interventions* (pp. 1–12). Emerald Group Publishing Limited.

Ertmer, P. A. (1999). Addressing first-and second-order barriers to change: Strategies for technology integration. *Educational Technology Research and Development, 47*(4), 47–61.

Ertmer, P. A., Ottenbreit-Leftwich, A. T., Sadik, O., Sendurur, E., & Sendurur, P. (2012). Teacher beliefs and technology integration practices: A critical relationship. *Computers & Education, 59*(2), 423–435. doi:10.1016/j.compedu.2012.02.001

Estapa, A. T., & Tank, K. M. (2017). Supporting integrated STEM in the elementary classroom: A professional development approach centered on an engineering design challenge. *International Journal of STEM Education, 4*(6), 1–16. doi:10.1186/s40594-017-0058-3

Francom, G. M. (2020). Barriers to technology integration: A time-series survey study. *Journal of Research on Technology in Education, 52*(1), 1–16.

Giovanni, A. (2020). Curriculum innovation with Universal Design for Learning, *Education Sciences & Society, 11*(1), 90–103.

González-González, C. S. (2019). State of the art in the teaching of computational thinking and programming in childhood education. *Education in the Knowledge Society, 20*, 1–15.

Griffiths, A. J., Nash, A. M., Mauphin, Z., & Mathur, S. K. (2020). Her voice: Engaging and preparing girls with disabilities for science, technology, engineering and math careers. *International Electronic Journal of Elementary Education, 12*(3), 293–301. Doi: 10.26822/iejee.2020358223. https://digitalcommons.chapman.edu/education_articles/244/

Hall, T. E., Hughes, C. A., & Filbert, M. (2000). Computer assisted instruction in reading for students with learning disabilities: A research synthesis. *Education and Treatment of Children, 23*(2),173–193.

Harper, K. A., Kurtzworth-Keen, K., & Marable, M. A. (2017). Assistive technology for students with learning disabilities: A glimpse of the Livescribe pen and its impact on homework completion. *Education and Information Technologies, 22*, 2471–2483. doi:10.1007/s10639-016-9555-0

Huang, Y. M., & Liang, T. H. (2015). A technique for tracking the reading rate to identify the e-book reading behaviors and comprehension outcomes of elementary school students. *British Journal of Educational Technology, 46*(4), 864–876. doi:10.1111/bjet.12182

Individuals with Disabilities Education Improvement Act of 2004, 20 U.S.C. § 614 et seq.

Israel, M., Jeong, G., Ray, M., & Lash, T. (2020). Teaching Elementary Computer Science through Universal Design for Learning. In *Proceedings of the 51st ACM Technical Symposium on Computer Science Education* (pp. 1220–1226).

Israel, M., Ray, M. J., Maa, W. C., Jeong, G. K., eun Lee, C., Lash, T., & Do, V. (2018). School-embedded and district-wide instructional coaching in K-8 computer science: Implications for including students with disabilities. *Journal of Technology and Teacher Education, 26*(3), 471–501.

ISTE Standards for Educators. (n.d.). Retrieved from https://www.iste.org/standards/for-educators

Jingrong, X., Basham, J. D., Marino, M. T., & Rice, M. (2018). Reviewing research on mobile learning for students with and without disabilities in k-12 educational settings. *Journal of Special Education Technology, 33(1)*, 27–39. doi:10.1177/0162643417732292

Katzenmeyer, M., & Moller, G. (2009). *Awakening the sleeping giant: Helping teachers develop as leaders*. Corwin Press.

Kasch, H. (2019). Innovative inclusive educational technology in language classrooms and learner perspectives: A study of nine learner narratives. *Interactivity, Game Creation, Design, Learning, and Innovation* (pp. 660–670). Springer.

Kennedy, M. J., & Boyle, J. (2017). The promise and problem with technology in special education. In J. M. Kauffman, D. P. Hallahan, P. C. Pullen (Eds.), *Handbook of special education* (2nd ed., pp. 606–614). Taylor & Francis.

Kim, M. K., McKenna, J. W., & Park, Y. (2017). The use of computer-assisted instruction to improve the reading comprehension of students with learning disabilities: An evaluation of the evidence base according to the what works clearinghouse standards. *Remedial and Special Education, 38*(4), 233–245.

King-Sears, P. (2020). Introduction to remedial and special education's special issue on universal design for learning. *Remedial and Special Education, 41*, 191–193.

King-Sears, M. E., & Johnson, T. (2020). Universal design for learning chemistry instruction for students with and without learning disabilities. *Remedial and Special Education, 41*, 207–218.

King-Sears, M.E., Johnson, T.M., Berkeley, S., Weiss, M., Peters-Burton, E.E., Evmenova, A.S., Menditto, A., & Hursh, J.C. (2015). An exploratory study of universal design for teaching chemistry to students with and without learning disabilities. *Learning Disability Quarterly, 38*(2), 84–96.

Kiru, E. W., Doabler, C. T., Sorrells, A. M., & Cooc, N. A. (2018). A synthesis of technology-mediated mathematics interventions for students with or at risk for mathematics learning disabilities. *Journal of Special Education Technology, 33*(2), 111–123.

Koba, M. (2015). Education tech funding soars—but is it working in the classroom? Retrieved from http://fortune.com/2015/04/28/education-tech-funding-soars-but-is-it-working-in-the-classroom/.

Leaman, H., & Corcoran, R. (2018). Teacher action research in elementary social studies: Use of iPads in 6th grade geography instruction. *IE: Inquiry in Education, 10*(2), 5, 1–11.

Leinonen, T., Keune, A., Veermans, M., & Toikkanen, T. (2016). Mobile apps for reflection in learning: A design research in K-12 education. *British Journal of Educational Technology, 47*(1), 184–202.

Lim, C. P., Zhao, Y., Tondeur, J., Chai, C. S., & Tsai, C. C. (2013). Bridging the gap: Technology trends and use of technology in schools. *Educational Technology & Society, 16*(2), 59–68.

Lindsay, S. & Hounsell, K. G. (2017). Adapting a robotics program to enhance participation and interest in STEM among children with disabilities: a pilot study. *Disability and Rehabilitation: Assistive Technology, 12*(7) 694–704. doi:10.1080/17483107.2016.1229047

Liu, F., Ritzhaupt, A. D., Dawson, K., & Barron, A. E. (2017) Explaining technology integration in K-12 classrooms: A multilevel path analysis model. *Educational Technology Research and Development, 65*(4), 795–813.

Livescribe 3 Smartpen (2016). https://us.livescribe.com/

Mackenzie, B. (n.d.), Ontario's Upper Grand District chooses Chromebooks to help students with disabilities build confidence in learning. Retrieved from https://edu.google.com/why-google/case-studies/upper-grand-district/?modal_active=none

Mackiewicz, S. M., Wood, C. L., Cooke, N. L., & Mazzotti, V. L. (2011). Effects of peer tutoring with audio prompting on vocabulary acquisition for struggling readers. *Remedial and Special Education, 32*(4), 345–354. doi:10.1177/0741932510362507

Marino, M. T., Gotch, C., Israel, M., Vasquez, E. III, Basham, J. D., & Becht, K. M. (2014). UDL in the middle school science classroom: Can video games and alternative text heighten engagement and learning for students with learning disabilities? *Learning Disability Quarterly, 37*, 87–99. https://journals.sagepub.com/doi/10.1177/0731948713503963

Markworth, K. A., Brobst, J., Ohana, C., & Parker, R. (2016). Elementary content specialization: Models, affordances, and constraints. *International Journal of STEM Education, 3*(1), 16.

McLeskey, J., Barringer, M-D., Billingsley, B., Brownell, M., Jackson, D., Kennedy, M., Lewis, T., Maheady, L., Rodriguez, J., Scheeler, M. C., Winn, J., & Ziegler, D. (2017). *High-leverage practices in special education*. Council for Exceptional Children and CEEDAR Center.

Meyer, A., Rose, D., & Gordon, D. (2014). The UDL Guidelines: A framework for Implementation. *Universal Design for Learning, Theory and Practice*, CAST Professional Publishing, 109–126.

Microsoft Education Team. (2018). Modern methodologies for classroom IT management: Change management and adoption for education technology. Retreived from https://educationblog.microsoft.com/en-us/2018/01/modern-methodologies-change-management-adoption-edtech/.

Molenda, M., & Januszewski, A. (2008). Educational technology: A definition with commentary. *Association for Educational Communications and Technology* (AECT).

Morrison, J., Wolf, B., Ross, S., Risman, K., & McLemore, C. (2019). Efficacy study of Zearn Math in a large urban school District. *Center for Research and Reform in Education.* Retrieved from https://jscholarship.library.jhu.edu/bitstream/handle/1774.2/62395/Zearn%20Math%20Final%20Report.pdf?sequence=1&isAllowed=y

Moyer-Packenham P.S., & Bolyard J.J. (2016). Revisiting the definition of a virtual manipulative. In P. Moyer-Packenham (Ed.), *International perspectives on teaching and learning mathematics with virtual manipulatives* (pp. 3–23). Springer. doi:10.1007/978-3-319-32718-1_1

National Governors Association Center for Best Practices & Council of Chief State School Officers. (2010). *Common core state standards.* Authors.

National Governors Association Center for Best Practices & Council of Chief State School Officers. (2010). *Common Core State Standards for English language arts and literacy in history/social studies, science, and technical subjects.* Authors.

Oculus (2019). Mission: ISS retrieved from https://www.oculus.com/experiences/quest/2094303753986147/

Office of Science and Technology Policy (2019). Progress report on the federal implementation of the STEM education strategic plan. Retrieved from https://www.whitehouse.gov/wp-content/uploads/2019/10/Progress-Report-on-the-Federal-Implementation-of-the-STEM-Education-Strategic-Plan.pdf

Ok, M. W., Rao, K., Bryant, B. R., & McDougall, D. (2017). Universal design for learning in Pre-K to grade 12 classrooms: A systematic review of research. *Exceptionality, 25*(2), 116–138.

Okojie, M. C., Olinzock, A. A., & Okojie-Boulder, T. C. (2006). The pedagogy of technology integration. *Journal of Technology Studies, 32*(2), 66–71.

Ozdemir, M., Shafin, C., Arcagok, S., & Demir, M. K. (2018). The effect of augmented reality applications in the learning process: A meta-analysis study. *Eurasian Journal of Educational Research, 74,* 165–186. https://eric.ed.gov/?id=EJ1181457

Purcell, K., Heaps, A., Buchanan, J., & Friedrich, L. (2013). *How teachers are using technology at home and in their classrooms.* Pew Research Center's Internet & American Life Project.

Rao, K., Ok, M. W., & Bryant, B. R. (2014). A review of research on Universal Design educational models. *Remedial and Special Education, 35*(3), 153–166.

Rao, K., Ok, M. W., Smith, S. J., Evmenova, A. S., & Edyburn, D. (2020). Validation of the UDL reporting criteria with extant UDL research. *Remedial and Special Education, 41*(4), 219–230.

Rappolt-Schlichtmann, G., Daley, S. G., Lim, S., Lapinski, S., Robinson, K. H., & Johnson, M. (2013). Universal Design for Learning and elementary school science: Exploring the efficacy, use, and perceptions of a web-based science notebook. *Journal of Educational Psychology, 105*(4), 1210.

Rello, L., Pielot, M., & Marcos, M. C. (May 2016). Make it big! The effect of font size and line spacing on online readability.In Proceedings of the 2016 CHI conference on Human Factors in Computing Systems. (pp. 3637–3648).

Reich, J., Levinson, M., & Johnston, W. (2011). Using online social networks to foster preservice teachers' membership in a networked community of praxis. *Contemporary Issues in Technology and Teacher Education, 11*(4), 382–397.

Rodriguez, C. D., & Cumming, T. M. (2017). Employing mobile technology to improve language skills of young students with language-based disabilities. *Assistive Technology, 29*(3), 161–169. doi:10.1080/10400435.2016.1171810

Root, J., Cox, S. K., Saunders, A. F., & Gilley, D. (2020). Applying the universal design for learning framework to mathematics for learners with extensive support needs. *Remedial and Special Education, 41,* 194–206. doi:10.1177/0741932519887235

Rose, D. H., Hasselbring, T. S., Stahl, S., & Zabala, J. (2005). Assistive technology and universal design for learning: Two sides of the same coin. *Handbook of Special Education Technology Research and Practice,* 507–518. Center for Applied Specila Technology.

Ross, S. M. (2020). Technology infusion in K-12 classrooms: a retrospective look at three decades of challenges and advancements in research and practice. *Educational Technology Research and Development,* 1–18.

Samuel, N. O., Israel, M., Arnett, H., Bievenue, L., Ginger, J., & Perry, M. (2020). Understanding instructional challenges and approaches to including middle school students with disabilities in makerspace activities: A cross-case analysis. *FabLearn 2020.*

Schreffler, J., Vasquez, E., III, Chini, J., & James, W. (2019). Universal Design for Learning in postsecondary STEM education for students with disabilities: A systematic literature review. *International Journal of STEM Education, 6*(8), 1–10. doi:10.1186/s40594-019-0161-8

Scherer, M. J. (1996). Outcomes of assistive technology use on quality of life. *Disability and Rehabilitation, 18*(9), 439–448.

Snodgrass, M. R., Israel, M., & Reese, G. C. (2016). Instructional supports for students with disabilities in K-5 computing: Findings from a cross-case analysis. *Computers & Education, 100*, 1–17.

Stetter, M. E., & Hughes, M. T. (2010). Computer-assisted instruction to enhance the reading comprehension of struggling readers: A review of the literature. *Journal of Special Education Technology, 25*(4), 1–16.

Taylor, M. S. (2018). Computer programming with Pre-K through first-grade students with intellectual disabilities. *The Journal of Special Education, 52*(2), 78–88.

Texthelp (2020). Read & Write. https://www.texthelp.com/en-us/products/read-write/read-write-prof/

Tychsen, L. & Foeller, P. (2020). Effects of immersive virtual reality headset viewing on young children: Visuomotor function, postural stability, and motion sickness. *American Journal of Ophthalmology, 209*, 151–159. https://www.ajo.com/article/S0002-9394(19)30381-2/fulltext

UDL-IRN (2011). *UDL in the instructional process. Version 1.0.* Author. Retrieved from https://udl-irn.org/wp-content/uploads/2018/01/Instructional-Process.pdf

Vasquez, E., & Marino, M. T. (2020). Enhancing executive function while addressing learner variability in inclusive classrooms. *Intervention in School and Clinic.* 10.1177/1053451220928978

Weng, P. L., Maeda, Y., & Bouck, E. C. (2014). Effectiveness of cognitive skills-based computer-assisted instruction for students with disabilities: A synthesis. *Remedial and Special Education, 35*(3), 167–180.

Wood, S. G., Moxley, J. H., Tighe, E. L., & Wagner, R. K. (2018). Does use of text-to-speech and related read-aloud tools improve reading comprehension for students with reading disabilities? A meta-analysis. *Journal of Learning Disabilities, 51*(1), 73–84.

Wu, P. H., Hwang, G. J., Yang, M. L., & Chen, C. H. (2018). Impacts of integrating the repertory grid into an augmented reality-based learning design on students' learning achievements, cognitive load and degree of satisfaction. *Interactive Learning Environments, 26*(2), 221–234. 10.1080/10494820.2017.1294608

Zhang, M., Trussell, R. P., Gallegos, B., & Asam, R. R. (2015). Using math apps for improving student learning: An exploratory study in an inclusive fourth grade classroom. *TechTrends, 59*(2), 32–39. doi:10.1007/s11528-015-0837-y

24

Supporting Inclusion and Inclusive Schools

Bob Algozzine, Fred Spooner, James McLeskey, and Nancy L. Waldron

AUTHOR NOTE: BOB ALGOZZINE, PROFESSOR EMERITUS EDUCATIONAL LEADERSHIP, UNIVERSITY OF NORTH CAROLINA AT CHARLOTTE; FRED SPOONER, SPECIAL EDUCATION, UNIVERSITY OF NORTH CAROLINA AT CHARLOTTE; JAMES MCLESKEY, SCHOOL OF SPECIAL EDUCATION, SCHOOL PSYCHOLOGY, & EARLY CHILDHOOD STUDIES, UNIVERSITY OF FLORIDA; NANCY L. WALDRON, SCHOOL OF SPECIAL EDUCATION, SCHOOL PSYCHOLOGY, & EARLY CHILDHOOD STUDIES, UNIVERSITY OF FLORIDA.

Inclusion is a goal (i.e., an end toward which we extend effort) and an intervention (i.e., an action we take to achieve a goal) that promotes educational and other opportunities and experiences for people with disabilities that are the same as those for people without disabilities. Opining for and against changing special education and how people with disabilities are educated has been around for many years (cf. Dunn, 1968; Fuchs & Fuchs, 1994a,b,c; Kauffman, 2015; Kauffman et al., 2019; Lipsky & Gartner, 1987; Osgood, 2005; Ysseldyke et al., 2000). The previous chapters provide syntheses of research and the wisdom from practice regarding a variety of topics related to effective inclusion and the extent to which this knowledge has been and can continue to be translated into positive school, community, and societal outcomes in inclusive schools. In talking about how to finish the book, we came up with a three-part story about supporting inclusion. In the first part (pp. 505–510), we reiterate the limited state of educational *progress* and outcomes in America's schools despite considerable and continuing local, state, and national efforts to make them better. We then focus on what is known about why goals are sometimes not achieved and why innovations, implementations, and small- and large-scale program, practice, and product interventions *fail* (pp. 510–512) before sharing thoughts on what we believe we all can do to promote *conditions for change* (pp. 512–517). Our intent is not to review or represent everything written about the condition of education or special education and the continuing laments for why goals remain unreachable or why interventions fail. We are not promising guarantees or absolute directions for change, but more providing a reasoned perspective on what has passed as a base for sharing ownership and acceptance for the problem and for setting a future course for effective inclusive schools and how they might improve outcomes and life opportunities for individuals with disabilities and their families, neighbors, and peers.

Shining a Light on Education Progress

The National Assessment of Educational Progress (NAEP) is the only testing program that measures what U.S. students know and can do in various subjects across the nation, states, and in some urban districts. Also known as the Nation's Report Card, these data have provided information about how

DOI: 10.4324/9781003043874-24

students are performing academically since 1969 (NAEP, 2020a) and current performance is presented in two ways (NAEP, 2020d, 2020e):

1. The NAEP average scale score (SS) represents how students performed on each assessment. Scores are aggregated and reported at the student group level for the nation, states, and districts. They can also be used for comparisons among states, districts, and student groups.
2. NAEP achievement levels are performance standards that describe what students should know and be able to do. Results are reported as percentages of students performing at or above three achievement levels (e.g., SS for *Fourth Grade Reading Basic* = 208, *Proficient* = 238, and *Advanced* = 268). Students performing at or above the *Proficient* level on NAEP assessments demonstrate solid academic performance and competency over challenging subject matter. It should be noted that the *NAEP Proficient* achievement level does not represent grade level proficiency as determined by other assessment standards (e.g., state or district assessments).

NAEP (2020b, 2020d) assessment results are reported as averages on a 0–500 scale (reading, mathematics, US history, and geography) or on a 0–300 scale (science, writing, technology and engineering literacy, and civics). The scale scores are derived from student responses to assessment questions and summarize the overall level of performance attained by that student. Scale scores for individual students are not reported, but summary statistics describing the performance for groups of students (e.g., demographic, gender, race/ethnicity) are reported.

Are Students Performing Better Now than in the Past?

As illustrated in Figure 24.1, the trend in reading performance for elementary-, middle-, and secondary-aged students has been flat despite the rhetoric, policies, and large-scale federal initiatives that promised change with terms like "revolution," "reform," and "recovery." Gaps in performance noted in earlier chapters for different groups of students and over time appear similarly unmoved by promises, planners, and promoters for change (see McFarland et al., 2019, p. 93, Figure 3).

Intractability of Achievement Gaps

In 2019, all students at grades 4 and 8 in both mathematics and reading had higher scores overall and at five of six selected percentiles (all except for the 10th percentile in reading) compared to the first assessments in the early 1990s; however, compared to 10 years ago, scores at both grades in both subjects were lower or not significantly different for lower-performing students (i.e., those at the 10th and 25th percentiles) (NAEP, 2020c). A decade earlier, Murphy (2009) argued that closing an achievement gap is complex for a host of reasons, starting with "...decisions about the types of measures to use to chart the gap, carrying through to ways to measure and interpret scores, and ending with questions about the effectiveness of varying strategies" (p. 8). And, like most who opine eloquently about and "admire" more than solve intractable problems, he ended his article with potential and promise: "Over the last decade, we've been able to forge important "principles of work" that *need to be followed* if gap-reduction efforts are to be effective" (p. 12, emphasis added). Considering the continuing absence of gap-reduction evidence, it seems safe to conclude that the important principles of work promised to make a difference have not been followed or, if they have been followed, have failed to deliver as promised.

In 2015, the average reading score for White fourth-grade students was 26 points higher than the average score for their Black peers. This 26-point score gap was not significantly different compared to the score gap in 2013, the previous assessment year, but was narrower than the 32-point score gap in 1992, the first reading assessment year. The 24-point score gap between the average reading

Almost 50-Year Trends for Average NAEP Reading Scores

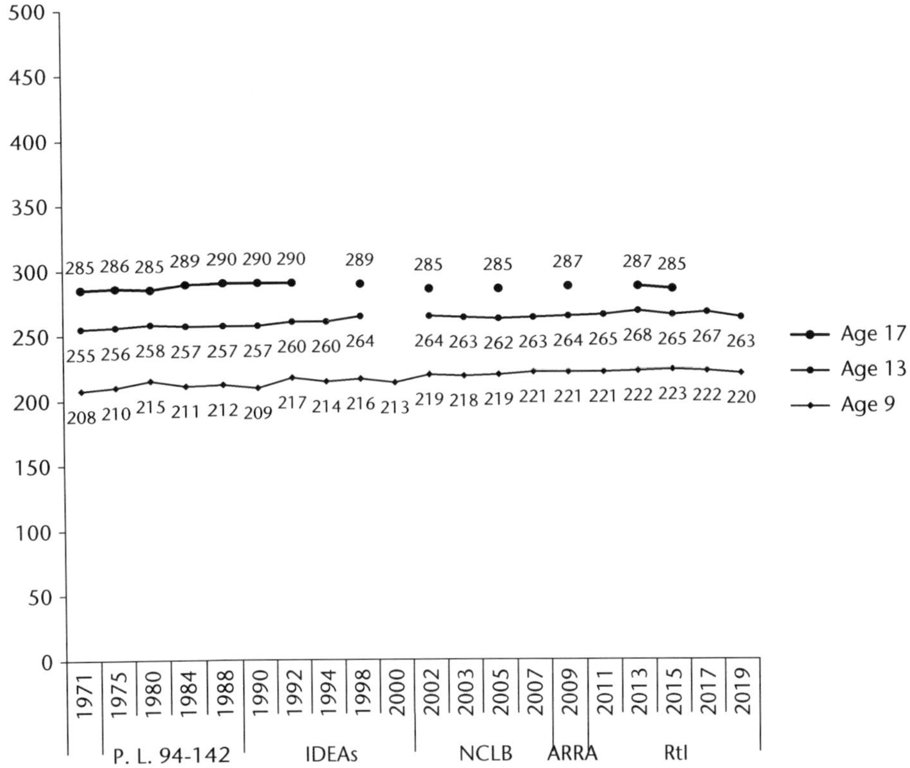

Figure 24.1 50-Year Trends for Average NAEP Reading Scores

Note. Compiled from multiple NAEP and other sources.

scores of White and Hispanic fourth-grade students in 2015 did not differ significantly in comparison to either 2013 or 1992. Similarly, the 7-point gap between the 2015 average scores of male and female students did not differ significantly compared to either 2013 or 1992 (The Nation's Report Card, 2020). Clearly, differences in standardized test performances have been resistant to change across notable and significant demographic groups in America's schools.

Are Conditions for Students with Disabilities Better Now than in the Past?

> Let us stop being pressured into continuing and expanding a special education program that we know to be undesirable for many of the children we are dedicated to serve. (Dunn, 1968, p. 5)

Prompted in part by problems lamented by Dunn, the Education for All Handicapped Children Act of 1975 gave great hope for an important change in the condition of special education (Ysseldyke et al., 2000). Heralded as "the end of the quiet revolution" (cf. Abeson & Zettel, 1977; Weintraub, 1977), the purpose of the legislation was to "assure that all handicapped children have available to them, within the time periods specified, a free appropriate public education which emphasizes special education and related services designed to meet their unique needs. (Public Law 94-142,1975, Sec. 3, c)" (Abeson & Zettel, p. 122).

Movement related to access to education has been well-documented in required monitoring reports to Congress on the implementation of the act and its reauthorizations (cf. U. S. Department of Education, 2020). For example, a recent annual report (OSERS, 2018) depicts progress in (1) providing a free appropriate public education (FAPE) for children with disabilities under IDEA, Part B, and early intervention services to infants and toddlers with disabilities and their families under IDEA, Part C; (2) ensuring that the rights of these children with disabilities and their parents are protected; (3) assisting states and localities in providing for the education of all children with disabilities; and (4) assessing the effectiveness of efforts to educate children with disabilities. The "summary and analysis" parts (Section I and II) of the report include national data on infants and toddlers, children ages 3 through 5, and students 6 through 21 served under IDEA. The "findings and determinations resulting from reviews of state implementation of IDEA" section of the report (Section III, pp. 201–230) includes descriptions of the plans that must be in place and reports that must be filed for "...the Department...to make an annual determination of the extent to which [states and jurisdictions] are meeting the requirements and purposes of...IDEA" (p. 203); and, the final sections (IV-VI) include descriptions of funded research, studies and evaluations, and assessments (pp. 231–272). As has long been the case (cf. Algozzine, 1991), the message on "implementation" is long on compliance-driven accountability data (e.g., numbers and percentages of students with disabilities "being educated" by whom here, there, and everywhere, descriptions of and dollars allocated and spent for research, evaluation, and assessment activities) and short on results-driven accountability data (e.g., numbers and percentages of fourth-grade children with disabilities scoring at basic or above on the NAEP in math and reading).

Interestingly, results from large-scale evaluations are less than complimentary of the power of heavily promoted interventions (e.g., Response to Intervention: RTI) to move the special education outcomes needle. For example, Balu et al. (2015) presented data showing that "... early-grade elementary students at the margin of being considered at risk by current screening measures failed to benefit from Tier 2 or Tier 3 intervention services provided to them. In first grade, these students actually fell further behind their counterparts who, because they scored just above the cut point on the screening variable for intervention, were placed to receive only Tier 1 services" (p. 93). In a critique of this work published in *Exceptional Children*, Fuchs and Fuchs (2017) used a popular explanation for unpopular findings and argued that many of the participating schools "...were not conducting RTI in a manner supported by research and policy" (p. 255). In the end, much of what has been promised, promoted, and provided as "...necessary if special education is to strengthen its capacity to meet the needs of the students with most significant learning needs..." (Fuchs et al., 2018, p. 130) has been around for many years and has failed to deliver predicted or desired change; and, the tarnish and letdown have not gone unnoticed (cf. Anastasiou et al., 2017; Artiles, 2011, 2019; Kauffman, 1993; Kauffman et al., 2017, 2019; Skiba et al., 2016).

Intractability of Achievement Gaps for Students with Disabilities

Schulte and Stevens (2015, p. 370) observed that "[t]he academic achievement of students with disabilities (SWDs) has been a long-standing concern (McDonnell et al., 1997; Wagner et al., 2006)." Stevens et al. (2015) observed gaps that were relatively stable over grades between students without disabilities and students in specific disability groups. Schulte et al. (2016) reported a pattern of "stable differences" and concluded that "growth sufficient to have an impact on...achievement gaps does not routinely occur in typical educational practice" (p. 925). In a meta-analysis of 180 effect sizes from 23 studies, Gilmour et al. (2019) found that students with disabilities were "1.17 standard deviations, or more than 3 years, below typically developing peers" (p. 329).

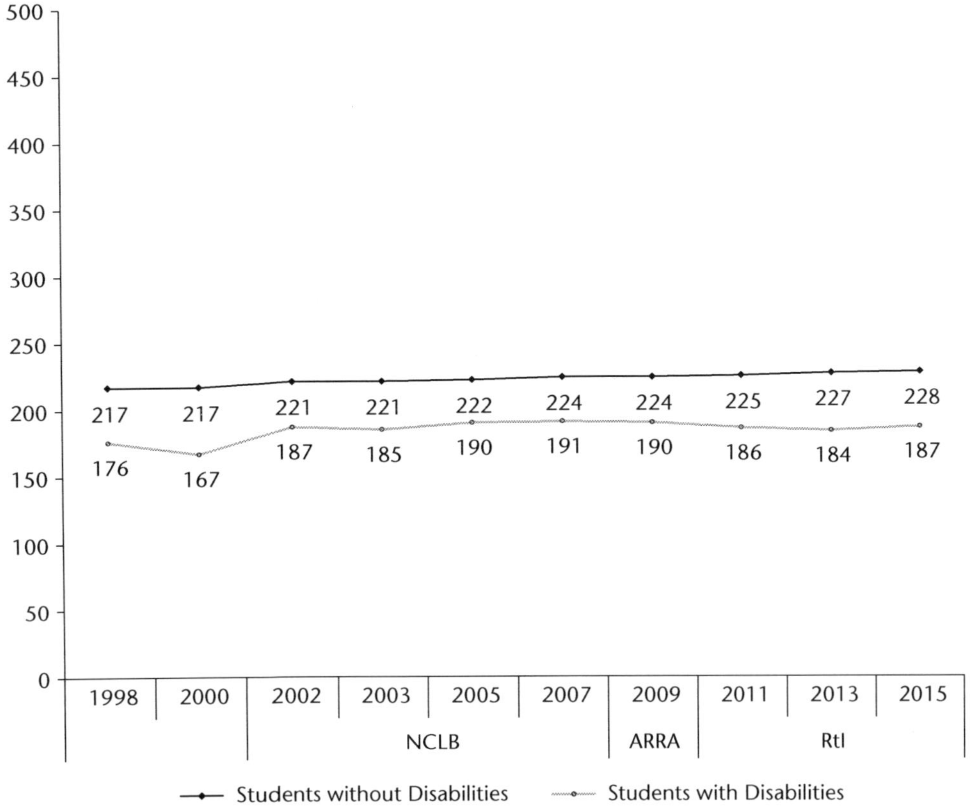

Figure 24.2 National Assessment of Educational Progress (NAEP) Reading Scale Scores of 4th-Grade Students with and without Disabilities: Selected Years, 1998–2015

Note. Compiled from multiple NAEP and other sources

It Is All in How You Look at It

"The good news: Students with disabilities who took a state general assessment in reading began with lower average Grade 3 reading comprehension scores, but across Grades 4–7, *made average annual gains similar to students without disabilities.* (National Center on Assessment and Accountability for Special Education, 2017). Put another way, if achievement growth across elementary and middle school grades is similar between students with disabilities and students without disabilities, it is not good news that the gap or difference in average reading scores for students identified with and without disabilities appears unchanged (see Figure 24.2) by big ideas, promises of reform, or passage across grades. There is little progress in running to stand still but to signal a need for change.

Looking Beyond Achievement

Sadly, conditions that Dunn wrote about many years ago persist. For example, at a recent symposium, special education professionals and others explored why "significant disproportionality" is "an important topic for all of us as we work to ensure that children with disabilities, regardless of race or ethnicity, are provided educational services and accommodations that enable and prepare them for post-school education and career opportunities" (OSEP, 2017, February 8). In a literature and practice too vast for review here, the continuing and unrelenting nature of the "over-representation/overidentification/disproportionality" problem and its intractability is evident in multiple perspectives of professionals in diverse organizations (cf. Camacho & Krezmien, 2019; Cruz & Rodl, 2018; Heller et al., 1982; MacMillan & Reschly, 1998) as well as in the Department of Education's recent ruling postponing the date for compliance with its significant disproportionality regulations (U. S. Department of Education, 2018a, 2018b) and in reactions to the delay (Diament, 2018). We do not know why all the rhetoric, reflection, and labor has left the problem of disproportionality largely unchanged for more than fifty years; and, more importantly, why special education is still failing to deliver as promised and the promises remain the "solutions" that drive a disconnected, discriminatory, and dysfunctional educational system of professional preparation and school- and community-based instruction that continues unsupported by evidence of change.

Why Goals are Sometimes Not Achieved and Why Interventions Fail

> We have met the enemy and they are us. Pogo by Walt Kelly
>
> The goal of implementation is to have practitioners (e.g., foster parents, caseworkers, therapists, teachers, physicians) use [interventions] effectively. To accomplish this, *high-fidelity practitioner behavior is created and supported by core implementation components* (also called "implementation drivers"). These components are staff selection, pre-service and in-service training, ongoing coaching and consultation, staff performance evaluation, decision support data systems, facilitative administrative supports, and system interventions. (Fixsen & Blase, 2009, p. 2, emphasis added)
>
> Overall, tensions seemed to stem *not from opposition or resistance* to [the intervention] but from *poor applica*tion of the [intervention] principles in their building—by the team, the administrators, and/or colleagues (Tyre et al., 2020, p. 102, emphasis added)

Could it be simpler? You see a need and set a goal for change, implement an intervention promised to bring about that change and if it does not work, you blame the implementers and/or the drivers, not the intervention; and move on to the next promise, proposal, or plan. For example, when responsiveness to intervention (RTI) became popular but requirements for successful implementation resulted in "inefficiencies in its application", proponents offered "...research-backed guidance for designing more effective and efficient (next generation, if you will) multilevel prevention—an approach [they call], Smart RTI" (Fuchs et al., 2012, p. 264). When a large-scale federally-funded evaluation of response to intervention practices for elementary school reading (cf. Balu et al., 2015) failed to find reliable differences between comparison students in Grades 2 or 3, RTI promoters characterized the work as "fundamentally flawed" (Brasher, 2017) and criticized it for having "...too many conceptual and methodological limitations for its findings to be taken at face value" (Fuchs & Fuchs, 2017, p. 259). They took the opportunity for criticism as a chance to advance the idea that simpler (not simple) frameworks, like "embedded RTI" (Fuchs & Fuchs, p. 264), may encourage more educators to implement RTI's important components with fidelity to remedy the more than twenty-year lack of "...authoritative guidance about whether this complex, challenging, and, many would say, necessary school reform is an effective means of improving students' academic outcomes" (p. 260).

And know that those who tag failure differently (e.g., claiming the intervention or what is being done is the problem) risk living professional lives as special education pariahs. For example, as a basis for promoting yet another reason for failure in special education, Fuchs and Fuchs (2015) opined that "Ysseldyke and associates' articles in the 1980s deepened skepticism among many stakeholders about the validity of the LD construct, if not about the meaningfulness of high-incidence disabilities more generally" (p. 106). In the introduction to a special issue of *Learning Disabilities Research and Practice* promoting "a renewed focus on intensive intervention," Fuchs et al. (2018, p. 129) connected the study to a "widespread underestimation of the severity of these children's learning problems and the failure by educators to come to their educational rescue" (p. 129) and in efforts to address the "abysmal school performance" of millions of America's children (p. 126).

In an article included in the special issue, Al Otaiba et al. (2018) reported small positive effects for reading comprehension favoring the treatment group and negligible effects on measures of vocabulary, fluency, and word reading for a subset of fourth graders with substantial reading comprehension deficits who participated in a larger two-year randomized control trial that tested the efficacy of multicomponent reading intervention. Interestingly, this effort to implement intensive interventions resulted in outcomes that made students appear more similar than different after receiving or not receiving them:

> On average, all students did grow from fall to spring, but...did not close the reading gap; group differences and related effect sizes were negligible for vocabulary, fluency, and word reading; [and,] effect sizes...were only on researcher-made measures rather than standardized measures, which precluded evaluating whether growth indicated a closing of the reading gap with peers. (Al Otaiba et al., p. 163).

As in prior studies similar in design and outcome (cf. Wanzek et al., 2016, 2017), the intervention was not more effective than "business-as-usual" for improving vocabulary, fluency, or word reading. In discussing the lack of meaningful differential effects after participating in "...an average of 94 well-implemented small-group intervention sessions" in their study, Al Otaiba et al. shared a loosely-coupled taxonomy of ways (e.g., increased *dosage, alignment, attention to transfer, comprehensiveness, behavior supports, individualization*) that "...schools and teachers could further intensify this intervention, or other similar intervention" (see pp. 164–165, emphasis in original).

Why would practitioners fail to implement interventions as intended (i.e., *as supported by research and policy*) and why would administrators or their colleagues accept the *poor application of intervention principles* or fail to provide and support *implementation drivers*? Why would interventions fail to be implemented with the *intensity* necessary to bring about change?

Over time, researchers have looked to practitioner opinions to learn about interventions and infer why they may fail. For example, in a research synthesis of "...attitudes toward teaching students with disabilities in their general education classes," Scruggs and Mastropieri (1996) found that about two-thirds of teachers reported supporting inclusion, but the primary implications of the work derived from the consistent findings related to areas of support needed to make it happen:

- Time—an hour or more per day to plan for students with disabilities.
- Resources
    - Training—systematic, intensive professional development, either as part of their certification programs, as intensive and well-planned on-site presentations, or as ongoing consultation.
    - Personnel—assistance to carry out mainstreaming objectives. This could include a one-half time aide and daily contact with special education teachers.
    - Materials—adequate curriculum supplies and other classroom equipment appropriate to the needs of students with disabilities.
- Structure—class size should be reduced, to fewer than 20 students, if students with disabilities are included.

- Consideration of severity of disability—Teachers are more willing to include students with mild disabilities than students with more severe disabilities, apparently because of teachers' perceived ability to carry on their teaching mission for the entire classroom. By implication, the more severe the disabilities represented in the inclusive setting, the more the previously mentioned sources of support would be needed. (p. 72)

The more things change, the more they stay the same and sometimes provide guidance for moving forward. Charlton et al. (2018) interviewed state leaders to document perceptions of key features associated with changes in practice. Participants identified "…multidisciplinary leadership, access to professional development, consistent language and/or practices, consultation with external partners, and a focus on student outcomes in evaluation and planning" as helping categories and "…competing philosophies, high personnel turnover, varying levels of readiness, and inadequate data systems…" as hindering categories (p. 191). They also identified access to personnel with high-level training and access to more effective interventions on the items they wished had happened or could happen in the future. In recent research, Kern et al. (2020) found that although teachers and staff rated the acceptability of practices that they implemented favorably, use of the interventions was low even when data indicated need, resulting in large variability in effects across treatment students.

Years of research have indicated that a few factors are consistently identified as slowing implementation of small- as well as large-scale interventions. Years of practice have also shown that focusing on some or many of these factors is not speeding the implementation of small- or large-scale interventions or change and moving forward is not a simple matter of doing this or that. So, nearly "…two decades after RTI efforts began, we have no authoritative guidance about whether this complex, challenging, and, many would say, necessary school reform is an effective means of improving students' academic outcomes" (Fuchs & Fuchs, 2017, p. 260). And, as documented in reports to the nation on the condition of education and reports to federal policy makers on progress in providing a free appropriate public education for individuals with disabilities, the lack of evidence of moving the achievement outcomes needle is real, continuous, and difficult to ignore.

Thinking about Conditions for Change

> Nations thrive when they develop "inclusive" political and economic institutions, and they fail when those institutions become "extractive" and concentrate power and opportunity in the hands of only a few. (Friedman, 2012)
>
> In a recent issue of the *Journal of Positive Behavior Interventions*, leaders in schoolwide positive behavior interventions and supports (SWPBIS) identified implementation science as a direction for the field. Adults charged with implementation are of increasing interest to researchers, with published studies of staff behavior, social validity, and fidelity doubling in the past decade (Clarke et al., 2018). This suggests a shift from identifying evidence-based practices to how such practices are perceived and *implemented*. (Tyre et al., 2020, p. 93, emphasis added)

Educational researchers have long been concerned with the reach and relevance of their work and what has come to be known as the "research-to-practice gap" (cf. Bloom, 1966; Farrell et al., 2021; Franke & Davis, 1931; Heller, 2021; Kezar, 2000; Krathwohl, 1969; Preston, 2021; Scates, 1948; Snow, 2016; Vanderlinde & Braak, 2010; Woody, 1924). For example, in the Presidential Address to the Educational Research Association in 1923, the Assistant Superintendent of Milwaukee Schools W. W. Theisen noted that the "findings of research must be translated into simple lessons for the teacher" but the primary contribution of much of the then-contemporary work was in "pointing out problems" (p. 307, 314). More recently, the gap between research and practice has been lamented in writing focused on implementation science in general (Fixsen et al., 2005; Wallace et al., 2008), how to build local effectiveness predictions (Joyce & Cartwright, 2020), and inclusion specifically (Grima-Farrell et al., 2011) as well as in articles addressing "…key considerations essential to successfully implementing and sustaining validated practices to support teachers in addressing the needs of [all] students within our school systems (Grima-Farrell, 2018, p. 89).

Much like those who try to explain why interventions fail, most scholars attribute the gap between research and practice to "individual, organizational, and external factors" like administrator and staff attitudes, beliefs, and training; contextual fit with extant structures, practices, programs, and supports; and, existing and potential local, state, federal funding, policies, and programs (see Gotham, 2006, pp. 607–608). Others take a different path.

> We want to reiterate that perfect fidelity is not possible. Educational settings are so complex that reporting how interventions were implemented in a study likely leaves out details that could be relevant. More importantly, aiming for fidelity is very often not the best way to implement an intervention. Given the significant differences across students and contexts, even if the target closely resembles the study along visible dimensions, producing positive effects in new settings will very likely require adjustments. Appreciating this, Nuthall (2004) observed that "the contextual details that [have] been eliminated from these studies in order to make the results generalizable are what teachers needed to know in order to…apply the results" (p. 286)" (Joyce & Cartwright, 2020, p. 1071).

Much research shows that some interventions "work" only in the context of a small- or large-scale "controlled" study and that when attention and resources move to the next big thing, business-as-usual prevails; that despite providing high ratings on social validity about interventions, many participants subsequently and freely produce a litany of reasons for not implementing them; that while a critical determiner of the continuing success of an intervention is the extent to which it is implemented as intended, evaluating and adjusting treatment fidelity is often ignored in monitoring implementation efforts; and, that most studies occur in settings that are not authentic or representative of real-life places where academic and social behavior are occurring and where changing them is the expected outcome of instruction.

By many standards, Positive Behavioral Interventions and Supports (PBIS) is a framework that has been successful in improving behavioral outcomes across states, districts, and schools (see Chapters 7 and 20). What can we learn and possibly reverse engineer based on what has made PBIS successful? Perhaps the most important overarching insight is that systemic change is foundational for success (Scaletta & Hughes, 2020; also see Chapter 20). Classrooms, grade levels, schools, districts, and states are systems that are comprised of interdependent components that make up a unified whole. Changing any part of these systems requires attending to context and ensuring that there is an infrastructure in place to support the changes; and this then requires actively and continuously engaging people in planning, implementing, and evaluating solutions (Fixsen et al., 2005; Fullan, 2016; Sarason, 1971, 1990; Sarason & Doris, 1979; Scaletta & Hughes, 2020).

We addressed the importance of systemic change in Chapter 1, and this topic is also addressed in Chapters 20 and 21, so we will not reiterate that information here. Rather, we will address additional findings from Scaletta and Hughes related to the successful implementation of the PBIS framework that could be beneficial in supporting the success of other far-reaching interventions such as inclusion. These findings included providing strong, shared leadership from administrators and staff, establishing practices that leverage teachers as powerful service providers, and actively engaging stakeholders in the intervention efforts. We believe there is no magic, mystery, or duplicity related to these findings. To bring about change, we believe that we need to accept that we have a problem and commit to changing it. To move in the right direction, we need to shift from trying to repair, renovate, or revise exclusive promise-based practices that have not worked to embracing a rebuild grounded in components of school improvement that Scaletta and Hughes, as well as Bryk and colleagues (Bryk, 2010; Newman et al., 2001) and others (Fullan, 2016; Sarason, 1990; Sarason & Doris, 1979), have found effective in bringing about both small- and large-scale change:

1. *Leadership* that reflects shared decision-making and engagement that actively provides resources to ensure that teachers have professional development and coaching to support change.
2. *Instruction* that reflects the what (e.g., curriculum, high expectations for student learning) and how (e.g., strategies and tactics, formative and summative assessment) of effective teaching.
3. *Collaboration* that reflects shared beliefs and actions among administrators, teachers, students, families, and communities.

Focusing on Leadership

> "[P]olicymakers seem to find meaning in stating the problems [with schools], but they do not find (or do not seem to look for) much meaning in engaging people in the solutions." (Fullan, 2016, p. 7)

In a collection of articles in *Kappan* (cf. Heller, 2021), professionals provided perspectives on the disconnect between research and practice and Farrell et al. (2021) suggested that providing opportunities for researchers and practitioners to talk about research, sharing a "productive stance on partnering," and understanding the importance of organizational conditions that support policy changes "…can contribute to meaningful shifts in school district policies and practice" (p. 39). A consistent finding related to successful school improvement across general and special education has been the importance of strong, supportive leadership that begins with the principal but is also shared with teachers and other school stakeholders (DeMatthews et al., 2020; Hitt & Tucker, 2016; also see Chapter 2 in this handbook). The findings from Scaletta and Hughes (2020) revealed that as the development and implementation of SWPBIS were initiated, principals sought to actively engage teachers in leadership roles while recognizing that leadership would have to be distributed across teachers and other school staff to address the substantial demands of using SWPBIS successfully.

While principals were influential supporters of this initiative, they did not take on the lead role on the leadership team but rather took a participatory and guiding role. This provided an opportunity for teachers to take active leadership roles as chair of the leadership team and as leads on subcommittees that addressed areas such as developing schoolwide systems and practices, tailoring SWPBIS to the unique context and culture of the school, and developing and using a schoolwide data system to make decisions. As Hitt and Tucker (2016) have noted, when teachers perceive that their contributions as leaders are valued, "…they then become more accepting of the invitation to innovate and transcend" (p. 536). Shared leadership is thus a key to ensuring strong support and a high level of engagement from teachers, as well as sufficient leadership to support the demands of successfully implementing and sustaining a major change initiative.

In addition to shared leadership, principals also engage in a range of activities to make sure that teachers and other stakeholders know that SWPBIS or any other major initiative is a schoolwide priority and that school administrators will provide the necessary support to ensure the success of the initiative. For example, the Scaletta and Hughes (2020) investigation found that principals actively modeled support for SWPBIS, allocated resources to support critical needs, worked to remove barriers and buffer teachers against factors that could interfere with effectiveness, and provided release time to leadership team members to accomplish tasks. A major area in which principals provide support for SWPBIS and other initiatives is providing high-quality professional development to make sure that teachers and other stakeholders understand, support, and are were well prepared to enact the different components of the change initiative. Research on the role of principals in supporting school improvement and enhanced student outcomes have consistently revealed the importance of ensuring that teachers are provided high-quality professional development (e.g., coaching, communities of practice) to prepare teachers and other professionals well as they enact new initiatives (DeMatthews et al., 2020; Hitt & Tucker, 2016).

DeMatthews et al. (2020, p.550) remind us that the public school system in the United States is "...far from perfect but...increasingly focused on inclusive education" and point out that "[p]rincipals play a critical role in creating effective inclusive schools for students with disabilities around the world." In addition to establishing an inclusive vision, principals in inclusive schools create opportunities for teachers to learn together and create communities of practice that support evidence-based instruction. Of course, in the end, principals focus on supporting instruction and teachers focus on delivering it.

Focusing on Instruction

In a recent position paper on Career Technical Education (CTE) for the Division of Career Development and Transition (DCDT), Harvey et al. (2020) reviewed the "great potential" in using CTE and summarized recommendations for "how this might be accomplished" in areas related to policy (e.g., align practice with quality, access, and equity standards), personnel and professional development (e.g., ensure knowledge of good pedagogy), and research (e.g., conduct high-quality research) (p. 71). As with most papers of position, the purpose was not to achieve the great potential but to "...broadcast and amplify the critical need for better-articulated policy, proactive professional development and personnel preparation with intensive collaboration...for special education professionals, and more rigorous research to identify effective practices..." (p. 75).

The Office of Special Education Programs (OSEP) supports programs to attract, prepare, and retain effective personnel—general and special education teachers, early childhood personnel, and related services providers. This is an area that is important for schools, states, communities, businesses, districts, and professional organizations and one that disproportionately affects children with disabilities and their families due to many unfilled positions and high attrition rates. Supporting teachers requires building the local knowledge and skills needed to provide effective instruction for children with disabilities.

We believe that high fidelity broadcasting of needs that require attention and/or for more intensive intervention and/or more rigorous research to bring about change has been a futile effort at best. As evidenced by a history of change now mired in what some believe reflects failure and abysmal outcomes, clearly identifying and admiring problems and waxing eloquently or otherwise about the potential, promise and insignificant progress are not enough.

The first step in solving a problem is admitting that there is a problem. The placemat for making a difference begins with questions that can be answered.

- Do we have a problem? What is it?
- What is our goal for change? What will "intervention" and implementation fidelity look like? What will improvement look like?
- Do we have sufficient and critical "skin in the game" (i.e., ownership, interest, and engagement in achieving the goal)?
- When is the time to change?

"[G]ood teaching is good teaching and...there are no boundaries on where it can occur..." (Ysseldyke et al., 2000, p. 200) or how to or who can make it happen (Algozzine & Maheady, 1986). In previous chapters, we set the context for tiered academic and behavior instruction driven by high functioning data teams supported by high-leverage practices that can be used to focus on teaching and monitoring relentlessly until fidelity and/or outcome data illustrate that it is time to change. We believe that unified and systematic implementation of these frameworks and interventions represents a right start for improving district-, school-, and classroom-levels of inclusion.

The Institute of Education Sciences (IES) is the statistics, research, and evaluation arm of the U.S. Department of Education. In addition to collecting, analyzing, and disseminating data on the "condition of education" (see "Shining a Light on Education Progress" earlier in this chapter), the agency performs other types of work, including developing and providing resources to support the use of data in decision making. For example, working collaboratively with a panel of experts, the IES What Works Clearinghouse (WWC) developed the criteria for a rating of effectiveness for intervention, including graphic or other evidence of outcomes resulting from the systematic implementation of an intervention across at least three observations or data collections (Beretvas et al., 2015). In the context of ownership and independent public schooling, the science here can be translated into simple guidance for deciding if inclusion efforts are working. Using a panel of local stakeholders (i.e., administrators, teachers, staff members, students, families, community members, policy makers, and other professionals), identify an intervention with contextual fit likely to bring about the desired change. For at least three assessments, a document that the core features of the intervention have been systematically implemented as intended and the extent to which desired outcomes are being achieved. If the intervention does not bring about change, ensure that it has been implemented as intended before moving to something new. As appropriate, build a portfolio of "what works" and celebrate achievements and progress regularly with stakeholders.

Focusing on Collaboration

In Chapter 17, Ryndak and colleagues eloquently set forth goals, indicators, and aspects of effective collaboration. These statements are based on IDEA goals about the ability of every student to gain educational benefit in the least restrictive environment. There are three indicators that could be used to evaluate the effectiveness of the endeavor. First, students are engaged, making progress in the general curriculum, and participating in grade level general education classes and other contexts. Second, students are engaged in relationships with their grade-level peers. Third, students are engaged in endeavors within their general education class, school, and home communities. For collaboration to be effective, these values must be shared among administrators, teachers, students, families, and communities.

The big idea that is reflected is that we are all in this together, working towards common goals and objectives for the benefit of the children that are served in schools. Effectively serving all of the children means serving ALL OF THE CHILDREN, including those with severe disabilities. ALL MEANS ALL! From the perspective of those involved with typically the most disenfranchised students, those with severe disabilities, those which are the focus of Chapters 13–19, is that much progress has been made, but there is still a lot of work that needs to be completed to facilitate these students learning side by side with their typically developing peers. For example, two investigations across the course of the last 15 years (Kleinert et al., 2015; Smith, 2007) suggest that less than 11% of students with intellectual disability are included in general education environments. This 11% figure is for students with intellectual disability at all levels, so those with severe disabilities, those whose needs require more support, more intensive instruction would be found in those general education settings at a much lower percentage.

Ryndak et al. (2014) suggest that students with severe disabilities are typically found in the most segregated placements and that educational policies have not been developed in such a way to ensure inclusive placement. Morningstar et al. (2016) suggest that there are positive outcomes for students with severe disabilities in inclusive contexts, but limited studies point to inclusive education as a moderate predictor of post-school success for employment, postsecondary education, and independent living. Efforts need to continue that promote active engagement with evidence-based practices, capacity building at the system level, school and classroom level, and the continuous documentation of student learning and development.

From an instructional perspective, there is ample evidence that students with severe disabilities can learn academic skills (e.g., reading, Browder et al., 2006, 2009; mathematics, Browder et al., 2008, 2018; Spooner et al., 2019; and science, Knight et al., 2019; Spooner et al., 2011), and several evidence-based practices have been validated among them, including embedded instruction (Hudson et al., 2013) and peer supports (Brock & Huber, 2017). The combination of embedded instruction delivered by peers (e.g., Jameson et al., 2008; Jimenez et al., 2012) can be a successful delivery strategy for general education contexts.

For progress towards including all students in general education environments to have the opportunity to participate and benefit from that context, placement should translate into active participation, accommodations should translate into action, and collaboration should reflect shared beliefs among administrators, teachers, students, families, and communities. It would appear the evidence is accruing to make this possible, but to date the limited investigations documenting this success have not tipped the scales to make inclusive practices adopted on a large-scale basis in our nation's schools. We believe a relentless focus on collaboration, effective instruction, and leadership will shift the balance and inclusion will become a part of a valued history rather than a continuing goal and unfulfilled promise.

Conclusion

> Cutting a bunch of teenagers loose on a computer was the idea of the Mothers' Club at Lakeside School in Seattle. The mothers decided that the proceeds from a big rummage sale should go to installing a terminal and buying computer time for the students. Letting students at a computer was a pretty progressive idea in the late 1960s—and a decision I'll always be grateful for.
>
> *Bill Gates, The Road Ahead, p. 1*

Acknowledging problems in the state of educational progress and performance (e.g., achievement and other outcome "gaps") and the continuing failure of large- and small-scale "reforms" in America's schools is necessary to address and fix them (Harper, 2015; Quinn, 2020). Recognizing and promoting the need for education change in general as well as for transformation in special education and how people with disabilities are educated has been around for many years (cf. Sarason, 1990; Sarason & Doris, 1979; Ysseldyke, 2001, 2005; Ysseldyke et al., 1983, 2000); and the balance sheet from all the effort is not impressive. While resharing opinions and admiring the problem remain as predictable messages being disseminated, a pervasive "failure to move the needle" persists.

The need for change is irrefutable and undeniable. The practice of replacing failed interventions with iterations and promises more like what failed than different is not going to bring about change. If you want schools where students with disabilities are valued and active participants, identify what they need to succeed in academic, social, and extra-curricular activities with their same-age neighbors and peers; have people with skin in the game teach and support them; and continuously evaluate your efforts as a basis for deciding when and if it is time for a change. We do not know if this will work, but in the name of progress, it may create a "tipping point" when society in general and education, in particular, achieves a desired but as yet unattained goal by adopting a rare but righteous practice. And if the goal seems too far away, think of what has not passed and mercifully try another way.

References

Abeson, A., & Zettel, J. (1977). The end of this quiet revolution: The Education for All Handicapped Children Act of 1975. *Exceptional Children*, 44(3), 115–128.

Al Otaiba, S., Petscher, Y., Wanzek, J., Lan, P., & Rivas, B. (2018). I'm not throwing away my shot: What Alexander Hamilton can tell us about standard reading interventions. *Learning Disabilities Research & Practice*, 33(3),156–167.

Algozzine, B. (1991). Observations to accompany analyses of the *Tenth Annual Report to Congress. Exceptional Children*, 57(3), 271–275.

Algozzine, B., & Maheady, L. (1986). When all else fails, teach! *Exceptional Children*, 52(6), 487–488.

Anastasiou, D., Morgan, P. L., Farkas, G., & Wiley, A. (2017). Minority disproportionate representation in special education: Politics and evidence. In J. M. Kauffman, D. P. Hallahan, & P. C. Pullen (Eds.), *Handbook of special education* (2nd ed., pp. 897–910).: Routledge.

Artiles, A. (2011). Toward an interdisciplinary understanding of educational equity and difference: The case of racialization of disability. *Educational Researcher*, 40(9), 431–445.

Artiles, A. J. (2019). Fourteenth Annual Brown Lecture in Education Research: Reenvisioning equity research: Disability identification disparities as a case in point. *Educational Researcher*, 48(6), 325–335.

Balu, R., Zhu, P., Doolittle, F., Schiller, E., Jenkins, J., & Gersten, R. (2015). *Evaluation of response to intervention practices for elementary school reading* (NCEE 2016-4000). U.S. Department of Education, Institute of Education Sciences. Retrieved from http://ies.ed.gov/ncee/pubs/20164000/pdf/20164000.pdf

Beretvas, T., Bleeker, M., Furgeson, J., Hedges, L., Horner, R., Hitchcock, J., Kratochwill, T., Monahan, S., & Schulte, T. (2015). *Key criteria used in WWC reviews of single-case design research*. Institute of Education Sciences.

Bloom, B. (1966). Twenty-five years of educational research. *American Educational Research Journal*, 3(3), 211–221.

Brasher, J. (2017, September 11). *RTI is getting a bad rap, say education researchers. Research News @ Vanderbilt.* Retrieved from https://news.vanderbilt.edu/2017/09/11/rti-is-getting-a-bad-rap-say-education-researchers/

Brock, M. E., & Huber, H. B. (2017). Are peer support arrangements an evidence-based practice? A systematic review. *The Journal of Special Education*, 51(3), 150–163.

Browder, D. M., Ahlgrim-Delzell, L., Spooner, F., Mims, P. J., & Baker, J. N. (2009). Using time delay to teach literacy to students with severe developmental disabilities. *Exceptional Children*, 75(3), 343–364.

Browder, D. M., Spooner, F., Ahlgrim-Delzell, L., Harris, A., & Wakeman, S. (2008). A meta-analysis on teaching mathematics to students with significant cognitive disabilities. *Exceptional Children*, 74(4), 407–432.

Browder, D. M., Spooner, F., Lo, Y.-y., Saunders, A. F., Root, J. R., Ley Davis, L., & Brosh, C. R. (2018). Teaching students with moderate intellectual disability to solve word problems. *The Journal of Special Education*, 51(4), 222–235.

Browder, D. M., Wakeman, S. Y., Spooner, F., Ahlgrim-Delzell, L., & Algozzine, B. (2006). Research on reading for students with significant cognitive disabilities. *Exceptional Children*, 72(4), 392–408.

Bryk, A. (2010). Organizing schools for improvement. *Phi Delta Kappan*, 91(7), 23–30.

Camacho, K. A., & Krezmien, M. P. (2019). Individual- and school-level factors contributing to disproportionate suspension rates: A multilevel analysis of one state. *Journal of Emotional and Behavioral Disorders*, 27(4), 209–220.

Charlton, C. T., Sabey, C. V., Dawson, M. R., Pyle, D., Lund, E. M., & Ross, S. W. (2018). Critical incidents in the scale-up of state multitiered systems of supports. *Journal of Positive Behavior Interventions*, 20(4), 191–202. 10.1177/1098300718770804

Clarke, S., Zakszeski, B. N., & Kern, L. (2018). Trends in JPBI publications, 1999-2016. *Journal of Positive Behavior Interventions*, 20(1), 6–14.

Cruz, R. A. & Rodl, J. E., (2018). An integrative synthesis of literature on disproportionality in special education. *The Journal of Special Education*, 52(1), 50–63.

DeMatthews, D., Billingsley, B., McLeskey, J., & Sharma, U. (2020). Principal leadership for students with disabilities in effective inclusive schools. *Journal of Educational Administration*, 58(5), 539–554.

Diament, M. (2018, July 13). *Ed department sued over delay of special education rule. Disability scoop.* Retrieved from https://www.disabilityscoop.com/2018/07/13/ed-department-sued-sped-rule/25280/

Dunn, L. M. (1968). Special education for the mildly retarded—is much of it justifiable? *Exceptional Children*, 35(1), 5–22.

Education for All Handicapped Children Act of 1975, Pub. L. No. 94-142, 89 Stat. 773 (1975).

Farrell, C. C., Wentworth, L, & Nayfack, M. (2021). What are the conditions under which research-practice partnerships succeed? *Kappan*, 102(7), 38–41.

Fixsen, D. L., & Blase, K. A. (2009, January). *Implementation: The missing link between research and practice*. NIRN Implementation Brief #1. The University of North Carolina. Retrieved from https://files.eric.ed.gov/fulltext/ED507422.pdf

Fixsen, D., Naoom, S., Blase, K., Friedman, R., & Wallace, F. (2005). *Implementation research: A synthesis of the literature*. University of South Florida, Louis de la Parte Florida Mental Health Institute, National Implementation Research Network. Retrieved from https://nirn.fpg.unc.edu/resources/implementation-research-synthesis-literature

Franke, P. R., & Davis R. A. (1931). Changing tendencies in educational research. *Journal of Educational Research*, 23(2), 133–145.
Friedman, T. L. (2012, March 31). *Why nations fail. The New York Times Sunday Review Opinion*. Retrieved from https://www.nytimes.com/2012/04/01/opinion/sunday/friedman-why-nations-fail.html
Fuchs, D., & Fuchs, L. S. (1994a). Inclusive schools movement and the radicalization of special education reform. *Exceptional Children*, 60(4), 294–309.
Fuchs, D., & Fuchs, L. S. (1994b). Sometimes separate is better. *Educational Leadership*, 52(4), 22–26.
Fuchs, D., & Fuchs, L. S. (1994c). *What's "special" about special education? A field under siege*. Retrieved from https://files.eric.ed.gov/fulltext/ED379817.pdf
Fuchs, D., & Fuchs, L. S. (2015). Rethinking service delivery for students with significant learning problems: Developing and implementing intensive instruction. *Remedial & Special Education*, 36(2), 105–111.
Fuchs, D., & Fuchs, L. S. (2017). Critique of the national evaluation of response to intervention: A case for simpler frameworks. *Exceptional Children*, 83(3), 255–268.
Fuchs, D., Fuchs, L. S., & Compton, D. L. (2012). Smart RTI: A next-generation approach to multilevel prevention. *Exceptional Children*, 78(3), 263–279.
Fuchs, D., Fuchs, L. S., McMaster, K. L., & Lemons, C. J. (2018). Students with disabilities' abysmal school performance: An introduction to the special issue. *Learning Disabilities Research & Practice*, 33(3), 127–130.
Fullan, M. (2016). *The new meaning of educational change* (5th ed.). Teachers College Press.
Gates, B. (1995). *The road ahead*. Viking Press.
Gilmour, A. F., Fuchs, D., & Wehby, J. H. (2019). Are students with disabilities accessing the curriculum? A meta-analysis of the reading achievement gap between students with and without disabilities. *Exceptional Children*, 85(3), 329–346.
Gotham, H. J. (2006). Advancing implementation of evidence-based practices into clinical practice: How do we get there from here? *Professional Psychology: Research and Practice*, 37(6), 606–613.
Grima-Farrell, C. (2018). Bridging the research-to-practice gap: Implementing the research-to-practice model. *Australasian Journal of Special and Inclusive Education*, 42(1), 82–91.
Grima-Farrell, C., Bain, A., & McDonagh, S. (2011). Bridging the research-to-practice gap: A review of the literature focusing on inclusive education. *Australasian Journal of Special Education*, 35(2), 117–136.
Harper, S. R. (2015). Success in these schools? Visual counternarratives of young men of color and urban high schools they attend. *Urban Education*, 50(2), 139–169.
Harvey, M. W., Rowe, D. A., Test, D. W., Imperatore, C., Lombardi, A., Conrad, M., Szymanski, A., & Barnett, K. (2020). Partnering to improve career and technical education for students with disabilities: A position paper of the Division on Career Development and Transition. *Career Development and Transition for Exceptional Individuals*, 43(2), 67–77.
Heller, K. A., Holtzman, W. H., & Messick, S. (Eds.). (1982). *Placing children in special education: A strategy for equity*. National Academy Press.
Heller R. (2021). Editor's note: The beginning of a beautiful friendship? *Kappan*, 102(7), 4.
Hitt, D., & Tucker, P. (2016). Systematic review of key leader practices found to influence student achievement: A unified framework. *Review of Educational Research*, 86(2), 531–569.
Hudson, M. E., Browder, D. M., & Wood, L. (2013). Review of experimental research on academic learning by students with moderate and severe intellectual disability in general education. *Research and Practice for Persons with Severe Disabilities*, 38(1), 17–29.
Jameson, J. M., McDonnell, J., Polychronis, S., & Riesen, T. (2008). Embedded, constant time delay instruction by peers without disabilities in general education classrooms. *Intellectual and Developmental Disabilities*, 46(5), 346–363.
Jimenez, B., Browder, D. M., Spooner, F, & DiBiase, W. (2012). Inclusive inquiry science using peer-mediated embedded instruction for students with moderate intellectual disability. *Exceptional Children*, 78(3), 301–317.
Joyce, K. E., & Cartwright, N. (2020). Bridging the gap between research and practice: Predicting what will work locally. *American Educational Research Journal*, 57(3), 1045–1082.
Kauffman, J. M. (2015). Opinion on recent developments and the future of special education. *Remedial & Special Education*, 36(1), 9–13.
Kauffman, J. M., Anastasiou, D., & Maag, J. W. (2017). Special education at the crossroad: An identity crisis and the need for a scientific reconstruction. *Exceptionality*, 25(2), 139–155.
Kauffman, J. M., Schumaker, J. B., Badar, J., & Hallenbeck, B. A. (2019). Where special education goes to die. *Exceptionality*, 27(2), 149–166.
Kauffman. J. M. (1993). How we might achieve the radical reform of special education. *Exceptional Children*, 60(1), 6–16.

Kern, L., Evans, S. W., Lewis, T. J., State, T. M., Mehta, P. D., Weist, M. D., Wills, H. P., &Gage N. A. (2020). Evaluation of a comprehensive assessment-based intervention for secondary students with social, emotional, and behavioral problems. *Journal of Emotional and Behavioral Disorders*, 29(1), 1–12.

Kezar, A. (2000). Understanding the research-to-practice gap: A national study of researchers' and practitioners' perspectives. *New Directions for Higher Education*, 2000(110), 9–19.

Kleinert, H., Towles-Reeves, E., Quenemoen, R., Thurlow, M., Fluegge, L., Weseman, L., & Kerbel, A. (2015). Where students with the most significant cognitive disabilities are taught: Implications for general curriculum access. *Exceptional Children*, 81(3), 312–328.

Knight, V. F., Wood, L., McKissick, B. R., & Kuntz, E. M. (2019). Teaching science content and practices to students with intellectual disability and autism. *Remedial and Special Education*, 41(6), 327-240.

Krathwohl, D. (1969, February). *Educational research: Perspective, prognosis and proposal.* Presidential Address, American Educational Research Association.

Lipsky, D. K., & Gartner, A. (1987). Capable of achievement and worthy of respect: Education for handicapped students as if they were full-fledged human beings. *Exceptional Children*, 54(1), 69–74.

McFarland, J., Hussar, B., Zhang, J., Wang, X., Wang, K., Hein, S., Diliberti, M., Forrest Cataldi, E., Bullock Mann, F., & Barmer, A. (2019). *The Condition of Education 2019* (NCES 2019-144). National Center for Education Statistics.

MacMillan, D. L., & Reschly, D. J. (1998). Overrepresentation of minority students: The case for greater specificity or reconsideration of the variables examined. *The Journal of Special Education*, 32(1), 15–24.

McDonnell, L. M., McLaughlin, M. J., & Morison, P. (Eds.). (1997). *Educating one and all: Students with disabilities and standards-based reform.* National Academy Press.

Morningstar, M. E., Allock, H. C., White, J. M., Taub, D., Kurth, J. A., Gonsier-Gerdin, J., Ryndak, D. L., Sauer, J., & Jorgensen, C. M. (2016). Inclusive education national research advocacy agenda: A call to action. *Research and Practice for Persons with Severe Disabilities*, 41(3), 209–215.

Murphy, J. (2009). "Closing achievement gaps: Lessons from the last 15 years. (Cover story). *Phi Delta Kappan*, 91(3), 8–12.

National Assessment of Educational Progress. (2020a). *About NAEP.* Retrieved from https://nces.ed.gov/nationsreportcard/about/

National Assessment of Educational Progress. (2020b). *Results by student group.* Retrieved from https://www.nationsreportcard.gov/reading_math_2015/#reading/groups?grade=4

National Assessment of Educational Progress. (2020c). *Results from the 2019 Mathematics and Reading Assessments.* Retrieved from https://www.nationsreportcard.gov/mathematics/supportive_files/2019_infographic.pdf

National Assessment of Educational Progress. (2020d). *Scale scores and NAEP achievement levels.* Retrieved from https://nces.ed.gov/nationsreportcard/guides/scores_achv.aspx

National Assessment of Educational Progress. (2020e). *The NAEP reading assessment levels by grade.* Retrieved from https:/nces.ed.gov/nationsreportcard/reading/achieveall.aspx#2009_grade4

National Center on Assessment and Accountability in Special Education. (2017, December). *Did you know? Reading.* Research Note No. 1. Author. Retrieved from www.ncaase.com

Newman, F., Smith, B., Allensworth, E., & Bryk, A. (2001). Instructional program coherence: What is it and why it should guide school improvement policy. *Educational Evaluation and Policy Analysis*, 23(4), 297–321.

Nuthall, G. (2004). Relating classroom teaching to student learning: A critical analysis of why research has failed to bridge the theory-practice gap. *Harvard Educational Review*, 74(3), 273–306.

Office of Special Education and Rehabilitative Services (OSERS). (2018). *40th Annual Report to Congress on the Implementation of the "Individuals with Disabilities Education Act," 2018.* Author.

Office of Special Education Programs (OSEP). (2017, February 8). *Symposium on Significant Disproportionality.* Author. Retrieved from https://osepideasthatwork.org/osep-meeting/significant-disproportionality

Osgood, R. (2005). *The history of inclusion in United States.* Gallaudet University Press. Available online: http://gupress.gallaudet.edu/bookpage/HIUSbookpage.html

Peurach, D. J., Cohen, D. K., Yurkofsky, M. M., & Spillane, J. P. (2019). From mass schooling to education systems: Changing patterns in the organization and management of instruction. *Review of Research in Education*, 43(1), 32–67.

Preston, T. (2021). A look back: Research meets practice, again and again in *Kappan*. *Kappan*, 102(7), 5–7.

Public Law 94–142. 1975, November 29). *Education for All Handicapped Children Act.* (see Education for All Handicapped Children Act of 1975).

Quinn, D. (2020). Experimental effects of "Achievement Gap" news reporting on viewers' racial stereotypes, inequality explanations, and inequality prioritization. *Educational Researcher*, 49(7), 482–492.

Ryndak, D. L., Taub, D., Jorgensen, C. M., Gonsier-Gerdin, J., Arndt, K., Ruppar, A. L., Morningstar, M. E., & Allcock, H. C. (2014). Policy and the impact on placement, involvement, and progress in general education: Critical issues that require rectification. *Research and Practice for Persons with Severe Disabilities*, 39(1), 64–74.

Sarason, S. B. (1971). *The culture of the school and the problem of change*. Allyn and Bacon.

Sarason, S. B. (1990). *The predictable failure of educational reform: Can we change course before it's too late?* Jossey-Bass, Inc.

Sarason, S., & Doris, J. (1979). *Educational handicap, public policy, and social history*. Free Press

Scaletta, M., & Hughes, M. T. (2020). Sustained positive behavioral interventions and supports implementation: School leaders discuss their processes and practices. *Journal of Positive Behavior Interventions and Supports*. doi:10.1177/1098300720924350

Scates, D. (1948). On our research the answers hinge. *Phi Delta Kappan*, 30(4), 120–123.

Schulte, A. C., & Stevens, J. J. (2015). Once, sometimes, or always in special education: Mathematics growth and achievement gaps. *Exceptional Children*, 81(3), 370–387.

Schulte, A. C., Stevens, J. J., Elliott, S. N., Tindal, G., & Nese, J. F. T. (2016). Achievement gaps for students with disabilities: stable, widening, or narrowing on a state-wide reading comprehension test? *Journal of Educational Psychology*, 108(7), 925–942.

Scruggs, T., & Mastropieri, M. (1996). Teacher perceptions of mainstreaming/inclusion, 1958-1995: A research synthesis. *Exceptional Children*, 63(1), 59–74.

Skiba R. J., Artiles A. J., Kozleski, E. B., Losen, D. J., & Harry, E. G. (2016). Risks and consequences of oversimplifying educational inequities. *Educational Researcher*. 45(3), 221–225.

Smith, P. (2007). Have we made any progress? Including students with intellectual disabilities in regular education classrooms. *Intellectual and Developmental Disabilities*, 45(5), 297–309.

Snow, C. E. (2016). The role of relevance in educational research, as viewed by former presidents. *Educational Researcher*, 45(2), 64–68.

Spooner, F., Knight, V., Browder, D. M., Jimenez, B., & DiBiase, W. (2011). Evaluating evidence-based practice in teaching science content to students with severe developmental disabilities. *Research and Practice for Persons with Severe Disabilities*, 36(1-2), 62–75.

Spooner, F., Root, J. R., Saunders, A. F., & Browder, D. M. (2019). An updated evidence-based practice review on teaching mathematics to students with moderate and severe developmental disabilities. *Remedial and Special Education*, 40(3), 150–165.

Stevens, J. J., Schulte, A. C., Elliott, S. N., Nese, J. F. T., & Tindal, G. (2015). Growth and gaps in mathematics achievement of students with and without disabilities on a statewide achievement test. *Journal of School Psychology*, 53(1), 45–62.

The Nation's Report Card. (2020). *2015|Mathematics & Reading Assessments*. Retrieved from https://www.nationsreportcard.gov/reading_math_2015/#reading/gaps?grade=4

Theisen, W. (1923). Recent progress in educational research. *Journal of Educational Research*, 8(4), 301–314.

Tyre, A., Feuerborn, L., Beaudoin, K., & Bruce, J. (2020). Middle school teachers' concerns for implementing the principles of SWPBIS. *Journal of Positive Behavior Interventions*, 22(2), 93–104.

U. S. Department of Education. (2018a). *A proposed rule by the Education Department on 02/27/2018*. Author. Retrieved from https://www.federalregister.gov/documents/2018/02/27/2018-04102/assistance-to-states-for-the-education-of-children-with-disabilities-preschool-grants-for-children

U. S. Department of Education. (2018b). *A rule by the Education Department on 07/03/2018*. Author. Retrieved from https://www.federalregister.gov/documents/2018/07/03/2018-14374/assistance-to-states-for-the-education-of-children-with-disabilities-preschool-grants-for-children

U. S. Department of Education. (2020). OSEP's Annual reports to Congress on the implementation of the *Individuals with Disabilities Education Act (IDEA)*. https://www2.ed.gov/about/reports/annual/osep/index.html

Vanderlinde, R., & Braak, J. (2010). The gap between educational research and practice: views of teachers, school leaders, intermediaries and researchers. *British Educational Research Journal*, 36(2), 299–316.

Wagner, M., Newman, R.S., Cameto, R., & Levine, P. (2006). *The academic achievement and functional performance of youth with disabilities: A report from the National Longitudinal Transition Study–2 (NLTS2)*. SRI International. Retrieved from https://files.eric.ed.gov/fulltext/ED494936.pdf

Wallace, F., Blase, K., Fixsen, D., & Naoom, S. (2008). *Implementing the findings of research: Bridging the gap between knowledge and practice*. Education Research Service.

Wanzek, J., Petscher, Y., Al Otaiba, S., Kent, S. C., Schatschneider, C., Haynes, M., Rivas, B. K., & Jones, F. G. (2016). Examining the effects of a standardized treatment for fourth graders with reading difficulties. *Journal of Research on Educational Effectiveness*, 9(Sup 1), 45–66.

Wanzek, J., Petscher, Y., Al Otaiba, S., Rivas, B., Jones, F. J., Kent, S., Schatschneider, C., & Mehta, P. (2017). Effects of a year-long supplemental reading intervention for students with reading difficulties in fourth grade. *Journal of Educational Psychology*, 109(8), 1108–1119.

Weintraub, F. J. (1977). The end of this quiet revolution: The Education for All Handicapped Children Act of 1975 (Editorial Comment). *Exceptional Children*, 44(2), 114.

Woody, C. (1924). A survey of educational research in 1923. *Journal of Educational Research*, 9(4), 357–381.

Ysseldyke, J. (2001). Reflections on a career: 25 years of research on assessment and instructional decision-making. *Exceptional Children*, 67(3), 295–310.

Ysseldyke, J. E. (2005) Assessment and decision making for students with learning disabilities: What if this is as good as it gets? *Learning Disabilities Quarterly*, 28(2), 125–128.

Ysseldyke, J. E., Algozzine, B., & Thurlow, M. (2000). *Critical issues in special and remedial education*. Houghton Mifflin.

Ysseldyke, J., Thurlow, M., Graden, J., Wesson, C., Algozzine, B., & Deno, S. (1983). Generalizations from five years of research on assessment and decision making: The University of Minnesota Institute. *Exceptional Education Quarterly*, 4(1), 75–93.

Index

Italicized and **bold** pages refer to figures and tables respectively, and page numbers followed by "n" refer to notes.

Made in the USA
Monee, IL
13 September 2026

62978984R10313